MONITORING CHILDR

MONITORING CHILDREN'S RIGHTS

Edited by

EUGEEN VERHELLEN

University of Ghent, Children's Rights Centre, Belgium

MARTINUS NIJHOFF PUBLISHERS

THE HAGUE / BOSTON / LONDON

Library of Congress Cataloging-in-Publication Data

Monitoring children's rights / edited by Eugeen Verhellen.
        p.   cm.
    "Contributions made and discussed at the European Conference on
Monitoring Children's Rights, December 1994"--Preface.
    Includes index.
    ISBN 9041101616 (alk. paper). -- ISBN 9041101624 (pbk. : alk.
paper)
    1. Children (International law)--Congresses. 2. Convention on the
Rights of the Child (1989)--Congresses. 3. Children's rights-
-Congresses. 4. Children--Legal status, laws, etc.--Congresses.
5. Child welfare--Congresses.   I. Verhellen, Eugeen.
K639.A55   1994
346.01'35--dc20
[342.6135]   95-43186
ISBN 90-411-0161-6
ISBN 90-411-0162-4 (pbk)

Published by Kluwer Law International,
P.O. Box 85889, 2508 CN The Hague, The Netherlands.

Sold and distributed in the U.S.A. and Canada
by Kluwer Law International,
675 Massachusetts Avenue, Cambridge, MA 02139, U.S.A.

In all other countries, sold and distributed
by Kluwer Law International,
P.O. Box 85889, 2508 CN The Hague, The Netherlands

Printed on acid-free paper

Printed in the Netherlands

Table of Contents

3. Childhood Policies and Monitoring Children's Rights

4. International Monitoring Procedures

5. Regional and National Implementation of the Convention on the Rights of the Child

6. The Role of NGOs in Monitoring and Implementing the Convention

7. National Monitoring Mechanisms: the Role of Ombudswork

10. Residential Care

11. Health care

12. Exploitation of Children

13. Street Children

14. Children in Armed Conflict

APPENDICES

Preface

This book contains the contributions made and discussed at the European Conference on Monitoring Children's Rights, organized by Gent University's Children's Rights Centre in December 1994.

Most European countries have already ratified the 1989 UN Convention on the Rights of the Child.

The Convention provides a framework for monitoring implementation of its provisions. Article 43, for instance, provides for a Committee on the Rights of the Child to be set up. This Committee is to be made up of ten members acknowledged as having expertise in the field covered by the Convention. The Committee started work on February 27th 1991. The reports which article 44 requires States Parties to draft at regular intervals must be submitted to this Committee.

Every two years the Committee submits a report on its activities to the UN General Assembly, via the Economic and Social Council.

The aim of the Conference was to discuss in a wider scientific forum the results of interdisciplinary research into monitoring. Two monitoring issues had to be tackled, with particularly emphasis on the reporting system: *what* to report and *who* reports? Eugeen Verhellen's contribution forms an introduction to these seemingly simple questions.

What to report deals with the content of the reports. We know little about children. This lack of knowledge becomes especially apparant in two areas.

First of all children are rarely represented as a separate category or class in demographical statistics. This demonstrates the fact that they are "invisible" to society. When they are counted, it is always "in relation to" adults. There is no real ethnography of children themselves.

Secondly we know very little about how children interpret certain events and give meaning to them. And in any case, we have a tendency to consider such processes as not (yet) important. What children really know, what they are capable of and who they really are remains largely a mystery. The child as a "meaning-maker" remains mostly a mystery to us.

E. Verhellen (ed.), Monitoring Children's Rights, xiii–xv.
© 1996 *Kluwer Law International. Printed in the Netherlands.*

We find an analysis of this question in the texts of Jens Qvortrup, Ferran Casas, Målfrid Grude Flekkøy and Nigel Cantwell.

Who reports deals with the more formal and procedural aspects of reporting. The Convention stipulates that there is an obligation for States Parties to submit reports. Many people are critical of this procedure. Must this really be left to the governements involved? What role can be played by NGOs? What part can children themselves play? What is the practical use of these reports? What national or regional (European) models can be developed to improve monitoring?

These and other questions are dealt with in the texts of Johan Vande Lanotte and Geert Goedertier, James R. Himes and Marta Santos Pais.

Over the last few years there have been many changes in the field of children's rights. Recommendation 1121, adopted by the Parliamentary Assembly of the Council of Europe in 1991, contained the suggestion that an Additional Protocol to the European Convention on Human Rights be drawn up, dealing specifically with children's rights. Were this provision is to be adopted by the Committee of Ministers, we might see the beginning of a totally new European monitoring framework.

There is also the draft European Convention on the exercise of children's rights, which will probably be discussed by the Parliamentary Assembly in mid 1995.

Developments in the Council of Europe will be dealt with in this book by Pascale Boucaud.

For the European Union, Juan Bandrès Molet will analyse EP Resolution A3-0172/92, which proposes a European Charter on the Rights of the Child.

Apart from suitable monitoring mechanism, there is also the self-executing force of the Convention, making it directly enforceable in national courts. Many European countries have this mechanism in national legal systems. What part can national courts play? What might be the role of the European Court of Human Rights? The extremely important issue is discussed in the texts of André Alen and Wouter Pas, Jean-Pierre Rosenczveig and Maud Buquicchio-De Boer.

Although the children's rights monitoring system plays a central role, it cannot be analyzed in isolation. Philip Alston therefore looks at monitoring against the wider background of human rights instruments.

Hans Van Loon makes an excellent attempt to draw together the different strands, asking a number of new questions and pointing to a number of new challenges.

The reader will find all these texts collected in the first part of this book, which attempts to describe the inner workings of the monitoring concept, on the basis of the above-mentioned simple questions.

The second part of the book is totally different in nature, containing the selected papers presented during the Conference's workshops. We were very pleased to find that so many people had answered the call to put forward a paper about the Conference's theme.

Given the diversity of these texts, the Editor had to conclude that they could not be edited into a coherent entity. Nevertheless, in view of their authors' serious commitment and their rich variety, it was decided that they should be published.

As set forth in Article 42 of the Children's Rights Convention, there is an important task for States Parties to "... *make the principles and provisions of the Convention widely known, by appropriate and active means...*" This publication can only be a modest but meaningful contribution to this international obligation.

As pointed out by several contributors, the dissemination of information and knowledge on children's rights is indeed a very important condition for adequate monitoring. Let us consequently hope that this book, in the words of one of the authors, "... *will really help (us) a lot in the promotion and advocacy of children's rights.*" It can perhaps even be regarded as a modest reaction to the present threat to human rights.

I owe a debt of gratitude to a number of people, who have contributed greatly to the preparation of this book. I would particularly like to thank Karl Hanson and Kathy Vlieghe for their patience and invaluable support.

May 1995   EUGEEN VERHELLEN

List of Contributors – Part ONE

André Baron Alen is Professor of Constitutional Law, Political Institutions and Federalism, at the Catholic University of Leuven, Faculty of Law, Belgium. He is assessor at the Legislation Section of the Council of State.

Philip Alston is Professor of International Law at the European University Institute in Florence, Italy. He is also Senior Fellow at the UNICEF International Child Development Centre and, since 1991, chairperson of the United Nations Committee on Economic, Social and Cultural Rights.

Juan Maria Bandrés Molet is a Lawyer and Ex-Member of the European Parliament. He is at present the Chairman of the Spanish Committee for aid to refugees (CEAR), San Sebastian, Spain.

Samir Sanad Basta is former Director of the UNICEF Office for Europe, Geneva, Switzerland (now on Sabbatical).

Pascale Boucaud is Professor in Law at the Catholic University of Lyon, France. She is Director of the Human Rights Institute of that university. She is also consultant and expert within the Council of Europe.

Maud Buquicchio-de Boer is Secretary to the First Chamber of the European Commission of Human Rights, Strasbourg, France.

Nigel Cantwell is a Consultant for Unicef, Geneva, Switzerland. He is Co-founder and former Secretary-General of Defence for Children International. He has been actively involved with the development of international children's rights standards and their implementation.

Ferran Casas is Professor at the University of Barcelona, Department of Social Psychology, Spain. He is chairperson of the Project on Childhood Policies of the Council of Europe.

Målfrid Grude Flekkøy is a clinical psychologist. She is affiliated with the Nic Waals Institute, Oslo, Norway where she is doing clinical work with children, youth and families, and teaching in-service trainees specialised in child psychiatry. She was Norwegian Ombudsman for Children 1981–1989. She has also been a Senior Fellow at Unicef, International Child Development Centre, Florence, Italy. She is currently doing research at the University of South Carolina, Institute for Families in Society, U.S.A.

Geert Goedertier is research associate at the University of Ghent, Faculty of Law, Belgium.

James R. Himes is Director of UNICEF Innocenti Centre, (International Child Development Centre) Florence, Italy. The Centre undertakes applied research and promotes policy analysis and training in selected areas of concern.

Wouter Pas is research associate at the Catholic University of Leuven, Faculty of Law, Belgium.

Jens Qvortrup is a Senior Research Fellow at the South Jutland University Centre, Childhood Unit, Esbjerg, Denmark. He is Co-director of the Childhood Programme, European Centre Vienna. He is President of 'Sociology of childhood' under the International Sociological Association.

Jean-Pierre Rosenczveig is President of Children's Court of Bobigny-Paris (Tribunal pour Enfants de Bobigny). He is Secretary General of COFRADE (Conseil français des associations pour les droits de l'enfant) and Administrator of the "Centre International de l'Enfance", Paris, France.

Marta Santos Pais is Rapporteur of the United Nations Committee on the Rights of the Child and Senior Legal Advisor for Human Rights in the Office of Comparative Law in Lisbon, Portugal.

Johan Vande Lanotte is Professor in Law at the University of Ghent, Faculty of Law, Belgium. His main area of work is Belgian Constitutional and administrative law and the European Convention on Human Rights.
He is at present Belgian Minister of Internal Affairs.

Hans Van Loon is First Secretary of the Hague Conference on Private International Law, The Netherlands.

Eugeen Verhellen is Professor at the University of Ghent, Belgium. He is the director of the Children's Rights Centre of that University.

List of Contributors – Part TWO

Bruce Abramson is a human rights attorney, Geneva, Switzerland.

Luisa Maria Aguilar is a permanent representative to the European institutions of the International Catholic Child Bureau (ICCB) in Brussels, Belgium. She is Director of the European Consortium "Communication between adults and children."

Pilar Arnaïz Sanchez is Professor at the University of Murcia, Department of Special Education, Spain.

Gill Barn works for The Save the Children Fund, United Kingdom and European Programmes Department, U.K. She is project co-ordinator of the Participation Unit.

Deepak Kumar Behera is Reader and Head at the Sambalpur University, Department of Anthropology, Orissa, India.

Josiane Brigot is president of Themis and of the youth magistrates court in Strasbourg, France.

Marianne Borgen is a sociologist. She has been the Head of Division in the office of the Commissioner for Children's Rights since 1985, Barneombudet Oslo, Norway.

Jan Bosmans is the Director of De Waaiburg, a non-profit organization which organizes several residential provisions for special youth welfare, Geel, Belgium.

Maria Bouverne-De Bie is Professor at the University of Ghent, Faculty of Psychology and Educational Sciences, Department Agology, Belgium.

E. Verhellen (ed.), Monitoring Children's Rights, xix–xxvi.
© 1996 *Kluwer Law International. Printed in the Netherlands.*

Teodor Bulenda is Assistant Professor at the Warsaw University, Institute of Social Prevention and Resocialization, Department of Criminology & Criminal Justice. He is a lawyer in the Office of Spokesman for Civil Rights, Poland.

Geert Cappelaere is a research associate at the University of Ghent, Children's Rights Centre, Belgium. He is consultant for the United Nations.

Isabelle Cherney is a psychology major at Creighton University in Omaha, Nebraska, U.S.A.

Katherine Covell is Professor at the University College of Cape Breton, Department of Behavioural and Life Sciences, Sydney, Nova Scotia, Canada. She is a specialist in developmental psychology whose research focus is the development of social understanding.

Elżbieta Czyż is the children's rights programme co-ordinator of the Helsinki Foundation for Human Rights and The Committee for the Protection of Children's Rights, Warsaw, Poland.

Giedra Dagiliene is advisor for children's rights of the Lithuanian children's rights protection committee, Vilnius, Lithuania. She was initiator and member of the voluntary advisors Committee for monitoring article 44 of the UN Convention on the Rights of the Child.

J. Christopher Daniel is Professor of Social Work at the Madurai Institute of Social Sciences where he is involved in teaching, research and social work practice. He is the founding Honorary Executive Director of the Goodwill Social Work Centre, a non-governmental development and research organisation in child, youth and women development, Madurai, India.

John Decoene is criminologist and is working in the Committee for Special Youthcare of Ostend, Belgium.

Rudy De Cock is social worker and ombudsman of "Kind en Gezin" ("Child and Family") for the province of West-Flanders, Belgium.

Koen De Feyter is a lecturer in International Law at the University of Antwerp, Faculty of Law, Belgium.

Marc De Staercke is president of the European Federation of City Farms, Brussels, Belgium. The European Federation of City Farms is a non profit youth organization created in October 1990 as a confederation of the European City Farm movement.

Lea Dherbecourt is a retired nursery school teacher, Antwerp, Belgium.

Maud Droogleever Fortuyn is co-ordinator at the Children's Rights Shop in Amsterdam, The Netherlands.

Simone Ek was one of the NGO drafters of the UN Convention on the Rights of the Child in Geneva. She is at present co-ordinator of Rädda Barnen, Stockholm, Sweden.

Willy Faché is Professor at the University of Ghent, Faculty of Psychology and Educational Sciences, Department of Cultural, Social and Leisure Agology, Ghent, Belgium. He was the founding director of the first Youth Information and Counselling Centre in Belgium and Director of the Flemish Federation of Youth Centres.

Annie Franklin is Assistant Divisional Director for Save the Children (North and East Division), Leeds, U.K.

Bob Franklin is Reader in Sociological Studies at the University of Sheffield, U.K.

Anne-Marie Frédéric is a retired Professor. She is the founder and chairperson of GREMA, Groupe de Réflexion sur les Risques de l'environnement Urbain et les Minorités Atopiques, Brussels, Belgium.

Céline Giroux is Vice President of the 'Commission de Protection des Droits de la Jeunesse', Montréal, Canada.

Ilka Grigorova is Office Manager of the Centre Children at Risk and secretary of the Association Children at Risk, Sofia, Bulgaria.

Lennie Haarsma is working as a lawyer for a national institute for methodological development in Utrecht, The Netherlands. She is currently working on projects on child abuse and children's rights.

Jamila Hamid is a staffmember of the National Cooperation Moroccans and Tunesians, Utrecht, The Netherlands. She is a specialist in women and youth affairs.

Brian Howe is Professor at the University College of Cape Breton, Department of Politics, Government and Public Administration, Sydney, Nova Scotia, Canada. His area of specialty is human rights legislation, commissions and policies.

Peter Idenburg is Director of the International Dialogues Foundation, The Hague, The Netherlands. He organised a conference on the Rights of Children in Armed Conflict.

Annette Jacob is social-worker, sociologist, and "chargée de mission" of the Lyonnaise Society for Children and Adolescence, Lyon, France.

Philippe D. Jaffé teaches at the Faculty of Psychology and Educational Sciences, and works at the Institute of Legal Medicine, University of Geneva, Switzerland.

Mary E. John is Professor at the University of Exeter, School of Education, U.K. She is a developmental psychologist whose principal research interests are in the transformation of power relationships.

George Kent is Professor in Political Science at the University of Hawaii, Honolulu, Hawaii.

Leyla Khalfallah is a laywer and president of Defence for Children International (DCI), Tunesian Section.

Marian Koren works as a researcher at the Centre for Libraries (NBLC) in The Hague, Netherlands.

Andrzej Kremplewski is assistant at the Warsaw University, Institute of Social Prevention and Resocialization, Department of Criminology & Criminal Justice, Poland. He is affiliated with the Helsinki Foundation for Human Rights, Poland.

Alena Kroupová is Director of the Human Rights Education Center at Charles University, Prague, Czech Republic. She is dealing with the status of children in the transitional period and has worked out the Czech project "School of tolerance, mutual cooperation and personal responsibility".

Claude Lelièvre is the General Delegate of Children's Rights and Youth Aid in the French Speaking Community of Belgium.

Adam Łopatka is a full Professor in Law at the Polish Academy of Sciences, Institute of Law Studies, Warsaw, Poland. He was the chairman of the UN Working Group drafting the UN Convention on the Rights of the Child.

Marie-Françoise Lücker-Babel is a lawyer working at the Swiss Section of Defence for Children International (DCI), Geneva, Switzerland.

Virginia Maxim is a researcher at the Rumanian Institute for Human Rights, Bucarest, Rumania.

Brian Milne is a social anthropologist who has studied street children and child labour in the developing world and in Europe. He now works as a research consultant and advisor for children's rights. He is also a member of the UK Section of Defence for Children International (DCI).

Helena Molander is a children's human rights lawyer and the Children's Ombudsman of the Mannerheim League for Child Welfare in Finland. She is chairperson of DCI-Finland and the ECPAT representative. She is now doing research on child pornography.

Irina Moroianu Zlàtescu is Executive Director of the Rumanian Institute for Human Rights. She is Professor for human rights at the Faculty of Law, "Spiru Haret" University, , Faculty of Law, Bucarest, Rumania.

Frans Nederstigt studied political and legal sciences at the Law Faculty of Leiden University in The Netherlands. Nowadays he works as a scientific researcher in the Projeto Legal of the Brazilian NGO I.B.I.S.S., Rio de Janeiro, Brazil.

Maria Nikolova is Technical Assistant in the Centre Children at Risk, Sofia, Bulgaria.

Ioan Oancea is head of the Training Department of the Rumanian Institute for Human Rights, Bucarest, Rumania.

Lynette Ochola is head of the Undugu society, Nairobi, Kenya.

Arian Pano is doing research or more specific fieldwork and is affiliated with the Human Rights Albanian Helsinki Committee. He runs the Human Rights of Children Project which has been carried out by students activists of this Committee, Tirana, Albania.

Zoran Pavlović is a senior researcher at the Institute of Criminology at the Faculty of Law in Ljubljana, Slovenia. His research interests include children's rights, child maltreatment and victimology. He is a member of the Commission on the Rights of the Child in Slovenia and president of the newly established Society for Prevention of Child Abuse and for Family Support.

Lilian Peeters is member of the steering Committee of the conference on the Rights of Children in Armed Conflict, International Dialogues Foundation, The Hague, The Netherlands.

Nancy Walker Perry is Professor of Psychology at Creighton University in Omaha, Nebraska, U.S.A.

Anne-Marie Poreye-Thys is a social worker and runs psychological and analytical training. She is responsable for 'Télé-Accueil', Brussels, Belgium. Deputy-director of an organisation for abused children.

Cynthia Price Cohen is Executive Director of ChildRights International Research Institute, New York, U.S.A.

Nielle Puig-Vergès M.D., Ph.D., practices at the Hospital 'La Salpétrière', Paris, France. She is Director of Doctoral Research and scientific supervisor of the GRECC-AP (Research Group on Comparative Clinical Epistemology and Psychotherapeutic Applications = Groupe de Recherches d'Epistemologie Clinique Comparative et d'Applications Psychotherapeutiques).

Panayot Randev is the Co-ordinator of the CAR Project, Institute of Psychology-BAS. He is President of the Association of Professional Psychologists in Education (APPE) and of a coalition of 12 NGOs – Association Children at Risk. Office Manager of the Centre Children at Risk, Sofia, Bulgaria.

Ludwig Rech is Professor and affiliated with the European Federation of City Farms, Dilbeek, Belgium.

Darija Remeta works at present at the Government Office for Victims of War, as Head of the department for children victim of war, Zagreb, Croatia. She is a member of the Committee for the coordination of relief and health care for children in exceptional circumstances and of the Croatian Comittee for children's rights.

Hélène Rey Wicky is a researcher at the University of Geneva, Faculty of Psychology and Educational Sciences, Switzerland.

Nelia Sancho is the Vice President for Asia of Defence for Children International (DCI). She is also the Executive Director of the Streetchildren and Childworkers Support Center – The Philippines, (SCWSC-Philippines, Inc.). Her experience in developmental work spans more than twenty years which includes women organizing, community development work, children's rights advocacy and international networking on women and children's issues.

Richard Sancho Andreo is the director of THEMIS, a non-profit making organization which advises young people and defends their rights, in Strasbourg, France.

Angelo Saporiti is Professor at the University of Malise, Campobasso, Faculty of Economics, Italy.

William Schabas is Professor and Chair of the Law Department, University of Québec at Montréal, Canada.

Jane Green Schaller is the Professor and Chairman of Pediatrics at the Tufts University School of Medicine, Boston, USA. She is also Pediatrician-in-Chief of the Floating Hospital for Children at the New England Medical Center, Boston.

Marc-G. Schweitzer M.D., Ph.D., practices at the Hospital 'La Salpétrière', Paris, France. He is Director of research and the scientific supervisor of the Ethics and Health Law section of the GRECC-EDS (Research Group on Comparative Clinical Epistemoloy = Groupe de Recherches d'Epistemologie Clinique Comparative).

Lieve Stappers is a lawyer and affiliated with the Centre Childhood and Society, Meise, Belgium.

Marja Strojin is the director of the Counseling Center for Children, Adolescents and Parents, Ljubljana, Slovenia. She is a member of different NGOs and vice president of the UNICEF National committee of Slovenia. She has been for 20 years engaged in children's rights through everyday experience with regard to the psychosocial problems of children.

Moulay Hasson Tall is educator and affiliated with Defence for Children International (DCI), Section Mali.

Félicité Talon Ahouandogbo is chairperson of Defence for Children International (DCI), Section Bénin, Cotonou.

Göran Therborn is Professor of Sociology at the University of Göteborg, Institute of Sociology, Sweden. He is working in the fields of comparative crossnational macrosociology, public policy and social theory.

Laura Theytaz-Bergman is a human rights lawyer and Co-ordinator of the NGO-Group for the Convention on the Rights of the Child, Geneva, Switzerland.

R.N. Trivedi is a Senior Advocate and former Advocate General, Uttar Pradesh, Lucknow, India.

Ankie Vandekerckhove works in the legal service of Child & Family, focusing on matters of family law and children's rights, Brussels, Belgium.

Lieven Vandenberghe is Administrator-general of Child & Family, Brussels, Belgium.

Jan Van Gils is the director of the Research Centre Childhood and Society, Meise, Belgium.

Anke van Keulen is affiliated with the Project agency 'MUTANT', an agency for innovation in methodology and management, Utrecht, The Netherlands. She is a specialist in methodical work with (im)migrant parents and children, intercultural management and support in child care.

Jeroen Van Nieuwenhove is research associate in Constitutional Law at the University of Leuven, Faculty of Law, Belgium.

Jan Van Susteren is Director of Bureau INSTAP, Oosthuizen, the Netherlands. He developed on the basis of his experiences the method "Working with Meeting Points".

María Eugenia Villareal is president of Defence for Children International (DCI), Section Guatemala.

Edu Willemse is a staffmember of the International Dialogues Foundation, The Hague, The Netherlands.

Dieter Windels is a social worker and works at the University of Ghent, Faculty of Psychology and Educational Sciences, Department of Orthopedagogics – Special Education, Belgium.

PART ONE

SAMIR SANAD BASTA

Foreword

> Using children as a cutting edge of human rights generally, in our many ongoing efforts in diverse fields of development, would contribute more to international peace and security, and more to democracy, development and the environment – more to preventing crises and conflicts – in a shorter period of time at a far lower costs than any other set of doable actions aimed at remedying global problems on the threshold of the 21st century.
>
> (James P. Grant's address to the World Conference on Human Rights, Vienna, 21 June 1993)

I think that Mr. James P. Grant, our Executive Director, would agree that despite great advances in reaching some of the goals of the World Summit for Children, never before have so many people been talking about the importance of respecting the rights of the child and yet never before have certain children's rights been so widely and so openly violated. And when rights are violated, the first step has been taken on the parth to social unrest and internal strife. This in turn will cause a regression in many of the educational and health goals to which UNICEF has committed itself.

Although monitoring alone cannot hope to stem the tide of children's rights violations, effective and independent monitoring nonetheless plays two essential roles in international efforts to protect and assist children:
– it tells us what is happening,
– it makes children rights better known, for monitoring and advocacy must come together.

Monitoring is traditionally implemented at many levels: *international* with the mechanisms set in place by the United Nations, *regional* with for instance the European Strategy for Children that is currently being developed, *national* with governmental plans of action, and at *sub-national* level with NGOs, grassroots organizations and communities. However, this order could and should be made more flexible. Why should NGOs only monitor at sub-national level? Why are regional bodies *not* more interested in monitoring

E. Verhellen (ed.), Monitoring Children's Rights, 3–5.
© 1996 *Kluwer Law International. Printed in the Netherlands.*

individual child rights? The essential point is that we should decide on *who* should monitor *what*. Specific countries may necessitate specific teams of experts while others, already having a good NGO base, may not need outside expertise. It would perhaps be desirable to draw up a list of priority countries. Another important issue is whether basic rights such as access to optimal health care and education should not first be in place before we jump to the monitoring of other rights.

Among the various mechanisms set up to undertake monitoring at the international level, the most promiment is the Committee on the Rights of the Child with which, taking advantage of its strategic location in Geneva, the UNICEF Office for Europe has built a close working relationship. In conjunction with the Centre for Human Rights. Our Office offers constructive input and assistance to the Committee. In particular, we have raised funds for increased administrative support to enable the Committee to review more State reports at each session. The UNICEF Office for Europe is also in the process of assisting the Centre for Human Rights to establish a data base on children's rights initially with the main aim of servicing the Committee but ultimately available to all concerned organizations.

As well as the Committee on the Rights of the Child, a special mention should be made of the work of the Special Rapporteur on the Sale of Children, Child Prostitution and Child Pornography. His resignation – instigated essentially by the lack of resources put at his disposal to enable him to carry out his mandate effectively – was a great loss for the cause of children and we very much hope that his successor will be provided with the necessary resources.

UNICEF National Committees, most of which are in Europe, also play a very important role in the monitoring of children's rights by virtue of their autonomy and sometimes provide inputs to pre-sessional working groups for the Committee on the Rights of the Child as to develop questions to governments at the official sessions.

Many mechanisms and bodies have been set up within the United Nations system which include as an implicit or explicit aspect of their mandate consideration of children's rights: for example, the Committee set up to monitor the Covenants on Economic, Social and Cultural Rights and on Civil and Political Rights, and the Working Group of the Sub-Commission dealing inter alia with sexual exploitation of children and child labour. Unfortunately, their work is not well known and needs to be consolidated and followed up by greater political will. The question again is why is their work not better known?

It is essential also that a knowledge base should be created to avoid duplication and increase effectiveness. UNICEF and its various partners, UN bodies, NGOs and academic institutes are presently working to establish and information exchange network which will help rationalize and reinforce the work of all concerned. A directory providing basic information on the work being done within Europe on the Convention on the Rights of the Child is in preparation.

In Juni 1994, following a meeting with the Social, Health and Family Affairs Committee of the Council of Europe, parliamentarians, eminent child experts, United Nations agencies and NGOs, a declaration was adopted, that called upon the 32 member states and 9 observer nations to put children first and to fully implement the Convention on the Rights of the Child through 14 specific fields of action. This European Strategy for Children should help at the European as well as international levels to implement and monitor child rights. It is to be based on a comprehensive analysis of regional concerns, to establish achievable goals and objectives and to identify identicators for progress – which will assist in monitoring how well Europe is doing on child rights. Europe is now facing escalating divorce rates, increasing rates of unemployment, of child proverty, of drug and alcohol dependency and of teenage suicide. In addition, laws on immigration and minotity discrimination cry out for better monitoring. These issues and others must be tackled comprehensively and systematically. A thorough and disaggregated analysis of the situation in each country is needed to help us define comprehensive national child policy action plans.

The development of this Strategy has already inspired national action such as a round table organized by the National Children's Bureau, London, and at the beginning of December 1994 experts participating in Madrid in a conference organized by the Council of Europe on the evolution of the role of children in family life agreed to cooperate in drawing up a first outline of the European Strategy for Children which will also serve as a model for other parts of the world. Each region may also have to specialize in and about why certain articles are the most violated (although all must initially be monitored). In some countries, particular attention may be given to the ostracization of gypsies, in others to the lack of equal opportunities for girls.

We must also remember that 1995 will be the start of the Decade of Human Rights Education and we should ask ourselves how these rights should and will be monitored.

EUGEEN VERHELLEN

Monitoring Children's Rights

INTRODUCTION

On November 20th 1989, the UN General Assembly without a dessenting vote adopted the Convention on the Rights of the Child. By September 2nd 1990, less than a year later, it has already entered into force, having been ratified by the required number (20) of States Parties pursuant to article 49, 1. Little more than five years later, the Convention had entered into force in most UN member states. Universal ratification, called for by the World Conference on Human Rights (Vienna 1993), is not far off. Only a few number of countries have not yet ratified it, which is unique in the history of human rights instruments. It is therefore reasonable to assume that there is broad consensus in the international community on starting to take the position of children in society seriously. In other words, although the Convention is a victory in itself, it is also a starting point for more work to be done.

Extremely intense political, social and scientific efforts to improve the position of children are converging rapidly, centered on the Convention on the Rights of the Child. Indeed, the same applies to efforts by the scientific community, since the Convention, by virtue of its comprehensive nature, covers all areas of society, and therefore also touches upon branches of science essential to children. Improving the position of children has thus become an interdisciplinary activity.

However the unique success of the Convention, which has made it a pole of attraction, has also led to an increased burden being placed on monitoring provision. The situation is such that it forces us as a matter of urgency to explore, develop and implement guarantees of effective monitoring of implementation of the Convention's provisions. In the end, rights are only effective when implemented.

There is a whole range of systems for providing guarantees on children's rights. They can be subdivided into what we might call the *legally binding* and the *socially binding* systems of guarantees.

All monitoring derives its binding nature, i.e. its authority, from the quality requirements it imposes, which must be of the highest order.

E. Verhellen (ed.), Monitoring Children's Rights, 7–19.
© 1996 *Kluwer Law International. Printed in the Netherlands.*

I. SOCIALLY BINDING MEASURES

International conventions are part of so-called hard law, i.e. they are binding. In an international context, however, there are often limits to their enforcement. This applies to the Convention on the Rights of the Child. There is a danger that the Convention will be interpreted as a declaration (of intent), the consequence being that it does not bring to light contradictions in the social landscape in which it is to be implemented. Tensions only emerge through implementation of the Convention. Serious implementation will therefore require enormous effort.

Generating more respect for children and thus improving their living conditions is described in the Convention as a *continuous* task. Viewed in this light, *reporting* can have an important part to play. It must take place initially after two years, and thereafter every five, which means it is a useful way of focusing society's attention and debate on children's rights in the country concerned. Reporting is therefore a means of actively improving the position of children.

The moral authority of this sort of monitoring, and therefore the guarantee that rights will be implemented, depends on the quality and effectiveness with which it is carried out. The international community has paid attention to monitoring quality requirements in the Convention on the Rights of the Child itself. Article 43, 2 states that the Committee on the Rights of the Child, which is to be established, shall consist of 1) experts of high moral standard and 2) recognised competence in the field covered by the Convention 3) who shall serve in their personal capacity. So far, in its actions, the Committee has met these quality requirements.

The care with which the Committee analyses country reports is therefore an important contribution to practical implementation of children's rights.

This does not change the fact however that two questions which concern reporting still await an answer: *how* is reporting carried out and by *whom* and *what* should the report contain.

A. How and by Whom

Formally speaking, according to article 44, 1 and 2, , states are accountable to the Committee for implementation of the Convention, in the same way that they are responsible for implementing children's rights contained in the Convention. This brings about a strange – but in international conventions not unusual – situation where states have to exert control over themselves and thus become judge and jury!

Although it is therefore perfectly feasible for a state to allow a civil servant or an interdepartmental group of civil servants to staple a report together at random, such an approach would show considerable lack of respect.

While formally reporting is an obligation on the authorities, implementation and monitoring are the responsibility of *everyone*. There is therefore good reason to believe that a broad base within society for the monitoring exercise may constitute in itself a major contribution to practical implementation of children's rights. The Convention itself provides a number of reference points. First of all there is the extremely significant *obligation to provide information* in article 42. Knowledge of children's rights is obviously the first guarantee of practical implementation. Moreover there is the obligation, derived from the Convention, to involve the public at large in implementation and monitoring.

Indeed, according to article 44, 6 states have to make their reports widely available to the public in their own countries.

If we accept that a broad base within society for monitoring is of such importance, organising it cannot be left to chance. This is why monitoring has to a matter for an *independent* body, a standing monitoring structure (SMC). The Convention describes rights mainly in terms of objectives and guidelines, rather than clearly defining them. Therefore continuous dialectic action has to remain possible.

Traditional mechanisms for exerting influence, such as the right to vote, lobbying, market mechanisms, etc. do not apply in the case of children. Children therefore need a new, distinct system of monitoring, and new ways of protecting their interests. The state has to take into account a whole range of interests, not always consistent with each other and in some cases, even conflicting with the interests of children.

NGOs, which were very much involved in drawing up the Convention, have already indicated their intention of keeping a close eye on reporting quality. They can do so under the terms of article 44, 6, referred to above, which requires states to make their reports widely available in their own country. The Committee on the Rights of the Child has also decided to promote this watchdog function and to be prepared to accept criticism as well as additional information from NGOs.

Indeed, a variety of proposals have been made designed to make full, organised and constructive use of commitment in society to the cause of children's rights for the purpose of monitoring implementation of the Convention. Following the example of the International Committee on the Rights of the Child, a national committee could be set up in each country. Such committees could even be created at every relevant policy level within the state, going right down to local level.

In this context the question arises of the *quality requirements* to be met by such bodies if they are to establish themselves as permanent and authoritative, and to be in a position to continue focussing attention on children's rights in their own country.

In different ways, these committees should also be a forum for children to express their views, if children are really to be encouraged to *participate actively* in all sorts of councils, and to make their voices heard in all areas relevant to them. First and foremost children wish to be respected. As far as children are concerned, the right to respect and to full citizenship is still not the norm. Many structural changes are still needed if this is to change.

Self-organisation for example, although a right granted by the Convention, poses legal problems. Children cannot exert their right to independence and self-determination.

However children do turn out to have a number of specific qualities which can be used. It is of great significance that respect for children's views, as described in article 12, is considered by the Committee on the Rights of the Child as a general principle. Article 12 gives children who are capable of forming their own views the right to express those views in all matters affecting them. It also states that due weight is to be given to those views. To ensure practical implementation of this right, the article states that children shall be given the opportunity to be heard in any judicial and adminstrative proceedings affecting them. Therefore there can be no doubt that children should also have a voice in monitoring implementation of the Convention.

Various models have already been worked out to organise monitoring children's living conditions and implementation of the Convention.

1. The state draws up the reports (as stated in the Convention) and a standing monitoring committee (SMC) examines them carefully and suggests critical questions to the international Committee of Experts monitoring the Convention;
2. The state draws up the reports and a standing monitoring committee (SMC) examines them critically and suggests improvements to the reports and to children's living conditions;
3. The state draws up the reports and invites a standing monitoring committee (SMC) to suggest improvements to the reports and to children's living conditions;
4. The state invites a standing monitoring committee (SMC) to monitor children's living conditions closely (this would bring about a situation of parallelism with the international committee) and to draw up the report *jointly*;
5. Within states parties this kind of structure could be set up at various policy levels: national, regional and local.

Whichever model is chosen, the question always arises as to the quality of monitoring both as a process and as a product (see below C.). Continuous and close monitoring of children's living conditions is in fact essential if these living conditions are to improve. It is also a condition which has to be met, to carry out the obligation contained in article 44,1 (reports to be drawn up initially after two years and then every five years) of describing the state of play in the country involved.

B. Content

There is not only the formal issue of who should draw up the report, there is also the question of what the *content* should be. One would expect there to be an easy answer to this question. However there is not. We do not have comprehensive knowledge of children. In fact, our knowledge of children is rather limited.

First of all there is insufficient knowledge of *children as meaning-makers*. In fact, we know very little of how children interpret events, of how they make meaning. Research still has to get off the ground. We can even go further and say that simple demographical data are often unavailable or out of date. This is where it would be possible to involve children in research on children (children as research subjects). Indeed, according to articles 12 and 13 of the Convention, children have the right to make their views known. Moreover, in combination with article 17, as users of information, they have the right to know what information has been collected concerning them and they have the right to make their views on this information known.

Secondly, we have only limited knowledge of *children as a permanent social group*. Research from the point of view of adults, but using the child as unit of observation (an ethnography of children), will contribute to better understanding of, and debate on, children's structural position in society. Information which we do have is fragmented, because it only contains data which is considered relevant from the viewpoint of adults.

For a long time, it was assumed we knew a lot about children, but gradually we are beginning to realise our knowledge is only partial and concerns mostly problem areas. It is difficult to obtain information which has particular relevance from the point of view of the child. In this area our knowledge is limited.

C. A National "Standing Monitoring Committee": Tasks and Quality Requirements

Whichever of the above-mentioned models (supra A.) is chosen, a "Standing Monitoring Committee" will have to carry out some important tasks and comply with strict quality standards. This has been examined in a study carried out with the support of the King Bauduin Foundation in Belgium. Below we shall give a brief description of its conclusions regarding these tasks and the quality requirements.

1. Tasks

Promoting *children's themes* in society as a whole can be regarded as a primary and global description of the tasks of an SMC.

The SMC has a *structural* task to carry out, which has to cover both the substructure and the superstructure.

The objective should be not only to *change the law*, but also to bring about in-depth *cultural changes*, i.e. changes in *mentality* and in the views of the population.

Ideas rooted in the consciousness of the public at large are of immense importance in improving children's living conditions. The most important ways of influencing public opinion are by disseminating information and by taking well-founded positions.

The attitudes of the public at large are of immense importance in determining whether and how children's living conditions can be improved. The most important ways of influencing public opinion are dissemination of information and putting a case to back up one's arguments.

However, legislation is also important, since in our culture legislation is regarded as the real means of influencing living conditions. Besides dissemination of information and putting forward arguments and concrete policy proposals, lobbying is another important means of influencing legislation and policy. Changes in the law are needed, inter alia, to increase children's access to the court, to enable them to defend their own rights and be heard. It is always useful to link changes in the law to information on the reasons why the changes are needed.

Improving legal protection and promoting practical enforcement of children's rights by children themselves are other priorities, in view of the structural function of the SMC. Children themselves implementing fundamental freedoms is a novelty in the Convention. Being able to claim the exercise of rights means, first of all, knowing that they exist. In this area there is still a great deal to be done.

The different components of this structural function are *interactive* and *interdependent*.

The Convention's provisions are abstract. As we have already pointed out, this means that the Convention can be read as a statement (of intent). The consequence is that the Convention does not reveal tensions in the society in which it is to be implemented. The tensions are only revealed when the Convention is implemented. Serious implementation of the Convention will therefore require considerable effort. It can be a task for the SMC to keep highlighting this arduous social obligation.

The SMC must be a *vehicle for children themselves* to express their views, rather than seeking to speak for them. The child, as a structural entity, is as much a part of society as any other group. And yet children are usually regarded as "on their way" to being integrated in society, a society of adults. If children are regarded as structural entities, the group of which they form part must be defined according to some common factors in the way they live. Even if the power difference between children and adults were to disappear, children and adults would still hold views characteristic of their group, because of their different social roles. The concepts and views of children differ from those of adults, but no longer be considered inferior. We must consider, however, to what extent it is possible to involve children in efforts to promote their rights in a society which believes that children should "be seen but not heard".

This is why methods have to be developed, allowing children to tell their own story using their own concepts.

Support for parents will also be a priority of the SMC. In fact, anything which can be done to enable parents to function more effectively as parents will ultimately be beneficial to their children.

An approach based on *principles* and not on individual cases must constitute the most important characteristic of the SMC. In such a context, individual cases can be dealt with only where they are representative of "all" children in share similar circumstances. An approach based on principles makes it possible to look beyond potentially emotionally charged situations. Monitoring children's interests must therefore take place *collectively*.

The SMC has to ensure that *all relevant policy levels* are covered. Many problems are global, but global policies are still few and far between. The Convention can be regarded as a plea for such policies.

Children have to know and understand the Convention. Promoting children's understanding can be a task for a SMC, and also increasing *public awareness* of the need for greater respect for children's rights. It is hardly surprising that some people should doubt the need for monitoring the way children live. The argument for this point of view is that parents are best placed to ensure respect for children's rights and interests, and that we already have a well-structured network of (welfare) provisions, which should ensure that there is adequate monitoring of children's living conditions. But reality shows these arguments to be incorrect.

2. Quality Requirements
If a SMC is to do all this, it must comply with strict quality-criteria.

a) General Quality Requirements
The monitoring mechanism, provided for by the Convention, can become an effective tool for implementation, provided it integrates the four basic strategies of ombudswork for children.

1. The intention of article 44, 6 is to provide a broad foundation for monitoring within society. The *development of networks* in the field of children's rights is encouraged and regarded as an important quality requirement for monitoring. Networks, both of children and of adults, are extremely important for keeping up the momentum and focussing our attention to and action on children's rights. Networks are essential as sources of information, as support for individual initiatives and as instruments to ensure a smooth and rapid exchange of information. Children must also be put in a position to share their experiences with other children, and particularly with children from other cultures.

2. At the moment the issue of children's position in society is receiving a great

deal of attention. More and more interest is shown in the rights of the child. We can learn a lot from the experience derived from adult projects aimed at improving the position of children. This is the kind of project we most frequently encounter and is very much in line with the spirit of the Convention (the best interests of the child being the guiding principle). Proper monitoring must take into account the experience of *child advocacy*.

3. Our attitude to children appears to have considerable impact on the way we interpret children's rights, and assess the need for policy changes. Our child image determines our reaction to practical situations. At the moment in the West child images seem to be undergoing change. Data on the child as a social category and on children's views are therefore urgently needed. The *study of the child* will therefore be another important requirement for proper monitoring. The monitoring body will be faced with a number of difficult questions: is the child a person, in legal terms, or an object of others' desire and power? Should we regard the child as a creature to be protected by society, or as a partner with a full right to participate? Do we not all need protection, without this being regarded as a reason to deny us the right to participate? While the right of children to protection and well-being does not affect the balance of power between adults and children, freedoms do. A very solid case will therefore have to be put together if these rights are ever to be implemented in practice.

Present child images can roughly be subdivided into three categories, each stressing different actions to be taken:
- childhood can be considered as forming part of the private sphere and as a transition to adulthood. Here the stress will be on protection.
- children can also be regarded as a separate group, a permanent stratum of society. In this approach, childhood is seen as a social and political phenomenon and the focus is on the balance of power between adults and children. Policy will be directed at promoting independence.
- the intergenerational perspective stresses the need to study and balance the needs and views of different generations. Policy will therefore attach equal importance to protection and independence.

4. One of the changes in our child image which seems to be taking place is an increase in attention to children's assertiveness and participation, leading to more stress on the views and feelings of children themselves. Decision makers will have to start thinking about the need to promote children's participation. Experience acquired in the context of children's *self-organisation* will therefore be invaluable for monitoring.

The above-mentioned quality requirements are already in use in the strategies of the children's rights movement. They are also regarded as key strategies in ombudswork. In order to assist implementation and thus contribute to improving the position of children in society, these four key elements will also have to be called on when monitoring the Convention.

b) Specific Quality Requirements
1. Official status
Conferring official status would indicate acknowledgement of the need for special attention to the rights of children, and of the importance of the subject matter. It would equally demonstrate that the monitoring body was acknowledged as a permanent interlocutor.

2. Stability
Stability can be achieved by anchoring the monitoring body in legislation, and by clearly defining its powers.

3. Authority and credibility
Authority must be founded on quality: the monitoring body must display high standards of competence and performance. Its affirmations must be based on fact, not on hearsay, intuition or individual opinion. Making no statement at all is preferable to one with no basis in fact. Cases must be built on data obtained from multi-disciplinary research. Obviously this approach requires a great deal of factual knowledge. Wherever necessary, scientific help should be sought.

4. Impartiality and independence
The monitoring body must deal exclusively with the rights of the child. The rights of the child have to be its focus, aim and sole point of departure. There must not be a hidden agenda, and no other interests can be allowed to play a part. The debate must be lively and objective. Other interests should not be served under the guise of promoting children's rights. Conflicts of interest must be avoided at all costs. There must be no party political interference. Involvement in disputes within individual families is also ruled out. The greatest possible autonomy and independence is essential. Nobody must be in a position to prevent the monitoring body dealing with a case. Autonomy need not, however, stand in the way of state recognition, which is desirable as an indication that the state also takes the view that monitoring children's rights is a necessity. Appointment of the monitoring body by an independent institution, such as Parliament, would offer immense advantages, guaranteeing both its autonomy and its authority. However, official recogniton must not result in financial dependence. The monitoring body must be guaranteed proper funding, and sufficient staff to do its job properly.

5. Accountability
Autonomy does not preclude accountability. However the monitoring body must be accountable only for fulfilling its general obligations and must be accountable directly to Parliament.

6. Comprehensive nature
The activities of the monitoring body must cover the whole of society, i.e. every aspect of the situation of children. The aim must be to achieve a full,

integrated picture. In each and every case, the best interests of the child must be the prime consideration. Drawing up a list of potential tasks would serve only to limit its scope.

7. Approachability and openness

If the monitoring body is to function as a catalyst and enhance the debate in society, it must be an open institution, which can be approached directly. It must have regular contacts with individuals and organisations. Everybody, even the civil service, must have the right to approach the monitoring body in an informal manner. The monitoring body must also take into account the views of children themselves. Approachability and openness are all the more important in view of the monitoring body's task of being the voice of the child. It must be an open and friendly institution rather than an anonymous bureaucracy. It is also important for children to be put in a position to participate fully in monitoring the way they live.

8. Purposefulness

The number of activities is less important than their purpose. Activities have to aim at achieving practical results for children. This will require perseverance.

9. Broad powers

Among other things, the monitoring body must have far-reaching powers of inquiry, and therefore must have easy access to files and information. It must be able to require official bodies dealing with children to hand over information on request. If necessary confidentiality must be waived. The monitoring body must also have the right to be heard in all administrative activities relevant to children. Furthermore, it is important for the monitoring body to have full right of initiative, including that of making declarations on any subject at any time.

10. Confidentiality

If necessary, the monitoring body must have the right to protect its sources.

11. Relationship with the media

The monitoring body must pay special attention to its relationship with the media. It is important for it to become known in the right way, i.e. as a civic institution, concerned with human rights and dealing with children's competence rather than with problem cases. Such efforts must be ongoing and directed at each new generation, using inter alia the mass media in an attempt to target specific groups (parents, professionals, adults, etc.).

12. Realism

Ideal solutions may not be attainable, which is why they meet only with general public indifference. A realistic attitude has far more chance of achieving an impact.

13. International co-operation
It goes without saying that children's living conditions are not determined solely by what happens in their own country. To function effectively, what is done locally must go hand in hand with, and be inspired by, what is being done world-wide.

The quality requirements resulting from this study may well turn out to be very useful in stimulating national and regional (i.e. European) discussion on ways of using the Convention pro-actively, and particularly on monitoring.

II. LEGALLY BINDING MONITORING

We have shown above how the specific monitoring mechanism, described in articles 42 to 45 of the Convention, can result in socially binding measures.
Despite the fact that this kind of monitoring offers ample opportunity to mobilise impressive social forces in favour of children's rights and that it is still the most dominant monitoring instrument in the international sphere, we should not forget that there are also a number of legally binding forms of monitoring which can be used in the implementation of children's rights. Here too the binding character of monitoring is dependent on its quality. In this case however the fundamental principles of the legal system (principle of legality, principle of proportionality, etc.) ensure the quality of effective monitoring. If necessary, individual citizens can use the powerful authority of States and sometimes international bodies to enforce their rights. Therefore legal forms of monitoring are extremely powerful. However one has to ask oneself to what extent legal forms of monitoring fit in with the objective of achieving progress in implementation of children's rights. Since the Convention does not itself provide such legal forms of monitoring, they can only apply in individual States Parties. This is where several aspects come into play. I will examine three of them.

A. *Self-executing Force*

There are only a few countries which have a so-called "monistic system", and consider the law as a whole. This legal system contains the principle of self-executing force, meaning that if provisions from international conventions meet a number of criteria, citizens can invoke them directly in court merely on the basis of the ratification of the conventions by their country. In the area of self-executing force there are many developments regarding the Convention on the Rights of the Child. Rulings, both recognising and contesting the Convention's self-executing force, are being handed down (cf. France, Belgium).
Does the nature of the Convention's provisions allow them to be self-executing? As we know the Convention contains both provisions on first

generation human rights (political and civil rights) and provisions on second generation human rights (social, economic and cultural rights). These generations differ in nature and traditionally apply different monitoring systems. What significance might be ascribed to concepts such as "standstill" in view of the Convention's self-executing force? This issue, which is primarily a legal and technical matter, is being hotly debated at the moment.

B. The Incorporation of Provisions in Domestic Law

And there is more: states may also incorporate international treaty provisions in their domestic law.

This happens mainly in those countries which have a "dualistic legal system". In these countries international provisions apply only when they have been incorporated into domestic law.

But in other countries with a monistic system or which have intermediate systems, the incorporation of international treaty provisions in national law is often considered the most unambiguous way of implementing them. Despite this there does not seem to be a systematic approach to this issue and many questions remain unanswered.

Which domestic law provisions refer to the Convention on the Rights of the Child? To what extent have these proved successful in achieving progress regarding implementation of children's rights? Has the criterion of the comprehensive nature of the Convention been met? Should there not be a "child impact assessment" in every legislative procedure? Which other domestic law provisions can be regarded as implementing provisions of the Convention, without there being explicit reference to it? What links of this kind have been present in reports submitted to the Committee on the Rights of the Child? What links have been made in case law and jurisprudence?

These questions indicate that urgent systematic research will be necessary to stimulate effective monitoring.

C. Guarantees Offered by Other International Instruments

The wording of some provisions of the Convention is regarded as too general to allow legally binding forms of monitoring.

Although the Convention can be considered a comprehensive instrument, in which, in other words, all aspects and areas of children's life are covered, other international provisions can also be used effectively to implement children's rights. Over the last few years children have been making increasing use of the European Convention on Human Rights (ECHR). This is an extremely powerful international instrument which can be used for monitoring children's rights, as it recognises the individual's right to complain. Which elements from the Children's Rights Convention can use binding guarantees taken over from the ECHR? To what extent has there been a follow-up to Recommendation

1121, which provides inter alia for an Additional Protocol to the ECHR? What other international instruments may also be used to support the Convention? We are thinking of possibilities such as conventions from the The Hague Conference on International Private Law, e.g. the Convention on International Adoption.

CONCLUSION

There can therefore be no doubt that monitoring, both in its legally binding and in its socially binding aspects, is indeed the Achilles' heel of the Convention, but it also allows for a pro-active approach to practical implementation of children's rights. Ongoing and dynamic monitoring can be a powerful impetus to making systematic progress in this area. All groups in society, and particularly scientists, must do their bit. The Convention (article 44,1) calls for progress in ensuring that the rights it enshrines can be enjoyed, which means academics too have a job to do. An interdisciplinary approach is needed first and foremost. The debate on monitoring the Convention may in this way expand into an attractive and exemplary debate on human rights conventions in general. If the quality of democracy is to be enhanced such debates are urgently required.

PHILIP ALSTON

Establishing Accountability: Some Current Challenges in Relation to Human Rights Monitoring

I. INTRODUCTION

Although the focus of the present volume is on the monitoring of children's rights, it is appropriate for that topic to be examined in a broader perspective within the overall framework of the international human rights system. In that setting, those who are primarily concerned with children's rights have some things to learn from their counterparts in other areas of human rights and many things to teach them. This paper cannot seek to deal comprehensively or even systematically with the challenge of human rights monitoring. Instead, the focus is on several specific challenges which are of particular current interest within the United Nations framework.

Such a focus is inevitably rather narrow. This is not in any way meant to imply that this is where the real centre of attention is, or should be. Indeed, there is no doubt that it is the national level which offers the greatest potential and has the most important role to play in the monitoring of human rights. This is very well illustrated by both the "four-step implementation strategy" and the list of the different dimensions of monitoring provided in the excellent contribution to this volume by James Himes.[1] For the most part, however, those broader issues will not be addressed in the present paper.

II. "MONITORING" AND THE ROLE OF THE TREATY BODIES

It is symptomatic of the ambivalence of governments towards international monitoring that the Convention on the Rights of the Child, which effectively constitutes the state of the art in terms of human rights treaties, does not contain any clear, explicit statement of the role to be played by the Committee on

---

[1] Himes, James R., Monitoring Children's Rights: Cutting Through the Confusion and Planning for Effective Action, this volume, 113-127.

E. Verhellen (ed.), Monitoring Children's Rights, 21–31.
© 1996 *Kluwer Law International. Printed in the Netherlands.*

the Rights of the Child. Article 43 of the Convention indicates that the Committee is to be established "[f]or the purpose of examining the progress made by States Parties in achieving the realization of the obligations undertaken" in the Convention. Beyond that indication, the nature of the Committee's overall role is to be deduced from the means by which it is to accomplish this "examination" of progress. Thus, States parties must submit to it "reports on the measures they have adopted which give effect to the rights recognized herein and on the progress made in the enjoyment of those rights" (art. 44(1)). The reports are to "indicate factors and difficulties, if any, affecting the degree of fulfilment of the obligations under the ... Convention" and should "also contain sufficient information to provide the Committee with a comprehensive understanding of the implementation of the Convention in the country concerned" (art. 44(2)). The Committee is also empowered to "request from States Parties further information relevant to the implementation of the Convention" (art. 44(4)) and to submit "reports on its activities" to the General Assembly (art. 44(5)).

A further indication of the Committee's role is provided by article 45 which enables it: to invite UN agencies and other bodies to provide it with expert advice, to request that specific studies be undertaken for it by the Secretary-General, and most importantly, to make "suggestions and general recommendations" based on information received pursuant to articles 44 and 45. The *chapeau* under which these activities are listed provides an indication of the overall purposes for which they are to be undertaken. They are "[i]n order to foster the effective implementation of the Convention and to encourage international co-operation in the field covered by the Convention" (art. 45).

Thus the Convention does not use the term "monitoring" nor any of the other roughly equivalent terms that have come to be associated with the functions performed by what are known in human rights circles as "the treaty bodies". What then are the reasons for, and the significance of, this lacuna?

What is most striking about these formulations is the extent to which the terms used are determinedly neutral. Thus for example we see the use of:

- *"fostering" effective implementation* (instead of, for example, "ensuring", or "actively promoting", or "overseeing" etc.),
- *examining the "progress made"* (as opposed to "monitoring compliance with obligations"), and
- *considering "factors and difficulties"* (rather than "identifying violations", or "ascertaining that a State party is genuinely unable to fulfill its obligations").

One reason why such terms are used is the obsession within the United Nations arena with precedents. Another is simply political. The precedent dimension derives from the unwritten, but nonetheless iron, rule that once a particular formulation has been agreed upon in one United Nations context, it must be used in another, no matter how inappropriate that may be, unless the proponents of change can mount an overwhelming case in favour of innovation. In the case of the Convention on the Rights of the Child the early texts envisaged either no, or at best minimalist, monitoring. By the time that issue came to be dealt with in the Working Group there had been a financial crisis in the United Nations, the sessions of some United Nations bodies had been cancelled (notably that of the Sub-Commission on Prevention of Discrimination and Protection of Minorities), two of the treaty bodies were in financial difficulties (the Committee against Torture and especially the Committee on the Elimination of Racial Discrimination), and there was little appetite either for expenditure or innovation. The easy path of following the precedents was followed and the terminology used was adapted only slightly from that used in what was generally perceived to be the weaker of the formulations used in the two Covenants – that of the International Covenant on Economic, Social and Cultural Rights.[2]

The political reason for choosing that option related essentially to the reluctance of governments to spell out the extent to which the Convention on the Rights of the Child was seen to be introducing a more demanding, more authentic element of international accountability than is specifically provided for in other existing instruments. Thus the language used amounts to an acknowledgement of the general principle of accountability combined with a preference for avoiding the need to define its nature and limits.

As a result of the relative unhelpfulness of the formulations used, there are three possible sources which can help us to understand the limits and possibilities of the notion of "monitoring" as it applies to the Convention on the Rights of the Child.

A. *The Views of Governments*

The first consists of the views expressed by individual governments and the decisions taken by them collectively in relation to the powers of the Committee. While such views and decisions cannot formally bind the Committee, they help to set the context and perhaps even the parameters within which the Committee's own approach will be formulated. But in practice this source is of limited assistance. States rarely pronounce themselves on what they see as the legitimate or appropriate limits to the Committee's powers. One notable exception was the spirited, negative response by Germany and a small handful of other countries to the General Comment adopted by the Human Rights Committee in 1984 in which nuclear weapons were characterized as being "among the greatest threats to the right to life".[3]

---

[2] Although, it should be noted that, apart from the specific issue under review, the Convention does innovate in several important respects, notably in relation to articles 42, 45.

[3] General Comment 14 (23) of 1984, on article 6 of the Covenant. UN doc. HRI/GEN/1/Rev.1, p. 18.

Another potential source of feedback is the Meeting of States Parties to the relevant Convention or the Covenant on Civil and Political Rights. But these are held irregularly and their competence has so far been auto-restricted to dealing with largely procedural rather than substantive matters (which, I might add, is how it should be).

The resolutions adopted by the Commission on Human Rights, the Economic and Social Council and the General Assembly provide another opportunity for States to express their views. For the most part, however, these resolutions have rarely purported to limit the powers of committees. While it could be argued that they do so by default, in the sense that what is not generally endorsed is discouraged, this is almost certainly overstating the importance which States parties to the relevant treaties attribute to such relatively pro forma resolutions. They are probably of greater significance in relation to administrative and financial issues than to the substantive question of defining the boundaries of monitoring. Except for the almost violent reaction of the General Assembly to the suggestion by the Committee on the Elimination of Discrimination against Women that the impact of Islamic principles on women's rights be studied, it is difficult to recall any particular rebukes handed out by the political organs to the treaty bodies. While this degree of relative autonomy is entirely appropriate, it means that the views of States are usually not going to be a very fertile source from which to identify what are perceived to be the appropriate limits to monitoring.

B. Notions of Accountability in Other Areas of International Law

A second possible source is the broader overall monitoring framework which has been developed in other areas of international law. In other words, we might assume that what governments have been prepared to accept in fields such as the environment, social development, economic policy or disarmament can provide guidance as to the general assumptions that might underlie their acceptance of accountability obligations in the human rights field generally, and specifically in relation to children's rights. In fact, however, such an inquiry into the transferability of concepts and assumptions from one arena of international accountability to another yields rather curious results.

Perhaps most importantly for present purposes is the fact that determinedly different terminology is used in each area. Thus, in the area of weapons control and disarmament (such as the 1992 Chemical Weapons Convention), the international community's functions are often encapsulated in the term "verification". One meaning of this term is, according to the Oxford English Dictionary, "[t]he action of establishing or testing the truth or correctness of a fact, theory, statement, etc., by means of special investigation or comparison of data." It thus has the connotation of being an occasional rather than a continuing process and of assuming that their is a single truth which, as a factual matter, is capable of being definitively ascertained, or verified.

In relation to international labour standards, the International Labour Organization (ILO) has chosen the term "supervision" to describe its accountability functions, although on occasions it has also slipped into the terminology of verification.[4] In its 1994 report, the ILO Committee of Experts on the Application of Conventions and Recommendations states that "there can be no development of international labour standards without effective supervision of it application" (p.13). There is, however, no technical definition within the ILO which indicates the precise parameters of such supervision. *Oxford English Dictionary* definitions of the term include: "[g]eneral management, direction, or control; oversight, superintendence" and "[t]he action of reading through for correction, revision by a superior authority". Some of the elements in these definitions, such as "control" or "correction by a superior authority" would almost certainly be rejected by States if put forward by way of explanation of the principles underlying the ILO's supervisory process. Moreover, the characterisation of some of the ILO's labour standards activities as "supervisory" (such as the "general surveys" drawn up under article 19 of the ILO Constitution, or the "direct contacts" undertaken between the ILO and governments to assist in the implementation of obligations under relevant Conventions) is regularly challenged within the ILO Conference.[5] The conclusion to be drawn is that the content of "supervision" within the ILO context is something that must be deduced on the basis of what the Organization actually does (or, less charitably, is able to get away with), rather than of any pre-agreed definition.

Finally, in the area of economic policy, an entirely different term is applied, openly and with relative specificity as to its content, by the International Monetary Fund (IMF). Under Article IV of its Articles of Agreement the IMF is mandated to "exercise firm surveillance over the exchange rate policies of members" and to adopt "specific principles for the guidance of all members with respect to those policies". The principal *Oxford English Dictionary* definition of "surveillance" is the: "[w]atch or guard kept over a person etc., esp. over a suspected person, a prisoner, or the like; often, spying, supervision; less commonly, supervision for the purpose of direction or control, superintendence". While many of these terms would be considered to be too strong by Fund officials, the IMF's own analyses do not seek to portray the exercise as merely one of dialogue and an exchange of views. While regular meetings with government officials of the State concerned serve to elicit the necessary information, the relevant report is prepared by the staff of the IMF. At the individual country level, IMF surveillance is said to:

---

[4] See e.g. "The ILO's role in relation to structural adjustment, including collaboration with the Bretton Woods institutions", ILO doc. GB.261/ESP/1/1, Nov. 1994, para. 16: "It is simple enough to verify ... whether basic labour rights are respected ...".

[5] See, e.g., "Report of the Committee on the Application of Standards", International Labour Conference, Eighty-First Session, Geneva, 1994, 25 *Provisional Record* 13–14.

encourage countries to adopt appropriate economic policies consistent with the member's obligations under the Articles of Agreement so as to provide the basis for sustained noninflationary economic growth. The exercise of surveillance can help to identify issues and problems in a timely manner so that suitable corrective measures may be adopted and, in this way, periods of tension avoided.[6]

In response to pressures from various sources, notably including UNICEF (through the work of Giovanni Andrea Cornia, Richard Jolly and others), the focus is no longer exclusively on macroeconomic policy:

> Relevant structural policies are also examined if these are germane to macroeconomic developments and policies. In recent years, surveillance has taken more account of such topics as regional, social (poverty), industrial, labor market and environmental issues, if these have important implications for macroeconomic policies and performance.[7]

In rather dramatic contrast to terms such as "verification" and "surveillance" we come then to the focus of this paper, "monitoring". The *Oxford English Dictionary* definition captures rather well the essence of the concept as currently applied in the human rights area. A monitor is "[o]ne who admonishes or gives advice or warning to another as to his conduct". "Also (*rare*), one who advises another to do some particular action, an instigator". The general usage of the term to monitor is said to be: "to observe, supervise, or keep under review; to measure or test at intervals esp. for the purpose of regulation or control". This definition seems quite accurate, at least until the final phrase which moves us closer to the assumptions that seem to underlie some of the other concepts, perhaps even including "supervision".

The predictable response of an international lawyer (and perhaps even of one whose vision has not been so distorted!), is to say that the nature of the accountability function inevitably varies with the subject-matter and does little more than reflect the objective requirements that apply in relation to each area (distrust in relation to armaments; the overriding exigencies of economic cooperation in the monetary area, etc.). Hence the foregoing survey of the different terminology employed in different contexts would be seen to be no more than a re-statement of the obvious. What I wish to suggest, however, is that such a response takes far too much for granted in terms of assuming that the status quo has a clear, appropriate and perhaps even inevitable logic to it. Rather, in many respects, a closer probing of the assumptions that underlie the choice of terminology will reveal a set of value judgments that may or may not withstand careful scrutiny from a distance.

This is not the place to develop this analysis further by seeking to identify the relevant values, but the point I want to make is that we should not assume that there are "natural" or "inevitable" limits to either the extent and reach,

---

[6] "Global Changes Underscore Role of Surveillance, *IMF Survey*, August 1994, 7 at 8.
[7] Ibid.

or to the form and methods, of holding States to honour their obligations in relation to human rights. It must suffice to emphasise that our predominant focus should not be on "monitoring", whatever that might mean in a particular context at a particular time, but rather on the principle of accountability. If international human rights law has contributed anything over the past half century it is the twin concepts of the rule of law (in the sense of spelling out specific standards which give content to an otherwise potentially open-ended and amorphous philosophical debate) and the accountability of governments to the international community for the way in which they treat (or permit others to treat) those individuals for whose well-being they are ultimately responsible.

C. The Approach of Other Treaty Bodies: A Process of Continuous Evolution

The third, and by far the most important source which can help us to understand the limits and possibilities of the notion of "monitoring" children's rights, is the overall monitoring framework developed by other treaty bodies and acquiesced in, to use minimalist language, by States.

Experience has shown that international procedures designed to promote respect for human rights have, in most cases, taken a lengthy period of time to attain a level of effectiveness that might be considered satisfactory. The UN's system for monitoring States' compliance with their human rights treaty obligations is no exception in this regard. For twenty years after the convening in 1970 of the inaugural session of the first such treaty body the principal pre-occupation of the expert members of what are now six separate committees, was to establish often rather rudimentary procedures which, while enabling the committees to perform their basic functions, would not make governments feel ill at ease. Indeed the argument was often heard that procedural development needed to be very gradual and avowedly non-threatening so that more governments might be convinced to submit themselves to the relevant monitoring arrangements. As a result, progress was relatively slow and by no means systematic or continuous.

In recent years, however, and indeed only just pre-dating the establishment of the Committee on the Rights of the Child, the work of the various treaty bodies has undergone a radical, but little noticed, transformation. This "quiet revolution" stems not so much from the perseverance or determination of the relevant committees but rather from a conjunction of events well beyond their control. The end of the Cold War has been the principal factor enabling the treaty bodies to transcend the ideological debates that often threatened to paralyse their work[8]. This development has, of course, been of major

---

[8] Indeed, it has frequently been remarked that the absence of United States experts from the committees throughout this period was a blessing in disguise. At least in this respect, the very belated recent moves by the United States to join the treaty system are perfectly timed.

importance in encouraging various States to participate in the treaty system of which they had previously been very wary. But, from the perspective of the treaty bodies, an even more important consequence of the end of the Cold War has been the ability to achieve a consensus on major procedural innovations which were previously blocked. Fortunately East-West tensions have not been replaced by any particular North-South tensions, as has occurred to some extent in other human rights fora. Another key factor favouring a more active role for the treaty bodies is the increasingly more direct, intrusive and sustained media coverage (what might be called the CNN – Cable News Network – phenomenon) of situations involving major denials of respect for human rights.

But while these external factors were probably indispensable catalysts to the changes that are occurring, they would not have been sufficient in themselves. The other essential ingredient has simply been a growing maturity on the part of the key actors. States parties have gradually begun to take their reporting obligations more seriously and have generally come to accept that the committees can and should act in an objective and non-adversarial, but nevertheless probing and forceful, manner. The prevailing ethos within the committees themselves has also attained a significant degree of maturity. Over time, important differences in terms of values, priorities, and perceptions of the appropriate role of monitoring have been greatly reduced. As a sense of shared responsibilities has developed, the impact of potentially divisive factors (nationality, regional affiliation, religion, political ideology etc) has diminished. Similarly the principle of consensus decision-making has tended to be applied in a constructive and sufficiently flexible manner, thus avoiding the pitfalls of a rigid approach to consensus which is capable of conferring a veto power on each member.

This vital evolutionary capacity can best be illustrated by reference to an issue which is of fundamental importance in relation to the Convention on the Rights of the Child. It is the question of reservations by States which limit the obligations they undertake by virtue of becoming a party to the Convention. As a result of sometimes rather sweeping and often very vague reservations by a raft of States, both the Committee on the Elimination of Discrimination Against Women and the Committee on the Rights of the Child have been faced with a major dilemma. By virtue of having developed essentially in the context of reciprocal relations between two or more States designed to further their own interests, traditional international law relating to reservations is at best unhelpful when applied to the human rights field.

Until recently, this had led to a certain paralysis on the part of the treaty bodies as well as of governments. It was assumed that, in the absence of specific provisions in the various treaties for determining the validity or otherwise of a given reservation (or other statement having the same effect), there was little that could be done beyond issuing general appeals to the States concerned to reconsider their approach. Thus, for example, the 1992 Meeting of the Chairpersons of the various treaty bodies, which distinguished itself from previous similar gatherings by focusing determinedly and critically on the issue, observed that "the number, nature and scope of ... reservations ... is cause for alarm". It therefore proposed that, in appropriate cases, the relevant treaty body should request, through the General Assembly or ECOSOC, an advisory opinion from the International Court of Justice. This was a comparatively creative approach but it was already clear even at that time that it had little prospect of being taken up and that the Court was, in any event, not especially well situated to resolve the overall problem. Moreover, resort to it would involve taking one reservation at a time rather than being able to present a cross-section of reservations of different types. The Meeting also suggested: that a study be undertaken by the Sub-Commission on Prevention of Discrimination and Protection of Minorities "of issues of incompatibility arising out of the reservations that have been made..."; that States should "keep the number and scope of ... reservations to a minimum" and should regularly review them; and that each treaty body should always address the issue of reservations in its dialogue with the State party.

But despite the attempted comprehensiveness of these responses to the problem, the fact remains that they proceeded from a premise that has since been shown to be incorrect, or more accurately, one that was able to be overcome. That was that the committees themselves were powerless to do much beyond treating the reservations as *faits accomplis* while at the same time making grumbling noises of greater or lesser volume depending on the circumstances. Happily, however, the situation has evolved dramatically as a result of a General Comment adopted in November 1994 by the Human Rights Committee.[9] The Comment is lengthy, complex and wide-ranging and cannot be reviewed in detail here. In essence, however, it responds to the entirely unsatisfactory nature of traditional international legal doctrines governing reservations by rejecting their applicability to human rights treaties. According to the Committee, "human rights treaties ... are not a web of inter-State exchanges of mutual obligations". Rather, because they "concern the endowment of individuals with rights", the "principle of inter-State reciprocity has no place", except perhaps in relation to inter-State complaints.[10] This analysis leads the Committee to conclude that it is the Committee itself which must determine the compatibility of any specific reservation with the object and purpose of the Covenant. This conclusion is justified on two grounds. The first is that "this is an inappropriate task for States parties [themselves]

---

[9] "General comment on issues relating to reservations made upon ratification or accession to the Covenant or the Optional Protocols thereto, or in relation to declarations under article 41 of the Covenant", General Comment No. 24 (52). UN doc. CCPR/C/21/Rev.1/Add.6 (2 Nov. 1994).

[10] Ibid., para. 17.

in relation to human rights treaties" and the second is that "it is a task that the Committee cannot avoid in the performance of its functions".[11]

If I may be permitted a brief aside at this point, it is fascinating to speculate as to the political winds that assisted the Committee to reach unanimous agreement on this General Comment. In recent years the biggest problem in relation to reservations has come from governments which have sought to limit their obligations by virtue of reservations making the entire treaty in question subject to the Koran. Leaving aside any potentially significant consequences of such an approach, particularly for women, the major problems from a legal perspective were the totally open-ended nature of the reservation and the element of auto-determination which implied that the State itself would make the relevant determinations of compatibility. The general result of the proliferation of such reservations was to place an Islamic cloud over any discussion of the reservations issue in general. Any attempt to address the issue could be portrayed as a covert assault on Islamic approaches to human rights, which more or less stalled attempts to find a solution. Happily, the United States then came to the rescue by ratifying several instruments, including the Civil and Political Rights Covenant in particular, subject to a series of reservations and understandings which, when taken as a whole, amounted to an assertion that the treaties were virtually, or at least by self-definition, consistent with United States law such that no changes to the latter were necessary or even foreseeable. This immediately transformed the reservations issue into a relatively non-partisan one and provided an important impetus for Third World and other members of the Human Rights Committee to seek to adopt a comprehensive solution to the full range of problems. Moreover, the United States even provided an incentive to the Committee to move rapidly by having an expert elected to the Committee, as from its first session in 1995. It is perhaps not surprising then that the Human Rights Committee was able to bring its efforts to fruition in November 1994.

III. CONCLUSION

To return to the main theme of this paper, the relevance for present purposes of the reservations example, which the Committee on the Rights of the Child should certainly be urged to follow, is twofold. In the first place it demonstrates that the treaty bodies have considerable scope to develop the evolution of their jurisprudence and procedures in response to specific concerns that are not directly dealt with in the text of the treaty itself. The second is that there is a presumption that States parties, in establishing a monitoring mechanism, intended to establish an effective means for achieving accountability in relation to the obligations contained in the Convention. It is therefore no longer acceptable to ask simply whether the procedures laid down are capable of

---

[11]   Ibid., para. 18.

achieving that goal and, if they are not self-evidently adequate, proceeding to accept large gaps in the fabric of accountability. Instead, the relevant committee is called upon to develop the threads (and doctrines) which are necessary to weave a whole cloth of State accountability. This is not to suggest that the treaty bodies can, or indeed should, have the final word. In matters such as the appropriate response to over-reaching reservations the debate will continue within the Human Rights Committee as well as in other fora (such as the General Assembly and the Commission on Human Rights) and it is through the interplay of the different positions and interpretations that a legally and politically acceptable balance can be struck.

JENS QVORTRUP

Monitoring Childhood: Its Social, Economic and Political Features

INTRODUCTION

When I began my sociological research on childhood – a few years before the adoption of the UN Convention on the Rights of the Child – I had to inform myself also about the legal situation of children. I nurtured the perhaps naive idea that children were human beings, and even if I knew about the Declaration of the Rights of the Child from 1959, I found it interesting also to see how children were represented in the "real" human rights document, namely the Universal Declaration of Human Rights of 1948.

Indeed, I did find a few remarks about children, e.g. article 25(2) stating that "motherhood and childhood are entitled to special care and assistance", but the article which I found particularly interesting and revealing was article 2, which says the following: "Everyone is entitled to all rights and freedoms set forth in this Declaration, without distinction of any kind, such as race, colour, sex, language, religion, political or other opinion, national or social origin, property, birth or other status". The word *everyone* is substantiated in the preamble, which talks about the "recognition of the inherent dignity and of the equal and inalienable rights of all members of the human family...".

Since nobody, I am sure, will contest the assumption that children belong to "the human family", one has a right to expect that the Declaration is valid for both adults and children. However, article 2 gives you doubts that this really is so, because *age* is not explicitly mentioned among those statuses, which give entitlement to the rights and freedoms set forth in the Declaration. A benign interpretation might suggest "age" to be included in the residual category "other status", although one wonders if such an important variable, which typically belongs to the standard set of variables, has not been weighed by an international group of jurists, politicians and diplomats and found wanting. Rather, the inclusion of age may have been found disturbing and dangerous, since it would have amounted to acknowledging children equal and inalienable rights.

E. Verhellen (ed.), Monitoring Children's Rights, 33–48.
© 1966 *Kluwer Law International. Printed in the Netherlands.*

It is not only the inauguration of both the 1959-Declaration and the Convention on the Rights of the Child of 1989, which appears to confirm the suspicion that children are regarded as a special kind and therefore not really included in the human family, since these documents are not specifying any of the articles of the Universal Declaration, but lead their particular and autonomous life; indeed, the quoted lines from article 2 of the Human Rights Declaration are even reiterated in the Preamble of the Convention on the Rights of the Child. The suspicion is also supported by, I believe, all national legislations, which stipulate a particular regulation on children in their laws on majority.

The point I wish to make with those introductory words is not that the placement of children and adults in different legal departments is right or wrong. It is rather, simply, to draw your attention to it as a fact – a fact which is significant in the sense that adults by that, perhaps unwittingly, seem to be reserving for themselves the notion of the human family, and as an indication of a growing trend towards separating childhood and adulthood. These ideas are not as innocent as they may appear. They reflect the way in which children are perceived as members of society and, in general terms, adult attitudes to childhood; and thus it generalises the question of discrimination, which in the Convention merely focuses on discrimination *between* children. Should one not also think of discrimination between adults and children as a problem?

As far as attitudes of adult society are concerned it is interesting to look at national legislation. At least in my country, Denmark, the majority law includes two categories of persons, who do not enjoy majority status. One group are children, of course, from 0–17 years; the other category refers to those adults who have been deprived of their majority, for instance insane, psychic ill persons, drug abusers and alcoholics. From a legal point of view it is important to note that the case of the latter must be considered on an individual basis, judged by the court. If they are not found capable or competent to act as expected of an adult, a number of their fundamental human rights entitlements are taken away from them and they are, so to say, relegated to childhood status. As Rodham has said it: "Except for the institutionalized, who live in a state of enforced childishness, no other group [than children] is so totally dependent for its well-being on choices made by others" (Rodham, 1974, p. 7).

The placement of children as legal minors is different from that of individual adults deprived of their majority, i.e of their adult status; children are placed as a category, i.e. without individual consideration. They are excluded from a number of rights, which otherwise is regarded as "equal and inalienable for *all members* of the human family" – not explicitly because they are lacking capability or competence, because this has not in any case been tried, but in reality because of their young age. I do appreciate the advantages for authorities and adult society in general of these stipulations: they are practical and very convenient; they are saving society from much effort in finding out who among children were actually competent as citizens. But inconveniences cannot in a just society be used as an argument for exclusion and discrimination. The question is furthermore if this collective assessment and treatment of children, while taking for granted that they without exception are incompetent citizens, accords with our thrust in a just society based on an individualistic ethos. Or is it an expression of ageism, and thus that even the Convention – contrary to its main tenets – harbours some "ageistic" prejudices?

Hillary Rodham – now better known as Hillary Clinton – has argued that the presumption of incompetence, which results in children's exclusion from full citizenship, is almost as arbitrary as the exclusion of any other category of persons. "The first thing to be done", she writes, "is to reverse the presumption of incompetence and instead assume all individuals are competent until proven otherwise" (quoted by Lasch, 1992, p. 75).

Now, it is quite obvious that the separation of children and adults into two distinct legal departments is not without reason – apart from practicalities and conveniences. The main reason is, that children because of their vulnerability are assumed to be in need of protection. The law is protecting children from dangers and it is protecting others from dangerous children. This argument makes sense, given the world as we know it, and given we take for granted that the serious business of adults is the more important part, which children are supposed to adapt themselves to; and given, finally, that we take *ad notam* that adults actually are stronger and more powerful, which in a state of absolute equality might be detrimental for children, because, as Marx said, equal rights under unequal conditions are actually unequal rights.

The protection of the vulnerable can however be seen in another context. Child-protective laws that exclude children may also be interpreted as laws which actually have as their main rationale to keep children outside what may be perceived as a vulnerable adult society: our highly complex society with its extremely expensive equipment, with its precarious financial balances, with its striving towards exploiting every minute and each and every bit of resources in its search for productivity, efficiency, and accumulation, with its frail political balances between a number of different interests – such a society cannot afford the intrusion of children into its vulnerable arenas, because it might jeopardise both the economic fabric and the social order. In this sense the protective argument may as well be an argument for protecting society against disturbing and noisy children.

Without venturing this argument at all, protection is instead and *expressis verbis* garnished with paternalistic overtones. Children are excluded for their own good – and with this reason at hand no further justification for their exclusion seems needed. As already Blackstone argued more than 200 years ago: Children are within the "empire of the father", and therefore their privileges come from their incapacity. "Infants have various disabilities; but their very disabilities are privileges" (Blackstone, 1979, p. 441 and 452). This is a classical way of formulating a paternalistic attitude in the sense that a shortcoming is turned into a privilege in the eyes of the paternalists. "Paternalistic arguments generally hold that those marginalised on paternalistic grounds are finally the beneficiaries of their exclusion, while the benefactors are burdened with responsibility and the exertion of power" (Qvortrup, 1990, p. 16).

At the beginning of this century the American sociologist William I. Thomas formulated what he called "the four wishes", the fulfilment of which he found fundamental for any human being: "the desire for new experience; the desire for security; the desire for response; and the desire for recognition" (Thomas, 1966, p. xxxix and 117ff). Thomas had not children in mind, but in my view these four wishes are as relevant for children as for adults, and one might ask if the Convention meets these wishes as far as children are concerned. It has become popular in connection with the Convention to talk about the three Ps – protection, provision and participation. The three Ps and Thomas' four wishes do not completely coincide, but it is worthwhile to have both in mind when monitoring the Convention. Thomas' desire for security covers, I suggest, both the Convention's claims for protection and provision, while the desires for new experience, for response, and for recognition specify the claim for participation.

What I shall do in the following is to discus what can be done from a sociological point of view in terms of reporting about children's life conditions. Monitoring is obviously much more than simply quoting the national legal text of children's rights and see to it that it coincides with the Convention. State Parties are in article 44 of the Convention requested to report "on the measures they have adopted which give effect to the rights recognized herein and on the progress made on the employment of those rights", and also to report about "factors and difficulties, if any, affecting the degree of fulfilment of the obligations under the present Convention".

These requirements shall of course not be interpreted in absolute terms in such a universal document, and therefore I believe that article 4 is important to understand the scope of them, when it is written that "State Parties shall undertake all appropriate legislative, administrative, and other measures, for the implementation of the rights recognized in this Convention. In regard to economic, social and cultural rights, State Parties shall undertake such measures to the maximum extent of their available resources and, where needed, within the framework of international co-operation".

This article seems to presuppose that the respective nations share their resources in an equitable way among their citizens, inclusive intergenerational distributions; given the harsh reality of inequality between nations, the article is also an encouragement to wealthier nations to support children in less wealthy nations.

The meaning of a just distribution of resources – be they legal, economic, social or cultural – between generations is in the first place not given once and for all; to a large extent it depends on traditions, norms and morals in a given society. The Convention has however provided us with instruments for coming to terms with what we should be looking for. Most certainly, the Convention's requirements of the State Parties to report about the situation of children also presupposes current investigations. Have we actually undertaken measures to the maximum of our available resources, as far as economic, social and cultural rights are concerned?

What can, from a sociological point of view, be done to meet such requirements of a reporting system? As a sociologist I shall refrain from giving any legal answers, but instead make an effort to answer the following questions, which are more or less coinciding with Thomas' demands: What are children's rights to be *represented*? What are children's rights to *acknowledgement*? What are children's rights to *distributive justice*? What are children's rights to *political constituency*?

I. THE CHILD'S RIGHT TO BE HEARD – CHILDHOOD'S RIGHT TO VISIBILITY

It is one of the main tenets of the Convention to make sure that children are heard, that they be given a voice. This is explicitly stated in articles 12 through 16, which deal with the child's opinion, freedom of expression, of thought, conscience and religion, of association, and protection of privacy. Such claims are foreseen to be affirmed on an individual basis – the *child* should be heard in "any judicial and administrative proceedings affecting the child", as article 12,2 says – and may be realised for instance in the court room, in medical consultation, in schools and other institutions. But I believe that this right to have a voice should be extended so as to make it more effective, in a way however that is neither foreseen nor in contradiction with the Convention, but rather in line with its spirit. Children's voice should be envisaged also on behalf of *children as a collectivity*. As I shall demonstrate, to make children visible and heard as a collectivity is a most pertinent demand, if we wish to come to terms with the life conditions of children. In the Convention this obligation on the State Parties is not made clear, but merely alluded to in article 17 about children's access to appropriate information and in particular its letter (a), in which mass media are encouraged "to disseminate information and material of social and cultural benefit to the child", and in article 19 (about protection from abuse and neglect) it is in §2 proposed to establish programmes "for identification, reporting, referral, investigation, treatment, follow-up of instances of child maltreatment described heretofore, and, as appropriate, for judicial involvement". Even in the implementation articles (42 through 45) it is only in the very last sentence and, as it were, the very last resort, recommended that studies on specific issues relating to the rights of the child may be undertaken.

As already said, I am convinced that systematic and current investigation programmes set up with the purpose of reporting about children's general and specific conditions is in line with the aims and spirits of the Convention. But it has not been clearly demanded, on the contrary, I am afraid that such programmes are partly hindered by the Convention's bent towards being preoccupied with the rights of the individual child rather than – or in addition – being explicitly interested in the common and general conditions of all children, or – if you like – with childhood as it is socially, economically and culturally construed.

To be heard and to have access to information is indeed a right which is appropriate for the individual child; but not only that. To give a voice to children is also a matter of obliging authorities to actively seek current and up-dated information in a much broader way than it happens today; it is also the right and the obligation of schools and other institutions to demand insight in children's life worlds as they actually are and with a view to what they should be; and it is a right also for parents and parents' organisations to have access to easily available information about how their children lead their life both from a general point of view and as far as more specific conditions are concerned.

One can only support the Convention's encouragement to "the mass media to disseminate information and material of social and cultural benefit to the child", but one must in this context ask from where the mass media obtain their information if not from studies and investigations – unless we are supposed to rely on what the mass media collect themselves on a day to day basis – maybe partly from what happens to be available in terms of research conducted beyond the systematic provided by the Convention's framework.

In the research in which I have been involved, we have been very interested in giving children or childhood a voice in the sense that children must them-selves be represented. We have not in this connection spoken about rights of the child in a legal sense, neither has it been a must that each child literally speaking should be given a voice. What we have talked about has rather been the need to provide children and childhood with *conceptual autonomy*. This is not in the first place a recipe to revolutionise children's worlds in economic or political terms, and it does not require new legal measures; it only requires new administrative and research practices. Nevertheless it is likely to have consequences, that may not be welcomed by everybody, since it necessarily will impinge on sacrosanct relationships.

II. CHILDREN'S RIGHTS TO REPRESENTATION

The idea of providing children with conceptual autonomy is as straightforward as it is farreaching: it simply means that it is children we are focusing on, studying, investigating, counting and not anybody else related to them, if it is the life conditions of children we are interested in. To ears unexperienced in those matters, such a claim may seem self-evident. But it is not. As a matter of fact it threatens first of all the role of the family as a representative of the child. And in practical terms the demand is paramount to recasting the existing practice of most statistical offices, other governmental reporting agencies as well as a good deal of research.

The Convention clearly states the child's right as an individual. It has a right to an identity, i.e. a name, a nationality, and family ties. In reality, however, the family gains a preponderant position whenever children are reported about by authorities. The general appreciation of the family as a haven of security and love for a child, the recognition of parental responsibilities and of parents as children's guardians are typically translated into letting parents represent children; or to let "the family" do it – which amounts to the same, since "family" most often but mistakenly is seen as synonymous with parents (cf. expressions like "the family must cooperate with the school"; "the family must socialise its children"; "the family is responsible for the children"; etc.). And this tendency is not suspended even if the individual child in the wake of the Convention is given the right to express its own views about its very own particular circumstances – a right which by the way is very important.

It is far from accidental that the notion of familialisation of childhood has emerged recently. On the one hand it is a positive phenomenon in the sense of giving children protection and provision within the orbit of the parental house; on the other hand it may imply a growing invisibility of children in two ways: firstly, the familialised child may be referring to the continuing and possibly increasing dependency of children on families, i.e. parents, despite the fact that more and more children are away from parents and home during large parts of the day; or as Makrinioti says, familialisation refers to "the fusion of childhood into the family institution to such an extent that it defines an inseparable unit, which hampers the social visibility of its weaker part on its own" (Makrinioti, 1994, p. 268); secondly, it may refer, in Oldman's words, to "the systematic *refusal* on the part of authorities to 'open up' the privacy of the family and subject it to the public gaze" (Oldman, 1991, p. 10). A familialised perspective is due to hide a number of aspects of childhood – either because it is seen as wrong or threatening from ideological points of view that authorities intrude in the privacy of the family, or because it financially may reflect the "unwillingness to devote public resources to the systematic recording of family matters" (Oldman, 1991, p. 10). Familialisation thus represents a double attack on the visibility of children – one based on an old family ideology, and another based on monetary considerations. In both cases it jeopardises monitoring tasks as desired by the Convention, while it must also be said that the Convention is evading this problem, because it typically presupposes a coincidence of parents' and children's interests.

What is it, then, that is hidden? Hidden is first of all a number of facts about children's own lives and relationships that are badly needed if we want to know about children's life situation and conditions. This concerns for instance family relationships such as number of siblings, experience of separation or divorce of parents, number of children living in families which receive public support, number of children exposed to parents' unemployment, housing conditions of children, poverty or affluence of children relative to other social groups, and many other issues. Such are data which in most countries are not systematically and currently recorded as far as children are concerned; typically only families or parents are counted, and the failure to count children themselves leads to often grossly distorted impressions of children's own lives. From our study the example has become almost classic, that current statistics based on the family as the unit of observation gives the impression that around half of children are single children without siblings while counting children themselves proves that more than 80 percent of all children have at least one sister or brother. As far as trends in marriage, cohabitation, separation and divorce are concerned and their consecutive pluralisation of family forms, we know much more about adults than about children. It is agreeable that the Convention in article 9 proposes ways and means for those children who have already arrived in a situation of parents' divorce, but there is also a dire need to know more about the scope of the problem, its societal background – in terms of for instance individualisation, secularisation, gender equality, full time participation in the labour market of both parents etc.

In terms of income a family oriented statistic tells us that families with children are relatively well off, while using children as unit of observation proves that children in general terms belong to the lower economic echelons. I will return to this later on.

But hidden is also the time use of children and their activities at home; in numerous surveys it is taken for granted that parents use time on children, that children are consuming parents time, as if children were doing nothing themselves. In terms of the Convention's wish to grant children an identity, it would seem important to recognise children as individuals or persons rather than reducing them to items on parents' time budgets; it would seem reasonable to acknowledge that children's activities have a worth in their own right. In general, one might express the desire to know more about intra-family distribution of both activities, consumption and privileges. I am afraid that such a desire will not in the first place meet understanding; on the other hand it is based on the fact that we hardly know anything about such matters, and secondly I would suggest it to be in line with the Convention's claim to secure children's identity and individuality.

Since children are increasingly leading their lives outside the family home, it becomes accordingly more and more important also to make sure that their rights are represented here. But we are to a large extent ignorant about children's rights in many of their out-of-the family arenas. Let me illustrate this suspicion with reference to a discussion in Denmark two months ago (autumn 1994). It was already well-known that the standards of school buildings left much to be desired and in particular were reparations not up to date; often schools are dull, they lack painting, etc. Now some cases were brought to the fore that a number of teachers felt ill because of bad interior climate in the schools – to an extent that some of them had to take leave of absence for several months; dry-rot was detected in roofs and walls and unhealthy humidity affected those teachers. But what about the children? Physicians had to admit that no children were examined, that no studies had been made about how children were affected, and moreover it also became clear that no body existed in our system which permitted children to complain, since only employees have a right to complain by their employers.

Of course one might say that parents should be responsible, and that they should have revealed some hidden illnesses in their children; and of course we have in principle a medical system for school children, which by the way is not functioning, because it has been more or less starved of resources. In my view, the example is of principle importance. Despite the fact that children are much more numerous in schools than adults, and despite the fact that children are forced to stay daily in school at least as long time as adults, children do not have any rights with reference to the token argument that they are not employed, and they are not as a collectivity insured against neither short nor long term consequences of damages that may be inflicted on them.

Children are in other words hidden in such serious matters, because they are without representation, and because they have no rights, they are not recorded; they are even without a right to complain and possible injuries have no repercussions for anybody, because no one is responsible in legal terms (besides perhaps the parents); they are defenceless vis-a-vis authorities who must cut expenses somewhere, and children's arenas are thus convenient targets.

State Parties which have signed the Convention recognise according to article 24 "the right of the child to the enjoyment of the highest attainable standard of health and to facilities for the treatment of illness" and also endorse that appropriate measures be taken as far as prevention of illnesses are concerned. Perhaps the mentioned example may make State Parties responsible according to article 19, which obliges them to "take all appropriate legislative, administrative, social and educational measures to protect the child from all forms of physical or mental violence, injury or abuse, neglect or negligent treatment, maltreatment or exploitation including sexual abuse, while in the care of parent(s), legal guardian(s) or any other person who has the care of the child". But this article is, as it is typical for the Convention, individualising the problem while talking not only about the child, but also alluding to different categories of guardians to whom responsibilities may be delegated.

What is needed here is indeed a monitoring system, which makes sure that the well being of children is safeguarded even in all those increasing arenas outside the home, where children are collectively present; one must fear that not only schools but also other institutions, premises of sportclubs and other of children's leisure organisations, playgrounds etc. are in a similar bad shape – but only moral and political pressures may be of help to alleviate the situation, because no one is legally forced. The particular guardians of children may be living perfectly up to their responsibility, and yet children may be neglected for other reasons.

I am afraid also that children in many other contexts are similarly left unprotected by the law – the irony is however that children may be left vulnerable under the very pretext of being protected, because one wants to shield them from being involved in adult-like frameworks, legally and organisationally. It is for instance known that children, at least in my country, who work for money outside schools have much fewer rights than adult workers, who are encompassingly protected through their union membership, for instance. The reason seems to be that children are not supposed to be members of unions, they are not supposed to work gainfully at all, and therefore they can neither strike, be protected against dismissals, be compensated and many other things, which are self-evident rights of adults. But the fact is that children are nonetheless working, and as long as they do that they should be granted at least as many rights as adults; otherwise we are making ourselves victims of our own wishful thinking. Similarly children must in schools and other institutions be given legal protection against unhealthy buildings even if they are for formal reasons lacking entitlements as employees. Children are actually attending schools, and it seems to be a bad joke to keep them outside typical adult protection under this pretext.

III. CHILDREN'S RIGHTS TO ACKNOWLEDGEMENT

The example about the interior climate in schools illustrates not only children's lack of representation, but also that their position is not conveyed the *acknowledgement* it deserves; children appear to be less important than adults because it is not acknowledged that they – exactly as adults – have to stay in schools not only for their own sake, but indeed also for the sake of society; one therefore might expect that this fact, which is not likely to be contested by anybody, would entail greater responsibility from authorities in terms of granting children a right to be protected and to complain. The example also illustrates that it has not been sufficiently appreciated that children are as a matter of fact to a large extent beyond the reach of parents' insight and control; their new role and its consequences thus must be overseen by somebody in *locus parentis*, and it is in my view a good example of new circumstances that must be monitored in the wake of the Convention; it obliges in other words monitoring bodies to be inventive and attentive to the new life worlds of children, which are developed in society.

We are, as adults, still largely caught in partly outdated prejudices about children's life worlds, their new circumstances and expectations. The other example mentioned earlier about children's work after schools may illustrate this. We are rightly – in a global perspective – concerned about exploitation of children through forced employment under dangerous and unhealthy conditions; it is likely that article 32 about child labour in the Convention was formulated with these sad realities in mind. The situation is however another one in Europe; nevertheless has the European Union recently decided to restrict labour conducted by children after their school hours – not because the documents presented by the European Union in any way demonstrate insight in this problem, but because one wants to protect children and perhaps make the schooling of children more effective.

Now in terms of what I call children's rights to acknowledgement, one has to ask also other questions. One should also make an effort to understand why many children in even rich, developed nations are looking for paid work. Our knowledge about this is not very good, but from the studies we know about it is fair to conclude that children look for jobs for mainly three reasons: they want to earn money themselves; they are seeking new experiences; they wish greater independence. When children mention these reasons for taking a job, one is permitted to suggest that they have been found wanting by children in their daily scholarised and institutionalised life offered to them by adult society. In turn we can translate children's reasons to work into the following questions: Does their wish for money mean that children claim a right to be consumers? Does their wish for new experiences (cf. one of Thomas' four wishes above) indicate that schools are not providing them sufficient and satisfying options for exploring the world on their own? Finally, is their wish for greater independence reflecting big children's dissatisfaction with being forced to negotiate with parents about things which they feel they can manage themselves? As a fourth point, let me add that it can be documented that what children earn are often quite important contributions to many family incomes.

What I am arguing is, that from a monitoring point of view it is decisive also to know about children's own desires even if they may run counter to adults' interests or prejudices. I have elsewhere argued extensively for the thesis that school work can be seen – historically, logically, and in terms of its economic worth – as the modern form of child labour. This view is not recognised by society or by adults in general – far from it – on the contrary, schooling is rather seen as a gift to children, as an expense on public budgets. On this background we as adults appear to expect children to be grateful for the opportunities provided to them. But this adult interpretation is not necessarily one that is shared by children themselves, and if this is so we have a problem in terms of not being in harmony with children's own opinions, as stipulated in article 12 of the Convention, even if this opinion is expressed in aggregate terms as a result of particular studies.

To put it clearly: a child has a right with the Convention in its hands to complain about bad working conditions; but is the Convention instrumental for children to complain about their missing opportunities to work, to be consumers, to be independent?

Even if most adults are not prepared to adopt the radical solution to compensate children in monetary terms for their school labour, there remains the question if we are generally speaking acknowledging children for what they actually achieve in schools in terms of contributing to production and accumulation of knowledge; there remains the question if we fulfil their desire for new experience, and if children as adults have rights as consumers in a society in which the business sectors in a most aggressive way have children as a target. Probably most adults would opt for minimising children's role as consumers in order to protect them; but firstly can we be sure that the real reason is not rather that parents want to control children's behaviour; and secondly, would an exclusion of children from the market not be tantamount to limiting their experiences as consumers? Actually, there are studies which seem to conclude that children's responsibility as consumers increase, if they have to spend money, which they have earned themselves.

Everyone will accept with acclaim that children must not be exploited, and that children need to be educated; monitoring tasks as far as the relevant articles of the Convention are concerned should however also look at the background and the consequences. We do know – unfortunately – about examples of idealistic aims to save children which in reality have turned into moral crusades against children and their independence. I guess this is also what Verhellen is alluding to when he writes that child-protection has sometimes been "regarded as a 'political' instrument to preserve the existing social and economic order" (Verhellen, 1994, p. 54).

IV. CHILDREN'S RIGHTS TO DISTRIBUTIVE JUSTICE

The term distributive justice corresponds in the popular interpretation of the Convention to one of the three Ps, namely "provision" and in terms of Thomas' four wishes to "the desire for security". I have preferred "distributive justice" because it is more instrumental for envisaging the position of children in the outcome of struggles over societal resources in general. Both "provision" and "security" are more defensive terms, indicating the responsibility of some parties – in the first place the parents, in the last resort the political authorities – to make sure that at least some economic minimum standard is safeguarded for children.

From a monitoring point of view it is important to obtain information about the general situation of children compared with other age groups as far as available resources are concerned. When – as in article 27 about standard of living – parents are foreseen to have the primary responsibility to "secure, within their abilities and financial capacities, the conditions of living necessary for the child's development", we are in reality accepting inequality among children as a fact depending on parents' abilities and financial capacities – although State Parties are called upon to provide support in emergency cases. This is to be sure the more realistic alternative and somehow in contradiction with the Convention's perspective to prevent discrimination between children. From a monitoring perspective the other alternative might however be useful, that children are depicted as a collectivity so as to demonstrate how this population group is foreseen, when societal resources are shared. It is true that the struggle over economic resources between social classes must be fought in other arenas and with other means, but if we wish to understand ourselves as children's advocates we do not have to accept that children must be victims of such class struggles or struggles between different interests. It is likely that we cannot do much about it, but what can be done is in any case to make sure that it is *known* how resources are distributed between generations, which is the overlooked perspective of preventing discrimination between generations. This is the first condition for actions for change. It is sometimes said, that parents who get children must accept a lower standard of living as long as they have children. In my view this is not a natural law, but what is worse is that this argument in fact condemns children to lead a life in relative deprivation, because practically all children live together with those parents who are asked to assume a lower living standard, and thus also forced to share this lower living standard. A political demand for providing equally for children might have farreaching consequences.

Against the standard argument that children are supposed to be dependent on their parents' financial capacities, one should raise the additional question if children have claims on their own – as human being – to lead a life under decent material conditions. It seems to me that the familistic argument about children as first of all members of a family and dependent on parents have taken the upper hand compared with a concern for children and their material well being.

What we know about these matters is, that children as a population group – that is, compared with other age groups – have experienced a relative worsening of their economic situation. In a long term perspective this has been documented for the USA by Coleman (1990), and in recent decades we dispose of a number of studies which almost unanimously but with large variations demonstrate that children's economic situation has deteriorated in relative terms in industrial countries (see for instance Sgritta, 1994; Wintersberger, 1994). The reasons for this development are varied, but one of them is the changing age structure of our populations. This is further substantiated by the fact that in generational terms it is adults, whose children have left the home, who are best off.

We are, given such data, left with the impression that children are expensive, and that may be one reason why we are reluctant to have children in the same numbers as before. There is some irony in this impression, since data show that children as a collectivity occupy relatively less resources than adults and old aged. One problem in this context is of course that this discussion is seen merely from the point of view of the family economy (the familialised child once again!), and this is increasingly problematic as children are more and more becoming participants in extra-familial settings. If we therefore turn, as we must, to the relationship between children and the public purse, the question is if children are also here seen as a liability?

In the first place, as already said, children are or should be deserving people alone because they are human beings; besides that, secondly, I have indicated that children in schools are conducting useful activities of great importance for society, and thus from this point of view should be regarded as assets in any calculation concerning public budgets; as a matter of fact, children are nonetheless regarded as an expense in general, and even education is seen as a drain on social resources; thirdly, it can be documented that even on public budgets children are not particularly expensive compared with adults – if at all – and with distance much less expensive than old people (Qvortrup, 1994). Such data can of course be interpreted differently, but the gist of the matter is, that there is a need in any monitoring activity to explore much more thoroughly into these issues. There is a lot of taken-for-granted stuff, benign paternalism and ideological inheritance in our ways of dealing with children's position, including many formulations in the Convention.

Nevertheless, I believe that the Convention remains a useful tool if interpreted with good will by its Committee and by State Parties. When, in article 4 it is said that "In regard to economic, social and cultural rights, State Parties shall undertake such measures [i.e. appropriate legislative, administrative and other measures] to the maximum extent of their available resources", it is in any case open for interpretation what that means. As far as children are concerned – and beyond the orbit of the family – one could for instance return to the example about school buildings. Does this article not oblige State Parties to act as defenders of children's right to decent and healthy institutions even if this advocacy might interfere with interests of others struggling to take up the same societal resources?

In other words – providing for children in a just way is not merely an obligation for parents, but as well a claim on State Parties to make sure that children are foreseen in an equitable way compared with other age groups.

V. Children's Rights to a Political Constituency

The defence of children's rights as they are found in the Convention is totally left to adults; it may be answered that children – or rather the child – have got the right to express themselves. But the reality is of course that without adults to interpret and advocate, children would be left in the lurch. The much more so since children do not have a political constituency; the Convention has not explicitly provided them with political rights, even if it neither explicitly denies them such rights.

To the extent that the Convention does not foresee political rights to children it may be beyond its monitoring obligations and prerogatives to deal with the issue; nevertheless, I believe it is of some interest in order to place the whole complex in its proper context to do so – at least if the idea is to promote children's interests in society.

The most severe problem for children in political terms is their diminishing influence in view of the demographic development. The ageing of society, which in a few decades will leave us with much more old people than children, will in democratic societies like ours in Europe turn the political attention away from children – the much more so since children are not voters themselves. Projections show that around year 2030 the median voting age will be 50 years – which means that half of all voters will be above grandparent-age. This is not to say that grandparents are less child friendly than others, but it only means that a political pressure towards favouring middle and old age groups will become more outspoken.

In my country there are children in merely every fourth of all households, and less than 30 per cent of all voters live together with children; and we cannot even be sure that parents in all cases will be supportive of what one might call children's interests, because the new generations of adults have many other interests than those concerning the family – in accordance with the secular trend towards individualisation.

It is as mentioned likely to be beyond the competence of the Convention to deal with such issues, but they are in my view nevertheless of urgent importance for the future of childhood. If one is to speculate, there may be the following proposals to be discussed.

The first and the most radical – and as a consequence of what Rodham has suggested, as quoted at the beginning of my paper – would be to grant children all rights, including the right to vote. Since this is completely unrealistic, the second proposal may be more eatable, but probably still unappetizing, namely to make sure that parents obtain as many extra votes as they have children.

My third proposal to enhance the political concern for children would be to expand the responsibility for children beyond the family and even beyond the state and municipalities. We need in my view to discuss the importance of children for various interest groups, for business, for unions, for employers' organisations, etc. Sometimes it happens that factories and other firms establish their own kindergartens, and we also see other indications of a recognition of the importance of children beyond the parties we normally oblige. Because we are clinging to an ideology of the family which came into being a century ago, we have brought ourselves in a situation, which the German sociologist Kaufmann (1990) has described as a "structural disregard" and a "structural indifference" towards children – i.e. that normal interest groups and pressure groups do not really – and are not supposed to – care about children, and the political system allows them not to care under the pretext that merely parents are responsible.

I do not opt for widening private arrangements, but for encouraging State Parties to bind business and pressure groups to become partners of a common commitment and responsibility for children, given my contention that childhood is an interest for them as much as for other parties in society.

CONCLUSION

My task has been to develop some monitoring aspects from a sociological point of view. My main message has been to encourage monitoring bodies to take a broader view while considering the trends in the development of childhood in general, and first of all to draw on experiences from children's arenas outside the family. My message also includes a call for making current and encompassing investigations about children's life world as a basis for creating a more well informed verdict about children's actual situation.

I trust that the tool is there; the Convention is an instrument which can be used to invite and request much more information than we dispose of so far. Using the Convention as a platform may be our best chance for not only collecting more insight to the advantage of children and their life worlds, but also for creating pressure groups which on children's behalf have so far been disgracefully weak.

REFERENCES

Blackstone, William (1979) *Commentaries on the Law of England.* Vol. I (A facsimile of the First Edition of 1765–1769). Chicago: University of Chicago Press.

Coleman, James S. (1990) *Foundations of Social Theory.* Cambridge, Mass.: The Belknap Press of Harvard University Press.

Kaufmann, Franz-Xaver (1990) *Zukunft der Familie.* München: Beck.

Lasch, Christopher (1992) "Hilary Clinton, Child Saver." In *Harpers Magazine*, October, pp. 74–82.

Makrinioti, Dimitra (1994) "Conceptualization of Childhood in a Welfare State: A Critical Reappraisal," pp. 267–283 in Qvortrup et al. (1994).

Oldman, David (1991) *Childhood as a Social Phenomenon. National Report. Scotland.* Eurosocial Report 36/9. Vienna: European Centre.

Qvortrup, Jens (1990) *Childhood as a Social Phenomenon: An Introduction to a Series of National Reports.* Eurosocial Report 36/1990, Vienna: European Centre.

Qvortrup, Jens (1994) *Børn halv pris – Nordisk barndom i samfundsperspektiv* (Children Half Price – Nordic Childhood in Societal Perspective). Esbjerg: South Jutland University Press.

Qvortrup, Jens, Marjatta Bardy, Giovanni Sgritta and Helmut Wintersberger (eds.) (1994) *Childhood Matters: Social Theory, Practice and Politics.* Avebury: Aldershot.

Rodham, Hillary (1974) "Children Under the Law." In *The Rights of Children*, Harvard Educational Review, Reprint Series No. 9, pp. 1–28.

Sgritta, Giovanni B. (1994) "The Generational Division of Welfare: Equity and Conflict", pp. 335–361, in Qvortrup et al. (1994).

Thomas, William I. (1966) *On the Social Organization and Social Personality. Selected Papers.* Edited and with an Introduction by M. Janowitz. Chicago/London: The University of Chicago Press.

Verhellen, Eugeen (1994) *Convention on the Rights of the Child.* Leuven/Apeldoorn: Garant.

Wintersberger, Helmut (1994) "Costs and Benefits – The Economics of Childhood," pp. 213–247, in Qvortrup et al. (1994).

FERRAN CASAS

Monitoring Children's Rights and Monitoring Childhood: Different Tasks?

"The Convention is an instrument which can be used to invite and request much more information than we have so far". By this statement, with which I fully agree, Jens Qvortrup focusses on a crucial point: Information is the basis of knowledge, and we do not have enough information on childhood reality, on the new worlds children know (their universes of experiences, their cultures).

Knowledge may be acquired in many ways, from basic research and consideration of theory in various disciplines, and also from an evaluation of what has been done.

While information on the situation of children is available from many sources, the Convention on the Rights of the Child establishes only one procedure for monitoring implementation of the rights recognized in it, i.e. national reports by States Parties (art. 44), though UNICEF and other UN agencies and bodies may also be invited to submit reports (art. 45) on matters falling within the scope of their activities.

In practice, the Committee on the Rights of the Child has suggested that national reports should be drawn up in cooperation with national NGOs, has given more detail on procedures, and relies on input from international NGOs. But even so, the risk inherent in being "judge and jury", as pointed out by Verhellen (1994) must not be underestimated, because in any case national reports are mainly written by governmental bodies.

A report written by a State Party, however rigorous, is unlikely to be scientific, which does not diminish its potential value. The Convention is the first integrated international instrument involving action for the benefit of children. Precisely because it is a political instrument, the reports on its implementation by the States Parties probably tell us much more about childhood policies than about the situation of children. Is that wrong? I would only say, for now, that all information may be relevant, depending on our purposes.

The work of monitoring what is in the Convention itself – as well as the goals of the World Summit for Children – has revealed a number of new information needs, particularly on indicators of economic, social and cultural

E. Verhellen (ed.), Monitoring Children's Rights, 49–56.
© 1996 *Kluwer Law International. Printed in the Netherlands.*

aspects of child welfare. Some areas are particularly new (how to monitor children's freedoms in articles 12 to 16?), and some academic bodies and international networks (e.g.: Childwatch International) have already described these information needs as a considerable challenge (Casas, 1994).

Qvortrup, in my opinion, has concentrated a good part of his paper on several areas not covered by the Convention. He has adopted a scientific approach to the analysis of what is missing which is most enlightening. I would subscribe to many of his conclusions. They show us the *broader context of childhood reality* in our societies, which entails looking beyond the Convention.

Having said that, I think we must also consider some practical questions:
a) Even assuming we all agree with this analysis, is anybody really in a position to ask States Parties to report on matters not explicitly covered by the Convention? Is it not more realistic to concentrate on obtaining reliable reports on implementation of what States have signed up to, at least as a starting point?
b) Are we in a position to ask anybody else to report on these other areas, so that so far hidden aspects of children's worlds can be brought to light? Is that a task for NGOs, for academic bodies, for all of us? If many agencies are involved, how can we organize more efficiently?
c) Is it our ultimate aim to compare reports and thereby get a better view of reality? Or are there more fundamental objectives involved, e.g., making adults more conscious of the need for children's issues to be given higher political priority? If so, who should take the lead in such activities, and how can they be promoted?

Qvortrup's words show an obvious awareness of the situation. "Only moral and political pressure may be of help to alleviate the situation, because no one is legally forced". Reporting is, then not all we need to do, unless reporting is considered sufficient moral and political pressure – which I frankly doubt.

A monitoring system cannot operate in a vacuum, which will work well automatically, even if we manage to design an "excellent instrument to monitor", and make use of it completely neutrally, independently, and without outside pressure. A monitoring system provides an opportunity to interact with public opinion, with people's beliefs, to change the psycho-social context of "childhood" in which children live – and a key function of reporting is probably that of using reports as a means to an end. But we need to bring in new users of these tools, and new concepts of what a report could be, when we consider children.

If we regard reports as genuine monitoring instruments, one report per country (or two or more, even if from different perspectives) cannot give us enough information to monitor many things we would like to. Of course, published reports may play interesting roles in society. But what we really want is not just to *monitor*, but to monitor children's reality *on its way to somewhere*, in some *direction* we can define with goals. Goals must be conceived, and to become childhood policy goals, they must be shared by a number of relevant people (including children), in a position to exert pressure on decision-makers.

Children's rights included in the Convention may be regarded as a "defined direction"; but probably not all the implicit goals are clear enough, explicit enough or shared enough. There is still a good deal of work to be done on this.

We may take a somewhat different view, and feel that what the Convention says is not enough or appropriate enough. We may think we need another Convention or other international instruments. But equally many aspects of our current thinking may yet prove beyond the bounds of what can be done by means of a Convention (at least as things stand in the international arena).

I completely agree with Qvortrup that we need to "expand the responsibility for children beyond the family and even beyond the state and the municipalities". But I am not entirely sure whether that is a real proposal, or just a wish, an aspiration. I believe that much of what we wish for in fact involves creating a new climate for the benefit of children in our society, a new culture for children and with children. I may be wrong; but I suspect States Parties are unlikely to start working on that direction just now, because of lack of public interest ("low social intensity") in improving children's quality of life.

A new culture means, of course, putting new and different information and perspectives into the system of analysis, as well as generating fresh debate and new scales of values quite unlike those already under discussion. In our "technologically advanced societies" this can't be done without the media. But how to involve the media? We need the media to discuss not only each country's report (are they doing that?) but also alternative reports, not to mention what we are hoping to achieve for children's quality of life and our future society. Wishes and aspirations for children are aspects of the social context children live which it is difficult to ask anyone to report on.

We live increasingly in a society dominated by icons. We must use the language of images to reach people. If we want to change the social climate on behalf of children, we must "get in there" get to know the rules of the game and change things from the inside. We need to "translate" our theoretical reflexions and scientific findings from text into image. We may all find it very difficult to persuade the media to say what we would like them to say. But it is a real challenge we meet if we are to achieve anything in practice.

Social representations of children are not static, they are changing because of media influence on society; but they are probably going in a different direction from the one we would like to see; at least the "child" we see on television is hardly ever the "real" child, and yet both adults and children are interiorising the television child in real life as "the norm", and sometimes as aspirations (Casas, 1994c, d).

The "visible" child on television (indeed we often hear that what is not on television actually does not exist) forms a contrast to the growing invisibility of children rightly emphasized by J. Qvortrup, as result of "familiarisation" of childhood. At a different level, we see that *childhood policies have usually also been invisible*, hidden policies in many countries and intergovernmental organizations. We have heard about policies for education (or schools), the family, social and cultural policies and so on. In each of them some areas related to childhood, but very often nobody had an overview, or overall responsibility for political actions to benefit children. Children were pupils, sons and daughters, poor, ill, and so on... but not "just children".

I believe it is not by chance that, alongside the discussion of the Convention, and indeed after its approval, a number of national and international agencies tabled new ideas on the topic of childhood policies (e.g.: Council of Europe Project III.8 on Childhood Policies). The Convention required politicians to ask what, overall, had been done for children. Since there was often no-one who could give the full picture they needed to assemble information rapidly. For the first time, serious questions were asked about the coherence of political actions related to children (e.g.: Social Security policies in European countries).

The Convention puts pressure on States Parties to take an overall view of their "real" childhood policies, and how children's rights can be related to past, present and future childhood policies.

Of course, it is assumed that any coherent action affecting reality will be based on systematic knowledge of that reality. For that reason, the Committee rightly requested States Parties to include in their reports statistics providing information about the situation of children in each country. This should be considered only a starting point, because, as we know very well, many aspects of reality do not show up in statistics. And, in any case, any data from reality need a theoretical framework within which they can be interpreted.

This is what Qvortrup has offered us, i.e. a good range of theoretical considerations giving us potentially new and more profound ways of interpreting children's reality. He has also told us that we need more research to develop such interpretations appropriately.

I would like to stress that we must also keep in mind the need to go deeper into the relationship between research and political action in relation to children (including research resources, researcher's status, real impact of evaluative research, and so on; Casas 1994b) and I would also like to pursue his proposals, to which I broadly subscribe, though, because of my psychosocial background, my concepts and definitions may be slightly different.

I totally agree that a large number of the current images of childhood in our western societies have been built up in contrast to our images of what an adult is i.e. through a process of intergroup category differentiation. An important characteristic of such processes is that they emphasize intergroup differences and intragroup similarities (Casas, 1994c).

Table 1. Social representations of children and childhood

Figurative nucleus:	"NOT-YETS" – Not-yet adult – Not-yet responsible – Not-yet capable – Not yet with the same rights – Not-yet with enough knowledge – Not-yet with collective aspirations – Not-yet...
Attitudes:	"HIGH CONSENSUS AND LOW INTENSITY" – "Common sense" – Atomistic thinking – No personal involvement – Feelings of social responsibility missing – ...
Information:	OFTEN MISSING FOR CONCRETE SOLUTIONS – Not paying attention to such information – Information not internalised – ...

In this process some so-called "common sense" beliefs (Purkhardt, 1993) acquire a deep cultural meaning and become shared social representations by the adult-group. Social representations, according to Moscovici (1981) are structured around a figurative nucleus, which has an organizational function and is very resistent to change. Taking some ideas from Qvortrup (1987) and Verhellen (1992), a tentative design of our social representations of children and childhood may be as shown in Table 1 (Casas, 1994d).

I have said "our" very consciously. We all, even researchers, have difficulty in changing the paradigms through which we perceive the realities of childhood, partly because we also contribute to the dynamics of intergroup category differentiation. As scientists we have also made it difficult for the voice of children to be heard. For years, methodological considerations have been adduced to argue that information given by children is unreliable. Only in the very recent years have things started to change (see, for example, Garbarino, Stott et al., 1989).

The social representation of children as "not-yets" is so deeply rooted that, even when scientists have defined children's competences, social skills or capability to deal with responsibilities, as a process, still legislators (though they seem to have understood the point last century) have apparently proved unable to the task of "translating" the idea of process into legal language (Casas, 1993). Law, at least in the Latin tradition, is a question of acts, of being responsible or not (of categories), and it cannot accomodate the notion of the individual particular process.

The second generation of human rights, as stated by Verhellen (1992), means a proactive political compromise. To be proactive with rights related to freedoms (meanly art. 12–16) may be perceived as conflicting with the dominant social representation of not-yets, involving category differentiation. Protective policies throw up no contradictions with intergroup relations, one of the groups being considered "not-yet"; but "promotive" policies do involve contradictions with such policies. Promotive policies are founded on aspirations, mainly on collective aspirations; and children are considered "not-yet" to have *rights to collective aspirations*.

On the one hand I agree with Qvortrup's implicit position that monitoring children's rights means, in the end, monitoring childhood, which in turn implies knowledge of the reality experienced by children as a collective group. On the other hand I wonder if the change of perspective implied is too much to expect in the short term, because of the deeply rooted representations of childhood that must be changed, and not only in the minds of our politicians. Sometimes, when major change is required, society's reaction may be somewhat violent, and even counterproductive.

It might, perhaps be better strategically, if we were to focus for the time being on "monitoring children's rights", as a first stage, as there is still so much to be done in that stage. At least in our European societies, we can work towards the other goals, simultaneously, provided we do not lose sight of the long term, overall perspective which demonstrates that they belong to the same cluster of coherent actions and goals.

We can only expect major changes in the policies of States Parties (and their reporting systems) once children's rights now ratified have been to some extent absorbed; at which point we could create the conditions and make a case for broader reporting and more profound change. This does not mean we drop or put off our major goals, particularly in the international arena. We must work intensively for a more positive social climate towards major childhood policies, particularly those which are not just protective, but designed to promote an improvement in the way children live.

On the other hand, while I am entirely in favour of collective analysis of the situation of children and of collective action for children's rights, I do not like the idea of losing the capacity to defend the individual child. I don't think these two ideas are necessarily mutually exclusive. The language of the Convention is clever on that point, in my opinion: "the child" may have individual and collective meaning at the same time. When legal action must be taken, I think each individual can be an example for many others of how to defend a child's rights (we have interesting European jurisprudence at that level; see Verhellen, 1992). A hypothetical children's collective participation system does not need to duplicate adult participative systems where individual participation is not possible most of the time; new technologies, which children handle so well, can be helpful in articulating individuality and collectivity in new ways to enable participation. Finally, adults' social representations have consequences both at the individual and at the collective level, and it is important to bear this in mind. In conclusion I would like to summarize my personal views in five points:

1. All over the world improvements must be made in our capacity to monitor implementation of the children's rights clearly specified in the Convention, particularly in and with States Parties. Reports by States Parties are a valuable, albeit not exclusive, source of information.
2. We must interpret what is written in the Convention as fully as possible, in the best interests of the child, and ask all States Parties for coherence.
3. We must work for a broader monitoring system world-wide of hidden aspects of childhood reality and matters related to children. To that end we must be able to call on the full support of NGOs and academic bodies. Our social representations of children and childhood impose limits even on scientific activities, which must be overcome. Such efforts go beyond the Convention as such.
4. We must work to change attitudes and deeply rooted social representations of children, childhood and childhood policies, to create new social climates on behalf of children. For that purpose we need to cooperate fully with the media. The contribution of the media to monitoring is very important.
5. All these levels can be and must be developed at the same time, with those willing to cooperate in each one.

It is not easy to transform knowledge into action, or information into policy. Among other things, it requires an open dialogue between those who produce information and those who use it.

We need increased cooperation across the traditional borders between government, NGOs and academe to identify all possible ways of supporting implementation and monitoring of the Convention. And additionally, we need to draw together all efforts and capabilities to improve children's quality of life, even beyond the Convention.

REFERENCES

Casas, F. (1993) "Imputabilidad y responsabilidad: Los niños como actores desde la mirada de los adultos." *Anuario de Psicología Jurídica, 3*, 55–71.
Casas, F. (1994a) The Role and Responsability of Institutions in Supporting the Implementation and Monitoring of the Convention on the Rights of the Child. Séminaire pour l'Europe du Sud *L'Enfance: Les Droits retrouvés*. Venezia, 23–26 march 1994.

Casas, F. (1994b) "Social Research and Policy Making." In M. Colton et al. (Eds.): *The Art and Science of Caring*. In press.

Casas, F. (1994c) Social Representations, Children, Media and Children's Rights. *XIII Biennial Meeting of ISSBD*. Symposium on Social/Psychological Implications of the Global Implementation of the U.N. Convention of the Rights of the Child. Amsterdam, 29 June 1994.

Casas, F. (1994d) "Images and Social Representations of Children's Problems in the Media." *XIII World Congress of Sociology*. Bielefeld, 19 July 1994.

Garbarino, J., Stott, F.M. et al. (1989). *What Children Can Tell us*. Chicago: Jossey-Bass.

Moscovici, S. (1981) On Social Representations. In J.P. Fargas (Ed): *Social Cognition: Perspectives on Everyday Understanding*, 181–209. London: Academic Press.

Purkhardt, S. (1993) *Transforming Social Representations; A social Psychology of Common Sense and Science*. London: Routledge.

Qvortrup, J. (1987) "Childhood as a Social Phenomenon: An Introduction to a Series of National Reports." *Eurosocial, 36*.

Verhellen, E. (1992) Los derechos de los niños en Europa. *Infancia y Sociedad, 15*, 37-60.

Verhellen, E. and Spiesschaert, F. (1994) *Children's Rights: Monitoring Issues*. Gent: Mys & Breesch.

MÅLFRID GRUDE FLEKKØY

Children's Participation and Monitoring Children's Rights

I. A PIONEERING STEP

Jens Qvortrup is a man with a remarkable devotion and sense of purpose. With his collaborators in several countries, he has set about changing the map of childhood. This means, of course, that the group is taking a new look at the landscape, for a new map cannot be made without a truer perception of the country itself. It also means that they must try to convey to others the newer, truer landscape they perceive.

The main principle involved in acquiring a different perception of the landscape comes from changing the focus, the very distance from which the landscape is perceived. In what we might call "Pre-Qvortrup" statistics, adults perceived children as the astronauts on the moon perceived the world. Then the concern arose, in Jens Qvortrup and his colleagues and in others concerned with the visibility of children, e.g. the Norwegian Ombudsman for Children. Moving from the distance of the moon, they wanted to see the children themselves, looking at childhood more from the child's own level. They no longer only asked how many members the family might have, but started to wonder how e.g. the changing size of the family would affect its younger members.

The level, and so the perceived elements, must change as children grow. The child may look bigger as he grows, but adults hardly recognize as well the fact that the child's perceptions might be of adults diminishing gradually in size. The world, fairly stable to the grown-up viewer, also expands around the growing child. Each child will, as Qvortup says, experience his individual childhood, but for children at approximately the same age in approximately the same culture, there will be common denominators, enabling us to describe childhood as a phenomenon, the children as statistical members of a cohort, the cohort with specific characteristics of its own. This *variety* of childhoods has not yet been clearly described, but it seems clear that the common denominators, the collectivity is the sum – or more than the sum

E. Verhellen (ed.), Monitoring Children's Rights, 57–65.
© 1996 Kluwer Law International. Printed in the Netherlands.

– of individual childhoods. Thus, as Qvortrup so eloquently points out, it is of special interest to study how the political, economic and demographic changes in society have their impact on childhood, how attitudes to children and childhood have changed, for better or for worse. This, I believe, is a most important contribution of the Qvortrup research. It means that childhood can no longer be considered only a period transitional to becoming adult. It means that children can no longer be considered a marginal group within society, but as equal members of the human race even from birth. Thus statistics must count children as individuals, not only as "dependents". We can no longer only count the number of divorces or of unemployed adults, but must also consider how many children are divorced from their parents, how many children have unemployed parents or working mothers. We can no longer state categorically that children are un-productive, expensive, or burdensome, because we have to look at these issues from the children's point of view, to see what they are actually doing, actually producing. Children do not only *take* time, they *spend* time, they do not only cost money, public funds as well as the family's income, they are investments in the future of that same society.

II. THE NEXT STEP

So what is the next step? To me, as Qvortrup also indicates, it is obvious that we must re-set our sights once more, to include the views, perceptions, experiences and opinions of the children themselves. Let me introduce the importance of this by giving you an example. In Scandinavian statistics, Swedish children are supposed to have a better quality of life than Norwegian children, because the Norwegian children more often than their Swedish counterparts must share a room with another person. But if we ask the children themselves what sharing a room actually means to them, I am sure we will get different answers from children of different ages. Small children may *prefer* to share the room of their parents, while teen-agers probably would prefer not to do so. For preschool and school-age children the question might depend on who they share with. It might be O.K. to share with a sibling, or it might not. One 12 year-old girl loved sharing a room with her baby sister. Unknown to their mother, the baby even shared her bed when the little one woke at night, giving the elder a feeling of competence, as well as warmth. In other cultures sharing the sleeping space will make an assumption of quality of life meaningless. And even in Scandinavia changes take place which may influence the experience of room-sharing. Thirty years ago an average apartment had one large and one or two small bedrooms, the parents as a matter of course taking the larger one. Now it is more common that the parents leave the larger room to the children.

Apart from the obvious inherent importance of asking the children themselves, the UN Convention on the Rights of the Child places an obligation on all of us to monitor and implement the participation rights of the child. Participation rights include the rights to information, the freedom to express opinions and have a say in matters concerning the child's life. Further the Convention gives the child the right, with increasing maturity, to increasingly participate in activities of society and take a part in decisionmaking in the family, in school and in the widening circle of local community. We cannot monitor the implementation of the Convention without including participation rights as well as the rights to survival, protection and development. And more important, we cannot truly monitor implementation of participation rights without the participation of the children.

"The evolving capacities of the child" implies that it is *reasonable* that children gradually take over more responsibility in matters concerning them. The concepts of "the best interests of the child" (which change with age) and a scientific knowledge of "the evolving capacities of the child" are crucial in this connection. With the rights of children to participate in decision-making, it will be of particular importance to focus research on the child's evolving capacities from a positive point of view, to try to determine which decisions children should or can make at different stages of development, what kinds of responsibility they are able to and can benefit from having and how their decisionmaking and responsibility-taking capacities can be encouraged, supported and enhanced. While we *should* not assume incompetence, we *cannot* assume competence until proven otherwise, as suggested by e.g. Hilary Clinton. We must find out which competencies or part-competencies children have and gain as they grow.

There are arguments used against participation rights that we do not hear concerning other types of rights. One of these is that children must earn the right to exercise these rights or that they must be mature enough to have "the right" opinions or to make "the right" decisions. These are conditions adults would object to if applied to them and disregards the fact that children need time to learn, to gain experience through the "immature" decisions before they can be expected to take on full responsibility for decisions with far-reaching consequences. This, however, does not mean that they should not – on their own level, start exercising these rights from birth on. In fact, they do. The baby's influence on parental decisions is from birth un-planned and unconscious. But from birth on each baby starts to learn which behaviors will have an influence on his or her parents' behavior. To be properly considered "exercise of participation rights" this infant expression must be met with adult respect for the dignity and integrity of the child. Based on the research of Bowlby and of Brazelton, Koslowski and Main 1974, Stern 1974, it is clear that "The infant is an active and often *controlling* participant in the interaction process" (Goldberg 1982, my emphasis). The infant's part in the process is far more complex than researchers realized 20 years ago, with the infant as well as the adult capable of matching the pacing and rhythms of each other's behavior and making adjustments that are self-correcting for the interaction system. This in turn will sustain the infant-parent dyad. "A well-functioning parent-infant dyad generates confidence and competence in its members" (Goldberg 1977, Lewis and Goldberg 1969) that become resources for coping with new challenges.

The types of process resulting from individual child-parent interactions vary with "the type of child", "the kind of parent" and the resulting infant-parent dynamics (Thomas, Chess and Birch 1968, 1970) But it is not unreasonable to believe that by the age of 8–14 months the child knows how to influence the activities of adults.

Self-assertion, the drive towards self-determination, self-control and independence dominates much of the child's behavior during the second year. Learning where the limits are in the physical world and in relationship to decisionmaking, to other people, can be frustrating, but necessary.

To be able to participate in an active, conscious way with other people in a democratic, decision-making process, children must be able to comprehend that the other may have different points of view, different feelings and different reactions than their own. As long as the child is truly egocentric (in the classical Piagetian meaning) there would be no reason for the child to even consider such possibilities, in making his/her own decisions or in accepting/not accepting the decisions of others. More recent research has demonstrated that the child's abilities to think about their social worlds, to understand or consider others' thoughts, intentions and feelings appear far earlier than Piaget led us to believe. Piaget and his co-workers concluded that perspective-taking ability develops in three sequential stages, with egocentrism dominating until the age of six. By splitting the concept of perspective-taking into cognitive perspective-taking, affective perspective-taking and spatial perspective-taking, differences have been demonstrated in the age-levels at which these appear and in how the different aspects develop. By simplifying and making more familiar the original Piaget spatial task, Borke (1975) and Flavell (1978) have demonstrated some degree of spatial perspective-taking in three- and four-year-olds. As with spatial perspective-taking, different levels of cognitive role-taking skill have been described. Selman (1976) has recorded what he calls "egocentric roletaking" in children at age three years, when the child can understand that others may have distinctive thoughts and feelings, but cannot yet distinguish between his own and others perspective of the same experience. The child at this stage judges that others will view this experience in the same way as he does, moving at age six to a stage where he can make the distinction between self-centered and other-centered viewpoints, but without the ability to interpret either his own actions or thoughts from the *other's* viewpoint. This stage has, however, been demonstrated in four-year-olds (Marvin, Greenberg and Mossler 1986) in experiments that demand less verbal proficiency or in other ways are more experientially direct and concrete for the child. In much the same way affective perspective-taking has been demonstrated in three-to-four year-olds. (Dickson, Lieber and McIntyre 1976).

By age eight to ten years, the child can think that others think of the self in particular ways and realizes that the other person's perspective can have implications for how that person behaves towards him. (Selman 1976) Interesting results of recent studies of "deprived" environments (Parker et al 1988) in developing countries, aimed at identifying the strengths of these environments, conclude that "Opportunities for play with peers and older children with minimal adult interference enhance the development of self-reliance, self-control, cooperation, empathy and a sense of belonging". Adults are useful as consultants, models and teachers. But children need a spectrum of different social learning situations, a continuum from solitary play (or even boredom) to the peer-group (without adults) to the mixed age-group even with adults as equal members, to adult-led groups and the close-knit stability of the family, spanning generations.

The point of the above discussion has been to demonstrate that while there does not exist a total understanding of capabilities and competence in young children, the capacities of children have clearly been under-estimated, perhaps in particular in areas that are important for social functioning, i.e. for participation. Also, developmental knowledge is necessary if we are to include the children as informants, to be able to formulate our questions, tailor our research in a way that gives meaning for the children themselves. In conclusion at this point it is evident that important prerequisites for participating in other-related decision-making are present in children at a much younger age than believed just a few years ago. Thus we can also conclude that if the situation is tailored to suit the child, even three-year-olds can voice an opinion. On the other hand, perhaps we need to ask the children themselves in which fora they would want to participate. The issue of voting rights, for instance, is not in my opinion an either-or issue. Perhaps we should e.g. make distinctions between local and national elections or between the right to vote and the right to be elected. Perhaps there is a balance here between the right to participate and the right to protection? Or a difference between what adults think and what the children/young people themselves think and want? Have we asked them if they want the right to vote and at which age?

III. WHY IS PARTICIPATION SO IMPORTANT?

Participation is important from the sociological as well as the psychological point of view, for the development of the individual child as well as the democratic development of our world.

The right to participate, to give views and opinions, does *not* mean having to take responsibility for choices with consequences the young person cannot understand or cannot handle. Here there is a delicate balance between the rights to develop and participate and the right to protection. Successful decision-making and respected opinion-stating can be very important for the development of the child's "sense of self", and "identity". This is important because recently, investigators (Rutter 1979, 1987) have identified the child's "sense of self" as a key determinant for successful developmental outcomes – in developing as well as in industrialized communities. Children with positive feelings of self-esteem, mastery and control can more easily manage stressful experiences. This in turn leads to more positive reactions from their environment. They show initiative in task accomplishment and relationship formation. Even in stressed families, one good relationship with a parent reduces psychosocial risk. For older children a close, enduring relationship with an external supportive adult may provide a protective function.

Children need to acquire the skills and competencies that will prepare them for a wide variety of possible futures. Communications skills and social skills will be important regardless of many other things. Future adults will need persistence and courage, flexibility and creativity, self-confidence and responsibility, as well as imagination and faith. One way to give them this is by believing in children, by trusting in the evolving – not lacking – competence of children. We know that children who are active in decisionmaking, who learn from their own experience as well as by seeing adults spending time and energy involved in "causes", because they believe they can contribute to making a change, are less prone to depression, hopelessness and suicides. (Raundalen, M. & Raundalen, T.S. 1984; Escalona 1982; Schwebel 1982). Starting with having some impact in their own families, learning that they can make a difference in the neighbourhood, in their organizations and schools, their faith in the possibilities for change, their courage to try, their persistence in the face of the odds grows with them. This encourages development of personality characteristics important in any future society, particularly as the need to cooperate with people of different cultural backgrounds increases.

IV. PRINCIPLES FOR NATIONAL MONITORING MECHANISMS

As mentioned, I do not believe we can properly monitor implementation of the Convention without the views and opinions of children. The examples given have, however, mostly concerned individual children within the context of their families and near social institutions, such as the schools. Do we, then, have any experiences that can illuminate the children's individual and collective impact, if the opportunity exists, on the governing bodies of society? We have episodic information, e.g. from Brazil or from local communities. But we also have the experiences of formalized and permanent structures. These exist in societies with an Ombudsman for Children or a similar institution, the first one created in Norway in 1981. The majority of existing models function in industrialized countries. But even in developing countries it seems that the some guiding principles are applicable. A study of the existing institutions shows which principles are important all over the world. Some of the principles could admittedly be extremely difficult to apply and would in many countries represent more long-term goals. They should however be applicable in many countries. While seven such principles have been formulated, I shall present only three here, perhaps the ones most important to be effective transmitters of attitudes, problems, and opinions of the children themselves.

A. It Should Be a Voice for Children

giving a possibility to monitor how children see their world and have an impact upon it. An Ombudsman Office also implicitly gives the children the *right* to complain, because it provides the means to do so, e.g. for pupils in the school system. Thereby they also gain representation and thereby a strengthening of their rights. Serving as a "voice" or channel of communications between children and the health, welfare and education systems, the judiciary, the local planning boards and, in general, any area of government where decisions affecting children are being made, an Ombudsman Office:
 – transmits information from children;
 – makes the needs and rights of children publicly known;
 – imparts to children information they need to know, making sure that children are aware of the Convention and its relevance to their daily lives;
 – ensures that the literal voices of children are heard - that is, that the concerns and opinions which children themselves have actually expressed are taken into consideration.

B. It Must Be Accessible to the Population, Preferably Including Children Themselves

Access to such an Office should be as direct and easy as possible. Children and families should be able to relate easily to it. The fact that the Office is open to children themselves must be widely publicized. In Norway, when we started, we were so efficient in this respect that many adults thought *only* children could use the Office. We had for instance a caller who claimed to be six years old, but used such adult language that we asked her age. She turned out to be 72 years old. This access could be facilitated by identifying the structure with a person or, in some situations, with an institution or an organization which is widely regarded as an identifiable body related to children's issues, with a non-bureaucratic approach.

Our experiences in 1981–1989 were that children are eager to use the Office and presented a wider variety of issues than did adults. During the years after 1989 the number of calls from children has multiplied dramatically. However, when establishing such a service, consideration of quality and quantity must be considered. A greater number of calls, recorded, may not increase the number of problems or issues raised. If the individual call is not met with a personal conversation, the service may well lose a valuable opportunity to acquaint itself with the child's thinking, motivation and possibilities for – with help – dealing with the issue in question.

C. It Should Be Close to the Decision-making Bodies Concerned with Conditions that have an Impact on Children

Existing national ombudsman structures have all been established in small, democratic, homogeneous countries. Yet closer analysis has shown that these factors are not decisive for whether or not such mechanisms can be set up. The size of a country, its political system, cultural traditions, organizational structures and the total situation of children will all influence the choice of methods for improving or monitoring conditions for the younger population. Apart from the need in some countries to establish branches on sub-national levels to be close to the decision-making levels, mechanisms may consist of groups of organizations or one organization can be authorized by the national government to serve as the Ombudsman for Children.

In view of the participation rights of children, established by the Convention, it would seem increasingly difficult to exclude children entirely when models for monitoring are planned. It is important that children know about their rights and can give information about how their rights are protected. But it is also important for the development of children and young people that they have opportunities to be heard, to give opinions and to participate in the decision-making process. In my own experience children as young as 4 could and did call the Ombudsman. Children of school age raised issues which eventually led to legislative amendments. One child told us that she dreaded her 10. birthday, because after that mother could no longer stay at home when the child was ill. This has been changed. Another child raised the issue of visitation rights to grandparents or stepparents, an issue which has recently been picked up again by a group of grandmothers. In general children would point to a much wider variety of issues and problems than the adults did, partly because of the children's different point of view. Thus children also have experiences and information not shared with the adults.

I believe, then, that:

– Monitoring the participation rights of children cannot be done without listening to the children themselves.
– Our thinking about competence cannot be an either-or issue. The need for new research is a demanding one, but one that will not only provide new knowledge about child development, but also have a direct, strong and necessary impact upon attitudes to and perceptions of children.

— We are doing *children* a grave injustice if we do not encourage participation, as well as doing the future of our world a disfavour.

REFERENCES

Bowlby, J. (1969) *Attachment and Loss*. Vol.1.*Attachment*. New York: Basic Books.
Bowlby, J. (1973) *Attachment and Loss*. Vol.2. *Separation, Anxiety, and Anger*. New York: Basic Books.
Bowlby, J. (1980) *Attachment and Loss*. Vol. 3. *Loss, Sadness and Depression*. New York: Basic Books.
Brazelton, T.B. (1982) "Early Intervention: What does it Mean?" In Fitzgerald, H., Lester, B.M. and Yogman, M. (Eds): *Theory and Research in Behavioral Pediatrics*. Vol. 1. New York: Plenum.
Brazelton, T.B. (1982) "Early Intervention: What does it mean?" In Gunzenhauser (Ed) *Infant Stimulation: for Whom, what Kind, When and How Much?* New Jersey: Johnson and Johnson, Pediatric Round Table: 13. Johnson and Johnson Company.
Brazelton, T.B., Koslowski, B. and Main, M. (1974) "The Origins of Reciprocity: The Early Mother-Infant Interaction." In (M. Lewis and L. A. Rosenblum (Eds): *The Effect of the Infant on its Caretaker*. New York: Wiley.
Dickson, E.B., Lieber, L.E. and McIntyre, C.W. (1982) The Development of Cognitive, Affective, and Perceptual Role-Taking Skills in Early Childhood. (unpublished, referred to in Moore, S.G. and Cooper C.R. (Eds): *The Young Child*. Washington D.C.: National Association for the Education of Young Children).
Escalona, S. (1982) "Growing up with the Threat of Nuclear War: Some Indirect Effects on Personality Development." *American J. of Orthopsychiatry, 52 (4)*, 600–607.
Flavell, J.H. (1978) "The Development of Knowledge about Visual Perception." In C.B. Keasy (Ed): *Nebraska Symposium on Motivation*. Lincoln, Nebr.: University of Nebraska Press.
Flekkøy, M.G. (1991) *A Voice for Children: Speaking out as their Ombudsman*. London: J. Kingsley Publishers.
Flekkøy, M.G. (1991) *Models for Monitoring the Protection of the Rights of the Child*. (mim.report), UNICEF/Firenze, 1991.
Goldberg, S. (1977) "Social Competence in Infancy: A Model of Parent- Infant Interaction." *Merrill-Palmer Quarterly, 23*, 164–177.
Lewis, M. and Goldberg, S. (1969) "Perceptual-Cognitive Development in Infancy: A Generalized Expectancy Model. A Function of Mother-Infant Interaction." *Merrill-Palmer Quarterly, 15*, 81–100.
Marvin, R.S., Greenberg, M.T. and Mossler, D.G. (1976) "The Early Development of Conceptual Perspective-Taking: Distinguishing among Multiple Perspectives." *Child Development, 47*, 511–514.
Parker, S., Greer, S. and Zuckerman, B. (1988) "Double Jeopardy: The Impact of Poverty on Early Child Development." *Pediatric Clinics of North America, 35 (6)*, 1227–1240.
Raundalen, M. and Raundalen, T.S. (1984) *Barn i Atomalderen*. Oslo: Cappelen.
Schwebel, M. (1982) "Effects of Nuclear War Threat on Children and Teenagers: Implications for professionals." *American J. of Orthopsychiatry, 52 (4)*, 608–618.
Selman, R.L. (1976) "Social-Cognitive Understanding: A Guide to Educational and Clinical Practice." In T. Lickona (Ed): *Moral Development and Behavior*. New York: Holt, Rinehart & Winston.
Thomas, A., Chess, S. and Birch, H.G. (1968) *Temperament and Behavior Disorders in Children*. New York: New York University Press.
Thomas, A., Chess, S. and Birch, H.G. (1970) "The Origin of Personality." *Scientific American, 223*, 102–109.

NIGEL CANTWELL

Monitoring: Back to Basic Questions

Qvortrup's contribution to the debate on monitoring is – characteristically – quite stimulating. At the same time, my initial reaction was extremely hesitant. On reflexion, I have to say it still is.

But first the good news. We can no doubt all agree on the basic aims that Qvortrup is pursuing. Thus, probably no-one will have a major problem with at least the overall justification of what he calls the "conceptual autonomy" of childhood – what I would rather call "starting from where the child is". Indeed, if the reality of children's issues and situations is obscured by data secured from a family-based approach, for example, it seems both feasible and desirable to propose a shift. If we are monitoring the situation of children, then we have to start from the standpoint of those children, not that of their families or any other setting in which children may find themselves. Equally, children require a direct and indirect voice in policy-making at all levels; this is what Qvortrup would term "political constituency". Children must be recognised and respected as human beings – Qvortrup's "right to acknowledgement". And clearly a certain level of resources must be devoted to meeting the needs of the child population, in other words a form of "distributive justice".

What does concern me deeply, however, is the substance that Qvortrup gives to these aims, and many of the arguments he puts forward in their favour. An approach on these lines is to me tantamount to shooting ourselves in the foot. If such arguments were to be heard outside the hushed walls of academic fora, they would constitute an open invitation to totally discredit the rights of the child and the Convention in the eyes of the public, including decision-makers and policy-makers. The results of all the efforts made to date – and not without success – to secure acceptance of the concept of "the human rights of the child" would immediately be jeopardised.

Take, for example, his assertion that the "familialised" (as opposed to child-focused) approach stems from some sort of naive belief that the family is only a source of good and happiness. Put this together with his statement that the child's "right to acknowledgement" is denied because of parents wanting to "control" their children's behaviour (is it not rather that parents want to be aware of what their children are doing and to guide them – in complete accord with the Convention – as necessary and appropriate?). The result is an "anti-family", "anti-parent" message in complete opposition to all our efforts

E. Verhellen (ed.), Monitoring Children's Rights, 67–72.

to demonstrate that the Convention and the rights it contains are not inspired by such an approach – nor could or should they be.

The family simply happens to be the smallest unit in society with primary responsibility for the child and where, it is hoped, that child will in principle be in a position to develop "fully and harmoniously". No-one would try to contend that this hope is always fulfilled. But at the same time, it would seem to be erroneous, from a children's rights point of view, to create dissent within the family structure. Indeed, during the International Year of the Child, we documented that what children wanted most of all was not some kind of precocious autonomy but quite simply parents who had sufficient time and resources to care, listen and understand...

Regrettably, many other arguments used by Qvortrup have a similarly aggressive or unnecessarily provocative vein that is out of tune with both the spirit and the letter of the Convention. In order to "acknowledge" children, do we really have to envisage paying them a salary to go to school? Is it productive – in the context of monitoring the Convention, at least – to bring up the idea that children might "claim a right to be consumers"? What is a realistic reaction to the affirmation that a child's standard of living should not depend on his or her parents' income?

On the question of "political constituency", Qvortrup thankfully agrees that giving votes to children is probably not feasible, at the present time at least. I would add that children are not calling for a system that allows them to vote for a given political party every five years. They are simply and logically looking for channels and structures through which their concerns will be taken seriously by policy-makers. The alternative that Qvortrup suggests – allowing parents an extra vote per child – is surprising given the fears he expresses elsewhere about parental desires to control their children. Where is the child's access to a political constituency under that system?

Overall, then, I do not believe that Qvortrup's arguments – regardless of one's opinions as to their justification – provide guidance as to what we should be monitoring in the field of children's rights. A dose of realism and objectivity is required. Whilst I fully agree with, for example, Verhellen that in practice the Convention is *more* than a legal instrument, and has become a veritable mobilising tool[1], this has only proved possible precisely because it *is* at the origin a legal instrument. It therefore has to be monitored from a legal standpoint, not on the basis of individualistic interpretation or projection. Monitoring children's rights means monitoring those contained in the Convention, respecting the spirit and letter of the provisions. We have to distinguish very clearly between monitoring the rights of the child and monitoring childhood.

At this point, let us briefly recall the fact that the Convention is not revolutionary, but evolutionary. It did not fall from the sky onto an unsuspecting

---

[1] Verhellen, this volume.

world on 20 November 1989, but was the result of developments in international human rights law and thinking on children's issues that had been taking place for several decades – at least 70 years on the international level. And as a human rights instrument, it essentially creates obligations on governments.

The rights that these obligations imply are interdependent and mutually reinforcing. However much we are tempted, for our own analytical convenience, to categorise rights in one way or another, it must always be remembered that the Convention is a whole, and has to be read as such. In this respect, I beg to differ with the proposal made by Samir Basta[2] that we should prioritise certain rights for monitoring purposes: no right is inherently more important than any other, even though in given circumstances we may have to place more emphasis temporarily on ensuring respect for a limited number.

Why are we so concerned about monitoring this particular Convention? I find it disturbing to note that, notwithstanding the experience of several decades of promotion and protection work based on international human rights instruments, monitoring the Convention on the Rights of the Child has apparently given rise to ardent feelings that we do not possess the basic knowledge or correct approaches that will enable us to do it effectively. What could make this Convention so special in objective terms?

Of course this Convention is unusually comprehensive in nature and deals with several issues never previously tackled in hard international human rights law: adoption, traditional practices harmful to health, administration of juvenile justice and – explicitly and uncompromisingly at last – many aspects of what we have come to term "participatory" rights. But neither its scope nor the innovative nature of certain of its provisions seems to me to justify such trepidation.

In the first place, the fact that there now is a Convention and that it contains what it does is, precisely, the result of a monitoring process. We may have carried out the exercise haphazardly, pragmatically and almost without realising it, but carry it out we did, and it gave rise both to recognition of the need for a treaty and to acknowledgement that its provisions had to cover such and such issues and phenomena in such and such a way. The Convention is not perfect, of course, but its existence and the generally-accepted adequacy of its approach and coverage bear witness to the fact that, overall, we knew – or came to know – what was needed and why.

We had found out, first of all, that the contemporary body of international law was not sufficient as a basis for dealing with the problems that we could see children having to face. We noted that the somewhat vague 1959 Declaration, containing no State obligations, was ineffective as a tool. As a result, we supported efforts to secure a full-fledged and all-encompassing Convention.

---

[2] Basta, this volume.

Then we documented the fact that abuses of intercountry adoptions were increasing and warranted special protective measures; that children were being unreasonably deprived of their liberty; that arbitrary decisions were being made about their future, in the absence of consultation with them; that they were being forced to fight in wars, to sell their bodies, to forego basic education and to attempt to survive in situations of utter destitution. As a result, we tried – with some success – to ensure that the content and spirit of the Convention reflected these concerns.

Now, surely, all we need to do is to follow developments in these different areas, in the same way as those organisations that monitor respect for the International Covenant on Civil and Political Rights or the Convention against Torture. But this, according to some, is too simplistic an approach. We have to look again at what we should be seeking out when monitoring children's rights.

Deciding what we must monitor means first of all being certain that we agree on what monitoring means and why we do it.

Alston has noted that the real aim of monitoring is "pursuing the accountability of governments"[3], and this is certainly a basic element. At the same time, he has admitted that there is no single view of what monitoring is. The report of the Global Seminar on Monitoring organised by the UNICEF International Child Development Centre in Florence in May 1994 confirms the view that such agreement does not yet exist. All sorts of conceptions of the content and form of monitoring still abound. More helpfully, however, the report informs us that, etymologically, "monitoring means information-gathering for the purpose of reminding or warning, which may include admonition". In other words, it is a dynamic, on-going and pro-active process of collecting data that can be brought to the attention of the appropriate decision-makers. It therefore goes hand-in-hand with advocacy. We carry it out to effect change, in a kind of circular pattern:

- we set out to identify and document problem areas, and to determine obligations in their regard;
- then we advocate for, and propose, appropriate responses that may be legal in nature and/or on the level of policy and practice;
- if and when we secure the changes, we continue to document the effects of these responses; and
- the whole process is set in motion again.

The two most important implications of this process are, in my view, that:
- obviously, credible advocacy has to be based on credible monitoring, and this leaves little room for the interference of personal attitudes and interests;
- the data we gather must be useful for reaching goals that are desired, desirable and feasible. This feasibility depends on the following factors,

---

[3]   Alston, this volume.

which are not only of unequal significance but indeed vary in importance according to the specific situation concerned:

- financial ramifications;
- existing elements of justification (accepted standards, etc.);
- potential political (and/or, in some cases, administrative) will;
- the pre-disposition of the public or of the most concerned sectors thereof;
- the propensity of goal achievement to be formulated in strategic terms.

In keeping with this approach, the kind of situations that Defence for Children International (DCI) has been monitoring, both through its International Secretariat and, nationally, through its Sections, have tended to be very concrete and basic in nature.

Thus, how many children are in prison, who are they, why are they there, under what conditions and with what consequences? When the conclusion is, in a given country, that most detained children are simply on remand before trial, that they are accused of trivial offences, are at high risk of being subjected to physical and sexual assault, are deprived of their right to education, and – what irony – do not in the end receive custodial sentences, it is possible to point to the standards being violated and to begin formulating a strategy to deal with the problem. In this case, that strategy will no doubt have to contain an element of public information, since the general population is not always especially favourable towards a less repressive approach towards the juvenile offenders in their midst – witness the not infrequent remark that "human rights activists are always defending criminals". Law-makers and decision-makers may also have to be strongly encouraged, in various ways, to take the appropriate steps. In terms of the list of "feasibility factors" set out above, this leaves us with "financial ramifications".

In the case of institutional treatment – or, less euphemistically, deprivation of liberty – the financial arguments (cost per day of keeping a child in a closed facility) have in fact been quite widely used. In general, however, monitoring organisations have not been renowned for estimating the costs of the measures they oppose and propose, let alone proceeding to a full-fledged cost-benefit analysis. In terms of the subject of this section – "what is to be monitored?" – clearly one answer is that "cost-effectiveness" has to be added to the list.

Monitors must systematically and continuously ask the classic kind of questions that are mentioned above in relation to children in prison – how many, who, why, with what results – when looking at a whole series of situations, ranging from non-registration at birth, child labour, sexual exploitation and abuses of inter-country adoption through to lack of access to education and health services, inadequate standard of living and removal from parental care. These questions are so basic and well-known that, if it had not been for Qvortrup's presentation, I surely would not have felt it worthwhile to recall them here. But I do so deliberately because I fear that they may be unwarrantedly marginalised and discredited as boringly uninventive in the face of a "brave new world of ideas" for monitoring. This "new world", in my view, in many instances tries to turn the Convention into something it was neither intended to be nor should be allowed to become, and frankly stretches the concept of "what should be monitored" beyond reasonable limits.

Whilst appreciating the stimulating nature of Qvortrup's paper, and his well-known commitment to the cause of children's rights, I would therefore simply plead that the healthy aim of provoking debate not be allowed to endanger what has been acquired – with some difficulty – to date and to complicate unnecessarily what we have to do in the future in monitoring compliance with the Conventon on the Rights of the Child.

JOHAN VANDE LANOTTE and GEERT GOEDERTIER

Monitoring Human Rights: Formal and Procedural Aspects

INTRODUCTION

1. On November the 20th 1989, exactly thirty years after the adoption of the "Declaration of the Rights of the Child" (November 20, 1959), the General Assembly of the United Nations unanimously adopted the "Convention on the Rights of the Child". Whereas the Declaration of 1959 was only a statement of principles in which 10 main guidelines on the protection of the child were put forward,[1] the Convention of 1989 constituted a legally binding instrument. In some forty articles, certain civil, political, social, economic and cultural rights of the child were guaranteed. The Convention entered into force on the 2nd of September 1990 having been ratified by 20 countries.

2. A treaty is a legally binding instrument. The agreeing countries undertake to fulfill the obligations of the treaty. To ensure the actual implementation of the agreement there are many possible means of control. The effectiveness of a treaty will largely depend on the chosen control system: a treaty is as effective as its monitoring system.[2] This choice will be largely determined by the general aims of the treaty concerned. A system of control may indeed be purely sanctioning, but it may also have a stimulating, informative or helpful effect.

3. In this text we will discuss the monitoring system of the Convention on the Rights of the Child, as drawn up in articles 42 to 45. This system, like every other monitoring mechanism, was established to verify the effective compliance of the States Parties with their legal international obligations.

---

[1] On the Declaration of the Rights of the Child of 1959, see: Veerman, P., *The Rights of the Child and the Changing Image of Childhood*, Dordrecht/Boston/London, Martinus Nijhoff Publishers, 1992, p. 159–180; Verhellen, E., *Convention on the Rights of the Child*, Leuven/Apeldoorn, Garant, 1994, p. 59–64.

[2] Verhellen, E., *op.cit.*, p. 77.

E. Verhellen (ed.), Monitoring Children's Rights, 73–111.
© 1996 *Kluwer Law International. Printed in the Netherlands.*

The States Parties are monitored by an international medium to see if they fulfill their established legal obligations. In this way the monitoring system is a judicial mechanism. From the relevant articles, the "travaux préparatoires" and the viewpoints adopted by the Committee on the Rights of the Child with respect to these, it appears, however, that more is expected from the monitoring system. It is hoped that the monitoring system will actively contribute to the improvement of the position of the child in general and that it will give occasion to a broad, social discussion within the various countries themselves. From the study of the Conventions' articles and the working methods of the Committee, it will be clear that the Convention on the Rights of the Child offers many possibilities for the fulfillment of these objectives.

4. The framework in which the Convention on the Rights of the Child is situated, deserves to be outlined before further examination of the monitoring system. The Convention on the Rights of the Child is, after all, only one instrument enacted by the United Nations concerning human rights. Alston writes "(...) si chaque régime conventionnel doit être examiné individuelle-ment compte tenu de ses normes et de ses procédures propres, les divers régimes ne peuvent pas être, à certains égards, envisagés indépendamment les uns des autres ou hors du programme plus large concernant les droits de l'homme dans lequel ils s'intègrent".[3] This especially applies to an evaluation of the monitoring system for two reasons. On the one hand, the former human rights treaties often serve as an inspiration for the newer treaties. On the other hand, more and more people wish to coordinate the several procedures and organs, which were developed to monitor human rights, thus creating a more effective and more efficient unit.[4]

I. The Implementation of Human Rights

A. *The Activities of the UN Concerning Human Rights*

5. Traditionally, there are a number of phases recognized in the activities of the United Nations with respect to the human rights issue.[5] In the first phase (from 1947 to 1954) the "standard-setting" was most important. In

---

[3] Alston, Ph., *Application effective des instruments internationaux relatifs aux droits de l'homme, y compris l'obligation de présenter des rapports à ce titre*, A/44/668, para./9.

[4] See for example Nowak, M., 'Proposals for Improving the UN Human Rights Program-me", *NQHR 2* 1993, p. 153–162.

[5] See among others Alston, Ph., "Appraising the United Nations Human Rights Regime", in *The United Nations and Human Rights – A Critical Appraisal*, Alston, Ph. (ed.), Oxford, Clarendon Press, 1992, p. 3; Dormenval, A., *Procédures onusiennes de mise en oeuvre des droits de l'homme: limites ou défauts?*, Paris, Presses Universitaires de France, 1991, p. 6; Parmentier, S., "Mensenrechten in de jaren negentig", in *Mensenrechten tussen retoriek en realiteit – Tegenspraak Cahier 14*, Parmentier, S. (ed.), Ghent, Mys and Breesch, 1994, p. 7–8.

the second phase the promotion of human rights formed the most important agenda-point (1955–1966). In the third phase attention was drawn mainly to the protection of human rights. Since the end of the eighties the efficiency and the effectiveness of the monitoring of the implementation of human rights comes more and more on the agenda of the United Nations: "In the 1990's the pre-eminent human rights concern of the international community will be the establishment and development of effective procedures and mechanisms for sustained monitoring and for rapid and constructive responses to violations".[6] This concern appears, among others, in the agenda of the "World Conference on Human Rights", which took place from the 14th to the 25th of June 1993.[7] It is however clear that this evolution does not give an overall image of the human rights activities of the United Nations. The setting of standards, promotion and protection remain important UN-activities, which for example is clear from the recent Convention on the Rights of the Child.

6. The recent attention drawn to the efficiency and effectiveness of the monitoring procedures is explained by the fact that the United Nations, after a period of upwards development, now has reached a point of reflection where the objectives and means of the human rights program must be evaluated.[8] Parmentier speaks of the "mid-life crisis" of the United Nations.[9,10] This

---

[6] Alston, Ph., "Preface", in *The United Nations and Human Rights – A Critical Appraisal*, Alston, Ph. (ed.), Oxford, Clarendon Press, 1992, V. See also the study carried out by Alston, by order of the General Assembly of the U.N.: "De quelque manière que l'on qualifie la situation présente, il est admis en général que le système de surveillance créé par les instruments des Nations Unies relatifs aux droits de l'homme est parvenu à un point critique. Si l'on veut assurer son succès dans l'avenir, il faut reconnaître la gravité des problèmes actuels, réaffirmer l'importance cruciale du régime conventionnel dans son ensemble et poursuivre avec énergie et détermination la recherche de solutions créatrices et efficaces. Il ne faudrait pas pour autant s'engager dans cette recherche sans reconnaître qu'une oeuvre très considérable a été accomplie jusqu'ici et qu'il importe de procéder avec finesse et perspicacité de manière à ne pas sacrifier l'intégrité fondamentale du système, et en particulier son aptitude à sauvegarder les droits de l'homme, à des notions illusoires de rationalisation et de rendement. En d'autres termes, dans cette époque de crise ou de défi, il faut voir aussi une époque où s'ouvrent des possibilités de réforme et d'amélioration constructives" (Doc. A/44/668, para. 8). See also: Opsahl, T., "Instruments of Implementation of Human Rights", *Human Rights Law Journal* 1989–10, p. 14.

[7] In this respect, see Boerefijn, I. and Davidse, K., "Every Cloud...? The World Conference on Human Rights and Supervision of Implementation of Human Rights, *NQHR 4* 1993, p. 457–468; Vienna Declaration and Programme of Action, UN Doc.A/Conf.157/23, 12 July 1993; published in *NJCM-Bulletin* 1993, 716-738.

[8] Parmentier, S., "Internationale controle en implementatie van mensenrechten", in *Belgen over mensenrechten – Een bijdrage tot de Wereldconferentie Mensenrechten, Vienna, 14–25 juni 1993*, Brussels, Ministerie van Buitenlandse Zaken, Buitenlandse Handel en Ontwikkelingssamenwerking, 1993, p. 26.

[9] Parmentier, S., *op.cit.*, p. 26.

[10] A similar evolution does not only appear within the framework of the United Nations but also within the Council of Europe. See: Roucounas, E., "The reform of the human rights institutions of the Council of Europe", in *The reform of international institutions for the*

development is sharpened, according to the same author, by a number of important political developments on a world-wide level. After the fall of the Berlin wall, the international authorities did not appear to be able to guarantee human rights in Eastern Europe that has now become the battle field of ethnical conflicts and civil wars. Neither in the young democracies of Latin-America (not to speak of Africa) does respect for human rights appear to gain support without problems.[11] The UN had to face very recently its failures in dealing with the events in Somalia and Rwanda.

7. The attention paid to the monitoring of the implementation of human rights is mainly focused on two topics: (1) the important increase in the number of UN control bodies and (2) the functioning (or malfunctioning) of the several control bodies and monitoring methods.[12] It is indeed the case that more and more control mechanisms and control bodies have been established since 1947. Some consider this increase as a positive development, whereas other people think that this increase has led to less clarity and a lower efficiency.

8. Recently, a lot of attention is being paid to the efficiency of the monitoring systems. This is why this study aims to screen the monitoring mechanisms of the Convention on the Rights of the Child. Before this study is undertaken, however, we must state that it will never be possible to completely examine to what degree a control system can have a positive influence on human rights: "too many factors influence progress in human rights to make it possible to document precisely the role of international supervisory systems".[13] The Convention on the Rights of the Child does however offer us, thanks to its recent development, a good opportunity to find out what the United Nations have already learned from the past and how the efficiency of the supervisory systems can be increased in the future.

---

protection of human rights. First International Colloquium on Human Rights. La Laguna, Tenerife, 1st – 4th november 1992, La Laguna University, Brussels, Bruylant, 1993, p. 213–249; Carrillo Salcedo, J.A., "Vers la réforme du système européen de protection des Droits de l'Homme", in *Présence du droit public et des droits de l'homme. Mélanges offerts à Jacques Velu*, Brussels, Bruylant, 1992, p. 1319–1325; Meyer-Ladewig, J., "Reform of the Control Machinery", in *The European System for the protection of human rights*, Macdonald, R.St.J., Matscher, F. and Petzold, H.(ed.), Dordrecht, Martinus Nijhoff Publishers, 1993, p. 909–926.

[11]   Parmentier, S., *op.cit.*, p. 26.

[12]   Parmentier, S., "Internationale controle en implementatie van mensenrechten", in *Belgen over mensenrechten – Een bijdrage tot de Wereldconferentie Mensenrechten, Vienna, 14–25 June 1993*, Brussels, Ministerie van Buitenlandse Zaken, Buitenlandse Handel en Ontwikkelingssamenwerking, 1993, p. 26. See also the study by Philip Alston, carried out by order of the General Assembly of the UN (*Application effective des instruments internationaux relatifs aux droits de l'homme, y compris l'obligation de présenter des rapports à ce titre*, Doc. A/44/668).

[13]   Virginia A. Leary, "Lessons from the Experience of the International Labour Organisation", in *The United Nations and Human Rights. A Critical Appraisal*, Alston, P. (ed.), Oxford, Clarendon Press, 1992, p. 595.

B. The Implementation of Human Rights on Both a National and an International Level

9. A treaty is an agreement made between States. From a judicial point of view, a State fulfills its international obligations towards other States and not towards individuals; the State is not responsible to the victim of the violation, but to other States Parties.[14] The provisions of a treaty can nevertheless have their influence on the national legal system. As far as States with a dualist constitutional system are concerned, a provision of a treaty can only acquire a judicial meaning in the national legal system once the provision is transformed into national law. In those States with a monist constitutional system however, the treaties are directly integrated into the national legal system. International provisions can moreover gain a self-executing character in the latter type of countries. This implies that individuals can appeal to the provisions of a treaty when appearing in a national court.[15]

10. The implementation of human rights accepted in international treaties is basically a national concern.[16] This is only natural for those States with a dualist constitutional system. Indeed, the provisions of a treaty must always be converted into internal law before they can have any legal meaning in the internal legal system of the country. The implementation, however, is also basically a national matter for those countries with a monist constitutional system. It is indeed the case that not all provisions of a treaty can acquire a self-executing character. The ratification of a treaty does not only involve the obligation of a State to enter the provisions in national law (as far as this is necessary), but the State is also obliged to attune its national policy to the ratified provisions of the treaty.

11. As a result, the implementation of human rights is first of all a matter of national legislation and policy. However, lots of mechanisms have been developed on an international level to make sure that the States do actually comply with their obligations. Implementation is consequently not a purely national but also an international matter. The term implementation is usually applied in this second meaning, i.e. regarding the international mechanisms that have the actual realization of the standards concerning human rights as

---

[14] Dimitrijevic, V., "The Monitoring of Human Rights and the prevention of human rights violations through reporting procedures", in *Monitoring Human Rights in Europe. Comparing International Procedures and Mechanisms*, Dordrecht/Boston/London, Martinus Nijhoff Publishers, 1993, p. 1.

[15] For the self-executing character of the UN-Convention on the Rights of the Child, see the contribution made by André Alen and Wouter Pas in this volume.

[16] Zwaak, L.F., *International Human rights procedures – Petitioning the ECHR, CCPR and CERD*, Utrecht, Ars Aequi Libri, 1991, p. V; Opsahl, T., "Instruments of Implementation of Human Rights", *Human Rights Law Journal* 1989–10, p. 32: "One should never forget that national implementation must be the alpha and omega".

their main objective.[17] The role played by these international procedures is subsidiary in relation to the implementation of human rights by the national authorities.[18]

12. These international procedures have different objectives and functions. On the one hand, there are procedures through which legal enforcement of human rights is made possible on an international level. This is the less developed kind of procedure within the United Nations. Parmentier states that only the procedure for the International Court of Justice matches this description to a certain degree.[19] This category is more extended on a regional level. The European Court of Human Rights is for example qualified to pronounce judgments that are binding for the States that have recognized the legal power of the Court. A person who cannot enforce his rights before a national judge can hence appeal to an international judge.

13. The intention of the other procedures is not to judicially enforce human rights on an international level but to check and encourage the implementation by the States. UN activities concerning human rights are characterized by an amalgamation of similar procedures, such as: reporting procedures,[20] country procedures,[21] thematic procedures,[22] communications procedures[23] and confidential procedures such as e.g. procedure 1503.[24] Van Boven makes

---

[17] Parmentier describes the implementation as the whole of mechanisms that intend to put the standards regarding human rights into practice and that contribute to the actual realization of human rights (Parmentier, S., *op.cit.*, p. 32). See for a similar definition: Opsahl, T. "Instruments of Implementation of Human Rights", *Human Rights Law Journal* 1989–10, p. 14.

[18] "(...) although international control procedures are no substitute for means and methods of national implementation of human rights, international procedures have an important subsidiary or supplemental role to play" (Van Boven, T., "The international system of human rights : an overview", in *Manual on Human Rights Reporting* (Doc. HR/PUB/91/1), New York, United Nations, 1991, p. 10).

[19] Parmentier, S., *op.cit.*, p. 28.

[20] The reporting procedure is laid down in Article 40 CCPR, Article 17 CESCR, Article 9 CERD, Article 18 CEDAW, Article 19 CAT and in Article 44 CRC.

[21] The intention of country procedures is to thoroughly examine flagrant violations of human rights in a certain country. This can be realized by delegating special rapporteurs to the country concerned or by founding a permanent working group (e.g. the "Ad hoc Working Group of Experts on Southern Africa').

[22] Thematic procedures are applied to examine the violation of certain human rights (such as torture, religious intolerance, ...)

[23] See for example the Optional Protocol to the Covenant on Civil and Political Rights. Within the framework of the United Nations, the term "communications" is used instead of "complaints". Opsahl describes the term "communications" as a UN-eufemism for "complaints" (Opsahl, T., "The Human Rights Committee", in *The United Nations and Human Rights – A Critical Appraisal*, Alston, Ph. (ed.), Oxford, Clarendon Press, p. 419).

[24] By application of procedure 1503, the Sub-commission on Prevention of Discrimination and Protection of Minorities and the Commission on Human Rights discuss violations of

a distinction between the regular and the special supervisory procedures.[25] The reporting system is a regular supervisory procedure. Thematic procedures, country procedures, communications procedures and procedure 1503 are special procedures.

14. Not only a great number of methods but also a large collection of bodies that are active in the field of human rights can be distinguished within the United Nations. Alston classifies these bodies, depending on their judicial basis.[26] He comes up with two kinds of bodies. On the one hand, there are the so-called "Charter-based organs". The 6 principal organs, the functional commissions of the Economic and Social Council and the sub-commissions founded by these functional commissions are classified in this group. The other group consists of those bodies that were established through specific treaties. This group constitutes the so-called "treaty-based organs". The latter group has gone through a huge expansion over the past thirty years and contains (among others) the following organs: the Committee on Elimination of Racial Discrimination, the Committee on Elimination of Discrimination against Women, the Human Rights Committee, the Committee against Torture, the Committee on Economic, Social and Cultural Rights and the Committee on the Rights of the Child. The "treaty-based organs" have a number of characteristics in common and, according to Alston, mainly distinguish themselves from the "Charter-based organs" as far as their mandate and attitude with regard to the States are concerned.[27] The "treaty-based organs" bear the responsibility for monitoring the implementation of the provisions of the treaties concerned. The "Charter-based organs" have a much broader mandate to promote awareness, to foster respect, and to respond to violations of human rights standards. The 'treaty-based organs" mainly take a non-conflicting stance vis-à-vis the States Parties, whereas the "Charter-based organs" take strongly conflicting stances whenever needed.

15. The UN human rights apparatus hence consists of a rather opaque ensemble of procedures and organs. Quantity does however not necessarily entail quality. On the contrary. "The main difficulty is created by the pluralism of the systems. Many organs apply similar rules in a different manner. The same rule is interpreted differently. This creates a lack of confidence on the part of all those who place their trust in human rights",[28] as Ermacora states. The recent

---

human rights behind closed doors. A list of the countries discussed is published afterwards. Possible recommendations may however be made public.

[25] Van Boven, T., *op.cit.*, p. 8.

[26] Alston, Ph., "Appraising the United Nations Human Rights Regime", in *The United Nations and Human Rights. A Critical Appraisal*, Alston, Ph. (ed.), Oxford, Clarendon Press, 1992, p. 4–5.

[27] Alston, Ph., *op.cit.*, p. 3–5.

[28] Ermacora, F., "The reform of the human rights institutions of the United Nations", in *The reform of international institutions for the protection of human rights. First International*

attention paid to the improvement of monitoring systems has therefore a lot to do with the vaguenesses and overlaps that have arisen due to the extension of the control organs and monitoring systems. This is exactly the reason why a more intensive coordination is more and more being advocated.[29] Some people even advocate a complete reform of the reporting procedures by means of a fusion of all the different reporting obligations into one single reporting obligation. In the latter case, the monitoring would be taken care of by one monitoring organ. As a result, the various "treaty-based organs" could be dissolved.[30]

16. According to Meron, the United Nations' human rights system is characterized by a weak and sporadic implementation.[31] This shortcoming could, in his opinion, be remedied by a precise formulation of human rights: "The weaker the implementation system, the greater the importance of a more precise formulation of human rights instruments".[32] An exact and clear formulation could indeed ensure that the provisions concerned acquire a self-executing character. Individuals would thus be able to enforce their rights in national court. It goes without saying that this is not possible for all rights and freedoms. This situation is in most cases only feasible for civil and political rights. More problems will rise when social, economic and cultural rights are concerned.[33] A precise formulation of these rights will in many cases turn

---

Colloquium on Human Rights. La Laguna, Tenerife, 1st – 4th november 1992, La Laguna University, Brussels, Bruylant, 1993, p. 140.

[29] See for example Van Boven: "In order to maintain consistency in the interpretation of standards and in the assessment of facts and information, and with a view to avoiding duplication and confusion, there is much need for co-ordination between the various coexisting procedures and mechanisms. This co-ordination should be a constant concern of international secretariats and of the control mechanisms themselves" (Van Boven, T., *op.cit.*, p. 10). See also: Doc. A/44/668, *Application effective des instruments internationaux relatifs aux droits de l'homme, y compris l'obligation de présenter des rapports à ce titre*

[30] Nowak, M., "Proposals for Improving the UN Human Rights Programme", *NQHR 2* 1993, p. 158.

[31] Meron, Th., *Human rights law-making in the United Nations – A critique of Instruments and Processes*, Oxford, Clarendon Press, 1986, p. 2.

[32] *Ibidem*

[33] "Now it is agreed that the economic, social and cultural rights set out in the other Covenant are to be implemented progressively. Indeed, it would obviously be impossible for a number of them – the right to work, for example – to be implemented immediately and completely anywhere. Civil and political rights, on the other hand, are as a general rule capable of immediate application, and a State should put its laws and administrative practice in compliance with the Covenant before ratifying it" (Robertson, A. H. and Merrils, J.G., *Human rights in the world. An introduction to the study of the international protection of human rights*, Manchester, Manchester University Press, 1989, p. 42–43).

out to be impossible, since the economic possibilities of the potential States Parties must be taken into account.[34]

17. The nature of the rights that will constitute the subject of the implementation will also have to be taken into consideration when choosing a monitoring system. Civil and political rights can be formulated in a more precise way. The development of a "more jurisdictional" monitoring system will therefore not be excluded. A stimulating monitoring system will rather be opted for when the treaty contains social, economic and cultural rights. This became clear, for example, in the two Covenants of 1966. Valticos states: "The difference between the procedures laid down in the two Covenants has been explained by the fact that the Covenant on Civil and Political Rights involves precise and immediate obligations, whereas that relating to economic, social and cultural rights is considered to be aiming at promoting the progressive observance of the recognized rights to the extent that the means available to the State permit. A procedure for consideration of claims had not, therefore, seemed appropriate for rights of this kind".[35]

18. The above shows that the way in which implementation is carried out on the national and international levels cannot be separated from both the nature and the formulation of the rights to be implemented. It is within this framework quite understandable that the monitoring system of the Convention on the Rights of the Child, that comprises both civil and political rights on the one hand and social, economic and cultural rights on the other hand, is based on a reporting obligation for the States involved.

II. THE MONITORING MECHANISM OF THE CONVENTION ON THE RIGHTS OF THE CHILD

A. *General philosophy of the monitoring mechanism*

19. The monitoring mechanism of the Convention on the Rights of the Child is included in articles 42 to 45. The authors of the Convention did not consider it appropriate to develop a chastising and reprimanding control system. The stances taken by the non-governmental organizations, organized in an 'ad hoc group', had a lot to do with this. The 'ad hoc group' indeed wished to create a 'positive atmosphere' surrounding implementation. The monitoring

---

[34] This does however not exclude social and economic rights from acquiring a self-executing character. Indeed, some social and economic rights can entail a so-called "standstill"-obligation. Within this respect, see the contribution made by Prof Dr A. Alen and Wouter Pas.

[35] Valticos, N., "International Mechanisms for the Protection of Human Rights", in *International Law: Achievements and Prospects*, Bedjaoui, M. (ed.), Dordrecht/Boston/ Londen, Martinus Nijhoff Publishers, 1991, p. 1152.

system had to be based on the idea of mutual help, support and co-operation.[36] This is why a complaints procedure was not developed in this convention. A monitoring mechanism, based on a reporting obligation for the States, was opted for. The Committee that was founded for this purpose does not only act in a controlling but also in an advising way. The dynamic character of the implementation system of the Convention was stressed more than once in the course of the 'travaux préparatoires'. For example: there were originally two proposals regarding the description of the general task of the Committee on the Rights of the Child: 1st 'monitoring the implementation of the provisions of the obligations undertaken in the present Convention'; and 2nd 'examining the progress made by States Parties in achieving the realization of the obligations undertaken in the present Convention'. The authors finally adopted the second proposal since the dynamic character ('examining the progress') of the obligation to report would thus be explicitly entered in the Convention.[37]

20. The States Parties do not only have the obligation to report but also an obligation to inform. Article 42 says that the States are to make the provisions of the convention public, both to adults and to children.[38] A real and actual exercise of rights by children presupposes in the first instance a certain knowledge of these rights. This is why it is of paramount importance to inform children of their rights on the one hand and to raise public awareness relating to a larger respect for the rights of the child on the other hand. This obligation to inform, which is an essential part of the provisions of the Convention, is quite original since the other treaties on human rights never mentioned a similar dissemination duty.[39] Moreover, article 44 § 6 obliges the States to put their reports at the disposal of everybody in their country. The population, the non-governmental organizations and other associations will thus be well-informed. This will enable them to contribute strongly to the improvement of the effective application of the Convention. The Committee was moreover resolved to encourage the States to publish the results of the dialogue with the Committee: "Recognizing the importance of this measure to encourage popular participation and to achieve a comprehensive national approach to the implementation process of the Convention, (...), the Committee decided

---

[36] See Verhellen, E., *op.cit.*, p. 82. The author points out that the idea of mutual help, support and co-operation is at the same time explicitly comprised in the substantial provisions of the Convention itself. Article 4, dealing with the economic, social and cultural rights, mentions that the States, whenever necessary, can look for the means to realize these rights, within the framework of the international co-operation.

[37] Detrick, S. (ed.), *The United Nations Convention on the Rights of the Child. A Guide to the "Travaux Préparatoires"*, Dordrecht/Boston/London, Martinus Nijhoff Publishers, 1992, p. 539.

[38] Article 42: "States Parties undertake to make the principles and provisions of the Convention widely known, by appropriate and active means, to adults and children alike".

[39] Except a number of humanitarian conventions, that are applicable in situations of armed conflict.

to encourage States Parties to inform it about the steps taken to ensure the widespread dissemination of the results of the dialogue with the Comittee".[40] The report drawn up by the States is to mention in which way their information duty is accomplished. The 'concluding observations' on the reports of those countries that have not yet (sufficiently) published the provisions of the Convention, clearly show that the Committee considers this duty to inform as an essential part of the obligations entailed by the Convention.[41]

B. The Committee on the Rights of the Child

1. The Foundation of the Committee

21. By virtue of Article 43 of the Convention, a Committee on the Rights of the Child was installed to assess the progress made by the States regarding the fulfillment of their obligations. The 'travaux préparatoires' of the Convention show that not every country gave their downright approval to develop a specific children's committee. A lot of countries were indeed aware of the problems (such as financial implications,[42] problems due to vagueness and overlaps, strains put on national administrations, ...) that are implied by an increase in the number of control organs within the United Nations. As a matter of fact, it was the Belgian delegate who suggested leaving the monitoring of the implementation of the Convention on the Rights of the Child to the existing Committees. He more specifically meant the monitoring organs of the two Covenants of 1966.[43] Poland had suggested having the reports examined by a 'Group of Governmental Experts', founded by the Economic and Social Council.[44] These proposals arose as a consequence of the recent concern regarding the increase in the number of UN organs that are to monitor human rights.

22. Neither proposal was adopted, however. The foundation of a separate Committee on the Rights of the Child was finally opted for. This Committee

---

[40] CRC/C/20, para. 29.

[41] See for example the 'concluding observations' on the reports of Bolivia (CRC/C/20, para 44), Viet Nam (CRC/C/20, para. 67), Costa Rica (CRC/C/20, para. 137), Peru (CRC/C/20, para. 75) and Egypt (CRC/C/16, para. 108).

[42] In the course of the 'travaux préparatoires', a lot of attention was paid to the financial implications of the increase in the number of committees (see Detrick, S. (ed.), *op.cit.*, p. 555 and following).

[43] Detrick, S (ed.), *op.cit.*, p. 555.

[44] The Polish proposal was formulated as follows: "1. Reports submitted by the States Parties to the present Convention under article 22 shall be considered by the Economic and Social Council, which may bring its observations and suggestions to the attention of the State Party concerned and of the General Assembly of the United Nations. The Council may also request a State Party to submit additional reports on specific issues relating to this Convention. To assist it in its task, the Economic and Social Council shall establish a Group of Governmental Experts entrusted with the responsiblility of examining the reports submitted by States Parties. ..." (Detrick, S. (ed.), *op.cit.* p.552).

is financed through the UN-budget.[45] The argument that no UN-body has an overall view on the rights of the child has had a decisive influence on the discussion.[46]

2. The Composition of the Committee

23. The Committee on the Rights of the Child, just like the other 'treaty-based organs', consists of "experts of high moral standing and recognized competence in the field covered by this Convention" (in casu the rights of the child). The Committee consists of 10 members. It is thus, together with the Committee against Torture, the smallest of the 'treaty-based organs'.[47] Article 43 provides a specific procedure for the election of the Committee members.[48] The first election of the Committee members took place between the 27th of February and the 1st of March 1991.[49] The members of the Committee are elected for a period of four years. The term of office of five of the members[50] who were elected during the first elections comes to an end after two years. The Committee (or at least half of it) can thus have a different

---

[45] A lot of discussion on the manner of financing has arisen in the course of the "travaux préparatoires". Some countries, such as the United Kingdom and the United States of America, advocated financing by contributions made by the several States Parties. Other countries in their turn adhered to financing by the United Nations. This is why paragraph 12 of article 43 has remained between square brackets for a long time. Financing via the budget of the United Nations was finally opted for: 'With the approval of the General Assembly, the members of the Committee established under the present Convention shall receive emoluments from United Nations resources on such terms and conditions as the Assembly may decide' (art. 43, § 12).

[46] "One representative expressed her belief that neither in the United Nations system nor among the non-governmental international organizations was there at present a legal entity which had an overall view of the rights of the child: it therefore believed that if it proved possible to establish a committee of specialists in this branch of the law, with expert knowledge of the serious problems that affect childhood today and with moral and legal authority to approach any governmental or private international agency to draw attention to the shortcomings in respect of children in the area of their different specialities (...), such a committee could be of considerable benefit to children and young people, in other words, minors" (Detrick, S. (ed.), *op.cit.*, p. 539).

[47] The Committee on Elimination of Racial Discrimination, the Human Rights Committee and the Committee on Economic, Social and Cultural Rights each consist of 18 experts. The Committee on Elimination of Discrimination against Women consists of 23 members.

[48] The procedure can be roughly outlined as follows: 1° Each State Party of the Convention may nominate one person from among its own nationals. The Secretary General of the United Nations invites the States Parties to submit their nominations within a period of two months. He is to do so at least four months before the elections actually take place. 2° The Secretary General draws up an alphabetical list of all nominated persons, mentioning the countries they were nominated by. This list will then be submitted to the States Parties of the Convention. 3° The elections are held at a meeting organized by the Secretary General. All States Parties are invited to this meeting. At least two thirds of the States Parties must attend the meeting. To be elected, a candidate must obtain an absolute majority of the votes of the attending delegates of voting States. Those who have the most votes are elected.

[49] CRC/C/7, para. 3.

[50] These five members are appointed by the President of the Meeting by means of a lottery.

composition every two years. The members are eligible for re-election if they are renominated (art. 43, § 6).[51]

24. The experts act in their personal capacity and are hence not dependent on the State of which they have the nationality (art. 43, § 2): "(...) the Committee members are solely accountable to the children of the world".[52] It is for this reason that the Committee decided that the members will not participate in the discussion on the country report of their own government.[53]

3. Official and Informal Meetings

25. Initially , the Committee would meet once a year. The duration of the sessions is determined by a meeting of the States Parties of the Convention (art. 43, § 10). During its first session (1991) the Committee already noted that one session a year would not do to meet its objectives: "It was noted, for example, that the initial reports of some 100 States Parties would need to be considered by the Committee between 1992 and 1996, before the second periodic reports became due, and that a single annual session of three weeks duration would clearly not permit timely and thorough action on those reports even if the Committee devoted its time exclusively to that one activity. Additionally, the Committee would be unable to effectively address its other important responsibilities including those regarding technical assistance under article 45, the consideration of special studies and other reports submitted to it, the formulation of general recommendations on the implementation of the Convention, and the formulation of general comments to assist States Parties in fulfilling their reporting obligations".[54] This is why the Committee deemed it necessary to ask the General Assembly to authorize the Secretary General to organize at least two meetings a year. Moreover, the Committee asked the General Assembly's permission to found a 'Pre-sessional Working Group'.[55] This 'Pre-sessional Working Group' would examine the country reports for a first time two months before the session would actually take place. Some questions regarding the country reports would be drawn up. These possible questions could then be put to the representatives of the States concerned. "This would facilitate the task of States Parties by providing advance notice of the principal issues arising from the examination of their reports and would significantly

---

[51] Six women and four men were elected at the first elections. Their countries of origin were the following: Egypt, Burkina Faso, Barbados, the Phillipines, Sweden, Portugal, Russia, Brazil, Zimbabwe and Peru. The female Brazilian member was replaced by a male Brazilian member at a second round of elections (CRC/C/10, para. 5). The terms of office of 4 of the five members that expired at the 28th of February 1993 were renewed for another four years. The male Brazilian member was replaced by a female Brazilian member.

[52] CRC/C/10, para. 33.

[53] CRC/C/10, para. 33.

[54] CRC/C/7, para. 5.

[55] CRC/C/7, *Recommendation concerning sessions of the Committee or its subsidiary bodies*

improve the efficiency of the reporting system".[56] The 'Pre-sessional Working Group' could also pay some attention to the international co-operation and the technical support, as dealt with in article 45 of the Convention.[57]

26. Nevertheless, the main problem of the Committee remained the lack of time. Indeed, the Convention on the Rights of the Child had, in a very short period, become the UN convention with the largest number of ratifications. It was in the course of their fourth session (1993) that the Committee decided to organize a special session in 1994.[58] At a fifth session (1994), the Secretary General was asked to organize a meeting of the States Parties at which the duration of the meetings would be discussed. He was at the same time asked to increase the number of both the annual sessions and of the meetings of the 'Pre-sessional Working Group' from two to three.[59]

27. In spite of these administrative troubles, the Committee did not throw in the towel. The Committee itself took the initiative to promote both its activities and the children's Convention. Indeed, apart from the official sessions, the committee has organized a number of informal regional meetings.[60] These meetings intend to promote the provisions of the Convention on a regional level, to encourage international co-operation in the field of children's rights and to offer its members the opportunity to examine the situation of the rights of the child on the spot.[61] The Committee on the Rights of the Child thus became the first UN human rights body to study the situation of human rights on the spot in certain countries. "The regional meetings had constituted an innovative method of work and might be regarded as a first step in action by any treaty body useful tool for better promotion of children's rights".[62,63] The Committee does however stress the fact that the regional informal meetings have no control function at all: "It was important to bear in mind that the Quito

---

[56] CRC/C/7, para. 12.

[57] The General Assembly of the United Nations has approved both demands of the Committee in resolution 46/112.

[58] CCR/C/20, *Recommendation 1*

[59] CRC/C/24, *Recommendation 1*

[60] The first meeting was held in Quito, Ecuador between the 1st and the 5th of June 1992. The meeting was organized and financed by UNICEF and the Human Rights Centre (CRC/C/10, p. 1). The second meeting took place in Bangkok, Thailand, between the 23rd and the 29th of May 1993 (CRC/C/20, paras. 143–149).

[61] CRC/C/10, para. 34; CRC/C/20, para. 143.

[62] CRC/C/SR.29, para. 7.

[63] It was at their second session (1992) that the Committee decided to call the attention of the "Fourth Meeting of persons chairing the human rights treaty bodies" to this work method: "The innovating experience of holding informal meetings at the regional level should be brought to the attention of the Fourth Meeting, in view of its relevance as a means to promote greater awareness of the Convention on the Rights of the Child and its system of implementation, and to provide the Committee with a deeper knowledge and better understanding of the realities of a region" (CRC/C/10, *Recommendation 5*).

meeting had not been a monitoring operation by the Committee but simply an educational and training exercise. In future meetings, that fact should be made clear at the outset".[64] By means of listening to children on the spot and by getting in touch with non-governmental organizations, the Committee has given shape to one of the most important reasons of the Convention's existence: the participation of the children themselves.[65]

C. The Reporting Procedure

1. The Content of the Reports
a. Article 44 of the Convention

28. In accordance with article 44 of the Convention, the States are to regularly report on the measures they have taken to protect and promote the rights of the children and on the progress they have made with regard to the enjoyment of the rights concerned. This reporting obligation is to be complied with for a first time within two years after ratification of the Convention. Afterwards, a report is to be submitted once every five years. The reports are addressed to the Secretary General. He then communicates them to the Committee on the Rights of the Child. The States have the obligation to make sure that the reports are publicly available in their own country (art. 44, § 6).

29. The Convention does not give a clear definition of what exactly is to be included in the report. According to the first paragraph of article 44, the following is to be mentioned: "the measures they have adopted which give effect to the rights recognized herein". This is of course not sufficient. At the same time, information is to be given on "the progress made on the enjoyment of those rights". It is hence not sufficient to list the measures taken; it also has to be checked to what degree these new measures (and the already existing regulations) have contributed to the actual enjoyment of human rights. This does not only force the States to take measures, but also to assess the effect of these measures and to check whether they really contribute to the realization of the rights of the child.

30. Within this framework, the second paragraph of the same article specifies that the reports are to mention the factors and the possible difficulties that have their influence on the compliance with the obligations entailed by the Convention. States that, in one way or an other, experience some difficulties with the implementation of the Convention, have the opportunity to communicate these troubles to the Committee. The Committee will then give its advice on the matter concerned. Article 44 mentions that the reports are

---

[64] CRC/C/SR.29, para. 14.

[65] Reid, R., "Children's Rights: Radical Remedies for Critical Needs", in *Justice for Children* Asquith, S. and Hill, M. (ed.), Dordrecht/Boston/London, Martinus Nijhoff Publishers, 1994, p. 21.

to contain sufficient information in order to provide the Committee with a comprehensive understanding of the implementation of the Convention in the country concerned. In order not to strain the States too much, the third paragraph of Article 44 finally stipulates that a State, which has submitted a comprehensive initial report to the Committee need not, in its subsequent reports repeat basic information previously provided.

31. In spite of all these stipulations, this matter remains rather vague. How are the reports to be drawn up? How exhaustive and specific should the reports be? How is it to be checked whether progress has been made relating to the enjoyment of human rights? When is the information considered to be sufficient as implied by article 44, § 2? The Committee on the Rights of the Child drew up some "general guidelines" on the 15th of October 1991 in order to better specify the requirements for the reports. The States are to meet these guidelines when drawing up their reports.[66] The introductory part of the report is to be based on the so-called 'consolidated guidelines'.[67] In the introductory part the States should inform the Committee about the population and the general institutional and judicial framework of the country. The description of this institutional framework is allowed to be the same for each report under an international treaty on human rights.

b. The General Guidelines
32. According to the 'general guidelines' the report is to be split up into eight sections. This classification entails that the articles of the Convention are grouped per topic. A similar approach does not only offer the advantage that the Committee will receive better-structured reports. It also facilitates the participation of specialized agencies and non-governmental organizations that are well-skilled in certain aspects of the Convention on the Rights of the Child.[68] However, the Committee did stress that this classification is not a classification based on the importance of the rights. All rights remain equally important. The eight sections of the report are listed below:
  1. *General measures of implementation:* this section is to contain the description of the measures taken by the States to harmonize national law and policy with the provisions of the Convention. At the same time, all mechanisms that have been or that will be established on a national or a local level for coordinating policies relating to children and for monitoring the implementation of the Convention are to be described. The way in

---

[66] *General guidelines regarding the form and content of initial reports to be submitted by States Parties under article 44, paragraph 1 (a), of the Convention* adopted by the Committee at its 22nd meeting (first session) on 15 October 1991 (CRC/C/7, Annex III).

[67] HRI/1991/1. See also *Manuel relatif à l'établissement des rapports sur les droits de l'homme*, New York, Nations Unies, 1992, p. 33–34.

[68] Goodman, D., "Analysis of the first session of the Committee on the Rights of the Child", *NQHR 1* 1992, p. 50.

which the report will be made public in the country concerned and the way in which the population will be informed of the provisions of the Convention are to be mentioned as well.

2. *Definition of the child:* the States are asked to inform the Committee about what is meant by child (art. 1 of the Convention) in their legislation.

3. *General principles:* the States are to supply all useful information concerning the non-discrimination principle (art.2), the best interest of the child (art.3), the right to life, survival and development (art.6) and respect for the views of the child (art.12). The Committee considers the above four principles as essential provisions, that are, as it were, incorporated in each other provision of the Convention.

4. *Civil rights and freedoms:* this section contains information on the civil rights and freedoms of the Convention.[69]

5. *Family environment and alternative care:* the rights of the child in relation to his or her family are to be described in this section.[70]

6. *Basic health and welfare:* this section contains information on a number of social and economic rights of the Convention.[71]

7. *Education, leisure and cultural activities.*[72]

8. *Special protection measures:* this section is split up into four sub-sections. The four sub-sections concern: (1) children in situations of emergency; (2) children in conflict with the law; (3) children in situations of exploitation (including physical and psychological recovery and social reintegration) and (4) children belonging to a minority or an indigenous group.

33. It should be noted that States are asked to describe the mechanisms at national or local level for coordinating policies relating to children and for

---

[69] Specifically: name and nationality (art. 7), preservation of identity (art. 8), freedom of expression (art. 13), access to appropriate information (art. 17), freedom of thought, conscience and religion (art. 14), freedom of association and of peaceful assembly (art. 15), protection of privacy (art. 16) and the right not to be subjected to torture or other cruel, inhuman or degrading treatment or punishment (art. 37).

[70] Specifically: art. 5 (parental guidance), art. 18, § 1 and 2 (parental responsibilities), art. 9 (separation from parents), art. 10 (family reunification), art. 27, § 4 (recovery of maintenance for the child), art. 20 (children deprived of a family environment), art. 21 (adoption), art. 11 (illicit transfer and non-return), art. 19 (abuse and neglect, including physical and psychological recovery and social reintegration), art. 25 (periodic review of placement). The States are also to supply the Committee with the necessary information on the way in which the "best interest of the child" and the opinion of the child are being taken into account.

[71] This section concerns the following articles: art. 6, § 2 (survival and development), art. 23 (disabled children), art. 24 (health and health services), art. 26 and 18, § 3 (social security and child care services and facilities) art.§ 1 to 3 (standard of living). Within this framework, the States are to describe a.o. the infrastructure of their health care policy.

[72] The Committee asks the States to supply some information on the provided infrastructure when carrying out their policies regarding education, including vocational training and guidance (art. 28), aims of education (art. 29) and leisure, recreation and cultural activities (art. 31)

monitoring the implementation of the Convention. Sections 6 (basic health and welfare) and 7 (education, leisure and cultural activities) also mention a similar monitoring mechanism. The Convention does not explicitly mention a similar national monitoring and coordinating mechanism. It is however obvious that when the States take the reporting seriously, a national follow-up is indispensable. This is especially so since the States, in accordance with article 44, are not only supposed to give information on the measures taken but also on the progress that was made concerning the enjoyment of the rights of the child. Moreover, several 'concluding observations' on the country reports, show that the Committee sets great store by a national follow-up structure of this kind. The countries are either congratulated with the existence of a national follow-up structure, or they are urged to organize one.[73]

34. The success of the reporting procedure largely depends on the clearness of the guidelines.[74] When drawing up these guidelines, the Committee is to take into account the two following important elements: (1) on the one hand, the reports are to be sufficiently detailed and elaborated in order to enable the Committee to thoroughly evaluate the situation of human rights; (2) on the other hand, the Comittee is to take into account its own possibilities and workload. Indeed, reports that are too detailed can give rise to some problems when the Committee tries to get an overall view of the situation of the rights of the child in the country concerned. As a consequence, the dialogue with the delegate of the State will not turn out to be very efficient. However, in the opinion of several authors, the general guidelines set by the Committee still lack some specification. Abramson, for example, states: "One glaring inadequacy of the guidelines is that they do not ask States for any information on spending. Even the most elementary questions about what percentages of the budget go to children's health or education are omitted. States merely "are encouraged" to provide relevant statistical information and indicators. The State is given total freedom to decide what is relevant".[75] This

---

[73] See for example the "concluding observations" on the reports of Bolivia (CRC/C/16, para. 29), Viet Nam (CRC/C/16, para. 62), the Russian Federation (CRC/C/16, para. 85), Egypt (CRC/C/16, para. 96) Peru (CRC/C/20, para. 58), Sudan (CRC/C/20, para. 110) and Costa Rica (CRC/C/20, para. 123).

[74] Goodman, D., "Analysis of the first session of the Committee on the Rights of the Child", *NQHR 1* 1992, p. 51.

[75] Abramson, B., "First State reports: Sunny and... cloudy", *International children's rights monitor* 1993, Vol. 10, nos. 1–2, p. 23. See also: Goodman, D., *op.cit.*, p. 51; Theytaz-Bergman, "Adjustments urgently needed. Fourth session of the Committee on the Rights of the Child", *International children's rights monitor* 1993, vol. 10, no. 4, p. 22; Smith, J., "The Committee on the Rights of the Child", *NQHR* 1994–3, p. 322; Himes, J.R., "Reflecting on indicators concerning the rights of the child – The development and human rights communities should get their acts together", in *Innocenti essays No 5. The United Nations Convention on the Rights of the Child: Three Essays on the Challenge of Implementation*, Unicef, Florence, 1993, p. 20.

situation has led to a large diversity in the quality of the reports.[76] The Committee was pleased to see that the bulk of reports met the quality standards. Nevertheless, some reports turned out to contain insufficient information.[77] When the country reports lack the most elementary information – such as the percentages of the Gross National Product that go to children's health care or education – then the Committee cannot but spend most of the meeting on the gathering of additional information. Thus, only little time remains to hold a debate. Nevertheless, the gaps in the guidelines are quite understandable. Indeed, at the time when these guidelines were drawn up, the Committee did not have a clear view on what the reports and the 'constructive dialogue' would lead to. It is obvious that the Committee will derive the necessary and useful lessons from the initial reports of the countries. With this regard, it was decided to add a commentary to the guidelines, asking the States for a number of supplementary specifications.[78] Moreover the Committee will have to set up a monitoring-strategy, as well as appropriate indicators to measure achievement in the progressive realization of economic, social and cultural rights.[79] After all, monitoring doesn't only imply a supervision of the States, but also a measurement of the progress made on the enjoyment of the human rights.

2. The Study of the Reports by the Committee
a. The Pre-sessional Working Group

35. The Committee decided during its first meeting that each report should be responded to within one year after submission.[80] In view of the very large number of reports and the limited time for meetings, this requires a thorough organization of the activities.

36. The Committee considers the reports in two steps.[81] In a first stage, the reports are studied by a Pre-sessional Working Group. This meeting is held behind closed doors. Some key questions, that will afterwards be presented to the delegate of the State concerned, are raised. The resulting questionnaire is sent to the State in order to enable the representative to prepare himself for the Committee's dialogue, thus avoiding the possibility that the repre-

---

[76] On the first reports, see: Abramson, B., "First State reports: Sunny and ... cloudy",*op.cit.*, p. 22–37.

[77] See the concluding observations on the reports of Rwanda (CRC/C/20, para. 139), Sudan (CRC/C/16, para. 111), Peru (CRC/C/20, para 56) and Indonesia (CRC/C/20, para 37).

[78] Theytaz-Bergman, L., "Out of time. 5th session of the Committee on the Rights of the Child", *International children's rights monitor* 1994, Vol. 11, No. 1, p. 10.

[79] See: Himes, J.R., "Reflections on indicators concerning the rights of the child", *op.cit.*, p. 13–20.

[80] Hammarberg, T., "Justice for Children through the UN-Convention", in *Justice for Children*, Asquith, S. and Hill, M. (ed.), Dordrecht/Boston/London, Martinus Nijhoff Publishers, p. 69.

[81] CRC/C/10, para. 39.

sentative would make no reply to the questions of the Committee and that additional time would be unnecessarily lost. Another advantage of this way of proceeding is that non-governmental organizations can be efficiently involved in the implementation process. The Committee has stressed that the contributions made by non-governmental organizations are to be submitted before the pre-session starts. When doing so, the Committee members have the time to examine the remarks delivered by the non-governmental organizations and to compare these to the reports drawn up by the several States.

37. In the opinion of Abramson, this way of working (the study of the reports by the Committee in two steps) has only been successful to a minor degree. This is due to the fact that the Pre-sessional Working Group has had to spend too much time gathering additional information.[82] It is however the gaps in the guidelines that have caused this problem.

b. A constructive dialogue

38. The Committee examines the reports submitted by the various countries on the basis of the Pre-sessional Working Groups' preparations and the contributions made by the non-governmental organizations. In the first instance, the Committee's experts consider the reporting as a means of coming to a constructive dialogue with the States. It is not only the Committee's intention to check what rights the States have not implemented, but also to check whether those that have been implemented so far have been done successfully.[83] It is, however, not easy to have a profound and constructive interview on the basis of the – in most cases – exhaustive and complex reports within a limited period. The quality of the dialogue will always depend on several elements: the quality of the report, the document knowledge of the Committee's members, the relevance of the questions asked, the available time, the priorities set, ... The ability of the representatives of the States is an important condition for a constructive dialogue. Hence, the Committee has more than once stressed that the States should delegate expert representatives in order to hold as efficient a dialogue as possible.[84] Apart from some exceptions,[85] the Committee seemed to be pleased with the delegates representing the several States.

39. On the one hand, and as a result of the discussion of the first reports, it was clearly seen that the Committee's way of proceeding is at some points in need of improvement. On the other hand, and in view of the large number of ratifications of the Convention on the Rights of the Child, it was also obvious that the Committee does not have sufficient time at its disposal to hold a dia-

---

[82] Abramson, A., "First State reports: Sunny and ... cloudy", *op.cit.* p. 26.

[83] Goodman, D., *op.cit.*, p. 48.

[84] CRC/C/10, para. 40; Theytaz-Bergman, L., *op.cit.*, p. 22.

[85] See for example the "concluding observations" on the El Salvador report (CRC/C/20, para. 77).

logue with the States. The Committee, being aware of this problem, has taken a number of measures to spend the time available as efficiently as possible. It was in the course of the fifth session (1994) that the Committee decided to spend at the most 9 hours on the discussion of each single country report.[86] This measure is at present probably a necessary evil if the Committee wishes to limit the backlog to a minimum. But then again, the Committee should not forget its own basic principle: the first objective pursued through the reporting is to come to a constructive dialogue with the States. As a matter of fact, the study of the reports is the first and foremost task of the Committee. In some cases, and in the opinion of Theytaz-Bergman, the time limit has had some baleful influences on the Committee's activities: "This (the time limit) proved to be disastrous in the case of Mexico where the Committee barely had time to even touch upon the serious problems that the country is facing including street children, torture and the uprising in the Chiapas region".[87]

40. In order to loose less time, the Committee has requested the States to write down their answers to the questions of the Pre-sessional Working Group and to send them to the Committee[88] beforehand. The gaps in the report could in this way be treated in writing. This way of proceeding did not turn out to be very efficient. Indeed, most of the States did not have sufficient time (only 1 month) to prepare the additional information. This is why the answers were not submitted before the day of the session.[89] Moreover, there is a real danger that the States will ask to postpone the discussion on their reports, because they have to give additional written information.[90]

41. Considering that the Committee's composition and the UN budget are limited, it is obvious that the Committee will never be able to examine each single aspect of the implementation of the Convention. This is why the Committee will have to get their priorities right and why they will have to deal thoroughly with flagrant problems. These will obviously differ from country to country. Priorities will also have to be established when drawing up the questions of the Pre-sessional Working Group. Reporting could for example be restricted to certain aspects of the Convention, thus facilitating a thorough examination. A following report could then deal with other aspects, including a follow-up of the previously examined report. This way of proceeding does bring along the disadvantage, however, that the interrelations between

---

[86] Theytaz-Bergman, L., *op.cit.*, p. 11.

[87] Theytaz-Bergman, L., *op.cit.*, p. 11; Smith, J., "The Committee on the Rights of the Child", *NQHR* 1994–3, p. 322.

[88] Theytaz-Bergman, *op.cit.*, p. 10.

[89] Mexico, Namibia, Romania and Belarus did comply with the request of the Committee but were not able to submit their written answers until the session actually took place. The information was moreover written in their own languages. Hence, the Committee members were not able to understand the information given. (Theytaz-Bergman, L., *op.cit.*, p. 10).

[90] Smith, J., "The Committee on the Rights of the Child", *NQHR* 1994–3, p. 321.

the several rights undertaken in the Convention will be paid less attention to.[91]

c. Concluding Observations

42. The deliberation over the reports results in 'concluding observations'.[92] As pointed out in article 45 of the Convention, the Committee is indeed allowed to formulate suggestions and general recommendations, based on information received pursuant to articles 44 and 45. These suggestions and recommendations are sent to any State Party concerned and reported to the General Assembly. The information will possibly be accompanied by comments, if any, from the State parties (art. 45, d). The 'concluding observations' enter the Committee's main points of discussion. The Committee also indicates the topics that require a special follow-up. Thus, the documents constitute the basis for the discussion of the reports that follow. The 'concluding observations' are always structured in one and the same way: (1) introduction; (2) positive aspects; (3) factors and difficulties impeding the implementation of the Convention; (4) principal subjects of concern; (5) suggestions and recommendations.[93]

43. The exact formulation of the 'concluding observations' is a very important condition for the success of the reporting procedure. On the one hand, the 'concluding observations' encourage the States to take their reporting obligation seriously[94] whereas, on the other hand, the credibility of the Committee will in the long run be determined by the contents of the observations regarding the dialogues and the reports. 'Concluding observations' that are drawn up too cautiously may lead to the indifference of States with regard to the Committee's recommendations. But then again, the Committee is to make sure that the 'concluding observations' do not turn into convictions. Indeed, the Committee does not have the authority to do so.[95] It is not only the formulation of the 'concluding observations' but also the follow-up of suggestions and recommendations that is of paramount importance if the Committee wishes to encourage the States to take their reporting duties seriously.[96]

---

[91] CRC/C/16, annex VIII.
[92] CRC/C/10, para. 41.
[93] CRC/C/10, para. 42.
[94] Goodman, D., *op.cit.*, p. 52.
[95] Abramson, A., "First State reports: Sunny and ... cloudy", *op.cit.*, p. 24.
[96] The Committee has emphasized that a follow-up of the suggestions and recommendations is really necessary (CRC/C/20, nr. 28). See: "*Follow up to the consideration of initial reports by States Parties to the convention of the Rights of the Child as at 24 February 1994*"(CRC/C/27, annex).

d. The Evaluation of the Operating Procedure of the Committee when Examining the Reports

44. The above clearly indicates that a Committee on the Rights of the Child can also have its teething problems. The cause is to be found in the large number of reports to be dealt with and in the limited meeting time. The Committee is well-aware of this and has made one of its members responsible for the preparation of a "working paper". This working paper is to contain the ways in which the activities can be better organized.[97] When it is assumed that the Committee cannot possibly carry out an in-depth study for each report, then it is absolutely recommendable to establish priorities. Pursuing one's priorities often results in incompleteness. But then again, when the monitoring system of the Convention on the Rights of the Child is considered rather as an awareness-raising process than as a purely judicial tool, then there can hardly be any objections at all.

3. The "Positive Atmosphere" Surrounding Implementation: "Cooperative Attitude"[98]

45. As we have already pointed out above, the expectations of the implementation mechanism are high: indeed, the implementation system is to be more than just a control mechanism. This turns out among other things in article 45 of the Convention. This article adds an original procedure to the reporting mechanism. The monitoring of the implementation of the rights is to be accompanied by help and support: "(...) the Convention envisages a much more active role for the Committee with respect for technical advice or assistance than is the case with other human rights treaty bodies".[99] The authors of the Convention have seized the reporting procedure as a tool in order to act in an advisory or assisting way wherever needed. They do so on the basis of the information given in the reports: "The aim is that the Committee – together with the reporting government and any aid agencies involved – should attempt to define the problems and discuss what remedies are necessary".[100]

a. From Reporting to Development Aid

46. As article 44, § 2, points out, the reports are to indicate the factors and possible difficulties that have their influence on the compliance with the obligations implied by the Convention. Reports showing a need for technical advice

---

[97] The "working paper" is adopted as annex VIII with CRC/C/16. The following suggestions are, amongst others, formulated: the organization of an additional yearly session, in order to enable the Committee to spend two entire sessions on the study of the reports, and one session on specific topics, work organization, technical support, ...; increase the number of Committee members to 18; only discuss the country reports for a certain period; restrict the time of discussion for each report; install sub-committees.

[98] Verhellen, E., *op.cit.*, p. 82.

[99] Goodman, D., *op.cit.*, p. 44.

[100] Goodman, D., *op.cit.*, p. 44.

or technical support can be sent to specialized agencies, UNICEF, and other competent bodies. The Committee can possibly add remarks and suggestions (art. 45,b). The Convention on the Rights of the Child goes a step further than other treaties. The reports cannot only be transmitted to a larger number of organs, it is moreover the Committee itself that decides whether the reports will be transmitted or not. The Covenant on Political and Civil Rights (art. 40, § 3) and the Covenant on Economic, Social and Cultural Rights (art.16, § 2, b) also provide the opportunity to submit the reports to specialized agencies. However, for these two Covenants, it is the United Nations Secretary General who is to take the initiative. It is obvious that the procedure adopted by the Convention on the Rights of the Child is less complex. However, in order to optimally seize this opportunity, it is necessary to inform the Committee of the existing programs concerning technical assistance on a national level and of the problems involved.[101] Here again, the "general guidelines" are not sufficiently elaborated on. Whenever a specific technical assistance program is recommended, the Committee will always encourage the State concerned to discuss the suggested program with the aid agency.[102] When drawing up the "Rules of Procedure", the Committee on the Rights of the Child was also resolved to closely follow the transmitted reports. Doing so, they would see what kind of technical help was rendered and what progress was made (rule 74).[103]

47. Article 4 of the Convention also embodies the idea of mutual help and support: "(...) With regard to economic, social and cultural rights, States Parties shall undertake such measures to the maximum extent of their available resources and, where needed, within the framework of international co-operation". No other Convention on Human Rights links the reporting with development aid to such a large extent.[104] But then again, development aid is often used to enforce respect for human rights.[105] "The link established by the Convention between the reports by the states and discussions about development aid may become a dynamic element in aid policies".[106] States can ask for help through their reports. At the same time, they can prove that they respect human rights. Moreover, through the "concluding observations" of the Committee on the Rights of the Child, States are encouraged to look

---

[101] CRC/C/16, para. 140.

[102] CRC/C/16, para. 144.

[103] Goodman, D., *op.cit.*, p. 53.

[104] Hammarberg, T., *op.cit.*, p. 70.

[105] Within this respect, see: De Feyter, K., "Mensenrechten and ontwikkelingssamenwerking", in *Tegenspraak Cahier 14. Mensenrechten tussen retoriek en realiteit*, Parmentier, S. (ed.), Ghent, Mys and Breesch, 1994, p. 88–105.

[106] Hammarberg, T., *op.cit.*, p. 72.

for, or to render, international assistance.[107] This way, the reporting procedure can develop into an important basis for well-founded development policies. The main condition is that the States release the necessary information on their expense policy. It is indeed important for the aiding States to know the priorities of the States that call for assistance and where exactly their money goes to. The guidelines relating to this matter still need further elaboration.

48. One has to be rather cautious when linking respect for human rights with development aid. According to De Feyter development aid soon adopts a compulsive character if the donor and the receiver do not share the same beliefs towards human rights.[108] Still according to the same author, there will arise no problems when development aid is joined to respect for human rights by the States. Indeed, by ratifying the Conventions on Human Rights, the State has assumed a judicial obligation to achieve the realization of human rights. When, on the contrary, cultural traditions are envisaged, De Feyter thinks it advisable to act cautiously, due to the fact that donor and receiver might possibly have differring opinions on human rights. This is even more the case when principles such as "the best interests of the child" are under discussion. After all, the ideas about what is or isn't in the best interests of the child differ depending on the cultural tradition.[109]

b. A Broad Basis for Participation
49. The cooperative spirit of the Convention is also seen in the fact that the specialized agencies, UNICEF and other United Nations organs have acquired the right to be represented at the deliberation on the application of those provisions that fall within the scope of their mandate (art.45, a).[110] What's more, the Committee can invite the specialized agencies, UNICEF and other competent bodies that turn out to be useful, to give their expert advice on the implementation of the Convention. They can also be asked to submit reports. In view of the workload and the limited financial resources of the Secretariat,[111] the Committee will have to use this possibility efficiently in

---

[107] See for example the "concluding observations" on the reports of Sudan (CRC/C/20,nr.119), Peru (CRC/C/20,nr.73), the Russian Federation (CRC/C/16,nr.88) and Viet Nam (CRC/C/16,nr.65).

[108] De Feyter, K., *op.cit.*, p. 97.

[109] See: Alston, Ph. (ed.), *The best interests of the child – Reconciling Culture and Human Rights*, Oxford, Clarendon Press, 1994, 297 pages.

[110] This opportunity was indeed used. See for example CRC/C/10, paras 7–10; CRC/C/16, paras. 7–10; CRC/C/20, paras. 5–9; CRC/C/24, paras. 4–8; CRC/C/29, paras. 5–9. The Committee also wants to get involved in the activities of other bodies (see CRC/C/24, *Recommendation 3*).

[111] CRC/C/10, paras. 27–28.

order to be well-informed.[112],[113] The 'travaux préparatoires' clearly show that the term 'other competent bodies" is to be understood in the broadest sense of the word.[114] It was in the course of the first session (1991) of the Committee on the Rights of the Child that a delegate from Defense for Children International suggested a whole range of 'other competent bodies': amongst others non-governmental organizations,[115] the Organization of African Unity, the Organization of American States, the Council of Europe, ILO, national research instititutions,...[116] Thus, the Convention constitutes a broad basis for the participation of all kinds of organizations in the implementation process. In view of the increase in the number of treaties on human rights, of control bodies and control procedures, both within the United Nations and on a regional level, the Convention on the Rights of the Child offers an important opportunity to come to a certain degree of coordination and co-operation.[117] The explicit inclusion of this matter is an important and innovative aspect of the reporting procedure. The success will however depend on the way in which the Committee uses the opportunities offered by the Convention. This is why it will be essential to develop procedures that can effectively guarantee this co-operation: "In regard to the work of the Committee, members pointed out that there should be effective coordination in the provision of relevant information from governmental and non-governmental sources on the imple-

---

[112] It was undertaken in the Rules of Procedure (rule 37(2)) that all reports and documents drawn up by the specialized agencies, UNICEF, and other competent bodies will be transmitted to the members of the Committee. It was also decided that the Committee is allowed to decide to send those documents to the States and to other participants in the activities of the Committee.

[113] See a.o. CRC/C/10, *Recommendation 2*: "The Committee on the Rights of the Child, (...) Encourages United Nations bodies, specialized agencies and other competent bodies, in order to foster the effective implementation of the Convention, to provide the Committee with relevant information concerning each State Party whose report is scheduled to be considered by the Committee".

[114] Detrick, S. (ed.), *The United Nations Convention on the Rights of the Child. A Guide to the "Travaux Préparatoires"*, Dordrecht/Boston/London, Martinus Nijhoff Publishers, 1992, p. 582.

[115] Non-governmental organizations are being recognized more and more as valuable participants in the implementation of human rights: "The Committee on the Rights of the child recalled the recognition paid by the World Conference on Human Rights to the important role played by non-governmental organizations in the effective implementation of the Convention on the Rights of the Child" (CRC/C/20, nr. 170). At its fourth session (1993), the Committee held a working meeting with the Coordinator of the NGO Group on the implementation of the Convention on the Rights of the Child in order to discuss the possible contributions of the national non-governmental organizations within the framework of the implementation of the Convention (CRC/C/20, nr. 172).

[116] Goodman, D., *op.cit.*, p. 44.

[117] The Committee has in its turn decided to follow-up the activities of the other human rights treaty bodies and of the other United Nations meetings relevant to its work. At the same time, the Committee hopes "that adequate resources will be provided to enable the Committee to develop effective communication and dialogue with other human rights bodies and to participate in United Nations meetings relevant to its work" (CRC/C/10, *Recommendation 4*; CRC/C/16, *Recommendation 3* and CRC/C/20, *Recommendation 4*).

mentation of the Convention in submitting reports".[118] There was a lot of attention paid to this topic at the first session of the Committee (1991).[119,120] The Committee listened for two days to the co-operation suggestions made by UNICEF, ILO, World Food Program and NGO's. The representatives of the different organizations proposed the following ways of cooperation:
- provide information and documentation to the Committee;
- assist the Pre-sessional Working Group during the formulation of questions that are posed to the government's representatives;
- give advice about technical assistance to the Committee and the countries, if their reports indicate such a need;
- draw up reports about certain themes on the rights of the child and send them to the Committee;
- assist the Committee during the formulation of "general comments" about articles of the Convention.

The different ways how the cooperation can be realized, were also discussed. It was suggested, among other things, to found a "technical advisory group".[121] This group would consist of representatives from specialized agencies, UNICEF, other United Nations bodies and other competent bodies. Goodman sticks to the opinion that this technical advisory group would create lots of opportunities to steer the participation in the right direction. Still according to the same author, this group could act as the link between the Committee and the participating organs.[122] The technical advisory group could for example assist the Committee when determining what organ is specifically skilled in a certain topic or in the situation of the children's right in a certain country. Hence, a similar structure would entail the advantage that the Committee would be able to determine in a fast and efficient way what organ can make a positive contribution to the Committee's activities.[123] Under the influence of the Convention on the Rights of the Child and the Committee on the Rights of the Child, more and more attention is given within the UN

---

[118] CRC/C/7, para. 15.

[119] Goodman, D., *op.cit.*, p. 57.

[120] During its fourth session the Committee decided to arrange a meeting with the specialized agencies in order to discuss the possible ways of cooperation (CRC/C/20, para. 161). During this informal meeting four themes were discussed: 1) the installation of a common information centre; 2) the organization of conferences and visits to countries or regions, where in one way or another special attention has to be given to the rights of the child; 3) the Committee's "concluding observations" about reports of the countries, should be observed by the other UN-bodies and specialized agencies and should be taken into account when taking measures that are within their competences (more specifically, measures to set up programmes of technical assistance); 4) the cooperation with NGOs has to be regarded seriously, given their contribution to promotion and protection of the rights of the child.

[121] See also: CRC/C/10, para. 39.

[122] Goodman, D., *op.cit.* p. 60.

[123] For the preparation of the study of the first country reports, the pre-sessional working group was assisted by a similar "informal technical advisory group" (CRC/C/16, para. 13; CRC/C/20, para. 14).

to the ways of cooperation. Especially with regard to the installation of a common information centre, the Committee turns out to play a pioneering role within the UN.[124]

D. Other Activities of the Committee

1. Urgent Actions
50. During the second session (1992) the members of the Committee agreed upon the fact that the Committee, apart from the periodical study of the country reports, should also be authorized to undertake urgent actions in serious situations.[125] It was nevertheless stressed that the urgent actions ought to embody the spirit of the constructive dialogue. The Committee will therefore take a non-conflicting attitude regarding this matter. Moreover, a number of conditions will have to be met, before the Committee will be allowed to take so-called "urgent actions":

– The action is to be based on reliable information. This information can be passed on by anybody (e.g. non-governmental organizations), provided that it is accurate and trustworthy: "The situations justifying the urgent procedure would either be brought to the attention of the Committee by United Nations bodies and other competent bodies, or taken up ex officio by the Committee".[126]
– A violation of the rights undertaken in the Convention is to be involved. The problematic situation is to fall within the jurisdiction of one of the States Parties.
– The violation concerned must be blatant. There must be a real danger that more violations will take place. It must be possible to avoid a deterioration of the situation by taking the urgent action. The Committee has charged a working group with the further and more detailed development of the procedure.[127]

51. The "urgent actions"-procedure is considered to be a part of the obligation to report:[128] indeed, the Committee can ask a State at any time to draw up a report relating to the implementation of a specific provision of the Convention or to provide additional information.

---

[124] "(...) il (the Committee) a souligné qu'il était particulièrement encourageant de voir que les droits de l'enfant avaient préparé la voie à un dialogue constructif entre les différents organes des Nations Unies, les organisations non gouvernementales et le Comité dans un domaine aussi crucial que celui de l'information" (CRC/C/24, para. 148).

[125] CRC/C/10, para. 54–58; Abramson, B., "Un immense défi. Deuxieme session du Comité des Droits de l'Enfant", *Tribune internationale des droits de l'enfant*, 1992, Vol. 9, Nos. 3–4, p. 24.

[126] CRC/C/10, para. 55.

[127] CRC/C/20, para. 156.

[128] CRC/C/10, para. 56.

52. Heedful of the co-operation idea, the Committee planned to pass on serious violations of human rights, that fall within the competences of other organs, to the organs concerned.[129] This has happened for example with a request for urgent actions (November 16, 1993) made by the Government of the Federal Republic of Yugoslavia.[130] The Government asked the Committee to examine the violations of the Rights of the Child in Yugoslavia as a consequence of the sanctions imposed by the United Nations. The Committee passed the case on to the Special Rapporteur on the former Yugoslavia, since it did not have sufficient information on this matter at its disposal.

53. The "urgent actions"-procedure authorizes the Committee to take actions, even if no report was received from the State involved. In this way, the Committee can also offer their services at any moment between the consecutive reports. Although the Committee considers the urgent actions procedure to be an essential part of the obligation to report, the procedure could also be considered an alternative to the communications procedure. Indeed, the Committee has stressed that, apart from the United Nations organs, also other competent bodies can pass on blatant violations of the Rights of the Child to the Committee. Since non-governmental organizations are generally accepted as competent bodies, they have the possibility to lodge a complaint with the Committee. But then again, it remains unclear in which cases the Committee will declare a request for urgent actions admissable.

2. *Studies on Topics Concerning the Rights of the Child*

54. Article 45 (c) states that the Committee may recommend to the General Assembly of the United Nations to request the Secretary General to undertake on its behalf studies on specific issues relating to the rights of the child.[131] The Committee has given this provision, in connection with art. 45 (a) a broad interpretation.[132] They can also ask specialized agencies, UNICEF, and other bodies to carry out studies.[133] According to the Committee, similar studies "would contribute to an increased awareness and better understanding

---

[129] CRC/C/10, para. 57.

[130] X, "Federal Republic of Yugoslavia. Urgent Action requested", *International children's rights monitor* 1993, Vol. 10, no. 4, p. 25.

[131] For example, the Committee has recommended to the General Assembly of the United Nations to request the Secretary General to carry out a study on "children in armed conflicts" (CRC/C/16, *Recommendation 1*). At the same time, the Committee has stressed once more the "co-operative idea': "for this purpose, the Secretary General might wish to invite the co-operation of relevant specialized agencies, other United Nations organs, non-governmental organizations and the International Committee of the Red Cross" (*Ibidem*).

[132] CRC/C/10, para. 59. According to art. 45 (a), the Committee can ask any other organization for their advice and ask them to pass on reports.

[133] Goodman, D., *op.cit.*, p. 54.

of the provisions of the Convention and their implementation throughout the world".[134]

55. During its first session (1991) the Committee also decided to dedicate one day of each session to the study of a well-determined topic. The following topics have already been discussed: children in armed conflicts[135] and economic exploitation of children.[136] During these topical days the Committee listens for example to representatives of intergovernmental and non-governmental organizations.[137]

56. The topical days constitute an important aid to come to a uniform interpretation of the provisions of the Convention on the Rights of the Child. This is more than ever the case when new developments in the area of human rights are concerned.[138] The Committee will use these topical days as the basis for the publication of "general comments" on specific articles undertaken in the Convention.[139] What's more, these topical days can lead to the formulation of additional protocols of the Convention. For example, the study day on "children in armed conflicts" has led to a proposal for an optional protocol.[140]

III. THE EFFECTIVENESS OF THE REPORTING PROCEDURE

A. The Limitations of the Alternatives

57. From a judicial angle, a State fulfills its international obligations towards other States and not towards individuals.[141] Nevertheless, it is obvious that States will not be eager to lodge complaints relating to violations of human rights in other States. The States will usually only do so when the viola-

---

[134] CRC/C/10, para. 59. See also CRC/C/16, para. 147.

[135] CRC/C/10, paras. 61–77; CRC/C/16, paras. 173–180. See also: Abramson, B., "Un immense défi. Deuxieme session du Comité des Droits de l'Enfant", *op.cit.*, p. 24.

[136] CRC/C/20, paras. 186–196.

[137] Theytaz-Bergman, L., *op.cit.*, p. 24.

[138] Goodman, D., *op.cit.*, p. 47.

[139] During its sixth session the Committee decided to postpone the formulation of "general comments". Two reasons were given for this: on the one hand the Committee has at present an excessive workload and on the other hand the Committee wants to gain more experience with regard to the articles eligible for a general comment (CRC/C/29, para. 184).

[140] See annex VII, CRC/C/16. The Secretary General was asked to pass the proposal on to the Commission on Human Rights (CRC/C/20, *Recommendation 5*). Initiatives were also taken to set up an additional protocol concerning the sale of children, child prostitution and child pornography (CRC/C/29, *Recommendation 3*).

[141] Dimitrijevic, V., "The Monitoring of Human Rights and the prevention of human rights violations through reporting procedures", in *Monitoring Human Rights in Europe. Comparing International Procedures and Mechanisms*, Dordrecht/Boston/London, Martinus Nijhoff Publishers, 1993, p. 1.

tion is very blatant, when they can gain profits (e.g. economic interests), and when they themselves will not suffer from any negative consequences.[142] Even when the Convention provides a specific procedure, then interstate complaints can only offer little guarantees against the violation of human rights. The interstate complaints procedure of the Covenant on Civil and Political Rights has so far never been applied.[143]

58. The alternative would be to give the individual, who is the victim of a violation of human rights, the right to lodge a complaint with an international organ. This procedure cannot sufficiently guarantee an implementation of the human rights as broad as possible. Dimitrijevic lists a number of limitations of the individual complaints procedure[144]

- It is useless to lodge an individual complaint when the right involved cannot be judicially enforced, e.g. certain social, economic and cultural rights.
- When the convention concerned provides a gradual implementation, then an individual complaints procedure cannot easily be followed, since States cannot (or very hardly) be held responsible for the fact that they have not yet achieved the realization of the ideal human rights situation.
- States take a very reluctant stance towards individual complaints mechanisms.
- Human rights are in most cases not violated by the State but by individuals or groups of individuals.
- According to Dimitrijevic, the main reason is that complaints procedures can never cover the entire range of human rights. "A modern human rights treaty aims at a generally favorable human rights situation, which includes creating the necessary conditions for the enjoyment of human rights and the elimination of factors that lead to violations. If a state is remiss, this very often cannot be related to an individual "victim" such as, for instance, when the cost of human life becomes low due to disease, uncontrolled and unrestricted use of dangerous installations and noxious substances, terrorism, poor police protection and other circumstances and the right to life is thus threatened and violated".[145]

---

[142]   Dimitrijevic, V., *op.cit.*, p. 2.

[143]   The States also seem to take a rather reticent stance with regard to interstate complaints as far as the European Convention on Human Rights is concerned (Bossuyt, M., "De werking van het VN-Comité mensenrechten", in *De Betekenis van het Internationaal Verdrag inzake Burgerrechten en Politieke Rechten voor de interne rechtsorde*, Interuniversitair Centrum Mensenrechten (ed.), Antwerp/Apeldoorn, Maklu uitgevers, 1993, p. 11).

[144]   Dimitrijevic, V., *op.cit.*, p. 3–4.

[145]   Dimitrijevic, V., *op.cit.*, p. 4.

59. With regard to the two first limitations quoted by Dimitrijevic, a certain evolution should be noted. More and more attempts are made to increase the normative character of the economic, social and cultural rights. In this way the Committee on Economic, Social and Cultural Rights reflected its view in a 'general comment'[146] on the normative nature of the economic, social and cultural rights. According to the Committee the Covenant does impose various obligations which are of immediate effect. Moreover the Committee stresses that "(...) suggestions that the provisions of the Covenant are inherently non-self-executing would seem to be difficult to sustain".[147] Moreover the Committee itself seems to advocate the installation of a complaints procedure.[148] According to the Dutch Committee of Jurists for the Human Rights a complaints procedure is precisely required to expose the normative implications of the Covenant.[149] The Dutch Jurists' Committee thinks that the juridical nature of the economic, social and cultural rights constitutes no impediment for the installation of the complaints procedure.

60. Even if the first two impediments quoted by Dimitrijevic should somewhat be toned down, the other impediments still keep their value. Especially the small policy nature of the complaints procedure prevents a broad implementation of the human rights. Opsahl therefore states that the complaints procedure can only be a secondary aim.[150] The author pleads for the installation of complaints procedures at a regional level and not so much for universal complaints procedures. For this the following reasons are given: "(...) the Committee will never be able to control violations in all parts of the world through complaints procedures. It would not be practical to develop its machinery to the extent which this control would require, since this would include hearings, fact-finding, visits, investigations, use of many languages, etc.".[151] Yet regional complaints procedures also offer the advantage that cultural traditions which seem to be inconsistent with human rights can be judged in a more pragmatical way.

61. In order to achieve an implementation as complete as possible, the States can pass on their monitoring function to an international organ. The interna-

---

[146] General Comment nr. 3, *Report on the Fifth Session* E/1991/23, Annex VI.

[147] Alston, Ph., "The Committee on Economic, Social and Cultural Rights" in *The United Nations and Human Rights – A Critical Appraisal* Alston, Ph. (ed.), Oxford, Clarendon Press, 1992, p. 495.

[148] *Report of the Seventh Session* E/1993/22, Annex IV.

[149] NJCM-Commentaar inzake de versterking van het respect voor economische, sociale en culturele rechten, *NCJM – Bull 19–3* 1994, p. 291.

[150] Opsahl, T., "The Human Rights Committee", in *The United Nations and Human Rights – A Critical Appraisal*, Alston, Ph. (ed.), Oxford, Clarendon Press, 1992, p. 440. See also Opsahl, T., "Instruments of Implementation of Human Rights", *Human Rights Law Journal* 1989–10, p. 29.

[151] Opsahl, T., "The Human Rights Committee", *op.cit.*, p. 440.

tional organ then examines the international human rights situation based on the reports that were submitted by the several States. These reports explain how the international obligations have been complied with. The main advantage of this kind of control is that the casuistic approach is no longer used. As a consequence, all human rights are getting a chance.[152]

B. The Limitations of the Reporting Procedure

62. Following the creation of more and more procedures to guarantee human rights within the United Nations and the regional organizations, such as the Council of Europe, the Organization of American States (OAS) and the Organization for African Unity (OAU), the positive character of the reporting procedure was more and more emphasized.[153] The obligation to report aims at a better international co-operation in the field of human rights. The stress was put more and more on the fact that the reporting ought to achieve the realization of a "constructive dialogue" between the States and a committee consisting of experts. Thus, the reporting procedure is not conceived as a contradictory procedure.

63. There are a lot of doubts about the use and effectiveness of reporting procedures. The States' reports – it is said – are drawn up by national "officials", who try and draw a picture as positive as possible of the situation in their countries. Moreover, they will hardly ever draw the Committee's attention to flagrant violations of human rights. According to Robertson and Merrils, this criticism is justified to a certain extent. They add that the reporting system as such does not constitute an effective measure of control.[154] Theodor Meron puts it in a more lyrical way: " (...) the reporting system, to paraphrase the title of Jacques Brel's play, is alive, but not well".[155]

64. Robertson and Merrils think moreover that the efficiency and the effectiveness of the reporting system are largely dependent on the way in which

---

[152] Dimitrijevic also advocates a further development of the reporting procedures within the framework of the Council of Europe (Dimitrijevic, V., *op.cit.*, p. 10–11).

[153] Alston, P., "The purposes of reporting" in *Manual on Human Rights Reporting* New York, United Nations, 1991, p. 12.

[154] Robertson, A.H. and Merrils, J.G., *Human Rights in the world – An introduction to the study of the international protection of human rights*, Manchester/New York, Machester University Press, 1992, p. 41.

[155] The author quotes the following paragraph taken from a report by the Committee on Elimination of Racial Discrimination: "... only the five of the 63 reports received during the year were submitted on time or before the deadlines provided for under article 9, paragraph 1, of the Convention. The rest were submitted after some delay, ranging from a few days to nearly six years. In the case of 39 of the reports received during the year, 1 to 11 reminders had been sent to the States Parties concerned before their reports were submitted" (Meron, Th., *Human Rights Law-making in the United Nations – A critique of Instruments and Processes*, Oxford, Clarendon Press, 1986, p. 237).

the national reports are dealt with after submission: "What matters is how they (the national reports) are dealt with after they have been received. That is to say, whether there is an opportunity for critical examination, for drawing attention to gaps or inaccuracies in the information provided, and for comparing official statements with other sources of information on the same subject".[156] The authors think that there are some four additional conditions that determine the effectiveness of the reporting system: (1) the co-operation of the authorities involved regarding the completeness of information; (2) the possibility to receive further ('and perhaps less flattering') information from other responsible sources; (3) the examination of gathered information by independent authorities or people; (4) a body's right to pass on suitable remarks and recommendations to the States concerned in view of the improvement of the law or the practice of human rights in the country involved.

65. It is remarkable that the authors pay this much attention to the gathering of additional information. The usual criticism is strongly countered by the possibility of the examining body to acquire additional information.[157] For example, the official report can be compared to the information submitted by non-governmental organizations. This can give rise to the examining body asking the official authorities for additional information.[158] It can also lead to a reaction to a number of "less flattering" data of the non-governmental organizations. What's more, the States Parties cannot back out of their obligations implied by the Convention by submitting reports that contain no relevant information: additional information can, after all, be requested. Mostly, representatives of the States are invited by the monitoring body to be present at the discussion of their reports, which gives cause for dialogue, whereby further clarifications and specifications of the country report will be discussed.[159] Much will depend however on the manner in which the monitoring body makes use of the provided procedure.

66. Robertson and Merrils examine the reporting system purely from the point of view of control by the international organ. It is clear, however, that the reporting also has, in another way, effects concerning the application of the convention in question. The reporting obliges the States to check, within an arranged time limit, the national legislature and practices on the principles of the convention in question. Or, as Theodor Meron points out: "The task of preparing reports focuses the attention of national administrations on weak points in internal compliance with international human rights obligations and

---

[156] Robertson, A.H. and Merrils, J.G., *op.cit.*, p. 41.

[157] Opsahl, T., "Instruments of Implementation of Human Rights", *Human Rights Law Journal* 1989–10, p. 29.

[158] Opsahl, T., "Instruments of Implementation of Human Rights", *op.cit.*, p. 20–21.

[159] Meron, Th., *op.cit.*, p. 237.

encourages improvements".[160] The States are in this way obliged to evaluate themselves, within a stipulated time limit. Furthermore, when bodies other than the official ones – we think for example of the NGOs – get the chance to study the country reports critically, the system can give cause to a broader discussion and consciousness in the country concerned.

67. According to Zwaak the effectiveness of a legal, international instrument can be worked out in two ways: (1) the universality, specifically the extent to which the convention is accepted by a large number of countries and by public opinion; and (2) the readiness of the States to implement the provisions of the convention.[161] In connection with the first factor, it has to be observed that the reporting mechanism has a stimulating effect. The reporting procedure is, after all, a non-contradictory procedure, so that countries will more quickly ratify a convention in which a reporting procedure is provided than a convention in which a communication-procedure is accepted. The universality is not only concerned with the number of ratifications but also with the extent to which the rights in question and the general freedoms are accepted by public opinion. Since the reporting obligation forms a sound basis for coming to a social discussion within the different States, the public opinion too will become conscious more quickly of the importance of the concerned rights and freedoms.

68. Zwaak's second criterion regarding the effectiveness of a human rights treaty deals with the willingness of the States to implement the treaty. The reporting procedure has got a stimulating effect within this framework too. Indeed, the States are periodically obliged to make a self-evaluation and to check whether their country's legislation and practice meet the stipulations put forward in the convention. But then again, this is at the same time the weak point of the reporting procedure. The international controlling body cannot enforce the "concluding observations". The good-will of the States themselves will therefore be a decisive factor for the success of the reporting procedure. This second criterion, adopted by L.F. Zwaak, is consequently not only a standard to measure the effectiveness of a treaty, but also a standard to measure the effectiveness of the reporting procedure. The degree in which the States take their reporting obligation seriously will be decisive for the use and effectiveness of the reporting duty: " (...) il semble exister une corrélation positive entre l'efficacité des systèmes de présentation des rapports et la mesure dans laquelle les Etats parties prennent au sérieux leurs obligations en la matière".[162]

---

[160] Meron, Th., *op.cit.*, p. 227.

[161] Zwaak, L.F., *International Human Rights Procedures. Petitioning the ECHR, CCPR and CERD*, Nijmegen, Ars Aequi Libri, 1991, p. V.

[162] A/44/668, *Application effective des instruments internationaux relatifs aux droits de l'homme, y compris l'obligation de présenter des rapports à ce titre*, para 35.

69. It is however to be said that some States are not so fussy about the timely submission of their reports.[163] Belgium for example, submitted its initial report regarding the Covenant on Civil and Political Rights after a delay of more than three years[164] and its report regarding the Covenant on Economic, Social and Cultural Rights after a delay of almost 10 years.[165] On the 1st of June 1988, there was an overall backlog of 626 reports.[166] The heavy workload implied by the draft of these reports is usually mentioned as the main reason for this delay.[167] Moreover, States have had to draw up increasingly more reports for the last couple of years. It is consequently harder for the national administrations to submit the various reports in due time. The United Nations themselves are also well-aware of this problem. By order of the General Assembly, Alston has formulated a number of proposals within this respect.[168]

70. Another often voiced criticism on the reporting procedure concerns the fact that the controlling body is only authorized to act when it has a report at its disposal: "(...) it has compelled treaty bodies to behave, in situations where allegations of massive human violations were made, as if nothing had happened and to wait for years until the time for the submission of the report was due. Even when a government declared a state of emergency and then derogated some rights under the human rights treaty and duly notified the United Nations, the treaty body was supposed to remain inactive, not to speak of the more frequent *de facto* states of emergency".[169] Some evolutions have however occurred in this field. When dealing with the situation in the former Yugoslavia, the Human Rights Committee has asked the governments of Croatia, Bosnia-Herzegovina and Yugoslavia, to urgently submit some specific reports on the implementation of certain articles of the Covenant on Civil and Political Rights.[170] At that moment, Bosnia-Herzegovina and Croatia had not yet submitted their initial reports (and still had some time left to do so). Yugoslavia had just submitted its third report. During its sixth session

---

[163] See Meron, T., *Human rights law-making in the United Nations. A Critique of Instruments and Processes* Oxford, Clarendon Press, 1986, p. 237–238.

[164] Bossuyt, M., "De werking van het VN-comité mensenrechten", in *De Betekenis van het Internationaal Verdrag inzake Burgerrechten en Politieke Rechten voor de interne rechtsorde*, Interuniversitair Centrum Mensenrechten (ed.), Antwerp/Apeldoorn, Maklu publishers, 1993, p. 16.

[165] E/C.12/1994/7, p. 1–2.

[166] A/44/668, *Application effective des instruments internationaux relatifs aux droits de l'homme, y compris l'obligation de présenter des rapports à ce titre*, para. 34.

[167] Dimitrijevic, V., *op.cit.* p. 14; Meron, T, *op.cit.* p. 238.

[168] A/44/668, *Application effective des instruments internationaux relatifs aux droits de l'homme, y compris l'obligation de présenter des rapports à ce titre*.

[169] Dimitrijevic, V., *op.cit.*, p. 15.

[170] CCPR/C/SR.1178/Add.1, para. 5. Within this respect, see Dimitrijevic, V., *op.cit.*, p. 16.

the Committee on Economic, Social and Cultural Rights went even further. The Committee requested the Dominican Republic "to suspend any actions which are not clearly in conformity with the provisions of the Covenant, and requests the governement to provide additional information to it as a matter of urgency".[171] So the Committee did not only ask for additional information, it also requested the State to stop the activities that were inconsistent with the Convention. Within this framework, the Committee on the Rights of the Child decided at its third session that it is authorized to undertake urgent actions under serious circumstances.

71. Although the reporting procedure is not even close to perfection, it still appears to be the main method to keep on calling the people's attention to human rights through a non-casuistic approach. The effect of a similar procedure cannot be expected to show in the short run and is therefore to be assessed in the long run. Opsahl writes: "The long-term task of uniting nations in the cause of human rights should be seen in the first place as the constructive one of promoting respect of human rights and securing their observance. That is, after all, what the Universal Declaration calls for. It is, therefore, perhaps more important to convince and influence States than to condemn and expose them".[172] An important condition for the success of the reporting procedure is that the participants take their tasks seriously. More publicity will also be required concerning the activities of the Committee in order to increase the efficiency of reporting. The concluding observations issued by the Committee should give rise to a debate within the involved States. This task does not only concern the NGOs, but also the academics. If as much attention would be paid to these "concluding observations" as to for example the "views" of the Human Rights Committee, then a reporting procedure can also be accompanied by a certain "mobilization of shame".

IV. THE EVALUATION OF THE MONITORING SYSTEM OF THE CONVENTION
ON THE RIGHTS OF THE CHILD

72. When studying the monitoring mechanism of the Convention on the Rights of the Child from a judicial angle, and when checking the degree to which the victim of a violation of human rights can call in the support of the Committee to cease the violation, one cannot but conclude that the control mechanism of the Convention offers only few possibilities. The meaning of the Convention however, is not in the first instance a judicial one. Opsahl thinks that all convention-based systems within the UN emphasize the promotion of human rights more than the protection of victims of potential human rights

---

[171]   X, "The Sixth session of the UN Committee on Economic, Social and Cultural Rights", *NQHR 3* 1992, p. 318–319.

[172]   Opsahl, T., "Instruments of Implementation of Human Rights", *op.cit.*, p. 28.

violations.[173] It is rather a political instrument than an ensemble of judicially enforceable elements. Thomas Hammarberg, member of the Committee on the Rights of the Child, states: "The Convention will in all probability result in increased political attention being given to children and young people. The Convention can from now on serve as an "agenda" for the discussion of the actual circumstances of children. The process required by the Convention, whereby reports have to be submitted on a regular basis and discussions held, should lead to regular examination in every country of issues relating to children and young people".[174]

73. The Convention on the Rights of the Child will, in the first instance, give rise to a change in attitude. Children are for the very first time in history seen as subjects of rights and no longer as objects of legal protection. The "implementation" of this viewpoint cannot occur just like that by means of legislation or regulation. A lot more is needed to do so and the effects will only show after quite some time. "Looking at legislative changes and economic issues is not enough because implementation is ultimately shaped by attitudes. The starting point of dialogue is the State's attitude towards children, and what the State is doing to change the public's attitude".[175]

74. In our opinion, the monitoring system of the Convention offers a wide range of possibilities to implement the change in attitude mentioned above. The States are obliged to regularly submit their reports to the Committee. The reporting duty of the State could result in a discussion in the country concerned, in which several participants could be involved. The Convention appears to stimulate a similar discussion by obliging the States to make their reports public in their country and to make the provisions of the Convention widely known to adults and children.

75. It is not only at a national level that a debate is pursued. The Committee on the Rights of the Child invites States to hold a dialogue on the reports they have submitted. They can always call in the technical assistance of the Committee. There is moreover a wide range of opportunities for other interested organizations and bodies to participate. This well-developed opportunity to participate constitutes an innovating aspect of the implementation process within the United Nations. What's more, it can give rise to a better-coordinated and more uniform approach and interpretation of human rights. The Convention explicitly links development aid with respect for human rights. It can therefore develop into a new and dynamic element in development policies.

---

[173] Opsahl, T.

[174] Hammarberg, T., *op.cit.*, p. 72.

[175] Abramson, B., "First State reports: Sunny and ... Cloudy", *op.cit.*, p. 26.

76. The Committee organizes regional informal meetings and, by doing so, gets in touch with children living in problem areas, with regional non-governmental organizations and government leaders. This way of working strongly contributes to the promotion of the Convention on the Rights of the Child and stimulates the awareness-raising process.

77. However, all of the above does not mean that the Convention on the Rights of the Child would have no judicial meaning at all. Some rights are undoubtedly eligible for a self-executing character.[176] The Convention can moreover serve as the starting point for further national or international standardization: "The Convention could also serve as a starting-point for further standard-setting within the field of children's and young people's rights. (...) The Convention is obviously not a final product. Instead, it should be seen as the first and important milestone".[177]

---

[176] See the contribution by André Alen and Wouter Pas in this volume
[177] Hammarberg, T., *op.cit.*, p. 72.

JAMES R. HIMES

Monitoring Children's Rights:
Cutting Through the Confusion and Planning for
Effective Action

I. NEED FOR CONCEPTUAL CLARITY

In any gathering on the subject of monitoring human rights involving specialists from fields outside that of international human rights law, I think it is
useful to begin with an effort to ensure, not necessarily that we all agree on
the definitions of our terms and relevance of our conceptual frameworks, but
at least that we understand how we are using our terms and concepts.

The paper on "Monitoring Human Rights: Formal and Procedural Aspects"[1]
by Johan Vande Lanotte and Geert Goedertier left me uncertain about their
definition of "monitoring" and how broad a concept of monitoring systems
they see as critical to the analysis they have undertaken. The Introduction
to their paper almost equates "implementation systems" and "monitoring
processes":

> In this text we will discuss the monitoring system of the Convention on
> the Rights of the Child, as drawn up in articles 42 to 45. This system, like
> every other monitoring mechanism, was established to verify the effective
> compliance of the States Parties with their legal international obligations.
> The States Parties are monitored by an international medium to see if they
> fulfill their established legal obligations. In this way the monitoring system
> is a judicial mechanism (no. 2).

From the point of view of an organization such as UNICEF, which is becoming
heavily involved in supporting both the *implementation* and the *monitoring*
of the Convention on the Rights of the Child (CRC), I would strongly prefer
to maintain as clear a distinction as possible between these two concepts,
recognizing that they do overlap.

---

[1] The citations in this commentary refer to the contribution of Vande Lanotte and Goedertier
in this volume.

E. Verhellen (ed.), Monitoring Children's Rights, 113–127.
© 1996 *Kluwer Law International. Printed in the Netherlands.*

The same authors note that, as used in a legal sense in an international treaty, "implementation" relates to the actual fulfilment of the obligations of the States Parties to a treaty as specified (often rather ambiguously) in that treaty. But, they also note that the "implementation of human rights accepted in international treaties is basically a national concern" (no. 10). It is somewhat less clear, either in the paper being reviewed or in the CRC, what precisely is meant by "monitoring". That omission strikes me as significant, especially since the authors draw attention to Philip Alston's statement that "In the 1990's the pre-eminent human rights concern of the international community will be the establishment and development of effective procedures and mechanisms for sustained monitoring and for rapid and constructive responses to violations" (no. 5).

In seeking a useful definition of "monitoring" for our purposes, the standard dictionary entries are reasonably helpful: *Webster's* appears particularly pertinent: "to watch, observe or check esp. for a special purpose" and "to keep track of, regulate, or control [an] operation". *Oxford's* adds an important dimension, drawing on the Latin root, relating to "warning" or "admonition", even citing an example of a "monitory" as "a bishop or pope's letter of admonition".

In an *Innocenti Global Seminar* held in Florence in May 1994, on the subject of "Monitoring the Rights of Children,"[2] we found it useful, in a sense, to bring both the *Webster's* and the *Oxford* connotations into play: (a) a more empirical and somewhat technical notion of monitoring as "measuring" or systematic observation (linked to mechanisms for planning, regulating or control); and (b) a "watchdog" and warning function, which could be either more positive and encouraging or more "enforcement" or sanction-oriented depending on the nature of the monitoring process involved. I will return to this distinction later.

I hope we can begin by accepting the premise, which I think is implicit in the paper being reviewed, that it makes little sense to assess international human rights implementation or monitoring mechanisms in a manner divorced from the actual national and subnational contexts in which these rights are either fulfilled or not – in the lives of real people and real communities. If so, then we certainly should not restrict the concept of "implementation" to the more formalistic reference to certain articles in a convention simply relating to "implementing" that convention, in a procedural sense. In the human rights field we urgently need to get much closer to "implementation" as defined, to return to *Webster's*: to "carry out, accomplish; esp. to give practical effect to and ensure of actual fulfilment by concrete measures". It follows from that definition that "implementation" necessarily concerns us with actual *impacts* on people, not just the results of *processes* in terms of systems development. This approach then strengthens our concern for monitoring as "measurement"

---

[2] Black, Maggie, *Monitoring Children's Rights, Innocenti Global Seminar - Summary Report*, UNICEF International Child Development Centre, Florence, September 1994.

and as an organized process of sustained systematic observations regarding those actual impacts.

II. MANAGING AND MONITORING HUMAN RIGHTS WORK BY OBJECTIVES

It will come as no surprise that someone writing about children's rights from a UNICEF perspective will wish to insist on the importance of setting clear, verifiable and preferably time-bound objectives to guide the work which we support, which is largely in developing countries. We also have a firm principle in our work that effective programming, including in the area of children's rights, must be based on an initial *situation analysis*, combining as thorough a set of baseline data as can be obtained plus an ongoing analysis of the data, hopefully providing clues to immediate and underlying causes of problems which need to be addressed in the programmes being developed. An effective system of monitoring progress in achieving a programme's objectives or goals must be based on a combination of initial baseline data and analysis plus an agreed set of objectives to be achieved in a given period of time. Otherwise we are simply flying blind.

Some human rights advocates are wary of applying these sorts of planning tools to the field of human rights. I can understand part of their concern. Particularly in fundamental areas of civil and political human rights, one could imagine the force of human rights activism becoming dulled by the necessity of going through an extensive process of data gathering and other elements of a good situation analysis when the immediate "situation" concerns egregious rights violations such as torture, summary executions, genocide, or rape as an instrument of state terrorism. It is also obviously inappropriate, legally as well as morally, to set "time-bound goals" for the progressive elimination of these practices – however pragmatic one is forced to be in assessing how long it may take, in fact, to achieve their elimination.

In the overwhelming majority of cases concerning children's rights, however, I would argue that there is considerable relevance in the "planning/implementing/monitoring" model of serious development cooperation work. An abbreviated version of this model, as applied to the implementation of the CRC, is presented in Annex 1. A main reason for the relevance of this approach, particularly for low-income developing countries, is the obvious importance for children of the economic and social rights (concerning child survival and development linked to major progress which must be attained especially in the fields of health, education and nutrition). These are precisely the areas where both the CRC and the realities of economic and other constraints require progressive achievement of rights within certain limitations of available resources.

But many areas of children's rights which might be classified as more in the civil and political rights domain, concerning protection and participation rights, also lend themselves to the "progressive achievement" strategy which, in turn, gives rise to the need for devising an appropriate "planning/implementation/monitoring" approach to fulfilling these rights. The work of Philip Alston and colleagues,[3] which our Centre in Florence has sponsored, on the "best interests of the child" principle, as stated in Article 3 of the CRC, provides many examples of issues, especially in traditional cultures of Africa and Asia, where considerable time will be needed to achieve a "reconciling of culture and human rights" in critical areas such as early marriages, child labour and custody of children at risk. These are also areas where the tools of "monitoring as measurement" are much weaker than in fields such as health and education. But I would argue that work on the protection and participation rights of children can proceed in a way which allows the setting of "verifiable" if not always "quantifiable" goals for the systematic monitoring of progress in attaining these goals. Problems such as child marriage and child labour clearly fit, though not without substantial problems, in this framework. Other matters, including the child's right to freedom of expression or association and access to information, involve even more complex challenges of verifiability and monitoring. But that complexity should not be turned into reasons to avoid the responsibility we all share for devising monitoring tools and mechanisms which are appropriate to these sensitive areas of children's rights to participation. The alternative, I fear, is to leave these rights to the realm of noble intentions and very little action.

III. MONITORING CRC IMPLEMENTATION AND MONITORING THE NATIONAL PROGRAMMES OF ACTION FOR CHILDREN

Some 150 countries, including 21 in Europe, are in the process of preparing or have finalized their National Programmes of Action (NPAs) for Children following commitments undertaken at the 1990 World Summit for Children at the United Nations. Robert Ledogar has written an important paper on "Implementing the Convention on the Rights of the Child through National Programmes of Action for Children."[4] He notes that the most complete of these NPAs are ideal as a framework for monitoring many of the provisions of the CRC, not only because they provide the basis for the accountability associated with time-bound objectives, but also since they specify strategies, programmes, budgets and monitoring mechanisms needed to achieve these objectives.

One major advantage which the better NPAs have over human rights conventions such as the CRC, as well as the monitoring Committee's guidelines for reporting on progress, relates to the matter of costs and financing. Those

---

[3] *The Best Interests of the Child: Reconciling Culture and Human Rights*, Oxford University Press, UK, 1994.

[4] *International Journal of Children's Rights*, Vol. 1, Nos. 3–4, 1993, pp. 377–391.

NPAs which have good cost analyses provide a much-needed basis for assessing how a country's resources are currently being allocated and how much should be expected of that country in meeting the requirement of Article 4 of the CRC. That Article, it is recalled, provides that, with regard to economic, social and cultural rights, "States Parties shall undertake such [implementation] measures to the maximum extent of their available resources and, where needed, within the framework of international co-operation." For developing countries, it is essential to determine what level of commitment of a country's own resources should be considered adequate in order, among other outcomes, to provide a rationale for determining a reasonable level of foreign assistance. For industrialized countries, the issue is more one of intersectoral comparisons of resource commitments: is enough being done for children in comparison with the claims on a country's resources from other groups? In either case, the NPAs can serve as an important basis for serious analysis of the commitment countries are making – or not making – to fulfil their obligations under the CRC.

Ledogar also points out that "One of the most hoped-for dividends of the NPA process is the improvement in national systems and capacities for monitoring progress toward child survival, development and protection goals."[5] Improvements which are "rights-oriented" will help ensure not only that data needed for monitoring are reliable and timely but also disaggregated to highlight important disparities, including by age, gender and ethnicity. For developing countries, it is often essential for the international community to provide special assistance for strengthening national capacities for monitoring progress in meeting the goals of both the NPAs and the CRC (and avoiding costly duplication of efforts between the two processes). For most industrialized countries, capacity-building is less the need than generating the political commitment to devise and strengthen monitoring systems which are sensitive to the special situations of children and youth. Lesson-learning exchanges among countries can help in the development of more reliable and cost-effective systems than often prevail at present.

Data collected and analysed as part of the NPA monitoring process are, like the States Parties' reports on the CRC, expected to be made public. Activist organizations, international and national, need to press governments to ensure this commitment is met. Information of this sort can become a powerful tool for mobilizing public opinion and political support for the objectives of the NPAs and the CRC. Organizations such as UNICEF can help to provide both technical assistance for the improvement of the "tools" and added international publicity for the results. UNICEF's new annual publication, *The Progress of Nations*, including revealing "league tables" and "national performance gaps", is intended to become a highly visible and widely disseminated reminder to the world of both progress and failures by countries in meeting

---

[5] *Ibid*. p. 386.

the obligations to which they are committed. A more technical and detailed example of a monitoring report, at a regional level, is the semi-annual series on "Central and Eastern Europe in Transition", produced by our Centre in Florence.[6]

Certain rights recognized in the Convention, including sensitive areas such as the sexual exploitation, trafficking and torture of children, are not normally going to be emphasized, if mentioned at all, in NPAs. "Since NPAs are official documents, it is likely that the monitoring of these subjects will tend to be weakest in the countries where the problems are greatest."[7] Problems of this sort draw attention to the importance of taking full advantage of the (hopefully coordinated) monitoring processes offered by both the NPAs and the CRC, exploiting the most promising openings for work on sensitive issues wherever they may appear.

This concern for sensitive issues brings me to the subject of the different ways, for different purposes, which the CRC can be used as an instrument for the implementation and monitoring of children's rights.

IV. THE CRC: A POLITICAL, PLANNING OR LEGAL INSTRUMENT?

One of the reasons why there seems to be considerable confusion surrounding the terms "implementation" and "monitoring" in the CRC (and more broadly in human rights circles) is the fact that there are very different viewpoints and expectations regarding how the CRC should be used to promote and protect children's rights most effectively. It is not surprising, for example, that the UN Centre for Human Rights, UNICEF, Defence for Children International (DCI), and a national children's bureau would identify quite different ways of utilizing the Convention in their regular work for children. The Vande Lanotte/Goedertier paper recognizes this possibility in a positive way: "From the study of the Conventions' articles and the working methods of the Committee [on the Rights of the Child], it will be clear that the Convention ... offers many possibilities for the fulfillment of these objectives" (no. 3). The authors note that while the implementation system of the Convention is "a judicial monitoring mechanism", the "meaning of the Convention, however, is not in the first instance a judicial one. (...) It is rather a political instrument than an ensemble of judicially enforceable elements" (no. 72).

I see no problem, quite the contrary, with the fact that there are many and diverse ways in which the CRC can be used by different groups, at various

---

[6] Regional Monitoring Report No. 1, *Central and Eastern Europe in Transition: Public Policy and Social Conditions*, UNICEF International Child Development Centre, Florence, Italy, November 1993; Regional Monitoring Report No. 2, *Central and Eastern Europe in Transition: Public Policy and Social Conditions, Crisis in Mortality, Health and Nutrition*, UNICEF International Child Development Centre, Florence, Italy, August 1994.

[7] See note 4 *supra*, p. 386.

levels (community to international) to advance the cause of child rights and promote the well-being of children. In the work of our Centre in Florence, we have found it helpful, in fact, to distinguish between three different types of approaches to using the CRC: (a) as a political, promotional or advocacy tool; (b) as a tool for policy planning and programming; and (c) as an instrument for legal action. Annex 2 describes these approaches in more detail.

What is worrisome is not the multiple uses of the CRC, or other human rights conventions, but rather the tendency for these different approaches to get confused and for inappropriate channels to be chosen for the approach in question. Politicians, for example, rarely make good judges, and judges should try to stay out of politics, at least while they are "on the bench". Journalists are often talented, courageous and effective in uncovering and publicizing gross violations of human rights, but they are typically less concerned than the judiciary with due process of law or than policy makers should be with how to address the underlying causes of these violations. Different institutions concerned with the effective implementation of the CRC, with different strengths and weaknesses, need to consider how they can best contribute to meeting the many challenges of implementing and monitoring this complex international treaty. And they should not pretend they are institutions different from what they are.

Curiously, in my view, there has been a tendency thus far to emphasize the political and advocacy or social mobilization role of the CRC almost to the exclusion of serious attention to this Convention as a legal instrument entailing binding commitments by States Parties.

This neglect is particularly odd in the context of Europe and other industrialized countries where well-developed, often-activist and independent judiciaries, as well as the existence of an institution such as the European Court of Human Rights, would lead one to expect that the potential power of the CRC (and appropriately harmonized national legislation) as a *legal tool* would be more recognized. Part of the reason for this apparent neglect is undoubtedly an understandable degree of scepticism about "enforcing" human rights commitments at the international level. At the national and subnational levels, moreover, there is growing concern with the "limits of legal intervention" when it comes to sensitive issues of family and family/community relations. Drawing largely on the experience of the United Kingdom, Michael King and Judith Trowell, in their book *Children's Welfare and the Law*,[8] have forcefully argued against what they see as a growing "legalization" and dominance of the legal profession in matters of child and family welfare and protection. These and other legitimate concerns notwithstanding, they could, in my view, result in our overlooking major opportunities for creatively and strategically combining the forces of the political, "development planning", and judiciary worlds to achieve far more effective implementation and monitoring of the

---

[8] Sage Publications, UK/USA/India, 1992.

CRC than would occur if any one of these three spheres of interest ends up dominating the process. Again, however, considerable attention needs to be given to the most appropriate roles to be played by each set of key actors.

Let me cite one example of considerable relevance to UNICEF's work. Vande Lanotte/Goedertier refer to Meron's observation that the UN human rights system is characterized by weak and sporadic implementation and call for a more precise formulation of rights in order for judicial remedies to be more readily available, especially in national courts. Vande Lanotte/Goedertier state that this approach "is in most cases only feasible for civil and political rights. More problems will arise when social, economic and cultural rights are concerned. A precise formulation of these rights will in many cases turn out to be impossible, since the economic possibilities of the potential convention partners must be taken into account" (no. 16).

I certainly agree that in many legal systems it will be difficult, if not impossible, to address through the judiciary instances of "violations" (or failure to meet reasonable standards) in the areas of economic and social rights. We should, however, certainly push on the matter of legal action and judicial remedies wherever possible – and my view is that there are more possibilities in the field of children's rights than have been adequately explored. It is a different matter, however, to retreat on this judicial front because of an alleged inability for the rights in question to be formulated precisely. I would argue that in the area of children's rights, at least, it will be much easier to reach agreement on precise formulation of certain economic and social rights than in many of the areas of "participation" rights, which fall more in the conventional categories of civil and political rights. For example, Article 28 of the CRC is quite clear in requiring States Parties to "Make primary education compulsory and available free to all."[9] This provision is certainly less ambiguous than many provisions in the field of children's civil rights, such as the provision in Article 40 of the CRC providing that children accused of criminal offences be "treated in a manner consistent with the promotion of the child's sense of dignity and worth". Phrases such as "consistent with the evolving capacities of the child" in Article 14 and other provisions concerning participation rights are certainly full of ambiguities. The provision regarding compulsory primary education is, quite wisely, made contingent on the "progressive" achievement qualifier. But that qualification must not be allowed to weaken the commitment. It merely adds a time dimension, linked also to the question of "available resources", to the challenge of devising a reasonably precise formulation of the States Parties' obligations.

There are many examples at the national level of courts requiring various governmental jurisdictions to undertake actions, within specified time peri-

---

[9] For anyone who finds, incidentally, economic and social rights such as free, compulsory primary education not especially relevant in the European context, let us keep in mind that many of these provisions are likely to pertain to marginalized minority groups such as Gypsies or the children of "undocumented" immigrant groups.

ods, which could be considered (although the determinations are not generally caged in this language) as meeting appropriate standards for the fulfilment of economic and social rights. Decisions of state courts in the United States, for example, finding discriminatory practices in the provision of funding for public schools in different districts, have required educational authorities to correct specified inequities within judicially determined time periods. Even in very low income developing countries, especially in South Asia, we are beginning to see activist judges requiring municipalities, states and other jurisdictions to alter their budgetary priorities to meet certain minimum standards in areas of crucial importance to children such as public health, water and sanitation.[10]

The point I would like to emphasize here, in terms of our procedural CRC monitoring concerns, is threefold: (1) there are judicial as well as other actions and remedies at the national level which can be of considerable importance in implementing international legal instruments providing critical rights for children, including economic and social rights; (2) especially when resource limitations are significant obstacles to the fulfilment of these rights, reasonable goals and time periods need to be established for compliance, and provisions must be established for the sustained monitoring of the steps being taken to achieve compliance; courts can and should play a part in such monitoring; (3) although an international treaty monitoring body such as the UN Committee on the Rights of the Child cannot of course get involved in the details of in-country monitoring, it can "monitor the monitoring", i.e., monitor the processes (including judicial processes) whereby States Parties are seeking to achieve effective implementation of the CRC's provisions. This monitoring should include, in my view, an attempt over time to encourage the development of appropriate legal precedents, or good case law, to help to ensure that national and local courts, through their normal actions or through more innovative processes such as social action litigation and public interest law, are exercising their full potential to put into practice, at the national and subnational levels, the provisions and standards of the CRC.

---

[10] In *Ratlam Municipality v. Vardhichand*, for example, the Supreme Court of India upheld a municipal Magistrate's decision requiring the town of Ratlam to begin immediately to take action to correct a serious local problem of industrial and human waste pollution. Finding the municipality's financial and other reasons for inaction unacceptable, the Supreme Court's ruling directed the State Government to take immediate action to stop the industrial pollution and required the Municipal Council within a period of six months "to construct a sufficient number of public latrines for use by men and women separately, provide water supply and scavenging service morning and evening so as to ensure sanitation". The Court added "We have no hesitation in holding that if these directions are not complied with the Sub-Divisional Magistrate will prosecute the officers responsible." What more can be asked by way of enforcement of economic and social rights! Regarding this case and similar examples of social action litigation in India, see Ajit Kumar Sengupta, "Indian constitutional jurisprudence on human rights: creating national conditions for development", in Subrata Roy Chowdhury, *et al.*, eds., *The Right to Development in International Law*, Martinus Nijhoff Publishers, 1992, pp. 213–229.

V. MONITORING GOVERNMENTAL ACTIONS VS. MONITORING SOCIETAL
ACTIONS

We are indebted to Vande Lanotte and Goedertier that they have drawn attention, particularly in their section on "The effectiveness of the reporting procedures" under the CRC, to the importance of not leaving the formal monitoring
process exclusively in the hands of the governments and inter-governmental
bodies directly concerned. They emphasize the importance of critical and
independent examinations of the reports of the States Parties, identifying gaps
and inaccuracies in the information provided and facilitating comparisons of
official information with that of non-governmental sources (nos. 57–71).

I would simply add that the Committee on the Rights of the Child should
also, in refining its procedures for monitoring the CRC, recognize that, just
as governments cannot be expected to report fully and "objectively" on their
progress in implementing the CRC, neither can governments be expected to
be able to take all the actions which will be necessary to ensure a society's
eventual compliance with the CRC's provisions. In no area of human rights
more than children's rights is it so important to involve non-governmental
groups, starting of course with families, but more broadly to include the
full range of institutions of the "civil society", in the implementation of this
innovative Convention.[11] This fuller societal participation is important not
only because of the inherent importance of participatory processes (including
those involving children) in this Convention, but also in terms of the provision
of Article 4 regarding implementation, including that provision's reference to
"available resources" and to "international co-operation".

As we have argued elsewhere,[12] a full and constructive interpretation of the
concept of "available resources" needs to move beyond the notion of focusing only on the financial resources of governments to a more far-reaching
interpretation, explicitly recognizing the availability and potentially increasing significance of resources – economic, human and organizational – at all
levels of society, from the family to the international level. The broadening
of the concept of "available resources" beyond governmental budgets enables
us to devise implementation strategies which are far more powerful, as well
as more realistic, than those involving only governmental plans and programmes. In these days of severe burdens on governmental budgets, however,
and heavy pressures from international institutions and from market forces
to cover more and more costs of public services through "cost recovery" and

---

[11] Child labour is a prime example of a major human rights violation which cannot be
effectively addressed without the cooperation of both the public and private sectors, as well
as trade unions, the media and activist NGOs. Formal legal approaches to dealing with child
labour historically have been of limited effectiveness.

[12] Himes, James R., *Implementing the United Nations Convention on the Rights of the
Child: Resource Mobilization and the Obligations of the States Parties*, Innocenti Occasional
Papers, CRS 2, UNICEF International Child Development Centre, Florence, Italy, November
1992.

user fees, this broader approach involves substantial complexities in terms of effective monitoring. It suggests the need not only for monitoring progress in the fulfilment of the provisions of the CRC, but also for attention to questions such as how this "progress" has been financed and whether the distribution of the burdens is equitable and non-discriminatory. While I agree with the comment in the Vande Lanotte/Goedertier paper (no. 34) that the Committee needs to insist on more information about governments' expenditures relating to their CRC obligations, it is probably unrealistic to expect that answers to these broader issues of resource allocation and distribution of costs could be dealt with adequately in the States Parties' reports. The Committee, however, and other bodies concerned with the CRC should seek to use and encourage analyses by other institutions, including international and regional development banks, university research centres, and agencies such as ILO, UNICEF, UNDP and WHO which have the capacity to undertake work of this sort. The idea of creating a Technical Advisory Group (no. 49) for the Committee to assist it on matters of this sort is surely worth serious consideration.

CONCLUSIONS

The paper presented by Vande Lanotte and Goedertier provides a fair, if not entirely complete, assessment of the strengths and weaknesses of the formal monitoring mechanism established in the CRC. Since this paper was prepared for a section on "Formal and Procedural Aspects of Monitoring", it could not be expected to delve too deeply into some of the more interesting prospects for relating formal to less formal monitoring approaches. A "hybrid" strategy of mixing formal and informal approaches may be especially promising in monitoring the Convention as a political and advocacy tool, as well as in terms of using more formal or "measurement/observation" types of monitoring to feed information to monitoring systems performing more of a "watchdog" function, including by non-governmental institutions. For the watchdog role to be effective, a significant amount of autonomy from the regular agencies of government (including inter-governmental organizations) is essential. That autonomy can at times be achieved in the formal governmental sector, as in the case of ombudsman or public defender institutions in some countries. But, especially important in countries where a strong commitment to human rights is lacking, watchdog roles also need to be played by activist NGOs, religious groups and the media, among other institutions of the "civil society".

In reviewing the vast scope of the many provisions of the CRC, one cannot help but be struck by the daunting task facing the Committee on the Rights of the Child and its major partners. Finding innovative ways to provide additional and sustained support to this Committee, blessed so far with strong membership and an admirable *esprit de corps* (which could wane, however, with time), will be essential to its effective functioning in future years. The support provided to the Committee by the UN Centre for Human Rights, including for information processing and analysis, also requires strengthening. Better ways must be found to improve the flow of information, professional commentary and advisory services from the most relevant UN agencies, including UNICEF, to the Committee.

I would suggest that, to encourage and coordinate this additional support which is urgently needed by the Committee, a consortium of major sponsors, including a sizeable group of committed donor governments but also with NGO participation, be established to provide ongoing supplementary support to the implementation and monitoring mechanisms of the CRC. A number of governments in this region and other European organizations, including the Council of Europe, are well placed to assume a leadership role in this regard.

Beyond financial support, the Committee itself will also need, as the Vande Lanotte/Goedertier paper suggests, "to establish priorities" (no. 44) and to focus on a limited number of issues where they feel that concerted international action can make a significant difference. The Committee, in my view, cannot afford, at least with its current level of resources, to become heavily involved in dealing with very many actual violations of children's rights, however flagrant. It will necessarily have to direct most of its limited time and energies largely to the *processes* of monitoring, especially in terms of the quality of the formal reporting process and "monitoring the monitors". While also concerned with monitoring the CRC as a political and a planning tool, as described in Annex 2, the Committee is a formal body in international human rights law; accordingly, it should not neglect its responsibility to monitor the major legislative, legal reform, enforcement provisions and judicial decisions of key importance around the world in terms of advancing children's rights.

Finally, I agree most heartily with the Vande Lanotte/Goedertier suggestion (no. 33) that the Committee and its allies need to exert strong pressure on the CRC States Parties to establish or strengthen a "national follow-up structure". I doubt that a single "follow-up" institution will be advisable in most cases, especially if one considers the importance of both "monitoring as measurement" or observation, and monitoring as a "watchdog" or warning function. Certainly in the European context, hopefully also extending to Central and Eastern Europe (where the needs are urgent in some cases), the "ombudsman for children" concept, well analysed by Målfrid Grude Flekkøy of Norway[13] is one important element of this national structure.

---

[13] *A Voice for Children: Speaking Out as their Ombudsman*, Jessica Kingsley, UK, 1991.

ANNEX 1

A Proposed Four-step Implementation Strategy for the Convention on the Rights of the Child (CRC), Especially for Country-level Action

Situation Analysis

The essential first step in developing an implementation strategy for work in child rights is to ascertain, as precisely as possible, the nature of the existing situation with respect to each right, in order to identify more clearly the problems that need to be addressed. Good baseline data, appropriately disaggregated (including by categories such as gender and ethnicity needed to identify patterns of discrimination) are essential to an effective system of monitoring compliance with the Convention's provisions. Participatory planning approaches, especially important in the area of children's rights, need to involve households and communities in the situation analysis process. Children and youth can be effectively involved as well, helping them to develop their capacities to responsibly exercise their rights to participate as young citizens in society. It should be kept in mind, however, that high professional standards need to be applied in ensuring that data gathered meet reasonable standards of reliability and comparability.

Goal and Standard Setting

Effective planning for action in the human rights field, as in other areas of public policy, requires the setting of standards and agreement on goals; rights (especially economic, social and other rights requiring achievement "progressively") need to be converted into verifiable goals or objectives, achievable within agreed time frames. Some goals, such as universal primary school enrolment, can be quantified more easily than others, e.g., eliminating "discrimination of any kind". But specific and even binding standards have been set by legislatures and courts even in the more difficult areas. Goals and standards are much more likely to be viewed as legitimate, and indeed as "rights", if a broad and genuine consensus in society is reached regarding these goals. Once again, children should be a part of that emerging consensus.

Plans and Programmes of Action

Different countries have widely varying approaches to social or development planning, but most systems (including various international systems) have some capability of developing concrete plans or programmes for action to achieve agreed goals. Countries which have developed strong National Programmes of Action (NPAs) following the 1990 World Summit for Children, including cost estimates and financial plans, have a good basis for implementing many of the key provisions of the Convention. One of the advantages of the Summit and NPA commitments to children, from the perspective of the Convention, is that they can be used to provide concrete and verifiable indicators of whether a State Party is meeting the minimum core obligations, including financial commitments, central to the achievement of the survival and development rights of children. Attention must be given to a broad array of legislative, administrative, judicial, regulatory and other measures at all levels of government, needed to achieve the goals or attain the standards which have been agreed. For many of the objectives linked to the Convention, goals and specific measures to realize them need to be developed, whenever possible, at the municipal and other levels of government closest to families and children. Plans can include an active role for the private or non-governmental sector. Realistic plans and programmes must recognize clearly that fulfilment of nearly all rights has significant resource implications. Feasible measures for the mobilization of all "available resources" – economic, human and organizational – need to be specified, including through international cooperation where required.

Monitoring Compliance and Enforcement
A mix of official and non-governmental monitoring mechanisms (national and international) is important to help ensure that goals are being reached and the legal rights and duties of all relevant parties are recognized, understood and enforced. Understanding rights needs to reach the level of communities, families and children. Monitoring, which must also reach those levels to be useful, is much more effective when based on widespread popular understanding of the relevant goals and rights. Especially at the international level, a non-adversarial "constructive dialogue" among the relevant parties, led by the UN Committee on the Rights of the Child, is likely to be the most accepted form of monitoring. At the national and subnational levels, however, strong incentives, including financial incentives, for compliance, as well as significant penalties for non-compliance, will be essential complements to an effective system of monitoring progress in achieving the agreed child rights objectives, as provided in the Convention.

An approach of the sort described, adjusted to the circumstances and capacities of different countries, can help ensure that the progressive achievement of the goals of the Convention on the Rights of the Child leads to more than just another illusory utopia in the realm of human rights.

Source: Himes, James R., "The UN Convention on the Rights of the Child: More than a New Utopia?" in *Innocenti Essays*, 5, 10–11. Florence: UNICEF ICDC.

ANNEX 2

Monitoring the Protection of Child Rights

In a number of meetings of UNICEF and other colleagues concerned with the implementation of the Convention on the Rights of the Child (CRC), it has been found useful for various purposes to think of the Convention in terms of three different types of practical uses for human rights instruments of this sort:

1. As a *political, promotional or advocacy* tool: Using the CRC as an additional weapon both: (a) for generating increased political commitment to children; strengthening and broadening alliances and networks to advance children's best interests; and to motivate the public to be concerned for children's well-being – on the positive side of the ledger; but also (b) for drawing attention to shortcomings, criticizing, and even shaming violators of children's rights ("the organization of shame" in the language of human rights activists).

2. As a tool for *policy formulation and programming*: Taking advantage of the CRC as an opportunity, especially for "development agencies", child service organizations and NGOs which have not traditionally been involved in human rights work, to use this Convention as a way to broaden their framework for their regular policy and programme development, implementation, monitoring and evaluation efforts. How this can best be done will depend on the objectives and operational style of the organization concerned. For UNICEF, it has been proposed that a four-step implementation strategy could be adopted, based heavily on the regular country programming process which characterizes UNICEF's cooperation with developing countries. (See Annex 1.)

3. As an instrument for formal *legal action*: Initiating legislative or legal action, including through law reform, improved enforcement or the legal representation of groups of children and/or their families whose rights have been violated. This latter approach, little developed in most countries, might involve (depending on local legal possibilities and practices): social action litigation, class action suits, or "public interest law", as well as more conventional legal aid for marginalized groups or individuals. Efforts to achieve constitutional and other legislative reform, for purposes of compliance or increased compatibility with the CRC, are likely in some legal systems to involve a combination of formal "legal action" with the two other types of tools mentioned above.

As with all typologies, this rough threefold distinction will apply with different degrees of relevance to different social and political contexts. The "fit" is presumably best in more democratic systems, characterized *inter alia* by an independent judiciary and a reasonable degree of open political space for non-governmental organizations and the press. It is proposed, however, that some rough breakdown of this sort will be especially useful to help guide the work of organizations, at the local to the international level, which have some capacity for work on children's rights in more than one of these three areas of a broad implementation strategy.

MARTA SANTOS PAIS

Monitoring Children's Rights
A View from Within

Following the contribution of Vande Lanotte and Goedertier on the "Formal and Procedural Aspects of Monitoring", it may seem interesting to describe the activities developed by the Committee on the Rights of the Child in its four years of existence, as perceived by a member of this monitoring treaty body. It is therefore a view from within, coloured by optimism and guided by the search for the continuous improvement of the situation of children and the effective realisation of their rights.

When the Convention on the Rights of the Child was adopted in 1989 by the General Assembly[1] it was hard to guess or to anticipate the impact this international instrument would have in the future. It was the outcome of a long negotiation and it constituted a natural progress as a new instrument in the field of human rights. But would it mean something more? In particular when the monitoring of the rights of the child is at stake, what has been, or may be, different from the traditional approach followed by other human rights instruments?

To address such questions it seems important to recall the main elements that colour the philosophy of the Convention, to look into the general principles that inspire its implementation and to consider the way its monitoring system works.

I. THE PHILOSOPHY OF THE CONVENTION ON THE RIGHTS OF THE CHILD

The Convention on the Rights of the Child is an expression of some nuclear philosophical values. In fact,

- the Convention reaffirms the universality of children's rights;
- the Convention is a source of inspiration and a reference for action;
- the Convention promotes consensus and is based on a transparent and participated process;
- the Convention is a tool for advocacy;

---

[1] The Convention was adopted by General Assembly Resolution 44/25, of 20 November 1989.

E. Verhellen (ed.), Monitoring Children's Rights, 129–143.
© 1996 *Kluwer Law International. Printed in the Netherlands.*

- the Convention sets the framework for international cooperation and technical assistance;
- the Convention promotes a holistic and multidisciplinary approach to the rights of the child.

A. The Convention Reaffirms the Universality of Children's Rights

The Convention reflects a compromise between different legal systems and cultural traditions, in the respect for universally recognised human rights.

As the Commission on Human Rights reflected in 1988, such was the challenge faced by the drafting group – to bear in mind the solutions followed by the national legislation, prevailing cultural values, specific needs of the developing countries, but to achieve the universal recognition of the rights set forth by the Convention.[2]

Today we can say that the challenge was gained and that diversity and national specificity have paved the way to universality![3] This reality is undoubtedly confirmed by the unprecedented number of ratifications to the Convention, made by countries from all regions of the world.[4] They have in fact thereby expressed a solemn political commitment to effectively realise the rights of children in an atmosphere of dialogue and solidarity, as well as to adopt all necessary and appropriate measures to that end, bringing national law and practice in line with the Convention. States parties have furthermore pledged themselves to always apply the most conducive norm in this process, even when it derives from relevant international law.[5] And last year, at the World Conference on Human Rights, held in Vienna, they have accepted the call to integrate the Convention on the Rights of the Child into their national action plans.[6]

B. The Convention is a Source of Inspiration and a Reference for Action

Thus, the Convention has gained an undeniable value as an ethical reference, an inspiring guide for action and as a legal framework for the promotion and protection of the rights of the child, both at the international and national levels.

The wide political relevance of the Convention is reaffirmed by its constant inclusion in the international agenda. The rights of the child became a systematic subject for discussion and a source of inspiration, as the World

---

[2] Resolution 1988/75 of the Commission on Human Rights, adopted on 10 of March 1988.

[3] As recognised by the Final Document of the World Conference on Human Rights, I, paragraph 5.

[4] By January 1996, 186 States had ratified or acceded to the Convention on the Rights of the Child.

[5] See article 41 of the Convention on the Rights of the Child.

[6] Final Document of the World Conference on Human Rights, II, paragraph 47.

Summit for Children, held in September 1990, clearly showed and the World Conference on Human Rights so openly reaffirmed. That is why universal ratification of the Convention is a shared and consensual target and so close to reality.

This is also the reason for the Vienna World Conference to recommend that human rights and the situation of children be regularly reviewed and monitored by all relevant United Nations system organs and mechanisms and by the supervisory bodies of the Specialized Agencies, and the implementation of the Convention be a priority in the United Nations system-wide action.[7]

At the same time, this also explains the reason why the international campaign for protection of the rights of the child goes hand in hand with the national implementation system. In fact, States are called to integrate the Convention on the Rights of the Child into their national action plans, and to adopt all the necessary measures to ensure the effective implementation of the Convention.

Moreover, as recognised by the World Conference on Human Rights the comprehensive national approach in the implementation process adopted by the Committee on the Rights of the Child, should be encouraged. Such an approach will allow for the international community to assess the national reality and to launch programmes of technical assistance and advice, namely through the action of the Committee on the Rights of the Child. These Programmes will in turn be of decisive importance to strengthen the national capacity to find the best solutions and policies for existing problems or setbacks. Similarly, the international community and the Committee on the Rights of the Child will be in a position to bring pressure on the national authorities to ensure the constant improvement of the strategies defined and of the situation of children.

C. The Convention Promotes Consensus and is Based on a Participated Process

Having been adopted by consensus, the Convention promotes action and encourages alliances around children and children's rights, both at the national and international levels.

1. For this reason, the rights of the child are envisaged not in opposition to the rights of adults, not as a conflictual alternative to the rights of parents, rather affirmed as individual rights inherent to the human dignity of every person.

The child is therefore seen not only as the vulnerable human being needing a special assistance and protection, but also as the subject of fundamental rights and freedoms, – the right to express views and to see those views taken

---

[7] Final Document of the World Conference on Human Rights, II, paragraph 51.

into consideration, of being informed and consulted, of sharing decisions together with adults In a word, having the right to participate in the decision making process affecting his or her life as well as the freedom of making free choices.

2. Similarly, the Convention has a non adversarial approach to children's rights. Thus, the implementation provisions, while underlying the Government's accountability for the policies pursued, stress the need for dialogue, rather than a punitive attitude.

And this is exactly the inspiring attitude of the Committee on the Rights of the Child. It encourages an open discussion with States in order to understand the country's reality, to identify difficulties and to be in a position to assist in the search for the best solutions to promote and protect the rights of children. In fact, its purpose is not to simply condemn, accuse or of being confrontational.[8] That is why it attaches such a great deal of importance to formulating suggestions and recommendations to States parties following the examination of their periodic reports.[9]

The same philosophy inspires the transparency ensured to the implementation process – in fact, in the light of article 44 paragraph 6 of the Convention, States parties reports are to be made widely available to the public in their own countries, thereby offering the opportunity to encourage popular participation and pave the way to a follow-up system.[10]

Moreover, the Convention appeals for advocacy for children's rights as a means to promote the deep understanding of its principles and provisions, – among professional groups, non governmental organisations, families and, in a very special way, among children themselves, by means they may really understand. It becomes therefore an essential tool for changing attitudes, creating awareness, preventing violations of children's rights.

At the same time, this prevailing spirit of consensus strengthens the important international trend to build a movement of solidarity and aid for the development of programmes designed to strengthen the realisation of the rights of the child. It therefore also sets a framework for international cooperation and technical assistance.

---

[8]   See in this spirit the General Guidelines regarding the form and content of initial reports to be submitted by States Parties under article 44 paragraph 1 (A/47/41, Annex III), paragraph 4.

[9]   Convention on the Rights of the Child, article 45 d) and the second Report of the Committee on the Rights of the Child to the 49th session of the General Assembly (A/49/41), paragraph 359 to 361.

[10]   See also First report of the Committee on the Rights of the Child to the General Assembly, in the light of article 44 paragraph 5 of the Convention – A/47/41, Annex III, paragraph 11; Second report of the Committee to the General Assembly (A/49/41), paragraphs 366 to 371, and in particular paragraph 370.

D. The Convention Implies Accountability for the Rights of the Child

It is important to stress, however, that, while promoting consensus, the Convention does not reflect apathy or a simple and welcomed lip-service to children. In fact, each State party has a particular responsibility in the realisation of the rights of the child. The State is expected to act, to adopt all necessary and appropriate measures in order to respect the exercise of children's rights. It is also expected to ensure the conditions for those rights to be fully enjoyed by each child without discrimination of any kind.[11]

The adherence by States, as well as by international organisations and national bodies to this project imply a necessary commitment and willingness to work towards such a goal. It becomes therefore natural and at the same time essential to assess and evaluate measures undertaken with a view to regularly review and monitor the situation and the rights of children.

E. The Convention Promotes a Holistic and Multidisciplinary Approach to Children's Rights

The Convention has set up a holistic approach to the rights of the child. In an innovative way, civil, political, economic, social and cultural rights are included in the same text, all being recognized as necessary for the full and harmonious development of the personality, and inherent to the human dignity of the child.

Let us recall, however, that the Convention has intentionally not established any hierarchy, or given any priority, to the implementation of some rights in detriment of the others. In fact, the same essential importance is recognised to each one of them, in the respect for all the others.[12]

That is why it becomes so important to be aware of the comprehensive reality before studying any specific situation, or considering any strategy to implement policies for children. Only this approach will allow to address problems in an integrated manner, to seek for appropriate solutions and to study the underlying causes of problems affecting children and the enjoyment of their rights.

That is also the reason to gather complete data on each and all fields covered by the Convention, both those which are traditionally considered as measurable and those of qualitative nature; and by the same token, to take into account the reality at the regional, national and local levels. The importance of this comprehensive approach was revealed in some of the reports examined by the Committee, particularly in cases where decentralisation and regionalisation policies have been followed. Although intended to ensure autonomy

---

[11] See in this regard articles 4 and 2 of the Convention on the Rights of the Child.

[12] See in this context the General Guidelines regarding the form and content of initial reports to be submitted by States Parties under article 44 paragraph 1 of the Convention (A/47/41, Annex III), paragraph 8.

and allow for creativity in the different regions, provinces or local authorities, such an approach has also raised some difficulties.

In fact, it became sometimes hard to assess the real general national situation through an effective system of evaluation and monitoring, to coordinate actions clearly inspired by a shared philosophy, or even to overcome existing social and economic disparities, in fields as important as the ones of education or health.

The holistic approach followed by the Convention gives way to the building up of a spirit of partnership among all institutions and entities working with and for children, Governmental departments, National institutions, non governmental organisations or international bodies.

In a lively way, the indivisibility of the rights of the child paves the way to an effective interaction between the different sectors and bodies intervening in the field, either when considering strategies for implementing the Convention, launching campaigns of advocacy and training or when establishing programmes of technical assistance. Thus, the Convention has also introduced a new methodology for action!

This explains the reason for each State party to be expected to provide the Committee on the Rights of the Child with a comprehensive understanding of the implementation process, as stated in article 44 paragraph 2 of the Convention.

This is why the Committee is so interested in receiving information not only on the measures adopted by the Government itself, but also on the process followed in each country to bring the Convention into reality – namely on the role played by NGOs and other important national institutions in the realisation of the rights of the child – including courts, the Parliament, Ombudspersons, Human Rights or Children's Commissions. Such information will make it possible for the Committee to understand the extent to which popular participation and public scrutiny of the government policies are encouraged, or to phrase it in a different way, how far the realisation of the rights of the child has become a priority and a commitment for the society as a whole.[13]

This further explains the importance attached to the pre-sessional working group organised by the Committee to prepare the consideration of States parties reports. Taking place two to three months in advance to the formal meeting, the pre-sessional working group allows for the *identification of the main areas* that would need to be further discussed with representatives of the reporting State, as well as for the consideration of *questions relating to technical assistance and international cooperation.*[14]

---

[13] See the General Guidelines regarding the form and contents of initial reports to be submitted by States Parties, First report of the Committee to the General Assembly (A/47/41, Annex III), paragraphs 3 and 9 b).

[14] See Second Report of the Committee to the General Assembly (A/49/41) paragraphs 357 and 358.

During this pre-sessional meeting, the Committee bases its study of the States Parties reports on the information contained in the country file organised by the Secretariat.[15] The file is intended to give an overall picture of the country under examination, its human rights and children's rights situation and compiles all relevant information available from all sources, including NGOs.

To allow the Committee to clearly understand the reality in the country concerned, and to be in a position to better assist the Government through the suggestions and recommendations it will later formulate, it has proved to be extremely useful to cooperate closely with and benefit from technical advice of the representatives of United Nations bodies (UNICEF, ILO, WHO, UNHCR, ...) and of relevant competent bodies, including national institutions or NGOs.

The participation of NGOs has shown to be of a decisive relevance, in particular in the light of their organisation as a NGO Group on the implementation of the Convention, which interacts with the Committee on an on-going basis, either in the preparation of the examination of States Parties reports, the discussion of working methods or during the thematic discussions held by the Committee on specific topics or rights covered by the Convention.

The recognition of the importance of this process was curiously stressed during the very first meeting held by the Committee – in an informal meeting organised in May 1991, the very first of the kind organised by a treaty body in the history of the United Nations.[16] In the report then prepared, it was recognised that the cooperation between the Committee and United Nations organs, Specialized Agencies as well as competent bodies, was in fact guided by the provisions of article 45 of the Convention. In that spirit, it was suggested to establish a Technical Advisory Group composed of individuals belonging to those bodies, with a view to assist and advise the Committee on a continuous basis, including in the collection and dissemination of information on the rights of the child.[17]

II. GENERAL PRINCIPLES

The Convention stresses the importance of inspiring fundamental principles in the process of realisation of the rights of the child. Such principles constitute a constant reference for the implementation and monitoring of children's rights.

---

[15] See Second Report submitted to the General Assembly (A/49/41), paragraphs 355 and 356.

[16] See Marta Santos Pais "The Committee on the Rights of the Child", in ICJ The Review no. 47/1991.

[17] See the Summary of the Informal Meeting of the Committee on the Rights of the Child, held in Geneva from 21 to 24 May 1991, prepared by Hoda Badran and Marta Santos Pais, Members of the Committee on the Rights of the Child.

Non discrimination, best interests of the child, participation of children as well as the right to survival and development are in fact underlying values that should guide the way each individual right is ensured and respected. And they are decisive criteria to assess progress in the implementation process of those same rights – this explains the special attention paid by the Committee to these general principles during the consideration of States Parties reports.

A. Non-discrimination

Non discrimination[18] means that no child should be injured, privileged, punished or deprived of any right on the ground of his or her race, sex, language, religion, political or other opinion, social or ethnic origin, property, birth or other status. This principle implies therefore that girls and boys, rich or poor children, living in urban or rural areas, belonging to a minority or an indigenous group should be given the opportunity of enjoying the same fundamental rights recognised by the Convention.

Yet, we realize that vulnerable groups of children often constitute an invisible reality (working children, domestic servants, children involved in prostitution or affected by an armed conflict) or at least where a precise assessment is lacking (children placed in institutions, children who are forced to live and/or work in the street, children who are abandoned or who are not registered and therefore not even recognised as persons).

This situation shows the importance of establishing a system of information and the use of disaggregated data which may help identifying and assessing how different groups of children live, while allowing for the consideration of the best possible ways to overcome the problems that are affecting the enjoyment of their fundamental rights.

However, we are still confronted with *legislative solutions* which don't fully take this principle into consideration, as it is often the case of the different minimum age for marriage between boys and girls, a distinction which is purely based on an alleged notion of physical maturity.

In other cases, specific positive measures have to be considered to address the situation of children in a disadvantaged situation, handicapped children who become marginalised and often lack special care; unaccompanied minors seeking asylum or family reunification, who are systematically ignored. In other cases, there is a need to bridge social and geographical disparities prevailing in the country, as in the case of children living in rural areas or of children belonging to minorities.

B. The Best Interest of the Child

The second principle is the best interests of the child, a criterion which should be considered as the *primary consideration* in all actions concerning children,

---

[18] See article 2 of the Convention on the Rights of the Child.

whether undertaken by private or public welfare institutions, administrative authorities, courts of law or even legislative bodies.[19] A principle that should also be the guiding reference for the way parents exercise their responsibility of upbringing and ensuring the development of the child.[20]

This principle should inspire all decisions taken and affecting the life of the child, prevailing in the case where there is a conflict between the interests of the child and of those who are responsible by him or her, namely the parents – as often is the case of the right of the child to education and the interest of the parents to benefit from the economic support of the child through his or her employment[21]; or between different rights of the child, as in the case of the right to be cared by the parents and the right to be protected against situations of abuse or neglect caused by the parents; or the right to work, in the light of article 32 of the Convention, but not to perform a hazardous activity or any other that might be harmful for the child's development, health or education.

The best interests of the child should also play an essential role when the allocation of resources is at stake. As stressed by article 4 of the Convention for the implementation of economic, social and cultural rights the allocation of resources should be made to the maximum extent possible. And this is a way of clearly reflecting the principle of "first call for children" at the budgetary level, to be applied both for national policies and for international aid development programmes.

This principle implies that policies for children should be given priority but also that there is a need to have a clear picture of the way the budget reflects this same priority – be it the central, regional or local budget. It further ensures consistency to the policies adopted at the different levels, it allows to overcome possible disparities between different regions in the country, between urban and rural areas, majority and minority groups, etc, and it addresses the area of international development aid.

Once again, it becomes obvious how important it is to benefit from an effective system of information, evaluation and monitoring, based on the identification of specific policies, projects or programmes addressed to children.

C. Participation of Children

Participation of children is probably one of the basic challenges set by the Convention on the Rights of the Child, either at the legislative level or in practice, within the family, the school system or in the community. It shows that no implementation system may be carried out and be effective without

---

[19]   See article 3 of the Convention on the Rights of the Child.

[20]   See article 18 of the Convention on the Rights of the Child.

[21]   This reality was reflected in reports submitted by some Latin American countries, where, according to the labour code a special authorisation is allowed for children to work below the minimum age of access to employment based on the need of the family.

the intervention of children in the decisions that affect their lives. They have a word to say, they should be listened to and taken seriously into consideration, they should be able to influence decisions and supported in the process of becoming active, tolerant and democratic.[22]

Participation implies information and awareness on the rights of the child, building the capacity among children of expressing opinions and taking free decisions. And it further implies training and mobilisation of others to learn to give children that chance, building together a spirit of democracy.

Yet, very often the legislation does not reflect this opportunity and there is no tradition to make it work. It becomes therefore essential to study positive experiences, to support research projects in this field, to create spaces for children to intervene without just being used for the benefit of others. And to allow for a system which is open to reflect the perspective of children on the way their rights are being promoted and protected, and their effective participation ensured.

D. The Right to Survival and Development

The fourth general principle is the one of survival and development.[23] It means ensuring the right to an adequate standard of living in the full respect for the child's human dignity, the right to the highest attainable standard of health, to information and education in the basic knowledge of preventive health care, nutrition and environmental sanitation... Areas which have been traditionally considered as measurable and where the goals of the World Summit for Children together with the national plans of action play a decisive role.

And still to gain another and deeper challenge of self-betterment of the child, ensuring the capacity of developing talents and abilities to their fullest potential, giving the child this essential feeling of belonging to a world made of solidarity where there will be no place for indifference towards mimetism inside extreme poverty.

For this principle to be respected it becomes essential to identify for example the number of children living below a minimum poverty line. It will be therefore of decisive importance, for instance, to establish an effective system of birth registration – yet, such a system is lacking for so many children around the world, because they are living in rural areas, in countries where the number or training of registration officers is insufficient or in cases where the law does not provide for any legal status in case of abandonment of children.[24]

---

[22]   See Convention on the Rights of the Child, article 12.

[23]   See Convention on the Rights of the Child, in particular articles 6, 24, 27 and 28.

[24]   When such a problem is identified in a country it becomes essential to consider the capacity of the international community to launch a chain of solidarity to assist in the realisation of the rights of the child, namely by shaping adequate programmes of aid and technical

III. THE MONITORING SYSTEM: THE REPORTING SYSTEM OF THE CONVENTION

For the purpose of examining the progress made by States parties in the real-isation of the rights recognised in the Convention, a Committee on the Rights of the Child has been established. Composed of ten independent experts, serving in their personal capacity, its mandate derives from the provisions and principles of the Convention. As recognised at the second session of the Committee, its members do not represent their country, Government or any other organisation to which they may belong and are solely accountable to the children of the world.

The Committee was entrusted with important tasks in the field of the promotion and protection of the rights of the child, both being essential to its monitoring functions.

Some are designed to ensure a better understanding of the provisions and principles of the Convention – as it is the case of the formulation of general comments or general recommendations, or the organisation of days of general discussion, (three have already taken place on the involvement of children in armed conflict, on the economic exploitation of children and on the role of the family in the promotion of the rights of the child). Or still to request for studies on the rights of the child, in the light of article 45 c) of the Convention – as it was the case of the impact of armed conflicts on children's rights.[25]

Similarly, the organization of informal regional visits[26] has given an addi-tional opportunity for the Committee members to promote a greater awareness of the principles and provisions of the Convention and of the work developed by the Committee. It is furthermore an extremely effective way of acquiring a deeper knowledge and understanding of the realities of each region and country, thus contributing to a better preparation and a more accurate con-sideration of the States parties reports. But the experience has also proved that such visits may constitute a meaningful follow-up to the examination of a report by the Committee, as it was clearly the case of Viet Nam. More-over, it is interesting to mention in this context that in a recent meeting, the Committee further decided to consider undertaking missions by some of its members to particular countries, with a view to encouraging universal ratifi-cation of the Convention, to contributing to its effective implementation, or to ensuring a follow-up to the discussion of a particular State Party report by the Committee.

Some other tasks are specifically linked with the activities of the Com-mittee as a supervisory body, monitoring the way States parties implement

---

assistance, including through training activities with a view to strengthening the national capacity.

[25] See Second Report of the Committee to the General Assembly (A/49/41), paragraphs 536 to 559 and first recommendation adopted at the 7th session of the Committee (CRC/C/33).

[26] Three informal meetings have already taken place in Latin America, Asia and Africa.

the Convention through a system of a constructive dialogue, in order to help identifying difficulties, pointing to possible solutions or mobilising resources.

And in this framework, the Committee is entrusted with a decisive and important function – the promotion of international co-operation and solidarity, and the consideration of forms of technical assistance and advice. The Committee is in fact well placed to play a catalysing role in this area, encouraging a combined action between States, United Nations bodies and other competent bodies, including NGOs, with a view to foster the implementation of the Convention.

Every State undertakes to submit to the Committee periodic reports on the different measures adopted to give effect to the rights covered by the Convention.

These reports should contain sufficient information to provide the Committee with a comprehensive understanding of the implementation of the Convention in every country concerned. Comprehensive in the sense that it covers *all the areas* of the Convention and that it should reflect the way the *different concerned entities, of public or private nature*, at the central, regional and local levels are involved.

Reports are therefore expected to provide information:
– on the diversity of measures adopted, in order to bring the national law and practice in line with the provisions of the Convention and to ensure a growing and dynamic improvement of the level of implementation (art. 44 par.1);
– on the progress made in the enjoyment of the rights of the child, that is also an *evaluation of the effect of the measures* adopted (art. 44 par. 1);
– as well as on the factors and difficulties that may have affected the degree of fulfilment of the obligations undertaken by the State under the Convention (art. 44 par. 2).

In a word, they are intended to ensure a periodic assessment of the reality.

In order to assist Governments in the preparation of their reports, the Committee on the Rights of the Child adopted General Guidelines on initial reports of States parties, to be submitted within two years of the entry into force of the Convention.

These reporting guidelines are intended to provide guidance to each State party in the preparation of its initial report, minimising the risk of *insufficient information* and ensuring *consistency and uniformity* to the form and contents of the report. In view of their thematic approach, they furthermore constitute an important reference to *collect information on*, and to *ensure consistency to*, the implementation process of the different rights recognised by the Convention.

But Guidelines are also designed to underline the relevance of the reporting process and emphasise that it is not a simple formal obligation. Through reporting, States are reaffirming their *international commitment* to respect and ensure the rights of the child, as well as establishing an open and *mean-*

ingful dialogue with the Committee on the Rights of the Child. But States are furthermore expected to regard the process of preparing a report as a particular important occasion for conducting a comprehensive review of the various measures undertaken to harmonise national laws and policies with the Convention, and for ensuring a periodic monitoring action.

The Convention sets the rule for this periodicity in article 44.[27] Yet, it allows the Committee to ask, in the light of the specific reality of a country, for additional information or for a progress report before that time-limit.[28] By the same token, it explains how decisive it may be for the Committee to request for specific information in urgent situations where the rights of the child may be at stake or run the risk of being deteriorated.[29] The reporting system will enable the identification of existing problems, the consideration of new policies and the establishment of new targets.

Such an occasion should thus be used by Governments to monitor their own achievements. But it should further be used to launch a movement of social mobilisation for children's rights and to encourage public scrutiny of the Government's policies.[30]

For this reason, the Convention has included an innovating follow-up system, by which States are to make their reports widely available to the public in their own countries.[31] In the same line, the Committee systematically recommends in its concluding observations that States Parties further ensure the widespread dissemination of the results of the dialogue held with the Committee,[32] that is, of the evaluation this international body made of the national reality and of the commitment of the Government.

Such a measure will reflect the transparency of this process. Both of the supervisory function of the Committee on the Rights of the Child and of the Government policies. It enables the recognition of progress or failure and paves the way for attracting support for the areas where a particular need is felt. It will still contribute to ensure a wider popular participation, providing an opportunity for governmental officials, private institutions and independent advocates to act together, or in a complementary way, to achieve the common goal of improving the level of implementation of children's rights.

---

[27] The intial report should be submitted two years after the entry into force of the Convention in the State Party concerned; the following ones, every five years.

[28] This has already been the case when the Committee considered the reports submitted by Sudan, Indonesia and Colombia, where only *initial observations* were first adopted, allowing for the conclusion of the examination at a later stage in the light of additional information provided on specific areas; in the case of Pakistan the Committee decided to ask for a *progress* report within two years, in order to assess the follow-up ensured to the recommendations formulated by the Committee during the consideration of the initial report.

[29] See Secong Report to the General Assembly (A/49/41) para.372 to 381.

[30] See General Guidelines regarding the Form and Content of initial reports, paragraph 3.

[31] See Convention on the Rights of the Child, article 44 paragraph 6.

[32] See Second Report of the Committee to the Genral Assembly (A/49/41) para. 370.

It is in this context that some States have established a national focal point on the Rights of the Child, for co-ordinating policies relating to children and for monitoring the implementation of the Convention – a measure to which the Committee on the Rights of the Child has attached a particular interest in its guidelines and in the consideration of the initial reports of States Parties. In fact, isn't it true that the essential aim of the international monitoring system is to strengthen the national capacity to ensure and monitor the realisation of the rights of the child?

In the periodic reports the national reality should be described with *objectivity* and the information provided should be based on *reliable, complete and specific data* – *complete* in the sense that it should cover *all the areas* reflected in the Convention, at the central, regional or local levels; *reliable*, since it should be objective, accurate and not politicised; *specific* for identifying disaggregated data and meaningful indicators to consider each of the rights recognised by the Convention.

It seems important to recall in this framework the instrumental role that may be played by the concluding observations adopted by the Committee following the examination of the States parties reports. They are a public document which constitutes a portrait of the nature of the dialogue held with the Governmental Delegation, and by the same token a general evaluation of the report and of the implementation process in the country. They indicate therefore the positive developments, the factors and difficulties and the areas of concern identified by the Committee. They further include a set of suggestions and recommendations addressed to the State Party, highlighting the areas where a specific follow-up will be required, including through programmes to be implemented in cooperation with NGOs or in the framework of international assistance.

The concluding observations are a relevant public document which will naturally be the starting point for a future dialogue with the State and a decisive encouragement for a wider national debate on policies designed to promote and protect the rights of the child.

For this system to work, the availability and accuracy of data concerning the implementation of the rights of the child become essential. In fact, in order to ensure a real evaluation and monitoring of the policies designed to implement the Convention on the Rights of the Child, and to prevent the misuse of existing resources or the inappropriateness of the measures undertaken, every State has naturally to carefully and seriously study its specific reality. Only this way it will be in a position to ascertain the kind of strategy it should adequately and realistically envisage, the benchmarks it should identify to ensure progressive betterment in the enjoyment of children's rights.

However, challenges still lie ahead, since:
– some fields covered by the Convention are traditionally considered as *not measurable*, therefore not benefiting from any particular evaluation,

of statistical or other nature, as it is often the case of civil rights and freedoms or the right of participation;
- some others are not even seen as *meaningful* for children, – it seems sufficient to think about the impact of homelessness or unemployment on the level of enjoyment of the rights by children to realise that only the vague impact on the family or on adults is assessed;
- in some other cases, data exist but are *not easily accessible*, – for the lack of timely collection and publication of disaggregated data, or for the non existence of compiled data, in a comprehensive manner that may reflect the action of all the different institutions involved.

And we could also mention those extreme, although still common cases where the use of statistics is guided by political considerations, leading to criteria which are intentionally chosen to ensure a certain picture of the reality, or to circumstances where the lack of data in a particular field is considered to clearly reflect a reality where problems "obviously" do not exist.

What has been said shows the importance of establishing a system of information which will not be only dependent on Governmental sources, but which will also rely on data gathered by International Organisations, Research Institutes and non governmental organisations, extremely well placed to build a non politically-oriented memory of the implementation process. A system which may be reliable and effective. Being aware that by assessing the reality, as well as by identifying the existence or lack of progress, one is not expressing an attitude of political opposition, rather indicating a serious willingness to contribute to the improvement of the reality. It is in fact and simply a healthy sign of a responsible reinforcement of, and participation in, democracy!

PASCALE BOUCAUD

Recourse Procedures Against the Violation of Children's Rights in European Countries

How can a child denounce and act against violations of the rights which have been acknowledged both by international and national texts and which are imposed upon member states of the Council of Europe?

Traditionally, there is a recourse procedure within the framework of the Council of Europe based on the European Convention for the protection of rights and fundamental freedoms. The positive results of this type of action will be dealt with first.

But since the International Convention on Children's Rights has come into force, the Council of Europe has been trying to prepare a more specific Convention to further reinforce the implementation of the international convention within its member states, at least as far as some of the provisions are concerned.

These projects will be examined later.

I. Individual Recourse for Minors, Based on the Violation of the European Convention on Human Rights and the Protection of Fundamental Freedom

This convention, signed on 4 November 1950 came into force on 3 September 1953.[1] It set up a Commission and a Court.

An individual can apply to the first body, the Commission, against a State if the State in question, in pursuance of article 25 has recognised the competence of the Commission. Today 31 members of the Council of Europe have made this acknowledgement.

But can a minor apply directly to the Commission himself?

The Commission does not supply a precise indication; the Commission has however accepted it since a petition in 1977.[2] This petition was applied

---

[1] 32 signatory states; 31 ratifications: Austria, Belgium, Bulgaria, Cyprus, The Tchec Republic, Denmark, Finland, France, Germany, Greece, Hungary, Ireland, Islande, Italy, Liechtenstein, Luxembourg, Malta, the Netherlands, Norway, Poland, Portugal, Rumania, San Marino, Spain, Slovenia, Slovakia, Sweden, Switzerland, Turkey.

[2] Petition no. 6753/74, Judgment of 19 December 1977, D.R. 2., p. 118.

E. Verhellen (ed.), Monitoring Children's Rights, 145–158.
© 1966 Kluwer Law International. Printed in the Netherlands.

by a young 14 year-old girl whose parents had forced her to return home after running away with her boyfriend. Yet most of the applications are made by the parents themselves or by associations, non-governmental bodies.

A. Children before the European Commission and Court

For some years now the European Commission and Court of Human Rights are increasingly having to decide cases in which children have been the victims of violations of the European Commission, which has given rise to a series of interesting court cases. At this point it appears important to give some examples before examining the effectiveness of the procedure.

1. The European Commission and its Court have received several applications about equal rights for children, regardless of their family situation at birth (legitimate, illigitimate, abandoned, adopted).

They considered that the need for explicit recognition of maternity outside wedlock "derived from a refusal to acknowledge fully" maternity from the moment of birth: the difference between the ways in which the affiliation of children born out of wedlock and that of children born in wedlock is established "lacks objective and reasonable justification".

Two cases were of particular interest as they have led to changes being made in the internal law of the country concerned. The first example is the Marckx against Belgium case.

A journalist and single mother, Paula Marckx, found out at her daughter's majority that the latter, a natural child, had no official maternal affiliation and, consequently, no rights because her mother had omitted to recognise her at birth. In a judgement on March 13th, 1979, the Court pronounced that such a situation did not respect the right to family life and considered it discriminatory.[3]

As a result of this judgement Belgium changed its legislation on this particular point on March 31st, 1987. Voluntary acknowledgement by a mother is no longer necessary for affiliation on the mother's side to be established.

After this case, the Committee of the Ministers of the Council of Europe adopted the European Convention on the legal status of children born out of wedlock.[4] This convention has two objectives:
  – to give children born out of wedlock the same legal status as children born in wedlock;
  – to lead to a harmonisation of the legislation in the various states concerning filiation.

---

[3] Marckx v. Belgium, Judgement of 13 June 1979, series A, vol. 31.

[4] European Convention on the legal status of children out of wedlock, signed in Strasbourg on 15 december 1974; came into force on 11 august 1978; ratified at 1 january 1988 by mine states: Austria, Cyprus, Denmark, Luxembourg, Norway, Portugal, Sweden, Switzerland, United Kingdom.

In this convention the principle of "mater semper certa est", meaning that maternity is established by the mere fact of giving birth or delivery, is recognised for all children. The convention provides two ways of evidencing or establishing paternal affiliation: voluntary acknowledgement and judicial decision. It does indicate, however, that any legal restriction on the establishment of paternity must be regarded as incompatible with the convention; and that recognition should not be opposed or contested unless the person seeking to recognise, or having recognised, is not the biological father.

More recently in the Johnson v. Ireland case,[5] the European Commission of Human Rights adopted a report in which it stated that the "policy of non-recognition of the reality of the family ties of a child born out of wedlock, in contradiction to the legal position of a child born in wedlock" represented "a failure by the state to provide a framework for the proper ordering of relations between the illigitimate child and its parents". Ireland was thus forced to alter its legislation: a bill introduced before Parliament on May 9th, 1986, attempted to solve the problem of paternal affiliation by presuming that the father – except for evidence to the contrary - was the person recorded as father in the register of births. Besides the natural father could ask for the joint-guardianship of the child before the judge. In this case the natural father and the mother would be entitled to the same rights and they have the same responsibilities as married parents.

Even more recently, in the Kroon and others v. the Netherlands case a petition was submitted to the Commission by Mrs Kroon, Mr Ali Zerrouk and Mr Samir M'Hallem Driss. Mrs Kroon had married Mr M. in 1979. The latter disappeared leaving no trace even to this day. Mrs Kroon then established a permanent relationship with Mr Zerrouk with whom she had a son, Samir M'Hallem Driss. Mrs Kroon, however, remained legally married to Mr M. until the annulation of their marriage one year after Samir's birth. A petition for Mrs Kroon to enable Mrs Kroon to declare that Mr M. was not Samir's father and to obtain the recognition of the biological reality was rejected by the registrar's official. The Amsterdam district court also dismissed the claim, and its decision was confirmed by the Court of Appeal and the Supreme Court of Appeal. In the petition brought before the Commission the applicants complained about the impossibility for Mr Zerrouk and Mr M'Hallem's family ties to be recognised by Dutch law on the account that, at the time of Samir's birth, Mrs Kroon was married to another man. The applicants considered this a violation of their right to a family life in breach of article 8. They also claimed to be the victims of discriminating treatment since Mrs Kroon's former husband could disown Mr M'Hallem Driss whereas she had no possibility whatsoever to contest her ex-husband's paternity. The Commission pronounced in its report of April 7th, 1993, that there had been violation of article 8.

---

[5] Johnston v. Ireland, Application no. 9697/82; report of the European Commission of Human Rights of 5 March 1985.

2. The Commission then had to take cognizance of a series of cases concerning the extent of a minor's rights and fundamental freedoms.

On that point it may be noted that the International Convention on Children's Rights uses word for word articles from the European Convention on Human Rights and Fundamental Freedoms, such as freedom of thought, conscience or expression, as well as articles concerning the protection against invasions of the privacy of persons.

It is in this way that the European Commission decided that an adolescent should have a say in decisions affecting him, e.g. the choice of school or the choice of the religion in which he is to be brought up. But as long as their children remain in infancy parents retain the right to determine the nature of their children's education in accordance with their own religious and philosophical convictions. The competent authorities, however, should take the greatest care to ensure that at this level the religious and philosophical convictions of the parents do not deprive the child of care and medical services to the detriment of the child's health and development.

In the Hoffman v. Austria case[6] the European Court of Human Rights pointed out a violation of the Convention in a judgement pronounced by the Austrian Supreme Court. The latter had committed the children of a seperated couple to the father's care because the mother belonged to the religious community of the Jehovah's Witnesses. According to the European Court of Human Rights, "considering, in order to evaluate the children's interest, the possible negative repercussions of the mother's religion, the Supreme Court established a discriminatory difference of treatment in the absence of any objective and reasonable justification, for, if the aim pursued is the protection of the child's health and rights there is no reasonable link of proportionality between the means and the end - a distinction essentially grounded on religious considerations which is therefore inacceptable since husband and wife are entitled to fudamental equality, notably regarding parental rights". In this case, the judges in the national court took into account the practical consequences of the Jehovah's Witnesses' religious convictions: the rejection of holidays like Christmas and Easter traditionally celebrated by the majority of Austrians, the opposition to blood transfusions and more broadly speaking, the position of a social minority living according to its own distinct rules. But the mother, Mrs Hoffman, had declared she was willing to let her children spend holidays with their father, a Catholic, and to authorise blood transfusions in accordance with the national law. Moreover, the psychological expertise tended to prove that the children, who were very young at the time, and their mother had a very good relationship and that Mrs Hoffman demonstrated a particular aptitude to take care of them. The only defensible solution, which the European Court adopted, was the a priori assumption that the religion of the parent or the religion which he wants to share with his child is of no importance, as long as

---

[6]   Hoffman case v. Austria, Judgment of 23 June 1993.

no inevitable and immediate physical or intellectual consequences impairing the child's development can be ascertained in concreta. These circumstances may derive from the religion itself if its precepts are particularly harmful to health or education. They may also arise from the religious practices of the parent responsible for the child.

The Hoffman law-case should avoid having to establish a degrading list in each religion of taboos and prohibitions which are likely to cause psychological or moral disorders in a child. That sort of research might even concern the most influential religions in Europe.

3. Article 8 of the Convention could also be used to protect a child against invasions of his privacy, such as the searching of his room or the inspection of his private mail. This article was also used by a child placed under the care of social services and who asserted his right to have access to his administrative file.

This is the Gaskin v. UK case.[7] In the United Kingdom, minors depending on local authorities and who are committed to the care of foster families are the object of a confidential file which retraces the various stages of their placement in child welfare. In this case, John Gaskin, claimed the right of access to his personal file in order to sue the local authorities for neglectfulness and retributory damages, but the competent courts partially denied him this right. The European Court declared that the persons in a similar position had a fundamental interest, protected by the Convention, to obtain information enabling them to learn and understand their childhood and formative years. If, as in the United Kingdom, the access to these documents depended on the consent of the informers, the principle of proportionality required that an independent body took the final decision. The Court therefore concluded that the procedures followed in this particular case had not respected John Gaskin's private and family life. The applicant received five thousand pounds in retributory damages for the affective distress and anguish produced by the lack of procedure. He also obtained eleven thousand pounds to cover costs and expenses.

A rule adopted on April 1st, 1989, prior to the announcement of the judgement, now compels social services to give everyone access to their personal documents, except for medical data or information which would identify a third party not consenting to its the communication.

4. The Commission and the Court were also led to pronounce on the irregular detention of minors, a violation of article 5, paragraph 1 and 4, of the European Convention on Human Rights.

In the Bouamar v. Belgium case,[8] Mr Bouamar, a seventeen year old Morrocan citizen, was temporarily placed in a borstal nine times because it was impossible to find a person or an institution likely to take him in. In all, Mr Bouamar had been deprived of freedom for 119 days. As Belgium

---

[7] Gaskin case v. United Kingdom, Judgment of 7 July 1989.

[8] Bouamar v. Belgium case, Judgment of 29 February 1988.

had opted for a system whereby juvenile offenders are monitored, the Court declared that this state was to set up an appropriate infrastructure to carry out its functions. The detentions that Mr Bouamar had undergone were therefore irregular and constituted a breach of article 5, paragraph 1 and 4.

5. The Commission and the Court also had to pronounce on the violation of article 3 in the European Convention of Human Rights which prohibits inhuman and degrading treatment.

This is illustrated in the M.N. v. France case when an application was submitted against France by M.N., an Algerian citizen. The applicant was born in 1960 and was resident in Paris. He had lived in France since the age of four. He had been deaf and dumb since birth. He was educated in various special institutions and received vocational training as a house painter. He stated, however, that he did not have a good knowledge of sign language and that he was illiterate. Since 1977, the applicant had been the subject of criminal proceedings, convicted of theft, violence and collective rape. On August 21st, 1987, the Minister of the Interior made out a deportation order against the applicant on the grounds that he had five convictions for theft, attempted theft, criminal damage and participation in collective rape. The order was adopted in accordance with article 25 of the order of November 2nd, as amended by the Law of September 9th 1986. The order stated that "having regard to this conduct, the presence of this alien on French territory constitutes a threat to public order". On January 30th 1992, the applicant was taken to the Préfecture, where he was arrested for the purpose of being deported to Algeria. On October 28th 1992, the Administrative Court in Paris dismissed the applicant's appeal on the grounds that "having regard to the applicant's serious criminal record and the gravity of the facts known, his presence on French territory constitutes a grave threat to public safety". The court concluded that the impugned decision "did not infringe the applicant's right to a family life in a way that is disproportionate to the aims for which it was taken".

Before the Commission the applicant claimed that, on account of his handicaps, his deportation to Algeria would expose him to treatment prohibited by article 3 of the Convention, which provides that "No one shall be subjected to torture or to inhuman or degrading treatment or punishment". The Commission recalled that the applicant had the level of conception and communication of a child of seven or eight and that his understanding of the world remained rudimentary.

It is true that the applicant had been able to establish certain contacts with other persons in France, but it followed from the evidence provided by the parties that his family remained his sole relational environment. If he were removed from that environment the applicant would consequently be left to his own devices in an environment he did not know, and it was reasonable to fear that he would have particularly serious, if not insurmountable difficulties in adapting to that environment. If the applicant were deported in the above-mentioned circumstances it was likely that this would cause him to experience feelings of fear and anguish that would humiliate and degrade him and break down his physical and mental resistance. Accordingly, the enforcement of the order to deport the applicant would constitute inhuman treatment, contrary to article 3 of the Convention.

6. Finally, the European Commission and Court have received frequent applications concerning refugee or immigrant children.

The Commission has received frequent applications concerning the refusal of residence permits to individuals whose expulsion has affected children directly, or indirectly, in violation of article 3 of the Convention.

In one such case, a Syrian family from Lebanon, applied for a residence permit in Sweden. The Swedish immigration authorities rejected the application, and the authority responsible for enforcement of the expulsion order took them into custody. The family took refuge in a monastery. The police reacted by taking the youngest of the children, Abdulmassih Bulus, who was still a minor, into custody. Relatives took him into charge. The child's lawyer Sgoner requested the aliens police not to enforce the expulsion order, citing the child's poor state of health and the new information as regards the family's political situation if it returned to Lebanon. To avoid deportation, the child was moved from family to family. The expulsion order could no longer be enforced once two years had passed. Since Abdulmassih's health was giving cause for concern, the immigration authorities issued him, his mother and his sister with residence permits entitling them to remain in Sweden for one year. The Commission heard the petition and the case ended fortunately on a happy note: all the family were granted residence permits and the Swedish government paid for the return journey of the two brothers who had been expelled. The Commission has also recognised the right of a child one of whose parents was alien to his country not to be expelled for the non-renewal of the latter's residence permit.

The Berrehab v. the Netherlands case is an illustration.[9] Being married to a Dutch woman, Mr Berrehab was able to obtain a Dutch residence permit. The couple had a daughter but divorced two years later. Consequently, Mr Berrehab was not allowed to renew his residence permit. He was therefore expelled and encountered many difficulties to obtain a visa every three months in order to exercise his right to visit his child. The Court considered it was not competent to judge Dutch immigration policy in its self. It could only examine the litigious interferences preventing the petitioners to maintain their relationship. The court pointed out that Mr Berrehab and his daughter had been very close to each other for some years and the refusal to issue Mr Berrehab an independent residence permit and his subsequent expulsion were a threat

---

[9]   Berrehab case v. The Netherlands, Judgment of 21 June 1988.

to their ties. Mr Berrehab consequently obtained a residence permit as well as the amount of twenty thousand Dutch florins as amends.

Another illustration is the Chahal v. UK case. Here the Commission recognised the right of a child to join his father, a Turkish citizen who had been living in the Netherlands for ten years. After the Dutch government had granted the child a residence permit the father withdrew his complaint.

B. Children Represented by their Parents

In certain cases, a child may be represented before the Commission by his parents who will attempt – either to defend him against a third person – or to obtain compensation.

1. Defense against a Third Person

It could be the case of defending a child against certain institutions. In many cases the authorities decide to remove a child from his family. The parents undergo the decisions without being heard and have no possibility to contend them. The European Court of Human Rights already has had the opportunity to lay down a number of general principles in this area.

The European Court considers that the removal of a child from its family by force or subsequent measures, such as refusal by the authorities to indicate his whereabouts, might in itself constitute a violation of the right to family life.

In one of the cases involving the United Kingdom,[10] the European Commission noted that, although the local authorities' first duty was to protect the welfare of the child its discretionary area "also included the question of how fully and when the applicant and his wife should be informed that options were being discussed, and of his participation in the discussion and knowledge of the decisions taken".

The parents may also defend their child against an education they deem contrary to their philosophical or religious convictions.

In the Karnell and Hardt case,[11] the parents complained that compulsory religious instruction in state schools prevented them from bringing up their children in accordance with their own convictions. But in January 1973, before the Commission had had the time to pronounce a judgement it was informed that the applicants intended to withdraw their application, since an order by "the King in Council" on December 28th 1979 had remedied the situation. That same day an order was issued to amend the general school curriculum and provide that religion be taught as a seperate subject and integrated with other subjects in classes where certain children were dispensed from following religious instruction under the Swedish Education Act. The Commission

---

[10] Application no. 9726/81, c.v. United Kingdom.

[11] Karnell and Hardt case v. Sweden. Press Communique of 7 June 1973, no. C(73) 8.

accordingly decided to strike this application off the roll of court (May 28th 1973).

2. *To obtain compensation for their child*

The European Commission and Court of Human Rights have received several applications concerning the infliction of corporal punishment on schoolchildren.[12] The Court condemned the state concerned to modify the internal regulations in schools and to pay the victims retributory damages.[13]

The parents' petition, however, in favour of their child may conflict with the interest of the child which is considered higher.

The Commission and the Court have already had to deal with cases of such conflicting interests. Petitions to the Commission based on article 8 of the Convention have been submitted by adolescents against their parents while the latter have also been referring to this article asserting their right to the respect of family life.

Hopefully these few examples will have illustrated the effectiveness of recourse before European authorities, especially when a child's or an adolescent's civil rights and fundamental freedoms are at stake.

The regional implementation of this petition procedure is based on the violation of rights as stipulated in the European Convention of Children's Rights. But the effectiveness of these regional procedures is far greater than the mode of enforcement implemented by the Convention on Children's Rights adopted by the General Assembly of the United Nations. It is felt however that a more specific European text to complete the European Convention on Human Rights, especially as far as social and cultural rights are concerned, would reinforce the effectiveness of the implementation of the International Convention of Children's Rights within the European context.

II. At the present moment there are two projects for an European Convention on the exercise of children's rights

A. *The First Project has been Prepared by the European Committee on Juridicial Cooperation for the Direction of Legal Affairs in the Council of Europe*

Its first article makes its scope of application clear:

> This Convention shall apply to children who have not reached the age of 18 years. The object of the present Convention is, in the best interests of children, to promote their rights, to grant them procedural rights and to facilitate the exercise of these rights by ensuring that children are

---

[12] Campbell and Cosans Case, Judgment of 25 February 1982.

[13] Aurairay, Townend and Brant v. United Kingdom; application no. 9303/81.

themselves or through other persons or bodies, informed and allowed to participate in the proceedings before a judicial authority affecting them. For the purpose of this Convention, the proceedings before a judicial authority affecting children are family proceedings, such as those involving the exercise of parental responsibilities, in particular, residence and access to children.

This project is limited therefore to family proceedings before an authority affecting children. It is for the contracting states then, to make a clear notification of the three different types of family proceedings where the Convention would apply. But in this context, what new rights have been recognised for a child?

- The right to receive all relevant information and to be consulted and express his or her views.
- The right to apply in person or through other persons or bodies for a special representative in proceedings, before a judicial authority affecting a child where, by internal law, the holders of parental resposibilities are precluded from representing the child as a result of a conflict of interest between them and the child.
- Parties "shall" consider granting children additional procedural rights, in particular:
  · the right to apply to be assisted by an appropriate person of their choice in order to help them express their views;
  · the right to appoint their own representative;
  · the right to exercise some or all of the rights to such proceedings.

Does not this last provision risk creating inequalities between children seeing as the granting of additional rights is still not compulsory for contracting states?

Besides we could query the existence of the novelty compared to the rights already stipulated in article 6 of the European Convention for Human Rights, if it were not for these proceedings called 'additional'. The project also affects the role of the national authorities in charge of assisting in the context of these family proceedings.

Before taking any decisions the authority shall:

- examine to see if sufficient information is available in order to take a decision, in the best interest of the child, and if not, elicit additional information, especially from the holders of parental responsibility;
- consult the child in person in appropriate cases, and if necessary, in private, either her/himself or through other persons or bodies judged fit to do so, unless it was felt to be contrary to the interests of the child;
- to duly consider the views expressed by the child.

The only really important innovations relating to the role of these national authorities bear on three points:

- automatic referral: in proceedings affecting children, the authority, in serious cases determined by internal law where the welfare of the child is threatened, has the right to make an enquiry immediately;
- prompt action to avoid any delay;
- the existence of proceedings to ensure rapid execution of decisions.

In order to control the observance of this Convention it has been moved to set up a standing committee in charge of any matters relating to the Convention. According to the text, the Committee can, in particular:

- consider any relevant questions concerning the interpretation or implementation of the Convention. The Standing Committee's conclusions concerning the implementation of the Convention may take the form of a recommendation;
- propose amendments to the Convention;
- provide advice and assistance to the national bodies and promote international cooperation between these bodies;

Each body may be represented on the Standing Committee by one or more delegates. Each Party shall have one vote. Any state which is not a Party to this Convention may be represented on the Standing Committee by an observer. The Standing Committee shall be convened by the Secretary General of the Council of Europe. It shall meet whenever one-third of the Parties or the Committee of Ministers of Europe so request.

Our main disappointment lies exactly in these limits and restrictions of the Committee's powers. Its intervention will never be direct, its comments will never have the same effectiveness of a sanction like the judgements made by the European Court for Human Rights. In fact, it will have no more power than the Committee for Children's Rights in the UNO. It will even have less power since the scope of intervention for this Convention is limited to the context of family relations. Consequently, we may wonder what the point is of having this text which intended to be a text on the "exercise of children's rights". That is the reason why a second proposal can be put forward.

B. Project for a monitoring system to be implemented within the framework of the Council of Europe

1. The project for an European Convention for Children's Rights should not only concern the exercise of rights but it should also complete the European Convention on Human Rights in certain areas, which are in fact covered by the International Convention on Children but are not protected enough within the framework of the Council of Europe.

As for the issue, first of all, of attributing legal status to a child, there is a loophole concerning the right to a nationality. In many situations, the provisions in national or international law do not suffice in order to avoid statelessness. In these conditions it seems important that a provision be established whereby:

> if, at the time of his her birth in the territory of one of the High Contracting Parties, it is not possible to attribute any nationality to the child, he or she shall be entitled to the nationality of the place of birth.

As for the very worrying issue in Europe of children working, we regret that the project previously referred to makes no mention of it. Article 32 of the International Convention of Children's Rights is, however, the only article in the text demanding the Contracting states to provide appropriate punishment or sanctions in order for its actual implementation to be enforced. In these conditions, it would be important to add a specific provision to limit, through sanctions, the work of 15 year old minors; some derogation could be allowed for children employed in work which does not harm their health, morality or education.

Another important area has not been dealt with in the project presented by the Division of Legal Affairs: that of the right of access to appropriate health care. At a time when more and more impoverished families in Europe no longer have access to social services, this requirement seems fundamental to us. It is unrealistic to want to picture a Europe with childhood at two speeds:
- that of rich chidren whose only problem lies in family relations;
- that of the rest who will have no support in the context of employment and illness.

It is true that these last points relating to protection in work and health are provided for in the European Social Charter, but, unfortunately, the latter does not have more effectiveness in its implementation than the International Convention for Children's Rights.

Finally, a last area remains uncovered in the project presented above: that of the penal liability of a minor and his or her imprisonment. A very important debate does, in fact, exist on the consequences of minors' imprisonment and on alternative forms of punishment. It might be a good opportunity to harmonise the different European legislation on this point by stating that: "the penal liability of a minor is fixed at 13 years and imprisonment shall remain an exceptional measure before the age of 16".

2. The one or two areas to be covered by the new project could be completed by the proposal made by the Division of Legal Affairs of the Council of Europe, especially those areas which affect the right of a child to be represented before judicial authorities and the automatic referral on behalf of the competent authority.

In order to enforce these children's rights we propose adding a new protocol to the European Convention on Human Rights rather than setting up a new Convention.

Within this protocol, a new section would relate to the rights completing those already set forth in the European Convention on Human Rights and its additional protocols, some of which shall be taken from the European Social Charter. A second section would concern the procedure for enforcing those rights when the petitioner is a minor. To ensure the observance of the commitments devolving on the High Contracting Parties under this Protocol, there shall be set up:

- a Committee of ombudsmen, hereinafter referred to as "the committee",
- a special Children's Division of the European Court of Human Rights.

The Committee should consist of a number of ombudsmen equal to that of the High Contracting Parties, elected for a period of six years. Any High Contracting Party may refer to the Committee, through the Secretary General of the Council of Europe, any failure to respect the provisions of the Convention and this Protocol which it deems can be imputed to another High Contracting Party.

The Committee may receive petitions in accordance with the provisions of articles 25 and 27 of the Convention from:

- the minor concerned;
- the minor's legal representative or ad hoc administrator in the event of a mentally disabled minor;
- a non-governmental association or organisation.

When it is the minor who lodges the petition directly without any intermediary, the rule that all domestic remedies must have been exhausted should be applied only in cases where it was in the minor's own power to have recourse to these remedies in the State concerned.

Without prejudice to the admissibility of the petition, the Committee may decide on temporary protection measures to prevent any irreparable harm to the minor.

The Committee should propose conciliation and a friendly settlement.

If the State concerned rejects an out of court settlement, the case could then be heard before a special division of the European Court for Human Rights, called "the Children's Division". It does not seem useful, in fact, to set up another authority when the Council of Europe already has a very effective Court at its disposal. This Division would follow the same procedure as the Court. It could be established that the hearing be held in camera. This special Division of the European Court for Human Rights would deliver enforceable orders just like the other orders from the Court itself.

On the other hand, it appears preferable for the additional Protocol relating to children's rights not to be open for signature and ratification by other states than the member states of the Council of Europe. This is another possibility, and we have noted it, put forward in the project presented by the Direction of Legal Affairs. But is it not preferable for the states in question to prove their real desire to observe the democratic principles and the fundamental rights by adopting new constitutional or legislative texts which would allow them to enter the circle of the member states?

To conclude, we feel that it would be a good thing if a certain unity existed within the Council of Europe as far as the adoption of this text is concerned. This text must also be based on what already exists and strive to be, above all, effective.

JUAN MARIA BANDRÉS MOLET

Towards a European Law on Children
The European Charter of Rights of the Child

The very fact of giving me the opportunity to write this article makes me think that the work accomplished by the European Parliament, is not really as remote and distant from the European citizins as it sometimes seems to be, at least not for people who are interested in important human themes. I suppose that the fact of being the rapporteur and thus the author of the "European Charter of Rights of the Child", adopted by the plenary session of the European Parliament on 8 July 1992, has contributed to my elaborating the principles of this charter.

Since 1990, when I became involved in the European Parliament with the situation of children in Europe and in the world, my desk became littered with testimonies and shocking reports.

Those testimonies and reports told me that dozens of millions of children die because of malnutrition and neglect in the poorest regions of the world. That child labour increases in the world and that these children's condition deteriorates. And that this problem also exists in Italy, in Portugal, in Greece and in every country of the prosperous European Union.

The most developed countries do not escape. In the United States, the violation of the law on child labour increased by about 250 percent, between 1983 and 1990.

Such facts indicate that the pace of the economic growth does not always assure the satisfaction of elementary needs of the whole population. In numerous industrialized countries and in other developing countries, the poorest 20 percent of the population does not benefit from this growth. The benefits of a possible growth generally are so unequally divided that the poorest take no or very little advantage of those benefits.

As we already stated, millions of millions of children die in the third world due to the lack of sanitary education, due to diseases, which can be avoided by health education, according to a report elaborated jointly by the WHO, UNICEF and UNESCO.

And even if they are not sufficiently proven, we could go on mentioning vehement suspicions about the use of children for illegal organ transplants in Haiti, in some capitals of Latin America or in Albania. Or about the illegal

E. Verhellen (ed.), Monitoring Children's Rights, 159–164.

and clandestine adoption of children by questionable people, which actually happens in a lot of countries.

Or clearing the streets of big cities in Central and Southern America. The tourist authorities of the USA only have to declare Bogota, Lima, Sao Paulo or Rio de Janeiro as dangerous cities or merchants, with the help of the police, when off duty, give free play to the chase of children. Of course a chase of street children who survive by begging, theft or prostitution and who therefore disturb peaceful tourists.

But it is true that, in spite of this dark situation and in spite of all the drawbacks we have gone through, we managed to make for humanity, and thus for children, more progress in the last fifty years than in the two preceeding millennia. Since the end of the second world war, the actual average profits have more than doubled in the developing world; infant mortality has been reduced to less than half; the average life expectancy has increased by about one third; the ratio of the educated child population in the developing world has risen from less than half to more than three quarters of the whole child population.

Our present decade offers a real chance to achieve some important progress contrary to what we can describe as the last great scandal: the persistency of malnutrition, diseases and illiteracy which cannot be avoided and which keep on casting a shadow over the lifes and the future of one fourth of the children in the world: the poorest.

If we don't take the measures, necessary to protect life, health and a normal development of millions of children, it will not be due to economic incapacity, but particularly because it concerns the children of the poor, of this part of the population which not only lacks in purchasing power, but also in political influence and which does not have the capacity to attract the attention of the media.[1]

UNICEF is very clear. If we don't overcome the poverty, the malnutrition, the illiteracy and the diseases of the world's children, it has to be made clear that this is not caused by a lack of possibilities, but because we have not given priority to this matter.

But referring to our so called advanced societies, we have to recognize that child abuse is under a social taboo which is very difficult to change. The cases for which the judicial system comes into action are extreme and obviously represent a very small percentage of the total number of cases, probably a lot more important, which actually happen.

All over the world, but also in Europe and even in our surroundings, sometimes due to our silence, children suffer from the consequences of the incomprehension, the selfishness, the indifference, the lasciviousness or the cruelty and brutality of adults.

---

[1]   State of the World's Children, Unicef, New York, 1993.

Therefore it is important that the institutional authorities provide judicial mechanisms to protect children from this so dark reality.

It is as necessary as the existence of civil non governmental organizations, which deal with those questions as their main objective or in a collateral way, because all the judicial and legal systems, all the important and solemn speeches, all the international conventions and charters of rights are useless without generous people who are ready to use them and put them into practise. To come finally into action in favour of the children.

The European Parliament must have thought about something we just said, when in 1990, it decided to write partial and cyclical declarations on childhood, to draw up and yes even to adopt a "European Charter of Rights of the Child".

We have to recognize that Parliament has already shown some concern about children, on several occasions. In May 1986 about children in hospital,[2] in May 1989 about the abduction of under-age children[3]; in April 1989 it paid explicitly attention to children within the scope of the Declaration of fundamental rights and freedoms[4]; in July 1990 it adopted a resolution on the Convention on the Rights of the Child, urging the Member States to ratify the Treaty[5] and later, in December 1991, it adopted another resolution on the problems of children in the European Community.[6] Not so long ago, a Commission adopted a draft report on the abduction of children[7] and that same day, the Committee on Legal Affairs and Citizens' Rights asked me to draw up a resolution on the adoption of foreign children,[8] which unfortunately I have not been able to finish until the end of the legislative term of June 1994. But Parliament still needed a document, if possible an imperative one for the Member States, that "adapts the United Nations Convention to the judicial, economic and demographic situation of Europe". And it was this agreement of Parliament asking me to draw up the European Charter of Rights of the Child,[9] which obviously is not the charter of rights of the European child, but the charter of rights of the child in Europe, which is of course not quite the same. And that was the start of what probably will be the most passionate parliamentary adventure of my political carreer.

---

[2] Resolution of 13 May 1986 on a European Charter for children in hospital, OJ No C 148, 16.6.1986, p. 37.

[3] Resolution of 26 May 1989 on the abduction of children, OJ No C 158, 26.6.1989, p. 391.

[4] Resolution of 12 April 1989 adopting the Declaration of fundamental rights and freedoms, No C 120, 16.5.1989, p. 51.

[5] Resolution of 12 July on the Convention on the Rights of the Child, OJ No C 231, 17.9.1990, p. 170.

[6] Resolution of 13 December 1991 on the problems of children in the European Community, OJ No C 13, 20.1.1992, p. 534.

[7] E.P. 201–667

[8] B3–1500/92

[9] B3–0035/90

For almost two years I worked with dozens of organizations that take care of children in Europe and elsewhere. I exchanged ideas with tutors, doctors, educationalists, psychologists, child psychiatrists, lawyers and judges sitting in juvenile courts. I travelled all around Europe and South America and I talked as much as possible with the children themselves. Those children who rightly complain because we ignore them, because we are not interested in them because they do not vote or because they are not able to write in newspapers.

Afterwards I drew up a document, that in principle deserved to be approved of by the Committee on Legal Affairs and Citizins' Rights, followed by a draft resolution, which respected the essence of the matter but which the heart of the Committee almost completely rejected. We listened to the opinion of the Committee on Women's Rights. The draft then was amended and eventually it was presented to the plenary session which finally adopted almost unanimously the text of 8 July 1992. That day Parliament gave attention to childhood. And the European Parliament recognised that children also in Europe are being physically and morally abused, are exploited at work, are the object of sexual abuse, are prostituted, beaten and killed. Consequently the representatives of more than 300 million of European citizens, by a dramatic appeal to the responsibility of the great of the earth, remind us with the charter that the rights of the child cannot be violated but that unfortunately this happens every day. The most important regulations of the Charter are the following:

- The appointment of a children's ombudsman at national as well as at Community level, without excluding the Autonomous Communities.
- It is necessary to introduce specific legal Community instruments, derived from the Convention on the Rights of the Child, to deal with the special problems that European integration will create for under-age children and for which there are no provisions in the legislation of the Member States.
- The Charter asks that, as soon as all Member States have ratified the United Nations Convention on the Rights of the Child, the European Community should also become party to it.

As to the 45 rights stated by the Charter, these are the most important ones:
- No discrimination on the basis of his or her parents' nationality, family background, sexual orientation, race, colour, sex, language, social origin, religion, belief, state of health or other circumstances.
- The right to life, to a name and a nationality and to know certain circumstances regarding his biological origin.
- The right to have parents, or if he has no parents, to persons or institutions to replace them and to maintain direct and permanent contact with both parents if the parents are divorced, legally separated or live apart. Appropriate measures must be adopted to prevent either of the

parents or a third person from abducting children, unlawfully holding them or failing to hand them over. Likewise any child who has one or both parents in prison must be allowed to maintain contact with them.

— The right to move freely throughout the territory of the Community, to leave it and to return when he wishes.

— The right to physical and moral integrity. Special protection shall be given to any child who suffers torture, ill-treatment, brutality or exploitation.

— The right to conscientious objection and no child under the age of eighteen shall be obliged to participate in armed conflicts.

— The right to freedom, to legal security, to freedom of expression, conscience, thought and religion.

— The right to have his own culture, to practise his own religion or beliefs and to use his own language.

— The right to leisure, play and sport.

— The right to health, to be protected from sexual illnesses and drugs. The right to benefit from social services and the right to social security. The specific rights of handicaped children are also included.

— The right to receive education which includes free and compulsary primary education. The right to receive appropriate sex education and information. Children's education must, as well as preparing them for working life, also encourage the development of their personality and promote respect for human rights and the national cultural differences of other countries or regions and the eradication of racism and xenophobia. A child's schooling may not be affected or interrupted because of an illness which is not contagious for other children.

— Every child shall be protected from pornographic and violent messages.

— The right to be protected against all forms of sexual slavery, violence or exploitation. Appropriate measures shall be taken to prevent any child from being abducted, sold or exploited for the purposes of prostitution or pornography in the territory of the Community and to prevent anyone within the Community facilitating or endorsing the sexual exploitation of children outside the territory of the Community.

— For purposes of criminal law the age of eighteen shall be considered the minimum age of criminal responsibility.[10]

— Children from third countries, whose parents lawfully reside in a Member State of the Community, and refugees or stateless children recognized as such who reside in that Member State, must be able to enjoy the rights listed in this charter.

These are the main parts of the document which has no legal value. It is not a directive, it is not a Community law. It can not even be one because it not only

---

[10] I have not been able to follow closely the application of the Charter in the whole Community, but I can announce that the bill of the new Spanish criminal code includes this important declaration of the European Parliament.

contains questions reserved for Member States, but also questions of Community jurisdiction. But, it has the value and the authority of a Community law because it is a demand of the almost unanimous European Community towards its members to introduce norms in their internal legislation and community laws which represent the voice of the Community legislator.

Even if, at first sight, the non imperative character of the resolution may be a disillussionment, we may not underestimate the value of these important programmed documents containing principles "de lege ferenda" because they serve not only as orientation for the ordinary legislator, but also as explication criterion for the judicial or administrative authorities and pave, probably, the way towards a more perfect future from the judicial point of vue, and finally towards a society being more fair and having more respect for the rights of the child.

We adults have to be aware of the fundamental role we have to play: we have to make it easier for children to run their own lifes and we have to favour their total personal development. Therefore we have to change the small and limited idea we have of children. Children are real persons, and no objects we have to train for the future.

We cannot use children for political, economic, ideological or religious purposes, but we have to reinforce and appreciate their contributions and facilitate their creativity and originality. Accepting a child's contribution means accepting a general transformation of society. We have to change the relationship adult/child from a relationship based on power into one based on aid and respect.

Finally, we do not make a concession to children, but we recognize their right and their capacity to participate as a person, because they are persons.

Considering all we just mentioned, what counts most is that we all together are capable of creating a social conscience to judge this intolerable situation.

If we will have succeeded, even if it will take a lot of time, even if it will be very difficult and our effort will have to be constant and sustained, I will think that people finally heard the frightening cry of Parliament in July 1992, which is in fact the priviliged echo of the crying children and of the call of several honest people who are concerned about those who do not have a voice and I will think that society will have one reason less to feel ashamed.

We will continue our work as we are doing it now and I hope that some people in Europe and all over the world will stand up and get organized to realize one day what might have been only the dream of a poor lonely member of Parliament in Strasbourg, in the summer of 1992.

ANDRÉ ALEN and WOUTER PAS

The UN Convention on the Rights of the Child's Self-executing Character

I. SELF-EXECUTING CHARACTER

A. Concepts

Analysing the "UN Convention on the Rights of the Child's Self-executing Character" is not an easy matter. The concept "self-executing" is not simple and straight-forward and there is no generally accepted definition in law or jurisprudence. Furthermore its meaning is determined by the domestic (constitutional) law of each legal system. As Professor Brownlie rightly puts it: "the whole subject resists generalisation, and the practice of states reflects [in the final analysis] the characteristics of the individual constitution".[1]

1. The concept "self-executing character" has to be looked at in the context of the relationship between the international and national legal system. The main source of international law is the law of treaties. Here the contracting parties are legal persons under international law: States (and possibly also international organisations or members of a federal state). When treaties are concluded, it is in principle States which mutually take obligations upon themselves. However, these obligations under international law can have consequences for a State Party's domestic legal system. In order to fulfil its obligations under international law, a State will often have to adapt its own domestic legal system. This may be done in different ways, to be determined by domestic or constitutional law. In general, international law does not involve itself with this directly.

2. These domestic constitutional rules, which allow a treaty to have domestic effect, can be systematically ordered on the basis of the answer to the question whether the treaty, under certain circumstances, forms part directly of

---

[1] Brownlie, I., quoted in Drzemczewski, A., *European Human Rights Convention in Domestic Law. A comparative Study,* Oxford, Clarendon Press, 1983, 39.

E. Verhellen (ed.), Monitoring Children's Rights, 165–186.
© 1996 *Kluwer Law International. Printed in the Netherlands.*

the domestic legal system or has to be transposed into national law using a national legal source. This classification based on the way a treaty has to be incorporated into national law, can be defined as the question of a treaty's *"direct"* or *"indirect applicability"*.[2]

3. In comparative law, three categories can be distinguished.[3] To the first category belong those States which form the pure *"dualistic school"*, such as the United Kingdom, Denmark,[4] Ireland, Iceland, Norway, Sweden. In principle, in these countries a clear distinction is made between domestic and international law. An obligation undertaken under international law has effect in the domestic legal system only after it has been transposed into national law. For instance, in the UK an "Act of Parliament" adopting the content of a treaty's provisions is required before the treaty becomes part of domestic legal system.[5] In other words, magistrates never apply treaties, but only the most recent national legislation. The effect and meaning of a treaty only derive from domestic legal provisions.

---

[2] Iwasawa, Y, "The Doctrine of Self-Executing Treaties in the United States : A Critical Analysis", *Virginia Journal of International Law*, 1986, 643–645 uses the expression "domestically valid". Bossuyt, M., "The direct applicability of international instruments on human rights", in *L'effet direct en droit belge des traités internationaux en général et des instruments internationaux relatifs aux droits de l'homme en particulier*, Brussels, Bruylant, 1980, 80, in this context talks about "directly" and "indirectly applicable". Other authors treat this issue by examining "l'introduction dans l'ordre juridique interne", decisive for whether there is "applicabilité directe" (i.e. what we will call "self-executing character") or not. See Verhoeven, J., "La notion d'applicabilité directe" du droit international",*ibidem*, 249, nrs. 6–8, and Velu, J., *Les effets directs des instruments internationaux en matière des droits de l'homme*, Brussels, Swinnen, Prolegomena, 1981, nrs. 3–4. Nevertheless, Verhoeven does talk about "l'applicabilité immédiate" (p.14) (Bossuyt uses "immediate effect", p.80, footnote) to indicate certain acts by international organisations, which require no further international (e.g. ratification) or national (e.g. approval) action to be incorporated into the domestic legal system (see in particular EC decisions and regulations). Given the objective of this contribution we will not enter into further detail on this issue.

[3] Jacobs, F.G., and Roberts, S. (eds.), *The effect of treaties in domestic law*, London, Sweet & Maxwell, 1987, XXIV–XXVI. See Iwasawa, Y., *op.cit.*, 638.

[4] Hofmann, R., "Das dänische Gesetz vom 29.April 1992 zur innerstaatlichen Anwendbarkeit der EMRK", *Europäische Grundrechte Zeitschrift*, 1992, 253–256.

[5] English magistrates are not required to apply international treaties, as long as they have not been laid down in Acts of Parliament, and more recent Acts of Parliament can invalidate a treaty, even though English magistrates will always attempt to interpret more recent Acts of Parliament in such a way as to make them compatible with treaty law : Bradley, A.W., "The legislative Supremacy of the United Kingdom Parliament", *Tijdschrift voor Bestuurswetenschappen en Publiek Recht (T.B.P.)*, 1989, 445–452; Jacobs, F.G., "The Convention and the English Judge", in *Mélanges en l'honneur de G.J. Wiarda*, Cologne, Carl Heymanns Verlag, 1988, 273–279. This "incorporation" has not yet taken place for the ECHR : see LAWS, J., "Is the High Court the Guardian of Fundamental Constitutional Rights?" *Public Law*, 1993, 59–79.

The second category consists of countries with an *intermediate system*, such as Germany,[6] Italy and Austria.[7] In these countries a treaty has to be "transformed" into a national law, but as soon as this has happened, the treaty as such (i.e. as international law) is applicable in the domestic legal system. As of that moment in fact the same rules apply as in the third category of countries, which have a system of "direct applicability".

4. In this third category of countries this "transformation" is not necessary. They belong to the so-called *"monistic school"*, which sees the law as a whole. International legal rules are therefore part of that one legal system which applies to all legal subjects of that country. This is the case in France, Luxembourg, the Netherlands,[8] Switzerland, the United States[9] and also Belgium.[10] It has to be pointed out that in these countries too often an act of Parliament is required. However "approval" by Parliament is only required to allow the State to validly conclude a treaty. In France for instance certain treaties can only be ratified after consent by a statute.

5. It is only when this preliminary question has been answered, concerning the introduction of a treaty, i.e. whether the international obligation forms part of the domestic legal system, that the issue of a treaty's self-executing character can be raised. A treaty provision, an international obligation, is self-executing when a legal person can invoke the international norm directly in a national court. The magistrate can apply the treaty provision in an individual case, without reference to a domestic law. After parliamentary consent, apart from ratification, no further act by domestic state bodies is required to give effect to the international provision.[11]

---

[6] Hilf, M., "Relations between Constitutional Law and International Law", in *Rights, Institutions and Impact of International Law according to the German Basic Law. The Contributions of the Fed. Republic of Germany to the Second World Congress of the International Asociation of Constitutional Law*, Starck, C. (ed.), Baden-Baden, Nomos, 1987, 180.

[7] Bleckmann, A., "Verfassungsrang der Europäische Menschenrechtskonvention ?", *Europäische Grundrechte Zeitschrift (EuGRZ)*, 1994, 150–151.

[8] Contra : Brouwer, J.G. , "Nederlands gedachten over de grondwet en het Verdrag", *Rechtskundig Weekblad (R.W.)*, 1992–1993, 1366–1370.

[9] *"and all treaties made, or which shall be made, [...] shall be the Supreme Law of the Land;"* : Article VI, paragraph 2 of the American Constitution. Bungert, H., "Einwirkung und Rang von Völkerrecht im innerstaatlichen Rechtsraum. Ein Vergleich des deutschen mit dem US-amerikanischen Recht", *Die öffentliche Verwaltung*, 1994, 797–806, I and II ; Paust, J., "Self-executing Treaties", *American Journal of International Law*, 1988, 760–783.

[10] See the important ruling "Fromagerie franco-suisse Le Ski" by the Court of Cassation (Cass., 27th May 1971, *Pasicrisie*, 1971, I, 886). With this ruling the Court carried out a "jurisprudential or tacit revision of the Constitution" by rejecting traditional "dualism". See Salmon, J. , "Le conflit entre le traité international et la loi interne en Belgique à la suite de l'arrêt rendu le 27 mai 1971 par la Cour de Cassation", *J.T.*, 1971, 535.

[11] It should also be pointed out that the notion "self-executing character" is applied more and more often in relation to (domestic) constitutional provisions (see Vanwelkenhuyzen, A.,

6. Before we start examining the concept "self-executing character" in depth, it is worth taking a look at terminology. What we call *"self-executing character"*[12] in English, is translated as *"unmittelbare Anwendbarkeit"* [13] in German. In French both *"effet direct"* and *"applicabilité directe"*[14] are used.

B. Consequences of the Self-executing Force

Whether the self-executing character of international legal rules is recognised or not has important practical effects.

7. It happens quite regularly that States take upon themselves international obligations, but refrain from taking the necessary measures to implement them or procrastinate. If a treaty provision has "self-executing character", private individuals do not have to wait for such measures, but can invoke the treaty provision directly in a domestic court. The self-executing character of a treaty therefore allows a legal person to obtain rights and obligations out of a norm which has been mutually accepted by States. Hence the self-executing character of a treaty is a form of protection of the individual. The legal subject is put in a position to monitor a State's actions or absence of actions. This way human rights treaties in particular gain considerable force.

8. A comment has to be made here on the hierarchy of legal norms. In a monistic or quasi-monistic system, a magistrate may be confronted with a treaty provision with self-executing character which conflicts a national norm. In various legal systems international law norms occupy the same hierarchical position as laws.[15] Therefore they take precedence over lower norms and earlier legislation. However, because they only have the same rank as laws, they have to give way to more recent legislation. In principle however, magistrates try to avoid conflicts by interpreting more recent legislation in conformity with the treaty.

"L'application directe et l'effet indirect des normes constitutionelles" in *Rapports belges au XIe Congrès de l'Académie internationale de droit comparé*, Brussels, Bruylant, 1985, 95–115).

[12] Bossuyt, M., *op.cit.*, 80 ; Paust, J., *op.cit.* ; Iwasawa, Y., *op.cit.*, 635–642, 692 suggests "directly applicable".

[13] Verdross, A. and Simma, B., *Universelles Völkerrecht. Theorie und Praxis*, Berlin, Duncker und Humblot, 1984, par. 864.

[14] Velu, J., *op.cit.*, passim ; Verhoeven, J., "Applicabilité directe des traités et 'intention des parties contractantes'", in *Liber Amicorum E.Krings*, Brussels, Story-Scientia, 1991, 895–905 ; Krings, E., "La mise en oeuvre de la Convention des Nations Unies sur les droits de l'enfant en droit interne", in *La Convention sur les droits de l'enfant et la Belgique*, Meulders-Klein, M.T. (ed.), Brussels, Story-Scientia, 1992, 71–86.

[15] Jacobs, F.G. and Roberts, S. (eds.) *op.cit.*, XXVIII.

An international norm's self-executing character does therefore not necessarily give it precedence over other norms. In Belgium however international norms do take precedence, as a consequence of a ruling by the Court of Cassation. In the Belgian legal system, hierarchical precedence of an international norm is linked to its self-executing character, even regarding more recent laws.[16] In France the precedence of treaty law has in the meantime also been accepted.[17]

9. In summary if a treaty has self-executing character it contains rights and obligations which private individuals can invoke directly in a national court. The fact that a treaty norm which has self-executing character directly results in rights and obligation, without the intervention of a state body, does however not imply that state bodies cannot act to implement the treaty, in order to reinforce it. The most important examples in Europe of international treaties which have self-executing character are the EC-treaties (included all secundary community legislation), the European Convention for the Protection of Human Rights and Fundamental Freedoms (ECHR) and the International Covenant on Civil and Political Rights.

C. The Criteria Applying to Self-executing Treaty Provisions

10. A treaty provision is self-executing in as far as it can be invoked in a national court where the magistrate can use it as the basis for his ruling in a particular case.

What we have to examine here is the State's policy freedom; in other words how much room for manoeuvre does the state have (to act or avoid action) when implementing the treaty? The State has to comply with its obligation. This does obviously limit its discretionary power. The question is therefore: how much freedom of action do States have when complying with their obligations. It is the limitations to a State's freedom of action which have direct effect:[18] infringements of obligations as a consequence of exceeding available margin of appreciation (by acting or failing to act) will lead to sanctions in

---

[16] This principle was adopted by the highest court in the above mentioned Le Ski ruling. Velu, J., *"Contrôle de constitutionnalité et contrôle de compatibilité avec les traités"*, *J.T.*, 1992, 729–741 and 749–761, nrs. 33-35 and Masquelin, J., *Le droit des traités dans l'ordre juridique et dans la pratique diplomatique belge,* Brussels, Bruylant, 1980, nrs. 323–324.

[17] See: Polakiewicz, J. and Jacobs-Foltzer, V., "The European Human Rights Convention in Domestic Law: The Impact of Strasbourg Case-Law in States where Direct Effect is given to the Convention", *Human Rights Law Journal*, 1991, 75–76 ; Benhamou, Y., "La Convention de New York du 26 janvier 1990 sur les droits de l'enfant, le droit international et le droit français" annotation under Cass. fr., 15th July 1993, *La Semaine Juridique*, 1994, 83–88.

[18] Compare "La règle directement applicable ne saurait laisser à l'Etat de pouvoir discretionnaire", Ganshof van der Meersch, W.J.. "Le juge belge et le droit international", *Revue belge de droit international (R.B.D.I.)*, 1970, 413 ; "Non-self-executing rules strictly must consist of rules of two kinds: those not creating any obligations for the State but merely

court. The concept "self-executing" implies that the judge has to determine what lies within his own competence and which issues are within the discretionary power of the legislator and the authorities.[19] Hence there will be degrees in the self-executing nature of treaties[20] (see also D).

11. Whether or not a treaty is self-executing has to be determined by the national judge.[21] He has to decide whether a case can be resolved directly on the basis of the international treaty, or whether there are different possible solutions, from which a choice has to be made by a state body (in principle the legislator). In principle this is the freedom of every domestic judge, even if he has to take into account rulings by higher courts. The specific situation of EC law and of the ECHR should also be pointed out. The Luxembourg Court of Justice in particular has laid down the extent of the self-executing nature of EC legislation.[22]

Let us now take a look at *the criteria* which determine a treaty's self-executing character. We can distinguish two criteria : an objective and a subjective criterion. Usually these criteria are regarded as cumulative conditions for a treaty to be self-executing. The Belgian Court of Cassation put is as follows : the notion direct applicability[23] of a treaty with regard to the citizens of a State Party implies that the obligation of the State is fully and clearly expressed and that the States Parties intended to make granting subjective rights to persons and imposing obligations on them the object of the Treaty.[24]

12. The *subjective criterion* is founded on the intention and aim of the signatories of the international treaty.

---

allowing for discretionary power, (and those which, although they creat obligations, cannot be implemented because the necessary organs or mechanisms have not been developed)" *Conforti*, B., *International Law and the Role of Domestic Legal Systems*, Dordrecht, Martinus Nijhoff Publishers, 1993, 27.

[19] This avoids problems concerning the separation of powers.

[20] Cf. "A proper understanding of the possibilities for direct applicability [...] can only be established by approaching the problem as a matter of degree [...]" : Scheinen, M., "Direct applicability of economic, social and cultural rights : a critique of self-executing treaties" in *Social Rights as Human Rights. A European Challenge*, Drzewicki, K., Krause, C., and Rosas, A., Åbo Akademi University, Åbo, 1994, 85.

[21] Verhoeven, J., "La notion d'applicabilité directe" du droit international", *op.cit.*, nr. 18.

[22] O'Neill, A., *Decisions of the ECJ and their Constitutional Implications*, London, Butterworths, 1994, Chapter 2, 2.2.1.

[23] The Court of Cassation uses the term "direct applicability" to indicate what we call "self-executing character".

[24] Cass., 21th April 1983, *Revue critique de jurisprudence belge (R.C.J.B.)*, 1985, 22 with annotation Waelbroeck, M., "Portée et critères de l'applicabilité directe des traités internationaux".

In a 1928 Permanent Court of International Justice advisory opinion on the jurisdiction of the courts in Danzig[25] the issue of the self-executing nature of international treaties was dealt with for the first time by an international public law forum. The opinion established the traditional doctrine that the "intention of the contracting parties" is decisive. If the parties expressly agree and declare that the obligations they have entered into are self-executing, then this obviously is the case. However in most cases the intention of the contracting parties is not clearly expressed.[26] In those cases the treaty has to be interpreted to determine the intention of the contracting parties.

It has to be pointed out that in the case of a multilateral treaty one can often not expect or assume that the contracting parties had a clear intention regarding the self-executing nature of the treaty, since there may be contracting parties who do not have the notion "self-executing treaty" in their domestic legal system (for instance because they first have to transform a treaty into national law).[27] Moreover, when interpreting a treaty, judges have to follow the guidelines laid down in article 31, §1 of the Vienna Convention. According to this article, a treaty shall be interpreted in good faith in accordance with the ordinary meaning to be given to the terms of the treaty in their context and in the light of its object and purpose. The European Court of Justice, for instance, has considerably extended the self-executing nature of EC legislation on the basis of its context, background and nature. The intention to make EC norms self-executing is assumed and the Court only has to examine whether the norm is sufficiently clear and unconditional not to require further legislative action before it can be applied by the judge.[28]

13. This brings us to the *second criterion, which we consider decisive, i.e. the objective criterion.* This criterion implies that the wording, the text, has to be examined to establish whether the State's obligation is sufficiently clear and exact (i.e. self-sufficient) to be applicable by a judge. The fact that treaty provisions are worded in such a way that they address States parties is in itself not sufficient for it to be not self-executing.[29] The content and nature of the obligation are decisive.

---

[25]   PCIJ 1928, Serie B, nr. 15, 17.

[26]   Iwasawa, Y., *op.cit.*, 651 and 654.

[27]   Bossuyt, M., *op.cit.*, 82.

[28]   According to the Court of Justice the spirit, the general scheme and the wording of a norm have to be taken into consideration: C. o. J., 5th February 1963 (Van Gend & Loos), 26/62, *ECR*, 1963, 1–30.

[29]   Iwasawa, Y., *op.cit.*, 684. Compare also C. o. J., 5th February 1963 (Van Gend & Loos), 26/62, *ECR*, 1963, 13: "the fact that under this article it is the Member States who are made the subject of the negative obligation does not imply that their nationals cannot benefit from this obligation".

The "nature" of the obligation is in fact the discretionary power which state bodies keep in complying with the obligation. In a ruling concerning free primary education the Belgian Council of State states that the issue [...] is not whether the Covenant on economic, social and cultural rights grants subjective rights to private citizens which they can claim in court, *it is to verify whether the Belgian legislation is compatible with the purpose which is laid down clearly and precisely in article 13, 2, a of the Covenant.*[30]

The nature of an obligation, as expressed sufficiently clearly in a provision which has been formulated in a complete and precise manner, is decisive. This has to be the basis of the judgement the magistrate makes to decide on the self-executing character of a treaty, even if the contracting parties were not clear in their intention.[31] This does however not mean that the subjective criterion is of minor importance. The contracting parties are perfectly free to totally exclude the obligations of the treaty being invoked directly in court. In that case the "treaty" becomes merely a declaration of intent.[32]

14. Finally it has to be pointed out that a treaty is not only self-executing when it confers rights to private individuals, but also when, on the basis of the treaty, magistrates have to decide on the legality of an administrative act.[33] An example of this can be found in extradition treaties. The provisions of these treaties are not generally regarded as conferring rights to private individuals. A judge can however check whether extradition in a certain case is compatible with the provisions of the treaty and the State's obligations.[34]

---

[30] C. o. St., 6th September 1989 (M'Feddal), nr. 32.989, with report and opinion Dumont, M., *Administration Publique - Trimestriel*, 1989, 276, and comment Leroy, M., *Revue trimestrielle des droits de l'homme*, 1990, 184.

[31] Cfr. C. o. St., 4th July 1989 (V.Z.W. Crasc), nr. 32.945 ; " bien que les hautes parties contractantes n'aient pas exprimé d'intention à ce sujet, les règles portées par l'article 6 [de la Convention pour la répression de la traite des êtres humains et de l'exploitation de la prostitution d'autrui] doivent être considerées comme d'application directe en raison de l'objectif de protection des droits fondamentaux qu'elles poursuivent, de leur caractère complet et suffisamment précis et des conséquences immédiates qui peuvent en être déduites pour les particuliers".

[32] A treaty provision forcing states parties to undertake all necessary measures to execute the treaty, is in itself not a sufficient expression of the intention not to make the treaty self-executing: Iwasawa, Y., *op.cit.*, 648–661.

[33] Cfr. Ergec, R., "Le minerval exigé des élèves étrangers et les effets directs des droits économiques et sociaux", comment under Cass., 20th December 1990 (Najimi), *Revue de jurisprudence de Liège, Mons et Bruxelles (J.L.M.B.)*, 1991, 1206–1211, espec. nrs. 6, 11 and 14.

[34] Jacobs, F.G. and Roberts, S. (eds), *op.cit.*, XXVII.

D. Degrees of Self-executing Character

We already know that there are degrees to the self-executing nature of a treaty, depending on the discretionary power remaining for the state.

15. Thus it is possible for a *positive obligation* (an obligation to act) of a State to be self-executing.

This is the case for instance of article 8 of the ECHR, which deals with respect for family life. The State has the obligation to abstain from arbitrary interference in its citizens family life. However, besides this negative aspect, respect for family life can also result in a number of positive obligations for States parties. According to a ruling by the European Court for Human Rights, respect for family life also means that when States parties legislate on the legal ties between unmarried mothers and their children, they have to act in such a way that those involved can have a normal family life.[35]

The fact that the State has some discretionary power in doing this does however not mean that the obligation is not self-executing. The legislator may have the choice between different options, but judges have to refuse to apply those options which are in contradiction with the obligation. The judge has to look for a solution using existing rules which are in conformity with the treaty.

16. The so-called *standstill obligation* which can be derived from certain treaty provisions is a special way in which treaties can be self-executing.[36]

When the State undertakes to achieve a certain objective, it cannot do away with that which has been achieved already (i.e. the existing protection[37] of certain rights). The positive obligation which the State has accepted, gives it much discretionary power, but only in a positive sense. It also results in the obligation not to undertake anything which goes against the fulfilment of the obligation (negative obligation). We find an example of this in rulings of the

---

[35] Following this reasoning the old Belgian legislation was considered in breach of article 8 of the ECHR, in that, besides producing the birth certificate of an illegal child, it imposed other conditions (recognition by the mother or a procedure to legalise the child) in order to establish a legal link between mother and child: European Court of Human Rights, 13th June, *Marckx, Serie A*, vol. 31. See Bossuyt, M., *R.B.D.I.*, 1980, 53–81, and *R.W.*, 1979–80, 929–970; Rigaux, F., *Annales de droit*, 1979, 369–383, and *J.T.*, 1979, 513–524.

[36] Cfr. Ergec, R., *op.cit.*, 11, 12 and 14.

[37] Opinion differ on the point in time when this "existing protection" has to be considered : either the date of entry into force of the treaty or the date of its signature: see Ergec, R., *op.cit.*, 1210–1211.

Belgian constitutional court (Court of Arbitration)[38] and the Belgian Council of State[39] concerning provisions of the International Convention on Economic, Social and Cultural Rights on free education (art. 13,2). Article 13 does not impose the obligation on States parties to provide free education immediately, but to make efforts in that direction. According to the above-mentioned Belgian courts, a law undermining existing free education by introducing school fees for children of parents who are not Belgian and who do not live in the country, would be in contradiction with the international treaty and can therefore not be applied.

17. The two above-mentioned aspects (the self-executing nature of positive obligations and the standstill effect of positive obligations) crop up mainly in the context of *social and economic fundamental rights*. Social and economic fundamental rights are those rights which allow the individual to enjoy personal and social fulfilment, and which impose on the State an obligation to act.[40]

Social and economic fundamental rights are self-executing in the sense that they impose certain objectives on the States, limiting their discretionary power. Moreover, in fulfilling their social and economic obligations, States have to respect the principle of equality. Acts by the public authorities which cannot be examined by the courts on the basis of a social and economic fundamental principle, can be judged on the basis of their conformity with the ban on discrimination.[41]

E. Conclusions

18. It is clear that the role of the judge is decisive. It is the judge who has to interpret the treaty text and who has to decide whether domestic legal norms are to be applied. The judge is not limited in this either by the intentions of the contracting partners (in as far as they have not expressly excluded the possibility of the treaty being self-executing), or by they intentions of the national legislative assemblies, as demonstrated in parliaments preparatory work.

19. The judge's dynamic roles thus also creates the possibility for views on the self-executing nature of a treaty provision to evolve. Article 3 of the

---

[38] Court of Arbitration, nr 33/92, 7th May 1992, *Belgisch Staatsblad (B.S.)*, 4th June 1992, with comment De Feyter, K., *Tijdschrift voor onderwijsrecht en onderwijsbeleid (T.O.R.B.)*, 1992–93, 247.

[39] See footnote 30.

[40] Van Boven, T.C., "Les critères de distinction des droits de l'homme" in Vasak, K., (ed.), *Les dimensions internationales des droits de l'homme*, Paris, Unesco, 1978, 53.

[41] Cfr Nederlandse Hoge Raad, 7th May 193, *NCJM-Bulletin*, 1993, 694–696, with comment Heringa, A.W., 696–699.

First Protocol to the ECHR is an example of this. This article states that contracting parties undertake to hold free elections at reasonable intervals by secret ballot, under conditions which will ensure the free expression of the opinion of the people in the choice of legislature. Because this provision has been phrased as an obligation for States to act, it had been assumed in case law that private individuals could not directly invoke this provision in court.[42] However the European Court of Human Right has given this article a different interpretation. The Court confirms that the States have a large degree of discretionary power, which does however not allow them to undermine those rights or to make the provision ineffective. This is why citizens can enforce their active and passive right to vote.[43]

20. Thus judges use the self-executing character of treaties in a dynamic and innovative way to improve the legal protection of citizens in respect of the state and its bodies, particularly by giving them the possibility to enforce respect for their fundamental rights and freedoms in court.

One must however not be blinded by the self-executing character of international treaties. In many cases the legislator still has to act. While judges may set limits to the legislator's discretionary power, treaty provisions require practical legislative implementation. This also improves legal certainty. Thus while we have mentioned the fact that article 8 of the ECHR is self-executing in its positive obligations, the Belgian legislator rightly decided to amend Belgian Civil Law to enshrine the principal of equality of all children regardless of whether they are born within wedlock or not.[44] Moreover treaty provisions which are not self-executing are also important. Judges can use treaty provisions, which are mere declarations of intent, as guidance in the interpretation of domestic legal norms. This is the so-called interpretation "in conformity with the treaty".

II. THE UN CONVENTION ON THE RIGHTS OF THE CHILD

21. In part one we have demonstrated that the issue of the significance of an international treaty for the domestic legal system involves three separate aspects: the applicability of a treaty, its self-executing character and its place in the hierarchy. All of these aspects are determined by the domestic law of each state. It is therefore all but easy to discuss an international treaty's self-executing character in abstract terms without referring to a particular legal system.

---

[42] See for instance Velu, J., "Les effets directs ...", *op.cit.*, 27.

[43] European Court on Human Rights, 2nd March 1987, *Mathieu-Mohin en Clerfayt, Serie A*, Vol.113. See De Meyer, J., "Electoral rights", in Mac Donald, R.ST.J. e.a. (eds.), *The European System for the Protection of Human Rights,* Dordrecht, Martinus Nijhof Publishers, 1993, 553–569.

[44] Law of 31st March 1987, *B.S.*, 27th May 1987.

Concerning the first aspect, "direct applicability", in the following analysis of the UN Convention on the Rights of the Child[45] we shall assume that the Convention, like in Belgium, is directly applicable in national law, in conformity with the domestic legal system.

Next we can look at the actual issue which we shall examine: the degree to which the provisions of the Convention are self-executing, and therefore do not require further executive measures on the part of the competent state bodies and can be directly enforced in court.

A. International Enforceability

22. We have already pointed out the importance of a treaty's self-executing nature, particularly with regard to improved legal protection, in part 1 (nr. 7). The issue of self-executive character, and therefore of the domestic enforceability of treaty law provisions, is particularly important in the case of the Convention on the Rights of the Child, given the fact that its enforceability in international law is practically inexistent.

The Convention's monitoring mechanism involves no more than the obligation for States parties to report to the Committee on the Rights of the Child. This procedure is based on the idea that implementation of the Convention has to be monitored in a "positive spirit", with a "constructive and aid-oriented thrust" and a "strong emphasis on the need for international solidarity, co-operation, dialogue and technical assistance in fostering implementation".[46]

The Convention's voluntary nature is to do with the fact that the Convention did not only come about to counteract possible infringements of children's rights, but also to act in favour of more respect for children.[47] In the same spirit the Convention imposes the obligation on States parties to make its content widely known to all legal subjects (article 42).

---

[45] Hereafter called "the Convention".

[46] Veerman, P.E., *The Rights of the Child and the Changing Image of Childhood*, Dordrecht, Martinus Nijhof Publishers, 1992, 208–209.

[47] Verhellen talks about "defensive/re-active" and "offensive/pro-active" : Verhellen, E., *Internationaal, regionaal and nationaal beleid*, Gent, Centre for the Rights of the Child, 1990, 88. For the same reason, the Convention allow farreaching reservations, without imposing strict conditions like other human rights conventions, in order to allow as many States as possible to become party to the Convention ; Verhoeven, J., "La mise en oeuvre de la Convention des Nations Unies sur les droits de l'enfant. Observations en droit des gens", in *La Convention sur les droits de l'enfant et la Belgique*, Meulders-Klein, M.T. (ed.), Brussels, Story-Scientia, 1992, 62. Cfr. Bisset-Johnson, A., "What did States really agree to?" *The International Journal of Children's Rights,* 1994, 399–411.

Although the reporting system also has a number of advantages,[48] from a legal and normative point of view this monitoring mechanism must be regarded as very weak.[49] Unlike the ECHR and the International Covenant and Civil and Political Rights, the Convention does not contain the right for States Parties or individuals to submit complaints to an independent body against a State which infringes its treaty obligations. Individuals (i.e. anybody younger than 18) who want to complain about infringements of the Convention, can only do so internationally by political action, such as lobbying via NGO's or the media.

Hence the importance of the self-executing nature of a Convention. The question is therefore whether a private person can take a State Party to a national court for negligence or breaches of the Convention, or whether, in any given country, the Convention is no more than a means of exerting political pressure.

B. The Self-executing Nature of the Convention – General Observations

23. One characteristic of the Convention on the Rights of the Child is its so-called comprehensive nature. The Convention is designed to protect the child, in all aspects and everywhere. This is why the Convention does not distinguish between different kinds of fundamental rights, but intends to demonstrate that they are equally important and even interdependent.[50] Thus in the Convention we encounter both traditional civil rights and economic, social and cultural rights. Or, looked at from the point of view of the objectives, provisions aimed at giving children rights to self-determination as well as the right to be protected.[51]

---

[48] See Alston, P.: "[...] the reporting process is able to focus primarily on the positive rather than the negative dimensions of international human rights co-operation": Alston, P., "The purposes of reporting", in *Manual on Human Rights reporting*, New York, UNO, 1991, 13. Compare Verhellen, E., "Het toezichtmechanisme in de UNO-Conventie inzake de rechten van het kind: een pro-actieve benadering", in *De kant van het kind – Liber Amicorum Miek de Langen*, Arnhem, Gouda Quint, 1992, 93–104.

[49] Verhoeven, J., "La mise en oeuvre de la Convention des Nations Unies sur les droits de l'enfant. Observations en droit des gens", *op.cit.*, 69–70.

[50] Verhellen, E., "Kinderrechten in Europa" *Panopticon*, 1993, 188–207; Buirette, P., "Réflexions sur la convention internationale des droits de l'enfant", *R.B.D.I.*, 1990, 54–73: "Les droits contenus dans la Convention se renforcent mutuellement et forment un tout".

[51] For more information on this subdivision according to objectives: Deli, D., *De privaatrechtelijke positie van de minderjarige bij het stellen van rechtshandelingen: een proeve tot hervorming van het bestaande recht in het licht van de gewijzigde maatschappelijke context*, Dissertation, Antwerp, UIA, 1993, 883–894.

This inherent complexity[52] at the heart of the discussion of the nature of the Convention does not make analysing its self-executing nature any easier. In its opinion on the bill granting parliamentary approval to the Convention, the Belgian Council of State points out that there are both provisions which meet "generally accepted criteria" on the self-executing nature of conventions and provisions which impose the obligation on States Parties to introduce legislation to implement the Convention.[53]

This corresponds more or less to the traditional distinction between civil and political rights on the one hand and fundamental social or economic rights on the other. So far these different categories of fundamental rights have been dealt with in separate international treaties with different legal implementation techniques. Thus the ECHR and the International Covenant and Civil and Political Rights contain traditional defensive rights, implying prohibitions or negative obligations for the State. The European Social Charter or the International Covenant on Economic, Social and Cultural Rights on the other hand contain fundamental social and economic rights, thereby imposing the obligation to act on the authorities.

In the first part we have pointed out that traditional fundamental rights may also involve positive obligations for the State, while fundamental social and economic rights, through the notion of standstill, may be self-executing and may also imply negative obligations (nrs. 15–17). Therefore to analyse the self-executing nature of the Convention, it is not sufficient to make use only of the traditional distinctions. What must be examined is the extent to which, in view of the intentions of states parties and the wording of the provisions (nrs. 12–13), domestic judges may settle disputes directly on the basis of the Convention, or whether national legislation is required. We have already pointed out that in this the domestic judge has the final say (nr. 11).

24. As far as the intentions of states parties are concerned, as we have already said (nr. 12), it is not always possible to determine unambiguously what they may have been. However the transition from a declaration of intent (i.e. the 1924 Geneva Declaration and the 1959 Declaration on the Rights of the Child[54]) to an internationally binding convention would seem to indicate that

---

[52] "Il est rare de voir un tel imbroglio d'obligations (des Etats contractants, des parents) à l'égard des enfants (mais aussi des parents) [...]": Meulders-Klein, M.T., "Les droits civils de l'enfant" in *La Convention sur les droits de l'enfant et la Belgique,* Meulders-Klein, M.T. (e.d.), *op.cit.,* 130, nr. 65.

[53] Opinion by the section legislation of the Council of State (6th March 1991), *Doc. Parl.,* Chambre, 1990–1991, nr. 1568/1, 24.

[54] League of Nations, *Declaration of Geneva, O.J.,* spec. suppl. 21, 1924 : resolution 1386 in 14 U.N. GAOR Suppl. (nr. 16), *U.N.Doc.,* A/4059 (1959) .See Veerman, P.E., *The Rights of the Child and the Changing Image of Childhood, op.cit.,* 155–159 and 159–181.

it was definitely not states parties' intention to make of the Convention a non-self-executing text.[55]

Some people believe, however, that such an intention can be deduced from the fact that the Convention repeatedly addresses states parties, and imposes obligations on them. This, they feel, is demonstrated by expressions, such as " States Parties undertake to", "shall assure", "shall ensure", "recognize", "shall respect", etc.[56]

We find this reasoning in a ruling by the French Cour de Cassation (march 10th 1993): "les dispositions de la Convention [...] ne peuvent être invoquées devant les tribunaux, cette Convention, qui ne crée des obligations qu'à la charge des Etats Parties, n'étant pas directement applicale en droit interne."[57] However we feel this approach to be unsubtle and incorrect.[58] It is in the nature of a treaty to address states parties and to impose obligations on them (nr.13). What matters is the nature of the obligation, and its stringency. It is therefore impossible to make global, general statements of the Convention's self-executing nature.[59] When examining the different provisions of the Convention we moreover find that the wording used differs from case to case. Many articles are worded in vague and general terms. This is not surprising,

---

[55] Alen, A., w.c.o. Clement, J., "Van 'belang van het kind' naar 'recht van het kind'", in *XXXste verjaardag van de Universele Verklaring van de Rechten van het Kind*, Brussels, A.M.A.D.E., 1989, 95.

[56] Bossuyt, M., "La Convention des Nations Unies sur les droits de l'enfant", *R.U.D.H.*, 1990, 143 ; Pouleau, V., "Propos sur l'applicabilité (directe?) de la convention des droits de l'enfant dans l'ordre juridique belge", *Revue trimestrielle de droit familial*, 1991, 497, footnote 12, 501, 503, nr. 12 : "Il ne peut être question, pour ces dispositions, d'effet direct, celles-ci s'adressant aux Etats signataires [...]", and 506 ; Krings, E., *op.cit.*, 86; Verhoeven, J., "La mise en ouevre de la Convention des Nations Unies dus les droits de l'enfant. Observations en droit de gens", *op.cit.*, 67 : Benhamou, Y., *op.cit.*, 86.

[57] Cass. fr., 10th March 1993, *Recueil Dalloz Sirey*, 1993, 361, with comment Massip, J.; confirmed in Cass. fr., 2nd June 1993: see Dekeuwer-Défossez, F., *Recueil Dalloz Sirey*, 1994, *Somm.*, 34. In later rulings (Cass. fr., 15th July 1993 and 13th July 1994) the Cour de Cassation confirms its position but with a nuance: "... il résulte du texte même [...] que, conformément à l'article 4 [de la Convention], ses dispositions ne créent d'obligations qu'à la charge des Etats, *de sorte qu'*elles ne peuvent être directement invoquées devant les juridictions nationales" (italics added). See Massip, J., *Recueil Dalloz Sirey*, 1994, *Juris.*, 191–192; Benhamou, Y., *op.cit.*, 83 in *La Semaine Juridique*, 1995, nr. 2, 17.

[58] Neirinck, C. and Martin, P.-M., "Un traité bien maltraité. A propos de l'arrêt Le Jeune" *J.C.P* , 1993, I, 3677 ; Rondeau-Rivier, M.-C., "La Convention des Nations Unies sur les droits de l'enfant devant la Cour de cassation : un traité mis hors jeu", *Recueil Dalloz Sirey*, 1993, *Chron.*, 203–206 : Wacongne, M., comment under CA Paris, 27th November 1992, *Recueil Dalloz Sirey*, 1994, *Somm.*, 36–37.

[59] "[La Cour de cassation] aurait dû, article par se demander ceux qui étaient directement applicables et ceux qui nécessitaient une adaptation [de la législation]": Moneger, F., *Rev. dr. sanit. et soc.*, 1993, 536. Contra: Massip, J., *Recueil Dalloz Sirey*, 1994, *Juris.*, 192 who is of the opinion that such an approach "aurait été de nature à donner lieu à une casuistique et à des difficultés d'application que la Haute juridiction a sans doute estimé opportun d'éviter".

given the fact that the Convention is the result of intense and arduous negotiations between representatives of different political, philosophical, religious
and legal systems. Therefore it has to be taken into account that many articles
of the Convention are compromise texts.[60] Obviously this does not make
analysing the scope of the provisions of the Convention any easier.

C. Provisions of the Convention Taken Over From Other International Law Treaties

25. First of all, the Convention contains a number of provisions which (in
some cases partly and often with a different wording) repeat fundamental
rights from the ECHR and the International Covenant on Civil and Political
Rights.

This is the case particularly of the right to life (article 6); the ban on torture and inhuman or degrading treatment or punishment (article 37 a); the
right to personal liberty and safety (article 37 b); the right to a fair trial particularly in penal cases, with respect for the principle of legality (article 40);
the right to respect of privacy (articles 7, 8 and 16); the right to freedom of
thought, conscience and religion (article 14); the right to freedom of expression (article 13 and 17);[61] the right to freedom of assembly and of association
(article 15). The special protection of people belonging to a minority, taken
over from the International Covenant on Civil and Political Rights, is also
covered by the UN Convention (article 30). There shall be no discrimination
against children by States Parties as regards respecting and guaranteeing the
rights laid down in the Convention (article 2).

The self-executing nature of the provisions of the ECHR and the International Covenant on Civil and Political Rights is generally accepted.[62] It can
therefore reasonably be assumed that the corresponding provisions in the
Convention on the Rights of the Child are also self-executing.[63]

26. We must now consider the issue of the relationship between, on the one

---

[60] Explanatory memorandum to the Belgian Bill on approval of the Convention on the
Rights of the Child, *Doc. Parl.*, Chambre, 1990–91, nr. 1568/1, 4–5.

[61] With regard to art. 12 of the Convention: see nr. 30.

[62] Polakiewicz, J. and Jacob-Foltzer, V., "The European Human Rights Convention in
Domestic Law: The impact of Strasbourg case-law in states where direct effect is given to
the Convention", *Human Rights Law Journal*, 1991, 65–85 and 125–142: Velu, J., *Les effets
directs des instruments internationaux en matière de droits de l'homme, op.cit.*

[63] See e.g. Verhoeven, J., "La mise en oeuvre de la Convention ..." *op.cit.*, 67 and the
afore-mentioned opinion by the Belgian State Council (nr. 23, footnote 53). However see also
Pouleau, V., "A propos sur l'applicabilité (directe?) ...", *op.cit.*, 82 and 85, recognising the
self-executing nature only of articles 37 and 40, §1 and §2: Krings, E., *op.cit.*, 82 and 85,
recognising the s nature only of articles 6, 37 and 40, §1, §2 and §3.

hand, existing instruments designed to ensure protection for the fundamental rights of each individual and, on the other hand, the Convention, which deals specifically with children.

One of the main criticisms levelled at the Convention was that it might undermine the fundamental and universal nature of human rights.[64]

However the UN Convention should be regarded as complementary to existing international provisions and interpreted as dovetailing with existing human rights protection. In other words, it does not take the place of other international conventions, but adds to them. As a consequence, if protection on the basis of other international treaties goes beyond that of the Convention, the other international treaties take precedence (article 41).[65] This may be the case, for instance, for the right to freedom of religion, which is protected to a lesser degree in the Convention.[66]

In practice, the afore-mentioned provisions will play only a limited role, despite their self-executing character, since a minor will first of all invoke the ECHR or the International Covenant and Civil and Political Rights, which are much better known and contain the right of an individual to complain.[67] This will be even more so if a Protocol is added to the ECHR, specifically protecting children's fundamental rights.[68]

However, there are circumstances in which the UN Convention on the Rights of the Child reinforces the protection offered to children and minors by the

---

[64] Rietjens, P., "Situering van het VN-Verdrag inzake de Rechten van het Kind in de bredere context der internationale mensenrechteninstrumenten: al dan niet noodzaak tot een aparte Conventie ?", in *Rechten van het Kind. Lezingenbundel 2*, Verhellen, E. (ed.), Gent, Center for the Rights of the Child, 1992, 23–36. Stöcker, H., "Diskussion: Die UNO-Kinderrechtekonvention und das innerstaatliche Recht. Schlußwort" *Zeitschrift für Familienrecht*, 1992 even talks about "die Profanierung der Menschenrechte zum Schaugeschäft und zu einer die Sonderinteressen schirmenden Schaufassade ...".

[65] Verhoeven, J., "La mise en oeuvre de la Convention des Nations Unies sur les droits de l'enfant. Observations en droit des gens", *op.cit.*, 67.

[66] The UN Convention does not protect the right of the child to freedom of religion. The islamic delegations were of the opinion this would be in contradiction with the Koran, which would recognize this right only for adults: Cohen, C.-P., "Introductory note", *International Legal Materials (I.L.M.)*, 1989, 14550–1451.

[67] On the protection of minors by the ECHR and through the European Court on Human Rights: Buquicchio-de Boer, M.F., "Children and the European Convention on Human Rights" in *Protecting Human Rights: The European Dimension, Studies in honour of G.J. Wiarda*, Cologne, Carl Heymanns Verlag, 1988, 73–89; Boucaud, P., "Le Conseil de l'europe et la protection de l'enfant",*Dossier sur les Droits de l'homme*, nr. 10, 1989.

[68] See Council of Europe, *Parliamentary Assembly*: Report on the rights of children of november 6th 1989, doc. 6142; Recommendation 1121 (1990) on the Rights of Children, point B; European Parliament Resolution A3–0172/92 on a European Charter of Rights of the Child, *O.J.*, 1992, C241/67–73.

ECHR, which is self-executing in most Council of Europe member states. Article 7 of the UN Convention grants children the right to registration, and to a name and nationality[69]. Article 12 of the Convention recognises the right of the child to express its views freely in all matters affecting it (see nr. 30).

27. The UN Convention on the Rights of the Child also contains a number of provisions which correspond to provisions of the European Social Charter and the International Covenant on Economic, Social and Cultural Rights, such as the right to health (article 24), to social security (article 26), to an adequate standard of living (article 27), to education (articles 28 and 29). In article 4 States Parties undertake to take all appropriate legislative, administrative and other measures to implement these rights.

In general these provisions are considered not to be self-executing,[70] but, as we have pointed out above, this requires qualification, in that these provisions may lead to a standstill obligation (nrs. 16 and 17). An example, based on article 29 of the Convention, will demonstrate that these provisions can indeed, within certain limitations, be invoked in national courts. This article states that education shall be directed to the development of respect for a child's cultural identity, language and values, for the national values of the country in which the child is living, as well as the country from which he or she may originate, and for civilisations different from his or her own (article 29, §1, c). One might be forgiven for assuming that this provision has a purely political significance.[71] This is correct in the sense that children or their parents cannot go to court to demand a particular curriculum. But if the authorities were to impose a curriculum infringing article 29, then in our view they could be taken to court.

D. Some Specific Provisions

28. We shall now examine those provisions of the Convention which are specifically focused on the issue of children. We will deal with a number of these provisions and examine their self-executing nature, without however being able to be complete.

29. One of the most important provisions of the Convention is article 3,

---

[69] See also article 24, International Covenant and Civil and Political Rights.

[70] Once again we discover that the self-executing nature of international treaties is a dynamic notion and that each treaty provision has to be considered on its own merits, taking into account practical circumstances. The Belgian Court of Arbitration and the Dutch High Council have in fact recognised the self-executing character of article 6 of the European Social Charter (the right to strike): Court of Arbitration, 15th July 1993, nr. 62/93, *B.S.*, 5th August 1993 and High Council, 30th May 1986, nr. 12698, *Nederlandse Jurisprudentie*, 1986, 2546–2551.

[71] Veny, L., "De implementatie van de internationale verdragen in de Belgische rechtsordening" *T.O.R.B.*, 1992–93, 309, NR. 17.

§1 stating that in all actions concerning children, undertaken by an institution whatsoever, the best interests of the child shall be a primary consideration. This general guidance as to the child's best interests is repeated explicitly in a number of specific provisions: a child shall not be separated from his or her parents against their will, except when competent authorities determine, in accordance with legislation or procedures in force, that such separation is necessary in the best interests of the child (article 9). The two parents are jointly responsible for the upbringing and development of the child, and the child's best interest must be their basic concern (article 18). In the system of adoption the best interests of the child must constitute a constant(article 21).

The rule whereby "the best interests of the child" must be the primary consideration can be looked at in two ways: as an objective which the state undertakes to pursue (see article 21), but also as a negative obligation, i.e. not to do anything which would go against "the best interests of the child".

A Belgian court case will serve as an example.[72] A minor was "abducted" by her Belgian parents from the Dutch foster family, where she had been placed by a Dutch juvenile judge 4 years previously. In accordance with the European Convention on recognition and enforcement of decisions concerning custody of children and on restoration of custody of children (1980), the Belgian judge must recognise and execute the decision of the Dutch judge. However the Belgian judge did not, instead requesting the Dutch judge to carry out a new enquiry. He made his request on the basis of articles 3 and 9, § 3, of the Convention, feeling that it must be established whether, in view of the present situation, placement with foster parents and therefore separation from the parents was in the best interests of the child. In applying other (in this case international) provisions, the Belgian judge used the "best interests of the child" as a negative criterion, self-executing and therefore taking precedence: measures applied to children may not be in conflict with the actual interests of the child.

We feel that in this case the Belgian judge applied the self-executing nature of the Convention correctly. The fact that the notion "best interests of the child" is not a strictly defined criterion, therefore requiring interpretation and practical application, does not prevent it from being self-executing, but obliges the judge to weigh the interests involved and thus determine its content *in concreto*.[73]

---

[72] Court Kortrijk, 8th December 1992, *Journal des Droits des Jeunes (J.D.J.)*, 1993, nr. 126, 33 with comment Cappelaere, G., Verhellen, E. and Spiesschaert, F.

[73] The fact that the conclusion which was drawn by the Belgian judge after weighing the interests of the parties may be open to doubt, does not change the fact that the self-executing nature of the Convention was correctly applied.

30. Other noteworthy provisions in the Convention are those regarding the right of the child to be heard in legal proceedings, a major innovation in many countries.

They appear in articles 12 and 9, § 3, of the Convention. A child capable of forming his or her own views has the right to express those views freely in all matters affecting him or her, the views of the child being given due weight in accordance with the age and maturity of the child (article 12, § 1). For this purpose, the child shall, in particular, be offered the opportunity to be heard in any judicial or administrative proceedings affecting him or her, either directly, or through a representative or an appropriate body (article 12, § 2). In proceedings concerning the separation of a child from his/her parents for whatever reason, all interested parties shall be given an opportunity *to participate in the proceedings and make their views known* (article 9, § 2).

In many court cases in France[74] and Belgium[75] the obligation to hear the child is considered sufficiently clear and precise. There is, for instance, a recent ruling by the Belgian Cour the Cassation, in which the court implicitly recognises that article 9, § 2, of the Convention can (in general) be invoked directly.[76] Therefore the judge must obey the Convention, even where it conflicts with current legislation, and must hear the child.

This does not alter the fact that the Convention does not provide practical instructions on how to apply the right to be heard. For instance, who is to be considered suitable to hear the child? How has the child to be heard? And when is the child capable of forming his or her own views?[77] These are

---

[74] With the exception of the Cour de Cassation: see footnote 57. Bv. CA Paris, 27th November 1992, *Gazette du Palais*, 11–15th April 1993, 22–26; see footnotes 58 and 59.

[75] E.g.: Mons, 20th April 1993, *J.L.M.B.*, 1993, 784, with comment Panier, C.; Cappelaere, G., Spiesschaert, F. and Verhellen, E., "Het VN-Verdrag inzake de Rechten van het Kind en de partijbekwaamheid van minderjarigen", *Tijdschrift voor de Rechten van het Kind*, 1993, nr. 3, 23–25 (in this ruling the court does not only accept the right to be heard, but also the right to make a voluntary appearance in court to implement it); Crt. Liège, 7th March 1994, *J.L.M.B.*, 1994, 521, with footnote Panier, C.; Crt. Nivelles (Summ. Proc.) , 21th May 1993, *J.L.M.B.*, 1993, 1278; Crt Brussels (Summ. Proc.), 10th September 1993, *J.D.J.*, 1993, nr. 128, 30–31; Crt Liège (Summ. Proc.), 22th November 1991, *J.L.M.B.*, 1992, 146 with comment Panier, C. (in this ruling art. 12 of the Convention was applied before the Convention had entered into force in Belgium); Gent, 13th April 1992, *R.W.*, 1992–1993, 229, with comment Cappelaere, G., Verhellen, E. and Spiesschaert, F. Contra: the Antwerp Court of Appeal which explicitly denies "the self-executing nature of the Convention in domestic law", without however giving its reasoning: Antwerp, 14th April 1994, Kinderrechtengids, 3.1, 3–6.

[76] Cass., 11th March 1994, *Kinderrechtengids*, 3.1, 3–6.

[77] See Liège, 24th June 1992, *J.L.M.B.*, 1992, 957–959, in a case concerning deprivation of parental authority, the decision was taken not to hear the child because it was not yet capable of judging its own interests and wishes nor of expressing them. We can also refer to rulings by the Council of State which declared admissible an appeal by a minor on condition that he had the necessary discernment to exercise his rights : R.v. St., 22nd February 1989 (Van Eynde and Collier), nr. 32.054, *J.L.M.B.*, 1989, report Kreins, Y., with comment Panier, C., and *J.T.*,

questions to which the Convention does not provide the answers.

This is precisely why many authors make the case for the legislator[78] to resolve all practical problems of organisation and implementation of a minor's right to speak (or to be heard). The fact that this is a delicate area, where some[79] fear that parents and children may find themselves in conflict, or where children may fall prey to manipulation, is an extra argument for intervention by the legislator. However, intervention by the legislator may not, in any circumstances, involve detracting from the right contained in the UN Convention.[80]

E. Conclusion

31. As we have repeatedly said, it is impossible to make general statements about the Convention's self-executing nature. We would go further, and say that, were we to seek to examine the self-executing nature of all the Convention's provisions, and attempt to draw conclusions with international validity, this would indicate a false understanding of the notion.

The self-executing nature of a treaty depends not only on the legal system where it is to be applied, but also on the material right involved. In fact, research into the self-executing nature of the Convention will be carried out in the first place in the courts,[81] in the different areas of law, such as youth protection, criminal law, family law, etc., on which the UN Convention has a bearing. This is one of the reasons why the notion is still evolving rapidly.

Many provisions will require action by national authorities (the legislator in particular), who will have considerable leeway in defining "appropriate" measures to take. Examples are article 11, concerning the illicit transfer of children abroad; article 13, concerning the protection of children against the use of drugs; article 34 concerning sexual abuse of children and articles 32, § 2 and 36, obliging States Parties to take measures to protect the child from dangerous or harmful work or exploitation.

Other obligations are clear and precise enough to be invoked directly in

---

1989, 676, with comment Rigaux, F. (compare also the ruling of Council of State, 7th October 1988 (Stoquart), nr. 30.985).

[78] Deli, D., *op.cit.*, nr. 78; Cappelaere, G., e.a., *op.cit.*, *R.W.*, 1992–1993, 230 ; Adriaenssens, K., "De rechten van het Kind", *R.W.*, 1991–92, 1116–1117.

[79] Pouleau, V., "A propos de la Convention des droits de l'enfant. L'enfant, sujet de droits: enfin une réalité ?", *J.T.*, 1990, 617, nrs. 10–11, 69–70; Krings, E., *op.cit.*, 84.

[80] Deli, D., *op.cit.*, 570, nr. 78.

[81] "Encore faut-il préciser que tel article de la Convention, immédiatement applicable dans certains cas, ne le sera plus dans d'autres: s'il avait fallu ici, non pas entendre mais créer le droit du mineur à la sécurité sociale, un texte de loi eût été nécessaire..." Wacogne, M., comment under CA Paris, 27th November 1992, *op.cit.*, 36.

court. Sometimes this is the case for only a part of a provision, such as article 38, § 3, which is self-executing in its first sentence (ban on recruiting anyone under the age of fifteen into the army), but probably not in its second sentence (States Parties shall "endeavour" to give priority to those who are oldest, when recruiting children between 15 and 18).

32. If this contribution demonstrates that it is impossible to draw general conclusions concerning the Convention's self-executing nature, but that there are different techniques for making use of most provisions and that nothing stands in the way of conferring self-executing nature on several provisions, then we have achieved our aim.

JEAN-PIERRE ROSENCZVEIG

The Self-executing Character of the Children's Rights Convention in France

It has fallen to me to discuss the excellent report by André Alen and Wouter Pas on the legal efficiency of the UN Convention on the Rights of the Child. This is no easy task. Still, I shall do my best, and try at the same time to indicate some avenues potentially open to those who deal with this area on a daily basis.

What I have to say is inevitably affected by my background, or perhaps I should say backgrounds, and this should go some way towards explaining any ambiguity or what one may perceive as shortcomings in this submission.

I am President of the Deuxième Tribunal pour enfants de France in Paris (juvenile court). I am, then, a lawyer, but, first and foremost a judge, i.e. a legal practicioner. At the moment I am dealing with 1.000 cases of children and young people in danger of becoming delinquents. Often the same children and young people are involved in several cases. In other words, I think I can say that I am in touch with reality, or at least with the reality of situations encountered at the sharp end.

I also act as coordinator for 85 associations, which have got together to promote actively respect in France and by France of the UN Convention on the Rights of the Child. In 1988 I contributed to setting up this group, which became COFRADE in 1993, at the request of the French section of the ICCB and of the French UNICEF Committee. It became the interlocutor of the French authorities and, under the patronage of Marie Paule Eisele, it gained the ear of the Experts Committee in Geneva. We took steps to make sure the Convention was publicised, and to ensure the adaptation of domestic law. We have made it our job now to ensure obligations undertaken are fulfilled. Thus in France analysis of the report to the Committee of Experts took place under our critical eye.

In other words, I shall approach the subject as a militant lawyer, a lawyer, in other words, who, unlike others, will not hesitate to show his lack of neutrality.

I must add that, in the last ten years I have had some say in how of our system of child protection is implemented and in adapting juvenile law to the Convention.

E. Verhellen (ed.), Monitoring Children's Rights, 187–197.
© 1996 *Kluwer Law International. Printed in the Netherlands.*

So I have put my (visiting) cards on the table, although I should not forget to mention my contribution to the journal "Droits des Jeunes", published in Belgium at the behest of Jean-Pierre Bartolomé, the driving force behind the Services Droits des Jeunes in Wallonia.

In my text, I shall be addressing three aspects in varying degrees:

1. I will react to the theoretical and conceptual ideas in Alen and Pas' remarks;
2. I will describe, in more detail, the legal – and therefore political – debate in France, echoing Alen and Pas' testimony on the Belgian situation, and developing their final question a little further;
3. Finally, I will look into certain extra-legal aspects of the Convention's self-executing nature.

I. A VERY SUBJECTIVE EXAMINATION OF THE CONCEPTS IN THE ALEN/PAS ANALYSIS

I particularly enjoyed the rare quality and lucidity of Alen/Pas' legal analysis of what is essentially a dull subject matter.

Non-lawyers might be put off by the necessarily technical nature of this exposé on international public law.

However, they will be aware of the importance of this analysis – demonstrated also by the French situation, which I will describe below – given the controversy surrounding the Convention's impact. The least one can say is that there are those who would like to consider the Convention as more a statement of principle than a binding text.

In my opinion, these issues are no longer just a matter for politicians. From often contradictory and/or cynical motives, they did their bit, signing and ratifying the Convention. Now it is up to the courts, and resistance is far from overcome! The game is on, and it can be won if we prepare well in advance by bringing about the necessary balance of power.

I have already remarked that I have rarely read a more lucid treatise on the subject of the self-executing effect of international conventions.

I have certainly never come across anything as precise in France, and it makes me think that our judges at the Cour de Cassation cannot have either, or they would not have handed down the rulings of the last two years. Let me briefly summarise the most telling points made by Alen/Pas:

1. The reminder that in the majority of states with a constitutional model, a treaty which has been duly ratified – by either law or referendum – has, at the very least, constitutional or even supra-constitutional value. In any event, it takes precedence over all existing and future legislation which might conflict with it or cover less.

I would like to point out that in France, in 1994, after the adaptation of the Maastricht Treaty, the Congress had to meet in Versailles to change the Constitution of 4th October 1958.

Being Cartesian in my logic, I have to conclude that, in countries like Belgium and France, treaties – in this case the Convention on the Rights of the Child – take precedence over the constitution in the hierarchy of legal provisions.

Better still, a treaty becomes domestic law. This is all too often forgotten. It does not stand outside national law, it is part of it. Under normal circumstances, pre-existing law should not need bringing in line with the Convention. In reality however there will be points which must be specified. In fact the Convention itself often requests states to this.

And you will have taken note of the other fundamental idea that treaties take precedence over the law if they are more favourable to those involved. Thus there is nothing to prevent states from having legislation more favourable than the Convention. We all know how important this argument was during the debate on the Draft European Directive on Child Labour!

2. A second idea in Alen and Pas' text to be kept in mind in the present debate: the self-executing nature of treaties applies to different degrees depending on the room for manoeuvre left to the state.

So much the better if the text involved is precise enough to create a subjective right, and especially if it concerns an objective the state has taken it upon itself to achieve, without quantifying it or setting a deadline. In that case, the state's practice must not conflict with this general objective.

The importance of this assertion, which I had not come across before, is clear when one takes into account the emphasis the Convention places on social, economic and cultural rights for children, besides the civil and political rights.

3. A third essential idea: while stating that certain provisions may be self-executing and be invoked by anyone in a court of law – and in France the articles on freedom of expression have had an extraordinary impact – it is important to remember that:

– There may be a need for legislation to establish a framework for enforcing of rights recognised in the Convention ... which must not however hamper implementation of the Convention! Thus when in France the right of a child to be heard in court is made dependent on the judge's approval, a purely fictitious right is created. Freedom of expression in court – in this case of children – exists or does not exist! Its existence should not depend on the good will of a judge. It is a fundamental principle; a major human right.

– In the end it will be up to the judges to guarantee respect of the rights and freedoms recognised by the Convention in practice. Real rights do not exist unless there can be recourse to the law when they are violated!

I note in passing that, on the subject of children's rights to be heard in court, Belgian law is more favourable than the French.

II. JUDGES' ATTITUDE TO THE CONVENTION

We should not conceal the fact that we are going through a bad patch in France as a consequence of a number of rulings by the Chambre Civile de la Cour de Cassation in July 1993 and by the Chambre Sociale in July 1994.

Alen and Pas mention these at the end of their text.

The Committee on the Rights of the Child also expresses its concern about the recent decisions adopted by the Cour de Cassation in its Concluding Observations on the French report of 22nd April 1994.[1]

I will briefly go over the rulings by the Cour de Cassation, and attempt to look beyond the controversy they caused. How is this attitude to be explained? And especially how are we to judge their impact bearing in mind the imminent need to answer a number of fundamental questions. First and foremost, I would like to remind you of two essential facts:

1. The first follows on from Alen/Pas' remarks on the Belgian situation. France stated only one reservation on article 30, when in April 1994, in our report to the President of the Republic and to the Haut Conseil de la Population et de la Famille, we drew up a list of some ten points in our legislation which could not be adapted in the short term. We were thinking particularly of articles 2, 12, 14, 15, etc.

2. The second is a reminder of the extraordinary reception accorded to the Convention in France, generating considerable optimism, but also some consternation among neo-philosophers, in family movements and among the followers of a line of thinking based on article 371 of the Civil Code, which states that "at whatever age, the child must honour and respect its parents."

A. *The Cour de Cassation Causes Trouble*

Throughout the period since public debate on the Convention started in 1988, no voices have been raised in protest when it has been stated in public that the Convention would be binding on the state, and even self-executing.

Rulings by the Cour de Cassation in 1993 therefore came as a profound shock. We assumed, at first, there had been some mistake, as even the authors admitted[2]. Real jurisprudence by the bench, in other words.

The provisions of the Convention on the Rights of the Child cannot be invoked in court, given the fact that this convention ... cannot be applied directly in domestic law.

In several rulings in 1993 and 1994,[3] the Première Chambre Civile of the Cour de Cassation therefore weakened the force of the Convention, deciding

---

[1] CRC/C/15/Add. 20 of 25 April 1994 Also published in extenso with a critical examination of my critical remark in JDJ no. 136 (June 1994)

[2] Note MASSIP, Dalloz 1993 p.361.

[3] Iere Civ. 10th March 1993 and 15th July 1993.

that the provisions of the Convention were binding only on the state, and that where there were no domestic implementing provisions, judges could not apply them directly. In other words, judges were to be considered as bound only by national legislation.

This approach baffled and even shocked lawyers, who had traditionally been taught that treaties take precedence over the law and that judges can indeed refer to them directly.

B. The Majority of Lawyers Take the Cour to Task

There was a barrage of criticism of the Haute Juridiction.[4] The only positive comments were made by Benhamou and Massip, the latter having presided over the hearings in the Première Chambre Civile when the first two rulings were made.

The Cour de Cassation was accused of having applied an approach which was too general and of having thereby overlooked the complexity of the Convention and the heterogeneity of its provisions.

Certain provisions are in fact by their very nature precise enough to be self-executing, while others do require implementing texts. Each provision must be considered on its merits. This is the traditional view of lawyers who have to make a judgement on the self-executing nature of international provisions.

In a memo to the Commission Nationale Consultative des Droits de l'Homme, Braunschweig and de Gouttes recall these principles. As the diplomats they are, they try to be fair to the Cour de Cassation: the Convention imposes obligations on the French Government and the Cour did not intend to contest this principle. In stating that the Convention imposes obligations only on the state, the Cour implicitly confirmed that the French State had the obligation of implementing the Convention.

In the view of the two consultants, to say that the Convention imposes obligations on the French government means that

> a state which has ratified a convention has the obligation of taking all necessary steps to ensure that it can be implemented effectively and that the rights which are recognised therein are guaranteed. If the state has to change its legislation to bring it into line with the convention, it has to do so before or simultaneously with ratification of the convention itself.

They added that

> if the state does not adopt the necessary texts to adapt its legislation or adopts unsuitable texts, its responsibility in international law is at stake and a complaint can be made by another state party to the International Court

---

[4] *"Un traité bien maltraité : à propos de l'arrêt Lejeune"* par Claire NEIRINCK and Pierre-Martin MARTIN, Semaine juridique JCP 1993, 3677, p. 223; *"La convention des N.U. sur les droits des enfants devant la Cour de Cassation : un traité hors jeu"* M.CL. RONDEAU-RIVER, Dalloz 1993. Chr. p. 203; J. RUBELLIN-DEVICHI, JCP 1994, ED. G. 1994.I.3729, Nr. 1.

in The Hague for non-compliance, providing the state involved recognises the Court's competence.

To return to my analysis of the rulings, I have noticed, to my satisfaction, that lately the court seems to have started qualifying its earlier opinion and is no longer using the sweeping statement made in March 1993, which seemed to indicate that all the Convention's provisions were of the same ilk. Note has been taken! Now all we have to do is decide which provisions are "self-executing".

For Braunschweig and de Gouttes articles 3–1, 7–1, 12–2, 13, and 16, for instance, should all fall into that category. To avoid controversy they then recommend that the government take the necessary steps, as it has done for article 12 (Law of 8th January 1993). This however is easier said than done, as the Convention is richer than is generally thought.

However we would be in a more comfortable position had the Cour not sown the seeds of doubt.

From the words of Alen/Pas, I conclude that criticism of the Haute Juridiction was also echoed abroad, particularly in countries with a Latin legal culture.

C. And Despite this Barrage of Criticism, the Cour de Cassation Persists and Even Manages to Discourage Certain Lawyers...

We had been hoping to put the errors of the past behind us, but the Chambre Sociale, in a ruling handed down on 13th July 1994 (CPAM de Seine et Marne vs Ponnau) carried on where the 1ère Chambre Civile had left off and quashed a ruling by the Cour de Paris, which granted social security benefits to a young girl on the basis of her parents's cover, referring to the Convention, despite the fact that the Social Security Code contained an age limit which would have disqualified her. We again find the same reasoning, which says that

the provisions of this Convention ... cannot be invoked directly in domestic courts.

It is worth quoting the grounds for this decision, which are extremely succinct:

It follows from article 4 of the Convention that its provisions engender obligations only for States Parties, and thus cannot be invoked directly in domestic courts.

We should also note the fact that this ruling by the Cour de Cassation is not noticeably modified by the more traditional stance taken by the Conseil d'Etat on 17th February 1993.

D. As Long as Lower Court Judges keep up the fight...

Whereas some people might have concluded from all this "that the Convention had been sidelined in court", to our satisfaction judges continue to refer to it in their rulings. Judges feel they retain the freedom to interpret the law and more particularly the Convention, and do not hesitate to do so in practice.

Thus, on 13th June 1994, the Tribunal Correctionel in Rennes did not find against a young woman from the Ivory Coast, who had refused to comply with an expulsion order by the Prefect, with the excuse that the State had not put her in a position to leave the country with her 5 month old baby, which had been taken into care at birth.

Let us first take a look at the legal background to the case:

According to article 11–5 of the new Criminal Code, courts administring the criminal law are qualified to decide on the legality of administrative acts, where they affect the outcome of a criminal case they are called upon to examine. Part of the Convention on the Rights of the Child, also known as the New York Convention of 26th January 1990, can be considered such an act. Effectively, when article 4 of the Convention states that "States Parties shall undertake all appropriate legislative, administrative, and other measures for the implementation of the rights recognized in the present Convention" this provision does not appear to prevent certain articles of the text from being self-executing; the self-executing nature of treaties stems from a general principle concerning the inclusion of treaties into the domestic legal system (article 55 of the Constitution and rulings by the Chambre Mixte of the Cour de Cassation). This principle and consequent rules governing the self-executing nature of treaties, apply to all the provisions of the Convention which do not refer to a sovereign initiative of the signatories and are comprehensive and precise enough not to need implementing texts based on domestic law.

The Tribunal Correctionel has no qualms about invoking the European Convention on Human Rights and the UN Convention, particularly article 9, complementing article 7 – a child shall not be separated from his or her parents against their will – in refusing to find the young mother guilty. It is interesting to note that in fact in the case in question the juvenile court had not even been consulted when the expulsion order was issued.

The position of judges is clear. One feels that they are aware of the Cour de Cassation's position but do not share it:

Article 9 of the Convention on the Rights of the Child contains provisions which are precise enough to be directly applicable by administrative bodies and domestic courts. (...) These parts of the Convention are no less precise than provisions of the Civil Code, such as articles 372–2 and 375–3 for instance.

Conclusion: because necessary precautions were not taken to ensure that the mother was not separated from her child – and vice versa – the expulsion order could not become the basis for criminal proceedings:

In the light of what preceded, a prefect intending to expel a foreign father or mother must ascertain whether the child or children can leave France with the person expelled if the latter wishes this to happen, or that direct contact remains possible, all of this with the proviso that the child's best interests are safeguarded.

For its part, on 29th July 1994, the Tribunal de Coutances, in a ruling concerning parental authority after divorce, stated that

the criterion of the best interests of the child, referred to in the Convention (...), which, since it has been ratified by France, the judge must apply by virtue of article 55 of the Constitution, requires that parental authority be conferred on one of the child's parents.

Taking everything into account, it becomes clear that it is high time the Cour de Cassation Toutes Chambres Réunies adopted another position, more in line with... tradition.

E. A Legal Text which Confuses the High Magistrates

How to explain the attitude of the French Cour de Cassation? First of all, they have not listened to Alen and Pas. I believe that the civil law specialists of the Cour de Cassation are not versed in international law. I, myself, have taken particular note of the fact that even where provisions are not self-executing, it must still be established that the state has taken all necessary steps to move in the direction indicated by international law!

I therefore recommend that, without delay, the excellent legal analysis of Alen/Pas be widely distributed in France.

There are, then, deficiencies of a technical nature, but we have to dig deeper to get to the root of the problem if we are to understand fully the resistance still to overcome. What has gotten into the Cour de Cassation?

The primary consideration underlying the attitude taken by the Cour de Cassation is, without any doubt, concern that lower court judges might give their own interpretation of the Convention in order to advance children's rights, potentially leading to excesses, such as the decision in 1991 to allow a child to become a litigant in his parents' divorce proceedings.

In 1991–92, for lack of clear texts on the hearing of children in matrimonial cases, different and contradictory rulings were made: most judges allowed the child to be heard and assisted by a lawyer, but others refused and insisted on waiting for a domestic text. And then there was the case of the judges in Saint Brieuc and Montpellier who, in 1991, allowed cases brought by children, refusing to follow their parents to Indian ashrams.

Order had to be restored! What would happen if any judge could refer directly to a text which is in fact a real legal treasure-chest? If children cannot be separated from their parents, does that not mean that foreign parents must be allowed into France if their children are there already?

One essential fact about the Cour de Cassation which is often overlooked, i.e. that it rules on facts rather than points of law. By this I mean that before changing its jurisprudence, the Cour de Cassation tries to give fair consideration to the political, social and human aspects of the case in question. This does not mean the Cour de Cassation is always "re-active" in its approach. Quite the contrary. In the past it has proved it can be quite inventive, using a Napoleonic text, for instance, to find a legal solution to compensate victims of road accidents, or to compensate both wife and concubine.

It is clear that the idea of the child as a person with rights of his own, which he can also exercise, irritates certain High Magistrates, who follow in the footsteps of the great lawyers who left their mark on their era. We need look no further for the reasons behind the reservations of certain judges at the Cour de Cassation, who, in a manner rather surprising for lawyers of that quality, continue to refer to the New York Convention, signed on 26th January 1990, though the Convention was ratified by France on 6th September and entered into force on 7th September 1990!

And then there is the original and heterogenous content of the Convention, which may have confused the honourable magistrates of the Supreme Court, who specialise in civil law.

It has been pointed out that on economic, social and cultural rights, states' obligations concern objectives and means of achieving them, rather than rights in practice. We frequently find expressions in the text, such as "*to the maximum extent possible*", "*States Parties shall use their best efforts*", etc. which further qualify the scope of certain provisions.

As a global text the Convention covers all rights: civil, economic, social cultural and political. In fact this is the main original feature of this text.

In international conventions civil and political rights are, by their very nature, self-executing. The right to a name, a nationality, freedom of expression, etc. do not require that a number of conditions be fulfilled before they can be applied.

In the case of economic, social and cultural rights, however, one can do little more than convince states to commit themselves to objectives and attitudes to be adopted. Hence the feeling after reading the text that there are several levels of rights being defined in it, and this has led some people to say that the text is a mixture of legal, philosophical and political considerations.

Would it have been possible to avoid some degree of abstraction in a text which sought to be universal, conceived not only for all the peoples of the planet but to be implemented throughtout the world? It was necessary to take into account cultural differences and especially levels of economic development.

This was the challenge facing the initiators of the Convention: convincing states to commit themselves to objectives and mobilising the economic and technical solidarity necessary to bring about the economic conditions indispensable for putting into practice rights conferred on children and families.

Those countries which can fulfil their obligations will do so, but they may also have to help other States Parties and to this end are to establish international co-operation. France itself is hardly in a position, as things stand, to guarantee a place in a child care centre for every child (article 18). Despites our efforts over the last decade, we shall still have to invest substantial amounts if we are to attain the objective we have committed ourselves to via the Convention, given a current shortfall of places estimated at 350.000. These "practical" constraints inescapable even in a rich country like France are obviously going to weigh even heavier on many other countries. Realism and the desire to make progress in conferring rights under the Convention created the need to find a compromise between a statement of principle without any binding force and the granting of positive rights which clearly cannot be put into practice at the moment.

Article 4 speaks for itself:

> In regard to economic, social and cultural rights, States Parties shall undertake such measures to the maximum extent of their available resources and, where needed, within the framework of international co-operation.

It is easy to be mean-spirited, and to suggest that States have no difficulty in signing up to ambiguous obligations, further qualified by phrases open to interpretation such as "to the maximum extent of their available resources", when their subsequent behaviour is a matter of record, dictated either by lack of funds or a failure of political will. But that is to see only part of the text. As a whole, it remains difficult to ratify and in fact some States have neither signed nor ratified it.

We need only look at the example of the US, where it is well known that the argument of federal structure is used to hide a fundamental problem. The US has many difficulties in implementing the Convention's provisions: death penalty applied to minors, limitations in their health and social security legislation, etc.

Criticism of the Convention is partly justified, but should not be generalised, for fear of jeopardising its impact the world over.

F. Summary

The rulings by lower court judges I have reported on, bode well for the future, when certain key-questions will inevitably have to be resolved in court.

Leaving aside the issue of social and economic rights (income, housing, etc.), I would like to give two very telling examples:
- Article 6 and the right to know one's parents: the provisions, contained in the law of 8th January 1993, legalising "anonymous" deliveries, i.e. where names of parents are withheld, are contrary to the Convention.
- "Wearing the veil" at state schools. I feel – with a number of others – that the circular from the Education Ministry (September 1994) is in breach of article 14–3, which states that freedom to manifest one's religion or beliefs may be subject only to such limitations as are prescribed by law and necessary to protect public order. If there is no proselitism or

provocation, the Conseil d'Etat will have to quash decisions to expel children. It has already done so in the past. The 1989 ruling is clear.

III. Extra-legal Monitoring of the Convention's Self-executing Nature

We all know how important NGOs are when it comes to ensuring implementation. They can question the authorities when they feel the Convention is not being properly implemented or that there are infringements. Moreover they can – or, should I say, must – keep the flame of the Convention burning when it looks as though it is flickering and may even be extinguished completely.

The farcical consultations we had this year around 20th November between the authorities and COFRADE have shown once again that for there to be a dialogue there has to be common purpose.

Whether by accident or political change of heart, our objectives were far from attained: those who were politically responsible failed to appear or even send a political message, ministers were lukewarm to indifferent, civil servants informed at the last minute, etc.

So much for the consultations the authorities boasted about in their submission to the Committee on the Rights of the Child in April 1994! And the blame does not lie with the administration, which has played by the book, but with the politicians who still seem to feel that to talk about children's rights is somehow attacking the family!

But we, the associations, must also take our share of the blame: we have to change the balance of power in our countries to force the authorities to listen to our criticism. But, technically and in terms of human resources, we are not always geared up to do battle.

To keep the flame burning, must we therefore invest particularly in information and training for legal professionals (lawyers, judges) so everybody starts invoking the Convention of their own accord. This year we have made a start: 800 lawyers have been trained in or at least made aware of children's rights and will now contribute to the recognition of new rights. I should add that we also have to ensure that the Convention has sone impact on education and can contribute to changes in attitude. If teachers and social workers start making use of it, they can change a great deal in the way they do their jobs.

I don't have time to go into the approach of the Association La Vie au Grand Air, led by P. Verdier, which tries to apply to the hundreds of children resident in its establishments a number of key articles of the Convention, such as article 6 on establishing the identity of each child, and others on respect for privacy or the right to have a relationship with their parents.

Is this not the best way to ensure implementation of the Convention?

MAUD BUQUICCHIO-DE BOER

The Direct Effect of the European Convention of Human Rights and the Rights of Children

INTRODUCTION

The question of direct effect of the European Convention of Human Rights is not a question which the European Commission or Court of Human Rights is particularly concerned with. Their role is to examine whether in a given case a violation of the Convention has occurred, irrespective of the question whether that violation has occurred as a result of the direct effect attributed to the provision concerned or whether the alleged violation is the result of the application of domestic law alone.

It concerns the Convention organs only to the extent that, where Convention law is part of domestic law, as a result of the requirement to exhaust domestic remedies, the domestic authorities may have addressed the Convention argument, which can be of interest to the Convention organs. In those countries where Convention law is not part of the legal system that element is lacking: in order to satisfy the condition of exhaustion, it suffices to invoke the Convention argument in substance, basing it on equivalent notions of domestic law.

The duty to incorporate the text of the European Convention of Human Rights could arguably be based on the text of its first Article which reads:

> The High Contracting Parties shall secure to everyone within their jurisdiction the rights and freedoms defined in Section 1 of this Convention.

More plausibly, the above provision should merely be read as obliging the Convention State to give full effects to the rights guaranteed by the Convention, leaving the question as to the means to be employed to the discretion of the State concerned. The latter interpretation is confirmed by the case-law on Article 13 of the Convention, according to which this provision does not lay down for the Contracting States any given manner for ensuring within their internal law the effective implementation of the Convention.[1]

---

[1] No. 11603/85, Dec. 20-1-1987, D.R. 50, p. 228.

E. Verhellen (ed.), Monitoring Children's Rights, 199–210.

The question of direct effect does not only concern the Convention as such, but also the interpretation given to the provisions by the Convention organs. In this respect, the question is closely related to that of the execution of the Court's judgments, the supervision of which does not lie with the judicial Convention organs, but with the Committee of Ministers.

However, a State, having been found to have acted in breach of the Convention, which does not take the necessary action to remove the source of the violation, may again be answerable for a breach of the Convention in a fresh application.

The failure to apply a judgment of the European Court delivered against Austria in which a breach of Article 10 of the Convention had been found as a result of the applicant's conviction for defamation,[2] has given rise to a new application before the Commission, the Austrian Supreme Court having rejected a plea of nullity for the preservation of the law with a view to having quashed the judgments at issue in the case in which the European Court had found a breach. While rejecting the Government's argument that the case was inadmissible for being substantially the same as the case previously examined, the Commission nevertheless rejected this application considering that the mere refusal by the Supreme Court to reopen the proceedings did not affect the applicant's situation to such an extent that it could be regarded as a new interference.[3]

The fact that the Convention, in a number of Member States, is not part of the domestic law does not necessarily mean that it has no effect whatsoever. Case-law in the United Kingdom has witnessed the striking down of secondary legislation (Prison Rules) by reference to basic rights of the prisoner. Reference to Strasbourg case-law was made to endorse the conclusion reached on the basis of domestic law . The decision stated "This decision (judgment of the European Court in the case of Campbell),[4] although not directly binding in England, reinforces a conclusion that we have arrived at in the light of the principles of our domestic jurisprudence.[5]

The cautious way in which reliance is being made in the United Kingdom on Convention case-law may well be explained by the desire to avoid criticism that judges take the place of the legislator and thereby provide munition to those who oppose incorporation.

Given the fundamental nature of the rights in the Convention, there is no reason why minors should constitute a separate category of holders of these rights, which pertain to "everyone" within the jurisdiction of the Member States. The Convention itself makes reference to the status of minors only exceptionally : in Article 6 an exception to the general rule of public hearing

---

[2] Eur. Court H.R., Oberschlick judgment of 23 May 1991, Series A No 204.

[3] No. 19255/92, dec. 16.5.1995, DR 81A, p. 5.

[4] Eur. Court H.R., Campbell judgment of 25.3.1992, Series A No 233.

[5] Regina v. the Secretary of State for the Home Department, ex parte Leech, Court of Appeal 19.5.1993.

is permitted in the interests of juveniles, whilst Article 5 para. 1 (d) provides for a deprivation of liberty either as a protective measure or in the context of criminal proceedings (cf. below).

Another matter is of course the procedural and psychological hurdle for young people to avail themselves of Convention rights or of rights in general. As far as the proceedings in Strasbourg are concerned, the Commission has made it clear that mere lack of years does not constitute an obstacle for bringing applications.

A parent can in principle make an application to the Commission on behalf of his or her child although this opportunity is qualified in certain cases by the status of the parent's legal relationship with the child in domestic law. Where under national law a parent no longer exercises parental rights, the Commission requires clear evidence of the child's wish to be represented by that parent in proceedings under the Convention. Such situations have arisen, for example, where a parent wished to challenge a custody or care arrangement on behalf of the child affected by it.[6]

A number of rights in the Convention are of particular relevance to children. I will deal with three of them in examining the question whether these rights, by their nature, lend themselves to producing direct effect, namely the right to respect of private and family life (Article 8), the right to liberty (Article 5) and the right to a fair trial (Article 6).

What follows is an analysis of the question whether these provisions, from an objective point of view, lend themselves to direct applicability. It does not address the question by which States the Convention has been incorporated in domestic law and by what means.

This survey is by no means exhaustive. The question whether any legal norm is capable of producing direct effect depends on the nature of the norm and the way it is formulated. Some of the Convention rights are of such an absolute nature, such as the right not to be tortured or not to be subject to inhuman or degrading treatment (Article 3), that the question whether it is capable of producing direct effect is not worthy of any legal argument.

I. Private and Family Life

Article 8 of the European Convention of Human Rights provides as follows:

1. Everyone has the right to respect for his private and family life, his home and his correspondence.
2. There shall be no interference by a public authority with the exercise of this right except such as is in accordance with the law and is necessary in a democratic society in the interests of national security, public safety or the economic well-being of the country, for the prevention

---

[6] No 8045/77, Dec. 4.5.79, D.R. 16, p. 105.

of disorder or crime, for the protection of health or morals, or for the protection of the rights and freedoms of others.

In the well-known Marckx judgment the European Court of Human Rights has qualified the nature of the obligations flowing from this provision: in addition to the primarily negative undertaking to refrain from interference the Court emphasized that there may be positive obligations inherent in an effective respect for family life.[7]

In order to comply with the above Convention norm, the State concerned may, in a given case, be required to take positive action, in particular by way of legislation.

At first sight this duty seems to be difficult to reconcile with the concept of direct effect, the characteristics of the latter being precisely that no further action is called for and that the individual concerned may benefit from the protection offered by this provision in the domestic legal system without any further legislation. Sir Gerald Fitzmaurice's dissenting opinion to the Marckx judgment clearly reflects this approach. Emphasising the distinction between family *life* on the one hand and family *law* on the other, he heavily criticised the Court for having included the latter concept in the former and, in doing so, for having wanted to substitute itself to the Belgian legislator.

The problem was again highlighted in the aftermath of the Marckx judgment. Ms. Vermeire, excluded from the estates of her deceased grandparents because of the illegitimate nature of the relationship between her and the deceased, brought a succesful action to claim a share in the estates, before the domestic (Brussels) court of first instance. The lower court indeed considered that the prohibition on discrimination between legitimate and illegitimate children as regards inheritance rights was formulated in the Marckx judgment sufficiently clearly and precisely to allow a domestic court to apply it directly in cases before it.

This decision was however overruled on appeal and by the Belgian Court of Cassation, who considered that, given the fact that the Belgian State had various means to choose from fulfilling its obligations in this area, the provision was no longer sufficiently precise and comprehensive and had to be interpreted as an obligation to act, the responsability for which was with the legislature and not the judiciary.

The European Court of Human Rights did not share this interpretation. An overall revision of the legislation with the aim of carrying out a thorough-going and consistent amendment of the whole of the law on affiliation and inheritance on intestacy, was not necessary at all as an essential preliminary to compliance with the Convention as interpreted by the Court in the Marckx case. The freedom of choice allowed to a State as to the means of fulfilling its obligation under Article 53 of the Convention, so the Court held, cannot allow it to suspend the application of the Convention while waiting for such

---

[7]   Eur. Court H.R., Marckx judgment of 13.6.1979, Series A No 31.

a reform to be completed, to the extent of compelling the Court to reject in 1991, with respect to succession which took effect on 22 July 1980, complaints identical to those which it upheld on 13 June 1979, when it delivered the Marckx judgment.[8]

The Supreme Court of the Netherlands, as early as 1980, i.e. only one year after the Marckx judgment, had followed the same approach, by applying the Convention directly as interpreted by the European Court of Human Rights in the Marckx judgment, the interpretation being regarded as an authentic one.[9]

The above controversy is perhaps not so fundamental as it looks. In the first place the dividing line between positive obligations and negative undertakings inherent in Article 8 is not always so clearly defined: measures to place children into public care must of course be regarded as an interference with the parents' right to respect for family life. On the other hand the claim of the same parents under the same provision to a right of access may as the case may be raise issues as to the respect of positive obligations of the State in this area.

Moreover, whereas the Court in the Marxck's case, having found that the Belgian legal system showed lack of respect for the applicants' right to respect of family life, did not pursue further the question whether there could be any justification therefore in terms of para. 2 of that provision, it adopted a slightly different approach in a number of subsequent cases.

In determining the question whether or not in a particular case a positive obligation existed, the Court has regard to the fair balance to be struck between the general interest of the community and the interest of the individual, the search for which balance, so it argued, was inherent in the whole of the Convention. In other words, the "classic" proportionality test applied under para. 2 of Article 8 in order to assess the justification of an interference by positive action, was applied in just the same way, in order to determine the existence of the failure to comply with a positive obligation, i.e. an obligation to act.

One of the cases in which this approach was adopted by the Court concerned the United Kingdom.

The applicant had spent his entire childhood with foster parents, having been placed first in compulsory and then in voluntary public care from the age of one until he attained the age of majority. He contended that he had been ill-treated in care and wished to obtain details of where he was kept and by whom and in what conditions in order to overcome his problems and learn about his past.

Under the applicable regulations in the United Kingdom it was the practise of the local authorities to keep a case-record in respect of every child in care.

When he was 20 years old the applicant, wishing to bring proceedings against the local authority for damages for negligence, made an application

---

[8] Eur. Court H.R., Vermeire judgment of 29.11.1991, Series A no. 214-C.

[9] N.J. 1980, no. 480.

for discovery of the local authority's case-record made during his period in care. This application was rejected by the High Court and leave to appeal was refused by the House of Lords.

In the proceedings before the Commission and the Court in Strasbourg the question arose whether the above refusal constituted a breach of the applicant's right to private life under Article 8 of the Convention.

The local authority's main argument in objecting to discovery was that it would be contrary to public interest: the principal contributors to those case records were medical practitioners, school teachers, police and probation officers, social workers, foster parents etc.. Their contribution to the case-records was treated in the strictest confidence and it was in the interest of the effective conduct of the care system that such records should be as full and frank as possible. If discovery were ordered, the public interest in the proper operation of the child-care service would be jeopardised since the contributors would be reluctant to be frank in their reports in the future.

The Commission considered that, since the information compiled and maintained by the local authority related to the applicant's basic identity, and indeed provided the only coherent record of his early childhood and formative years, the refusal to allow him unimpeded access to the file constituted a (positive) interference with the applicant's right to respect for his private life, which had to be justified under para. 2 of Article 8.[10]

The Court followed a different approach. Notwithstanding the margin of appreciation left to the State, the Court found that a legal system fails to respect the above principle of proportionality, when it does not provide for an independent authority to decide whether access should be granted in cases where a contributor fails to answer or withholds consent.[11]

It follows from the above that, even where a breach consists in the failure by a State to secure, through its legal or administrative system, the right to respect for private life, Article 8 is capable of producing direct effect: what matters is that States are under a duty to respect private life. That must also be the claim of the individual before the domestic courts.

Positive obligations are obligations for the State to act. The necessary corrollary for the individual is a claim towards the State that the latter fulfills its obligation to act, failing which the State must be found in breach of its Convention-obligations.

The next question is of course what the reaction of the domestic court is. The latter may be hesitant to take the place of the legislator, often inspired by a concern for (or excuse of?) legal certainty. If that is the case, the case may be brought before the Convention organs. The case of Vermeire mentioned above is an example thereof.

Where an interference with a right consists in positive action, the outcome of the so-called proportionality test under para. 2 of Article 8 may vary

---

[10] Gaskin v. the United Kingdom, Commission Report 13.11.87 Series A No 160, p. 28.

[11] Eur. Court H.R. Gaskin judgment of 7.7.89 Series A No 160.

according to the subjective interpretation by the national judge, having regard to the particular facts of the case at issue. Whilst the substantive norm contrives to confer direct effect, whether containing positive or negative obligations, its acceptable limitations are also defined by the Convention organs through its case-law on the justification issue. In the light of the case-to-case approach applied by the Convention organs the jurisprudence in this area conveys a method but does not secure a particular result.

The following example may serve as an illustration. It concerns the case of a young Moroccan national, whose deportation was being ordered from Belgium , since his presence on Belgian territory was regarded as a serious threat to the Belgian public order, following his conviction for a series of criminal offences.

The applicant's claim to stay in Belgium was based on the following considerations:
– his youth (20 at the time of the deportation order)
– he arrived in Belgium at the age of 2
– his whole family lived in Belgium
– he was learning a trade
– he was unfamiliar with his country of origin and its language
– his social readaptation was proceeding well, as evidenced by the fact that the prison leave granted to him on two occasions had not given rise to any incident.

The Belgian courts, including the Conseil d'Etat, upheld the deportation order. In balancing the applicant's interest in maintaining a family life against the public interest in the prevention of disorder and crime, the Belgian judicial authorities relied in particular on the large number of offences, the severity of the sentences imposed and a risk of his reoffending and concluded that the applicant's presence on Belgian territory was unacceptable.

The Court's conclusion was different. Its evaluation of the criminal offences was more indulgent. Moreover, while applying the same criteria, it placed greater emphasis on the applicant's family situation, the fact that he had received all his schooling in French and that his country of origin was as good as unknown to him. It therefore concluded that Article 8 had been breached by the Belgian State.[12]

The above example shows that, whereas Article 8 para. 1 is undoubtedly capable of producing a direct effect, so are the restrictions under paragraph 2 on which the Government may rely. The outcome of the proportionality test varies in each case, depending on the factual circumstances of the case and the subjective interpretation given by the national authorities concerned.

---

[12] Eur. Court H.R., Moustaquim judgment of 18.2.91, Series A No 129.

II. DEPRIVATION OF LIBERTY

Another area of law in the Convention, which may be relevant to children concerns the right to liberty. As mentioned above, the drafters of the Convention have included an explicit reference to the case of minors where deprivation of liberty is concerned. The norm in Article 5 is the right to liberty for everyone and deprivation of liberty is only permitted under certain conditions, listed exhaustively. Article 5 para. 1 (d) allows States to detain a minor, inter alia "for the purpose of bringing him before the competent legal authority". In the context of criminal process deprivation of liberty, in general, is governed by Article 5 para.1 (c) to be read in conjunction with Article 5 para. 3 of the Convention which together provide for a number of safeguards against arbitrary deprivation of liberty. The question therefore arises why is it that deprivation of liberty of minors should obey to different and apparently more lenient rules than that of adults? Does this distinction reflect the desire by States to exclude children from the process of ordinary criminal justice and place more emphasis on welfare and educational considerations?

The Convention organs have sofar provided little guidance to the domestic authorities to their difficult task in tackling the competing interests between the latter desire and the legitimate claim by a child to security of person.

In the case of a child of ten and a half years who complained to the Commission of having been detained for a few hours at a police station with two fellow pupils in order to be questioned in relation to thefts that had occurred at school, the Commission dodged the issue by answering that the above did not constitute deprivation of liberty within the meaning of Article 5 para. 1 of the Convention.[13]

Whilst the above decision may be acceptable in the light of the particular circumstances of the case (short duration, cell unlocked), the same approach seems to be much more questionable in a case involving Denmark arising out of the placement of a twelve year old boy in a psychiatric hospital ward.

The boy was born out of wedlock and the mother had custody and care of the child. After having spent a summer holiday with his father the boy, then 8 years old, refused to return to his mother. Having been placed in a children's home, he disappeared from the home and returned to the father. Father and child then went underground until the father was arrested on a charge of kidnapping. The social authorities, with the consent of the mother, placed the child in the Department of Child Psychiatry in a county hospital, from which he absconded and returned to his father. The boy and father remained in hiding for more than three years. Following a court hearing in the framework of proceedings instituted by the father in order to have the custody rights transferred to him, the father was arrested again and the child was placed in a children's home. Subsequently the mother, advised by the social authorities and with the recommendation of the family doctor, had her son admitted to

---

[13]   No 8819/79, Dec. 19.3.1981, D.R. 24, p. 158.

the child psychiatric ward of a State Hospital. Eventually the father's request to have custody tranferred to him was successful and the boy went to live with him.

The Government maintained that there was no deprivation of liberty because the child was subject to parental authority and that a placement in a hospital with this authority is a voluntary placement, even if the child disagrees. The applicant argued that children have an independent right to protection and are not completely subject to the authority of their parents.

The Commission shared the applicant's view that the rights of the holder of parental power vis-à-vis his or her children are not unlimited and do not involve unrestricted power of decision over the child and its personal conditions. An examination of the case-file revealed a normally developed 12 years old boy capable of understanding his situation and to express his opinion clearly. The Commission concluded that the placement against his will in a psychiatric ward which lasted over a period of several months, amounted to a deprivation of liberty which could not in any way be justified.[14]

For the Court however the hospitalisation of the young boy did not amount to a deprivation of liberty within the meaning of Article 5, but was "a responsible exercise by his mother of her custodial rights in the interest of the child".[15]

The above decision was far from unanimous (9 to 7), the dissenting judges having basically followed the Commission's line. The Court's qualification of the events is all the more surprising taking into account the fact that the Danish courts ultimately awarded custody to the father, which decision can only have been taken with due regard to the child's best interests.

What conclusions can be drawn from the above in answer to the question whether Article 5 produces direct effect?

In Denmark the Convention had at the time of these decisions not been incorporated into domestic law and the domestic authorities examined the above-complaint only in the light of applicable domestic law.[16] The fact that the two judicial Convention organs, the Commission and the Court came to opposite conclusions, does not mean however that no direct effect can be attributed to Article 5. In fact statistics tend to show that this provision is frequently invoked before the domestic courts in those countries where Convention-law is part of the domestic legal order. It is clear however that the benefit of the direct effect of the Convention norm decreases proportionally with the increase of room for interpretation. The clearer the wording of the Convention norm, the more ready it is for domestic consumption.

---

[14] Nielsen v. Denmark, Comm. Report 12.3.87, Series A No. 144, p. 37.

[15] Eur. Court H.R. , Nielsen judgment of 28.11.88, Series A No 144.

[16] The Convention has been incorporated into Danish Law by Act No. 285 of 29.4.1992 with effect as from 1.7.1992.

III. Fair Trial

The third area of law in which specific issues have arisen under the Convention for children is the area of administration of justice. The provision in the Convention dealing with fair trial is Article 6. One of the ingredients of fair trial is the impartiality of the judge determining the charge. The Convention organs have developped substantial case-law concerning this aspect of fair trial. According to that case-law the existence of impartiality of Article 6 para. 1 must be determined according to a subjective test, that is on the basis of the particular conviction of a particular judge in a given case and also according to an objective test, that is ascertaining whether the judge offered guarantees sufficient to exclude any legitimate doubt in this respect.

In the Netherlands criminal procedure applicable to juveniles is regulated quite differently from that concerning adult law. The underlying principle of juvenile criminal procedure is that it places much emphasis on protection and education and that it tries to establish links with the protection of juveniles in civil law in which the juvenile judge is empowered to order various protective measures.

It reflects also the concern to ensure in the interest of the children an optimal coordination of the various decisions which can be taken in respect of them aiming at their protection. It is for this reason that the juvenile judge is also the central actor in juvenile criminal procedure. In the first place he is involved in the decision whether or not to prosecute a minor. Decisions to drop charges against a minor can only be taken after consultation with the juvenile judge. The same judge is also the central figure in the investigation phase. He has all the powers of an investigating judge (obtaining evidence, hearing witnesses, obtaining expert opinions etc.) and takes all the decisions concerning detention on remand. His decisions in this respect can only be reviewed by himself. Subsequently, sitting as a single judge, he conducts the trial and gives judgment.

The above procedure gave rise to an application in Strasbourg. The applicant, a young man of 15 at the time of the events, was tried and convicted by a juvenile judge on a charge of rape. The day before the trial was to take place the applicant's lawyer challenged the judge on the ground that he was not impartial, since he had taken a number of decisions in the pre-trial phase. His challenge of the judge was rejected first by the same judge and subsequently by the Regional Court. The latter Court considered in detail the relevance of the Strasbourg case-law and in particular the judgment of the Court in the De Cubber case[17] in which the Court had considered that the successive exercise of the function of the investigating judge and first-instance trial judge by the same person was in breach of Article 6. The Regional Court was of the opinion that there was a fundamental difference between the position of a Belgian investigating judge and that of a Netherlands juvenile judge, particu-

---

[17]   Eur. Court H.R., de Cubber judgment of 26.10.84, Series A No 86.

larly as far as their independence was concerned. It further held that the above judgment did not imply that the performance of the functions of investigating judge and trial judge in the same case constituted a breach of Article 6 in all circumstances. The applicant was eventually tried and committed to an institution for the psychiatric treatment of juvenile offenders.

In the proceedings in Strasbourg the applicant complained of the lack of impartiality of the trial judge invoking Article 6 of the Convention , as the latter had dealt with his case throughout the proceedings, i.e. during the pre-trial phase as well as the trial. He pointed in particular to the fact that the same juvenile judge had ordered his detention on remand on four occasions. These decisions implied in his view that this judge had already reached the conclusion at that stage that there were "serious indications" that the applicant had committed the crime of which he stood accused.

The Court avoided giving a general appraisal of the compatibility of the above procedure with Article 6 of the Convention but limited its examination to the question whether in the case in point the applicant had legitimate doubts as to the judge's impartiality.

As far as the detention-decisions were concerned the Court noted that in finding that there were "serious indications" (ernstige bezwaren) against the applicant, the judge had merely ascertained whether there was a prima facie case against the applicant, who had moreover admitted the charge. Apart from the detention-decisions, the judge had made no other pre-trial decisions than allowing a request by the prosecution for a psychiatric examination of the applicant, which the latter had not contested.

Considering moreover that the applicant had been assisted throughout the proceedings by a lawyer there could be no question of intimidation suggested by the applicant . The Court concluded that the applicant's doubts as to the impartiality of the judge were not objectively justified and that Article 6 had *not* been breached.[18]

It is interesting to note that a proposal for the amendment of the law was sent to the Dutch Parliament in 1989, the gist of which is to remove from the juvenile judge the functions of investigating judge and reviewchamber. The juvenile judge is however to retain the power to order initial detention on remand.

The last feature corresponds to case-law of the Netherlands Supreme Court. In a judgment of 15 March 1988 the Supreme Court decided, with reference to Article 6 of the Convention, that the fact that an investigating judge who had not carried out any preliminary investigations but had given the order for initial detention on remand did not jeopardise his independence.[19]

On 13 November 1990 the Supreme Court decided however that a juvenile judge who had instituted a preliminary investigation as an investigating judge lacked impartiality if "he previously had dealings in the same case aimed

---

[18]   Eur. Court of H.R., Nortier judgment of 24.8.93, Series A No 267.
[19]   NJ 1988, no. 847.

at the collection of evidence, either as an investigating judge in the course of the preliminary investigation or in another way during the investigations preparing the case".[20]

The above approach by the Netherlands Supreme Court is very much in line with that adopted by the Strasbourg organs under Article 6 as shown in the above Nortier case, i.e. the question of impartiality within the meaning of this provision must be assessed on the basis of the facts of each case. Nevertheless the national courts in carrying out the above assessment are guided by the above-mentioned principles established by the Convention organs for the interpretation of Article 6.

CONCLUSION

In conclusion it is fair to say that basically all substantive Convention provisions are capable of producing direct effect.

The question to what extent children may draw benefit therefrom in those States where Convention law forms part of domestic law, is very much a question of subjective appreciation. Nihil obstat.

---

[20] NJ 1991, no. 219.

HANS VAN LOON

Synthesis of the Discussions at the European Conference on Monitoring Children's Rights

It is a daunting privilege for me to draw up the Summary Report of this European Conference on Monitoring Children's Rights.[1] It is a daunting task because of the variety of themes and approaches of this Conference: no one can claim to master all of them fully, and certainly not I as a relative outsider in many respects. The discussions between specialists in child research, child development, in international human rights and constitutional law have been in themselves very enriching and have underlined the multidisciplinary character of our topic and indeed, as Marta Santos Pais has emphasized, of the *United Nations Convention on the Rights of the Child* (CRC) itself. It is a privilege, however, to present this synthesis, for one whose prime focus is on, as many still see it, the somewhat esoteric field of private international law, an area which until recently few would have associated with that of human rights, and children's rights in particular. That is now rapidly changing, thanks to the CRC, because of growing common interests of the two disciplines, especially in children and families on the move: problems of international child support, custody of children, child abduction, adoption and legal status of refugee children. In several of its articles (11, 2, 21 (e), 27(4)) the CRC calls upon States to become Parties to international agreements on these matters and, because of the unprecedented success of the CRC, this has given a "children's rights aura" to the Conventions drawn up by the Hague Conference and other organizations on these topics. The co-operation which has developed with the Committee on the Rights of the Child, UNICEF and NGOs has been for me and my colleagues at The Hague very stimulating and encouraging.

The European Conference had three themes: (1) What are we monitoring?, (2) How do we do it?, and (3) a special aspect: Can the CRC be relied upon before the national courts?

---

[1] Held at Ghent (Belgium) from 11 until 14 December 1994. For the texts of the papers commented, see Part 1 of this volume.

E. Verhellen (ed.), Monitoring Children's Rights, 211–221.
© 1996 *Kluwer Law International. Printed in the Netherlands.*

I. What are we Monitoring?

Jens Qvortrup presented a paper in which he, deliberately, took a radical perspective: he went to the roots and questioned the basic assumptions underlying our accepted perceptions and attitudes towards children. What are these perceptions and what attitudes follow from them? Or, vice versa, what are these attitudes and how do they condition our perceptions? His answer is: (1) that children tend to be approached by adults in terms of what they miss – i.e. the capabilities of adulthood – rather than in terms of what they positively contribute as children, as human beings in their own right; and (2) that this "not yet" syndrome has been institutionalized by society, formalized and crystallized in laws which either declare children as a category incapable of performing certain acts, or simply ignore children (as shown by the lack of regulations for certain forms of employment of children, e.g. domestic servants).

Qvortrup, as a sociologist, questioned in particular the collective and institutionalized "not yet" syndrome. One of its symptoms is that it causes children to be eclipsed behind the concept of the "family", which is generally used as the basic parameter for demographic statistics, social research and policy. However, this tends to obscure essential facts about children's lives: e.g. if in demographic statistics one counts only families, half of the children have no siblings, if one counts children, the figure is only 20%. There is a need, then, for what Qvortrup calls the autonomy of the concept of "child" and "childhood" – not to be confused with the concept of autonomy of the child, as Nigel Cantwell stressed. This conceptual autonomy of childhood, also emphasized by Eugeen Verhellen, will then lead to new ways of collecting statistics, new directions for research, new orientations for policy and a critical examination of existing laws, which is particularly important in view of the diminishing demographic significance of children in the ageing population of Europe.

So far, all members of the panel agreed, but a lively discussion took place on some of the consequences Qvortrup drew from his analysis, in particular his criticism of the CRC for not going far enough in according "distributive justice" and political rights to children. Nigel Cantwell warned that defenders of children's rights should remain realistic and credible, which is best done by insisting on the implementation by States of their obligations under the CRC rather than by demanding radical changes going beyond the Convention.

To this sociological perspective Ferran Casas added the social-psychologist's view, by pointing out how deeply rooted the invisibility of children is in our collective consciousness (or unconsciousness), making it particularly resistant to changing the idea of some scientists that information given by children is not reliable, or the view that children should not be interviewed. Casas highlighted in this respect the responsibility of the media, both negatively in that they tend to reinforce the "not yet syndrome", and positively as a powerful tool for change to make children visible again.

Målfrid Flekkøy, as a psychologist, further added a dynamic developmental perspective of evolving capacities of the child. She presented the results of recent research showing that there is not such a thing in the life of a child as "the age of reason". Rather, it is the case that a child's intellectual and emotional capabilities, as well as the child's capacity to participate in the making of decisions, (1) evolve progressively and (2) moreover that this progressive evolution starts at birth. However, if this development is to be successful, it is essential that the child be heard, may give opinions and participate in decisions.

All this I think was interesting in itself but all the more so where Målfrid Flekkøy pointed to a number of practical implications which are, in fact, potentially quite powerful and indeed radical. That her paper did not provoke a debate in the panel whereas Qvortrup's radicalism did, is I think for three reasons. The first is that she offered a perspective which is not simply a reversal of the "not yet syndrome" into a "children-should-have-all-the-rights-of-adults" recipe, but a more, as one might call it, "functional" view in which the rights given to a child are adapted to various steps of the child's development. The second reason is that rather than seeing participation and protection as opposites – protection having the smell of "paternalism" – she favoured an approach based on combining the two. The third reason is that while Qvortrup appeared critical of the CRC because of what he saw as "taken for granted stuff" and "benign paternalism", Målfrid Flekkøy suggested that the functional approach could be applied right now, within the framework of the Convention, referring as she did to her experiences in Norway as the first ombudsman for children.

In my view, this new developmental approach faces us with enormous challenges, precisely because the balance of "capacity to participate" and "need for protection" will not only vary per individual child, but will also depend on the age group – and Målfrid Flekkøy told us that even the voice of a three-year-old may be heard "if the situation is tailored to suit the child". Think of conflict situations in the family: divorce and kidnapping by one of the parents, when a child may be exposed to heavy psychological pressure from the two opposing sides. Giving "due weight", as Article 12, 1 of the CRC requires, to the child's view in such situations will be a very delicate operation.

Nigel Cantwell finally reminded, as Marta Santos Pais and others did, that the CRC should be read as a whole and that no single fundamental right is more fundamental than others. I agree, although I could imagine that there are circumstances where a State is in such difficulties that one has to accept that that State may, temporarily, derogate from certain of its obligations under the Convention but then still not from others (e.g. prohibition of torture, cf. Article 15 of the European Human Rights Convention). Certainly, from the point of view of systematic monitoring of the Convention, it would be disastrous to favour certain rights and not others; this would be tantamount to allowing States to determine the scope of their accountability for those "less important" fundamental rights. One would, therefore, hope that the Committee will never, e.g. in order to reduce the pressure of its workload, draw up a hierarchy of children's rights.

II. FORMAL AND PROCEDURAL ASPECTS OF MONITORING

While the focus of the paper presented by Vande Lanotte/Goedertier was on the monitoring and implementation of the CRC, we were also offered, for purposes of comparison, examples of monitoring systems in the regional European context, in particular that of the *European Convention on Human Rights and Fundamental Freedoms* (ECHR).

Both the CRC and the ECHR are human rights instruments which apply to children but their scope and international monitoring systems are quite different. As Vande Lanotte/Goedertier pointed out, there is a relationship between the nature of the human rights guaranteed by these texts and the fact that the ECHR, essentially limited to civil and political rights, has a (quasi-)judicial machinery in Strasbourg for individual complaints, while the CRC, also including social, economic and cultural rights, has "only" a system of periodic review of reports submitted by States Parties. Why is that so? The answer is *not* that social and economic rights are not "rights", nor, as James Himes stressed, that they are necessarily always less precise (think of the obligation to provide for compulsory and free primary education for all (Article 28 CRC)). These are rights which in most States can only be implemented step-by-step depending on progressively available resources and evolving conditions for which a judicial monitoring system is less appropriate. This, as well as political reasons, also determined the fate of the civil and political rights in the CRC.

A reporting system such as provided for by the CRC also exists for other international conventions; but this one is very special. Marta Santos Pais explained its nature and philosophy. Its purpose is co-operation, not sanctioning; it stresses the need for dialogue rather than a punitive attitude. Co-operation and dialogue provide the second reason why this system is so special – not just to States, but beyond their governments and bureaucracies to the civic society, including children. A unique feature of the Convention is that it requires States: (1) to inform adults and children of children's rights under the Convention (Article 42) which is basic for advocacy of children's rights, and (2) to make the reports widely available to adults and children in their country (Article 44 (6)). As Himes pointed out, it is here that the reporting system can be turned into a potentially very powerful political instrument at the national level because this enables people to participate; it subjects States to public scrutiny.

Let us now return to international monitoring. The Committee thus entertains a "constructive dialogue" with the State Parties which is unique and,

I think, can only work so well because children's rights are relatively less controversial than adults' rights. It is fascinating to see how the Committee has managed to give meaning to this concept of constructive dialogue, despite serious practical constraints – in part the result of its success in terms of frequency and number of ratifications (there is a constant danger for the Committee to become the victim of its own success). One feels that the Committee is also constantly monitoring itself, its own way of operation, improving working methods, actively seeking co-operation with other organizations, including the Hague Conference on Private International Law, to provide a broad basis for participation.

Hardly had the Committee been created when it decided to meet more frequently than once a year as originally foreseen. The next innovative step was the creation of the "pre-sessional working group" two months before the official meeting to give advance notice to States on the principal problems raised by their reports so as to make the discussions at the formal session more meaningful. Next, the Committee drew up its "general guidelines" to assist States in the preparation of their reports, but with the additional advantage of facilitating participation by other organizations and NGOs. One important and again innovative feature of the guidelines is that States are asked to describe the mechanisms which they have adopted for the co-ordination of activities concerning the rights of the child and of the monitoring of their compliance with the Convention. To give an example, closer to home, the Committee will now, in the context of Articles 11 (2) and 21 (e) of the Convention, encourage States to become Parties to the Hague Conventions on Child Abduction and Intercountry Adoption. I might suggest that a similar question be put in the context of Article 27(4) concerning international child support in relation to the 1973 Hague Conventions on the Law Applicable to and on the Enforcement of Decisions Relating to Maintenance Obligations.

Heartening is also the link made by the Committee between the reporting system and Article 4, which urges States to seek international co-operation, where needed, to help them implement the social, economic and cultural rights of children. States may ask for assistance through their reports and the Committee's comments may help States to be more successful in obtaining development aid. An interesting perspective here would be international co-operation to find the best child care alternative for abandoned and institutionalized children in many countries in Africa, Asia, Latin America and Eastern Europe, in the context of Articles 20 and 21 of the CRC and of the new *Hague Convention of 29 May 1993 on Protection of Children and Co-operation in Respect of Intercountry Adoption*.

It is interesting to see how the Committee, as Vande Lanotte/Goedertier indicated, in its "urgent action procedure" bends the reporting systems somewhat in the direction of a quasi-judicial examination, especially in case of violations of civil and political rights. I might add the "informal regional visits" (the successful visit to Viet Nam concerning juvenile justice was mentioned), and one can only be deeply impressed by the way the Committee has in record time demonstrated an amazing degree of organizational creativity. There may be reason, as Vande Lanotte/Goedertier suggested, to adapt or improve the pre-sessional working group or the general guidelines, but on the whole the system has been remarkably productive and the Committee deserves our full co-operation, support and encouragement. One senses that there is a strategy behind the Committee's monitoring policy and, as Marta Santos Pais clearly explained, this strategy has everything to do with the Convention's philosophy. The Committee is guided by the four underlying principles of: (1) non-discrimination, which makes it particularly attentive to the "invisible" marginalized children that do not appear in official statistics (street children, domestic servants, child prostitutes); (2) the best interest of the child, which also has implications for the allocation of money to investment in resources for children (the Committee presses governments to give priority to policies for children and to account for that in their budgets, both at the central level and at the less visible local level); (3) participation, a particular challenge because it is here that, consistent with what one saw in the context of the first theme, lack of awareness and resistance are considerable because participation means that adults admit being criticized by children; and finally (4) survival and development (this probes the Committee to urge States and communities to define measurable standards for the progressive improvement of health systems, etc. in particular, in the context of national action plans). Above all, there is this inspiring vision of unity in diversity: all the children of the world, each according to their own needs, have rights that must be recognized, respected and fulfilled.

As Philip Alston emphasized, the Committee has a very strong supporter in UNICEF and, as James Himes pointed out, UNICEF sees the CRC as an important tool for: (1) advocacy (the mobilization of shame); (2) programming; (3) legal work. As far as programming is concerned, the UNICEF Center in Florence has developed a four-step implementation strategy, in particular for developing countries, which includes the setting of measurable, time-bound standards. This strategy has proved to be important for the realization of economic and social rights in the framework of national action plans.

Interestingly, for a lawyer like myself, Himes, Alston and also Cantwell stressed the importance of the CRC as a legal tool, an instrument for social change. Himes suggested that more emphasis be given to the use of court action and legislative reforms. Alston also stressed the empowering function rights for children. What I also sensed in these comments was a note of caution to the Committee: "you are doing a marvellous job, but please do concentrate on monitoring the Convention as a human rights instrument. See yourselves as a catalyst to encourage others e.g. States, NGOs and individuals to react to the many flagrant violations of children's rights, otherwise you will become too heavily politically involved and you may put the constructive dialogue at risk". The difficulty here, I think, is that the Committee needs to maintain the dialogue both with governments and with the population. For a dialogue one needs credibility in the eyes of both and there may well be a conflict of credibilities.

Pascale Boucaud and Juan Bandrés Molet brought us back to monitoring within Europe. Pascale Boucaud examined the international individual petitions procedure before the European Commission and the European Court of Human Rights in Strasbourg. As we have already seen, the ECHR deals almost exclusively with civil and political rights for "everyone within [the] jurisdiction" of a Contracting State. What is the significance of this system for the protection of children's rights? Although formally a judgment of the Strasbourg Court only concerns the defending State (Article 50 (ECHR)), in actual fact these decisions have had an impact on other States as well. A series of highly important and bold judgments of the Court concerning Article 8 (ECHR) have changed the landscape of family law in Europe and have considerably strengthened children's rights. The famous *Marckx* case against Belgium in 1979 put an end to discriminatory treatment of children born out of wedlock, not only in Belgium but also in the Netherlands and elsewhere. It is also interesting that the Court has condemned measures of expulsion of family members with whom a child had developed a close relationship: human rights law may so interfere with migration law (*Berrehab* v. *The Netherlands*). Since a number of rights of the European Convention have been literally taken over in the CRC (e.g. the rights to freedom of thought, conscience, religion and expression, and the right to respect for one's private and family life), it would seem important for the Committee to follow closely the Strasbourg case law. A case in point is the judgment concerning *John Gaskin* versus *the United Kingdom*, where the Court liberally acknowledged a right of access of a child to personal data concerning the child's origin, based again on Article 8 of the ECHR.

I think Kerstin Ekman and Pascale Boucaud deserve our sympathy and support for the idea of a Protocol to the ECHR, which would fill certain gaps in that Convention as well as supplement the CRC, such as the right to a nationality and protection against child labour. This is a matter in which the Committee, as a "monitor of monitors" (Himes), may take an interest. That may also be the case for the European Charter for Children in Europe, adopted by the European Parliament, about which Bandrés Molet has spoken.

III. Self-executing Character of the CRC

The third theme, the self-executing character of the CRC, is obviously a lawyer's delight but it is much more than that. It is of crucial importance that wherever possible children's rights be enforced by the courts in each State Party. It means extending a State's accountability at the national level;

it adds to the acknowledgement of children's rights as rights, of children as persons as Jean-Pierre Rosenczveig stressed; it empowers children; and it may have a multiplier effect on the information about children's rights. From this perspective, it is disappointing that when ratifying the Convention some countries, such as Germany, made statements to the effect that they consider that the CRC cannot be relied upon by individuals in courts, and also, that the French *Cour de cassation* categorically declined to accept the direct applicability of the Convention's provisions. This is disappointing because, as Alen/Pas emphasized, (1) not all the rights of the Convention should be put in the same box, and (2) domestic courts are very well able to distinguish between those provisions capable of having direct effect and those which are not because, in essence, this is a matter of interpretation a court's function *par excellence*.

It is true that not all constitutional law systems admit that treaty provisions, even if they are formulated in a clear and precise manner and do not require any further legislative measures at the domestic level, may be applied by their courts. This is the case, in particular, of the United Kingdom constitution, and of other, "dualist" systems following that model, where the effect of a treaty depends upon a process of transformation, on a legislative act which purports to incorporate the treaty. In many other, "monist" constitutional systems, however, a treaty which has been approved by the State and which has entered into force on the international plane automatically becomes part of the law of the State, without any separate act of incorporation being required. This is the case at least for Belgium, France, Luxembourg, the Netherlands, Portugal, Spain, Switzerland, the United States, the Latin American States, Japan and former dependencies of France and other countries mentioned.

It is in the countries of the latter category that courts may apply the norms of a Convention directly, provided they meet certain criteria regarding precision, clarity and capability of producing immediate effect. As Maud Buquicchio concluded, all of the articles of the ECHR that confer rights are capable of producing direct effect. The case law of the Strasbourg Commission and Court has comforted courts in European States adhering to the "monist" approach in giving that direct effect to the substantive provisions of the ECHR. But what about the CRC?

As Alen/Pas points out, there is no *general* answer. There are articles in the CRC (those on civil and political rights on life, personal security, right to family life) which were literally taken over from the ECHR. Does it make sense, in a "monist" system such as France or the Netherlands, to say that the same right to family life which can be enforced by a national court when it is found in the ECHR, cannot be enforced by that same court if it is included in the CRC? No, says Alen/Pas, and I agree. What about social, economic and cultural rights, many of which are also found in other Conventions? Those rights are generally not considered to be self-executing. There is one important exception, however, and that is that individuals may rely on such articles (e.g. an article which provides primary education for all) in a case where a State would go against such a treaty norm (e.g. when it would exclude certain children from an existing right to primary education for all – the so-called "standstill" effect). Alen/Pas suggests, therefore, that the social and economic rights of the CRC should have a similar effect. That is a little more subtle, but again I would agree in principle. Finally, there are other provisions which are not taken from other Conventions but which are of crucial importance to children. Here I am more hesitant than Alen/Pas, at least with respect to the self-executing character of Article 3 (1), the best interest of the child. There is no question that this is a fundamental principle, one that, as Marta Santos Pais explained, underlies the Convention as a whole. But that is just the point: it is not an (absolute) rule. There are other important principles . The CRC itself recognizes (in Article 18) that parents have primary responsibility for the upbringing of their child; it is not enough to establish that a child would be better off with other parents in order to terminate the care of the original parents. I also disagree with the decision of the Belgian Court of *Courtrai* (*Kortrijk*) quoted in Alen/Pas' paper which overlooks the fact that the Child Abduction Conventions are based on a general principle i.e. that kidnapped children should be returned except in narrowly defined circumstances. Refusing (or delaying) their return just because their "best interest" in a specific case might militate, in the eyes of the court of the jurisdiction to which the child has been illegally removed, in favour of the child staying in that jurisdiction, would undermine the very system of the worldwide Hague and the regional European and Inter-American countries; it is for a very good reason that Article 11 of the CRC itself encourages States to accede to these instruments.

This does not remove, however, from my agreement in principle with the approach taken by Alen/Pas and we should accept that there are provisions in the CRC which lend themselves to being invoked by or on behalf of children before the courts. The Belgian courts have been courageous and one would very much hope that the French *Cour de Cassation* would revise its categorical denial of the self-executing character of the Convention, the more so because that might inspire courts in countries that have copied the French "monist" system, e.g. in Africa, to follow that example. I understand that there is hope. I think the Committee of the CRC might be well advised to take, at some point, a look into this. The question is not new to the Committee, as Marta Santos Pais pointed out. Would it not be possible for the Committee to draw up a tentative list of those articles which it feels are, from an objective point of view, self-executing? The Committee might then suggest, in consultation with countries which accept the idea of direct effect of treaty norms, that their courts apply these articles directly.

CONCLUSION

Some years ago, when the CRC was not yet completed, I wrote an article on the draft Convention[2] in which I concluded that the Convention would probably long depend for its efficiency on other international instruments such as the Covenants of the UN, the ECHR, the ILO Conventions and Hague Conventions. I tended to see the Convention as a "not yet" Convention. I did not need to wait long to discover that I had underestimated the Convention's potential because the negotiations on the new *Hague Convention on Protection of Children and Co-operation in Respect of Intercountry Adoption*, which we started negotiating at The Hague in 1990, received a considerable impetus from the CRC. Nevertheless, this Conference has also shown that the CRC and its Committee should not be seen in isolation but as the focal instrument and body in a network of instruments and bodies dealing with children's rights. When we look at Article 32 on child labour, we should think of the ILO and its Conventions. When we look at Article 22 on refugees, we should remember UNHCR and the 1951 Refugee Convention and its 1967 Protocol, but also the Red Cross, the ECHR, and the Hague Convention on Protection of Minors. In many ways, the CRC is a gateway which opens our eyes to children's rights protected in other Conventions, as well as in domestic law. Children's rights are out there, sometimes hidden in adult's rights, and the CRC helps us to notice or rediscover and re-assert them.

Of monitoring we learned that there are many forms (formal, informal, international, national, regional and local) which are most effective when used in combination, but also in an intelligent manner: go to the news media, to the politicians, to court, but don't go to the media for a judgment or to court for political advice. Most importantly, we realized once more that monitoring is no one person's privilege. Everyone is at least potentially involved, in particular children themselves. Participation by children in the various avenues for monitoring children's rights is empowering and reinforces those rights.

My third conclusion is that there is a need for close co-operation. The Convention has a formidable potential and has given rise to expectations worldwide. We must help the Committee not to frustrate those expectations. There are also, as yet unthought of, new opportunities for co-operation in children's matters between East and West, North and South; not just at the governmental level, but also at the level of the civic society. If you have an organization for protection of children's rights in Europe, why should you not look for a partner in Eastern Europe, Africa, Asia, or Latin America?

I have been asked, at the request of one of the workshops, to transmit their deep concern about perhaps the most invisible of the invisible: children at war, who are increasingly victims and – a new phenomena – targets of hostility; children in former Yugoslavia, in Rwanda, in situations where all our

---

[2] "Der Entwurf einer Konvention über die Rechte des Kindes im Kontext anderer internationaler Übereinkommen" in *Forum Jugendhilfe*, Vol. 3/4, 1988, p. 28.

Conventions and monitoring systems fall short, despite incredible work by professionals and volunteers alike. Let us not forget those children and those courageous people who are out there trying to help. Let us hope that Conferences such as these may help, just a little, to reinforce the idea that children are human beings and vulnerable human beings, in need of special assistance and protection, but also subjects of fundamental rights and freedoms.

PART TWO

MARIA BOUVERNE-DE BIE

The Monitoring of Children's Rights in Relation to Youth Cultures

The monitoring of children's rights focuses on two key problems concerning the monitoring mechanism and in particular on the reporting system, viz. *what* is to be reported and *by whom*? The frame of reference to look for an answer for these questions is the "children's rights movement" and is based upon an image of children as (growing up to be) autonomous, competent and responsible persons. This image is not empirical but *normative*: it concerns a pedagogic norm which will have to be realized in different ways according to the concrete situations and positions in which children and young people find themselves and with the contribution of *adults*. In this respect the striving for children's rights links up with a central theme from which *education* has departed for time immemorial, viz. helping children and young people to grow up to personal autonomy. The monitoring of children's rights therefore also involves the evaluation of educational practices, also from the point of view of children and young people themselves. The debate on youth cultures offers some clues in this respect.

I. THE TERM "YOUTH CULTURE"

Just like the term "children's rights" the term "youth culture" suggests that children and young people form a group that can be distinguished from other groups in society. This suggestion can be criticized; the differences in mutual situations in which children and young people find themselves might eventually be bigger than the differences between children and adults. In relation to education the term "youth culture" is nevertheless clarifying, because it draws attention to the experience of young people themselves: to the way in which they account for what they experience. Making this experience socially visible demands the fulfilment of a number of minimum conditions, viz. that young people, from a stuctural point of view, are for a long period of time as young people involved with each other, in other words that they have a particular social situation in common – and that they have to solve mutual problems in this mutual situation. As a result of these structural

E. Verhellen (ed.), Monitoring Children's Rights, 225–240.
© 1996 *Kluwer Law International. Printed in the Netherlands.*

conditions also adults play an inherent active part in the construction of youth cultures.[1]

II. The "Social Specifity" of Youth

The first condition to be able to talk about "youth culture" is that education is organized in such a way that there is a defined youth period; this definition is usually the delineation of a period of minimum school age. In most western countries this process was executed round the turn of the century and actually realized after the First World War. The existence of a defined youth period enabled and enables young people to acquire "room for themselves" and to go by both their contemporaries and adults for their development. "Being young together" became a social phenomenon and led to considering "youth" in terms of "youth existence" , i.e as a proper historical-social space. This youth existence is traditionally divided into three domains: the socalled first, second and third environment. The *first environment* contains the world of the family, relatives and other possible intimate relations with adults. The *second environment* contains the broad field of institutionalized interventions (from the authorities) with regard to youths and aims at the development of their competence to function socially. To the second environment belong first of all the school and following naturally from that youth protection and youth help.

The *third environment* is considered to be the source of the *social specifity* of youth. It concerns the terrain on which young people, apart from the interventions from the first and second environment, maintain and cultivate an own terrain.[2]

This notion of youth existence in terms of first, second and third environment led to the arising of an *ideology of youth*, from which it is attempted to weld diverse aspects of youth existence into a *global image* of "the" youth, which determines the *expected* and eventually also the *actual* behaviour of youths. From this ideology of youth the image of youth is historically-sociologically[3] framed: young people are, *different* than adults, seen as pre-

---

[1]   J. Janssen & J. de Hart, Jeugdcultuur: een kind van haar tijd, in : Jeugd en Samenleving, 21e jrg., 1991, nr. 2/3, pp. 68–85.

[2]   J. van Hessen & C. Klaassen, Jeugd in verleden en heden, Een historisch-sociologische benadering, in : C. Klaassen, Jeugd als sociaal fenomeen, Identiteit, socialisatie en jeugdcultuur in theorie en onderzoek, Amersfoort, Leuven, Acco, 1991, pp. 1O5–128.

[3]   As opposed to the opinion of young people as "constructed reality" which says – following a.o. Ariès – that youth is a recent "discovery" and even "in-vention", the historical-sociological approach assumes that the formation of a definition of youth is a historical constant in the approach of the human life cycle. Thus the concept of youth is to be seen as a *process of sedimentation*: also in the current youth order one finds relicts of earlier times. In this way four themes can be distinguished within the ideology of youth, viz. * the *charismatic* theme, derived from the religious world. In this theme youth is seen as pre-eminently enthusiastic,

eminently "idealistic", a "promising" future, "more sincere" and "more creative" than adults.

This ideology of youth was strikingly present in the pedagogic appreciation of the youth movement for example – in western countries the most dominant form of youth work during the interbellum and until the fifties. Young people were encouraged to *organize* themselves in the youth movement, and from the experience of being young together to prepare themselves for the building of a harmonious society.[4] In numbers the youth movement only reached part of the youth, especially middle class young people, who were on average member of a youth movement for a couple of years. The *influence* of the youth movement however was more far-reaching; within the notion of the third environment the youth movement stressed its distinctive features as being *ideal-typical* for youth existence and young people who did not take part in it were problematically pointed to as "non-organized youth".

III. YOUTH AS AREA OF TENSION

Also nowadays the image of "the" youth is to an important extent ideologically framed; the – sometimes very heated – discussions about the "rudderlessness" or the "commitment" of today's youth respectively show this. This kind of discussions are based upon the premise that young people develop a specific style of personality originating from an individual appropriation of youth existence in a particular time. The "youth movement youth" from the fifties thus stands for a different type of youth than what present young people model for. This premise is based upon a relatively narrow basis of perception, viz. upon those situations in which young people draw attention to themselves by presenting themselves *in a striking manner* (with regard to adults) and by acting as a *group*. On the other hand for the large majority of youths the youth period passes little noticed because of the bounds with the world of adults through family, school, work and spare time and because of the social control resulting from these. Youth cultural behaviour is therefore often "negociated behaviour": leaving behind relations of *independence* and learning to take up *responsibilities*. Youth cultural behaviour is not merely

---

idealistic, committed and prepared to go to great lenghts; * the *progressive* theme, derived from the Age of Enlightment, and in which youth stands for a promi-sing future, a better world; young people have the task to do everything better than adults; * the *non-conformistic* theme, derived from Romanticism. In this theme youth is seen as more pure and sincere than adults. The youth does not adapt to, on the contrary resists to the world of adults which compromised itself; * the *activism* theme, derived from the middle classes, and in which youth is seen in terms of great deeds, decisiveness and sense of initiative. Young people are a guarantee for creative unrest and rational sense of enterprise. see : J. van Hessen & C. Klaassen, Jeugd in verleden en heden, *op.cit.*, p. 112.

[4] see for example, K. Schweizer, M. van Lieshout, I. van der Zande (red.), Van de straat. Een beeld van honderdvijftig jaar jeugdcultuur in Nederland, Amersfoort, Academische Uitgeverij Amersfoort/Jeugd en Samenleving, 1993.

as the ideology of youth suggests the expression of collective experiences, in other words a *reaction* of young people to their surroundings. Youth culture might just as well be the expression of individual fantasy: the emotion young people experience from dressing in a particular way, adopting an attitude and forming an image of themselves with regard to other young people and with regard to the surroundings.[5] In this respect "youth" does not as much refer to age group and/or population category as to the *social organization* of this group.[6]

In this light youth cultures are not merely to be seen as the expression of the character of an age. They just as much indicate the areas of tension which – i.c. young – people experience in this day and age and they provide us with an image of the possibilities and difficulties people experience to make their lives concrete. An as concrete and empirical as possible view on these areas of tension, possibilities and difficulties is an important element in the monitoring of children's rights on several levels.

First of all: both the cultural behaviour of young people itself and the social framing of youth existence through the ideology of youth indicates which borders are drawn for and by young people between independence and responsibility, or in respect of the monitoring of children's rights: how the socalled objective and subjective rights of children are weighed against each other.[7] Analyses of youth cultures might provide an entrance to make these abstract rights concrete and to bring out into public discussion their checking standards.

Secondly analyses of youth cultures may contribute to the refinement of the theme of children's rights in its own right. The significance of the children's rights theme lies in the attention for the *interaction* between pedagogic normation and juridical regulation and jurisdiction regarding the position of children and young people in our society. In other words the attention goes to an analysis of *society* from the frame of reference from "right, room and

---

[5] S. Frith, The sociology of youth, Ormskirk, Causeway Press ltd., 1984, p. 31.

[6] S. Frith, The sociology of youth, in : M. Haralambos (ed.), Sociology, New Directions, Ormskirk, Causeway Press, 1985, pp. 304 e.v.

[7] Under the objective rights we understand the "well-being rights" and "protection rights" of children and young people, i.e. rights where the "interest" and not in the first place the "right to self-decision" of the child or young person prevails, and which involve a duty from adults to do something (well-being rights) or to neglect something (protection rights). The subjective rights of children contain their "claiming rights" to maintenance, care, education, etc., their "freedom rights" to opinion, acquisition of information..., their "jurisdiction rights" to act factually and judicially (e.g. as concerned party in a dispute) and their "immunity rights" to fysical and psychic integrity, to privacy and to non-intervention.

see : K. Raes, De morele betekenis van het vertoog over de rechten van het kind, in : E. Verhellen, e.a., (red.), Kinderrechtengids (KIDS), Commentaren, regelgeving, rechtspraak en nuttige informatie over de maatschappelijke en juridische positie van het kind, Gent, Mys & Breesh, sept. 1994, dl. 1–1.1., pp. 41 e.v.

respect".[8] for children. When unlinked from this social analysis it is not inconceivable that the theme of children's rights itself acts as a theme of youth ideology, the concept of youth being framed in terms of a generally assumed autonomy and competence. Such framing leaves unnoticed the concrete, often very different situations in which young people grow up and in which processes of *social inequality* play an important role. Not all young people (and not all adults) experience the same possibilities towards autonomy and responsibility. In this respect the research of youth cultures provides important indications, a.o. in the difference that is made between socalled "youth subcultures" and "youth countercultures",[9] thus drawing attention to the central meaning of both the home environment and the level of education in young people's mode of living and possibilities of action. Here home environment and level of education are more than simply "explanatory factors". They also indicate within which *limitations* and by means of which *instruments* young people attempt to give meaning and form to their own situations from often *contradictory* feelings and considerations. These contradictions show a – in certain respects poignant, c.q. cynical.[10] – paradox, viz. that youth cultural *resistance* in its class and sex specific aspects eventually unwillingly leads to the *reproduction* of existing relations.[11] The differences according to home environment and level of education, a constant in consecutive youth cultures.[12] refer to a difference in social position and hence a difference in *experience*: to give meaning to your personal life as an individual is a highly appreciated value if it is also possible to live through it as a factor of experience.[13] With respect to the monitoring of children's rights this means that the debate on the *individualized rights* of children can and may not be unlinked from this context either and must be related to the discussion on the

---

[8] M. De Winter, De kwaliteit van het kinderlijke bestaan, Bunnik, Landelijke Vereniging voor Thuiszorg, 1990.

[9] Under "youth *subcultures*" we understand youth cultures borne by young people from the working class; these youth cultures maintain a close bound with the culture of their parents. The term "*youth counter cultures*" stands for youth cultures developed by young people from the middle class and with a higher education; these youth cultures to a lesser extent lean against the parental environment and are developed on the basis of intellectual selfconsciousness, see : R. Abma, Jeugd en tegencultuur, Een theoretische verkenning, Nijmegen, Sun, 1990.

[10] see for example, W. Vollenbergh, De tijd van negeren is voorbij. Een conferentie over omgaan met extreem-rechtse jongeren, in : Jeugd en Samenleving, 22e jrg., 1992, nr. 11, pp. 690-695.

[11] D. van Zuilen & C. Klaassen, Jeugd tussen systeem en leefwereld, de CCCS-benadering van jeugd, in : C. Klaassen, Jeugd als sociaal fenomeen, *op.cit.*, pp. 63–82

[12] see : D. Matza, Subculturele jeugdtradities, in : Jeugd en Samenleving, 16e jrg., 1986, nr. 8/9, pp. 483–5O7 (Dutch translation of : Subterrean traditions of youth, in : American Academy of Political and Social Science, 1961, 338, pp. 1O2–118); D. Matza, Position and behaviour patterns of youth, in : E. Farris (ed.), Handbook of modern sociology, Chicago, 1962, pp. 191–216.

[13] see for example, H. De Witte, Conformisme, radicalisme en machteloosheid. Een onderzoek naar de sociaal-culturele en sociaal-economische opvattingen van arbeiders in Vlaanderen, Leuven, Hiva, 1990.

conditions on which these rights can be made concrete. Here the debate on the "rights of children" touches at its closest the debate on the development of the welfare state, i.e. not merely the debate on equal chances of participation of children and adults but at the same time also the debate on the *solidarity* to be accomplished in a society in order to make these chances of participation effective. Finally: as a pedagogic norm the theme of children's rights provides a frame of reference for a respectful contact with children and young people. The checking of existing educational practices to this norm is an *intervention* in the frames of integration that people form going about with each other and which must be legitimized as such. It is an absolute requirement that a pedagogic relation between children/young people and adults is realized, just as its consistent application in practice is an absolute requirement. With respect to the checking of the application remains the tension between a norm laid down from a "child oriented" point of view and the support and security which educators themselves (first of all parents) may experience. This tension deserves the necessary attention, because it stresses the necessity of linking up the theme of children's rights towards again the very different concrete situations in which it is applied – such as situations of poverty – as well. To put it differently: in this light the theme of children's rights is a theme *within* the debate on human rights rather than a particularization of the latter.

IV. YOUTH AS "IDEAL" VERSUS YOUTH AS "PROBLEM"

Analyses of youth cultures may also provide an important entrance towards the realization of the collective rights of children, i.e. those rights which can only be realized as a collective good, such as the right to peaceful and safe surroundings, the right to child-loving public areas... It concerns those rights which are vital for the chances of development of children and after all of: all vulnerable groups in society, because they involve the development of values which can only exist as "shared values": values such as tolerance, participation, community spirit.[14] It also concerns those rights which are under pressure in both the debate on human rights and the debate on the modernization of society – including recent developments in the welfare state. After all, whilst the classic basic rights grant citizens an atmosphere of liberty, the rights to collective goods – the socalled social basic rights – on the other hand involve claims to the achievements of the authorities. In this light the attention for social basic rights has been described as a *"breach of democracy"*, i.e. as a dynamic which fundamentally thwarts an unequivocal and universally applying formulation of human rights, because

---

[14] K. Raes, De morele betekenis van het vertoog over de rechten van het kind, *op.cit.*, p. 41.

it forces a society to constantly and incessantly revise the conditions for a *worthy existence*.[15]

In this light analyses of youth cultures point out that the socalled "social specifity" of youth is not unequivocally approached. The as said before ideologically framed image of young people (and of children) raised a.o. in the media and in pedagocic and/or political discussions varies between two main types: "youth as ideal" and "youth as problem".[16] Notably the image of "youth as ideal" especially pops up in times of booming economy and is borne by studying young people. The image of "youth as problem" especially pops up in times of slowing economy and is borne by employed and unemployed young people with on the whole little education. "Youth as problem" refers to concern about the comings and goings of the "youth growing up", their behaviour, political opinions, leisure time activities, etc. It always concerns behaviour and/or situations considered to be problematic, behaviour with a high news value which gets broad (media) attention. The varying representation of young people as "ideal" or as "problem" is expressed both on the level of concrete educational practices and on the level of formation of theory thereof. The "support with the growth towards personal autonomy" – as the core of the pedagocic task – was in most western countries during the postwar period considered as a shield against the "modern" world; therefore provisions got above all the character of precautions and warnings. Youth cultures – in those days especially borne by "non-organized" (i.e. not belonging to a youth movement) and usually employed young people – were, when involving an acceptation of the "modern" values, looked upon with distrust. Adults found it difficult to deal with these "nozems" and "blousons noirs". In the following decades this idea of protection was increasingly criticized in favour of a more emancipatory approach: young people did not need to be protected from social dangers, on the contrary they had to be supported to oppose to them in a critical manner. The "resistance of the youth" – as expressed in youth cultures borne by studying young people this time (provos, hippies,...) was tolerated, even positively appreciated from this point of view.

Recently youth existence in the western world is approached in a more differentiated manner and is seen rather as a moveable social landscape formed by a range of youth activities. Also in the formation of theory the difference between first, second and third environment is used to a lesser extent and the line of thought is one of a *two way traffic* between young people and their surroundings, young people being seen as an *experience subject* that experiences the spatial context as an everyday, enduring and spatially definable

---

[15] J. Fierens, Droit et pauvreté, Droits de l'homme, sécurité sociale, aide sociale, Bruxelles, Bruylant, 1992.

[16] S. Frith, The sociology of youth, in : M. Halalambos (ed.), Sociology, New Directions, Ormkirk, Causeway Press ltd., 1991, pp. 303–368.

environment. However, it is important that also in this approach.[17] there is an explicit reference to the impact of young people's home environment on the growth towards, but also on the formation of personal autonomy. In other words also here the above mentioned constant in the youth cultural debate, viz. young people's *level of education* in connection with their home environment, is presented as an important dividing line between young people. For the debate on children's rights this means that the question of how the striving for children's rights relates to other dividing lines, e.g. criteria such as social class, sex or ethnic group, is raised again.

V. INDIVIDUALIZATION VERSUS PLURALIZATION

The approach of young people as experience subjects also refers to the changing – and as a society modernises: increasing – impact of non-intentional processes of socialization. This puts the traditional pedagocic line of thought under a lot of pressure. Whilst before, for example in the third environment concept, one could assume that it was desirable and possible to offer children and young people in the family, at school and in leisure time a "controlled living environment", one must now increasingly take into account the "broader environment". In this especially anonymous "educators" are pre-eminent, viz. the mass media and the industry, which comply rather with the demands of the market than with pedagocic aims.[18] Thus intentional educational interventions get a mere private meaning, which must be balanced not only against the

---

[17] This approach is described as "living environment approach" and contains in youth research on the one hand a *development theory* (Bronfenbrenner) which focuses on the contextuality of the personality development, and on the other hand a *"socialization theory"* (Baacke) which focuses on stimulating influences from the environment on young people's socialization. Thus a number of socalled "social-ecological zones" are distinguished, which young people can acquire during their socialization: – the first zone, the socalled ecological centre, consists of the everyday, immediate environment, generally the young person's home environment. Characteristic are the close emotional relations and direct contacts. The cultural and material possibilities of the ecological centre are very important for the kind of experiences that young people can have. – The second zone is the socalled ecological proximity, consiting of the young person's living environment and his home environment. In this "neighbourhood" he experiences the first extern relations and he finds the first playmates. Here young people come across each other and find fixed meeting places. – The third zone is formed by the ecological sectors, being the school, the company, the youth centre ... This zone is defined by function specific relations; one comes there at specific times and with a specific purpose and one is confronted with function specific expectations. – The fourth zone is the ecological periphery, being the contacts one has with a.o politics, mass media, theatre, shopping centre, regions where one spends his holidays... As this ecological periphery is bigger and more stimulative for a young person he will be able to gain more experiences. In other words young people's action radius increases as they move more and more often in the direction of the periphery.

see : F. van der Linden & C. Klaassen, Jeugd in context, De sociaal-ecologische benadering, in : C. Klaassen, Jeugd als sociaal fenomeen, *op.cit.*, pp. 129–148.

[18] H. Giesecke, Pedagogiek als beroep. Grondvormen van pedagogisch handelen, Voorburg, De Meerval, 1990, p. 8.

influence of contemporaries but also and not in the least against the cultural effects of the market. As a consequence of this the pedagogic formation of theory and practice in the approach of young people generally tends to stress the support of young people's autonomous possibilities of development: young people must learn to design and plan their lives and in doing so have to go by their own insights, wishes and accomplishments and have to examine the possibilities to realize these and take them up. That goes for everybody regardless of background, sex and preferences. Class, sex and ethnic criteria are especially seen in relation to individual chances of development; provisions are seen as correcting in this respect. The "(growth towards) personal autonomy" is then no longer formed from a fixed religious or moral truth, but from a pluriform and universal system of human rights. This development is generally described as the *individualization* of society: the waning of the normative power of social environments and cultural traditions in favour of an increased rationality in planning and directing civilization processes. As a result of this the individual gets more opportunities to form his life: with regard to educational opportunities, leisure possibilities and material position most Western children and young people are doing much better than before. The striving for children's rights links up with this tendency towards individualization and offers young people more opportunities to *behave* as and be *recognized* as *right subjects*. However, individualization also involves higher *demands to competence*, which is expressed by the asessment that young people do not always experience this new form of own responsibility for failure or success as an enrichment, but very often as an area of tension or even as a burden.

From a youth cultural point of view the area of tension between greater individual possibilities but increasing demands to competence finds in the western world expression in the development of a *prolonged youth phase* or "post-adolescence". From the point of view of society this prolonged youth phase is characterized by contradiction: from a social-cultural point of view young people are tackled about independence earlier than before, which is expressed in a style of education more based on consultation. From an economic point of view young people find themselves longer than before in a position of dependence as a result of the participation in education lasting longer and the introduction to the employment market becoming more problematic and drawn out. The contradictory character of the youth phase demands that young people prepare themselves for a future which is at the same time utterly open: young people who are at school encouraged to choose ambitious fields of learning are at the same time told that they need not/cannot make any fixed and structuralized plans for the transition to professional practice and thereafter. "Drawing up a life plan one takes into consideration some *restraint and flexible cautiousness*. A condition to be able to do that is to stabilize oneself in a certain way as an emancipated personality, to look for something to hold on to, without being thrown back on a certain occupational bio-graphy and a certain life path. One has to hold back a trump card and keep it for the right moment. One constantly has to choose between provisional commitment and non-specific readyness to commitment. *The personality builds a potential* that for want of surveyable circumstances can get a considerable meaning for the self-image. Each further step is coupled with knowledge of possible *alternatives*. The social understanding that it might also be different is inevitably present".[19] This development involves that the youth period is to a lesser extent then for example in the fifties and sixties determined by the *collective* resistance of young people against the adult world but increasingly by the *individual* claiming of more independence and equality with regard to adults. Young people increasingly consider their youth as something with a value in its own right and as being legitimized by the present, not by what it means for future "adulthood". The term "post-adolescence" expresses both this individual positioning and the tension that young people experience between their own desires and the life routes that are mapped out for them. Youth culturally this is expressed in a form of consciously "postponing" adulthood in the traditional sense and in the interpretation of the youth period in terms of the making of a "life design": young people are thinking about the purpose of their lives and are defining this purpose for the different terrains of life (work, school, family); they try to plan and realize these purposes and thus map out *route* to realize their life design. This development is (for the time being) especially borne by young people with a generally higher education and especially coming from higher social environments, in which moreover an open style of education based on consultation prevails.[20]

With respect to children's rights these developments raise an important field of attention.

To a certain extent this field of attention links up with the above mentioned questions about the relation children's rights-social inequality. The tendency towards individualization in the western world, including the striving for children's rights is formed in a period in which the in western countries relatively steady development of economic growth and social well-being is stagnating and the social inequality between both population groups and regions is increasing. The future is increasingly seen as determined by a large social, ecological, economic and political pressure with as key words: affection of the environment, new poverty, violence, pressure to perform, drug abuse, etc. In other words the individualization of society involves *pluralization*, i.e. the maintaining of different forms of social inequality, such as discrimination on ethnic grounds, inequality in participation in education according to the social stratum of the home environment, forms of sex specific role

---

[19] W. Fuchs-Heinritz, Jeugd als statuspassage of geïndividualiseerde jeugdbiografie ? in : Jeugd en Samenleving, 20e jrg., 1990, nr. 7/8, pp. 451–473 (cit. p. 468).

[20] M. Matthijs, Mythe van de jeugd, 1. Cultuur en leefwereld, Groningen, Wolters-Noordhoff, 1993, pp. 61–64, with reference to : J. Zinnecker, Jugend und Jugendkultur im Gesellschaftlichen Wandel, in : Jugendkultur 1940-1985, Opladen, 1987, pp. 309–380.

socialization, regional differences. This pluralization indicates that next to "winners" in modern society there are also "losers" and that minorities are marginalized and isolated. With regard to young people this development is expressed in the problematic nature of the situation of for example young people with little education, "teenage drop outs", etc.[21] Whilst the theme of children's rights provides the *theoretical borders* or in other words *the frame of reference* from which children's and young people's personal autonomy can be realized, the *factual realization* of this autonomy can not be seen apart from the above mentioned *solidarity* which a society must be able/willing to establish in order to realize these theoretical borders for everybody and for a society as a whole. With respect to the monitoring of children's rights this means that a manageable balance must be found between the refinement of the theoretical borders and the effects of their actual application in the area of tension individualization-socialization. On the other hand, the waning pedagocic autonomy in favour of an increasing influence of the broader environment means that the question about the relation between children's rights and this broader environment must be raised. In this respect it has been pointed out that there are three types of "child", according to the spheres of influence children and young people are involved with. From the "*traditional*" child – i.e. the child seen from the family – originated with the introduction of the socalled children's laws (prohibition of child labour, compulsory education, child and young people protection) round the turn of the century the "*public child*" – i.e. the child surrounded by steadily increasing institutions and experts who from a normative frame of reference take care of its well-being. The present period is said to be characterized by the creation of the "*commercial child*", in other words children adressed as consumers of goods and services, but above all: children adressed socially and emotionally as a group with its *own* opinions and desires, which can be fulfilled by the commercial supply of goods and services, but which not necessarily comply with the values which are presented by intentional education.[22] The connection to the debate on youth cultures here lies in the question how much room children are offered to other than "commercialized" and i.c. "mediatized experiences".[23] as well, and in the question which cultural contents that add *meaning* to existence are offered to them. With regard to the debate on

---

[21] R. Bendit, W. Gaiser & U. Nissen, Gevaren en kansen in de moderne verzorgingsstaat. Opgroeien in de Duitse Bondsrepubliek, in : Jeugd en Samenleving, 23e jrg., 1993, nr. 2/3, pp. 67–89.

[22] R. Liljeström, The public child, the commercial child and our child, in : F. Kessel & A.W. Siegel (eds.), The child and other cultural inventions, New York, Praeger, 1983, pp. 124-157.

[23] Young people's desire for "non-mediatized experiences" is strikingly expressed in e.g. the novel "La dérive des sentiments" (Dutch title : Gevoelens op drift) by Yves Simon. In 1991 the novel was awarded the Prix Médicis and became a cult book among the French youth, who seemed to recognize themselves in the text made up of loose fragments and in the end in the description as a "rudderless generation" : a generation hoping for utopias but not really expecting them, because they are cut off from the historical construction of a humane society.

children's rights this means the question is raised of how this debate can contribute and does contribute to both the realization of these cultural contents and to young people's *ability* to form these cultural contents. In other words in this line of thought the monitoring of children's rights is framed in a broader *cultural reflexion*, in which the connection is made of the social position of young people, c.q. desirable and necessary changes of the latter, with how young people themselves experience that position and with the discussion on the *meanings* offered to them in this experience.

VI. SUCCESION OF THE GENERATIONS

The experience of young people themselves, the way in which they experience their time and environment is central in the concept of *generation* as elaborated by Karl Manheim.[24] According to Manheim the concept of "generation" contains three levels of distinction, viz. the generational position (being born in the same year and the same national context or language community), the generational coherence (taking part in mutual fortunes) and the generational unity (processing the mutual fortunes into a mutual consciousness). These levels of distinction indicate that especially the *social dynamics* provide the form and contents of the concept of generation: biological generations come "alive" on the basis of the given social stimuli. In this respect the generations have a media-ting function between social changes and the existing cultural heritage; when social changes occur rapidly more adaptations are necessary and the generations will succeed one another faster. In other words generational units involve a new treatment of the existing cultural heritage; therefore not only the "new" must be seen in a generation, but also the social and intellectual movements in which the generations join up.

Young people look *differently* at reality than adults who will tend to keep looking at the changing historical reality from the existing frames of thought. However, *differently* does not equal "more progressively": the radicality of young people may exist in for example returning to older cultural forms. In this respect not so much the contradiction between the generations ("the generation gap") deserves attention, but the difference in orientation itself: each generation creates as it were its own "*opponent*". At the same time there is an *interaction* between the generations; this interaction is bigger as social dynamics are bigger: in dynamics of rapid changes the older generation is forced to be more open to the influences of younger generations.

Using Manheim's apparatus of concepts one can distinguish three consecutive generations in western civilization in the period after World War II, each of which is characterized by a breach in problem consciousness with regard to

---

[24] R. Abma, Jeugd en generatie, De generatiesociologische benadering, in : C. Klaassen (red.), Jeugd als sociaal fenomeen, *op.cit.*, pp. 14–29.

the previous generation.[25] The generation of the forties – the socalled *recon-struction generation* – is dominated by reconstruction. This reconstruction does not only stand for the recovery of the devastation of war, but fundamentally also for a strong acceptation of and orientation to the economic values of production and consumption and making career, simultaneously with a reserved attitude towards the political-cultural orientation with which the previous generation – the socalled war generation – had grown up. This reserved attitude induces to speak of the "sceptic generation" (H. Schelsky, Die skeptische Generation, 1963). The generation of the sixties – the socalled *generation critical of the social structure* – manifests itself in a period in which the rise of welfare has reached a top and the expansive growth of production and consumption is almost self-evident. The problem consciousness of this generation focuses on aspects connected with this growth and experienced as being negative, especially the alienation and social inequality that spring from them. The protest against them results in all sorts of emancipatory movements and in questioning the prevailing performance mentality and economic relations. The generation of the eighties – the socalled *unbound* or *rudderless* generation.[26] – can boast the cultural achievements of the previous generation, viz. the destruction of order systems and fixed value frames in favour of bigger possibilities for participation and alternative value orientation. However, on the economic level the performance mentality and the balance of power are less broken down than ever: economic growth in the West is stagnating, there is high persistent (youth) unemployment, the differences between poor and rich are increasing, there are more fluxes of migration as a result of which cities are becoming more multicultural, the welfare state is under pressure, both on the level of the social right dimension and on the level of solidarity, the social basis that enables the elaboration of social rights.[27] The younger generation is confronted with the task to determine an own attitude towards all this: "The success of the generational unit of the sixties lies in the cultural domain: the destruction of order systems; it is their failure that they did not break down the regularities of the economic-political system. The lesson of both results seems to be the core of the generation consciousness of the eighties generation: stand up for yourself. In a cultural climate which lacks obligatory cultural models, there is room to develop an own value and norm system and behavioural orientations; in combination with an economic climate in which you have to fight for a job such room easily results in a

---

[25] M. Matthijssen, Het probleem van jong zijn, in : C.J.M. Corver & M. Elchardus (red.), Sociologisch en antropologisch jaarboek 1989, Brussel, reeks Tijdschrift voor Sociologie, 1989, pp. 195–214.

[26] see note 23 : Y. Simon, Gevoelens op drift, Rijswijk/Antwerpen, Goossens/Manteau, 1993.

[27] G. Engbergsen, De weg naar Anomia, Armoederegimes en levenskansen, in : G. Engbersen, A.C. Hemerijck, W.E. Bakker, Zorgen in het Europese Huis, Verkenningen over de grenzen van nationale verzorgingsstaten, Amsterdam, Boom, 1994, pp. 113–141.

mentality of standing up for yourself; especially when the political climate is one of dismantling social securities and systems of care in the public sphere and appealing to individualization in a caring society".[28]

Concrete research on the specific orientation of generational relations shows that the rough image is often misleading. For example the reports on an increasing extent of "standing up for yourself" on the basis of emipirical research must be strongly relativized: the generation of the eighties is less individualistic than believed, to a large extent tends to consider society as a community and is clearly prepared to commitment which is not free of obligations.[29] However, with regard to the theme of children's rights insight in the "succession of the generations" is once again an argument to put and keep putting the striving for and monitoring of children's rights in the framework of a fundamental reflexion on the close relation between education and culture and on the mea-ning of education in the humanization and democratization of society.[30] The significance of the theme of children's rights in this discussion is: making the *trust* in children and young people socially visible and form adults' commitment to actually talk to young people about this striving for humanization and democratization. The question of *what* has to be reported with regard to the monitoring of children's rights and by *whom* thus becomes, in relation to youth cultures, a question of how *humane* and *democratic* a society develops *in connection with* children's and young people's opportunities for development. With respect to the *what* this means that the monitoring of children's rights may not be categorical – in other words the institutionalization of the theme of children's rights itself must be avoided. With respect to the *by whom* the situating of the monitoring of children's rights within the striving for humanization and democratization means that children and young people themselves must be recognized as concerned party, also in the monitoring mechanism.

VII. THE MONITORING OF CHILDREN'S RIGHTS IN RELATION TO YOUTH CULTURES

With respect to a concretization of the monitoring mechanism the *participation* of children and young people is thus central. The participation of children and young people is first of all central with regard to the choice and elaboration of the *themes* to be reported. As far as the choice of the themes is concerned, these can be linked up with the themes which (also) prevail in *youth cultures*, e.g. with respect to the present western world themes such

---

[28]   M. Matthijssen, Het probleem van jong zijn, *op.cit.*, p. 209.

[29]   M. Elchardus & P. Heyvaert, m.m.v. M. Scheys, Soepel, flexibel en ongebonden. Een vergelijking van twee laat-moderne generaties, Brussel, VUB-Press, 1990, pp. 199–222.

[30]   see : K. Mollenhauer, Vergeten samenhang, Over cultuur en opvoeding, Meppel/Amsterdam, Boom, 1986.

as social isolation, poverty, security, living together in a multicultural society, labour and unemployment, education. Important is that the necessary instruments are available to grasp these themes. This requires investment in historical, social and pedagocic research on how society develops and how this affects the social position of also young people. A specific point of attention is the question of what young people forming *society* might experience regarding the way adults go about with each other and with young people, in other words regarding "citizen's values" such as respect, responsibility, plurality, solidarity... [31] With respect to the *elaboration* of these themes, this must be related to the point of view of children and young people. As being a child and being a young person and children's and young people's living conditions are fundamentally determined by the same economic, political and social forces that create the framework of adults' lives, it is appropriate to regard the reporting on children's rights and the reporting on human rights, including the way in which these are expressed in a social policy, not as separate but as *inherently* connected matters. In this respect the monitoring of children's rights specifically involves that in the debate on human rights and in the debate on social policy – very topical in the western context: the debate on the development of the welfare state – the position of children is made explicit.[32]

The participation of children is also central with respect to the formation of the monitoring mechanism itself or with respect to who reports. Concretely this means possibilities must be found to actively involve children and young people with policy and provisions, not only as a short term aim (for example within the framework of school projects and or youthwork projects), but as an essential striving for change of the *relation* between children, young people and society towards a more respectful contact.[33] Therefore it is necessary to describe the concept of participation not merely in terms of "taking actively part in" – but also in terms of "having part in", or in other words not only the ways in which young people can be involved with the planning and execution of policy must be examined, above all possibilities for consultation of and deliberation with young people about the *execution* of policy must be looked for.[34] This broadening of the concept of participation is necessary

---

[31] M. de Winter, Kinderparticipatie : er gaat een wereld voor je open, in : Jeugd en Samenleving, 24e jrg., 1994, nr. 1, pp. 14–27

[32] J. Qvortrup, Het kind zijn als sociaal verschijnsel, Inleiding op een reeks nationale rapporten, in : E. Verhellen, e.a. (red.), Kinderrechtengids (KIDS), Commentaren, regelgeving, rechtspraak en nuttige informatie over de maatschappelijke en juridische positie van het kind, Gent, Mys & Breesch, 1994, Deel 1.1.-1–37.

[33] M. de Winter, Kinderparticipatie : er gaat een wereld voor je open, *op.cit.*, p. 24.

[34] Different forms of participation are thus distinguished, being
– asking for and receiving information about the policy;
– consultation : the organization of involvement meetings and i.c. of the possibilities of response to policy execution;
– deliberation : the creation of permanent deliberation structures, i.c. regular surveys of opin-

because – i.c. young – people must be able to look upon themselves as serious discussion partners who are also *taken seriously*. Being able to take part in a society's regulations and provisions – the understanding that they go "for you too" and that this rule is complied with – forms the heart of a democracy[35]. The monitoring of children's rights with children and young people themselves through information and co-partnership and above all through systematic consultation and deliberation about the daily execution of policy and provisions might be an important instrument to accelerate that heart's beat to a more optimal tempo.

ions, wishes and problem perceptions and provoke reactions with regard to contents;
– co-partnership : participation in policy deliberation
for this distinction, see : J.L. Hazekamp, J. van der Gauw & J. Nutjens, Jongeren doen mee aan beleid. Verslag van een onderzoek naar politieke participatie van jongeren op lokaal niveau, Den Haag, Vereniging van Nederlandse Gemeenten, 1993.

ISABELLE CHERNEY and NANCY WALKER PERRY

Children's Attitudes Toward Their Rights

An International Perspective

Only during the past two decades has the issue of children's rights gained serious international attention from researchers, advocates, and public policy makers. During that time, increasing awareness of children's developmental needs and rights has led to a global move toward giving children and adolescents a greater degree of autonomy in the decisions affecting their own lives (Billick, 1986). The United Nations' (1989) Convention on the Rights of the Child, which established international guidelines regarding children's rights, added impetus to that growing movement, and recommended that children be educated about their rights. In order to provide appropriate educational programs, however, we first need to know what children understand about their rights.

According to Rogers and Wrightsman (1978), two fundamentally different orientations toward children's rights exist. The *nurturance* orientation stresses society's obligations to make decisions in the best interests of children and to protect children from harm. Thus, the nurturance orientation essentially is paternalistic (or maternalistic) in that what is deemed good or desirable for the child is determined for the child by authority figures (such as parents, teachers, or governments) rather than by the child. The *self-determination* orientation, on the other hand, stresses the importance of allowing children to exercise control over various facets of their lives, including making autonomous decisions about what they want and need, even when those decisions might conflict with the views of adults charged with the children's care.

Adults have not been reluctant to express their preferences regarding children's rights orientations, with those views typically reflecting various social groups' agendas. According to Feshbach and Feshbach (1978), "rights are intimately related to the specific legal and social structure of a society, e.g., the right to privacy, the right to an individual versus a group-based choice. Needs are more universal and are less subject to negotiation, e.g., the need for food, shelter, caring, protection from physical and psychological abuse" (p.6). However, few researchers have asked children themselves what they think about their rights. Melton (1980), the first to elicit information about children's rights directly from children, found that both developmental factors and socioeconomic status influence children's conceptions of their rights.

Based upon Piagetian and Kohlbergian theories, Melton (1980) reasoned that "children will be more likely to assert rights for themselves as they grow older and as they develop more mature moral judgments" (p.186). He proposed a three-level progression of children's conceptions of their rights. At Level 1, children cannot differentiate between what actually happens to them and what they should be entitled to. Children who reason at this level believe that adults have more rights because they are physically bigger and "able to do more things and that children have rights only if adults allow them" (pp.186-187). At Level 2, children perceive rights as being "based more on criteria of fairness and competence to exercise self-determination than on what authority figures actually allow children to do" (p.189). Thus, at Level 2, children's views toward their self-determination rights become more positive. At Level 3, justifications for rights are based not on fairness or competence but rather on abstract universal principles such as the right to privacy, to freedom of speech, to autonomous decision making, and so forth.

Melton (1980) found that children from families with higher socioeconomic status (SES) typically achieved Level 2 reasoning several years earlier than did Low-SES children. In addition, High-SES children tended to espouse more positive attitudes toward children's rights approximately two years earlier than did their lower-status peers. Melton concluded that Koocher (1979) was correct in asserting that "children reared in the less entitled groups may grow up to see themselves as having fewer rights, less access to self-actualization, and less opportunity for self-determination" (p.91).

Melton (1980) also considered the effects of ethnicity, age, school system, and gender on children's conceptions of their rights; however, none of those variables significantly reduced the variance in the stepwise regression analysis he performed. Melton concluded that those variables were less potent predictors of children's attitudes toward their rights than were school grade and socioeconomic status.

Consideration of Melton's work suggests a *socioeconomic explanation* for differences in same-aged children's conceptions of their rights. According to that view, socioeconomic status should be a potent predictor of children's attitudes, with High-SES children espousing more positive views toward self-determination than Low-SES children.

However, we assert that Melton's socioeconomic explanation is too simplistic. In contrast to the socioeconomic hypothesis, therefore, we offer a *cultural explanation* which suggests that cultural values play a central role in influencing children's conceptions of their rights.

For example, some cultures – such as that of the United States – place a primary value on the autonomy of the individual member, whether adult or child. US children are taught values of self-reliance, assertiveness, competition, and individuality (Sigel, 1988). School children learn that the United States Constitution guarantees its citizens certain rights and freedoms, and that children are duly empowered to assert their own needs via enacted legislation that assigns them legal rights. Because such values typically are consistent with the self-determination orientation, one might expect US children to favor self-determination rights regardless of socioeconomic status.

Other cultures place higher priority on the nurturance orientation. For example, European cultures tend to reflect the views of such philosophers as Hobbes, Locke, and Mills that children have no natural rights and no rights by social contract because they lack the ability to make covenants with other members of society and to understand the consequences of such contracts. Thus, the European view stresses that children need to be protected against the possibility of injury from themselves and others. In western Europe, therefore, it might be reasonable to assume that children would tend to favor the nurturance orientation over the self-determination orientation.

National philosophy is one factor that may influence children's conceptions of their rights. Another factor is the amount of exposure children have to real-world experiences. According to the cultural explanation, children who have more opportunities to be "out in the world," and therefore to make autonomous decisions, should favor more self-determination rights. Thus, both children who have more liberal educational experiences and those who are "street-wise" should advocate for more self-determination rights than those who live in more sheltered, protected environments with fewer opportunities to make their own decisions. As one social anthropologist noted, "if we are looking at less developed societies in general, particularly where we find children with increased responsibilities, we are likely to find that in differently defined roles or age sets and genders there are far more rights, freedoms, and a great deal more opportunity for self-determination" (B. Milne, personal communication, August 7, 1994).

Our study investigated cultural and socioeconomic influences on children's perceptions of their rights. Our hypothesis was that because different cultures encourage varying amounts of autonomy during childhood, cultural values also should affect children's perceptions of their rights.

I. METHOD

A. Subjects

Eighty-seven 11- to 13-year-old children from Switzerland, Canada, and the United States participated in our study. All children were in the sixth or seventh year of school.

The European sample consisted of 46 children attending school in Geneva, Switzerland. The European children represented the following cultural groups: Swiss French, Swiss German, German, and English. The European sample consisted of relatively affluent children from moderate- to high-SES families, with most attending private schools.

The Canadian sample consisted of 12 children living and attending public school in a rural area of Alberta, Canada. The Canadian children, all Caucasian, came from moderate-SES families.

The US sample consisted of 29 children living and attending school in the state of Nebraska. The US children, all from Low-SES families, represented the following ethnic groups: Anglo-, African-, Hispanic-, and Native-American.

B. Materials

We used the Children's Rights Interview (CRI) developed by Melton (1980) (see appendix). The questionnaire consists of two parts.

Part 1 asks four preliminary questions: (a) What is a right? (scored on a 3-point continuum as incorrect, a correct example, or the correct definition of a right), (b) Who has rights? (analyzed by frequency distribution), (c) Do children have rights? (scored as yes, no, or unsure), and (d) Should children have rights? (also scored as yes, no, or unsure).

Part 2 consists of 12 conflict-laden vignettes. Vignettes involve rights to information (#1), to expression and due process (#2, 3, 6, 7, 8, 11), to make treatment decisions (#4, 5, 12), to work (#9), and to privacy (#10).

Each vignette is followed by a question designed to test whether the child will or will not assert a right for the child described in the story situation. Replies to the vignettes are scored on a 3-point scale indicating the degree to which the child advocates the expression of a right by the child in the story. A score of +1 indicates that the child advocates, or leans toward advocating, expression of a right for the child in the vignette. A score of zero denotes that the child either advocates equally positive and negative positions, or gives no opinion. A score of -1 means that the child opposes, or leans toward opposing, expression of a right for the child in the vignette. Thus, the total score for the 12 vignettes in Part 2 ranges from +12 to -12.

C. Procedure

For the European sample, we translated Melton's interview, as well as the necessary consent forms, from English into French and German.

After obtaining permission from the parent and child, each child participated in a personal interview in his or her preferred language (English, French, or German). The researcher read each question aloud to the child, and recorded responses on audiotape. All verbatim responses then were transcribed, and those in French and German were translated into English. Another researcher, who was blind as to the child's SES and cultural group, scored the interview responses and performed the data analysis. We used the same interviewing, transcription, and scoring procedures for the North American children whose interviews were conducted in English.

We calculated frequency distributions for the questions in Part 1. We analyzed the total score for Part 2 as a global measure of children's attitudes toward their rights. We also inspected scores on an item-by-item basis. Our between-subjects variable was home country (Switzerland, Canada, USA).

II. RESULTS

Part 1

Fifty-seven percent of the children correctly defined or explained the meaning of a right (58% Swiss, 58% Canadian, 55% US); an additional 31 percent (32% Swiss, 0% Canadian, 41% US) gave a correct example of a right.

Of the total sample, 67 percent said that everyone has rights (70% Swiss, 100% Canadian, 85% US). Thirteen percent of the total sample indicated that only authority figures or "some but not all" individuals have rights (24% Swiss, 0% Canadian, 4% US). Twenty percent gave responses that fell into neither category.

Overall, 83 percent of the children interviewed felt that children do have rights (89% Swiss, 100% Canadian, 66% US), whereas 91% believed that children should have rights (87% Swiss, 100% Canadian, 93% US). Interestingly, but not surprisingly, the low-SES ethnic US children were least likely to believe that children actually are accorded rights.

Part 2

A one-way ANOVA for total score on Part 2 produced a significant difference among the samples, $F(2,84) = 3.36, p = .04$. On average, High-SES European children advocated for more rights ($M = 5.5$) than did Low-SES US children ($M = 4.1$) or Moderate-SES Canadian children ($M = 3.4$). Fisher's PLSD revealed a significant difference between the Swiss and Canadian samples, mean difference = 1.87, $p = .03$. This finding favors the cultural explanation over the socioeconomic explanation.

We also performed a repeated measures analysis of variance (ANOVA) with country as the between subjects variable and questionnaire items as the repeated measure. The main effect for country resulted in a significant effect, $F(2,83) = 3.9, p = .02$. On an item-by-item basis, High-SES European children were more likely to advocate for their rights ($M = .46$) than were low-SES US children $M = .35$) or Moderate-SES Canadian children ($M = .26$).

The main effect for questionnaire item was highly significant, $F(11,913) = 52.0, p < .0001$. This result suggests that children did not advocate indiscriminately for rights; rather, they distinguished between those rights

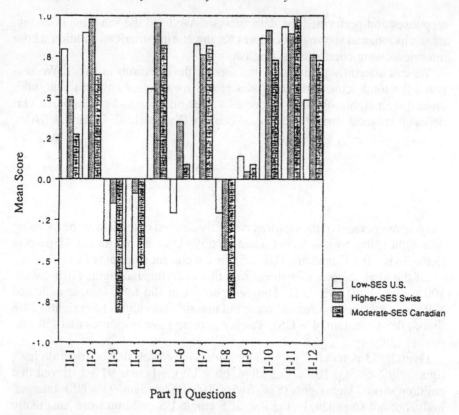

Fig. 1. Children's rights favored and opposed by children from three sociocultural groups. One case was omitted due to missing values.

they believed they were entitled to exercise and those they felt they were not yet ready to handle.

The interaction effect for country and item also was significant, $F(22,913) = 2.0$, $p = .004$. This result indicates that, on average, European, Canadian, and US children responded differently to certain items. (See Figure 1.) A series of one-way ANOVAs revealed where the three samples agreed and differed.

The three samples did not differ significantly in their responses to eight of the 12 vignettes. Swiss, Canadian, and US children of various socioeconomic levels agreed that children should be able to see their school records (Swiss $M = .50$, Canadian $M = .33$, US $M = .79$), to play undisturbed (Swiss $M = .76$, Canadian $M = .83$, US $M = .83$), to not divulge their private thoughts (Swiss $M = .91$, Canadian $M = .75$, US $M = .86$), to receive due process in disciplinary hearings (Swiss $M = .89$, Canadian $M = 1.00$, US $M = .93$) and to talk to a doctor without parental consent (Swiss $M = .76$, Canadian $M = .75$, US $M = .48$). Children from each country also agreed that children should not be allowed to vote (Swiss $M = -.44$, Canadian $M = .-75$, US $M = -.21$), nor should they be allowed complete autonomy in choosing their own classes in school (Swiss $M = -.15$, Canadian $M = -.75$, US $M = -.38$). In addition, all samples were ambivalent about whether children should be permitted to work (Swiss $M = .04$, Canadian $M = 0.8$, US $M = .14$). Several children from each group indicated that permission should hinge on the nature of the job and the maturity level of the child.

Four vignettes elicited significantly different responses from the three groups. Although all samples tended to favor children's rights to choose their own living arrangements following a divorce, the Canadian sample ($M = .67$) was significantly less likely to advocate that position than were the Swiss children ($M = .98$), $F(2,84) = 3.2$, $p < .05$. The US children advocated a position closer to that of the Swiss children ($M = .90$), but not statistically different from the other groups.

No group favored children's right to refuse a vaccination, but the Swiss sample ($M = -.09$) held that view significantly less strongly than did the US group ($M = -.55$), $F(2,84) = 3.1$, $p = .05$. In other words, the US children were more likely to say that doctors should be permitted to force children to have a vaccination. The Canadian children's position ($M = -.42$) was intermediate, not differing significantly from either the Swiss or US views.

All groups believed that an injured child should be treated by a physician even if the child's parents could not afford to pay for the treatment, an expression of children's right to be nurtured. However, consistent with the cultural explanation, the Swiss children ($M = .96$) were significantly more likely to hold that view than were the US children ($M = .55$). The view of the Canadian children ($M = .83$) did not suffer significantly from that of either of the other samples.

The most disparate views involved the vignette that asked whether a school principal should have the right to censor a child's newspaper story expressing disagreement with the school rules. Consistent with the cultural explanation, the Swiss sample tended to favor the authoritarian view ($M = .35$), whereas the US children mildly advocated freedom of expression ($M = -.21$). The Canadian children were neutral on that topic ($M = .09$).

III. DISCUSSION

Although the children in our sample came from disparate socioeconomic and cultural backgrounds, it is clear that their responses to the CRI vignettes tended, on the whole, to be more similar than different. Of course, the cultural distinctions between European and North American children likely are less pronounced than the distinctions between those groups and children from other parts of the world such as Asia, Africa, and South America. Whether our findings apply to children from those regions is, at this point, unclear.

What we do feel confident in concluding from our initial studies is that twelve-year-old children do not advocate indiscriminately for rights. Instead, they distinguish between those rights they believe they are entitled to exercise and those they feel they are not yet ready to handle. Twelve-year-old children in our sample seemed to recognize that most children have neither the judgment nor the experience of adults and could hardly be expected to judiciously exercise all adult prerogatives. At the same time, however, our study participants recognized that children are not merely objects or helpless organisms. The children in our sample believed that children should be empowered to make autonomous decisions if and when they are capable of doing so.

In addition, it is clear to us that the factors entailed in considering children's perceptions of their rights are complex and cannot be dealt with independent of developmental, cultural, and socioeconomic contexts. Our results suggest that, to some degree, children's perceptions of their rights do vary as a function of SES and culture, among other factors. More complete information about cultural and socioeconomic influences would be useful in guiding efforts to educate children about their rights.

In order to obtain that information, we must explore a number of thorny questions. For example, what roles do parents from various cultures play in educating their children concerning their rights? Do they teach their children about self-determination, or do they prefer to protect them from both harm and autonomy?

How do different school systems educate children about their rights? Do children who are exposed to theoretical teaching about their rights learn to advocate more self-determination rights than children who do not have such opportunities?

Do children who learn about their rights through practical experience advocate for more autonomy than their more sheltered counterparts? Is such practical experience good or bad for children's development? For example, street children do not have the opportunity to choose their own way of life. Economic, social, environmental, and psychological issues drive them away from home and into potentially dangerous and violent situations, so their nurturance needs often are sorely neglected. The responsibilities faced by these children may indeed make them autonomous decision makers, but those same responsibilities are developmentally inappropriate.

To what extent should children be empowered? Is it the case that more is better? Certainly as much depends on the child's age, maturity, and skills of judgment as on the particular issues in question. Implicit in the act of empowering children are the assumptions that children are to be heard, that their opinions are valid and valued, that both they and their parents are esteemed as persons important to the process of decision making, and that what they say will have a bearing upon and may influence the final decisions that are to be made. What should be the fulcrum point in balancing the rights of children and their parents?

In order to answer those questions, more complex research designs should be employed in a series of investigations. We recommend that low-, moderate-, and high-SES samples from cultures around the globe should be included in further analyses. In addition, we believe that Melton's Children's Rights Interview needs to be revised. The vignettes presented in the CRI involve situations that cannot be applied to all cultural groups. Moreover, the instrument simply asks whether a child has a right in a given situation, rather than considering such factors as the age, experience, and developmental maturity of the child in each vignette. Finally, children of various ages, as well as the parents of those children should be included in the research samples.

We believe it would be a fruitful endeavor to continue investigating children's perceptions of their rights using updated instruments and methods with a broader representation of children's groups. The knowledge obtained should be useful in appropriately educating children about their rights.

Acknowledgment

The authors are grateful to Michaela Culver and Tonia Nicholls who assisted in interviewing children for this project, and to J. Don Read who obtained permission to interview the Canadian children. The authors wish to acknowledge grant support for this project provided by the Creighton University Graduate School.

REFERENCES

Billick, S. B. (1986) "Developmental Competency." *Bulletin American Academy Psychiatry Law, 14 (4)*, 301–308.

Feshbach, N.D., & Feshbach, S. (1978) "Toward an Historical, Social, and Developmental Perspective on Children's Rights." *Journal of Social Issues, 34 (2)*, 1–7.

Koocher, G.P. (1979) *Child Advocacy and Mental Health Professionals*. In P. A. Vardin and I.N. Brody (Eds): *Children's Rights: Contemporary Perspectives*. New York: Teachers College Press.

Melton, G. B. (1980) "Children's Concepts of Their Rights." *Journal of Clinical Child Psychology, 9*, 186–190.

Rogers, C. M. & Wrightsman L. S. (1978) "Attitudes toward Children's Rights: Nurturance or Self-Determination?" *Journal of Social Issues, 34 (2)*, 59–68.

Sigel, I. (1988) "Commentary: Cross-cultural Studies of Parental Influence on Children's Achievement. *Human Development, 31*, 384–390.

United Nations (1989). *Convention on the Rights of the Child.*

APPENDIX CHILDREN'S RIGHTS INTERVIEW

Part 1: General Questions

1. What is a right?

2. Who has rights?
3. Do children have rights? What rights?
4. Should children have rights? Why or why not? If so, what rights?

Part 2: Vignettes

1. Joe knows that he has a chart in the school office, and he wants to know what it says about him. The teacher told Joe that he is not allowed to see his own chart. Should there be a rule or a law that the teacher can keep Joe from seeing his own chart? Why?
2. Mary's parents are getting a divorce. Her mother wants Mary to live with her, but her father wants Mary to live with him. Should there be a rule or a law that Mary could decide by herself with whom she will live? Why?
3. In Jane's school, everyone has to attend a science class. Jane doesn't like science, though, and she thinks that she shouldn't have to take it. Should there be a rule or a law that Jane can take any subject she wants to? Why?
4. Joan went to the doctor, and he told her that she should take a shot. Joan said that she would not take one. Should there be a rule or a law that the doctor can make Joan take a shot even if she doesn't want to? Why?
5. Jim hurt himself while playing ball, and he was taken to the hospital. The people at the hospital said that they couldn't help him because his parents didn't have enough money to pay for his care. Should there be a rule or a law that a doctor would have to help Jim even though his parents couldn't pay for it? Why?
6. Mark wrote a story for the school newspaper. In his story he said that he didn't like the school rules. The principal told him that he couldn't print his story. Should there be a rule or law that the principal can decide if Mark's story will go into the newspaper? Why?
7. David and Mike are both 6 years old. They were playing soccer and some 10-year-old kids came by. The bigger kids told David and Mike that they would have to leave because they weren't old enough to play. Should there be a rule or a law that David and Mike can stay? Why?
8. Some people think that there should be a law that kids could vote for the political leaders. Do you think there should be such a law? Why?
9. Linda wanted to work in Mr. Smith's grocery store. Mr. Smith said that she was not old enough to have a job. Should there be a rule or a law that kids like Linda can't work in a job? Why?
10. Betty kept a diary, and she said that nobody else could read it, not even her parents. Should there be a rule or a law that Betty's parents see her secret, even though she wants to keep it from everyone? Why?
11. Larry got into a fight at school. The teacher said that he would have to do extra homework for school. Larry said, "Wait! You have to hear my side of it first." Should there be a rule or a law that the teacher can punish Larry even if he hasn't had a chance to tell his side of it? Why?
12. John wanted to go to a doctor to talk about some things that were bothering him, but his parents would not let him. Should there be a rule or a law that John could go to a doctor for help even if his parents didn't want him to? Why?

KATHERINE COVELL and BRIAN HOWE

Perspectives of Canadian Youth on Children's Rights

I. BACKGROUND

On December 13, 1991, Canada ratified the UN Convention on the Rights of the Child. In 1992, in preparation for the implementation of the Convention, the Government of Canada provided substantial funding to promote the Convention and to increase public awareness of, and support for, children's issues. The basic objectives were to foster positive public attitudes and values regarding children's rights, and to make the Convention an integral part of Canadian life (Canada, 1994). How successful that will be is yet to be determined. An important element of eventual success will be the extent to which children and youth themselves understand and value their rights. As they are affected by laws dealing with their rights, and as youth often provide the impetus for social change (e.g., Wohlfield & Nevitte, 1990), their understanding and support is vital. What is the likelihood that the current cohort of Canadian youth will impel political agendas concerned with children's rights?

This paper reports on our studies of the perspectives of Canadian youth on children's rights. We examined the extent to which youth value children's rights, their beliefs about rights and their basic knowledge of what rights Canadian children currently have. These three components – values, beliefs, and knowledge – are those expected to jointly determine the likelihood that youth will be the driving force for successful long-term implementation of the UN Convention. The assessment of the views of youth should also provide information of relevance for education such that their rights can be meaningful to them.

II. AGE OF UNDERSTANDING

The philosophical issues surrounding the possession of rights, rights understanding and rights knowledge have been addressed elsewhere (c.f., Gewirth,

E. Verhellen (ed.), Monitoring Children's Rights, 251–262.

1982). However, it is important to emphasize that in the absence of knowledge and understanding, a child's rights may be only nominal. A child may have the right to be free from abuse, but in the absence of understanding of what that right means or how to exercise it, may not be able to prevent parental abuse. For example, in many schools, children are taught a phone number (abuse helplines) to call if parents are abusive. But anecdotes about young children who have used child abuse helplines when asked to clean their rooms demonstrate clearly the need for greater understanding. Knowledge that helplines exist, and knowledge of how to use them, must be accompanied by understanding of what is and is not appropriate parental behaviour.

Whereas even young children can understand and exercise some rights, their knowledge tends to be limited, and domain specific. Generally, developmental psychologists believe that the ability to understand rights in an adult-like fashion is present after about age 15. At this time, the child is able to understand abstract concepts, future implications and possible outcomes of events or behaviours, and is able to engage in relativistic assessments of beliefs systems (e.g., Fischer, 1980; Selman, 1980). During the same developmental period is the crystallization of identity which includes the formulation of a values system (Erikson, 1968; Marcia, 1991), and the questioning of social and legal systems (Piaget, 1932). As thought becomes increasingly adult-like, adolescents' comprehension of social issues increases, their needs change, and their goals become more defined (Beech & Schoeppe, 1974). It is at this developmental stage, also then, that we would expect adolescents to articulate their beliefs about what rights should exist for children, and whether currently existing rights are adequate or appropriate. For these reasons, we used age 15 as the minimum age for the participants in our studies.

III. THEORETICAL PERSPECTIVES

According to social science literature, the extent to which adolescents value rights for others is primarily a function of the socialization experiences of the cohort. However, it is suggested in other literature that rights orientation may also vary with sex. The reasoning for both expectations is as follows. According to Inglehart (1977), building on the needs theory of Maslow (1970, 1972), values reflect socioeconomic conditions, most particularly the conditions that prevail during adolescent development. Those whose development is in a relatively affluent environment have a sense of security about their futures that promotes "post-materialist values". What is valued are freedom of speech, protecting the environment, peace, equality rights and so forth. In contrast, those who grow up in socio-economic environments that promote insecurity and concern about the future support "materialist values" such as financial well-being and law and order. Considerable empirical data support Inglehart's assertions. For example, an examination of changing values from

1968 through 1990 (Santrock, 1993) suggests a large overall increase in the value given personal financial well-being. Most researchers find that those who were adolescent through the 1980s show a decreased concern with the well-being of others – especially for the disadvantaged, those most in need of rights protection (Astin, Green, & Korn, 1987; Astin, Korn & Berz, 1990). And recent studies show adolescents to be apathetic about such values as world peace, but show significant concern for personal goals (e.g., Covell, Rose-Krasnor & Fletcher, 1994; Schatz, & Fiske, 1992). In general, the data suggest that self-fulfilment and self-expression may now be the most characteristic of many youth (Conger, 1988).

Yet there is evidence also in the other direction. Research indicates that Canada increasingly is a rights conscious and rights supportive nation (e.g., Sniderman et al, 1987). With respect to children, this is reflected in juvenile justice legislation in 1984, the *Young Offenders Act*, in the ratification of the UN Convention in 1991, and in the creation of the Children's Bureau to monitor and coordinate federal programs and policies for children. Research also indicates that Canadian youth may be even more rights supportive than are adults (Bibby & Posterski, 1985). For example, they appear more supportive than adults of rights associated with multiculturalism and bilingualism, and less prone to prejudice and discrimination. This suggests that despite adverse economic conditions, youth may continue to place high value on rights, perhaps even more so than their parents.

The second variable that may affect adolescents' attitudes toward children's rights is sex. Gilligan (1982, 1990) has argued that moral reasoning differs between the sexes, with males emphasizing justice considerations and females showing care considerations. Gilligan's assertions predict that males may be less supportive than females are of rights for children because the justice perspective is focused on the right of the individual to be autonomous. The care, or female, perspective recognizes the need for protection and nurturance, and emphasizes relationships. In accord with Gilligan's theoretical predictions are empirical findings such as those of Furnham (1985). In a study of adolescents' socio-political attitudes, Furnham found that females were significantly more positive than were males in attitudes toward equality issues. However, such sex differences are not always obtained (e.g., Smetana, Killen, & Turiel, 1991).

The importance of adolescents' attitudes toward children's rights is seen in the relation between attitude and behaviour. Glover (1991), among many, notes the striking evidence of the influence of values and political attitudes on behaviours such as participating in civil rights activities. Similarly Serow and Dreyden (1990) found students' community service to be predicted by attitudes. We believe then, that a positive attitude toward children's rights among the current cohort of Canadian youth, together with knowledge of rights, will allow, if not promote, the successful implementation of the UN Convention.

IV. THE STUDY

There were three phases to the study which was conducted between June and September of 1994 in Nova Scotia, Canada. Questionnaires were used to assess basic knowledge of what rights exist and rights values; interviews were held to assess beliefs about rights, and knowledge of what to do when rights are violated. Copies of the questionnaires, the interview protocol, scoring and coding details, are available from the authors upon request. The respondents to each part of the study, were high school students between the ages of 15 and 18. The students were drawn from across the three education levels in the system – the technical, regular and university streams. The term "children's rights" was used to include rights for those up to age 18 years. Rights were examined in three domains: (1) legal (e.g., right to a lawyer), (2) social-economic (e.g., right to health care), and (3) basic protection (e.g., right to protection from physical and sexual abuse).

V. RIGHTS KNOWLEDGE AND BELIEFS

A. For basic knowledge of existing rights for children and related law, a questionnaire was used. The questionnaire comprised 30 statements in each of the legal, physical abuse, sexual abuse, and social-economic domains, and two general questions about the UN Convention. Sample statements were: "Parents are allowed to spank their children as a form of discipline" and "Juvenile prostitution is against the law". Each statement was to be marked true or false. The statements were pilot tested for clarity and understanding. The questionnaire was completed by 56 females and 66 males aged 15 to 18 years (average age 16 years 9 months). A MANOVA (rights domains by sex) showed that overall, knowledge of existing rights was greater with regards to protection from sexual and physical abuse than it was in the legal and social economic domains. However, sex differences were obtained also with females showing more knowledge than males in the two abuse domains, and males showing more knowledge than females in the legal and social-economic domains. Scores and statistics are presented in Appendix 1. The responses to the statements on the UN Convention indicated no sex differences in knowledge.

Most of the adolescents were aware that the children's rights specified in the Convention apply to Canadian children (70%); however, only 59% were aware that Canada has ratified the Convention.

B. Individual telephone interviews were held with 49 male and 51 female adolescents to assess further their knowledge and beliefs about rights. The age range of these adolescents was 15 through 18 years with an average for both males and females of 16 years, 3 months. The interview protocol was designed to assess for each of the domains described above, the adolescent's beliefs about what rights should exist, and what action could be taken when a child's rights were violated. Within the domains of legal, abuse and social-economic rights, the issues were drawn from the articles of the Convention and the existing Canadian legislation. At the completion of the interview, the adolescents were asked their overall opinion about the state of children's rights in Canada.

A content analysis of responses with subsequent analyses of the qualitative data (none of which showed any significance) and MANOVAs performed on the quantitative data (see Appendix 2 for a summary of the quantitative data) yielded the following.

In the domain of *legal rights*, the adolescents were asked questions in the areas of a) children and youth in trouble with the law, and b) children caught in parental custody disputes. There were no sex differences in their beliefs here. Fifty-seven percent of the adolescents believed that those under 18 years should in general be treated differently from adults when in trouble with the law, although many of them added qualifiers for those who were repeat offenders or who committed more serious crimes. When asked what age they thought children should be treated as adults before the law, the average age given was 14 years, 6 months.

Considerable concerns were expressed about the welfare of children whose parents are engaged in custody disputes. Overwhelmingly, the adolescents suggested children should have their own court appointed and government paid lawyers to represent their interests. The concerns and the suggestions are exemplified in the response of one 18 year-old male "With the parents' lawyer, they'd be doing what the parent wants – there should be someone appointed by the court to make a neutral decision for the child and child welfare should pay; if the parents paid they might have influence." The adolescents also believed that children should have choice in custody disputes from an average of age 9 1/2 years. When asked what action could be taken when a child's rights in legal proceedings were violated there was very limited knowledge of appropriate action. Most of the respondents either believed nothing could be done, or suggested some type of help might be available, but they were not sure what, or how to access it.

In the domain of *abuse*, we asked about physical punishment, and protection from involvement in, or access to, pornography and prostitution.

Although few of the adolescents (8%) believed that teachers should be allowed to use physical punishment under any circumstances, a surprising number (55% of the boys and 41% of the girls) believed it was alright and even sometimes desirable for parents to physically punish their children. Nonetheless, if families were consistently abusive, most of the adolescents believed that children should have the right to live elsewhere (96%), and even legally divorce their parents (78%).

Most of the adolescents believed that they should make their own decisions about involvement in prostitution after age 17 years, but appreciated the benefits of legislation preventing younger teens and children from sexual exploitation. Many expressed derision about trying to protect children from access to pornography citing its widespread availability, but did suggest that it would be desirable to avoid exposure to "hardcore" before the age of 16 years. The need for better sex education was emphasized here also with the suggestion that the best role for governments in the area of protection from sexual exploitation would be in the provision of education rather than in weak (and unsuccessful) attempts at protection. Knowledge of where to seek help and of what type of help is available for those who are sexually or physically abused was quite high among both males and females. Many reported knowing phone numbers for help lines. Such numbers are widely advertised, successfully it seems, through schools and in the media.

The most salient finding in the domain of *social-economic* rights was the underlying distrust many adolescents had of parents. Fifty-three percent of the adolescents suggested solutions to child poverty that, in essence, described a guaranteed annual income to children, to be received directly by the child (some suggested as young as 3 years!), not the child's parents. Many of those who believed money should go to the parents when the child was younger than 16 years also said that there should be regular monitoring of the family's spending and child care, if necessary bringing in third parties such as social workers to resolve spending conflicts between child and parent. Typical responses in this area were "(Give the money) to children after 5 or 6 (years) but not to the parents -some take the cheque and use it for something else" (female age 17) and "(when parents use money for themselves at the expense of the child) the kid should be able to report them and the parents should have charges laid against them. I'd like to see that." (male age 16). A few adolescents also suggested that governments should ensure employment for parents rather than social assistance. Knowledge of what to do when rights in this area were violated was, again, very limited.

When we compared beliefs and knowledge across domains we found that there was a significant difference by domain in beliefs about what age a child should be given adult-like choices, from age 9 in custody disputes to 17 in prostitution. We also obtained significant domain differences in knowledge of what to do when rights are violated, with the least knowledge in the legal and social-economic areas, and the most in physical or sexual abuse situations. There was, however, also a significant difference by sex in knowledge. Across domains, girls evidenced less knowledge of how to deal with violated rights than did boys. When given the opportunity to express their general rights related concerns, 73% of those interviewed expressed concerns. Most of their comments fit into one of four general categories. Interestingly, a full 51% expressed strong concerns about the current *Young Offender's Act*. They complained of its leniency; they wanted harsher treatment for juvenile offenders, and they wanted the names of offenders publicized. Their attitudes could well be related to the concerns expressed by a further 18% about discriminatory treatment by adult authorities, being harassed by police, and being stereotyped as delinquent. Together, the comments indicate that many adolescents are angry about discrimination on the basis of age. They want greater differentiation, with the "good kids" being treated with more respect, and the "bad kids" being punished. Few (19%) of the adolescents expressed a desire for more autonomy; they wanted the decision making age lowered for smoking (the age has recently been raised), drinking, driving, and leaving school. The remaining comments were that there is too much support for pregnant teens, that the drinking age should be raised, and that legislators should disallow funding cuts to education.

VI. RIGHTS VALUES

Rights values were assessed with a two part questionnaire, which was completed by a further 50 males and 78 females aged 15 through 18 years. Although current social and economic conditions are relatively poor, as noted previously, it is also the case that not all families are negatively affected by current economic policies. Thus it would be inappropriate to treat adolescents as an homogenous unit in this regard. To determine if current social and economic conditions do indeed influence adolescents' attitudes toward rights for others, one part of the questionnaire was a scale which measures awareness of limited access to opportunity (LAOS), (Landis, Dinitz & Reckless, 1963). The scale arguably is the most age appropriate measure of the sense of security Inglehart (1977), described to be predictive of values. The scale items measure the extent to which adolescents perceive themselves to have access to opportunity for educational and occupational development. In past research, the scale has been found to be predictive of adolescent values (e.g., Cernkovich, 1978; Short, Rivera, & Tennyson, 1965). Further, research has demonstrated a link between perception of future opportunities, especially occupational opportunities, and current concerns or attitudes (Nurmi, Poole & Kalakoskis, 1994; Poole & Cooney, 1987).

The other part of the questionnaire comprised 35 statements about rights in the general domains of social-economic, individual, collective, and children's rights. The inclusion of the various domains of rights was to allow for comparison of support for rights for children with those already in existence for adults under the Canadian Charter. Social-economic rights described rights to social welfare programmes, healthy environments, education and health care. Individual rights described rights to freedom of speech, democratic participation, equality of opportunity in employment, and in treatment before the law. Collective rights described the rights of minorities and women; for example, the rights of natives to self-government, and of women to abuse centres. The children's rights, drawn from the UN Convention, were, again, in the areas of protection from physical and sexual abuse, legal rights and social-economic rights. Each statement was accompanied by a 5 point likert-type scale on which the importance of that right was to be indicated. Age and sex of the adolescents also was asked for.

The importance ratings were summed within rights domains and MA-NOVAs yielded the following significant findings. (Data are presented in Appendix 3) There was a main effect of sex, with females rating each domain of rights as being of greater importance than males. There was also a main effect of domain; post-hoc analyses (all post-hocs were planned comparison t-tests for the differences among means) indicated that importance ratings differed significantly among all domains with social-economic rights being rated the most important followed by children's rights, individual rights, and collective rights respectively.

Within the domain of children's rights, there was again a sex difference, a main effect of sub-domain, and a sex by sub-domain interaction. In essence the data indicated that with the exception of legal rights, females are more supportive than are males of children's rights, and that both males and females show more support for rights offering protection from abuse than for legal and social-economic rights.

Correlations performed on the rights importance ratings and the LAOS scores showed the following. Both males and females who perceived limited opportunities for their futures were significantly less likely to assign importance to individual, social-economic, or children's rights. The lack of a significant correlation between collective rights and LAOS may be attributable to the relatively low level of support for collective rights that was shown.

VII. SUMMARY AND IMPLICATIONS

The major findings of our studies suggest support among the current cohort for the rights specified in the UN Convention may depend on sex, education, and sense of security.

In accord with the theoretical predictions of Gilligan (1982, 1990), it was found that across domains girls value rights more than do boys. However, with the exception of protection from abuse, girls' knowledge of rights is less than boys, particularly with respect to actions that can be taken when rights are violated. This latter may result from socialization patterns that promote more independence among males and help seeking behaviours among girls, or it may result from males generally showing more political interest and knowledge (Furnham, 1985). Or the sex difference in knowledge may be related to differential needs and concerns: statistically, females are more likely than are males to need help in abuse situations. Further research is needed here.

The success of educational programs in both promoting support for rights, and in making rights meaningful to those who hold them, is seen in the data obtained for the domain of protection from physical and sexual abuse. This is the area of rights which has received the most attention in schools and the media. There was greatest level of knowledge of the basic law here, and what to do when rights are violated. There was agreement that protection was needed, and the right to protection from abuse was highly valued.

The need for education was clear in the social-economic domain. Although rights were valued in this domain, knowledge was very poor. Many adolescents assumed rights exist that do not; for example, most believed that children have a right to dental care, to daycare, and to freedom from poverty. But no such rights exist in Canada at this time. Legal rights, also, were in general less well known, and less valued. This may reflect the cynicism underlying the broad consensus among our sample that there were insufficient rights for victims (e.g., children caught in custody disputes), insufficient rights to protect against discriminatory treatment on the basis of age, and excess rights for juvenile offenders. Appropriately designed educational programs should sensitize youth to which rights remain needed by children, and why rights are necessary in certain areas (e.g., *Young Offender's Act*). It is perhaps obvious that accurate knowledge and understanding of existing rights and related law is a necessary precondition of striving for change. But education alone may be insufficient.

In accord with the theoretical predictions of Inglehart (1977), a sense of security about the future predicted valuing rights. The relation between perception of educational or occupational opportunity and support for rights suggests that it may be unlikely that this cohort will provide much impetus toward strong commitment to the Convention in Canada. Continuing high levels of unemployment, together with higher education costs, suggest that a large portion of youth may be faced with limited opportunities for the future.

The successful implementation of the Convention ultimately will require a social environment which promotes opportunities and hope for the future among youth. Such an environment requires an array of social and economic policies which are committed to pursuing goals such as full employment, accessible education, and so forth (c.f., Howe, 1994). Policy makers, for example, cannot be content to allow high levels of unemployment, as has been the case in Canada since the late 1970s. If children develop in a social and policy environment sensitive to their psychological and material needs, they then are more likely to value the rights of others.

ACKNOWLEDGMENT

We gratefully acknowledge the cooperation and assistance of Mr Angus McMullin, Cape Breton District School Board in obtaining the adolescents for our studies; the dedication and tireless efforts of our research assistant, Jenny Ramsey; and the funding provided by the Research Committee of the University College of Cape Breton.

APPENDIX 1

Rights Knowledge: Questionnaire Data

Mean scores

RIGHTS DOMAIN	FEMALES	MALES
legal	4.01	4.16*
sex abuse	5.07	4.65
physical abuse	5.34	4.95
social-economic	2.98	3.27

*maximum score = 7

Main effect of domain: $F(3,118) = 87.07, p < .001$
Sex X domain interaction: $F(3,118) = 3.46, p < .02$

APPENDIX 2

Rights Knowledge: Interview Data

Mean age at which adult-like rights should be granted

RIGHTS DOMAIN	FEMALES	MALES
legal(crime)	14.9	14.75
legal(custody)	9.14	10.33
abuse(prostitution)	17.77	16.92
abuse(pornography)	16.08	15.50

Main effect of domain: $F(3, 98) = 4.93, p < .03$

Knowledge of appropriate action when rights are violated

RIGHTS DOMAIN	FEMALES	MALES
legal(crime)	1.04	1.29*
legal(custody)	.63	.82
abuse (sexual)	1.45	1.61
abuse (physical)	1.25	1.59
social-economic	1.24	1.31

Main effect of sex: $F(1,98) = 4.63, p < .03$
Main effect domain: $F(4,98) = 17.82, p < .001$

* responses were coded as:
    0 = don't know or there's nothing that can be done
    1 = unspecified help would be sought
    2 = appropriate action described

maximum score = 2

APPENDIX 3

Rights Values Data

*Mean Importance Ratings Given to Rights**

RIGHTS DOMAIN	FEMALES	MALES
Social-economic	43.30	40.44
Children	40.72	37.38
Individual	39.71	34.89
Collective	31.28	26.82

* ratings summed: maximum score 50

Main effect of sex: $F(1,126) = 22.89, p < .001$

Main effect of domain: $F(3,124) = 11.01, p < .001$

*Main Importance Ratings Given To Children's Rights**

SUB DOMAIN	FEMALES	MALES
Physical abuse	4.30	3.99
Sexual abuse	4.22	3.61
Social-economic	4.08	3.68
Legal	3.81	3.74

* ratings averaged: maximum score 5

Main effect of sex: $F(1,126) = 12.56, p < 0.1$

Main effect of domain: $F(3,124) = 9.00, p < 0.1$

Sex X domain interaction: $F(3,124) = 6.47, p < 0.1$

Correlations between laos and rights ratings

Individual rights r	$= -.241, p < .01$
Social economic rights	$= -.231, p < .02$
Children's rights r	$= -.241, p < .03$

REFERENCES

Astin, A.W., Green, K.C. and Korn, W.S. (1987) *The American Freshman: Twenty-year Trends*. Los Angeles: UCLA Higher Education Research Institute.

Astin, A.W., Korn, W.S. and Berz, E. R. (1990) *The American Freshman: National Norms for Fall 1989*. Los Angeles: UCLA Higher Education Research Institute.

Beech, R.P. and Schoeppe, A. (1974) "Development of Value Systems in Adolescents." *Developmental Psychology*, 10, 644–656.

Bibby, R.W. and Posterski, D.C. (1985) *The Emerging Generation*. Toronto: Irwin Publishing.

Canada (1994) *Convention on the Rights of the Child: First Report of Canada*. Human Rights Directorate, Department of Canadian Heritage.

Cernkovich, S.A. (1978) "Evaluating two Models of Delinquency Causation." *Criminology, 16,* (3), 335–352.

Conger, J.J. (1988) "Hostages to the Future: Youth, Values, and the Public Interest." *American Psychologist, 43,* 291–300.

Covell, K., Rose-Krasnor, L. and Fletcher, K. A. (1994) Age Differences in Understanding Peace, War, and Conflict Resolution. *International Journal of Behavioural Development,* 17(4), 717–737.

Erikson, E.H. (1968) *Identity: Youth and Crisis.* New York: Norton.

Fischer, K. W. (1980) A Theory of Cognitive Development: The control and construction of hierarchies of skills. *Psychological Review, 87,* 477–531.

Furnham, A. (1985) Adolescents' Sociopolitical Attitudes: A study of sex and national differences. *Political Psychology, 6,* (4), 621–636.

Gewirth, A. (1982) *Human rights: Essays on Justifications and Applications.* Chicago: University of Chicago Press.

Gilligan, C. (1982) *In a Different Voice.* Cambridge, MA: Harvard University Press.

Gilligan, C. (1990) "Teaching Shakespeare's Sister." In C. Gilligan, N. Lyons, and T. Hanmer (Eds): *Making Connections: The Relational Worlds of Adolescent Girls at Emma Willard School.* Cambridge, MA: Harvard University Press.

Glover, R. (1991) "Value Selection in Relation to Grade in School and Stage of Moral Reasoning." *Psychological Reports 68,* 931–937.

Howe, R. B. (1994) "The Case for a Canadian Social Charter." In M. Charlton and P. Barker (Eds): *Contemporary Political Issues.* Toronto: Nelson Canada.

Inglehart, R. (1977) *The Silent Revolution.* Princeton: Princeton University Press.

Landis, J. R., Dinitz, S. and Reckless, W.C. (1963) "Implementing Two Theories of Delinquency: Value orientation and awareness of limited opportunity." *Sociology and Social Research, 47* (4), 408–416.

Marcia, J. E. (1991) "Identity and Self-development." In R. Lerner, A.C. Petersen and J. Brooks-Gunn (Eds): *Encyclopedia of Adolescence.* Vol 1. New York: Garland.

Maslow, A.H. (1970) *Motivation and Personality.* New York: Harper Row.

Maslow, A.H. (1972) *The Farther Reaches of Human Nature.* New York: Penguin.

Nurmi, J.E., Poole, M.E. and Kalakoskis, V. (1994) "Age Differences in Adolescent Future-oriented Goals, Concerns, and Related Temporal Extension in Different Sociocultural Contexts". *Journal of Youth and Adolescence, 23* (4), 471–478

Piaget, J. (1932) *The Moral Judgment of the Child.* New York: Harcourt Brace Jovanovich.

Poole, M.E. and Cooney, G.H. (1987) "Orientations to the Future: A Comparison of Adolescents in Australia and Singapore." *Journal of Youth and Adolescence, 16,* 129–151.

Santrock, J. W. (1993) *Adolescence,* Madison, WI: WCB Brown and Benchmark.

Schatz, R.T. and Fiske, S.T. (1992) "International Reactions to the Threat of Nuclear War: The rise and fall of concern in the eighties." *Political Psychology, 13,* 1–29.

Selman, R.l. (1980) *The Growth of Interpersonal Understanding.* New York: Academic Press.

Serow, R. C. and Dreyden, J. I. (1990) "Community Service among College and University Students: Individual and Institutional Relationships. *Adolescence, 25* (99), 553–567.

Short, J. F., Rivera, R. and Tennyson, R.A. (1965) "Perceived Opportunities, Gang Membership and Delinquency." *American Sociological Review, 30,* 56–57.

Smetana, J. G., Killen, M. and Turiel, E. (1991) "Children's Reasoning about Interpersonal and Moral Conflicts." *Child Development, 62,* 629–644.

Sniderman, P., Fletcher, J., Russell, P. and Tetlock, P. *Attitudes Towards Civil Liberties and the Canadian Charter of Rights.* Institute for Social Research, York University.

Wohlfield, M.J. and Nevitte, N. (1990) "Postindustrial Value Change and Support for Native Issues. *Canadian Ethnic Studies, 22* (3), 56–68.

WILLY FACHÉ

How to Develop a Participatory, Comprenhensive and Coherent Youth Policy?

In this chapter we will explore a model of what we name a participatory, comprehensive and coherent youth policy and review the instrumentarium for the implementation of this kind of youth policy. The ideas developed in this paper are based on:

1. a comparative research of the youth policy literature in European countries;
2. the experience of implementing the proposed instrumentarium in collaboration with the Youth Council of the Flemish Community from 1985 till 1987 (Faché, 1987);
3. the first round of our European survey who was sent out by the Standing Conference of Local and Regional Authorities of Europe of the Council of Europe in 1987.

We shall first examine the different components of the concept comprehensive and coherent youth policy and review the instruments for such a policy. Afterwards we shall discuss at length the concept of participatory youth policy and its implementation.

I. THE CONCEPT OF COMPREHENSIVE AND COHERENT YOUTH POLICY

Traditionally, areas of policy are identified functionally and not in terms of target groups. Various departments look after the needs of the entire population: one department looks after the education needs, another the housing needs, etc. In other words, a sectorial approach is used.

With respect to some categories of the population, however, we can discern a specific attention in the governmental policy. The policy attention for some social categories is characterised by specific laws and regulations, and by specific provisions over which a great deal of money is spent. This social category as policy target group determines sometimes also the governmental structure. In various countries, a categorical policy attention is given to ethnic minorities, elderly, the handicapped and young people.

The degree to which a social category gets a specific policy attention depends upon normative ideas. A high degree of specific attention is justified

E. Verhellen (ed.), Monitoring Children's Rights, 263–279.
© 1996 *Kluwer Law International. Printed in the Netherlands.*

when a group in its situation is sharply different from the rest of the population, if there is a specific need for help in such a situation and if the group does not dispose of the necessary resources to meet his needs.

There is a growing awareness that governmental policy – not only in the areas of education, health and recreation, but also in areas such as housing, labour, environment and other areas concerned with the political, legal and economic position of the young – should be systematically evaluated for their compatibility with the needs and specific situation of young people. In other words, there is a growing awareness that young people merits explicit attention in all fields of governmental involvement, and that a comprehensive youth policy is justified (Faché, 1981).

This specific policy attention to young people can find expression in each of the policy departments separately. There is also another approach possible: the policy attention to youth is the responsibility of one single department, i.e. a department for young people.

We do not opt for one single department – i.e. a youth department – but for a youth attention spread over many departments. The effect being that a comprehensive youth policy does not require an upheaval in administrative organisation and the specific competence of each department can be used in developing a youth policy (Faché, 1984).

But the coherence and consistency of an inter-sectoral youth policy will remain unsatisfactory as long as it is developed solely by each of the separate government departments. In order to make a coherent youth policy, all policy actors need to develop a common view on youth policy and continual coordination is necessary.

II. THE INSTRUMENTS FOR A COMPREHENSIVE AND COHERENT YOUTH POLICY

For the realisation of a youth policy as briefly described above, the following instrumentarium appeared necessary:
  a. a youth-impact survey of governmental regulations and decisions which explicitly or implicitly affect the world of the young people;
  b. foundation statement regarding youth policy;
  c. a co-ordinating authority for youth policy (i.e. Minister for young people) (Faché, 1984 and 1987).
We will now successively discuss each of these tools.

A. A Youth-impact Survey of Governmental Regulations

In almost every area of policy there are made regulations and taken decisions that specifically and explicitly are intended to affect the lifeworld of the young people. There are also made a number of regulations that not specifically concern young people, nevertheless considerably affect the lifeworld of young people. Our research (Faché, 1987) give evidence that policymakers do not always realise the impact of their decisions (possibly in combination with decisions taken by other policymakers) on the young people. On top of this we find opposing and overlapping regulations. A survey which detect and inventory all youth relevant regulations and indicate per regulation the targetgroup, the aims, and the impact on the lifeworld of young people could identify regulations requiring adjustment or harmonization. This survey will be also a valuable instrument when we subject new policy proposals at a youth-impact analyses. Finally, problems which transcend any one area of policy and require comprensive and fundamental measures could come to light. For example, with respect to youth unemployment, regulations do not suffice. Only "interdepartmental" action can lead to results in this respect.

By publishing the youth-impact survey, non-governmental organisations (for example a youth council) may make policy makers, who proclaim not to be involved in youth policy, aware of the "side effects" their policies have on the young people and insist on adjustment or harmonization of their regulations.

In collaboration with the Youth Council of the Flemish Community we designed a method for a youth-impact survey of governmental regulations (Faché, 1987).

B. A Foundation Statement Regarding Youth Policy

In order to further the coherence of various governmental regulations, an "interdepartmental" instrument in the form of a foundation statement regarding youth policy is essential. Main lines and priorities of youth policy are stated herein. The main lines could constitute the aims, objectives, principles of execution and political instruments for youth policy. The foundation statement is not a detailed policy document. A foundation statement should however lead to such an annual policy document for each governmental department.

On the basis of the foundation statement (prepared by the co-ordinating authority for youth policy) policy actors can debate on possible courses of action with regard to future youth policy, and state priorities. Ultimately, it will contain the politically most important choices. A foundation statement on youth policy also provides one with a frame of reference on the basis of which decisions are made with regard to policy changes, or about new developments, and it stimulates the placing of youth problems in a contextual sense. It provides a point of reference for the execution of youth policy and permits insight into a larger context on the basis of which political mesures receive their legitimacy.

The aims and objectives towards a comprehensive and coherent youth policy are an essential part of a foundation statement.

A pluralistic welfare state does not have a dominating ideology from which universally accepted policy aims and objectives may be derived by the government. In our welfare state various frames of reference co-exist.

If one were to list the "official" aims as stated in youth policy papers, and the aims inspiring those directly involved, it will become apparent that some of these aims place us in a dilemma. For example the following aims form a dilemma: "the stimulation of self-reliance" and "protecting the young". It is very clarifying to formulate the objectives in terms of a dilemma. In discussions on future youth policy real choices can become evident.

The weight attributed to the individual objectives also determines also the scope of the youth policy. Should the emphasis lie on "protection and education" then youth policy is restricted to school, youth work and youth protection. If, for example, we want to promote equality then this entails that we should consider the causes of inequality which usually lie outside the welfare sector.

All governmental departments should co-operate in producing a mutually agreed foundation statement on youth policy. The introduction of a foundation statement on youth policy makes it possible to arrive at a coherent youth policy without putting together the various policy units which are involved in youth policy into one youth department.

This procedure has no consequences for the present organisational structure. The strength of segmented policy making, namely the knowledge of the area of policy together with the intrinsic expertise, should be preserved.

C. A Co-ordinating Authority for Youth Policy

Next to a foundation statement on youth policy, which is an interdepartmental instrument for a coherent youth policy, it is necessary to set up a separate policy institution with political power. The primary responsibility of this institution is to draw attention of all policymakers to the interests of the young people, to initiate, to co-ordinate and to monitor the development of a comprehensive and coherent youth policy.

Why is it necessary to have a such separate policy institution when every governmental department must take account of the interests of the young? Present policy shows clearly that the interests of the young people are not sufficiently taken into account in each of the governmental departments nor do the young people participate in policy-making processes.

Particularly in areas of policy where young people, together with other population groups, are the target-group of policy, they are all to easily overlooked or not taken seriously. Thought for the needs of young people does not come by itself within a sectorial policy (for example, housing, employment policy).

III. THE CONCEPT PARTICIPATORY YOUTH POLICY

In the majority of the European countries, society's responsibility is seen as limited to the improvement of individual well-being and socialisation of the young. However, changing concepts about the role of young people in society have, since the seventies, resulted in advocating not to restrict society's responsibility in this sense, but to extend it into giving the young the possibility of developing their own ideas about the future of society, of sharing power with other groups in society as a whole.

A. Empowering Young People

The concept of empowerment is defined in the literature in various ways. But the common underlying assumptions are, that individuals understand their own needs better than others understand them, and that the individual should have the power both to define his/her own needs and to act upon that understanding (Rappoport, 1981; Freire, 1983, Cochran and Woolever, 1983). But differences in definitions involve whether empowerment is a state or a process, and whether empowerment as a process involves only change in individuals or also in mediating and controlling structures (Cochran, 1987). We refer in this context to empowerment as a process.

Those authors defining empowerment as a process are themselves in some disagreement over what unit(s) in society should be the focus of efforts to empower: changes in individuals, mediating structures (as neighborhood, voluntary associations) or controlling structures (as school and workplace) (Cochran, 1987).

Virginia Vanderslice (1984, quoted in Cochran, 1987) has presented an evolving definition of empowerment which takes into account the writings of those earlier thinkers. She refers to empowerment "as a process through which people become more able to influence those people and organizations that affect their lives and the lives of those they care about". In addition to the assumptions common to all those working with the empowerment concept, Vanderslice stresses as a goal the making of "meaningful changes in institutions", and argues that in order for such a goal to be reached the empowerment process must include people working together on behalf of something greater than themselves as individuals.

Vanderslice refers to empowerment as a developmental process, and even identifies some steps in that process. Yet empowerment must involve more than the normal course of development, if it is to make a unique contribution to practice, and improve the human condition. What distinguishes the empowerment process from those engaged in by individuals in the normal course of living? Developmentalists are interested in understanding how individuals proceed from one developmental stage or phase to another, and the changes that occur throughout this life course. Those involved with the empowerment process assume that development occurs, but recognize and systematically acknowledge those obstacles to development which operate outside the spheres of influence of the developing individual. Such obstacles include social class structure, structural differentiations by race and gender, and perhaps even the influences of bureaucratization upon individuals and groups (Vanderslice, 1984, quoted in Cochran, 1987).

According to Cochran (1987) an entire "school" of theorists (such as Willis, 1983; Anyon, 1980) "has emerged during the 1970s and 80s around the general thesis that schools and workplaces are organized to maintain power differentials based upon historically and biologically defined differences in class, gender and race. For individuals assigned less value by those criteria the unequal distribution of resources based upon such discrimination represents an obstacle which stands in the way of full development throughout the life span." "Developmental psychologists do not, as a rule, give such impediments to development a central place in their inquiries. They are more likely to "control them away". The proposition offered there is that such obstacles are indeed central to the empowerment concept, although not always explicitly acknowledged as such. The proposal is that empowerment only becomes germane to the developing individual when barriers to the normal course of development are encountered, the removal of which are beyond the present or future capacity of that person as an individual. These obstacles are the raison d'être of the empowerment process, and therefore progress in overcoming them must be seen as the basic purpose underlying that process." (Cohran, 1987).

Useful for understanding the concept of empowerment in this context is according to Cohran (1987, quoting Girous, 1983) the theory of "resistance", which "celebrates a dialectical notion of human agency that rightly portrays domination as a process that is neither static or complete". Giroux argues that in all societies where structural inequities exist there is resistance to those structures. It follows that the empowerment process must, to be complete, provide an outlet for those energies of resistance in the service of overcoming obstacles to the realization of full developmental potential.

From the previous discussion, Cochran (1987) has distilled the following definition of empowerment, which we find relevant in qualifying youth policy: "Empowerment is an interactive process involving mutual respect and critical reflection through which both people and controlling institutions are changed in ways that proivde those people with greater influence over individuals and institutions which are in some way influencing their efforts to achieve equal status in society".

Currently young people experience powerlessness through their status as young people – by exclusion from decision-making processes, for example in schools, or, on a wider basis, by their exclusion from the political process. Moreover, this powerlessness is often overlaid by other categories, most notably social class, disability, etnicity, and gender – which interact with generation to produce a matrix of power/powerlessness.

In the last two decades we have, according to Stein and Frost (1992), become used to understanding gender, etnicity, disability, and to a lesser extent sexual orientation as indices of the unequal distribution of power in a stratified society. Equal opportunities policies have become a familiar vehicle for attempts to tackle such inequalities. This conceptual framework has not been applied to "generation" in such a rigorous manner. "Generation" is understood by Stein and Frost (1992) as a system through which young people experience negative attitudes, policies, and practices which act in an discriminatory manner against them. As with racism and sexism this is manifested in both individual practices and attitudes and in instutional forms. Children and young people experience inequality according to social class, gender, ethnicity, and disability, but their experience cannot be fully understood unless generation is conceptualized as a comparable indicator.

Seen in this way generation becomes a crucial political field of play – comparable to those other fields we are more used to understanding as political.

What sort of theoretical framework do we need in order to achieve change?

For Stein and Frost (1992) it follows "that empowerment acts as an effective framework for understanding policy and practice development with young people. In order to establish why empowerment is an important concept we will first have to argue that the emphasis on children's rights, often regarded as the "radical" perspective, is an inadequate conception both theoretically and practically."

"First, arguments for children's rights are often proposed in a legalistic and paternalistic manner – something that adults should legislate for on behalf of children and young people. In this sense children's rights are contradictory as they exclude children and young people from the process of improving their own lives."

"Second, rights arguments have a tendency to stop once they have achieved the aim of reaching the statute book. The best example of this is the legislation designed to stop discrimination on grounds of gender or ethnicity. Such legislation, while a symbolic advance in its own right, has patently failed to eliminate such discrimination. In order to work, such legislative changes have to have an impact on material reality as well as on the state books."

"Third, rights in relation to young people tend to be framed indivually; "the child shall have the right to...". Effective change for children also requires collective action and organisation."

Youth policy should therefore be one which is empowering young people. If one is attempting to move towards empowerment of young people as a goal of youth policy then powerfull participation of young people in policymaking-processes is essential.

Participation is far from a simple concept, it is indeed a complex one. Participation means many things to many people. The concept of participation seen from the viewpoint of individual citizens who are affected by policies or receive services, may well differ from those who make policy and provide services.

B. *Different Perspectives on Participation*

To consider these different perspectives on participation is very important, because they affect the various attempts made to empower people in the policy-making process and in the provision of a number of services. We will first consider the viewpoint of individual citizens. Boaden et al. (1982) formulated three perspectives.

"First, participation in service provision can be seen as a means by which individuals may protect their rights as consumers of public goods and services. Just as the consumer has rights which protect his interest in relation to services and goods provided in the market place by the private sector, it is argued that he should have his interests protected in relation to those goods and services for which there is either no market or where the state has replaced the private sector as provider. In other words, the public should be protected as consumers of public goods, and participation in decisions about the nature and delivery of such goods is one way to do this."

"A second mass perspective on participation might best be described as the right to consultation. From the point of view of the individual citizen, it is important to have the opportunity to express his opinion and put his point of view to those in authority. He wants to be consulted on those matters which affect him, particularly those which do so directly and in the immediate future. Proposals for new roads, reorganisation of schools and the closure of hospitals are examples of occasions when those affected will not only want to express their views but will expect to be able to do so."

"A third individual perspective on participation involves the idea of people sharing in the processes of policy-making and service provision so that they may determine or share in the determination of policy and service content. This is a perspective adopted by many radical advocates of participation who believe that people have the right to decide for themselves the factors which shape their own local issues and problems can be resolved by all local inhabitants coming together to settle differences. Such a view of participation involves some transfer of power from existing elites or policy-makers to the wider community, as well as involving much wider and more frequent interaction among those concerned." Boaden et al. (1982) used the concept of "interactive participation" to describe this kind of participation.

So far we have considered three perspectives on participation from the point of view of those who are affected by policies and receive services. The perspectives of those who make decisions and provide services, may well differ from those of individual citizens.

"The first of these elite perspectives stresses the value of participation as a legtimating device, securing support for those in authority and for the taking of particular decisions about policy and service. Much of the participation in relation to structure plans is of this kind: publicity campaigns for proposals, public meetings, surveys and the like. These make the public feeling it has been involved, but largely leave the decision-makers to do as they like. Other examples can be found in housing and transportation and we would conclude that this mode of participation is most heavily favoured by those in authority locally. It involves minimal action, secures support for their proposals; and for very little effort enjoys high symbolic value. The authority is able to point to a range of visible activities and often to quantifiable involvement without real threat to the prevailing distribution of power." (Boaden, et al. 1982).

"Groups and individuals drawn into this mode of participation often find themselves subject to the criticism levelled at community participation. Many of the methods used in legitimating participation lend themselves to the charge that groups have been co-opted or become incorporated. The problem for groups in the community is that failure to respond to opportunities of this kind makes it difficult for them to exert any influence at all. Often the same techniques serve different participatory ends, and it is the conflict of intention between decision-makers and participants which is problematic. Channels of influence viewed from below are often no more than channels of support when viewed from above." (Boaden, et al. 1982).

The second elite perspective points to the utility of participation as a way of improving policies and services. This instrumental view of participation is frequently used by professional officers involved in policy-making and service provision to justify quite elaborate exercises in participation. Information collection describes this form of participation which is usually practised through sample surveys, public meetings, consultative committees and the like.

Clearly these methods provide information often not available in any other way and from sources which do not usually contribute to decision-making. If officers can digest and use it, such information may well improve decisions. What it may also do, given the organisation of much participation in the public sector, is enhance the power of professional officers in relation to their elected "masters". Councillors often counter such officer attempts to use information in this way by pointing to their own extensive sources of such information. Their daily contact with the public, their frequent surgeries for constituents, their exposure to the views of party members, and their involvement in some participatory exercises, allow councillors to argue from their own well-informed base. Whatever the outcome of the dialogue between officers and members, and our review suggests they are usually in agreement, both the use of information and the decision-making remain in their hands. There is no third perspective from the elite point of view to match the mass perspective which favours a shift of power. Elites do not favour such transfers.

They are concerned to improve their capacity through the acquisition of more information and to reinforce decisive positions through popular support. They are not about to give power to the people. In this regard they enjoy powerful control over the means of access to decisions about public services and can often screen out contributions after they have been made. Of course, the decision-makers do not eliminate all external views. Rather they operate selectively so that only a limited range of views are heard. This practice raises important questions about the bias inherent in the choices wich decision-makers make about who will be heard." (Boaden, et al. 1982).

The different perspectives on participation adopted by both elites and general public affect the various attempts made to increase public participation.

In our European survey (Faché, 1988) this becomes apparent in the different new ways and means by which participation of youth in local government is encouraged.

When we want to empower the young people in policy-making processes than consultation and interactive participation as described above are the right perspective on participation.

C. Non-manipulative Participation of Young People

Taking into account the long debate about the merits of "real" participation contrasted with socio-technical" participation in organisation-theory, one has to bear in mind that the mere fact of formal participation does not suffice to gain influence in an organisation. On the contrary, giving for example youth some possibility to elect their own representatives in schools, universities, political youth groups, can according to Hartmann and Trnka (1985) be taken as a way to manipulate the young people and to turn their activities to areas of minor importance for society. The reform of universities in some countries might serve as an example of such a manipulatory effect of increased participation, in which student representatives were accepted on all decision-making levels. At the same time, students had to accept more rigid study programmes for which they shared responsibility, as they were taking part in the decisions. When criticised, teachers and administrators could always refer to student-representatives for having approved course programmes. Participation of young people, therefore, contains the notion of a non-manipulative voluntary engagement of youth in policy-making processes which is contrasted with other forms of participation based on manipulation, coercion or renumeration.

IV. INSTRUMENTS FOR A PARTICIPATORY YOUTH POLICY

In this section we will identify some of the implementation issues and programmatic challenges in applying the empowerment concept at the local community level.

First of all the participation of youth people in decisionmaking processes relating to affairs which affect their lifeworld must be guaranteed by law.

A. A Legal Liability to Inform and to Consult Young People

A major way for citizens to influence the policy is by electing their representatives. There are two aspects of this indirect democracy; relating to (1) those who represent, and (2) those who are allowed to elect the representatives. As far as those two aspects are concerned, some ameliorations have been proposed to achieve greater involvement of young people in the decision-making relating to community affairs. One of the proposed measures in different countries concerns the lowering of the age at which youngsters are allowed to vote, and at which they are allowed to run as a candidate for a political function. Another measure that has been proposed is that a certain number of seats would be reserved for young people.

Moreover, government must be legally liable to inform and to consult young people in all governmental decisions related to youth. No single fundamental policy decision should be made by the government without previous consultation of concerned parties. Not just those the policy measure is aimed at, are concerned parties, but also those affected by the measure in one way or another. With each policy proposal the interested parties change. The body with the decisive power in policy making carries full responsibility to determine who is consulted, when and how. For that very reason the governing body can be called to account. By not explicitly stating in a law who should be consulted a large degree of flexibility is maintained within the development of the consultation principle, and provision is made for a variety of consultation practices (such as innovative approaches). This consultation system is to support as well as correct the representative democracy (Faché, 1981).

Permanent advisory councils (for example a youth council of which the membership composition does not vary per policy issue) are not in a position to exhaustively realise the consultation principle as previously defined. Such bodies are less problem related than is usually supposed. They are indeed made up of concerned population categories but that does not imply they are capable of overseeing each policy issue from the relevant viewpoint. Because the concerned population categories may vary per policy issue (Kuypers, 1978). The problem-solving ability of permanent advisory councils is therefore, by definition, limited.

A prerequisite for truly participation by citizens is an adequate exchange of information. A democratic state system presupposes the duty to inform.

This entails: giving information to citizens with regard to policy proposals as well as the consultation procedure (who, when and how shall be consulted), and finally about the policy decision and the motivation thereof.

The authorities are responsible for on the one hand the completeness and the reliability of the information provided, and on the other hand for the availability and accessibility (also readability) of the information for the public, and finally for the time of circulation of the information.

By means of a legal liability to inform and consult, the authority may be answerable to her obligation, should she for example fail to involve young people in the relevant consultation processes. This occurs frequently. For example authorities have advisory councils for the environment, education and housing policy on which young people are not invited to participate.

As far as young people may join in with public participation procedures together with adults, actual experience shows that they frequently do not come to the foreground. This is no excuse however not to proceed with the demand for direct involvement of young people in participation processes. However, this negative experience does provide us with a motive to search for ways in which to equip young people better in order that they may take part in the development of policy and the participation processes on equal par with other citizens. A support structure for youth participation at different levels could be one way of achieving this (see later).

So far we have considered a legal obligation for the government to consult and inform young people. But legal obligations are also necessary to guarantee participation in services' policies. Some countries do have such legal obligations. In this way for instance, a "Schulordnung" (1 October 1975, § 49–53) put into effect this obligation for educational matters in the Canton of Basel Stadt (Faché, 1988).

In Austria the law even stipulates that companies with at least five young workers under eighteen should establish a young workers' representative council (§ 132 Als. 1 Art. VG: Jugendversammlung, ein Wahlvorstand für die Wahl des Jugendvertrauensrats und ein Jugendvertrauensrat).

B. Examples of Participation of Young People in Policy Making Processes at Local Level

It does not suffice for the government to acknowledge the right of participation of young people; it is equally necessary for the local state (and also for the other levels) to implement measures which support and foster this participation.

In all countries there are successful examples of empowering young people by achieving greater participation of young people. We will describe them concisely (see: Faché, 1988).

Young People's City Council

In Filderstadt (Kreis Esslingen), a young people's city council was elected by youngsters between 14 and 18 years old. One out of four of the young people that were entitled to vote chose twenty youngsters from among the 49 candidates. The sucessful candidates have a seat on the young people's city council for a period of two years. This council is entitled to discuss and advise on all matters that concern young people. Each proposal of the young people's city council, however, has to be approved by the adult council.

In Epinal the "Conseil des Jeunes" is elected in an entirely different way. Each secondary school and all the quartiers of the city choose their two respresentatives (one boy, and one girl) who have to be between 13 and 17 years of age. Each school and each quartier, however, decides for itself how it will elect its representatives. At the beginning of a new school-year, the council is composed anew. As a whole, it consists of 42 young people. The "Conseil des Jeunes" functions in the same way as an adult city council.

Dialogue Between Young People and City Councillors
In Weingarten, youngsters have been offered the opportunity to discuss youth problems in a city-council meeting twice a year since 1978. Also in the city of Rastatt such discussions are organised under the name of "Der Gemeinderat steht Rede und Antwort".

Representatives of Young People in Special Committees of the City Council
In numerous cities youth-organisations and local youth-councils are invited to appoint representatives to consult with the youth committee of the city council for the purpose of giving their views and experience on matters being considered by the committee.

Youth Forum
In Basel, Innsbruck, Pforzheim and Norwich, there are annual youth forums. To such a youth forum all the city's young people receive an invitation; it gives them the opportunity to exchange ideas and discuss issues, especially important youth issues. Young people have the opportunity to let know their problems and visions to the city council members.

In Grenoble the children of the highest grades in primary school (9–11 year-olds) were granted a single opportunity in the city-council hall to pick one out of five youth projects proposed by the council, viz "Une maison des métiers".

Youth Council at the Local and National Level
Numerous cities and governments have functioning youth councils, that consist of youthwork representatives. Most of these councils deal mostly with problems with respect to youth work.

C. A Support Organisation for Youth Participation

In addition to the different ways of empowering young people mentioned above we advocate a "support organisation for youth participation" with the following composition and tasks at the local and national level alike.

The participation of young people in policy making processes requires for young people to have the knowledge and the skills to participate. To enable young people to take really part in policy making processes well-prepared and equiped with policy proposals, a support system is needed that offers young people the possibility to:
- learn to think constructively and discuss;
- develop a vision on youth issues and the problems of particular youth categories;
- (re-)define (policy) problems;
- test the strength of new ideas in relation to various policy issues;
- draft and develop alternative policy proposals;
- to show up that so-called imposed external constraints on policy making are in reality sometimes restrictions which those in position of political power have chosen themselves.

In short, we are concerned with a support organisation where young people can increase their competence for participation, and where youth policy proposals can be developed by young people. These activities would enable young people to take part in policy making processes well-prepared and equipped.

Why is such support system necessary for young people? The young people need, more than other population categories, an organisation which stimulates and supports the intended activities again and again, because young participants in policy making situations are continuously being replaced by new ones. Young people are members of the category "youth" for a relatively short timespan only.

The above mentioned objectives of the proposed support organisation, the continuous replacement of the young participants, and the ever freshly presented youth issues require an organisational structure made up of project teams and a co-ordinating body, with the following composition and tasks.

The project teams must remain open to new members. For each youth issue an equivalent project team should be instituted. Each youth issue should be examined from all the relevant angles in these project teams. The project issues and the composition of this project teams will change continuously.

The co-ordinating body (where the youth officer takes a seat as discussed later) shows greater continuity than the project teams, and its duties are:
- (to stimulate) the constitution of project teams per youth issues;
- to provide technical service to project teams;
- to co-ordinate the project team activities by supporting a structured exchange of information and by stimulating co-operation;
- to follow the political agenda;
- to guard the government observing its liability to inform and consult youth people.

This co-ordinating body is not meant to be the (communication) channel along which exchange of information (such as policy proposals) between project teams and government must pass. The obstruction of the communication channel between support organisation and government by overloading the co-ordinating body should be avoided.

An important problem within the support organisation is: who decides which youth issues come up for discussion in the project teams, in other words who decides upon the agenda? This question refers to the following obstacles.

— How can we prevent a divergence between the problems experienced by the youth population (population agenda or public agenda) and the problems being discussed in the support organisation (agenda of the support organisation) and by the local and national authorities (the political agenda)?

— How can we prevent a divergence between the problems being discussed in the political system (e.g. the central government) (political agenda) and those in the support organisation?

Determining the agenda can be described as a process whereby demands of various groups in society are being translated into agenda points which compete for attention from the public (public agenda), from members of the support organisation (support structure agenda) and/or the governing body (political agenda). Such a process can follow three paths:

— the first path is taken by groups in society (for example young inhabitants of a city neighbourhood or young actiongroups) who previously had little or no contact with governing bodies, taking the initiative to publicly discuss their problems in the shape of action points (conversion from group agenda to public agenda), and subsequently try to get their action points placed on the political agenda, whether or not via the youth participation support organisation, thus making them action points on which political decisions (for example in municipal councils) will be based;

— a second path is for members of the support structure to place (youth) problems they detect in society (and which possibly they themselves are confronted with) on the agenda of a project team of the support organisation. Youth policy conferences, hearings and the like, can bring quite a few (youth) problems out in the open;

— there exists a third path. Points on the political agenda are also placed on the support organisation agenda. That is the reason why the support system for youth participation should at all times be aware of the political agenda (amongst others making use of the governmental duty to inform and consult).

From the short overview of the function, activities and structure of the support organisation for youth participation, the need for professional assistance from a youth officer becomes apparent.

D. A Youth Officer With Responsibility for Participation

According to a first view youth participation is the responsibility of everyone who is involved in the provision of youth services and policy-making.
According to a second view one youth officer on the local and national level
must have this responsibility. It could be suggested that the designation of
an officer might result in others feeling that they had a lesser or negligible
role, and this is clearly undesirable. However, the converse danger is that
while everyone is responsible and no-one has a specific role, the commitment
remains a general aspiration and few steps are taken to achieve it in practice.
The main duties of the youth officer responsible for youth participation are:

– Developing, implementing and monitoring participation policy. This
  involves among other things: the development of a support organisation for youth participation; together with the local and national authorities responsible for youth policy, take care of the effectuation of the
  governmental information and consultation liability.
– Making sure that in all areas of policy the interests of young people are
  actually taken into account.
– Evaluating of the governmental foundation statement regarding youth
  policy, in co-operation with the support organisation, and (in the event
  of the government failing in this respect) developing a proposal for a
  foundation statement.

REFERENCES

Berger, P. and Neuhaus, R. (1977) *To Empower People*. Washington, American Enterprise
    Institute.
Boaden, N., M. Goldsmith, W. Hampton and P. Stringer (1982) *Public Participation in Local
    Services*. London, Longman.
Cochran, M. and Woolever, F. (1983) "Beyond the Deficit Model." In Sigel, I. and Laosa, L.
    (Eds.): *Changing Families*. New York, Plenum Press.
Cochran, M. (1987) Empowering Families: An Alternative to the Deficit Model. In Hurrelman,
    K., e.a. (Eds.): *Social Intervention: Potential and Constraints*. Berlin, W. de Gruyter.
Faché, W. (Ed.), Gemeentelijk jeugdbeleid. Gent, Rijksuniversiteit, Studiegroep Jeugdwel-
    zijnsbeleid, 1981.
Faché, W. (1984) De taak van de jeugdconsulent in een maatschappelijk geïntegreerd en
    samenhangend jeugdbeleid. *Jeugd en Samenleving, 14(5)*, 320–337.
Faché, W. (1987) Een maatschappelijk geïntegreerd en samenhangend jeugdbeleid. In: *Jeug-
    draad voor de Vlaamse Gemeenschap*, Vierde Jaarverslag, juni 1986-juni 1987. Brussel,
    Ministerie van de Vlaamse Gemeenschap, 49–64.
Faché, W. (1988) Participation of young people in the political process. General Report.
    Strasbourg, Council of Europe, Standing Conference of Local and Regional Authorities
    of Europe.
Freire, P. (1983) *Pedagogy of the Oppressed*. New York, Seabury Press.
Hartmann, J. and Trnka, S. (1984) *Towards a Concept of Democratic Youth Participation in
    Society*. Uppsala, Uppsala University.
Kuypers, G. (1978) Beginselen van beleidsontwikkeling, Deel II.

Leene, G. and T. Schuyt (1981) Generale beleidsivisie en lokale praktijken. *Tijdschrift voor Agologie, 11*, 222–247.

Rappoport, I. (1981) "In Praise of Paradox." A social policy of empowerment over prevention. *American Journal of Community Psychology*, 9(1), 1–25.

Stein, M. and N. Frost (1992) "Empowerment and Child Welfare." In: J.C. Coleman and Ch. Warren-Adamson (Eds): *Youth Policy in the 1990s*. London, Routledge.

LENNIE HAARSMA

Children's Participation in Residential Care

There are a number of reasons for paying explicit attention to the position of young people in residential youth care. (a) Young people in residential youth care are dependent on professionals and find their freedom restricted to some extent; (b) they are often insufficiently informed about their rights and duties, or they think they only have the formal right of complaint; (c) young people in residential youth care are prepared for active participation in society.

This article is based upon the participation rights of the UN Convention and deals with the results of a small-scale practical study. Cees Senten and I interviewed educational workers, young people and managers of institutions of residential care. We compared some examples about children's participation with the participation Ladder of Roger Hart. At the end of the article I shall mention some conclusions.

I. Participation in Residential Care in Connection to the UN Convention

The UN Convention is based on the assumption that children have rights, they have rights on parents' and care providers' duties and on the role government has in enabling children to function as mature citizens.

However, the Convention also deals with these points in concrete terms. I consider four articles in particular to be especially relevant to this article's subject. Article 12 gives children the right to express their views in matters which involve the children themselves. With respect to residential youth care, this right plays an important role in a number of areas: from the registration of young people to the arrangements made with them on leaving the institution.

The article that gives young people the right to obtain and impart information (I am referring to article 13), is particularly relevant with respect to information on the treatment and the opportunities for complaint within the institution.

Article 14, which concerns freedom of thought, conscience and religion, is relevant as well within youth care: a clear example is the young person's own opinion on problems during an intake interview.

The right to freedom of assembly and association, as laid down in article 15, is reflected in the existence of youth councils and residents' councils.

E. Verhellen (ed.), Monitoring Children's Rights, 281–285.

II. Findings from Actual Practical

Educational workers play a vital role within residential youth care in taking young people seriously in daily practice. After all, it is their attitude which to a large extent determines whether young people feel safe, encouraged or understood. But these professionals cannot cope on their own. The management will have to create conditions, including an overall vision on young people, the creation of a culture within the institution and the explicit development of consultation and participation opportunities for young people. It will also be necessary to focus on expertise improvement on the part of the educational worker. Without this support, even the most committed and well-motivated group leaders will not be able to cope for long.

What, in 1994, is daily practice like with respect to young people's rights, in particular young people in an institution? What are the views of managers? What problems do educational workers experience in daily practice, and what experiences do young people themselves have with participation? To me, these were good reasons for studying daily practice and conducting interviews on those three levels.

A. *The First Level: The Educational Workers*

What would be the best way of discussing with educational workers, their role and attitude towards children, and their views on young people's rights and duties? We found a solution by discussing these matters with some of them on the basis of their daily experiences. We put several questions to them. These questions were:
- In what way do you implement the UN Convention participation rights in daily practice?
- In daily contacts with young people it is important for them that there are clear rules. How do you develop these rules, and what role do young people play in this development?
- No doubt you occasionally experience conflicts in daily practice. Could you indicate what practical solutions are effective?
- We would like to present you with a few questions/comments from children themselves. What would be your response?

Don't be inconsistent: it confuses me and I will only try even more to have my way in everything.
Don't give the feeling that my mistakes are sins. I will have to learn to make mistakes without getting the feeling I'm an idiot.
Don't ever think that is is beneath you to apologize to me. An honest apology gives me a good, warm feeling.
Don't forget that I can thrive without a whole lot of understanding and encouragement, but I shouldn't need to tell you about that.

What strikes you when you talk to educational workers about their contacts with young people in daily practice? Do they also take the view that it is quite an effort to take children seriously. And what did they answer?

They think it one of the professional's duties to make young people aware of the fact that all people have rights; they must indicate clearly what these rights mean in concrete terms. They consider it as their task to teach children that they have to be aware of the rights of others in relation to their own rights and their limits. Professionals see it as their duty to prepare young people how to deal with their rights in society. From the point of view of the professionals' attitude, they think it important that they themselves can make mistakes and they have to learn to apologize to the youngsters. They distinguish different rules for individual age categories. They think it important to monitor daily practice in close consultation with the young people involved themselves.

B. The Second Level: The Young People Themselves

We talked to representatives of two youth councils. The youth council we consulted first has existed for more than twenty-five years. The second youth council had been set up more recently. We used the following questions:
   – What is your opinion about the youth council in your institution? Can you tell me about some of the things the council discusses?
   – Do you feel you're taken seriously by the staff in your institution? Can you give an example?
   – Do you represent any other young people within your institution, and how do you inform them about what has been discussed in the council?
   – What subjects do you discuss within your own group, and what subjects are discussed in the youth council?
   – Would you find it useful to exchange experiences with young people from other institutions?
What were the answers of the young people?

They make differences between what is discussed within the group and what is discussed in the council. Broadly speaking, the group discusses rules and conflicts within the group. The council discusses less personal matters such as food, lighting, procedures about e.g. inspection of files, wishes with respect to sports and the leasure programme etc.

They meant one characteristic of being taken seriously in the council: the fact that direct answers are given to questions and that promises are kept. The young people feel they are treated on a basis of equality, and they feel they are involved in all sorts of areas.

The youngsters themselves admit to having been changed by the council. They became less aggressive and learned to express their views. In the exchanges with other youth councils they tell they are proud of their institution. Furthermore, it has an inspiring effect for them to hear how other young people run their councils.

C. The Third Level: The Managers

Managers have to create conditions for the participation of children's participation. The following answers were used in the interviews:

- Are the staff and managers of your institution aware of the UN Convention on the rights of the child. Does the Convention offer you any practical opportunity?
- What is your institution's view on participation by young people within the institution. Do you have any written rules and regulations?
- In what way are young people within your institution involved in care, both in formal procedures such as the right of complaint, right of inspection etc. and in more informal ways?
- How does your institution deal with drawing up rules in daily contacts with young people? Does your institution have a particular view on the desired attitude the worker should adopt in his/her contacts with the young people?
- What, in your opinion, should be done to improve young people's participation within your institution as far as the formal position is concerned; in informal forms of consultation with young people and in daily contacts with young people?

What was the opinon of the managers?

Managers know the UN Convention; they try to implement some aspects in their own institution. Mostly they focuss on the formal position of youngsters: the right of the child to complaint and the right of inspection of files. They sometimes talk about factual implementation. They balance between protection and self determination rights of children. They think the attitude of the educational worker in relation to participation of the youngsters is very important.

III. WRITTEN EXAMPLES ABOUT CHILDREN'S PARTICIPATION AND ROGER HART

We used the participation ladder of Roger Hart as a tool to promote discussion about participation in residential care.

We selected the four following written examples: a declaration of intent from twelve institutions; a young people's statute for a medium-sized institution; an information magazine for young people and their parents and a young people statute from a regular institute. Most of these examples are developed by managers.

In comparing our findings with the Hart's participation Ladder, stage 3 and (occasionally) stage 4 appear to occur most frequently. Many questions remain, however, on how participation is given concrete shape in actual practice. What is striking is that adults have a key position and that in most cases one can speak of one-way traffic.

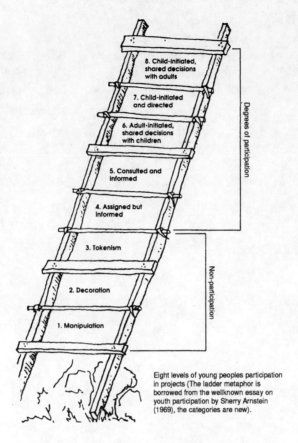

Eight levels of young peoples participation in projects (The ladder metaphor is borrowed from the wellknown essay on youth participation by Sherry Arnstein (1969), the categories are new).

Fig. 1. Roger Hart's Participation Ladder.

Involvement and consultation, yes, but the adults have the privilege of initiative. I am painting a somewhat positive picture here, because these examples are taken from institutions which do take young people's rights seriously. My fear is that rather a large number of institutions are still in stage 3, that of tokenism.

CONCLUSIONS

Interviews and written examples gives me the impression that children's rights get more attention than before.

It is my conviction that all participants have their own task in translating children's rights into attitude in their own practice. Exchanging experiences with other institutions, more training and research will be needed.

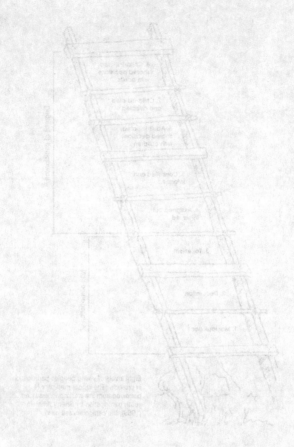

ADAM LOPATKA

Appropriate Direction and Guidance in the Exercise by a Child of the Rights to Freedom of Expression, Thought, Conscience and Religion

The general need to examine the progress made by States Parties in achieving the realization of the obligations undertaken by the Convention on Children's Rights, led to the establishment of the Children's Rights Committee. The Committee can make suggestions and general recommendations based on information received from a State Party and from specialized agencies, the UNICEF and other competent bodies. The Committee estimates whether a given State Party properly fulfils obligations stated by the Convention, including those covered by Articles 13 and 14.

However, in order to come up with adequate and reasonable evaluation of realization of the obligations, one has to apprehend the contents of the mentioned articles. Also, accurate assessment of the ways obligations are realized requires numerous other elements, as for example, complete information on the factual situation of a child, awareness of the history of the country under consideration, changes the country is undergoing in the areas the Committee might be interested in, etc. Proper evaluation is also based on skills and personalities of the Committee members. Nevertheless, the first and most significant factor here is the essence of the norm according to which the Committee will appraise the progress accomplished in the process of realization of the mentioned freedoms, and especially the way this norm is supposed to be applied with regard to European countries.

I. RIGHT TO FREEDOM OF EXPRESSION

In general, with reference to every single human being this norm is described by Article 19 of the Covenant on civil and political rights, whose parties are all European countries. According to this Covenant, everyone shall have the right to hold opinions without interference, and also that everyone shall have the right to freedom of expression. The exercise of the latter carries with itself special duties and responsibilities. It may, therefore, be subject to certain restrictions. The Covenant clearly states these restrictions. The

E. Verhellen (ed.), Monitoring Children's Rights, 287–292.
© 1996 *Kluwer Law International. Printed in the Netherlands.*

European Convention for the protection of human rights and fundamental freedoms, whose party consists of all European countries today, also declares (Article 10) that everyone has the right to freedom of expression. Only the number of restrictions of the exercise of this freedom is larger than that stated in Article 19 of the Covenant. Neither the Covenant nor the European Convention distinguish between the ways freedom is used, with regard to whether someone is a child or an adult.

Article 13 of the Convention on Children's Rights applying exclusively to a child, that is to every human being below 18 years of age, basically repeats the contents of Article 19 of the Covenant. The Convention, however, introduces additional limits to freedom every child deserves (Article 5). It states, for instance, that a State Party shall respect the responsibilities, rights and duties of parents or other persons legally responsible for a child, to provide appropriate direction and guidance in the exercise of this right by a child. It has to be realized in a manner consistent with his/her evolving capacities.

This means that a child also has the right to freedom of expression. It indicates, too, that the freedom of a child is much more restricted than that of an adult's. Freedom of a child is limited by those responsibilities, rights and duties of parents. This extra restriction is based on the fact that a child, by reason of his/her physical and mental immaturity, needs special safeguards and care. It is obvious though, that freedom of expression of a teenager and that of a newborn differ. A child who is almost 18 years old should have an opportunity to exercise his/her freedom in nearly the same way as an adult. The Convention on Children's Rights, as we all ought to remember, imposes an obligation on a State Party to assure a child who is capable of forming his/her own views – the right to express them freely in all matters affecting him/her. At the same time the Convention requires that the views of a child be given the weight in accordance with the age and level of maturity of a child.

The above resolution implies that both – appropriate direction and guidance – should be most convenient for a child. They should represent the level of minimal necessity, and not the level of what is maximally permissible. It also has to be emphasized here, that the best interests of a child should always be of primary consideration. It is specifically important that a child is not discriminated with regard to political views or other opinions expressed by him/her.

It is worth noting that in the process of formulating the Convention, the Danish delegation underlined that the rights of a child to express his/her opinions should not be understood in the way that a child has a right "to express his/her opinion in matters concerning his or her own person".[1] Having agreed with the above notice, most delegations participating in drawing up the Convention decided not to specify subjects or ideas on which a child can have freedom to express his/her opinions. On the contrary, it appeared

---

[1] "Legislative history of the Convention on Children's Rights" (1978–1989), Article 13 (Freedom of expression), UN Centre for Human Rights.

necessary to complete the article with: "freely in all matters". The intention of the authors of the Convention is to assure a child possibly the greatest respect of his/her autonomy and personality. Specifying responsibilities, rights and duties of parents to guarantee a child appropriate direction and guidance, the Convention does not place a child and his/her parents in opposition. It assumes that parents, following the natural feeling of love to their child will provide him/her with the best direction and guidance in the matters of his/her interest exactly from the parents. The only obligation of the state is to respect the responsibilities, rights and duties of parents. However, in case of disregarding the rights of a child by parents, also, when they fail to give him/her appropriate direction and guidance, or, worse still, abuse their parental rights thus limiting the freedom of expression of a child, the state has an obligation to step in for the good of a child.

It has to be stressed when evaluating the realization of the right of a child to freedom of expression, that every new generation perceives and estimates the world in its own specific way and is eager to mark it with its peculiarity. This tendency should by all means be respected by parents or people taking care of a child. The Children's Rights Committee cannot neglect this aspect either.

II. RIGHT TO FREEDOM OF THOUGHT, CONSCIENCE AND RELIGION

The Covenant on civil and political rights declares (Article 18) that everyone shall have the right to freedom of thought, conscience and religion. The Covenant specifies the essence of this freedom and forbids the use of any type of violation in this matter. It also defines the boundaries of manifesting one's religion or belief. It additionally says that the States Parties to the Covenant undertake to have respect for the liberty of parents, and, when applicable, legal guardians, to ensure the religious and moral education of their children in conformity with their own convictions. The same article, as we can see, specifies that everyone shall have the right to this freedom, although at the same time saying that this does not apply to children, since it leaves the decision – as to the kind of religion and morality in which a child is to be brought up – to parents. European Convention for the protection of human rights and fundamental freedoms (Article 9) uses almost the same words to formulate the right to freedom of thought, conscience and religion as the Covenant. Coincidentally, it forgets to mention the respect for the liberty of parents to ensure the religious and moral education of their children in conformity with their own convictions. One may presume that the Convention using the expression "everyone" includes children into the group to whom the right applies.

The Convention on Children's Rights (Article 14) declares that States Parties shall respect the right of a child to freedom of thought, conscience and religion. Thus, it states *expressis verbis* that the right applies also to a child. It is a novelty, indeed, which marks great progress. At the same time, however, the Convention sets clear limits to the range of applicability of the right to a child. Despite the notion illustrated by Article 5 referring to responsibilities, rights and duties of parents, the Convention introduces Article 14 para 2 which declares that States Parties shall respect the rights and duties of parents to provide direction to a child in the exercise of his/her right. Guidance, which conveys persuasive meaning rather than that of direction, is however not mentioned here. Placing the regulation in this article against the contents of Article 5 would seem redundant. It results however from a determined stand of Islamic countries as well as Holy See, which believe that a child should not have the right to freedom of thought, conscience and religion, and underline the liberty of parents to take decision for a child. The adherents of this opinion suggested that the Convention should also state that "States Parties shall respect the liberty of a child and his/her parents to ensure the religious and moral education of a child in conformity with convictions of their choice".[2] Despite great influence that this standpoint had on the purview of Article 14, it has not been accepted. The delegate of Holy See, supported by the representative of Italy, made an announcement to the protocol that although the above mentioned resolution was not included in the Convention, he understands that "the right to religious and moral education must be respected by states". Instead, it was made obligatory by the Convention that the direction shall be used "in a manner consistent with the evolving capacity of a child". This means that direction of parents referring to a child's right to freedom of thought, conscience and religion varies depending on the age of a psychically sane child.

Both the Covenant on civil and political rights and the Declaration on the elimination of all forens of intolerance and of discrimination based on religion or belief interdict any coercion which would impair freedom to have or to adopt a religion or belief of his choice. The Convention on Children's Rights lacks this resolution, which implies that it permits cases when especially a small child may be forced to adopt a religion or belief chosen by his/her parents. It has to be emphasized that in Islamic countries the decision in this matter is taken exclusively by the father, instead of both parents as is demanded by the Convention. The only curtailment that the Convention provides for the possibility of applying coercion is the regulation demanding respect of the evolving capacities of a child. While discussing the project of Article 14 the delegate of the USA proposed that the "education be in conformity with both the parents and the child's convictions". Other delegates stressed the necessity of having "due regard for the importance of allowing a child to develop the skills and knowledge required for an independent adulthood". It was also

---

[2] All quotations included here come from "Legislative history of the Convention on Children's Rights" (1978–1989), Article 14 (Freedom of thought, conscience and religion), UN Centre for Human Rights.

noticed that "protection from the state given to the family must be equally balanced with the protection of a child within the family".

Article 14 of the Convention on Children's Rights, contrary to the Covenant on civil and political rights and other international instruments dealing with the right to freedom of thought, conscience and religion, does not say that everyone has the right to manifest his/her religion or belief in worship, observance, practice and teaching. Nevertheless, no one working on the article questioned the pronouncement of the Swedish delegate that there was consensus "on the understanding that this right should include freedom to manifest one's religion or belief in the form of worship, observance, practice and teaching". It means that the Convention grants a child freedom of religion or belief in all and only the above forms. It clearly indicates that the objective scope of a child's freedom is neither narrower nor broader than that of any adult's. It also indicates that this direction of parents may refer to all and only those symptoms of freedom.

When evaluating the realization of the Convention's resolutions, it has to be specified to what extent the right to freedom of thought, conscience and religion applies to a child. The answer seems to be as follows: a child undergoes the same limitations in manifesting his/her religion or belief as an adult. Moreover, a small child is totally limited by his/her parents' decisions, who act according to their responsibilities, rights and duties in relation to their child. An older child who develops normally is also subject to additional restrictions from the side of his/her parents. However, the substance and form of the restrictions should consider the evolving capacities of a child. Obviously, an European child has a great chance to expect respect of his choice of religion or belief than a child in many other countries of the world. It is most significant that the direction of parents is the implication of agreement of both mother and father, and is not based exclusively on the father's will.

The Convention grants a child the right to freedom of thought, conscience and religion. It is a remarkable step forward towards general respect of a child's personality. With relation to a small child, however, this regulation practically does not work. Nevertheless, proclaiming this right is very important. When, in face of difficulties with laying down the purport of Article 14 of the Convention a few delegations suggested that perhaps regulating the right to freedom of thought, conscience and religion should be given up, their proposal was voted down. With relation to an older child, the above regulation has a clear meaning, since parents while providing direction have an obligation to respect the evolving capacities of a child.

Conceding the right of giving direction to parents has a natural justification. Exercising this right, which for parents is also a duty, should be consistent with the sense and spirit of the Convention that aims at increasing respect of a child's autonomy and personality. A highly influensive role in this matter lies in the hands of legislature and politics of the Convention's States Parties.

The way of comprehending the resolutions of the Convention is demonstrated in the Polish law on educational system dated September 7, 1991. It states that public primary schools introduce the course "religion" as requested by parents, and secondary schools either at the request of parents or students themselves. The first variant applies to children under 15 years of age, and the other to teenagers between 15 and 18 years of age. For young people over 18 religion is an elective subject.

Unfortunately there are countries (for example Pakistan, Djibouti, Indonesia, Holy See, Maldives and others), which in spite of having ratified the Convention on Children's Rights refuse to consider and apply the resolutions referring to the freedom of thought, conscience and religion as well as freedom of expression.

The Children's Rights Committee, which will monitor and estimate the way obligations included in the Convention are exercised by various countries, has a great chance to become an advocate of proper exercising by a child the right to the both discussed freedoms. The Committee may do this by criticising unnecessary restrictions imposed by parents that adversely affect the extent to which children use this right, or by promoting cases when parents allow rational liberty in applying the rights by a child according to his/her evolving capacities and taking into consideration the best interest of a child.

BRIAN MILNE

Children's Participation: How far Can Children be Involved?

The most exciting century in recorded human history is drawing to a close. Humanity has achieved a great deal of scientific and technological progress, yet failed to meet many of the expectations of those who predicted an age of peace and universal egalitarianism. Not only have we seen the "war to end all wars" at the beginning of the century, but also the first ever truly definable "world" war in the middle. Some nations' whole superstructures were virtually destroyed and populations decimated, often the result of actions that took hours or even minutes and were the product of the economics and politics of war that cared little for life. It did not discriminate between military or civilian, male or female, old or young, rich or poor. It produced a technology of mass destruction with maximum efficiency. The aftermath found much of the world in social and economic chaos. That war saw a tide of change in its wake.

Out of the chaos rose the United Nations and its agencies, mostly new, some carried over from the League of Nations, to draw all nations together. It also saw the adoption of some of the most significant human rights documents that form the basis of many ideas those of us concerned with children's rights were to pursue. Some weeks after my own birth in 1948 the world was given a *Universal Declaration of Human Rights* by the United Nations, nine months later the *Geneva Conventions* by a Diplomatic Conference in Geneva. Both were based on previous attempts to protect human life and dignity that had failed. Between them they set out to ensure safety and security of peace and social justice. Whilst one endowed us with the promise of freedom, equality and brotherhood as a single human race without distinctions based on race, colour, sex, belief, etc., the other regulated war to protect not only those involved actively in hostilities but also civilians, most explicitly women, children up to age 15 years, the infirm and the elderly. The *Geneva Conventions* were added to by protocols in 1977. Included in the first Protocol are two Articles that specifically state how children must be protected.

In the spirit of contradiction inherent in the nature of theory and practice in all human activities, the standard these two great legal instruments set the world has probably seen more war, violence and injustice than ever before

E. Verhellen (ed.), Monitoring Children's Rights, 293–303.
© 1996 *Kluwer Law International. Printed in the Netherlands.*

using more powerful and sophisticated means of destruction and manipulation than before. As ever, it is the most vulnerable who have no right of opinion about these contradictions, as too those who are killed and injured without legitimate cause for their inclusion in all manner of conflicts, deprived of dignity and a decent standard of living by the same greed for wealth and power of a minority as ever before. Equality and the end of prejudicial treatment of all people is still an ideal rather than a standard.

These opening paragraphs set a depressing agenda for any consideration of children's rights. However they are our reality and since we do not work in an ideal world, but one that confronts us constantly with new problems, we must constantly refer back to them to understand why things do not happen instantly a new international treaty enters into force.

In this modern age we should expect to be free and equal in dignity and rights, should enjoy an adequate standard of living, the right to work or be protected by social security if we cannot, and enjoy many other social and economic rights too numerous to list here. Other charters, declarations and conventions reinforce earlier treaties. At the beginning of 1976 the *International Covenant on Economic, Social and Cultural Rights* came into effect, followed within three months by an *International Covenant on Civil and Political Rights*. The Universal Declaration and two Covenants effectively form the basis of all concepts of rights that are either acceptable or extendible to the diverse peoples, cultures, ideologies and religions found within membership of the United Nations.

Since the 1948 Universal Declaration, about 25 conventions, covenants and protocols to those treaties have been carried over from before the UN's formation or adopted and come into effect since. A recent one brings us together here. The *Convention on the Rights of the Child* has now reached six years of age. The vast majority of nations have signed, many ratified and now working toward eventual implementation. In 1989 when the Convention was adopted by the General Assembly of the UN, probably nobody expected it to come into effect as quickly as it did. There was probably even more scepticism than enthusiasm from observers, however we have seen major abstainers from the process of development of the Convention in the 10 years from 1979 to adoption come to be key players in the promotion of the Convention. Indeed even UNICEF, one of the UN's early offspring, has raised itself from very low to very high profile and is now extremely encouraging in its efforts to promote children's rights. Compared with the 46 years until exactly one day before this Conference began, the fulfillment of the Universal Declaration's promise seems to pale into insignificance compared with the vigorous progress of the Convention over little more than six years.

Few parts of the Convention receive greater attention than those articles that encourage children's participation. Having recently examined the topic in depth, including indirect input from children dating back to the time when the Convention was still new and still not come into effect, I have first hand experience that tells me some very remarkable things about children's so-called participation.

Firstly, how do we define it? Imagine someone approaching any one of you in the street and asking *"Would you like to participate?"*. If you thought quickly you would naturally ask: *"Participate in what?"*. This is how the use of the word *participation* tends to stand alone in common children's rights use. It is not explicit. I have come to understand it to mean participation in democratic processes or citizenship. Given the civil legal status of children, that is a limited concept since it usually means little to fully franchised adults to begin with.

Secondly, participation is defined by adult standards and is usually organised and overseen by adults. The inclusion of children's opinions as per *Article 12* of the Convention seems mostly to consist of asking children whether they enjoyed what they were doing afterwards. Adults are setting parameters for participation to limits they assume for children. The more informed I become, the less convinced I am that children have gained much ground at all.

Thirdly, things that were common practice before the life of the Convention seem to be regarded as outside the sphere of interest of people examining participation as they understand it according to *Articles 12-15*. There is, thus, no tradition of participation we can refer to because the "clean slate" approach dictates what participation will be rather than what it is or has been. That is slowing down rather than encouraging progress.

Fourth, no sooner had the topic become "important" than we had a model thrust upon us that is becoming the norm we are expected to work to. The "Ladder of Participation" in Roger Hart's Innocenti Essay *Children's Participation: From Tokenism to Citizenship* has been with us since March 1992. In no way do I understand Hart to have thrust a model upon us. He tells us *"The Ladder of Participation is designed to serve as a beginning typology for thinking about children's participation in projects"* (Hart, p. 8). He could not be more specific: *"beginning typology"*. Neither Hart nor UNICEF can be called to account for the assumption that we now have a model and that those of us who do not work comfortably within such rigid frameworks are accumulating unwanted photocopies of something we are told is "the" model, that we have been aware of for four years and are no longer interested in. Perhaps at this early stage in the exploration of children's participation, conservatism and profound lack of imagination have already penetrated our sphere of interest. Interestingly, and referring back to my last point, Hart very carefully includes pre-Convention examples of participation. I am, of course, aware of the contradictory way people select and reject artefacts for their own explanations of things that have already been explained perfectly well. I wonder if anybody has asked for children's opinions on this subject? Whilst I do not personally use models and what I consider to be inflexible control groups, I do not entirely object to their use. Social psychologists often say how much they dislike them, however they are often virtually compelled to use them in order to be taken seriously within their own discipline. However I do feel that they often determine how and how far children will participate in research and certainly do not use children as researchers. In that respect one step on Hart's ladder, number three – *tokenism*, is as far as participation extends. Hart includes that in the "non-participation" bracket. In terms of children's true position we need to carefully rethink beginning typologies and models to measure participation that really do incorporate children actively.

Fifth, the Convention is itself somewhat limited in scope. Whilst account has been made of Islamic *Sharia* law, it is so obviously culturally based on "Western" values that when we consider a single dimension like children's participation we do so within cultural bounds. We must also bear in mind that no UN treaty exists in isolation. Let us consider, for instance, cultural implications. The Convention includes cultural exceptions in *Articles 29* and *30*. Assumed standards should therefore conform to instruments like the *International Convention on the Elimination of All Forms of Racial Discrimination* and ILO's *Convention Concerning the Protection and Integration of Indigenous and Other Tribal and Semi-Tribal Populations in Independent Countries*. We cannot assume that because the Convention leads us to believe ages 0 to 18 are childhood, except in countries where majority is attained earlier, that it is as "black and white" simple as that. Coming from an anthropological background I cannot see what can be achieved by imposing those values on traditional societies where initiation into adulthood often follows reproductive and physical maturation cycles. If girls become women with the menarche or boys become men after their first hunt, then those are traditions we have no moral right to interfere with. Indeed, those children often enjoy all privileges of adulthood far earlier than supposedly "civilised" children. It is also ridiculous to assume that they are being deprived of childhood.

The same applies, broadly speaking, to universal concepts of education as most people understand them in *Article 28*. Compulsory primary education means little if literacy plays no role in learning how to find food because you are a hunter-gatherer in a preliterate society. Children's work is even more contentious because of its different position within economic activities that do not conform to what we consider conventional models. I cannot begin to do complicated cultural issues justice here. What we should bear in mind, is that very few people in traditional societies live in total isolation today. If they wish to change their way of life they are perfectly entitled to. Information is available when they need it. What we should not do is impose education because we feel it is the "right thing" since the outcome would be that children could no longer participate in society within their own traditions but in something that draws them toward our way of life with all the promises of exploitation and poverty that the so-called modern world has to offer. In short, participation must be allowed to be what it is in its own setting and not what we want it to be.

My sixth and final point raises two exclusions in international instruments generally. Children are only notionally included because even where the words *all human beings*, *everyone*, or other means of being all inclusive occur, they are usually followed by lists of qualifiers. Examine those lists and race, colour, gender, language, religion, etc., will consistently reappear. Although there is the open phrase "other status", the specific term "age" is virtually universally excluded. In other words, it is hard to see how it can be categorically proven that children are included. Then, and this is my central concern henceforth, in all economic respects children are exempted from protection by omission. Where they are specifically included is as already stated, in the 1977 Protocols to the Geneva Conventions, a treaty that hardly concerns itself with any economic issues. Therefore, apart from protection in war and what is in the Convention on the Rights of the Child, children have little going for them.

In the abstract for this paper, I said that my title is intended to tantalise rather than set an agenda. I go on to say that an agenda itself depends on developments beyond the Convention that would begin to give children all necessary components of participation in democratic processes. Indeed my whole rather disparaging overview of children as they stand on a sand of exclusion rather than a bedrock of inclusion in international treaties is itself only a reflection of a far deeper pit of despair we can look into. Whilst many of us come to a conference to look at how children's rights are being monitored, we do so with mainly preconceptions based on inclusions. Those inclusions may well encompass things that are not happening or are even bad for children as well as those moving children's access to rights forward. The exclusions are beyond our remit, therefore we ignore them. Today, and neither for the first nor last time, I throw down the gauntlet of challenge to achieve those forgotten elements in the spirit of the Polish government's proposal to the UN Commission on Human Rights in 1978 that a convention on the rights of the child be adopted.

The Convention makes a lot of assumptions about the world and some kind of optimal democracy as we understand it in the West at its core. One very attractive aspect of the Convention is that it is also what I would like to see for all people. Behind the façade of children's rights a unique expression of rights that should be enjoyed by all human beings throughout their lives is ever present. Very little modification would be required. Often only words *child* or *children* would need to be replaced. As a document to express our social conscience in a truly democratic world we would ideally live up to all standards expressed. I have never been comfortable with the distinctions *adult* and *child* anyway since they determine how we perceive fellow human beings. Since life is a continuum between birth and death that is unique to each person and contains so many different life events, it seems almost irrelevant that the arbitrary use of age as a means of classification exists at all. However, the critical point here is democracy itself. We perceive it as something pure and unassailable, the *raison d'être* for civil, social and human rights, well-being of humanity and how we practice those values. It is a limited, idealised democracy because it is confined to a version that has largely been constructed around affluent, usually peaceful capitalist societies.

Whatever it is, it is not as inclusive as usually implied, since the level of enjoyment of democracy we attain is usually governed by our relative wealth and access to power. The richer a person, the more freedom and power he or she will tend to enjoy. Some people are therefore more equal and powerful than others. In some democratic countries bankrupts and the homeless are excluded from certain economic, social and political privileges alongside criminals and the insane. Children are also excluded by omission usually and by statute often. They do not have civil, social or economic rights comparable with those of adults. The Convention goes some way toward inclusion in civil and social rights, giving some protections they have hitherto lacked. Apart from brief mention of social security (*Article 26*) and protection against economic exploitation (*Article 32*), no serious consideration of children's economic situations exists.

Can children ever be fully participant in democratic processes without enabling and protective economic rights? The answer is simple. They cannot without wealth that means they could compete for a share in the power that holds them back. Whilst adults retain power over children and withhold wealth there is no need to even consider addressing the matter at all. Without a number of additional rights that will probably never happen. Those additional rights would allow them access to some of the key institutions of modern democracy in capitalist society that invite participation in many democratic processes.

Many of the social and economic indicators we use to measure and monitor children's welfare and access to increased rights reproduce capitalist instilled notions based on adult economic activity. However, they exclude children from major indicators such as GDP and GNP although they are part of national and global economies. Many children work, many others are wealth creating consumers and savers. Unless money is removed from circulation by hiding it under one's mattress it is part of an economy, whilst goods and services remain available and are used an economy is functional. Children are an extremely large part of the world's population and whilst they need food, clothing, shelter, use fuel, energy and other resources, are an important part of the world economic system. Yet that is a sphere where they have no rights and very little influence on market forces beyond the amount of goods and services they consume. In national as well as international legislation children are excluded by laws that protect control of finance, goods, services or any other assets. Until either majority or other stipulated ages they are denied the right to own property, control resources or even regulate their investments. Let us look at some simple examples of the greater problem.

During the first half of this century a new phenomenon stole the imagination of the world. The moving picture. Cinemas became a means of reaching large audiences with highly profitable entertainment. Stars sometimes enjoyed relatively short careers but the higher their box office standing, the higher their performance fees and the richer they became. Child stars were especially popular in the 1920s and 30s. One of the most popular ones illustrates how children were completely economically powerless. Because Jackie Coogan was so exploited and before he had reached an age when he could enjoy any of the fortune HE had earned, he was virtually penniless. His case made international headline news and held the attention of readers for months. In 1938, aged 23, he filed a law suit against his parents to recover what was left of four million dollars he had earned during the 1920s. His earnings had been used by his parents without need to ask his opinion or consent. When the court decided in his favour in 1939 he received half of the remainder of his dead father's estate (what was left of his own income). It was a mere $126,000. When the case was filed, stepfather Arthur Bernstein responded with the words *"He'll not get a penny from us, the law is on our side. Lawyers tell his mother and me that every dollar a kid earns before he is twenty-one years old belongs to his parents."*

In 1938 a limited legal protection henceforth known as the *"Coogan Act"* (The Child Actors' Bill) was passed under section 36 of California's Civil Code to protect children's assets until maturity. In 1939 the act was extended by what became known as the *"Shirley Temple Amendment"* to include already running contracts (Edwards, pp. 116-8). Whatever the law did to protect children's assets in the long term, it continued to allow adult control and use of most of the child's wealth whilst they were still definably minors. There were, of course, no guarantees that badly judged investment or use of funds would not entirely lose fortunes without children's consent or knowledge. This single example, whilst set in California, has remained one of the best examples of universal lack of will to incorporate children into the economic world more than half a century on. Bernstein's words are, broadly speaking, still true. Whilst age 21 now generally reads 18, the legal status of children is that they are subordinate to their adult caretakers who control their economic lives. In national and international law, neither constitutionally nor in any other civil codes, where finance, ownership and such issues are addressed are children included because majority defines the point in time when persons may represent themselves in civil law. If we very closely scrutinise what this really means then we would see that if parents fall heavily into debt, and have bankruptcy proceedings issued against them, their children's assets may well be seized. For much of childhood children may have bank accounts but whilst they can pay in what they wish, they often require parental permission to draw funds. Parents often have open access to those accounts. One could go on listing what children are not allowed without adult intervention.

There is a paradox in that at present I occasionally work for the UK census office as a researcher on a Labour Force Survey whilst also researching child labour in the UK for the DCI/ISPCAN International Working Group on Child Labour. One of the objects of the Labour Force Survey is to use a sizeable sample to make a reasonably accurate picture of economic activities in the UK. It examines what people are doing by profession or other activity (or inactivity), home ownership, incomes, etc. It includes all members of each household but unless residents are aged 16 or above does not list their economic activities. Indeed even when aged 16 and into adulthood, if residents are students and have part-time work that is not included if it is only definably casual. Temporary, seasonal, part-time and all other legitimate economic activities of children are excluded. Yet I have sat in homes whilst collecting data where children went off to do or came home from newspaper delivery rounds, have also had children imagining I would ask them the same questions as over 16s, thus begin to tell me about Saturday jobs, holiday jobs on farms and so on. The computer programme I use does not ask me to collect that data, therefore I listen impassionately, unable to use it because of regulations that force me to observe full confidentiality of all members of each household chosen by the government for this particular survey.

Compared with what a number of recent researches on child labour, including the IWGCL, are finding the Labour Force Survey is missing a quite significant sector of the economically active population. Indeed, exceptionally children may even be main breadwinners in a few homes, but government surveys cannot accommodate that possibility. In the many other countries where labour force surveys are carried out, and India springs immediately to mind here, children's economic activities are included. The UK government's attitude to social legislation within the European Community that would protect young workers mirrors a more universal lack of will to give children economic protection. At the same time, our government, like others here in Europe, is considering similar new laws to the Harkin Bill in the USA that is probably far more punitive than protective of children's economic roles in developing countries. It appears an almost universal blind spot. Protection of economic rights rather than prohibitions would surely, amongst other important questions, open new channels to finding ways of abolishing exploitative child labour.

I now return to the UN, diplomatic and other charters and conventions I began with. Age is not one of the listed criteria in those treaties and whilst we may interpret texts to be inclusive because it is not considered necessary to state the obvious, there are people with legal and political skills who use exclusions to advantage. Pair this possibility with citizenship and full economic rights in constitutional law almost universally keeping economic power in adult hands. Then, and this is where justification could so easily be found to state a case for continued exclusion, the Convention on the Rights of the Child does not even begin to offer economic rights to children.

Capitalism may rest assured that one of its most valuable assets is well protected. Economic child will not become a threat to adult wealth and power in the immediate future and therefore their enjoyment of democracy is further denied. It is not in the best interest of adults to even consider giving children what morally belongs to them because that would begin to undermine their absolute control. After all, women have gained much ground in the twentieth century. Should the joint, economically powerful force of women and children ever challenge the might of the few immensely wealthy men who control world finance, it may lead to an age of reason in which social justice and peace might just take precedence over injustice and war.

Of course there are other battles to be won. Having mentioned women I am reminded that there are gender issues to be addressed. Girls are less likely to be heard than boys in many cultures, even in the "modern", liberal and secular West. This deserves special attention. Then the whole question of *informed consent* and whether we should go to children first and, with their approval, seek consent from adult caretakers or approach the adults first. That is an interesting debate in itself since it describes one of the greatest barriers to cross. Whilst children still "belong" to parents or other caretakers and this is clearly stated in law, children's participation in almost everything depends on the goodwill and permissions of the adults who do not feel threatened by young people.

I imagine the cultural questions could be dealt with comparatively easily. Such things do not usually threaten anybody. Whilst our experience of Bosnia, Rwanda and other inter-ethnic wars tell us a great deal about the pitfalls involved in trying to separate different societies within modern nation states that wish to redefine themselves as what they once were and would like to be again, we should thereby learn that trying to integrate distinct groups into a single society offers no guarantees for success. Non-intervention probably lessens the burden of responsibility for the success of children's rights. I do not think the extension of enabling and protective rights is as simple. Enforcement of the Convention on the Rights of the Child and imposition of adherence to its articles offers only the imperialism of doing things "our" way and not an ideal solution. A great deal has still to be learned about how, when and where things fit in the scheme of things at present as against a future where things are constantly changing. It may be that some articles need to be rewritten or annexed and that additional protocols will extend the catalogue of rights and how we give rights to children. All of this will take time. I am not considering these possibilities from the point of view of children's liberation or some other kind of idealised libertarian position. It is purely a pragmatic view based on my strong views on what democracy should be and what I generally accept it not always is.

It may be that underlying all else, the Convention on the Rights of the Child is designed only ever to reach the stage of *tokenism* on its own version of the ladder. Perhaps full rights for children are considered undesirable and people like myself have too much faith in the Convention however much we point out its imperfections. Whatever the case may be, neither people who share my critical view nor myself are arguing for universal egalitarianism from birth to death. The burden of responsibility itself would be too much to thrust on children without learning a great deal more about the pace at which they believe they would prefer to be given rights. There are some things we need to give renewed thought to in order to bring children's participation in citizenship and democracy forward.

It is not a new idea. In essence Eglantyne Jebb was proposing it within the notion of child welfare in the 1919 Declaration of Child Rights for which she is credited as being the prime mover. In about 1920 Janusz Korckzak more elaborately explained that he believed that children had *not yet spoken* but were *still listening*. How prophetic of Article 12 of the Convention children now have. But how sad that it was nearly 60 years before the notion and almost 70 years before the reality of a somewhat muted but nevertheless genuine voice for children came to be. Sadder too that little original thought appears to have expanded beyond the ideas of those visionaries.

There is still a great deal of room for expansion of what we already have until the Convention and the practice of children's rights by young people themselves becomes the norm. A great deal of stress, probably far too much at that, is placed on political rights rather than the token value, as it stands, of any child's right to express an opinion as a representation of some kind of participation. What really matters is how far children wish to be involved in *any* rather than pushed into *all* issues. But it is above all quite clear that only if economic rights are taken seriously, given due and full consideration and ever become one of the issues in which they can stake a claim that then, and only then, can we seriously turn again to the question of children's participation and ask: How far can children be involved?

REFERENCES

Edwards, Anne (1989) *Shirley Temple: American Princess*. London: Fontana.
Hart, Roger A. (1992) *Children's Participation: From Tokenism to Citizenship*. Innocenti Essays, No. 4. Florence: UNICEF ICDC.
International Committee of the Red Cross (1987). *Protocols Additional to the Geneva Conventions of 12 August 1949*. Geneva: ICRC.
International Committee of the Red Cross (1989). *The Geneva Conventions of August 12 1949*.Geneva: ICRC.
International Labour Organisation (1957). *Convention Concerning the Protection and Integration of Indigenous and Other Tribal and Semi-Tribal Populations in Independent Countries* (ILO Convention 107). ILO, Geneva.
United Nations (1948), *Universal Declaration of Human Rights*. New York, UN.
United Nations (1965), *International Convention on the Elimination of All Forms of Racial Discrimination*. New York: UN.
United Nations (1966). *The International Covenant on Economic, Social and Cultural Rights*. New York: UN.

United Nations (1968) *The International Covenant on Civil and Political Rights*. New York: UN.

United Nations (1960) *Optional Protocol to the International Covenant on Civil and Political Rights*. New York: UN.

United Nations (1989). *The Convention on the Rights of the Child*. New York: UN.

GILL BARN and ANNIE FRANKLIN

Article 12 – Issues in Developing Children's* Participation Rights

The Experience of Save the Children in the UK

INTRODUCTION

Save the Children is the UK's biggest international children's charity. It was set up 75 years ago by the woman who wrote the first charter of children's rights – Eglantyne Jebb. As a result, Save the Children has always viewed itself as a "rights-based" organisation. However, it has never attempted seriously to involve children themselves in decision-making within the organisation.

Save the Children recognised the centrality of Article 12 of the UN Convention. It also felt that as a children's rights organisation it should seek children's own views and opinions on its current practice and future plans. It has established a Participation Unit to promote children's participation at all levels in the organisation.

As part of its development of this new Unit, the Fund undertook a survey of all of the projects it runs in the UK, to examine the current level of participation by children. This was followed up by a survey of other organisations – around the UK and Europe – to enable us to set our work into a broader context.

This paper reports on the findings of both the internal and external surveys and on the progress made by the new Unit in promoting participation. It describes briefly the level of children's legal rights to participation in the UK generally and highlight the – many – areas in need of improvement.

I. ARTICLE 12

1. States Parties shall assure to the child who is capable of forming his or her own views the right to express those views freely in all matters affecting the

---

* The term "children" is used throughout this paper to mean all people under eighteen years of age

E. Verhellen (ed.), Monitoring Children's Rights, 305–316.

child, the views of the child being given due weights in accordance with the age and maturity of the child.

2. For this purpose, the child shall in particular be provided the opportunity to be heard in any judicial and administrative proceedings affecting the child, either directly, or through a representative or an appropriate body, in a manner consistent with the procedural rules of national law.

It is widely accepted that Article 12 of the UN Convention on the Rights of the Child is one of the three key articles. A child's right to participate in matters which affect it is acknowledged to inform most other articles and to be a prerequisite to the achievement of many other rights detailed in the Convention. (The two other key articles are seen as Article 2 – "non-discrimination" and Article 3 – "best interests of the child").

To achieve realisation of Article 12 demands considerable work at a number of levels. First the child's status must be raised to ensure that their opinion is listened to. Second, legislation must change to establish this right in key areas of children's lives. Third, children must receive support to enable them to understand their rights; to express themselves or to use an advocate. Fourth, institutions and organisations must consider carefully how best to improve children's rights to participate and change their own practice to enable this to happen. It is this last point, in respect of Save the Children's attempts to involve children, which this paper addresses.

II. Children's Participation in the UK

The simplest description of the current state of children's participation in the UK would be that it is non-existent. And, while not wholly true, it is largely the case. The main exception is under The Children Act 1989, which gives children – who are mature enough – the right to have their views taken into account in legal proceedings regarding family breakdown and related matters. Children have few if any participation rights in other legislation. A good example is education, where acts regulating children's schooling regularly refer to parental rights, but never to children's rights. Children have no legal right to a say in their schooling and no right to complain about it. Similarly they have no right to a say in their home and family environment (except when they are in care) unless their parents grant it to them.

Britain is, and seems always to have been, a child hating society. There is fear of children which is deep rooted. Children are not welcomed in adult society and parents are judged for bringing their children to places not designed for them, e.g. restaurants. The fear worsens as children grow up and the group many Britain's fear most is adolescents, particularly boys. There is a rich history of hating those most oppressed by society. None of this suggests that proposals to strengthen children's rights would be welcome and of course, they are not. For example, exposure of child abuse in schools has brought a backlash from teachers that they are at the mercy of children's lies. This has been a major topic at teachers' unions' annual conferences and the media have been more than ready to add their weight to the teachers' side. The British obsession with criminal justice, especially as it relates to the young, is another good example of an anti-rights approach. The "bring back the birch" brigade typifies many people's attitude to young people in trouble and the mass hysteria generated by the James Bulger murder trial also exemplifies a desire to view children as inherently evil.

The UK may not be untypical in these attitudes, indeed its colonialism has left an inheritance all over the world. It is however difficult for promoters of children's rights to make much progress in this environment. Some achievements have been made nonetheless. In particular, The Children Act 1989 stated clearly that children are not the possessions of their parents and that their views should be listened to. Most progress on children's rights has occurred in the "care field" mainly in response to atrocities in institutional care. This has led to a rapid growth in the employment of children's rights officers by social services departments. It is in this area too that most work has been done on complaints procedures. Some charitable and voluntary organisations have also developed a stance on children's rights, in particular the establishment of the Children's Rights Development Unit to monitor government progress in implementing the UN Convention, has done much to raise the profile of the issues a develop thinking among professionals.

Other positive changes also appear to be taking place in broader society: there is less smacking of children in public at least and the anti-smacking lobby is no longer presented as a "lunatic fringe"; there is more sympathy for the difficulties of being a parent; there has been a growth in schools councils, etc, although there is no regulation to ensure student representation; a major TV station has recently run a series of programmes about children, which involved children in production; etc.

There is still much to campaign about however, and this is no more evident that in the UK Agenda for Children: the alternative to the official government view of progress in implementing the convention in the UK. The UK Agenda, collated and published by the Children's Rights Development Unit is over 300 pages long and details where the UK needs to improve to meet the Conventions requirements for improvements in children's rights. The Agenda is set out under fourteen heading and each demonstrates the lamentable progress made by the UK government to date.

III. SAVE THE CHILDREN'S PARTICIPATION WORK

Throughout the decades since Save the Children (SCF) was set up in 1919, it has organised and delivered emergency relief; provided services at home and abroad; promoted improvements in services for children in need; and developed sustainable, community based initiatives. In all this work SCF has sought to uphold people's right to a say in their own lives. However, it must be acknowledged that until recently it made little effort to promote children's right to a voice, only that of their parents.

Save the Children's founder, Eglantyne Jebb, established the organisation in response to the state of children in Europe after the First World War, She soon recognised the need to be secular; the importance of politics; and the need to be rights based. It was she who drafted the first charter of children's rights in 1923 which laid the foundations of the 1959 UN Declaration and the current Convention. So SCF has long history of rights based work, but it was the emphasis placed on participation in the Convention which led to a review of children's participation in the organisation itself.

SCF's UK Department decided that if it was to promote children's participation to other agencies then it must also do more internally to involve children in its own organisation. This led to the development of the Participation Unit and the work described below. As Eugene Verhellen states in his introductory chapter to "Children's Rights: Monitoring Issues", "efforts have to be undertaken *at every level*, ..., to set up bodies, with a broad base in society, whose task is to monitor and *promote* implementation of children's rights." SCF approached this task by surveying its own projects to discover the extent and level of children's participation across the department. It then decided to resource a special unit to work across the department to promote children's participation at every level in the organisation. One of the Unit's first tasks was to survey what other organisations were doing to promote children's participation, so that SCF could set its own work in context and share its experience with others engaged in similar processes.

A. *The Participation Unit*

The overall aim of the Participation Unit is "to develop full participation of children and young people in decision making processes in Save the Children". The objectives of the Unit are to:

1. Improve practice on participation by advising, encouraging and supporting staff, children and young people and other project users in their initiatives.

2. Identify and develop a range of approaches and styles of practice on participation appropriate to the different developmental stages of children and young people.

3. Develop a written policy on participation; to implement it and to regularly review its operation.

4. Design relevant mechanisms and forums to enable children and young people to have a voice and be consulted regarding Save the Children planning, policy and practice, within agreed boundaries which are understood by all.

5. Integrate an anti-discriminatory approach into all participatory practice.

6. Enable information exchange and develop resources which support practice on participation.
7. Raise awareness across the Fund of children's and young people's participation rights.

B. The Structure of the Unit

The Participation Unit is a national unit serving the UK & European Programmes Department; its office is based in Leeds. There are six divisions within the department – North & West, North & East, Scotland, Northern Ireland, London and Wales and so being based in Leeds (in the North & East Office) is very central to all the other divisions.

The Unit has four staff: a Project Co-ordinator, Development Worker, Information Worker and Project Administrator. A steering group has been set up to help the Unit focus on the development of participation within UK and European Programmes Department, as a pilot for the organisation as a whole. The group, which has a membership of practitioners, managers, policy staff and young people, meets bi-monthly. In keeping with its UK and European wide brief, it meets in a different region on each occasion, to maintain visibility and provide cost effective opportunities for project visits at the same time.

With the help of the steering group, we have planned our work programme for the next year. This includes work with specific projects on areas of participation, both at training, development and information levels. These will be individual pieces of work which aim to bring about positive change (in practice) in the way children and young people participate in the projects/divisions. Innovative approaches will be piloted, since currently SCF knows of no "right way" to tackle this issue. The steering group will guide the team on its priorities and ensure a balance in its work, in terms of age range, context and departmental coverage.

C. Getting Started

Most of the Unit's staff started work in spring 1994 and began by visiting projects to develop a picture of the level of participation. They also began at once to contact divisions (within the UK) and to make contacts with other key people within SCF, e.g. Overseas Department, Staff Development, Personnel, Policy, Information Technology and other sections at HQ. The next task was to set up our own systems in terms of administration and monitoring our work.

One of the tasks the Unit undertook within its first few weeks was to find definitions of "participation", as well as "process", "development", "decision", "rights", "resources" and "raise awareness". This not only stimulated our own thinking but helped us consider ways we may communicate such concepts to others, both children and adults.

The aims of our induction visits to projects and divisions were to:

1. Introduce ourselves
2. Update projects/divisions on the Unit's progress
3. Find out about projects'/divisions' work on participation
4. Listen to any ideas for or expectations that projects/divisions have of the Unit.

The nature of the visits so far have been variable, sometimes meeting mainly managers, sometimes project workers and other times meeting people who use projects. Issues and questions that have arisen during the visits have been consistent. These are:

– that resources are needed to support participation
– that participation with early years groups needs particular attention
– how far is the organisational prepared to change?
– how representative can participation be?
– how best can children and young people be involved in the recruitment of staff?
– should children and young people be paid for their time?

Several requests have also been made during the visits for support with developing participation work and there has been discussion of best ways to work with projects/divisions on this.

D. Newsletter

We have produced newsletters (every 2 months) which have been circulated across the department. Content includes information on events that have taken place; articles on a particular division's or project's work on participation; forthcoming events; publications; resources; a "did you know" column; and an ongoing competition to try and involve children and young people on the design of the Unit's logo. One of our discussions for a future steering group is how to make the newsletter accessible to children and young people and how and whether to distribute it outside the Fund, (these newsletters are currently only distributed internally).

E. Developing Participation Practice

The Unit has become involved with the North & West Division, working with them to evaluate their Manchester Young People's Forums in terms of young people's participation.

The aim of these forums, which are being held over a one year period, is to develop opportunities for young people to discuss and work together on issues that matter to them. The first forum on was planned to coincide with the Global Forum on Cities and Sustainable Development and focused on young people and their environment. Future forums will be on Drugs, the Police and finally, Racism. The forums are a joint venture between the Fund and Manchester City Council's Youth Service. The first event was very successful, being well attended and having different young people involved, as well as providing many learning points for all the organisers. The Unit has been involved in planning and reviewing meetings for the events so far and will be producing an interim (largely descriptive and observational) report after each event. At the end of the year after the four events have taken place the Unit will produce a larger report with more analyses on levels of participation and recommendations which the Forums hope can be presented to Manchester City Council. Being involved in the Manchester Young People's Forums is also a learning experience for the Unit in terms of existing practice of developing participation and particularly participatory evaluation.

F. Survey and Research Work

An internal, telephone, survey of children's participation in Save the Children's UK projects was undertaken and updated in 1993. The aim of this survey was to establish the 'state of play' on participation at the time within the department. Participation had been developing at a project level for some time and it was considered useful to have a clearer idea of what the current practice was across divisions/projects.

Therefore the purpose of the survey was to provide the UK and European Programmes Department with an overview of children's involvement in decision making at project level. The survey sought to seek some indication of:

1. Potential models of good practice.
2. The degree of variation between and within specific programmes areas (e.g. early years, youth work, community health).
3. A clearer understanding of the obstacles to greater participation.

Shortage of staff and time pressures prompted a telephone survey. The worker conducting the survey asked a series of agreed questions and recorded the answers on a form, which she then collated.

The questions asked are listed in appendix 1 at the end of this paper.

71 projects were telephoned and gave responses for the survey. These were from all UK divisions and include a variety of projects. The results now constitute a baseline against which future progress may be measured. They have been used by the Participation Unit to gain a snapshot of what is already happening in terms of practice on participation.

Few projects have demonstrated any clarity about the nature of participation, rather they have seen it as a 'good thing' and attempted to incorporate it into their work. Further, most of the examples only consider participation for children in terms of their status as consumers. Of course it is right that they should do so, but if Save the Children is to consider children and young people's participation across the department it needs to be much clearer about what participation involves and also consider the participation of children as its primary *constituency* as well as its consumers. This is an important distinction, since acknowledging consumer rights requires us to ensure proper participation of users whether children or adults, but involving our constituents requires that children are consulted and have opportunities to participate appropriately in respect of the rights we promote on their behalf.

As well as surveying our own projects, it was always intended to undertake a further piece of work with other agencies to set SCF's work in context and to identify organisations with whom we can learn and exchange information. The Unit has established this research project as one of its first pieces of work.

The aims of this research are to:

1. Contribute to the development of practice in this area through the sharing of experience and recording of the lessons learnt.
2. Identify models of good practice which can be replicated or form the basis for new initiatives.
3. Identify the variety of approaches to participation for which practice experience already exists.
4. Motivate, stimulate and encourage those wishing to develop participation by the presentation of practical examples of successful initiatives.

The Unit collected/collated lists of possible children's organisations throughout the UK and some overseas, through our various information contacts. It was agreed to research as wide a range of organisations as possible on issues such as environment, homelessness, health, education, arts, children and young people, as well as researching agencies specifically aimed at working with oppressed groups ie, girls and young women, black and ethnic minorities, disabled children, lesbians and gay men.

The second part of our research brief is to identify a small number of agencies (10–15) and their models of working from the questionnaire sample to then research further as case studies.

These more detailed case studies would look at models of successful working in respect of:

– the nature and scope of participation
– mechanisms for facilitating participation
– obstacles encountered in developing participation
– support offered to participants
– the views of children and staff about their experience of participation work
– the role of wider organisational structures and processes on the pace and nature of participation

It is hoped to be able to highlight examples of good practice in such areas as respect for equal opportunities training and support codes of good practice, publications, policy development and formats and procedures for enabling participation. Such case studies may also include unsuccessful models where such examples highlight problems, pitfalls and learning points in developing participation. Again this sample will include a range of types of organisations and issues they are working on.

From our lists and contacts we identified 350 organisations/agencies/projects which offered us the above range. We drafted a letter and a questionnaire with support from the UK Policy Division. Although some questionnaires were returned after the deadline we have in total received 116 completed forms from a wide range of organisations. Much of the data on these will be analysed quantitatively using SPSS computer package. However, we although the analysis is not complete, we are already aware that there are many responses that do not fit neatly into the categories offered on the forms. Participation is clearly not an easy concept or practice to describe, define or be concise about or ask research questions about. The initial analysis of the sample is beginning to emerge as follows:

1. Most respondents have an interest in or commitment to participation of children and young people in their organisation and many more are seeking to formalise that by means of policy or written statements.

2. Ways of communicating this stance on participation to children and young people include:
   - word of mouth
   - posters
   - leaflets
   - talks
   - videos
   - at introduction to project
   - training
   - mailings
   - meetings
   - children's and young people's forums
   - special events
   - guides for children and young people

3. Ways that children and young people contribute to decision making in organisations already include:
   - involvement in decision making
   - involvement in day to day planning
   - children and young people's representatives at meetings
   - children and young people's forums
   - involvement led by adults
   - involvement led by children and young people
   - involved in planning special events
   - involvement in management
   - involvement in evaluation and/or research
   - involvement in budgets

4. Reasons for children and young people not being involved include
   - children and young people too young
   - children and young people not primary "client" group
   - work is with carers
   - must hold the adult responsible
   - no formal commitment
   - organisational blocks
   - informal commitment only

5. Models/theories that organisations find helpful on participation
    – Freire
    – Boal
    – Hart
    – Lovett
    – Alinsky
    – Hallet
    – Hawker
    – Croft/Beresford
    – Gordon
    – Summerhill
    – Many other individually developed models relating to specific practice in organisation eg, respect for children and young people, collaborative working between children and adults, peer education etc.
6. Successes in encouraging/doing work on participation include
    – fun
    – learning
    – theory into practice
    – accessability to all groups
    – meaning of participation for the organisation
    – children and young people directed work
    – adult events
    – adult awareness
    – changing organisational structure
    – more participation
    – participation training
    – children and young people involved in planning
    – preparation for world
    – children and young people developed materials
    – support children and young people
    – reciprocity between children and young people
    – resourcing children and young people
7. Less successful work on participation includes
    – changing organisation
    – participation in organisational structures
    – making time needed
    – sticking to budgets
    – working with organisations/practitioners
    – work with carers
    – accessability of groups
    – communication issues
    – facilitating children and young people
    Several organisations say they are "still learning" under this question.

8. What organisations have learnt from their successes and difficulties on participation:
    - need time
    - need skills/training for children and young people
    - need skills/training for practitioners
    - importance of participation for children and young people
    - difficult to evaluate
    - tokenism
    - hierarchical/organisational blocks
    - adults to facilitate not lead
    - many definitions of participation
    - needs planning
    - needs commitment to children and young people participating
    - children and young people own forums
    - provide resources for children and young people and practitioners
    - participation as end in itself
    - difficult to sustain
    - practice and learn
    - open door – children and young people decide when to participate
    - children and young people involvement in planning
    - enjoyable
    - productive
9. Changes that have been made in organisations because of participation work include:
    - organisation more committed
    - more children and young people friendly resources
    - organisation opening/participation of aims
    - more children and young people participation

Most organisations are keen to stay in touch with the Unit and exchange information and ideas on participation. Once we have followed up more information from the questionnaires generally in terms of materials, training packs, policies etc as well as other contacts, we hope to have a wide range of information and resources available to others involved in the work. There is no doubt that we will find many examples and models of good practice on participation and be able to network about these through our newsletter.

We are currently identifying/selecting the sample for case studies which we will carry out over the next month or so. There is an extremely exciting and diverse range of organisations to choose from, ranging from a children's zoo, youth theatre, training organisations, young peoples self-organised groups.

APPENDIX 1

Questions – Internal Telephone Survey

1. Can you identify specific decisions in which children and/or young people have had an opportunity to influence the outcome?
2. Can you identify specific opportunities which the project has used to encourage the involvement of children and/or young people?
3. Are there any regular meetings/occasions at which children and/or young people are able to comment on or influence the running of the project?
4. To what extent would you say children and/or young people can influence the day to day work of the project?
   Very much
   A lot
   Slightly
   Not at all
   (PROBE for examples)
5. Does your project do any work to build the confidence of children and/or young people and to enhance their personal or social skills in ways that might help them to become more involved?
   No
   Yes (specify how)
6. Do you offer specific training which might enable children and/or young people to become more involved in the running of your project? (e.g. assertiveness, use of the telephone, letter writing.)
   No
   Yes
7. In your view what are the main difficulties in encouraging greater participation by children and/or young people in your project?
   Focus of project
   Lack of time
   Don't know any effective methods
   Staff resistance
   Other (please specify)
8. What would be most helpful to you in enabling you to involve children and/or young people more in decision making in your project?
   Seminars/workshops to share experience
   Visits to other projects
   Resource materials (videos, leaflets, etc)
   An advisor/development worker
   Creation of some "space" to do it
   Other (please specify)

BOB FRANKLIN

Children's Right to Participate in Decision Making

A *Case Study of Ravenswood Primary School Council Newcastle upon Tyne, England*

Education, institutionalised in school life, is a major focus for children's early lives. Children's experiences of school, however, are differently constructed expressing the divergent gender, class, ethnic and even historical locations of particular individuals. Life for the children who attend Grange Hill Comprehensive in the British television programme of that same name, for example, is very different to the school experiences of Billy Bunter at Grey Friars recounted in the humorous novels authored by Frank Richards; both differ again from Tom Brown's schooldays or the educational regime provided by Miss Jean Brodie. But underlying this diversity school imposes a common experience on children. They are subject to the arbitrary decision making of adults (whether teachers or governors), have no voice in deciding which subjects they will study (curriculum design) or in what ways (choice of pedagogic style) and are not involved in the judicial and punitive systems of the school although they are frequently on the receiving end of such systems. In brief children are encouraged to be the passive recipients, not the active consumers and co-constructors, of education. It is remarkable how many schools manage to metamorphose what should be the engaging and stimulating experience of education, into an authoritarian drudgery which alienates some of their most intellectually curious and gifted students. It is a particular sadness that British law requires children to spend eleven of their first sixteen years in such a disempowering and alienating environment.

Luckily, some schools are changing. This chapter examines children's involvement in decision making via their membership of the school council at Ravenswood Primary School, Newcastle upon Tyne in the North east of England. The discussion is in three sections. First, the various strands in the debate concerning children's right to participate in decision making are reviewed. Second, the structure, organisation, composition, election procedures for membership, aims, objectives and recent achievements of the school council will be outlined. Finally, children's involvement in the Council will be assessed using Hart's ladder of participation. My broad argument in the chapter is that children possess the competencies necessary for decision

E. Verhellen (ed.), Monitoring Children's Rights, 317–326.
© 1996 *Kluwer Law International. Printed in the Netherlands.*

making in certain areas and that the major obstacle to children's enhanced participation is the absence of appropriate institutional mechanisms. Schools are an obvious forum in which children should possess a greater voice since they constitute by far the largest consumer group of the institutions' services. Children's participation in decision making at school, moreover, provides a useful experience from which they can learn and develop their decision making competencies even further.

I. Children and Participation The Debate

The argument for denying participation rights to children has two inter-related strands. First, it is alleged that children are not rational or capable of making reasoned and informed decisions. Rights to autonomy in decision making grow with maturity. The philosopher John Locke stated the matter unequivocally. "We are born free as we are born rational" he claimed, "not that we have actually the exercise of either; age that brings one brings with it the other too" (Locke, 1964:326). Second, children lack the wisdom born of experience and consequently they are prone to make mistakes. By denying them the right to participate and make decisions for themselves, society is engaging in nothing more objectionable than protecting children from their incompetencies. These two strands were cogently interwoven into a classic statement and defence of paternalism by the Master of the Rolls in Re S ([1993] 2 FLR 437). "... a child is, after all, a child" he claimed. "The reason why the law is particularly solicitous in protecting the interests of children is because they are liable to be vulnerable and impressionable, lacking the maturity to weigh the longer term against the shorter, lacking the insight to know how they will react and the imagination to know how others will react in certain situations, lacking the experience to measure the probable against the possible".

Both objections to children's participation claims can be met either positively or negatively; ie, by asserting that children do possess the qualities which critics allege that they do not or, by conceding that if children do lack the skills and qualities necessary for participating in decision making, they lack them to no greater degree than adults who are not, on this ground, disqualified from participation. Advocates of children's rights offer a number of arguments.

First, they suggest that children do reveal a competence for rational thought and do make informed choices. Children who have been sexually abused, for example, have to make a very complex assessment of the consequences for their family of disclosing that abuse. In these circumstances children display remarkably sophisticated skills in decision making and evaluating outcomes. Second, the argument which suggests that children are likely to make mistaken choices, because they lack experience of decision making, rests on tautology and a confusion. The tautology is evident. If children are not allowed to make decisions because they have no experience of decision making, how do they ever get started? This is catch 22. "Even children, after a certain point, had better not be *treated as children*", Feinberg remarks, "else they will never acquire the outlook and capability of responsible adults" (Feinberg, 1980:110). There is, moreover, nothing wrong with making mistakes; we all do it. Mistakes can provide positive opportunities to learn from our experiences. Children, like adults, should be allowed to learn from their mistakes?

The confusion in the argument is also clear. It does not follow that children should not make decisions simply because they might make the wrong ones. It is important not to confuse the right to do something with doing the right thing. As Dworkin argues, we often accept that adults have the right to do something which is wrong for them (Dworkin, 1977:188). Smoking offers an obvious example.

But even if it was conceded that children are not competent decision makers, it could still be argued that they lack these competencies to no greater degree than adults. Since adults are not excluded from participation in decision making on this ground, the exclusion of children represents a case of double standards. There is ample evidence of the inadequacy of adult decision making; history reflects a catalogue of adult blunders. War, inequality, famine, racism and injustice are merely some of the fruits of adult deliberation. To deny children the right to make mistakes would deprive them of a right which adults have exercised extensively. It would be hypocritical.

But if paternalists wish to insist that the possession of certain competencies is the criterion for participation, then it is a criterion which argues for the exclusion of adults as well as children. Presumably the paternalist intention is not to exclude children from decision making merely because they are children, since this is not an argument but simply another tautology. Their argument about age-related rights regresses eventually to a debate concerning competence and, on this reasoning, it is not children who should be denied rights but all incompetent people – without regard to their age. Argued consistently, the paternalist position risks excluding adults as well as children and leads to unacceptably elitist conclusions.

Finally, the denial of participation rights to children is unfair because children can do nothing to change or ameliorate the conditions which exclude them. If the grounds for exclusion were ignorance, then the ignorant might endeavour to become wise. But young people cannot prematurely grow to the age of majority even if foolish enough to entertain such an ambition. Nor is the allegation of inequity met by the suggestion that the denial is temporary since children eventually become adults and acquire the appropriate status and rights. The argument here rests on a confusion between particular children and children as a social group. An individual child matures to adulthood, but this does not alter the status of children as a social group; 13 million people in the UK who are denied the right to participate in making decisions about important matters in their lives.

In summary the argument for denying participation rights to children on the grounds that they are not rational and lack experience, has been strongly contested by libertarians. Under pressure, three additional arguments have been offered.

First, it is argued that children should not possess participation rights because they are incapable of what the German philosopher Kant called "self maintenance"; what might now be described as "self sufficiency" (Kant, 1887:118). But the criterion of self maintenance fails to distinguish adults from children; it merely distinguishes between those who capable of self sufficiency and those who are not. It might, however, be used to justify excluding people who are disabled, sick and older people, as well as people who are unemployed, from participating in decision making. Each of these groups could be judged to be incapable of self maintenance. But it is surely a dubious moral claim to suggest that anyone who lacks self sufficiency should be subject to the intervention of others in their affairs and denied autonomy rights?

A second argument suggests that the advocacy of children's rights is antipathetic to adult rights and threatens to diminishes adults' "genuine' rights claims" (Heartfield, 1993:13); children's rights are bogus – a trojan horse. Children's rights are demands for protection either by parents or by the state in the guise of "super parent". But for adults, democratic rights are, above all else, the "right to independence from the state ... Whenever the spurious notion of children's rights is invoked we can be sure that an attack on the real freedoms of adults is not far behind" (Heartfield, 1993:14). But this argument is wrong headed on two counts. First, children's rights have never been reducible to claims for protection, but have always embraced claims for participation rights. Children want the same autonomy rights that adults enjoy. Second, the argument blames the victim. If children's claims for rights were being used to undermine adult rights, the appropriate strategy would be to criticise the state which was seeking to reduce adult rights, rather than to attack children whose rights entitlements are already considerably less than those of adults.

A third argument is based on what might be termed "future oriented consent" or what Archard calls the "caretaker argument" (Archard, 1993:51–57). The argument suggests that a parent (or some other rational adult) has a right to restrict a child's freedom and to make decisions in a child's best interest, on the understanding that the child must eventually come to acknowledge the correctness of the decision made on their behalf. A child, for example, may not wish to attend school, but education is essential if that child is to develop into a rational and autonomous adult. A parent is therefore entitled to override the child's current wishes to guarantee their future independence. It is precisely because the caretaker argument places such a high value on individual autonomy and critical rationality in decision making that intervention in children's affairs is judged permissible. As Archard notes with an evident sense of irony, "the caretaker thesis thinks self determination too important to be left to children" (Archard, 1993:52).

Dworkin suggests that these parental interventions constitute "a wager by the parent on the child's subsequent recognition of the wisdom of restrictions. There is an emphasis on ... what the child will come to welcome, rather than on what [s]he does welcome" (Dworkin, 1971:119). This is no mean trick. As Archard points out, the caretaker must not only choose what the child would choose if competent to make the choice autonomously, but also have regard for the interests of the adult which the child will become. "The caretaker" Archard claims, "chooses for the child in the person of the adult which the child is not yet but will eventually be" (Archard, 1993:53). There are two difficulties here. If the justifiability of the intervention depends on future consent, there is no way of judging at the time of the intervention whether it is appropriate. But the more serious objection is that the intervention by the adult might generate "self justifying" rather than "future oriented" consent. The consent of the child at some future date may simply be a product of the very process of intervention. The benchmark of successful brainwashing is that the person violated in this way is happy and confirmed in their new beliefs. If Freud was correct to suggest that the child is father to the man, then on this account the man may be substantially fashioned by the caretaker. The caretaker argument may amount to little more than a vicious circle of self justifying adult intervention in children's lives.

Libertarians like Holt have little time for caretakers. They argue that children possess the competencies necessary to make decisions about important matters in their lives and should be allowed to participate in making those decisions. The U.N Convention offers some endorsement for this view. The Ravenswood school council offers an obvious example of children's deliberative and participant competencies.

II. RAVENSWOOD SCHOOL COUNCIL

The Ravenswood School Council was initiated by the Head teacher who suggested the idea to students in a morning assembly. The children approved the suggestion and the Council was established in 1992. The Council's composition and functions, as well as some of its initial achievements, are detailed below.

The Council's constitution offers a model for democratic organisation and procedure. Its 16 members include two teachers, two members from each of the year 5 and year 6 classes (nine and ten year olds), two members from the School Association (parents), with the head and deputy head teacher being advisory members. The children enjoy a clear majority of the members of the Council which is highly significant because decisions also reflect simple majority.

The ten pupil members are elected by a simple plurality in a competitive vote. Each class group must elect one male and one female representative, with all members of the class being eligible to vote; all candidates must be nominated and seconded. The younger children are not permitted membership of the Council but retain a voice in school affairs, albeit vicariously. Each Council member is allocated a number of junior classes (their "adoptive classes") and charged with the responsibility of canvassing the views and opinions of these younger children and articulating them in Council. The issues arising in these consultative meetings form a major component of the agenda for Council meetings. In this way, the younger children are not precluded from participation although it is indirect. Representatives are also given the responsibility of communicating Council discussions and decisions to the younger children and have routine consultative meetings with them. They also issue bulletins, newsletters and minutes recording Council decisions.

The overall purpose of the School Council is expressed with admirable lucidity by a young student. "The School Council" he claims, "is a group of children trying to improve the school in different ways, trying to make it better for the children".[1] More specifically, the Council fulfils four important functions. First, it offers a channel of communication and potential redress for children's grievances. It also allows and promotes the articulation of grievances which otherwise might not be expressed; "you can talk to the representative of the school council about things you might not want to discuss with a teacher". Second, the Council forms part of the decision making process within the school. Some very significant areas of decision making such as curriculum concerns are beyond the Council's remit, but it does address important issues such as bullying (see below). Third, it provides a forum for debate and discussion in which young people are consciously encouraged to participate. Since even the youngest children can raise issues with their representatives, the children control the agenda for meetings which can range across any relevant topic. Fourth, the Council targets and tackles issues of particular concern to its members. The major focus of Council concerns has been the issue of bullying within the school. Students argue that they have achieved considerable success in reducing, if not eliminating, bullying. A threefold strategy has been adopted. Representatives have visited their adoptive classes (the younger children) and discussed the issue with them, notices about bullying and discouraging bullying have been posted around the school and instructions have been posted in every classroom advising children how to react if they are bullied or invited by others to bully a third party. It is uncertain whether the success in eradicating bullying, which is

---

[1]   Quotations by students are taken from a video entitled "Power To The Pupils". The video, which was scripted and produced by four students (Jessica Ross, Julie Tomkins, Joseph Wear and Laura Wigg) from Ravenswood School, is a documentary account of the School Council.

claimed by the children, has been sustained. But what seems incontestably clear is that the Council facilitates students' identifying and tackling issues which they consider to be central to nurturing their well being at school. This is also clear in their priorities for allocating their annual budget of $1,000.

A first priority was expenditure to purchase and fit mirrors in the toilets and locks on the toilet doors. It is perhaps symptomatic of the lack of regard for the sensitivities of children which institutions can express, that locks were not fitted to toilet doors prior to the children's request. Other expenditure priorities included the purchase and installation of bench seats in the playground, painting the markings of a football pitch on the school yard, the purchase of table tennis equipment and the establishment of a club; the setting up of a computer club. Hardly the radical, irrational or mistaken choices heralded by the paternalist opposers of participation rights for children. On the contrary, these seem eminently reasonable decisions, well suited to the requirements of the young people and taken on the basis of a highly democratic procedure in which every child can participate. If only adult decision making was so well ordered and egalitarian.

But the question of tokenism and manipulation of the students by the teachers and other adult Council members must be considered. The Council, however, enjoys in-built structural safeguards designed to protect the young people from manipulation by adults. It is, for example, understood that teachers have a distinctive interest to promote. One student who was asked about the role of the teachers in the Council makes explicit the respective roles of the participants and the communities they represent; "the teachers" role is to represent the teachers as the children's role is to represent the children and the parents role is to represent the parents'. Teachers cannot simply force through their agenda. The children constitute a majority and all issues can be pressed to a vote if they cannot be resolved by discussion. It would be naive to imagine that structural safeguards can wholly prevent adult manipulation of children, but to assert that this must inevitably occur on every occasion when young people and adults work together, is to succumb to a dreadful scepticism, pessimism and determinism. Such a position, moreover, fails to address the issue of how children's participation is ever to get underway. There must be a starting point, no matter how inadequate. As long as the starting point for children's participation does not compromise the terminus, attempts at manipulation can be addressed *en route*.

III. THE SCHOOL COUNCIL: PARTICIPATION AND HART'S LADDER?

More recently the debate about children's participation has tended to move away from questions about whether children have a right to participate in decision making, to consider and attempt to construct analytical models designed to measure and assess children's participation.

Hart has developed an eight level "ladder" to represent children's participation (Hart, 1992). The various "rungs" of the ladder are not incremental, deterministic or sequential stages through which participation must progress but, to adopt a different metaphor, yardsticks against which to measure the extent and quality of children's participation.

The first three rungs of the ladder – manipulation, decoration and tokenism – more accurately express children's *involvement* rather than *participation* in a particular enterprise. "Manipulation", for example, may reflect the involvement of children as consultants in a project where they are not given any feedback. Flekkøy offers the example of opinion polls which use children as their respondents (Flekkøy, 1992:124). "Decoration" expresses those involvements of children which stress their "decorative character". The parading of children in T shirts bearing slogans which the children may not have chosen is an obvious example here; arranging for children to sing or dance at conferences is similarly "decorative". Tokenism describes children's notional involvement in conferences or other events, when there has been no attempt to consult the group whose composition the child "representatives" are intended to reflect. In summary, these first three rungs of Hart's ladder do not signify participation but manipulation, decoration and tokenism. But how remarkable to even calibrate the ladder in this way and discuss such forms of involvement as if they might constitute participation. Imagine sticking a rosette on a dog, a monkey or a child, or taking any of them (or all three of them) on a demonstration and describing such passive, ill informed and non deliberative acts as "participation".

In truth there are only five rungs of genuine, but graded, participation. The first form of activity which approximates participation is labelled "assigned but informed". Here, a project is chosen and planned by adults but the participating children understand and endorse the objectives and fulfil a meaningful role in achieving them. "Consulted and informed", "adult designed with shared decisions with children", "child designed and directed" and "child designed with shared decisions with adults" express the increasing possibilities for children's participation. It is instructive of children's limited participation in decision making, even in institutions such as schools where children are crucially significant and should be centrally involved, to lean the ladder against the institution and see how few rungs children are able to climb.

The School Council seems to reflect a form of participation which Hart would describe as "adult designed with shared decisions with children"; rung six of the eight rung ladder. A giddy height indeed. The Council seems to be an admirable introduction to participation in decision making for children who are quite young. It does not seem to be tokenistic. The decisions which the children at Ravenswood School have taken, as well as the priorities they set for themselves, signal the seriousness of purpose which they invest in the Council and their competencies to resolve issues which concern them. Their competencies will undoubtedly grow as they acquire greater experience. The

Ravenswood School Council offers a useful illustration of children's ability to climb ladders of participation. Paternalists warn of the dangers of allowing children to participate; given opportunities such as the school council to express their competencies, children will prove them wrong.

A final parting shot at Hart's ladder is irresistible. What seems so problematic about the ladder is that Hart is content to be purely descriptive rather than prescriptive. The ladder seeks simply to classify forms of participation (some of them pretty dubious); like a latter day Comte, the whole exercise seems to centre round the construction of taxonomies.

It might be helpful, however, to come at the problem from another direction. Instead of trying to identify those factors which disallow participation (lack of rationality, lack of information, manipulation by others) and showing how they disqualify young people (although never adults), it might be more useful to attempt to construct a model of "perfect participation" – rather like a model of "perfect competition" in economic theory. The ideal conditions for participation could be established and the ability of different groups to meet them considered. The model would adopt the classic 19th century "liberal" assumptions about human capacities and propensities. People are rational, defined as the ability to relate means to ends in a certain way; irrationality, prejudice and emotions do not intrude on their decision making logics. Peoples' decision making is informed and based on the fullest possible knowledge of alternatives and possibilities. People have sufficient resources of time, information and competence to adjudicate authoritatively on all issues. People are autonomous agents not only in their actions but also in constructing their thoughts and opinions. They are not for example, manipulated in their ideas by popular culture or the mass media. People are able to identify their particular interests and will pursue them rationally. There are no social circumstances or pressures which "blind" them *to* their interests nor compel them to be blinded *by* their interests. Such assumptions are of course naive and anachronistic. Yet we continue to apply them solely to children and then exclude them from decision making when they cannot comply with their unrealistic expectations. But who could meet such expectations?

REFERENCES

Archard, D. (1993) *Children: Rights and Childhood* Routledge, London
Dworkin, R. (1977) *Taking Rights Seriously* Duckworth, London.
Feinberg, J. (1980) "Legal Paternalism." In *Rights, Justice and the Bounds of Liberty: Essays in Social Philosophy*. Princeton University Press, USA.
Flekkoy M. (1992) "Closing Address To The Second International Congress on Ombudswork With Children." In Droogleever-Fortuyn, M and M. de Langen (Eds): *Towards The Realisation Of Human Rights For Children*, DCI Amsterdam, pp 120–131.
Franklin, B. (Ed) (1986) *The Rights of Children*. Blackwells, Oxford.
Hart, R. (1992) *Children's Participation from Tokenism to Citizenship*. Innocenti Essays No 4 UNICEF, London.

Heartfield, J. (1993) "Why Children's Rights are Wrong." *Living Marxism*, October, pp 13-15.
Holt, J (1975) *Escape From Childhood*. Penguin.
Kant, I. (1887) *The Philosophy of Law*. T and T Clark London.
Locke, J (1964) *Two Treatises of Government*. In P. Laslett (Ed). Cambridge University Press.

ZORAN PAVLOVIĆ

Children's Parliament in Slovenia

I. INTRODUCTION: WHAT MAKES A HEALTHY FAMILY, ORGANIZATION, SOCIETY?

Before I can describe and present a string of events, or rather a process of "Children's Parliament" in Slovenia, that has been taking place yearly since 1990 (which was also the year of the first session of the first adult multi-party parliament in Slovenia) I feel it necessary to outline briefly some kind of theoretical framework. Namely, an inspiring book attracted my attention at the right moment (as it usually happens), which has "forced" me to formulate the starting-point question in the following manner: "How well the Children's Parliament in Slovenia reflects the "mental health" status of our society, and how much can it contribute to its improvement?"

Robin Skynner and John Cleese begin their book Life and How to Survive It[1] by summarizing what is known about the characteristics of the most mentally healthy individuals and families.

- The first feature of these happy families is their basic positive and friendly, "Affiliative Attitude", which they share not only amongst their members but radiate to their social and natural environment as well.
- While the "Affiliative Attitude" reflects and also provides ground for the basic security and acceptance of the family's members, the second surprising feature is a quality of independence in their loving relations, which allows them both intimacy and separateness, and to move easily between the two; this quality depends on the individual's sense of own identity, but again, it also supports it.
- the third is the family structure of authority, with the parents in a strong and equal coalition, prepared to lay down the law if they have to, but always consulting fully the children first; being always fully consulted, children seem to be more willing to accept authority and "command", when necessary.

---

[1]   Robin Skynner / John Cleese: *Life and How to Survive it.* Mandarin Paperback, London 1994. 422 p. (first published by Methuen London, 1993)

E. Verhellen (ed.), Monitoring Children's Rights, 327–345.
© 1996 *Kluwer Law International. Printed in the Netherlands.*

- the next is the family's very free and open communication, based on the children's sense that no feelings they experience are unacceptable or forbidden, giving a feeling of freedom and lots of fun and high spirit; where there is no taboo on experiencing feelings, it is much easier to learn how to control them (when their expression is inappropriate) and so to gain social competence without sacrificing a full feeling of self.
- the fifth is their ability to perceive the world very clearly and realistically, based on the fact that they can accept all their own feelings and therefore don't need to project them onto other people.
- and finally, they can cope quite readily with change, because they have a realistic view of the world and mental maps that represent it, and because they have access to a variety of sources of emotional support: from good relationship that the family members enjoy with each other; from good connections in the community, due to their friendly behavior in the past. And also, they seem to be particularly good at drawing support from some kind of transcendental value system, a set of values and beliefs which gives a sense of meaning and purpose that goes beyond just the welfare of themselves, or even of their family. Often, the "transcendent" values are not so much religious as connected with some broader humanitarian cause.

All these features are obviously interconnected, they support and amplify each other; even more, a progress achieved at any of them is likely to enhance the well-being of the whole system.

Skynner and Cleese then proceed to show how the very same characteristics apply as indicators of "mental health" of social organizations and institutions (like schools and companies, with which they deal specifically), and finally, of a society as a whole, or its large subsystems. Doing this, they add some other related features that seem to be specially relevant to the subject matter. Regarding organizations, such a health-displaying and health-enhancing feature seems to be the willingness of the leadership to delegate as much power as possible down the levels of hierarchy, retaining only those decision-making powers they cannot delegate, and keeping strict control over a very limited number of critical regulators. Also, in an atmosphere of open communication, a reasonable amount of mistakes is expected to occur; if concealed, they make a system rigid and distrustful; if openly recognized, they enable the whole system to learn faster. Open communication also enables that the intelligence of the whole system is used!

Regarding society, and particularly its value system(s), societal myths held a prominent place. "Myth" is understood as an abstract bit of common condensed wisdom, which fills in a blank in our mental map of the world, which we, being limited empirical creatures, cannot draw out relying only on our experience. Myths are ideas and stories that enable human beings to cooperate and work together as a society. A value of a particular myth must be assessed by asking, how effective it is in helping to integrate human behavior

(individuals to become more integrated, groups to become more cooperative). Skynner and Cleese point at the two aspects to that effectiveness:
- how *inclusive* is the myth? Is it just helping some people to integrate and cooperate better, but excluding others?
- how *persuasive* is the myth. How much does it actually affect people's behavior?

II. CHILDREN IN A SOCIETY

Skynner and Cleese explicate in detail how all this applies to children in families, and the schools, naturally; but they do not say much about the position of children, as a social group, in society. Well, can the criteria of healthy family, organization, society be applied to the position of children in a society? It does not hurt to try.

Certainly, a relatively healthy society feels "affiliative", loving and caring towards its offspring. Only in the times of extreme adversity, which tend to severely damage integrity of individual and of social bonds, are children in jeopardy of being deprived of the last expressions of altruistic behavior of adults, and so of being effectively abandoned.

However, the quality of love for children can vary enormously. While having their survival effectively protected, they very seldom seem to be treated with respect as separate individuals with their inborn plan of growth that they need to follow, but rather as an extension of what the adults have achieved, or what they have not achieved in their lifetime. Being accepted as members of a society (although not fully valid ones), they will serve as a material for biological, emotional and spiritual reproduction of what is already there, and have their rights to an open future in many ways denied. Less "communal" and more exaggeratedly individualistic society can, on the other hand, allow a child to "take risks" and get a feeling of "separateness", for sure, but without providing a "safety net", a secure feeling of belonging somewhere, which is a necessary precondition for a courage to be "separate" to develop, and for exploring possibilities in a relaxed manner, because mistakes are allowed. That is the reason why such societies, instead of producing a variety of well integrated life styles, tend to "clone" identical anxious "individuals".

Some societies may foster strict authoritarian attitude, develop very dependable, maybe even fair set of rules and sanctions, but without much incentive for children to participate or be even consulted about anything. It is hard to imagine a feeling of self as being valuable to develop under such conditions. Others may foster delegating the power "down" to the extent of abdication of the parental responsibilities. While it would be probably "healthy" for a society to include children into its definition of who are valid subjects of democracy (so that it can use intelligence *of the whole system*), it is not likely to be healthy to forget to what extent children are genuinely dependent on adults, to what extent they need them as "auxiliary organs", before they develop sufficient skills and internalize mental maps complete enough to enable them to proceed on their own, in a mature way. Certain amount (but only certain amount!) of self-discipline is needed, as a requisite of social competence, so that we can participate constructively and share in the good sides of living in society; before self-discipline is accomplished to a sufficient extent, external agents of control are necessary. However, "healthier" society will do better job in judging "how much" is necessary and "how to do it" than a less "healthy" one.

It is easy to lose balance on any of these dimensions. For example, a desire to protect childhood from the vices of the corrupted world and to equip children with sufficient knowledge to cope in an increasingly complex society has driven children in our society into isolation from adults, into a separate world of learning. Desire to protect them from exploitation has ended up in depriving children of any substantial opportunity to test themselves in the world of work. They start learning about responsibility only after they "finish school", which comes late, and tends to come even later. They have an "open future", but they are hardly ready to take part in it competently, apart from their academic skills. On the other hand, there are societies where children make valuable contribution to their family's economy, but it unfortunately often means that they have to participate in a very inappropriate kind of work (if not prostitution), they are deprived of proper educational opportunities, and, effectively, their right to an open future also ends up being denied.

The "healthiness" of an open communication with children, as a social group, must be obvious. To be realistic about its own qualities, a society must be open to all its members, everybody must feel to be a part of it. A society must learn how social groups understand and feel about their position, how they experience social realities, and it should adjust to the needs of the most vulnerable, children being among them. We have to re-learn, again and again, what it means to be a child in an adult world, and believe them when they talk about their families, peers, schools, work, about their joys and hardships of their lives. Obviously, we have to create channels through which their voice will reach decision-makers; open communication must not be limited only to the child's home. As parents, we learn from our children about intensive emotions, about the joy and sorrow of life, about fun, about excitement and pride in learning and achievement, about gratefulness, about unconditional love, and many other things. They force us to learn about new dimensions of responsibility. There is a lot that we can learn from children as a society as well. Taking seriously their needs and their point of view would sober us up and teach us better than getting repeatedly stuck on our often petty and envious business.

The world is changing rapidly. How are societies to get ready for the inevitable changes? For one thing, they should better be realistic about what they really are and how its social groups feel about living in a given setting.

They should better rely on the intelligence of the whole system and not just the wisdom of the chosen few. They should open up to the messages from "the bottom". They should "produce" competent, compassionate yet independent, pro-social yet separate individuals. It is hard to prepare a society for a specific challenges, simply because we do not know what is coming. However, if we raise our children with an intention to make them healthy, competent, confident individuals, they will probably grow up to be just the kind of persons a society will need to face the challenge: well rooted in the culture, yet flexible enough to adjust their mental maps, when necessary. We must value the child for what she/he is, without calculating if she/he will carry on our mission in this world; if we actually commit ourselves to our children just for the sake of their happiness, they will probably eventually do their best to make sure that our most honest efforts were not in vain. We must teach children about the value of tradition, for its condensed wisdom, but also give them a feeling of entitlement to change it to make things better. We are capable of raising children more healthily that we are ourselves, if we accept their feelings and give them opportunity to learn to handle them; if we make them not just to accept the rule, but also allow them, eventually, to understand the value and the meaning of it; if we teach them not only the value of achievement, but also allow them to experience the value of solidarity with other human beings and other living creatures.

To be able to use the intelligence of the whole system, society should foster persuasive, inclusive rather than exclusive myths. So, what about the myth of "children's rights", is it such a myth?

It certainly includes *children*, but it can be understood in so many different fashions, depending on the "mental health" level of the particular group or society. It can be understood as a call for the protection, or just the opposite, for liberation of children, and many other things. If we fall out of balance, we will lose from the picture a specific nature of the child as a human being, person in permanent development and change, in need of belonging, protection, assistance, support and tolerance for his/her mistakes, as well as in need of respect of his/her individuality and his/her point of view, freedom of feeling, of exploration, of going away and coming back, of acquiring his/her own independent empirical experience. A balanced and integrated view of the child's nature opens a possibility for a better integration for a care-giver as well, and of the society. Fragmented view leads to a one-way communication and one-way process of giving-and-taking, to the feeling of a zero-sum game, where one must lose for the other to gain, to a myth of children's rights as an exclusive one.

Living with a child may make an adult's life more difficult or at least more complicated, but definitely richer. An adult may have to give up some of his/her comfort, but in return, he gets full wealth of new life unfolding right in front of him/her, whatever one makes of it, after all. And for society, a life without children would equal to imminent death. If the myth of "children's rights" did not mean a better quality of life also for parents, kindergarten, school and all other levels as well, because of everything children give and teach us, it would not really be inclusive. We want to see it as an inclusive myth, indeed, as a new positive utopia, a hope for a better future for everybody. Yet, we so often make it be a zero-sum game, whenever we make it sound that being pro-children's rights means being against somebody else's rights or interests.

Therefore, the "children's rights" myth has powerful potentials of becoming an inclusive myth, but there are still lessons to be learned before it actually does.

On the other hand, is it a persuasive myth?

The UN Convention on the Rights of the Child comes readily into the picture at this point. It has been signed and ratified by so many countries by now that it looks like a best possible confirmation of the persuasiveness of the myth. Yet, do all these countries take children's rights really seriously? Did they not, during the World Summit on Children in 1990, discuss the Gulf crisis behind the curtains? Didn't they sign the Convention because it sounded nice at the time, while making significant reservations, to preserve national legislation intact? Well, even so: the Convention itself and the international process related to it will probably *persuade* countries to take it seriously. Some of them may not have meant it seriously at the time, but they have officially involved themselves into certain commitments. Gradually, as monitoring mechanisms evolve and mature, international persuasiveness of the myth will grow as well as the international pressure to initiate real changes. It may be a slow process, but nevertheless bound to have profound impact, on the involved particular societies, and on the meaning of universality of human rights as well.

How about "democracy", is that a persuasive and inclusive myth? It is certainly persuasive, as recent history of Eastern and Central Europe clearly displays. But is it inclusive?

There have always been people and forces who find it their vocation to drive somebody out of the participation in public affairs, or out of the country, or out of the Earth. Because they were of the wrong skin color, wrong place of birth, wrong age, wrong gender, or wrong whatever. Democracy has, historically, hardly been an inclusive myth. Yet, gradually, the inclusive understanding seems to be prevailing – at least as long as a society is doing relatively well. In the times of adversity the majority usually puts some tighter control on women, foreigners, maybe even handicapped, certainly over children (maybe just for their safety reasons...) and therefore gives a "decisive decision-making" priority over slow and bothersome process of "inclusive democracy", where everybody must be consulted before the elected representatives can formulate a compromise.

Without children, democracy is not inclusive. They are explicitly excluded from the right to vote, for example. This fact alone must not necessarily present a tragedy for children, as long as they are fully consulted in their healthy families and as long as their parents or other care-givers genuinely represent children's interest in the public affairs. However, just in case all this did not work so ideally, it sounds wise to invent some other channels to be used by children, when they want to communicate something to somebody in charge outside their immediate family (or the school, for that matter), or when they simply want to communicate their point of view of some significant matter. We all, in our different roles, often can profit more from having access to some civil pressure groups who advocate our interests, and to the media, than from merely relying on our power to give our vote away every four years to a political party, who can turn out not to have our benefit at its heart at all. Yet, we are not willing to give our right to vote away, are we? Just that we realize that it is not sufficient; we can use all means to control the people in power we can invent. Even having some of them available, it does not work perfectly, but better system is still to be invented. Children also need to get access to as many modalities of participation as possible – if democracy is to be an inclusive myth.

III. CHILDREN'S PARLIAMENT IN SLOVENIA

I think it is a very promising sign for the future of democracy in Slovenia that the Children's Parliament started in the same year as the "big" one, first multi-party State Assembly, in 1990. I like to think that it happened because the people in power shared the same inclusive notion of democracy with people who actually initiated the Children's Parliament, the organization called "Association of the Friends of Youth of Slovenia" (AFYS). They shared the conviction that everybody's intelligence was needed, and that the children definitely must have their opinion on the significant public issues heard. The Association was very serious about that all from the beginning; it is hard to say whether the politicians, the hosts of the Children's Parliament, were equally serious. If they were not, they certainly did not show their amusement.

To be quite frank, I was rather skeptical about the whole idea in the beginning. I thought that the adults were trying to use just another gimmick for making themselves look good and fell good about themselves, while manipulating children into thinking that they were able to influence something and even make some decisions while concealing actual lack of power of children as a social group. Even if my concerns had been quite adequate, the process in the following years outgrew them.

The children we are talking about are students of the higher classes of the eight-year elementary school, 13 to 15 years old, but there are always also some younger than that, and some middle school students as well.

So there they were on 19 October 1990, 105 kid-representatives of 44 (out of 65) municipalities in Slovenia, discussing environmental issues with the president of the adult parliament, prime minister, ministers for education and for social affairs, "Green" and several other parliament members and a number of other officials. In the beginning, it was not even called "Parliament". It was "a meeting" of children and high political officials. It was actually because of what had happened the first time that the term Parliament was attached to the process.

It must be mentioned at this point, that the session in the building of the Slovenian Parliament (State Assembly) represents in fact only the final act, which is nevertheless the most ceremonious part of a much longer process. It starts at the school level, where children first accumulate relevant knowledge about the given problem and then become involved in a discussion, based on the theory and of course on the empirical evidence, as they experience it in their everyday lives. It would not make much sense to choose a theme for the Parliament that would bear no significance to children's everyday experience. A couple of students are chosen to represent the school at the Parliament at the municipality level; there, a couple of students are elected to represent municipality at the State level.

A. 1990 – "Environment"

In 1990, the theme of the Parliament process was "Healthy and Safe Environment for Children". Children displayed a considerable level of awareness and understanding of serious ecological problems threatening our planet, as well as of concrete ecological "bombs" in their own community; indeed, they composed a pretty comprehensive list of the main ecological problem areas in Slovenia! Another sub-topics was really unsafe road traffic in Slovenia, which takes regularly about 500 lives yearly (per 2 million inhabitants), and about 50 of those are children, i.e. two classes, every year. They also spoke about the school as their living environment and pointed out how neglected and poor many of these environments were, and they also tackled a number of related issues among which they, at the end, chose a topic for the next parliament.

The overall atmosphere was not too optimistic, it was rather depressing and accusing – accusing adults, of course, for such a state of affairs. They demanded serious changes, but they were not able to see themselves as a competent agents of change. When they were invited to participate at sessions of some political bodies which would discuss their demands, a girl said explicitly that they had no intention of attending some tiresome meetings; they formulated their requests and expected politicians to do their job and to report to the next Children's Parliament!

The present adult politicians were discussing and replying in a friendly and frank, although somewhat sweet and over-flattering tone; they also made promises – not just because of the presence of the media, I believe ...

The proceedings (magnetogram, a full transcription of the meeting's record-ings) of the Parliament were published by the AFYS, accompanied by twelve short scholarly papers by adult experts, on pollution-related health hazards, on the child in the road traffic, and on the school-related stress of children.[2]

I think "environment" as a subject of the first Parliament was a very good choice. As children are our positive future, pollution is our negative future. Although we adults often seem to think that "we'll be well dead before it really hits", we do care for our children and the future of the planet just enough to make pollution we create also our problem to solve. Children's basic message at the Parliament seems to have been: "We want to have a future, but we don't seem to have any!" The adult reply seems to have been: "We hear and understand what you are saying. We accept our responsibility and promise to take care of it." This was a kind of inter-generational alliance for the future, a sound basis for the development of the second Parliament in 1991. It was decided to be on "free" or "leisure time" of children and youth, which is really a traumatic issue of a modern world. In a way, environmental issues are easy to discuss. It is a real problem, yet so complex that when nothing improves it is hard to point a finger to the "guilty" party. Even a whole international community seems to be rather helpless! But if children and youth are not happy and constructive when they have all chances of being – in their leisure, free time – the causes must be somewhere really close; it must be caused by the way we communicate with each other, how we live our lives, what we, old and young, do to each other. It is about the "health status" of the society, therefore an inter-generational discussion on the subject must be a real test of how meaningful their endeavour is.

B. 1991 – "Leisure Time"

Many things happened between two Parliaments. Although environmental issues are a way to ask about your future, it was not the "top" "future" issue at the time in our country. In 1990, the former federation of Yugoslavia (SFRJ) was already in a deep trouble and its the future, of its federal parts and of all of us was tremendously uncertain. A girl at the first Children's Parliament actually challenged the president of the (adult) Parliament about his personal attitude regarding Slovenia as an independent state. After he had offered a very fair and honest reply (saying that we must create such a homeland for ourselves in which will would be the masters of our own destiny, but we must be aware that in the modern world nobody is alone, everybody must cooperate with the neighbors in a co-dependent world), the subject did not return.

At the time, very few seriously considered a possibility of a real war. Yet, in 1991, it happened. First in Slovenia (after the Declaration of Independence), very soon it moved to Croatia and then it blasted in Bosnia and Herzegovina

---

[2] *Otrokom varno in zdravo okolje.* Zbornik. Informacije 5/1990, Zveza prijateljev mladine Slovenije, Ljubljana, november 1990. 132 p.

in the Spring of 1992; three years later we still see no end or solution to it. Hundreds of thousands of refugees moved in the reverse direction, from the war areas to the safe areas of Croatia, to Slovenia and further west and also out of Europe. This was all beyond our worst nightmare that we had just months earlier. The memories and vicinity of on-going war, plus all the economical and other difficulties a young country needs to face, caused a lot of anxieties among people; children were not spared from it. Child welfare organizations got involved in the work with refugees, adult Parliament was preoccupied with the new Constitution of Republic Slovenia, which was finally adopted by the end of 1991. Children's Parliament had to wait. But it was not forgotten; commitments were there, and a wish to continue, so it was actually held on 28 February 1992. That is another good sign for the future of democracy in Slovenia: children were not put aside, they were invited for further consultations, even in the hardest times, just a little later than planned!

One would not expect such a thing as Children's Parliament to develop in time, because the majority of the actors change from one to another. But, social processes seem to have this ability to actually have an evolution even when all the actors change in a rather short time, as is the case with the members of the social group "children".

The second parliament was actually a step further. For one thing, the government actually provided a report on the realization of the commitments to the first Parliament. It was able to present only a few actual accomplishments in that short and hard time, but it was ensuring that the government was taking seriously all the children's request and was preparing intensively further measures for improvements.

It was just the second Parliament, so it was still not completely certain, how real it was and to what extent or if was just "make believe". At that moment, I think, children decided to test their power. There was a vote on the government's effectiveness. *Nobody* thought the government had been very successful, but only a few assessed is as unsuccessful. The majority opted just for the moderate "successful".

There was a separate report on the specific progress in the area of ecology (by a member of the "Green" party, at the time also a member of the collective presidency of the Republic), which was quite optimistic, and did not provoke much discussion.

And then, there was a report of the minister of education on the efforts of the government in the area of schooling. For whatever reason, his report was faced with discontent. Children felt that the minister was not replying to their questions. Speaker after speaker requested *concrete* answers.

Children, reflecting general anxious state of the society, came to the Parliament to complain, and they used the opportunity well. They had the power to choose, and they chose to be unsatisfied and also to show it. Talking about the trauma of leisure time, they mainly attacked *school* for not fulfilling its task. They expressed their feeling that everything was actually *better* a couple of years earlier, that the school was cutting on extracurricular activities, that there are to few facilities (like gyms and pools) and those existing were in a poor shape, that the teachers are just about to start striking because of their poor salaries. Moreover, overall, school was not efficient and was taking much more of the students' time and energy than necessary. There were very few constructive suggestions for the improvement. It seems to me that the children just wanted to see whether they would be allowed and accepted if they were just angry, anxious and unsatisfied. And the good thing is, they were. Not an easy job for a minister of education, though. The Children's Parliament became quite serious.

If the basic message of the first Parliament had been "We want to have future", the message of the second was, I feel: "Take care of us. We are entitled."

Through their complaints they were really saying to adults, you promised so many things, yet you have let us down. Many of us feel lonely, and many of us are not self sufficient, not even (or maybe *the least*) in our "free" time. This society devotes to little time, money and attention to our needs and doesn't provide sufficient assistance to our development.

Again, the good thing was, the adults did not reply, "that is not the truth, you ungrateful, selfish little brats". They really said, "we hear what you are saying; we thought we were doing our best, but we will try to do better; but you need to be patient, our resources are limited, we cannot make it over night". Children were allowed and accepted for their negative feelings and complaints, in a fair parliamentary discussion. The adults argued their point of view honestly, showed personal feelings and concern, and the Parliament was a success. It created very solid ground for further development, and it also created a list of demands for the government to be fulfilled in the following year(s). Not surprisingly, the children decided to devote their next parliament to the school.

AFYS published the magnetogram of the meeting, accompanied with fifteen scholarly papers on the problems of the "free" time of children and youth.[3] Several public debates on the subject were organized in the following months.

C. 1992 – "Friendly School"

In a booklet following the third parliament (held on time in December 1992) AFYS published magnetogram again, but this time accompanied not by scholarly contribution but by the translation of the UN Convention on the Rights

---

[3] *Prosti čas mladih*. Zbornik. Strokovni teksti, magnetogram in sklepi drugega otroškega parlamenta. Informacije ZPMS št.1/1992. Ljubljana, junij 1992. 160 p.

of the Child, the report of the organization on its activities in 1992 and its plans for 1993.[4]

The president of AFYS in the introduction to this publication summarized several qualities of the third Parliament in a brief yet significant manner. The following sentences relate a good deal of the "behind-the-curtain" process: "The Association of the Friends of Youth of Slovenia is particularly pleased by the ever improving cooperation of the local authorities at the local Parliaments (presidents of municipal governments and parliaments). Accepting an initiative of AFYS, parliaments were even organized in some municipalities where we no longer have our committees. In some places, parliaments motivated revival of our branch. We estimate that we have overcome fears and prejudices that with this activity AFYS wants to continue a political manipulation of children, following this or that ideology. A conviction is firmly established now that AFYS is just a non-governmental and non-partisan organization of people with different world views and aspects, joined by the common interest of acting for the welfare of children and youth."

In the beginning, it was not completely clear whether the Parliament was or was not a manipulation of children, even to the organization that was standing behind it. There was a lot of discussion going on in the organization over this matter. The focus was on the "big event"; the organization did not have much influence on the process of preparation at the lower levels and was not sure how much the children were actually representing children's interests and how much they would just read a message that was written by some school- or community-related adult, who wanted to send a message to the Capital through the children's mouth.

But after two quite successful attempts it became much clearer that the Parliament really has powerful potential of opening a dialogue between authorities and the authentic voice of children, even when we take into account the fact that children at this age need an adult assistance in all stages of the process and that they still carry written (adult-assisted) notes with them to Ljubljana. There was a new confidence that the children's voice does come through.

Adults at many levels started taking the whole process more seriously; the organization noticed improved cooperation of the local authorities. The starting points of the process gained in importance, and consequently the role of mentors at the school level as well. AFYS started organizing seminars for mentors (teachers or school counselling staff) to prepare them for the role of mediators, involving experts in the subject matter of the particular Parliament.

These changes reflected immediately in the work of the third Parliament. One of the most important features was, the children, being previously accepted even when they were not pleasing the adults, became much more cooperative and realistic in their discussions and demands. They had much better

---

[4]   *Otrokom prijazno šolo.* Zbornik. Informacije ZPMS št.2/1993. Ljubljana, april 1993. 102 p.

insight into issues which could and should be dealt with at the school level, which they needed to discuss with the local authorities, and which they really needed to address to the State level politicians. They gained in self-confidence and in feeling that the Parliament may bear some concrete fruit after all.

(Of course, not everything suddenly worked perfect. About one third of municipalities still did not have a representative at the "big" one; about the cooperation of local authorities one girl at the Parliament said that they were there only as long there were representatives of the media present, then they left them to talk amongst themselves.)

In his Introduction, the president of AFYS also wrote: "All of us who follow the work of the Parliament from the very beginning, appreciate continuing growth of the quality of young representatives' discussions. The third Parliament particularly excelled with the spontaneous performances of the representatives, who did not read texts written by their mentors. This did not mean that these performances were not carefully prepared and thoughtful."

The children also gained their sense of power. A girl said at the third Parliament, with a nice touch of humour: "We had elections in Slovenia.[5] Therefore, the old parliament has gone, while the new one has not started working yet. Our, Children's Parliament, which has a session today in the building of a Slovenian State Assembly, is at present the highest body of the Republic Slovenia, composed of representatives, elected by children all around Slovenia!"

The third Children's Parliament worked under the title "Friendly School to Children". Children spoke about the material standards of schooling, but even more about the interpersonal relations in the school and about the quality of the curriculum. They had a lot of concrete suggestions. Instead of complaining, they were describing difficulties in a more matter-of-fact manner, and pleaded for faster modernization of the school (there was a lot of talk about computers). While asking adults (teachers) to be fair, they were quite willing to recognize their own role in making the school "friendly", their obligation to behave correctly and to do their part of the job. One of them said: "We too often misunderstand democracy as anarchy." Several "integrative" subjects were recurring repeatedly: suggestions for a tolerant dialogue, for better communication between the school and parents. Words like "independent work", "cooperation", "solidarity with less affluent", "relaxed atmosphere", were not uncommon. The children would themselves ask speakers not to repeat what had already been told.

As already mentioned, they often clearly expressed their understanding, which issues can be resolved at the school level, even when they mentioned them at the Parliament, while they addressed adequate requests to the State officials. They included requests for more money to be invested in the young

---

[5] It was just after the second multi-party elections to the State Assembly.

generation, but also for more rational curriculum and more effective teaching methods, with more field work, modern equipments etc.

The minister of education and his team replied very clearly and efficiently to the children's questions and discussions. There was no conflict. The minister was not the same one as a year earlier; maybe the new one was a better communicator, but the children were certainly more ready to listen, because they had acquired the confidence that they would be heard. Even more: the children themselves often expressed optimism, they had noticed things "to be moving" and they were quite satisfied with some of these "moves", although the majority of the schools were just the same poor old ones, while there were only several new schools with nice gyms opened in the meantime.

Remembering our question about the "mental health" status of our society and the role of the Children's Parliament in it, I must say I do not find it surprising that the person, who moderated the third Parliament, exclaimed enthusiastically at one point: "I must admit that I am surprised by the profoundness and vision displayed by the young representatives. I think this country has a truly great future!"

Looking for the "basic message" of the third Parliament, I think it is: "If you are fair, we can do our part. We can live together well." The climate had obviously considerably changed, but I think the messages from the first two parliaments should not be forgotten. They requested future for themselves and they wanted to be taken care of before they agreed to cooperate.

Encouraged by the level of dialogue, while being quite critical regarding their own conduct and very concerned about bullying, smoking and drinking of some of them, they decided to address these particularly difficult issues at their next Parliament.

D. 1993 – "For Friendship Without Violence"

Why should these issues be particularly difficult?

The Parliament started in 1990 by establishing a coalition between children and adults, against a "common enemy", deadly pollution and dangerous road traffic. Next, children felt free to put adults on the "other side" and address their complaints to them. Next, while keeping adult on the other side and still addressing demands, they offered cooperation. Now, with violence as a main subject of forthcoming session, titled "For Friendship – Without Violence", they had to face the fact that "they", the children, are not a homogenous group of people; they were about to divide themselves to "good" and "bad" kids.

At that time the adult community was also quite alarmed by the cases of violence against peers in and out of our schools, and still is. The school came into the focus of public attention, while the school itself felt rather helpless. The police were specially concerned about the first appearances of organized groups, lead from behind by young adults, intimidating younger children for money. A big auditorium, where AFYS organized a public panel discussion on the subject, as a part of the preparation of the mentors, was overcrowded. Although I never considered myself to be an expert in bullying (or any other form of deviance of children and youth, for that matter), I was, as a researcher at the Institute of Criminology, invited to chair that panel. After the event, a number of schools from Ljubljana and vicinity invited me to visit them and to give a lecture or have a talk with the teacher and parents. Their concerns were genuine and these evening talks were very interesting.

One school invited me to help them conduct their school Parliament. That was, unfortunately, my first "first hand" experience with this process at the school level, and the only one, so far. I was, as could be expected, pleasantly surprised. Some students read their very well-prepared reports on the subject as a theoretical framework for the discussion. There was a lot of open discussion; the teachers, some present parents and a member of local authorities, cooperated nicely. Some of the children tried to simplify the issue; some of them suggested the "bad" children really needed some kind of help; the others would like them punished or somehow excluded. But some other children made their best to keep in balance both sides of the story, which was painful, because the children obviously needed to be protected from the bully, who was one of them and himself a child. Talking about bullying with an adult does not only mean overcoming the humiliation of the victim, but also betrayal of the peer. The children became soon aware of the dilemma (even if they had not had any bad experience themselves) and did not look very convinced when they were told to consult a teacher or a school counselor if they were attacked or pressed for money, for the reasons of his own safety and because of the fact that it is easier to help a bully if he is stopped early.

It was impossible not to notice that the "bad" children were not there, at the school Parliament. They probably self-excluded themselves in the very beginning of the whole process. There were some children outside, throwing snowballs in the window. Maybe they were just younger kids amusing themselves. But more likely they were of the same age as those inside, but they did not "belong" into this nice, smart, cooperative crowd.

At the "big" Parliament in December 1993, the difficulty became even clearer. Many blamed society for violence, smoking, drinking and drug abuse among youth, the culture of alcohol and violent movies, bad adult models (even drinking and smoking teachers were mentioned), many were discussing family reasons for deviant behaviour, but many were also simply blaming it on the "bad children", just that nobody knew exactly what to do with them. To be fair, there were many proposals regarding *prevention*. They called on the families to devote more attention to children; they wanted the school to be a positive experience for everybody, so that nobody would need to seek affirmation in a negative way; some described good experiences, like class excursions, which helped to integrate the class better and lower the level of violence; most of all, they wanted more cooperation between students and teachers; they also demanded more control, in the school, and by the police.

At this Parliament the children actually exposed their vulnerability. I think the basic message was: "Protect us." But it was not just, "you, good people, protect us, good children, from the bullies, drugs and alcohol". It also meant "protect us, good and bad children, from yourselves. Change your ways."

I am not sure whether this message came through to the adult ears. It only occurred to me after reading the magnetogram over and over again and remembering the atmosphere in the assembly hall.[6] But maybe the children have found their own way to make it come through, eventually, and to help adults to change. At the end they had to decide on the subject for the next session. There were several proposals, among them one that sounded really attractive: love. What are the things that make our life easier and help us cope? That would be something very different from hard thinking about the dark sides of life. But they explicitly refused it and decided to talk about relations and communication between students and teachers, plus the students' school-related stress. I think they did that because they wanted to create another opportunity to do a little bit of complaining, but also an opportunity to make some real impact. Maybe they will talk about love some other time; now they want to improve adults.

I feel it to be a good judgement. The subject of violence made them to face their vulnerability and a lack of power. They had to call adults for help. That is fair. Violence, drug abuse and drinking are issues out of their power; they definitely demand very active and firm adult approach. Here they can do their part and cooperate if the adults change. They can try to help them change. I think they are right. A good school parliament with a lot of open communication may be just the right thing to help integrate the school. In fact, I think it is already happening.

The adult State officials made very valuable contributions again, and displayed sincere and honest attitude. The president of the State Assembly addressed the children in the beginning; the president of the Republic send a message and apologized for his absence; the minister of education presented a realistic report on the progress on the "friendly school" project from the last session and answered, together with his team, many questions during the debate. They ensured that the kind of school that the ministry envisions will also greatly reduce tension and consequently violence as well. The minister of interior affairs assured the young representatives that the police was concerned about the violence among youth and was also very active. They both called the children to actively cooperate with the school in fighting undesired conduct of their peers.

Finally, I must say a word on the afterthoughts that this session initiated in my mind.

---

[6] This time I happened to be in charge of 'technical assistance' to the Parliament. Apart from the children's presiding board, there is always an adult person who technically leads the discussion. The proceedings of the fourth Parliament have not been published yet.

Some kids are more cooperative than others. Some are more rebellious than others. It may be their inborn character, but it certainly is a different kind of experience they have with adults that must be held accountable for this diversity. The process of the Children's Parliament attracts the more cooperative ones. (At least at this age. Later, in middle school, they are much more capable of organizing themselves independently from adult assistance.) Is it possible that we are actually doing a bad favour to these good children, by involving them into the adult way of resolving problems? We often hear from experts that some kind of rebellion against the previous generation is necessary for the formation of one's individual identity. Are we not making it even harder for the good children if we teach them that everything can be nicely "talked out"? They will find it hard to rebel anyway. Should we pull them even further from their naughty peers? These are going to have a lot of fun in their youth. The majority of them will mature to become good and responsible people, but will retain the capacity for fun and will understand children and youth. Well, the majority of the good ones will find some reason to rebel, eventually, and get even with the bad ones, but, paradoxically, the good experience of the Children's Parliament may not exactly help them in their development.

On the other hand, if the adults want to hear the authentic voice of the children, they should not listen only to the good ones and pretend that they hear them all. As we all know, some children are very hard to reach. Yet, we must try. Not just because of the Parliament, of course. But if the school takes care that everybody is "in" and belonging safely to the school community, it will be easy to include everybody's point of view into a discussion on important matters, important for children, that is. To reach more difficult children we may need to use some different methods; sitting and talking may be too much hard work for some of them. Whatever we can do to include them, we must do it. Articulation of children's point of view is not valid as long as we exclude some or many of them, or they self-exclude themselves. More integrated process may help the good and the bad equally.

On the other hand, people in power, who sincerely want to learn from children, should not just wait for them to come and speak out their problems in a mature parliamentary manner. They should come at least half-way down to children's level and learn in the children's natural environments and re-learn some of the "childish" ways of conveying messages. At least some of them already do, but that is already quite different story, not the story about the Parliament. Still, even the Parliament itself could profit from some non-verbal means of communication, drawings, posters, dramatizations of the topics...

Something else has been bothering me: when we finally sort out all the problems and everybody is well integrated, in a perfect world, what will children then rebel against? And if there is nothing to rebel against, how will they form their identity? Have no fears, I hear everybody saying, there will never be a perfect world. Then why are we working so hard? Why don't we go have some fun – with children?

CONCLUSION

While looking forward to the session on "Communication between Students and Teachers"...

In four years the process of the Children's Parliament has firmly established itself and has become a good tradition. Of course, there is still work to be done. It has not reached all schools in Slovenia, not even all municipalities. In the schools, it has not reached all students of the higher grades.

I have discussed already why I think it should reach all students. But why should it reach all schools?

When the focus of the process was on the Parliament on the State level and everything leading to it was a preparation for the "real" event, a sample of children was sufficient to convey their message to the people in power. However, the focus has been shifting gradually. With improving cooperation of the local authorities children have been becoming more aware of the "school issues", "municipality issues" and the "state issues". With the new subject of communication between students and teachers the focus has definitely shifted to the school level. There will the main part of the Parliament be taking place in 1994. There is no reason why some schools, children and staff, should benefit equally from such a useful discussion without leaving the other schools behind.

That does not mean that the rest of the process in no longer necessary. Very probably the discussion in the schools will reveal certain structural problems which may make improvements of communication difficult (although I hope that the adults will not be excusing themselves on the "real world" too much). They can address such issues to municipal authorities, who are responsible for schools. There they will be told which problems can be helped with at the local level and which are out of their powers. Again, a voyage to the capital will be quite necessary.

After all, they also have to review the work of the government in the last year. What has it done about violence, alcohol and drugs? They will certainly want to hear about progress made regarding the "friendly school", ecology, road traffic, and opportunities for spending a quality leisure time, as well. And they will discover new issues to talk about, in the years to come.

Reading the transcripts of the first four Parliaments and writing about them, I tried to present them as a social process in evolution. I tried to read between the lines a lot, to find the underlying emotional message of children to adults, and their replies. I believe different reading than mine is quite possible, because it is a very complex process and many messages were actually sent, some more effectively than others.

According to my understanding, the children were saying, "we want a future", "take care of us", "we can do our part", and "adults, change!". I am looking forward to seeing what will be the shift this year. If may easily happen to be: "You see, we can help you and teach you something!"

JAN VAN GILS

Social Participation: Beyond the Effect of Sweetness, with Illustrations from the Project Snater

In this contribution we would like to locate and frame children's social participation, based on practice and study.

The practice to which I refer is of many kinds. First of all there is Snater, which is a project concerning children's rights, and existing for two years now. In the second part of our contribution, this experience of Snater will be dealt extensively. Beside that, there were various projects of input around playareas, policy plans of youth work, children's provincial councils, children's town councils,... Finally, there was also the European Week of the Child and Youth in Barcelona last Summer, where we were involved intensively concerning the forming of the concept and the evaluation. Beside that, there is also the scientific work with researches into "how do children feel about family", "how do children experience sports"? We can't go into this within the scope of this contribution, but the starting points of these researches will be mentioned: the experience of the child and the communication about it with society.

I. CONSULTATION – PARTICIPATION – SOCIAL PARTICIPATION

Although the words "consultation" and "participation" are mostly used,, we prefer the term "social participation" when we talk about children's communication with society and in society.

The term consultation doesn't emphasize this two-way intercourse enough. It emphasizes the contribution of one of the partners, but doesn't mention anything about the other partner. So, it suggests that the other partner listens and doesn't take part in what is happening. The term participation also emphasizes the person of the participant more than the participation in what is happening. Besides, the terms consultation and participation both refer to formal processes of decision-making like those built up in the world of adults, for instance consultation in processes of area planning, consultation in traffic planning, participation councils in the education, ... The term social participation emphasizes the communicative happening between the participants

E. Verhellen (ed.), Monitoring Children's Rights, 347–356.
© 1996 Kluwer Law International. Printed in the Netherlands.

and society more; that is why we feel that "social participation" is a term of equal value.

A. *The Location of the Child in our Society*

It is necessary to have a good view on the location of the child in our society in order to situate this social participation well. And this location is in one word: ambiguous.

On the one hand, society has a lot of attention for the child: it organizes and/or gives grants for the education, it takes care of the family allowance. There is social security which makes medical assistance realizable, ... On the other hand, society doesn't really take the child seriously: it has no place whatsoever in the democratic process of decisionmaking, neither in its immediate surroundings (school, district, community), nor on higher political levels. The children are well taken care of, but they are not appreciated for their own contribution.

Another ambiguity parallels the first one. On the one side, children are being isolated from social life. One creates a separate child's world with schools, nurseries, youth work, ... where the characteristics of the child are focused, together with the development within the peergroup. On the other side, children are part of a world of adults. One presumes for instance that they participate in the traffic. One also handles the same media for children as for adults (television-programming, magazines,...).

So children are rarely "well" integrated in social life.

The isolation of the children is the result of the awakening of their own character and of their vulnerability. Before this awakening by the Aufklärung, children were fully integrated in the world of adults, they were little adults.[1] After the discovery of the child, people wanted to protect it from the dangers and threats of the adult's world: they made specific institutions and specific laws for children.

Childlabour was forbidden and going to school became obligated. Youth movements and other organizations of youngsters were created: playgrounds, youth centres, ... All these initiatives created a world without risks and without responsibilities, where children could play safely, where they could develop themselves and where they could be happy: these were initiatives of adults; children were patronized.[2]

These initiatives, as well on the socio-cultural level as well as on the level of welfare, have considerably contributed to the improvement of the life conditions of children and in that way they were helped to develop themselves at their own pace.

On the other hand, children were isolated because of this.

---

[1] Ariès P., 1987, De ontdekking van het kind, Dasberg L., 1984, Grootbrengen door kleinhouden

[2] Baeten W., 1993, Patronaten worden chiro

The construction of the children's paradise, the created youth land, allows children to grow up far away from the dangers of the world, but at the same time the children alienate from society. School prepares them for the social life later on, but this preparation remains very abstract: it can be compared to learning how to swim on dry land. The complete reality, the engagement, the responsibility, the concrete result of the initiatives, all these things are being missed. A lot of pedagogics tried to meet this fundamental criticism on the education. The reality of life, the connection with the world, world orientation, ... these are all very important themes, but the fear exists that unworldly education is structurally connected to the way the education is being organized. That is why a big part of the children's life goes by in the waiting room of life. They say: "You will get to know the real life later. Now you are too young to understand, it is too early to explain, but later ...".

Next to this pedagogic youth land there is a non-pedagogic land of recreation with, among other things, traffic , media, fun-parks. This land doesn't make a difference between children and adults. One tries to make that land pedagogic and tries to incorporate it with the youth land, but without a lot of success: children are given reflecting bands, but they don't get a separate lane. Sometimes children are offered separate television-programmes, and even a separate channel, but the number of these programmes is certainly diminishing. Children are also watching the so-called family programmes. The funfairs, subtropical holidayparks, and even the zoo don't make a difference at all. If a distinction is being made, they often have pedagogic motives for it (see the separate children's broadcast on television), but usually the pedagogy can't be found in these areas of life. Here it often concerns the recreational sectors which are connected to the collective leisure activities of parents and children. And in families that are continually getting smaller, children and adults are becoming more and more dependent upon themselves.

Next to the youth land and the land of recreation, there is the world of labour, the world of the hard reality. It is very obvious that the labour situation of the adults remains very distant from the children. Firm walls are standing between both worlds. Nevertheless children show interest and we can draw that conclusion in view of the successful annual organization of Roefel, the day of the child, which gives children a chance to explore the world of adults, more specifically the world of labour.

It wouldn't be correct to conclude from this description of the life situation of the child that children were much better off in the past. But the conclusion might be that one has to strive after the preservation of the advantages of this children's land and moreover after the integration of the children in the social life. More space must be created for social participation.

B. Three Good Reasons for the Promotion of Social Participation

There are a lot of good reasons to promote social participation: we will talk about three of them.

1. The Right of the Child to Participation

In the United Nations' Convention about the rights of the child, three kinds of rights can be distinguished: the rights to care (education, health care, ...), the rights to protection (ill-treatment, exploitation, ...) and the rights to participation.[3] Concerning the participation rights, especially the articles 12, 13, 14 and 15 are important. These articles state that the child must be able to express and organize itself freely. They also state that the child must be heard in all procedures that concern the child.

These rights are warrented by the law in every country that has subscribed to that Convention. And even though it is difficult to enforce these rights in concrete situations, the subscribing countries have become engaged to realize, among other things, this right.

2. Society Can't Permit Itself Anymore to Ignore its Most Dynamic Group, Especially When The future of This Group is at Stake

Our society has big problems such as ecology, peace, food supply and health in the Third World, ...

"Instant" solutions for these problems don't exist, it is, for whole mankind including children, more a matter of searching solutions. Besides, children are strongly interested for several reasons. First of all, they feel a certain involvement in these problems: they know these problems better and better because of the television and the education, which becomes de facto more global. Moreover, they express their solidarity with people who are living in regrettable circumstances. Next to that, they are concerned about their own future: what will the earth and the world they live will look like after the resignation of the present politicians in charge? From this point of view, children show a lot of interest for peace problems and ecology. It is therefore necessary to give children a chance to contribute to the solution of these problems. They won't find immediate radical solutions – solutions are being built while acting, while digging themselves in the problems. And they can apply their achieved knowledge later on.

3. There isn't More Efficacious Learning Process, Nor a More Concrete Education Than the One Taking Place in The Middle of Society

Children miss out on very interesting learning and development opportunities because they are being socially isolated. The sometimes hard, but especially realistic school of life is very remote from our education school. There chil-

---

[3] See E. Verhellen, 1991, *Conventie van de rechten van het kind*

dren can learn what they need, what they have to know to be able to live better in certain circumstances. In this way, they learn that they can see the results immediately; they learn that learning is interesting; they learn how to learn. In this way social participation offers interesting learning opportunities.

C. How Can We Work at the Social Participation?

1. No Imitation of the World of Adults
The participation of children will always remain children's participation: children may not be treated as adults, but always as young people in complete development. Their participation will therefore be characteristic but nevertheless as valuable as the one of adults.

An example from traffic: traffic is the organization of the mobility of people. If this organization wants to meet all people, it has to take into account the characteristics of the children (but also of the old and the disabled people) and it is obvious that their physical abilities are very much different from those of adults. If traffic treated everybody the same, it would favour the ones with power, those who are healthy, and that is an unjust organization.

The participation of children should not be organized in the same way as the one of adults (supposing that this participation of adults is well-organized). The question is: how can children's participation be organized, respecting the characteristics of the children?

Nevertheless, it must be obvious that the answer can't exist of a battery of methods and techniques. Certain things can't be solved with a few tricks, because the poor participation of children is strongly connected to their social position: the change of implicit structures of a society takes time and no procedures and techniques are therefore sufficient. That is a second reason why the imitation of the adult's world doesn't solve much. Children's councils, children's municipal councils, children's elections, children's representatives aren't the final objective of participation, they are at the most an intermediate stage. They are valuable because they make the expression of children possible. They are provisional because they don't contain a communication between equal partners. Social participation wants to make ànd expression ànd communication possible.

2. The Ability to Express Themselves
One must be able to express oneself when one wants to communicate. What children think and feel is valuable enough to be stated, because it contains a social participation.

Why is the children's telephone so important? Well, it becomes more and more self-evident that children use the telephone to talk about their needs to unknown but competent people. Therefore children's magazines are important; not only magazines for children, but preferably magazines by children. More and more magazines provide space for the opinion of children, for their worries, for their questions. More and more radio and television programmes offer children the opportunity to speak. More and more children become the interlocutor and they also offer the themes and ideas for the arrangement of the programme. This mainly concerns specific children's programmes. So children get a chance to express themselves and listening adults are offered the opportunity to get used to children with an opinion.

Scientific research which allows children to speak, also contributes to this "expression". This research sees the child not just as a social category, or a unit of observation.[4] Nor has this scientific research been set up to test pedagogic, psychological or sociological hypotheses, but concerns research which wants to track down the frames of reference of the children themselves. The interest for, for example the sociological research concerning children may be big,[5] research from the point of view of the child remains rather rare.[6] It doesn't belong to the scientific most appreciated lines of research either, because it mainly concerns and provisional necessary qualitative and descriptive research. The description of the way children look at various aspects of their own life and of society, nevertheless offers important information to improve the communication with children. When the children, as a social group, become known, communication with them will facilitate.

3. Social Participation

Social participation means that children are considered to be people of age who can participate in social life. They are allowed to talk, but especially to join, to help constructing the social event.

It isn't about having a seat for children at meeting-tables where they can help to decide. No, it is more about being involved in and contributing to social processes in a full manner.

Firstly, it isn't about the installation of a family council in the life of the family where decisions are made; it is much more important that children are present if decisions which concerns them are being made: that they are there, participate in the discussion, argue with the others. Their arguments won't often be strong enough, and won't even be taken into consideration in a few cases, but one learns to participate like that: live and learn.

---

[4]   Qvortrup J. e.a.,1994, Childhood matters. Social Theory, Practice and Politics

[5]   See the success of the XXXIth International Sociological Association, Committe on Family Research Seminar concerning: Children and Families: Research and Policy in April 1994

[6]   We did such research into the global situation of the child's life and the spending of time and the experience of time. Van Gils Jan, 1992, Wie niet weg is, is gezien. Hoe beleven kinderen het gezin, de school en de vrije tijd? Van Gils Jan, 1992, De tijdsbesteding, de tijdsbeleving en de opvoeding op woensdag. At this moment a research is going on with 10 year olds concerning their experience of sports and there is a European research into the opinions of children about the family.

Secondly, the school council with representatives from all classes isn't the summit of participation at school. It is much more important that what happens daily in class can also give a direction to learning: to the subjects, the methods, the organization. A relation of equality with the teacher is therefore necessary and learning becomes a social event.

Thirdly, the children's municipal council isn't the end, but it comes down to the fact that children, like citizens, must learn to reach for their pen in order to make their wishes public. They must learn to make a call to the mayor when public transport is concerned. Officials and politicians shouldn't put them on to the youth service or the children's telephone, but they should listen to their problems and solve them like they do for every other citizen.

Social participation can't be reduced to a democracy of councils. Social participation means being a part of the community: being able to use the street, the bus, the post office, the municipality. It means taking part in the decisions on the daily routine, there where you live.

We give a few illustrations on the basis of Snater.

II. SNATER

Snater is a collective noun for various groups of children who occupy themselves with the rights of the child in a concrete and practical manner. It is the intention to enlarge the children's possibilities to contribute to living together and to convince the society of the value of this contribution.

Snater wants to help children in:
— distinguishing their own problems or their own approach of problems;
— forming a group around this subject and in formulating their own ideas about it;
— making an active contribution concerning this problem;
— informing the public opinion about the importance of this contribution.
Snater started in 1992 as a small scale experiment with about 10 adults and 25 children between the age of 8 and 17.

Four groups of children looked into various themes like media and children, divorce and children, school and children, and the launching of a magazine about children's rights. These groups worked with variable success, and after a year of meetings, actions and visits, the experiment was evaluated in order to start the second stage. These were the conclusions:

— the participating children were very enthusiastic and they were motivated for the project;
— choices have to be made concerning the intended age group;
— it is better to determine the themes first and search for children afterwards (the determination of the themes in consultation with the children asks a lot of time);
— it is important to stimulate the action more than the discussion;

- the groups must organize themselves locally so that children can reach each other easily;
- the support of groups is necessary. At the same time, this is delicate so that the guides need to be well formed.

In the schoolyear 1993–1994 the project Snater was supported by 6 organizations: UNICEF, "Kaderschool Don Bosco", The Children's Telephone, "St.-Kamiel Bizaar", "Zonnige Uren" and The Centre of Research Child and Society. The Foundation King Boudewijn was involved in the starting stage. These organizations looked for local groups and looked after them, they followed the actions.

The suggested working-themes were: children and traffic, children in the Third World and children and their differences. The target group: the age of 9 to 14. They worked from September untill May.

Finally 10 groups started and they worked on the following themes: a refugee family in the village, the organization of life in the own children's home, the life in institutions and a group of children of the Fourth World worked around the Third World. There was a group of little ones (5–6 years old) and a group of teen-agers. The other groups worked with 9 to 13 year olds. The evaluation learns us:

- that children are very motivated for this kind of activities because of the formation of groups and the possibility "to let themselves be seen, to let themselves be heard";
- that children achieve concrete results which are important for society;
- that the global animation is important and that it gives some identity: stickers, a little magazine, the end-happening;
- that it is of no use to set a working-period (from September untill May): children must be able to organize themselves when they think it is necessary and for as long as they think it is necessary;
- that it is very hard to find organizations who are willing to support the project;
- that it is difficult to find competent guides and moreover, they want constant supervision.

The next stage is the stimulation of the children's organization so that they can play an active role in society. This stimulation will take place on a larger scale. We highly prefer to do this in co-operation with other organizations of/for children. We want to extend a permanent guidance for children who want to organize other children with regard to specific problems. We want to help them in their search for an appropriate guidance, and in their expansion of all sort of actions concerning their theme. So we might give them information about responsible authorities, about reaching the press,... Another important mission is to anchor the project socially: it may not be a unworldly, marginal happening. At this moment we are still looking for the necessary means to achieve this goal.

III. The Situation of Snater in the Context of Social Participation

The question is how we can get beyond the effect of sweetness[7] with a project like Snater and how we can actually contribute to the social participation of children.

Initiatives like children's local councils and children's consultation now have a certain sympathy in the eyes of the general public because it is sweet to watch the children imitate the world of adults.

In Snater also, children act in a certain way which can sooner be expected from adults. Moreover, one can get stuck in this sweetness effect. To avoid this, it is very important to dose the contribution of the adults well so that it is to a large extent an initiative of the children. The arrangements concerning the themes, the timing and the working-schedule must be characteristic to the children. The guidance must be very subtle.

A second trap that needs to be avoided is the one of elitarism. Such projects often demand so much guidance that it becomes impossible to spread them on a large scale. Such an intensive guidance can be necessary in the early stages, in order to be able to describe the guidance well. But in the phase of implementation, such projects must be able to function with a minimum of guidance because of a very efficacious coaching.

With Snater, a working method has been developed, which contributes to the social participation of children, provided that the mentioned traps are avoided. Snater contributes to the social participation of childeren because of the following characteristic features: Snater aims at the assistance of children so that they can organize themselves in their daily environment working around themes from their own world of experience. It concerns:

- *children*: the age ranges between 4 and 18;
- *to assist*: subtle guidance is necessary to give cohesion to the group, to deliver them a referenceperson and to supervise the task;
- *to organize themselves*: children organize themselves for as long as they think it is necessary, with the persons who they think are necessary and in the way they think it is necessary;
- *in their daily environment*: children organize themselves in their daily environment in order to be able to communicate smoothly with each other and other partners (e.g. adult responsibles);
- *to work*: the "action-dimension" is very important as well for the gathering of information (e.g. children really live a day in a children's home) as for the determination of the intention: one wants to change something, it certainly isn't a gathering of children without engagement;
- *around themes of their own world of experience*: children must be confronted with themes which occur in their daily existence, they must be real.

---

[7] Kinderinspraak. Theme number NUSO-magazine, March 1984.

Snater will be superfluous when the social participation will be optimally realized. Snater offers a working-frame and some support during the period that the active presence of children in society isn't self-evident. This can be explained by the weak social position of the children in this intermediate period.

ANKE VAN KEULEN and JAMILA HAMID

Marriage: That's Your Own Choice!
Morroccan Youngsters and the Choice of a Partner

INTRODUCTION

A group of young people that is hardly ever or not at all allowed to speak when it comes to rights of children and youngsters is the group of *migrant young-sters* in West European countries. This group of migrant children and young-sters, parents of which came as working migrants, citizens of ex-colonies or refugees, has probably even less say about their own lives than the group of youngsters indigenous to these countries. Often, there exists a standard image of migrant youngsters. They are regarded as a group that causes trouble and lags in development. In most cases, there exists no interest in what these youngsters themselves wish and how they would like to interpret their rights.

Since the sixties and seventies working migrants and citizens of excolonies live in most West-European countries. In the Netherlands the Moroccans are one of the three largest migrant populations. The Moroccan community in the Netherlands comes from the most backwarded region in Morocco: the Rif mountains in the north-eastern part. Most Moroccans of the first generation are illiterate farmers. Their children – migrated to the Netherlands on an early age or born in the Netherlands – visite now-a-days Dutch schools and often speak even better Dutch then their home language. These children and youngsters of the second generation are more integrated in Dutch society then their parents and most of them want to spend their lives in the Netherlands.

An example of how Moroccan youngsters wish to express their rights is the project *"Marriage: that's your own choice!"*. It focusses on how Moroccan youngsters think about marriages and the choice of a partner, what rights they have and what bottlenecks they encounter. Who, in the end, chooses the new partner in a culture where the arranged marriage is common practice, what influence do youngsters themselves have on this? The report *"Marriage: that's*

E. Verhellen (ed.), Monitoring Children's Rights, 357–366.
© 1996 *Kluwer Law International. Printed in the Netherlands.*

your own choice!" came into being by means of interviews and discussion meetings with youngsters, completed with literature.[1]

The project is carried out by the National Co-operation for Moroccans and Tunesians (SMT), a national body for public participation and Project agency MUTANT (bureau for innovation in methodology and management).

What do Moroccan youngsters expect of marriage? What should their ideal possible partner be like? How do parents view the marriage of their sons or daughters? Who, in the end, chooses the new partner, what influence do youngsters themselves have on this?

A lot of Moroccan youngsters would like to express the choice of their possible partner in a manner different than their parents wish. This has become clear from the sources used in this research: interviews with youngsters, research results and outcomes of discussions led by youngsters.

In this article the outcomes and results of the research wil be presented, combined with the recommendations directed to institutions.

Starting-point of the report *"Marriage: that's your own choice"* is *to take the youngsters seriously*: what do youngsters themselves want if the choice of a possible partner is involved? Most Moroccan youngsters have the wish to organize their own lives and at the same time they do not wish to break the ties with their parents and family. There are a number of impediments in Dutch society that make it difficult to realize this. In order to take away these impediments a number of recommendations is made directed to the government, institutions for education or aid and the Moroccan community.

I. Marrying-off, Arranged Marriage or One's Own Choice?

Most Moroccan youngsters find *marrying-off* old-fashioned, something they disapprove of. Their definition of marrying-off is: the parents choose a partner for their son or daughter, the youngsters cannot, or hardly, participate in this choice, and both youngsters do not, or hardly, get to know each other before the wedding. This form of choosing a partner occurs in the Netherlands; a small amount of youngsters do not object to this form, but in many cases this form leads to serious problems (especially, girls running away from home).

In the case of an *arranged marriage* the parents inquire beforehand after the situation and family of the future partner, and propose to the girl. The girl has the possibility to refuse. This form of choosing a partner occurs frequently in the Netherlands and in Morocco. Most youngsters agree that parents have something to do with the choice of their partner.

---

[1] Trouwen doe je zelf. Marokkaanse jongeren en partnerkeuze. [Marriage: that's your own choice. Moroccan youngsters and the choice of a partner.] Anke van Keulen/Project agency MUTANT, Publ. Cooperation for Moroccans and Tunesians (SMT), Utrecht, the Netherlands, 1994.

A part of Moroccan youngsters, both in Morocco and in the Netherlands, view the choice of a partner as *their own choice*. The youngsters themselves have chosen each other, they get to know each other and then they pass on their wishes to their parents (mothers). The parents then together discuss and arrange the marriage "in the Moroccan style". Youngsters plead for more and better communication within the family.

II. INDEPENDENCE

During their upbringing Moroccan girls are mostly prepared for their task as future woman, mother and wife. Qualities as modesty and obedience are particularly emphasized. The restrictions imposed on girls especially relate to going out with boys, very often also on going out with girls and a ban on sexual contacts with boys. This all for fear of the girl's virginity, the mutilation of which is seen as a great disgrace for the family. The upbringing of Moroccan girls in the Netherlands is in many cases much more rigorous than in Morocco. Many girls name marriage as an uncertain factor in their plans for the future. A part of the girls can be influenced by the parents and the upbringing, and this group will then work less hard to finish education successfully and work towards economic independence. A large part of the girls reconciles itself to the facts; one of the consequences of this is the high number of drop-outs among Moroccan girls.

Although a growing number of Moroccan youngsters marry at an older age because of their studies, enforced marriages at very young ages still occur. A girl of the age of under eighteen is still very young and impressionable to be able to consider a decision of that kind or refuse it. When she is older (older than 18) she will probably have more maturity and self-awareness, because of study- or work experience, to accept or refuse a marriage proposition of her parents.

III. MOROCCAN PARTNER?

The parents as well as the youngsters generally favour a Moroccan partner. The reason for this is that they will have the same culture and background and/or the same Islamic background.

Marriages between *Moroccan boys and Dutch girls* do occur; the boy falls in love with a Dutch girl, and presents the parents with the fact that he wants to marry her. Moroccan parents sooner accept a mixed marriage of their son than of their daughter. The standard that a Moroccan woman should marry an Islamic man is generally accepted. For Moroccan girls who sometimes think about the possibility of marrying a *Dutch man*, the topic should be more open to discussion.

IV. PARTNER FROM THE COUNTRY OF ORIGIN

In principle, Moroccan youngsters living in the Netherlands should be able to marry a partner from Morocco.

Restricting immigration by means of restricting the *forming of families by the Dutch government* particularly affects youngsters from ethnic minorities. To have a partner come over out of the country of origin, one has to dispose of sufficient income and housing. Due to the high unemployment figure among Moroccan youngsters they will have great difficulty in meeting this requirement. This restriction imposed by the government is not only unjust but also unnecessary:
- the group of immigrants that enters the country for forming Turkish and Moroccan families is relatively small;
- the right to individual freedom in the choice of a possible partner is affected;
- the measure has a dicriminating effect, particularly towards migrant youngsters.

A partner from the country of origin is sometimes a wish of both youngsters and parents. Moroccan youngsters in Morocco very much like to marry Moroccan boys or girls in the Netherlands, partly also to be able to come to Europe in a legal way. Imams could play an important part in making this way of contracting marriages, in which sometimes large sums of money are involved, open to discussion.

When a partner is taken from the country of origin to the Netherlands, this can sometimes lead to problems of adaption. The difference in cultural knowledge puts heavy pressure on the newly-married couple. It is advisable to call in bureaus for newcomers to guide the new partner in co-operation with the partner living in the Netherlands. Many youngsters foresee these problems and therefore do not desire a partner from the country of origin. They would rather marry a Moroccan youngster from the Netherlands, but Moroccan boys and girls do not find many suitable places for meeting each other.

A form of marrying-off that seriously contravenes the rights of the girl is the *enforced marrying-off in the country of origin*. Usually during a holiday period in Morocco the wedding ceremony is celebrated against the wish of the girl and afterwards she will stay with her partner to live in Morocco. Why do parents do this to girls? One of the most important reasons is that the parents think that the girl "has gone astray" in the Netherlands, and they expect that the girl will start to behave – in their view – respectably again, because of her marriage and stay in Morocco. Sometimes, economic interests are involved in the marriage. In the holiday period many girls fear these enforced marriages; they themselves cannot leave the country anymore, because the father keeps all the official papers with him. When, after her marriage, a girl stays to live in Morocco, her right to a residence permit lapses. Only under very limited conditions can she again receive a permit. Poignant examples are known of girls who out of fear for being married-off in Morocco ran away from home or went into hiding, and examples of girls who returned to the Netherlands illegally.

V. TENSION BETWEEN AUTHORITY AND FREEDOM

Upbringing and choice of marriage are based on certain values and standards. Children and youngsters partly take over the values and standards of their parents, partly those of society around them (via school, neighbourhood, media). This then also holds true for the way in which Moroccan youngsters deal with marriage and choosing a partner: they are provided with values and standards by their parents, and they are influenced by the values and standards prevalent in the Netherlands. A part of Moroccan youngsters comes into conflict: they want to express marriage and the choice of a partner in a manner different than their parents wish.

In Moroccan families where conflicts between parents and children have not mounted, youngsters (both boys and girls) strive to achieve a *balance* between respect for their parents and being able to choose themselves. This can create a tension between "authority and freedom". Most youngsters do not want to offend or hurt their parents. Central values that the parents believe in – religious obligations, Islamic code of behaviour and standards, maintaining a form of parental authority and marrying a Moroccan partner,– are recognized by many youngsters, but interpreted in a different manner. All youngsters wish to give their own interpretation to their lives, different from their parents and more oriented towards the Dutch situation.

There are youngsters who succeed in remaining in contact with their parents, to convince them of certain necessary changes in traditions and standards. There are parents who see the necessity of a behaviour oriented towards Dutch society, and who give the youngsters some room for a kind of autonomy.

There is also a group where the contact between parents and youngsters has been seriously disturbed. Many youngsters are not accepted in Dutch society and vent their tensed emotions at home with the family. Many parents fail in continuing to keep up with their children, they are afraid and disappointed.

A great number of Moroccan fathers have usually lived separated from their families for about 10 to 15 years, before family reunion started. Due to this long separation, a great (emotional) distance grew between fathers and children.

At the same time many fathers (parents) suffer great disappointments with regard to migration: their dreams have not come true, they feel they are not wanted and discriminated against in the Netherlands and they fear the Dutchification of their children. As a reaction many hold on to habits and rules from the fifties and sixties; habits that are also very much out of date in

Morocco as it is today. Because of this, the method of upbringing the parents use is not successful in the Dutch situation. Moreover, information about upbringing that Dutch families do receive via, for instance, the health centre, magazines and television is often lacking in these families.

VI. THE ROLE OF THE ISLAM

Marriage within the Moroccan community is closely linked up with the various opinions about the relation between men and women. Both in the Moroccan community as in Dutch society there are movements that regard the culture and the traditional ideas about this relation as characteristic for the Islam.

In order to promote the emancipation of youngsters, especially girls, it is important to break through this static view. The Islam – experienced according to this view – needs innovation.

Most youngsters that have grown up here find this experience of the Islam very strange, particularly when marriage and the choice of a partner are involved. They are therefore facing a difficult choice: choosing that what their fathers present as God's word and come into conflict with society around them, or refuse to obey it and live on with a heavy feeling of guilt because they "are no longer Muslim".

In such a situation, youngsters do not know how to act and there is no place they can go for support and advice.

It is important that parents and youngsters know that the Islam is a very dynamic religion which can easily be absorbed in the new environment where it arrives. This holds particularly true for the wordly part of the religion where the mutual relations between people are indicated in broad outline. The ecclesiastical part, also called the unchangeable values (among other things the five pilars of the Islam), determines the relation between the individual and God. This part concerns much more the individual, which should not restrict the emancipation of the Muslim-youth in the Netherlands.

VII. RELATION BETWEEN BOYS AND GIRLS

Possibilities for Moroccan youngsters to get to know each other and socialize with each other *in a friendly manner* are hardly or not at all present in the Netherlands. In Morocco youngsters meet at secondary schools, universities, in libraries and on the streets. Mixed activities organized by the school have become quite common in Morocco during the past few years, in the smaller cities and the Rif-area, too. This provides youngsters with opportunities to get to know each other, make friends and get to know possible partners.

In the Netherlands, this opportunity does not exist. A lot of Moroccan boys and girls go to technical and vocational training for 12–16 years old which is for the greater part education divided on the basis of sex. The girls hardly or not at all get permission to visit mixed activities outside the school, for instance, a course, a community centre, a sports club. *Many Moroccan boys* in the period before their marriage choose to have contact with girls outside the Moroccan community with whom they can go out and have sexual contacts. Almost all of them wish to marry a Moroccan woman that is a virgin. The inconsistency of this idea and the inequality of it between boys and girls is ignored by most boys or viewed as something which is "just the way it is".

Among Moroccan youngsters hardly any change can be detected with regard to *role patterns* between men and women. Two examples illustrate this.

On the one hand, many young men accept the partner chosen by their parents. Even if the girl is against the marriage, and the boy knows this, in many cases he will obey to his parents wish. He does not see that this goes against his own interest and that of the girl, since chances of tension within the marriage and chances of divorce are high.

On the other hand, Moroccan boys make a big difference between Moroccan and non-Moroccan girls, particularly when sexual contacts are involved. They apply the standard of virginity to their sisters, nieces and other women in the Moroccan community and keep close control on its observance. At the same time they do not apply this standard to themselves, nor to the girls outside of their own community.

Both examples – marrying-off and virginity – clearly show that Moroccan boys can be *an impediment for the emancipation of Moroccan girls*. Instead of mutual solidarity within the group of Moroccan youngsters, this leads to discord between boys and girls.

VIII. RECOMMENDATIONS

A. *Recommendations Directed to the Government*

1. In the case of enforced marrying-off in Morocco, there should be more possibilities for Moroccan youngsters to return to the Netherlands. The Dutch government should allow youngsters who have been victimized in this way to have a new right to a residence permit when they return to the Netherlands.
2. A co-operation agreement should be effected between the European Union and Morocco in which is laid down how young Moroccan girls can be protected from being married-off against their wish. In this agreement can also be laid down how information can be exchanged between Morocco and the countries involved of the European Union, aiming at offering help to girls who have been married-off during a family visit in Morocco. The Netherlands should act as a pioneer in this.

3. For the Moroccan youngsters living in the Netherlands it is recommended to maintain the official Dutch age for marriage and to acknowledge the marriage only from the age of 18 onwards. This to protect particularly young girls from being married-off before they are 18.

4. To prevent girls being taken away from school in order to get married, it is necessary that the Compulsory Education Law is observed for one hundred per cent. Schools should quickly notice signals of absence and pass these in time to the respective civil servant of the local authority. School absenteeism and failing to observe the Compulsory Education Law should not be tolerated.

5. As appears from the literature, a large part of the Moroccan boys have rather conservative ideas. The boys should gain more understanding of the present men-women relationships. For this reason the government should stimulate projects which are aimed at the emancipation of boys. In schools, too, (during sociology classes and the like) attention should be paid to this.

6. Among youngsters there is a need to experience an Islam that is directed to the situation here and now, which is tuned to the present Dutch society. In order to help achieve this, the education of Muslim hadjis is an important instrument. The government should stimulate initiatives in this field.

7. It is recommended to start an information centre about the Islam which can function independent of the governments of the countries of origin. This centre has as its task to present information to Muslims (the young and the old) and non-Muslims with the assignment: increasing knowledge and understanding of the culture and religion of the Islam, observing the area of tension between standards and values of the older Muslims and those of Western society. The centre can also function as a place of reference for both individuals and institutions which need answers or help with respect to conflicts connected with cultural differences.

B.   Recommendations Directed to Institutions and the Moroccan Community

8. In order to give youngsters greater understanding and knowledge of a renewed experience of the Islam, Dutch schools should pay attention to the Islam within the subject "religious and spiritual movements". The Muslim spritual framework educated here can play an important part in this.

9. It is absolutely necessary that schools start to pay attention to the skill "dealing with differences (of opinion)", within society as a whole as well as within their own community or family. Such a skill should initially enable students themselves to solve the problems resulting from a possible collision between the various standards and values. For this improving the expertise of teachers is highly important.

10. A large part of Moroccan girls have not learned (in their upbringing) the skill of fighting against decisions with which they do not agree. This is also true for the choice of a partner or marrying-off. The consequence of this is that they marry a partner they do not want. Within education this skill (to be able to assert your own interests) should be given extra attention. There are various projects running in primary and secondary education aimed at learning to make your own decisions. Stimulating a positive self-image is also part of this. In some projects the mothers of the girls are emphatically involved. Also, information about the economic independece of girls has been tuned to migrant girls in the form of projects. In all these projects aimed at enlarging the self-awareness and the possibilities for choice of the girls, there could be a lead to one's own choice in marriage.

11. School contacts and/or social workers should be appointed to schools, so that youngsters can go there with their problems. This will particularly help the girls to improve learning how to deal with their problems and to seek less often outward flights in marriage.

12. The bureaus for newcomers can play an important part in the care and guidance of possible partners from the country of origin. To prevent the newly-married couple from getting problems with the great differences between them in knowledge of the Dutch culture and language, both partners need to be involved in the guidance.

13. Institutions for aid, such as relief centres for girls and consultancy centres for the young, should be better informed about "marriage and the choice of a partner within the Moroccan community". Among other things, this knowledge is necessary to be able to point out to the Moroccan youngsters their rights as these exist within their own culture. Methodologies need to be developed in order to be able to deal as effectively as possible with youngsters that get into problems at this point.

14. It is possible to work in a much more preventive manner towards both parents and youngsters in order to prevent problems. Before great contradictions or conflicts between youngsters and parents arise, youngsters should work on creating an atmosphere of openness between them and their parents. In this, both parties will have to learn to show understanding for each other's points of view. On the one hand, youngsters should realize that they are responsible for their own lives and, on the other hand, that their parents, too, feel responsible for their lives. It demands a great deal of tact and skill to learn to voice one's own opinion. Centres for the young, institutions for aid and educational institutions can be good trainings for learning these kinds of manners between youngsters and parents.

15. Institutions (schools, childcare centres, health centres) should extend their accessability and tune their way of working to a multicultural society. Through this, among other things, Moroccan parents will be more easily involved in the upbringing of their children out of doors. Parents

should gain an understanding of how the responsibility of the parents for the upbringing should be realized in Dutch society. Here is meant the responsibility at large that is expected of parents here. In order to get this idea across, it is important that parents are involved in the activities of their children in an early stage: at the playgroups, at primary school, at the sports field, etc.

16. The possibilities for mutual contact between Moroccan youngsters should be extended. This can, for instance, be done by stimulating taking part in existing facilities, such as sports club, libraries, socio-cultural activities etc. Also, there should be more youth workers appointed to this institution, particularly in places where a high number of Moroccan people live.

17. Parents and youngsters should be more informed about the contents of the Islam, about the border between religion and tradition and about the possibilities of living your life as a Muslim in Dutch society. Youngsters, too, should gain more in-depth knowledge of the present developments around the Islam. This will give them more possibilities for living their lives in harmony with society around them. Thus it should be known that the Moroccan marrital law entitles the girl the right to be heard about her future husband and to refuse the possible partner. Moroccan parents (and elderly) should know about this right and respect this right of the young. Marrying-off violates this right and could have legal consequences for the parents, if the girl or boy files a complaint about this.

Moroccan parents should also be more aware of the fact that forcing their daughters or sons to marry partners from the country of origin which they do not, or hardly, know contravenes the Islam. (Religious) leaders within the Moroccan community can play a part in warning about these practices. And Moroccan youngsters should be more informed about the risks and problems which marrying a partner from the country of origin can involve.

The chair in Islam at the University of Amsterdam can be seen as an attempt in this direction and also as a means to break open the traditional ideas about the Islam. But this positive movement should go beyond the University.

18. In order to make the topic "marriage and the choice of a partner" open for discussion within the Moroccan community, the use of their own media is one of the most important means, since it reaches most of the target group. It is therefore recommended to maintain the Moroccan media, on the radio as well as on television. In the media various aspects related to the choice of a partner could be discussed. Furthermore, attention can be given to the consequences of the enforced choice of a partner. Such as: divorces, problems related to not acknowledging Dutch divorces by the Moroccan government, run-away problems and the like.

ANGELO SAPORITI

Evaluating the Process of Monitoring Children's Rights

INTRODUCTION

The European Conference on Monitoring Children's Rights is addressed to analyze the mechanisms delegated to check the effective implementation of the Articles of the United Nations Convention on the Rights of the Child. As it is pointed out in the final announcement of the Conference, it

> ... will focus on two key questions concerning the monitoring mechanisms and especially on the reporting system. *What* is to be reported and *by whom*.

This paper represents a modest effort to approach the topic of "monitoring children's rights" from a methodological point of view bringing it into the wider context of the "evaluation studies".

Political, judicial and institutional actions, as well social investments can improve social status and living conditions of children. Children's needs, however, compete with those of many other constituencies of society, and available resources are limited. A rational analysis of the measures already undertaken, or to be undertaken, to meet the needs of children will help us to make them more effective and efficient.

To this end, I suggest referring to the theoretical and methodological framework of the "evaluation analysis" – that is, a set of assumptions, theoretical tenets, methodologies and technical procedures worked out to assess the effectiveness (and the efficiency) of social programs.

The Convention is not, of course, a true social program. My point, however, is that the Convention could be assimilated to a social intervention, although having its own peculiarities. Starting from this assumption, the paper explores the possibility of evaluating the monitoring process of children's rights according to the criteria governing the field of "evaluation".

Of course, this is a very first and general attempt in the field. It is open to every kind of criticism and suggestion.

E. Verhellen (ed.), Monitoring Children's Rights, 367–375.
© 1996 *Kluwer Law International. Printed in the Netherlands.*

I. Monitoring and Evaluating Children's Rights: A Possible Link

According to the English dictionary, the transitive verb "to monitor" means, *inter alia*:
- to observe or to inspect (*what?*), especially for a special purpose (*what for?*);
- to regulate or control the operation of (*whom?*) (that is, a machine or process).

Translated into our subject these meanings become:
- to observe or to inspect actions undertaken in the area of the rights of the child (*what*) in order to *evaluate* their protection and promotion (*what for*);
- to control and regulate the actions of all the "bodies" contributing to the improvement of the respect of the rights of the child (*whom*).

Combining both meanings, we have:

> *Monitoring children's rights*
>
> =
>
> *evaluating social programs aimed to make effective (and efficient) the respect of the rights of children*

II. Monitoring Children's Rights as a Social Program

We already dispose of a tool to evaluate social programs. "Evaluation" is a scientific discipline applied to a variety of problems – economic, social ecological, and so on. Two questions arise, however.
1. Can we apply the theory and methodology of evaluation analysis to the field of monitoring children's rights?
2. If such is the case, can we learn some lesson on the subject from a quite well-established tradition of study and research?

To answer the previous questions we must first define The Convention on the Rights of the Child as a social program. We define:

> *The Convention = social program*
>
> =
>
> *any collective effort undertaken by a public and/or private body to better the living conditions of children*

In the remaining part of the paper I shall try to compare the *ingredients* of a social program to the content of the Convention. To properly evaluate a social program eight ingredients of the program should be known. I shall present each of them separately. Then I shall see what the Convention says about them, and finally I shall make a very short comment on each one.

A. *To Define as Clearly and Uniformly as Possible the "Target" of the Program that is, the Human Beings the Social Program is Addressed to*

The Convention is clear on this point. Its target is the "child" – that is,

... every human being below the age of eighteen years... (art. 1).

On the other hand, the Convention is not uniform on the very same point:

... unless, under the law applicable to the child, majority is attained earlier (art. 1).

Comment
 – The target is not fully applicable to situations in which there isn't yet a reliable system of demographic registration.
 – Differences in the definition of the "child" make more difficult cross-national comparisons. This holds true within a single country as well, when different kinds of "majorities" are attained at different ages.

B. *An Understanding of the Living Conditions of Children*

The Convention translates the concept of living conditions of children into a number of rights children should be entitled to. The Convention is very extensive in declining all rights corresponding to the different aspects of children's life. They can be divided as follows:[1]

1. General rights. These include the right to life, ..., freedom of expression, ..., the right to information...
2. Rights requiring protective measures. These include measures to protect children from economic and sexual exploitation....
3. Rights concerning the civil status of children. These include the right to acquire nationality, ..., to remain with the parents...
4. Rights concerning development and welfare, including the child's right to a reasonable standard of living, ..., to health and basic services...
5. Rights concerning children in special circumstances, or in "especially difficult circumstances". They apply, ..., to handicapped children, refugee and adopted children...

---

[1] V. Muntarbhorn, "The Convention on the Rights of the Child: reaching the unreached?", in The Rights of the Child, *Bullettin of Human Rights*", 91/2: 66–67

Comment

The list of the rights children are entitled to is really exhaustive, and the scope of the Convention is clearly stated: The Convention is aimed to meet almost every aspect of children's lives. However, a number of questions arise in this respect:

1. is there any priority among all these rights?
2. if so, is this priority the same in every country?
3. is there any "correlation" between different rights?

From a general and abstract point of view I think it is quite easy to give an answer to these questions at least as far as a number of countries is concerned. However, from my present point of view a *multipurpose* program is much more difficult to evaluate than one stating a single scope or few scopes. It would be much easier to produce statements on the effectiveness of the Convention, both within and between countries, focusing the process of evaluation on those few purposes of the Convention deemed to be the most relevant ones.

C. A Standard of "Goodness" or "Welfare" with Reference to Children – that is, a Standard to Measure the Fulfilment of a Scope

The Convention does not specifically indicate *standards* for all rights. Obviously we could assume that *some rights have to be considered as universal standards themselves*. The same, however, cannot automatically be assumed to apply to most of these rights, especially to the economic, social and cultural ones. It is clearly stated in the Preamble:

> *Taking due account* of the importance of the traditions and cultural values of each people for the protection and harmonious development of the child ... (Preamble)

On the other hand, The Convention refers to the States Parties for the determination of what should be considered as an appropriate fulfilment of the rights of children:

> *States Parties* shall ensure that the institutions, services and facilities responsible for the care or protection of children shall conform with the *standards established by competent authorities*... (art. 3, emphasis added)

Comment

For the purpose of valid and reliable evaluation it is necessary to fix clearly the *standards* a course of action has to conform to. Such standards must take into account both the gradients of the existing different situations within and between countries and, above all, a realistic possibility of reaching them. This is not an easy task. The right of a child to not be in poverty is just a case in point. For some countries "poverty" is synonymous of starvation and death; for others it means "inequality" in the sharing of both material and "relational" resources. Sometimes the two meanings of the concept of poverty can be applied to the same country.

D. To measure, assess the status of children's rights – that is, to work out a valid and reliable set of indicators informing on the actual living conditions of the children

The Convention doesn't say anything about this.

Comment
For evaluation purposes we need know as many as possible of the characteristics of the target population. We need them especially to identify the very same target population, and to assess the effects of a given course of action. This need has been formally recognized and advocated by the Committee on the Rights of the Child:

> ...the use of appropriate indicators could contribute to a better assessment of how the rights covered by the Convention were guaranteed and implemented and to an evaluation of progress achieved over time towards the full realization of those rights. It was stressed that the Convention covered a whole range of civil, political, as well as economic, social and cultural rights and that there was therefore a need for a right-by-right approach in order to determine what kind of indicators would be relevant for each of the rights set out in the Convention. Indicators constituted an important component offering the Committee the possibility to assess the progress achieved by the States parties .[2]

Indicators of children's rights are not only needed to evaluate the implementation of the Convention; they are also methodological tools suited to anticipate *children's demands* and possible areas of failing respects of their rights.

To both ends – *post hoc* evaluation and forecasting – such indicators should meet basic requirements such as validity, reliability, sensitivity, comparability, accuracy and disaggregation (*ivi*). The indicators should not be developed and organized, however, as a list of quantitative measures and qualitative statements. To be effective for the purposes set out by the Committee they should form an "informative system" i.e., a set of coherent information sufficiently structured and functional to the inspection and evaluation of the social program carried on. They should also be suited to the operational planning of future course of actions.

In developing such set of indicators we have to keep in mind that an indicator *never* has an informative power *per se*. Its value stems from its

---

[2] *Report from the 2nd Session, 28 September - 9 October 1992*, CRC/C/10, quoted in Childwatch International Research Network, *Indicators for Children's Rights. Proposal for a Project to identify and develop Indicators for the use in monitoring the Implementation of the Convention on the Rights of Children*, 29 November 1993, typescript: 4

being coherently suited to a plan of "social accountability" or to a course of action.

E. To have a deep and full knowledge of the resources (human, financial, as well as in kind resources) brought in the whole process – that is, to evaluate a social program we need know its inputs

The Convention is rather hazy on this point. It refers to various specialized agencies and other organs of the United Nations such as the International-al Labour Organization (ILO), the World Health Organization (WHO), the United Nations Educational, Scientific and Cultural Organization (UNESCO), the United Nations Children's Fund (UNICEF) and the Office of the United Nations High Commissioner for Refugees (UNHCR), as well as a wide range of non-governmental organizations (NGO). It refers also to the very same Committee on the Rights of the Child and to experts but, above all, to the States Parties and to international co-operation:

> States Parties shall undertake all appropriate legislative, administrative, and other measures for the implementation of the rights recognized in the present Convention. With regard to economic, social and cultural rights, States Parties shall undertake such measures to the maximum extent of their available resources and, where needed, within the framework of international co-operation (art. 4).

Comment

A well planned social program can fail in meeting its ends because of a shortage of input resources. On the other hand, the outputs of a social program could be the best *given a certain amount of input resources*.

Available resources are far from infinite. We must always choose between two or more options within a framework of a given amount of resources. Some of the most powerful tools of evaluation analysis and methodology require the measurement of the costs of such resources. *Cost-benefit* analysis and *cost-effectiveness* analysis, for instance, refer to approaches for comparing the costs and outcomes of various alternatives under policy considerations.

In some areas of the rights fostered by the Convention, it is very difficult both to identify the input resources and to assess their cost. However, with no (or scanty) knowledge on how much a social program invest in terms of human, financial and in kind resources, it becomes arduous to evaluate its outcomes.

F. An organizational and operational structure – that is, a functioning apparatus to finalize the mobilization of the resources to an end

The Convention doesn't prescribe any specific *modus operandi* for the implementation of the rights of the child. However, the Convention itself is an outward manifestation of an already established and functioning organization. Furthermore, to the same end the Convention refers to other well-tested agencies and other organs and to international co-operation. The "reporting system" envisaged by the Convention (art. 44) to check the progress made on the implementation of the rights of the child can be considered, on the other hand, as a component of that *modus operandi*. At any rate, the paramount organizations and operative structures deputed to undertake the necessary courses of action are those of the States Parties.

Comment
The outcomes of social programs depend also on the good running of the machine as a whole. Evaluation analysis clearly distinguishes between two models: the *black box model* and the *process model* (see on page 374).

G. The political and administrative (bureaucratic) framework within which the social program is embedded

The Convention is itself a "political" agreement between the States Parties. Apart from that, however, it seems to take explicitly into account this point at the international level. Part III of the Convention regulates the signature, ratification, reservations and amendments, as well as the denouncing of the Convention – it recognizes, in other words, the different political interests and attitudes of the States Parties. This holds true implicitly at the national level too. Referring to the States Parties as the first subjects in charge of the implementation of the rights of children, the Convention seems to recognize implicitly the role played by their political, organizational and administrative interests and processes.

Comment
The process model highlights a relevant aspect of social programs. As they have been previously defined, social programs are planned and implemented within a political and an administrative (bureaucratic) framework. Such a framework – characterised by different values, political and administrative interests – can affect a social program in two different ways. First, it can affect the very same outcomes of the program. Secondly, it can affect the use of the results of the evaluation analysis. As a matter of fact, most of the more recent literature on evaluation is focused on the political processes governing the implementation of social programs.

H. The extent and quality of participation of the target population

The Convention is oddly silent on this point. In stating the rights of the child the Convention recognizes children's active role as inherent to some of them:

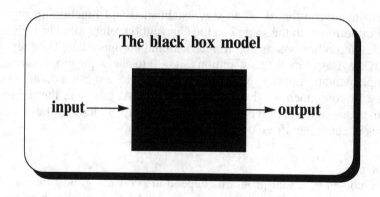

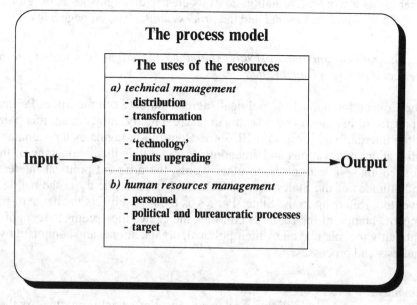

States Parties shall assure to the child who is capable of forming his or her own views the right to express those views freely in all matters affecting the child (art. 12, §1).

For this purpose, the child shall be in particular provided the opportunity to be heard in any judicial and administrative proceedings affecting the child, ... (*ibid.*, §2).

The child shall have the right to freedom of expression... (art. 13, §1).

It doesn't recognize, however, any active role to the children in the implementation of its ends. Such a role is instead mainly attributed to the family and to other adult subjects.

Comment

A social program can end in failure simply because the "target" is not co-operative, or simply because people don't share the ends of the program. The extent and quality of the target's involvement can help us to understand why a social program is successful or fails to meet its ends, completely or partially. A co-operative target population can also help us to understand the weakest points of the program and, consequently, to modify them.

III. Concluding Remarks

For evaluation purposes the Convention on the Rights of the Child can be assimilated to a social program although with various qualifications.

In my view, however, those qualifications do not pertain to the "rationale" behind the Convention or to its scope. They refer rather to the exceptional complexity of the problem the Convention is addressed to, and to the scarcity of the resources necessary to solve it.

These difficulties should not prevent us from evaluating the various aspects of the Convention – its content, the way it intends to accomplish its goals, its actual working, as well as the very same goals. To this end much more information than now available is required. In this respect the increasing number of movements and international networks strongly claiming for the development of a systematic and comprehensive set of indicators on children's living conditions is encouraging.

However, the need to cover such a knowledge-gap should not be considered as an end *per se*, an academic or scientific goal. Rather it is instrumental in making ready more effective and efficient tools for the use in monitoring and implement the Convention on the Rights of the Child.

GÖRAN THERBORN

Child Politics: Dimensions and Perspectives

The richness, the variety and the rapid growth of the field is what strikes a mature social scientist, whose own children are now entering adulthood, looking into the issues of child politics from experiences of other areas of social analysis. As this new field of social action has been laid out by lawyers and practitioners, it poses new challenges to sociologists and political scientists interested in social conditions, public policy, and social change.

I. "THE CHILD" AND ITS POLITICS: AN INTRODUCTORY CONCEPTUAL NOTE

Neither "child politics" nor "child policy" is an expression frequently in use and self-evident to all competent speakers. Even analysts of politics or policy may still spend their entire life without using one or the other.

"Child" and "childhood" are social typifications. They refer to a set of people, children, and an age, childhood, as having something identifiably characteristic and significant in common, regardless of their parents and their gender, for example. The typification may have a variable distinctiveness in different languages. In some languages, for instance in Spanish, there is a distinction between children as offspring ("hijos") and children as an age-group ("niños").

It was the consolidation of the first wave of nation-states towards the end of the 19th century, which established the modern conception of "child" and "childhood". Freedom from labour and the duty to learn then became normal features of young people's lives. At about the same time other significant aspects of the modern status of childhood came into place, a general exemption from normal sanctions against crime, a status protected from legitimate sexual advances, and a condition having the right to protection from physical violence and maltreatment even from family members.[1]

Together, these various pieces of legislation gave an abstract, general meaning to the word "child". They had a number of different concrete origins, but the historical context of the constitution of modern childhood is clear enough.

---

[1] See further G. Therborn, "The Politics of the Childhood: The Rights of Children in Modern Times", in F. Castles (ed.), *Families of Nations*, Aldershot, Dartmouth, 1993, pp. 247ff.

E. Verhellen (ed.), Monitoring Children's Rights, 377–391.
© 1996 *Kluwer Law International. Printed in the Netherlands.*

Modern childhood was a creation by the nation-state, against the threatening encroachments of the market (for child labour) and against the sovereignty of *patria potestas*, of paternal power and the seclusion of the family.

The *politics* of childhood, however, has a very different history than the social construction of the latter. "Politics" is not the same thing as "policy", although only English and Dutch among Western European languages have two words to express the distinction.[2] "Policy" refers to a set of measures, defined either by the intentions of the actor – "our policy is ..." – or by the area of application, "foreign policy", "domestic policy", etc. "Politics", on the other hand, refers to a human activity having two characteristics. First, politics is a kind of action that bears upon a collectivity, large or small, organized or unorganized. Second, politics refers to actions bearing upon a collectivity which do not follow directly from given rules, of jurisdiction or administration. Politics refers to debating, promoting, or resisting prescribed and non-prescribed decisions and to making non-prescribed ones.

II. Vagaries of the Politics and Policies of Childhood

The constitution of childhood established a set of basic rules, but did not give rise to any institutionalized politics and policy of childhood. The immediate, not very illuminating, reason for that was that "childhood" and "children" were not conceived as one type or field of public concern. There were education, of various levels, housing and hygiene, disease, public health, and care, immorality and crime, poverty and the social question. There was population, with regard both to quality and quantity, and there was the family, circumscribed by Holy Scriptures and their contemporary guardians, the foundation of social authority, and the procreator of populations of soldiers and workers. All these areas of politics and policy affected children, but few politicians and political organizations had any ideas of child politics and child policy.

The modern nation-state accorded children a special, protected legal status, but adult politics could make no political sense of children. True, they could be politically mobilized, as scouts/guides, young Christians, balillas, Young Eagles, pioneers, etc., in a number of variants, religious, nationalist, Fascist, Social Democratic, or Communist, but only as future adults. The policy areas affecting children were those of policy for adults, current or coming.

This blindness to children was part of a broader pattern, of a one-gender, one-generation politics carried out overwhelmingly by middle-aged males. Latin and Balkan Europe excluded women altogether from politics till the end of World War II, and in the first two thirds of this century the only first rank female politicians in the developed world were revolutionaries without power,

---

[2] "Politiek" and "beleid" in Dutch. The French gendered distinction between "le politique" and "la politique" covers the distinction only partly. To "make politics" is "faire de la politique" in French.

Dolores Ibarruri, Alexandra Kollontay, Rosa Luxemburg, Clara Zetkin, and a few others of the same kind.

Now, banners of collective concern for children have been raised outside the mould of institutionalized male politics. Where have they come from, and what has been their outcome? These are questions of the history of contested politics, which still remains to be written. But some contours may be sketched here.

Until the recent breakthrough, there seem to have been three major forces concerned with children as a topic of public concern. One was *philanthropy*, which was also the major entry of women into public policy-making, until a couple of decades ago. Save the Children Fund, founded in London just after World War I and spreading from there across the world, is perhaps the best example. A strength of ideologically committed philanthropy was its internationalism, present in the very original concept of Save the Children – reaching out to the children of the defeated national enemy. Eglantine Jebb and Save the Children managed to get the League of Nations to issue, in 1924, a declaration of children's rights.

The most important institutional effect of child philanthropy took place in USA, where class politics was less developed and middle class women were more autonomous than in Europe. In 1909 there was organized a White House Conference on Dependent Children, which led to a series of decadal summit conferences on children, till the last one in 1970, replaced in 1980 by one on Families, and in 1990 by nothing of the sort. The US Federal government in 1912 also set up a Children's Bureau, unique of its sort, which for a while looked heading for a major career of policy-making. That impetus petered out in the interwar period, with the polarization of class politics, and the Bureau itself was phased out in the 1970s.[3]

Then there were two professional concerns. One came from *medicine*, which provided much of the discourse on social issues in late 19th and early 20th century, focusing on hygiene, medical enlightenment, disease prevention, corporeal care and fitness, eugenics. In the beginning of the 20th century the new medical specialty of pediatrics emerged. Child medicine provided key figures of child politics both in Europe and in South America. In Europe there was, ahead of others, Janusz Korczak, a Polish-Jewish physician (b.1878) who wrote about children's rights since the 1910s, who played an important part in the Geneva Declaration of 1924, and who was gassed to death in 1942.

Most institutionally successful were the initiatives of some South American physicians, of Argentina, Uruguay, and Brazil, who started a still going periodical series of American Child Congresses, from 1916, and a Interamerican Child Institute in Montevideo, set up in 1926, inspired by a Belgian office of the time. Psychoanalysis and eugenics were important original sources of inspiration. The first demand of the first Congress was "the introduction of

---

[3] On the early, "maternalist", context of the Children's Bureau, see T. Skocpol, *Protecting Soldiers and Mothers*, Cambridge Mass., The Belknap Press, 1992, ch. 9.

sexual education in the schools", a demand soon attenuated in euphemistic terms. After underlining the importance of maternal breastfeeding, the third demand call for measures "to protect the race against physical and mental degeneration".[4]

However, the moving force was pediatrics, in Buenos Aires, Montevideo, and Rio de Janeiro, and the guiding spirit of this movement was Dr. Luís Morquio of Montevideo. It was mainly because of him, that the American Child Institute was set up in Montevideo. In the second half of the 1930s, after the death of Morquio, physicians began to withdraw from the Panamerican child movement. The torch was handed over to another professional group.

After philanthropy and medicine, *law* and lawyers have played a special part in the history of child concern. It was they who took over the major international childhood movement, the American congresses, from the 1930s and on. But the legal look at children has mainly been the very special one of the criminal lawyer. Juvenile delinquency and children at moral and legal peril became the main preocccupation of people concerned with children in the Americas. The vista of the juvenile court justice became the predominant perspective.

Also in the states of Europe, "child care" and "child protection" were, at least until the late 1960s, legal terms referring to children trespassing the law, or at risk doing so.

None of the three, philanthropy, pediatrics, and penal law, has been able to assert itself, neither alone nor in common, as a mainstream political discourse. In fact, with the expansion of the welfare state after World War II all of them lost ground relatively, private philanthropy to public rights and services, medical discourse of social science, and law to economics and politics. In that sense, there is a clear historical discontinuity between the first waves of child concern and the current. On the other hand, from a child's point of view, it is clear, that all the mentioned endeavours have borne heavily upon the trajectory of modern childhood.

III. THE FORCES OF THE BREAKTHROUGH

The particular dynamics of current child politics is indicated by the source of the UN Convention on the Rights of the Child, i.e., a regime now defunct and discredited, Communist Poland. In 1978, the Polish government of Edward Gierek presented to the UN a draft proposal for a UN convention of children's rights.[5] It took a decade to get through, and there were many hands on it, but

---

[4] *l. Congreso Americano del Niño*, Washington D.C., Unión Panamericana, 1950, pp. 13–14.
[5] The Polish proposal was co-sponsored by Austria, Bulgaria, Colombia, Jordan, Senegal, and Syria.

the original initiative was guided to completion through the UN labyrinth by a Polish jurist, Adam Lopatka.[6]

Today's new child politics and child policies owe the weight they have to three forces mainly, the relative importance of which is hazardous to disentangle. Most visible in any case and the main provider of focus are the new *international law and politics on human rights*. Human rights got onto the world stage in the end phase of the Cold War, with the Helsinki Declaration in 1975 of the Conference on Security and Cooperation in Europe. The Polish initiative was intended to take the Western Cold War wind out of the human rights issue. The US Carter Administration pushed a human rights discourse vigorously. Other international organizations were considerably activated in the field of human rights from the mid-1970s, for instance the Council of Europe and its Commission and Court on Human Rights. The Child Convention of 1989 was elaborated within the UN Commission for Human Rights. A crucial role was played by individual representatives of small countries, such as Finland, Norway, Portugal, and Venezuela.[7]

This was a different legal perspective from that which had come to dominate the postwar Latin American child congresses. For all their awareness of the causality of poverty and marginalization – most clearly expressed in the Santiago de Chile congress in 1973, just before the coup –, the latter perspective was focused on issues of social control, of the abandoned, "antisocial" children, i.e., of Others. Human rights, which also became an important part of Latin American politics in the 1980s, directed attention to the rights and needs of all children, including my own.

The Child Convention is not only a solemn declaration of intent, although there is no court for it. There is a certain bite to it, in the form of the elected autonomous Committee on the Rights of the Child, to which the convention states undertake to submit regular reports, which may be, and are, the object of hearings.

Furthermore, through an activist interpretation of "international co-operation", as mentioned in articles 4 and 24, backed up by commitments from the Unicef and, secondarily ILO and WHO, poor countries have been giv-

---

[6] Cf. "The times have changed: Questions to Adam Lopatka", *Eurosocial* 45 (1993) pp. 139–40. The initiative was strictly political, coming from Gierek and the Politburo of the Communist party, not from the professional milieux in Poland (Adam Lopatka, oral communication 14.12.94). On the other hand, there was a Polish interest in a convention on the rights of children indedependent of the turbulent history of Polish Communism. Already in 1959, when the UN adopted a Declaration on the Rights of the Child, Poland, then governed by Waldyslaw Gomulka, had expressed interest in a convention. N. Cantwell, "The Origins, Development and Significance of the United Nations Convention on the Rights of the Child", in S. Detrick (ed.), *The United Nations Convention on the Rights of the Child. A Guide to the "Travaux Préparatoires"*, Dordrecht, Martinus Nijhoff, 1992, pp. 20–21.

[7] Cantwell 1992 op. cit. p. 23; Thomas Hammarberg, interview 9.2.1995. The UK, the Netherlands, Costa Rica, and Eastern European countries such as GDR and the USSR were also active. The US entered at a late stage only, on the issue of child soldiers.

en reasons to expect problems reported to the Committee may bring forth international assistance.[8]

Although a treaty between "State parties", the Convention on the Rights of the Child has become something more than a state and an inter-state affair. As such, it should be seen in a broader pattern of contemporary politics. We may call it *international NGO politics*. (NGO is a typical part of the jargon, meaning "non-governmental organizations"). I use it here to refer to politics by or through international state organizations, the effectiveness of which largely and deliberately depends on the mobilization of non-governmental organizations, and/or by non-governmental organizations effective operating across state boundaries.

This is not a completely new phenomenon. The International Labour Organization in Geneva, set up after the First World War, has worked in a similar way for a long time. On the other hand, NGOs as a social type did not exist, and only a small set of well-defined players with given roles – unions and employers' associations – took part. On a large scale, international NGO politics dates only from the 1970s.

United Nations special conferences, "years", and "decades" have provided a major impetus. The Environmental Conference in Stockholm in 1972, the Women's Year of 1975, the Women's Conference in Mexico, and the 1976-1985 "Decade for Women" opened a new era of international politics. In 1976 the UN General Assembly decided to declare 1979 the Year of the Child, entrusting Unicef to direct the organization of it. That year a UN commission was entrusted with the task of writing a convention on the rights of the child.

From 1983 non-governmental organizations were de facto drawn into the process of convention drafting. The Unicef, originally skeptical of the convention proposal, provided logistic support for the setting-up of an NGO Ad Hoc Group working on convention drafts. Three NGOs in particular were active and influential, Defence for Children International, the International Catholic Child Bureau, and Save the Children.[9]

NGOs have been drawn into the monitoring system of the Convention. Governmental reports are supplemented by reports from the Unicef office and, in particular, from coalitions of concerned NGOs of the country in question.Their, usually, more critical reports are also officially received by the Committee, which may then ask the government in question to react to statements of the non-governmental report.[10]

---

[8] A recent list of sixteen countries in need of international assistance, ranging from legal advice and help in bridging law and practice to general support for children in "especially difficult circumstances". United Nations, CRC/C/37. Donor countries are also regularly asked by the Committee on the place of children in their aid programs.

[9] Cantwell 1992 op. cit. pp. 24–25; Simone Ek oral communication (13.12.95); Hammarberg, interview.

[10] I would like to express my gratitude to the International Department of the Swedish Save the children, and to Alfhild Petrén, Eva Geidenmark, and Inger Östergren in particular, for

What are the characteristics of this new kind of politics?

1. It has an internationally set agenda, but deals explicitly (also) with internal affairs of state-bounded societies.
2. It operates through international state organizations, such as the UN and its special organs, but usually with specially concerned minor states, such as, e.g., Poland, Canada or Sweden, playing key roles as initiators and practical organizers and implementers. It is this imbrication with interstate organizations that makes internationally active NGOs political – and not only providers of transborder charity –, and which makes domestic civil society activism international.
3. To the traditional means of peaceful interstate politics, diplomacy and covert operations, international NGO politics has added civil society sensitization and mobilization through public communication and public money. – The international agenda also means mass media focus and, very importantly, that money is available, for writing papers, making speeches, going to conferences, doing research, publishing things. In the Third World, where there are usually little resources for any civic undertakings, that is especially important.[11] But the effects of media and money are clearly discernible also in rich nations with rich civic cultures, such as the one this writer comes from.
4. The objectives are societal change as well as state change, i.e., affecting the legislation and the policies of the latter is not seen as the only road to the change of social behaviour and socal relations.

This is a kind of politics going clearly against the classical nation-state politics, of "national self-determination", "national sovereignty", and "non-interference in internal affairs". Nevertheless, it has so far been relatively non-controversial. One reason for that is most probably that international NGO politics has created – or, more cautiously and correctly, has been part of the creation process of – new areas of politics, never recognized by the classical nation-states, "women" (the rights and status of women), "children", and "the environment". The global agenda has also been sustained by regional endeavours, most importantly in the EC/EU, but also by looser regional groupings, like the OAS, the OAU, and the Arab League.

The historical context of the new politics is the wide and vast movement of emancipatory efforts which developed in the course of the 1960s, and which is known, at least in Western Europe and in the Americas, as the "movement of 68". This new international politics is perhaps the major form in which the movement survived the defeats of the second half of the 1970s and the surge of neoliberalism. It is also difficult to see how it could have developed without the partial defrosting of the Cold War in the mid-1970s.

---

their cooperation and letting me have access to their excellent archive on the Convention and its Committee.

[11] The crystallizing importance of the International Year of the Child was underlined to me in several expert interviews in South America, undertaken in September-October 1994.

However, the breakthrough of child politics and child policy depended crucially also on a force much more specific than human rights and international NGO politics. That is on *Feminism*, in the broad oecumenical sense of a movement asserting women's rights. Women spearheaded the new international politics and provided a model of mobilization, more so, it seems, than the Environmental Conference.

The rise of women made two central contributions to the emergence of child politics. One was of *visibility*, the other of *conceptualization*. Women's fights for and entry into participation in public life, in the labour market, in public debate, in places of power made children more visible to public discourse, because of the handed-down special relationship between women and children. "Child care", parental leave and other arrangements making it possible both to have children and a public life became important political issues. More women MPs and other politicians tended to mean more attention to the situation of children in all walks of life.

One aspect of the importance of gendered language, which the women's movement highlighted and deconstructed concerned the "family". Most pertinent to our concerns here was the refusal to take the latter as given collectivity, as "the foundation of society" as much constitutional discourse had. The "family" was *individualized*, comprising individual members, who had but who should not have unequal rights and powers. This individualist egalitarianism (or egalitarian individualism) first and most explicitly asserted the individuality of the woman. But in doing so, it undermined the patriarchal collectivism of the family, and opened up a space for discussing the individuality and the rights of the child as well.

"The family" has in public discourse usually been a traditionalist and patriarchal concept. The classical ideological split was nicely expressed in the names of two major Austrian organizations around family-child policy issues, the Catholic "Family Association" and the Socialist "Friends of Children".[12] Since the late 1960s, the more child-oriented view has had the upper hand also in European Christian Democracy. In 1969 the retiring CDU Secretary of the Family A. Brauksiepe argued for a turn in family policy, for encouraging a family in which "its individual members, the wife and the children as well as the husband, [are enabled] to develop their individual personalities", and for "the protection of children against the misuse of parental power". The 1976 family policy program of German Christian Democracy proclaimed that "the well-being of the child is the primary goal of family policy".[13]

"Children" did not win everywhere, though. Richard Nixon's effective veto killing the Comprehensive Child Development Act, adopted by Congress

---

[12] E. Krebs and M. Schwartz, "Austria", in S. Kamerman and A. Kahn (eds.), Government and Families in Fourteen Countries, New York, Columbia University Press, 1978, pp.199–200.

[13] F. Neidhardt "The Federal Republic of Germany", in S. Kamerman and A. Kahn (eds.), Government and Families in Fourteen Countries, New York, Columbia University Press, 1978 p. 223; cf. Krebs and Schwartz 1978:187.

in 1971 is an important counter-example.[14] President Nixon's veto was formulated with an unusual vehemence, "for the Federal Government to plunge headlong financially into supporting child development would commit the vast moral authority of the National Government to the side of communal approaches to child rearing over [and] against the family-centered approach."[15] The growing weight of Christian fundamentalism in the US, in particular as a vote-getter for the Republican party, with its ideology of "the family" as a patriarchal collective, is apparently the major reason why USA has not ratified the UN Convention on the Rights of the Child.[16]

The point in this context is that "the child" had to emerge out of the shadow of "the family". To the extent that that succeeded, Feminism was the major force de-collectivizing the latter. So far, children as well as women have been only modestly successful. Child policy and politics are still rather rare as explicit phenomena, usually overshadowed by "family policy" or, in some countries, by Ministries and policies of "Youth".

IV. THE RIGHTS OF THE CHILD AND THE POLITICAL SOCIOLOGY OF CHILD POLITICS

What chances do the new rights and the new politics of the child have, in affecting children's lives? In a way, that is a question only a prophet could answer. But the social scientist might at least indicate some of the conditions, risks or opportunities, and issues. They may be grouped into four dimensions, the relation of the national to the international, the social meaning of law, the power of legislation, and the patterning of politics.

The Convention on the Rights of the Child has been a great and rapid sucess in terms of national ratification. By November 11, 1994, i.e., about five years after its adoption, 166 states had ratified it. Only nine months were required for it to enter into force, when twenty states had ratified it. A number of the first round of due official reports is in and has been treated by the Committee on the Rights of the Child, subject to quite penetrating hearings in fact.

It has been followed up on a regional level, by an African Charter of the Rights and Welfare of the Child (of 1990) and by a resolution of the European

---

[14] The bill had not been non-controversial in Congress and in public debate, and its multi-faceted and complicated proposals – of federal support for child development services and day-care – involved many issues. But the idea of a broad federal program had ample congressional support, and the most divisive issue in the congressional stage had been, as so often in welfare state history, the organisation of implementation.

[15] The rationale for Nixon's veto seems to have been his need to appease the far right, who were up in arms against Nixon's opening to China. American child policy was no more than trading money. G. Steiner, The Children's Cause, Washington D.C., The Brookings Institution, 1976, ch. 5.

[16] On the agenda of the Democratic Clinton Adminstration, children happened to come after the very controversial issue of homosexual rights in the military, which stalled the former issue, till it became politically impossible after the November 1994 Congress elections.

Parliament on a European Charter, calling for, among other things, UN ratification, an Ombudsman, and certain specified orientations of policy. Moreover
by regional meetings of the monitoring Committee in Latin America, Africa,
and Asia.

The World Summit on Children in 1990 adopted a set of basic developmental goals with regard to children, of health, nutrition, education etc. With
a view to implementing national programmes of action were to be set up. By
July 1993 86 states had set up such programmes, according to a Unicef survey.
Their main significance has been in countries of the Third World, where the
plans have been tied in with international co-operation and assistance. To the
extent that they play any role, these plans seem to run parallell to, rather than
integrated with, the monitoring of the Convention.

All this is by any standard of international politics an impressive result.
The Convention is expressed with an explicit recognition of the global variety
of cultures as well as of national resources. The developmental goals are
humanly elementary, and therefore easy to accept in principle from vastly
different perspectives on human life and on human society.

However, this does not mean that the *national-international relationship*
has ceased to be a problem and certainly a variable. Even national polities
with the same kind of regime and at comparable level of socioeconomic
development should be expected to vary in their responsiveness to and in
their concern with international conventions and declarations. The national-
international variable will take on different values, according to domestic
commitment to international social issues, and to national dependency on
international organizations and on committed foreign states.[17]

A perusal of the parliamentary records for the first 3–4 years of a small
number of Northern and Western European countries[18] shows considerable
differences with regard to children's rights and the UN Convention. Sweden
forms a group apart among its neighbours. Swedish MPs are very interested
in children's rights as a general topic, and in the the UN Convention. Each of
the four parliamentary years 1990/91-1993/94 there are a number of motions
about the Convention, about domestic adaptions to it, about monitoring and
following up, about Sweden pushing other countries to ratify the Convention
and to live up to it, etc. Most of these are "heavy" party motions, signed by
the leaders or by other frontbench members of all the political parties, except
the two most conservative ones, from which individual members occasionally
show up. There were also many motions calling for a Children's Ombudsman,
an office which was set up by a government bill in 1973.

---

[17] Other dimensions are conceivable, but I doubt whether they will have equal power of
discrimination. Whether an international convention automatically has the status of national
law is one candidate. But in such an internationally committed country as Sweden, the value
on that axis is zero.

[18] Denmark, Finland, France, Germany, Norway, Sweden, the UK.

In Denmark, Finland and Norway, by contrast there was little interest. In Finland there were unsuccessful motions for an Ombudsman, but for the rest silence prevailed, as far as more general issues of children's rights, national and international, were concerned. (It should, of course, not be forgotten, that Norway on its own had pioneered a clause of territorial and housing planning legislation that children's interests had both to be represented and to be paid attention to as well an Ombudsman, decided in 1981).

The German Bundestag of 1992–94 registered only two references to children's rights, one about the government report on the Convention in Germany, the other a motion on "ecological children's rights". Children's rights, and the UN Convention, were given a certain attention by the House of Commons in 1989–90, very little or none since then (survey ended in January 1994). Also the French National Assembly, which was preoccupied with children's rights and with "politique de l'enfance" in 1989 and in 1990, soon lost interest, and avoided the issue in 1991–93.

Now, all the above-mentioned countries have ratified the Convention. The most powerful country of the world, the USA, has not. The 1994 elections there make it unlikely, that the US will ratify within a near future. – Nor have the Netherlands ratified the Convention, by February 1995, which is surprising (but probably not definitive), even in view of both still remaining conservative familism and of the often slow parliamentary process of the country.[19]

Two kinds of questions are pertinent here. What determines the national-international relationship in the child context? How will the national-international variable affect children's rights?

The former is primarily determined by two factors, by domestic commitment to social internationalism and by external dependency. Neither is very firmly and anciently established, and both are open to governmental change. However, in recent decades certain patterns have become discernible.

For instance, among larger rich, stable democracies France has a universalistic tradition, shared by most of the right and the left, but largely egocentric. When President Mitterand said in June 1989, "I want France to be one of its [i.e., the Convention's] first signatory countries and the work of adapting our domestic law to be completed successfully", he gave a personal touch to this universalistic tradition.[20] Japan has a consistently national political and cultural orientation, with little interest in international non-economic issues as well as with little international penetrability. Japan ratified the Convention late (April 1994) and little effect is to be expected. US politics is constantly divided between an egocentric liberal universalism and a conservative isola-

---

[19] I have not had access to the Dutch parliamentary record for recent years, but a check with the officious parliamentary yearboek *Parlement en kiezer*, Leiden, Martinus Nijhoff, indicates little Dutch parliamentary concern with children in 1989–93.

[20] The French Report to the UN Committee, UN CRC/3/Add.15 4 June 1993, p. 4. France was also rather cooperative with and higlevel represented for the UN Committee hearing.

tionism, of which the latter currently has the upper hand. Attenuated forms of a similar left-right divide appear to characterize Germany and Britain. The latter has under Thatcherism, both with and without Mrs T, taken a haughty *noli me tangere* attitude to international social concerns, whether in the EU, the WTO, and at the January 1995 hearing before the UN Committee on the Rights of the Child.[21]

Among the smaller nations, some have been more internationally committed than others, on global social issues, that is. Canada, the Netherlands, Norway, and Sweden are the countries most frequently encountered in Third World projects without any ex-colonial background. Most relevant here, though, is a general tendency for small, rich states to be cooperative with and responsive to international organizations.

Dependent countries are, first of all, poor countries, and among poor countries foreign aid-dependent countries. In other words, sub-Saharan Africa, islet republics in the Pacific and the Caribbean, Latin America, to a variable extent.

Among nationalistically governed economically rising countries, as well as among isolationist poor countries, we should expect the Convention to have little impact, on the East Asian "Tigers" and on Argentina, on inward-looking dictatorships, like Myanmar, for instance.

On the national-international dimension alone, we should expect a divergent effect of the Convention, and of international child politics generally, among the rich countries, but rather a convergent one among poorer countries, and between poor and rich countries. The socially internationalist developed countries, or regimes of such countries, tend to have been more concerned with the rights and needs of children in the past, and they will now be given an extra impetus. Among the less developed countries, on the other hand, the positive dependency effect should tend to benefit (many of) the poorest countries. The Convention, its assistance apparatus, and aligned NGOs should have a strongly positive effect also on other, economically growing less developed countries with a socially oriented government, such as Chile.

The Convention will probably contribute to lessening the overall gap between rich and poor countries. But the net effect of commitment and dependency upon global convergence or divergence of children's situation and prospects looks impossible to calculate at this point. Given the prevailing ideology about the Convention, it should be emphasized, that this means, that a divergent effect of the World Convention is not to be ruled out.

The Convention is a law-like norm, and may therefore for our purposes here be treated as a law. Then, a fundamental tenet of the sociology of law had better not be forgotten: *the meaning of law is variable*. Rwanda, for instance, ratified the UN Convention on the Rights of the Child on January 24th 1991. Did that make any difference to the disasters that befell Rwandan children

---

[21] The sessions are open to the public, and my graduate student Kristina Bartley attended the January 1995 session.

in 1994? Probably not.[22] The input of children's rights into the Brazilian Constitution of 1988 and the new Statute of the Child and the Adolescent, adopted by the Brazilian Congress in 1990 have probably had more impact, at least changing the official discourse of a democratically rather stabilized country.[23] On the other hand, any tangible effects on the situation and the risks of poor children in Brazil would be hard to find. The massacre on street children outside the Candelâria Church in central Rio de Janeiro, most likely by policemen, took place afterwards, in 1993.[24]

Generally speaking, this sad truth tends to hold, the more good laws are needed, the less value laws tend to have. Or, more bluntly, the more misery there is, the less do laws count. The richer a country is, the better its society is organized, the more its laws are applied.

However, this does not necessarily mean that the UN Child Convention has a Matthew Effect, giving more to those that already have. There are variations in the meaning of law at equal levels of development. Among the Scandinavian countries, for instance, it is a common understanding among social scientists, that laws, and governmental decisions generally, carry more weight, are more strictly applied in Sweden, than in the other countries. Similarly, in South America it seems that Chile is more legally serious than the other countries.[25]

Further, and above all, a public law establishes rights, which, if not necessarily applied, can at least be legitimately *claimed*. The international NGO politics of children's rights creates claim rights of civic organizations, and foci and yardsticks of social research and public debate. How much impact such claims and findings will have depends, ceteris paribus, on how integrated or segmented a society is. But given a certain amount of political liberties, their effect is likely to be significantly deviant from zero.[26] And in many countries of the Third World, for instance in the Philippines, in Senegal, and in Central

---

[22] Rwanda submitted a meagre, exclusively legalistic report to the Committee, which took it up in October 1993, i.e., before the massacres of 1994 but with a civil war already raging. But the Committee then suspended the meeting, requesting more information, within one year. But in the following year Rwanda went into the abyss.

[23] Cf. Unicef, *The Convention: Child Rights and UNICEF experience at the country level*, Florence 1991, pp. 35ff; M. Cury et al. (eds.), *Estatuto da criança e do adolescente comentado*, Sâo Paulo, Malheiros editores, 1992.

[24] The UN Committee reacted to the shootings, by a letter to the Brazilian government. (Thomas Hammarberg interview.)

[25] During the dictatorship Chile had its toll of killings as well. But a much larger proportion than in the other countries of the Southern Cone seem to have been killed after some semblance of procedure, however military, secret, and summary. Exiled Senators continued to receive their pensions.

[26] An example is the study, directed by Francisco Pilotti, for the Inter-American Child Institute, of the situation of the children in Chile, *Infancia en riesgo social y políticas sociales en Chile*, Montevideo, Instituto Interamnericano del Niño, 1994, presented with considerable fanfare in Santiago de Chile, in the presence of the Minister of Justice and other high government officials.

America, NGO child politics is making a very important contribution to the constitution of an active civil society.

A third dimension bearing upon the operation of international rights and politics of children is the sheer *power of legislation*, however seriously intended and applied, in bettering children's lives. Put in this way, it's clear from the outset, that many very important aspects of a child's life are not (directly) amenable to legislation. This holds most obviously, of course, for those dependent upon parental care and love. True, the latter may be made easier or more difficult by political decisions. Parental care was, for example, made more difficult by the recent British EU veto of unpaid parental leave for fathers, characterized by the UK employment Minister, Mr Portillo, as "immensely disruptive and destructive".[27]

Legislation may govern the rights and obligations with regard to existing resources. But it is rather powerless in the face of changes of the resource base. Russia, to take only the two largest heir of the former USSR, has ratified the UN Convention. The current meaning of law in the ex-Soviet countries may be open to debate, but that is hardly the reason why the conditions of children have declined since the ratification of the Convention. Infant mortality has risen, under five mortality has risen, the rate of immunization has gone down, pre-primary enrolment rate has declined, etc.[28] Article 24, 2, a of the Convention calls on State Parties "To diminish infant and child mortality". The Russian state is in fact increasing both. But at least non-lawyers would probably hesitate to call that a breach of the Convention. The Russian delegate to the hearing on Russia told the UN Committee that "Russia's children had become hostages of the economic reform under way".[29]

Technically, the costs of decline may be regulated as well as the dividends of growth. The expression of Article 4 of the Convention is appropriate here, as the Committee is trying to bring across in its hearings, of measures to implement the Convention "to the maximum extent of their available resources". But international child law and politics have not been designed to cope with social decline, and the latter is governed by larger forces than that of law.

Finally, there is the purely *political* dimension of child politics. It needs to escape from its two traditional locations, on the margin or in the realm of symbolism. From the symbolic politics of baby-kissing and from the corner of marginal affairs far away from "high politics". The symbolic significance of child politics is not to be neglected though. Bernard Shaw once said he had no enemies under seven, and the plight of children has sometimes been singled out by social policy lobbies as important targets, as, e.g., the British Child Poverty Action Group.

---

[27] *Financial Times* 23.9.1994 p. 16.

[28] Unicef, *Public Policy and Social Conditions*, Florence November 1993, pp. 84ff.

[29] UN Press Release HR 3288 21 January 1993 (Morning).

In the longer run of child politics, the latter has to get incorporated into the domestic mainstream, and to be at least recognized by the mainstream monitoring of world development, e.g., by the World Bank. For that international NGO politics is not enough. However internationally committed or dependent, nation-states have their primary domestic agendae. NGOs tend to imply NCOs, non-central organizations, however dedicated and competent in their area of operation. But the mainstream follows its own, specific course. True, certain themes have become common, for the time being, like daycare of children, from France to Finland, and also child benefits. Others are very special, such as the British preoccupation with the Child Support Agency, and its task of cashing in child support money from absent fathers, or the German concern with the pensions rights of parents and non-parents.

The cause of children will have to be attached to one or several of the conflicting major political causes of the country, be it "development", "welfare", "solidarity", "participation", "emancipation", "opportunity", or something else.

The UN Convention may be a catalyst, but something else has to be catalyzed into action.

V. CODA

International child politics should be studied not only for the sake of children. It has also a great deal to teach social and political scientists, about opinion formation, the functioning of law, the interrelationship of national and international politics and legislation, and the dynamics of social change. There is a rich potentiality for a stimulating encounter between specialists of the field and general social scientists and lawyers.

BRUCE ABRAMSON

The Invisibility of Children and Adolescents

The Need to Monitor our Rhetoric and our Attitudes

Despite the nearly universal ratification of the Convention on the Rights of the Child (CRC), the sad fact remains that children and adolescents are invisible. Even in human rights advocacy, and this includes CRC advocacy, too often either young people do not exist or some aspect of their humanity is denied. This paper will examine quotations taken from the human rights community, identifying turns of speech and clichés that, despite their good intentions, make children and adolescents invisible.

The CRC campaign for human rights is a reform movement, and changing behaviour requires changing attitudes. We must also recognize the socio-political implications of reform. Young people under 18 make up almost half of humanity, a half which is virtually powerless in relation to the other half. To ensure the well-being of children and adolescents in light of this imbalance of power, we must identify attitudes and practices which cause invisibility. We must monitor ourselves as well as governments, attitudes as well as behaviour.

I. "MEN AND WOMEN" AND "THE MAJORITY"

Human rights issues are often portrayed in language which totally excludes children and adolescents. Several quotations illustrate the problem: (a) "A national climate conducive to human rights [can] only be created through a broadly based participation of both men and women in the political, economic, social and cultural development of a society on a democratic basis"; (b) "Women are half of humanity"; and (c) "the majority of [South Africa's] population have never participated in the decision-making process of their country solely because of their race".[1]

Quotation (a) fails to include young people, while (b) and (c) could only be true if children and adolescents did not exist. What these "men and women" and "majority" statements have in common is that they project a vision of human rights in which young people play no part.

---

[1] These and the following quotations are from NGOs, the UN (agencies, treaty-monitoring bodies and their members, etc.) and, in one case, a diplomat at a human rights conference. Citations are not given because the purpose is to illustrate language usage, not to call attention to authors individually.

E. Verhellen (ed.), Monitoring Children's Rights, 393–402.
© 1996 *Kluwer Law International. Printed in the Netherlands.*

II. "WOMEN AND CHILDREN"

When young people do get mentioned it is frequently in the phrase "women and children". This expression has been used so often and so carelessly that it has become a cliché. The trouble with clichés is that they stifle our thinking; as George Orwell put it, they choke our minds "like tea leaves blocking a sink".[2] It is now time we took a fresh look at the "women and children" cliché. The expression is not "women and their children" nor even "mothers and children". The expression usually treats the two groups as a single unit, as in "the situation of women and children" instead of the plural, "situations". Also, the CRC makes no reference to "women and children". These observations lead us to ask, what is it that makes some advocates join these two demographic groups into a unit?

What typically unites women and children is the imagery of weakness. This image is often only implied, but sometimes it is made explicit as in these quotations: (a) "women and children were abused, being the most helpless and vulnerable"; and (b) "[structural adjustments cause a loss of] protection affecting the weakest sectors – women and children".

The image of children as weak – as fragile or vulnerable – has obvious advocacy value for its emotional appeal, but "women and children" is still a cliché that presents a false picture of the young people covered by the CRC. First, there is lateral falseness when the one dimensional picture ignores other qualities of the individual child or children as a group. "Children are fragile, dependent and developing". These are the reasons why they are entitled to the special treatment of the CRC, as UNHCR explains in *Refugee Children: Guidelines for Protection and Care*. While the portrait of women as weak is often objected to because it denies strengths, the fixation on the fragility of children misses their developmental needs. For example, a "feeding programme" for malnourished infants might take care of physical weakness but still neglect the developmental needs for stimulation and emotional attachment.

Second, there is vertical falseness. With its underlying image of weakness, "women and children" invokes images of small children, the ones under 5 years of age that are typically in the care of their mothers or other females. This image excludes the majority of people covered by the CRC. A picture of teenagers, especially 16 and 17 year olds, does not spring to mind when we read "women and children", for example.

The third problem is contextual falseness. The CRC recognises the human rights of individuals, but it also emphasises relationships. As stated in UNHCR's *Guidelines*, "Children must always be seen in the context of their families and community". The phrase "women and children" does not fit the conceptual framework of the CRC, nor does it correspond to real life. When it

---

[2] "Politics and the English Language", from G. Orwell, *Shooting an Elephant and Other Essays*, (Secker and Warburg, 1950), p. 94.

comes to programming, for example, the "w & c" approach to young people produces marginalisation. In the reports of UN special rapporteurs, the splitting of "the situation of women and children" from the main discussions give the impression that human rights are primarily men's issues. Also, the discussions under the "women and children" sections inevitably become distorted because children and adolescents are not seen in the context of family and community. (One report even put the "situation of women" as a sub-category of "the situation of children"!)

George Orwell's observation about clichés is instructive: "the decline of a language must ultimately have political and economic causes". The monitoring of CRC rights requires us to look behind the rhetoric for the political and economic forces at work. A paragraph from a human rights publication illustrates the point:

> Certain groups of women are particularly vulnerable to infringement of their sexual integrity. One such group is refugee women. At least 75% of the world's 18 million refugees are women and children; in some countries women and children make up 90% of refugees. Refugee women are too often victims of rape and other physical and sexual abuses, and have special needs of human rights protection.

This paragraph is about women, not children. The article in which the paragraph appears is also about women, as shown in the title, "Empowering Women", and the conclusion, "Now is the time for a political approach – by having women in positions of power dealing with human rights and other political and public issues". It is clear that the only reason that children were mentioned in the middle of the paragraph was to give the impressive figure of 75% and the overwhelming number 90%. Children have been used here like the butcher's thumb on a scale.

Part of monitoring the CRC movement is monitoring the rhetoric. As the above quotation illustrates, it is easy for clichés about children to slip by us without our noticing how young people are being used in the pursuit of other agendas.

III. "THE CHILD"

The CRC is the manifesto for a movement that will greatly improve the welfare of young people, but some of its language unfortunately works to produce invisibility. The problems relate to the term "child".

The CRC often uses "child" as a singular noun, but in three articles it is used incorrectly as a plural. Article 17 says, in part, "To this end, States Parties shall ... encourage the mass media to disseminate such information and material of social and cultural benefit to the child ... ". Since television, magazines and the like are not directed to specific individuals but to groups, "the child" is used here as a collective noun. (See also Art. 3(1) and (2) and

Art. 19: compare to Art. 33). In other Articles where "the" is used instead of "each" or "every", "the child" suggests a plural meaning (e.g. Art. 7; compare to the correct usage of "the" in Art. 9.1).

Even the title, "Convention on the Rights of the Child", seems to convey a plural meaning. This becomes apparent when we compare it to other treaties, such as the Convention on the Elimination of All Forms of Discrimination against Women, the African Charter on Human and Peoples' Rights, and the Declaration on the Rights of Disabled Persons. Who would have tolerated using "the Woman", "the African", or "the Disabled Person"? Reducing a whole group to one is offensive: the diversity within the group is denied, stereotypes are fostered, and the depersonalised one becomes a thing.

Some advocates have picked up on the plural usage in the CRC, using "the child" as a collective word, often turning it into the personification, The Child. When they do this, they treat 2.5 billion people as an object, and unless they use "the woman" and other words similarly, they are practising double standards.

IV. INVISIBILITY OF ADOLESCENTS

"Child" is defined in the dictionary as a person who has not reached sexual maturity. Upon puberty, the person becomes an adolescent, and is often called a young man or young woman. After adolescence comes adulthood. This linguistic division between child, adolescent and adult reflects divisions of development that are universally recognised. All this the Convention ignores by defining rights in terms of "child" while extending coverage up to adulthood.

Adolescents are excluded by "child" similarly to the way that women are excluded by "mankind", "man", "he", and "his". The Universal Declaration of Human Rights and the two Covenants of 1966 used these masculine words to include females, as did the Declaration on the Rights of the Child. Today these words are seen by many as excluding females, not legally, but in a socio-political sense.

The negotiators of the CRC rejected these gender-excluding words, using the more cumbersome "he and she", "him and her", and "his and her". However, in using "child" instead of "child and adolescent" or "minor", double standards were applied to age-exclusion. Ironically, one price adolescents are paying for CRC coverage is their visibility.[3]

---

[3] There is a major difference between using "he", "chairman" and "mankind" generically to include females and using "child" to include adolescents. In the former cases, everybody can tell by the context when the generic meaning is intended. While some people may be offended, no one is confused because the traditional generic meaning is understood by everyone. The same cannot be said when a word is given an artificial meaning. When a beverage that is sold as "orange juice" contains no orange product but just artificial colouring and flavouring, the

V. "INFANTILISATION" OF ADOLESCENTS

Article 1 says: "For the purpose of the present Convention, a child means every human being below 18 years unless ... majority is attained earlier". Strictly speaking, this does not say that adolescents are children. Many human rights advocates are now treating adolescents as children, and they point to Article 1 for justification. But when we look closely at the legalistic language we see that the Convention is being misunderstood and misrepresented.

The Convention started out to be only about children's rights but later in the negotiations a decision was made to extend coverage to 18. This created a discrepancy: draft article 1 was extended to cover minors ("18 years unless ... majority is attained earlier"), but the rights were still defined in the rest of the draft articles in terms of "child". Rather than change "child" to "minor" or use other words, the discrepancy was resolved by using legalistic language to create an artificial definition of "child": "For the purpose of the present Convention, a child means ... ".

The words, "a child means", do not define real-life adolescents as children; the phrase is only a stipulation that "child" in the text is not to be understood in its ordinary meaning but by the artificial definition in Article 1. In paraphrase it is saying, "Whenever you see the word 'child' in the text, translate it as 'minor' according to Article 1". It is not saying, in paraphrase, "Whenever you see a 17 year old, you are looking at a child". The phrase, "a child means", is defining a word in a text, not flesh and blood human beings. The CRC, therefore, does not say that adolescents are children.

The objective of Article 1 is to identify the class of persons who get CRC rights, not to change language. When a State enacts legislation to implement the CRC it can still use "minor" or "juvenile", for example. This is the significance of the legal phrase, "for the purpose of the present Convention": the purpose is to give an artificial definition to the word "child" in the text of the CRC; the purpose is not to change the meaning of that word as it is otherwise used in society. The intention of Article 1 is to give CRC rights to minors, not to get governments and the public to call all minors "children".

What we are seeing is a distortion of Article 1 during the course of advocacy. One publication, for example, says, "Article 1 of the Convention recognises every human being below the age of 18 years to be a child, unless under the law applicable to the child, majority is attained earlier". This is not true. "Recognise" means "to identify from past experience or knowledge", "to acknowledge the validity of".[4] Adolescents are not children, and the CRC

---

practice is condemned as consumer fraud. When a government reports that its military has carried out a "pacification" exercice where the reality is that civilians have been bombed, the language is a deception. In both cases, the objective is to obscure the truth. In the same way, advocacy which uses "children" to refer to adolescents is manipulative.

[4] *The American Heritage Dictionary of the English Language*, (Dell Publishing, 1970).

does not "recognise" that they are. This publication spreads a myth about what the CRC says, and it is a myth that "infantilises" adolescents.

"Children's rights" is not synonymous with "CRC rights" because "children" does not include adolescents: as discussed above, neither the dictionary nor the CRC says that adolescents are children. People are free to change language, of course, and those advocates who are using "children's rights" as a synonym for "CRC rights" or "children" to include adolescents, are doing just that. Since the CRC gives an artificial definition to the word "child" only as it is used in the text, those advocates who are using "child" to refer to real-life persons above the age of puberty are going beyond the CRC's definition. Despite their good intentions, these advocates infantilise adolescents when they call them "children".

The practice of using "girl" as a synonym for "woman" illustrates infantilisation. Decades ago the feminist movement made it a goal to stamp out this practice because it dehumanises on two levels. To treat an adult as a child ignores the adult's capabilities and stifles fulfilment of potential. To systematically treat members of a group as children is a political act of subjugation. The emerging practice of calling adolescents "children", of speaking of CRC rights as "children's rights", dehumanises adolescents in the same two ways.

History illustrates the politics of infantilisation. Sexism and racism, and to a large extent imperialism, are based on theories of inferiority, and these theories have often compared the subjugated groups to children. A "scientific" book in 1850 justified slavery by an analogy to children: "We have been irresistibly brought to the conviction that in intellectual power the African is an inferior variety of our species. His whole history affords evidence that he is incapable of self-government... Our child that we lead by the hand, and who looks to us for protection and support is still our blood notwithstanding his weakness and ignorance". In 1978, Herbert Spencer, one of the giants of anthropology, wrote: "How races differ in respect of the more or less involved structures of their minds will best be understood on recalling the unlikeness between the juvenile mind and the adult mind among ourselves, which so well typifies the unlikeness between the minds of savage and civilized". At the turn of the century, President Taft promoted imperialism in the Pacific by calling the Filipino people America's "little brown brother".[5]

Those advocates who label everyone under 18 or the age of majority as "children" are going a step further than the racist quotations, but it is a giant step. The above quotes only compared non-Caucasian adults to children in an *analogy*. These advocates are *defining* adolescents as children.

Reform movements are basically one of two types: either movements for moral improvement or movements to empower some down-trodden group. The "children's rights" movement is usually presented as a moral improvement campaign. The ultimate message is that adults have to be more sensitive

---

[5] Quotations in this paragraph are cited in T. Gossett, *Race: The History of an Idea in America*, (Schocken Books, 1965), pp. 63, 149, 155.

to the needs of children and less selfish in meeting those needs, which, in formal language, becomes the best interests rule of Article 3. It is easy to see why the moral improvement approach is so common. The public's image of children is that they are innocent and helpless; they are to be cuddled, nurtured and protected. The objective is to get adults to do a better job of meeting the fundamental needs of children, not to give children power. There is one serious consequence to the moral improvement approach, however: because adults typically believe that children are not capable of claiming legal rights on their own behalf, most people who say "children's rights" probably mean "right" in a metaphorical sense, in the same way that "animal rights" is metaphorical, rather than in the legal sense that adults have rights.[6]

Adolescents are not children. Young people under 18 marry, have children, make medical decisions, work, pay taxes, engage in politics, and vote (beginning at 16 in Brazil). They drive cars, fly aeroplanes, attend universities, create art, make scientific discoveries and open businesses. Young men and young women under 18 do virtually everything that people over 18 do. Nothing magical happens on the 18th birthday. Culture rather than innate capacity accounts for the variation in what older adolescents actually do in any given society.

The CRC recognises the capabilities of adolescents in two ways. First, it allows States to drop the age of majority below 18, thereby cutting off all CRC rights of adults under 18 years of age.[7] Second, Article 12(1) recognies a right to personal autonomy, that is, a right to make one's own decisions, that operates on a sliding-scale according to "age and maturity". If a young person's "age and maturity" render that person capable of making a particular decision, then the "due weight" requirement would entitle the young person to make the decision. If maturity is such that restrictions can be imposed, such as requiring consultation with an adult or an adult holding veto power, then adults cannot act arbitrarily in administering those restrictions. By linking decision-making to maturity, Article 12(1) is an empowerment article.

The CRC campaign can be, at least in part, an empowerment movement for adolescents. The more autonomy a young person has in the exercise of CRC rights, the less the rights are metaphorical and the more they are legal rights like those adults have under the International Covenant on Civil and Political Rights.

Here lies the dilemma. One image that adults often have of adolescents is that they need to be controlled. Decisions that teenagers make can be threatening to adults, particularly when it comes to sex, violence and drugs. There is so much tension already between autonomy and control that the

---

[6] The moralistic approach also tends to underestimate the capacity of children to make decisions. Some CRC advocates are now working to overcome the assumptions about the incompetency of children.

[7] Article 37 (a) prohibits States from imposing capital punishment on adults under 18 even though these same adults have no CRC rights under Article 1.

prospect of empowering adolescents is not a comforting thought for many people.

When it comes to implementing Article 12, everything will depend on how accurately the young person is seen. Making assessments about maturity on an individual or group basis can be so delicate that the determing factor will be the adults' attitudes rather than objectively determined facts. The more that adults see adolescents as larger-sized children, the less of a role adolescents will be granted in decision-making under Article 12. This is why infantilisation is a political issue.

Human rights advocates are free to chose their vocabulary. Although the Covenants of 1966 define rights using "he", "his rights", "his life", and so on, advocates are free to say "she and he" and "his and her". In advocating for the CRC, they are free to explain the artificial definition of "child" in Article 1, or they can create myths. They can say either "children's rights" or "the rights of children and adolescents", just as they please. They are legally free to speak as they wish, whether their rhetoric enhances or diminishes the rights of others. The point is that human rights advocates have choices, and the choices they make will be shaped by their attitudes.

Monitoring the CRC includes monitoring how adolescents are portrayed and how Article 1's artificial definition of "child" is presented to the public. It also includes monitoring the political and economic forces behind the rhetoric.

VI. "CHILD SOLDIER"

Talks are now underway about creating a new treaty to supercede CRC Article 38 in order to ban the practice of "child soldiers". Some proposals would prohibit both the voluntary service and conscription of everyone under 18. Since recruitment of persons under 15 is already illegal, these proposals are really about 15, 16 and 17 year olds. And since some of these proposals cover everyone under 18 regardless if they have attained the age of majority, the ban could apply to persons who are legally adults. Discussing these proposals in terms of "child soldiers" ignores the fact that these people are older adolescents or adults, which in turn obscures the legal and policy issues.

First is the issue of participation under Article 12(1). While banning conscription protects liberty, banning voluntary service restricts freedom of choice. Since restricting a person's autonomy would be a "matter affecting" that person, superceding the CRC raises three legal issues regarding participation: (i) Do people who hold CRC rights have a right under Article 12(1) to participate in UN and State forums when the proposal to supercede Article 38 is under consideration? (ii) Is there an obligation to assist their participation? (iii) Can a CRC article be lawfully superceded in the absence of meaningful participation of those who hold CRC rights?

Second is the issue of cutting back on substantive CRC rights. One of the reasons that underage soldiers give for joining the military is necessity. When civilians are routinely attacked by soldiers, paramilitaries and bandits, some young people join as a means of defence against attacks. The right to life under Article 6 inherently entails, one may argue, the right of self-defence. When the scope of the right to self-defence is defined by what is reasonable under the circumstances, joining a military unit and even some participation in combat could sometimes be justified. Genocide or attacks against undefended villages might give rise to such situations, for example. In those cases where self-defence would be justified, a total ban on voluntary service would restrict the right to life.

Once CRC rights have been recognised, subsequent action to restrict them raises additional issues: (i) Are there sufficient policy reasons to justify restrictions? (ii) Is there a right to participate under Article 12(1) when the matter under consideration is the restriction of rights? (iii) If a new treaty were to restrict the exercise of any CRC right, would the treaty have to be ratified by all present parties to the CRC? (The answer to the last question would be "yes" under the Vienna Convention on the Law of Treaties, Art. 30 and Art. 41).

None of the above issues need to be taken seriously if CRC rights are metaphorical instead of legal. Nor need they be considered if the persons to be affected are children rather than adolescents and adults. Only where the persons affected are competent to make decisions for themselves are the issues serious, and herein lies the political significance of "child soldiers". In the racist quotations above, inferiority or incompetency was never proven factually but assumed in the imagery which depicted the people as children. Likewise, a young person's incompetency to make decisions about superceding CRC Art. 38 or about joining the military is decided beforehand by calling that person a "child".

The cliché "child soldier" also obscures the fact that almost all soldiers are males. In *A History of Warfare*, military historian John Keegan states: "Warfare is, nevertheless, the one human activity from which women, with the most insignificant exceptions, have always and everywhere stood apart. Women look to men to protect them from danger. ... Women have followed the drum, nursed the wounded [and given other support, but they] do not fight. ... If warfare is as old as history and as universal as mankind, we must now enter the supremely important limitation that it is an entirely masculine activity.[8]

The real-life problem is one of "boy-soldiers" or young men under 18 volunteering or being conscripted. The gender issue, however, goes much deeper than actual participation in combat. Because the child rearing practices which prepare males for the role of warrior begin at a very early age, the

---

[8] (Hutchinson, 1993), p. 76.

differences in the socialisation of boys and girls raises gender discrimination issues under Article 2. "Child soldier" makes the gender issue invisible, and when gender discrimination is actively looked for in other areas of life while being ignored here, the problem of double standards appears once again.

CONCLUSION

Our rhetoric both reflects and perpetuates the invisibility of children and adolescents. The examples that have been presented illustrate the need for CRC advocates to monitor both their rhetoric and their attitudes.

GEERT CAPPELAERE

Possible Optional Protocols to the UN Convention on the Rights of the Child

Improving or Undermining the Convention and its Monitoring? The Case of Child Prostitution, Child Pornography and Sale of Children

INTRODUCTION

Child prostitution, child pornography and sale of children have very recently become phenomena of concern in many (political) fora. The social awareness about the existence and about the impact of those phenomena is increasing worldwide. However, despite a number of important pioneering studies, we have to observe that today still little is known about (sexual) exploitation of children.[1] There is hardly any systematic information on the situation worldwide. Often the focus seems to be limited to harsh expressions mostly in developing countries, to sensational events or to related phenomena such as paedophelia.

In the spring of 1994, the United Nations Commission on Human Rights decided to establish an open-ended intersessional Working Group responsible for elaborating, as a matter of priority and in close collaboration with the Special Rapporteur on the Sale of Children, Child Prostitution and Child Pornography and the Committee on the Rights of the Child, *guidelines for a possible draft optional protocol* to the Convention on the Rights of the Child on the sale of children, child prostitution and child pornography, as well as the *basic measures* needed for their prevention and eradication.[2]

---

[1] R. O'Grady, The child and the Tourist, Stockholm, Ecpat, 1992; R. O'Grady, The rape of the innocent, Auckland, Pace Publishing, 1994; F. Bruce, The sexual exploitation of children, Geneva, Bice, 1991; M.F. Botte, J.P. Mari, Le prix d'un enfant, Paris, Laffont, 1993.

[2] U.N. Commission on Human Rights, Resolution 1994/90, Paragraph 17 entitled "Need to adopt effective measures for the prevention and eradication of the sale of children, child prostitution and child pornography". The Economic and Social Council, in its Resolution 1994/9 authorized the establishment of an open-ended working group which met for the first, time in Geneva from 14th till 25th November 1994. The report of this first session has been adopted by the U.N.-Commission on Human Rights at its fifty-first session (February – March 1995/ Document E/CN.4/1994/WG.14/CRP.3rd – 20th December 1994).

E. Verhellen (ed.), Monitoring Children's Rights, 403–430.
© 1996 *Kluwer Law International. Printed in the Netherlands.*

In the meantime the Commission on Human Rights has decided to establish another Working Group as well in order to elaborate, as a matter of priority, *a draft optional protocol* to the Convention on the Rights of the Child on the involvement of children in armed conflicts.[3]

The difference in the formulation of the mandate of both Working Groups (guidelines for a possible draft optional protocol vs draft optional protocol) is important, as it reflects a big discussion within the Human Rights Commission on the necessity of an optional protocol on sale of children, child prostitution and child pornography. In order to avoid a vote on a children's issue (!), the mandate of this Working Group was negotiated for a long time until a consensus was achieved.

The disagreement on the necessity of an optional protocol on child prostitution, sale of children and child pornography had to a certain extent to do with the amount of already existing national and international provisions in this field. Therefore we begin our article with a survey of some of those existing provisions.

In a third part we will discuss the activities at the first session of the Working Group and its outcome.

Finally, we will give some own reflections regarding the discussion on monitoring children's rights in general.

I. ANTECEDENTS – EXISTING LEGAL FRAMEWORK

In his first report, the Special Rapporteur on Child Prostitution, Child Pornography and Sale of Children searched for an answer on what the existing legal framework was regarding these phenomena. His conclusions were quite clear: "...one should note that the legislative framework already exists...many of the international laws concerned take a "stick" approach of either regulating or prohibiting practices. Moreover they tend to be targeted to the protection of the child and punishment of the exploiter."[4]

Traffic in persons and prostitution have indeed already for a long time been phenomena of primary concern within the United Nations system. For example in 1949, only 4 years after the organization was established, the UN adopted the International Convention for the Suppression of the Traffic in Persons and of the Exploitation of Prostitution of Others. Traffic and exploitation of prostitution were also considered under the 1956 Supplementary Convention on the Abolition of Slavery, the Slave Trade and Institutions and Practices similar to Slavery. We could also mention here the 1923 International Convention for the Suppression of the Circulation and the Traffic in Obscene Publications, the "Convention Internationale relative à la Répression de la

---

[3] U.N. Commission on Human Rights, Resolution 1994/91

[4] "Sale of children", Report submitted by Vitit Muntarbhorn, Special Rapporteur appointed in accordance with resolution 1990/68 of the Commission on Human Rights. United Nations, Economic and Social Council, E/CN.4/1991/51, 28th January 1991.

Traite des Blanches" (Paris, 4th May 1910), the "Arrangement international en vue d'assurer une protection efficace contre le trafic criminel connu sous le nom de traite des Blanches" (Paris, 18th May 1904) or the "Convention internationale pour la suppression de la Traite des femmes et des enfants" (Genève, 30th September 1931).

But as the Special Rapporteur also points out: these conventions are not self-contained and should be placed in the setting of all the existing human rights instruments, including inter alia, the 1948 Universal Declaration of Human Rights, the 1966 Covenants on Civil and Political Rights and on Economic, Social and Cultural Rights, including also regional instruments such as the European Convention on Human Rights.

Only recently the concern for (sexual) exploitation has been expressed in very concrete and particular actions (c.q. legal instruments) for children. One could say that only recently the existence of social phenomena such as prostitution, pornography or trade in human beings has been considered amongst children too.

A. The UN Convention on the Rights of the Child (1989)

1. The Convention[5]
The UN Convention on the Rights of the Child was adopted unanimously by the UN General Assembly on November 20th 1989, exactly 30 years after the adoption of the Declaration on the Rights of the Child, and 10 years after the International Year of the Child. Less than one year later it entered into force, on September 2nd 1990. At the moment more than 95% of UN member States have already ratified this Convention.

The Convention can be regarded as a historic milestone. On the one hand, it is the culmination of a difficult struggle over a decade, aiming at improving children's situation in society; on the other hand, it is the beginning of a new way of dealing with children, enshrined in hard law by the international community. Since the turn of the century, law has reflected our relationship with children, founded on a view of them as creatures who are "not yet human beings", which has led to them being considered as mere objects of law. Over the last decade, however, more and more criticism has been levelled at this child-image. Gradually, but with increasing insistence, voices have been heard emphasizing that children are in fact first and foremost human beings, and that therefore our relationship with them has to be based on respect for them as people. In legal terms this means that children are to be regarded as individuals with fundamental human rights. This new child-image is becoming even more forceful and hence the present situation has become confused and, at times, even paradoxical. Indeed our relationship with children is still based on the dominant child-image, while, simultaneously, the new one is gaining influence.

---

[5] E.Verhellen: "Convention on the Rights of the Child", Leuven, Garant, 1994.

The Convention on the Rights of the Child reflects this situation. It reemphasizes that children too are bearers of all human rights (civil, political, economic, social and cultural rights) and moreover, they have, because of their particular vulnerability, the right to special protection.

2. *Child Prostitution – Child Pornography – Sale of Children*

The entire Convention is of course very relevant, also in the context of child prostitution, child pornography and sale of children. The children concerned by those phenomena should be considered first of all as human beings. Their exploitation is of course a reason for giving them extra attention.

With respect to this particular vulnerability, articles 11 (illicit transfer and non return), 16 (protection of privacy), 19 (protection from abuse and neglect), 21 (adoption), 22 (refugee children), 32 (child labour), 34 (sexual exploitation), 35 (sale, trafficking and abduction), 36 (other forms of exploitation) and article 39 (rehabilitative care) can especially be focused upon.

The articles directly concerned with child prostitution, child pornography and sale of children are articles 34 and 35.

3. *Article 34*

Article 34 reads as follows:

> States Parties undertake to protect the child from all forms of sexual exploitation and sexual abuse. For these purposes States Parties shall in particular take all appropriate national, bilateral and multilateral measures to prevent:
> a. the inducement or coercion of a child to engage in any unlawful sexual activity;
> b. the exploitative use of children in prostitution or other unlawful sexual activity;
> c. the exploitative use of children in pornographic performances and materials.

When we consider the "Travaux Préparatoires" on this particular article of the Convention, a number of interesting observations can be made.

The protection of children against sexual exploitation and their protection against sale and traffic was initially considered in one and the same article. The mere fact that children are also sold or trafficked for other reasons than sexual exploitation explains why finally, it was decided to elaborate two seperate articles. The problem of sale or traffic of children is wider in scope than that of sexual exploitation. Children are subjected to sale or traffic for many reasons: economic exploitation, sexual exploitation and sexual abuse, as well as for reasons of adoption or labour.[6]

---

[6] S. Detrick: "The United Nations Convention on the Rights of the Child.", Dordrecht, Martinus Nijhoff Publishers, 1992, p. 430.

Sexual exploitation was initially considered also with other forms of exploitation. The initial proposal read: "The States Parties to this Convention undertake to protect the child against all forms of exploitation, particularly sexual exploitation..." The Working Group however decided to consider the different forms of exploitation separately. Therefore the initial proposal gave rise to three articles (34, 35 and 36) with the provision of economic exploitation (child labour) already adopted before.

Reference was also made to the International Covenant on Economic, Social and Cultural Rights (1966) and its article 10 in which *social* exploitation is considered. It was said that it would be a step backwards with regard to the Covenant, if the Convention on the Rights of the Child wouldn't consider social exploitation either. Without mentioning it explicitly, social exploitation is now considered under article 36: "other forms of exploitation".

A clear distinction was made between sexual abuse within the family, considered under article 19 of the Convention and sexual exploitation outside the family. Sexual exploitation having a more commercial connotation...[7] Interesting too is the fact that in the final text, no reference is made anymore to the inclusion under "appropriate measures" of penalties or other sanctions to ensure the effective enforcement of the article. It is however not clear why this initial provision was deleted.

Some member States wanted to condemn explicitly the printing, distribution and sale of pornographic photography and materials. While no delegation had opposed to the substance of the proposal, a majority supported the view that the prevention of those activities was covered in the text of article 34.

A last but certainly not the least important observation has to do with the discussions on what should be considered unlawful within the sexual activities of children. A number of member States clearly emphasized that "the purpose of the article was *not to regulate the sexual life of children but rather to combat the sexual exploitation of children* on the basis of concrete examples". One of the main questions debated in this respect was whether or not children's sexual practices could be lawful. It was said for example that the Convention could not declare unlawful sexual practices between husband and wife under the age of 18.

4. Article 35
Article 35 of the Convention reads:

States Parties shall take all appropriate national, bilateral and multilateral measures to prevent the abduction, the sale of or traffic in children for any purpose or in any form.

It might be important to remember that the issue of sale of children was considered in a separate article because the phenomenon is not exclusively linked to child prostitution and child pornography (cf. supra).

---

[7] S. Detrick, op.cit.,p. 434.

B. *A Special Rapporteur on the Sale of Children, Child Prostitution and Child Pornography from 1990*

At its 46th session, the Commission on Human Rights adopted a resolution on "Sale of Children", recommended by the Sub-Commission on the Prevention of Discrimination and the Protection of Minorities.[8] By this resolution, the Commission on Human Rights decided a.o. to appoint a Special Rapporteur to consider matters regarding the sale of children, child prostitution and child pornography, including the problem of the adoption of children for commercial purposes. On September 10th 1990 Vitit Muntarbhorn was appointed as Special Rapporteur. In the beginning of 1995, he was replaced by Ms. Calcetas-Santos. The mandate concerns adoption, bonded labour, child prostitution, child pornography and organ transplantation.[9]

Up to now the Special Rapporteur has presented 5 reports.[10] A questionnaire has been sent to all UN member States and 4 field visits have been made (Nepal, The Netherlands, Australia and Brazil). It is not the intention of this text to examine these reports in detail. We have to limit ourselves to a number of summarizing observations which are made throughout the reports.

Throughout the reports, a large number of recommendations are made concerning[11]:

1. Social mobilization/education/sensitization
2. The Child/Community/Social Welfare
3. Development strategies
4. Legal measures
5. Law enforcement
6. Research/information collation
7. International cooperation/coordination
8. National cooperation/coordination
9. Adoption

Key-issues in those different recommendations are:
- the attention for both, the structural "demand" for children and the structural "supply" of children;
- a permanent attention for the root causes, such as poverty, the fragmentation of the family, gender discrimination, cultural practices such as the persistent point of view that children are the chattels of their parents;

---

[8] Sub-Commission Resolution 1989/42 Commission Resolution 1990/68 Economic and Social Council Decision 1990/240

[9] "Sale of children". Report submitted..., op.cit., p. 4.

[10] E/CN.4/1991/51   E/CN.4/1992/55   and   Add.1   E/CN.4/1993/67   and   Add.1 E/CN.4/1994/84 and Add.1 A/49/478–5 October 1994

[11] Recommendations by the Special Rapporteur on the Sale of Children, Child Prostitution and Child Pornography. A thematic analysis 1991–1994. Geneva, NGO Group for the Convention on the Rights of the Child, Sub-group on sexual exploitation, November 1994.

– the need for a multi-faceted and comprehensive approach; the need for a pro-active rather than a re-active approach;
– laws alone will never eradicate and/or prevent the phenomena ("it requires a whole variety of social, economic, political and budgetary interventions to bolster the law as a means to an end and not an end in itself"[12]);
– the observance of poor implementation of legislation;
– the importance of the non-governmental sector.

The first Special Rapporteur resigned from his post in October 1994. The lack of resources put at his disposal was one of the main causes.

C. Programme of Action for the Prevention of Sale of Children, Child Prostitution and Child Pornography (1992)

1. Background

The UN Commission on Human Rights, in its Resolution 1989/35, endorsed the programme of work of the Working Group on Contemporary Forms of Slavery for the period 1989–1991. This programme of work[13] included 3 main themes to be discussed in the successive years: prevention of the sale of children, of child prostitution and of child pornography (1989); eradication of the exploitation of child labour and debt bondage (1990) and prevention of traffic in persons and of the exploitation of the prostitution of others (1991).

The Working Group on Contemporary Forms of Slavery, having examined at great length the main theme of the 1989 session, concluded that urgent action was required to prevent these abuses and proposed a (draft) programme of action for prevention of sale of children, child prostitution and child pornography.[14] Parallel and complementary to the formulation of this (draft) programme of action, the Working Group at the same time recommended the appointment of a Special Rapporteur of the Commission on Human Rights to consider matters regarding the sale of children, child prostitution and child pornography, including the adoption of children for commercial purposes (cf. supra).

"The deep concern being expressed about the information on world-wide occurrences of the sale of children, child prostitution and child pornography and the call for measures to prevent these practices by United Nations human rights bodies, should be viewed in conjunction with the greater international attention focused on children's rights in general."[15] In its comments on the draft Programme of action, Defence for Children-International expressed

---

[12] "Sale of children." Report..., op.cit., p. 6.

[13] E/CN.4/Sub.2/1988/32

[14] E/CN.4/Sub.2/1991/41 and Corr.1

[15] Report of the Sub-Commission on Prevention of Discrimination and Protection of Minorities An analytical summary of comments received by the Secretary-General on the Draft Programme of Action for prevention of sale of children, child prostitution and child pornography E/CN.4/1991/50, 28th January 1991, p. 3.

the feeling that "it might be premature and somewhat illogical to proceed with the approval of a Programme of Action in this field prior to becoming aware of the findings of the Special Rapporteur (...). We would therefore urge that the Commission on Human Rights postpone any decision in this regard until the Special Rapporteur's conclusions and recommendations can be incorporated."[16]

However, this important remark was not taken into consideration nor by the Sub-Commission, nor by the Human Rights Commission. The Programme of Action was finally adopted in 1992.[17]

The decision of the Commission of Human Rights included 2 Programmes of Action. Besides the Programme of Action for the Prevention of the Sale of Children, Child Prostitution and Child Pornography, a Programme of Action for the Elimination of the Exploitation of Child Labour was adopted. Moreover, at the same meeting of the Human Rights Commission, it was decided to extend the mandate of the Special Rapporteur on Sale of Children, Child Prostitution and Child Pornography for another 3 years. The Special Rapporteur initially being nominated for a period of 2 years (cf. supra).

2. Content

The Programme of Action contains different chapters, each of them indicating an area of major concern for the prevention and the eradication of the phenomena. Without going into detail, we want to list here the different chapters and to present some of the concrete provisions.

a. General. "The sale of children, child prostitution and child pornography cannot be justified by reason of poverty or underdevelopment. Besides the long-term action required to treat the underlying causes and thus prevent these phenomena in the future, it is essential that States take urgent and immediate measures to reduce the dangers that children face" (article 10).

b. Information. "...teaching that culture and traditions which encourage these forms of child abuse are contrary to international norms for the protection of children" (article 12f).

c. Education. "All educational efforts should be based on universal ethical principles including the recognition of the integrity of the family and of every child's fundamental rights to the integrity of his or her own body and the protection of his or her own identity..." (article 21).

"In all educational measures, care should be taken to avoid both underplaying and sensationalizing these issues..." (article 23).

---

[16] E/CN.4/1991/50/Add.1, 30th January 1991, p. 6.

[17] Decision of the Sub-Commission on Prevention of Discrimination and Protection of Minorities (Decision 1991/113 of 29th August 1991); Decision of the Commission on Human Rights (Decision 1992/74 of 5th March 1992).

d. Legal measures and law enforcement. "The Convention on the Rights of the Child provides protection against trafficking in, sale and sexual exploitation of children. States are encouraged to become parties to the Convention at the earliest possible date. For its implementation within States, national institutions composed of representatives of public agencies, non-governmental organizations and associations should be established to coordinate action and to protect children and their rights" (article 27).

"States are urged to take all necessary measures to ensure that persons involved in trafficking in, sale or sexual exploitation of children are punished or extradited to other countries" (article 30).

e. Social measures and development assistance. "...Priority should be given to formulating a family policy to prevent abuse and to policies aimed at improving the social, economic and working conditions of girls and women in general, and of the poorest girls and women in particular. Local community-based projects, including collective self-help projects should also be encouraged" (article 32).

f. Rehabilitation and reintegration. "Rehabilitation and reintegration programmes using an interdisciplinary approach should be established to assist children who have been victims and their families..." (article 34).

g. International coordination. "A special intergovernmental task force should be set up at the regional level to assist Governments in devising ways and means of checking the phenomena...; national level commissions should plan new measures to address these problems in cooperation with concerned non-governmental organizations" (article 36).

h. Trafficking in and sale of children. This chapter includes particular attention for child abduction (article 38), transplantation of organs (article 39), refugee children (article 40) and adoption (articles 41–42).

i. Child prostitution. This chapter includes attention for incest and sexual abuse within the family, as a possible cause of prostitution (article 46), sex tourism (articles 47–48) and the possible problems with military bases or troops stationed on foreign territory (article 49).

j. Child pornography. "States who have not yet done so are urged to enact legislation making it a crime to produce, distribute or possess pornographic material involving children" (article 53).

k. Follow-up. "States are invited to consider this Programme of Action in relation to the Plan of Action for Implementing the World Declaration on the Survival, Protection and Development of Children in the 1990s and to the implementation of the Convention on the Rights of the Child" (article 57).

States are moreover requested to inform periodically the Sub-Commission on the Prevention of Discrimination and the Protection of Minorities, of the measures adopted to implement the Programme of Action and on the efficacy of such measures. The Sub-Commission has to submit every two years a report to the Human Rights Commission. The Commission will examine the question of the implementation of the Programme of Action in order to evaluate the progress made (cf. infra).

3. Monitoring

At its fiftieth session, the UN Commission on Human Rights discussed for the first time the reports submitted by different States (21 in total), UN bodies (3) and other intergovernmental organizations (1) and non-governmental organizations (1).[18]

The different reports especially tell us about the existing or draft legislations and the jurisprudence in the different countries. Hardly anything is said about the phenomena themselves. However, it is confirmed that:

- the phenomena do exist, but are hardly discovered and thus little is known. In Brazil for example, the phenomenon of sale of children for the purpose of adoption was raised officially in 1973; in Sri Linka the same phenomenon has been known for about 20 years;
- the phenomena are universal; some States firmly claim the non-existence in their country (e.g.Iraq); It is also interesting to quote the Bolivian report here: "Le délit de vente d'enfants n'existe pas dans la législation bolivienne. La pratique a cependant été dénoncée par certains organes de presse, qui ont publié des articles selon lesquels des "ventes" se produiraient dans la plus grande clandestinité lors de la remise d'enfants à des couples étrangers. Toutefois ces articles n'ont pas été corrobés par le dépôt de plaintes en bonne et due forme....".[19]
- often, appropriate legislation is (totally) absent; in a number of countries, new legislations (have been) are being developed recently (f.ex. Germany, Brazil);
- little is done about prevention while mere repression seems very ineffective;
- international agreements are important; note however that e.g. Argentina raised objections against paragraphs b), c), d) and e) of article 21 of the Convention of the Rights of the Child, because of their "non applicability in those countries where no mechanism exists for the legal protection of children concerned by international adoption".

---

[18] – United Nations, Economic and Social Council, 8th July 1993, E/CN.4/Sub.2/1993/31 – United Nations, Economic and Social Council, 23th June 1993, E/CN.4/Sub.2/1993/31/Add.1

[19] U.N. Document E/CN.4/Sub.2/1993/31/Add.1, op.cit., p. 6

D. Other Recommendations of United Nations Bodies

1. Introduction
The phenomena of sale of children, child prostitution and child pornography are directly or indirectly object of still many other recommendations of UN bodies or international UN-related intergovernmental initiatives.

2. The World Declaration on the Survival, Protection and Development of Children and Plan of Action
In 1990 the United Nations Children's Fund organised a "World Summit for Children". On 30th September 1990 an important number of Heads of State agreed on a "World Declaration on the Survival, Protection and Development of Children" and a "Plan of Action for Implementing the World Declaration". The Declaration and the Plan of Action take into consideration, though only indirectly, the phenomena of sale of children, child pornography and child prostitution (see e.g. the chapters on child health, on children in especially difficult circumstances and on alleviation of poverty and revitalization of economic growth).

Articles 8 and 9 explain the overall opportunity for the World Declaration as follows:

"Together, our nations have the means and the knowledge to protect the lives and to diminish enormously the suffering of children, to promote the full development of their human potential and to make them aware about their needs, rights and opportunities. The Convention on the Rights of the Child provides a new opportunity to make respect for children's rights and welfare truly universal.

Recent improvements in the international political climate can facilitate this task. Through international co-operation and solidarity it should now be possible to achieve concrete results in many fields – to revitalize economic growth and development, to protect the environment, to prevent the spread of fatal and cripling diseases and to achieve greater social and economic justice. The current moves towards disarmament also mean that significant resources could be released for purposes other than military ones. Improving the wellbeing of children must be a very high priority when these resources are reallocated."

The Plan of Action enumerates concrete short- and long-term steps to be taken in order to achieve the set goals by the year 2000. All of them can be relevant for our subject but we find no concrete strategies exclusively linked to the prevention and eradication of child prostitution, child pornography and sale of children.

3. The Committee on the Rights of the Child
At its fourth session, the Committee on the Rights of the Child devoted its 95th and 96th meetings, on 4th October 1993, to a general discussion on

the economic exploitation of children. "The decision to consider this topic reflected the importance of the issue in the framework of the promotion and the protection of the rights of the child, the urgency of creating awareness and raising concern at the growing number of children in situations of economic exploitation, the need for integrated and concerted action by Governments, United Nations bodies active in the field of the rights of the child, as well as the decisive role the Convention of the Rights of the Child could play in that regard."[20]

A set of recommendations have been adopted for follow-up initiatives, designed to improve the system of prevention, protection and rehabilitation regarding children in situations of economic exploitation, including the phenomena of child prostitution, child pornography and sale of children. Maybe we can limit ourselves here to the very challenging introduction to these recommendations:

"The general discussion on the economic exploitation of children reflected the important holistic approach to the human rights of children stressed in the Convention on the Rights of the Child. In this spirit, the Committee on the Rights of the Child recalls that all rights are indivisible and interrelated, each and all of them being inherent to the human dignity of the child. The implementation of each right set forth in the Convention, as is the case of the right to be protected from economic exploitation, should therefore take into account the implementation of, and respect for, all the other rights of the child."[21]

The same ideas will be repeated in the Committee's comments on a possible draft optional protocol to the Convention on the Rights of the Child (cf. infra).

4. UN Commission on Crime Prevention and Criminal Justice

The issues of sale of children, child prostitution and child pornography are also considered within the UN bodies dealing with crime prevention and criminal justice.

In the field of Juvenile Justice, the United Nations adopted a number of standards and guidelines laid down in 3 documents:
- The Standard Minimum Rules for the Administration of Juvenile Justice (the "Beijing"-rules)[22]
- The Guidelines for the Prevention of Juvenile Delinquency (the Riyadh-guidelines)[23]
- The Minimum Rules for Juveniles Deprived of their Liberty[24]

---

[20] United Nations General Assembly, Document A/49/41 See also Report of the fifth session of the Committtee of the Rights of the Child. Document CRC/C/24 of 8th March 1994.

[21] A/49/41, op.cit., p.3

[22] General Assembly Resolution 40/33

[23] General Assembly Resolution 45/112

[24] General Assembly Resolution 45/113

Though these standards mainly deal with the juvenile delinquent, some of the provisions of e.g. the Guidelines for prevention are relevant for the phenomena of sale of children, etc. Article 26 of the Riyadh-guidelines states: "Schools should serve as resource and referral centers for the provision of medical, counselling and other services to young persons, particularly those with special needs and suffering from abuse, neglect, victimization and exploitation."

In 1990, at the 8th UN Congress for the Prevention of Delinquency and Treatment of Offenders, two other resolutions were adopted more directly linked with the child-victim. One resolution deals with "Domestic violence"[25]; the other is entitled "Instrumental use of children in criminal activities".[26] This last resolution mainly stresses the importance and the urgent necessity of information gathering on the issue, emphasizing that "categories of children such as those who are runaway, vagrant, wayward or streetchildren are targets for exploitation, including seduction into drug trafficking and abuse, prostitution, pornography, theft, burglary, begging and homicide for reward."

An expert meeting was held in Rome, from 8th – 10th May 1992, where an important number of recommendations were adopted in order to give a more concrete impetus to the prevention and eradication of the instrumental use of children in criminal activities. For example in pursuance of General Assembly Resolution 45/115, operative paragraph 1(c) by which Member States and the Secretary-General were requested to take measures in combatting criminality in view of ensuring that appropriate sanctions are applied against adults who are the instigators and authors of crimes, rather than against the children involved who themselves are victims of criminality by virtue of their being exposed to crime, it was recommended that:

(i) in all aspects of the criminal justice system, promotion should be encouraged of the regard of a child as a human being and a member of society with full human and legal rights, and not simply as an object of care, protection and control...; (...)

(vi) ways should be found to make legal aid and assistance more accessible to child victims of exploitation; (...).[27]

Another expert meeting on the application of human rights standards in the field of the administration of juvenile justice, held in Vienna from 30th October till 4th November 1994, also considered the phenomena of sale of children, child prostitution and child pornography. Chapters IV and V of the Recommendations resulting from this meeting of experts deal especially with "Instrumental use of children and juveniles by adults in and for criminal activities" and "Exploitation of children". Another chapter of a more general concern ("Coordination and technical cooperation") also implies important recommendations for the policies concerned here. For example the urgent

---

[25] General Assembly Resolution 45/114

[26] General Assembly Resolution 45/115

[27] "Uso dei Minori in Attivita Criminali", in, Esperienze di Giustizia Minorile, 1992, Anno XXXIX, 1992, nr. 2.

need was recognized for close cooperation between all bodies and mechanisms concerned with the field of juvenile justice, including the Committee on the Rights of the Child, the Crime Prevention and Criminal Justice Branch, the Centre for Human Rights and Unicef.[28]

The IXth UN Congress on Crime Prevention and Treatment of Offenders, to be held in Cairo from 29th April till 8th May 1995 has on its agenda a particular interest in the issue of victims of crime. A draft resolution is being prepared by Belgium on "Elimination of violence against children", focusing on the child as victim of crime in general and therefore also on the phenomena of sale of children, child prostitution and child pornography.

E. *Other Relevant International Instruments*

1. Introduction
Sale of children, child prostitution and child pornography have not exclusively been dealt with within the United Nations. Many other international bodies have (recently) also taken these phenomena directly or indirectly into consideration.

We give here only a few examples.

2. The Hague Conference on International Private Law
The Hague Conference on International Private Law is an intergovernmental organization, founded in 1893 in view of "the progressive unification of private international law" (art. 1 of its statutes). 63 States are actually member of this organization. The first international convention on private international law concerning minors is "The Treaty on the conflict of laws and jurisdiction concerning guardianship of minors" (1900). Conventions which are of direct interest for our theme here are "The Convention on competent authorities and applicable law in child protection" (1961, own translation of the only in french existing official text; this convention is under review for the moment); "The Convention on Jurisdiction, Applicable Law and Recognition of Decrees Relating to Adoptions" (1965), "The Convention on the Civil Aspects of Child Abduction" (1980) and the very recent "Convention on International Co-operation and Protection of Children in Respect of Intercountry Adoption" (1993).

International adoption is one of the items of particular concern in the discussions on sale of children. The Hague Convention of 1993 does not aim at creating new rights for the children concerned. It rather aims at better organizing the cooperation between States involved in a case of international adoption. The Convention contains a preambula and 6 chapters. One of the objectives is: "to establish safeguards to ensure that intercountry adoptions take place in the best interests of the child and with respect for his or her

---

[28] "Children in detention: application of human rights standards" Vienna, Federal Ministry of Environment, Youth and Family, 1995.

fundamental rights as recognized by international law" (art. 1,a). Article 4 determines the conditions which should be met in a case of international adoption: the child has to be adoptable; the adoption has to be in the interest of the child (placement of the child within the State of origin has been given due consideration); the persons, institutions and authorities whose consent is necessary for adoption, have been counselled...and duly informed of the effects of their consent; the consents have not been induced by payment or compensation of any kind;... The consent of the child can also be requested (art. 4,d): "...have ensured, having regard to the age and the degree of maturity of the child, that (1) he or she has been counselled and duly informed of the effects of the adoption and of his or her consent to the adoption, where such is required, (2) consideration has been given to the child's wishes and opinions, (3) the child's consent to the adoption, where such consent is required, has been given freely and unconditionally, in the required legal form and expressed or evidenced in writing, and (4) such consent has not been induced by payment or compensation of any kind."

Every contracting State has to charge a Central Authority with the coordination of the international cooperation. The Central Authority has "to provide information as to the laws of their State concerning adoption..."; "to keep one another informed about the operation of the Convention..." This Central Authority, or organizations recognized by the contracting State, will also be in charge of the practical realization of an international adoption (art. 6–13).

The fourth chapter of the Convention deals with the procedure: the different steps to be taken when adults want to adopt a child from another country. The sixth and last chapter contains a number of provisions which are of importance for the legal protection of children to be adopted. For example article 32 states: "No one shall derive improper financial or other gain from an activity related to an intercountry adoption".

For the moment, only four States, Mexico – Romenia – Cyprus – Sri Lanka, have ratified the Convention.

3. Interpol

At the opening ceremony of the new Headquarters building of the Interpol General Secretariat in Lyons in 1989, the President of the French Republic expressed his concern about the violations of the rights of the child. This led to the adoption, a few days later, of Interpol General Assembly Resolution AGN/58/RES/15 which states that the General Secretariat, in close cooperation with the appropriate United Nations bodies, should carry out a study in view of proposing measures to improve international co-operation on offences against minors.

In view of the fact that so little information was available on this particular problem[29], the General Secreteriat prepared a questionnaire on the subject

---

[29] "It is clear that most offences committed against children, such as maltreatment or sexual abuse, are not international *per se*. Consequently, the General Secretariat is seldom

and circulated it to member States. It included questions on the scale of the problem; on methods used to prevent and identify offences of this nature, and on specific programmes being adopted by various countries in connection with offences against children. Replies were received from 53 member States. A number of specialists from different countries were invited to study the replies (27th – 30th October 1990). They produced a set of recommendations based upon answers to the questionnaire, and based on their own expertise. Since it was the first time that the ICPO-Interpol was dealing with the subject of child victims and, indeed, with the subject of victims at all, the aim was to formulate recommendations that covered all the various aspects of the problem.

The Recommendations were adopted by the ICPO-Interpol General Assembly at its 61st Session (November 1992). The Resolution contains 3 main chapters (I. General considerations; II. Recommendations on general and preventive measures and III. Recommendations on Law Enforcement measures). We give here some examples of the concrete provisions:

I.B. "The approach of combatting offences against children should be victim-oriented".

II.A.1. "It is recommended that each ICPO-Interpol member country keeps statistics on child victims..."

II.B.1. "Prevention measures must not place a burden on children or encroach their rights."

II.B.3. "The ICPO-Interpol is asked to establish contacts with the United Nations to examine the possibilities of co-operation in matters relating to the prevention of crimes against children."

II.C.6. "It is strongly recommended that national police forces appoint at least one specialist liaison officer whose duties would include:
  – guaranteeing and protecting the rights and interests of children throughout the proceedings,
  – acting as intermediary for the flow of information between national and international agencies."

II.D.1. "Every police officer should receive training on human rights and basic training on dealing with child victims."

II.E.2. "Member countries are urged to conduct research on unreported offences against children."

Chapter III deals with particular problems such as child pornography, sex tourism, international adoption, child prostitution,...

---

provided with relevant information on that particular domain. Furthermore, offences of a more international nature, such as trafficking in children for adoption purposes and child pornography, are also scarcely reported to the General Secretrariat. This may be because the information is communicated bilaterally without passing through the General Secretariat; it could also be due to a lack of awareness or even interest on the part of some member States. The General Secretariat is endeavouring to obtain as much information as possible from other sources such as non-governmental organizations and the media, in order to gain a clear picture of the situation." ICPO-Interpol, 61st General Assembly Session, Dakar 4th – 10th November 1992, Report on Offences against Children, p. 1 (Doc. AGN/61/RAP. No. 16).

After the adoption of this resolution by the ICPO-Interpol General Assembly, a Standing Working Party was established which has already gathered 6 times. In close cooperation with the United Nations Human Rights Center and the United Nations Crime Prevention and Criminal Justice Branch, a training programme for law enforcement officials on "Juveniles, Human Rights and the Administration of Criminal Justice" is being prepared.

4. Council of Europe
a. Introduction.   The Council of Europe is an intergovernmental organization, established in 1949. Every European country can become member of the Council if it accepts the principles of individual and political freedom and respect for the law and if it guarantees the human rights and the fundamental freedoms on its territory. The European Convention on Human Rights (4th November 1950) is without any doubt its major realization up to now. The Convention guarantees the classical human rights, i.e. the civil and political rights. They are object of a juridical control through the European Commission and the European Court on Human Rights. Today, the Council of Europe counts 33 member States.

The Council of Europe has also been active in the field of the rights of the child and juvenile justice, and mainly within this context it has been involved in the issues of traffic in children, child pornography and child prostitution.

Some of the recommendations/resolutions of the Council of Europe have a binding character for its member States (cf. the European Convention on Human Rights or the European Social Charter). Some other conventions are also relevant for the problems of sale of children, child prostitution and child pornography. For example the "European Convention on the Adoption of Children" (1967) or the "European Convention on the Repatriation of Children" (1970). Other provisions are rather recommendations. Both, the Committee of Ministers and the Parliamentary Assembly have adopted recommendations directly concerned with sale of children, child prostitution and child pornograghy.

b. The Parliamentary Assembly.   In 1987, the Parliamentary Assembly discussed a comprehensive study made by one of his members (Mr. Stoffelen) on the traffic in children and other forms of child exploitation.[30] The study itself was a consequence of Recommendation 1044(1986) on International Crime in which the Parliamentary Assembly recommended the Council of Ministers to invite the governments of the member States to co-operate in a study of and action against the trade in children. The report itself is very interesting because it contains an important chapter on the factual situation concerning trade in children and other forms of exploitation of children. It was one of the first more or less comprehensive studies ever made on the subject.

---

[30]   Council of Europe, Parliamentary Assembly, 10th September 1987, Doc. 5777.

However not without difficulties.[31] The study dealt with trade in children for various purposes: (illegal) adoption, prostitution, pornography, child-labour and slavery-like forms of exploitation.

This study finally resulted in a Recommendation of the Parliamentary Assembly.[32] Some of the provisions are claiming an overall and pro-active approach of the phenomena, e.g. "to inform educators and youth of the rights of the child and incorporate human rights education in school curricula at all levels". Others are linked to a more particular problem such as "the elaboration of a code of conduct and guidelines for individuals proposing to undertake the interstate movement of unaccompanied minors" or "condemn any policy of commercial or industrial competition based on exploitation of child labour, and ensure that the activities of national and international agencies working in the field of development are designed in such a way as to have a positive effect on the rights and the interests of children throughout the world".
Some other relevant recommendations of the Parliamentary Assembly are:
  – Recommendation 561(1969) on the Protection of Minors against Ill-treatment;
  – Recommendation 874(1979) on a European Charter on the Rights of the Child;
  – Recommendation 1121(1990) on the Rights of Children;
  – Recommendation 963(1983) on Cultural and Educational Means of reducing Violence.

c. The Committee of Ministers.   In 1991, the Committee of Ministers adopted a Recommendation on Sexual exploitation, Pornography and Prostitution of and Trafficking in Children and Young Adults.[33] One of the considerations for this recommendation is "that sexual exploitation of children and young adults for profit-making purposes in the form of pornography, prostitution and traffic of human beings has assumed new and alarming dimensions at national and international level". This consideration has to do with a study on the phenomena carried out by a group of experts in the member States of the Council of Europe.[34]

---

[31] "During the preparation of this report I discovered how difficult it was to gather information on this subject. It seems as if the problem is scarcely heard of in our member States. One might be inclined to conclude that, apart from the attention drawn to a specific incident once a year, the problem hardly exists." Council of Europe, Doc. 5777, op. cit., p. 3. A comparable observation was made in a more recent study of the Council of Europe on streetchildren. Council of Europe, 1994.

[32] Council of Europe, Parliamentary Assembly, Recommendation 1065(1987) on the traffic in children and other forms of child exploitation.

[33] Council of Europe, Committee of Ministers, Recommendation R(91)11

[34] 'Sexual exploitation, pornography, prostitution and traffic involving children and young adults' Council of Europe, 1993. Also this study starts with the observation that: "Ce n'est que récemment que l'exploitation et l'abus sexuels d'enfants et de jeunes adultes ont été reconnus comme problèmes sociaux qui appellent une action urgente aux plans national et international.

Recommendation R(91)11 counts 3 chapters. The first chapter deals with recommendations at a national level. A distinction is made between General Measures (public awareness, education and information; collection and exchange of information; prevention, detection and assistance; criminal law and criminal procedure), measures regarding pornography involving children, measures regarding the prostitution of children and young adults and measures regarding the trafficking in children and young adults. The second chapter deals with international aspects and the third with research priorities.

Some recommendations:
- "to provide for special conditions at hearings involving children who are victims or witnesses of sexual exploitation, in order to diminish the traumatising effects of such hearings and to increase the credibility of their statements while respecting their dignity";
- "to encourage and support the setting up of mobile welfare units for the surveillance of, or establishment of contact with, children at risk, particularly streetchildren, in order to assist them to return to their families. If possible, and if necessary direct them to the appropriate agencies for health care, training or education";
- "to introduce rules on extraterritorial jurisdiction in order to allow the prosecution and punishment of nationals who have committed offences concerning sexual exploitation of children and young adults outside the national territory, or, if applicable, review existing rules to that effect, and improve international co-operation to that end".

Some other recommendations/resolutions of the Committee of Ministers which are relevant for our subject, are:
- Recommendation R(79)17 concerning the Protection of Children against Ill-treatment;
- Recommendation R(85)4 on Violence in the Family;
- Recommendation R(87)21 on Assistance to Victims and the Prevention of Victimization;
- Resolution (77)33 on Placement of Children;
- Recommendation R(90)2 on Social Measures concerning Violence within the Family.

F. Non-governmental Initiatives
Non-governmental organizations have played and still play a very important role in the process of raising social awareness on phenomena such as sale

---

De fait, dans ce domaine, toutes les phases dans l'évolution d'un problème social, identifiées par les spécialistes en sciences sociales, se sont succédé. Il y a eu, tout d'abord, la phase de la négation ou de la minimisation du problème ... La deuxième phase a été celle où l'exploitation et l'abus sexuels d'enfants et de jeunes adultes sont attribués à quelques déviants ... La troisième phase consistait à faire des reproches à la victime ... Enfin, certains pays ont atteint la phase finale où il y a émergence de groupes de pression et de mouvements sociaux luttant contre l'exploitation sexuelle d'enfants et de jeunes adultes. Ils contribuent largement à sensibiliser le législateur, les autorités chargées de l'application de la loi et le grand public." (pp. 17–18) of children, child prostitution and child pornography. International organizations such as Defence for Children-International, Rädda Barnen, ECPAT (End Child Prostitution in Asian Tourism)[35], Terre des Hommes, the International Catholic Child Bureau and International Abolitionist Federation have brought the issues to the attention of the large public and of the national and international authorities.

Defence for Children-International, Terre des Hommes and the International Abolitionist Federation are involved in a criminal proceeding against the author of the Spartacus guide[36], as civil party for the children concerned. The criminal proceedings started in November 1994 in the Criminal Court of Turnhout (Belgium).

In 1996 ECPAT organizes a World Congress on Child Prostitution, Child Pornography and Sale of Children in Sweden.

II. The Mandate

A. The Mandate

After this rather large introduction, giving however only a brief and far from complete overview of existing international proposals for policy and even binding legal instruments aiming at the prevention and eradication of child prostitution, child pornography and sale of children, we concentrate again on the decision of the UN Human Rights Commission to establish a supplementary Working Group for studying new options for policies in this field. The Working Group had the following mandate:

    a. elaborating *guidelines* for a *possible* draft optional protocol to the Convention on the Rights of the Child on the sale of children, child prostitution and child pornography

    b. elaborating *basic measures* for the prevention and eradication of these phenomena

    c. – as a matter of priority

    – in close cooperation with the Special Rapporteur on Sale of Children, Child Prostitution and Child Pornography, and the Committee on the Rights of the Child.

B. The Opinion of the Committee of the Rights of the Child[37]

The Working Group had to work in close cooperation with the Committee on the Rights of the Child and the Special Rapporteur on Sale of Children, Child Pornography and Child Prostitution.

---

[35] Ron O'Grady: "The rape of the innocent", Auckland, Pace Publishing, 1994. Ron O'Grady: "The child and the tourist", Stockholm, Ecpat, 1992.

[36] The Spartacus guide is a guide with relevant information on where one can find homosexual- and children-prostitutes worldwide.

[37] Doc. E/CN.4/1994/WG.14/2/Add.1, pp. 9–10.

The Committee explained its view in a preparatory document sent to the Working Group. The Committee stresses the importance of a holistic approach of the rights of the child as the Convention on the Rights of the Child puts forward. The principles underlying the Convention are, for the Committee, an important tool in the efforts for preventing and eradicating the phenomena of sale of children, child prostitution and child pornography. The nearly universal ratification of the Convention is an extra element for an effective (international) policy.

The Committee concludes that it is very stongly convinced that priority should be given to the reinforcement of the application of already existing international standards.

The Special Rapporteur did not express his views to the Working Group through a separate document. His first reports could (should) entirely have been taken into consideration.

III. The First Session of the Working Group[38]

A. Date and Venue
The first session of the Working Group was held in Geneva (Palais des Nations) from 14th till 25th November 1994.

57 countries were represented, 3 United Nations bodies (UNICEF, UNHCR, UNESCO) and 9 Non-Governmental Organisations in consultative status with the UN Economic and Social Council.

Mr. Ivan Mora Godoy (Cuba) was elected Chairman-Rapporteur.

B. Guidelines for a Possible Optional Protocol
Guidelines were developed with respect to the *substance* of a possible optional protocol and with respect to *procedural* requirements.

1. Substance. Three documents were presented to the Working Group: a document prepared by the French delegation, one by the Australian delegation and one by the Chairman-Rapporteur.

The French proposal, after it was redrafted in guidelines[39], was considered as the guiding document.

The final document contains 7 chapters and 3 additional provisions (on Non-discrimination, Reservations and Reporting). The different chapters deal with:

---

[38] Doc. E/CN.4/1994/WG.14/CRP.3–20 December 1994.

[39] The initial French proposal was entitled "Projet de Protocole Facultatif relatif à la lutte contre la vente des enfants, la prostitution des enfants et la pornographie impliquant des enfants" and was composed of a preambula and 14 articles. Several delegations pointed out in the general debate that the mandate of the Working Group was not to elaborate a draft optional protocol but only guidelines and that their governments were still opposing against such a protocol. The French delegation redrafted therefore its proposal in guidelines.

I. INTRODUCTION
II. DEFINITIONS
III. IMPLEMENTATION OF PERTINENT INSTRUMENTS
IV. PENALIZATION – COMPENSATION AND PROTECTION OF CHILDREN
V. INTERNATIONAL COOPERATION AND COORDINATION
VI. ASSISTANCE AND REHABILITATION
VII. INFORMATION – EDUCATION AND PARTICIPATION

The final document was adopted ad referendum with a number of guidelines in brackets on which no consensus was obtained.

The chapter on penalization gave rise, as could be expected[40], to the heaviest discussions. The final text reads:

> 1. Les Etats s'engagent à prévoir des infractions pénales appropriées pour prévenir et sanctionner la vente d'enfants, la prostitution et la pornographie impliquant des enfants, selon leur gravité.

> 2. The States should address the problem to ensure that such offenders can be prosecuted either in the country where the offence was committed or in the country [where the perpetrators reside] or are nationals [or where the child victim is a national]. A corporation or other legal person can be prosecuted if consistent with the legal system of a State. This would require consideration by States of measures to prosecute [with due regard to the double criminality rule] their own nationals [or residents] for offences committed outside their territories or develop appropriate arrangements for extradition.

> 3. The States give due regard to the necessity or appropriateness of possibly expanding the scope of seizure and confiscation of proceeds of, and all equipment and other property used in the sale of children, child prostitution and child pornography, belonging to any natural person or [legal entities] or organizations responsible for these offences (...)

2. Procedural Guidelines

a) Two proposals were presented to the Working Group, one by the United States of America and one by Belgium. Both proposals were combined and read as follows:

  1. The provisions of any protocol should be clearly complementary to existing norms or instruments, or should define existing standards in a clearer or more binding fashion;

---

[40] Cf. the similar problem with the Convention for the Suppression of the Traffic in Persons and of the Exploitation of Prostitution of Others (1949), which can explain its limited number of ratifications, even today.

2. The provisions of any protocol should be adopted by consensus, if possible;
3. The contents of any protocol should be closely coordinated with the relevant work of the United Nations bodies and other international organizations involved in law enforcement and crime prevention;
4. Any protocol must use terms with clear and mutually understood meanings, so that the requirements of the protocol can be enacted into national legislation where required;
5. Any protocol should enjoy the greatest possible support of the Committee on the Rights of the Child;
6. Any protocol should enjoy the greatest possible support of major non-governmental organizations involved in protecting children and promoting their rights;
7. Any protocol should contribute to, and not detract from the United Nations' holistic approach to the problem of sexual exploitation of children;
8. Any protocol should be consistent with other efforts aiming at international cooperation in the field of protection of children;
9. Any protocol should be based on a sound understanding of the factual circumstances related to the sale of children, child prostitution and child pornography.

b) The need, and therefore the elaboration of procedural guidelines can be explained by the concern of a number of member States for an inflation of international instruments. A concern shared by the United Nations General Assembly itself in its Resolution 41/120 entitled "Setting international standards in the field of human rights". The importance of this Resolution was several times repeated also on other occasions.[41]

Also this resolution emphasizes that priority should be given to the effective implementation and monitoring of existing instruments. Only when those are proven to be clearly inappropriate, insufficient or ineffective, possible new standards could be taken into consideration.

c) The final text adopted ad referendum reads as follows:
1. A possible optional protocol should be developed in conformity with the guidelines contained in General Assembly Resolution 41/120 entitled "Settling international standards in the field of human rights".

---

[41] See e.g. the Vienna Declaration and Programme of Action, as adopted by the World Conference on Human Rights on 25th June 1993: "The World Conference on Human Rights, recognizing the need to maintain consistency with the high quality of existing international standards and to avoid proliferation of human rights instruments, reaffirms the guidelines relating to the elaboration of new international instruments contained in General Assembly resolution 41/120 of 4th December 1986 and calls on the United Nations Human Rights bodies, when considering the elaboration of new international standards, to keep those guidelines in mind, to consult with human rights treaty bodies on the necessity for drafting new standards..." Doc. A/CONF.157/23 – 12th July 1993.

2. A possible Protocol should make existing standards more effective.
3. A possible Protocol should be closely coordinated with the relevant work of the UN bodies and other international organizations involved in law enforcement and crime prevention.
4. A possible Protocol should attract broad international support and, to the greatest possible extent, take into account the views of relevant UN mechanisms and bodies and Non-Governmental Organizations concerned with the Sale of Children, Child Prostitution and Child Pornography.
5. A possible Protocol should reflect the factual circumstances related to sale of children, child prostitution and child pornography."

C. Basic Measures

During the first session, hardly any attention was given to this second aspect of the mandate "to elaborate basic measures for the prevention and the eradication of the phenomena".

A number of member States however recalled the importance of all the already existing recommendations and provisions in this field. The problem is, for these Sates not the lack of ideas about measures but rather the lack of effective implementation of the measures.

On the initiative of Belgium, a text has finally been adopted by the Working Group which emphasizes, as a matter of priority, the urgent and permanent need of the effective implementation on an international and national level of all the already existing proposals for basic measures for the prevention and the eradication of the phenomena of sale of children, child prostitution and child pornography. The text also requests that all the necessary means are immediately made available, at a national and international level, and through international cooperation for implementing those measures. The effectiveness of the measures should be evaluated permanently.

D. The UN Commission for Human Rights

The United Nations Commission for Human Rights considered the conclusions of the Working Group at its 51st session.

Cuba and the European Union introduced resolutions at this session which were directly relevant for the future work of the United Nations in the field of sale of children, child prostitution and child pornography.

The resolution presented by the European Union aimed at an extension of the mandate of the Special Rapporteur on Sale of Children, Child prostitution and Child Pornography with another 3 years.

Central in the Cuban proposal was the request that "the established open-ended intersessional Working Group of the Commission on Human Rights elaborate, as a matter of priority and in close cooperation with the Special Rapporteur and the Committee on the Rights of the Child, and on the basis of the guidelines submitted in its report, a draft optional protocol to the Convention on the Rights of the Child on the Sale of Children, Child Prostitution and Child Pornography, that will meet for two weeks before the 52nd session of the Commission on Human Rights".

The European and the Cuban proposal both were adopted by the UN Human Rights Commission. It has to be mentioned however that a vote was necessary before the Cuban resolution was adopted. Most of the developed countries withheld their votes[42].

IV. SOME OBSERVATIONS AND CONCLUDING REMARKS

A. Is There a Need for an Optional Protocol?

1. Are the Phenomena Increasing?
A first element which could explain the need for an optional protocol on sale of children, child prostitution and child pornography to the United Nations Convention on the Rights of the Child, could be the increase of the phenomena themselves. As we stated already in the introduction, there are probably too few indications which could prove this beyond any doubt. There is indeed more than enough evidence that the phenomena are important as well in quantity as in quality, but there is a lack of systematic and permanent information (gathering) which could allow us to make firm general statements about the phenomena or to make comparisons over time and/or space. As it is the case for many harsh situations children are facing, we are only very recently "discovering" phenomena such as sexual exploitation of children. The raise of the social consciousness however may not be confused with a possible raise of the phenomena themselves.

Of course it is important to have the possibility and all the means to prevent and to eradicate those situations we are already aware of today. We will study hereafter the pros and the cons of an optional protocol in this respect. However, if the international community wants to combat the phenomena of sale of children, child prostitution and child pornography in depth and not only on an ad hoc basis, policy should be based on well-founded and comprehensive information and knowledge. The establishment by the United Nations of a Special Rapporteur on Sale of Children, Child Prostitution and Child Pornography can be an important step towards a more comprehensive knowledge of the phenomenon. But also the Committee on the Rights of the Child, UNICEF and non-governmental organizations can play a crucial role here. Indeed, the Committee for example has through its duty of monitoring the application of the Children's Rights Convention, a privileged view of the overall situation of children worldwide and of the (legal) possibilities for improving the situation of children, also of those children in especially difficult circumstances.

---

[42] United Nations Economic and Social Council Doc. E/CN.4/1995/L.11/Add.6

2. Is There a Lack of (Legal) Provisions?

In point 2 of this article we presented a summary of existing (legal) provisions aiming exclusively or mainly at preventing and eradicating the phenomena of child prostitution, child pornography and sale of children. It is rather amazing to see how many intergovernmental and international bodies have already paid so much attention to the phenomena and have elaborated such an important number of policy recommendations. It is therefore not surprising to see that the Working Group decided, with respect to the second part of their mandate ("to elaborate basic measures") to reemphasize all those measures proposed already in one or another context rather than searching for new ones. It may be clear that there already exists an important (legal) framework which can allow (even compel) States to tackle immediately the phenomena of child prostitution, child pornography and sale of children, if they are willing to do so. It will be difficult probably fo find any new or other "magic" measure, which was not yet proposed. Besides those measures focusing particularly on the mentioned phenomena, it is important to take into consideration also those provisions aiming at improving the overall situation of children. Of course we should quote here once more the importance of the Convention on the Rights of the Child. It is maybe a bit early to believe that the Convention itself and all the other recommendations for preventing and eradicating the phenomena are ineffective or insufficient. A bit too early because these (legal) instruments are hardly adopted by the international community and hardly known to all the persons and institutions concerned.

3. Is There a Lack of Implementation and Effective Monitoring?

The main problem might be not the lack of measures but rather the lack of implementation and effective monitoring of what already exists. However this problem seems to exceed the policies for preventing and eradicating child prostitution, child pornography and sale of children. It seems to have more to do with international policy in general, and with the functioning of intergovernmental organizations such as the United Nations. Are we not looking for a nice excuse when we intend to draft an optional protocol on child prostitution, child pornography and sale of children? A new positive element for our image, telling the world that we are very busy coping with the problems, sitting in Geneva drafting nice intentions? For still how long will the community accept that the role of the international organizations is mainly focused on or limited to law-making, while very few is changing in the every day reality. It might be very important to think about new or existing mechanisms for implementing and monitoring the effective realization of all those beautiful intentions expressed once before. The question is whether or not an optional protocal can be of any help here.

4. Is There a Lack of Cooperation?

An important element for the process of implementation and monitoring is cooperation and networking. It is surprising to see that many organizations have developed, sometimes simultaneously, proposals for combatting child prostitution, child pornography and sale of children without any consultation or even without knowing the mutual initiatives one from another. This problem too goes certainly beyond dealing with child prostitution, child pornography and sale of children. Cooperation and networking are rather structural challenges which exceed probably the possibilities of an optional protocol.

B. What Could Be the Advantages of an Optional Protocol?

Most of the existing measures at the level of the United Nations are translated in recommendations rather than in binding provisions. The United Nations Convention on the Rights of the Child being an important exception. An optional protocol could therefore help in making recommendations more binding for the member States or making the existing binding articles of the Convention more precise and complete. However the "Travaux Préparatoires" of the Convention learn us that quite a number of member States had problems with a too precise formulation (cf. the withdrawal of the provision aiming at introducing penalties or other sanctions to ensure the effective enforcement of article 34 on sexual exploitation). Is there a will to do better now ? In any case, the first session of the Working Group proves that an important number of resistances do persist. One of the questions will thus be how to avoid on the one hand years of negotiation or, on the other hand, a text which is far from being precise or complete and therefore gives room for very different interpretations?

But even if the United Nations succeed in drafting a precise, complete and binding text, it will depend on the member States if they are willing to approve and to ratify the text. We should ask ourselves if sufficient member States will be immediately ready to ratify the protocol so that it can enter into force soon after its adoption.

C. What Could Be the Disadvantages of an Optional Protocol?

A first and foremost biggest disadvantage might be that it might harm the holistic approach of the problems children are facing which underlies the United Nations Convention on the Rights of the Child. For example if one considers the root causes which explain and support the existence of phenomena such as child prostitution, child pornography and sale of children, one will see that not first of all a very specialised policy or one or another very particular measure will help to cope with them but rather an integrated social policy or a drastic change in the overall way of dealing with or looking at children.

Taking into consideration that the claim for an optional protocol has probably more to do with a growing social awareness about child prostitution, child pornography and sale of children rather than with an alarming increase of the phenomena themselves, it might be interesting to warn for a possible war on priorities amongst the defenders of children's rights. And this also could be an important threat for the so challenging and for us so necessary holistic approach of the problems children are facing.

Another disadvantage of an optional protocol might be that it hampers a quick and necessary response to what we know already today about the phenomena. As we said before, there are quite a number of indications for a probably slow and difficult drafting process. The means the United Nations and the member States are investing in this process will not be spent somewhere else. This maybe soft argument is however an important element in reality. It is for example surprising that one and the same United Nations give little or no support to the Special Rapporteur on Sale of Children, Child Prostitution and Child Pornography while 2OO.OOO USD can be spent for a session of a Working Group which should "reinvent" basic measures and "think about" guidelines for a possible draft optional protocol.

D. The Question of an Optional Protocol and Monitoring Children's Rights

If we consider, after the adoption of the United Nations Convention of the Rights of the Child, that the main challenge on the agenda for children is the implementation and the monitoring of their rights, then we should be rather reluctant with respect to any effort for the elaboration of an optional protocol to the United Nations Convention on the Rights of the Child. The development of new future instruments may not withdraw our attention from the immediate and effective realization of existing provisions. Instruments such as the UN Convention on the Rights of the Child with a nearly universal ratification could be, too quickly and in the middle of the still living euphoria, reduced to a nearly empty box. Certainly children are not served with such a prediction...

KOEN DE FEYTER

The Prohibition of Child Labour as a Social Clause in Multilateral Trade Agreements

INTRODUCTION

Early 1994, the International Confederation of Free Trade Unions proposed the insertion of a social clause into the General Agreement on Tariffs and Trade and similar international agreements. The following text was put forward:

> The contracting parties agree to take steps to ensure the observance of the minimum labour standards specified by an advisory committee to be established by the GATT and the ILO, and including those on freedom of association and the right to collective bargaining, on the minimum age for employment, discrimination, equal remuneration and forced labour.

The proposed advisory body would be able to recommend measures to a government not fulfilling its obligations, and indicate a specified period of time[1] for compliance. At the same time, the International Labour Organization would offer technical assistance (to be funded by a new international social fund). At the end of the period, the advisory body would prepare a further report, either stating that the country was now fulfilling its obligations, or noting progress, or noting failure to implement the recommendations. At the very least a government would need to demonstrate its recognition of the problem, and present proposals to bring about improvement. If it did not, trade sanctions, in the form of increased tariffs to be levied by all GATT members on the offending country's exports, would be applied. In the WTO framework, the final decision would probably rest with the General Council, consisting of representatives of all contracting parties.

No social clause was in fact included in the Final Act embodying the results of the Uruguay Round of Trade Negotiations (which includes the revised General Agreement on Tariffs and Trade),[2] but the issue was put on

---

[1] The ICFTU paper proposes two years.
[2] For the text, see *International Legal Materials*, 1994, 1–152.

E. Verhellen (ed.), Monitoring Children's Rights, 431–444.
© 1996 *Kluwer Law International. Printed in the Netherlands.*

the agenda of the Preparatory Committee for the World Trade Organization.[3] In addition, the 1994 International Labour Conference decided to set up a working party of the ILO Governing Body[4] to discuss the issue. The debate on the insertion of social clauses in international trade agreements is therefore only in its initial phase.[5]

This paper looks at the appropriateness of attempting to enforce one particular right, the prohibition of child labour, by using trade agreements to ensure observance. Factors taken into account include the restrictions of current monitoring mechanisms, the status of international law on linkages between human rights and trade, the universality and legal nature of the norm under review, including the consequences of the resource implications of the abolition of child labour, and the practicability of sanctions. The paper only deals with the prohibition of child labour, not with social clauses generally.[6]

I. CURRENT MONITORING MECHANISMS

Those who argue in favour of recourse to trade mechanisms to ensure implementation of the prohibition of child labour, often hold that current international monitoring mechanisms in the human rights area lack sufficient tools. Specific human rights mechanisms need to be supplemented by mechanisms sanctioning those rights in other areas of international relations such as development assistance, peace and security, or, as in this case, trade. Only then, it is argued, may enforcement become a reality.

---

[3] The Preparatory Committee for the WTO was established by a decision of 14 April 1994 at the Marrakesh Ministerial Meeting, when the Final Act of the Uruguay Round was signed. The Preparatory Committee is to "perform such functions as may be necessary to ensure the efficient operation of the WTO immediately as of the date of its establishment...". See *Gatt Focus*, May 1994, no. 107, 10.

[4] The Governing Body is the executive organ of the ILO. It meets frequently between annual sessions of the Conference and consists of government, employer, and worker representatives.

[5] In February 1994, the European Parliament adopted a report on the introduction of social clauses in the unilateral and multilateral trading system (European Parliament doc. RR/243/243101 (6 January 1994) – Rapporteur: A. Sainjon). The Report called for an extension of the exception clause in Article XX(e) of GATT to allow for a ban based on disrespect of minimum social rights, including the prohibition of child labour. The North American Agreement on Labour Cooperation, adopted in the framework of NAFTA (North American Free Trade Agreement, *International Legal Materials*, 1993, 289 and 605), provides for a settlement mechanism for disputes involving a Party's alleged persistent pattern of failure to effectively enforce labour laws with respect to health and safety, child labour and minimum wage, relating to a situation involving mutually recognized labour laws and the production of goods or services traded between the Parties.

[6] The same test applied to some of the other social rights proposed for insertion in a social clause may yield different results. The resource implications of respect of the right to freely establish trade unions, are very limited; ILO Convention No. 97 on the freedom of association has been ratified more widely than the Minimum Age Convention; and the cultural diversity argument carries little weight in that context.

The continuing prevalence of child labour round the world may be seen as evidencing the weakness of current monitoring mechanisms. This test may, however, be too harsh. The relevant norms on child labour are to a certain extent open-ended (see *infra*); perhaps progress is the more relevant success criterium. Secondly, any international interference in this area, whatever its form, may have its limits. The abolition of child labour not only requires political will at the level of the national State, but also change at the societal level: child labour often persists within the informal (sometimes family-based) economic sector. Perhaps the capacity of international actors to foster change in such circumstances should not be overestimated.

The international human rights mechanisms involved with child labour include the UN Committee on the Rights of the Child, the UN Committee on Economic, Social and Cultural Rights and the International Labour Organization monitoring system.[7]

The supervisory activity of both above-mentioned UN treaty mechanisms relies to a great extent on the examination of reports regularly submitted by the State parties on the measures they have adopted to give effect to the rights recognized in the conventions. The committees may request additional information (*e.g.* when non-governmental sources point out deficiencies in the official reports), and issue recommendations. Child labour is, of course, only one of the issues addressed in the treaties, and may not be the focus of discussions.

The UN Committee on Economic, Social and Cultural Rights has gradually instilled more vigour into its exchanges with governments. Upon a discussion of a national report, the Committee publicly adopts so-called concluding observations, which have become increasingly bold in identifying impediments to the implementation of the Covenant.[8] Some of these concluding observations have taken on the issue of child labour.[9] The UN Committee on the Rights of the Child has benefitted from the experience of its sister body, and has adopted a similar approach.[10] In addition, both bodies regular-

---

[7] Other international monitoring mechanisms partly dealing with forms of child labour include the UN Working Group on Contemporary Forms of Slavery, the UN Committee on the Elimination of Racial Discrimination, or the UN Committee on the Elimination of Discrimination against Women.

[8] For an overview of the present working methods of the Committee, see Committee on Economic, Social and Cultural Rights, *Report on the Eigth and Ninth Sessions*, UN doc. E/C.12/1993/19, paras 22–52.

[9] Two recent examples include the concluding observations on the initial report of the Socialist Republic of Vietnam (see UN doc. E/C.12/1993/19, paras 131–142). In the Committee's view, "particular efforts" were to be made "to solve the problem of school absenteeism and the concentration of child labour at the expense of school attendance". With regard to the situation in Mauritius, which has so far failed to submit a report on its implementation of the Covenant, the Committee noted "with regret that Mauritian child labour legislation is not strictly enforced" (see UN doc. E/C.12/1994/8, para 12).

[10] Including the adoption of concluding observations, *e.g.* in its concluding observation on the initial report of Egypt, the Committee recommended a revision of national legislation on

ly engage in so-called 'general debates' on specific issues. In October 1993, the UN Committee on the Rights of the Child thus discussed the right of the child to be protected from economic exploitation, which includes the child labour issue.

In the run-up to the World Conference on Human Rights, the UN Committee on Economic, Social and Cultural Rights proposed that a complaints procedure (in the form of an optional protocol), permitting communications by individuals or groups alleging violations of the rights recognized in the Covenant be added to its monitoring machinery. The Committee argued that a system for the examination of individual cases was essential if economic, social and cultural rights were to be treated as seriously as they deserved to be,[11] thus implying some dissatisfaction with the limited means currently at its disposal. The World Conference encouraged the UN Commission on Human Rights to examine the possibility of adding optional protocols to the Covenant, but this has not yet been followed up by a governmental initiative.[12]

State Parties desiring help in meeting their obligations under the conventions may turn to the UN Centre for Human Rights in order to apply for advisory services. The Centre has, however, so far not built up much expertise in devising such services in the field of economic, social and cultural rights.[13]

The International Labour Organization has set up a general reporting system which applies to all ILO Conventions.[14] State reports are first examined in closed session by a Committee of Experts on the Application of Conventions and Recommendations. The Committee may address direct requests for further information to the States concerned and adopt observations on lack of implementation. In the Committee's report, each Convention is reviewed separately.[15] The most serious cases identified by the independent experts

---

the minimum working age, and ratification of ILO Convention no.138. See Committee on the Rights ofthe Child, *Report on its Third Session*, UN doc. CRC/C/16, para 107.

[11] See Committee on Economic, Social and Cultural Rights, *Report on the Seventh Session*, UN doc. E/C.12/1992/2, annexes III and IV.

[12] See World Conference on Human Rights, Vienna Declaration and Programme of Action (12 July 1993), art. II, 75.

[13] On the advisory services program, see Gomez del Prado, J.L., "Preventing Human Rights Violations: Advisory Services and Technical Assistance", International Institute of Human Rights (ed.), *Collection of Lectures. Twenty-Third Study Session*, 1992, 46 p.

[14] See extensively: Betten, L., *International Labour Law*, Deventer, Kluwer, 1993, 396–414, Leary, V., "Lessons from the Experience of the International Labour Organization" in Alston, P. (ed.), *The United Nations and Human Rights. A Critical Appraisal*, Oxford, Clarendon Press, 1992, 580-619. Virginia Leary qualifies the UN system for the implementation of economic and social rights as "incipient".

[15] In its section on ILO Convention No. 138 on Minimum Age, the 1994 Report of the Committee of Experts raises issues about the conformity of national legislation in Belarus and the Dominican Republic. The report notes that, in addition, requests regarding certain points were directly addressed to Antigua and Barbuda, Belgium, the Dominican Republic, France, Guatemala, Malta, Niger, Romania, Spain, Sweden and Venezuela. See International Labour

are consequently discussed by a committee of the ILO's Annual Conference, the Conference Committee on Standards, a large political body with a tripartite composition. The Committee's report, which is up for adoption by the plenary, may note failures to implement ratified conventions.

The ILO Constitution, in addition, provides for a complaints procedure, allowing 'representations' by employers' and workers' organizations alleging a violation of a Convention to which a State is a party, or 'complaints' by Member States to the same effect. Both are examined by the ILO Governing Body, which in the latter case, may appoint a Commission of Inquiry; the Commission prepares a public report including recommendations. The so-called 'direct contacts' procedure allows for missions by ILO officials or independent experts to States facing difficulties implementing ILO Conventions. The missions are carried out at the request of the State, or upon a proposal by the Secretariat, the International Labour Office. Lastly, the ILO has a long tradition of providing technical assistance, specifically to developing countries, in overcoming difficulties in implementing labour standards.

Reporting procedures are part and parcel of a mobilization of shame approach. Governments do not enjoy criticism on account of the persistence of child labour before an international monitoring body, but whether they care enough to redress the situation, depends on the prestige of the monitoring body, – the ILO may be in a somewhat more comfortable position here –, and on the priority the State gives to both the eradication of child labour in its domestic policy, and to its human rights image generally in its foreign policy.

Monitoring bodies examining reports exercise pressure, but not force. State cooperation remains vital. This is equally true in the area of technical assistance, which will only materialize, if the State concerned agrees. Complaints procedures are more adverserial, but even then an element of voluntary State compliance with decisions remains. Traditional UN human rights mechanisms are inadequate in establishing real State accountabiity. That may be different if the State is made to pay – in economic terms – for the positions it adopts.

II. Linking Human Rights and Trade

Few rules govern trade sanctions for human rights purposes in international law. The issue of linkages was arguably the main current running through the debates at the World Conference on Human Rights, but there was little agreement, and as a result the Vienna Declaration and Programme of Action, which was adopted by consensus, does not take unequivocal positions on the relationship between human rights and trade, development cooperation or peace.

Conference doc. 81 III (4A), 500–501. For a general review of the Committee of Experts' case law on child labour, see Betten, L., *op.cit.*, 301-308.

The Declaration does call upon States "to refrain from any unilateral measure not in accordance with international law and the Charter of the United Nations that creates obstacles to trade relations among States and impedes the full realization of human rights...".[16] The text was a Cuban initiative, directed against the trade embargo imposed by the United States. The text may be taken to imply that free trade relations are beneficial to the realization of human rights. But in many ways it is not relevant to our discussion here: sanctions as in the ICFTU proposal would not be unilateral, would be based on an international treaty, and aim at the realization of minimum social rights.

Another, hugely ambivalent provision appears to deal with conditionality in general. The text recognizes that democracy, development and respect for human rights are interdependent and mutually reinforcing, and goes on to state that "in the context of the above, the promotion and protection of human rights and fundamental freedoms at the national and international levels should be universal and conducted without conditions attached".[17] Government delegations made it clear that they had very different understandings of what the text meant; and on that condition the provision was adopted.[18] Donors explained that the text required States to promote and protect human rights unreservedly: respect for human rights should not be made conditional on economic improvement. Recipient countries on the other hand clarified that the provision meant that States should abstain from setting conditions, *e.g.* in the areas of development cooperation or trade, when promoting human rights at the international level.

With international palaver in such dire straits, it may be useful to briefly distinguish positive and negative linkages between human rights and trade, – the carrot or the stick approach.[19] Positive linkages come in two forms: a) when improvements in human rights are rewarded by granting additional trade benefits to countries, and b) when funding is provided by trading partners to projects specifically directed at an improvement of human rights (along the lines of the technical assistance to be provided by the ILO in the ICFTU proposal). Negative linkages sanction lack of improvement in human rights

---

[16] World Conference on Human Rights, Vienna Declaration and Programme of Action (12 July 1993), art. I, 31.

[17] World Conference on Human Rights, Vienna Declaration and Programme of Action (12 July 1993), art. I,8.

[18] In *Through the Looking-Glass*, Alice objects to this approach when Humpty Dumpty explains to her that words mean what he chooses them to mean: "The question is", said Alice, "whether you can make words mean so many different things". "The question is", replies Humpty Dumpty "which is to be master – that's all" (Lewis CARROLL, *Through the Looking Glass*, Oxford, Oxford University Press, 1990, 190). Humpty Dumpty, of course, is right. An ambivalent text simply shifts the debate from adoption of wording to interpretation. Those who become masters will determine at a later stage what its meaning is.

[19] Compare, at more length: De Feyter, K., "Mensenrechten en Ontwikkelingssamenwerking" in Parmentier, S., *Mensenrechten tussen Retoriek en Realiteit*, Gent, Mys & Breesch, 1994, 87–105.

by penalizing exports, either generally, or specifically of products produced in violation of international standards.[20] Quite often, both types of linkages are combined, as is the case in the ICFTU proposal.[21]

Although not undisputed, positive linkages (and, of course, in particular type a) often prove acceptable to developing States. The controversy rages about negative linkages: conditionality in the narrow sense.

III. The Prohibition of Child Labour as a Universal Norm

Noting for now that the negative linkage between trade and human rights is controversial as a method of international implementation, it is helpful if the human rights norm which is to be implemented is beyond such controversy, and is deemed universal. If all partners in a multilateral trade agreement have acknowledged, be it at a human rights forum, that each of them is under an obligation to abolish child labour, raising the issue at the trade forum may be less problematic.

The establishment of human rights norms as universal is fraught with difficulties, because the method chosen implies a position on the sources of human rights. Immediately the spectre of the debate on whether human rights derive from natural law, positive law or from shared values and customs within different societies appears.

The positive law approach has its advantages in that it is practical[22]: if universality is established on the basis of the worldwide recognition by States of international human rights obligations, it is feasible to derive from the rate of ratification of treaties or by analyzing customary law (admittedly, not necessarily easy), to what extent a norm has achieved universality.

A summary review of the major international norms on the abolition of child labour now follows. Article 10, para 3 of the International Covenant on Economic, Social and Cultural Rights protects children and young persons from economic and social exploitation, by requiring that States *i.a.* prohibit their employment in work harmful to their health and development and "set age limits below which the paid employment of child labour should be prohibited and punishable by law". The provision does not itself define such an age limit. The Covenant has been ratified by 127 States.[23] Article 32 of the UN Convention on the Rights of the Child, in a very similar context, requires

---

[20]   In the same country, labour conditions may differ considerably depending on the sector or area. The ICFTU proposal does not specify whether it favours a general or a specific negative approach.

[21]   Compare EC Council of Ministers for Development Cooperation resolution on human rights, democracy and development (28 November 1991).

[22]   The approach is, on the other hand, limited, *e.g.* because it takes the legitimacy of governments, and, more generally, the validity of normative processes within the United Nations for granted.

[23]   All figures on ratifications as of 31 December 1993.

States to "provide for a minimum age or minimum ages for admission to employment",[24]. The Convention has been ratified by more than 155 States.

Both treaties deal with a vast number of rights, and it is unlikely that the decision on ratification depended on the provision under review here. The rate of ratifications of the ILO treaties which deal specifically and in a more detailed manner with child labour is significantly lower. The original Minimum Age (Industry) ILO Convention No.5 (1919) stipulating that children under the age of 14 years shall not be employed in industrial undertakings, other than those in which only members of the same family are employed, was ratified by 71 States.[25] The 1973 Minimum Age ILO Convention No. 138, the ILO's current central standard on the issue, refers to a minimum age for employment in all sectors of the labour market. Its basic principles are as follows: States "undertake to pursue a national policy designed to ensure the effective abolition of child labour and to raise progressively the minimum age for admission to employment or work to a level consistent with the fullest physical and mental development of young persons". That minimum age shall not be less than the age of completion of compulsory schooling, and, in any case, not be less than 15 years. Developing countries may initially specify a minimum age of 14 years. ILO Convention No. 138 was ratified by 46 States.[26]

Although there is a wide range of ratifications of both UN Conventions, the norm on child labour in those treaties is open, in the sense that States are free to determine themselves what constitutes child labour; when that authority is taken away from them, as in the relevant ILO Conventions, the rate of ratifications drops. In conclusion, universal agreement on the prohibition of child labour depends on the majority of national States' refusal to allow international bodies to define what constitutes child labour in their own country.

A different approach to universality focusses on prevalent moral values in different societies; it is not so much concerned with what States declare at intergovernmental fora, but with what societies regard as essential. Dundes

---

[24] Thomas Hammarberg, in noting that Article 32 allows for different minimum ages depending on the nature of the job, states: "The point is that there should be a conscious policy in this field and that children's health and possibilities for education should not be undermined". See Hammarberg, T., "The Rights of the Child in Developing Countries: International Norms and Procedures for Real Change?", *Human Rights in Developing Countries Yearbook 1994* Deventer, Kluwer, 1994, 16.

[25] And later denounced by 23 States, upon ratification of a successor ILO Convention.

[26] Algeria, Antigua and Barbuda, Azerbaijan, Belarus, Belgium, Bosnia Herzegowina, Bulgaria, Costa Rica, Croatia, Cuba, Dominican Republic, Equatorial Guinea, Finland, France, Germany, Greece, Guatemala, Honduras, Iraq, Ireland, Israel, Italy, Kenya, Kirghizistan, Lybia, Luxembourg, Malta, Mauritius, Netherlands, Nicaragua, Niger, Norway, Poland, Romania, Russia, Rwanda, Slovenia, Spain, Sweden, Tajikistan, Togo, Ukraine, Uruguay, Venezuela, Yugoslavia and Zambia.

Renteln has discussed the abolition of child labour from this perspective[27]. She points out that in many societies child labour is not only an economic necessity, but is also perceived as natural and moral: children derive a status within society from the work they perform. Since the concept of childhood varies accross cultures, the assertion that there is a universal standard prohibiting child labour betrays an ethnocentric inspiration.

As Dundes Renteln explains, this does not mean that external criticism is impossible,[28] as long as one is honest about the local source of the criticism rather than to pretend that it is universal. Surely, however, when it is acknowledged that the society in which child labour prevails does not perceive of the practice as a violation of human rights, special care should be taken in determining the form external pressure for change should take.

IV. LEGAL NATURE OF THE PROHIBITION

The choice of the method of implementation is not only dependent on the universal character of the norm, but also on the legal nature of the norm generally.

In its proposal on the social clause, the ICFTU specifically refers to the relevant ILO standards. ILO Convention No.138 obliges States to pursue a policy to ensure the effective abolition of child labour. It does not require States to immediately abolish child labour upon ratification; it aims at progressive realization in stead.

Immediate abolition is difficult, because in many cases the State will not be the employer; abuses are committed by private persons, which may include relatives or members of the same local community: children in domestic service are a case in point. The State's factual control over the labour market may be limited, *e.g.* the impact of simply outlawing child labour may be counterproductive, in that it makes child labour invisible, rather than disappear, unless the State is able to follow-up its prohibition, *e.g.* through a well-organized labour inspectorate. Whether that is available in many developing States is in some doubt. It is equally doubtful whether many developing States are willing or able to compensate families for the loss of income they sustain if abolition of child labour is effectively implemented.

The 1983 Report of the Director-General of the ILO which deals with child labour therefore goes to great lengths to explain that abolition will take a long time, since it is dependent on an improvement of standards of living generally, a development policy focussing on (adult) employment, an effective social security system, the improvement of the educational system

---

[27] See Dundes Renteln, A., *International Human Rights. Universalism versus Relativsm* Newbury Park, Sage Publications, 1990, 59–60.

[28] Dundes Renteln, A., *O.c.*, 77–82.

etc.,[29] all of which require considerable resources. In the transitionary period, the objective should be to limit child labour and to ensure that the conditions of such work are favourable. Another recognition of the resource implications of the abolition of child labour is the allowance for developing countries to set a slightly lower initial minimum age for employment than that allowed to developing countries.

Nevertheless, the Convention does impose some obligations which are of immediate effect. Apart from the formal requirement to set a specified minimum age,[30] an obligation of progressive realization minimally implies an immediate obligation not to retrograde: any lowering of the minimum age for employment would thus be difficult to justify.[31]

Clearly, a rapid abolition of child labour requires priority spending, which is considerably more difficult in States or societies where resources in general are scarce.[32] This does not imply that the goal should be abandoned, but it does raise the issue of international responsibility. Perhaps such responsibility should not stop at monitoring and scrutiny, but should equally involve duties to assist States which can show that resources are demonstrably insufficient at the national level to realize what is internationally required. At a less ambitious level, it suggests that this is an area in which monitoring and assistance should go together.

In conclusion, however, ILO Convention No. 138 is primarily conceived for the purposes of reviewing national policies pursuant to child labour. The ILO's reporting procedure reflects the nature of the norm under review: the international body's aim is to persuade States to devote more resources (both intellectual and material) to the gradual abolition of child labour, in the context of a general improvement of working conditions. For the international body to be able to monitor (lack of) progress, the existence of a forum for *systematic* dialogue at regular intervals is vital, and this is what the ILO has created. In addition, technical assistance is offered.

Is there any role for trade sanctions in such a set-up? In the ICFTU proposal sanctions would apply when a government had failed to make adequate efforts

---

[29] In the International Covenant on Economic, Social and Cultural Rights there clearly is a link between the aims of the abolition of child labour and the provision of free education (art. 13, ICESCR). Children should be able to go to school, not be forced to work. But even if education is free, school transport or books may not be. In practice therefore, compulsory education may increase the pressure on children to work.

[30] One would expect, however, that most ratifying States would have fulfilled this obligation before ratification, although disputes may still arise about whether the minimum age applies generally.

[31] Compare the UN Committee on Economic, Social and Cultural Rights' General Comment No. 3 (1990) on the nature of States parties obligations under the Covenant, para 9 in UN Committee on Economic, Social and Cultural Rights, *Report on the Fifth Session*, Annex III.

[32] Tomasevski has asserted with some vigour that data on the economic development and resource availability of the least developed countries show that they do not generate sufficient resources to enable governments to implement their human rights obligations. See Tomasevski, K., *Development Aid and Human Rights*, London, Pinter, 1987, 98.

to implement the GATT/ILO recommendations: "The trade sanction would operate as the ultimate penalty for non-cooperation".[33] The government needs to demonstrate political will to bring about change. What appears to be sanctioned therefore is not so much the actual persistence of child labour, but the non-fulfillment of the obligation to cooperate with the monitoring body. In other words, trade sanctions would apply when the government concerned refused to enter into the systematic dialogue provided for within the international framework. A clear example would be a case in which a government, after two years, had given no response at all to the panel's recommendations. If sanctions are applied in such a way, they are not inconsistent with the very gradual approach subscribed by the norm under review: co-operation, willingness to discuss at the international level is a pre-condition for the gradual approach to work.

V. SELECTIVITY AND EFFECTIVENESS OF SANCTIONS

Two further difficulties with any type of human rights conditionality are now discussed briefly. The questions are whether a non-selective approach in applying sanctions is really feasible, and secondly, whether sanctions are effective in realizing the norm under review.

If sanctions are to be applied, they need to be applied consistently, on the basis of an agreed criterium, *i.e.* failure to co-operate with the monitoring body, or alternatively (as in the NAFTA Agreement on Labour) failure to effectively enforce (inter)national child labour laws. Other considerations, such as the importance of the target country as a market for imports, or the need to protect domestic labour markets and prevent delocation of industries to the target country should not be relevant.[34] In practice, these may be difficult to exclude, particularly if the final decision on sanctions is taken by a political body, such as the WTO General Council.

Another aspect of selectivity is the limitation of the clause to social rights. According to United Nations dogma, all human rights are equally important, indivisible and interdependent. So why limit trade sanctions to disrespect of social rights? Why not equally include the possibility of trade sanctions when childrens' rights in the area of physical integrity are violated? Some of the most serious violations of their rights occur when children are in prison, or in refugee camps, or during armed conflict.

It may be argued that trade fora are particularly capable to deal with social rights, as there is a direct link between trade and social conditions. The preamble to the Agreement establishing the World Trade Organization thus recognizes that the relations between the parties in the field of trade and

---

[33] ICFTU, *The Social Clause: Rationale and Operating Mechanisms*, 3.

[34] Compare Goutier, H., "Social Clauses in Trade. Protecting the Rich or Helping the Poor?", *The Courier*, no. 145, May-June 1994, 95–97.

economic endeavour "should be conducted with a view to raising standards of living, ensuring full employment...".[35] In the area of positive linkages, trading partners may therefore wish to specialize in funding projects specifically directed at improving social rights. In the area of sanctions, however, little justification can be found for taking into account violations of only category of human rights, while ignoring the other.

A final question is whether trade sanctions will help the abolition of child labour. The resource implications of abolition have already been pointed out, and it is questionable whether reducing the target State's income from exports, by compelling it to increase its labour costs, is helpful in this context. The concern is raised in the UN Secretary-General's report on An Agenda for Development, which is under review at the 1994 session of the UN General Assembly.[36] The report states that the expansion of international trade is essential to economic growth, and recognizes that difficult access to the world trading system is an enormous obstacle to development: "At present, the system often discriminates against the developing world by limiting its advantage in low labour costs, while the price of many primary commodities has tended to decline". Seen from this perspective, social clauses further impede the access of developing States to the world trade system. In addition, it has been pointed out that negative conditionality runs counter to the spirit and principles of GATT: the system is geared towards eliminating, rather than adding barriers to trade.[37]

The underlying assumption that access to the world trade system is beneficial to the developing States may be challenged. It has *e.g.* been argued that the World Trade Organization is geared to the interests of the developed States. If it is in the interest of (some) developing States to remain outside of the system, however, clearly social clauses will not work as an instrument of leverage in their respect. Social clauses can only be effective, if developing States perceive of access to the world trade system as a benefit.

The 1994 Report of the Director-General of the ILO includes a chapter on social clauses.[38] The report puts forward a propasal which, in contrast to the insertion of social clauses in trade agreements, aims at reinforcing ILO procedures. The report suggests that a special procedure be set up which would analyze the evolution of social progress in the light of the freeing of international markets and the internationalization of the economy. The ILO

---

[35] But note that the language of social *rights* is avoided. For the text, see Agreement establishing the World Trade Organization (15 December 1993), *International Legal Materials*, 1994, 15.

[36] See UN doc. A/48/935 (6 May 1994), paras 53–54.

[37] See Van Liemt, G., "The Multilateral Social Clause in 1994", ICDA (International Coalition for Development Action) paper, August 1994, 8 p. The author also points out that social clauses tend to focus on labour standards in the manufacturing sector for export only (since they are part and parcel of a multilateral trade agreement), while many offences occur in firms working entirely for the domestic market.

[38] See International Labour Conference doc. 81 I (1).

would review whether States sufficiently use the benefits they derive from the liberalization of world trade for the purpose of realizing ILO norms. In return, parties ratifying the proposed new Convention would agree to renounce from unilateral measures restricting trade on the basis of lack of respect for labour standards. In addition, practical assistance to developing countries would be increased through the creation of an international fund, to be set up in cooperation with GATT. As an example, the report suggests that increased pressure on developing countries to progressively abolish child labour should be accompanied by simultaneous assistance in setting up educational facilities for children.

CONCLUSION

This text has raised a number of concerns at the insertion of the prohibition of child labour as a social clause in multilateral trade agreements. Since there are few rules governing the subject in international law, – primarily for lack of agreement within the international community on linkages between human rights and trade –, the focus has been on the appropriateness of the insertion of such a clause.

The abolition of child labour has received significant, but not universal recognition as an international human rights norm. Cultural differences on the perception of childhood within societies remain. Consequently, special care should be taken in determining the form external pressure on such societies should take. As a starting-point, the emphasis should be on monitoring and assistance, rather than on sanctions.

The need for assistance follows from the nature of current international norms on the subject. These either leave the determination of the minimum age to the national State, or allow for progressive realization, mainly in recognition of the resource implications of the abolition of child labour. Consequently, if the international community is serious about its concern for rapid abolition, the resources available at the international level for this purpose should be increased. A positive linkage between human rights and trade should therefore be made, through the provision of funds by trading partners for projects specifically directed at improving working conditions for children or providing the socio-economic conditions in which child labour can be abolished.

The establishment of new barriers to trade, on the other hand, through the imposition of a negative conditionality, reduces the prospects for economic growth in the countries concerned. Economic growth is in itself insufficient to realize the abolition of child labour (it does not ensure that the government will adopt of social development policy), but is a pre-condition.

Monitoring implies a dialogue between the relevant international expert bodies and the States and societies in which child labour persists. Both within the relevant ILO and UN frameworks, States are under an obligation to enter into such a dialogue. Difficulties arise when States refuse to honour that obligation. Most often the same States will also be lacking in political will to take action on child labour domestically.

Clearly, there is a need to reinforce current monitoring bodies in the area of economic, social and cultural rights when States fail to co-operate. The means at the disposal of these bodies should be increased, including the legal and political consequences of their reports and observations. With regard to the abolition of child labour, the reinforcement of specific human rights monitoring bodies, along the lines already proposed by the relevant bodies, is an alternative preferable to the imposition of trade sanctions. One possibility is the addition of individual complaints procedures to both the International Covenant on Economic, Social and Cultural Rights and the UN Convention on the Rights of the Child.[39] Another interesting avenue is how direct access for children (adolescents) to international monitoring bodies can be organized: perhaps the procedures adopted by the UN Committee on the Rights of the Child are too much a carbon copy of those adopted by existing human rights bodies. More thought could be given to what type of unique procedure could result in directly empowering children at the international level.

---

[39] The European Court and Commission on Human Rights have built up interesting case-law in the area of children's rights, *e.g.* see Buquicchio – De Boer, M., "Children and the European Convention on Human Rights" in Matscher, F., Petzold, H. (eds.), *Protecting Human Rights: the European Dimension*, Köln, Carl Heymanns Verlag, 1988, 73–89.

LEYLA KHALFALLAH

Impressions en Marge d'une Session du Comité des Droits de l'Enfant

INTRODUCTION

Cette contribution n'a pas la prétention d'être le remède à ce malaise que nous ressentons tous à un moment donné de notre action. Nous adultes intéressés par les sujets que nous fûmes, mais que nous ne sommes plus, à savoir les enfants.

Cette contribution est simplement un modeste témoignage d'un malaise que j'ai moi même ressenti lorsque j'ai eu la possibilité d'assister en tant qu'observateur d'une organisation non gouvernementale (Défense des Enfants-International DEI) à la quatrième session du comité des droits de l'Enfant qui s'est tenue au cours du mois de Janvier 1994 au palais des Nations à Genève.

J'ai cru au départ pouvoir enfin cerner de près les mécanismes internationaux de contrôle de la bonne application par les états parties à la convention relative aux droits de l'enfant.

Ma formation de juriste et ma profession d'avocate ont contribuées à cette déformation intellectuelle qui accorde une place importante à la notion de contrôle.

Mon appartenance au mouvement "Défence des Enfants-International, DEI" qui s'est fixé comme but principal lors de sa création en 1979, d'assurer sur le plan international une action continue et concertée afin de promouvoir et de protéger les droits de l'enfant, a encore accentuée cette déformation.

Cette déformation s'est confirmée aussi par le sérieux et le professionnalisme des experts du comité des droits de l'enfants: leur savoir faire et leur tact sont pour beaucoup dans la réussite des travaux du comité, et une preuve matérielle de la nécessite de l'existence de pareille institution.

J'ai cru enfin trouver raison à mon action!

Mais mon optimisme béat s'arrête là, pour laisser place à ce malaise, ou le goût de l'inachevé qui s'est installé au fur et à mesure du déroulement des travaux du comité. Les raisons de ce malaise?

Elles étaient malheureusement concrètes et diverses, et réunies, m'ont emmené, à poser la fatale question que se pose à un moment ou à un autre

E. Verhellen (ed.), Monitoring Children's Rights, 445–451.
© 1996 *Kluwer Law International. Printed in the Netherlands.*

toute personne qui milite pour les droits de l'enfant: à savoir la raison d'être du comité.

Mais, heureusement que l'action de terrain nous a rendu plus lucide: Car quelque soit le degré d'utilité d'une institution, du moment qu'elle parvient à résoudre fut ce les problèmes d'un enfant, cela justifie déjà son existence.

Le comité du droit de l'enfant apporte une contribution tangible pour l'amélioration des droits de l'enfant: encore faut-il le rendre plus performant et plus efficace: mettre en évidence ses faiblesses, c'est déjà une étape vers sa consécration, le doter de plus de moyens matériels et humain, assurer une meilleure collaboration avec les ONG en les reconnaissant comme une nécessité absolue au contrôle de l'application de la convention et non comme de simples figurants, garantir enfin une information accessible à tous: c'est justifier l'existence du comité et anéantir ce fameux malaise qui nous harcèle.

I. Des Moyens à la Mesure des Aspirations

D'après la convention relative aux droits de l'enfant dans ses articles 43 et 44 le comité des droits de l'enfant est constitué de dix (10) experts de "Haute moralité et possédant une compétence reconnue dans le domaine visé par la convention" (article 43).

Ce comité est chargé de suivre de près les progrès réalisés par les états qui ratifient la convention ou que y adhèrent dans l'accomplissement de leurs obligations.

Il peut en outre, demander aux états parties de compléter les renseignements fournis dans leurs rapports et peut également formuler des suggestions ou recommandations.

Est-ce que le comité des droits de l'enfant a les moyens matériels et humains pout accomplir son travail? Comment se présente dans la pratique cette tâche colossale?

Si nous nous référons à l'alinéa 11 du article 43 de la conventions, nous ne manquerons pas de remarquer que la dite convention a entendu doter le comité de "certains" moyens pour l'accomplissement de sa tâche.

Toutefois, nous ne manquerons pas aussi de constater la formulation très vague et très peu contraignante de cet alinéa quand il stipule que "Le secrétaire générale de l'organisation des Nations Unies met à la disposition du comité le personnel et les installations qui lui sont nécessaires pour s'acquitter efficacement des fonctions qui lui sont confiées en vertu de la présente convention".

D'après la formulation de ce texte nous pourrons imaginer aisemment les difficultés que peuvent rencontrer les membres du comités dans l'exercice de leur fonction, surtous, si nous avons une idée, même approximative, des rouages de l'administration onusienne.

Nous ne manquerons pas de réaliser alors qu'être expert au comité des droits de l'enfant n'est pas une fonction de tous repos:

Avoir un secrétariat exclusif au comité, et un local adéquat pour ses réunions, ses archives et ses documents, n'est pas une mince affaire même au sein de la plus haute instance Internationale qu'est l'ONU!

Que dire alors de l'engagement des dépenses qu'engendreraient le recours à des experts pour les études ou enquêtes?

Le comité doit pour ce faire "recommander à l'assemblée génerale de prier le secrétaire général de procéder pour le comité à des études sur les questions spécifiques touchant les droits de l'enfant" (article 45-C).

Que de complications et que de perte de temps qui ne nuit en fait qu'à l'enfant, pourtant objet et raison de tout cet arsenal juridique!

Certes, le centre pour les droits de l'Homme fait ce qu'il peut pour faciliter la tâche du comité. Mais est-ce suffisent? Est-ce que la solution ne se trouverait par ailleurs, dans un autre local avec un personnel "personnel" au comité et un budget propre et ce pour pouvoir mener à terme une action efficace et rationnelle? Qu'en est-il maintenant de la partie apparente de l'iceberg à savoir, les réunions publiques du comité des droits de l'enfant?

Les conséquences du manque des moyens matériels et humains sont mises en évidence et se répercutent nécessairement sur le bon déroulement des travaux du comité.

En effet, celui qui compte assister aux sessions publiques du comité doit avoir le coeur solide et une endurance de sportif de haute compétition pour emboîter le marrathon des réunions.

Il aura alors a suivre l'exposé du rapport de chaque état partie, les questions des membres du comité, les réponses du responsable étatique, et enfin les suggestions et recommandations du comité.

Le tout au cours d'une seule journée ou avec plus le chance, et grâce au débit lent d'un représentant étatique, deux journées.

J'ai trouvé tout simplement choquant que la plus haute instance de contrôle de la convention des droits de l'enfant se penche sur les problèmes de l'enfance d'un pays donné, en une seule journée, et ce, sans parler bien sur des pauses cafés, pauses déjeuners et des retards accumulés ... est-ce normal?

Le but ici, n'est nullement de mettre en question la compétence des experts, loin de là, mais d'attirer l'attention sur cette anomilie pour leur rendre justement la tâche plus facile et plus efficace.

En effet, pratiquement, matériellement, logiquement, humainement cette tâche est impossible à réussir dans les conditions actuelles. Je ne connais pas les raisons de ce manque de temps, de cette course infernale de cette course infernale, mais je les imagine mien qu'en connaissant les hautes responsabilités des membres du comité, pour la plupart des ministres, ambassadeurs, hauts responsables dans des institutions gouvernementales et non-gouvernementales. Or, réunir ces compétences, compte tenu de leurs disponibilité respectives, et celle au palais des Nations, sans parler bien sur du travail de préparation des dossiers et de collecte d'informations, qu'ils doivent accomplir avant les réunions, devient nécessairement une tâche des plus ardues. Quelle solutions devant pareilles contraintes?

Une disponibilité entière des membres du comité, et la possibilité pour eux de se décharges sur d'autres experts nationaux pour le traitement des rapports nationaux pourrait peut-être tempérer ce marrathon et permettre à tous de souffler!

Toujours est-il que dans les conditions actuelles du travail du comité des droits de l'enfant, nous réfléchirons beaucoup à envier les honorables membres du comité pour la position qu'ils occupent.

Car, faire partie de ce comité, nécessite, outre les qualités "d'honorabilité et de compétence" des qualités certaines de funambules capables de jongler avec le manque de temps et les contraintes matérielles de toute sorte.

II. *Pour la Réhabilitation du Rôle des ONG*

Il est indéniable que les créateurs de comité des droits de l'enfant n'ont pas prévu d'en faire une institution renfermée sur elle même. De ce fait ils lui ont accordés certaines "libertés" tout en prenant le soin de surveiller ses "fréquentations". D'une autre manière, ils lui ont choisis ses partenaires.

Ainsi, et pour promouvoir l'application effective de la convention et encourager la coopération internationale, le comité des droits de l'enfant peut inviter les institutions spécialisées, le fond des Nations Unies pour l'enfance (UNICEF) et les autres organismes compétents qu'il juge appropriés, à donner des avis spécialisés ou des rapports sur l'application de la convention dans les domaines qui relèvent de leur mandats respectifs, ou dans les secteurs qui relèvent de leur domaine d'activité.

En outre, le comité transmet, "s'il juge nécessaire" aux institutions spécialisées, à l'UNICEF, et autres organismes compétents tout rapport des états parties contenant une demande ou indiquant un besoin de conseil ou d'assistance technique, accompagnés le cas échéant des observations et suggestions du comité et touchant la dite demande ou indication (article 45, a et b de la convention). Il apparaît de la lecture de cet article deux constations:

1. Le souci de faire participer les institutions des Nations Unies aux travaux du comité : ce qui est tout a fait normal et logique: l'apport de ces dernières est considérable.
2. Un silence voilé sur la collaboration avec les organisations non gouvernementales ce qui a normal et incompréhensible.

Certes, le texte parle d'organismes compétents, appellation bien vague qui peut ne pas englober les ONG, si "les membres du conseil le jugent nécessaire"!

Cette situation précaire des ONG au niveau du texte l'est aussi au niveau de la pratique: le malaise ressurgit alors, imperceptible lors des réunions du comité. Les membres des ONG sont mis à l'écart sans droit à la parole et exclus de certaines réunions auxquelles assistent pourtant les institutions des Nations Unies.

Et même quand les représentants de ces ONG essayent de traverser ce mur il n'est pas évident qu'ils y parviennent. J'ai moi-même essayé d'établir les contacts avec les membres du comité; ils étaient bien sur très ouverts et avaient la modestie des grands mais je devais savoir garder mes distances en ma qualité d'observateur d'une ONG!

Et c'est là que j'ai ressenti une fois de plus l'incompréhension du rôle effectif des ONG dans les instances non seulement nationales qu'internationales.

Une fois de plus, je me suis heurtée en tant qu'observateur d'une ONG à l'exclusion: bien sur la notion d'exclusion est très vaste puisqu'elle peut être aussi bien physique que morale.

J'ai eu le sentiment qu'une maille sautait dans ce processus de contrôle. Et j'avais la désagréable certitude que même au niveau de cette haute instance internationale qu'était le comité des droits de l'enfant, les ONG ne sont pas considérées comme une nécessite absolue au contrôle et comme une liaison indispensable entre le comité et la réalité de chaque pays, ou comme un miroir duquel se reflète justement cette réalité:

Les ignorer, les cantonner dans un rôle négatif, les soustraire à la collaboration pour des raisons d'éthique (ne pas provoquer la susceptibilité des états-concernés) ou pour soi-disant les protéger (notamment dans les pays en développement) c'est tout simplement amputer le comité d'une source d'information fiable capable de faire le contrepoids avec le discours officiel très souvent en langue de bois. En écartant les ONG, le comité des droits de l'enfant se détacherait de la réalité pour devenir un rassemblement de sages "honorables et compétents"!

Certes, il y a la coalisation des ONG qui s'est plus ou moins imposée pour participer aux travaux du comité soit au niveau de la préparation ou lors des réunions publiques, mais il n'est pas évident que les ONG nationales en fassent partie ou connaissent même son existence.

Nous posons par là un problème pas des moindre, celui de l'information.

III. *Une Information Fluide et Accessible*

Nul ne conteste que l'information est devenue aujourd'hui une arme redoutable, parfois à double tranchant, mais indispensable à toute action économique, politique, sociale ou culturelle. C'est pourquoi, il s'avère urgent que le comité des droits de l'enfant soit sensible à cette nécessité, en utilisant "cette arme" dans l'intérêt suprême de l'enfant.

Certes, de part la convention, le comité n'a pas une obligation d'information à l'égard de ses partenaires, mais son travail serait plus rationnel s'il est connu par les intéressés notamment les ONG.

Bien sur, la politique actuelle en matière d'information consiste plutôt en la recherche de cette dernière, mais, il est parfois des contraintes qui justifieraient l'inversement de cette règle.

En effet, une ONG de la Colombie a malheureusement des occupations beaucoup plus urgentes et vitales que de chercher à connaître les rouages de fonctionnement du comité des droits de l'enfant.

Ce n'est pas une excuse, mais il y a parfois des priorités qui s'imposent, comme par exemple "l'opération nettoyage des rues"!

Dans ce cas, il appartient, à la partie la plus diligente de se faire connaître ou du moins de se rendre accessible aux ONG par une information fluide et accessible. Autrement son travail n'aurait aucun sens en restant méconnu de la quasi majorité des ONG nationales.

Et croyez-moi, ce ne serait sûrement pas les états concernés (surtout s'ils sont en voie de développement et pas particulièrement friands du culte de la liberté d'expression et d'information) qui se dérangeraient pour informer leurs ONG de la date de présentation du rapport national ou encore "d'assurer, comme le stipule la convention, une large diffusion dans leurs pays respectifs de leur rapport". Or, cette étape au niveau du contrôle est vitale pour rationaliser le travail du comité.

Certes, ce dernier est déjà submergé par le volume du travail, serait-il alors plus judicieux de penser à créer des comités nationaux des droits de l'enfant, indépendamment des états concernés et plus accessibles aux ONG nationales? Le résultat serait certainement bénéfique pour tous les intéressés:
- Décharger le comité d'un volume de travail considérable ce qui permettait à ses membres d'être encore mieux informés.
- Permettre aux ONG nationales de collaborer directement avec le comité, et se tenir informé.
- Eviter la langue de bois choisie par certains états comme moyen de communication avec le comité en les obligeant à être plutôt critiques sinon positifs.

Ainsi, nous pourrons peut-être caresser l'espoir d'approcher des buts essentiels de la création du comité des droits de l'enfant, à savoir faire de lui un forum international ou les parties concernées s'échangeront les idées pour définir les dangers qui menacent le bien être des enfants, de chercher des solutions pratiques à des problèmes spécifiques, de mobiliser les ressources humaines et financières nécessaires à la solution de ces problèmes, de sensibiliser et d'intéresser davantage le public à la protection et à la promotion des droits de l'enfant. Ce n'est certes pas une mission impossible.

- Si l'on reconnaît enfin le rôle important des ONG dans les processus de contrôle en tant que nécessite absolue à la rationalisation du travail du comité.
- Si l'on dote le comité de plus de moyens matériels et humain afin d'assurer sa tâche dans les meilleures conditions et les meilleurs délais.

– Si nous réfléchissons sur la nécessité de trouver d'autres institutions pour décharger le comité d'une partie du travail et de rendre ainsi le contrôle plus pratique et surtout plus accessible à tous.
– Si enfin nous imaginons l'intervention des "sujets" de tout cet arsenal juridique a savoir les enfants, en leur donnant enfin, comme le stipule la convention la possibilité de faire entendre leur voix en tant qu'êtres humains à part entière.

Réaliser ces objectifs, c'est donner enfin un sens à notre action et rendre possible "une surveillance propre et efficace des acquis de l'enfant".

ELŻBIETA CZYŻ

Process of Implementation of the Convention on the Rights of the Child in Poland

Poland signed and ratified the Convention on the Rights of the Child. It has been in force since 7th July 1991. Before ratification, a scientific conference on "The Convention on the Rights of the Child versus Polish Law" was held at the Polish Parliament (Sejm). It was stated there that generally, Polish legislations (except for few and less important rules) were in accordance with the contents and requirements of the Convention, and it could therefore be ratified.

Indeed, the basic assumptions of the Convention, i.e. the principle of equal treatment in relation to law, family autonomy (respecting rights and responsibilities of both parents), the principle of the well-being of the child and the principle of the welfare state are in agreement with the assumptions of the Polish Family Law. This statement does not entitle one to claim that Polish Law is in accordance with the Convention. However, any detailed investigation has not been conducted so far. The matter of compatibility of Polish Law with the Convention was commented at the Supreme Court on the occasion of answering the Supreme Court President's question on how (taking into consideration article 21 of the Convention) to deal with an adoption case if the applicant is a resident of a foreign country. Answering this question at the Supreme Court a resolution was passed demanding consideration of the relevant provision of the Convention as the Polish Law does not contain particular normalizations regarding foreign adoptions. It has been acknowledged that the state law contains some gaps which enables courts to apply the Convention resolutions directly. Considering the problem of the application of the Convention by courts, it has been claimed that the Constitution of 1952 did not contain any regulations with regard to the application of international conventions. What is more, it did not point out any ways of transformation of treaty norms into inner norms.

Constitution amendments introduced in 1992 (article 33) allow for international agreements to be ratified and renounced by the President. Any ratification of international agreements that requires serious financial liabilities or necessary changes in legislation must be accepted by Parliament (Sejm). There is no uniform view regarding the relation between treaty law and inner

E. Verhellen (ed.), Monitoring Children's Rights, 453–455.
© 1996 *Kluwer Law International. Printed in the Netherlands.*

law. Some people claim that international agreements become part of the Polish legal system at the time of its ratification and publication in Dziennik Urzedowy. In case of conflict with inner regulations the international agreement has priority over inner law. The relation between the norms of the Convention and inner law is to be solved in the future Constitution of the Republic of Poland and in the Act regarding international agreements. Suggested solutions emphasize the priority of treaty law over inner law. The fact that the Parliament (Sejm) agreed to ratify the Convention on the Rights of the Child and that it was published in Dziennik Ustaw mean that the Convention may be applied by courts as legislative acts with all the resultant consequences. It should be emphasized that the stipulating character of the Convention resolutions (states *assure*; they *will undertake* the right steps; they *will respect* and so on) make their direct application more difficult. The provision in the Act on the System of Education of 1991 may be treated as the indication of the implementation of the Convention. Its preamble says "Education in the Republic of Poland is common welfare of the society; it is guided by principles included in the Constitution of the Republic of Poland and the recommendations included in the Declaration of Human Rights, the International Treaty of Civil and Political Rights and the International Convention on the Rights of the Child. Articles 35 point b and 36 point 1 of the general school statutory say that the pupil is provided with the right to corporal immunity and respect for his/her dignity, that is connected with the ratification of the Convention.

Unfortunately the recording of rights does not guarantee their compliance, and that is why it is necessary to introduce some means for their execution. Generally, Polish law is compatible with the fundamental regulations of the Convention. However, there are many regulations relating to the child's rights and personal freedom which do not exist in Polish law. In some cases it is only the lack of appropriate provisions, in others the lack of adequate interpretations that have not been applied so far. For example, article 12 of the Convention states that the child has the right to shape his/her opinions and express them in any judicial and administrative proceedings affecting the child. The child may be represented by his/her spokesman or may participate in the above mentioned proceedings himself/herself. Polish law provides for the minor to be heard at some proceedings concerning the child. For example, children are not allowed to express their will in divorce cases (the problem of choosing the parent, a guardian taking direct care of the minor, the problem of contacts with that parent who does not take care for the child directly). In practice, the child's right to have contact with both parents is often broken. The Family and Guardianship Code contains the provision of the right of both parents to raise the child but there is no provision about the right of the child to have contact with both parents (article 9, 2 and 3 of the Convention). The next example is the right to identity including the right to surname (article 8 of the Convention). The Polish Civil Code (article 23) says that every person has the right to protection of his/her freedoms, for example, his/her surname. Simultaneously the Family and Guardianship Code provides for the change of children's names and surnames without their agreement. Only 13-year-old children are asked to give their consent. It is obvious that mostly children who are small and unaware of their rights are adopted. As there is a regulation that says that "every person has the right to protection of his/her freedoms" no particular legal changes should be introduced except the appropriate interpretations of the existing ones.

The Helsinki Foundation for Human Rights together with the Committee for the Protection of Children's Rights and the Polish Foundation of Children and Youth tried to present the legal situation of the child considering a few fundamental rights (the rights of the child in family, school, hospital, court, educational centre and so on) and compare them with the Convention standards. Preliminary analysis prove that protection of the child's rights, especially personal rights and freedoms, are insufficient. In our opinion thorough analysis of Polish civil, penal and administrative law would be worth analysing with regard to their potential of protecting the rights of the child.

Summing up, we cannot say that the Convention has been implemented into inner law as any activities with regard to this process have not been undertaken so far. However, we may underline the positive effects of the ratification of the Convention. Discussing the child's rights, especially his/her personal freedoms, is a new phenomenon in Poland and is undoubtedly connected with the ratification of the Convention. Although the records in the Education System Act and General School Statutory referring to the child's right to dignity and corporal immunity are still imperfect, they prove that some evolution has begun with respect to children's rights. Lately, the possibility of appointing a ombudsman for children's rights has been considered. According to the opinion poll by OBOP 60% of the inquired into that matter state that such institution is necessary in Poland.

NOTE

This text was written in 1994. In 1995 the provisions about adoption in the family code were changed. New legislation is more compatible with the provisions of the convention. For example: the judge must ask the child under 13 years old for his/her consent for adoption and for the change of the name if the child understands his/her situation properly.

GIEDRA DAGILIENE

The UN Convention on the Rights of the Child in Lithuania

In 1988, together with the expressive movement for independence of Lithuania, parents of Lithuanian children started an uprising for the rights of their children and family.

We called upon the Government to make it possible for children to grow up in their families, and not in institutions. Delegations of mothers went to the Ministries and the Government with declarations and signatures. Some of our demands were fulfilled. Mothers can stay at home with their children until the children are three years old. Also financial assistance was delivered from the State's budget for children up to 1.5 years old. The working place for mothers must be preserved, which means a guarantee for the mothers' pensions.

We were only mothers, and not lawyers. The lack of information about our rights made it necessary for us to analyze the structure of services for children and families. We must study the actual laws and international regulations if we want to change something by legal reform through political process.

At first the main attention was devoted to grasping the new situation and collecting information about the conditions of children in Lithuania from different Ministries. We found very formal statistics, and insisted on obtaining more information. Uniting people who hold the same view and keeping contact with society required much effort. The main task was to identify current problems of children, to attract society's and Government's attention, to initiate amendments of laws – the Constitutional law at first.

The following topics are being discussed at the Ministries, the Government and the Committees of the Seimas of the Republic of Lithuania:
- military service and civil service;
- child care;
- the adoption of orphans;
- board schools reform for abandoned children;
- food supply in schools and special food for babies;
- the prevention of children's invalidity;
- the prevention of youth delinquency;
- cruel behaviour towards children, including sexual abuse;
- the abolishment of corporal punishment.

E. Verhellen (ed.), Monitoring Children's Rights, 457–461.
© 1996 *Kluwer Law International. Printed in the Netherlands.*

Round table discussions with different organizations, municipal workers and political leaders responsible for solving the problems were established.

The main means undertaken were publicity and initiatives at all levels. Difficulties were encountered in creating basic material and in other areas. Unwillingness to accept the new wave was expressed by idle, ignoring suggestions and even by slander. The most active members of the Lithuanian Committee on the Rights of the Child, women-mothers, families and youngsters had to overcome many obstacles standing between Lithuania and the rest of the world, e.g. they had to resist blackmail. Initial attempts to create an economically independent organization could not be realized in this period.

Some main difficulties, due to growing inflation and lack of knowledge, could only be overcome by consistent work and the dissemination of true information about the situation of children in the country. At the same time we tried to find ways of how to solve current problems in the light of the articles of the Convention.

A child is a developing human being, and his or her needs are as important as those of adults. The events of life taking place around children also have enormous effects on how they will behave in future society. Today the main attention is devoted to political events that confront people with each other. If adults do not have time for their children, it is difficult to expect love and understanding in solving State matters. The movement for mother, child and family rights had to concentrate on concrete activities.

Due to the efforts of the Swedish organization *Rädda Barnen* and the personal efforts made by Karin Soder, Thomas Hammarberg and Lenart Lindgren, a similar organization, called the Lithuanian Save the Children (Gelbekit vaikus) was established in Vilnius, the Capital of the Republic of Lithuania. The organization established her legal status in 1991.

People having different political views and religious convictions became active members of the organization. The general aim now becomes more apparent: the conditions of children must virtually be changed and their living standards have to be improved by applying complex means, with an emphasis on legal means.

Although the relations were not constant, Rädda Barnen Sweden was the only reliable support for the newly created structure dealing with children's rights.

After the Lithuanian independence from the Soviet regime on 11 March 1990, during a period of four years of democracy development, 20 new organizations for child care were established and 100 national standing public societies seeking to develop complete programmes for children. There are nearly 2000 institutions for child care and disabled persons care in Lithuania, but family needs are still our first attention.

The Human Rights Committee at the Supreme Council of the Republic of Lithuania was the first structure at the Highest level where voluntary advisors on children's rights had a possibility to influence State policy. After proposals by several NGOs the Lithuanian Government, understanding that there are many children in Lithuania living in very hard conditions, acceded to the UN Convention on the Rights of the Child on January 6, 1992.

Notwithstanding the consciousness of individual politicians, it was possible to influence Lithuanian policy only by drastic means. So was part 14 of the Family and Marriage Code, regulating adoption and foster care, approved after a struggle of two years. We disclosed illegal foreign adoptions with the support of the Procurator, bringing into light a complete chaos in the system of child and foster care. Even taking into consideration the fact that individual politicians were persuaded that it is possible to establish a National Adoption Centre, the Seimas of the Republic of Lithuania did not take any global decision. Other laws and regulations were not parallelly changed. The court will now urgently look at the requirements of law, but municipal services can take care of themselves. It is too difficult to control the whole situation, i.e. to control information about children who need a family and of families who can adopt children in the native country. After the new Adoption Law, intercountry adoption became more effective, but still there is no possibility to control the process. Parental training for instance is something we can only dream of.

The Constitution of the Republic of Lithuania was adopted by the citizens on 25 January 1992. The 3rd part regulates relations between the State and society.

- Article 38: "The family shall be the basis of society and State. Family, motherhood, fatherhood, and childhood shall be under the care and protection of the State..."
- Article 39: "The State shall take care of families bringing up children at home and shall render them support in the manner established by law. The law shall provide for paid maternity leave before and after childbirth, as well as for favourable working conditions and other privileges. Children who are under age shall be protected by law."
- Article 41: "Education shall be compulsory for persons under the age of sixteen..."
- Article 42: "Culture, science, research and teaching shall be unrestricted."
- Article 44: "Censorship of mass media shall be prohibited ..."
- Article 45: "Ethnic communities of citizens shall independently administer the affairs of their ethnic culture, education, organizations, charity, and mutual assistance. The State supports ethnic communities..."

After the Constitution, the Citizenship Law was the most important message solving national relations and youth rights.
- Article 8: "Citizenship of children whose parents are citizens of the Republic of Lithuania: A child, both of whose parents at the moment of his or her birth were citizens of the Republic of Lithuania, shall be a citizen of

the Republic of Lithuania regardless of whether he or she born on the territory of the Republic of Lithuania, or beyond its borders."

– Article 9: "Citizenship of children one whose parent is a Citizen of the Republic of Lithuania: A child, one whose parent at the moment of his or her birth was a Citizen of the Republic of Lithuania, shall be a citizen of the Republic of Lithuania, if: 1. he or she was born on the territory of the Republic of Lithuania; 2. he or she was born beyond the borders of the Republic of Lithuania permanent place of residence on the territory of Republic of Lithuania. If at the moment of the child's birth one parent was a citizen of the Republic of Lithuania, and both parents had a parental place of residence beyond the borders of the Republic of Lithuania, the citizenship of the child, until he or she is 18 years of age, shall be established by the parents' agreement. A child, one of whose parents at the moment of his or her birth was a citizen of the Republic of Lithuania, and the other parent was either a person without citizenship or unknown, shall be a citizen of the Republic of Lithuania regardless of his or her place of birth."

– Article 10: "Acquiring citizenship of the Republic of Lithuania by children whose parents are persons without Citizenship: A child, whose parents are persons without citizenship and permanent residents in Lithuania, shall acquire citizenship of the Republic of Lithuania."

– Article 11: "Citizenship of children whose parents are unknown: A child found on the territory of the Republic of Lithuania, both of whose parents are unknown, shall be a citizen of the Republic of Lithuania, unless there are grounds for him or her to acquire a different status...".

So all children including national minorities have the same rights.

The new economical and social situation, established after a four-year period of changing society, demands new initiatives.

The mass media reveal more facts concerning children's rights violations by individuals and state.

Twenty charitable organizations dealing with specific problems of children gathered for round table discussions. The informational booklet about the Convention and the work of Save the children was spread.

Voluntary advisors of the Committee for monitoring article 44 have written proposals to the highest institution, the President of the Republic of Lithuania, and reminded that it was time to submit the initiative report to the UN Committee on the Rights of the Child.

The *General Guidelines regarding the form and content of initial reports to be submitted by States Parties under article 44, paragraph 1 (a), of the Convention on the Rights of the Child* was distributed to all institutions dealing with this matter.

We understand the limited possibilities imposed by the budget when unemployment is as high and the health care sector is dealing with extremely hard circumstances.

Under the pressure of NGOs, the Government wishes to establish a Children's Rights Service under the Ministry for Social Care. During 1992-1994 the professional experts and voluntary advisers have prepared several drafts of regulations and a status for this institution. The opinion that the Children's Rights Service must implement the UN Convention in Lithuania became more and more widespread.

According the recommendations of Rädda Barnen and Defence for Children International, the group of voluntary advisers has prepared a questionnaire for NGOs following the *General Guidelines*, and distributed this document among different organizations as well as to the highest levels of decision-making institutions. Thirty commissioners are competent and ready to write an alternative report and comment on the Governemental report.

The draft Bill of Children's Rights and Protection Law has been prepared by a working group under the Justice Institute. The experts would like to know the opinion of NGOs and also that of parents and young people.

Of course we will need examples and technical assistance from international bodies. The material obtained from the Ghent Conference will be the basis of our continuing work.

PANAYOT RANDEV, ILKA GRIGOROVA and MARIA NIKOLOVA

Children at Risk and Defence of their Rights in Bulgaria (The CAR Project)

I. THE PHILOSOPHY OF THE CAR PROJECT

During the last decade, and especially in the last 3–4, years the situation of Bulgarian children is in evident aggravation from all possible perspectives – medical, social, behavioural, legal, educational, moral, etc. There is evidently a need for a new social mechanism and specially for a new monitoring system, for dealing with the growing (as quantity and as gravity) concern of child-related problems.

With a grant from the German Marshall Fund of the United States, the Association of Professional Psychologists in Education (APPE) started in February 1994 a one-year project named "Raising public awareness and setting up central informational system and office on children's rights, child abuse and children at risk in Bulgaria" (CAR Project).

The immediate objectives of the CAR Project are:

1. To set up a central information system and a consultative office on children's rights, child abuse and children at risk.
2. To elaborate and implement a system of collecting, classifying, storing, verifying, analysing and distributing the information, and to offer different informational and consultative services to all persons and organisations (state, local, NGO, etc.) which need (or may be interested in) such information, advice and support.
3. To keep journalists from different mass media (newspapers, magazines, journals, radio and TV) interested in and acquainted with the facts, concepts, preventive strategies and different activities concerning children's rights, child abuse and neglect and different groups of children at risk using awareness meetings and seminars. The journalists interested in this will be invited to participate in network or lobby on those problems and to be part of media campaigns on children's rights and child abuse.
4. To evaluate the needs for such an informational and consultative system and those services, and to evaluate the first year of this system, as well as the possible directions and forms of its development.

In May 1994 the APPE established the Centre "Children at Risk".

E. Verhellen (ed.), Monitoring Children's Rights, 463–474.
© 1996 *Kluwer Law International. Printed in the Netherlands.*

II. GENERAL FRAMEWORK OF THE CENTRE "CHILDREN AT RISK"

The Centre is an independent non-governmental substructure of APPE for activities, projects and social entrepreneurship in the field of children at risk (medical, social, legal, educational, behavioural, ethnic, ecological, religious, transport, etc.), child abuse and maltreatment and for effective advocacy and defence of children's rights. The philosophy of the Centre is an eco-systemic approach.

At present, there are 3 professionals and 12 volunteers engaged at the Centre and the subjects are persons from 1 to 18 years. The clients can be children, adolescents, parents, specialists, administrators, the state, the community or private organisations or institutions.

The main functions of the Centre are: Information; Consultation and counselling; Mediation and moderation; Advocacy; Education (awareness and training); Research.

The main principles of the Centre are: Client-centred; Eco-systemic approach; Neutrality; Volunteer (benevolent, non-profit); Explicity; Involvement; Confidentiality; Demonstrative (pilot/model).

The introduction of the concepts "Risk" and "Children at Risk" (medical, social, behavioural, ecological, legal, transport, political, moral, multiple, etc.) *is a useful and common methaphor* for professionals, citizens and administrators and a conceptual, administrative, legal and financial *framework* for awareness, understanding, management and evaluation of the activities (work, projects, programmes, etc.) in this field. Through the paradigm "Children at Risk" "*re-labelling*" or "*positive reframing*" of children, their families, institutions, specialists, approaches, and working with them becomes possible. This re-labelling can permit and facilitate processes of their change and development, as well as the process of internationalisation of the Bulgarian legal system, practice and socio-cultural attitudes and stereotypes. This can facilitate using and introducing international experience and integration within European and global structures.

Through the paradigm "Children at Risk" we put accent on the *process* of increasing or decreasing the risk, on the real *effectiveness* of our work, on its limitation and disappearance, on *our own role* in this process, and not on self-sufficient verbal or practical activities, without clear and measurable social outcomes.

From an eco-systemic point of view, it is necessary to shift our focus from analysis and solving of concrete cases toward a catalysation of a new and holistic social mechanism that deals with a whole spectrum of problems related to children and their families, because, as it is well-known from the system analysis – a partial solving of the whole problem is better than a holistic solving of the partial problem.

If we use Figure 1 we can say that there is an urgent need to reorient or shift our present focus from A and C (and corresponding social institutions

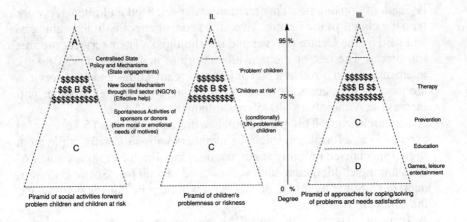

Figure 1.

and legal, administrative and financial regulations) to B, e.g. re-thinking, re-viewing the A and C through the prism of B:

The main 3 levels of work of the Centre "Children at Risk" are:

1. *Work with a concrete case (case study)* – by phone, face-to-face communication, analysis of documents and articles in media, letters from or to different organisations, mediation between two sides in conflict, etc.;
2. *Work with small and medium groups* of parents, children and adolescents, specialists, administrators and others who have common problems – self-help groups, support groups, forming interests or pressure groups, seminars, groups for peer counselling, etc.;
3. *Macro-social interventions* – information in media or media campaigns, lobbying in parliament, in ministries and other state or municipal institutions, monthly public trials, creating local and national data base, annual reports, annual awards, etc.

At this stage of development, the Centre "Children at Risk" has the following structure:

1. A Team for Management and Co-ordination of the Centre and the CAR project. The members of this team are: the co-ordinator, the office-manager and one Technical Assistant. Each of them has a job specification. They are engaged between 4 and 8 hours daily in the Centre and are paid.
2. A Team for First and Direct work with clients (hotline and face-to-face communication). This team includes 12 volunteers (specialists, parents, students, retired professionals) and its role is to establish (by phone or face-to-face) contact with clients. They are engaged between 4 and 12 hours weekly in the Centre and are volunteers.

3. A Team of consultants. This team offers specialised and intensive work with the clients of the Centre. Two of the consultants are directly engaged and paid by the Centre (lawyer and psychologist). Their services are free for clients. The rest of the consultants (up to now more than 10) work independently in governmental or private organisations and their services are paid by the clients themselves. In the near future their number will increase very rapidly (to 40–50 consultants).

4. A Research team. This team (which will consist of 10–15 persons, at present, is at a formation stage. Its members will work without payment in two specialised monthly seminars: one, for "Interdisciplinary study of risks among children and adolescents", and second for "Social Entrepreneurship". Some members of this team will help in statistical study and the data base of the Centre;

5. A Team of Experts. The aim of this team is to be a resource for other Centre's teams. Its members will be leading Bulgarian professionals in this field. This team is in process of formation. Until now there are 3 members of this team. They will be also evaluators of the work of the Centre.

For a better level of quality of the services of the Centre Temporary Guidelines of its activities were established. These Temporary Guidelines are formulated in a 10-page document. There are 13 principles of the Centre, 17 rules of the work and 7 steps in working with clients.

III. THE FIRST 6 MONTHS OF THE FUNCTIONING OF THE CENTRE (MAY-DECEMBER 1994)

The Centre started this work at the end of May. All telephone calls and face-to-face meetings in the Centre "Children at Risk" were registered in specially prepared data sheets. For the first 6 months (1.6.-1.12.1994) of the activities of the Centre "Children at Risk" there were more than 700 telephone calls.

1. Approximately 100 calls were from journalists;
2. More than 150 were calls from specialists (psychologists, doctors, social workers, educators, jurists, etc.). They expressed their interest for the work of the Centre and some of them offered themselves or their organisations to support the work of the Centre.
3. 458 persons asked the Centre "Children at Risk" for information, consultation and help. We call them "clients" of the Centre. 278 persons (61%) were from other Bulgarian towns and 180 (39%) were from Sofia. 306 (67%) came for face-to-face conversation in the Centre for more intensive communication. More than 75% of the clients were women (mothers, wives, grand-mothers), and the rest were men. Approximately 65% of clients define the problem as their own, 25% as joint with another person, and 10% as problem of other persons.

Until the present, the following groups of problems arise from the data accumulated after 6 months of work of the Centre "Children at Risk":

A. Legal problems	*48 cases (10.4%)*
1. Child abuse (physical, sexual, emotional)	16 cases (3.5%)
2. Legal aspects of adoption	11 cases (2.4%)
3. Juvenile delinquency	8 cases (1.75%)
4. Non-payment of money for children after divorce	8 cases (1.75%)
5. Kidnapping	2 cases (0.4%)
6. Disappeared/burned child	1 case (0.2%)
7. Father to whom mother does not permit to meet his son for 1 year	1 case (0.2%)
8. Child from a mother with AIDS is not permitted to enter school	1 case (0.2%)
B. Social and economical problems	*211 cases (46.1%)*
1. Non payment of child compensations (specially for unemployed mothers)	81 cases (17.7%)
2. Grave living conditions and poverty	52 cases (11.4%)
3. Educational segregation (in selection procedures in schools)	19 cases (4.2%)
4. Problems of families with many children	18 cases (3.9%)
5. Problems of unemployed families	18 cases (3.9%)
6. Problems of families from Gypsy minority	7 cases (1.5%)
7. Beggars	6 cases (1.3%)
8. Closing educational and social child institutions	6 cases (1.3%)
9. Lack of vital drugs and food for children	4 cases (0.9%)
C. Behavioural and parental problems	*199 cases (43.5%)*
1. Behavioural problems of the children	67 cases (14.8%)
2. Parental problems	39 cases (8.6%)
3. Problems with adopted children	32 cases (7.0%)
4. Problems with parents in divorce	24 cases (5.2%)
5. Mental health problems	17 cases (3.7%)
6. Drug users	14 cases (3.1%)
7. Religious sects	6 cases (1.3%)

This classification is temporary (ad hoc). We have decided that after we will have accumulated 1,000 cases, their statistical analysis and theoretical interpretation, we will discuss a more precise classification, which will consider the empirical reality, the Bulgarian as well as the foreign classification of such problems. This classification must be multidimensional. The elaboration of such a classification itself is an important problem (conceptual, practical, legal, administrative, statistical, etc.) which needs time and efforts.

Apart from statistical data and analysis, there are unique and concrete cases. At weekly seminars of the collaborators of the Centre, (at the seminar usually attend between 10 and 15 persons) 17 specific and typical cases are presented and discussed. Four of these cases are analysed in depth more than one time and with participation of external specialists or persons in connection with the given case:

1. *the Case of Rosen*, a 4-year-old boy who died of a rare infection, but after negligence from different state institutions – foster home, emergency medical service of Sofia, municipality social assistance service, as well as police, journalists and doctors.
2. *the Case of Nadya*, a 14-year-old adopted girl, who lives in very grave family conditions – mother is invalid without income, uncle who sexually abused the girl. Nadya is a prostitute and drug-user with dependence on drugs and with several suicide attempts.
3. *the Case of the grandmother from Burgas*, who took care of 5 children from her 23-year-old daughter. One of the children possibly was sold because nobody knows were she is, and another child is on the way to be sold.
4. *the case of Rosina*, a 6-year-old girl who was kidnapped by bodyguards of her father after a divorce, while the court gave the parental rights to the mother. During the kidnapping she was interrogated by the police in Varna. The aim of this interrogation, which is illegal because of the age of the girl, was to prepare a document in which it was noted that Rosina did not love her mother and wanted to live with her father. This document was accepted by the court, which also means a violation of the law. A very similar case was the case of a 7-year-old boy from Lom.

To work with this amount of cases we need a number of volunteers. In several courses (in May, September and November) we train 51 persons. These volunteers receive short-term training (30 to 40 hours intensive course and 40–60 hours participation in weekly seminars on concrete case, e.g. the total training is 80–100 hours). We prepare them for work on the hotline or as a peer-counsellor and facilitators of self-help groups. This kind of work (group work) will be our focus in near future (1995).

IV. Analysing Publications about Children in the Written Media

The team of the Centre extracted 1,116 articles discussing child-related issues from the disposable written media (15 national daily and weekly newspapers) in the period between May 15 and November 31. The newspapers "24 hours" and "Standard" were present on daily base and other newspapers less frequently. These 1,116 articles were classified in 10 groups with the following distribution in numbers and per cents:

1. legal(crime)-related issues	304 articles (27.2%)
2. drugs-related issues	33 articles (2.9%)
3. religious sects-related issues	93 articles (8.3%)
4. social assistance-related issues	43 articles (3.9%)
5. health-related issues	75 articles (6.7%)
6. other risks-related issues	81 articles (7.3%)
7. education-related issues 227	articles (20.3%)
8. human development and creativity issues	31 articles (2.8%)
9. business-related issues	17 articles (1.5%)
10. foster homes and help-related issues	43 articles (3.9%)
11. donation-related issues	23 articles (2.1%)
12. other topics	146 articles (13.1%)

For example, we show statistics of the content of the first group of articles –
Legal(crime)-oriented. The subdivision of topics is as follow (N=304):

homicides of new-born	31 articles (10.2%)
suicides	17 articles (5.6%)
children killed by parents	5 articles (1.7%)
other types of child-related homicides	21 articles (6.9%)
disappeared children	8 articles (2.6%)
sexual abuse (incest and rape)	54 articles (17.8%)
prostitution	18 articles (6.0%)
physical abuse	32 articles (10.5%)
accidents	19 articles (6.2%)
property-related crimes	22 articles (7.2%)
other types of crimes	25 articles (8.2%)
child-related crimes abroad	41 articles (13.5%)
child-related state or other programmes	11 articles (3.6%)

At present we analyse these articles in depth under 13 criteria and we will
publish this statistical analysis in March 1995. For these reasons we will
analyse all 8 national newspapers on a daily basis for one month.

V. PUBLIC AWARENESS ACTIVITIES OF THE CENTRE

1. In 1994 the Centre "Children at Risk" organised 5 press conferences
   which were devoted to specific children's rights related issues or on
   specific dates (June 1st, 15 September, 10 December).
2. From October onwards a 30-minute weekly radio programme "Children
   at Risk" (for 40 weeks) will start at the National Radio in which we will
   invite representatives of different NGOs who work with specific groups
   of children at risk.

3. In 1994 representatives of the Centre participated in 15 radio interviews or shows, in 6 TV shows, and approximately 25–30 articles and information about Centre "Children at Risk" appeared in newspapers.

VI. Organising the Umbrella Coalition – Association "Children at Risk"

The Fist National Interdisciplinary Multisectorial Conference "Children at Risk" was organised by APPE with sponsorship from 6 Bulgarian Ministries in November 1993. More than 350 participants from approximate 100 state, municipal, professional and non-governmental organisations from all over the country took part in it. The APPE was the initiator and principal organiser of the inauguration at May 13, 1994 in the National Palace of Culture of the umbrella coalition of NGOs Association "Children at Risk" which include 12 NGOs (ranged from very large ones as Bulgarian Red Cross, with more than 200,000 members to small parent groups of children with leukaemia or muscle dystrophy with not more than 50 members) and a number of individual members (specialists, parents, administrators, journalists). Now the Association "Children at Risk" is in process of legal registration and we hope that in spring 1995 this will be happening;

Before and after the official opening of the Centre "Children at Risk" we established many contacts with a number of persons and institutions. Some of these were: Ministry of Education, Ministry of Health, Ministry of Justice, Ministry of Home Affairs, Ministry of Labour and Social Welfare, Ministry of Defence, Ministry of Transportation, Ministry of Telecommunications, Ministry of Culture, Municipality of Sofia, more than 20 newspapers and magazines, many schools, hospitals, social services etc., as well as with many leading professionals in different fields of science and practice. The Centre "Children at Risk" established very good contacts with students from the University of Sofia and from the New Bulgarian University, and more than 35 of them visited the Centre and are ready to be engaged as voluntary members.

Our aim is to establish and to help structuring the "Third sector" (NGOs, non-profit, non-governmental), especially in this part with regard to family, children, education, health care and social welfare and social work for children and their families as a model, in a way it can be a model for other parts of the Third sector (effective, pragmatic, open, human), creating examples of what we call "social entrepreneurship", based on modern business-like management of organisation of the work, as well creating "live systems" in the field of as work with children and their families.

VII. OUR PLANS FOR THE FUTURE

In the next pages we present in short our future projects in the following three years, by means of how we will realise as our "social entrepreneurship" approach.

1. Organising a travelling exposition (in the largest Bulgarian towns) and support activities (seminars, concerts, charity balls, etc.) on children at risk, children rights and the families and communities in which they live.
2. Creating a Centre for training and supporting young or adult volunteers, peer-counsellors and self-help groups to work with different groups of children, youth and families at risk.
3. Creating in the 10 largest bulgarian towns, a National Network of Regional Centres for Information, Consultation and Support for children at risk (hotline, consultation, library, data-base, self-help groups, etc.).
4. Initiating the National Network "Children at Risk and Children' Rights" of institutions, specialists, citizens, and teams, which will work on concrete projects or programmes.
5. Starting a Foundation "Child Wish" to help terminally or chronically ill children mainly not with money but by making direct or distant (by phone, post cards, etc.) meetings with famous Bulgarian or foreign personalities (in arts, science, sport, etc.).
6. Preparing a TV 30–40 minute serial "Children at Risk".
7. Starting publishing a journal "Children at Risk".
8. Starting monthly public demonstrative judge trials (role-played) concerned with concrete typical social (administrative, legal, financial, medical, educational, etc.) problems in connection with children at risk and their families. These public trials will be shown on TV in a compressed form – 45–50 minutes.
9. Establishing an Interdisciplinary Seminar and Research Centre for surveys, statistics and analyses of problems connected with children at risk (system of indicators, data-base of cases, statistical and science investigation for discovering specific patterns, factors, trends and future scenarios).
10. Establishing contacts (by postal mail, E-mail or personal) with major international and foreign national associations, foundations, institutes, agencies and other structures working or concerned with problems of children at risk, as well as including them as a part of different international networks.
11. Opening a shop (or chain of shops) for second-hand products or products which are created or produced by children at risk which can be sold at a very reduced price (2 or 3 times) to the persons with social or financial problems.
12. Starting a yearly competition and giving awards for activities, ideas, persons, projects, sponsors etc. in the field of work with children at risk

(near to 10 December – the World Day of Human Rights, especially of children's rights).

13. Starting the preliminary and preparatory work for creating a National Educational and Recreational Active (Theme) Park near Sofia (NORA-Park).

14. Starting a Junior School for Social Enterpreneurship for supporting adolescents to acquire skills to become effective social helpers and to become skillful in realising small social-oriented individual, group or community projects to help children from risk groups.

15. Initiation of a Fund "Children at Risk" for fund-raising for activities, projects and programmes which will be mainly preventive in nature in the whole spectrum of children at risk. For some years, step by step, this Fund can move from pure charity into insurance-based with parents, institutions, municipals and state as a clients.

16. Lobbying to establish a National Agency for Defence and Development of Children and for priority voting in the Parliament (the Laws concerning children and families) for equalising the Bulgarian laws and social practices and institutions with international norms and practices, in particular, with UN Convention of Rights of the Child.

Based on the text above, the reader can see that the activities related to the CAR project go beyond the initial relatively narrow objectives of the project. After approximately 1-year work on this project it became evident for us that if we want to be effective in our work with different groups of children at risk, as well as with persons who are connected with those children, we must differentiate and diversify our activities and increase the amount of material, financial and human resources which are devoted to these children. In our work in the following one "to" two years, with co-operation with our colleagues from coalition Association "Children at Risk" and from spectrum of other NGOs, we intend to combine 4 different perspectives:

1. Promotion of children's rights (mainly legal perspective).

2. Establishing, a now non-existing social mechanism for social work with children at risk and their families (social work and social welfare perspective).

3. Supporting community, institutional, family and individual efforts for child development (intellectual, emotional, personal, social skills, etc.) – (child development perspective).

4. Supporting individual and community efforts for development of conditions, infrastructure and specific forms of play, leisure, entertainment, spirit of enterpreneurship, both in adolescents, and in persons which live or work with them (social enterpreneurship perspective).

We think that specific organisational forms, projects, programs, institutions, etc... must be created for each of these perspectives, or for different combinations. This will a create social infrastructure which can be a good framework

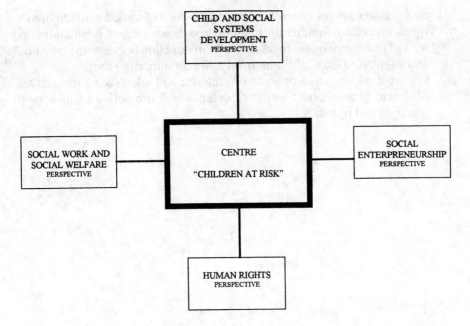

Figure 2. The socio-ecological space of possible perspectives for working with specific groups of children at risk, their families and different social institutions.

for effective work for fulfillment of the needs of children at risk. In Figure 2, the reader can see the possible social ecology of such organisations.

In Figure 2 we show that the main efforts in 1995 of the Center "Children at Risk" will be in a Human Rights perspective. This work will be carried out in the following 5 directions:

1. An analysis of Bulgarian legislation concerning children and a proposition of its changes in line with international legislation in this field. Several concrete activities here are: starting a campaign for public awareness about the UN Convention on the Rights of the Child; preparing and publishing a book on the UN Convention with its text, comments and cases and distributing this book among lawyers, social workers, administrators, school principals, journalists, as well as awareness seminars on the subject (this activities will be made in cooperation with other NGOs within collation of NGOs "Children at Risk".

2. Design and establishment of a nation-wide non-governmental system for monitoring children's rights within the framework of the UN Convention on the Rights of the Child (in cooperation with other NGOs).

3. Education for human rights with children within and out of school with accent on children's rights (emissions of TV, radio and written media, seminars for journalists, teachers, school principals).

4. Social advocacy for concrete, but typical, cases of violation of children's rights especially from minority group and disadvantaged populations, as well as joint activities with other NGOs in direction to overcome labelling and stigmatisation of children from different minority groups.
5. Concrete participative projects of children and adolescents themselves (different peer-to-peer forms) for defence and promotion of their own opinions and rights.

CYNTHIA PRICE COHEN

Monitoring the United Nations Convention on the Rights of the Child in a Non-party State: The United States

It is probably difficult for most people to understand why a country like the United States, which has always been known for its civil liberties and its support of rights and freedoms, has not yet ratified or even become a signatory to the United Nations Convention on the Rights of the Child.[1] This paper seeks to shed light on this question by providing insights into the workings of the American system and outlining strategies being used by children's rights advocates to promote the Convention's ratification and to implement the Convention's standards, even before the US becomes a State Party.

I. US FEDERAL SYSTEM

The United States is comprised of fifty separate states. While all of them are subject to certain constitutionally mandated federal constraints, each state has its own laws, system of taxation, and distinctive personality.

A. Demographic and Diversity Considerations

Approximately half of the states are larger than many European countries.[2] A comparison of population and geographic area in square miles between the United States and a randomly selected group of countries, based on the most recently available statistics, provides the following information:

---

[1] Convention on the Rights of the Child, G.A. Res. 44/25, 1 U.N. GAOR Supp. (No. 4a), U.N. Doc. A/144/149 (1989). On February 16, 1995, two months after this paper was presented in Gent, Ambassador Madeleine Albright signed the Convention on the Rights of the Child on behalf of the United States. This step was taken by the United States in response to a death bed letter to President Clinton from James Grant, former Executive Director of UNICEF, urging the US to sign and ratify the Convention.

[2] The author apologizes for not having had the time to do a full comparison of European countries and U. S. states.

E. Verhellen (ed.), Monitoring Children's Rights, 475–489.
© 1996 Kluwer Law International. Printed in the Netherlands.

Country	Population	Square Miles
Russian Federation	148,542,000	6,592,800
United States	248,709,873	3,618,770
Belgium	9,921,000	11,799
France	56,595,000	220,668
Netherlands	15,002,000	15,770
Spain	39,384,000	194,869
Sweden	8,564,000	173,731

The Netherlands is the most densely populated of these countries having almost 1000 residents per square mile. By comparison, the United States has only 68 residents per square mile, which is still greater than Sweden and the Russian Federation. Only the Russian Federation has more square miles of area than the United States, but with roughly half of the population. When one looks at these numbers in terms of a random selection of states, it is possible to get a better understanding of American diversity:

State	Population	Square Miles
California	30,379,811	158,706
Colorado	3,376,669	104,091
New York	18,057,602	49,108
Oklahoma	3,174,775	69,919
Ohio	10,938,800	41,330
Texas	17,348,206	226,807

Population density among the selected states ranges from 368 per square mile for New York to 32 per square mile in Colorado. In other words, there are some areas of the United States where population is fairly dense, but there are other vast areas of the US that are sparsely populated.

Although the United States is unified by a single, official language (English), many other languages are spoken throughout the country. Ethnic diversity reaches beyond cities and coastlines far into the interior of the United States. Thus, one can find enclaves of Germans, Italians, Czechs, Scandinavians, Mexicans, Latin Americans, Greeks, Jews, and Vietnamese scattered throughout the country, often in surprisingly remote places.

Each state is distinct, although there are some regional similarities. For example, cuisine varies among the states with a cluster of states known as New England (Massachusetts, New Hampshire, Rhode Island, Maine and Connecticut) being acclaimed for their sea food – especially scrod and lobster, while Louisiana is famous for its hot Cajun cooking, including blackened red-fish. Eating habits in states bordering on Mexico, such as Texas and New Mexico have been heavily influenced by Mexican seasonings and such dishes as chili and fajitas are found on most restaurant menus. Washington state is noted for its salmon, and California for its wine and its innovative use of fresh vegetables and herbs. These differences can be traced to two sources: geography, especially as relates to the availability of ingredients, and/or the tastes of the ethnic groups that settled there.

Food in Southern states that were part of the Confederacy before the Civil War, have a style of their own, a Southern grace and elegance and a cuisine that includes sweet potatoes and okra, vegetables originally cultivated by slaves from Africa. Western states tend to have a rugged "rough and ready" atmosphere, probably owing to the fact that these "wide open spaces," were part of the frontier and only came into existence as states around the turn of the century or after. Not surprisingly, since much of the West is cattle country, beef has an important place on the local menu. The influence of Native Americans is also becoming an important factor in American life. Previously confined to such states as Arizona, New Mexico, Oklahoma and the Dakotas, tribal leaders are expanding their influence and tribal activities are now taking place in many other states, such as New York and Connecticut. As yet, with the exception of Indian fry bread, their dietary habits have not become popularized.

Not only has the cuisine of states has been influenced by the national origins and customs of settlers, this is also true of the legal system. Everything from contracts to crime to marriage is governed by state law. What may be a capital crime in one state, may result in life imprisonment in another. What is a void marriage in some states, because of age or affinity, may be perfectly legal in another. The Northeastern part of the United States has been strongly effected by the laws of England, Spanish legal concepts have found their way into the laws of "border states," those which were at one time occupied by the Spanish and now share a border with Mexico.[3] Perhaps the most unique of the state legal systems is that of Louisiana, which has clearly evidences its roots in French law. It is this legal diversity which may interfere with efforts to have the Convention on the Rights of the Child ratified and may ultimately cause difficulty in successful implementation of the Convention in the United States.

---

[3] This difference is especially noticeable in the area of property law. Parts of the country influenced by the English are governed by a "title property" concept, while those with Spanish roots are governed by "community property." The difference is most apparent in cases of divorce. In "title property" jurisdictions the divorcing spouses own only that property to which they have formal title, meaning that it is listed in his or her name. In "community property" jurisdictions, all properties accrued during the marriage are the property of both divorcing spouses, regardless of who actually holds the title.

B. Federal/State Relationship

The United States Constitution consists of seven articles and a number of amendments, the first ten of which define the relationship between the federal government and the citizen and are known as the "Bill of Rights." The articles of the Constitution define the powers of the legislative branch, the presidency, and the judiciary, as well as the relationships between the states and between the states and the federal government. Although there are specific limitations on state power, such as prohibitions against treaty-making, issuing of money or collecting duties, except where a power has been expressly reserved to the federal government in the Constitution, all other powers belong to the states. In practical terms, the power of a state is the power to enact laws, to govern and to protect its citizens. Nevertheless, whenever there is a conflict between state law and federal law, federal law is supreme.

The relationship between the states and the federal government has been the basis for an enormous number of law suits. Because states have a tremendous reservoir of power, there are often conflicting opinions as to where federal power ends and the state's authority begins, a matter that must be decided by the federal courts. An example of this tension can be found in the control of commerce. Among the many powers of Congress is the power to "regulate commerce...among the several states."[4] Although the regulation of commerce is clearly a federal power, this language has been interpreted as meaning that whenever the commerce takes place solely within the state, where Congress has not taken action, it is open for regulation by the state government. Conflicts occur when the control of commerce within a state effects commerce in other states. For example, attempts at state regulation of child labor were seen by the Supreme Court as affecting interstate commerce. This was because children were a source of cheap labor, and where a state allowed children to work in factories, those factories were considered to have an unfair market advantage because the lower wages meant that there was a wider profit margin.

The Commerce Clause of the Constitution has been used as the basis for elimination of a number of social ills, such as gambling (interstate transportation of the instruments of gambling) and, more importantly, racial segregation. In the 1950s a series of Supreme Court cases cited the Commerce Clause as the basis for overturning state legislation permitting segregation in restaurants and motels.[5] The theory was that if black customers were excluded from these establishments, it would affect their freedom to travel and participate in commerce and that, therefore, desegregation could be advanced through federal regulation under the Commerce Clause. As can be seen from this illustration, limitations on state power come from two sources of the Constitution:

---

[4] United States Constitution, Article I x 8. To regulate commerce with foreign nations and among the several States and with the Indian tribes.

[5] These cases are known as Ollie's Barbecue and Heart of Atlanta Motel.

Congress, which has broad legislative powers and from the federal judiciary, which has the power to declare state laws unconstitutional.

While federal law tends to cover those concerns that affect the entire country, it is state law that governs most of the everyday life of the average American citizen. As stated above, state law controls everything from contracts to crime to marriage. The following list will give the reader some idea of the subject matter covered by broad reach of state legislation: contracts, business regulation and incorporation, inheritance, torts,[6] marriage, divorce, transportation, automobile registration, traffic regulations, sanitation, welfare, health, education, adoption, foster care, child custody, child abuse and neglect, child labor, pornography, crime, prisons, and juvenile justice. Nevertheless, under article IV of the United States Constitution, the laws and judicial rulings of one state must be recognized and upheld by all of the others. For example, the doctrine known as "full faith and credit" requires that a state recognize as legal a marriage that would be illegal under that state's law (such as a marriage between first cousins) provided it was legal in the state where the marriage took place.

Those who are familiar with the Convention on the Rights of the Child can see from the above list that if and when the United States ratifies the Convention, most of its implementation will take place at the state level. The main areas in which federal law will play a role is in the implementation of the civil and political rights that are protected by the Bill of Rights.

II. THE STATUS OF THE CONVENTION ON THE RIGHTS OF THE CHILD IN THE UNITED STATES

As of the time that this essay was written, the United States was one of fifteen of the world's nations that had yet to become signatories to the Convention on the Rights of the Child. Included in this group were: Andorra, Botswana, Krygystan, Kiribati, Malaysia, Oman, Saudi Arabia, Singapore, Solomon Islands, Somalia, Tonga, Tuvalu and the United Arab Emirates.[7] To an outside observer it is difficult to understand why a country as prosperous as the United States would be among these States.

---

[6] For those unfamiliar with American law, a tort is a "civil wrong." It is not a crime. It encompasses everything from negligence to libel and unlike a crime, the cause of action is brought by the injured party (in a crime it is the state that prosecutes) and a favorable judgement may result in an award of money damages. Unlike the European civil law system, the American common law system does not combine civil and criminal actions (delict), they are always kept separate, even if this results is two cases being brought in separate courts, but based on a single act.

[7] The following countries had signed, but not ratified: Haiti, Liechtenstein, Netherlands, Qatar, Samoa, South Africa, Switzerland and Turkey.

A. US Role in Drafting the Convention on the Rights of the Child

Lack of United States action toward ratification of the Convention becomes even less comprehensible to the observer, when one looks at the record of US participation in drafting the Convention. The text of more than half of the Convention's articles were effected by US input. Typically, US participation took one of two forms: comments and suggestions that ultimately affected the wording of the final draft of an article; or proposals for the texts of entirely new articles. The United States took part in the discussions and drafting of and ultimately influenced the wording of almost all of the Convention's substantive articles.[8] The following is a list of articles for which the United States made specific proposals and initiated the drafting:

---

article 3 (best interests of the child);
article 5 (parental guidance and the child's evolving capacities);
article 9 (separation from parents);
article 12 (child's opinion);
article 13 (freedom of expression);
article 14 (freedom of thought, conscience and religion);
article 15 (freedom of association and assembly);
article 16 (right to privacy);
article 17 (access to appropriate information);
article 19 (protection from abuse and neglect);
article 25 (periodic review of placement);
article 29 (aims of education); and
article 31 (leisure, recreation and cultural activities).

Of particular significance are articles 13-16. They are civil-political rights which are in the Convention solely because of the efforts of the US delegation. These are rather radical articles in that they grant to children rights not previously recognized under international law: the right to freedom of information, association, assembly and the right to privacy.[9] What is particu-

---

[8] For the full text of reports of the United Nations Working Group which drafted the Convention on the Rights of the Child for the years 1979-1989, see U.N. Doc. E/CN.4/1468 (1979); U.N. Doc. E/CN.4/L.1542 (1980); U.N. Doc. E/CN.4/1981/L.1575 (1981); U.N. Doc. E/CN.4/1982/L.41 (1982); U.N. Doc. E/CN.4/1983/62 (1983); U.N. Doc. E/CN.4/1984/78 (1984); U.N. Doc. E/CN.4/1985/64 (1985); U.N. Doc. E/CN.4/1986/39 (1986); U.N. Doc. E/CN.4/1987/25 (1987); U.N. Doc. E/CN.4/1988/28 (1988). For the report of the Working Group's second reading, which concluded with the final text of the Convention, see U.N. Doc. E/CN.4/1989/48 (1989). For an article by article compilation of the Working Group reports see United Nations Convention on the Rights of the Child, A Guide to the "Travaux Preparatoires," S. Detrick (ed.) (1992).

[9] Actually, the right to privacy is very controversial in the United States. It was more or less "created" by the justices in order to protect the right to contraception. It was reasoned that,

larly interesting about these articles is fact that, while most of these rights are clearly protected by the "Bill of Rights," the right to privacy exists only as a result of judicial interpretation. In addition, the status of children in relation to the "Bill of Rights" is not entirely clear under constitutional law, yet the United States proposed that they all be included in an international treaty on children's rights.

B. US Treaty Ratification Process

Considering the extent to which the United States was involved in drafting the Convention on the Rights of the Child, one would expect it to be among the first countries to ratify it. To understand why the US has not even signed the Convention, after such vigorous participation in the drafting process, it is helpful to know something about the US treaty ratification process.

Under the "separation of powers" doctrine, the Constitution states that it is the President who "makes" treaties, but only with the "advice and consent"[10] of the Senate. In practice, the President's treaty-making power is exercised in the following manner. The President asks the Department of State to study the treaty and to make recommendations as to what reservations, understandings and/or declarations (RUDs), if any, the US should attach when ratifying the treaty. The Department of State submits its findings to the President, who either follows the recommendations, ignores them, or makes his own modifications. He, then, transmits the treaty with his list of recommendations to the Senate for its "advice and consent" to ratification.[11]

The Senate's "advice and consent" is guided by the Senate Foreign Relations Committee. Once the Foreign Relations Committee receives the treaty, it may do one of two things. It may either take action on the treaty by holding a series of hearings and then making its own recommendations regarding RUDs and return it to the President for his signature. Or, it may do nothing and keep the treaty "in Committee" indefinitely. In the 1980s, President Jimmy Carter signed four human rights treaties: The International Covenant on Civil and Political Rights, the International Covenant on Economic, Social and Cultural Rights, the Convention on the Elimination of All Forms of Discrimination Based on Race (Racial Discrimination Convention) and the American Convention on Human Rights. The Covenant on Civil and Political Rights was finally ratified in 1992 and the Racial Discrimination Convention was ratified in 1994. However, the other two treaties still languish in Committee.

---

although privacy per se was not mentioned in the "Bill of Rights" (The first ten amendments to the U.S. Constitution), it was implied by the other enumerated rights and, therefore could be said to be part of the "penumbra" of rights emanating from those rights.

[10]   United States Constitution Article II §2.2

[11]   In the case of the Convention on the Rights of the Child, although the President had Ambassador Albright sign the treaty, he did not send it on to the Senate.

The United States instrument of ratification for the Convention Against Torture and Other Cruel or Degrading Treatment or Punishment (Torture Convention) was not deposited with the Secretary-General of the United Nations until 1994, many years after the Senate gave its "advice and consent." Possible future ratification of the Convention on the Elimination of All Forms of Discrimination Against Women (Women's Convention) was discussed on the floor of the Senate in the fall of 1994, but without reaching a decision.[12] Considering that it took the United States thirty years to become a Party to the Convention Against Genocide, it could be argued that the US human rights treaty ratification record is slowly improving.

As stated above, the treaty ratification process does not conclude with the Senate's "advice and consent." The treaty must go back to the President, for a final signature, only then is it deposited with the appropriate international body. In the case of human rights treaties, this may not be instantaneous. As previously noted, the US did not become a Party to the Torture Convention until many years after the Senate's approval. This is because the US takes the position that human rights treaties are not "self-executing." In other words, human rights treaties are enforced through national law and not directly through the treaty itself. There must be implementing legislation which puts the treaty into effect and the ratification process is not considered to have been completed until this legislation is in force. It took a number of years for the Torture Convention's implementing legislation to be drafted and put in place. Interestingly, US ratification of the International Covenant on Civil and Political Rights did not present this type of problem, because its rights were already protected by the US Constitution's Bill of Rights and, therefore, there was no need for additional legislation.

Clearly, the United States treaty ratification process is rather complicated and once the Convention on the Rights of the Child is signed by the President, its ratification will not be speedy. On the other hand, the fact that both President Bush and President Clinton have declined to even sign the Convention is difficult to explain. According to the rumors, both Presidents received a positive review of the Convention from the Department of State. President Bush's reluctance to sign has been linked to his fear of upsetting the country's Conservatives, in particular, the religious right. However, at that time, their exact objections were not entirely clear. Some allegations were made that linked the Conservative's objections to the Convention to the issue of abortion. Other allegations focused on the juvenile death penalty. Probably neither of these was entirely accurate.

Because President Bush was not known for his support of human rights, his lack of action was not surprising. But President Clinton's whole image has been one of sympathy to children's issues. Most child advocacy groups are very disappointed that President Clinton has failed to signed the Convention

---

[12] Women's groups have been pressing for its ratification to take place before the world conference on women's issues in Beijing.

on the Rights of the Child and send it to the Senate. Rumors about the basis for his inaction have linked this to women's rights issues. It is said that President Clinton decided not to sign the Convention on the Rights of the Child until the Women's Convention had been ratified. Considering the results of the recent US elections, in which conservative Republicans made major gains, this seems unlikely to happen at any time in the near future.

III. STATUS OF THE CHILD IN THE UNITED STATES[13]

According to a 1993 survey by the American Bar Association (ABA), poverty is one of the greatest problems faced by children in the United States. The survey points out that poverty effects all aspects of the child's life, including school performance and health. In support of its position, the ABA survey refers to 1991 statistics which indicate that 24% of American preschool children live in impoverished families. Moreover, this poverty is not limited to inner cities or particular ethnic groups, but can be found in every area of the country. Publicly, child poverty is often blamed on high divorce rates and single parent families. While there may be some support for these allegations, the fact remains that nothing is being done to ameliorate the problem. Repeated proposals for the establishment of minimum income benefits to prevent families from falling below the poverty level have never received the support necessary to result in legislation.

The ABA survey, *America's Children at Risk*, concludes with a list of twenty recommendations urging lawyers to work toward improving the circumstances of American children, both through legal representation and promotion of supportive legislation and administrative procedures. In addition to confronting child poverty, the ABA urges its members to use their skills as lawyers to represent children and their interests in legal cases concerning education, health, child abuse, foster care and juvenile justice.

Another disturbing report on the situation of American children was released in 1992 by the Children's Defense Fund (CDF). CDF is one of the leading national nongovernmental organizations working for children and has been spearheading the drive for US ratification of the Convention on the Rights of the Child. CDF's report, *America's Children Falling Behind: The United States and the Convention on the Rights of the Child*, was written as an example of the type of report that the United States will have to submit to the Committee on the Rights of the Child, if and when it ratifies the Convention. In its report, CDF spotlighted certain areas of the Convention where it felt that United States standards did not measure up. In addressing America's shortcomings, the following statistics were among those on CDF's list:

– Fourteen million American children live in poverty

---

[13] Parts of Section II were originally written for Children's Rights: An American Perspective in Children's Rights: A Handbook on Comparative Policy and Practice (Routledge, 1994).

– An estimated 10,000 children die each year from the effects of poverty
– The 1991 government report of 2.7 million cases of child abuse was three times greater than that reported in 1980
– The criminal laws of twenty-four states allow the execution of juveniles for crimes committed when they were under the age of 18
– At least 500,000 children and youths are deprived of their liberty as the result of juvenile crime
– Of the 7 million children in the US who work, 2 million of them do so illegally
– Children are rarely given a voice in judicial decisions concerning them in matters of foster care, adoption or custody.

It is important to note that while both of these reports evaluate the situation of children, they do not focus on this as an individual rights issue. The reports are primarily concerned with the child's quality of life and not with the child's right to be recognized as a person. This is significant for two reasons. First, because the traditional view of children's rights, as expressed in the 1959 United Nations Declaration of the Rights of the Child, has been one of care and protection or nurturance and not one of self-expression. Second, as will be explained later, the American view of rights is very narrow and can best be described as "claims by citizens for protection from undue interference by the State." It does not include "claims by citizens for benefits or services."

One explanation for the fractured picture of children's rights is that the United States has no overall children's policy. In fact, there is no single office or bureau within the federal government that is designated to deal with the interests of children, or even of children and families.[14] During the drafting of the Convention on the Rights of the Child, in order to be able to ascertain US policy on any given set of proposed articles, United States delegates found it necessary to consult with a variety of separate administrative agencies, in addition to conducting a review of Constitutional law.

A second element which exerts an influence on the children's rights picture is the fact that the United States is a notoriously litigious society. As a result, it has a tendency to define its law through litigation.[15] This is also true of rights. In America, rights are definitively upheld only through judicial decisions. This is not surprising, since reliance on judicial interpretation is characteristic of a particular school of American jurisprudence which takes the position that a law has no meaning until it has been interpreted by an

---

[14] Since the individual states are free to organize their services to citizens in any manner they choose, there are various policy models regarding service delivery at that level which are quite different from those of the federal government.

[15] This portent of things to come was foreseen by Alexis de Tocqueville, who noted in his book, Democracy in America, that the country had an extraordinary number of lawyers.

authoritative body.[16] Since, from the point of view of judicial interpretation, the subject of children's rights is relatively new, it will undoubtedly be some time before the concept will be fully developed and applied.

According to a recent survey, during the period between 1953 and 1992, the Supreme Court decided only forty-seven cases dealing with children's issues.[17] The majority of these feel into four categories: cases dealing with matters relating to illegitimacy; cases addressing the problem of parental control, especially in the area of underage abortion; cases relating to education and schools, including freedom of expression issues; and cases defining the parameters of juvenile justice standards, including the death penalty. Only a few of these can be said to have achieved "landmark" status. "Landmark" children's rights cases can be roughly divided into three groups: those which deal with the child in school; those which are related to the juvenile justice process; and those which have to do with other matters, such as the group of privacy cases, which upheld the right of young people to receive information about contraception and abortion and to be able to obtain contraceptives without parental consent.

Of all of the children's rights cases, the "landmark" case of In re Gault[18] is probably the most well known. Prior to Gault,[19] juveniles accused of committing a crime were given some sort of informal hearing in a family court setting. The Gault decision brought an abrupt halt to these inconsistent and unpredictable procedures, by upholding the juvenile's rights to counsel, to prior notice of charges, to remain silent, and to confront and cross-examine witnesses. A subsequent decision added the requirement that proof in juvenile hearings must meet the adult standard of "proof beyond a reasonable doubt."[20]

Oddly, this trend toward granting greater Constitutional protections to juveniles may have had an undesirable side effect. For a number of years, there has been a movement in this country toward granting "full" adult rights to accused juveniles. Consequently, it is becoming commonplace to "waive" juvenile cases into the adult system and to try juveniles as adult criminals, with adult responsibility and sentencing. While this process is usually limited to those juveniles who have committed very serious crimes, such as murder,

---

[16] An interesting example of the thinking of the school of jurisprudence known as America Legal Realism can be found in the essay, Path of the Law, by Oliver Wendell Holmes, 10 Harvard Law Review 459. (1907).

[17] Thirty-four of these were between the years of 1969 and 1986, when Warren Burger was Chief Justice. See Susan Gluck Mezey, Constitutional Adjudication of Children's Rights Claims in the United States Supreme Court, 1953-92, 27 Family Law Quarterly 307 (1993). Interestingly, Ms. Mezey did not consider Brown v. Board of Education, the 1954 case that struck down racial segregation in the schools, to be within her definition of children's rights.

[18] In re Gault, 387 U.S. 1 (1967).

[19] The move to handle juvenile cases outside the normal criminal procedures, in a special, informal process came about as a result of what is known as the "child-saving" movement of the nineteenth century.

[20] In re Winship, 397 U.S. 358 (1970).

the result has been that a large number of young people have received capital sentences and have been executed for crimes they committed while under the age of eighteen, which is a violation of international law.

Although Constitutional litigation can be time-consuming, it was, nevertheless, successful when used to establish the rights of blacks and women. However, it may not prove to be the best vehicle for promoting the rights of children. To a certain extent this is because the children's rights are such a patchwork quilt and the claims are so ill defined. Additionally, many of the rights claims of children, such as the right to an education, are not protected by the Constitution. While children's rights advocates will undoubtedly continue to pursue legal remedies as the only method currently available for legitimizing children's rights, there is no doubt that many unresolved children's rights issues could be more effectively settled through US ratification of the Convention on the Rights of the Child.

IV. PROSPECTS FOR UNITED STATES RATIFICATION OF THE UNITED NATIONS CONVENTION ON THE RIGHTS OF THE CHILD

Despite the fact that it has been five years since the Convention on the Rights of the Child was adopted by the United Nations General Assembly, most people in the United States have never heard of the Convention. While they may be familiar with the words "human rights," it is doubtful that the average person could give the name of even one international instrument protecting human rights. Perhaps most disturbing is the fact that human rights advocates themselves know very little about the content of the Convention and even less about its implementation. This means that if the Convention on the Rights of the Child is to be ratified by the United States, a major education program must be carried out. At the present time, the people who are most aware of the Convention are those who are against it.

A. Arguments Against the Convention on the Rights of the Child

A survey of the mail received by a select group of Senators shows that it is running 50:1 against the Convention.[21] There is a concerted effort being undertaken by certain national nongovernmental organizations to make sure that the US never becomes a Party to the Convention. These groups are well organized and their members regularly contact Congress about their opinions. They are primarily conservative religious groups who view the children's

---

[21] See unpublished paper by Susan Kilbourne, graduate student at the George Washington University School of Political Management.

rights as a threat to the family.[22] All of their objections to the Convention are based on fear.

There are several themes that run throughout the anti-Convention literature. There is a concern that ratification of the Convention on the Rights of the Child, since it is a treaty that is monitored by an international body, will undermine United States sovereignty. They claim that if the US ratifies the Convention, United States law regarding the parent-child relationship will be completely controlled by the United Nations. Of course, part of the problem is that Americans know so little about international law. They are probably unaware that, without surrendering its sovereignty, the United States ratified the International Covenant on Civil and Political Rights and will soon be submitting its first report to the Human Rights Committee.[23]

Interestingly, one of the claims these groups make is that if the United States ratifies the Convention on the Rights of the Child, the United Nations will send inspectors to tell them how to raise their children and to take their children away if they do not comply.[24] Again, this shows a lack of information and understanding of international law and how the United Nations works. These groups see the UN as a step toward "world government," a step that is much to be feared. There is no comprehension among Convention's detractors that the United Nations is not a world government but an organization of sovereign nations, all of which carefully guard their sovereignty.

They are similarly uninformed about the United States treaty-making process. They do know that under Article VI of the US Constitution a treaty, like federal law, is the "supreme law of the land." Based on this, they conclude that ratification of the Convention will override all existing law, including the United States Constitution. What they don't seem to know is that 1) no treaty can be superior to the Constitution and 2) the United States always implements human rights treaties through legislation. Therefore, while any federal legislation passed in connection with the Convention's implementation would supersede state law, it could not conflict with the Constitution.

Those who oppose the Convention make many allegations that show their naivete in regard to the workings of the state legal systems, as well. They claim, for instance, that if the US ratifies the Convention on the Rights of the Child a child would be able to bring a law suit against his or her parents to prevent them from sending him or her to religious school, or to sue them because he or she doesn't want to do school homework. Moreover, they

---

[22]   There is also one organization that promotes "home education" as an alternative to public school education which joins with the religious groups in their objections to the Convention as being anti-family.

[23]   Examination of the U. S. report by the Human Rights Committee took place in New York in March of 1995, without incident. In fact, it was not even mentioned in the newspapers!

[24]   To anyone familiar with the workings of the United Nations and the Centre for Human Rights, these claims are truly laughable. The U. N. is so understaffed that it couldn't take on a job like this, even if it part of the treaty's requirements.

argue that US ratification of the Convention will interfere with their parental rights and that it will make it impossible for them to prevent their child from obtaining and reading pornography or other materials that might be unsuitable for young children, or to prohibit their children from joining gangs.

The US legal system just doesn't work that way. First of all, the child would need an attorney to bring such a law suit and since lawyers expect to get paid for their services, it is unlikely that a dependent child would be able to pay the requested fee. Second, the American legal system has a strong prejudice against intra-familial law suits. Cases as frivolous as those outlined above, if they were actually brought before the court, would probably be thrown out by the judge. Third, a child could never use the Convention itself as the basis for a law suit, but could only sue on such implementing legislation as provided for such litigation and it is highly unlikely that such laws would ever be passed. In addition, there is nothing in the Convention that supports such claims. In fact, the Convention on the Rights of the Child is most supportive of the parental role in child-rearing, but of course, from the point of view of the child's right to parental care.

Obviously, all of the above allegations are baseless. Nevertheless, although the Convention-bashers are badly informed, they are well-organized and very vocal. They will make the ratification process much more difficult. What is unfortunate is that by letting fear overcome good sense, these family rights groups do not seem to realize that the Convention on the Rights of the Child gives them the very protection and support that they so desire. They are blinded by the fact that the Convention speaks in terms of the child's right to a nurturing family instead the rights of parents to care for their children.

B. Grassroots Efforts Toward Ratification and Implementation of the Convention Now

As can be seen from the previous discussion, proponents of the Convention have a large task ahead of them. In addition to trying to correct the mistaken information being distributed by opponents of the Convention, there is the very real problem of federalism and the diversity of state law. Even though a survey of state legislation indicates that most state law is in compliance with the standards of the Convention,[25] this can still prove to be a stumbling block once the Convention reaches the Senate for its "advice and consent," as rival Senators argue specific issues from their state's legislation.[26]

---

[25] See Children's Rights in America: U.N. Convention on the Rights of the Child Compared with United States Law, Cynthia P. Cohen & Howard A. Davidson, eds. (1990).

[26] One area in which there are certain to be conflicts has to do with the fact that some states allow application of the death penalty to juveniles for crimes committed when they were under the age of eighteen. Similarly, in some states juveniles can be incarcerated with adult prisoners if their crime was so serious that they are being tried as adults.

Frustrated with the President's lack of action, those who support its ratification are beginning to work together to organize a grassroots movement in favor of the Convention. The main coordinating body for this work is a coalition of nongovernmental organizations known as the National Committee for the Rights of the Child (NCRC). The NCRC has a nucleus of about thirty or forty active organizations, with a larger number of inactive supporting organizations. Member organizations are not limited to child advocacy groups, but include main stream human rights groups, as well as religious and educational institutions. Also among the groups participating in the NCRC are several organizations devoted to ensuring that the child has a voice in the development of children's rights standards.

NCRC members are undertaking a number of activities that are aimed at promoting children's rights in general, not only at broadening support for the Convention on the Rights of the Child. Among the projects being undertaken by the NCRC are the creation of a clearinghouse on children's rights information to enable members to keep track of one another's activities, establishment of a speaker's bureau, and the development of a general program to educate the public about the importance of children's rights and the benefits of Convention ratification. One of the main goals of these activities is to begin put in place a system that can monitor the Convention, once it has been ratified. In the meantime, the NCRC is urging organizations and local governments to begin implementing the Convention's standards NOW. In this way they will be adequately prepared to serve a watchdog function, after the Convention's ratification.

Because of the fact that so many of the Convention's rights are administered on a state level, energies are being directed toward convincing state governments of the befits of the Convention. For example, in the state of Vermont, a group of high school students successfully petitioned their state legislature to pass a resolution in support of Convention ratification. This model is being emulated by youth groups in other states, as well. As a result of youth action, some states have recently been convinced to declare a special "Children's Rights Day." Considering the child rights backlash that has been organized by religious groups, this was quite an achievement.

Although it is disappointing that ratification of the Convention on the Rights of the Child is taking so long, perhaps the delay actually works to the advantage of the Convention's supporters. It gives them time to organize and to counter negative information prior to Senate hearings on the Convention. In the interim, the NCRC and others interested in the rights of the child are doing what they can to close the information gap. Educators are working to create a children's rights curriculum and universities are holding symposia and conferences on the rights of the child. By the time the President gets around to signing the Convention and sending it on to the Senate, the NCRC and other children's rights advocates will, hopefully, have managed to ensure that the Convention is implemented swiftly and effectively.

MARJA STROJIN

Children's Rights in Slovenia

The National Commission for Children's Rights in Slovenia, as one of the Commissions within the NGO Association of Friends of Children, was established in November 1989.

In 1991 the Slovenian Constitution was proclaimed. The Commission proposed a paragraph concerning the special needs of children, which was accepted and introduced as par. 56 of the Constitution.

The Commission established the first SOS Children's phone and is working on building a complete network in Slovenia.

The Commission for children's rights has, as NGO, influenced the policy with respect to refugee children from Croatia and Bosnia. It supported establishing primary education before the financial support was approved from abroad (in 1992). At that time also its incentive was realised for supplying refugee children with 10,000 schoolbags.

The first aims of the Commission were to ratify the Convention on the Rights of the Child in the newly established State Slovenia and to introduce it to the people, especially children. At present we feel that a lot still has to be done despite the already accomplished work to make every child familiar with the Convention. We are currently trying to produce series of videos and written discussions and illustrations on paragraphs in the way close to the children's comprehension and interests.

To increase public awareness of Children's rights, each year a conference is held in Ljubljana, the Capital of Slovenia, dealing with a theme, a problem of general importance for children introduced to the open discussion by participating experts. The themes, in chronological sequence are as follows:

1990 Healthy and safe surroundings for children – encompassing physical and social aspects;

1991 Free time for children – with a critical view on excessive strain – especially with school work and lack of opportunities for satisfactory recreation;

1992 Legal aspects of children's rights with a critical approach to procedures and the accessibility to children;

1992 School, friendly to children;

E. Verhellen (ed.), Monitoring Children's Rights, 491–493.
© 1996 *Kluwer Law International. Printed in the Netherlands.*

1993   Children's rights in the hospital, with a special emphasis on allowing and encouraging the presence of parents in the wards;

1994   Children's rights at the parents' divorce, emphasising the child's needs and rights as the most important concern in the threatening situation, when each parent stands up for his (or her) aspect of the rights especially concerning the right to get the custody of the child.

Some of this themes conform with the children's suggestions for the annual Children's Parliament. These themes are being discussed by children in primary schools all over the country where the pupils under the supervision of mentors, sometimes also with participation of parents, prepare discussions, questions, remarks for municipal Parliaments and for the final appearance in the State Parliament. There have been Children's Parliament meetings on the following themes:

1991   Safe environment

1992   Free time

1993   Violence and prevention

1994   Power of a friendly word (improvement of communication with reference to the theme of the previous year).

To draw some conclusions on the work done, I think we can be happy with some achievements, although some very important problems still need attention. We have to do our best to find proper ways and methods which – in my opinion – will have to be searched for first.

The positive side is the large response of children throughout the country (by way of parliaments). The topic of children's rights is being popularised on each year's professional's open discussions. There have been published handbooks and leaflets. But the general impression is that this volume of work has to be transferred into such a form as to enable children to participate with equal rights. I'm approaching this problem from the psychological point of view, although legal, official and sociological aspects are very important as well.

The children are considered as a group of "not yets", but at the same time the research of contemporary social grouping reveals that the young are becoming a "group without generation", without "historic memory" and without the "future memory". When it seems necessary for the young to become in their rights more initiative and independent, the other side of the problem appears to become a danger of splitting young and the grown ups into two independent systems. I'm convinced that the need for understanding and coexistence is stronger than ever.

My basic assumption can be illustrated by outlining the work of the Children's Parliament in a way that would enlighten and help to a better understanding of my idea. The teachers/mentors should be educated for their role

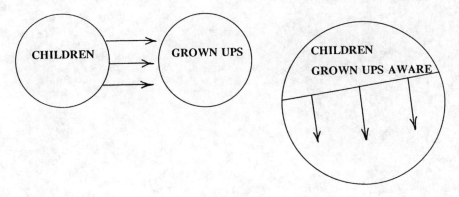

Figure 1.

together with pupils. The initiative should come from the pupils. We are nowadays acquainted with different techniques which could encourage the young to be active in making demands and passing their experiences. This co-education should implement procedures to enable the children express their needs, opinions and suggestions, whilst offered by grown ups their knowledge and strategies how to do it.

MARÍA EUGENIA VILLARREAL and GEORGE KENT

Regional Implementation of Children's Nutrition Rights in Central America and Mexico

In December 1992 in Rome, just before the International Conference on Nutrition, a Task Force on Children's Nutrition Rights was established. Functioning under the umbrella of the World Alliance on Nutrition and Human Rights, the task force promotes the strengthening of children's nutrition rights in local, national and international law. I serve as its Central America Coordinator. The Task Force eases and encourages a variety of activities such as research and lobbying on the issue, but its work centers on encouragingly the organization of national workshops on the theme. These national workshops are designed to launch locally-based long-term campaigns to strengthen children's nutrition rights, giving attention both to their articulation in the law and the effective implementation of that law. Individuals from both governmental and non-governmental organizations will be invited to participate.

The workshops will use a variation of the "triple-A-approach recommended by UNICEF:

> The three most important elements of this strategy consist of a continuous and self-refining process of Assessment, Analysis and Action (followed by reassessment, clearer analysis, more focused action, etc). The first step describes how information should be used. The second prides a guide for discerning what data should be collected. The third suggests the action to be taken (UNICEF,1992).

While UNICEF uses this approach to help communities and governments develop overall strategies for dealing with malnutrition, in these workshops the focus is narrowed to the ways in which children's nutrition rights, explicitly stated in the law, can be developed and strengthened.

The assessment of the situation will involve describing the current nutrition problems and responses to them, and will also require examination of existing law. Has the nation agreed to any of the mayor international instruments that affirm rights to adequate nutrition? Are those rights currently articulated in national law? If they are present in the law, are they clear and strong, or vague and abstract? Are children's nutrition rights actually implemented in practice? Are there measures of accountability to assure that food, health and care programs reach all who should be reached?

E. Verhellen (ed.), Monitoring Children's Rights, 495–502.
© 1996 *Kluwer Law International. Printed in the Netherlands.*

The analysis will explore explanations for why the nutrition situation is as it is, and why the law is as it is.

On the basis of these foundations, the workshops will then consider action, developing strategies for strengthening children's nutrition rights in the nation. The first stage will involve a brainstorming exercise in which many different kinds of approaches are considered, and then these will be reviewed and reformulated to shape concrete plans, with specific steps, and clear commitments by different individuals and organizations to follow through.

Task Force on Children's Nutrition Rights in Central America and Mexico. Malnutrition in Central America and Mexico is very serious:

 - It is one of the principle problems in the region and is associated with factors linked to poverty.
 - It is the major cause of avoidable children deaths and morbidity too.

The purpose of this task force is to promote children's right to adequate nutrition throughout Central America and Mexico, with full participation in that effort by national, regional and global organizations. The plan is that through concerted action, childhood malnutrition will be ended in the region.

This will be accomplished by:

 - Joining the efforts of national governments, public and private sectors, NGO's, regional and international organizations working in the areas of nutrition, food, health, human rights, children's rights and related disciplines.
 - Removing obstacles which hinder the realization of adequate nutrition for children.
 - Urging governments to introduce into their domestic law such measures as are needed for ensuring adequate nutrition for children.
 - Raising the level of priority for children's nutrition in the allocation of resources at the national level.

At the International Conference on Nutrition held in Rome in December 1992, governments of the nations of Central America and Mexico endorsed the World Declaration and the Action Plan for Nutrition, committing themselves to fight against hunger and all forms of malnutrition. Malnutrition in Central America requires urgent attention, and strengthening ongoing actions. Each country of the region must assume the political, judicial, economic, and social commitment to end malnutrition among children.

Regional organizations such as PARLACEN, INCAP, PAHO, UNICEF, can play major role in the effort to assure children's nutrition rights. They would work in the middle: directly with the countries of the region, linking them with the global international organizations. If the regional organizations took on the challenge, they could become world leaders in showing that it is possible, with concerted action, to end extreme childhood malnutrition.

Even though these countries are neighbours, they are different and they have different legislation. All the Central America constitutions include children's right to nutrition. Unfortunately, this legal formality does not solve the problem of malnutrition. There are legal loopholes; there are no common laws to give life to the Constitutional right the institutional frame does not respond to the laws; there are no mechanism for making the laws operational; there is no leadership to promote the implementation of children's right to adequate nutrition.

The workshop should have three major components: a review of the existing Situation nationally and regionally with regard to children's nutrition; a discussion of possibilities for improving the situation; and the formulation of a strategy for carrying out the campaign.

SITUATION

The core of the description should focus on children's nutritional status. What is currently known about the extent to which the nation's children are wasted or underweight? What are the infant and children's morality levels? What has been the pattern over time? Which of these data are available on particular areas of the nation, or on particular social groups?

The description of the situation should also provide an account of existing programs designed to alleviate children's malnutrition, whether these programs are sponsored by government agencies on nongovernmental organizations.

It is also important to look at existing law to see if there are elements that support the idea that children have a right to adequate nutrition. If it is present in the law, is it clear and strong, or vague and abstract. Is it actually implemented in practice? How? If not, why not?

Many different kinds of explanations for children's malnutrition may be offered. They may refer to the nature of the current political system, the motivations of particular political leaders, political and economic forces originating outside the nation, and so on.

This part of the workshop should bring a number of different explanations to light. Since several different kinds of understandings can be valid at the same time, the workshops should not get stuck in a debate over which is the one correct way to understand the situation.

In dealing with children's nutrition, it is not as important to decide who caused the problem or who is right or wrong about it as it is to agree on what should be done about the problem.

POSSIBILITIES

Once the workshop participants arrive at a shared understanding of the problem of children's nutrition in the nation, they should discuss what might be done about it. Many different kinds of ideas are likely to come up, but for the purposes of this workshop the focus should be on what can be done with the law: how can children's nutrition rights be more clearly articulated in the law, and how can that law be effectively implemented?

Even within this focus, there will be many possibilities for action. Proposals may range from improvements in the system for recording births and deaths to the development of elaborate new feeding programs. Simple things, like requiring regular measurement and recording of children's heights and weights, could be helpful. It is important to let the ideas flow, and not get into a premature debate about which are the good ideas. There needs to be a time for real creativity, without being stifled by criticism.

STRATEGY

Children's nutrition rights will not be strengthened simply by passing a resolution at the conclusion of a brief workshop. There will be a great deal of work to be done, in a sustained campaign. Different individuals and agencies will be able to contribute to the effort in different ways. The effectiveness of the campaign will be determined by how effectively they can work together.

Participants in the workshop should establish a shared vision of what might reasonably be accomplished to strengthen children's nutrition rights in the nation. This should be followed by discussion of what needs to be done to achieve the goal. Who needs to be convinced to do what? How might that be done?

Once it is clear what needs to be done, there should be some discussion of who will do it. Who will make which concrete commitments to do what over the few months following the workshop?

It may be that one group is interested in certain kinds of actions while others prefer a different approach. There is no need for everyone to agree to go down exactly the same path. Some may want to take small steps while others want to be bolder. Another group might want to provide support services for the campaign, organizing meetings and perhaps an occasional newsletter. Perhaps a number of different teams could work separately, but meet together from time to time and discuss ways in which their distinct approaches might complement and reinforce one another.

A regular schedule of follow-up meetings should be established to assess achievements, study obstacles, refine plans for the future, and constantly reinvigorate the campaign. No matter what particular shape it takes, those will not be easy campaigns, but the participants surely would agree that it is worth the effort.

ACCOUNTABILITY

While many countries have means for identifying malnourished children and have programs for providing services, if children are to have meaningful nutrition rights, there must also be strong mechanisms of accountability. There may be some informal monitoring of government performance by the mass media or by interested nongovernmental organizations, but the focus here is on means of accountability established by law. The workshop has to work on this, doing a national report about the legal aspects. We suggest that the report has to include the following questions:

1. Is there a clear law assuring children's right to adequate nutrition?
2. Has the government established appropriate service programs to prevent and to remedy malnutrition among children?
3. Are these service programs effective and adequate? are the programs satisfied with servicing some needy children, or are they obligated to find and serve all children who meet the eligibility criteria?
4. Is there a clear legal entitlement to services for all children? For children who are at risk of malnutrition? For children who are malnourished?
5. Are there any government agencies or advocacy organizations which regularly assess the performance of the service programs?
6. Is there any assured means through which a child could obtain adequate nutrition if all conventional means prove inadequate?
7. Are there accountability mechanisms, established by law, for guaranteeing that children receive the services they require to become adequately nourished?
8. Is there clear legal recourse for children who do not get the services to which they are entitled? For example, is there an ombudsman or some other designated individual to whom complaints may be taken? Is the complaint procedure straight forward, simple, accessible, inexpensive, fair, and safe to use?
9. Is there a record of cases in which complaints have been made and government has been legally required to respond to the needs of malnourished children?
10. Are the accountability mechanisms effective and adequate?

When a child is not adequately nourished, it is not only the child's family but the society as a whole that have failed that child. There should be mechanisms for calling governments to account and correcting that failure. If the law says that children are entitled to some particular service as a matter of right, the law also should establish an accountability mechanism to assure that the service is provided adequately and effectively.

An implementation mechanism for achieving a goal has both monitoring and response components. The monitoring component assesses the distance and direction from the goal, and the response component acts to move toward the goal. An automobile driver, for example, monitors through the eyes, and responds by pressing the pedals and turning the steering wheel. Where the goal is to improve children's nutrition, the monitoring element could use indicators such as food intake or anthropometric measures to assess the location and extent of malnutrition in the society. The response element would involve feeding, health and care programs targeted to where the monitoring component showed it was needed.

There are many ways in which such a system could go wrong. The monitoring component may measure the wrong things, or it may not be very sensitive. Or the responses may not work well. For example, income transfers to the family may be diverted to uses other than meeting the needs of the child. Government-funded school lunch programs that feed all public school students may feed many who don't need assistance, and thus may be unnecessarily costly. People who are technically entitled to a particular benefit may not know about it or may have difficulty accessing it. A child who is fed at a centralized feeding program may for just that reason get less to eat at home. An effective system would notice these problems, and make constant course corrections to navigate the system toward the goal. The design of a system for assuring children's right to adequate nutrition would have to be refined over time until it could be shown hat it really works.

Social service programs usually reach only some of the needy some of the time. Governments may boast about the number of individuals served, but they tend to be silent about the number of people who are needy but are not served. Accountability means paying attention to that shortfall. The obligation is not simply to provide some service, but to end the problem of malnourished children. Any government that really wants to end childhood malnutrition should be willing to make itself accountable for meeting that challenge.

Assurance that services will be provided results not simply from the creation of service programs (e.g., school lunches, nutrition education programs) but form institutionalized mechanisms to establish accountability. An *accountability* (or compliance) mechanism watches the implementation mechanism to make sure it does its job well. It is located outside the implementation mechanism, and may have its own separate monitoring procedures. A highway patrol officer is such a device, assuring that automobile drivers do what they are supposed to do. In the United States, there is a compliance monitoring procedure designed to assure that the states provide disabled children the educational services to which they are entitled under the law. If a government wants to assure that it will always be attentive to the concerns of children, it could pay for an independent Children's Ombudsman to handle complaints against the government (Flekkoy, 1991). Many different kinds of measures can be used to provide accountability (Rosen, 1989). The use, or threat of use, of the judicial system can be a potent means for keeping implementing agencies on track, but other more political means (such as public information campaigns through the media) may be used as well.

In general, if the system threatens to go off the tracks, the compliance or accountability mechanism sounds an alarm and takes action to correct the implementation mechanism. Accountability means there are independent observers of the implementation mechanism that have some capacity to take or call for corrective action if the system is not operating well. Ideally there should be explicit standards against which the accountability agency evaluates the performance of the implementing agency. The accountability agency is in effect a permanent auditor.

In a negative approach the accountability, a government agency assigned the duty of ending malnutrition could be sued or fined in some way for each severely malnourished child that is discovered, thus increasing its incentive to end childhood malnutrition. In a more positive approach, designated non-governmental organizations could be given an award or "bounty" of a small sum of money for each malnourished child they find and present for services. This sort of positive approach would engage nongovernmental organizations in a partnership with government in support of their larger common purpose.

One particular form of accountability mechanism is giving aggrieved parties themselves or their representatives a procedure for complaining and getting some remedy. Human rights in the laws rests on the principle *ubi jus ibi remedium* – where there is a right there must be a remedy. Article 8 of the Universal Declaration of Human Rights asserts that "everyone has the right to an effective remedy by the competent national tribunals for acts violating the fundamental rights granted him by the constitution or by law". Children's nutrition rights should be articulated in the law, together with a description of the means of legal recourse that are available if even a single individual's rights are violated. If you or your child don't get what you feel you are entitled to under the law, there should be straightforward, simple, accessible, inexpensive, fair, and safe means for pressing your claims. This legal recourse is essential for assuring the government's compliance with the law.

The implementation of the right to adequate nutrition is ultimately the responsibility of government at different levels, but it is also the responsibility of the community at local, national and international levels. Interested groups both within and outside government can watch the performance of service delivery agencies and call them to account as necessary, even if there is no explicit provision in the law for them playing that role. If the law says that every child has a right to adequate nutrition, any one who is concerned could help to see that the right is honored.

The meaning of hard rights and accountability can be understood by recalling the nature of contracts. Suppose you have a contract with me in which I promise to provide goods or services in exchange for a specified amount of money. Then a contract is not simply an articulation of claims; if it is legally binding it represents *enforceable* claims. If one of us is not satisfied, there is some third party to whom we can go to press for fulfillment of the contractual obligations. Similarly, a human rights regime can be understood as representing an implicit contract between citizens and government, comparable to that described by Rousseau in the *Social Contract* of 1762. If that contract is to be taken seriously, there must be some basis on which claims against the government can be enforced.

People in power may resist the articulation of specific rights because rights imply accountability – and political people don't like the idea of being called to account. Nevertheless, the argument is worth pressing. Talking about human rights does not mean much if it does not mean accountability.

REFERENCES

Carlson, Bevwerly A. and Wardlaw, Tessa M. (1990) *Global, Regional and Country Assessment of Child malnutrition.* New York: UNICEF.

Christensen, Cheryl (1978) The Right to Food: How to Guarantee. New York: World Order Models Project, working Paper Number Six, Institute for World Order, p. 33.

Eide, Asbjorn, Eide, Wenche Barth, Goonatilake, Susantha, Gussow, Joan and Omawale (Eds) (1984) *Food as a Human Right.* Tokyo: United Nations University.

Flekkøy, Målfrid Grude (1991) *A voice for Children: Speaking out as their Ombudsman.* London: UNICEF/Jessica Kingsley Publshers.

Flekkøy, Målfrid Grude (1991) *Models for Monitoring the Protection of Children's Rights.* Florence, Italy: International Child Development Centre.

INCAP (1992) *How INCAP supports Maternal and Child Health in Central America.* Guatemala City, p. 12–13–14.

INCAP (1991) *Informe anual.* Ciudad de Guatemala, pp. 21-51.

International Conference on Nutrition (1992) *Nutrition: the Global Challenge.* Rome: FAO/WHO Joint secretariat for the Conference, pp.3-6.

Kent, George (1994) *Children in Global Civil Society.* University of Hawaii: Department of Political Science.

Kent, George (1993) "Children's Right to Adequate Nutrition". *The International Journal of Children's Rights, 1,* 133-154. The Netherlands: Kluwer Academic Publishers.

Kent, George (1994) "The Roles of International Organizations in Advancing Nutrition Rights". *Food Policy, 19(4).*

Rosen, Bernand (1989) *Holding Government Bureaucracies Accountable,* Second edition. New York: Praeger.

UNICEF (1993) *El progreso de las Naciones.* New York: UNICEF, pp. 15-18.

UNICEF (1992) *Food, Health and Care*: The UNICEF Vision and Strategy for a World Free from Hunger and Malnutrition. New York: UNICEF.

LUISA MARIA AGUILAR

The Role of the NGOs in Monitoring Children's Rights

INTRODUCTION

The entry into force of the Convention on the Rights of the Child heralds a global approach to these rights, which include civil, political, economic, social, cultural and spiritual rights, all of which match the human dignity of the child and contribute to promoting his "higher interest".

The concept of the "higher interest of the child" is a theme permeating the Convention which enables it to be understood as a whole, and does not reduce it to its urgent or legal aspects. The child is regarded as a subject of law, not an object. This is a very important change in perspective; in order to apply it, a number of stages need to be passed through.

Since its approval in 1989, a lot has been done to publicise and disseminate the legal scope and symbolic value of the International Convention on the Rights of the Child. However, day-to-day experience shows us that there is a considerable gap between the legal dimension and reality. Enormous efforts must still be made in relation to education and dialogue, changing customs and mentalities in order to ensure that the Convention is applied and that it moves from a purely legal dimension to a real dimension, in which the child is effectively seen as an individual with rights and responsibilities. Action must be taken therefore to guarantee the effective exercising of the child's rights and, at the same time, to obtain a political commitment from governments regarding children.

In the context of the International Year of the Family (IYF) proclaimed by the United Nations for 1994, the ICCB wished to embark on a dialogue with other NGOs to assess the quality of the child's social environment from the point of view of his rights and to identify priorities for action in order to guarantee a family and community environment favourable to the development of the child.

This was the topic covered by the seminar on "The rights of children rediscovered?" organised by the International Catholic Child Bureau in Venice in March 1994 for the countries of southern Europe.

E. Verhellen (ed.), Monitoring Children's Rights, 503–507.
© 1996 *Kluwer Law International. Printed in the Netherlands.*

I. Moving on to Action

Why was this title chosen – "The rights of children rediscovered?" Had they gone astray? Had they in some way been lost? No. The aim was in fact to enable children to take over these rights, because most of the time it is adults who possess them (Aguilar L.M.).

This implies a process of recognition, assimilation and integration into daily life. It involves putting these rights into perspective in a social context.

Giving children their rights and responsibilities in fact implies participation, which in turn means partners, in other words a social context.

II. Towards a Real Children's Culture

How can we promote the conditions that will foster such a process whereby children appropriate their rights? How can we build a social environment propitious to the exercising of these rights?

In European society today, we can see that children are not valued as individuals, a shortcoming frequently reflected in a climate of implicit social violence which tends to ignore the higher interest of the child. When passing on values families, like institutions and the media, often neglect their responsibilities and their role as an educator. This situation certainly does not contribute to the full development of the child or facilitate responsible participation by him in society.

It is high time that a real children's culture emerged, in other words a culture where the child is a full individual.

This will require the highlighting of different social and legal contexts in Europe and the consideration of the problems, which vary depending on the country in question. In some cases, society does not recognise children as full individuals for cultural, social or historical reasons, and one can then speak of a need to "free" the child. In other situations, children enjoy freedom which all too often resembles abandonment and lack of interest. Between the "oppressed" child and the "liberated" child, there should be room for a child who is a partner within his family and community.

III. Main Guidelines

At this seminar, we identified several guidelines for action.

Learning: the need to listen. We are used to proposing models of action based on "the problem child" and his "shortcomings". The action concerned these situations. Thus we usually work with children without families, who do not go to school and have psychological and affective shortcomings.

Looking at the child as a subject and a person implies adopting a global vision, seeing the "child within a situation", in other words a child with problems or shortcomings but also with his own capacity to overcome these problems.

In order to be able to move on to a model of action which helps to reinforce the child's own capacities, *thanks to constructive interaction with his family and global environment*, it is necessary to get to know the child and his point of view, his "expectations", his sensibility. This involves "listening to him" and knowing how to read and interpret his messages.

The aim of listening to children is to ensure that "children can communicate with society and to prepare children for life in society" (Jan Van Gils).

The NGOs have a vital role to play in this: they must include the child's perspective in programmes, action models and child policy plans. They must contribute to the interaction between children and society and, above all, create the conditions that will enable such interaction to emerge.

Learning therefore implies "learning to learn", in other words training the various social players *to listen* and promoting the establishment of *forums* for listening.

At the same time it is necessary to encourage on the one hand the social partners to cover the issue of children, and on the other the media which could play a very important role in supplying information and, why not, in training and raising awareness among social groups. Finally support must also be given to professionals who work with children and who are often ignored or seen in a poor light.

Lastly, dialogue must be established at all levels: parents/children, institutions (schools and others), NGOs/media, in order to permit communication. Additional action by the social partners at different levels depending on their responsibilities is vital to implement these principles.

IV. WHAT KIND OF ACTION SHOULD BE TAKEN BY THE NGOS?

This vital complementary dimension paves the way for action by the NGOs, which might thus promote a favourable social climate for the child and ensure his integration into family life and society. The role of the NGOs therefore consists of several levels of action.

On a "micro" level, it covers all the initiatives aimed at improving direct dealings with children, teachers and social players, thus contributing to the change of perspective which we mentioned above.

On a "macro" level, the NGOs must increase their influence by means of policies on children and vis-à-vis decision-makers.

There are no legal rules in the European Union which define a concrete policy: issues concerning children are exclusively dealt with by national laws. Given this, significant progress could be achieved if the various national policies were coordinated and closer cooperation existed between international NGOs.

It is for government institutions, which are responsible for policy on children on a level much closer to reality, to supply a more appropriate legal framework to ensure that the rights of the child are respected and implemented.

In this process, the NGOs take on an important, practical dimension. Even without having direct powers as regards decision-making, their cohesion means that they can set down guidelines and reinforce coordination in order to achieve a social and political impact.

National and international NGOs, the proximity of the "area of action" and the placing in context of actions all facilitate a good perception of the ground to be covered in order to achieve a real improvement in the social environment of the child. This "ground" could be transformed into a policy on action.

At the same time, the task of raising awareness and identifying real needs, vis-à-vis inter-governmental and public bodies, will carry more weight since it will be better rooted in the local social and cultural setting: this might promote the implementation of more suitable action programmes.

Proposals aimed at creating forums for coordination and cooperation will acquire greater significance since these forums cover the two dimensions mentioned above: the improvement of the practical side and "field" action, and the definition of policies on a "macro" level.

A platform for coordination at national level and, possibly, at regional level, would have the following main objectives:
– to promote communication at the various levels
– to facilitate the exchange of experiences and information
– to identify and guarantee actions and initiatives which ensure an impact at social, political and institutional level, with a multiplier effect.

CONCLUSIONS

The implementation of the Convention on the Rights of the Child therefore consists (as demonstrated at the Venice seminar) of two separate stages, the scope and urgency of which vary depending on the country, or even the region within the country.
1. Children must be given their rights and responsibilities, which implies participation. This in turn implies a partnership relationship and a social context.
2. The implementation of these rights must be supervised, controlled and monitored. To do this, existing forums (observatories) where such monitoring can be conducted must be identified: these are intermediary forums which are vital to prevent and identify risks:
     – parents-children within the family
     – parents- teachers at school

– parents-institutions (medical, social and legal)
– public opinion-institutions
– media-family
– media-institutions
– media-media

This means that a new way of taking positive action in society is required: by means of dialogue, which implies monitoring, not as the rules of the road are applied with a legislator and a user.

It also implies a new relationship between persons which is not a balance of power. What is required here is love rather than tolerance, provided that love of children does not mean possession but a concern for their higher interest.

REFERENCES

Aguilar L.H. in collaboration with A. Felcher and J. Cots "What Policies for Children in Southern Europe?" ICCB, Geneve, Switzerland, 1995.
Van Gils J. in "Bulletin d'information ONG", No. 4, Council of Europe, Strasbourg, 1995.

SIMONE EK

Can we Make Reality of Children's Rights?
NGO Monitoring in Sweden

INTRODUCTION

On behalf of Rädda Barnen this paper contains a presentation on the status
of the UN Convention on the Rights of the Child, the NGO role in the
drafting process as well as the monitoring mechanisms in Sweden. This paper
also introduces the Swedish Children's Ombudsman and Rädda Barnen's
relationship to the Swedish Parliament to promote the rights of the child.

I. UNIQUE RESPONSE TO THE UN CONVENTION

The status of the child has been upgraded by the adoption of the UN Convention on the Rights of the Child by the UN General Assembly on November
20, 1989.

Sweden was one of the first countries to ratify the Convention on the
Rights of the Child. June 29, 1990. Sweden ratified the Convention without
reservation of any point and stressed that the national legislation is compatible
with the UN Convention on the Rights of the Child.

As for Sweden, the Convention came into force on September 2, 1990,
likewise for the UN after the ratification by the first 20 States Parties.

The World Summit for Children in September 1990 contributed with
demanding obligations on the States Parties. More than 70 Heads of Governments of States as well as some 90 other senior officials, were present to promote children's rights and support future annual reports on concrete National
Programmes of Action to be submitted to UNICEF. Prior to the World Summit
UNICEF initiated in the late 1980s regional seminars to increase awareness
of the UN Convention. NGOs can and should assist in asking for National
Programmes of Action in their respective country and discuss their possible
role.

By December 1994, 176 countries have either signed the Convention or
have become States Parties to it by ratification or accession. (167 States are

E. Verhellen (ed.), Monitoring Children's Rights, 509–515.
© 1996 Kluwer Law International. Printed in the Netherlands.

Parties and 9 signatories but still 14 countries are neither States Parties to the Convention nor have they signed it). UNICEF has called for universal ratification by the year 1995.

The UN Convention on the Rights of the Child has received a unique response since 1989 and its speedy ratification is unprecedented within the UN. All the joint efforts made by UN agencies, UNICEF and INGOs and NGOs have contributed to the speedy ratification of the Convention. It has also been beneficial to discussions on the status of other human rights treaties and have made people more aware about other existing conventions ratified or not ratified.

II. THE BASIC PHILOSOPHY OF THE UN CONVENTION

The Convention binds Sweden and other states, which are parties to the Convention, to a number of obligations i.e. to respect and implement this international legal document, where a vision of children as fellow human beings with their own rights are fundamental principles to decision makers and others. These principles are: To respect the rights of the child below the age of 18 years to highlight the principle of the best interests of the child as a fundamental principle in all actions concerning children (article 3 in the Convention).

The child should be respected and listened to. The child has a right to express an opinion and to have that opinion taken into account, in any matter or procedure affecting the child. The child's views should be given due weight (article 12).

No child should be discriminated against and the State has an obligation to protect children from any form of discrimination. The principle is that all rights apply to all children without exception and that the State must take positive actions to promote these rights (article 2).

The inherent right to life for children goes further than the right not to be killed. The State has an obligation to ensure to the maximum extent possible the survival and development of the child (article 6).

The State has an obligation to transform the rights in the Convention into reality "to the maximum extent of their available resources", which means to give children priority in planning of resources in the society and, where needed, within the framework of international co-operation (article 4).

These basic articles shall be combined with all other kinds of human rights i.e. economic, social, cultural as well as civil and political rights makes the Convention unique. In the Convention there are also articles concerned with humanitarian rights i.e. children with refugee background or children living in armed conflict (articles 22, 38 and 39). Together they make the UN Convention a very powerful treaty which require political courage and political will to enforce.

The UN Convention has an integrated approach and the different rights are not ranked in order of importance, instead they interact with one another to form part of the same whole. The Convention in its character is visionary and sets standards, outlines universal principles and norms for children as fellow human beings with their own rights. It also requires a new attitude towards children.

III. NGO Role in Monitoring

The Convention by its character and its very nature started a process for monitoring and discussion on how to implement the Convention and on the roles of States Parties, and NGOs and other competent bodies.

NGOs have a crucial role to play in the implementation of the standards and norms of the UN Convention on the Rights of the Child. The mobilization of children's rights movements is essential for the monitoring.

The independence and integrity of NGOs must be safeguarded and their role as watch-dogs is strengthened by relying on this international instrument to improve the rights of the child.

One NGO role is to remind politicians and decision makers and other authorities of their obligations.

Another role for the NGOs is that the implementation of the UN Convention depends to a great extent on the NGOs role as partners and spokespersons for the rights of the child. Articles 43-45 of the Convention contain principles and provisions for the implementation of the Convention and include NGO participation. NGOs could also assist in information and educational campaigns on the UN Convention.

IV. NGO Role in the Drafting Process in Geneva

In January 1983 in Geneva three NGOs (Defence for Children International, The International Catholic Child Bureau and Rädda Barnen International) took the iniative to call together NGOs who decided to set up the "Informal NGO Ad Hoc Group on the drafting of the Convention on the Rights of the Child". Some twenty NGOs were active and the network of interested NGOs grew over the years. Defence for Children International agreed to act as secretariat for the group.

The NGOs created a precedent in the UN by participating actively in the drafting process. Based on their knowledge and experience of children the NGOs made proposals and started open dialogues with government representatives and UN agencies on how to better protect children. These NGOs in Consultative Status with ECOSOC fullfilled a complementary role to the governments.

The fact that NGOs were part of the drafting of the UN Convention on the Rights of the Child has given them a special status explicitly in the Convention's articles which necessarily involves them later on in the process of implementation on the national level. This is the only human rights treaty which specifically gives NGOs a role in the monitoring procedure (article 44).

Some NGOs have in fact been part of the children's rights ideology, a philosophy already expressed in the 1924 Geneva Declaration (Dèclaration de Genève) and the 1959 Declaration on the Rights of the Child and The International Year of the Child in 1979. The 1924 and 1959 Declarations served as the springboard for the initiatives to draft the Convention.

V. THE STATUS OF THE UN CONVENTION IN SWEDEN

In 1983 a question was raised in the Parliament to the Swedish government "How does the Swedish Government want to stimulate a discussion related to the on-going drafting of the UN Convention in Geneva. (Mrs Kerstin Anèr, former MP and former president of Rädda Barnen.)

The response by the government was to establish a governmental group to assist the Swedish delegates participating in the on-going drafting of the UN Convention on the Rights of the Child in Geneva.

Since the Convention makes it the duty of the participating States to make its provisions and principles generally known to both children and adults in each individual country (Article 42), the Swedish government made special efforts. They have among other things earmarked for three years, 1990-1993, MSEK 30 (USS5.45m) from the State Inheritance Fund to enable voluntary organizations to publicize the provisions and principles of the Convention to the Swedish public. Some 40 NGOs and a number of institutions have received funds to disseminate information about the UN Convention.

VI. THE LEGAL STATUS OF THE UN CONVENTION IN SWEDEN

Before ratification Sweden ensured that its domestic legislation was in accordance with the provisions in the Convention. Sweden ratified the Convention without any reservations. Through the ratification of the UN Convention, Sweden has undertaken to respect the Convention as international law, binding Sweden to implement its provisions. In contrast to many other countries, international law is not directly applicable in Sweden. The courts are therefore not bound by the rules of the Convention as by Swedish law. But the principles in the UN Convention may be used in interpreting Swedish law, so that the interpretation is in accordance with these international obligations. These obligations are part of the considerations when new laws are drafted.

VII. THE CHILDREN'S OMBUDSMAN

The Swedish Government appointed on July 1st, 1993 an Ombudsman heading the Office of the Children's Ombudsman with a staff of 14. The office is a National Board under the supervision of the Swedish Ministry of Health and Social Affairs. The office has been set up to safeguard the interests of children and young people in Swedish society. The main task of the Children's Ombudsman is to monitor the implementation of the UN Convention on the Rights of the Child. The work of the Children's Ombudsman is divided into four specialist areas: the conditions in which children and young people, respectively grow up; psycho-social issues, child safety and social planning. The Ombudsman chairs a council of experts appointed by the Swedish Government. Cooperation with organisations and authorities which deal with questions concerning children and young people at all levels of society is a fundamental element of the work of the Office.

The Children's Ombudsman presented the first annual report on September 5, 1994 to the Government in which she high-lighted areas where it is felt that Sweden does not live up to the UN Convention. She suggested steps for bringing about improvement. The report is called "Hi there".

VIII. MONITORING MECHANISMS IN SWEDEN

A. *Swedish Parliament and Rädda Barnen*[1]

On May 22, 1992 a seminar took place, entitled "Children in especially difficult circumstances". This seminar was held in the Parliament, and was a cooperation effort between some Members of Parliament and Rädda Barnen. In connection with this seminar a network of Members of Parliament across the political borderlines was established. It called itself the Swedish Network of Parliamentarians for Children's Rights. On a regular basis Rädda Barnen is meeting with the Children's Network Group in the Parliament to discuss matters of concern for children.

Rädda Barnen is carefully following the debates in the Parliament. There are other possibilities also i.a. the Question Times, when Members of Parliament have the right to put questions to Members of the Cabinet. Normally a minister chooses to reply. NGOs cannot put questions, but we can discuss issues with the MPs and propose concerns to bring up, which they decide upon

---

[1] *Rädda Barnen and the UN Convention* Rädda Barnen's mandate is to implement the UN Convention on the Rights of the Child and to combine research and advocacy with concrete assistance programmes. *Rädda Barnen* is a Swedish non-governmental organization struggling to enforce the rights of the child in its programmes in Sweden and in some 20 countries in the world. It is a voluntary, democratic organization, with no party-political or religious affiliation, based on voluntary individual membership. Rädda Barnen has a total of 250.000 supporters.

at their choice. Rädda Barnen publishes a Newsletter regularly containing the latest news on childrens issues in the Parliament.

Over the next few years 1994 - 1998, we will map out the debates in the Parliament and what happens to motions and bills of interest to Rädda Barnen. We intend to present a report on Child Politics in Sweden from an NGO viewpoint.

Rädda Barnen as a popular movement is now looking into strategies to ask active Rädda Barnen members everywhere in Sweden to approach their local authorities and raise questions with those with political power. This would have even more of an impact on the implementation of the UN Convention at a local and regional level.

B. The NGO Child Convention Group in Sweden

In 1985 major child organisations initiated a seminar to start their work from a NGO point of view of the UN Convention. The group is called "The NGO Child Convention Group in Sweden". There was also a link between the NGO Group in Sweden and the Geneva Ad Hoc Convention group of NGOs. The purpose of the NGO Child Convention Group, a Network of some 40 NGOs, is to disseminate information about the UN Convention and monitor the implementation from an NGO viewpoint. This is carried out primarily by organising a Yearly Hearing in the first week of May questioning representatives of the Swedish government on how they implement and monitor the UN Convention in Sweden.

On May 5, 1993 the first Hearing ever held, was attended by five Ministers and one Under-Secretary of State and other officials from the government office. They replied to questions by the NGOs. Some 100 questions were compiled and put to them in a report prepared beforehand and sent to responsible ministries in order for them to prepare individual statements and replies to our questions.

On May 5, 1994 the second Hearing was held and a report compiled containing more than 100 questions to be put to responsible Ministries. Five ministries were represented by their Ministers, an Under-Secretary of State and Political Advisers, who attended this Hearing.

Reports from these meetings are also produced. The NGO Child Convention Group intends to submit a report to the UN Committee on the Rights of the Child in 1997 based on the yearly hearings from 1993 - 1997.

The Swedish government, which submitted its initial report in 1992, will submit its next report in 1997 to the UN Committee.

In December 1992 Rädda Barnen submitted its comments on the initial report by Sweden to the UN Committee on the Rights of the Child by a letter and a memorandum. Rädda Barnen participated as an observer at the UN Committee Meeting in Geneva when the Swedish report was examined.

In 1994 Rädda Barnen is chairing the NGO Child Convention Group and the secretariat is held by the Red Cross.

IX. Actions That Can Be Taken by NGOs

1. NGOs should inform themselves about the content and philosophy of the UN Convention on the Rights of the Child.
2. Document facts, carry out special investigations, studies and reports for decision makers to consider. Produce information and educational material for schools and adults.
3. Submit NGO comments and views to complement the report of the national government to the UN Committee on the Rights of the Child.
4. Make sure that the government reports are made public and distributed for discussions.
5. Mobilize and create networks of concerned NGOs. If possible, create NGO monitoring mechanisms.
6. Inform and put pressure on decision makers and lobby national and regional politicians. Ask for political will and courage and resources. Ask for a Government department with overall responsibility for children's policy and identify officials in the Government department. Strengthen the child's rights in your society. Map out national child policies.
7. Meet with parliamentarians and listen to the debates in Parliament. Ask for reports on government resources allocated for children, and maybe ask for a separate budget for children in your community.
8. Be watchdogs or spokespersons or ombudsmen for children and meet and assist children and young persons. Make sure children are aware of their human rights.

References

Initial report by Sweden to the UN Committee on the Rights of the Child CRC/C/3/Add.1 23 September 1992.
Swedish Government Bill 1989/90:107.

MARIE-FRANÇOISE LÜCKER-BABEL,
PHILIPPE D. JAFFÉ and HÉLÈNE REY WICKY

Pre-surveillance of Children's Rights

*The Project "IDÉE" Promoting Children's Participation in Geneva,
Switzerland*

The child's right to express his/her own views and to be heard is proclaimed in Article 12 of the 1989 United Nations Convention on the Rights of the Child. This right to meaningfully participate in all matters and proceedings that affect the child is one of the pivotal advances of the international treaty. As it is being implemented, this right stands out, one the one hand, as controversial in some professional and political circles and, on the other, as particularly complex in terms of its practical ramifications that largely transcend the legal field. Based on these observations, in 1993, at the initiative of the Swiss Section of Defence for Children International (DCI), the project "IDÉE"[1] was conceived in pursuit of two objectives:
- examine what it takes for a child to express him/herself freely under the best possible conditions, and
- promote this right in Geneva, Switzerland, where, for a variety of social, legal and political reasons, its implementation is rather arduous.

I. SWITZERLAND... LIGHT YEARS FROM THE 1989 CONVENTION

A major impediment is that Switzerland has yet to ratify the Convention on the Rights of the Child. This is often surprising to foreign observers given that, in practice, Switzerland has an established pro-Human Rights stance. In addition, Geneva hosts a multitude of relevant international governmental and non-governmental organizations and has a long tradition of scholarly innovation in the field of childhood, most recently due to the influential Piagetian school of thought.[2]

---

[1] In French, the acronym "IDÉE" means "IDEA". In English, "IDÉE" stands for "Introduction of the child's right to be heard and listened to".

[2] Ironically, much of Piaget's original theory of child development is based on a careful examination of the views and thought processes expressed by children themselves.

E. Verhellen (ed.), Monitoring Children's Rights, 517–523.
© 1996 *Kluwer Law International. Printed in the Netherlands.*

The tardiness in ratifying the Convention on the Rights of the Child is accounted for by several specific institutional brakes. Indeed, Switzerland's attitude with regard to international treaties at large, and Human Rights conventions in particular, is marked by three characteristics:

- Firstly, the federal system is somewhat cumbersome and implies consulting all the cantons, the main political parties, as well as any interest group that may be concerned by the international treaty;
- Secondly, there is a scrupulous caution to only enter into binding international treaties if the conditions they set can reasonably be met;
- Thirdly, in recent years, a majority of so-called "nay sayers" has turned down, via national referenda, various government proposals advocating joining the European Community, membership in the United Nations, contributing to an international peace force (blue helmets), etc.

It is thus with some reluctance that the Swiss parliament is considering the ratification of the Convention on the Rights of the Child. No decision is likely before 1996 and, should Parliament ratify the Convention, a referendum seeking to annul this decision can not be excluded. Even in the likely scenario that Switzerland ultimately ratifies the Convention, it will certainly emit a number of reserves, none of which at this point in time targeting Article 12. Finally, if ratification takes place, the right of the child to express his/her views and to be heard will have to await an overhaul of current Swiss law. In the meantime, this right will be upheld by current, and somewhat deficient legal texts mitigated, nonetheless, by the gradual creation of new jurisprudence. Although it is not enshrined in the Constitution, the right to be heard is an essential component of Swiss Human Rights law.

II. LITTLE ROOM FOR THE CHILD

Concerning the child specifically, Swiss law allows little opportunity for the child to express him/herself. Parents must "take into consideration his/her [the child's] opinion as much as possible for important matters" (article 301 alinea 2 of the Swiss Civil Code). In regulations governing divorce and post-divorce proceedings, listening to the child's views is not mentioned. Participation is guaranteed for older children in adoption procedures and may occur, under restrictive conditions, in some child protection cases and when a legal guardian is designated. An overview of Geneva's cantonal legislation indicates that child protection agencies must of course base decisions on the child's best interest, but are under no obligation to hear the child. In divorce proceedings, Geneva cantonal law even explicitly bars judges from inviting children to express their views directly.

If the Swiss legal landscape changes substantially, it will only occur in a fairly distant future and gradually in accordance with ongoing and planned revisions of federal law. In this regard, the federal government has stated two views that are particularly relevant:

- the right of a minor to be heard traditionally takes place via an intermediary representing him/her, usually the parents, sometimes a tutor;
- Swiss divorce law is being revised and initial drafts propose that, in case of a parental separation, the child has the right to be consulted directly or through an intermediary. The federal government has informed the cantons, sovereign in implementing child protection measures as well as civil, penal and administrative rules, that they will have to modify their legislation and introduce the children's right to participate... once the Convention on the Rights of the Child is ratified!

This absence of clear guidelines could, in our opinion, jeopardize the introduction of Article 12 of the Convention even once it is ratified. This concern is what motivates our initiative in Geneva and the creation of the Group "IDÉE".

III. THE ABSOLUTE NEED FOR ACTION

The Group "IDÉE" was created in reaction to perceived deficiencies in the social, legal and administrative structures of Geneva, a rather progressive jurisdiction by Swiss standards of about 400.000 inhabitants. We became rapidly convinced that little thought was given to the child's place in matters and procedures that affect him/her, and that even less consideration was given to his/her participation. Hence, the project "IDÉE" seeks to promote the implementation of Article 12 of the Convention on the Rights of the Child despite the fact that the Convention has yet to be ratified.

Membership in the Group "IDÉE" reflects the shared conviction that the project must be widely interdisciplinary. Current members are jurists, magistrates, psychologists, physicians, social workers, teachers and sociologists. Most are engaged in applied activities, many are also involved in graduate teaching and research. Members are co-opted and seek not to represent the institutions that employ them.

IV. THE FIRST ACHIEVEMENTS OF THE GROUP "IDÉE"

The Group "IDÉE's'" discussion and planning meetings produced considerable forward-looking headway which bodes well for tangible changes affecting children's lives:

1. Each group member has had to deal with the areas of expertise of the other members. While this may seem obvious, childhood is a conceptual field that draws the interest of many disciplines, each asserting a degree of knowledge. However, the various disciplines have not yet acquired how to share their knowledge in a truly interdisciplinary fashion. We feel that this aspect of children's rights remains largely ignored and deserves increased attention.

Indeed, for some (mostly jurists), the child's participation tends to be viewed as a right that should be prescribed so that all children may enjoy it in almost all situations. For others (mostly social scientists and physicians), children's participation is so complex that it should be rooted in individual considerations and examined in relation to the specific context in which it is to take place. While this example starkly contrasts viewpoints and perhaps underestimates collaborative potential, it underscores differences in methodology, epistemology, ideology, research methods, etc., that mark various disciplines, differences that deserve much more attention in the future if interdisciplinarity is a stated objective.

2. Despite these differences, group members fortunately discovered that they agreed on some important principles, chief among these that participation should not be token and that the child is entitled to quality and expert listening. Furthermore, the child's views and opinions should contribute meaningfully to the decisions that affect him/her.

3. To achieve these objectives, it is important to demystify what listening to the child entails and to create opportunities for the child to express his/her views and opinions with no untoward effects.

For example, the Group "IDÉE" became aware of strong opposition to the child being directly consulted in some proceedings. For some, listening to a child is too serious and delicate a matter to be undertaken by jurists, be they lawyers or judges. Indeed, some jurists argue that their professional training does not qualify them to listen to a child in a psychologically risk-free manner and that their direct involvement could be detrimental to the child.

Another view, often expressed by social workers, is that some forms of participation could cause the child to be caught in detrimental situations. Often cited is the loyalty conflict that may arise in a divorce proceeding, i.e., the child is put in a position of expressing a preference for one of his/her parents. In our opinion, this view rests on a misunderstanding of the Convention which does not seek in any way to relieve adults of decisional responsibility. In addition, Article 12 in fact specifies that a child's opinion should be taken into consideration (and not followed blindly) in accordance to age and maturity.

The objective of Article 12 is simply to allow the child to express his/her view, should he/she choose to, and thus be recognized and feel acknowledged in situations that are often rather painful. Several studies actually show that children who are allowed to speak up meaningfully during their parents' divorce proceedings demonstrate higher satisfaction indices years later when compared to children who have no say in the matter. These studies did not ask children to choose the parent they preferred but to more generally express their feelings and thoughts in the forum where decisions affecting them were being taken.

4. The Group "IDÉE" feels strongly that listening to a child should be centered on his/her person and not a function of who the "listener" is or what he/she needs to know. The child must have the opportunity to speak up or to remain quiet and not have to rely on someone's decision to grant him/her this opportunity.

V. THE COMPETENCY ISSUE

The Group "IDÉE" recognizes the close link established in Article 12 between the child's right to speak and his/her competency to do so in accordance with age and maturity. However, the Group contests the notion that competency to participate is a linear notion and can be prescribed according to a child's chronological age. In our opinion, competency relies on numerous abilities that a child applies in situations that are relevant to him/her. In other words, a child may be fully competent with regard to something that occurs in his/her daily life and not at all for something else occurring in the daily life of a much younger child living in a different cultural setting. Furthermore, competency should never be considered an all or none proposition. If it were expected that one be fully competent in all areas, most adults would not qualify.

We feel much more comfortable with North American law which views competency in a pragmatic manner: competency is evaluated based on the specific question that confronts the child and the judicial authority. It is child- and context-specific. For example, a child victim or witness may testify to events only if he/she can relate them in a fairly reliable manner.

In some cases, children as young as three have provided reliable and valid accounts of their abuse. It may not be exaggerated to conceive that an infant competently testify to his/her abuse based on somatic reactions or rejection attitudes when the abusive adult approaches him/her physically. These considerations raise the absolute need to work in a pluridisciplinary fashion, acknowledging and understanding the child's abilities, and using all available techniques that favor participation to the best of his/her ability. When needed, child specialists can help provide "translations" to understand the pre-verbal or the particularly emotional child and thus promote his/her own right to participate.

VI. THE GROUP "IDÉE'S" PROPOSALS AND ACTIONS

The Group has examined what actions to undertake to ensure participation. One of the first actions was to draw up a list of situations in which the child's views should be expressed. With this goal in mind, the Group has also already initiated meetings with several official representatives from pivotal institutions (e.g., the police, school authorities, civil courts, etc.) to jointly examine how they currently take into account the child's views and opinions. Further contacts are ongoing with other institutions (penal courts, health authorities, child protection agencies, etc.). Out of these meetings, the Group will produce a report that surveys the current practice as well as proposals promoting participation.

Other means of promoting children's participation are planed: navigation of the informal network of relations and information that Group "IDÉE" members have built; contacts with political and judicial authorities to encourage legislative changes; cooperation with other recent initiatives (e.g., a child's legal walk in set up by the local bar association); creation and participation in teaching activities in the field of children's rights.

Finally the Group hopes to set up a specialized unit linked to the courts which all children in some way or another confronted to the judicial system could consult[3]. This pluridisciplinary unit would offer the child information and advice on his/her right to participate, on how the judicial system works, who the main legal players are, what to say, when and to whom, what to ask and how, etc. In turn, the judicial system could itself use this specialized unit as a center which concentrates expertise on children and offers advice on how to respect their specificity and to act according to their rights and in their best interest.

VII. BEYOND THE CONVENTION...

The need to inform local Geneva institutions and authorities of the Convention on the Rights of the Child is in itself an important objective that the Group "IDÉE" feels necessary to undertake. Many of the encounters we have set up have made our counterparts curious about the relative novelty of children's participation and about what culturally close countries, such as France and Belgium, have achieved in this area.

In this way, we have paradoxically set up a sort of pre-surveillance scheme for the application of some aspects of the Convention. Of course, we call this pre-surveillance only because Switzerland has yet to ratify the Convention. But pre-surveillance nonetheless because our contacts with authorities and institutions have led them to feel evaluated with respect to a growing legal doctrine, i.e., children's rights. In turn, this will no doubt stimulate them to reflect on their own practice and ultimately to introduce changes that favor participation. We have noticed that the fact Group "IDÉE" is interdisciplinary and multi-institutional is an important credibility factor helping it accomplish its mission.

Curiously, the greatest challenge of the Group "IDÉE" does not rest in accelerating the inevitable greater consideration for the child's participation,

---

[3] Adapted from the model of so-called "family clinics" that exist in some jurisdictions of North America.

but the need to master the complexity of interdisciplinary thinking and action. To speak a common language regardless of professional background and to act with respect towards the differences is as necessary as proclaiming and promoting the rights of children.

NELIA SANCHO

Monitoring the Implementation of the UN Convention on the Rights of the Child

The Experience of Philippine NGOs

INTRODUCTION

In 1990, the Philippines ratified the United Nations Convention on the Rights of the Child, the fifth country in Asia to do so. In January 1995, the UN Committee on the Rights of the Child will officially review the first country report of the Philippine Government. In preparation for this, a new coalition of NGOs in the Philippines was organized in September 1993. This coalition, composed of all the major networks of child-focused NGOs and other international and local child-focused NGOs was organized specifically to monitor the implementation of the UN Convention on the Rights of the Child in the Philippines.

I. THE ROLE OF NGOS IN THE PHILIPPINES: DIVERSITY AND UNITY

In the last two Decades, NGOs in the Philippines have played a significant role in addressing the needs of Filipino Children. A vibrant and dynamic NGO community has actively worked for the protection of the rights of children through direct programmes and services, information, advocacy and organizing efforts. Renewed efforts to strengthen the NGOs – as organizations and in terms of improving the quality of programmes – are underway.

The Philippine NGOs are diverse in their origins, purpose, nature of operations, social and political orientation. Most of the child-focused NGOs in the Philippines have been established to provide some kind of service or programmes for children and families, there are some NGOs with a clearly religious or charitable purpose or fulfill welfare objectives. A good number of these NGOs were established two or three decades ago and were known as foundations, religious or civic organizations. While many of them worked

E. Verhellen (ed.), Monitoring Children's Rights, 525–535.
© 1996 *Kluwer Law International. Printed in the Netherlands.*

as welfare organizations committed to helping poor children, the work was perceived to be apolitical or part of a religious or philanthropic mission. They started to focus their attention on the needs of children in especially difficult circumstances e.g. streetchildren, only after 1986. Before that, many of them were involved in running institutions for abandoned children, some form of pre-school programs, or providing scholarships for poor children. They were organized into networks that were recognized by the government and often worked in partnership with the government agencies with the mandate to provide services for children. The credibility of these organizations among the private (i.e. business sector) and government sector made them more highly visible. It also gave them easier access to funding from church-based organizations or from churches themselves, from the business sector and other civic organizations, from international and governmental development agencies.

In the late 1970's up to the early 1980's, there were other types of child-focused NGOs which were organized specifically to draw attention to and respond to the needs of children in especially difficult circumstances. These NGOs were closely linked to the then emerging and strengthening people's movement that actively led the struggle against US-Marcos dictatorship. These NGOs were often composed of individuals and organizations from the various sectors – women, health, peasants, workers, educators, and other professional working with children – all committed to promoting a nationalist and democratic agenda for social development. Their objective was clearly to highlight the crisis that Filipino children were in because of the social, economic, and political crisis that the country was in. Thus, social and political action for children were closely linked to contribute to efforts to work for structural changes within a repressive and inequitable society. Working to improve the quality of the life of Filipino children especially the majority who belonged to the families who lived below poverty line clearly required a social movement from the perspective of these NGOs. From 1983 to 1985, these child-focused organizations started to organize themselves into multi-sectoral alliance that would work together to promote a progressive orientation to working with children across the socioeconomic classes but with special attention to the children in rural and urban poor and those affected by human rights violations. Understandably, many of those NGOs were in opposition to the Marcos government. Thus, it was almost impossible to work in partnership with government agencies which were strongly controlled and refused to acknowledged problems affecting Filipino children especially child prostitution, children in situations of armed conflict, the effects of internal corruption and repression, as well as foreign domination of the economy on the educational systems and the health delivery system. Much of the support for these more progressive child-focused NGOs came from development agencies in the North particularly from Europe who recognized the real problems in Philippine society.

These different alliances and networks of NGOs worked on parallel – sometimes even conflicting and competing – efforts during the late 1970's up to 1986. There was barely any interaction among them. But from 1986 to 1993, after the fall of the Marcos dictatorship, with the new political regime headed by President Corazon Aquino, some organizations from these different alliances and networks found themselves working along similar concerns e.g. streetchildren, child prostitutions, early childhood development, the promotion and protection of the rights of children, the rights and welfare of youth in conflict with the law. It was already acceptable to talk openly about the relationship between the social, political and economic conditions of the country and the difficult life situations of the majority of the Filipino children. Given the different political conditions, there were more opportunities and venues for cooperation – between NGOs as well as with government agencies. This is not to say, however, that the goals and purposes of all child-focused NGOs were the same. There continue to be a wide variety of NGOs based on their social and political orientation, and the nature of their operation but there are opportunities for crossing these dividing lines and cooperation on certain issues.

One such basis for cooperation is the shared concern for monitoring the implementation of the UN Convention on the Rights of the Child. Such is the significance of the UN Convention – it can and has been a rallying point for all concerned with children to work together to translate the Convention into reality for all the children of the world to enjoy the quality of life that they deserve and are entitled to. Thus, the basis for unity among the child-focused NGOs and government agencies in the Philippines can be this shared responsibility for monitoring the implementation of the UN Convention on the Rights of the Child.

II. THE PROCESS OF MONITORING THE IMPLEMENTATION OF THE UN CONVENTION

A. *Organizational Issues*
The Philippine NGO Coalition was conceived out of this realization that there must be a more systematic effort to monitor the implementation of the UN Convention. It was the scheduled submission of the Philippine government's report to the UN Committee on the Rights of the Child that gave impetus to the organization of the Philippine NGO Coalition. On September 1993, a two-day consultation was convened by the Council for the Welfare of Children, the national coordinating agency which is tasked with monitoring the implementation of the UN Convention and the Philippine Plan of Action for Children which was adopted after the World Summit for Children was convened in 1990. During this consultation, more child-focused NGOs were invited to participate and they articulated all their comments and reservations

about the government report. First, it was noted that the consultation with NGOs was already too late in the process of preparing the govenment report. However, the NGOs who attended the consultation convened by the Council for the Welfare of Children still communicated their observations and comments on the government report. By the time the revised government report was released, the NGOs who participated in this meeting convened by the government had already conceptualized and began the process of organizing the Philippine NGO Coalition which was intended to bring together all the child-focused organizations to begin serious and well-coordinated efforts to monitor the implementation of the UN Convention.

The Philippine NGOs were inspired and encouraged by the experiences of other countries and regions particularly in Latin America where NGOs worked together through national coalitions to jointly monitor the implementation of the CRC. The Philippine NGOs thought that the government's submission of its initial report to the Committee on the Rights of the Child presented a perfect opportunity to organize a national NGO Committee. We learned about these through our participation in the international efforts to promote children's rights which allow access to information about models for monitoring and strategies for promoting the CRC e.g. publications and materials from DCI, Radda Barnen, the NGO Group.

Some representatives of Philippine NGOs also had the opportunity to interact with some members of the UN Committee on the Rights of the Child from 1992 to 1993 and were encouraged by the insights and suggestions to work for a similar organization of child-focused organizations in the Philippines. It was also timely that at precisely the time that the NGO Coalition were deliberating on the immediate plans and discussing long-term possibilities, the Coordinator of the NGO Group who was based in the DCI Office in Geneva communicated with the head of the DCI-Phil. Section upon the suggestion of the International Secretariat of DCI. This gave us access to helpful information as well as critical encouragement as the DCI-Philippines was directly involved in the actual preparation and writing of the NGO Coalition report. It is clear that learning through participation within the international networks was a critical factor for initiating these efforts in the Philippines.

Working committees were formed with lead organizations identified to assume responsibility for the following tasks which were identified to be the immediate needs and objectives: organizational matters, research, committee to draft the concept paper on the NGO Coalition. These were the initial committees at the early stages of the Coalition. Meetings were convened with organizations rotating responsibility for hosting the meeting.

At the outset, the immediate objective was to study in greater depth the first government report which was submitted to the UN Committee on the Rights of the Child and to work on a separate report from the NGO Coalition for submission to the UN Committee.

B. Working Committees: Initial Activities of the Coalition
1. Research Committee.   The potential for generating information among the member organizations was immediately recognized by the leading organizations of the Phil. NGO Coalition. It was also important at this stage to admit the fact that among the weakest aspects of NGO work in the Philippines was careful and diligent documentation of programme activities, services and the situation of children in their own geographic areas. The research committee worked on designing an initial questionnaire for use by the local NGOs in reporting on the implementation of the Convention within the context of their own communities or geographical areas. The questionnaire was developed in two languages used in the country: Filipino and English. It was envisioned that translation into other major dialects would follow at a later stage. From the beginning it was envisioned that the questionnaire would serve as a diagnostic tool also to provide information about the extent to which local, grassroots-based child-focused NGOs were 1) familiar with the specific articles of the Convention and how these were implemented within their own contexts; 2) how the child-focused NGOs perceived their work with children and families in relation to the UN Convention. The process of retrieval of the questionnaires would also indicate how closely coordination could be achieved among NGOs especially given the distances that had to be covered from Metro Manila (the largest urban center where the organizing NGOs were based) and the different regions throughout the archipelago where the member organizations or partner organizations were based. This would give important information about the organizational strategies that would have to be addressed and developed.

Most of the questionnaires were retrieved but initial results indicate that many of the child-focused NGOs tend to see their work with children and families in a very particular and specific way, e.g. only early childhood development programmes or only streetchildren's programmes without making any connections with the specific articles of the UN Convention. The research committee of the NGO Coalition interprets this to mean that more in-depth studies on the specific articles of the Convention will have to be initiated and facilitated by the NGO Coalition for the member organizations. It was encouraging to note that the willingness to participate in the information-gathering process was apparent but there was also a need to provide technical assistance as articulated but the local NGOs during some of the regional consultations or in the retrieval process by the Secretariats of the alliances or networks or by the Reseach Committee.

This information-gathering exercise also generated a new interest in the UN Convention among child-focused NGOs beyond the awareness of the significance of the UN Convention. It was important to begin the process of exploring the role of NGOs in the monitoring process as well as in education and advocacy efforts on the UN Convention. This would entail developing new directions for working together within the networks and alliances they belong to as well as integrating the work on promoting the rights of children within their own programmes and organizational lives.

Another important and simultaneous data-gathering process was undertaken by the research committee in preparation for writing the supplemental report for submission to UN Committee on the Rights of the Child. This involved contacting specific NGOs for existing studies, researches, case studies, internal documentation on the work with children in their own areas. This data-gathering process generated valuable concrete information about the situation of Filipino children. Using the information in a way that indicates a clear connection with the specific articles of the UN Conventions was an important undertaking for the research committee. It also revealed the gaps in information about children as well as the work of NGOs i.e. what specific areas of work with children are currently covered by local NGOs and which areas are left unattended to and what are the reasons for these. For example, it was clear from the information generated that there was not as much work on child labor in the agricultural and manufacturing sector among NGOs compared to the informal services sector which was often in connection with streetchildren's programmes.

The next stage was the actual writing of the report which began with an in-depth study and analysis of the government's report. The fact that this had to be undertaken by representatives of each of the organizing NGOs of the coalition meant that arriving at a consensus on key issues to be raised and the manner of articulation of concerns had to be acceptable to all. Given the broad range of participating NGOs, it was anticipated that it could not be a simple process of writing a draft for approval by all, that thorough discussion would have to be the most important investment. This was a valuable exercise also in working together as a group so that the contents of the report would reflect the major concerns of the NGO Coalition.

When it was time to finalize the supplemental report, it was suggested by the research committee that only the organizations who actually agree with all the contents of assume that other organizations who did not have an opportunity to thoroughly study the supplemental report would be willing to affix their organization's name to the report. It was encouraging to note that more and more organizations wanted to register their agreement with the NGO report as it was circulated for validation and continuing consultation with them after the report was submitted to the Committee on the Rights of the Child in March and after the pre-sessional meeting in April of 1994.

2. Organizational Committee.   The organizational committee assumed the task of broadening membership to the coalition by other organizations who were not members of the networks and alliances which were already active in the coalition. They were also expected to inform other broader-based or other sectoral groups, educational organizations and institutions about the newly-organized NGO Coalition and its activities.

The other important organisational activity was the identification of NGOs in the Coalition who would work as convenors for the regional consultations that would be held in four regions to cover the major island groupings and the National Capital Region where there were many child-focused organizations. Two or three organizations volunteered to be convenors for each of the four regional consultations. Fund-raising efforts from a local grant-giving organization to cover the expenses for these regional consultations were initiated and support was given for four meetings, two of which have been held and two will be held early next year. The members of the Coalition Discussed the agenda for these consultations and informed one another about the developments in the preparation for the meetings as well as the details of the meeting. Given the broad geographical coverage of the work of the coalition, these regional consultations are important activities.

One of the major issues that needs to be addressed at this point is the organizational structure of the Coalition, the need to establish a more permanent Secretariat which can devote fulltime energies to coordinating the work of the NGO Coalition. At the same time, there is caution in discussing these issues so that the supportive role of the Secretariat in relation to the members of the NGO Coalition, the issue of representation of the NGO Coalition and the active participation of the member organizations will be insured in designing the organizational structure of the NGO Coalition. Given the fact that this is the broadest formation of child-focused NGOs in the history of NGO work for children in the Philippines, this is a process that requires careful decision-making that takes into consideration all the views of the coalition members. The issue of fund-raising for the needs of sustaining the activities of the NGO Coalition and the need to design a systematic and sustainable approach to monitoring the implementation of the UN Convention are the priority concerns at the moment.

The committee will eventually cooperate with the Research Committee in working on projects proposals and concept papers to address these important objectives for discussion with all the members of the Coalition.

Another current concern that coalition members are addressing is the issue of partnership with government in national work for the rights of the child. The recent decentralization process of the Philippine government offers many opportunities for NGO participation in monitoring and implementing the Philippine Plan of Action for Children (a national plan of action which is closely but not exactly correlated to the articles of the UN Convention) and the enforcement of revised national legislation to conform with the UN Convention at the local levels. At the same time the importance of defining these partnerships with government agencies at the national, regional, provincial and municipal levels require careful consideration for maintaining NGO autonomy and independence. It is a critical balancing-act and concrete strategies for NGO-GO partnerships that allow for critical collaboration efforts and participation in local government units specifically in organizing and activating the local, village-level Child Protection Councils will be an important topic of study in Coalition-led workshops in the immediate future.

One immediate result of the submission of the NGO report to the UN Committee is that the Philippine government has communicated with the NGO Coalition requesting for comments by the Coalition on the criteria for selection of the NGO representatives in the Council for the Welfare of Children. The Council has also requested for nominations of NGO representatives from the Coalition. This is an important development as the previous representatives were only from one network of child-focused organizations and so broader representation and consultation with other NGOs were not always possible nor undertaken. This was a key issue raised by the NGO Coalition in relation to the process of preparing the Philippine government's initial report on the implementation of the UN Convention. This indicates that the Philippine government recognizes the legitimacy of the newly-organized NGO Coalition as representing the broadest range so far of child-focused NGOs in the country. It is also an important indication of the government's openness to working with NGOs especially on the monitoring process as the Council for the Welfare of Children in the national inter-agency body tasked with monitoring the implementation of the UN Convention and the national plan of action for children. This is a valuable opportunity for NGOs to participate in defining the monitoring system for the entire country. The challenge is to remain independent so that the NGO Coalition can be free to serve as watchdog while being a partner of the government agencies in order to influence policy-making and monitoring processes of children's programmes and services for the implementation of the UN Convention. A most important challenge for the NGO Coalition, should it decide to nominate a representative to the Council for the Welfare of Children and define specific ways of working with government at the different levels, is to remain accountable to the member organizations they represent and especially to the Filipino children that they are committed to working with.

III. FUTURE DIRECTIONS FOR THE NGO COALITION

There are key issues that the NGO Coalition must address at this point if it is to effectively participate in national work for the rights of the Child. These are future directions that the NGO Coalition is seriously considering.

A. *Intensifying Organizational Efforts*
This entails continuing the regional consultations, defining agendas for these consultations and mobilizing the active participation of local NGOs in the work of the NGO Coalition. This is a trust-building effort among NGOs as well as serious education and advocacy efforts on the importance of the NGO participation in monitoring the implementation of the UN Convention.

Activating working committess of the Coalition and addressing the nature of the relationships between the proposed Secretariat and the members of the Coalition will also be important at this stage. The definition of leadership roles for the organizing NGOs and the other members of the Coalition will have to be undertaken. The concept of leadership as facilitating the active participation of member organizations and enabling them to assume leadersship roles on behalf of the Coalition, within the local, national and international levels is a direction that will be taken.

B. Designing Models for Monitoring the Implementation of the UN Convention

A systematic assessment of what is currently in place within the NGO community will have to be undertaken so that the design of a viable and effective monitoring system will be achieved. The NGOs at the local level must be actively involved in this process so that it will not be a view from the top but a realistic view from the ground, at the level closest to children and families and other institutions that work with the children or who are responsible for them. At this point there is no comprehensive study of the actual work or the extent of NGO work for children on a national level. This is also an important project for the NGO Coalition to undertake.

An important aspect of designing monitoring systems will be the identification of indicators that will be applied to specific articles or groups of articles on the UN Convention as it is implemented within the Philippine context. These indicators must be agreed upon as valid and viable among NGOs and discussion with the concerned implementing agencies of the government will have to be initiated by the NGO Coalition.

Part of the process of designing and beginning to set-up viable monitoring systems will be the identification of activities for integrating children's rights work within programmes and services for children and broader-based development efforts especially at the community level, launching and sustaining awareness campaigns, gathering and compilation of the data about the status of Filipino children, submission of reports to the government and the UN Committee on the Rights of the Child and coordination with other national and international bodies who may be helpful in promoting specific concerns for children.

C. Participation of the NGO Coalition or its Member Organizations in Policy-making and Reforms

Actively promoting a legislative reform agenda for Filipino children and monitoring the enforcement of national and local laws in support of children's rights will be a major undertaking of the Coalition. The Coalition can also initiate discussions with the concerned government agencies and intergovernmental bodies e.g. UNICEF, active in the Philippines about the relationship between the Philippine Plan of Action for Children and the UN Convention with the goal of expanding the Plan of Action to more closely approximate the articles of the UN Convention.

The NGO Coalition can also initiate discussions with the government on defining or redefining the relationships between government agencies or bodies such as the Council for the Welfare of Children and the newly-established Children's Rights Center under the Commission on Human Rights and the Special Task Force of the Department of Justice so that the existing public resources can be fully maximized, made more effective and unnecessary overlap in functions can be avoided. These government agencies are the officially recognized bodies which can be maximized for the monitoring process.

Some of the member organizations are already undertaking related projects and have already been invited to participate in government-organized Task Forces or consultation activities e.g. on the rights of children in conflict with the law, on the juvenile justice system, on child prostitution and other forms of child abuse, education of law enforcement agencies and officials on children's rights, in the IPEC-ILO Country Programme. DCI-Phil. was invited to represent the NGO Coalition and present the NGO supplemental report at the National Seminar Workshop on the Implementation of the UN Convention convened by the Council for the Welfare of Children in September 1994. Four of the leading organizing NGOs in the Coalition: Childhope, NCSD, Salinlahi, and DCI-Phil. participated in the IPEC-ILO National Planning Workshop also held in September 1994. These were opportunities to disseminate information about the new Coalition as well as the supplemental report which was also circulated by the Council for the Welfare of Children to all government agencies and units concerned with implementing the Philippine Plan of Action for Children.

Consulting with member organizations of the NGO Coalition and initiating information-dissemination activities to keep Coalition members informed about government efforts as well as to inform the government about the NGO work will be part of the approach for keeping the communication lines open between government and the members of the NGO Coalition. Technical assistance for members organizations on documentation activities as well as educational programmes on policy development for children's rights should be priorities in the near future. Workshops and training programmes will be organized for this.

It is clear that the birth of the Philippine National Coalition of NGOs for Monitoring the Implementation of the UN Convention is both a cause for celebration as well as a new challenge in working for the rights of childrens in the Philippines. The process of working together as much as the product of the collaborative work among Philippine NGOs are both equally important. One of the most important issues that will be addressed as the newly-formed coalition continues its work is the issue of the legitimacy of NGOs in the work for children's rights. As Prof. Hoda Badran, Chairperson of the UN Committee on the Rights of the Child, pointed out during the presessional meeting of the Committee with representatives from the Philippine NGO Coalition, this is one of the central issues that NGOs must now face. Legitimacy is earned rather than conferred or self-endowed. Ultimately, the legitimacy of the NGOs committed to promoting and protecting the rights of children in the Philippines and in other countries will depend on whether the children – active and equal partners in the work for children's rights – will validate the legitimacy of the NGOs. This will depend to a large extent on the quality of our work and how we can further the rights of the Filipino children to survival, development, and special protection while ensuring their active participation in all the processes involved in such an important undertaking that seeks to make the UN Convention a reality for the Filipino children.

LAURA THEYTAZ-BERGMAN

NGO Group for the Convention on the Rights of the Child

The NGO Group on the Convention on the Rights of the Child is a coalition of international non-governmental organizations, which work together to facilitate the implementation of the United Nations Convention on the Rights of the Child. The Group is composed of thirty-seven international non-governmental organizations with consultative status with ECOSOC. Although some of the member organizations focus on children's rights and child welfare, for many members, children are but one aspect of their mandate. These organizations include jurists, religious groups, women's rights advocates and educational associations. Participation in the NGO Group allows these organizations to engage themselves in discussions on children's rights issues without having to devote the necessary resources to follow these issues on a full time basis.

I. ORIGINS OF THE NGO GROUP

The NGO Group was originally formed in 1983 as the Informal Ad Hoc NGO Group for the Drafting of the Convention on the Rights of the Child. From 1983 until 1988, members of the NGO Group were actively involved in the drafting of the Convention. Members of the Group would meet twice yearly in private in order to analyze the text of articles of the Convention which had been proposed by the Working Group and to draft changes to these articles or to recommend the inclusion of new articles. Joint proposals on draft articles endorsed by approximately thirty NGOs were submitted to the Working Group. This cooperation not only allowed NGOs to present a unified front to the Working Group but also allowed them to have a considerable impact on the shaping of the final text of the Convention. Nigel Cantwell, Secretary of the NGO Group, has written that "it was the breadth of the expertise on which the NGO Group could draw, combined with its cohesion and careful preparation, that largely explains how it had an impact in so many of the fields covered by this unusually comprehensive treaty."[1]

---

[1] Nigel Cantwell, "The Origins, Development and Significance of the United Nations Convention on the Rights of the Child" in *The United Nations Convention on the Rights of*

E. Verhellen (ed.), Monitoring Children's Rights, 537–540.
© 1996 *Kluwer Law International. Printed in the Netherlands.*

Once the Convention on the Rights of the Child was adopted by the General Assembly in 1989, the intention was to dissolve the NGO Group as its reason for existing was officially over. Due to the fact that article 45 of the Convention states that the Committee "may invite...other competent bodies...to provide expert advice on the implementation of the Convention", the NGO Group decided to reconstitute itself with a slightly different focus in order to assist in the monitoring and implementation of the Convention.

II. AIMS OF THE NGO GROUP

One of the major goals set by the NGO Group is to keep in regular contact with the Committee on the Rights of the Child in order to provide a focal point for two-way information flow between the non-governmental community and the Committee. The Coordinator of the NGO Group tries to identify possible contributions from the NGO community related to issues on the agenda of the Committee and to secure all relevant information from non-governmental sources. Members of the NGO Group are available to provide expertise on a wide range of topics and are able to act as a resource for information regarding State Party compliance with the standards of the Convention through their network of national affiliates. The Coordinator, similarly, keeps its members and their affiliates informed of the work of the Committee.

The Coordinator of the NGO Group also tries to ensure that the Committee on the Rights of the Child receives information from non-governmental sources for all countries on its agenda. The reports that governments submit under article 44 of the Convention tend to be fairly legalistic and usually present only the legal perspective as to the situation of children in their country without considering the practical implementation of these laws. This means that the Committee is often unable to obtain a complete view of the situation of children based solely on the government report. The consideration of non-governmental information is therefore essential to the monitoring process in order to ensure that the Committee receives a complete picture as to how the Convention is being implemented in a particular country.

III. NGO CONTRIBUTIONS TO THE REPORTING PROCESS

In order to determine whether the government report accurately reflects reality, the Committee welcomes written information from international, regional, national and local NGOs. The Committee seeks specific, reliable and objective information that deals with all the different areas covered by the Convention in order to effectively monitor its implementation in a country. The NGO Group promotes the preparation of alternative, complementary, or supplementary

---

the Child, A Guide to the "Travaux Préparatoires", ed. Sharon Detrick, Martinus Nijhoff Publishers, 1992, p. 25.

reports by NGOs that attempt to analyze the implementation of legislation in order to give an accurate picture of the practice in a country, provide information that complements or supplements the information provided in the government report and make concrete recommendations as to what can be done to improve the situation of children in their country. The NGO Group has prepared "A Guide for Non-Governmental Organizations Reporting to the Committee on the Rights of the Child" which provides information on the reporting procedure and the participation of NGOs in this process.

Based on written information provided in advance, the Committee may invite NGOs to participate in its pre-sessional working group in order to provide it with factual information on specific aspects of the implementation of the Convention in the country under consideration. Participation of NGOs at the working group allows Committee members to ask questions and to obtain a picture as to the true situation of children in a particular country. It helps Committee members to set priorities and to identify key issues for discussion with the government. The NGO Group may be able to provide limited funding in order to allow one representative from each country who has been invited by the Committee to participate in the working group to travel to Geneva.

IV. FOLLOW-UP AT NATIONAL LEVEL

The information presented both orally and in writing by NGOs has had a strong impact on the questions asked by Committee members and on the recommendations to governments. The NGO Group tries to ensure that once this whole process is complete, the results of the discussion (press releases, summary records, concluding observations) are transmitted to national level in order to ensure that they are disseminated widely within the country. Often in the United Nations system, information on human rights abuses is submitted only by international NGOs working in Geneva. Committees prepare recommendations based on an examination of a report that takes place in Geneva and the recommendations are disseminated to Geneva based NGOs. In this process, the national level is left out of the picture and the impact at national level is virtually non-existent. The NGO Group wanted to ensure that the voices of non-governmental organizations working at the national level directly with children were heard and that these NGOs were able to contribute effectively to this process.

NGOs can contribute to the implementation of the Committee's recommendations by periodically reviewing the measures undertaken, evaluating their success and adequacy and making suggestions for future action. They should also continue to monitor achievements and encourage public scrutiny of policies by identifying existing problems, considering new policies and establishing new targets. Finally, NGOs should investigate and report on violations of children's rights.

V. MONITORING THE IMPLEMENTATION OF THE CONVENTION

In order to facilitate contact between the NGO community and the Committee on the Rights of the Child, the NGO Group promotes the creation and development of national coalitions of non-governmental organizations working with children. A national coalition that is broad based and representative allows NGOs working with children to cooperate and coordinate their work in certain areas. It also allows for more effective monitoring of the implementation of the Convention at national level due to the specialist knowledge of coalition members and the variety of points of view that may be represented. In addition, alternative reports prepared by coalitions rather than individual NGOs are much more difficult to disregard or discredit. Governments can easily claim that information submitted by one NGO should not be taken seriously because that particular NGO is politically motivated, linked to the opposition, not reliable, or is basing its criticism on fantasy rather than fact. It is much more difficult for a government to discredit an alternative report prepared by a group of NGOs.

It is important that NGO coalitions are not only critical of the way in which a government is implementing the Convention, but should offer concrete recommendations or proposals for improving the situation of children in their country. They should strive to become partners in the monitoring process rather than parties to a conflict with the government. The Committee often recommends the establishment of a national monitoring mechanism in which NGOs are active participants.

Although there are no sanctions for non-compliance of its recommendations, the Committee does expect to see its concerns addressed in the next report submitted by the government. It is not possible, however, for the Committee to continuously monitor the implementation of the Convention. It can only emphasize the importance of a national discussion about the rights of the child, point out problems and suggest possible remedies. The Committee must therefore rely on domestic monitors in order to ensure that the Convention is being implemented in each State party. The development of sound national monitoring is essential in order to provide the strongest basis for effective international monitoring.

The creation of a movement at national level is the only way in which to improve the situation of children. The Committee cannot solve the problems of children in a specific country, it can only help to prioritize problems and offer suggestions for improvement at national level. Therefore, the need for continuous local monitoring by NGOs is essential. Although the Committee can pressure governments for change, the solutions themselves must come from national level. It is up to NGOs to get and keep children's issues on the national agenda.

MARIANNE BORGEN

Developing the Role of an Ombudsman

To work for Children's rights is to work on all political areas, on all levels of society. The UN Convention on the Rights of the Child (1989)is an important tool, and a very good basis for this work, therefore the Conference theme is essential. To focus on the monitoring process national and international , by asking the questions *what* is to be reported and *by whom,* set up several challenges to the monitoring bodies. Challenges to the official ones, like the Norwegian Ombudsman for Children, as well as the NGOs, and the possible coordination an collaboration between the different bodies.

The State Ombudsman for Children in Norway, was established in 1981.

Sweden got their official ombudsman for Children in July 1993 (Louise Sylwander) and Island will have their office from January 1995. Therefore we are know creating a nordic ombudsman board to discuss the work and to coordinate our work in connection with the UN Convention. I hope that we will be able to discuss the possibilities in Europe – for strengthening the Rights of Children, and find ways to collaborate and to coordinate our work.

INTRODUCTION: A SHORT PRESENTATION OF THE NORWEGIAN COMMISSIONER FOR CHILDREN

Since there exist many ombud-like bodies, it is necessary to find a consensus of the meaning of the term "Ombudsman" when describing an office or a spokesperson for children.

To be more specific about the official function of the Norwegian ombudsman, the Norwegian Ministry of Foreign Affairs has chosen to translate "Barneombud" (Ombudsman/person for Children) with "Commissioner for Children". The French translation is "Le Médiateur pour l'Enfance", the German is "Der Kinderbeauftragte", and the Spanish "el Defensor de la Infancia". Each of these approximate translations reflect different aspects of the Ombudsman role, as well as different socio-legal, political, and administrative traditions of the various languages and the countries from which they originate.

In Norway the term "Ombudsman" or "Ombud" is most commonly reserved for the national Ombudsmen (for Public Administration, Equal Status for

E. Verhellen (ed.), Monitoring Children's Rights, 541–554.
© 1996 *Kluwer Law International. Printed in the Netherlands.*

Women, Consumer Affairs, and for Children; a fifth is exclusively for the military services, and is therefore not "public").

"Ombud" is occasionally used as a synonym for "Ombudsman" in the same way that "chair" is used synomously for "chairman". Despite this practice "Ombud" as a term is not recognized by English language specialists.

The Public Ombudsman Offices were established and funded by the Storting (the Norwegian Parliament), their responsibilities described in the Acts for their respective Offices. Except by revoking or amending the Acts, the Storting cannot, however, instruct the Ombudsmen. They have therefore a rare independence in relation to administration – and are obligated to criticize even the Storting itself, if need be.

The Ombudsman Offices are required to propose amendments of law, regulations, and procedures, seeking to improve the situation for the groups with which they are concerned. Except for the Ombudsman for Children, the Offices are responsible for specific provisions of Norwegian legislation. The Ombudsman Offices for Equal Status and for Consumer Affairs were established to defend – and handle complaints – in connection with actual legislation in those two areas.

The Commissioner for Children is in a special situation compared to the other Norwegian ombud. The Commissioner does not work with, nor handle complaints related to a specific area of legislation. The Commissioner's responsibilities as spokesperson for children cover most areas of society, and involves, therefore, several judicial areas. The Commissioner's role as promoter and ensurer of children's interests apply to all areas of legislation that affect children.

The Norwegian Commissioner for Children was established to "promote the interests of children vis à vis public and private authorities and to follow up the development of conditions under which children grow up" (Act of the Commissioner for Children §3). The only prohibitions are handling individual conflicts within the family and issues which have been brought to court, until the court process has been completed. The Commissioner for Children must therefore keep an eye on all areas of society, give warning of developments harmful for children, and propose changes to improve their conditions. He (or she) must be alert to the consequences and implications for children in all parts of Norwegian legislation and regulations. The Office has no decision-making power and no right to rescind the decisions of other authorities. As a result, information, advocacy, and well-documented statements are its main tools. The Office seeks to increase public knowledge and influence the opinions and attitudes of others, in an effort to improve the situation of children.

I. The History

For countries who are thinking of establishing a Commissioner for Children it will be interesting to know something about the history of the Norwegian model.

A. The Idea and the Discussion

The idea of a special ombud for children – a Commissioner for Children, is a truly Norwegian idea. It was first launched in the late 1960's by Dr. Juris. Professor Anders Bratholm. He has since been called the father of the Commissioner for Children.

The first official proposal for a Commissioner came from the Child Act Committee, established in 1975. The Committee's task was to forward proposals for a law dealing with the relationships between children and their parents, as well as to discuss the question of a Commissioner for Children.

The Committee concluded that an independent agency, free to criticize both the authorities and private bodies was called for. The Committee proposed that an institution be created to safeguard children's interests – a Commissioner for Children.

The Commissioner for Children should, on his own intiative, or as a hearing instance protect the interests of children in connection with planning and study-reports. He/She should ensure that legislation protecting the child is observed, and promote children's rights under the law, especially children in institutions.

The proposals from the committee were sent for comments, and a working group was established in the Ministry. The Group concluded that a free and independent agency was needed, because children are not able to take up their own causes with the authorities or with public opinion. There were two models to choose from:
- a Commissioner who functioned as a protector of children's interests and rights;
- the establishment of an independent council, a State Children's Council which would follow developments pertaining to children's situation, and further children's interests with public and private authorities.

They recommended, however, that children's legal and judicial rights be part of the sphere of the Ombudsman for Public Administration.

B. The Establishing

The Ministry chose the first model, an ombudsman especially for children, a Commissioner for Children, on the grounds that an ombudsman would have more authority and real influence than a council or committee. The Ministry also felt that an ombudsman would be able to react much faster than a council, which would, after all, be limited to just a few meetings a year.

The Ministry also stressed the Commissioner's visibility as an institution for children and others who need an ombudsman's help in specific cases.

The Commissioner's relations to the Ombudsman for Public Administration, and other ombudsmen and councils, to Ministries, government, the Storting and the Courts were also discussed by the Ministry. Their conclusions were incorporated into the law proposal.

The United Nations International Year of the Child was a central factor in establishing the Commissioner for Children. Discussions in 1979 uncovered shortcomings and needs tied to public child-welfare. Although the proposal for a Commissioner for Children was forwarded earlier, the 1979-discussions were instrumental for achieving a political majority in the Parliament.

II. THE ACT

The preliminary work done, and later incorporated into the world's first law for a Commissioner for Children, bears evidence of being concerned with "principles". The Act has, over the years, become a tool that has given the Norwegian Commissioner for Children a respected as well as independent position in the State. The Act has also become a model for similar laws throughout the world.

The Act was forwarded by the Harlem Brundtland Administration late in 1980. The Parliament's Standing Committee for Administration and Consumer Affairs discussed the proposal and delivered its recommendation January 23, 1981. The act was passed by the Parliament March 6, 1981, and the world's first Commissioner for Children, Målfrid Grude Flekkøy, was appointed September 1. the same year.

The Act and instructions concerning the Commisssioner's work are attached. The main points are:

- The Commissioner shall be an independent spokesman for children in Norway. The Commissioner shall not be obligated by the Government or by the Ministry's professional viewpoints or priorities.
- The Commissioner is given a wide mandate to observe and work for improving children's living conditions, from 0–17 years old.
- The Commissioner can set his/her own professional priorities and working methods.
- The Commissioner has the right to see all documents in all cases dealing with children handles by the public authorities. The Commissioner shall also have access to all children's institutions.

The Act has proven to be quite helpful for the Commissioner's work, and has given the Commissioner the necessary freedom of action.

III. THE ADMINISTRATION AND THE BUDGET

The Office of the Commissioner for Children is formally administered under the Ministry for Children and Family Affairs.

The Commissioner is subject to the rules applicable to budget management in public and state services. Besides this economic and technical tie, the Ministry has no means to guide or steer the commissioner's activities. Professionally, the Commissioner is totally independent from the Ministry.

Professionally, the Commissioner is guided by the Act, and no authority can steer the Commissioner's professional judgements.

Through budget allocations, however, the Ministry can to a certain extent steer the Commissioner's activities, or rather level of activity. The Ministry proposes a budget to the Parliament, who passes it.

The Commissioner's budget goes entirely to wages and management. The Commissioner has no funds of its own for research, studies or measures for children.

The staff of the Commissioner for Children has increased from 3 to 6 permanent positions. Including temporary and part-time positions, the staff today numbers 11. These cover the fields of law, sociology, education, child welfare, medicine, culture and information, as well as the duties of a secretariat.

IV. THE ADVISORY PANEL

The Act stipulates that the Commissioner shall have an Advisory Panel, consisting of central persons, knowledgeable in child-affairs. When the Commissioner was established in 1981, the Council had an important, legitimate function. Central child-experts "protected" the Commissioner, and were also directly useful as advisors during this initial phase.

Since 1981, however, experiences with the Council have varied a good deal. A permanent council has proven to be a cumbersome system, a system that can be more of a strain to the Commissioner than an aid. Therefore, a permanently organized council is no longer a necessity. The Commisioner can himself choose weather he wants a permanent Council or not.

Today, the Commissioner works more with small working groups and round-table conferences, where professionals are invited to participate and to contribute suggestions, advice and guidance from case to case. This kind of ad hoc advisory system has proven to be just as useful, or more so, than a permanent organization.

V. THE PERSON AND THE OFFICE

The Commissioner for Children is organized in such a way that the way the spokesman role is performed is dependent on the individual holding the position of Commissioner.

One individual cannot hold the Commissioner-position for more than 8 years. The position is appointed to a term – 4 years at a time. The term idea also underlines the desire that different personalities, with different professional backgrounds, hold the position. The idea is that this will strengthen the Commissioner and make it a more effective service – developing and modifying so that all children will have an active and timely spokesman.

Up to now, two people have held the position of Commissioner for Children. These two, a woman(Målfrid Grude Flekkøy) and now a man(Trond Viggo Torgersen), have had different professional backgrounds and very different ways of fulfilling their functions as Commissioner.

Our experience after the first 13 years show that the institution has been marked by development and change. A central point through the years has always been to build an institution children trust, and that professional and political circles find credible. One goal is to produce such *well-founded and documented proposals and statements that decision-makers will find it difficult, or at least very uncomfortable to ignore the Commissioner's opinions.*

In order to achieve this, the Commissioner depends on a wide network among organizations and professionals that can be a support and allies in professional issues. Over the years, such a network has been carefully established.

In 1981, when the Commissioner for Children was established, there was som scepticism among professionals and politicians as to how this would develop. Today, the Commissioner for Children has become an accepted and respected authority. The press, politicians, Parliament and professionals, all contact the Commissioner for knowledge and information about children and their situation, as well as inviting the Commissioner to be an active participant in public debate.

Trond-Viggo Torgersen was appointed Commissioner for Children on 1 September 1989. He had wide experience in media, and had worked for 15 years in television. He was someone almost all children and youths already knew, because he had done several television productions for children. He is a doctor by profession.

The choice of a well-known person, with an active and professional relationship to the press, led to an even stronger focus on the Commissioner for Children than before. This again resulted in a substantial increase in the number of cases and complaints arriving at the Office. During the first 8 years, there were approximately 2-3000 cases, during the last few years the level has reached 10–12000.

The number of cases initiated by children has especially increased. This is one result of the *"Klar Melding"-system* established in 1989.

This is a system where anyone under 18 years of age can phone free to the Commissioners telephone answering service, and ask any question or present any kind of problem to the Commissioner. Many of these are taken up and answered in the Commissioner's weekly radio programmes. Earlier we had Television Programmes every second week, answering questions raised by children and giving them advise and discussing different aspects about children's rights.

VI. WHO USES THE COMMISSIONER?

Applications to the Commissioner for Children have increased considerably since 1981, when the Office was established. Since the change in Commissioners in 1989, both written and telephone applications have also increased.

A. *The Adult Applicant*

Adults who contact the Commissioner for Children do so for varying reasons: I.e. as politicians, as union representatives, as teachers, as researchers, as parents or grandparents.

Everyone who contact the Commissioner receives an answer, but many adults are referred further on, or their queries are shelved.

Adults who contact the Commissioner as private individuals are most often concerned with 2 problems:

– Dissatisfaction with a ruling by the child welfare authorities, placing a child/children under public care.
– Problems concerning children after a divorce.

These applications are generally referred to other authorities or are rejected because there is no reason or possibility for the Commissioner to get involved.

The Commissioner for Children assumes the role of general spokesman for childrens' needs in such cases, but should not, as I see it, get involved in individual cases except in very special circumstances where it is quite obvious that the child has been the victim of a judicial injustment. Only rarely are we contacted by those who *should*, namely the child or guardian who suffers because the public authorities have *not* interfered.

Besides these areas, adult contacts are spread over a wide range of subjects. Some ask for information and request speeches.

We also receive several inquiries relating to municipal planning, especially with respect to schools and plans for zoning and traffic.

B. *The Minor Applicant*

Everyone under 18 years of age who contact the Commissioner's Office, orally or by letter, can talk with a case-worker and get help. This can take the form of information on where to go further to get help, or information about their rights.

Children seldom contact the Commissioner on trivial matters. They are concerned with a wide range of issues, for example a dangerous play-area in their neighbourhood, lack of special education services, lack of supervision in foster-homes, unsatisfactory visitation conditions for children with a father in jail, or conditions for children in families with alcoholics. In such cases, the Commissioner acts in accordance to the law, or takes the case to higher authorities either as an individual case, or a case of principle. Such cases also form the basis for further reports from the Commissioner, or reports in collaboration with other bodies.

During the 13 years of experience the number of contacts from children has risen from approximately 200 pr.year to between 2–3000 contacts in the last years. Most of these children are between 10 and 14 years old, and there are more girls than boys in the group.

This is mainly due to the "Klar melding"-system.

Children can use the system just as adults can use the postal system. All contacts are treated seriously. From 1989 the Commissioner had weekly television shows. We made all together 150 TV programs. And now we have made over 65 Radio programs. We try to give the children guidance, answers and information about their rights. Most of the inquiries are collected together with other material, and form the basis for the Commissioners work. Children and youths are now really influential. Klar Melding is mainly used by 10–14 year-olds, but we hope to develop this further so that we also reach 14–18 year-olds.

We have seen that this system was very active for the first 4 years. Lately we have seen that the messages from children have decreased. The reason for this can be that after having stopped producing television programmes, the knowledge about the Commisioner aming children are smaller. We are therefore just now discussing several different ways of trying to increase the contact and the direct dialogue with children themselves.

To be an active spokesperson also for 14–18 year old ones give us new challenges, – and we have to use other methods in communication as well as in the monitoring process. We have during the last year given priority to work with questions concerning children between 14 to 18 years of age.

VII. Working Methods

The Commissioner's work is two-fold:
  – to approach the different levels of the power structure and confront them with problems, criticism and proposals for change;
  – to gather information through contacts with individuals applying to the Commissioner, through the research communities and through professional literature.

To achieve this, the Commissioner for Children must vary his working methods. For example we use traditional bureaucratic methods -writing formal letters and statements, as well as active lobbying in the Parliament and conscious use of the press and television.

A. *Information from Research and Public Contact*
The Commissioner has frequent contacts with all of the national professional bodies working with children and young people. Through contacts with research institutions,the Commissioner is able to collect much of the material used in its own appraisals.

The Ombudsman collects, coordinates and presents all available and reliable research data and statistics concerning minors in the booklet *Facts About Children in Norway*. Our extensive contact with research centers and the National Central Bureau of Statistics gives us a central role when it comes to collecting, distributing and using documentation on childrens living conditions. Norway has its own National Research Center and we are represented in the board of the national research program "Children, Youth and Family".

All in all this gives the Office a unique survey of the available knowledge of children and young people and thereby puts us in the position of challenging the authorities in fields where we lack knowledge or statistics. Our wish, or demand, for documentation has often led to action.

As mentioned before, contacts with the public are just as important, and it is often difficult to say what came first – the chicken or the egg. Sometimes it seems as if the Commissioner's actions lead to more people contacting the Office, while at others our actions are triggered by individual contacts.

In order to give an indication of how wide-spread our areas of interests are, we will list some of the more important areas we are engaged in:
 – Children and municipal planning
 – Rights of refugee children
 – Information to and about children's rights
 – School issues
 – Child-care institutions
 – Child welfare – especially concerning the new Act
 – Family judicial issues – especially concerning visitation and divorce issues
 – Sexual violence towards children, especially the penal aspects
 – Democracy and the young

B. *Contacts with Political Parties and the Storting*
Establishing the Commissioner for Children was a very controversial thing to do at the time. Today, 13 years later, there is no question whatsoever of dismantling the Commissioner. On the contrary, there is a wide consensus that the Commissioner fulfills an important function as critic and ensurer of

children's interests with respect to public administration and with respect to the general professional debate on children. Why?

Firstly, probably because the Commissioner is ensured by its own legislation, as well as by the long traditions and the good reputations that ombudsmen in general have in Norway.

Secondly, this is a result of the high moral and professional quality of the Commissioner's work. The Commissioner is often involved in political issues, but never involves himself in party-politics.

The Commissioner has been invited by the different political parties to talk about issues concerning children. The Standing Comittees in the Parliament have also been visited.

C. Contact with the Government and the Ministries

A commissioner for children as part of a state system is in many ways a contradiction. The Commissioner's main task is often to supervise and criticize its own administrative bodies. Our experiences here in Norway show, however, that this is fully possible.

Insofar as children's issues go, the Commissioner deals mainly with the following Cabinet Ministers:

Minister of Children and Family Affairs, Minister of Cultural Affairs, Minister of Education, Research and Church Affairs, Minister of Health and Social Affairs, Minister of Justice, Minister of the Environment.

In some cases, the Prime Minister is also contacted.

In some cases the Commissioner has supported government policies, while in others, the Commissioner has represented an uncomfortable opposition. It might be contended that this opposition has contributed to lack of support for government policy in the Storting.

D. Contact with the Municipal Level

The Commissioner has a lot to do with local politicians who need general information about children and young people in their work. The Commissioner's fact-booklet is widely used as a reference in municipal debates.

At this local level, children and young people have most opportunity to exercise their legal rights. This is especially true in issues concerning municipal zoning, school and education issues, and child welfare.

Many individual cases brought to the Commissioner are solved by referring the callers to the appropriate municipal authority. In other cases, just the fact that the Commissioner has the right to see all documents in a case often leads to a new and better review of the case in question.

E. Contact with the Unions and NGOs

The Commissioner's relations to the different professional unions (f.ex. teachers', child welfare workers, etc), and to the NGOs (f.ex. Save the Children, the Red Cross, and UNICEF) vary a great deal.

We feel that, generally, after an initial period with some conflicts, we have now found a working cooperation, where we benefit from each other's advantages and experiences.

This cooperation has led to a series of joint projects, such as a nation-wide contact-telephone for childdren, reference groups, seminars and joint reports.

The UN Convention was 5 years the 20th of November 1994. The 21 of November we established a Forum in Norway for the UN Convention. The Commisioner is having the secretarial functions for the Forum – and the Forum consist of several NGOs and Experts on the UN Convention. The idea of establishing a Forum, was because we needed a place to debate, discuss and coordinate the ongoing work according to the different convention areas. By the next report process to the expert committee in UN, we hope that this Forum also will be of great importance.

F. Contact with the Media

The Commissioner has extensive contacts with the media. There are weekly (sometimes daily, sometimes monthly) articles in the large national newspapers. In special instances, the Commissioner is also interviewed or referred to in news and current event programs.

First of all, this is a reflection of the media's relationship to the Commissioner. The media contact the Commissioner just as often as the other way around. In controversial cases, the Commissioner is often considered to be a more objective source than the Ministry. The Commissioner does not have to consider future elections or contributions, unlike politicians and humanitarian organizations, and is therefore often given the role of independent voice for children.

This is, of course, the Commissioner's strongest card in fighting negative (with respect to children) political forces; the threat of a negative press. At the same time this is where the most serious misunderstandings can arise.

It would seem that these dilemmas are unavoidable when you have a Commissioner invested with a lot of responsibility and very little formal authority. All in all, though, most would agree that even in cases where the Commissioner has balanced on the edge of exactness, the result has been a necessary and timely debate, leading to positive changes for children and young people.

It is difficult to measure the effects of the Commissioner's work. Many of the issues we work with are long-term in character, for example changing attitudes towards children and changing society's economic priorities to favor children.

Our experience is, however, that we have achieved changes and decisions for the good of children. Since 1981, there have been several central changes in legislation, strengthening children's rights, changes where the Commissioner has been a decisive factor. Through this work, the Commissioner has also achieved a decisive economic contribution to build up a good child welfare system.

In Norwegian society today, the Commissioner for Children is justified in its existence. Norway has ratified the United Nations' Convention on Children, and that has made it even more important to have a central "watch dog" and spokesperson for children. Unfortunately, children and youths' interests still often loose if there is a conflict with adults' interests.

VIII. Thirteen Years of Experience – a Summary

An Ombudsman for Children as part of a government system is in many ways a contradiction. The Ombudsman's main task is often to supervise and criticize the governing bodies. It is quite a challenge to keep issues and personalities separate from one another in order to keep the lines of communication open. This has been just as much a challenge for politicians and bureaucrats as for the Ombudsman.

Being a national body *without formal power*, the impact of the Ombudsman is not very easy to measure. Even so, the Ombudsman has had considerable influence in several cases using the tools he does have. With changing political situations, the Ombudsman has had a steady direction. Using statistics and research, together with advice from children and young themselves, we have analysed the children's situation and have fought against unfairness and discrimination of children. Children need strong spokespersons. They can not elect their politicians, are not automatically understood by or believed in the court system and not even automatically seen in a familiy lacking care. When it comes to choosing between welfare for children and adults – children often lose.

What can a Commissioner change? Of course, this is not very easy to answer. The Commissioner has no formal authority to change anything. Even so, the Commissioner has had considerable influence in several cases using the tools he does have.

It's easy to see that the Commissioner can be useful and important to individuals, but has the Commissioner had any real influence in a larger context? Are children in Norway better off with a Commissioner for Children than they were before? Some questions are apparent after 13 years of experience with a Commissioner for Children.

- Superficially, the Commissioner's work is coloured by the individual who is Commissioner at any given time. Underneath, a highly qualified staff with wide bureaucratic and professional ties is very important. No matter whose "personal touch" is at the surface, it is the basis for reactions that reflect the Commissioners work and quality.
- The Commissioner's work has many dimensions. I have mentioned the long-term dimension; influencing legislation, increasing competence and status are all important. Equally important, however, are the "day to

day" or "week to week" perspectives. The Commissioner must have the capacity to meet the press and headlines, and the politicians need for information. That is why the Commissioner has worked so hard to collect knowledge and facts – and has had them published in 1992's "Facts about Children and youth", a rewriting and doubling of an earlier publication "Facts about children in Norway."

– Last, and not least, is the opportunity to help individuals. Today, we focus on all of those under 18 years of age, and the adults who come to us with cases that are of more principle interest. Other cases are referred to other authorities, and many are turned down.

– The Commissioner for Children also gives preference to speeches at professional conferences, to visiting local municipalities and institutions for children and youths.

In Norwegian experience, the Commissioner for Children's largest asset is the effect of being an independent part of the system. Children and youth would surely have suffered more defeats in the different public arenas if the Commissioner for Children had not loudly championed their causes at the decision making levels. Our motto has become *"You can if you push!"*. Lacking any means of power, this is the closest the Commissioner for Children can come to a position of power.

IX. CHALLENGES SEEN BY THE OMBUDSMAN FOR CHILDREN IN NORWAY TODAY

The norwegian social democratic policy in Norway is in practical policy mostly good news for children. However, the Ombudsman is concerned with how these benefits are distributed and how they influence childhood itself. It seems that a right established on state level not necessarily reaches a child on the municipal level.

The above mentioned development trends also seems to influence on how politics are carried out. These complicated patterns create situations not necessarily beneficial to the child as an individual or childhood as a phenomena. Policy beneficial to children may at the same time be a substitute for adult needs. The following list of topics certainly brings forward new dilemmas for a welfare state such as Norway:

– The uneven decentralization of the welfare state
– The increase in parents' working hours and development in career plans for both sexes
– The increasing institutionalization and organization of the childhood
– The discovering of children lacking care without the possibility of giving necessary help to everybody
– The increasing amounts of refugees and asylum seekers in a changing Europe

- The internationalization of various media and thereby the availability to, and influence on, children and adolescents
- The internationalization of trade and politics influencing the national welfare policy

CÉLINE GIROUX

Commission de protection des droits de la jeunesse

Mécanisme national de surveillance des droits

La Commission de protection des droits de la jeunesse exerce depuis bientôt 20 ans un mandat unique au sein de l'appareil gouvernemental québécois. Placée aux confins de l'intervention sociale et de l'action juridique, la Commission de protection des droits de la jeunesse a reçu du législateur le mandat de veiller à ce que soient respectés les droits reconnus aux enfants par deux lois, soit la *Loi sur la protection de la jeunesse* et la *Loi sur les jeunes contrevenants*. Nous n'exerçons donc pas un mandat de surveillance générale sur tous les droits reconnus aux enfants par la Convention internationale, mais bien sur ceux reconnus par ces deux lois qui visent expressément les enfants en difficulté dont la situation est prise en charge par le système de protection de la jeunesse, c'est-à-dire les enfants les plus démunis de notre société. La Commission est dirigée par un conseil de 14 personnes et ses pouvoirs vont au-delà du pouvoir d'enquêter et de formuler des recommandations. En effet, elle peut saisir le tribunal de certaines situations, et celui-ci peut exiger l'exécution des recommandations formulées. En plus de son mandat de surveillance, la Commission collabore à des programmes d'information, réalise des recherches et joue un rôle de conseil auprès du gouvernement du Québec sur toute question touchant la protection des droits des enfants. Je reviendrai un peu plus tard sur ses différents pouvoirs.

Avant d'expliquer le fonctionnement de la Commission, je voudrais décrire le chemin qu'elle a parcouru au fil des dix dernières années et qui lui a permis de devenir un véritable organisme de surveillance des droits.

La Commission a été créée en 1975 par la *Loi sur la protection des enfants soumis à des mauvais traitements*. Elle portait alors le nom de Comité pour la protection de la jeunesse. L'adoption de cette loi visait à améliorer les services offerts aux enfants maltraités, c'est-à-dire les enfants soumis à des mauvais traitements physiques par suite d'excès ou de négligence. Le Comité agissait alors comme organisme de première ligne, car il devait recevoir et traiter les signalements concernant ces enfants. En 1979, entrait en vigueur la nouvelle *Loi sur la protection de la jeunesse*. Afin de mieux structurer les services accordés aux enfants en besoin de protection, cette loi créait dans chacune

E. Verhellen (ed.), Monitoring Children's Rights, 555–561.
© 1996 Kluwer Law International. Printed in the Netherlands.

des régions administratives du Québec un poste de directeur de la protection de la jeunesse. Celui-ci était, dès lors, chargé en exclusivité de recevoir les signalements, de les évaluer et de prendre en charge la situation des enfants dont la sécurité ou le développement étaient considérés comme compromis. Il ne s'agissait plus seulement des enfants victimes d'abus physiques, mais également d'enfants abusés sexuellement, négligés, ou qui présentaient des troubles de comportement sérieux ou encore d'enfants abandonnés. Les directeurs de la protection de la jeunesse et leur personnel étaient, et le sont encore aujourd'hui, rattachés au réseau des services sociaux. En vertu de cette loi, le Comité se voyait confier un nouveau mandat, celui de la surveillance générale de l'application de la loi et du respect des droits reconnus par celle-ci. Cinq années plus tard, soit en 1984, le législateur renforçait le pouvoir d'enquête du Comité et étendait son pouvoir de surveillance aux droits des enfants également reconnus par la *Loi sur les jeunes contrevenants*.

Si la loi adoptée en 1979 ne prévoyait pas la création d'une charte des droits de l'enfant, comme certains le souhaitaient alors, elle contient néanmoins, depuis son adoption, tout un chapitre, soit le chapitre II, qui s'intitule «Principes généraux et droits des enfants». Plus précisément, l'article 3 de la loi se lisait comme suit: «*Le respect des droits de l'enfant doit être le motif déterminant des décisions prises à son sujet en vertu de la présente loi*». Il s'agit de la concrétisation législative d'un changement majeur dans l'intervention sociale auprès des enfants qui reposait, jusqu'au début des années 1970, sur la recherche du meilleur intérêt de ces derniers.

Parmi les droits reconnus aux enfants par la *Loi sur la protection de la jeunesse*, citons le droit de recevoir des services de santé, des services sociaux ainsi que des services d'éducation adéquats compte tenu de l'organisation et des ressources des établissements, le droit d'être consultés et entendus avant qu'une décision ne soit prise à leur égard, le droit d'être préparés et informés avant un transfert de famille d'accueil ou de centre de réadaptation, le droit de pouvoir communiquer en toute confidentialité avec leurs parents, frères et sœurs, leur procureur et le juge du Tribunal de la jeunesse, lorsqu'ils sont hébergés en famille d'accueil ou en centre de réadaptation, le droit à ce que des mesures disciplinaires soient prises uniquement dans leur intérêt et conformément à des règles internes et le droit d'être hébergés de façon adéquate à leurs besoins. Par ailleurs, la *Loi sur les jeunes contrevenants* reconnaît, entre autres, le droit à la représentation par avocat à toutes les étapes de la procédure, le droit à la présomption d'innocence, le droit à la remise en liberté provisoire pendant leur procès pénal et le droit à une protection spéciale contre l'auto-incrimination.

En 1989, compte tenu de la nature de l'organisme et de l'objet de son mandat, le nom du Comité pour la protection de la jeunesse était remplacé par celui de Commission de protection des droits de la jeunesse.

Au Québec, la reconnaissance de droits spécifiques accordés aux enfants a accompagné le mouvement qui, au cours des 20 dernières années, a vu ces derniers passer du statut d'objets de droit, à celui de sujets de droit. Cette évolution s'est concrétisée par l'adoption de plusieurs autres lois, qui bien que de portée générale, touchaient les droits de tous les enfants. Je cite, à titre d'exemples, la Charte des droits et des libertés de la personne, adoptée en 1975, et la révision récente du Code civil du Québec, touchant directement les droits des enfants et renforçant leur statut de personnes de plus en plus autonomes. Ainsi, sans que l'on prétende que le Québec ait joué un rôle de précurseur à la Convention des droits de l'enfant adoptée par l'Organisation des Nations unies, l'on doit admettre qu'il s'est illustré dans la reconnaissance des droits des enfants. En outre depuis 1979, le Québec possède un mécanisme de surveillance des droits, entièrement distinct du réseau qui dispense les services de protection, et ce mécanisme porte actuellement le nom de Commission de protection des droits de la jeunesse.

Chez nous, la Commission s'inscrit dans la mission Justice du gouvernement et, comme la Commission des droits de la personne, elle relève du ministre de la Justice, tout en demeurant autonome et indépendante dans son fonctionnement. Ce rattachement au gouvernement lui assure une permanence non négligeable en ressources humaines et financières et lui confère des pouvoirs importants, conformément à une loi cadre. La Commission possède des bureaux qui couvrent toutes les régions administratives du Québec. Elle est composée de 14 membres nommés par le gouvernement du Québec et choisis parmi les personnes susceptibles de contribuer de façon particulière à l'étude et à la solution des problèmes de la jeunesse. Ces personnes, membres de la Commission et expertes dans différents domaines touchant l'enfance, agissent à titre personnel et jouissent d'une entière liberté dans l'exercice de leur mandat. En effet, les membres peuvent prendre toutes les décisions nécessaires pour faire corriger les situations de lésions de droit et formuler toutes les recommandations susceptibles d'assurer la protection des droits des enfants et ce, à l'abri de toute influence ou ingérence politique. Ces 14 membres, pris collectivement, forment la Commission.

Le président et le vice-président exercent leurs fonctions à temps plein, tandis que les douze autres membres ne font pas partie du personnel. Ils siègent sur demande à l'occasion de réunions régulières et d'enquêtes. Les membres de la Commission sont aidés dans leurs travaux par un secrétaire, un directeur des bureaux régionaux et une équipe d'une cinquantaine d'employés, techniciens et professionnels, parmi lesquels on retrouve des juristes, des criminologues, des sociologues et des psycho-éducateurs. Les employés sont nommés et rémunérés selon les dispositions de la *Loi sur la fonction publique* du gouvernement du Québec.

Conformément à son mandat, la Commission peut mener des enquêtes. Précisons que, dans le cadre de certaines enquêtes et lorsque la situation l'exige, il arrive exceptionnellement que les membres utilisent leur statut de commissaires-enquêteurs et détiennent alors le pouvoir de contraindre les personnes à témoigner. À l'issue des enquêtes, la Commission peut adresser des recommandations aux personnes, aux établissements et aux organismes visés par la prise en charge des enfants. Si les recommandations ne sont pas appliquées dans les délais impartis, la Commission peut alors saisir le tribunal et en demander l'exécution. Elle peut également prendre les moyens légaux qu'elle juge nécessaires pour que soient corrigée les situations où les droits des enfants sont lésés, au moment même où elle en est saisie. Dans l'exercice de ses fonctions, la Commission a accès à tout dossier pertinent au cas d'un enfant pris en charge par un établissement ou faisant l'objet de mesures de protection.

Nos requérants sont les enfants eux-mêmes dans près de 10% des cas. Les parents représentent près de 40% des personnes qui font appel à la Commission tandis que les avocats des enfants constituent 20% de l'ensemble. Les juges, les professeurs, les médecins, les membres de la famille élargie des enfants s'adressent aussi à nous dans de moindres proportions. En fait, toute personne qui juge nécessaire de le faire peut adresser à la Commission une demande verbale ou écrite. De plus, la Commission peut s'auto-saisir elle-même de situations où, à son avis, les droits d'un enfant ou d'un groupe d'enfants sont lésés.

La Commission est un organisme administratif, ce qui démontre bien la volonté du législateur de déjudiciariser le processus de correction des situations où les enfants sont lésés dans leurs droits. Ainsi, la Commission s'est dotée de mécanismes souples mais précis de réception et de traitement des demandes qui lui sont adressées, dans le but de corriger rapidement toute situation qui lèse les droits des enfants. La notion de temps chez l'enfant étant différente de celle de l'adulte, il est impérieux d'agir avec diligence dans ces cas.

Voici une description sommaire du cheminement des demandes d'intervention. Les demandes reçues sont acheminées au président de la Commission, qui les étudie. Lorsque le président a des raisons de croire que les droits des enfants sont manifestement lésés, il peut décider d'entreprendre une intervention correctrice immédiate pour faire corriger la situation ou saisir le tribunal, si l'intervention ne donne pas les résultats escomptés.

Par contre, si le président a des raisons de croire que les droits invoqués ont été lésés, il peut déclencher une enquête sur la situation dont il a été saisie. L'enquête est menée par trois membres de la Commission, dont le président. Ceux-ci sont assistés dans la collecte des données par des employés professionnels. L'enquête, qui n'a rien du formalisme de l'enquête judiciaire, se déroule de façon non contradictoire et dans le respect des règles d'équité. Toutes les personnes touchées ont la possibilité de se faire entendre. Au terme de l'enquête, si les trois membres concluent que les droits d'un enfant ont été lésés, ils peuvent formuler des recommandations sur les correctifs appropriés.

Voici un aperçu des problèmes courants auxquels nous apportons des solutions à la suite de la réception des demandes d'intervention:

- La direction de la protection de la jeunesse refuse de retenir le signalement du cas d'un enfant, ce qui de l'avis de la personne qui s'adresse à nous, met en cause la sécurité et le développement de celui-ci. À la suite de notre intervention, un nouvel examen a lieu.
- La prise en charge d'un enfant serait inadéquate, et celui-ci se trouverait toujours en danger. Notre intervention entraîne la reconsidération rapide du dossier.
- Un adolescent hébergé à l'extérieur de sa famille se plaint d'être dans l'impossibilité de communiquer avec celle-ci, par suite d'une décision des autorités chargées de sa protection. Notre intervention permet le rétablissement de la communication.
- Des parents affirment être mal informés de ce qui arrive à leur enfant qui a été confié au directeur de la protection de la jeunesse. Notre intervention assure une information adéquate aux parties.

Les initiatives de la Commission à l'égard des situations qui lui sont rapportées peuvent varier. Dans certains cas, nous adressons des recommandations individuelles ou collectives aux instances visées. Dans d'autres, nous procédons à des enquêtes approfondies sur différentes problématiques telles que les pratiques sociales dans les cas d'abus sexuels, l'existence et la qualité des rapports entre les composantes du réseau socio-sanitaire et les conditions d'hébergement temporaire des adolescents en attente de procès. Les enquêtes de la Commission peuvent amener à elles seules les responsables à améliorer certains aspects de leur pratique. Enfin, nous favorisons la concertation entre les différentes instances et les incitons à préciser les politiques existantes ou à en créer de nouvelles. Chaque année, nous profitons de la publication du rapport annuel de l'organisme pour rendre public nos observations.

Les pouvoirs et les responsabilités de la Commission ne se limitent cependant pas aux enquêtes et aux recommandations adressées aux personnes, aux établissements et aux organismes qui dispensent des services aux enfants. La Commission peut, en tout temps, faire des recommandations directement au ministre de la Santé et des Services sociaux, au ministre de l'Éducation, au ministre de l'Enseignement supérieur et de la Science et au ministre de la Justice. Ces pouvoirs permettent à la Commission de transmettre à ces derniers son avis sur toute question qui touche aux droits des enfants.

Au cours de la dernière année, la Commission a adressé des recommandations à plusieurs instances. Ainsi, la Commission a transmis au ministre de la Santé et des Services sociaux du Québec un document exprimant sa position sur les services de réadaptation dispensés aux enfants cris et inuits de la Baie-James et du Nord québécois. Dans cet avis, il était recommandé au ministre de définir, en concertation avec les représentants des Cris et des Inuits, des modalités d'organisation afin que les services de réadaptation soient dispensés par les services sociaux de ces communautés et ce, sur le territoire même de la Baie James et du Nord québécois.

Dans un autre ordre d'idée, la Commission a transmis un mémoire à un comité du Barreau du Québec chargé d'étudier la question de la représentation des enfants par avocat. Pour la Commission, les enfants, quel que soit leur âge, ont le droit d'avoir un procureur pour les représenter et celui-ci doit jouir d'une autonomie complète par rapport à toutes les autres parties à l'instance. Dans son mémoire, la Commission a soumis que la représentation des enfants soit on ne peut plus transparente et tienne compte ainsi du respect des enfants. Cette transparence doit s'appliquer tant à la désignation d'un procureur pour les enfants qu'à la détermination de la capacité de ceux-ci à confier un mandat et à l'exercice de la représentation des enfants qui sont incapables de confier ce type de mandat. La Commission a rappelé qu'il n'est pas souhaitable de fixer, de façon arbitraire, l'âge où les enfants peuvent donner un mandat à un procureur.

Parmi les autres responsabilités de la Commission, citons celle de mener des études et des recherches sur le respect des droits des enfants. La crédibilité de notre organisme dans plusieurs milieux repose sur cet aspect, que je ne saurais passer sous silence. La dernière recherche de la Commission portait sur la clientèle multiethnique des centres de réadaptation pour les jeunes en difficulté. Elle a permis d'établir la surreprésentation des enfants de certaines communautés culturelles dans les centres de réadaptation. Dans la foulée de cette étude, les membres de la Commission ont adopté plusieurs recommandations qu'ils ont adressées au ministre de l'Immigration et des Communautés Culturelles du Québec, au ministre de l'Éducation du Québec, aux autorités des centres de protection de l'enfance et de la jeunesse, aux directeurs de la protection de la jeunesse et aux associations des diverses communautés culturelles. Les autres recherches de la Commission qui ont précédé cette dernière ont porté, entre autres, sur les abus sexuels, les troubles de comportement à l'adolescence et les fugues du milieu familial.

La Commission collabore, de plus, à la réalisation et à la diffusion de programmes d'information destinés à renseigner la population en général et les enfants en particulier sur leurs droits. Depuis le début de son existence, elle a accordé une grande importance, d'une part, à informer les enfants de leurs droits et, d'autre part, à sensibiliser aux droits des enfants les divers intervenants dans les domaines de l'éducation, de la justice et des services sociaux. Par exemple, elle a publié en concertation avec l'Association des centres d'accueil du Québec, une brochure intitulée *Tu as des droits* destinée aux adolescents qui reçoivent des services dans les centres de réadaptation. Tout récemment, la Commission a aussi produit et diffusé une carte des droits, en collaboration avec deux autres organismes publics, soit la Commission des services juridiques et le Conseil permanent de la jeunesse, et un organisme communautaire le Regroupement des maisons de jeunes du Québec. Cette carte est facile à utiliser, et elle énonce dans des termes simples les droits des adolescents lorsqu'ils sont interpellés par la police. En conclusion, en vertu de son mandat, la Commission de protection des droits de la jeunesse possède des pouvoirs importants et elle peut exercer une influence réelle sur la situation des enfants qui relèvent de la *Loi sur la protection de la jeunesse* et de la *Loi sur les jeunes contrevenants*. En fait, la Commission est garante des droits de ces enfants. Dans les milieux de la justice et des affaires sociales du Québec, il est convenu qu'une telle instance de promotion et de surveillance des droits est indispensable et constitue un acquis majeur pour les enfants. Au fil des années, il nous a été donné de constater qu'il est essentiel de reconnaître par des lois, comme la *Loi sur la protection de la jeunesse* et la *Loi sur les jeunes contrevenants*, les droits fondamentaux des enfants et d'en assurer le respect dans la réalité par des dispositions précises. Bien que certains droits des enfants sont reconnus par la Convention, les chartes et les lois et, malgré les progrès accomplis année après année, la Commission doit intervenir régulièrement pour faire respecter ces droits des enfants et faire corriger les situations inacceptables qui y portent atteinte. L'expérience québécoise montre que, pour donner une portée véritable à l'exercice des droits des enfants, l'adoption de droits doit s'accompagner de la mise sur pied d'instances qui permettront aux enfants de revendiquer leurs droits et les faire appliquer. Car c'est par le respect de leurs droits, de tous leurs droits, que nos enfants, considérés comme des personnes à part entière, deviendront des êtres confiants et respectueux et des citoyens responsables.

Nous ne prétendons certes pas avoir de réponses à toutes les questions, ni de solutions à tous les problèmes. À l'instar de tous les autres, notre système est en progression. Je termine donc en vous affirmant que, au-delà des textes législatifs, des rapports à rédiger et des mécanismes de surveillance, il y a encore beaucoup d'éducation à faire sur ces droits, auprès des intervenants, des instituteurs et des parents. Ce type d'éducation permettra d'intégrer dans la vie de tous les jours l'exercice de ces droits et ce, dès la plus tendre enfance. Il est également de la plus haute importance de parfaire l'éducation des jeunes sur leurs propres droits, afin qu'ils sachent les faire valoir de plus en plus. C'est ainsi que nous serons davantage en mesure de prévenir plutôt que guérir.

CLAUDE LELIÈVRE

The General Delegate for Children's Rights and Youth Assistance: Evaluation of an Innovating Action in the French Community of Belgium

I. HISTORICAL SKETCH

On 26 June 1994, the Council of the French Community of Belgium adopts with unanimity the resolution on the rights of the child. This declaration stipulates in fine that "the Council of the French Community of Belgium takes the decision to impose the respect of children's rights as they have been determined by the "Declaration of the Rights of the Child" and to make all that is possible to promote the respect of these rights, for all children.".

In compliance with this resolution several proposals of decree have been put forward by members of the Parliament from all political sides:
- on 10 March 1987, the proposal appointing a Commissioner for children's rights;
- on 8 March 1988, the proposal with a view to the appointment of an Ombudsman for children;
- on 8 March 1988, the proposal creating a Mediator for children's rights;
- on 5 December 1989, the proposal creating a General Delegate for youth rights.

In December 1989, the United Nations unanimously adopt the International Convention on the Rights of the Child.

On 1 February 1990, the European Council invites the member-states to appoint a Special Mediator for children.

The decree of 4 March 1991 concerning youth assistance explicitly explains in its preamble that the Executive of the French Community must appoint someone to preserve the rights and the interests of all children and young people in order to enhance a better recognition of children and young people as law subjects who are able to take upon themselves responsibilities and duties: the General Delegate for children's rights and youth assistance, institution of the French Community of Belgium. The articles 1, 28, 32 and 36 of the decree of 4 March 1991 contain a reference to the General Delegate.

E. Verhellen (ed.), Monitoring Children's Rights, 563–574.
© 1996 *Kluwer Law International. Printed in the Netherlands.*

The order of 10 July 1991 of the Executive of the French Community institutes a General Delegate for children's rights and youth assistance.

At the end of 1991, Belgium ratifies the International Convention of the Rights of the Child.

On 8 July 1992, the European Parliament adopts a resolution on the European Charter for the Rights of the Child and asks its member-states to appoint a Defender of children's rights (ombudsman).

So, the French Community of Belgium has anticipated the wishes of the European Council and Parliament.

Claude Lelièvre has been appointed as the General Delegate for children's rights on 1 November 1991.

II. PRESENTATION OF THE INSTITUTION

A. *Mission: To enhance the Preservation of the Rights and Interests of Children and Young People*

The General Delegate is allowed, *among others*, to:
- spread information about the rights of children and young people;
- control whether the laws and the rules are correctly applied and, when necessary, to inform the King's Prosecutor;
- submit to the Executive any proposal with a view to adapting the rules in force and, to make all necessary recommendations;
- receive the information, the complaints or the requests for mediation concerning the preventions of the exercise of children's and youth rights.

B. *Scope of Application*

It concerns everybody below 18 years (children) as well as each person below 20 years (young person) for whom a special assistance has been requested from the Youth Assistance or Protection.

C. *Means of Action*

1. He can send to the authorities of the State, the Community , the Region, the Provinces or to any institution which depends of it, requests for interpellation and investigation.
2. Within the limits set by the Constitution, the laws and the decrees, he has a free access during the normal working hours to all the buildings of the Community public services or the private services benefiting by a subsidy of the French Community.
3. The managers and the staff of these services are obliged to communicate the files and the information requested by him, with the exception of the

files and information covered by the seal of medical confidence or about which they know as a result of their capacity as necessary confidants.

D. Composition of the Service

The General Delegate is seconded by a team of five assistants.

III. THE VERIFICATION OF THE CORRECT APPLICATION OF THE LAWS AND RULES – PRINCIPAL FILES

A. Savings-bank Books for Children Placed within the Framework of the Law of 8 April 1965 Concerning Youth Protection

The "Caisse Générale d'Epargne et de Retraite" has provided the General Delegate with a list of more than two thousand young people for whom a supplied savings-bank book has been opened by a placing authority. This enables the General Delegate to inform persons of full age who do not know that such a savings-bank book had been opened while they were still minors.

The General Prosecution of Mons regularly collaborates with the General Delegate to find the addresses of the young people mentioned on the lists transmitted by the "CGER".

A similar collaboration exists also with the "Caisse Privée banque".

B. Special Calls – Belgacom – 077 – Pornography through Telephone

As several complaints had been lodged regarding the 077-lines, the access of which was not denied to minors, the General Delegate has interpellated the involved authorities (General Prosecution, Minister of Justice, Minister of Communications, Belgacom).

The now existing O77-system enables a direct access for children to pornography without the possible interposition of the persons entrusted with the parental authority. As it is now, each child has the opportunity to dial the 077-number from a family phone and the bill is sent afterwards to the subscriber.

Furthermore, without the supervision of the contents of the messages by Belgacom, the child can through the 077-system, as a matter of fact, be used as a pornographic object by the pedophile.

The General Delegate has participated in the elaboration of a deontological code that is applicable to the information and telecommunications services. This code will impose rules in the contracts. There will also be penal repression.

C. Rules as far as the Transfer of Minors within the "Union Royale Belge des Sociétés de Football" is Concerned

The fact of registering in a football club entails an affiliation to the URBSFA. According to the statutes of the URBSFA, an affiliated player can obtain his assignment for another club if the payment of a training indemnity is made (17.000 Belgian francs a year).

Numerous countries of the European Community have adopted rules imposing to the sports federations the right for the minor to choose freely his sports club and to be transferred free of charge.

Nothing impedes the French Community to consider adopting rules as far as the transfer of minors within sports federations is concerned.

The General Delegate has already made several proposals on the basis of the results of a study by a technical group of the problematics of transfers:
- the editing of a collection of jurisprudence;
- the elaboration of rules with a view to promoting the educative aspects of sports;
- the institution of committees of conciliation within the sports federations.

IV. COMPLAINTS AND REQUESTS FOR MEDIATION

A. Individual Situations

First year
Amount of involved children: 98
Amount of situations: 115

Second year
Amount of involved children: 387
Amount of situations: 486

The situations taken into account in the statistics do not correspond with the huge amount of solicitations received by the General Delegate. In compliance with the action philosophy described at the beginning of this report, many intervening parties are immediately reoriented towards the competent services or authorities: "centres publics d'aide sociale" (public centres for social assistance), lawyers, advisors of Youth Assistance, communal authorities, Ministers... Such is the case when the person sends the request directly to the General Delegate without first consulting the competent service or authority.

The figures and descriptions of this table only correspond to *opened* files where there has been *written* intercession of the General Delegate without excluding a more important mediation action (interviews, movings, handing over of conclusions).

During the first year, 98 children had benefited from the intervention of the General Delegate for children's rights following an indication, a complaint or a mediation request. During the second year, the amount of involved children has risen to 387, i.e. four times more. The same tendency holds for the amount of handled situations (from 115 to 486).

Contrary to the first year, it should be noted that an ever increasing amount of children directly request the mediation of the children's mediator. The most active age section is the one between ten and fifteen years.

Two main types of situations stand out: the situations resulting from a separation or a divorce of the parents (33%) as well as those concerning children ill-treatment (29%). Then you have the problematic situations arising from the placing (14%) or, mutatis mutandis, the problematic situations arising essentially from the withdrawal of the child from his family.

When we analyse the diverse situations, we come to the conclusion that most cases of exposed ill-treatment concern the parents or relatives sensu largo. We also notice that the recourses of the grandparents, with respect to the custody or visit rights, can also sometimes be cumulated with the requests relating to the divorce of the separation. The denials or oppositions towards a measure entailing a family withdrawal are also numerous. Therefore, 80% of the situations treated by the General Delegate incriminate the family system sensu largo.

This entails that out of five situations treated by the General Delegate four relate to family problems or conflicts.

In this matter, it can also be useful to notice that there are many conflicts relating to grandparents, who even if they are not immediately part of the family cell, are nonetheless extremely present and active.

There is also another figure is worth of notice: 5% of the treated situations relate either to pedophilic facts, or to sexual abuse inside a family, i.e., for instance, much more than the total amount of the requests or complaints relating to education as such.

Worth of notice is also the complaints in the field of the integration of foreign populations almost exclusively concern either candidates for political asylum, or children in an illegal state.

Finally, the requests relating to lodging are often introduced by social helpers who notice that the child finds himself in a dangerous situation mainly becauase of the housing of the parents. So, it appears that, in fact, the difficulty to obtain a lodging is the main reason why the dangerous situation remains unchanged while the parents, even from the fourth world, show sufficient educational qualifications.

As far as the treatment of individual cases is concerned, the amount of complaints can sometimes be traced back to a legislative or regulation problem. So, the fact that the child is neither party nor heard during the custody or visit rights proceedings relating to a divorce can have an influence on the amount of complaints introduced with the General Delegate.

In such cases, the actions of the General Delegate should not amount to ever renewed intercessions. The analysis of these individual files must result in general proposals to modify the legislative and regulation bases in compliance with children's rights.

B. Service, Authorities or Blamed Standards

First year   26
Second year   37

It is a matter of information or complaints regarding a service, an authority or a legal or regulation stipulation without the direct implication of a child. The step taken has as main aim the defence of the collectivity without necessarily identifying an individual victim.

So, for instance, the case of the "Fonds 81" for the disabled refusing to take in charge the sudsidizing of foreign minors, either candidates for political asylum or political refugees, or illegal residents, living for less than five years in Belgium.

The tendency of the first year is confirmed. More than often the official authorities ask for the intercession of the General Delegate rather than individual persons: advisor for youth assistance, youth judge, residential or non residential service director, social helpers, district council for youth assistance... Working directly or upon denunciation on individual situations, these official authorities note dysfunctions or administrative or legal gaps and transmit the information about these to the General Delegate for children's rights in order to ask him to interpellate the responsible authorities.

Some associations leading an original fight against for instance kidnapping also ask the General Delegate to function as a go-between to get into touch with political authorities: i.e., either the member of the Executive, or the lawgiver.

The motivation of the steps taken by the administrative and judicial authorities is threefold. On the one hand, they can ask for the intercession of the General Delegate without delay and without particular administrative procedure, and on the other hand, there is no hierarchic formalism involved. Finally, anonymity is preserved if wished.

The actions or situations denounced by the professionals are often sustained by a juridical or regulation development. There are often alternative proposals. The General Delegate sometimes asks the professional who lodged a complaint to participate actively in the change, either through the elaboration of an explicative file, or through the implication in a workgroup that has been created on the initiative of the General Delegate.

Three files deserve a special attention and have seen precise actions of the General Delegate, as already mentioned: the unacceptable 077-system of Belgacom with pornographic vocation, the conflictual sportive transfers of "object-children" and, finally, the problems relating to the hearing of children in justice for their own cases.

V. MAIN GENERAL FILES

A. *The Problematics of Unaccompanid Minors which are Candidates for Political Asylum and of Illegal Resident Foreign Minors*

The General Delegate is asked to intervene in numerous situations of foreign young people or children waiting for a regularization of their stay or illegally residing in Belgium.

Thanks to a collaboration between the Deputy General Administrator of the Office for foreigners and the General Delegate, these individual situations are often examined.

B. *Workgroup Relating to Children of Separate Parents*

This group has been created as a consequence of numerous individual requests to the General Delegate with respect to problems encountered by children within the context of divorce or separation.

The workgroup is constituted of representatives of the judicial authorities, of the Ministry for Culture and Social Affairs, of the Administration for youth assistance as well as of other persons (lawyer, academic, psychologist, a meeting centre, a mediation service...).

This workgroup has given the General Delegate the opportunity to introduce a synthesis of his ideas and thoughts and has focused the attention of the Commission for Justice of the Senate and of the Minister of Justice on the topics of the hearing of children in all proceedings relating to them and of the revisability of agreements regarding children within the context of a divorce by mutual agreement.

C. *Taking Care of ill-treated Children, among Others Sexual Ill-treatment*

During a first phase, the General Delegate has instituted a pilot workgroup for taking care of ill-treated children. This group has in particular shown that a decree should be adopted with regard to the co-ordination of the struggle against ill-treatment of children.

During a second phase, the General Delegate has constituted a new workgroup with several persons who have shown their competence and their engagement in the struggle against child prostitution and paedophilia.

As a consequence of the meetings of this workgroup, a program to fight paedophilia has been handed over to the appropriate authorities. This program has also been commented before the parliamentary inquiry commission entrusted with the elaboration of a structural policy to facilitate repression and abolish slave trade.

In co-ordination with the associative movement, the municipalities ("communes") and the public sector, a campaign "Article 34" of the International Convention on the Rights of the Child has been launched, with three aspects of the fight against sexual abuse of children: petitions, sensitiveness and prevention.

VI. Conclusions

A. *The Priority: the Call of each Child*

The priority and fundamental action concerns the individual situations because they necessitate an immediate reaction and there can be no procrastination.

In 1992 already, it had been written, about the individual situations of which the General Delegate had to take care, that no sector was spared and that it appeared that the children were above all victims of conflictual family situations: ill-treatment, parent separation, withdrawal from the family environment.

For the second year, the fact that 387 children were taken in charge, living for the major part in 486 diverse situations, confirms from a larger sample the alarming conclusions of the first annual report. Out of five individual situations four relate to family problems.

Some children are ill from their family. And our society suffers from its actual helplessness in finding solutions.

When the General Delegate takes a call from a child, he is often struck by the outstanding faculty of analysis of their family situation they display, the lucidity in their suffering, as though this suffering revived in them a thousand times their ability for discerning.

What amazes too, is the use of exact, simple and at times terrific vocabulary to describe their unbearable situations.

What moves finally, is the straightforwardness and the confidence they show for one person, speaking face to face, and in a first meeting, but to them, he is the defender of children, their defence, their hopes. The little child in front of him speaks with candid yes about his loneliness, his problems or his misfortune and then looks with an interrogative eye in the deepest recesses of his to beg him to act imperatively.

So, the first thing is to believe them. Always.

Even if experience tells us that the grown-up of his environment is capable of being the conscious or unconscious perverse person who guides the revolts, the denials, the accusations, the complaints or the requests of the child.

B. Towards a Society that respects more strictly the Rights of Children

Fundamental is the mission of proposing reforms. These reforms are often the result of a thinking process following an analysis of individual situations.

At the end of the first year, several major society problems emerged from the totality of the problems considered: children of separated parents, ill-treatment of children, drug addiction among young people, juvenile delinquency, Aids, minority protection, the future of schools, the socialization of young people of foreign origin, assistance for childhood and infancy.

These problems should have entailed several priority reforms after the conclusion of the first report:

1. the form with a view to recognizing the child as a party within the framework of civil proceedings relating to their person and whose case has been laid before a police-court magistrate, a chambers magistrate and a youth judge;
2. the project of decree relating to the punishment of institutions, services and persons when they do not respect the legal stipulations of the decree of 4 March 1991 concerning youth assistance as far as the rights of young people are concerned;
3. the codification in an imperative legal text of all the rules of disciplinary right that have been enforced by the jurisprudence in the field of education and of teaching;
4. the project of decree concerning the co-ordination of the fight against ill-treatment of children...

As far as we know, the decree that could sanction in the field of youth assistance, the non respect of children's rights, has not even been proposed as a concrete project by the Minister entrusted with youth assistance since the Community Council for Yough Assistance has not been asked for an advice as foreseen in the evoked decree of 4 March 1991.

Still, this decree could be a model for the other sectors of childhood.

But the other advocated reforms have been given special attention and have resulted in several constructive steps.

First, in civil proceedings, texts have been passed to recognize the child as subject and actor of his own future.

Whereas the child is not recognized as a party in the law projct, it should nevertheless be noticed that, under certain circumstances, he will able to give his opinion in fields of personal interest.

Belgium has decided to abide by article 12 of the International Convention of the Rights of the Child. Is that enough?

On this point, the General Delegate keeps a vigilant eye and will continue to formulate other proposals relating to articles 931 (hearing of children) and 1288 (revising of the conventions concerning children in divorce with mutual agreement) of the judicial code, taking assistance of a workgroup he has instituted.

Then, as far as disciplinary right at school is concerned, the Minister of Education has, it is true, not introduced a legal text, but has, however, promulgated new rules and regulations for secondary schools in the French Community. These rules and regulations specify positively the rights and the obligations of the different parties: students, parents, teachers, directors, Minister and the responsibility of everyone is increased.

It is regretful that such an initiative cannot be extended to other networks. It is to be hoped that these regulations will progressively be taken as an example and that the jurisprudence will continue to perform its slow process of standardization of the rules.

Finally, in the field of ill-treatment, it is possible today to foresee very soon the elaboration of an efficient co-ordination of the fight against ill-treatment of children, as a consequence of the text of the Government of the French Community of Belgium.

This notion of general co-ordination is accompanied by that of denouncing ill-treatment and that of the co-ordination of individual cases.

The text still needs to be discussed for amendment with the advice of the Council of State and of the representative instances such as the Community Council for Youth Help and the Guidance Committee for ill-treated children.

When we come to make up the balance, it appears that things are moving in the right direction, even if an institution like that of the General Delegate is still of the opinion that there is too much time needed to come to a consensus enabling concrete results.

It is, however, not possible to conclude without dealing with the reform of the law concerning Youth Assistance introduced by the Minister. Even if his reform can globally be judged to be positive, it is impossible not to question, on the one hand, the fact of keeping in jail young delinquents of more than fourteen and, on the other hand, the disguised system of preventive detention organized in the public institutions of youth assistance of the Communities.

From this reality, the General Delegate will try to generate the appropriate reactions to avoid drifting and to obtain the effective repeal of article 53 as soon as possible.

Now, let's come to a last priority. Among the diverse proposals of the General Delegate, those relating to the fight against paedophilia deserve a close attention because they are the result of a long process of thought and of conclusions drawn by a great amount of people who join to break taboos and struggle against this curse.

Are we all not responsible of indifference and laxism because, up till now, our society has been unable to devise a global and co-ordinated policy of fighting paedophilia?

Among others, stunning and painful evidence has driven the General Delegate to create the workgroup on the problematics of paedophilia. The fact that the problem has deep roots and that there are numerous victims appears from what these little victims have experienced rather than the numerous affairs denounced in the mass media.

The action program that has resulted from these work meetings has been transmitted to the authorities who can change things.

Do they want to act? Are they able to do so? Will there be a positive result?

We shall help them because paedophilia is present everywhere: in the country and in the cities. All social spheres are involved: the poor and the rich, the intellectual and the manual.

Paedophilia is seldom ignored and isolated: it is part of a series of crimes against children.

It is an often repeated act, even when Justice has been made, and even when the therapeutists have done their job.

What we hope, at most, is to circumscribe the phenomenon.

To this end, the General Delegate for children's rights has taken in charge the co-ordination of the campaign "article 34" which aims at moving people to fight sexual abuse and sexual exploitation of children. More than 370.000 signatures have been collected on a petition campaigning for the struggle against paedophilia. This petition has been handed over to the King, the Prime Minister of the federal Government and to the Minister-President of the Government of the French Community of Belgium.

A large sensitization and prevention action will be set up during the autumn 1994, under the aegis of the Government of the French Community of Belgium.

To fight paedophilia, we must of course invoke and respect the International Convention of the Rights of the Child and, to that end, our legislation must be brought in compliance with these imperatives. It is however possible to go further than what is prescribed in the Convention in order to adapt and reform the laws, following, at least, the recommendations of the workgroup of the General Delegate that have obtained a large consensus.

Society could also acquire better and more arms to fight this curse: specialized treatment centres for paedophiles, control when recruiting in the sector of childhood, prolonged help to condemned people, multi-disciplinary teams for children victims of sexual abuse, specialized and approved therapeutists...

The awakening of the awareness of men and women towards the phenomenon of paedophilia requires more than a social epidermal reaction to mediatic incidents.

It not only requires reprobation or disgust towards mediatized affairs. It results from a more profound stream born of clear-cut decisions, as those of King Baudouin or King Albert II, emerging from actions that are eminently approved by our society, such as the action of Marie-France Botte. It is based on the recognition of the child as a subject of right in the International Convention of the Rights of the Child of 1989.

Thanks to the links now established, it appears impossible that the movement should stop and should not enhance constructive reforms for the child.

HELENA MOLANDER

A Child Against the State: Tasks of the Children's Ombudsman

> We must have the courage to speak up for children

I. ASSISTANCE IN INDIVIDUAL CASES

A. Why is an Independent Children's Ombudsman Needed?

Finnish children have many rights. Finland has modern legislation on children which emphasizes their right to special protection and seeks to safeguard their best interests. It grants children independent status and stresses the importance of hearing them where their interests are at stake. Finland also ratified the UN Convention on the Rights of the Child in 1991.

Finland is one of the five countries that in 1984 passed legislation prohibiting all violence against children, including corporal punishment. Corporal punishment in schools has been prohibited in Finland since 1914.

The work of the Children's Ombudsman, initiated by the Mannerheim League for Child Welfare in 1981, has shown that even modern legislation and effective institutions are not always enough to guarantee legal protection for children.

Some three hundred cases concerning the legal protection of children and young people come to the attention of the Children's Ombudsman annually. Aid has been sought from the Ombudsman in cases where the authorities have not heard a child in the way they should have, or when a child's rights have been violated and he/she has been left without legal protection.

There are special problems involved in implementing the basic rights of children. Numerous shortcomings remain in the systems for safeguarding the rights of children and the professional competence necessary to deal with certain crimes against children is inadequate.

Most of the crimes committed against children never come to the attention of the authorities and too many of the cases that do reach them are not handled properly. Officials may lack sufficient motivation to assist children or their professional competence may not be enough to solve difficult problems.

E. Verhellen (ed.), Monitoring Children's Rights, 575–586.
© 1996 *Kluwer Law International. Printed in the Netherlands.*

The bureaucracy sometimes attempts to conceal problems. The machinery designed to help children works against them; the result is clearly a situation of the child versus the state. For example the bureaucracy in Finland has done its utmost to conceal and cover up cases in which a person who has abused children sexually has served as a teacher or member of the care staff at a children's home. Pedophiles have been protected, even at the risk of serious violations of the rights of children.

In principle, the state should be disqualified from making a report to the UN concerning its own mistakes and negligence. It is obvious that the state will not tell everything in its report, and will attempt to embellish the situation. We also have to ask what is a reliable indicator of the mistakes and negligence.

At the individual level we have to ask, who the children can turn to when the bureaucracy fails?

One source of redress is the Children's Ombudsman, whose explicit duty is to assist in individual cases involving violations of the rights of children.

The work of the Children's Ombudsman for over a decade has clearly brought those cases to light in which the state's own machinery is ineffective. The Children's Ombudsman has brought two cases before the European Commission of Human Rights. The cases represent the ultimate "child versus the state" situation at the national level.

B. The Human Rights of Children

The Mannerheim League is an open civic organization that was founded in 1920. The League promotes and defends the rights of children with respect to society, health, economic security and education. The work of the Children's Ombudsman is a significant part of the League's total activities. The Ombudsman defends the human rights of children in practice.

The Children's Ombudsman sees that the following human rights of children and young people are upheld:
- the right to be heard whenever their own well-being is threatened;
- the right to a status of their own in court, defined in the law;
- the right to physical and mental inviolability.

C. The Children's Ombudsman Can Be Reached Easily

The Children's Ombudsman is available for telephone consultation at the Mannerheim League for Child Welfare on Mondays and Tuesdays, tel. +358–0-34811 470. The working methods will be explained below.

District counselling: the Ombudsman is available 2–5 times a year at the district offices of the League. District counselling has also included training and informative meetings for local mass media. The Mannerheim League has 13 independent districts in Finland.

The Children's Ombudsman can be reached also through the telephone counselling service for children and young people. Some 36,000 calls were made to the service in 1993 and 300 telephone counsellors have been trained. The service has a nationwide number 9800–20400, and counsellors are on duty in eleven cities.

D. Legal Help In Individual Cases

The mission of the Children's Ombudsman is to work consistently in the interests of children and to bring forward and emphasize the child's point of view, which is sometimes overlooked by adults. The Children's Ombudsman acts as the spokesperson for children. With respect to crimes against children, the Children's Ombudsman serves in the role of expert, particularly in cases of sexual abuse. The Children's Ombudsman promotes the rights of children and young people in the following four ways:

1. The Ombudsman gives legal aid in individual cases concerning children or young people, and thereby exerts a positive effect on official practice.
2. The Ombudsman seeks to increase general awareness of children's rights in society and draws attention to deficiencies in the legal protection of children.
3. The Ombudsman lectures and teaches on topics related to children's rights.
4. The Ombudsman makes initiatives concerning action needed to influence decision-makers and legislation.

The Ombudsman cooperates with various authorities.

The services of the Ombudsman are meant for both private individuals and authorities, and are available to everyone throughout Finland. They are also free of charge.

Children and young persons have a special position when they contact the Ombudsman. They have their own telephone consultation hour to facilitate contact.

When children and young persons contact the Ombudsman they also have a special position in the sense, that the Ombudsman is prepared to travel anywhere in Finland, even at short notice, to meet children and to provide them with concrete legal protection.

The work is confidential. The Children's Ombudsman is bound to professional secrecy by law and her own working rules. Approximately ten cases handled by the Ombudsman annually are reported by parties concerned to the mass media. The cases thereby become very public, and the Children's Ombudsman comments on the cases discretely and with respect to the rights of the child.

Below are the main types of cases handled by the Children's Ombudsman:
— Violence against children and young people;

- Sexual abuse of children and young people;
- Position and rights in school;
- Position and rights in various institutions: hospitals, children's homes, etc. (for instance the right to be in touch with relatives, freedom of opinion, contacts outside an institution);
- Position and rights in substitute care and in residential communities;
- Position and rights when parents divorce, particularly taking account of the opinions of children or young people with respect to meeting parents and other close persons, choosing a guardian and determining their best interests;
- Position and rights in a preliminary investigation by the police when accused or otherwise involved in legal proceedings, obtaining a legal adviser and a free trial;
- The validity of other official procedures in matters concerning children;
- Marketing that is injurious to the child or conflicts with good morals in some other way (for instance sex contacts via telephone);

In individual cases the significance and emphasis of the work of the Children's Ombudsman can also be divided into four main groups as follows:

1. Hearing the child. Has the child been heard in matters concerning him/her in accordance with the provisions of the UN Convention on the Rights of the Child?
2. The best interests of the child. Has all evidence of importance from the child's point of view been considered by the authorities when determining his/her best interests and have the relevant legislation and the UN Convention on the Rights of the Child been taken into account?
3. Offences against children as persons; mental and physical violence, sexual abuse and defamation. Have violations of law been adequately studied, has the child been protected against future violence, and has he/she received adequate care?
4. The position and rights of the child; in school and in institutions, particularly concerning children taken into care.

E. Methods Used by the Ombudsman

The methods vary as follows:
- legal advice
- guidance to the proper official and monitoring of the case
- monitoring; a contact person regularly informs the Ombudsman of progress in the case by telephone or letter and the Ombudsman takes action when needed
- discussions and meetings with contact persons and others involved, anywhere in Finland if the circumstances so require
- meeting with and listening to children and young people and making written statements of their views

- contacts with the officials necessary to make progress in a case
- participation in consultations with the authorities
- inviting the different parties to a consultation and thereby bringing the persons involved in the case together
- informing the child welfare authorities
- reporting an offence to the police
- making a written statement to the authorities or to the court
- serving as a witness or an expert in court
- serving as a counsel in court (rare)
- guidance and counselling in making a complaint occasioned by obvious official negligence (The Parliamentary Ombudsman and the Chancellor of Justice of the Council of State)
- undertaking special measures of legal protection, for instance an appeal to the European Commission of Human Rights (for example on February 8, 1993, the Commission of Human Rights was asked to express its opinion on whether it was in accordance with the conventions on human rights ratified by Finland to sentence a person to imprisonment for non-payment of fines that have been conditionally imposed because the rules of access have been broken).

F. Statistics on the Callers and the Types of Cases

The figures below are based on averages for 1991–1993. Most of the callers are adults. Children and young people make only slightly less than five per cent of the calls. However, in the contacts they have made, the violation in question has almost always been serious.

Number of cases:

1991	268 cases
1992	242 cases
1993	267 cases

Callers:

40%	the child's mother
10%	the child's father
10%	grandparents
15%	other relatives, foster parents and friends
5%	the children or young persons themselves
20%	lawyers and officials

Problems:

30%	sexual abuse of the child
15%	custody and the child's own opinion
13%	assault of the child

15%	conflict concerning the right of access to a child
10%	situation in child welfare (child taken into care or the possibility thereof, the legal status of a child living in a foster family)
5%	destructive circumstances for the child
2%	position and rights at school
10%	others

Sexual abuse is the most frequent problem. Although such cases account for one-third of the total, they take up approximately 70% of the working time when related lectures, training and interviews are included.

Children under ten years of age are involved in 80% of the cases. The rights of small children are apparently easy to violate because they are not always able to make themselves understood in the same way as older children and are therefore more vulnerable to threats aimed at preventing them from complaining about violations of their rights. In contrast, children over ten are able to express solutions to their problems verbally and can already look after themselves reasonably well. It is obvious, however, that when a young person is being abused or assaulted within his/her own family, situations in which help from the outside is required may well arise. In some instances the Children's Ombudsman has been the only individual whom the young person has had the courage to contact.

Every year there are 50–60 very difficult cases which require work over a long period of time. Such cases involve serious violations of the rights of children and require an unprejudiced attitude. Approximately one-fifth of these cases lead to a situation in which the Ombudsman is forced not only to provide legal counselling, but also to take more concrete action. This mainly means seeing and hearing the children and making active contact with different authorities.

There may be active consultation concerning these difficult and time-consuming cases and they may appear in the statistics as much as 2–3 years before they are finally solved. Conflicts concerning right of access to a child and involving conditional imposition of a high fine are examples. In such cases the children's own views have not been established.

G. The Children's Ombudsman appeals to the European Commission of Human Rights

On March 12, 1993, the President of the Republic of Finland pardoned the first custodian to whom a fine had been conditionally imposed. Before this, on February 8, 1993, the Children's Ombudsman had lodged a complaint concerning human rights against this decision to the European Commission of Human Rights, as imprisonment had been sought for the child's custodian as an alternative punishment due to failure to pay a conditionally imposed fine. The Ombudsman contended that the decision conflicted with the human rights agreements signed by Finland. After the complaint made by the Ombudsman the Ministry of Justice on its own initiative took measures to grant a pardon.

In April 1994 the Children's Ombudsman submitted another complaint to the European Commission of Human Rights of a case of child custody and right of access. The Children's Ombudsman contended that the child's obvious opinion had not been taken into account in the manner stipulated by the law and the UN Convention on the Rights of the Child.

H. The Children's Ombudsman sought aid from the Parliamentary Ombudsman to improve the legal protection of children placed in institutions

As she has been unable to influence the position of children in institutions, the Children's Ombudsman has directed two separate cases to the Parliamentary Ombudsman. Normally, the Children's Ombudsman has free access to a children's home at the request of a child or young person. The Children's Ombudsman has never been denied admission to institutions. However, more detailed explanations are now and then required. Such explanations can be demanded by the Parliamentary Ombudsman or the Chancellor of Justice.

If the Children's Ombudsman lacks adequate authority or the matter cannot for some reason be investigated as it should be, the Children's Ombudsman can request an examination from the Parliamentary Ombudsman or ask the person making contact to do so.

The Children's Ombudsman has been unable to acquire sufficient evidence on only a few occasions. These cases have concerned two child welfare institutions of different kinds. Both cases were resolved by the Parliamentary Ombudsman.

One of the cases was so serious that the Children's Ombudsman requested the Parliamentary Ombudsman to inspect the institution because children who had escaped complained about acts of violence against them. The request was made on June 17, 1991.

The Parliamentary Ombudsman considered the investigation justified and it was made on September 4–5, 1991 by an inspector from the Office of the Parliamentary Ombudsman, together with an inspector from the Department of Social Welfare and Health Care in the Provincial Administrative Board concerned. The Deputy Parliamentary Ombudsman also visited the child welfare institution on March 17, 1992.

After an extensive study of the case, the Deputy Parliamentary Ombudsman sent a 13-page decision on the matter, dated June 24, 1992, to the Children's Ombudsman. The decision discusses in detail the methods of punishment, sanctions and restrictions applied at the institution. These include limiting contacts, checking mail, separation from the other children, locking into his/her room, restricting freedom of movement and fines of 200 marks for escaping. The Deputy Parliamentary Ombudsman stated in his decision that the methods used by the institutions did not entirely conform with the goals of care and upbringing stipulated in the Child Welfare Act and Statute.

The Deputy Parliamentary Ombudsman informed the head of the institution in question about the deficiencies noted in the methods used.

In her complaint to the Parliamentary Ombudsman, the Children's Ombudsman insisted that the legal protection of children placed in institutions should be improved more extensively, and not merely in cases where complaints have been made. The Children's Ombudsman has for instance suggested that more information should be given to children placed in institutions on the measures they can take when their rights are violated.

A complaint against the official proceedings is the ultimate method, the use of which should be avoided if it is possible to solve the matter at a local level by the parties concerned by negotiating and with the required measures. If the authority concerned still does not investigate the case, a complaint must regrettably be made. This is the only way to improve the situation and the attitudes involved.

In the cases in which the Children's Ombudsman has consulted approximately 20 complaints are made annually to the controlling authorities due to neglect or to an error in official proceedings. The Children's Ombudsman does not, however, make the complaints herself, but instead directs clients to take action after other measures have not led to a decision that is fair and necessary from the child's point of view.

I. Hearing Children

The Children's Ombudsman herself rarely hears the children. This usually happens only when an authority totally neglects to hear a child or does so inadequately. In some cases the opinions of specialists do not include enough information.

In 1992 the Children's Ombudsman met a total of ten children in different parts of Finland. Their ages varied between 7 and 14. Hearing children almost always means that the Children's Ombudsman will later appear in court as a witness or that a written statement to the executive authorities will be required of her.

In 1992 the Children's Ombudsman was heard in court as a witness in the City Court of Turku (a nine-year-old girl), twice in the Rural District Court of Saarijärvi (an eight-year-old boy), twice in the Rural District Court of Hollola (an eight-year-old boy and a seven-year-old girl) and in the City Court of Lahti (a ten-year old girl, at the request of the prosecutor).

The Ombudsman delivered a written statement concerning the child's own opinion to the Provincial Administrative Board of Oulu. A ten-year-old girl had requested to live with her mother for years and eventually succeeded. The girl's own opinion was finally heard. The Children's Ombudsman visited Oulu on June 26, 1992 to hear the child in person.

On November 12, 1992 the Children's Ombudsman heard three pupils of the Samppalinna School in Turku who were on strike together with their entire class. The strike had even made the newspapers. The children complained of rough treatment, and together with their teacher, refused to attend the school. On November 12, 1992 there was a large hearing at which the school authorities of the City of Turku together with the children's parents and a few teachers attempted to find a solution and to save the class that had been abandoned. The Children's Ombudsman demanded that the pupils should be heard at the meeting, which then happened. The case has been resolved and the class is being taught by its own teacher, who had spoken for the pupils. For six months the teacher taught the class in a factory building without pay. The class has since been transferred to a new school.

On September 24, 1992 the Children's Ombudsman met a large group of children's parents at the North Karelia District Office of the Mannerheim League for Child Welfare in Joensuu. The authorities had not placed a child molester in proper care. The Ombudsman also invited the officials concerned to the district office to discuss co-operation. The child molester was eventually put into the care required under the condition.

J. A Finnish Example of so Called "False Allegation of Child Sexual abuse"

The Children's Ombudsman also defends the authorities when they come under attack while defending the rights of children.

Three hospital doctors in Helsinki "found it most likely that a 4-year-old girl had been sexually abused"; a medical report to the social welfare authorities on December 1 1988. With the assistance of a lawyer, the male suspect complained to the control authority about the opinion of the hospital doctors.

The control authority concluded that "the statement by the hospital team that sexual abuse is considered to have happened is a position too strong in view of the presented material". The three hospital doctors were disciplined by the control authority.

The hospital doctors were summoned to answer a claim for damages (500 000 FMK).

The doctors contacted the Children's Ombudsman. A statement was requested from professor Tilman Fürniss.

In a statement of 15 April 1992 professor Fürniss states among others: "In my opinion and from my experience the initial sequence of events in this case must raise not a vague but already a very strong suspicion of child sexual abuse".

Professor Fürniss analysed the four expert statements on which the Finnish control authority had based its decision to discipline the hospital doctors. According to professor Fürniss "the Finnish National Board of Health has accepted expert opinions which on one to two pages deal with one of the most complex professional issues in the overlapping field of medical, psychological, child-psychiatric, therapeutic and legal issues which have arisen over the last 20 years." Concerning the control experts professor Fürniss stated : "In my opinion the National Board of Health has either chosen experts of frighteningly low standards, who do not seem to be acquainted with up to date knowledge with regards to the diagnosis and intervention of sexual abuse of small children or who have not been given the entire material available or who did not care to evaluate the case in its entire complexity. He also stated: "It is in my opinion extremely disconcerting, how any professional body could responsibly draw a professionally binding decision on the bases of these reports."

Without the professionial help from professor Fürniss the above mentioned three hospital doctors obviously had been left without any guarantee of judicial relief in Finland. These kinds of cases are also known by the name of judicial murder.

II. Structural Work

A. *Making the UN Convention on the Rights of the Child Known*

The UN Convention on the Rights of the Child deals with the rights concerning the physical, mental and individual security of the child. One of the principal functions of the Children's Ombudsman is to make this convention known in conjunction with the cases handled, by providing information, making presentations and arranging training sessions.

The Convention has already been used as a basis for decision-making in courts of law.

B. *Public Debate*

The Children's Ombudsman has made the public aware of the shortcomings in the legal position of children through the media. Numerous interviews, particularly about abuse of children and violence directed against them, have been given. More than 300 interviews with the press, radio and television concerning the work of the Children's Ombudsman and the legal rights of children have been made in Finland.

C. *Legislation and Monitoring the Rights of Children on a General Level*

On the basis of concrete information received through her work, the Children's Ombudsman has also proposed amendments to the legislation. The Ombudsman is also responsible for issuing statements on proposed new legislation.

In conjunction with individual complaints, the Children's Ombudsman has requested the control authorities to take a wider stand on the status of children; for example in conjunction with a case involving a children's home, the Children's Ombudsman requested the Parliamentary Ombudsman to see that the legal rights of children in institutions are protected more effectively. This action on the part of the Ombudsman led to a review of procedures at several institutions.

On February 12, 1993 the Ombudsman sent a detailed memorandum to the Finnish Minister of Justice, which included a ten-paragraph proposal dealing with ways to improve the hearing of children's opinions and legal protection of children. The Children's Ombudsman proposed, for instance, that: 1) new documents should be designed with more space for notes on children's opinions (at present, one either ticks the appropriate box or there is a small space for notes on the child's opinions); 2) in cases dealing with children, an oral trial should be more common, also for the executive authorities; 3) if needed the social or other authorities should give a report under oath to the court of law; 4) thorough medical and psychological statements by specialists should always be required if assault or sexual abuse of the child is suspected.

D. Commercial Sex, Child Sex Tourism and Child Pornography

The Children's Ombudsman has long monitored advertising of telephone sex and intervened in marketing that is offensive to children. Thanks to the Ombudsman's efforts, many advertisements have been changed. The marketing for Nabokov's Lolita, for example, was changed in response to the demands of the Children's Ombudsman.

The Children's Ombudsman has also served as the ECPAT-coordinator, and the first seminar in Finland on child sex tourism was organized in autumn 1993 on the initiative of the Ombudsman. The Ombudsman has also worked actively to criminalize the possession of child pornography.

In cases of child pornography/pedophilia, the Children's Ombudsman works together with the police.

E. A Nationwide Children's Ombudsman Network

The Children's Ombudsman is presently training new attorneys for children in Finland. The goal is to develop a national network of legal counsels for children who would defend their rights more effectively.

F. NGOs, an Independent Children's Ombudsman and Supranational Control Are Needed to Safeguard the Rights of Children

Finland has only begun to realize the fundamental individual rights of children related to their personal security. The state is not sufficiently active in providing aid and information to children who are victims of crimes that are stubbornly concealed. How can the rights of children be secured when government officials do not help, even when assistance has been specifically requested from them?

An independent Children's Ombudsman is needed to safeguard the rights of children who remain beyond the sphere of official assistance. Moreover, professionals in various fields, as the example mentioned above concerning physicians shows, need legal counsel and support, especially when they themselves are victimized by a misdirected bureaucracy.

The state has not played an active role in providing children with information about their rights. Nor does it provide children with opportunities for help through a special telephone line. In Finland the Mannerheim League for Child Welfare has seen to this need since 1980.

There is evidence for arguing that the state is unable to be objective in reporting on its own actions to the UN; it should be disqualified from reporting its own errors.

The first report to the UN by the governmental working group was criticized by the Mannerheim League for Child Welfare in a statement to the press and the Government of Finland. After the criticism, a few positive additions were made to the final report to the UN approved by the Government of Finland on April 20, 1994. The Government promised to criminalize the possession of child pornography, something the Children's Ombudsman and the Mannerheim League for Child Welfare had long demanded. The Mannerheim League – as a non-governmental organization – will submit its own report to the UN.

It is of course extremely important that the Council of Europe provides supranational means to safeguard the rights of children when such means are not available in the child's own country. But it is also essential that the human rights bodies within the Council of Europe make use of the best expert aid available to ensure that the rights of assaulted and abused children are safeguarded in their decisions.

Action concerning the rights of assaulted and abused children should be taken as soon as possible and the decisions of the Council of Europe are not always quick enough to help every child in need. Supranational control should be expanded and developed so that concrete aid could be requested from the Council of Europe for children as soon as the national bureaucracy jams. This would guarantee independent aid to children in time.

Supranational and independent Children's Ombudsmen within the Council of Europe?

LIEVEN VANDENBERGHE and ANKIE VANDEKERCKHOVE

Monitoring Children's Rights: A Specific Task for "Child & Family"?

I. INTRODUCTION ON CHILD & FAMILY AND ITS OFFICIAL STATUS

People don't easily think of "rights" when they consider our main target group, babies and toddlers (and their parents). But ... they are children too so the UN Convention does indeed apply. This notion is becoming more important and real within Child & Family, focusing on this particular fraction of the child-population. In spite of the holistic approach, of which we are certainly aware, some rights will be taken into account more than others, due to the age limit of children up to three or six years old..

Child & Family is a flemish governemental agency with a mandate in the field of young children's mental and physical wellbeing and family support. In this context Child & Family works on different subjects. To name a few:
– preventive medicine for mother & child
– daycare
– child abuse
– adoption, etc...

Its official status brings along a strong moral authority. Lately Child & Family has taken more and more advantage of that authority to advise and signal the flemish authority on children's affairs, for example: regulating adoption-mediation, recommandations on unaccompanied refugee children, studies on the social and legal position of the child in the family as well as within our society.

II. ACHIEVEMENTS

For several years now, Child & Family has increased the study of children and children's topics on several levels and in several areas of its activities.

Every *year* Child & Family publishes a *report* in which data on young children are gathered. E.g.: how many children were born, how many children

E. Verhellen (ed.), Monitoring Children's Rights, 587–592.
© 1996 *Kluwer Law International. Printed in the Netherlands.*

are in daycare, how many children receive the basic vaccinations and so forth. These data give a clear view on the exact size of the young children's population and on changes within this population. This is a valuable source of information. With the increase in informatisation more data can be gathered and studied. Child & Family recently developed a child-data-base, on which we can design an efficient policy, based on actual needs and concrete figures. (All of this with respect of privacy-regulations of course).

Since '91 there is also an *annual report on child abuse and neglect.* Child & Family has been funding the flemish centres "Child in need", which use a uniform registration since '91. The centres have a mandate in the field of prevention of child abuse and they serve as a helpline for families, children, social workers etc. The centres have a uniform registration method and the facts and figures are gathered into an annual report by Child & Family. Although we still don't get hold of those cases which are not reported to these agencies, the number of known cases increases every year. This might be due to the fact that our policy on child abuse is a policy of multidisciplinary, family-oriented assistance instead of repressive action. This way, the taboo on abuse might slowly disappear, but still a large number of cases remain undetected. Based on the facts and figures, Child & Family works on child abuse policies with the ultimate goal to help disappear not only the taboo but the abuse itself.

In our work Child & Family focuses more and more on the actual intrest of the child and its family. Specific problems get a specific approach and the main perspective is always *the child's own family.* That is the basis we work from and we always try to keep the children in their families. Child & Family is investing thoroughly in family-support-systems so that children don't have to leave their homes, not even in dysfunctioning situations.

Next to this, Child & Family has been working for years (since 1919) in the field of *preventive medicine* for children and their mothers (free prenatal care, free vaccinations etc. ...).

Since '92 Child & Family also has an *ombudsservice.* In every provincial department an ombudsman was installed with several tasks:
– inform the public of Child & Family policy and decisions
– handle complaints
– advise on a more structural level and formulate long-term solutions, based on the questions and complaints that they receive.

Given the fact that Child & Family is active in the field of care for very young children, most clients of the ombudsservice are parents or other adults. Still, the ombudsservice works in the intrest of children and the UN Convention supplies them with the main guidelines.

Checking the Convention we will glance over several articles and how they are, or can be, implemented in the daily work of Child & Family. In this paper, we will only cover some topics at random.

III. THE UN CONVENTION ON THE RIGHTS OF THE CHILD: CAPITA SELECTA

A. Non-discrimination

All children are equal, also for Child & Family. What's more, this principle also implies specific care in specific cases and that is exactly what we do. If, for example, we look at minorities, we are working with intercultural workers for migrants and with experts by experience for the underprivileged families. Both the intercultural workers and the experts by experience have lived lives as respectively migrants and underprivileged people, so they know what problems those families are facing. They can "translate" their needs, explain their behaviour, and work from within Child & Family towards better, more adequate care for them. Special preventive-care-centres will be set up in the following years to come.

While all this may seem in favour of parents more than children, the effect on children in the long run should be greatly valued. By supporting the parents, those families may be able to break the vicious circle of generational poverty, bad housing, unemployment etc. and their children will have more opportunities later. Also, there is a stronger guarantee of the child's right to healthcare.

B. Intrest of the Young Child

The intrest of the child is the recurrent theme in all our activities.

A good example would be our quality-scales used in daycare-centres, funded and controlled by Child & Family. This scale is an instrument designed by Child & Family and the University of Louvain to check the quality of daycare facilities in order to fully guarantee an optimal upbringing of babies and young children. With "quality" we mean quality in a pedagogical sense: the main focus is on the young child, because daycare should indeed be more than "simply looking after" children. Priority is given to the needs of the child more than to those of parents or personnel.

The criteria are a.o. flexibility, individual approach, working towards independency, cooperation with parents, skills of personnel etc. The daycare-centres are continually checked by Child & Family on these criteria. The scale, result of scientific theory and daily practice, is the first european instrument to actually measure the daycare quality in an objective manner.

C. Responsability and Capacities of the Parents, Family Support

The family environment is very important for Child & Family, with respect for its own opinions, ideologies, habits etc. ... Social nurses of Child & Family pay home visits to every family in which a baby is born. This type of care is completely on a voluntary basis and free of charge. If the parents do not want it, our work is done, so to speak. However most young parents do appreciate it, especially with their first baby. They get basic information on the baby's health, development, behaviour, ... The advantage of this type of service is that it is not at all stigmatising. Child & Family is a well-know organisation and our social nurses visit all families, not because of a problem but because of a birth, a joyful occasion. But, at the same time, they are able to detect problems at an early stage and they will help the parents to overcome those problems, either on their own or with the help of more specialised professionals. This way they help and support the parents in caring for and raising their children.

D. Health Services

The legally formulated task of Child & Family concerning children's health shows similarities with art. 24 of the Convention.
   Child & Family activities in this field expand upon:
— prevention of perinatal death and prematurity
— child development, within the family as well as within society, in all its aspects (physical, psycho-motorical, social, affective, psychological, mental) with special attention for:
   · monitoring growth of babies, children;
   · prevention of developmental disorders and early detection of handicaps;
   · development of children with a handicap, sick children, migrant's children, children in underpriviliged families and children growing up outside the family home.
— psycho-social support and health support of parents, esp. the young mothers being pregnant, giving birth and after the delivery.

E. Adoption

Due to the Federal structure of Belgium the adoption legislation is situated on two levels. The adoption procedure, the conditions to adopt, the recognition of foreign adoptions, the admittance to Belgian territory is a federal (Belgian) competence.
   The two communities in Belgium, French and Flemish, are competent for the recognition and control of adoption agencies. Before 1989 anyone in Flanders could act as a go-between in an adoption.
   Since '89 however the recognition of these agencies is defined by the Flemish legislation in a rather detailed manner. In order to guarantee the well-being of the adopted child the adoption-agencies must prepare and evaluate the adoptive parents. A comprehensive study of the child must be made in collaboration with the competent authority in the State of origin. Child

& Family controls the financial situation of the agencies, the quality and methods of their work and the legality of their contacts in the State of origin.

Due to the different levels of competence in Belgium only a limited mumber of adoptions are mediated by an agency. A large majority are independent adoptions. For these adoptions there is no obligation of preparation and evaluation of the parents.

In collaboration with the federal authority and the French communitiy we are developing new legislation so that all adoptions will provide the same guaranties to every adoptive child. For these projects we are inspired by the Hague Convention on Protection of Children and Cooperation in respect of Intercounty Adoption, as well as by the UN Convention.

F. Refugees

Child & Family attended a european working seminar on unaccompanied refugee children and continues to take part in lobbywork on that subject. The result of that seminar was a set of recommandations for politicians. Child & Family has sent these to several national and all european politicians with a letter in which we urge them to put this matter on the agenda. We hope that the new european legislature will work on that in their harmonisation of asylum-procedures.

Also, in Flanders, our president of the Board of Directors has come forward in favour of refugees, be it illegal or not, and stated that all children and their parents have the right to basic health-care. At the consultation-bureaus of Child & Family no discrimination will be made for illegal refugees, so that they will at least receive basic vaccinations and guidance at birth.

IV. CHALLENGES FOR THE FUTURE

Child & Family uses the principles of the Convention in its range of activities and is planning on implementing the Convention even more in the near future.

We should do more in making the Convention know to the general public. Maybe our ombudsmen could work on this in the future. We also should consider to inform the parents on the Convention-principles by means of leaflets, during their visits to the consultation bureau, during the home visits of the social nurse.

We should also work together closely with other administrations and NGO's in setting up a national committee of experts, as it has been described by Prof. E. Verhellen. We encourage initiatives by the government on the installment of a children's ombudsman on a higher level, as independent as possible. Together with other experts, NGO's and universities, we should use all our knowledge and experience to help make that happen.

And finally, although we are on the right track, we must continue working on improving the child's position within society. We must systematically work on studies on children as a group, make child-effect-reports and put children on the map. There's more than enough of them and we can no longer ignore them simply because they have no political or financial power. They have power, as human beings and as legal subjects as described in the UN Convention.

JOSIANE BIGOT and RICHARD SANCHO ANDREO

Access to Legal Advice for Minors

Through the mass media and reports published by international organisations, we constantly hear how children's rights are being blatantly ignored all over the world. During this conference, however, we will hear information from committed people working in the field against all kinds of violence carried out against children. Being able to bring together adults committed to fighting against violence is indeed an encouraging sign but a few general questions still remain: How can we inform young people about their rights? How can we make them take an active part in this fight against violence? Legal advisory services are considered to be one of the most important factors allowing young people to acquire legal status; but how do they achieve this?

When THEMIS was set up in April 1990 in Strasbourg, France, its main aim was to provide a real and effective legal advisory service for children and young people providing them with clear information about their rights. All the founders of THEMIS, from all fields of work directly connected with child welfare (instructors, judges, psychologists, solicitors and teachers), had been motivated by one single observation: that it was difficult for a child to make himself heard in many areas of his life (at home, at school, in the courts or in normal everyday life) in a way which would respect both his opinions and his identity. The THEMIS project is based on the close relationship between two main ideas.

The first is the development of the social status of the child which has given him the right to contribute actively to social and educational programs and thus take part in local development. It is in this very special context and with a boost from UNESCOs International Year of the Child in 1979 that the first youth council was created in Schiltigheim.

The second is the obvious contribution that has been made in recent years by the social sciences and psychologists to listening to children as valued citizens.

In 1990 two further important developments strengthened the ideas behind the THEMIS project.

The first was the International Convention for Children's Rights included in the annexes of a government report on the participation of children in legal hearings which pointed out that it was necessary to reinforce the right of a child to be heard not only during judicial proceedings but also in all places

E. Verhellen (ed.), Monitoring Children's Rights, 593–595.

which contribute to his socialisation: in the family, at school and in normal everyday community life. It is important to note that this report enabled courses to be set up to train youth lawyers in this very specialised area which demands rarely taught legal knowledge and also training in social sciences. These experimental courses have been set up in around ten sites in France including Lille, Bordeaux, Lyons, Marseilles and Strasbourg.

Article 12 of the Convention puts forward the legal principle that any child capable of discernment should be able to freely express his opinion on any issue or legal or administrative procedure which concerns him, should be able to do this either directly or through a member of an appropriate organisation and should be able to see that this opinion has been taken into consideration. Based on this, the law passed on January 8th 1993 proposes the right of a child to be heard and defended before the courts.

The second major line of action taken by our association is also one of the objectives of the Policies on the Inner Cities in France which sets out to provide legal advisory services to underprivileged people. When we started this action we maintained, and we continue to do so, that children and young people were underprivileged because of the absence of legal counselling for them. This was especially the case in places considered priority areas by those responsible for the inner cities.

It is often said that young people either have too many rights or not enough but in such discussions it is usually enough to remind people that the absence of knowledge about rights and obligations is the main obstacle hindering their socialisation. We have to inform young people about their rights individually and in groups. If we don't, it will be impossible to help young people to integrate into society without helping them to resolve their conflicts with the law.

How does THEMIS achieve this?

When setting up a legal advisory service for young people, one main principle has to be adhered to: all action has to be voluntary, not legally imposed by educational or therapeutic legal injunctions. Only in this way can we provide the listening ear the children, young people or adults require and truly take into account their needs. We will only succeed if all action we undertake is centred around the individual (adult or minor) and guarantees anonymity whilst, at the same time, meeting all legal requirements. We respect the initiative and the decision to act taken by the person in need and we thus listen to him responsibly with respect right from the start.

At the outset it was decided that the rights of adults should never come into conflict with those of children but should be complementary and work together. For this, it is essential to create a partnership since adults are often just as powerless as children when faced with legal issues. In this way the law finds its place between the child's or young person's need for independence, his learning of responsibility and the necessity to protect him in the face of danger. The adolescent who asks for protection and adult intervention against drug dealers is often the very same adolescent mixed up in illegal dealings himself.

Despite these contradictions we must all realise that law is a tool, a means to get a better understanding of social laws. Explaining rights and giving guidance are tasks we carry out directly with young people and adults in the places where they live and work. We aim to bring together and facilitate communication between three different groups; (young people), adults and those in the legal profession (magistrates, the police, (youth lawyers) and educators). But law is much more than just a means of understanding each other, it is also a means of integration and allowing people freedom. Whether during individual consultations or when seeking legal advice from a youth lawyer it is always surprising to see how willing young people are to get involved in solving their case. We consider that a young person will be all the more able to understand his own act and any possible legal proceedings if he himself has the impression of being defended fairly.

Legal texts and practices are without doubt going to be greatly affected by the Convention on applying children's rights which is soon to be adopted by the Council of Europe. It will seek to promote their rights by introducing new legal procedures (draft of November 10th 1994).

We must not forget, however, that enjoying our rights requires us to have within our grasp all the legal information necessary to know our rights fully, implement them and have them accepted by everyone. This does not mean we are aiming to generate a mass of new regulatory legal texts, quite the opposite. We simply want to promote law as a guarantee of individual freedom which goes well beyond just French positive law and includes the principles contained in the European Convention on Human Rights.

This is why we believe that ignorance of the law is the reason so many young people simply drop out of society today.

MAUD DROOGLEEVER FORTUYN

The Role of the Children's Rights Shop in Monitoring Children's Rights

First of all I will go into some of the statements made in the announcement of the Conference Monitoring Children's Rights. This will enable me to make clear some viewpoints and working methods of the Children's Rights Shop.

In the announcement of the Conference Monitoring Children's Rights it is stated that we don't know very much about children. It says: "We know very little about how children, in their own minds, interpret events or give meanings to them. ... What children really know, are capable of and feel remains a complete mystery, because of their social status as "not yets", as they have been historically defined."

I. PARTICIPATION AND COMMUNICATION

You might say that this social status as "not yets" is – very generally put – reflected in the way adults usually talk with children. Even though the notion that children should be taken serious is more and more accepted – and is even becoming a norm – it seems adults have difficulty in really giving space to children's wants, believes and needs. The tendency is there to think for children, to believe that we, adults, know what's best for them. With the result that the so-called participation is a pseudo one; adults are listening to children but not integrating the information given to them in their subsequent actions.

The other point mentioned in the above quotation is that we know very little about how children interpret or give meaning to events. This statement can be disputed with reference to child developmental theories. I want to take another approach, namely that we can never tell for sure how the other person interprets events or interprets what is being said. Through communicating we can check if that what we intend te say is understood that way by the other. You could agree for the time being on the meaning of something. Adults, living in the same cultural context take it for granted that a lot that goes around there is understood in generally the same way by most participants in that context. If somebody from outside joins in, we know that we have to learn him or her various matters: how to use certain tools or systems, what

E. Verhellen (ed.), Monitoring Children's Rights, 597–601.
© 1996 *Kluwer Law International. Printed in the Netherlands.*

things or happenings mean, etc.. The same applies for children. You could see them as newcomers in society, in school, in the family. They have to learn what things mean, what one can do or not do, all kinds of implicit and explicit rules. Because they have less cultural bagage and because of their different perspective on the world (being smaller, being treated differently as children, knowing different things), they will generally give different meanings to events and to words of others than adults would do. But I want to go one step further. Adults as well as children take part in various social contexts. As a consequence, they all have different frames of reference. So different ways of interpretation exist between adults and children, between people actually. So I would say that the question of how children think is a fruitless one. There is not one way and we cannot find a theory or a way of interpretation that will be valid for all children, except very general statements. The statement that we principally cannot know how children interpret and give meaning to events is important enough in itself. This should be followed by saying that we can try to find out how a certain child thinks and we can try to help that child find it's way in society, in school or in family matters. In other words, I want to stress the importance of talking with children, a dialogue, to find out how a child in a particular situation sees its world.

What children are capable of – another question put in the announcement – is just as much a question that cannot be answered by a simple description or rule. When we think about what children do all over the world to stay alive and to meet their needs, we realize that children are capable of a lot, much more than is generally thought of. The circumstances, the conditions under which children grow up, have a very important influence on the behaviour of children. What the world, society, adults and other children offer them will help shape their behaviour. Society gives children opportunities to learn and to act. If it fits with their actual situation and needs, they will grasp the opportunity. That is where the responsibility of adults lies. What kind of society do we want? What kind of morals, standards? And what is the actual situation at hand? The answers to those questions give standards and directions to what and which competences we want to learn children. How they learn it is a complex question, as I mentioned before. But participation should certainly be part of the answer. And by presenting society as it is – that is, not a representation – gives children the opportunity to react on it by accepting it or trying to change it.

II. The Children's Rights Shop

After this introduction I want to go back to the theme of the conference. Art. 44 of the Convention on the Rights of the Child states that countries have to report the progress made in meeting the standards of the Convention. A key question is what is to be reported and by whom. I want to break a lance here for the voice and experiences of children themselves. Of course governments can report on how they changed laws and regulations to meet the standards of the Convention. And NGOs will no doubt be more critical towards the measures taken by the government. Jurists will get involved in very sophisticated disputes on the implications in the Convention that could lead to the conclusion that children should be able to put a case before a judge by themselves, etc.. But I haven't heard much yet on the subject of children reporting on how they experience their situation, how children feel that their rights are respected or trampled on. There are many ways imaginable on how to get this information. I want to focus here on the Children's Rights Shop as a source of information for anybody who wants to write a report on the effectiveness of the UN Convention. The advantage is that this will not give us some abstract information on what children think rights imply, but very factual information on the problems children meet when trying to realize their rights and how the law sometimes makes it impossible for children to reach a solution.

The Children's Rights Shop is a place where children, i.e. minors, can go to or which they can call if they have questions about or problems concerning their rights. Children can call anonymously if they want to and all the help they get is for free. Children who come to the Children's Rights Shop are helped to distilate from their problems the juridical questions. Sometimes these questions are part of a bigger or more complex problem. If these lie on a for instance a social, relational or psychological terrain, we will help find an organisation, such as the children's help-line or a Youth Advice Centre, that can help the child. The Children's Rights Shop only deals with juridical matters. Once the situation is clear we tell the child what it's rights are and which actions it can undertake. Sometimes that is not much for instance when children lack the possibility to realize their rights, in court. We sketch the child the actions it can undertake and the possible consequences – juridical, relational, social, financial – each choice implies. It's then up to the child to make the choice. Whatever choice it makes, we will help as much as we can with matters to do with rights and the law. Often this implies helping the child voicing its opinion to the judge. We do not undertake anything without the knowledge and the consent of the child. For us, the questions put by the child remains the central focus. Because of this working method, the child can formulate and explain to us the way he or she sees it's situation, what she thinks her rights are, what he wants to achieve. We can as far as possible help to realize the rights of children and at the same time learn them something about rights and law. Basic principles like the fact that "I have rights" implies that "you have rights too which I have to respect". Or that some problems cannot be solved by the law, for instance a fight with a friend or a lack of love or care from a parent. Children learn that undertaking action can be very effective or not so effective at all. Negotiations can come to a stand still or a judge may, after having heard the opinion of the child, decide something else anyway. But that's all part of the legal system which children have to learn to handle and understand.

The questions that children put to the Children's Rights Shop cover a wide range of subjects. A substantial part of the questions have to do with the divorce of their parents. Do they have a say in with whom they are going to live? How often can they see the other parent or do they have to see the other parent at all? Sometimes a child does not know its father, who left when the child was very young, but it still carries his name. Is it possible to get the name of mother? Children get kicked out of school. Sometimes that is quite understandible seen from the viewpoint of the teachers. But even if the child is a little bastard who fights with other kids all the time, walks around with too big a knive to be usefull for peeling an orange and paints the walls of the school in a maybe artistic but not planned way, it still has its rights. A youngster cannot be kicked out by the maths-teacher, and not without being heard, without a warning, without a letter to and talk with its parents. In such a case we can negotiate with the schoolboard and point out the rights of the child. To respect the rights of such a child seems very hard for certain grown-ups but I would say that especially for such a child a fair treatment could have a positive effect on him or her – besides the fact that the rights of each individual should be respected by governments, authorities and other individuals. This case also gives me the opportunity to point out something else. The last few years the Dutch government and public opinion complain about the present youth: there is supposed to be a lack of norms and morals. But if youngsters, like this boy, are not treated fairly, what kind of norms and morals will they learn?

Other problems the Children's Rights Shop is confronted with have to do with children who have run away from home or are turned out on the streets. Of these children the ones who are under 18 years of age have a hard time finding money to stay alive as minors in Holland have no or hardly any right to social security money and the minimum wages are very low. Children with parents from abroad have problems which often have to do with growing up in two cultures. Some girls should, according to their parents, get married young with a man of their parents choice. Scholing is not thought to be important. These girls have participated in the Dutch culture through school and want to keep on going there and marry a man of their own choice. They need to know about residence-permits, compulsory education, legal age to marry, etc. Especially at the Youth Advice Centres there has been a boom of these kind of questions.

Children who are sexually or physically abused also turn to the Children's Rights Shop. The advantage of the Children's Rights Shop for them is that we will not undertake anything without their consent. This way they keep control of the proceedings at least up to the point they choose which course of action they want to undertake. For instance: Anne, 17 years old, comes to the Children's Rights Shop. In the past she has been abused by the partner of her mother. Now, she wants justice to be done. Anne can go to the police, we can tell her what may happen once she has reported him. She could also start a civil procedure to ask for financial compensation. For this, she has to wait untill she is 18 years old, as minors cannot start such a legal procedure. The Children's Rights Shop can give her a name of a lawyer who can assist her in her case. Anne makes another appointment with us so she has time to think about what she wants to do.

It may be clear that I value the Children's Rights Shop as a juridical institution and a pedagogical one. As a juridical institution it helps children to realize their rights. By writing articles and reactions on Dutch law-making, the Children's Rights Shop also tries to improve the legal position of minors in general. The pedagogical worth of the Children's Rights Shop is the opportunity it offers children to get to know law and the juridical system and to get help to find their way within the system. This is of so much importance because in this way the gap between the "adult" society and children can be bridged, at least on this subject. And the bridging of this gap is needed because children come into contact with rights and regulations everyday – be it conscious or unconscious – and they have to learn about the juridical system, which forms an important part of a democratic society. It seems to me better to face this problem than to cover it up with rationalisations like "we know what is best for children". To make a last concluding remark I want to go back to the beginning of my paper. It is not enough to have a theory on how children think or interpret things. By talking to them we can find out how they experience their world and surroundings. What we need in the first place is an open mind, a will to listen and the flexibility to see things from a different viewpoint.

WILLIAM A. SCHABAS

The Death Penalty for Crimes Committed by Persons Under Eighteen Years of Age

INTRODUCTION

Article 37

States Parties shall ensure that: (a) No child shall be subjected to torture or other cruel, inhuman or degrading treatment or punishment. Neither capital punishment nor life imprisonment without possibility of release shall be imposed for offences committed by persons below eighteen years of age.

Convention on the Rights of the Child

Amnesty International reports that nearly half of United Nations member states have put an end to capital punishment, either *de facto* or *de jure*.[1] Among those that still retain the death penalty, human rights initiatives have focussed on limiting its use, restricting it to only the most serious crimes, and excluding from its scope certain groups, including children. In countries which have not yet abolished the death penalty, the prohibition on the execution of persons for crimes committed during childhood or adolescence is a widely recognized domestic norm. It is based on the notion of diminished criminal liability of juveniles. The general acceptance of this norm is reflected in its inclusion in article 37a) of the *Convention on the Rights of the Child*,[2] and many other multilateral human rights treaties.[3]

---

[1] Amnesty International, *Annual Report 1994*, London: Amnesty International Publications, 1994.

[2] G.A. Res. 44/25.

[3] *International Covenant on Civil and Political Rights*, (1976) 999 U.N.T.S. 171, art. 6 (5); *American Convention on Human Rights*, (1979) 1144 U.N.T.S. 123, O.A.S.T.S. 36, art. 4 (5); *Geneva Convention of August 12, 1949 Relative to the Protection of Civilians*, (1950) 75 U.N.T.S. 135, art. 68 (4); *Protocol Additional I to the 1949 Geneva Conventions and Relating to The Protection of Victims of International Armed Conflicts* (1979) 1125 U.N.T.S. 3, art. 77 (5); *Protocol Additional II to the 1949 Geneva Conventions and Relating to the Protection of Victims of Non-International Armed Conflicts*, (1979) 1125 U.N.T.S. 609, art. 6 (4).

E. Verhellen (ed.), Monitoring Children's Rights, 603–619.
© 1996 *Kluwer Law International. Printed in the Netherlands.*

However, the norm is not universally applied. In recent years, several states have sentenced to death and then executed individuals for crimes committed while under the age of eighteen.[4] Nine states, Barbados, Iraq, Iran, Nigeria, Pakistan, Bangladesh, Saudi Arabia, Yemen and the United States of America have, since the year 1980, executed individuals for crimes committed while under eighteen.[5] According to Amnesty International, only four states worldwide have engaged in juvenile executions since 1990: one person in Pakistan and one in Saudi Arabia in 1992, one in Yemen in 1993, and six in the United States of America.[6] A 1994 news report from Pakistan tells of a 12-year-old boy threatened with public hanging because he had defiled the name of the prophet, and had written derogatory phrases on the wall of a mosque.[7] Four juvenile offenders were executed in the United States in 1993.

According to Roger Hood's 1989 study of the death penalty, only forty retentionist states have legislation prohibiting execution for crimes committed while under the age of eighteen. Among those that do not, Professor Hood indicates South Korea, Burma, Sudan, India, Iran and Malaysia. Romania and Guatemala refer only to "minors", while Zimbabwe, Barbados, Bermuda, Belize, St Vincent and Trinidad and Tobago set an age limit of sixteen.[8] We have already qualified the norm as "widely recognized", but it falls far short of being universal in domestic law.

In the United States, of the thirty-seven states which allow the death penalty, only eleven have set eighteen as a minimum age, and most of them have done so only recently. According to Roger Hood's study, fifteen states have a minimum age between twelve and seventeen, and eleven states as well as the federal government have no limit at all.[9] The United States Supreme Court has suggested that the death penalty may not be imposed on persons for crimes committed while fifteen or younger, although in the deciding vote in

---

[4] The United States position has been criticized by the Parliamentary Assembly of the Council of Europe: C. of E. Doc. 5738. See also: U.N. Doc. E/CN.4/1991/36, para 514–520.

[5] Amnesty International, *United States of America: The Death Penalty and Juvenile Offenders*, London: Amnesty International, 1991, at p. 13; Amnesty International, *When the State Kills..., The Death Penalty: A Human Rights Issue*, New York: Amnesty International, 1989, at pp. 38-39; Nigel Rodley, *The Treatment of Prisoners Under International Law*, Paris: Unesco, Oxford: Clarendon Press, 1987, at p. 186; Amnesty International, "U.S.A.: Death penalty developments 1993", AI Index: AR 51/02/94, at p. 6.

[6] "USA: Death Penalty Developments", AI Index: AMR 51/05/95, January 1995, p. 12.

[7] Jennifer Griffin, "Is it a mosque or a state?", *Los Angeles Times*, March 20, 1994, p. M2. Note that Pakistan has been taken to task by the Committee Against Torture on the matter of juvenile executions: U.N. Doc. CRC/C/SR.133, para 10.

[8] Roger Hood, *The Death Penalty, A Worldwide Perspective*, Oxford: Clarendon Press, 1989, at p. 59.

[9] *Ibid* See also: Victor L Streib, *Death Penalty for Juveniles*, Bloomington and Indianapolis: Indiana University Press, 1987; Victor L. Streib, "Capital Punishment for Children in Ohio", (1984) 18 *Akron Law Review* 51; Victor L. Streib, "Death Penalty for Children: the American Experience with Capital Punishment for Crimes Committed While Under Age Eighteen", (1983) 36 *Oklahoma Law Review* 613.

that case, Justice O'Connor said that the minimum age should be left to the state legislatures and not to the Supreme Court.[10] In a subsequent case, the Supreme Court held that execution of individuals for crimes committed while aged sixteen or seventeen was not a violation of the *Bill of Rights*.[11] On a more positive note, recent surveys suggest that the United States public is not favourable to execution of juveniles.[12]

I. INTERNATIONAL HUMANITARIAN LAW

The first international legal norm limiting imposition of the death penalty for juvenile offenders appears in the *Geneva Convention of August 12, 1949 Relative to the Protection of Civilians*.[13] Article 68 (4) specifies that "the death penalty may not be pronounced on a protected person who was under eighteen years of age at the time of the offence". A protected person is an individual in the hands of a party to an armed conflict or an occupying power of which he or she is not a national.[14]

A provision restricting the death penalty in the case of civilians in occupied territories appeared in early drafts of the *Convention*. Specific reference to juveniles emerged at the 1948 Stockholm drafting conference. Resulting from a proposal by the International Union for the Protection of Children,[15] it stated that children under eighteen years of age could not be executed.[16] The Drafting Committee at the 1949 Diplomatic Conference changed the wording to exclude the death penalty for an individual under eighteen at the time of

---

[10] *Thompson* v. *Oklahoma*, 487 U.S. 815, 108 S.Ct. 2687 (1988).

[11] *Stanford* v. *Kentucky*; *Wilkins* v. *Missouri*, 492 U.S. 361, 109 S.Ct. 2969 (1989).

[12] Sandra Evans Skovron, J.E. Scott, F.T. Cullen, "The death penalty for juveniles: an assessment of public support", (1989) 35 *Crime and Delinquency* 546; J.L. Hoffman, "On the perils of line-drawing: Juveniles and the death penalty", (1989) 40 *Hastings Law Journal* 229; J.R.P. Ogloff, "The Juvenile death penalty: A frustrated society's attempt for control", (1987) 5 *Behavioural Sciences and the Law* 447; Norman J. Finkel et al., "Killing Kids: The Juvenile Death Penalty and Community Sentiment", (1994)12 *Behavioural Sciences and the Law* 5.

[13] *Supra* note 3.

[14] *Ibid.*, art. 15.

[15] Oscar M. Uhler, Henri Coursier, et al., *Commentary, IV, Geneva Convention Relative to the Protection of Civilian Persons in Time of War*, Geneva: International Committee of the Red Cross, 1958, at pp. 371-372.

[16] The "Stockholm draft" provided (Final Record of the Diplomatic Conference of Geneva of 1949, Vol. I, Berne: Federal Political Department, pp. 123-124): "Article 59. – ...The death penalty may not be pronounced against a protected person under eighteen years of age for any offence whatsoever."

the offence.[17] During first reading, the United States delegate "called for very careful consideration before such a sweeping provision was adopted".[18]

Article 68 (4) is often invoked to support the notion that the prohibition of juvenile executions is a universal norm because the *Conventions* have been ratified by virtually every state.[19] It is argued that no state could execute a juvenile within its own territory in peacetime if it undertakes not to do so in wartime in occupied territory.[20] The flaw in this argument is that states indeed make undertakings that are more generous to civilians in occupied territories, as can be seen from the other paragraphs of article 68. What was contemplated in article 68 is a more favourable regime for civilians in occupied territories than for those within the occupying state.

The inadequacies of the 1949 Geneva Conventions were addressed in the two additional protocols, adopted in 1977. Article 77 (5) of *Protocol Additional I to the 1949 Geneva Conventions and Relating to The Protection of Victims of International Armed Conflicts*[21] states that the death penalty for an offence related to the armed conflict shall not be executed on persons who had not attained the age of eighteen years at the time the offence was committed. Its scope is broader than the 1949 Convention because it applies to all persons "in the power of a party to the conflict", not only "protected persons".

The provision was first proposed at the 1972 Conference of Government Experts[22] and submitted without any substantive change to the 1974 Diplomatic Conference.[23] A Working Group settled on the age of eighteen because this was also used in a corresponding provision of draft protocol II.[24] The

---

[17]   *Final Record of the Diplomatic Conference of Geneva of 1949, Vol. III*, Berne: Federal Political Department, p. 141 (Annex 299). See also : "Letter of the International Union for Child Welfare", p. 131 (Annex 272)).

[18]   *Final Record of the Diplomatic Conference of Geneva of 1949, Vol. IIA*, Berne: Federal Political Department, 1950 (Summary record of nineteenth meeting of Committee III), at p. 673.

[19]   *Roach and Pinkerton* v. *United States* (Case No. 9647), Resolution No. 3/87, reported in: O.A.S. Doc. OEA/Ser.L/V/II.71 doc. 9 rev. 1, p. 147, *Inter-American Yearbook on Human Rights*, 1987, Dordrecht/Boston/London: Martinus Nijhoff, 1990, p. 328, 8 *H.R.L.J* 345.

[20]   Dinah Shelton, "Note", (1987) 8 *H.R.L.J.* 355, at p. 358.

[21]   *Supra* note 3.

[22]   International Committee of the Red Cross, *Conference of Government Experts on the Reaffirmation and Development of International Humanitarian Law Applicable in Armed Conflicts, Geneva, 3 May – 3 June 1972 (second session), Basic Texts I*, Geneva: International Committee of the Red Cross, 1972, p. 21; *Ibid II (Annexes)*, Geneva: International Committee of the Red Cross, 1972, p. 9: "Article 60 – Death penalty. In no case shall the death penalty be pronounced on civilians who are under eighteen years at the time of the offence..." I.C.R.C. Doc. CE/COM III/PC 14.

[23]   *Ibid.*, p. 22:

Article 68. – Protection of children ... "3. The death penalty for an offence related to a situation referred to in Article 2 common to the [Geneva] Convention shall not be pronounced on persons who were under eighteen years at the time the offence was committed."

[24]   I.C.R.C. Doc. CDDH/407/Rev.1, para. 64

original text had stated that the death penalty could not be "pronounced", but this was changed to "executed".[25] The provision was adopted by consensus in Committee III[26] and in the plenary Conference.[27] According to the Commentary on article 77 (5) prepared by the International Committee of the Red Cross, "...it can be said that the death penalty for persons under eighteen years of age is ruled out completely",[28] at least with respect to international armed conflicts.

A similar norm appears in article 6 (4) of *Protocol Additional II*.[29] At the 1972 Conference of Government Experts, draft article 6 dealing with children was submitted in two versions, one stating "fifteen" and the other stating "eighteen".[30] The experts in the Drafting Committee, with the exception of the United States,[31] agreed upon eighteen.[32] Pakistan later opposed the provision, arguing that such a stipulation would encourage rebels to force juveniles to participate in armed conflicts.[33] However, it was subsequently adopted by consensus in the plenary session.[34] The importance of the provision is that it extends the protection of juvenile offenders to non-international armed conflicts.[35]

II. THE INTERNATIONAL COVENANT ON CIVIL AND POLITICAL RIGHTS

The *International Covenant on Civil and Political Rights*[36] admits the death penalty as an exception to the right to life, but subject to several important limitations.[37] Article 6 (5) prohibits capital punishment "for crimes committed by persons below eighteen years of age". Article 6 is deemed a non-derogable

---

[25] I.C.R.C. Doc. CDDH/III/SR.59, para.17-18.

[26] I.C.R.C. Doc. CDDH/III/SR.59, para. 18.

[27] I.C.R.C. Doc. CDDH/SR.43, para. 55.

[28] Claude Pilloud, Jean Pictet, "Article 77 - Protection of Children", in Yves Sandoz, Christophe Swinarksi, Bruno Zimmermann, *Commentary on the Additional Protocols of 8 June 1977 to the Geneva Conventions of 12 August 1949*, Geneva: Martinus Nijhoff, 1987, pp. 897-905, at p. 904.

[29] *Supra* note 3.

[30] *Supra* note 22, I, p. 77, para. 2.153. It had been submitted by the drafting committee.

[31] I.C.R.C. Doc. CE/COM II/26. *Ibid.* p. 76, para. 2.149.

[32] *Ibid*, para. 2.155-2.156.

[33] I.C.R.C. Doc. CDDH/I/SR.34, para. 19. This view was endorsed by Nigeria, which suggested the age limit be reduced to sixteen.

[34] I.C.R.C. Doc. CDDH/SR.50, para. 78.

[35] Defined in article 1 of the *Protocol*

[36] *Supra* note 3.

[37] *General Comment 6(16)*, U.N. Doc. CCPR/C/21/Add.1, also published as U.N. Doc. A/37/40, Annex V, U.N. Doc. CCPR/3/Add.1, at pp. 382-3. See: William A. Schabas, *The Abolition of the Death Penalty in International Law*, Cambridge: Cambridge University Press (Grotius Publications), 1993.

provision, and it may not be suspended by States parties even in time of emergency or war.[38]

The original drafts of the *Covenant* established no special rule in the case of juvenile offences. At the fifth session of the Commission on Human Rights in 1949, Egypt proposed prohibiting the death penalty for offenders under the age of seventeen years,[39] an amendment whose purpose was to ensure the readaptation and rehabilitation of juvenile offenders.[40] China opposed the Egyptian amendment, which it felt would "overload the articles of the draft covenant with details",[41] and these views were endorsed by the chair, Eleanor Roosevelt.[42] In the Third Committee, which examined the death penalty provisions of the *Covenant* during its 1957 session, Japan[43] and Guatemala[44] attempted to address this matter again. Japan said its amendment was aimed at protecting the lives of children and young persons, who already enjoyed special protection pursuant to the draft economic, social, and cultural rights covenant.[45] The pitfall of Guatemala's amendment was, said Japan, that it suggested that the death penalty could be imposed after attaining the age of majority.[46]

Canada[47] and New Zealand[48] objected to mention of the term "minors", because it would be too difficult to agree upon the age.[49] The United Kingdom suggested the term "children and young persons" because it was more flexible.[50] Others proposed the term "juveniles".[51] Finland argued for reference to persons under eighteen, as this was the age used in the fourth *Geneva Convention*.[52] Australia liked the precision of the term "persons below eighteen years of age",[53]

---

[38] *Supra* note 35, art. 4.

[39] U.N. Doc. E/CN.4/SR.149, 68. See also the comments of the Uruguayan delegate, U.N. Doc. E/CN.4/SR.139, para. 28.

[40] U.N. Doc. E/CN.4/SR.149, para. 77.

[41] *Ibid*, para. 83.

[42] *Ibid*, para. 86.

[43] U.N. Doc. A/C.3/L.655 and Corr. 1: "Sentence of death shall not be imposed for crimes committed by minors, and shall not be carried out on children and young persons or on a pregnant women."

[44] U.N. Doc. A/C.3/L.647: "Sentence of death shall not be carried out on minors or on a pregnant women." This amendment was later withdrawn: U.N. Doc. A/C.3/SR.816, para. 19.

[45] U.N. Doc. A/C.3/SR.814, para. 19.

[46] *Ibid.*

[47] *Ibid*, para. 42.

[48] *Ibid.*, para. 49.

[49] *Ibid.*, para. 42.

[50] U.N. Doc. A/C.3/SR.730-738.

[51] U.N. Doc. A/C.3/SR.817, para. 40 (Saudi Arabia); U.N. Doc. A/C.3/SR.818, para 23 (Philippines).

[52] U.N. Doc. A/C.3/SR.819, para. 10.

[53] U.N. Doc. A/C.3/SR.817, para. 33.

Although the Working Party attempted to reach a compromise, there was no agreement on the proper formulation, and it submitted three alternatives to replace the controversial term "children and young persons": "minors", "persons below eighteen years of age", and "juveniles". For no apparent reason, the chairman suggested that the Committee vote first on the phrase "persons below eighteen years of age",[54] which was adopted in a very close vote.[55] No vote was taken on the other options, and there is no way of knowing which of the three alternatives was the most popular.

The provision as adopted is clear and poses no real problem of interpretation.[56] The periodic reports to the Human Rights Committee indicate general compliance with the norm,[57] although there are occasional examples of violation, where the age of majority is below eighteen years[58] or where there is no provision at all.[59] For example, the Cyprus Criminal Code sets a limit of sixteen years, but its representative told the Committee that the provision would be declared inoperative in view of its conflict with article 6 (5) of the *Covenant*.[60] Several states will not sentence a minor to death, leaving open the possibility of an individual over eighteen being sentenced for a crime committed while still a minor.[61] Sometimes, lengthy prison sentences are imposed

---

[54] U.N. Doc. A/C.3/SR.820, para. 19.

[55] *Ibid.* para. 21, by twenty one votes to nineteen, with twenty eight abstentions.

[56] In a Jamaican case, *Baker* v. *The Queen*, [1975] 3 W.L.R. 113, [1976] Crim.L.R. 49 (J.C.P.C.), domestic law providing that no sentence of death could be pronounced or imposed on a person under eighteen. Baker had committed a capital crime while under eighteen but was sentenced when over eighteen. On appeal to the Judicial Committee of the Privy Council, his argument that this violated the Constitution, which guaranteed him the right to the less severe penalty, was rejected.

[57] "Initial Report of Mongolia", U.N. Doc. CCPR/C/1/Add.38; "Initial Report of Morocco", U.N. Doc. CCPR/C/10/Add.10; "Initial Report of Japan", U.N. Doc. CCPR/C/10/Add.1; "Initial Report of Czechoslovakia", U.N. Doc. CCPR/C/1/Add.12; "Initial Report of the Byelorussian Soviet Socialist Republic", U.N. Doc. CCPR/C/1/Add.273; "Initial Report of Bulgaria", U.N. Doc. CCPR/C/SR.131, para. 30.

[58] "Initial Report of Morocco", *Ibid.*, sixteen years; Morocco was criticized in this respect by Bouziri, U.N. Doc. CCPR/C/SR.327, para. 8, Aguilar, U.N. Doc. CCPR/C/SR.327, 29, and Evans, U.N. Doc. CCPR/C/SR.328, para. 22. Also "Initial Report of Jordan", U.N. Doc. CCPR/C/1/Add. 56, where the age is unspecified; "Additional Supplementary Report of Jordan", U.N. Doc. CCPR/C/1/Add. 56, fifteen years; "Second Periodic Report of Iraq", U.N. Doc. CCPR/C/46/Add.4, sixteen years.

[59] "Initial Report of Canada", U.N. Doc. CCPR/C/1/Add.43, U.N. Doc. CCPR/C/SR.202, para. 6; "Initial Report of Saint Vincent and the Grenadines", U.N. Doc. CCPR/C/26/Add.4, U.N. Doc. CCPR/C/SR.953-954, U.N. Doc. A/45/40, para. 249, 266.

[60] U.N. Doc. CCPR/C/SR.166, para. 8; also U.N. Doc. CCPR/C/SR.166, para. 46.

[61] "Initial Report of Madagascar", U.N. Doc. CCPR/C/1/Add.14,; "Initial Report of Chile", U.N. Doc. CCPR/C/1/Add.25; "Initial Report of Jamaica", U.N. Doc. CCPR/C/1/Add.53; "Initial Report of Iraq", U.N. Doc. CCPR/C/1/Add.45; "Third Periodic Report of the Union of Soviet Socialist Republics", U.N. Doc. CCPR/C/52/Add.2 and 6.

as an alternative, a measure that lacks the horror of the death sentence but does little to further the principle of mitigated criminal liability.[62]

The United States of America ratified the *Covenant*, effective September 8, 1992, with a reservation to the capital punishment provisions of article 6.[63] Eleven European states have objected to the reservation.[64] Germany cites specifically the issue of juvenile executions: "The reservation referring to this provision is incompatible with the text as well as the object and purpose of article 6". Denmark's objection states that the reservation with respect to juvenile offenders constitutes a "general derogation" from the *Covenant*, which is prohibited by article 4 (2). France's objection states that the reservation respecting juvenile offenders "is not valid, inasmuch as it is incompatible with the object and purpose of the Convention". Similar statements appear in the objections of Italy, Portugal and Spain.

Although the right to life provision is non-derogable, reservations to specific elements of it have been made in the past without any objection, suggesting that states will tolerate minor reservations even to such fundamental norms.[65] Norway ratified the *Covenant* in 1972 with a reservation to article 6 (4), which deals with amnesty and pardon,[66] and which it later withdrew.[67] Ireland ratified the Covenant with a reservation to article 6 (5) that suggested its legislation was inconsistent with the *Covenant*. However, the reservation indicated that in practice the Irish government would take into account its obligations under the *Covenant*.[68] The Inter-American Court of Human Rights has also upheld the notion that reservations to discrete portions of non-derogable human rights norms may be acceptable, provide they do

---

[62] "Third Periodic Report of Senegal", U.N. Doc. CCPR/C/64/Add.5, para. 34, a sentence of ten to twenty years; U.N. Doc. CCPR/C/SR.289, para. 27 (Mali), twenty years; "Initial Report of Algeria", U.N. Doc. CCPR/C/62/Add.1, 80, a sentence of ten to twenty years; "Initial Report of Togo", U.N. Doc. CCPR/C/36/Add.5, ten years; "Initial Report of Libyan Arab Jamahiriya", U.N. Doc. CCPR/C/1/Add.3*, U.N. Doc. CCPR/C/1/Add.20, a sentence of not less than five years; "Supplementary Report of Denmark", U.N.Doc. CCPR/C/1/Add.19, life imprisonment (for military offences); "Initial Report of Democratic Yemen", U.N. Doc. CCPR/C/50/Add.2, three to ten years.

[63] United States, "Senate Committee on Foreign Relations Report on the International Covenant on Civil and Political Rights", (1992) 31 I.L.M. 645, p. 653, 14 *H.R.L.J* 77: "The United States reserves the right, subject to its Constitutional constraints, to impose capital punishment on any person (other than a pregnant woman) duly convicted under existing or future laws permitting the imposition of capital punishment, including such punishment for crimes committed by persons below eighteen years of age."

[64] Finland, Netherlands, Germany, Denmark, France, Norway, Belgium, Italy, Portugal, Spain.

[65] However, Belgium has suggested, in its objection to the reservation by the Congo to article 11 (imprisonment for debt), that any reservation to a non-derogable provision is illegal. The same view appears to be shared by Denmark, Norway, Spain, Portugal and Italy in their objections to the reservations made by the United States to articles 6 and 7 of the *Covenant*.

[66] (1976) 999 U.N.T.S. 297.

[67] U.N. Doc. CPR/C/2/Add.4.

[68] U.N. Doc. ST/LEG/SER.E/9, at p. 134.

not "depriv[e] the right as a whole of its basic purpose".[69] In its recent *General Comment* on reservations, the Human Rights Committee also recognizes that reservations to non-derogeable provisions are not *prima facie* inadmissible.[70]

Because of its broad scope, the United States reservation to article 6 of the Covenant is not one of these limited exceptions. The effect of the reservation is to deprive article 6 of its "basic purpose".[71] The objecting states have suggested that the United States remains a party to the *Covenant*, with the result that it is bound by article 6 (5) and may not execute individuals for crimes committed while under the age of eighteen.[72]

The controversial reservation will be examined by the Human Rights Committee at its New York session in late March, 1995. The Committee, in its *General Comment* on reservations has declared that it is prepared to rule on the legality of reservations during presentation of periodic reports. The *General Comment* implies that the reservation by the United States to article 6 (5) of the *Covenant*, with respect to the execution of individuals for crimes committed while under the age of eighteen, is illegal because it violates a customary norm. The *General Comment* could have been more explicit, for it refers only to a prohibition "to execute pregnant women or children", whereas article 6 (5) of the *Covenant* speaks of "crimes committed by persons below eighteen years of age".[73] The *Convention on the Rights of the Child* defines a "child", which is the term used in the Human Rights Committee's *General Comment*, as a person under eighteen.[74]

III. The Safeguards and the Beijing Rules

The "Safeguards Guaranteeing Protection of the Rights of those Facing the Death Penalty" were an outgrowth of the Sixth United Nations Congress on the Prevention of Crime and Treatment of Offenders, held in Caracas, in 1980. The Congress had failed to adopt a resolution on the issue of capital punishment that expressed the goal of "further restriction in the application of capital punishment".[75] In 1982 the Committee on Crime Prevention and Control prepared a series of draft "safeguards" that were to be respected where

---

[69] *Restrictions to the Death Penalty (Arts. 4 (2) and 4 (4) American Convention on Human Rights)*, Advisory Opinion OC-3/83, Series A, No. 3, at p. 61.

[70] *General Comment No. 24(52)*, U.N. Doc. CCPR/C/21/Rev.1/Add.6, para. 12.

[71] See William A. Schabas,"Les réserves des États-Unis d'Amérique aux articles 6 et 7 du Pacte international relatif aux droits civils et politiques", (1994) 6 *R.U.D.H.* 137.

[72] This is the only logical consequence of the European objections. it would be absurd to interpret these statements as meaning that the United States is bound by the *Covenant* except for the reserved provisions, because this is exactly the result that the United States has sought.

[73] *General Comment. 24(52)*, *supra* note 70, para. 8.

[74] *Supra* note 2, art. 1.

[75] U.N. Doc. A/CONF.87/C.1/L.1.

the death penalty was being imposed,[76] including the prohibition on execution for crimes committed while under the age of eighteen. The Committee adopted the "Safeguards Guaranteeing Protection of the Rights of those Facing the Death Penalty" at its March, 1984 session, proposing they be entrenched in an Economic and Social Council resolution.[77] The final version of article 3 stated that "persons below 18 years of age at the time of the commission of the crime shall not be sentenced to death".[78] The provision takes article 6 (5) of the *Covenant* a small step further, in that under the Safeguards, individuals may not even be sentenced to death for crimes committed while under the age of eighteen. The "Safeguards" were subsequently endorsed by the General Assembly[79] and by the Seventh United Nations Congress on the Prevention of Crime and the Treatment of Offenders, held in Milan in 1985.[80]

The "Beijing Rules", or "Draft United Nations Standard Minimum Rules for the Administration of Juvenile Justice", were adopted by the Interregional Preparatory Meeting of the 1985 Congress on the Prevention of Crime and the Treatment of Offenders, held at Beijing in May, 1984.[81] Article 17.2 of the "Beijing Rules" says "Capital punishment shall not be imposed for any crime committed by juveniles". The Commentary at the Congress adds: "The provision prohibiting capital punishment in rule 17.2 is in accordance with article 6, paragraph 5 of the International Covenant on Civil and Political Rights".[82] This is not quite accurate, because the term "juvenile" is defined as "a child or young person who, under the respective legal systems, may be dealt with for an offence in a manner which is diferent from an adult" (art. 2.2(a)), and the commentary adds that "juvenile" can encompass a wide range of ages, from seven years to eighteen years or above. The draft rules were studied by Committee II[83] and adopted by the Plenary Congress.[84]

IV. THE CONVENTION ON THE RIGHTS OF THE CHILD

The prohibition on execution of individuals for crimes committed while under the age of eighteen was reiterated in the *Convention on the Rights of the*

---

[76] U.N. Doc. E/CN.5/1983/2, chap. I, sect. A, para. 1, draft resolution I; also chap. V, 174.

[77] "Draft resolution VII", U.N. Doc. E/1984/16, U.N. Doc. E/AC.57/1984/18.

[78] U.N. Doc. E/1984/16, U.N. Doc. E/AC.57/1984/18. No summary records are kept of the sessions of the Committee.

[79] G.A. Res. 39/118, U.N. Doc. A/PV.101, para. 79, without a vote.

[80] U.N. Doc. A/CONF.121/22/Rev.1, pp. 83-84, 131-132. See also: U.N. Doc. E/AC.57/1988/9 and Corr.2.

[81] U.N. Doc. A/CONF.121/IPM/1, para. 55-56

[82] U.N. Doc. A/CONF.121/22/Rev.1, p. 34.

[83] U.N. Doc. A/CONF.121/C.2/L.1, sponsored by Australia, Botswana, China and India; U.N. Doc. A/CONF.121/C.2/CRP.1.

[84] U.N. Doc. A/CONF.121/22/Rev.1, 320, U.N. Doc. A/CONF.121/14.

Child.[85] A 1980 Working Party text included a rather summary provision dealing with criminal procedure, which specified that a child not be liable to capital punishment, and that "[a]ny other punishment shall be adequate to the particular phase of his development".[86] In 1985, Canada proposed the addition of a detailed provision guaranteeing the rights of a child upon being accused or convicted of a criminal offence.[87] Canada's text included a statement that no child could be sentenced to death. At the time, a "child" was defined in the draft *Convention* as being a person under eighteen, "unless, under the law of his State, he has attained his age of majority earlier".[88] The next year, Canada revised its proposal, rephrasing the provision and making a cross reference to article 6 (5) of the *Covenant*.[89] A competing Polish text stated that "no child shall be...sentenced to death".[90]

An informal Working Party formulated a text that prohibited capital punishment "for crimes committed by persons below eighteen years of age", removing any possible ambiguity relating to the definition of the term "child" and making the provision consistent with the *Covenant*.[91] The United States's representative objected to the draft paragraph, stating that reference to "persons below eighteen years of age" was too arbitrary, and proposed its deletion. The United States said that it did not consider the eighteen-year age limit to be "an appropriate general rule", but added that it would not insist upon an amendment which would block consensus, providing it be understood that the United States maintained its right to make a reservation on this point.[92] Amnesty International and the International Commission of Jurists opposed the United States on this point.[93]

In the 1986 Working Group, the Japanese representative questioned the phrase "or life imprisonment" and proposed its deletion.[94] According to the Working Group report, Canada sought to "accomodate" the Japanese position and suggested adding the words "without possibility of release" after the words "life imprisonment".[95] The Report indicates that the United Kingdom placed on record its reservation to the provision, but does not suggest why; presumably, the United Kingdom was troubled by the life imprisonment pro-

---

[85] *Supra* note 2.

[86] U.N. Doc. E/CN.4/1349*, article 20 (2).

[87] U.N. Doc. E/CN.4/1985/64, Annex II, p. 4.

[88] U.N. Doc. E/CN.4/1985/64, Annex I, p. 2.

[89] U.N. Doc. E/CN.4/1986/39, para. 90.

[90] U.N. Doc. A/C.3/40/3, para. 2.

[91] *Ibid.*, 93. The text read: "The following sentences shall not be imposed for crimes committed by persons below eighteen years of age: (a) capital punishment; (b) life imprisonment."

[92] *Ibid*, para. 105, 107. The United States made such a statement concerning the draft provision on more than one occasion. See, for example: U.N. Doc. E/CN.4/1989/48, 544.

[93] *Ibid*, para. 105.

[94] *Ibid.*, para. 104.

[95] *Ibid.*

vision, which is inconsistent with its legisation.[96] Eventually, the Working Group adopted the following text: "Capital punishment or life imprisonment without possibility of release is not imposed for crimes committed by persons below eighteen years of age".[97] The article was reviewed in a special Working Party session in late 1988. Besides the Working Group text, the Working Party had another version proposed by the Crime, Prevention and Criminal Justice Branch of the Centre for Social Development and Humanitarian Affairs, United Nations Office at Vienna, which revived the blanket prohibition on both capital punishment and life imprisonment: "The death penalty or a term of life imprisonment is not imposed for offences committed by children below 18 years of age."[98] A drafting group attempted to devise a compromise, but eventually submitted a text in which the reference to "without possibility of release" was square-bracketted.[99] During debate on the point, Austria, the Federal Republic of Germany, Senegal and Venezuela urged that the phrase "without possibility of release" be deleted, while China, India, Japan, Norway, the U.S.S.R. and the U.S.A. took the contrary position.[100] A suggestion that compromise be sought by simply removing any reference to life imprisonment, leaving the prohibition on the death penalty to stand alone, was opposed by Senegal, which said its omission would leave judges "at liberty to use life imprisonment as a substitute for capital punishment".[101] Eventually, those states that had fought to delete the square-bracketted reference to possibility of release withdrew their insistence, "[i]n a spirit of compromise".[102] The Working Party draft[103] was adopted by the Commission on Human Rights by consensus,[104] by the Third Committee in an unrecorded vote,[105] and ultimately by the General Assembly.[106]

Reservations are specifically permitted to the *Convention on the Rights of the Child*, providing they are not contrary to the "object and purpose" of the treaty.[107] Myanmar is the only state to have formulated a reservation to article 37a), but it was withdrawn after several oppositions were formulated.[108]

The unfortunate compromise in article 37a) allows for the possibility that children will be sentenced to life imprisonment and never released. Although

---

[96]   *Ibid*, para. 107.

[97]   *Ibid.*, para. 106. See also: U.N. Doc. E/CN.4/1988/WG.1/WP.1/Rev.2.

[98]   U.N. Doc. E/CN.4/1989/WG.1/WP.2.

[99]   U.N. Doc. E/CN.4/1989/WG.1/WP.67/Rev.1.

[100]   U.N. Doc. E/CN.4/1989/48, para. 541.

[101]   *Ibid*, para. 542.

[102]   *Ibid.*, para. 543.

[103]   U.N. Doc. E/CN.4/1989/48/Rev.1, p. 15.

[104]   U.N. Doc. E/CN.4/1989/L.88. The debates are found at U.N. Doc. E/CN.4/1989/SR.54, U.N. Doc. E/CN.4/1989/SR.55, U.N. Doc. E/CN.4/1989/SR.55/Add.1.

[105]   U.N. Doc. A/C.3/SR.44, 63, U.N. Doc. A/C.3/44/L.44.

[106]   U.N. Doc. A/44/PV.61, as G.A. Res. 44/25.

[107]   *Supra* note 2, art. 51.

[108]   Multilateral Treaties, U.N. Doc. ST/LEG/SER.E/10 (1993), p. 203.

the text speaks about the "possibility of release", this may well be subject to severe restrictions and even arbitrary discretionary authority. Such is the case in the United Kingdom, where individuals well into adulthood continue to serve life sentences for crimes committed while adolescents. They are sentenced to detention "at her Majesty's pleasure", which means that periodic review of such indefinite detention is undertaken on a purely discretionary basis. Two cases from the United Kingdom dealing with this situation recently came before the European Commission on Human Rights. The petitioners challenged the absence of a right of judicial review, and the Commission held that this constituted a violation of article 5 (4) of the *European Convention of Human Rights*. The Commission has decided to submit these cases to the European Court of Human Rights.[109]

The importance of the norm concerning execution of juvenile offenders in the *Convention on the Rights of the Child* cannot be underestimated. Of the nine states that have conducted such executions since 1980, Barbados, Iraq, Nigeria, Pakistan, Bangladesh and Yemen have ratified the *Convention* without reservation to article 37a), leaving only the United States, Saudi Arabia and Iran. The issue has arisen infrequently before the Committee on the Rights of the Child. In presentation of periodic reports, several states simply remind the Committee that they have abolished the death penalty.[110] Others note that their domestic legislation complies the Convention.[111] Some have stated that their legislation does not permit executions of "juveniles", but without providing details[112] The only suggestion of non-compliance is in Sudan's initial report, which declares "with the exception of offences punishable by penalties and sanctions, the death penalty may not be imposed on a person under the age of 18 or over the age of 70. A juvenile delinquent may be sentenced to death only for an offence punishable by penalties and sanctions, in accordance with provisions of Islamic law".[113] During discussion of the report, the issue of juvenile executions was not even raised by the Committee,[114] although it did express "its concern as to the issues of criminal responsibility".[115] With respect to the Egyptian initial report, which is silent on subject of juvenile executions,[116] the Committee said "[c]oncern is expressed, in general, as to

---

[109] *Hussain* v. *United Kingdom* (App. 21928/93), *Singh* v. *United Kingdom* (App. 23389/94) (unreported).

[110] "Initial report of Namibia", U.N. Doc. CRC/C/3/Add.12, para. 454; "Initial report of Sweden", U.N. Doc. CRC/C/3/Add.1, para. 83; "Initial report of El Salvador", U.N. Doc. CRC/C/3/Add.9, para. 194; "Initial report of Bolivia", U.N. Doc. CRC/C/3/Add.2, para. 92.

[111] "Initial report of the Russian Federation", U.N. Doc. CRC/C/3/Add.5, para. 162.

[112] "Initial report of Indonesia", U.N. Doc. CRC/C/3/Add.10, 107; "Initial report of Viet Nam", U.N. Doc. CRC/C/3/Add.4, para. 228.

[113] "Initial report of Sudan", U.N. Doc. CRC/C/3/Add.4, para. 228.

[114] U.N. Doc. CRC/C/SR.70, para. 42-48.

[115] "Preliminary Observations of the Committee on the Rights of the Child: Sudan", U.N. Doc. CRC/C/15/Add.6, 11; also U.N. Doc. CRC/C/16, para. 120.

[116] "Initial report of Egypt", U.N. Doc. CRC/C/3/Add.6.

the compatibility with articles 37 and 40 of the Convention of the juvenile justice institutions and the administration of justice system in so far as it relates to juvenile justice".[117]

<h2 style="text-align:center">V. The Juvenile Death Penalty in the Regional Human Rights Systems</h2>

The norm prohibiting juvenile executions is far less significant in the regional human rights systems. The *African Charter of Human and Peoples' Rights*, adopted in 1981 by the Organization of African Unity, makes no mention of the death penalty whatosever, although it does provide for a right to life, for a protection against inhuman treatment, and for procedural safeguards in criminal proceedings.[118] *The European Convention on Human Rights* enshrines the right to life, but also admits its major exception, the death penalty, and without any form of limitation or restriction. Practice has overstepped the *Convention*, and no death sentence has been imposed in a State party to the Convention for more than ten years (Turkey is the last recorded case). Furthermore, most parties to the *European Convention* are now bound by an additional protocol which outlaws the death penalty altogether in peacetime.[119] The Strasbourg organs have considered the issue of youth with respect to the death penalty in the *Soering* case.[120] In support of its position that prolonged detention on "death row" would violate article 3, the Court cited certain personal factors, including Soering's youth. Whether such a mitigating factor was merely obiter or a decisive factor in the Court's decision remains a matter of debate, and both domestic and international tribunals have divided views on this question.[121]

The *American Convention on Human Rights*[122] echoes the provision on juvenile executions found in the *International Covenant on Civil and Political Rights*. During the final stage of drafting, at the San Jose Conference in 1969, the United States urged deletion of the provision because it said "the proscription of capital punishment within arbitrary age limits presents

---

[117] "Preliminary Observations of the Committee on the Rights of the Child: Egypt", U.N. Doc. CRC/C/15/Add.5, para. 8; also U.N. Doc. CRC/C/16, para. 100.

[118] *African Charter on Human and People's Rights,* O.A.U. Doc. CAB/LEG/67/3 rev. 5.

[119] *Protocol No. 6 to the Convention for the Protection of Human Rights and Fundamental Freedoms Concerning the Abolition of the Death Penalty,* E.T.S. no. 114.

[120] *Soering* v. *United Kingdom and Germany*, Series A, Vol. 161, 11 E.H.R.R. 439, 11 *H.R.L.J.* 335.

[121] *Pratt et al* v. *Attorney General for Jamaica et al.*, [1993] 4 All.E.R. 769 (P.C.), 14 *H.R.L.J.* 338; *Kindler* v. *Canada* (no. 470/1991), U.N. Doc. CCPR/C/48/D/470/1991, 14 H.R.L.J. 307; *Catholic Commission for Justice and Peace in Zimbabwe* v. *Attorney-General et al.*, (1993) 1 Z.L.R. 242 (S), 14 *H.R.L.J.* 323; *Dame Joy Davis-Aylor*, C.E., req. no 144590, 15/10/93, D. 1993, IR, 238; J.C.P. 1993, Actualités no 43, [1993] *Revue française de droit administratif* 1166, conclusions C. Vigoreux.

[122] *Supra* note 3.

various difficulties in law". However, the United States couched its proposal in abolitionist terms, noting that such a provision weakened the text, given "the general trend, already apparent, for the gradual abolition of the death penalty".[123] The United States delegate subsequently withdrew this proposal during debate in Committee I.[124] Thus, the United States did not "object" to the norm prohibiting capital punishment for crimes committed under age eighteen. It subsequently signed the *Convention*, although it has yet ratified.

Barbados made a reservation to the *Convention* stating that "while the youth or old age of an offender may be matters which the Privy Council, the highest Court of Appeal, might take into account in considering whether the sentence of death should be carried out, persons of 16 years and over [...] may be executed under Barbadian law.".[125] No objections have been made to this reservation, tending to confirm the view of the Inter-American Court of Human Rights that reservations of this nature are not incompatible with the object and purpose of the *Convention*.[126]

The issue of juvenile executions has arisen within the Inter-American system under the regime of the *American Declaration of Human Rights* Subsequent to imposition of a death sentence, two American boys argued before the Inter-American Commission on Human Rights that article I of the *American Declaration*, which states laconically that "Every human being has the right to life...", constitutes a prohibition on executions for crimes committed while under the age of eighteen. They suggested that the instrument contained certain implied limits, including a prohibition on execution for crimes committed while under eighteen, if analysed in light of customary international law.[127] Referring to article 4 (5) of the *American Convention on Human Rights*, article 6 (5) of the *International Covenant on Civil and*

---

[123] O.A.S. Doc. OEA/Ser.K/XVI/1.1 Doc. 10 (Eng.), p. 9.

[124] O.A.S. Doc. OEA/Ser.K/XVI/1.1 Doc. 40 Corr. 1, p. 170. In *Roach and Pinkerton* v. *United States*, *supra* note 19, the United States contended that "the United States delegate at the drafting of the *American Convention* pointed out that the United States had problems with article 4 (5)'s arbitrary age limit of eighteen conflicting with its federal structure" (at 38(f)).

[125] O.A.S. Doc. OEA/Ser.L.V/II.71, Doc.6 rev. 1, at p. 58, (1983) 1298 U.N.T.S. 441.

[126] *Supra* note 70.

[127] See: Dinah Shelton, *supra* note 20; Dinah Shelton, "The Prohibition of Juvenile Executions in International Law", (1987) 58 *Revue internationale de droit pénal* 773; David Weissbrodt, "Execution of Juvenile Offenders by the United States Violates International Human Rights Law", (1988) 3 *American University Journal of International Law and Policy* 339; "Too Young to Die: International Law and the Imposition of the Juvenile Death Penalty in the United States", (1991) 5 *Emory International Law Review* 617; "The Execution of Juvenile Offenders: Constitutional and International Law Objections", (1991) 60 *University of Missouri at Kansas City Law Review* 113; "Thompson v. Oklahoma: The Role of International Law in Juvenile Death Penalty Litigation", (1989) 8 *Wisconsin International Law Journal* 165. See also, the reply to Professor Weissbrodt's criticism of the Inter-American Commission's report in Roach and Pinkerton by a lawyer for the Commission: Christina M. Cerna, "U.S. Death Penalty Tested Before the Inter-American Commission on Human Rights", (1992) 10 *N.Q.H.R* 155.

Political Rights, and article 68 (4) of the fourth *Geneva Convention*, they claimed that the travaux préparatoires of these provisions indicated they were norms of customary international law.[128]

The Commission concluded that it was convinced by the United States government's argument that there is no norm of customary international law establishing eighteen to be the minimum age for imposition of the death penalty.[129] In light of the widespread ratification of the *American Convention* and the *Civil Rights Covenant*, as well as state practice the Commission declared that such a norm was "emerging".[130] But it said that even if a customary norm did exist, it would not bind a state which had protested the norm.[131] With respect to the age of eighteen, the Commission noted that the United States had protested the creation of such a norm during the negotiation of various bilateral treaties, and that it had proposed to ratify the *American Convention on Human Rights* with a reservation to article 4 (5).[132]

The Commission recognized that there was a norm within the Member states of the Organization of American States, a norm that it went so far as to qualify as *jus cogens*, within the meaning of article 53 of the *Vienna Convention on the Law of Treaties*.[133] This norm prohibited execution of juveniles, but the Commission fixed the cutoff at some unspecified age below eighteen.[134] The Commission said it was "shocked" at Indiana's statute, which theoretically permitted a ten-year-old to be executed, but did not suggest at what point between ten and eighteen its shock would diminish to a threshold of tolerance.[135] It seems almost paradoxical to contend that a norm can be both so peremptory as to be qualified as *jus cogens* and at the same time to be so unclear as to be incapable of formulation!

CONCLUSION

This overview of comparative and international legal norms indicates that the prohibition on execution for crimes committed while under eighteen is a nearly universal norm. It highlights the value of international norms, because domestic legislation and practice is far from satisfactory. In some cases, States have openly declared that their own laws are inadequate, but that the international prohibition is hierarchically superior. Therefore, all but a handful of states are now bound by the prohibition on juvenile executions.

---

[128]   *Roach and Pinkerton* v. *United States*, *supra* note 19, at p. 37.
[129]   *Ibid*, para. 60.
[130]   *Ibid*, para. 60.
[131]   *Ibid.*, para. 52.
[132]   *Ibid*, para. 53. However, the United States had signed the *Convention* without any reservation.
[133]   *Ibid.*, para. 55-56.
[134]   *Ibid*, para. 57.
[135]   *Ibid.*, para. 58.

Considerable effort has been devoted by scholars to demonstrating that the norm is also customary. For international custom to bind states, both practice and opinio juris must coincide. Easy to demonstrate with respect to the growing number of States that accept the conventional norm,[136], it is harder to make the case for the United States and the others that continue to execute juveniles. Yet the issue is not without interest: the reservation by the United States to article 6 (5) of the *Covenant* is invalid if contrary to a customary norm.[137]

Theodore Meron has noted that "the invocation of a norm as both conventional and customary adds at least rhetorical strength to the moral claim for its observance and affects its interpretation".[138] Professor Meron speaks of a "tendency to ignore, for the most part, the availability of evidence of state practice (scant as it may have been) and to assume that noble humanitarian principles that deserve recognition as the positive law of the international community ahve in fact been recognied as such by states. The 'ought' merges with the 'is', the *lex ferenda* with the *lex lata*."[139]

Although eleven States objected to the United States reservation on the death penalty provisions of the *International Covenant*, nearly 120 did not. If a customary norm were being violated, would so many have remained silent? A more fruitful line of inquiry and action, in our view, is in demonstrating the illegality of the reservation from the standpoint of treaty law, with the consequence that the United States is in fact bound by article 6 (5) of the *Covenant*.

---

[136] R. Baxter, "Multilateral Treaties as Evidence of Customary International Law", (1965) *B.Y.I.L* 275.

[137] *North Sea Continental Shelf Cases (FRG/Denmark; FRG/Netherlands)*, [1969] I.C.J. Reports 198 (*per* judge Morelli).

[138] Theodor Meron, "The Geneva Conventions as Customary Law", (1987) 81 *A.J.I.L.* 348, at p. 350.

[139] *Ibid*, at p. 361.

R.N. TRIVEDI

Role of National Courts in Protecting Children's Rights

There is scepticism about what "monitoring" signifies in terms of children's rights.

It can not just mean collection, evaluation and submission of statistical data. For it were so, country after country, especially in the third world could cite as defense, lack of resources as the sole reason for not being able to ensure the full compliance of the rights.

It would appear that monitoring does not only convey accountability but also the proper apportionment and effective utilisation of the allocable resources. It also conveys creation of appropriate political and socio economic conditions, and empowerement of institutions involved in protection, preservation and promotion on the rights of the child.

Such empowerment has not only to be by positive measures e.g. legislation but ingenious empowerement by the institutions themselves by not letting its efforts and expectations being eroded and look beyond and reach out.

It also means accountability at all levels, including that of political will.

It is in this background that one has to construe some of the issues relating to the role of national courts in protecting children's rights.

I. ACTIVISM IN FILLING GAPS IN LEGISLATION

Although legislation itself is not sufficient to protect any rights, a legislative measure is the recogniton of a problem which requires to be remedied. Standard setting thus is the first important step towards alleviating wrong.

What happens when legislatures fail to enact a legislation or are compelled by extraneous factors to abandon steps towards legislating.

An important issue relating to children's rights is regulating inter-country adoption. Despite international covenants in that regard, in absence of such measures being included in the municipal law, it does not become enforeceable. The adoption of Children Bill, 1972 was introduced in the Upper House of Parliament in India, but was later dropped, presumably because of the opposition of Muslims that it was a step towards making uniform law for all

E. Verhellen (ed.), Monitoring Children's Rights, 621–625.
© 1996 *Kluwer Law International. Printed in the Netherlands.*

communities including Muslims. Another attempt was made in 1980 when Adoption of the Children Bill, 1980 was introduced in the Lower House of the Parliament containing a specific provision that it shall not be applicable to Muslims. However, it has not yet become law.

The Supreme Court of India in a landmark decision in Lakshmikant Pandey Versus Union of India A.I.R. (1984SC 469) has laid down detailed procedure relating to inter-country adoption. This is a classic case of judicial activism in filling gaps in legislation. The Courts in India have stepped in many areas where legislation is wanting. The legislatures may have political compulsions in being dissuaded from making legislations, the Courts, however, have not such compulsions except to uphold the Constitution. It is hoped that such activism would be displayed by other countries especially in the third world.

The Supreme Court of India went a step further in Sheela Barse Vs. Secretary Children Aid Society and Others [(1987) 3 SCC P.15] to observe that under the provisions of the Convention on the Rights of the Child adopted by the General Assembly of the U.N. to which India was a party it is obligatory for the Government of India as also the State machinery to implement the same in a proper way.

There is need for converting soft law into Hard Law.

II.   Socio-economic Causes of Acceptance of Violation of Existing Laws and Sensitivity of Personnel

It is trite that no legislation can operate either in vacuum or in absence of an environment conducive for its implementation. There is widespread acceptance of violation of laws protecting the interests of children due to socio-economic causes.

A.   *Employment of Children*

The non-enforcement of laws regulating, prohibiting or preventing child labour is accepted in the name of poverty.

The Supreme Court of India in the case of PUDR Vs. Union of India A.I.R. *1982 SC 1473* has laid down that prohibition against employment of children below 14 years in hazardous jobs could be imposed even in the absence of special legislation.

Sivkasi, in the Southern State of Tamilnadu in India has been the traditional centre for manufacture of match boxes and fireworks, employing large number of children. The factories with inadequate or no safety measures not infrequently are subjected to hazards of fire in which among others children are injured or killed. In the case of M.C. Mehta Vs. State of Tamil Nadu *(1991) 1 SCC 283*, the Supreme Court of India dealing with the problem, held that the children should not be employed in the manufacturing process but only in the process of packing and their wages should be 60% of the prescribed minimum of an adult. The Court further directed the State to improve the quality of life of such children.

Even in cases of selectively safe imployment areas for children, wages paid, dispute longer hours and greater productivity does not match with those given to adults for the same work. This, despite the state machinery in fixing minimum wages and charged with the obligation to enforce it.

According to some, child labour is the result of policy choices and thus change can be brought about by policy considerations.

B. Children in Custody

The custodial predicament of children is a sad story of executive non account-ability and near total desensitization of the personnel. There are innumerable instances of abandoned children, picked up from railway stations and kept in jail without trial, sometimes such a period exceeds the maximum period of conviction.

The Supreme Court of India after the political upheaval of 1984 following the taking over of the Sikh Holy Shrine (Golden Temple) at Amritsar, by the Indian Army had to deal with the arrest and continued detention of children who had gone as devotees or pilgrims, for alleged breach of peace. In a decision reported in Kamladevi Chattopadhya Vs. State of Punjab and another *(1985) 1 SCC 4* it directed the release of children, having found that there was no justification for their detention. The Supreme Court again in the case of Supreme Court Legal Aid Committee Vs. Union of India *(1989) 2 SCC 385* dealing with the question of Juvenile delinquents in jail, after having considered the lackadaisical efforts of the State Machinery, directed preparation of a scheme for monitoring the situation of juvenile delinquents.

Even in the jail instances of the abuse of the children by putting them to work without payment or sexual exploitation are not rare. This acceptance of the lot of the children cannot always be due to socio-economic causes but because of lack of humane treatment, understanding and compassion on the part of personnel responsible for their welfare. Instead of being given special attention because children cannot articulate and are not possessed of physical and intellectual capacity they are vulnerable and are treated as nobody's constituency. The Courts have intervened in such situations.

C. Education

Education, the lack of which to a great extent is responsible for perpetuation of poverty does not appear to have been treated with the priority which it deserves. Despite the constitutional obligation (Article 45) that the state shall endeavour to provide within a period of ten years from the commencement of Constitution (i.e. by 1960) for free and compulsory education to all children till they attain the age of 14, the literacy figure is anything but heartening. Today we have reached a state, if press reports are to be believed, that India has the distinction of having the largest population of Adult illiterates. The Central Education Advisory Board in 1986 allegedly during tea break at its conference decided to recommend that the constitutional mandate which had to be completed by 1960 should now be completed by 1995. Education should be given strategic priority as uprooting poverty should be preceeded by eradication of ignorance.

Article 28 of the Convention on the Rights of the Child, 1989 acknowledges every child's right to basic education. Something which is already there in the Indian Constitution (Art. 45), but the policy makers have to become sensitive to the continuous damage which is being caused to the development of the citizens of tomorrow. One should realise that education means knowledge and knowledge itself is power. As observed by John Adams "The preservation of means of knowledge among the lowest ranks is of more importance to public than all the property of all the rich men in the country". (Desertation on Canon and Feudal Law – 1765). The Supreme Court of India in the case of Unnikrishnan Versus State of A.P. *(1993) 1 SCC 645* expressed its dismay on the fact that even after 44 years of the Constitution the obligation under Article 45 has not been discharged by the State and was constrained to observe that allocation of available funds to different sectors of education in India discloses an inversion of priority indicated by the Constitution, and ultimately held that Child (Citizen) has a fundamental right of free education upto the age of 14 years.

It will be seen from the above that the Supreme Court has intervened in areas which normally should have been the exclusive domain of the legislature/executive, and exceptions apart (of the executive), has intervened in areas conservatively not falling strictly in the normal judicatory role of the courts.

D. Juveniles

In respect of neglected juveniles the power of police to take into charge is coupled with a social responsibility to enquire whether or not the Juvenile has a parent or guardian over him/her. In the case of Sunil Kumar Versus State *(1983) Cr. L.J.99)* the power of taking into charge was interpreted in terms of similar social input. In the case of Sanjay Suri Versus Delhi Administration *AIR 1988 SC 415* the Supreme Court laid down that it shall be obligatory for every magistrate or judge authorised to issue detention warrants to specify the age of the person to be detained and made it obligatory on the jail authorities not to accept any warrant of detention unless the age of detenu is given.

It has also been decided that wherever the juvenile courts are functioning a juvenile shall have a right to appear before such a court only, even in cases of offences which are punishable by death or imprisonment (Raghubir Versus State *1981 4 SCC 212*).

Despite the protection of Children ensured by the convention (especially Articles 26, 27 and 32) having been ratified by the Government of India and which is recognition of its political obligations, how far and how soon they are implemented would depend on the sagacity of the State and the plight of the children being given priority it deserves. Going by the past record, however, it does not appear realisable in the forseeable future.

III. Required Urgency and Tardy Procedures

Almost two generations of children of free India have had little succour from the consequences of poverty, lack of education disease and malnutrition and destitution. This sector has not been treated with urgency it requires and whatever measures are taken by the executive for their protection gets lost in bureaucratic maze.

The "delivery system" is woefully inadequate and for implementation of every legislation it is the police force which has been given the responsibility. Unfortunately there is a growing feeling that in addition to rampant corruption it is becoming highly politicized and instances are not rare when it is treated as an extension of the political party in power. In the circumstances the overburdened police force and still more overburdened judiciary, (most of the times without adequate number of personnel and infrastructural facilities) further retard even the tardy progress of the enforcement of the rights of the child. Unless revolutionary steps on war footing are undertaken, the improvement of the conditions of the Children would remain only a utopian dream. An element of shock needs to be generated to ensure faster implementation of the guaranteed protections. The children of today cannot be made to wait till tomorrow which is always convenient but which rarely seems to come.

IV. Absence of Data Storage

The obligations under the convention require constant evaluation and monitoring by states, of enforcement of the rights under the convention by the countries which have ratified it. This necessity requires setting up of infrastructural facilities on a decentralized basis to inspire any confidence. The public has to be taken into confidence about the steps which the government proposes to take in this regard. At present the efforts in this direction may not match the expectations of the convention. The NGOs have a great role to play by giving their inputs to ensure proper monitoring to make the convention a vibrant, living and organic document and not just a piece of paper on which promises are made and promises are made.

JOHN DECOENE and RUDY DE COCK

The Children's Rights Project in the Primary School "De Vrijdagmarkt" in Bruges

INTRODUCTION

Between October 1993 and June 1994 a project concerning children's rights took place in "De Vrijdagmarkt", a primary school which is part of the community education system (1) in Bruges. The initiative came from the Parents' Association (2) of the school. In the framework of this project, professor Eugeen Verhellen, head of the Children's Rights Centre in Ghent, was invited to give a lecture for teachers, principal and parents. His enthusiasm for the project was an important stimulus and support. He also suggested to put ideas and activities regarding the project on paper. The Parents' Association took his advice to heart. The following text is an attempt to give a brief summary of the aims, activities and evaluation of the project, including a number of observations.

I. Preparation of the Project

Every year the Parents' Association and teachers of "De Vrijdagmarkt" organise a cultural activity. In 1993 this took the form of a children's and youngsters' bookfair during which the children had the chance to meet some of the authors.

At the beginning of the schoolyear 1993–94 some members of the Parents' Association looked for an activity in which the child could take up an even more central position and in which the creativity of the child itself could be called upon. An exhibition to round off the event was considered.

During the planning of the project there were several sources of inspiration. For the past few years the teachers, principal and staff had paid particular attention to a childfriendly environment. This had created a school with a distinctive character: the teachers showed particular interest in the feelings, experiences and opinions of the children; they also paid attention to events which pre-occupied children. Via a number of practical arrangements they

E. Verhellen (ed.), Monitoring Children's Rights, 627–636.
© 1996 *Kluwer Law International. Printed in the Netherlands.*

made sure there was a space for the childrens' personal input. Other elements which directed the project: the fact that "Children's Rights" was a known topic with the teachers, directorate and parents (in Belgium the Convention on the Rights of the Child has been into force since 1992), the possible impact of children's rights on other ways of interaction with children, the fact that children's rights are of importance for both children and adults, the possibility to familiarise children with their rights in a creative way.

The Parents' Association attached a lot of importance to the overall involvement of the school in the project. All teachers were therefore asked if they would be prepared to engage all the children from their class creatively around the topic of childrens' rights during the academic year. The results of those activities would also be shown to the outside world.

The teachers and principal reacted enthusiastically to this request for the topic fitted in very well with their attempt to give the child a more central position within the school. From the onset of the schoolyear, a concensus was reached amongst the different adult partners involved in the project.

The teachers introduced the concept of the children's rights project in their classes, utilising their pedagogical experience and knowledge. The response from the children is clear especially from the results and effects of the project afterwards.

II. The Project

A. The Parental Workgroup

To accompany the project, a workgroup was set up within the Parent's Association, consisting of one teacher and four individual parents. The active presence of a teacher was of great importance. In that way the workgroup would obtain the necessary information concerning the progress of the project within the school and it would provide the possibility to check the fasibility of the ideas of the workgroup, taking the reality within the school into account.

The parental workgroup took on the following tasks: accompanying the project from a contents point of view, forming the link between the principal, teachers, parents and organisations which took part in the project (a.o. by organising regular discussions between all the parties involved) and being responsible for all kinds of practical matters (timing, materials for the classes, financial means, etc.). The workgroup put forward a number of principles for working out the project:

- The participation of the entire school would be persued, implying that an egagement of every teacher was expected.
- Each phase of the project would be supported by a consensus between the different actors within the school. This would imply a continuous dialogue between parents, workgroup and teachers. Via the latter the children would also get involved.

For the additional contents support of the project the workgroup called upon the "Kinderrechtswinkel" (Children's Rights Shop) located in Brugge. The "Kinderrechtswinkel" is set up within the "Jongeren Advies Centrum". Children can call upon this organisation for advice and support regarding their rights, they have a lot of information on this subject available, they organise courses. The "Kinderrechtswinkel" has also divised a course for teachers. That course was more or less intensively used during the project.

B. Aim
The general targets of this project were formulated by the parental workgroup as follows:
- Announcement of the children's rights to all children, teachers, directorate and parents.
- Allocation of space within the school to children's rights and more specifically to children's participation.
- Striving for a maximum level of participation and a consensus between the different actors involved.

For practical reasons and taking elements emanating from the discussions with the teachers into account, these aims were further described as follows:
- In each class (from nursery to last year at primary school) teachers and students are introduced to the Treaty regarding the Rights of the Child.
- Students and teachers look for their own interpretation of these rights and put them in their world of experiences.
- Teachers and students look for creative interpretations of the children's rights; children can express their rights in the form of drawings, collages, letters, poetry etc., according to their own choice.
- All these "creations" by the students will form part of an exhibition to which everybody is invited.
- All parents are informed about the progress of the project at regular intervals; in this way they too will be sensitised regarding the topic of children's rights.

C. Elaboration of the Project
1. Classroom Activities. The bulk of the project was made up by activities by children and teachers of different classes. Most teachers had already taken up children's rights more or less explicitly in their lessons and in their approach towards the children. One class had signed a petition in 1989, demanding the approval and acceptance of the Convention for children's rights. They presented all children's rights to their pupils and in view of the project let the children have their say when it came to chosing the right or rights which would be discussed.

It was considered important for children in the first year of nursery to be able to touch the pictures of the UNICEF exhibition and not only to look at them from a distance. They associated their own feelings with these pictures.

The teacher chose to work with the right to food because it is closely related to the first experiences of the child and because of the child's interest in food. The children made an enormous doll decorated with illustrations of food. Afterwards the right to play and recreation came up spontanuously.

The second year learned about the different forms of housing throughout the world. The children at nursery painted and played around with images of other children, houses, igloos and tepees.

The teacher of the third year looked for a theme related with the subject of children's rights that would interest the children. The theme "water" was dealt with in various ways. The children bought and sold water, played a watergame they had devised themselves, made small cups to drink water from, composed music and illustrated the theme.

In the first year of primary school the teacher noticed that children were interested in different rights: peace, love, protection, health care, education, play, a home... . The right to education was not so obvious. The teacher chose to focus on that right especially. The class visited a Medical Pedagogical Institution (3) for children with a mental deficiency and a youth centre was also involved. Parents and relatives were also involved in the project through assignments relating to education in their time.

The second formers learned about the differences between their lives and those of children in other countries. They also thought about their own world, about what is good and what could be done better. They gave each other suggestions on how to deal with difficult problems. Especially the freedom of speech was emphasised. They made an appointment with the mayor and read a letter to him expressing their own wishes and desires. This event even got into the papers and on local television.

The third form discussed the rights to information, protection, privacy and education. Two of the classes children were adopted and of different races. The class therefore chose to make adoption a central theme in the discussion about children's rights. Via the story of an Indian boy about the living conditions in India, the children compared their own living conditions, the rights attained and the rights which can still be improved, among others participation.

The children of the fourth form wrote letters to a UN soldier in the former Yugoslavia and to a school in Zimbabwe. Newspaper clippings were discussed. They visited a centre where children are placed due to family problems. They organised a role-play in which one team knew the rights and the other had to guess those rights.

The fifth and sixth formers made a collage and drawings related with children's rights. They also collected pictures of violations of these rights and situated them on a world map. They visited the "Kinderrechtswinkel" and learned about its activities.

2. Support Activities of the Parental Workgroup.   The parental workgroup organised more support activities in cooperation with the teachers. At the end of January 1994 during a talkshow, professor Verhellen gave attending parents information on children's rights, on the image of the child in society and the evolution of that image and on the movement for children's rights. He also presented a few major issues in his lecture: respect for human and children's rights as a guarantee for peace and democracy, a school where children learn to participate in decisions that concern them and a school where children's rights are put into practice. An exhibition of UNICEF was held in the school for 3 weeks. It was made up of pictures of children in different situations and from different parts of the world, illustrated with texts from the Treaty regarding Children's Rights. The exhibition was also the subject of a discussion between the parental workgroup and the teachers. The group noted that the pictures allowed enough space for different interpretations of children's rights. The group also mentioned that the application of these rights should be claimed throughout the world. The nature of the rights to be claimed, varies from country to country. The exhibition was important for the children because it formed the start of the project elaboration. The lecture and the exhibition were the components of the project's official start. All parents and third persons were extensively informed through the school paper, letters and by the press.

On two occasions the parental workgroup, the teachers, the principal and the "Kinderrechtswinkel" were consulted during the project. During the first meeting, at the start of the project, children's rights and various methods of approach were explored. This stage involved a number of teachers who already had some experience in working with children's rights. Interesting and practical ideas (such as applying these rights to everyday life, giving these rights a positive meaning, reflecting on the similarities between rights and duties) were interchanged. The second meeting saw the project considered in its entire form and the final decisions made for the school's day of children's rights. The teachers also got some support through regular informal meetings held with the workgroup during the project. These meetings were held during the break before the lessons and provided the opportunity of making an update on the situation, arranging practical matters and discussing problems. This gave the workgroup an objective view of the evolution of the project so that the demands of the teachers could be met.

The workgroup also negotiated with the Committee for Special Youth Care to raise the necessary funds. The Committee, an official department of the Flemish Community, has a double function: help out in difficult pedagogical situations in families and render advice on the prevention of these situations. The Committee financed the didactic costs of the project. It recognised the children's rights project for the prevention of children and youngsters problems. The age froup of 3 to 12 which the project was aimed at, was also considered important. The Committee decided to test the project's flexibility and promote it in other schools.

3. Children's Rights Day at "De Vrijdagmarkt". The project's official end for the schoolyear 1993–1994 was celebrated on 24 April 1994. The workgroup urged parents to organise fun activities using their own skills and those of all the children where possible. Everything the children had made in the course of the project on children's rights was exhibited and presented on that day. The exhibition was professionally set up by a student who was doing his thesis on the subject. The children also participated in all kinds of workshops together with parents, teachers and staff: they could improvise life among different cultures using make-up and clothes, prepare meals, work on animated films, listen to stories, build a small house and decorate the playground with wall paintings. The events of the day were covered bij the school's press featuring pupils as interviewers. The "Kinderrechtswinkel" provided balloons with cards for the children to let up. The children mentioned the right they gave preference to on their cards. The substantial involvement and effort of many parents during preparations and on the day itself provided a number of messages: recognition of the project for children's rights, belief in a child's possibilities, richness of differences between people (clothes, features...), importance of creativity.

D. Process Evaluation

The parental workgroup came up with the idea for the project's evaluation by the most important people involved in order to get some feedback information.

1. Evaluation by the Children. In June 1994 each parent of the workgroup had a complete school hour at his or her disposal in every class to discuss with the children their knowledge of their rights, a particular item which appaeled to most of them and their wishes for the future.

All children displayed sensitivity towards themes such as peace, injustice, war and hunger. Their answers also demonstrated that as children get older they show more interest in the world around them and make comparisons to their situation.

A returning factor in the evaluation was the need for children to represent their own ideas through for example the making of a film, to discuss the subject and to do something with it for example make a drawing. In the last forms this need was translated as a demand for more participation and involvement in the school's organisation.

The project itself and the children's rights day was evaluated in a positive way by the children. They were especially enthusiastic about the fact that they themselves could decide on which right to use and how they were going to represent it eventually. Visits to different institutions also made a lasting impression on the children.

2. Evaluation by the Teachers.   A co-worker of the "Kinderrechtswinkel" interviewed each teacher using a questionnaire drawn up in cooperation with the workgroup.

The evaluation showed the enthusiasm and energy with which the teachers worked on the project. Most of them were familiar with children's rights but it was the first time they had to work with the theme. All in all the teachers considered the different activities and the input of the parental workgroup as positive. All teachers were able to relate the situation to the child's world. They made sure that children in different forms could choose which rights to work with. The evaluation also showed that the teachers monitored the effect of working with children's rights by watching the relations between the children themselves: they have learned about each other's life and have gained in respect and understanding. The teachers did not speak to the children about these effects on relations, although they worked together with them or let them decide on the elaboration of the project. Its evaluation was not mentioned. The teachers chose to continue working with children's rights on special occasions and theme-wise per form.

III. Some Observations

As pointed out in the preparatory stage of the project, there were clear reasons why the topic of children's rights was decided upon for the project. The project itself brought about a number of experiences. Some of these are described below.

A. Children's Rights as the Title of a Project

Working around the topic of children's rights cannot be a non-committing activity. The subject deals with the being of a child itself and in that way directly appeals to them. Becoming aware of their rights has an influence on the relationship with people, children and adults, with whom they associate, it therefore also has repercussions on all possible structures with which they deal such as the school, the youth movement, etc.

The mutual relationships change which results into the need for new forms of communication. In that way the project was at the same time a contributor to this changing process which by no means ended with the termination of the project. Several parties involved would like to see a continuation of the process: the children in particular would like more and further participation. From the part of the teachers and parents there is, amongst other things, the willingness to redesign, together with the children, the playground of their school during the schoolyear 1994–1995.

B. A Positive Child Image

The description of the project continually stresses a positive child image: it called upon what children can do and provided opportunities for affirmation.

Much importance was paid to participation of the children, to their choices. They were stimulated to formulate their opinions. During the project, discussions took place between those involved regarding the topic of children's rights and its contents. This gave rise to a number of questions and reservations. Does freedom to express oneself imply that children always have to be put in the right? Do children's rights not receive too much emphasis? What about the obligations? Are children not overestimated? Both in its message to take children seriously as in the search for answers to all these questions, the project contributed towards a change of mentality regarding children and to the change of the child image which prevails in society.

C. Consensus

At the onset and throughout the entire project, much importance was paid to the establishment of a consensus between all those involved, both children and adults. That consensus was a prerequisite to start the project. This implies negotiations between directorate, teachers and parents, all those involved were asked to bring forward their point of view and everybody listened. That approach was ultimately an exercise in dealing with participation. It was also that way of communicating with each other as equals which the teachers attempted to pass on to the children as much as possible.

D. Children's Rights leading to other Topics

Via the subject of children's rights other related topics came up, such as dealing with one's own feelings and desires, concern for others, tolerance, realising that others have rights too. Several types of "being different" were also discussed: adoption, being handicapped, living in an institution instead of a family, colour of skin.

At the stage of the evaluation one of the teachers mentioned that one of her pupils had been placed in an institution by the juvenile court. This resulted in the boy being quiet and reserved. The discussions concerning children's rights gave rise to the teacher explaining the meaning of "being placed in an institution by the juvenile court". The class also visited the boy in the institution. The teacher noticed that from that time onwards the boy was accepted as one of the group in the playground. Another teacher noticed that a small minority of the children brought up the right to receive education. In that class there is a physically handicapped boy. The teacher used this argument to illustrate that all children deserve a proper education. The teacher with her pupils visited a Medical Pedagogical Institute so that they could meet peers in a different situation.

E. The Parents

As aforementioned, the idea of the project came from the Parent's Association, but the parental workgroup seized several opportunities to inform parents regarding the activities of their children in the project. A large number of parents showed, in different ways, a strong interest. Via the project, could they also be sensitised regarding children's rights and grew their involvement in the school activities.

F. The Project as a Preventive Measure

Taking the effects of the project into account, the workgroup believed that the project of children's rights can act preventively regarding matters which within the school context are experienced as problematic (truancy, school fatigue...). Another reason why the workgroup would like to recommend the project to others.

IV. Epilogue

The first version of the project description was put together by means of several notes taken during the project by the parental workgroup. The different parts of that text were discussed and revised within and outside the workgroup. That method resulted in a step-by-step composition of the entire text, like the project itself. Rudy De Cock and John Decoene were responsible for the final editing. The authors are grateful to all people with whom they discussed the project and to Kris Dockx for the english translation of the text.

APPENDIX

Explanation of Concepts

- The primary school consists of the 3 levels of primary and nursery education (age: 3 to 12). The Flemish Community is responsible for community education.
- The Parent's Association aims at organising activities for the benefit of the children and tries to get all parents involved.
- A Medical Pedagogical Institute (MPI) is an institution with boarding facilities for handicapped youngsters under 18.

Documentation

Below lists the literature regarding children's rights which was effectively used by children, teachers and parents.

Boden K., Decleir M., "Onderwijsbeleid en zeer kansarme jongeren. Onderzoek naar de concrete handelingsalternatieven voor een algemeen onderwijsbeleid ten aanzien van zeer kansarme jongeren", niet gepubliceerde tekst, 1988–1990.

"Kinderen hebben rechten (The world's children)", De Ruiter, Gorinchem, 1989.

"Kinderrechtengids KIDS", Centrum voor de Rechten van het Kind (U.Gent), Mys & Breesch, Gent, 1994.

Map voor leerkrachten, Kinderrechtswinkel, Brugge, zd.

Verhellen E., "Verdrag inzake de rechten van het kind", Garant, Leuven/Apeldoorn, 1993.

Van Gils J., "Wie niet weg is, is gezien. Hoe beleeft het kind zijn gezin, zijn school en zijn vrije tijd.", Koning Boudewijnstichting, 1992.

Van Gils J. en Dekeyser P., "Kinderen spreken met de samenleving. Een handreiking rond kinderinspraak en kinderparticipatie.", uitgave van het Onderzoekscentrum "Kind en samenleving" van NDO, Meise, zd.

"Voor alle kinderen. De rechten van het kind door Kermit de Kikker", een uitgave van Tijgerboek.

"Wat zijn je rechten?", UNICEF-poster, 1993.

MARC DE STAERCKE and LUDWICH RECH

The European Federation of City Farms and Working with Children

The social situation of children in the industrialised countries of Western Europe is affected by a typical ambivalence: on the one hand, especially during the last 20 years, children and young people have been increasingly able to strike out on their own and to choose an individual style of life. Training opportunities, general levels of information, mobility and comfort have been enhanced.

On the other hand, this increased individualisation has been dearly bought by severing social and cultural relationships and loss of integration in the extended family and the local neighbourhood. In spite of social, medical and economic progress, the number of children with social problems, psychological disorders and physical disabilities is growing in all West European countries.

For example, a study carried out in Nordrhein-Westfalen, Germany, has revealed that 48% of the 12–17 years olds often suffer from headaches, and more than one-third of the children and young people complained of nervousness, lack of concentration, lumbar pain and backache, stomach and sleep disorders. About 10% of all children suffer from an allergy, asthma, bronchitis or neurodermatitis. Such symptoms of ill-health suggest social and psychological stress factors, and are signs of bad living conditions. They should not be regarded as merely somatic complaints. The increasing number of children, who are violated and bullied and the increasing use of drugs by children, are indicative of current adverse living conditions.

In our view, children's lives are also determined by the following tendencies:
- The current social development leads, in the field of economics, to an increasing competitive struggle. Millions of children are affected by their parents' unemployment and poverty, and by having to rely on social security benefits. The consequences of this are unequal chances of development; isolation; increasing child labour and psychological and physical disturbances.
- In some European countries, in spite of the high percentage of divorces (in Germany 30%), one has to start from intact family structures. The

E. Verhellen (ed.), Monitoring Children's Rights, 637–639.
© 1996 Kluwer Law International. Printed in the Netherlands.

fundamental rights of children to good education and upbringing, participation and self-determination have often been disregarded. Children's
education is still considered a private matter, although families are less
and less in a position to fulfil the necessary conditions for the development of children. There are not enough educational institutions outside
the family (Kindergarten, crèches, city farms).

– School is still a focus of anxiety, discrimination and competitive spirit
  for most children. Parents' expectations of top performances in school
  work leads to a stronger competitiveness among the pupils. The pressure
  then leads to an excess of psychopharmacologic drugs and sets one pupil
  against another, thus destroying any solidarity.
– At a rough estimate 3%-5% of children are subject to sexual cruelty or
  are neglected psychologically and emotionally.
– The number of children killed or injured on the road, the environmental
  pollution, including air, water, ground and foodstuff, as well as the urban
  depopulation, prove that the right of children to a livable environment is
  terribly affected.
– Drug addiction and suicide of children are characteristic of the violent
  nature of our "civilised" society.
– During the last few decades children, their education, their play and
  learning have been separated more and more from daily and public
  life. Educational special environmental communes "Children's ghettos",
  partly provided with a programme and control, have arisen. Play and
  leisure are also regulated and commercialised more and more.
– Deserted cities, satellite towns and standardised leisure resorts offer little
  of what satisfies curiosity or promotes pleasure and discovery.
– Houses are often too small, especially for children's common games.
  There are hardly shops on the corners, where children could once evade
  the eyes and control of adults. Houses have been functionally appointed
  and geared to television, usually in the living room.
– Traffic density has reached such a level that it is almost impossible to
  play freely in the streets. In urban districts especially there are hardly
  any open sites which could serve as recreation areas.
– Especially city children are continually living in a second world of fiction
  and media information which television puts in front of them.
– Together with desensualisation and abstraction a worrying trend is also
  occurring in children's playing and learning: for example, commercial-
  isation of adventures and experiences, marketing of children's interests
  and wishes, sale of jokes and fascinating objects. This affects the children's own initiative and impairs their sense of self-esteem. Access to
  playing and learning is more and more regulated economically.

The trends mentioned refer to factors which are preventing children from
becoming free, self-confident and socially responsible adults. Children from
different European regions, city and country children, children from rich and

poor families, are all affected in quite different ways, but all of them are affected by these trends.

In all countries of Western Europe there are people who make a real effort to improve the living conditions of children. One practical example of this is the City Farm movement, which has developed in different ways according to the historical and social situation of each country, but all agree to these objectives:

- to give children their due place in modern society;
- to interest children, young people and adults of all ages in each other and get them to communicate;
- to encourage children to show their own initiative;
- to give children experience of nature and to foster ecological thinking;
- to boost the creativity and imagination of children;
- to bring children up to become responsible adults.

The individual national federations of City Farm have formed the European Federation of City Farms in order to learn from their common experiences (unity in diversity) and to look after children's interests in the right way.

LEA DHERBECOURT

Kitty 007

The Name by which Anne Franck Calls us to Hope and a Future

Monitoring the rights of children will always involve monitoring those of the most involved, namely the parent. This cannot be taken for granted – that would not only be doubtful, but untrue.

This is a professional stance, in view of the present situation for children. It depends on each specific field of work and comes over as controversial, as difficult. The vision of the parent and child will not be as specific for a nursery school teacher as for a teacher working with traumatised children. Her specific task does not require vision, but effective help; and respecting the rights of the child in the form of help is already a tall order.

The stance taken by the nursery school teacher, i.e. the more naive attitude of love and care, is in this sense all the more intriguing through the diversity apparent in the parent-child relationship and the consequences leading on from our starting position, which is not so automatic in its realisation.

The complexity of the various attitudes makes us want to quit, revolt, stick to the letter of the task, and though we try to understand, we remain inadequate in the face of rights or justice. With all of the consequences which this involves.

That this realisation leads to an all-consuming quest, self-analysis, exigencies, structures and the complexity of our present society is at once a torture, trial and liberation, which itself leads to the original, naive stance of "loving and caring, to respect and toleration".

Respect leads to the understanding, but not exoneration of human behaviour. Justice is much more complex than judgements and convictions; in the sense that it makes no sense, or becomes every bit as worthless as a critic without the faculty of self-criticism.[1]

In as far as I can squeeze this into a few sentences, I will try to describe my point of view.

In the past our socio-cultural structure has been evolving from absolute power to logical reasoning, in the spirit of the times, and to the delegation

---

[1] Nathan, Tobie L'influence qui guérit. Odile Jacob Paris 1994

E. Verhellen (ed.), Monitoring Children's Rights, 641–648.
© 1996 Kluwer Law International. Printed in the Netherlands.

and legitimation of power.[2] This contribution of power has grown from the seed-bed of knowledge and specialisms, and even then it was evident that this development answered to the vision and opportunities of the policy-makers of the times.

This is a factor which made possible the development from rights to power, to the power for rights, to the present right to think rights.[3]

Contrary to the past, we can say that the policy-makers have the right to gather information, needed for policy making and formulating preventative measures, from the workers in the field. This is happening already, though not in a comprehensive, systematic form.[4]

As a contradiction to the statement "to get something, give something in return"; a statement based on loyalty, flowing from the traditional right to power.

The deontology used in reports, with relation to over-structured, specialist knowledge, leads to both a splintering of the problem and a shift of the problems. Such schizophrenic situations have a paranoic effect and serve a misplaced loyalty. The present right to think rights will inevitably become entwined with the transmission of second fiddle values of education.

Under the present circumstances, these educational values, to reach consensus, are not definable because of the inequality in conditions.[5]

Though the expertise employed in questions and inquiries may have their value, they will never reach their desired goal without criticism or the chance for dialogue.[6]

The child, in its imposed yet uninhibited loyalty, must be taken as a yardstick, detector and touchstone by which to measure our own failures, guide our behaviour and correct our structural mistakes.

In our socio-cultural context, and with the emergence of the industrial revolution, the interpretation of children's needs has always rested on charity and protection. Whoever was being protected, and what was intended by recycling these children, is, I feel, clear to all of us.

In the spirit of those times account was indeed taken of the inequalities in conditions, but they were not distilled to the actual tenets of Christian belief, in which such a union was not possible, and by the left, which used economic

---

[2] Machiavelli, Niccolo, *De Heerser*, trans. F. Van Dooren, Publ. Athenaeum-Polack & Van Gennep/Amsterdam, 1991, 182 pages.

[3] Raes, Koen, *Het morele vertoog over de rechten van het kind*, Kinderrechtengids, Publ. Mys & Breesch, 1995. Verhellen, E., *Jeugdbeschermingsrecht*, Publ. Mys & Breesch, 1994. Van den Bergh, Bea, CBGS document, 1994.

[4] Centre for Children's Rights/Gent Koning Boudewijnstichting

[5] Lodewijks-Frencken, Els, *Op voeding aangewezen*, Publ. Nelissen/Baarn, Berne, E., *Games People Play*, Grove Press Inc. New York

[6] Crosbras Anne-Marie & J.-Marie, *Les sondages; principes et methode; que sais-je* Verhellen, E., Spiesschaert, *Ombudswork for Children*, ACCO Flekkoy, M.C., Cahier 13, Gent Willems, G. *Een parlementaire kinderombudsman*, Cahier 9, Gent

interests to legitimise their acts. That these things still persist cannot be put aside.

A democracy based on inequality, especially in terms of information and education, implies the rights of the strongest, and so does not deserve the name, and as such cannot therefore function. This must be plain to us all.

Through the State's ratification of the rights of the child we can now however suppose that this – the inequality in conditions – is roundly recognised as a part of the problem.

Contrary to the past, the child is ever more prone to becoming disposable, which bears the stamp of our culture as far as dealing with children is concerned.

The fact that this recognition of the problem leads to a real attempt to establish these rights is something which bodes well for the future.

In this spirit, and bearing the past in mind, the parent has never been given an honest chance to interpret these rights.

If now, however, they were deprived of the chance to exercise control, we could in fact talk of a status quo, and the meaning of the ratification would then escape me.

Nevertheless, it would be neither reasonable nor justifiable in all of these remarks to assign the social failings and their attendant problems to individuals or groups in society.

Our democracy is still in its infancy and the mistakes made due to the process of growth could be minimised with a more profound approach.

Where the rights of the child – the first precondition for human rights – are concerned, a little questioning on the matter reveals:

- ignorance about the exact content, and therefore a subjective interpretation;
- that the definition of these rights is not based on profound and honest thinking;
- that the present attention to children shows a manipulative perversity, by which mass-seducers attempt to steer the human soul towards financial gain, as a basic value;
- that the role of child psychology is reduced and commercialised by therapeutic processes, and lends no power by which to create conditions;
- that the economic context made all of this possible, but is not solely responsible;
- that the actual parent grew up under the same conditions and this is probably the most forceful argument for explaining current thinking, as well as a part of the problem.

In addition to these remarks, we can put the following statements forward:

The Changing Family Picture: the Possibility of Family Planning
Earlier, children entered families in a never-ending stream; this continuity has now been broken. As a consequence, tolerance in the mind of the adult has disappeared on the one hand, and on the other, it has led to an almost pathological attention to perfection and detail.

The Apparent Emancipation of Women
In this case too we can talk of a manipulation of the human soul, influenced in the main by all manner of women's magazines, which were well grounded in their own right to exist and prevent an economic backlash. Their assertion, by suggestion and generalities, that it is possible to make people and children to measure, by feeding subconscious thinking with elements of power, impotence and persistent hunger for more.

The One-parent Family
This has resulted from the subjective-defensive process of emancipation, the most important factor being the economic importance of women in the labour market. Because of this fact, on the one hand, the willingness and effort put into a full and meaningful parenthood became impossible and remained superficial. And on the other, we could say the opposite, that the mutual dependency of parents, with no more than a financial link between them, had a similarly devastating effect in the past. Regardless of the positions held on either side, where the consequences for the children themselves are concerned – from their behavioural need to find solutions to their problems themselves – we can draw our own conclusion from the mushrooming numbers of self-help groups.

Youth care
Under such conditions and circumstances youth care itself was affected and unable to put forward good human solutions because they were helping children with solutions from the "educational box of tricks". It is fair to put it that way, for there was no ill-will intended. The requirement and demand for an expansion of their fields of work can be seen as a move for survival and an act of self-confirmation, even as a sign of the superficial approach to the material and knowledge given them.

If, in the present situation, this argument were used as a means to limit financial support in the transitional phase, it would not only raise a question mark over the bad choice, but would also call into question the present will to act now.

There is also a lot to be done in the area of nursery schools and child care since there is some suspicion, almost taboo in these circles, fed by popular measures and statements by which the parent is ultimately soothed and prevented from a more animation-based education. Animation in this sense does not mean TV culture, I hasten to add.

When we look at these things we can again talk of a self-fulfilling and superficial attitude to children and the future.

In fact, this attitude uses the economic context as a sort of legitimation, and holds it responsible for defining educational responsibility and the needs of children. The fact that this is happening is not only reprehensible, but superficial where the definition of children's needs is concerned, even in this so-called specific environment.

The schools and the schooling system must also search their own consciousness.

The only conclusions we can reach are the following:
- Apparent solutions can never be corrected by superficial acts, nor by lack of insight nor by neglecting the specialised information available.
- Though these attitudes are the result of good intentions and have cost enormous amounts of money, the flux of initiatives has had negative effects and devastating consequences for human kindness. It is therefore easy to explain the refusal of some field workers to cooperate with official authorities or structures.
- In the welfare society in which we live, geared towards affluence, consumption and education based on animation, the cost of this narrow-mindedness, due to a lack of content and form, is that our youngsters are reduced to solving their problems for themselves, which tends to be rather negative.

True though it may be that we have managed to reduce child-mortality, we are heading the list for child suicides.

The drastically rising numbers of homeless people, the alarmingly high figure for youngsters on sedatives, using drugs and showing other self-destructive behaviour, and the growing aggression and criminality are not the usual signs associated with an improved quality of life.

If we think a little more deeply about the children's tendency to solve their problems themselves, we can talk of loyalty to elders.

In its turn, this loyalty is not rewarded by the same parent or elder, but rather, repression is the reply.

If it is ultimately the parent, who, under these circumstances and because of these single-minded conditions, turns out to be the victim of total chaos in this morass of power, impotence and forced discontent, this can hardly be surprising.

Because of this, the delegation of educational responsibility is not just the result of some form of logical thinking, but obviously an area manipulated by several pressure groups.

Unfortunately, the politicians are too wrapped up in newly discovered psychological market values, and this is why they legitimise the rejected or as yet undiscovered need for transaction between the various ministerial portfolios, and by so doing, unfortunately, neglect their emancipatory role – a precondition for and responsibility to democracy and the future. And much of this is to do with a lack of maturity.

In view of the ratification we can now put the demand for such a transaction forward.

I can now imagine that whilst all the parties are falling, a single group or individual will gain the monopoly to implement this surveillance.

At present it would be too much to expect an individual or group to have the power to define or sanction these rights on the basis of profound thinking.

Nowadays, sanctions hit only the children and can be seen as an act of pure violence which leads only to "would-be" solutions and "would-be" adjustments, with all the negative results for the individual and society as a whole.

Historical and recent events cannot be avoided and demonstrate that subjective-defensive thinking leads to nothing more than the naive, causal approach and serves only as a tool for self-fulfilment.[7]

It has been amply proved that the subjective-defensive way of thinking will ultimately call for a seizure of power.

However vast our vision or intelligence may be, when defining the rights of children we will be guided by the best pointer towards these rights – the child itself.

It is a question of giving the child the opportunity to formulate his feelings and desires and evolving from verbal to responsible assertion.

In this sense I feel that an ombudsman's office, adopted and elected by Parliament and given the appropriate competence, should be set up, whereby not only the children, but all of the parties involved in these rights can define the needs of children by means of transaction under conditions respectful of the human being. A body such as this is absolutely necessary.

As parents we have the responsibility of guarding and maintaining the right to peace, a fundamental element of all rights; and we must act on the advice of the various disciplines which have investigated and discussed the relevant conditions.[8]

A. Material programming which means
  – education based on knowledge, and
  – social exchange by giving a voice to all the parties involved in the reali-
    sation of children's rights.

B. Social programming linked by the following elements:
  – leisure: popularising intentions,

---

[7] Mandel Ernest, *Du facisme*, Publ. François-Maspero, Paris, 1974 Bednavik, Karl, *Gevaar-lijke Welvaart*, Publ. Erven J. Buleveld/Utrecht, 1958

[8] Berne, E., *Transactional Analysis in Psychotherapy*, Grove Press Inc./New York , 1961 Luce, R.D. and Raiffa H., *Games and Decisions*, John Wiley & Sons Inc.

- avoiding harmful situations: Ombudsman's Office, specialised and professional training,
- receiving incentives: mutual respect, efficiency (= cost savings), achievement of equilibrium,
- maintenance of this equilibrium.

In the light of the above suggestions I propose the following project:

KITTY 007
The name by which Anne Franck calls us to hope and the future

A. Contract, parent-State
- as an offer for popularisation; on birth or adoption
  Form: as a passport to adulthood
  Content: ratified text to be signed by the parent
- Free Phone number: as a means of obtaining information for children's
  rights
- Contract with the community: pages on which subsidised organisations
  can propose their intentions; in the light of the ratification this is a
  legitimate demand, a reference to parent and child
- White or blank pages, on which organisations can propose their intentions

B. Green number
This would allow everyone to collect information, make a complaint and
avoid "escape options" on an equal basis.
- This number could be introduced by delegation to individual or organised
  initiatives
- This would also provide an opportunity for commercial intentions, and
  will guarantee continuity through diversification.

C. Body elected by Parliament
- As an information and complaints service
- As an instrument to exercise control and evaluate individual and collec-
  tive efforts

For the future, we should focus attention on:
- Breaking the link between time at the nursery and educational standards.
  We should not forget that a childhood which ends to quickly leads to the
  undermining of the creative skills, skills which are needed in every stage
  of growing up.

- A schooling system in which these conditions for creativity are integrated with self-conduct through to social conduct and strategic conduct.[9]
- The fact that youth work itself will need to rethink its role and function, and must play an active role in learning to work cost-effectively.

---

[9] formulated by: Venger, Leonid, Soviet Psychology Dietvorst, C. and Mahieu, P., *Organisatiecultuur van scholen*, Publ. Samson H.D., Tjeenk Willinck: Alphen a/d Rijn, *De school staat niet alleen*, Koning Boudewijnstichting/Belgium, 1994.

MARY JOHN

Monitoring Children's Rights to Education

An Inter-agency Approach in the South West of England

This paper reports on work in progress in monitoring the obstacles to children's full entitlement within the educational process. Whilst it describes work that is being undertaken in a specific region of the United Kingdom, the issues this work raises are issues relating to social exclusion and the consequences of such exclusion early in life, which are of global, not just local concern. The present study is concerned with 'school-lessness', that is a study of children who for one reason or another are not at school. More fundamentally, we are trying to describe, possibility for the first time in the literature, the *culture* of school-lessness. There is little if any understanding of what children do all day if they do not go to school. On the basis of our early enquiries it seems that uncomfortably large numbers of children are in just such a situation yet we know little of their lives, least of all, from a child's point of view. In an earlier paper (John, 1993) some of the possible reasons for children's non-attendance at school and its impact on children's developing lives were explored. We have now gone beyond the identification of reasons why children may not be attending school to a much greater emphasis on the quality of their lives without school and how they themselves perceive these lives. Richard Scarry in a light-hearted way, illustrated for us in 'What Do People Do All Day?' with pictures and phrases many of us remember from our own childhood or from reading with our own young the sort of ideal world in which adults live and what they did with their time (Scarry, 1989). Light-heartedness apart, there has been no systematic attention, in a climate which increasingly recognises that a proportionately high number of children are not at school, to establish what are the experiences of these children and whether they are in any way educational. The way in which we are monitoring the child's right to access the educational process as laid down clearly in Articles 28 and 29 of the UN Convention is, rather perversely, by looking at the nature of the experiences that make up the lives of children who are *not* at school. In this work a team, made up of statutory and voluntary agencies and the Devon Youth Council (a council of young people themselves) are active participants. Our research has fallen into three distinct phases.

E. Verhellen (ed.), Monitoring Children's Rights, 649–666.
© 1996 *Kluwer Law International. Printed in the Netherlands.*

I. Phase One

A. *Housing*

The development of this study represents something of a detective story that it is quite instructive to follow. We started our enquiries at the instigation of a local group who were trying to set up a new Family Centre for children pre-school. We were invited to undertake some enquiries to establish whether or not there was a need for a further Centre. As part of these enquiries we started to look in detail at the lives of deprived young families with children of pre-school age. Our attention was immediately drawn to the housing situation of many of these young families. We became increasingly concerned about housing difficulties and the consequences of these for the child's physical and psychological health and the educational and recreational opportunities available for them pre-school. We felt that insufficient attention was being paid to inadequate housing from the point of view of the child's development. We, I am sure, like many other citizens in this area of the country, were astonished to find that the numbers of families living in very difficult housing circumstances in our city were very high. We began, therefore, to look in a lot more detail at this situation of young children who were 'statutorily homeless', that is, were living in temporary accommodation which typically is provided in houses with multiple occupancy, bed and breakfast accommodation in hotels, and a whole variety of makeshift arrangements whilst they wait on the housing list to be re-housed. We will return to our findings (Still and John 1993) later.

Simultaneously with our enquiries into the situation of young children living in temporary accommodation, we were becoming concerned about the number of young people sleeping rough on our streets. Ironically we had been holding in the University in 1992, a World Conference on Research and Practice in Children's Rights and we had had participants coming from Uruguay and Brazil to talk about their work with street children. In preparation for this, therefore, we began to look at what work was being undertaken with our own street children and became very interested in how they came to be there. This was a relatively new phenomenon in the South West of England and was giving rise to concern for a number of agencies. We began to feel that the two situations were possibly linked, that is that maybe some children living in difficult housing circumstances with little in the way of a stable family background and possibly an interrupted education eventually end up sleeping rough. At this stage these were suspicions only – we had no hard data to build this picture upon.

We have been working since then looking very carefully, not just at the situation of young children living in temporary accommodation but also at the lifespan development of such children. We began, therefore, to work with the various statutory and voluntary agencies around the theme of 'Home-lessness'. One of the things that was immediately apparent was that all of these agencies were themselves deeply concerned about fragmentation of effort and provision for such families. It is true that many of these agencies had done reviews of the service that they provided. These reviews were, in fact, not so much to see how things could be improved or better integrated so much as the justification for the funding for the continuance of that service itself. All of them complained that they did not know what other interested parties, active in this field were doing as there was little in the way of collaboration and information exchange between them.

A series of meetings were held at the University making it clear that our concern was the extent to which such young people were able to claim their rights under Articles 28 and 29 of the UN Convention, to access to the educational process. In these early meetings a large number of agencies took part (listed at the end of the article). These meetings were important in establishing joint concerns that rose above the self interest of any individual agency and in underlining and emphasising for us that a large problem in our city, was the impact that housing difficulties was having on children throughout the whole school age life span. These enquiries and discussions with interested agencies mark out Phase One of our research work with disadvantaged young people in our city. We were aware that the problem was, one which was not confined to the urban area of our Local Authority but that the problem was, if anything, even more acute in rural areas. In order to contextualise the work we were doing locally within the national picture, it is instructive to look at the situation on the basis of the national data available (which inevitably is several years out of date by the time it becomes available).

B. *The National Picture*

Looking at the country at large, at least 164,000 families in the United Kingdom are estimated to be without homes. In addition to this 170,000 households have been accepted as 'homeless', or threatened with 'home-lessness' taking the statutory definitions of this. 8,000 households outside the priority needs category were given advice and assistance in 1991, the date on which these figures are based. It is necessary for Local Authorities to provide temporary accommodation (in a Hostel, Bed and Breakfast, or a house unsuitable for *long*-term tenancy) while the case is being assessed and until long term can be arranged. At the end of 1991, 64,000 households who had applied to Local Authorities as homeless were in temporary accommodation at this time. This was an increase of a third on the previous year, and almost trebling since 1986. In 1991 Local Authorities in Great Britain accepted responsibility under the Home-lessness Legislation to secure permanent accommodation for 170,000 households. This is very much the same as in 1990, but an 18% increase on 1989. Of those in a 'Priority Need' category, over 66% had dependent children.

Poor housing inevitably causes stress and hardship for the family which is further exacerbated the larger the number of children in that family. The sort of situations in which these families have to live are cramped, have little in the way of privacy, have limited space for play for young children, and very little in the way of a quiet place for children to do their school homework. All of these aspects and many others beside lead to tensions within the family. Moreover, in houses in multiple occupancy there is no monitoring of who the other tenants in the house are. With housing being in short supply, and with new policies for moving the mentally ill into the community, it may mean that children are living in circumstances in which there are other stresses in the house and in which they may well be vulnerable in a whole variety of ways. This view of the unsuitability of such housing for vulnerable children is reinforced by the findings of the Policy Study Institute whose report on 'Home-lessness in Brent' paints the following bleak picture:

> What do we mean by social provision? One of the central conclusions of this report is that home-lessness as defined by the Housing Act and as experienced by the Borough of Brent is a child-centred problem without child-centred solutions. This has a number of important implications. First, many hostels are quite simply inappropriate places for children. Where mothers have to cook on electric hotplates on the floor in the same room as small children are learning to crawl, where families are not allowed to leave push-chairs in the hall but have to carry them up together with one or two children, the shopping and the laundry, where families are not allowed to use a telephone to call a doctor for a child, where mothers have to protect their school-age children from the clients of the hotel prostitutes, the management of home-lessness may need to change its emphasis from its concern with environmental health standards and may need to ask some questions on the standards of its homeless children". (Bonnerjea and Lawton (1987) *"Home-lessness in Brent"* Policy Studies Institute)

The problems are made even more difficult because outdoor play space is very limited and often unsuitable. The poverty of recreational provision is indicated in a study reported by the National Children's Bureau in 1992, by the fact that nearly three times as many mothers expressed a dissatisfaction with available amenities as were dissatisfied with housing conditions (33% compared with 12%): a recent Government study further corroborated these findings (Department of the Environment). This situation is likely to be worse for children living in deprived city areas where houses and flats are commonly without private garden or yard.

The National Children's Bureau point out that over-crowding and a lack of amenities have considerable and measurable effects on educational attainment, social adjustment and help. They indicate, for example, that at the age of 11 years, overcrowding was associated with a retardation of about seventeen months' reading age, and a further twelve months where amenities were lacking, giving a combined effect of almost two and a half years retardation.

Looking at this developmentally, they found out this effect is more marked than the effects of similar circumstances had been at the age of seven years (nine months' retardation in relation to overcrowding and nine months also in relation to amenities). Taken together the findings of the National Children's Bureau point to the three conclusions which were very important to us in our own studies.

Firstly, many children growing up in large families whose income is low are beset by multiple, interrelated and interacting disadvantages which have a detrimental effect on the level of the educational attainment, social adjustment in school and probably also on their physical development, particularly height. Secondly, these effects usually work in combination and are cumulative. Thirdly, their adverse influence seems to *increase over time* so that the gap between the most advantaged and the most disadvantaged groups grows wider as the child grows older. The National Bureau point out that their studies reinforce the commonly-held view that equality of opportunity will not come about through changes in secondary or higher education. Rather, the researchers suggest that it is during the *pre-school and early school years* ways must be sought to overcome or compensate for the effects of environmental disadvantages on children's development. They suggest that *limiting the initial gap* is likely to be the most effective way of reducing the gap at later stages. This work made it clear to us that in Phase Two of our own enquiries we must start looking at the effects of home-lessness on the educational achievement of such children, not just in their early years but as time went on. It was becoming clear to us that we should be thinking about undertaking a longitudinal study with all the difficulties that such studies involve.

C. The Local Picture

To speak of housing problems in the West Country takes everyone by surprise. To many outside the region this part of the country offers escape and relaxation. It is where people go on short recuperative breaks or relaxing holidays to enjoy excellent beaches, thatched cottages, cream teas, cider and, hopefully, sunshine! Tourism is the region's main source of income. It receives more than twice as many British visitors as any other region in the UK, and is one of the top three most visited regions amongst overseas tourists. In 1990, for example 11.5 million visitors spent a total of $1,859,000 in the counties of Cornwall, Devon, Somerset and West Dorset. The South West attracts not only visitors but migrants from other parts of the UK. Many have chosen to move here because it offers a pleasant environment in which to live and work and bring up a family, or spend one's retirement years. After East Anglia this region has the largest population growth of any region in the country, according to the 1991 edition of *Regional Trends* (Central Statistical Office), it went up by 6.2% between 1981 and 1989 (more than a million). Exeter itself, where our pilot work was undertaken in Phase One is a city with a population of 104,800 and housing problems exacerbated by student needs, high unemployment, a tourist trade and many young people arriving from inner city areas looking for seasonal work, of which there is in fact very little. Moreover, the local colleges, the University and the hospitals are also looking for more accommodation for their staff and students. In 1991 the Housing Action Group estimated that they were approaching 400 families that were truly (not just statutorily) homeless in Exeter. If this estimate is true, then it indicates a *figure of home-lessness proportionally higher than in London*. In 1992, the City recognised that there were in a particular area of the City at least 200 families in one room accommodation, some in divided rooms. There was, at the time, estimated to be 609 overcrowded households plus 788 concealed or shared households in the city. They also estimated at that time that 8% of the City's population lived in "Houses in Multiple Occupancy". In July 1992 there were 2,118 people on the housing waiting list of which 732 were families. Of these 732, 417 were on the Housing Priority List. 831 on the Housing Waiting List were single people of whom 125 were regarded as 'Priority'. It is worth commenting that the criteria for Priority status are becoming more stringent.

A local study undertaken by T Elliot (1991) on only six houses in Multiple Occupancy, found these to accommodate 35 children at risk of accident, infection, or underdevelopment, and her report paints a very disturbing picture of the home lives of these children.

> For example, M and her four children have been living in one attic room for over a year. Her three sons (two teenage and one five year old) share one bed behind a screen partition. The mattress and walls are damp and mildewed. Their sister sleeps on a camp bed by the cooker, and M on the bed-settee. There is no fire escape and no washing or drying facilities. The electrical appliances are in a dangerous state of repair and the communal kitchen ceiling is falling down. The bathroom is shared by 15 people and the children often find other people's excrement on the lavatory walls. Another family attending (a named Family Centre) was referred by the Health Visitor because of concerns about the young child's underdeveloped mobility. Within 3 weeks of attending the Centre the child was walking. She had not previously walked because there was literally no room to do so in the family's one room where there was about a inch gap between the bed, fridge, cooker and door. (Elliott, 1991 p. 4)

This study revealed a pressing need for further work with a larger sample and did not actually look at the school life of the children studied. From the point of view the Social Services, being 'homeless' is not a problem as far as their intervention is concerned, but problems arising from the home-lessness may come within their remit for intervention. Little systematic research has been undertaken to establish a picture of home-lessness from the point of view of the lives dependent young children and how *they themselves* view these lives.

Later on, responsibility for homeless single young adults lies uneasily between the providing groups in the City, the Social Services, Probation and the Health Authority. It seems that young people who are either on probation or pregnant stand a better chance of being found accommodation than young people who have to escape from abusive relationships at home and, therefore have become 'voluntarily' homeless. Many such young people are understandably reluctant to seek the necessary documentation from their parents to prove otherwise and are, moreover, not entitled to benefits from the state. In many other parts of Devon the problem of homeless young people has reached crisis proportions. In Torbay an Interagency Forum has just been established consisting of 30 different agencies working on the problem. In Plymouth activity is intense to deal with the escalating problems. It is clear that people in rural areas in Devon fare little better, as regards housing, and often migrate to the cities in search of work and accommodation. In Tavistock, for example, in the county, the *only* hostel for homeless young people is for people on probation. We have found it important in our work to examine the situation of young people identified by the Social Services 'at risk' across the county in both rural, urban and transitional (between the two) situations. Most of the data we have already examined is kept by the various statutory agencies. What appears to be missing is the *relationship* between data emerging from discreet sources and some sense of *historical* build up of the problems across all of these areas as evidenced in the individual lives of these young people and indeed the psychological fabric of those lives. We have continued looking at housing by undertaking extensive interviews with all the relevant statutory and voluntary agencies in the area.

II. PHASE TWO

A. Education: School Exclusion

In Phase 2 of our project we began to look more systematically at ways in which poor housing of the type we have described affects the child's educational achievement.

B. The National Picture

A recent report by Her Majesty's Inspectors of Schools (1992) indicated that their researches revealed that living in temporary accommodation disrupts children's schooling and adversely affects levels of achievements. This study found that the children had poor reading and oral skills and had a poor self-image. Secondary school children were at a disadvantage when it came to choosing options or choosing schools as they often arrive halfway through term. 'When these children meet a school system with opportunities and routines which rely on regular and consistent attendance, suitable achievement is often beyond their reach', it states in the report. Teachers are frustrated by pupils moving on again after they have spent time trying to help them and indeed the dearth of information about past achievements that is not passed from school to school. Pupils were often found to be listless from poor diet and suffered emotional problems that manifested themselves either in the child being withdrawn, tearful, aggressive or difficult. Elsewhere, (John 1993) the particular consequences of this for children with special educational needs has been examined in some detail.

The National Children's Bureau's research gives some hints as to the cause or the links here. They suggest that in such housing circumstances the child's need for security may remain unsatisfied because the parents' behaviour is unpredictable and contradictory. On the one hand they suggest, discipline tends to be autocratic, but physical punishment may at times be more of an outlet for parental anger and frustration, generated by the pressures of the daily struggle rather than a means of ensuring the child's conformity to particular standards of behaviour. The researchers suggest that discipline of this kind only succeeds in teaching the child to respect and use force itself. Even abusive verbal outlets coupled with all sorts of threats are more likely to make a child feel rejected that to enable them to understand that the parents are operating under a perpetual crisis of chronic frustration and uncertainty. The parents capacity to deal with such stresses is often so limited that they were found to be unable to give emotional support to their children. At times the children are in great need of such support just because even they are aware that family stability is so precarious. The researchers go on to point out further pressures as the children grow into adolescence as they become increasingly aware of how limited their chances are of escaping from multiple disadvantage. This material emerging from the studies of the National Children's Bureau clearly identifies the plight of some children living in temporary accommodation and the prognosis for their future.

In our own research one of the things that we explored was the extent to which children living in temporary accommodation appeared in the statistics for school exclusion. School exclusion in the United Kingdom at the present time is giving grave cause for alarm amongst a variety of professionals who work with the children. During the 1980s there was a spirit in education which emphasised the importance of inclusiveness, that all children whatever their backgrounds or abilities, intellectual, physical or emotional should have their educational needs met – these it was stressed should be met wherever possible within mainstream classrooms. The emphasis was on integrating all children within the classroom environment and where possible trying to provide for their particular needs within that setting. The 1981 Education Act emphasised the importance of this inclusive approach. 1986 however, marked a change of emphasis. The 1986 Education Act and the Elton Report (1986) spelt out a growing concern with the problems of discipline and behavioural difficulties amongst pupils in schools. Whilst the emphasis on integration is not entirely lost, nevertheless the need for preventative measures to reduce disruption and discipline difficulties in schools were stressed. It was made clear however, that some children might not be able to respond to these strategies and in such cases the particular remedy of 'exclusion' from school might need to be used. Under the 1986 Education Act three types of possible exclusion were identified, these being; 'fixed term' which was for under five days; 'indefinite' which was open-ended but was abolished by a later Education Act, in 1993, and 'permanent'. The provision for those excluded from school was to be either Home Tuition or small units to be provided for the few who were permanently excluded. In 1988 a further Education Act introduced Local Management of Schools. This meant the schools were going to be competing for pupils; were required to publish details for their pupil's educational achievements; budgets were devolved direct to schools such that schools were now set against each other in direct competition. The imposition of the National Curriculum and Standard Attainment Tests meant that school's performance results could be published for public scrutiny and comparison. This meant that schools were compared openly on one aspect of their activities i.e. academic attainment. Many schools argued that this was only one aspect of their effectiveness, that their personal care and teaching of children with differences and particularly those presenting with behavioural difficulties was not taken into account at all. Moreover as pupils became the selling point, for a school, it meant that pupils who were likely to present problems or to appear very poorly in the published statistics were not likely to be encouraged to be within the culture of the school. This has had consequences:

> The new anxieties of image and performance.. put back the clock. The spirit in our schools reverted to a pre-1981 state of intolerance and impatience towards difference and difficulty; of education for the norm, of selection criteria, ..., comparing individuals with others; of an narrow definition of what education was about. Moreover, with the emphasis on parental choice, this meant greater power to those parents who knew how to choose and felt empowered to make that choice. Some children have such a well co-ordinated parental lobby – the dyslexic, the physically disabled, those with partial sight, – but some do not. "Naughty" children are bad news in a market economy. No-one wants them. They are bad for the image of the school, they are bad for the league tables, they are difficult and time-consuming, they upset and stress the teachers. (Parffrey, 1993 p. 2)

The level of school exclusions in the United Kingdom gives grave cause for concern amongst many people who work with children, particularly as such levels started to include exclusions amongst children in their primary school years. The Government began to be active in trying to call a halt to such exclusions and started monitoring the statistics. The statistics for 1990–91, for example, 3000 children were reported having been excluded from school. The Department expressed doubt as to the accuracy of these figures.

Continuing work in the field, notably Margaret Stirling (1993) regarded this figure as a serious under-estimate. Even registered school exclusions in some authorities have risen at one stage by as much as 400%. One of the things that has happened since the Government starting actively monitoring school exclusion is that some of the problems have been driven underground in that children that are proving to be troublesome at school, it is suggested, are discouraged in a variety of ways from attending, particularly if they are towards the end of their compulsory education. The result of this is that they ceased to attend school and appeared in the statistics as 'truants'. It has now been suggested that schools should be forced to keep children and fined of they fail to do so.

C. The Local Picture

Given the national concerns about school exclusion of children presenting at school with emotional and behavioural difficulties, we found that it was not unlikely that some of the children in our city who are living in temporary accommodation would appear in the statistics of children excluded from school. We, therefore, started to look in detail at the school exclusion statistics. We did find remarkably high numbers of children in the primary school being excluded from school. Our earlier pilot indicated that disrupted housing might be associated with disrupted schooling to such an extent that some young children are not settled into a pattern of regular school-going in their early school life. Moreover, discussions with the personnel of one home for children in the residential care of the Local Authority revealed that all but one of these children were excluded from school and therefore children there were only receiving at that time 4 hours home tuition per week. We gathered enough data to raise anxieties about what was happening to children in temporary accommodation. Some of these children have to move frequently as temporary housing becomes available and lead quite unsettled lives at home both geographically and well as psychologically. Having collected data from several different domains, namely from the Housing Action Group and from the Education offices, we wanted to try to put together the meaning of the picture that we were assembling from these pieces. We were extremely fortunate that both the Director of Social Services and the Deputy Director of Education were both very concerned indeed about these issues. This meant that they worked closely with us, in establishing a series of meetings with their personnel, who they felt would be able to help us in establishing the meaning of some of the data we had collected.

The first meeting took place with 24 Head Teachers from primary schools in the city and its environs and a number of personnel from residential homes. We presented to them the data that we had accumulated and asked them to comment on what they felt was the single most important obstacle to the child's realising their rights as laid out in their Articles 28 and 29 of the

UN Convention. What we principally wanted to know was whether, in their view, they felt that there was any connection between a child's housing circumstances and their school performance and whether or not such behaviour had led in their experience to school exclusion. Moreover, we wanted to know something about their approach to the issue of managing emotional and behavioural disturbance at school. It was clear to us from looking at the collected statistics that schools in areas we would have suspected to have within their catchment area large numbers of children living in temporary accommodation, did not figure very predominantly amongst the statistics on school exclusions in the primary school. Other schools however, seemed to have very high numbers of children excluded from school and we wanted to understand, therefore, what lay behind these differences in practice. We wanted to know what in areas which, on the basis of our research, we felt were probably very challenging in terms of managing child behaviour at school, they were doing to contain and deal with the problems they encountered. To our astonishment, given the data that we had already collected, the general feeling of the meeting, with one or two notable exceptions, was that there was no connection whatsoever between housing problems and the sort of emotional and behavioural difficulties that led to school exclusion. They indicated most forcibly that this was not a problem they'd encountered and that they felt we, that is the researchers, were not in touch with the realities of what was happening in schools. This was difficult as, although we were not prepared to challenge schools directly, we had seen the statistics for school exclusions on a confidential basis, nevertheless what we were being told and what information we had gathered through looking at administrative records we could not reconcile. Apart from the Heads of the residential homes the teachers, generally speaking, felt there was no problem. We reflected on this after the meeting, and realised that it was not that there was no problem so much as they did not regard it as *their* problem. This intrigued us, as it demonstrated very forcibly to us the fragmentation of professional approaches to a common problem. In our initial meetings which we have referred to earlier in this paper with the various statutory and voluntary agencies concerned with homelessness, one complaint was the fact that there was poor communication between the services and that such fragmentation had been unconsciously encouraged by the repeated needs for each service to justify its own operation. This meant that each service tended to be looking towards their own need for resources rather than the need for collaboration with other relevant agencies.

Fortunately the meeting that we held under the auspices of our Local Education Authority with the Head Teachers was followed one week later by a meeting held with all the Social Service personnel that were involved in any way with families and young children or with young people. This meeting included the Youth Council itself which is a body in the County of Devon made up entirely of young people. The concept of the Devon Youth Council has been advocated and the organisation's needs to achieve representation through participation has been resourced appropriately by decision makers in this County.[1] The presence of the Council at this meeting was therefore important to us as a representative voice of young people in our Local Authority. The second meeting was important in that we put to the meeting the information that we had gathered at the previous one with Head Teachers. None of the participants at the second meeting seemed at all surprised. They indicated there were a number of reasons why the education personnel would not feel that this was a problem as follows:

1. The Education services would not regard this as their problem but as a 'Social Services problem' if a child was having difficulties as regards housing. They would not necessarily see that if these difficulties were manifesting themselves in difficult behaviour at school, that it was a problem that was something that they could take action about. This may be as a result of the narrowing of focus on the *educational* marketplace.

2. Many of the children living such difficult lives simply did not attend school on a regular basis and indeed, we were told that some of them had not even registered at school at all during the first few years of compulsory schooling. We established enough information in discussions with them to understand that there was a population of quite young children who had no experience of regular school attendance during the early years of compulsory school age.

Further enquiries and discussions with the local Adult Basic Literacy Project suggested to us that was possibly a further reason why young children living in difficult circumstances may not be attending school in these early years. These reasons are related to the mother's level of basic literacy. In our early enquiries we established that many teenage mothers had children who themselves became teenage mothers and many of these mothers had had disrupted schooling certainly in the latter part of their school life. The consequences of this disrupted schooling or abbreviated schooling had been that they had poor literacy skills. It was suggested to us therefore that some children did not attend school because the mother was unable to deal with the various administrative aspects of starting school and keeping the child at school, things like writing absence notes for a sick child, reading the parent-teacher newsletters and so on. They therefore, it was suggested, put off the child's registration at school for as long as they could.

On the basis of these two crucial meetings the emphasis in our research changed considerably. The discussions revealed that there were substantial numbers of young children who were not at school; there were large numbers of children who towards the end of the compulsory schooling period were living in difficult and very temporary circumstances who were also not attending school; that little was known about how either the young children or the older children spent their time. We have therefore on the basis of the

---

[1] A 'County' is a large administrative unit within England.

insights gained through working very closely with a large number of agencies in our local landscape established a project with which they fully co-operate which looks at the lives of children who are not at school.

III. PHASE THREE

A. *What do Children do all Day?*

The study we have now embarked upon has built upon our early enquiries and the co-operation we have received from all these local agencies. It is an accelerated longitudinal study of children who, for one reason or another, do not go to school. It has developed in all sorts of ways from the preliminary work we have done on the psychological "health" of young children living in difficult housing circumstances and school exclusion amongst young and older children. As we indicated earlier this preliminary work has been prompted by an interest in the life histories of "street children" of the South West and an attempt to look at possible developmental variables.

It is still suspected that housing circumstances will be a key variable in the present study although in this broader study other variables are not being eliminated. It is an "accelerated" longitudinal study as we are using the device of taking four samples of children at different ages as four "cross-sections" which we hope will inform each other. We hope that the study of each of these groups will contribute to some preliminary insight into what these children actually do all day as nobody seems to have clear picture of this. An early search of the literature of effectively 15 million publications revealed that no-one had yet published work on 'school-lessness'. We hope to establish the quality of the out-of-school experiences in the children's own eyes, giving us some broad picture of *the culture of school-lessness* across the whole school-age lifespan. The entire study remains framed within our concerns with monitoring Articles 28 and 29 of the UN Convention of Rights of the Child. We will be looking at the ways in which these rights are exercised. The research method in data collection centres around Article 12 of the Convention – the child's right to express an opinion, on matters that concern them and to have that view taken into account in decisions affecting them.

Given that our concern is with 'school-lessness' it might seem rather odd that included in our sampling, as described below, is a group of pre-school children. These four year olds provide the cohort for a traditional longitudinal sample which in a parallel study will follow these children through all the "cross-sections" in the present study (hopefully guided by our findings in these "sections") over the next ten years. In this way we will have data about particular age-groups and situations complemented, ultimately, by data about the continued development of individual children. The reasons for including pre-school children in a study ostensibly about schooling or lack or it, is to be found in the work of HeadStart and the National Children's Bureau researches which indicate long term effects of deprivation, or interventions in these early years. It is true that the early analysis of the HeadStart data did not seem to indicate that the experience of HeadStart interventions pre-school had little immediate effect on the child's performance in the first few years at school. Later follow-up of these children, however, indicates some remarkable differences among such samples compared with others who had not attended HeadStart Centres, particularly in relation to teenage pregnancy, drug abuse, youth crime. It was found that the HeadStart children figured much lower in these statistics than children from similarly disadvantaged backgrounds who had not had this experience.

The four cross sectional samples are as follows; each of these samples having subgroups of urban and rural children.

Group 1 two groups of children in the first year before they enter school. One of these groups is comprised of children living in temporary, inpermanent accommodation matched with children living in stable, if modest housing. This cohort is studied in the immediate present and was also be followed through over succeeding years to establish whether what we had hypothesised on the basis of reconstructions from our cross-sectional material holds good when the continuous development of the same individuals over time is monitored.

Group 2 consists of school aged children aged between 6 and 7 years who:
 – have never started school (compulsory school age in the United Kingdom starts at five)
 – do not attend school currently
 – have had disrupted schooling
 – have changed school frequently
   within this group we are differentiating groups for whom such changes are part of the pattern of their lives, e.g. children who have families who move frequently – such as service families, clergy, hospital doctors, banking personnel, etc.
 – children in short term situations such as children in hospital
 – children in the residential care of the Local Authority
 – children who are living in temporary accommodation
 – children in refuges and hostels

Group 3 focuses on those young people aged around 14 to 16 who for a variety of reasons find themselves "out of school". The source of school-lessness may be:
 – self inflicted, e.g. school refusal, school phobia
 – due to the formal procedures of "exclusions" being taken by the school and the Local Education Authority

– Home tuition due to illness or other circumstances

Group 4 consists of 14 to 16 year olds who are homeless and have ceased attending school.

B. The Aims of the Research

We are initially trying to establish some description of the children's informal experiences even before they start school and consider how these contribute to the process of education for self-reliance or making informed choices later in their lives. As the very young group will form the core of our longitudinal sample, we will eventually be able to undertake some life history and developmental analysis in addition to the cross sectional analyses that our ongoing accelerated longitudinal study will yield. We will look at what are the major characteristics of the child's life experiences in different groups and circumstances. A major emphasis will be on how the *children themselves* perceived their lives. Major questions we all address across all samples are:

What educational opportunities do these children have? In what way does this coincide with their entitlements?

Actualities
What form of schooling do they actually have / have had?
What do they do with their time? – What is the quality of that experience?
What is the nature of the peer group?
What they feel is important about what they do at the moment and what they would like to change?
How they see themselves?

The research team consists of: three members of staff from the School of Education, one of them with a background in Youth Work, one of them an Educational Psychologist, and one of them a Child Development Specialist; from the Department of Social Work we have a researcher with a background in working as a Social Worker with young families and a Senior Member of staff with a background in criminology; from the Local Authority we have Senior Management both from the Social Services and the Education Department. In addition we have representatives of various statutory and voluntary agencies. We would stress that the co-operation and collaboration with all of these parties has been a very important part of developing what is a challenging and important piece of work. Not only is the research breaking new ground in terms of collaboration, but also the research method is such that it is attempting to be innovative in collecting data which is sensitive and difficult to access.
The research method is largely qualitative, although some attempts will be made to collect quantitive data such that some sense of the size of the problem can be established. It would be important to know, for example, at any one

time what proportion of children of a particular school age are not at school. Whilst the size of the problem is clearly important, our primary concern is with the *nature* of school-lessness and what, if any informal educational experiences are part of that life. The methods used to access the child's world and their perceptions of that world involve a constellation of innovative methods providing a multi-perspective view by the following means. We will be keeping daily logs of children's activities ("diaries") and selected children will be shadowed. Some of their activities will be recorded on video tape and they will be asked to talk to us about what this video material means, that is interpret their own behaviour for us. We will also be using a semiotic method to identify the meaning for the child or some of the features of their life and environment so as to build up a picture of what the child does all day, and what the significance of these activities are for them. For the pre-school group we will also be establishing something about their hopes and fears about school – what they think school will be like, what they are worried about and the ways they feel it will change their present life. Some enquiries will be undertaken to establish whether or not they feel "safe" at present and also working with them to establish what they feel about themselves, what is "nice", what is "nasty" and what they wish for. These methods will be used particularly with the younger children. With the older children the video techniques are being used extensively and with great enthusiasm by them. They are also interviewing each other and the fact that some of their experience may cast some light on the work with the younger children is being used as a means to encourage them to help us with our enquiries.

C. The Child's Rights in the Research Process

A monitoring exercise of this kind, is highly dependent upon the goodwill, co-operation and, indeed, hard work of collaborating agencies. It also raises some challenging ethical issues. The project clearly involves some sensitive territory and requires a clear code of conduct in relation to the children is established as regards their continuing willingness to be involved and their understanding of what we are doing. We have also been anxious to establish quite clearly the constraints on the use of information relating the individual family / parent and that which is revealed during interviewing or shadowing of an individual child. In establishing these 'contracts' we have prepared a graphically illustrated booklet outlining that we are interested in building up a picture of what children do all day at various ages. This booklet is accessible to the young child and parent's with literary problems (the local Adult Basic Skills Unit have assisted here). Whilst the project has been agreed by the appropriate University ethics committees and procedures we have felt strongly that it is important in work of this kind that in enquiring into and monitoring the child's rights we do not in any way compromise those rights in our research procedures. The child's wishes, therefore, form the most fundamental guidelines for our research. Each child is our valued collaborator in the research process.

REFERENCES

Bonnerjea, S. and Lawton, D. (1987) *Homelessness in Brent*. London: Policies Studies Institute.

Elliot, T (1991) *Community Profile: Exeter North District*. Exeter: East Devon College (unpublished dissertation).

Elton Report (1986) *Discipline in Schools*. Report of the Committee of Enquiry. Chaired by Lord Elton, London: HMSO.

Her Majesty's Inspector Of Schools (1992) *Reported in "Exclusions: a Discussion Paper"*, November. London: Department for Education.

John, M.E. (1993) "Children with Special Needs as the Casualties of a Free Market Culture." *International Journal of Children's Rights 1* 1–22.

National Children's Bureau (1991) "Poverty and Family Support". Children Now. London: Joint Publication by the National Children's Bureau and the National Children's Home.

National Children's Bureau (1992) "Income and Poverty and Family Support" and "Children's Health". Children Now. London: Joint Publication by the National Children's Bureau and the National Children's Home.

Parffrey, V. (1993) Exclusion: Failed Children or Systems Failure? Paper given at the Annual Conference of Educational and Child Psychologists, British Psychological Society.

Scarry, R. (1969) *What do People do all Day?* New York: Random House.

Still, M. and John, M.E. (1994) *The Case for a New Family Centre*. Exeter.

Stirling, M. (1993) "Second Classes for a Second Class?" *Special Children, 66*, May, pp. 15–18.

APPENDIX

Statutory and Voluntary agencies who have worked with us so far:

The Education Department and Social Services Department Of Devon County Council

Shelter Housing Department Exeter City Council

Social Services (Childcare Purchasing Team)

Family Centre Architects

Health Visitors

Exeter Shilhay Community

Fairbanks Family Centre

Citizens Advice Bureau

Homeless Action Group

Palace Gate Centre

Justice and Peace Commission

Devon Probation Service

Relate

Dart

Careers Officer, DCC Education

Churches Day Centre Committee

Pupil Welfare Officer, South Devon

Devon Youth Council

Devon Community Education Tutors (Youth)
Youth Workers
Youth Work Officer
Children's Society
Youth Support Workers
Youth Justice Team, Plymouth
Detached Youth Workers
Wardens of a number of relevant residential establishments, Community Homes etc.
Various Child Care Teams in Devon
Managers of Children's Centres (for children in care)
24 Head teachers
2 Assistant Education Officers (Special Needs)
2 Senior Psychologists and Principal Education Psychologist
Senior Educational Welfare Officer East Devon

Other representatives from the NSPCC, Salvation Army, the Police and the Medical profession have indicated a desire to become involved.

MARIAN KOREN

The Right to Information – Too Vague to Be True?

Question-mark

Since the beginning of mankind a question floats around him. It is a sign, a mark that stays with him and appears at every birth. A question-mark: "Child, man, what do you seek?" And while the child is growing up, falls in love, has gladness and sorrow, the question-mark is always there. Sometimes it is very clear; at other times hardly seen or heard. But when man dies, the question-mark remains.

During the day human beings are busy. Children, and we ourselves, talk and work, laugh and cry. They don't give themselves a rest to ask themselves questions. But at some moments, when all movement stops, the question rises up before them, to remind them of something. Nobody can ask that question for another. Nobody can give the answer for another. Adult or child is irrelevant, they can only teach each other and learn not to escape but to face that question-mark in themselves. What do you seek in your desires, dreams and deeds? What do you seek?

This article[1] focuses on the fundamental aspects of the child's right to information, such as it is formulated in the UN Convention on the Rights of the Child. It will attempt to answer the following questions:
- What is the role of information in relation to the development of a child?
- What comprises a child's right to information as a human right?

---

[1] This paper is based on ongoing research about the significance of the child's right to information, which will result in a thesis to be upheld at the University of Amsterdam in 1996. It does not give any final definitions or statements, but reflects the state of the art, and welcomes reactions from various disciplines.

E. Verhellen (ed.), Monitoring Children's Rights, 667–679.
© 1996 *Kluwer Law International. Printed in the Netherlands.*

– What is the significance of the child's right to information?
– How to monitor the right to information?

At first sight this issue might seem to be too vague to be of substance. An in depth exploration of this right will add force to the applicability and the monitoring of the Convention.

I. The Role of Information in Relation to the Development of a Child

Would one be able to live without information?

It will not be possible to answer this question affirmatively in an age called "the information age". We are surrounded by numerous sources of information of various types and we function as a source of information ourselves. Information does not only include facts or knowledge, but also feelings, emotions, expressions, ideals. So information is important *in* our lives but also *for* our lives. Not only the processes in the brain and the mind, but all biological processes are described as information processes.[2] Life and information are closely related, especially when life still has to take shape. Information plays an important role in the development of children's lives. It supports their identity, personality and social participation. Some explanations:

Identity
By communicating with others children learn gradually about the world around them, their family, community and beyond. But they also learn about themselves as an encounter with another human being always works as a mirror. This information serves the child's identity; he knows who he is by saying and spelling his name. This name is related to the family and the community to which he belongs and whose culture he learns. Not knowing who his parents are, where they live or have lived, what they look like etc., means a lack of information which the child will try to fill by seeking the necessary information sooner or later, and if not possible, by compensating in behaviour. The existential questions of adolescents, not necessarily only adoptive children, witness the need of a human being to know and be sure about his descent, his roots and history of life.

Personality
The aim of growing up is not just achieving biological maturity or a certain age, it means becoming a true human being. The main question underlying all life development is: how to live and to develop qualities of a complete or perfect human being, such as dignity, honesty and carefullness. By exploring

---

[2] Thorenaar, W.S., *Vorm of inhoud. Over de verschillen tussen kunstmatige en biologische vormen van informatieverwerking*, Eburon Delft, 1992, p. 147–148.

this question a child develops his personality. By selecting, comparing and evaluating information from different sources his views and beliefs, his social and cultural experience, his taste and style of life are formed. In communicating with others he learns to give and receive information and how to make choices about what he will and will not communicate to others. Children mostly take over the norms and rules transmitted by parents, influenced in their turn by their parents and later experiences in society. Therefore the realization of values of a perfect human being depends very much on the actual behaviour of parents. How do they honestly try to realize this quality? The full development of a child's personality demands that in more or less traditional educational patterns some "spaces" should be left so that a child can decide for himself whether additional sources of information are needed.

Social Participation
Information is necessary in a complex society to survive, to fulfil primary needs such as housing, health, education and work. But survival is still far away from living as a perfect human being. Participation in social and cultural events depends on how young people are informed. What values are presented, that direct their needs and interests? The use of civil and other rights is unthinkable without having information about these rights and the way to use them. Respect and care for others and the environment are not possible without being informed about the values in different cultures, the consequences of exploitation of natural resources etc. Participation whether in family life or social life presupposes information. Otherwise decisions cannot be taken and children will be less able to influence their life circumstances. Recent research among Dutch youngsters shows that for most young people (12–21 years) their parents are the most important source of information for all aspects of life. They rely especially on their parents for information about education and society and turn to their mother for advice on relationships, sexuality and health. The informal network of parents, family and friends is primarily and far more consulted than the official information network of which teachers and libraries get the most requests for information.[3]

This short description makes clear how important information is in the development of children. But adults seem not always to realize this in their encounters, verbal and non-verbal, with children. Children don't want to be kept ignorant; they don't like to be just an object of conversation and regulation, but like to be active communicators themselves. If we want to see children grow up in harmony as true human beings, we have to offer them information which liberates them from dependence, which stimulates self-confidence and self-knowledge. Information which is useful and valuable can only be given by parents and adults who are honest in seeking and providing information themselves. In this way they can be models worthwhile to be

---

[3] Linden, F.J. van der, H. Guit, E. van Rooijen, *De vraag naar jeugdinformatie in feiten en cijfers. Kerngegevens uit een nationaal jongerenonderzoek*, Leiden, 1993, p. 210.

observed and imitated! Growing up as human beings children should be guaranteed to have access to the information which is necessary to be able to live as fully developed, perfect human beings. Is there a human right which supports this right to information?

II. A Child's Right to Information as a Human Right

The Charter and the Universal Declaration of the United Nations relate human rights to a spirit of peace, dignity, tolerance, freedom, equality and solidarity. These values can be regarded as qualities of full-grown human beings. Conventions, treaties and declarations are inspired by these sources. Both the Declaration and the Convention on the Rights of the Child show evidence of this spirit. The Convention links up with the general ideas about human beings and their growing up. It is a remarkable novelty that the process of maturation and gradual independence is acknowledged in the legal status of children. In the words of the Convention: "the evolving capacities of the child". It means that children will gradually be more involved in matters that concern their lives and that they will actively participate in decision-making.

The importance of the right to information is its encompassing role, due to the fact that information pervades all aspects of life. This is also recognized in the Convention where several articles refer to the right to information.

If one starts from the perspective of the child the right to information is an active right which supports the child's struggle to form his view of life and his role in the world. The right to information is for example related to the identity of the child. This not only includes a name and a nationality but also to know one's parents and be cared for by them, as stated in article 7. The idea was to ensure the psychological stability of the child, but protests during the drafting process led to a weakening of the obligation to ensure this right, by inserting "as far as possible" in the final formulation.[4]

Quite a number of rights dealing with the personality and participation of the child are formulated in the Convention although hardly elaborated for the situation of the child.[5] These rights include the right to express views freely in all matters affecting the child and the right to be heard in any judicial and administrative proceedings (article 12); the right to freedom of expression, which includes the freedom to seek, receive and impart information and ideas of all kinds (article 13); the right to freedom of thought, conscience and religion (article 14) and the right to privacy (article 16). All these rights are closely related to the right to information. To be able to form a view, to express an opinion, or to form a belief the child needs information. The

---

[4] E/CN.4/48, p. 18–22.

[5] See Van Bueren, G., "The struggle for empowerment: the emerging civil and political rights of children", in: *Selected essays on international children's rights*, Vol.1, Defence for Children International, Geneva 1993, p. 45–68.

right to expression and opinion presupposes the right to information. For instance, in confrontation with administrative and other authorities he needs to know about his rights and the consequences of communicating with these authorities.

The Role of the Media

The right to information is most explicitly formulated in article 17, which relates to the media. The two main parts of this rather large article are quoted:

> States Parties recognize the important function performed by the mass media and shall ensure that the child has access to information and material from a diversity of national and international sources, especially those aimed at the promotion of his or her social, spiritual and moral well-being and physical and mental health. To this end, States Parties shall:
> (a) Encourage the mass media to disseminate information and material of social and cultural benefit to the child and in accordance with the spirit of article 29;
> (...)
> (e) Encourage the development of appropriate guidelines for the protection of the child from information and material injurious to his or her well-being, bearing in mind the provisions of articles 13 and 18."[6]

Close reading of the text reveals that it is not literally the right to information, but the access to information which shall be ensured. This could make a difference: there is no right that any information required is given, but a child is free to seek and consult information available. The information must meet the qualification of diversity of sources and especially promote physical and psychical well-being and health. The value of the information supplied is to support the social and cultural benefit of the child. Reference is made to the purpose of education, formulated in article 29 which deals with: the development of the child's personality to his fullest potential; respect for human rights and fundamental freedoms; respect for other cultures and the preparation of the child for responsible life in a free society, in the spirit of understanding, peace, tolerance, equality of sexes, and friendship among all peoples. This formulation makes clear that the right to information is closely linked to a positive contribution of information to becoming a full-grown human being living according to valuable principles.

---

[6] A/Res/44/25. The text of the Convention can also be found in e.g. Van Bueren, G., *International documents on children*, Nijhoff Dordrecht, 1993.

Information Related to Educational Objectives

The close relationship between the right to information and the purpose of education is not surprising if one studies the Travaux Préparatoires[7] which reveal that the actual formulation[8] was mainly proposed by the Bahá'í Community, a religious NGO that promotes international understanding, world citizenship and stresses the importance of this education and supports the work of the United Nations.[9] [10] In a commentary on the proposal it is said: "Viewed positively, the mass media (in global terms, most notably the radio) provide the most potent means of conveying information to vast numbers of people. Appropriate information conveyed in this manner has the capacity to benefit children in a large variety of ways. Such information, disseminated in the appropriate languages, would be especially beneficial to children who live in remote rural areas and/or who are members of minority or indigenous people."[11] Tasks of the media would be to disseminate information to adults concerning child health, welfare and development; to support educational programmes; to promote the cultural heritage of the child and to inform the child of the wider world of which he is part.[12] Another proposal about the formulation of the aim of education (article 29) was put forward by Bahá'í as well. Bahá'í considers education as the most important means of improving the human condition, of safeguarding human rights and of establishing peace and justice on earth. But such education "cannot simply be academic education, or book-learning. The kind of education that is required is education of the character. It is not sufficient, for example simply to tell the child that he has a duty to respect human rights. What is required is guidance and training that will develop in the child qualities that are indispensable if the child is to become a promoter and protector of human rights."[13]

Dual Nature of Mass Media

In general there is a conflicting attitude towards information from the mass media, which is well reflected in article 17. On the one hand there is the

---

[7] Detrick, S.(ed), *The United Nation Convention on the Rights of the Child. A guide to the "Travaux Préparatoires"*, Nijhoff Dordrecht, 1992.

[8] E/CN.4/1983/62, Annex (E/CN.4/1983/WG.1/WP.2, WP.29).

[9] Information from Bahá'í brochures, like *The Bahá'í Belief*, Bahá'í International Community, London 1988; *The Promise of World Peace, a statement by the Universal House of Justice*, Bahá'í World Centre, Haifa 1985; and *Bahá'í Education*, Bahá'í Publishing Trust, London 1987[2].

[10] This is a clear example of the influence of NGO's in the drafting process of the Convention, as described in Cohen, C.P., Role of non-governmental organizations in the drafting of the Convention on the Rights of the child, in *Human Rights Quarterly*, Vol.12, no.1.

[11] E/CN.4/1984/NGO/2, p. 2–3.

[12] E/CN.4/1983/62, Annex II (E/CN.4/1983/WG.1/WP.2).

[13] Letter of Bahá'í International Community, undated, referring to their proposal about the aims of education (E/CN.4/1985/WG.1/WP.2).

view that one could learn a lot from the variety of programmes, articles and items which the mass media offer, on the other hand one rejects the presentation of violence, semi-pornographic scenes and misbehaviour. The supposed strong influence can work either way. Originally the draft contained only a regulation about the protection from harmful influence by the mass media.[14] But "one speaker felt that the mass media does more good than harm and therefore the article should be phrased in a positive way, rather than in terms of protecting children from the mass media. States parties should ensure freedom of information, so that children can take advantage of a diversity of opinion concerning all matters.[15] So article 17 stresses both the educational role which mass media should play, and encourages guidelines to protection of the child from injurious information. In its regulation the article even refers to the right to freedom of expression formulated in article 13 and to the primary responsibility of parents for the upbringing and development of their children in article 18. This could mean that the limits of guidelines for protection are formed by the freedom of the child to seek, receive and impart information and by the responsibility of the parents for bringing the child up according to the basic principle of what is in the best interests of the child.

III. THE SIGNIFICANCE OF THE CHILD'S RIGHT TO INFORMATION

The right to information, underlying so many important areas of life, is not only vast but also complicated as so many parties are involved: parents, state, other adults, mass media, and other institutions like public libraries. All have their task in ensuring that a child can realize his right to information.

Parents

The primary care for the child's right to information rests with his *parents*. It is part of their responsibilities relating to the guidance and development of the child. Not only in words but first of all in behaviour, in deeds and reactions an adult informs the child about activities and attitudes. If parents show respect for themselves and for others, a child will have less prejudices and keep an open mind. Children will only be informed if parents take time to listen to them, show interest in their questions and honestly try to answer them or to find out together. This should also concern questions of faith and belief, other cultures and lifestyles, habits and conscious acts, education and values of life. It is the duty of the parents to communicate with their children, also about rights and duties, smaller and bigger responsibilities and the underlying value of human dignity. They should offer possibilities for children to find

---

[14] E/CN.4/1349, p. 4.

[15] E/CN.4/L.1575, p. 19–20. (1981) The identity of this speaker is not revealed in the report. Nor is this the case in the report of the next year where the arguments were repeated.

out things themselves, to express themselves and to taste different sources of information. Children who have never seen a parent reading will hardly create reading habits, in spite of attempts to promote reading later on. Their efforts to form thoughts, ideas and opinions should be stimulated so that they can participate in making decisions about the activities of the family and about their own lives. The right to information presupposes the duty of parents to inform, but this cannot be done without honest and open communication. This includes information about the child's descent in an appropriate moment. Adopted children, children begotten with artificial means or those having lived in state care should not be left with secrets about their identity, however painful this sometimes might be for well-wishing adults. Honest communication is a better basis for reciprocal respect.

Other Adults

In certain circumstances there are *others* who should inform the child, either additionally or primarily. This is for instance the case when judicial or administrative proceedings take place. The child can only give his views when he has been clearly informed about this opportunity and his rights and has the feeling that he is listened to, that his words and feelings make a difference. The way the child is informed and listened to makes or breaks his belief in the judicial world and justice. In fact, the right to be heard would imply a duty to listen from the side of the authorities. This would mean that listening is an activity which requires one to be involved in the other and trying to understand what he tries to communicate.[16] In the specific case of a court investigation an extra effort is necessary as it cannot be expected that children speak in conformity with the usual language in a court. Little research has been done about communication in court[17] but it can be expected that practical application of communication science results can contribute to a human communication, where difficult decisions for the child are taken.

Another situation in which the child often seeks information is in hospital. He not only needs information about his medical data but also wants to be prepared in case of an operation, wants to know about diagnosis and prognosis and even about the process of dying.[18] As always, this information should be adapted to children's understanding, but their capability of dealing with the most difficult questions of life and death has often been underrated.

---

[16] idem, p. 54.

[17] See for one example, Atkinson, J.M., P. Drew, *Order in court. The organisation of verbal interaction in judicial settings*, Macmillan London, 1979.

[18] Theunis, M., "Rechten van het kind in het ziekenhuis: recht op informatie", in: E. Verhellen, F. Spiesschaert, L. Cattrijsse (eds.), *Rechten van kinderen. Een tekstbundel van de Rijksuniversiteit Gent naar aanleiding van de UNO-Conventie voor de Rechten van het Kind*, Gouda Quint, Arnhem 1989, p. 315–328.

The State

As in many other human rights, it is the duty of the *State* to respect the rights of the child and his freedoms to thought, conscience, belief, expression and opinion. Normally this means that the State should refrain from interfering. But it can be argued that the State also has a positive obligation in supporting the possibilities for children to seek information or to express their views. This would mean the establishment and supporting of children's rights service, advice and information services for children, free access to libraries and loans, workshops for children on topics of their interests. An important point is to relate the right to information to children's participation. This should not necessarily be a kind of "play parliament", but should first of all be a change of mind of adults who are going to decide about matters which also affect children. Communication opportunities for children will help to create more participation in decision making in their neighbourhood or organisations.

In general the State has the duty not to interfere in the life of the family and respect the privacy of parents and children. So the State should not prescribe what information parents have to give to children. But in last resort it is the duty of the state to control parents to take their responsibilities and to fulfil their tasks towards their children. The State has to ensure that the dignity of the child is respected by everyone.

Media

As article 17 states access to information should be ensured. As the relation between *mass media* and state is one of official distance, because of the freedom of expression and the free flow of information, the state's obligation cannot be formulated in strict terms. So the state's role is one of encouragement and stimulation towards the mass media. Of course some measures can be and should be taken. The production and distribution of children's books for example can be stimulated by creating libraries in countries where this service has not been sufficiently developed. Multicultural books and books in minority languages can be another aspect of this policy. The most important point is that the role of the media is related to an educational aim and the promotion of human rights. This can be a qualifying tool for the mass media and the productions which should be stimulated by the state. Both state and mass media should develop international co-operation in order to support the diversity of sources. Third World countries should profit from this regulation, which should be realized without "cultural imperialism".

In 1995 an international conference, has been organised by the Australian Children's TV-foundation, where a charter for children's television has been discussed. This charter attempts to protect the interests of children, stating that they "should have programmes of quality, which are made specifically for them, reflecting their particular needs, concerns, interests and culture, which do not exploit them." The importance and vulnerability of children's broadcasting are stressed.

Public Libraries

One of the public institutions which could be of main importance to support the child's search for information is the *public library*, which is freely accessible for everyone. The public libraries have subscribed to international values of democracy, equality and public access as formulated in the *Unesco Manifest of the Public Library* of 1972 which has been revised in 1994. There is no relation to the Convention although half of the library users are children. Amazingly enough, very few publications are dealing with the Convention's right to information and public libraries.[19] In an examination of the articles of the Convention related to access of information and freedom of expression Guggenheim found less protection for children's rights than adults rights in these areas. He also pointed to the fact that "school libraries are subject to greater restriction, based on content, than are public libraries, but schools are not permitted to remove books from their shelves because school officials do not approve the contents of the material contained in them."[20] In 1992 American Libraries started a campaign called "Your right to know: librarians make it happen". A background study dedicated to the youth's right to know concludes: "Youth's right to know is somewhat less firm than that of adults legally (...) It is important to remember that, despite the lack of absolute legal underpinning or definition, an implicit right can still exist. There are certain things a young person simply must know to survive, to grow up and to have a productive life in 21st century America."[21]

Research shows that children and young people have a lasting contact with libraries and that they go there especially for information on leisure time, social and juridical items, medical, relational and sexual aspects.[22] No doubt, libraries could play an important role in realizing the right to access of information not only by offering books for children, but also by developing their information seeking skills and by distributing information about the Convention. This presupposes that they accept the right to information as one of the human rights they serve.

---

[19]   A clear reference is found in the Japanese library magazine: S. Yammamoto, "Library activities and the Convention on Children's rights" [in Japanese], *Toshokan-Kai* (The Library World), Vol.43, nr.5 1992, p. 228–231.

[20]   Guggenheim, M., "The child's access to diverse intellectual, artistic and recreational resources", in: C.P. Cohen, H.A. Davidson (eds.), *Children's rights in America U.N. Convention on the Rights of the Child compared with United States Law*, American Bar Association, Chicago 1990, p. 289–302.

[21]   Chelton, K., "Youth's right to know: societal necessity or national oxymoron?", in: Curry, E., (e.a.), *Your right to know: librarians make it happen. Conference within a conference; background papers*, American Library Association 1992, p. 36.

[22]   see note 2, p. 224 and p. 210.

IV. HOW TO MONITOR THE RIGHT TO INFORMATION?

The monitoring mechanism of the UN Convention on the Rights of the Child is largely based on reports submitted by the State Parties who have ratified the Convention. "There is a need to carefully study the situation in each country, in order to see what kind of programme of action should be adequately and realistically considered, to ensure progressive betterment in the effective enjoyment of children's rights."[23] The nearest source of information are children themselves. As is stressed in the introduction of the conference theme: "We know very little about how children, in their own minds, interpret events or give meanings to them. In any event, we tend to dismiss such processes as not (yet) important." On the other hand the question arises as to how could children be involved in the monitoring of the Convention. A key could be found in the following points:

1. Children themselves should know about their rights. The Convention could be promoted as a kind of Children's Law, as has been done in Sweden.[24] Article 42 prescribes that the principles and the provisions of the Convention should be widely known. Attention should be paid to different forms of communication with children.
2. Adults living or working with children should be informed about children's rights and the actual existence of the Convention. Their important role in observing the situation for children and possible reporting to a NGO or ombudsorganisation should be stressed.
3. All adults, regardless of whether they have frequent or few contacts with children should be informed about the core of human rights in the case of children: children are human beings and should therefore be fully respected. Human rights are a means to exemplify human dignity in the relation between state and individual but also among individuals.
4. The value of the information given by children will increase as it becomes clear to them that what they think, feel, experience is valuable and important. This should always be the case. It would be dreadful if only adults had this attitude towards children, when a report has to be made! Children will clearly notice the difference in being listened to in a free communication, or in a more forced conversation.
5. National reports are only useful if they contain accurate and honest information. This can only be achieved if the sources of information are reliable. It involves attentive observation of all people involved and an honest evaluation of results.

---

[23] Santos Pais, M., "General introduction to the Convention on the Rights of the Child: from its origins to implementation", in: *Selected Essays on international children's rights*, Vol.1, Defence for Children International, Geneva 1993, p. 12.

[24] See for instance: *Barnens Lag, en skrift om FN:s konvention om barnets rättigheter*, Rädda Barnen, Stockholm 1993 and other informative and promotional materials from Rädda Barnen.

6. In order to be able to build up a view of the world, an identity and personality children need reliable sources, adults, who live and behave according to their own words and who stimulate children to inquire themselves. Most of all children need to learn to rely on themselves, which means that they can trust and feel free to express what they are experiencing.
7. The right to be heard should become more visible in judicial statistics, to broaden and ameliorate this right which presupposes correct and adequate information to the child.
8. In their duty to inform children parents should be supported by social institutions that perform their tasks based on the child's right to information.
9. A general institution where both parents and children have public access and can find reliable and additional information is the public library. It will help them in seeking, qualifying and selecting information according to their intentions.

No Excuses

The quick and broad ratification of the Convention could be odd. Are the formulated provisions so vague that necessary changes never become true?

It is important to notice for example that the heading of article 17 differs in the various drafts and in the final publications in different languages. The headings vary from "mass media", "Massamedien und Jugendschutz", "access to proper information", to "right to information" in Dutch. This variety shows that the matter regulated in article 17 can be and has been approached from different views and gives rise to different interpretations. The Council of Europe for example, clearly supported by the Convention, accepted a Recommendation concerning information and counselling for young[25] people, which led to the formulation of a Youth Information Charter by some youth organisations.[26]

One could criticize the fact that the right to information is so vague that it can hardly have any real or manageable meaning. This criticism is too easy and besides the point. One has to keep in mind the aim of the Convention: to formulate an international standard of human rights worldwide applicable to situations in which children without discrimination find themselves. It is true that the universality of human rights has been questioned (Vienna Congress 1993) but an alternative for letting human dignity survive even in difficult circumstances, has not been found, so the Universal Declaration remains the

---

[25] Council of Europe, *Recommendation* R(90)7 of the Committee of Ministers to Member States concerning information and counselling for young people in Europe, Strasbourg, 1990.

[26] *European Youth Information Charter*, Adopted in Bratislava (Slovakia on 3 December 1993 by the 4th General Assembly of the European Youth Information and Counselling Agency (ERYICA).

point of departure. And the Convention gives the guidelines for obligations to realize the provisions and rights formulated in a general sense.

What is needed is a general interpretation based on accepted concepts and derived from reliable methods. Such a general interpretation will be enough to be developed further in institutions working with or for children's rights. It is obvious that the application of a right to information cannot be the same in Third World countries and in Europe. In highly industrialized countries standards for human rights have to be high, which means that respect of children's rights in general is not enough. Where material needs are satisfied, there is an even greater duty to develop the inner life as a human being. That is the possibility which the right to information should offer to every child.

The Balloon

Slowly a balloon rises upwards. It floats over the top of the trees, over the hills. It goes straight up. The balloon is not red, not blue, you can look through it. The wind blows gently. Suddenly the winds sees something strange, it is round and surely no bird; it goes higher than the clouds. Such a thing he has never seen before! The wind comes closer, brushes past the balloon and asks:"Who are you? Where are you going?" The balloon rises higher and higher and keeps silent. The wind gets a little bit angry and cries: "What kind of empty thing are you? You are nothing. I blow you wherever I want!" And teasingly the wind begins to blow. The balloon goes up and down and keeps silent. The wind is astonished and holds its breath. He recognizes something in the balloon. Then, very softly, the balloon whispers: "I am not empty. In me it is full of life, in me is the longing for something which rises above all things. In me is the breath of a child."

ALENA KROUPOVÁ

Convention on the Rights of the Child

Education for the 21st Century

The transition from the communist totalitarian rules to democracy and thus also implementation of human rights to their full extent is a long and enormously difficult process which is unique in many respects because it is in fact taking place for the first time. *The confrontation of the past with the future needs a compromise solution to be sought for the present.*

The "post-communist" countries of Central and Eastern Europe – the Czech Republic among them – have taken the first steps towards democracy, but still have a long way to reach it. Not only the economic conditions are the obstacle but particularly *psychic and behavioural characteristics* that citizens adopted during the period of the totalitarian regime. Behaviour of the majority of them is far from the independent, tolerant and cooperative citizens. Besides that their way to democracy is coming up against newly emerging or previously neglected problems – many of them did not be expected.

The former CSFR, which has split in the Czech Republic and Slovak Republic by the end of 1992, was one of the first Central European countries which ratified the UN Convention on the Rights of the Child. Therefore the Czech Republic – since the beginning of 1993 – became a party of this Convention and undertook the obligations of the partners. Even in the past this country ranked among those where priority of children's interests was declared in the Constitution, in the Family Act and in social regulations. Yet, the true human rights of children, support for the development of the child as an autonomous individual possesing full rights and freedoms were practised only to a considerably limited extent.

The new Czech Government was convinced that safeguarding the rights of children as well as their protection declared in the UN Convention would not raise any problems because even in the past care for children enjoyed preference. The essential question, i.e. *the position of the child as the subject of the law or the subject of the educational process was mostly not raised at all.*

The compromise political solutions in the transitional period resort some time in *grossly simplified legal procedures*. And these may – and indeed in many cases do – produce new inequities which affect negatively the status

E. Verhellen (ed.), Monitoring Children's Rights, 681–689.
© 1996 *Kluwer Law International. Printed in the Netherlands.*

and position of children, too. It is no wonder that the UN Convention, in spite of its holistic approach, fails to cover this kind of cases.

Within this framework, there are two objectives for this paper:

1. To present information about the analysis of some of those problems in the Czech Republic which newly affect the life of children and implementation of the signed UN Convention on the Rights of the Child in the daily practice. These problems exist whereby the country is forced to resolve problems pertaining in economic, ecologic, legislative or social sphere and when new problems in the field of health care are on the rise.
2. To point out that the Convention on the Rights of the Child because of its synthetic characteristic can be used for human rights education purposes not only as one of the documents of the international law, but also as a living material for discussion among children and their tutors. We have in mind those kinds of discussions that should lead to the finding of the way for all of us to feel free, equal and selfconscious citizens of our planet.

I. NEW PROBLEMS IN THE PROCESS OF CHANGES

A. *Changing social welfare impact*

In the sphere of human rights and their implementation, the past situation of the Czech Republic was characterized by the *suppression of political and civic rights and freedoms.* This was "counter-balanced" by the emphasis on *egalitarian policies in the area of social welfare, particularly in the form of assistance to mothers taking care for small children.*

In fact, all those measures and regulations supported primarily women's employment. The number of children was a factor determining female retirement age and the number of years of employment required for the pension claim. Social as well as labour market legal norms not only encouraged women to work but simultaneously formed the legal basis for the duty to work practically throughout one's working age i.e. the period from compensation person's vocational training or school education (15 years age at earliest) until reaching the retirement age (53 – 57 years of age for women, 60 for men).

In the new situation, when voluntary care for household and children is not the reason for a person's punishment, former social assistance measures put women at a disadvantage. Unfortunately, up to now there is no governmental family policy able to promote equal status of women.

B. *Changing role of social legislation*

The period of transition to market economy is characterized *inter alia* by the fact that *former social measures and legal norms* and their not-yet-finished innovation *negatively affect labour market, particularly the position of young women*. Some of those problems were expected but their profundity and extent were underestimated. This is true above all with what concerns the increasing unemployment of well-skilled women. Female workers "aggravated" by the – up to now – valid social welfare protection, e.g. paid maternity leave up to three years of the child's life, are not being able to compete equally as their male collegues in the labour market.

This natural development in the labour market is not yet accompanied by the appropriate social legislation. The only visible provision is the *curtailment of flat-rate financial contributions* to families with small children and *destruction of the system of subsidized preschool and child-care facilities*. This development confronts citizens with problems for which they are not prepared and which in some regions create social tension. Unfortunately, the assistance of non-profit organizations, NGOs or trade unions in this sphere is not yet effectual, and increasing lack of appropriate preschool facilities practically sets women with small children aside the skilled employment.

C. Changing Value of Professional Skills

In the past for both boys and girls, *school education emphasized their role as members of labour force*, i.e. as workers and employees. It is no wonder, that this situation substantially affected – particularly women's – scale of values. This concept of the educational policy was accompanied with the *general phenomenon* in the Central and Eastern Europe way of life, i.e. that *women had children at a younger age* than their Western European counterparts. This often resulted in women being faced with the situation where raising small children fell in the same period as the need to concentrate on the development of occupational and professional skills. Such situation only reinforced the importance of providing adequate and cheap child-care facilities.

Two-earners income was for former way of life and in a prevailing number of the Czech families the necessity. Therefore, women very often resigned the higher education and preferred the low skilled job located in the neighbourhood of the preschool facility, i.e. *women's ability to make use of their higher professional skills strongly corresponded to the presence or absence of a small child in the family*. Findings of several surveys underlined that women really conceived employment outside the household as an economic necessity to ensure the family the appropriate standard of living as *the family, i.e. children ranked first and foremost for their interest*. During the last four years this situation is slowly changing. There is a visible decline in newly born children, particularly of 20-year-old mothers.

D. *Underestimation of education for democracy*

Other new unenvisaged problem is *a gap between proclaimed political will for human rights protection* e.g demonstrated by the ratification of all principal international covenants and the practical governmental policies neglecting *education for democracy, human rights, tolerance and international understanding as well as the acknowledgment of the legal status of nongovernmantal organizations* in the democratic society.

The totalitarian regime proclaimed economic, social and cultural rights as the fundamental ones which should be put above the political and civic rights, i.e. *equality being put above freedom*. This official policy caused in the minds of the people that the material aspects – even where values of rights and freedoms were concerned – had the priority. Human rights thus come to mean the Western way of life, i.e. high material standard of living. In a special case of UN Convention on the Rights of the Child, its provision regarding *the right of the child to an appropriate standard of living* is perceived not as a necessary complement of the fundamental human rights but as *an aspiration of material property irrespective of personal responsibility of one's fate and of rights and possibilities of the others*.

The deformed way of thinking requests special aproach to education for democracy, tolerance, human rights and international understanding. First of all, the new concept of teachers training should implement democratic teaching methods.

E. *Persisting lack of legal consciousness*

In the past, a lack of legal consciousness was the typical aspect of people's behaviour. The profundity of this educational aspect was underestimated. It is not only *the widespread ignorance of basic legal norms*, due to their practical inaccessibility and poor comprehension to the ordinary man, but indeed downright *disparagement of the significance of legal norms for the existence and development of the democratic society*. That together with deformation of people's minds and former long-term authoritative educational practice leads often to *the preference of traditional authoritative attitudes* in many spheres of daily life.

Besides, people's experience with the concept of *right* and *having a right to* causes the right to be seen as *claim or aspiration* on something, without making it clear that *rights involve also responsibility* which prevent them from infringing upon the equal rights of one's neighbours.

It is a real unpreparedness for freedom, the speed of changes in past four years, the fact that things develop often contrary to expectations that sometimes result in social confrontation and extensive ethnic and national conflicts.

II. EDUCATION FOR THE 21ST CENTURY

A. *School education for democracy, tolerance and human rights*

What concerns education, the Czech Republic has not yet carried out a comprehensive legal reform or articulated its overall concept of the State's role in the educational sector. However, many substantial changes are coming. It should be also noted that any established educational system undergoing fundamental change encounters numerous forms of inertia – new opportunities cannot be all seized at the same time, not every experiment can be a major success, and also many teachers find it difficult to break from long-term practice in both substance and methods.

Even if it cannot be said that the already realized changes and the already presented proposals for the reform of education system are consistently applying the approach to the child as an active self-conscious subject of the education process – as set in the Convention on the Rights of the Child – changes in the contents, methods, and means of education are pointed in this direction.

Education of national minority group children is provided either in standard schools on the basis of Czech as the teaching medium and the language of respective minority taught as an optional subject (German, Slovak), or through separate classes in standard schools or through independent schools. This is the case of Polish schools which are operated in North Moravia, where these schools (pre-school facilities, basic primary and middle schools, secondary schools) were in the previous year attended by some of 10,000 children.

The problem of *appropriate school education for Romany children* is not yet solved. In 1991, Romanies gained legal status of national minority. Romany language, unfortunately, does not yet exist in the written form and therefore Romany children in the first grade of primary school remain dissadvataged. They very often leave the standard school and continue in the special education. Alternative education is not yet frequent.

Special education for handicapped children is provided in the Czech Republic at all levels – from pre-school to primary and middle-school basic education, to secondary general, technical, or vocational education. The content and methods of this type of education are differentiated by the type of handicap – deafness, sight handicap, physical handicap, multiple handicaps, mental retardation, behavioural disorders and learning difficulties. About 3,4 per cent of all children under 18 years attended such special education schools or facilities in the year 1993.

Currently there is a strong movement favouring the *integration of handicapped children into standard schools*. The legal prerequisites for this have been already created. The main obstacles to practical implementation of such integration are not only a lack of appropriate technical equipment and architectural deterrents, but also the inadequate preparedness for this change on the part of parents (of both healthy and handicapped children), the general public, and teachers. The practice of separating handicapped children from others is still deeply ingrained. The implementation of alternative solutions – such as special or remedial classes in ordinary schools, different length of stay (selected hours), all-day medical care – should help to promote the further integration of handicapped children into the mainstream of the education system.

A school education system which corresponds to an understanding of human rights and   should follow the democratic example whereby *sensible and reasonable discussion*, based on respect for the individual, equality and freedom, should form the basis of classroom methodology. Understandably, such discussion can function efficiently within the framework of human rights implementation which means, however, certain personnel restrictions on expression and behaviour.

B. Educational role of the family

Speaking about children's education, we cannot forget *the educational influence of the family*. It is the family which is the first to shape or suppress the value of human dignity, mutual respect, as well as awareness of civic, family and individual identity and ideas of the way an individual should organize his/her life. As such, it is also the micro-society where the first application or violation of human rights, the formation of democratic or undemocratic attitudes takes place.

When analysing the present state of the family in the post-totalitarian country, clear distinction is mostly not possible to make between the general trends of modern society and the specific phenomena in family and social relations which are products of the communist system. *The cognitive insufficiency results inter alia* in – sometimes officially proclaimed – tendency *to return to the traditional patriarchal family model*. Restoration of the democratic, educational, emotional values of the family in the life of the individual as of the society seems to be *an urgent challenge of civic associations and non-governmental organizations* in all post-communist countries of Central and Eastern Europe in the next period.

C. Convention on the Rights of the Child as the basis for education for the 21st century

Within the PHARE Democracy Programme project "Towards Human Rights Education" the brief analysis of the UN Convention on the Rights of the Child as a fundamental document for human rights teaching, learning and training was completed. This analysis should be used as the teaching aid both for teachers as for students helping them to understand human rights, human duties and responsibilities.

The abstracts of the analysis could be referred as follows: *The Convention on the Rights of the Child* was adopted by the UN Assembly on 20 November 1989. Therefore it is not only in compliance with its subject (children from 0 to 18 years of age) but also to its own "age", the youngest in the line of principal international documents in the sphere of human rights. Up to the year 1993 the Convention was ratified by 174 UN member states, which is a substantially larger number than had been reached in cases of other international documents on human rights. In Europe all states joined this Convention.

Some of the principal characteristics of the Convention on the Rights of the Child partly differ and some are identical with other international treaties. The unique positive characteristic of the Convention on the Rights of the Child which differs from other human rights conventions is without doubt its *holistic approach* to the rights of the child. It forms *a complex of civic, political, economic, social and cultural rights in connection with the preservation of human dignity of the child.*

Therefore the document is not only *general* but at the same time *specific* – concentrating on a concrete social group. It is also a Convention *on the protection of the rights of groups* i.e. children and a Convention *against* their *discrimination.* All the rights in the Convention are at the same level – none has a more important place than others. (A similar endeavour can be seen in the approach of the European Convention on Human Rights, but its contents and range remain less complementary.)

The further list of contents demonstrates that the Convention on the Rights of the Child covers all aspects which have till now been globally known in the sphere of human rights protection.

UN Convention on the Rights of the Child protects rights to:
 - life, survival and development
 - a name, nationality and an identity
 - liberty and security of person
 - not to be abused and tortured
 - not to become a slave
 - human dignity
 - help and protection of national and international law
 - a fair and public hearing at courts
 - privacy of home and correspondence
 - protection in unlawful attack of honour and reputation
 - education
 - leisure, play, artistic and cultural activities
 - own property
 - adequate living standarts
 - marry and found a family
 - participation in civic life

Fundamental Freedoms:
- freedom of thought, conscience and religious belief
- freedom of opinion and expression
- freedom of peaceful assembly
- freedom of movement and residence

As can be seen from the former list the child in this Convention is an active subject, i.e. a citizen that has rights in all spheres and at all levels which concern him/her. In addition, a new aspect: *the right of the child to grow up in a family*, which is considered as the most natural environment for child's harmonic development and well-being.

The Convention cannot cover all the changes which occur in nowaday families and which often negatively affect children's lives. Therefore the ratification of the Convention poses a big social responsibility on States (Governments) for the life of children, *i.e. inter alia to guarantee appropriate living conditions for families with children* (even if such obligation is not an explicit part of the Convention). In the faremost consequences all UN member states which became parties of this Convention – without reservation of the described article – should revise their policies and programmes in all spheres concerning chidren and families. Even newly adopted social measures which concern families with children, if they are to be in compliance with the obligations ratified in the Convention, should be judged according to their effect on the life of children.

Nevertheless even the holistic conception of the rights and freedoms of the child anchored in the Convention show some unclear aspects in practical application. The most urgent tasks for all national legislations are those which emerge from *the definition of the child as a "human being from the age of 0 years to 18 years"*.

It is understandable that many rights and freedoms of children without the closer specification of the children's age group remain only on paper. However, direct admission of rights and freedoms for a concrete age group is not possible in this kind of international document. This was also one of the conclusions of the discussion within the experts of the Council of Europe. Therefore they recommended not to continue drafting a special European Convention on the Rights of the Child. Instead the *Council of Europe tries to formulate the principles of obligatory national policies for the welfare of children.* These policies should cover even the changing situations in families that endanger children and assure conditions for solving conflicts in favour of children.

The other, for implementation Convention on the Rights of the Child in daily practice, the big problem is *the absence of explicitly stressed responsibility of children* in applying their rights and freedoms while not being in collision with rights and freedoms of others. Although this aspect is common in promoting human rights through all international covenants, children's ability to *understand their rights and freedoms as their rights and duties* is particularly limited in European region (according to the traditional paternalistic understanding care for children in this part of the world).

The challenge of the Convention on the Rights of the Child is to help parents and educators to educate children as selfconscious, tolerant, responsible and sovereign citizens of the world of 21st century. The involvement to assist this positive process is an honest task for each of us.

REFERENCES

ABC Teaching Human Rights (1989) New York – Geneva: UN Press.

Kolektiv autorů (1992) *Výchova a práva dieťaťa*. Bratislava: ÚMC MŠ SR.

Kroupová A. (1993) *Children in the Time of Changes*. Praha: EIS UK.

Légeois J.P. (1987) *Gypsies and Travellers*. Strasbourg: Council of Europe.

Meodow R. (1989) *ABC of Child Abuse*. London.

Meron T. (1984) *Human Rights in International Law, Legal and Policy Issues*. Oxford: Clarendon Press.

Rozumíme lidským právum? (1994) Praha: SVLP UK.

Starkey H. (1991) *The Challenge of Human Rights Education*. London: CE ltd.

UN Convention on the Rights of the Child (1990) New York: UNICEF Press.

Williams J. (1985) *Our Freedoms Rights and Resposibilities*. UTD.

IOAN OANCEA

Les droits des enfants appartenant aux minorités nationales d'apprendre la langue maternelle et le droit d'être instruits dans cette langue – entre la lettre de la loi et la réalité de la société Roumaine

La Déclaration des droits des personnes appartenant aux minorités nationales, ethniques, religieuses et linguistiques, adoptée par l'Assemblée Générale de l'ONU en décembre 1992, dispose: "Les Etats devraient prendre des mesures appropriées pour que, dans la mesure du possible, les personnes appartenant à des minorités aient la possibilité d'apprendre leur langue maternelle ou de recevoir une instruction dans leur langue maternelle".

La Réunion de Copenhague de la Conférence sur la dimension humaine de la CSCE a adopté, en juin 1990, un document qui a inclus un chapitre substantiel relatif aux minorités nationales. Pour ce qui est de l'enseignement, le document susvisé mentionne que les personnes appartenant aux minorités nationales auront, outre l'obligation d'apprendre la langue officielle de l'Etat en question, la possibilité d'apprendre leur langue maternelle ou d'être éduquées dans cette langue.

En adoptant lors de sa réunion du mois de novembre de cette année la Convention-Cadre relative à la protection des minorités nationales, le Comité des Ministres du Conseil de l'Europe a aussi inclu dans ce document des prévisions concernant la reconnaissance du droit des personnes appartenant aux minorités nationales d'apprendre leur langue maternelle ainsi que des prévisions concernant les efforts déployés, dans le cadre de chaque système éducationnel, en vue d'assurer aux personnes appartenant aux minorités nationales des possibilités d'apprendre leur langue maternelle ou de bénéficier d'un enseignement en cette langue.

La Convention sur les droits des enfants – dont la mise en oeuvre fait l'objet d'analyse de notre Conférence – prévoit dans son article 30 que: "Dans les Etats où il existe des minorités ethniques, religieuses ou linguistiques ou des personnes d'origine autochtone, un enfant autochtone ou appartenant à une de ces minorités ne peut être privé du droit d'avoir sa propre vie culturelle, de professer et de pratiquer sa propre religion ou d'employer sa propre langue en commun avec les autres membres de son groupe".

E. Verhellen (ed.), Monitoring Children's Rights, 691–702.
© 1996 *Kluwer Law International. Printed in the Netherlands.*

Aux termes de l'article 2, paragraphe 1 de la Convention, la Roumanie – qui a ratifié la Convention le 28 septembre 1990 – s'est engagée à respecter les droits énoncés dans la Convention et à les garantir à tous les enfants, sans distinction aucune de race, couleur, sexe, langue, religion, opinion politique ou d'une autre opinion de l'enfant, de ses parents ou de ses représentants légaux, de leur origine ethnique ou sociale, de leur situation materielle, de leur naissance ou de toute autre situation.

La Constitution de la Roumanie, adoptée par un referendum populaire en décembre 1991 prévoit dans son article 20 que "Les dispositions consti-tutionnelles relatives aux droits et libertés des citoyens seront interprétées et appliquées en concordance avec la Déclaration Universelle des Droits de l'Homme, avec les pactes et les autres traités auxquels la Roumanie est par-tie. En cas de non-concordances entre les pactes et les traités portant sur les droits fondamentaux de l'homme, auxquels la Roumanie est partie, et les lois internes, les réglementations internationales ont la primauté".

En parlant de l'égalité en droits de tous les citoyens, basée sur le caractère unitaire et universel des droits et des libertés fondamentales, la Constitution de la Roumanie garantit cette égalité à "tous ses citoyens, sans distinction de race, de nationalité, d'origine ethnique, de langue, de religion, de sexe, d'opinion, d'appartenance politique, de fortune ou d'origine sociale" (article 4).

En ce qui concerne le droit à l'instruction, l'article 32 de la Constitution de la Roumanie stipule: "Le droit des personnes appartenant aux minorités nationales d'apprendre leur langue maternelle et le droit de pouvoir être instruites dans cette langue sont garantis; les modalités de l'exercice de ces droits sont déterminées par la loi".

En ce qui suit, je vous prie de me permettre de présenter quelques aspects concrets de l'organisation de l'enseignement pour les personnes appartenant aux minorités nationales en Roumanie.

I. LE RESEAU ET LA SCOLARISATION

Dans les localités à population appartenant aux diverses ethnies, l'Etat assure l'organisation et le fonctionnement de l'enseignement dispensé dans les langues des minorités nationales. Le système de l'enseignement pour les minorités nationales correspond à l'enseignement général de Roumanie, réglementé par un arrêté du Gouvernement et comprend: des écoles mater-nelles, des écoles primaires, des collèges, des lycées, des écoles profession-nelles et d'apprentissage et des écoles post-lycée.

Au cours de l'année scolaire 1993/1994, on a enregistré un nombre de 4.286.083 élèves et étudiants, (ce qui représente 18,8% de la population du pays) dont plus de 230.000 enfants, élèves et étudiants (5,5% ont fréquenté l'enseignement dans leur langues maternelles, autres que le roumain).

L'enseignement préuniversitaire comprend 28.941 unités, dont 2.807 fonctionnent en tant qu'unités ou sections d'enseignement dans les langues des minorités nationales (9,9%). Du total de ces unités et sections d'enseignement, 85,5% fonctionnent en langue hongroise.

L'enseignement dispensé dans les différentes langues maternelles est organisé tant en unités autonomes (1.350) qu'en sections roumaines -hongroises, roumaines-allemandes, roumaines-serbes, etc. (1.517). Tant dans les unités que dans les sections, le processus d'enseignement se déroule dans la langue maternelle. Dans les plus de 1.500 sections/unités mixtes, la base matérielle – salles de classe, laboratoires, bibliothèques etc. – est utilisée en commun, la direction de l'école est unique et une série d'activités extrascolaires sont organisées soit en roumain, soit en roumain et dans la respective langue maternelle.

Il est assuré aux élèves appartenant aux minorités nationales qui, selon leur désir ou celui de leurs parents, fréquentent des écoles où l'enseignement est dispensé en roumain, l'étude de la langue maternelle dans tous les cycles de l'enseignement: pour les classes I à IV, 4 heures par semaine et pour les classes V à XII, 3 heures par semaine. L'enseignement se fait par groupes composés de 15 à 30 élèves. Dans le cas où le nombre total des élèves désireux d'étudier la langue maternelle est au dessous de 15, des groupes de 7 élèves peuvent être organisés. Un groupe peut être composé d'élèves provenant de la même classe ou de classes différentes. Si les groupes sont composés d'élèves provenant de diverses classes, ils peuvent réunir des élèves des classes du même niveau ou du même cycle scolaire (I-IV, V-VIII, IX-XII).

Dans l'année scolaire 1992/1993, des 70.000 élèves qui fréquentaient les écoles où l'enseignement est dispensé en roumain, une partie étudiait également la langue maternelle (environ 20.000 Magyars, 1.000 Allemands, 8.064 Ukrainiens, 1.386 Russes-Lipoveni, 1.449 Turcs, 621 Polonais, 461 Bulgares, 55 Tsiganes etc.).

II. LE CONTENU DE L'ENSEIGNEMENT

Les plans d'enseignement, les programmes et les manuels scolaires nécessaires dans le processus didactique sont assurés par le Ministère de l'Enseignement.

Pour l'enseignement primaire, secondaire premier cycle et deuxième cycle sont élaborés des plans d'enseignement spéciaux, destinés aux établissements où l'enseignement est dispensé dans les langues des minorités nationales.

Dans le cycle primaire, 73,5% des disciplines prévues dans le plan d'enseignement sont enseignées dans la langue maternelle, dans les collèges 75,4% et dans les lycées, de 60,2% à 82,8%, en fonction du profil du lycée – humaniste, scientifique, industriel etc. L'enseignement de la langue maternelle et de la langue roumaine occupe une place importante dans les plans d'enseignement. Ainsi, dans les collèges et les lycées, l'enseignement de la langue et littérature maternelles occupe la même place que l'enseignement du roumain dans les écoles où la langue d'enseignement est le roumain. La bonne connaissance de la langue maternelle exerce une influence directe sur l'acquisition des connaissances dans toutes les disciplines scolaires, étant en même temps un moyen important dans la création de valeurs culturelles, de la littérature propre, ainsi que dans la réception des valeurs littéraires universelles.

L'assimiliation de la langue roumaine, langue officielle d'Etat, par tous les citoyens de la Roumanie constitue l'instrument qui assure les prémisses nécessaires à la coopération et à la communication entre les Roumains et les minorités nationales. La connaissance de la langue roumaine comme moyen de communication entre tous les citoyens de notre pays, sans distinction de nationalité, acquiert des valeurs particulières dans la réalisation de l'égalité des droits. C'est pour cela que la langue et la littérature roumaines sont des disciplines étudiées dans tous les cycles, formes et profils de l'enseignement préuniversitaire. Durant le cycle primaire le roumain est enseigné 19 heures, durant le collège 17 heures et durant le lycée 12 heures. Pour le collège et le lycée, le nombre d'heures est égal à celui prévu pour les écoles où l'enseignement est dispensé en roumain.

Les programmes de langue et littérature maternelles, par lesquels sont établis les objectifs et les tâches didactiques pour chaque classe et chaque niveau de l'enseignement, sont élaborés par le Ministère de l'Enseignement en coopération avec de nombreux groupes d'enseignants de tous les niveaux, des écrivains, des critiques littéraires etc. Tous les programmes de langues maternelles ont été révisés de manière substantielle pendant les années 1991 et 1992. Les programmes pour le cycle primaire et le collège prévoient des lectures littéraires dont la thématique est directement liée à la vie et à l'activité des enfants de cet âge. Ces lectures sont choisies dans le trésor de la littérature classique ainsi que des oeuvres littéraires contemporaines écrites dans la langue de la minorité respective.

Au lycée, l'étude de la littérature dans la langue maternelle se fait sur la base des principes linéaire et concentrique, de sorte que chaque élève prenne contact et acquière des connaissances sur les plus importantes oeuvres littéraires dans sa langue maternelle. Les programmes pour le lycée contiennent également les oeuvres littéraires écrites en Roumanie dans les langues des minorités nationales, oeuvres qui font partie intégrante de la culture de notre pays.

Un objectif de première importance de l'enseignement dispensé dans la langue maternelle – le développement des capacités d'expression – est réalisé par les leçons de rédaction, de grammaire ou celles qui traitent de problèmes d'orthographe et d'orthophonie ainsi que par les leçons de sémantique. Les exercices d'expression écrite visent la construction logique des propositions et des phrases, la corrélation entre le contenu de la proposition et la réalité etc. Les notions de langue sont généralement ordonnées sur la base du principe concentrique d'enseignement dans le cadre des divers niveaux scolaires, le bagage de connaissances des élèves s'enrichissant chaque année de nouveaux aspects. L'enseignement des notions linguistiques ne se réduit pas à l'explication des phénomènes grammaticaux, mais il est centré notamment sur des applications pratiques, faisant en même temps des références aux phénomènes de langue, tant sous leur aspect scientifique que sous l'aspect de la correction de l'expression.

Par l'enseignement et l'assimilation de la langue et de la littérature maternelles par les élèves on réalise – au delà des objectifs communs à toutes les disciplines scolaires – l'objectif spécifique de cette matière, c'est-à-dire susciter l'intérêt de tous les jeunes pour la littérature, développer leur capacité de réception du phénomène littéraire, la sensibilité pour le beau artistique, la capacité d'émettre des jugements de valeur sur une oeuvre d'art, en dernière instance, de faire en sorte que l'amour de la lecture les accompagne tout le long de leur vie.

Dans l'enseignement préscolaire et primaire, pour l'étude de la langue roumaine il y a des programmes spécifiques, au collège et au lycée les programmes sont uniques – les mêmes programmes, quelle que soit la langue d'enseignement.

Pour tous les élèves des écoles où l'enseignement est dispensé dans les langues des minorités nationales, les manuels en langue maternelle pour les disciplines prévues dans les plans d'enseignement sont assurés gratuitement. Dans les écoles en langues hongroise et allemande sont assurés des manuels en langue maternelle pour toutes les disciplines étudiées dans les classes I à XII, dans les écoles en langues serbe, slovaque et ukrainienne, pour les disciplines prévues dans les plans d'enseignement pour les classes I à VIII, ainsi que des manuels de littérature maternelle pour les classes IX à XII. Dans les écoles en langues croate et tchèque, sont assurés les manuels nécessaires aux élèves des classes I à IV, correspondant au niveau auquel l'enseignement est dispensé dans la langue maternelle. De même, sont assurés les manuels de langue et littérature maternelles aux élèves des écoles où l'enseignement est dispensé en roumain et qui ont demandé d'étudier la langue maternelle – turque, bulgare, polonaise, russe, romani.

Les manuels de langue et littérature maternelles et, selon le cas, de musique, sont élaborés par des professeurs qui enseignent dans les écoles où l'enseignement est dispensé dans les langues des minorités nationales ou qui font partie des chaires de langue et litterature maternelles des universités. Les manuels pour les autres disciplines (mathématiques, physique, chimie, biologie etc.) sont traduits du roumain. De même, sont élaborés des manuels spécifiques à l'enseignement de la langue roumaine dans les classes I à IV, avec des vocabulaires bilingues: roumain-hongrois, roumain-allemand, roumain-slovaque, roumain-serbe, roumain-ukrainien, roumain-tchèque.

L'édition des manuels revient aux Editions Didactiques et Pédagogiques où il y a deux rédactions pour les manuels en langues des minorités, avec deux filiales à Cluj-Napoca et à Timisoara.

Des quelque 1000 titres publiés pour l'enseignement préuniversitaire, plus de 330 titres de manuels sont destinés aux écoles où l'enseignement est dispensé dans les langues des minorités nationales. Pour l'année scolaire 1992/1993 ont été imprimés 95 titres, ayant un tirage de 631.460 exemplaires et pour l'année 1993/1994 ont paru 208 titres, ayant un tirage de 750.600 exemplaires.

III. LA FORMATION ET LE PERFECTIONNEMENT DES ENSEIGNANTS

Pour l'année scolaire 1993/1994 dans l'enseignement préuniversitaire fonctionnaient 262.771 enseignants, dont 16.022 dans les écoles en langues des minorités nationales (2.729 monitrices de maternelle, 3.630 instituteurs et 9.459 professeurs).

La formation des monitrices et des instituteurs s'effectue dans les écoles normales en langues hongroise et allemande, où, pour l'année 1993/1994 étaient inclus 2.150 élèves hongrois et 211 élèves allemands. Pour les autres minorités, il y a, périodiquement, des classes à profil pédagogique auprès de certains lycées. A présent, sont formés ainsi 150 élèves ukrainiens, 30 slovaques, 28 turcs, 82 russes-lipoveni, 55 tsiganes et 50 bulgares.

Le personnel nécessaire dans l'enseignement secondaire du premier et deuxième cycle (collèges et lycées) et de l'enseignement professionnel est formé dans les établissements d'enseignement supérieur de Roumanie. Les professeurs de langue et littérature maternelles, pour toutes les écoles en langues des minorités nationales, sont instruits par les professeurs spécialisés des universités de Cluj-Napoca, Bucuresti, Timisoara, Sibiu.

Dernièrement, un nombre important d'étudiants des diverses nationalités étudient à l'étranger: en Hongrie, Ukraine, Bulgarie, Slovaquie, Serbie, Croatie.

Le perfectionnement des enseignants ainsi que les épreuves des examens pour l'obtention des grades didactiques sont soutenus, sur la demande des candidats, dans leur langue maternelle.

Au niveau des établissements et sections scolaires, un nombre important d'enseignants provenant des minorités nationales occupent des fonctions de direction – directeurs ou directeurs adjoints. En fonction du nombre d'élèves et d'enseignants, dans certains inspectorats de département sont engagés des inspecteurs de spécialité provenant de leur minorité, y compris dans des fonctions de direction. Dans le cadre du Ministère de l'Enseignement il existe une Direction pour l'Enseignement des Minorités Nationales, où travaillent des spécialistes de diverses ethnies, chargés de la coordination et de l'orientation de l'enseignement dispensé dans les langues des minorités.

IV. Presentation de l'enseignement pour les minorites nationales

A. *La minorité hongroise*

Pendant l'année scolaire 1993/1994, l'enseignement dispensé en hongrois a été assuré à tous les niveaux scolaires (préscolaire, primaire, secondaire et universitaire) tant dans des écoles séparées que dans des sections de langue hongroise fonctionnant dans des écoles où l'enseignement est dispensé en roumain et dans les langues des minorités nationales.

Dans l'enseignement préuniversitaire le réseau scolaire contient, en tout, 2.451 établissements et sections scolaires. Le pourcentage des établissements et des sections où l'enseignement est dispensé en hongrois est de 8,5% du total du réseau scolaire de Roumanie.

Le réseau des écoles où l'enseignement est dispensé en hongrois détient un pourcentage de 8,7% dans l'enseignement préscolaire, c'est-à-dire 1.110 établissements et sections sur les 12.715 existant dans le pays; 8,95 dans l'enseignement primaire (classes I à IV), c'est-à-dire 547 établissements et sections sur les 6.160 existant dans le pays; 7,9% dans le premier cycle (collège) c'est-à-dire 602 établissements et sections sur les 7.639 existant au niveau national; 11,0% dans le deuxième cycle (lycée), c'est-à-dire 141 établissements et sections sur les 1.277 du pays; 4,5% dans l'enseignement professionnel et post-baccalauréat, c'est-à-dire 52 établissements et sections sur les 1.150 du pays.

Echelonnée en fonction de chaque niveau d'enseignement, la situation des enfants et élèves qui poursuivent des études en langue hongroise se présente comme suit: dans les maternelles il y a 48.192 enfants représentant 6,8% du nombre total d'enfants scolarisés à ce niveau; dans l'enseignement primaire et au collège (classes I-VIII) il y a 125.480 élèves représentant 5,0% de l'ensemble des élèves scolarisés à ces niveaux; au lycée il y a 30.450 élèves, soit 4,2% et dans l'enseignement professionnel, l'enseignement technique, l'enseignement post-baccalauréat et les écoles de contremaîtres il y a 7.170 élèves, soit 2,0%.

60.433 enfants et élèves d'origine hongroise fréquentent des classes où l'enseignement est dispensé en roumain. Ainsi, le nombre total d'élèves hongrois de tout l'enseignement préuniversitaire atteint 271.750, représentant 6,3% de l'ensemble des élèves de l'enseignement préuniversitaire de Roumanie. Par niveaux d'enseignement, la répartition des élèves de nationalité hongroise qui fréquentent des établissements ou sections où l'enseignement est dispensé en hongrois se présente comme suit: 77,8% du nombre total des élèves de nationalité hongroise étudient en langue maternelle; dans l'enseignement préscolaire, 85,4% sont compris dans des groupes d'enfants dont les activités se poursuivent en langue maternelle; dans les classes I à IV, 84,8% étudient en langue maternelle; dans les classes V à VIII, 80,4%; dans les lycées 69,0% et dans l'enseignement professionnel, l'enseignement technique, l'enseignement postbaccalauréat et les écoles de contremaîtres, 37,7%.

Le nombre d'enseignants qui assurent l'enseignement en hongrois atteint 14.565 dont 2.458 monitrices, 3.299 instituteurs et 8.808 professeurs et contremaîtres. Par rapport à l'année précédente le nombre d'enseignants a augmenté de 914. Du nombre total d'enseignants, 10.770 ont une formation adéquate à l'emploi, c'est-à-dire 74,0%, le restant des postes étant occupés par un personnel non-qualifié.

De la direction des 2.451 établissements et sections où l'enseignement est dispensé en hongrois font partie 1.462 directeurs et directeurs adjoints (1.243 directeurs et 219 directeurs adjoints) d'origine hongroise.

De même, les inspecteurs régionaux généraux des départements de Covasna et Harghita et un des inspecteurs généraux adjoints des départements Arad, Bihor, Brasov et Mures sont de nationalité hongroise. Plus de 60 inspecteurs de nationalité hongroise assurent la direction et le contrôle direct de l'enseignement de la minorité hongroise de Roumnie.

Dans le cadre de la Direction de l'Enseignement pour les Minorités Nationales du Ministère de l'Enseignement fonctionne un service chargé de l'enseignement dispensé en langue hongroise.

Les élèves bénéficient de manuels scolaires gratuits, quelle que soit leur ethnie.

B. La minorité allemande

L'enseignement dispensé en langue allemande comprend 302 établissements et sections, dont 12 établissements de plus par rapport à l'année scolaire 1992/1993 (162 maternelles, 123 écoles primaires et collèges, 14 lycées et 3 sections d'enseignement post-baccalauréat), où sont scolarisés 19.690 enfants et élèves.

Un nombre important d'élèves appartenant à la minorité allemande (plus de 5.000) apprennent dans des écoles où l'enseignement est dispensé en langue roumaine et peuvent étudier aussi, sur demande, la langue allemande comme discipline scolaire (4 heures par semaine dans les classes I-IV et, respectivement, 3 heures par semaine dans les classes V-XII).

Dans l'enseignement dispensé en allemand travaillent 1.123 enseignants (0,38% du total des enseignants de la Roumanie). Dans certains cas et notamment dans le milieu rural, l'encadrement des enseignants qualifiés dans les écoles où l'enseignement est dispensé en allemand est déficitaire. Conformément à l'accord conclu entre le Ministère de l'Enseignement de Roumanie et le ministère correspondant de l'Allemagne, en Roumanie plus de 40 professeurs allemands enseignent dans des écoles où l'enseignement est dispensé en langue allemande.

La direction de l'enseignement dispensé en langue allemande est assurée par des enseignants appartenant à la minorité allemande. L'inspecteur scolaire général adjoint du département de Timis et l'inspecteur général adjoint du département de Sibiu sont de nationalité allemande.

C. La minorité serbe

L'enseignement dispensé en langue serbe est organisé dans les départements de Timis, Caras-Severin et Arad et comprend 37 établissements et sections, fréquentés par 1.011 enfants et élèves. Le réseau scolaire comprend 15 maternelles, 20 écoles primaires et collèges et 2 lycées.

Dans l'enseignement dispensé en serbe il y a 108 enseignants (21 monitrices d'école maternelle, 28 instituteurs et 59 professeurs). A l'Inspectorat scolaire du département de Timis travaille un inspecteur de serbe. La formation des monitrices et des instituteurs se réalise dans l'Ecole Normale de Timisoara et la formation des professeurs de langue serbe dans les Universités de Bucuresti et de Timisoara. En même temps, il y a un certain nombre d'étudiants qui poursuivent des études en Serbie.

D. La minorité ukrainienne

Pour les élèves appartenant à cette minorité il y a 23 établissements d'enseignement préuniversitaire (10 écoles maternelles, 11 écoles avec les classes I-VIII et 2 sections de lycée) dans lesquels apprenent 778 élèves. Dans ces établissements l'enseignement est dispensé en langue ukrainienne étant assuré par 50 enseignants.

Pour les élèves de nationalité ukrainienne qui fréquentent les écoles en langue roumaine, on assure, sur demande, l'enseignement de la langue maternelle pendant 4 heures par semaine à l'école primaire et respectivement 3 heures par semaine au collège et au lycée. La plupart des élèves choisissent cette forme d'étude de la langue ukrainienne, leur nombre en étant une preuve. Ainsi, pendant l'année scolaire 1993/1994, 7.738 élèves étudient leur langue maternelle, dont 3.714 dans les classes I à IV et 4.024 dans les classes V à XII. Cette forme d'étude de la langue maternelle a connu une extension après 1990.

E. La minorité slovaque

L'enseignement dispensé en langue slovaque a un réseau stable et comprend 39 établissements et sections scolaires avec 1.355 élèves (12 écoles maternelles, 21 établissements avec les classes I à IV, 5 écoles générales avec les classes I à VIII et 1 lycée avec les classes I à XII dans la ville de Nadlac, le département d'Arad). Au lycée de Nadlac, il y a aussi une classe à profil pédagogique où sont inscrits 30 élèves provenant des départements dans lesquels il y a des écoles maternelles et des écoles primaires en langue slovaque.

Le processus d'enseignement est assuré par 141 enseignants.

F. La minorité tchèque

L'enseignement dispensé en langue tchèque comprend au niveau préscolaire et primaire 2 écoles maternelles et 5 écoles avec les classes I à IV où sont inscrits 204 élèves. Ces établissements sont situés dans le département de Caras-Severin, 15 enseignants y travaillent. Les élèves ayant achevé le cycle primaire poursuivent les cours dans les collèges où l'enseignement est dispensé en langue roumaine, mais, sur demnde, ils peuvent étudier aussi la langue tchèque comme discipline scolaire (3 heures par semaine), solution pour laquelle, pendant l'année scolaire 1993/1994, ont opté 191 élèves.

G. La minorité bulgare

Pour les enfants de nationalité bulgare il y a une école maternelle en langue bulgare, dans le département de Timis, fréquentée par 148 enfants, où enseignent 6 monitrices. Les enfants ayant l'âge scolaire apprennent dans les établissements où l'enseignement est dispensé en roumain et ils étudient, sur demande, leur langue maternelle. Le nombre d'élèves a atteint 612. Depuis 1990, il y a une tendance d'accroissement; c'est pourquoi, à part les groupes existant déjà dans le département de Timis, de nouveaux groupes ont été créés dans d'autres départements.

H. La minorité croate

Jusqu'en 1989, les élèves provenant de cette minorité fréquentaient les écoles où l'enseignement était dispensé en roumain et, sur leur demande, ils pouvaient aussi étudier la langue maternelle. A partir de 1990, dans le département de Caras-Severin ont été créées deux maternelles et deux écoles primaires (classes I-IV) où étudient 130 enfants, l'enseignement étant dispensé en langue croate. 439 élèves de nationalité croate qui fréquentent des écoles où l'enseignement est dispensé en roumain ont demandé d'étudier aussi la langue maternelle en tant que discipline scolaire (156 dans l'enseignement primaire et 283 au collège).

I. La minorité turque et tatare

Les élèves provenant de la minorité turque et tatare étudient leur langue maternelle en tant que discipline scolaire. A partir de l'année scolaire 1990/1991, des groupes d'étude ont été créés dans 44 écoles des départements de Constanta et Tulcea et il y a 52 enseignants. Le nombre d'élèves qui ont opté pour l'étude de la langue maternelle en tant que discipline scolaire dans l'enseignement primaire et secondaire atteint 1.682. De même, il existe trois sections d'enseignement préscolaire en langue turque, comprenant 116 enfants.

J. La minorité russe (Lipoveni)

Après 1990, pour cette minorité d'origine russe qui vit dans les localités des départements de Tulcea, Suceava, Constanta, Braila, Iasi et Botosani ont été créées des classes et des groupes d'étude de la langue maternelle (4 heures de cours par semaine pour les classes I à IV, 3 heures pour les classes V à XII) où sont compris 1.694 élèves.

K. La minorité polonaise

La minorité polonise vit dans le département de Suceava. Dans 7 localités de ce département il y a des classes ou des groupes d'élèves qui étudient leur langue maternelle (4 heures de cours par semaine pour les classes I à IV et 3 heures pour les classes V à VIII). Dans l'ensemble, ces groupes et classes contiennent 380 élèves.

L. La minorité tsigane

Comme importance numérique, la minorité tsigane occupe, conformément au recensement de la population de 1992, la troisième place.

Pour les élèves provenant de cette minorité il y a 8 établissements d'enseignement préuniversitaire où ils étudient, sur demande, la langue "romani". 375 élèves ont opté pour cette solution. Pour l'enseignement de la langue "romani" sont prévues 4 heures hebdomadaires dans les classes I à IV et 3 heures hebdomadaires pour les classes V à XII. Cette forme d'enseignement s'est développée des 3 classes existant pendant l'année scolaire 1992–1993 à 11 classes pendant l'année scolaire 1993/1994 (8 classes pour l'enseignement primaire et le collège et 3 classes pour le lycée).

55 élèves sont scolarisés dans les écoles normales de Bucuresti, Bacau et Tirgu Mures, auxquels on assure l'étude de la langue romani. Après le baccalauréat ces élèves vont enseigner en tant qu'instituteurs dans les localités où il y a une population tsigane.

* * *

Les événements de décembre 1989 qui ont déterminé la chute du régime dictatorial en Roumanie ont été suivis, surtout dans les districts avec une population hongroise majoritaire – Harghita et Covasna – par des actions de séparation des écoles, par la création de nouvelles unités scolaires, exclusivement sur des critères ethniques.

Les effets de ces actions se sont manifestés sous la forme de certaines tensions sociales, surtout au cours de l'année 1990.

Nous ne sommes pas encore en mesure d'apprécier si cette séparation a eu des effets bénéfiques sur la qualité de l'enseignement. Ce que l'on peut toutefois affirmer avec certitude c'est le fait que, du point de vue des relations interhumaines, de la promotion de l'esprit de tolérance, de l'amitié et de l'entente entre les personnes appartenant aux minorités et celles appartenant à la majorité ou n'a enregistré que des effets négatifs.

L'étude de ces aspects ainsi que de ceux concernant le mode d'intégration dans la vie sociale-économique des jeunes qui ont accompli leurs études dans les langues des minorités représentent des objectifs pour des recherches futures.

L'analyse du mode dont sont assimilées et mises en oeuvre les normes internationales concernant les droits des personnes appartenant aux minorités nationales ainsi que l'éducation en ce sens se retrouvent parmi les préoccupations de l'Institut Roumain pour les Droits de l'Homme, qui a élaboré à cette fin un programme d'actions au niveau national pour la période de la décennie, proclamée par l'ONU, de l'éducation aux droits de l'homme. Le programme comprend aussi un chapitre à part sur les actions destinées à soutenir l'éducation aux droits de l'homme dans l'enseignement pré-universitaire. Des activités de formation de formateurs, des symposions et autres manifestations en vue de la promotion d'une méthodologie adéquate pour l'enseignement de ces connaissances, ainsi que la réalisation de manuels et de materiels didactiques sont prévues à se dérouler dans le cadre de ce pro-gramme.

L'ensemble de ces activités est destiné à assurer une instruction adéquate aux enfants de la Roumanie, dans le but de les rendre capables de s'assumer les responsabilités de la vie dans une société libre, dans un esprit d'entente, de paix, de tolérance, d'égalité entre les sexes et d'amitié entre tous les groupes ethniques, nationaux et religieux ainsi qu'avec les personnes d'origine autoch-tone.

IRINA MOROIANU ZLĂTESCU et VIRGINIA MAXIM

Le Processus d'Enseignement aux Droits de l'Homme après 1989

L'éducation dans le domaine des droits de l'homme est devenue une préoccupation importante en Roumanie après 1989. Tous les efforts sont dirigés vers l'éducation, dans le but d'enseigner aux differentes catégories de la population pas seulment quels sont leur droits, mais aussi la manière dont ils doivent agir si ces droits leur sont violés, à qui s'adresser et, enfin, de leur enseigner que les droits sont toujours accompagnés par des devoirs, ainsi que par le respect des droits des autres. Les programmes éducationnels qui visent à préparer la population de se défendre contre les eventuelles violations des droits de l'homme constituent la préoccupation des organisations de caractère militant dans le domaine des droits de l'homme, mais il y a aussi des programmes educationnels destinés à ceux qui, en premier lieu, sont confrontés avec des problèmes reliés au respect des droits de l'homme – avocats, juges, procureurs, cadres de la police et des pénitenciers. Un place à part revient à l'enseignement, où l'attention est dirigée, d'une part, vers les enseignants qui ont la responsabilité d'enseigner les droits de l'homme et d'autre part, enfin, vers les programmes de l'enseignement des droits de l'homme conçus à l'intention des élèves.

Fondé par la Loi no. 9/1991, l'Institut Roumain pour les Droits de l'Homme déploie depuis plus de trois ans des activités relatives à l'enseignement aux droits de l'homme et à la démocratie, parmi lesquelles on peut compter des cours de formation de formateurs à l'intention des élèves de l'enseignement primaire et secondaire, des débats, séminaires, symposions et sondages d'opinion.

I. LE BUT ET LES MÉTHODES D'ÉDUCATION DANS LE DOMAINE DES DROITS DE L'HOMME ET DE LA DÉMOCRATIE

Les jeunes représentent le principal levier agissant à l'avenir pour créer une société tolérante, fondée sur une égale dignité de tous ses membres, opposée aux manifestations de racisme, de xénophobie, d'antisémitisme et en général, de toute intolérance. Ils doivent étudier les causes profondes de cette

E. Verhellen (ed.), Monitoring Children's Rights, 703–711.

intolérance, éliminer les préjugés et apprendre l'histoire en mettant en lumière les influences positives mutuelles entre les différents pays, religions et idées.

A cette fin, les programmes d'éducation des élèves visent:

1. l'assimilation des connaissances fondamentales sur la propre personne, sur les relations interhumaines et leur juste perception, leur signification, pour la vie dans le cadre de la société;
2. la connaissance, par les élèves, des droits et responsabilités contenus dans les documents internes et internationaux (déclarations, conventions, pactes, lois) destinés à réglementer les relations sociales;
3. la connaissance des principes de fonctionnement de l'Etat, des problèmes d'ordre global du monde contemporain, du spécifique de l'activité économique du vingtième siècle, dans le but d'une intégration consciente des jeunes dans la société moderne, démocratique;
4. la formation des pratiques civiques, l'enseignement au respect des normes, lois, traditions et du travail – dans le but d'une implication consciente et responsable des jeunes dans la vie de la société;
5. le modelage moral du comportement individuel, dans le but d'une participation efficace à la vie de la société démocratique.

Dans les programmes destinés à l'enseignement primaire et secondaire on a introduit comme discipline "La culture civique", qui comprend aussi des objectifs propres à l'enseignement, à l'aide desquels on attend de la part des élèves à:

– définir correctement les termes et les concepts propres au language de ladite discipline (tels que: peuple, ethnie, nation, patrie, nationalisme, etc.) et opérer correctement avec ceux-ci (en exemplifiant, en commentant des situations qu'ils auront vécues donc, dans de différents contextes),
– connaître, indiquer le fondement des similitudes et des différences entre les hommes et analyser l'être humain de la perspective de ses dimensions principales (homo: socialis, faber, moralis, loquens, ludens, etc.);
– analyser leur propre comportement au sein des groupes dont ils font partie;
– saisir la différence entre le comportement utilitaire et le comportement moral et décrire leur propre rôle dans l'épanouissement de leur personalité ainsi que dans le cadre de la société;
– être capables d'analyser les relations interpersonnelles et proposer des solutions dans une série de situations conflictuelles, réelles ou bien potentielles.

II. LES PROGRAMMES SCOLAIRES

En collaboration avec l'IRDO, le Ministère de l'Enseignement a élaboré pendant les années 1992–1993 et 1993–1994 des programes de culture civique pour les années primaires et pour les années d'études V-VIII. Pour les élèves des classes primaires, des cahiers d'éducation morale-civique ont été rédigés.

Les textes traitent de sujets tels que: l'état civil, l'identité du citoyen, la famille, ce que signifie l'action d'aider, comment on soutient un dialogue, ce que c'est qu'une collectivité, la bienséance, la planification du temps, le vote dans la classe, ce que c'est la patrie, les droits de l'homme, les droits de l'enfant, l'UNICEF, l'écologie, etc., textes accompagnés par des explications, des illustrations; les élèves ont a résoudre des exercices d'observation, de lecture,de discussion, de réflexion, ils sont incités à poser des questions, ainsi qu'á donner des réponses, entraînés à retenir l'essentiel; on leur présente des courtes histoires ou des blagues, toutes, sont autant d'occasions d'analyse à effectuer pour les élèves.

On leur apprend qu'ils ne vivent pas sur une île déserte, qu'on ne peut pas vivre sans les autres hommes, qu'une entente réciproque est nécessaire, ainsi que de l'amour, de la volonté d'aider.

En tant que discipline, "la culture civique" s'adresse à la réceptivité, propre à l'âge de 14–15 ans, vis-à-vis des problèmes quotidiens, à l'inclination naturelle du préadolescent de se rapporter à ceux qui lui sont les plus proches: la famille, les collègues, les professeurs, mais aussi à d'autres milieux, en saisissant peu à peu les relations sociales. Elle vise à contrecarrer les jugements catégoriques qui peuvent souvent marquer la vie et les choix d'un jeune, surtout lorsque le système informationnel, les medias devenues tout d'un coup explosives et, quelquefois douteuses – peuvent jouer un rôle négatif, grâce au fait que les élèves manquent encore de discernement dans leurs choix. Cette discipline n'a pas comme but de formuler des recettes, des matrices, mais vise la création voulue de situations mettant les élèves dans de différentes hypostases, en commençant par les plus simples ("qui suis'je?", "quelles sont les relations entre moi et les autres?"), jusqu'aux plus complèxes ("moi-le citoyen"), en l'entraînant - attentivement et activement – afin qu'il soit capable de saisir l'importance de chaque geste, acte fait pour chaque personne à part, mais aussi pour tous les autres, au milieu desquels il vit.

Les élèves aprennent au fur et à mesure, d'une manière cohérente,adéquate, quels sont leurs droits et responsabilités dans le système de droit civil, comment on prend des décisions, dans l'idée de l'intégration de leur propre personnalité dans la collectivité au sien de laquelle ils vont vivre, en tant qu'adolescents d'abord, en tant qu'adultes ensuite. Les programmes d'enseignement dont on a fait mention ont été axés sur les principes décrits plus haut, en utilisant des méthodes propres à l'enseignement, telles que:

– enseignement de classes théoriques;
– énumération des principaux instruments internes et internationaux;
– commentaires (élève-professeur, élève-élève), dialogue;
– analyse, explication des phénomènes, facteurs, attitudes;
– exercices (questions, exemples, tests);
– applications pratiques;

– autres méthodes au libre choix des professeurs;
– jeux, scénarios, enregistrements sur casettes audio/video.

Les conclusions de toutes ces activités apparaissent clairement,sans être impératives, ultimatives, de telle manière que les élèves soient capables d'arriver d'eux seuls (sans saisir le fait qu'ils sont dirigés avec discrétion), graduellement, à des jugements de valeur sociaux, moraux,civiques. Élèves et professeurs travaillent ensemble, étant en préoccupés à éviter la stéréotypie, l'habitude, l'ennui, l'aphatie, la lassitude.

Dans l'enseignement secondaire il existe un programme interdisciplinaire ayant comme objectif principal la formation de la conscience de soi-même de chaque élève – en tant que personnalité ouverte axiologiquement, de la perspective de l'assimilation de tels concepts, catégories, informations, capables de permettre à l'élève de réaliser son autointégration et autointrospection (de la subjectivité aux faits) et sa capacité d'agir et de corrélation, sur la base de critères de valeur scientifiques, humanistes et, surtout, moraux.

Ce programme interdisciplinaire vise les sciences socio-humaines: la psychologie, la logique, la philosophie, l'économie, la sociologie, l'histoire, la littérature, la geographie, la biologie et les langues étrangères.

Ainsi, parmi les objectifs de l'étude des disciplines socio-humaines dans le lycée, on peut compter aussi les suivants: la formation et la consolidation des attitudes de tolérance, la compréhension et le détachement critique face à la variété des phénomènes et interactions dans le domaine socio-humain, le développement des motivations et des disponibilités d'initiative, la participation responsable à l'action commune, sociale, le développement du dynamisme nécessaire en vue de l'intégration dans une société démocratique. Dans le programme des classes de psychologie on a inclu comme objectifs: la perception de l'importance de cette discipline dans l'analyse et l'explication du concept de "réalité hummaine", du mode de percevoir cette réalité et pour pouvoir déchiffrer les mécanismes du développement, pour être capable d'apprécier la contribution de la psychologie dans le processus éducationnel, ainsi que dans la formation, en tant que personne, de l'élève.

Parmi les objectifs spécifiques de la discipline sociologique on peut compter: la perception du sens et de la signification des concepts sociologiques, l'analyse des différents phénomènes sociaux. Dans le contenu du programme on retrouve de thèmes tels que: facteurs et conditions de la vie sociale,la dynamique de la société, l'action sociale, la dynamique de la société, l'action sociale.

La discipline "Economie" vise, entre autres:
– l'acquisition des capacités d'analyse et d'interprétation de la réalité économique,
– l'encouragement de la capacité d'adaptation consciente du propre comportement aux demandes de l'économie de marché.

Le programme contient aussi des thèmes tels que: l'Etat et l'économie, les problèmes globaux de l'économie mondiale – la crise alimentaire, le sous développement, la pollution.

Le programme des classes de "philosophie" entre autres:
- le développement des traits positifs de la personnalité (esprit de reflexion, esprit critique, la capacité de communiquer, dialogue et tolérance, équilibre psychique, discernement), le premier chapitre étant dédié à l'homme (concepts, homme et société, les droits de l'homme, applications).

La "littérature roumaine" vise la connaissance des valeurs de notre littérature, l'intégration de celles-ci dans le contexte de la culture universelle. En ce qui concerne les langues étrangères, leur étude doit conduire à un enrichissement des représentations culturelles, afin d'obtenir une vision d'ensemble sur les valeurs de ces cultures.

Le programme de la discipline de "l'histoire" se propose à faire connaître aux élèves les grandes valeurs de la culture mondiale et roumaine, leur enseigner dans quelle mesure les grands événements peuvent influencer l'histoire universelle, à les faire identifier correctement la marche générale de l'histoire, leur apprendre à identifier les périodes de progrès ou de régression au long de l'histoire. Un chapitre à part est destiné à l'évolution des relations internationales dans la période d'après la deuxième guerre mondiale: la guerre froide, l'ONU et son rôle, les alliances, les sources de conflits, les mutations dans le système des relations internationales après la chute du système communiste en Europe de l'Est.

Le programme de la discipline de la "géographie" se propose la formation d'une culture géographique en tant que partie de la culture générale. Il comprend des objectifs tels que:
- l'éducation dans l'ésprit des droits de l'homme, de l'égalité entre les nationalités;
- l'éducation en faveur de l'environnement, en faveur de la préservation d'un équilibre regional et planetaire, visant à une terre saine pour tous ses habitants;
- la connaissance des grands projets régionaux et planétaires qui vont améliorer la vie de l'homme;
- les modifications de l'environnement suite à l'intervention de l'homme;
- domaines prioritaires de la conservation et de la protection de l'environnement, la pollution.

Dans le programme des classes de "Biologie" il existe un chapitre d'écologie, où sont débattus des problèmes tels que: l'unité de l'organisme avec son milieu, la protection de la nature et de l'environnement, le mouvement écologique, les sources de la pollution – corps solides, matériaux plastiques, sonique, radioactivité, chimie et les effets de ceux-ci sur la vie.

Revenant aux programmes d'éducation civique, nous présentons en ce qui suit le contenu de ceux destinées aux années d'études VII et VIII pendant ces deux dernières années:

Pour l'année d'études VII
Chapitres:
    I Moi et les autres:
        – la propre identité;
        – les sentiments;
        – communication avec les autres;
        – prise des décisions;
        – relations interhumaines;
        – formes de relations interhumaines entre les jeunes(acceptation, tolérance, etc.);
        – modelage moral des comportements.
    II Groupe social, relations inter-groupes;
    III Activités sociales et leur importance;
    IV Individu, société, nation.

Pour l'année d'etudes VIII:
    I L'Etat;
    II La nation;
    III Les droits de l'homme;
    IV Formes d'organisation civile dans la société démocratique;
    V Facteurs pouvant saper la democratie;
    VI Activités économiques de l'individu et de la société;
    VII Problèmes courants de l'humanité.

III. Activités de l'I.R.D.O.

L'IRDO a initié un ample programme de formation de formateurs dans le domaine des droits de l'homme pour l'enseignement. Les chercheurs et les lecteurs de l'IRDO ont participé, en collaboration avec le Ministère de l'Enseignement aux 3 cycles de cours et seminaires destinés à instuire les enseignants:

7–11 decembre 1992: enseigner et apprendre les droits de l'homme dans l'enseignement primaire;

14–18 decembre 1992: enseigner et apprendre les droits de l'homme dans l'enseignement secondaire;

20–22 avril 1993: enseigner et apprendre les droits de l'homme dans l'enseignement primaire et secondaire – cours organisé pour les professeurs et instituteurs des districts de la Transsylvanie.

Les programmes ont inclu
- les termes et concepts sur les droits de l'homme, les droits de la femme, les droits de l'enfant;
- le droit à l'éducation;
- les normes internationales concernant les droits de l'homme;
- des cas pratiques à partir de la Convention sur les droits de l'enfant;
- la résolution des conflits dans la classe;
- l'enseignement pour les minorités ethniques, religieuses et linguistiques;
- des ateliers pédagogiques et échange d'expérience.

En 1994 l'IRDO a organisé le débat "L'enseignement des droits de l'homme – une modalité de preparer l'enfant pour s'assumer les responsabilités de la vie dans une société libre", avec la participation des responsables du Ministère de l'Enseignement, parlementaires, chefs de commissions, representants des ONG, des inspecteurs de disciplines civiques de tous les districts de pays et aussi un séminaire pour les inspecteurs des discipline civique de tous les districts de pays.

En collaboration avec la Radio, des exposés sur les droits de l'homme et de l'enfant ont été transmis dans le cadre de cours radiophoniques sur les droits de l'homme (La reconnaissance de la personnalité et des libertés fondamentales de l'enfant; les droits économiques et sociaux de l'enfant, éducation formelle et non-formelle de l'enfant). Un concours pour les enfants a été initié aussi en collaboration avec la Radio: "Les droits de l'homme commencent par les droits de l'enfant" qui s'est finalisé par une festivité au siège de l'IRDO.

IV. RECHERCHE SOCIOLOGIQUE DE L'IRDO

Pendant les années 1993 et 1994 l'IRDO a initié une recherche sociologique dans le but de se rendre compte du niveau des connaissances en cette nouvelle problématique dans le cadre de l'enseignement pré-universitaire; l'enquête s'est basée sur des questionnaires remplis par les élèves sous forme d'épreuve écrite.

Les réponses de 2136 élèves ont été étudiées: il s'agit d'élèves provenant de 43 lycées théoriques des principales villes répandues dans le pays; les classes comprises dans l'échantillon sont les classes VIII (classe terminale du gymnase) et XII (classe terminale du lycée). De cette échantillon ont fait partie 9 lycées hongrois et allemands.

Les 14 questions avec 56 variantes de reponses qu'elles ont généré, comprennent des réferences sur le dégré de connaissance des droits et des obligations de l'homme et particulierement sur ceux des adolescents, concernants leur obligativité et leur respect. On peut constater que les élèves ne perçoivent assez clairement l'obligation des écoles de leur transmettre suffisamment de connaissances en cette direction. Une analyse est faite des droits de l'homme les plus fréquemment mentionnés par les élèves. La seconde partie de l'étude est dédiée à un nécessaire tour d'horizon concernant des aspects de pédagogie des droits de l'homme, qui résultent des instruments et des recommandations internationaux adaptés à la strategie de l'enseignement dans notre pays.

V. Programme pour 1994–1995

A la suite de cette étude, ainsi que de l'expérience acquise pendant ces deux années d'activité, l'IRDO lance un Plan national d'actions destinés à appuyer l'enseignement aux droits de l'homme dans le cycle primaire et secondaire, comprenant les activités suivantes:

1. Elaboration d'un manuel des droits de l'homme pour l'enseignement secondaire, comprenant:

    A: Un court historique: faits et événements reliés à l'historie des droits de l'homme; les premiers documents qui font mention des droits de l'homme; la déclaration des droits de l'homme et du citoyen.

    B: La connaissance des documents contemporains:
    - internationaux: Déclaration universelle, Conventions et pactes internationaux et européens;
    - de la Roumanie;
    - organismes internationaux qui se préoccupent de la mise en oeuvre des droits de l'homme (ONU, UNICEF, UNESCO, etc.);
    - organisations gouvernementales et ONG du pays et de l'étranger (y compris les fondations, CIFEDHOP).

    C: La connaissance de quelques graves violations des droits de l'homme (guerres, apartheid, méthodes policières, brutalités), xénophobie, racisme, antisémitisme.

    D: Concepts fondamentaux des droits de l'homme (exemples, analyses, tests).

    E: Les droits de l'homme, leur développement, la démocratie: la tolerance et les consequences de l'intolérance; Les conflits et les tentatives de résolution.

    F: Les droits de l'homme (politiques et civils, économiques, sociaux et culturels; les droits individuels; les droits de l'enfant.

    G: Plan mondial d'action concernant l'enseignement aux droits de l'homme et à la démocratie; La décennie de l'éducation aux droits de l'homme.

2. La formation et l'éducation des enseignants: Perfectionnement des cadres dirigeants du Ministère de l'Enseignement:
    - spécialistes du Ministère, inspecteurs scolaires du Ministère et des inspectorats dans le territoire;

– professeurs d'éducation civique, éducateurs, les auteurs des manuels, des assistants sociaux

l'organisation de:

a) débats tels que: "L'enseignement des droits de l'homme – modalité de préparer les enfants en vue de s'assumer les responsabilités de la vie dans une société libre";

b) symposions "L'enseignement des droits de l'homme – objectifs et modalité de mise en œuvre"; "Aspects méthodologiques de l'enseignement des connaissances dans le domaine des droits de l'homme";

c) sondages d'opinion sur le mode d'assimilation par les élèves, des connaissances dans le domaine des droits de l'homme;

d) cours à l'intention des instuteurs et des professeurs (à Bucarest et dans le territoire) sur les thématiques:

– termes et concepts relatifs aux droits de l'homme et de l'enfant;

– normes internes et internationales concernant les droits des personnes appartenant à des minorités ethniques, linguistiques, religieuses;

– éducation dans un ésprit de tolérance, le combat des manifestations de xénophobie, racisme, antisémitisme;

– activités et ateliers pédagogiques, destinés à présenter l'expérience acquise dans l'enseignement de ces connaissances.

3. autres activités pour l'enseignement:

– publications des recueils de matériaux, guides méthodologiques, lectures, jeux, questionnaires, tests;

– initiation de concours à l'intention des élèves et professeurs (pour conception et réalisation de matériel didactique);

– émissions à la Télévision venant à l'appui des enseignants et des élèves;

– initiation d'une rubrique "Echange d'expérience" dans la revue "La tribune de l'Enseignement";

– réalisation dans les écoles, de vitrines de documentation sur les droits de l'homme et de l'enfant.

4. L'inclusion dans l'activité d'éducation des personnes provenant d'autres catégories d'activité, pouvant influencer le processus d'éducation, tels que: organisation et syndicats des enseignants, conseils de professeurs, d'administration de l'enseignement, organisations des parents, ONG, y compris des organisations des femmes.

Après un année de mise en oeuvre de ce programme, l'IRDO va initier un nouveau sondage parmi des élèves, afin de pouvoir évaluer les résultats de ce dernier avec ceux du premier sondage et de pouvoir évaluer l'efficacité de son programme d'éducation.

JAN BOSMANS

Implementation of Young People's Rights in Flemish Provisions for Special Youth Welfare

INTRODUCTION

In the reform of the Belgian State since 1980 the division of authority regarding youth protection law was a recurrent bone of contention. It took 5 decisions of the Court of Arbitration, one decision of the Council of State, an ammendment of the law and a number of decrees and implementing orders to render communal the youth protection existing since 1965.

An emancipatory assistance organized by the Flemish Community became the finality of our youth protection.

A brief analysis of several texts of a legislative or policy oriented nature shows that emancipatory thinking and acting next to strengthening of the legal status of minors have become key concepts in special youth welfare. The realization of these target concepts in practice demands that several conditions and instruments are established. Young people and families using special youth welfare need to have rights, need to be informed about them and need to be able to exercise or enforce them. Here the social worker and his provisions fulfill a key function as mediators of emancipation and legal protection.

Therefore the development of a number of structural instruments of a factual, legal and moral imperative and enforcing character in the organization of assistance is necessary. We will now go further into the development of:
- a statute for young people (right to information, concrete resident's rights, right to privacy, right to involvement and participation, right to complain);
- an elementary code of conduct for the social worker (involving several topics);
- the assistance relation through an assistance agreement;
- a permanent structure of follow up in the youth welfare sector.

E. Verhellen (ed.), Monitoring Children's Rights, 713–726.
© 1996 *Kluwer Law International. Printed in the Netherlands.*

I. Situation of Youth Protection Law in Belgium in the Year 1994: Welfare Outweighs Justice

As a result of the reform of the Belgian State in 1988 the Flemish Community was allowed the authority of youth protection (P. Senaeve and J. Peeters, 1994, pp. 26–57). After some legal disputes in the Court of Arbitration it became clear that the by now federal Belgian State only has a limitative authority specified with regard to contents in this matter and concerning:

- the civil rights regulations regarding the statute of minors and of their relatives;
- the criminal law regulations which describe behaviour inflicting on youth protection as a crime and define the description thereof as well as the penalty;
- the organization of the juvenile courts, their territorial authority and their judicial procedures;
- the statement of measures that can be taken with regard to minors who have committed an act described as a crime;
- the deprivation of parental authority and the monitoring of social security welfare and other social benefits.

Each part of youth protection which does not specifically belongs to one of the matters reserved for the federal authorities henceforth comes under the authority of the Communities.

As a result of this reform not only the *sui generis* character (regarding object, principles and methods) of the youth protection law in Belgium was stressed but also a stand was taken for the *assistance character* of the whole youth protection law. Legal measures are considered as modalities of assistance, their finality is based on education, counselling and assistance of minors. Their compulsory exertion is of a secondary and subordinate nature. It appears that "during the last 15 years the various Belgian legislators have often used intrinsic elements of discussion concerning the development of youth protection law (a repressive as opposed to an emancipatory approach) to fight out troubles concerning authority." (E. Verhellen, 1988, p.101). In 1994 it is save to say that the broad allowance of authority of the Belgian youth protection law to the Flemish Community has settled the fight for now in favour of the emancipatory and assistance oriented approach.

II. A Survey of Policy Intentions and Realisations with Regard to the Emancipation and Legal Status of Young People in Special Youth Welfare

A brief analysis of several texts of a legislative or policy oriented nature shows that emancipatory thinking and acting next to strengthening of the legal status of minors have become key concepts in special Youth Welfare. There now follows a survey of the most important texts and a concretization of applying items.

A. *The Decrete of the Flemish Community of June 27th 1985 concerning special Youth Welfare*

The Decrete has significantly changed the matters formerly exclusively regulated by the law of April 8th 1965 with regard to youth protection. (L. Dupont and C. Vanderauwera, 1988, pp. 35–40.) The concept of *welfare* henceforth replaces the concept of protection:

protection referred too much to care and keeping, to the responsibility of parents for their children. Welfare refers to assistance and support: it refers to a more equal attitude towards the target group. Responsibilities are no longer taken over, assistance does not as much has to lead to results rather as to respect, proximity and a mutual search for possibilities and the realization of oppurtunities.

The central concept in this respect is the *problematic educational situation*:

a situation in which the physical integrity, the affective, moral,intellectual or social opportunities towards development of minors are liable to suffer as a result of extraordinary events, relational conflicts or their living circumstances.

This decrete is characterized by four leading principles:
1. A strict division is established between voluntary accepted assistance and legal protection in order to give *maximum autonomy to assistance and service in a voluntary correlation*.
2. *Legal coercive measures are to be avoided* if a solution of the problem is possible within the framework of voluntary assistance by the obligatory calling in of the mediation commissions (R. Steyaert, 1985) as a link from voluntary to compulsory assistance.
   General *prevention* prevails and the least drastic measures have precedence as described in the *principle of solidarity*: in the event of an equal effect, that intervention must be given precedence which least deeply interferes with a person's private life.
3. Next there is the principle of *differentiation of the offer of assistance*. This differentiation is to allow an adequate response to each problematic situation. Through evaluation of the pedagocic concept and programme of the recognized provisions also a *quality control* of that offer of assistance is built in.
4. Although the Flemish Community is not authorized to affect the minor's civil rights statute, it was attempted within the framework of the emancipatory reform movement, which demands priority attention for the recognition of *minors' own legal status*, to allow actual rights to minors in assistance (J. Lenssens, 1990).

Henceforth minors until the age of 14 must be heard and from the age of 14 on they must express their agreement with the welfare or assistance offered to them. They are also given the possibility to have their right to assistance or their refusal thereof validated by the mediation commission.

As long as possible the self responsibility of the youngster and the families concerned is appealed to. Maximum terms are set concerning the duration of the measures.

Through the issue of regulations with regard to the arrangement of the visiting rights, correspondence, the educational regime and the pedagocic concept and programme in provisions of special youth welfare, the Flemish Community is able to guarantee the emancipatory character of the recognized assistance and service. Possibilities of placing young people are limited to the provisions recognized by the Flemish Community.

Furthermore a measure cannot be officialy changed without a question in this respect having been raised by one of the persons concerned apart from the juvenile judge himself. This explicitly involves the questions of the young people themselves. Neither can there be an official prolongation of the measures after the maximum terms have expired and the preparatory judicial procedures are limited to six months.

Finally, from 14 years of age on the minor himself can appoint a public or private credit institution to deposit money to to which he is entitled. The decrete also stipulates that each person who co-operates is responsible for the secrecy of the facts entrusted to him or related to it and is to respect the religious, ideological and philisophical persuasion of the families to which the minors belong.

B. In the Recommendation Concerning a Reformed Provisions Policy in Special Youth Welfare of November 16th 1990 the Recognition Commission calls the Emancipatory Procedure the Basic Condition for the Family Oriented Procedure, the differentiated Procedure and the Application of the Principle of Subsidiarity
A number of essential conditions for the emancipatory procedure are mentioned here (a.o. information about the client, continuity and co-ordination of the assistance, policy of prevention regarding escalations, individual phasing of the assistance custom-made, respect of basic rights by referents and social workers, a fundamental loyalty and dialogue with regard to the minor, parallel emancipatory procedures with the family, a large autonomy for the social worker, systematic and objective evaluation of the quality of the assistance).

C. The Policy Document of the Flemish Executive Concerning General Welfare Policy of July 10th 1991
This document also extensively draws attention to the legal status of the client in all sectors of social work. Although the sector of special youth

welfare does not come under it, it does show a lot of common ground with the general welfare policy

In it the policy option to strenghten the client's legal status is taken explicitly and clarified. Concretely this option is to lead to the elaboration of:

1. A generalizing use of the *assistance agreement*: first an admission and residence agreement will be imposed in all residential provisions, later it will be imposed in other forms of service. This agreement should be more than an inventory of legal rights and duties of the applicant for assistance and the social worker: it is to contain information about the service itself and about the contribution and co-operation that is expected from the applicant.

2. An *internal complaint procedure* will be introduced and if necessary a substitute defender must be able to assist or replace the client in formulating a complaint.

3. A *central ombuds service* will be established with a firm legal basis (obligatory announcement through provisions) and accessibility and with a mediator and signal function.

4. The introduction of real *legal procedure possibilities* against private provisions (cf. possibilities of appeal against decisions of the public welfare service).

D. The Order of the Flemish Government Concerning Conditions of Recognition and Norms of Subsidies for Provisions of Special Youth Welfare (and Additional Explanatory Memorandum)

This document of July 13th 1994 further devotes concrete attention to several rights of minors received or assisted by recognized provisions.

We here mention:

- several conditions for appointed staff (conduct, health, age, qualifications, multidisciplinarity, extra training, monitoring, presence);
- geographical distribution and proximity of several forms of work;
- only receiving minors, maximum capacity per department;
- minimal conditions for material infrastructure (kitchen, sanitary fittings, study, sleeping quarters, fire safety, room for living).
- practical guarantees for:
  · practice and pursuit of moral or religious beliefs
  · medical care
  · clothes
  · duration of assistance
  · nourishment
  · financial protection (deposit book from 12 years on, budget planning)
  · social legislation (prohibition to work)
  · psychological and orthopedagocic regulations
  · information at admission and departure

- · day schedule, free time, school, work
- · after care
- · right to pocket money
- pedagogic operation and climate (emancipatory, family oriented, social integration, stimulating contacts);
- the juvenile judge may not take any measures contrary to the recognized pedagogic concept or programme of the provisions;
- basic file (contents and cancellation, secrecy);
- drawing up a plan of actions (aims, terms, evaluation and means of assistance in consultation and concrete agreements regarding regime, visiting, correspondence);
- drawing up regular evolution reports;
- sanctions (adapted, education oriented, not physical, traumatising, abstaining from food);
- minors' basic rights to respect (Convention on the Rights of the Child, ECHR (European Convention on Human Rights), the counsellor as ombudsman).
- for the reception, orientation and observation centres there must be a security room for each six minors:
  - · purpose: security of minors and staff
  - · obligatory submission of security regulations for approval
  - · obligatory daily visit by management and doctor- psychiatrist
  - · obligatory security file for each minor, for each security (identity, duration, cause, those who decided,visiting)
  - · duty to report to referent;
- investigations must serve for orientation/observation;
- for some forms attainability outside the working hours;
- obligatory liability insurance;
- enforcement of right to subsistence level.

E. The Law of February 2nd 1994

Finally in the Law of February 2nd 1994, meant as amendment and adaptation of the Law on Youth Protection of 1965 ameliorations to the legal status of the minors concerned are introduced. We here limit ourselves to an incomplete enumeration:

- obligatory calling in of voluntary assistance in the event of a judicial measure of great urgency (involving notification of the possibilities to the parents);
- amelioration of the monitoring and the application of the part of the family allowance reserved for the minor;
- obligatory mention whether a youngster is placed in an open or a closed institution;
- possibility to apply for a reconsideration of the measure in the event of petitions;

- amelioration of the rights of the defence;
- obligatory cognizance of advice of qualified social service;
- limitation of the prohibition on freedom of movement of youngsters;
- limitation of duration of measure;
- limitation of and raising of defence rights in the event of provisional measures;
- amelioration of legal support (appointment of lawyer, access to file);
- conditions in the event of custody in a house of detention;
- summon duty from the age of 12 on in order to effectuate hearing right;
- in procedures concerning deprivation of parental authority the minor himself becomes party in the lawsuit if a provisional measure is demanded on his behalf;
- henceforth the same procedural guarantees apply for prolongation of measures as for the original decisions.

F. To Complete
We also mention:
- the *prohibition on publication and distribution of the report* of the debates in juvenile courts of the LYP (Law On Youth protection 1965);
- the *prohibition on publication and distribution of drawings, photographs and images* which might reveal the identity of the minors concerned in Youth protection (LYP);
- the introduction of an *optional possibility of hearing on the child's initiative* itself without age limitation (bill on divorce procedures);
- the introduction of a right *to communication,* alteration or removal of erroneous data in personal data processing (Law on Privacy of December 8th 1992).

All individual rights resulting from this law also apply for the client registration in special youth welfare (rights of the individual in the privacy law: information at the time of collection, information at first registration, knowledge of data on demand, right to amelioration, access to public register of registered personal data processing, complaint to commission, complaint to public prosecutor, possibility to petition lawsuit).

G. Conclusion to this Survey
It is save to say that the legislative and executive powers have gone to great lengths to work emancipatory in the promotion of the special youth welfare both on a federal and on a communal level. This is expressed on several levels and was probably also stimulated by the persisting conflicts of authority during the state reforms. On the Flemish side the law on youth protection has increasingly been undermined by a welfare and assistance line of thought. Of course, the freshly authorised Flemish authorities were bound to manifest themselves strongly in the area of special youth welfare.

Also the basic rights and legal status of the minors ending up in special youth welfare were given more attention and were even explictly included as an obligation for the recognized provisions.

These policy texts primarily create recognition, subsidies and procedure conditions to improve the emancipation and legal status of young people in provisions. However, by no means does this imply that young people can exercise or enforce these rights.

An evolution from protective law to legal protection and towards the development of a true emancipatory oriented assistance demands the fulfillment of several conditions.

III. CONDITIONS FOR AN EMANCIPATORY ASSISTANCE

A. *Emancipation of the Youngster (and his parents) as a Headword*

On many people the term emancipation has the effect of a bitter and sweet aperitif: it warms heart and mind, it sharpens the appetite for discussion and with some leads to enthusiasm or protest, with others to scepticism and resignation'.' (W. Leirman, 1977, p.42–85)

We must always speak about emancipation with at least two words: legal emancipation (or social-political emancipation) has a different meaning than social-pedagocic emancipation. Indeed, the concept of emancipation does not have a fixed definition: it is in essence a *target concept*, it is never completed and a description of it always gives it normative contents. (L. Walgrave, 1980, p.165) Therefore politics, law and pedagogics meet in this target concept. Therefore also an emancipatory interpretation of youth assistance and welfare cannot be imposed policywise. It is the result of a process of change in which the applicant for assistance and the social worker must find each other beyond all discrepancies.

After all, true emancipation presupposes an own insight in the situation and in the possibility to overcome and do away with any hindrances occuring as a result of self desired changes as exercise of power becomes superfluous. Therefore assistance in special youth welfare will engage in the creation of possibilities to increase knowledge and abilities in order to establish changes in practical experience and the own actions in social situations. (J. Fritz, 1979, p.21) In the end all social workers, services and provisions of special youth welfare will have to honour the same opinion on the aims of their assistance and its situation in the existing social structures.

B. *Wanted: Legal Protection*

Law belongs to the climate in which man grows up, it belongs to the elementary conditions of existence of man, it is a basic pillar of human sociability. That law is there for man, also means: law serves man". (J.M. Broekman, 1978,p.23)

An improved legal status of the youngster is not only necessary to guarantee a better access to all assistance services, it is also necessary to encourage their fighting spirit against side effects of the welfare model (viz. the impending chances of proliferation of the assistance and processes of problematization of situation and conduct) (C. Eliaerts, 1984,p.165). The youth protection law will only be over when it is obligatory to motivate the deviation of the child's rights (to self-determination) (C.Maes, 1994). If legal protection of children is actually presupposed as a strategy in the striving for respect for children, then a number of conditions must explicitly be complied with and be realized. (E. Verhellen, F. Spiesschaert and G. Cappelaere, 1994). For one thing children must have rights (legal status),they must be informed about them, they must be able to actually exercise them and to enforce them (legal access, legal ability and legal assistance).

Both for the realization of an emancipatory assistance and for the actual establishment of legal protection for young people in problematic eductional situations an important part is reserved for the social workers.

C. The Social Worker as Mediator of Emancipation and Legal Protection

It does not suffice to make institutions and legal assistance more accessible (and to develop them). One must go to those looking for legal assistance who are forgotten. Personal contact is of the utmost importance. Hence the capital role of those who professionally get in touch with the underpriviliged. They might be called the first mediators of the law.

"Mediator" because they are a link, a go-between, an intermediary. An active role is reserved for them in the distribution of information (C. Vanhuffel and F. Tanghe, 1990), the formulation of the allowed rights and protection of the interests of the youngster.

Under the influence of the presupposed policy principles and conditions the Flemish provisions issued their pedagogic concepts and programmes. Most of the time they explicitly paid attention to emancipatory accents and rules. They were mainly looked upon from a pedagogic point of view (individualization and phasation of the assistance offered) and formulated in group rules or rules of the house, methodics and procedures. Although the recognition commission calls the emancipatory procedure the basic condition for the family oriented and differentiated procedure, there is hardly any ennergy nor room provided for that.

Hitherto legal protection of young people has not been given a chance in Flemish provisions. The declarations of intention are there, concretization of young people's rights are mostly absent. Just as the family replacing line of thought is gradually replaced itself by a family oriented and family supporting procedure, the youth protection line of thought will have to make room for a legal protection line of thought in provisions. Therefore the development of a number of structural instruments of a factual,legal and moral imperative and enforcing character in the organization providing assistance is necessary. In the Waaiburg (residential and semi-residential provision for special youth welfare in 1986) for instance an intern basic memorandum was developed about the resident's rights in the Waaiburg. This was the result of a workshop "Interests and involvement of young people" and in the whole of the organization brought about a fundamental change in favour of the emancipatory support.

IV. IMPLEMENTING YOUNG PEOPLE'S RIGHTS IN SPECIAL YOUTH WELFARE

The law might be considered as an instrument to protect the interest of a person or of a group. Jurist and social worker hardly improve the world, if at all, but they are capable to *introduce structures* which can prevent or abolish the results of pernicious structures.

We wish to suggest to prime a procedure and line of thought in the Flemish special youth welfare in order to develop four instruments to systematically promote and elaborate the emancipation and legal protection of young people enjoying special youth welfare. In 1995 the workshop MINORIUS was set up in the bosom of the Verbond voor Jeugd- en Gehandicaptenzorg (VVJG) to this end. The name does not only refer to the law (ius) for minors (minor) but it aslo stands for the idea that no sound and logical argument (major -*minor*-conclusio) can be developed in youth welfare without legal protection of the young people concerned by the assistance organizations themselves.

These instruments need to comply with a number of general conditions. The following a.o. come to mind:

– they need to *integrate* the presupposed policy options and existing regulations (UN-Convention, ECHR, Laws, Decrete, Order and policy documents);
– they must be formulated *concretely and logically*, be pragmatic and usable;
– they must be a *proactive* instrument (not controlling or repressive) and must be considered (by the organization providing assistance) as a voluntary commitment;
– they must be put forward in *readable terminology*, presented and elaborated upon;
– they must be regularly checked and evaluated (in dialogue with young people). If this does not take place, these policy instruments will slowly die.

It is out of the question that these instruments are created only by and for special youth welfare, as assistance and welfare work are becoming a more and more integral and distinctive sector in our society. In this respect the specific will eventually have to be absorbed in the more general.

Nevertheless it is undoubtedly a good time to start this line of thought in special youth welfare: Flanders is authorized and opts for an emancipatory view on man in this sector.

We will now discuss the following four instruments: the assistance agreement; the charter of young people's rights; the code of conduct for the social worker and a permanent structure of follow up.

A. The Assistance Agreement lays down the Assistance Relation

Although the Policy Document on General Welfare mentions a general introduction of assistance agreements, we unfortunately enough do not find aything of the kind in the Order of the Flemish Government dated July 13th 1994. In practice, however, this was an increasingly occuring phenomenon.

The recognition, organization and financing of provisions for special youth welfare are increasingly planned and financed by the authorities. In those regulations indications and obligatory procedures are recorded to obtain a desirable assistance relation. The danger is that the care eventually overtakes the client and that provisions and assistance are arranged without the youngster or his family having any clear influence on the (increasingly standardized) events.

The only countermovement and legal protection for this is the more judicial and independent development of a legal relation between client and organization providing assistance through a assistance agreement.

We voluntarily agree here with J. Bartels (J.A.C. Bartels, 1984) who in Holland suggested to develop a named agreement of assistance in the civil law (with elements of administrative and civil law) and to legally base it.

This can undoubtedly be applied in voluntary assistance. As in youth welfare a judicial decision to exercise duress can legitimize an assistance relation, one must always consider how much "room" the client has to freely flesh out the contents of the assistance relation. That room is always there, because otherwise one must speak exclusively of exercise of duress (and in that case the Flemish Community as such cannot have any authority). Judicially spoken it is save to say that an assistance relation is a legal relation and that an assistance relation does not involve a commitment of result but of effort and means (however, commitments concerning specific performances and terms need to be respected by the social worker). A signed plan of action for example might link the client's right to autonomy and integrity to the offered assistance (regulated by the authorities but provided by a private legal person). Not complying with the agreement could be sanctioned (for the applicant for assistance: appeal to the judge, for the social worker termination of the agreement).

We regret this notable silence of the Flemish authorities about the introduction of the assistance agreement in special youth welfare.

B. *Young People's Legal Statute*

The purpose of this statute is to systematically and in a clearly understandable manner lay down the legal status of the youngster in asssistance. At the beginning of the assistance it must be clarified and given to the youngster (and/or to his parents). It is desirable to develop an own concrete statute for the parents: the parents' legal status can be easily distinguished from the youngster's. From an emancipatory point of view both need to be integrated for the social worker. For the client(s) these instruments are complementary. From a practical point of view we suggest the following division regarding contents:

- Right to Information;
  Items: information about how youth welfare works, why one is being assisted, that there is a preceding permission requirement, clarification hearing right, decision structure and decision possibilities of those concerned, extern possibilities to information and advice, proceedings and reporting, right to communication.
- The Concrete Residents' Rights
  Items: clarification of the social worker's procedures, clarification of the provision's educational regime (important matters or agreements (for all residents or individually) on e.g. pocket money, visits, going out, tv, group councel, school choice, contacts with friends, telephone, confidentiality of the mail, possibly socalled "security isolation", clothing, finance, medical care, day schedule, education and free time), clarification why something is not (or no longer) possible.
- Right to Privacy
  Items: personal attention and assistance, persuasion, respect, loyalty and trust, own means and goods, integrity, lockable closet, be able to be oneself.
- Right to Involvement and Participation
  Items: about contents of assistance, timing, procedures, concrete steps, termination or continuation of the assistance (e.g. dialogue in drawing up plan of action and assitance programme), deliberation with other residents.
- Right to Complain (to be distinguished)
  - internal possibilities to complain: suggestion box or anonymous complaints, open log with assistance, responsable or director, internal complaint committee
  - external possibilities to complain: consultant, inspection, external complaint committee, mediation commission; aid from confidential person

C. *The Code of Conduct for the Social Worker*

Because of the growing professionalization and power of the social worker, because of his growing (often individual) autonomy, because of the further interference of the authorities in the (complex) assistance relation, we think it is necessary to no longer depart from a silently supposed and morally funded code, but to strive for an elaborated code of conduct for social workers in special youth welfare. Eventually this might evolve to a normative (professional) norm.

The following topics might be given a chance:
- professional secrecy and discretion with regard to parents/youngster, a third party, employer, authorities, referent;
- carefulness norm;
- risks of stepping across the professional relation;
- right to assistance;
- guaranteeing the right to privacy, permission, loyal confidentiality, human relation development;
- distinction advice, research and assistance;
- respect for persuasion, self determination, participation.

D. The Permanent Structure of Follow Up (PSFU) in Special Youth Welfare
The Order of the Flemish government of July 13th 1994 provides as ombudsman for young people in provisions the consultant concerned. That is it. In my opinion follow up of emancipation and legal status of young people in provisions deserves more: also the referent himself needs to be the object of this. In this respect we gladly refer to the suggestions of Spiesschaert and Verhellen concerning the PSFU for the living conditions of children.

Also the introduction of a children's ombudsservice within Child and Family deserves inspiring attention in this respect.

It is desirable to prompt a deliberation and dialogue about this between all instances concerned so that a permanent support and evaluation of the line of thought and instruments can take place.

V. CONCLUSION: THE SOCIAL WORKERS OF SPECIAL YOUTH WELFARE FACING A DILLEMA

Good assistance is first of all emancipatory oriented and therefore not only a functional process (J. Bosmans, 1991). The growing importance of the financial-economic ratio and of the remediating and treatment oriented line of thought in the youth welfare sector, often forces counsellors to carry out a reduction of the social and emotional reality of the youngster (or his family as client system).

As a result of the predominating idea of the application line of thought, it is almost as if the application of certain methods of counselling constitutes the final sense of the assistance. This purely functional line of thought, which is concealed in a sentence such as "... something which is applied by somebody to somebody ..." is at odds with an emancipatory view of assistance.

From a pedagogic point of view emancipation both of those growing up and adults is a process of learning and education aiming to enable an increase of individual and social freedom. This freedom reveals itself in thinking, judging, deciding and conduct of client and social worker. Emancipation remains a target: each social worker will always be confronted with the choice to enlarge or to reduce the room for his client.

Good counselling presupposes a personal encounter based on trust between two people. The concept of encounter refers to the real involvement of two persons during the whole process of counselling. From the social worker's side this demands a professional and creative moment in which he subordinates his own living environment and personality to the purpose of the assistance.

A counsellor needs to work professionally and with the whole of his person in order to enable an open, empathic and emancipatory oriented encounter. Therefore he needs to find affiliation with a more encompassing and open attitude to life with regard to the own innner and outer world. Presupposing that assistance is not only an individual process but also has to change structural and material hindrances for the client group this is all the more difficult.

REFERENCES

J.A.C. Bartels (1984) *Hulpverleningsrecht,* Kluwer, Deventer.
J. Bosmans, *Op zoek naar een referentiekader voor sociaal-pedagogische hulpverlening aan jongvolwassenen in de bijzondere jeugdbijstand,* uiteenzetting voor het vijfjarige bestaan van JOBA, dienst BZW te Antwerpen.
J.M. Broekman (1978) *Recht en antropologie.* Antwerpen: SWU, p. 23.
L. Dupont en C. Vander Auwera (1988) *Het nieuwe jeugdrecht van de Vlaamse Gemeenschap. Teksten met inleidende commentaar.* Leuven: Acco, pp. 35–40.
C. Eliaerts, *Inleiding tot het jeugdbeschermingsrecht,* Gent, E. Story-Scientia, 1984, p. 165.
J. Fritz (1979) *Emancuipatorische groepsdynamica-plaatsbepaling, analyse, perspectief.* Bloemendaal: H. Nelissen, p. 21.
W. Leirman (1977) *Jeugd en emancipatie* in *Van onderzoek naar jeugdbeleid-stuurgroep jeugdonderzoek, ministerie van nederlandse cultuur en bestuur voor jeugdvorming.* Leuven: Acco, pp. 42–84.
J. Lenssens (1990) *Jeugd uit de marge, een uitgave van de Vlaamse Gemeenschapsminister van Welzijn en Gezin.* Brussel, 1990, pp. 10–15.
C. Maes (1994) *Rechten van het kind .... en verder,* in de Kinderrechtengids, Gent: Mys en Breesch.
P. Senaeve en J. Peeters (Eds.) (1994) *De hervorming van het jeugdbeschermingsrecht.* Leuven: Acco, pp. 26–57.
R. Steyaert (1985) *Ontwerpdecreet inzake de bijzondere jeugdbijstand. Memorie van Toelichting.* Brussel.
C. Vanhuffel (1990) *Armoede en rechtstoegankelijkheid. Armoede van rechtstoegankelijkheid* in F. Tanghe, *Recht en armoede,* Antwerpen, Kluwer, pp. 122–123.
E. Verhellen (1988) *Jeugdbescherming en de Staatshervormingen. Het wordt pas echt op de tanden bijten, of terug naar af.* Panopticon, p. 551.
E. Verhellen, F. Spiesschaert en G. Cappelaere (1994) *Van beschermingsrecht naar rechtsbescherming,* werktekst studiedag.
L. Walgrave (1980) *De bescherming voorbij-ontwerp voor een emanciperende jeugdcriminologie.* Antwerpen: Kluwer, p. 165.

TEODOR BULENDA and ANDRZEJ KREMPLEWSKI

Rights of the Child and their Protection in Polish Resocialization Institutions

INTRODUCTION[1]

The aim of this study is to present Polish legal regulations and practice related to the protection of rights of children placed in educational centres for youth ("ECYs"), houses of correction ("HCs") and penal institutions ("PIs"). It is based on reports prepared by the Intervention Bureau of the Chancellery of the Senate of the Polish Republic, the Helsinki Foundation for Human Rights and the Polish Ombudsman. The assessment of the status of children's rights is carried out against international standards (*UN Standard Minimum Rules for the Administration of Juvenile Justice* and *UN Rules for the Protection of Juveniles Deprived of their Liberty*). As a result of major changes of the Polish political system, works on reform of the whole legal system began in 1989. The reforms included regulations related to children and youth.[2]

I. TERMINOLOGY

There is no definition of the term "child" in the Polish legal system. There are, however, some other terms which are used apart from the term "child":

(a) "unborn child" (*nasciturus*);

(b) "minor" – a person under the age of 18;

(c) "juvenile" – 1) a person under the age of 18 showing symptoms of depravation, 2) a person of 13–17 who has committed a punishable act,[3] 3) a person under the age of 21, if educational or corrective measure (placement in a house of correction) has been applied;

---

[1] We should like to thank Prof. Andrzej Rzepliński and Dr Andrzej Rejzner (both from Warsaw University) for commenting constructively on earlier version of this study.

[2] E.g. a new act on educational system (1991).

[3] It is a criminal act committed by a juvenile. It is not an offence, since according to the Polish law a juvenile may not be considered responsible even if he is guilty. (Art.120(1) of the Polish Penal code).

E. Verhellen (ed.), Monitoring Children's Rights, 727–744.

(d) "young adult" – 1) a person of 15–18 which can be legally employed on an employment contract, 2) a person of 17–21 who has committed an offence.

In the Polish legal system (as in the *Convention on the Rights of the Child*), a child is every person under the age of 18; and that is what we mean by this term in this study.

By the term "resocialization institutions" we mean the following:

- educational and resocialization institutions for minors and juveniles – as defined in clause *(c)* 1) and 2);
- resocialization and revalidation institutions for minors and juveniles impaired physically or mentally;
- houses of correction for juveniles – as defined in clause *(c)* 2) and 3). (Exceptionally, also minors [as defined in clause *(d)* 2)] may be placed in all the above mentioned types of institutions .[4])
- penal institutions; in Poland persons who have attained the age of 17 (exceptionally, also those who have attained the age of 16) may be imprisoned.

II. LEGAL GROUNDS

The issue of children's rights and manner of their placement in resocialization institutions is regulated by several legal acts.

Protection of rights of the child (as of any citizen) is regulated by the constitution of 1952 ,[5] which states citizen's rights (social, economic, political and personal rights of a citizen) as well as guarantees of their practical implementation.

Principles of placement, stay and release of children from ECYs and HCs are regulated mainly by the following laws:

- Act of February 25, 1964 – Family and guardianship code (Journal of Law, No 9, item 59, as amended) ("F.& g.c.");
- Act of October 26, 1982 on proceedings in cases concerning juveniles (Journal of Law, No 35, item 228, as amended) ("A.p.c.j.");
- Act of September 7, 1991 on educational system (Journal of Law, No 95, item 425, as amended) ("A.e.s.");

---

[4] "With regard to a perpetrator who commits a less-serious offence after having attained the age of 17 years but before having attained the age of 18 years, the court instead of penalty shall apply the educational or corrective measures prescribed for juveniles if the circumstances of the case as well as the traits and personal conditions of the perpetrator warrant it" (Art.9(3) of Penal code).

[5] As provided in Art.77 of the Constitutional act of October 17, 1992 on mutual relations between legislative and executive authorities of the Polish Republic and on local governments (Journal of Law, No.84, item 426).

- Minister of National Education's ordinance of February 21, 1994 on types, organization and functioning of educational and resocialization institutions (Journal of Law, No 41, item 156) ("MNE's ord.");
- Minister of Justice's ordinance of May 7, 1983 on organization and principles of stay of juveniles in houses of correction (Journal of Law, No 26, item 126) ("MJ's ord.).

Principles of placement, stay and release of children from PIs are regulated by the following laws:

- Act of April 19, 1969 – Penal code (Journal of Law, No 13, item 94, as amended) ("P.c.");
- Act of April 19, 1969 – Punishment execution code (Journal of Law, No 13, item 98, as amended) ("P.e.c.");
- Minister of Justice's ordinance of May 2, 1989 on rules of carrying out penalty of deprivation of liberty (Journal of Law, No 31, item 166) ("R.c.pen.").

The above lists are not complete. There are some other acts related to those issues and some of them are mentioned below. It should be noted, however, that it is the internal rules of resocialization institutions that are of direct concern to a child. In practice, actions of administration are usually based on these rules; also pupils prefer to cite readily available internal rules than other normatives.

Such great number of legal acts results in practice in diametrically different methods of dealing with juveniles. Also, regulations are often incoherent.

III. ORGANIZATION OF RESOCIALIZATION INSTITUTIONS

Organization of various types of resocialization institutions (ECYs, HCs, Pls) is regulated by separate laws and varies considerably.

Educational centres for youth are a part of general educational system and are supervised by the Ministry of National Education .[6] In 1994, there were 48 such centres in Poland, with the the the total of 3450 pupils (see Table 1).

There is a separate statute for each institution, which determines the principles of admission and of dealing with pupils, the scope and methods of resocialization, organization of individual care, punishment and reward system, etc. (Art. 5(2) of MNE's ord.).

Houses of correction are managed by the Ministry of Justice. There are several types of HCs – depending on the degree of depravation, as well as physical and mental state of juveniles.[7] In 1994, there were 27 houses of correction in Poland, with the total of 1349 foster children (see Table 1).

---

[6] Apart from resocialization institutions, there are also some guardianship and educational centres, including: family children's homes, children's homes, rest centres and sociotherapeutic centres for youth (Art.2, part 1, section 1 of MNE's ord.).

[7] As provided in Art. 66 of MJ's ord. these are the following types of corrective institutions for juveniles: 1) for less depraved (limited supervision), 2) for those who require direct super-

Each house of correction is managed by a headmaster and has separate rules and daily routine.

Table 1. Houses of correction and educational centres for youth in Poland (on 12/31/1994)

	1985	1990	1992	1993	1994
Houses of correction	29	27	27	27	27
Wards	1470	1457	1462	1396	1349
Semi-liberty groups*	9	1	1	1	1
Wards	104	10	14	17	13
Educational centres for youth	49**	50	51	49	48
Wards	3891	3062	3250	2852	3450

*   educational experiment

** on 4/30/1985

Source: 1993 Year-book of Statistics, Warsaw 1994, p.92; information of Ministry of Justice and Ministry of National Education

Table 2. Juveniles placed in prisons and prisons for persons awaiting trial according to age (on 12/31/1994)

Age	Awaiting trial	Convicted	Total	Women
16–18 years	1193	443	1636	29
19–21 years	2577	3401	5978	111

Source: 1994 annual statistics of people awaiting trial, convicted and punished. Central Administration of Penal Institutions, Ministry of Justice, 1995.

There are special *penal institutions* for convicted young adults (Art.39(1.4) of P.e.c). However, young adult prisoners may also be placed in special units of other penal institutions. That also applies to juveniles who have attained the age of 16 .[8] In 1994, there were 1636 prisoners of the age of 16–18, representing 2.6% of the total of 62.719 prisoners in Poland (see Table 2).

Penal institutions are managed by the Ministry of Justice (precisely by the head of the Central Administration of Penal Institutions).

---

vision, 3) for those of high degree of depravation (strengthened supervision), 4) for mentally impaired, 5) for suffering from neuropsychosis or personality disorders.

[8] "A juvenile, who after attaining the age of 16 years shall commit a serious offence against life, a serious offence of rape, robbery, or a serious offence against public safety, or intentionally causes a serious bodily injury or a serious impairment of health may be subject to liability on the basis specified in this Code if the circumstances of the case as well as the traits and personal conditions of the perpetrator warrant it, and especially when previously applied educational or corrective measures have proved ineffective" (Art.9(2) of P.c.).

There are no private resocialization centres in Poland. It has been proposed, however, that some HCs and PIs should be turned private.

IV. CLASSIFICATION AND PLACEMENT OF CHILDREN IN RESOCIALIZATION INSTITUTIONS

A juvenile may be placed in an *ECY* by order of juvenile and family court as provided in A.p.c.j. (if the juvenile shows symptoms of depravation[9] or has committed a punishable act[10]) and F.& g.c. (if the interest of the child is threatened). The court does not specify the duration of stay in such institution, but the child should not stay there after he/she has attained 18 years.

Children may be placed in ECYs upon consent of their parents as well. Till March 1994, it was a school superintendent who was in charge of such decision; now, it is due to the head of an ECY .[11]

A juvenile may be placed in an *HC* by order of juvenile and family court (Art.7 of MJ's ord.). The court does not specify the duration of stay in such institution, but according to the Polish law the juvenile should not stay there after he or she has attained 21 years. A juvenile may be conditionally released by order of juvenile and family court, which shall consider his or her educational progress, as well as "positive prognosis" that upon release from an HC, the juvenile will comply with "legal order and principles of community life" (Art.86(1) of A.p.c.j.).

A juvenile is placed in a *PI* (in exceptional cases) upon imprisonment sentence of criminal court .[12] Period of detention is specified in the sentence. According to the law, a juvenile has a chance for a conditional early release after he or she has served 1/3 of the sentence (Art.90(2) of P.c.). Penitentiary court [13] is in charge of making such decision upon application of the juvenile himself, his counsel for the defence or the head of prison.

V. RIGHTS OF THE CHILD IN RESOCIALIZATION INSTITUTIONS

Growing interest of the public opinion in Poland in the issue of human rights has had positive effect on normalization of the legal status of children placed in resocialization institutions. There is a growing trend to word precisely

---

[9] A.p.c.j. does not define the term "depravation"; it just states its examples – "violation of the principles of community life, commission of a prohibited act, persistent evasion of compulsory education or vocational training, alcohol or drug abuse in order to intoxicate oneself, prostitution, vagrancy, participation in criminal groups" (Art. 4(1) of A.p.c.j.).

[10] See footnote 4.

[11] The number of children admitted in this way cannot exceed 15% of the total number of pupils. They stay in an ECY against partial payment.

[12] See footnote 8.

[13] Penitentiary court is one of the divisions of regional court.

rights and obligations of such children, as well as to treat them with respect for personal rights, both in legal theory and practice. According to the law, rights and obligations of children depend on the type of detention facility.

As provided in MNE's ord., children staying in *ECYs* have the right to:
- professional care, education and training;
- friendly and personal treatment;
- respect for human dignity, freedom of expression, including freedom of expression of religious beliefs or general outlook on life – as far as it does not infringe interests of other individuals;
- safety and protection against physical or mental persecution;
- use facilities of an ECY;
- visits of family members and friends [14];
- receive "pocket money".

Legal regulations related to organization and principles of stay of juveniles in *HCs* (MJ's ord.) do not provide a catalogue of personal rights *expressis verbis*. One can however derive from them that detained juveniles have the right to:
- receive clothing, shoes, school instruments and textbooks, means of personal hygiene and other personal items as required;
- full-day nourishment that satisfies the standards;
- use personal clothing and shoes according to principles set forth by educators' body;
- buy food and personal effects;
- receive parcels containing food and personal effects;
- receive money from their families and other persons or institutions;
- free medical care;
- communication with their family and other persons by means of correspondence [15] and mutual visits;
- contact with the defence counsel concerning court proceedings (inside the facility but in privacy);
- leave an HC for up to 42 days a year, depending on their conduct and "positive attitude towards work and education";
- religious practices and services, as well as possession of the necessary items of religious observance;
- complain about disciplinary sanctions to a judge sitting in a juvenile and family court.

---

[14] As provided in Art.18 of the standard statute for educational centres for youth (Annex 10 to MNE's ord.). The statute does not mention the right to correspondence, which is determined by internal rules of ECYs. The correspondence shall not be subject of censorship.

[15] Correspondence may be controlled by the head of HC or educational personnel authorized by him. It may be stopped and placed in an individual file, if its contents may bring about "negative effects on the process of resocialization" (*sic!*). Detained juvenile should be notified of stopping of his/her correspondence. "Official correspondence" may not be stopped (Art.23 of MJ's ord.).

Each ECY and HC has its own internal rules and daily routine. These rules and routines limit rights of juveniles set forth in acts and ordinances and at the same time extend their obligations. Sometimes, statutory rights of juveniles are considered to be an award .[16]

The issue of rights of juveniles placed in *PIs* is regulated mainly by P.e.c. As provided in Art 48 of P.e.c., a convict has the right to:

- proper nourishment, clothing, medical care and accommodation;
- communication with the outside world, especially with the family, by means of correspondence and visits;
- employment and relevant accident insurance;
- complaints to administration of PIs and penitentiary supervision authorities carried out in confidence;
- written requests and complaints to proper authorities; complaints to the court or public prosecutor should not be subject of censorship [17];
- use prison facilities and participate in cultural and educational activities.

Apart from the above mentioned catalogue of rights, according to P.e.c. the prisoner has the right to appeal to penitentiary court against any illegal decision of prison administration (Art. 14[1] of P.e.c.); he also has certain rights related to legal proceedings, including right to a counsel for the defence in executory proceedings (Art. 9(1) of P.e.c.). Rules of punishment execution determine the above mentioned rights more precisely and mention some other rights, including the right to:

- store documents related to legal proceedings in the confinement;
- possess food, means of personal hygiene and personal effects;
- religious practices as well as possession of the necessary items of religious observance;
- eight hours of sleep per day;
- everyday one-hour walk in the open air;
- education and vocational training.

As provided in the rules, some exceptions from the limitation of the rights may be carried into effect in case of young adult prisoners.

Persons placed in ECYs, HCs and PIs have also certain rights related to their status of learner, employee, patient etc., as provided in relevant regulations.[18]

---

[16] E.g. right of juveniles to contact with family by leaving a corrective institution for a visit to their home is only an award.

[17] As provided in internal regulations of prison management authorities, so called official correspondence (e.g. to the court or Spokesman for Civil Rights) may be handed by a convict to prison personnel in sealed envelopes.

[18] Including Act of June 26, 1974 – Labour code (Journal of law, No 24, item 141, as amended), Act of August 31, 1991 on health service institutions (Journal of Law, No 91, item 408) and A.e.s.

VI. MEANS OF LEGAL PROTECTION OF CHILDREN IN RESOCIALIZATION
INSTITUTIONS

Children placed in resocialization institutions (and their statutory representatives) have the following means of legal protection of their rights:
- requests, motions and complaints – made to the head of institution or supervisory authority;
- objections and complaints to the court;
- institution of criminal case;
- actions for indemnity or compensation of infringement of personal rights instituted to civil law court;
- individual complaints to Human Rights Commission on the basis of *Convention for the Protection of Human Rights and Fundamental Freedoms*.

VII. RIGHTS OF THE CHILD IN PRACTICE

A. Sources

The issue of observance of children rights in resocialization institutions will be discussed on the basis of materials of the Spokesman for Civil Rights ("SCR"), Helsinki Foundation for Human Rights [19] and Interventions Bureau of the Chancellery of Senate of the Polish Republic. These materials consist of reports on inspection of resocialization centres, selected examples of correspondence of juveniles with those institutions, photographical documentation and official documents issued by authorities responsible for protection of rights of juveniles. All these reports were prepared in the last three years.[20]

B. Monitoring

Monitoring methods were generally the same in case of all the above mentioned institutions; there were some differences, however, related to particular

---

[19] Executory body of Helsinki Committee – non-governmental organization, which has been operating in Poland since 1982.

[20] *Current state of affairs in respect of observance of basic personal rights in corrective institutions and homes for detained juveniles in 1993 and early in 1994*, SCR's Bulletin-Materials No 23, 1994 ("*SCR's report*"); *Houses of correction and homes for detained juveniles as seen by foster-children and educational personnel as well as analysis of organizational and legal system of these institutions* Senate Interventions Bureau, Warsaw, 1993 ("*Senate's report*"); T. Bulenda, A. Kremplewski, Z. Lasocik, A. Rzepliński, *Report on inspection of isolation institutions for juveniles and adult offenders* Warsaw, 1992 ("*1. Foundation's report*"); *Report on inspection of isolation institutions for juveniles and adults* (ed. A. Rzepliński), Warsaw, 1993 ("*2. Foundation's report*"); E. Bolewska, T. Bulenda, R. Musidłowski, *Information on current state of affairs in respect of observance of rights of juveniles placed in police stations for detained children*, SCR' Bulletin-Materials No 23, 1994; T. Bulenda, A. Kremplewski, *Report on inspection of 5. Public Educational Centre for Youth in Warsaw (at Strażacka street) – March 1994* (expert appraisement for Helsinki Foundation for Human Rights, typewritten copy).

techniques used and methods of "deeper" analysis .[21] Although Polish NGOs have played an important role as far as education and direct help is concerned, we will discuss only effects of their activities related to monitoring of resocialization and penal institutions.

Monitoring (which we ourselves call inspection [22]) of such institutions used to take several hours – depending on the size of the institution. It was carried out by two people in the following way: it used to begin with an initial conversation with the head of the centre (prison) about particular character of the institution, its personnel and wards, as well as relevant problems. It was followed by visits in rooms which we indicated; we had a chance to talk with wards and inspect documents. The inspection ended with a second conversation with the head of the institution about our doubts and initial assessment. Usually, we used to spend several hours in each institution – depending mainly on its size.

We used to carry out our inspection by means of inquiries and observation, making independent notes. Each person prepared its own written report and then the final version was prepared by one of us, which was later submitted to the head of the institution and supervisory authorities .[23]

The other institutions sometimes use some additional methods, e.g. interviewing of randomly selected wards (SCR) or anonymous polls (Senate Interventions Bureau).

C. Results of Inspection and Assessment of Observance of Rights of the Child

The detailed discussion of the issue of observance of children's rights will be carried out in the way it is presented in *UN Rules for the Protection of Juveniles Deprived of their Liberty.*

1. Records. Each institution keeps individual files of its foster-children, including their personal data and information about their placement and treatment in the institution. Requirements related to admission, registration and transfer of juveniles are generally met.

---

[21] SCR and Senate Interventions Bureau are entitled to monitor all types of detention facilities. Helsinki Foundation for Human Rights has a non-governmental status; thus it has to apply to supervisory authorities for a consent to enter into any particular institution.

[22] As associates of Foundation for Human Rights we took part in four inspections of such institutions: in western Poland – in May 1992, in southern Poland – in May 1993, in Warsaw – in February 1994 and in south-eastern Poland – in September 1994. T. Bulenda as a member of the team for detained persons in SCR's Bureau used to take part in inspections of police stations for detained children, homes for detained juveniles and houses of correction.

[23] We have monitored 4 prisons, 8 prisons for persons awaiting trial, 4 houses of correction, 9 educational centres for youth, 3 police stations for detained children, 1 rest centre, 1 asylum and 1 children's home. As associates of Helsinki Foundation for Human Rights (together with several other people) we have inspected the total of 31 institutions, in which juveniles may be placed according to the Polish law.

2. Classification and Placement.   Rules for classification and placement of children in resocialization institutions are usually observed. Children are separated from adults, and girls from boys. Due to legal regulations and actual situation, children and adults may stay together only in houses of correction and penal institutions. In case of HCs it applies to persons under the age of 21, only. In case of PIs, juveniles and young adults may be sometimes brought together with carefully selected adults for educational benefits.

Polish legal system provides regulations concerning special needs of girls. Proper conditions of their stay in educational centres and houses of correction are guaranteed.

3. Information about Rules Governing the Facility.   On admission, juveniles are informed orally about their rights and obligations. Usually, they are not given written copies of the internal rules. The rules are displayed in information boards. In many institutions, addresses of the governmental and non-governmental bodies to which the wards could apply are missing.

4. Accommodation.   With the exception for PIs, most buildings used by resocialization institutions have been adapted for this purpose. For example, 11 out of 34 houses of correction were built after second world war .[24] Therefore, many buildings do not meet standards for such institutions. In many cases, there are no proper classrooms, physician's offices, gymnasiums and sports fields .[25]

Room equipment is usually barely sufficient. There are some extreme cases of simplicity of rooms.

There are usually very large dormitories in institutions for children. Sometimes, there is nothing but beds (even up to 20) in the dormitories .[26] Personal effects are kept in other rooms (sometimes locked) or in a day-room which is accessible to everyone. It results in possible serious violation of the right to privacy.

Four meals a day are served in resocialization institutions. Usually, juveniles do not complain about nourishment. There were however some exceptions (complaints about insufficient quantity and monotony of food) .[27]

Juveniles have the right to receive clothing from the administration and they do receive it, if required. Generally, children use their own clothing; only

---

[24]   *Creation and application of law. Opinion of the Ministry of Justice* Warsaw, 1994, p.34.

[25]   E.g. houses of correction in Grodzisk and Trzemeszno are located in former prisons. Others are located mainly in old school buildings.

[26]   E.g. HC in Trzemeszno (*1. Foundation's Report*).

[27]   According to *SCR's report* 42% of wards of an HC in Poznań complained about it; according to *Senate's report*: 40% – in an HC in Barczewo, 30% – in an HC in Witkowo and 13% – in an HC in Danzig-Oliwa. And according to *1. Foundation's report* there was one institution where small food allowances resulted in children's undernourishment. The institution was finally closed after MNE's inspection.

exceptionally, they receive so called "official" clothing (it applies mainly to HCs and PIs).

5. Education and Vocational Training.   Administration of the resocialization institutions provides children with the opportunity to receive education and vocational training .[28] Most young people staying in resocialization institutions are educationally retarded .[29] Thus, special educational and teaching methods are required. Usually, education is limited to the level of primary school and basic vocational school. Most houses of correction have their own schools and workshops for vocational training. Otherwise, young people may use workshops outside the detention facility.

Selection of vocations is rather limited. Boys can usually choose between wood-worker, metal-worker, painter or mason, and girls between dressmaker, farmer, gardener or hair-dresser. Often juveniles would prefer other vocations, e.g. motor-car fitter or driver in case of boys. Choice of vocations has been further limited lately, due to liquidation of many vocational schools .[30]

6. Work.   Generally, juveniles have no opportunity to perform remunerated labour in ECYs and HCs. There are very few exceptions .[31] In such cases, wards usually spend earned money on recreational equipment (e.g. tables for table-tennis, T.V. sets, books). All protective standards resulting from labour law apply to those who are employed.

For their work in school shops, detained juveniles receive financial awards or remuneration.

In some educational centres, foster children receive pocket money; they can lose part or all of it in case of bad conduct.

In penal institutions, work is treated as one of educational measures. Employment is regulated by laws concerning imprisonment. Juveniles working in prisons receive remuneration themselves (it is not used for aims of the prison community).

---

[28] In Poland, compulsory education is limited to 8-year-long primary school. As provided in the Act on educational system, this obligation applies to children of the age of 7–17. As provided in regulations concerning children and youth in resocialization institutions, however, they are obliged to complete primary school and vocational training even if they have attained the age of 17.

[29] According to *SCR's reports* the retardation is 2–3 years on average. According to MJ's data, 90% of the juveniles to whom corrective measures had been applied were educationally retarded: 44.8% – 1–2 years, 22.4% – 3 years, 22.8% – 3 or more years. Often dyslexia or dysgraphia was the main cause of school difficulties. 15% of those juveniles were mentally retarded. (*Creation and application of law* p.35).

[30] Generally, it applies to factory technical schools. After privatization many enterprises close such schools – mostly for financial reasons.

[31] Due to high unemployment in Poland (3 mln people), work of detained juveniles is not very competitive.

7. Rest and Physical Training.   According to the law, detained juveniles have the right to rest and physical exercise. Observance of the right to physical exercise is different in institutions for juveniles and young adults. The worst situation is in PIs, due to their isolation function. Penal institutions with special units for convicted young adults have rather satisfactory (in comparison with "typical" PIs) facilities for physical recreation.

By means of physical activities, which are believed to be of therapeutic value, personnel tries to solve problems resulting from subculture and antagonisms between various groups of convicts. Generally, one of the educators – who is licensed to do so – is responsible for organization, planning and carrying out of sport activities. Physical activities have been always an important element of educational system in houses of correction. Therefore, there are various forms of sport activities available for juveniles institutionalized there.[32]

In ECYs right to physical exercise is implemented at school (compulsory classes in sports and the way the boarding-school of ECY is organized). Each educator is obliged to include time for sports and recreation when organizing children's activities. There are also special clubs for those interested in sports. Apart from routine physical activities (3–5 hours per week), ECYs organize school trips (mainly sightseeing tours).

8. Religious Care.   As a result of major political changes in Poland, which have taken place since 1989, foster-children have been given the opportunity to fully exercise their right to freedom of conscience and religion, including right to religious observance. Clergymen (mainly Roman Catholic and Orthodox priests), as well as representatives of other religious groups (Jehovah's Witnesses, Pentecost Church, Hare Krishna Movement, etc.) may freely visit resocialization institutions. Juveniles may attend religious services and meetings provided in the detention facility. As the need arises, they may go to a local parish church. There are also religion classes held in these institutions.[33] Every juvenile may receive visits from a representative of given church or religious group. He may also possess items of religious observance.

When questioned about it, juveniles complained neither about impediments and obstructions nor compelling to religious observance or education .[34]

9. Medical Care.   Right to protection of health is the one which is most frequently infringed. In many institutions, there are no physicians working

---

[32] A. Rejzner, *Psychomotor recreation in resocialization of juveniles.* Warsaw, 1980.

[33] Parents (if they have parental authority) are the ones to decide whether their children should attend religion classes.

[34] According to *SCR's report* those attending Mass represent rather small percentage of the total number of forest-children. Similarly, according to *Foundation reports* only a few dozen out of several hundred prisoners attend Mass in penal institutions.

full or at least part-time. The same goes for specialists, including psychiatrists. The best situation is in PIs.

Children often complain about superficial treatment and pharmaceutical shortages [35] as well as about long waiting time for medical aid [36] and improper attitude of doctors and medical personnel (disrespect, casual examination, suspicions that the child is pretending) .[37]

In Poland, rights of the patient were stated *expressis verbis* for the first time in 1991 .[38] Now, they have been slowly turning into practice in resocialization institutions. We believe that it is due to the fact that legal regulations concerning protection of health of children and youth do not correspond with actual opportunities to exercise these rights .[39]

Physical health of juveniles, however, is much better protected than their mental health. That has been partly due to the fact, that till recently, there was no act on protection of mental health .[40] There are no proper conditions for the rehabilitation of physically or mentally impaired.

But recently, individual and group therapy has become more frequent in resocialization institutions. There is a growing number of psychologists who begin to work with children and youth in ECYs and HCs.

Children who are alcohol- or drug-dependant undergo medical treatment in those institutions. More "complicated" cases are transferred to public hospitals.

10. Internal Freedom. Wards of ECYs and HCs may freely move about within the facility area. In some cases, dormitories are closed during the day and wards stay in classrooms or day-rooms. Such daily routines are closely related to the permanent control of movements of every ward.

In PIs, there are different rules concerning movement possibilities of juvenile prisoners. Only in some cases, confinements are open during the day, but nevertheless movements of prisoners are under intensive control.

Cameras are not used to control juveniles and adult prisoners in Poland.

---

[35] *SCR's report* pp.73–74.

[36] *2. Foundation's report, passim*

[37] *Senate's report* pp. 51–54.

[38] Act of August 30, 1991 on health service institutions (Journal of Law, No 91, item 408).

[39] E.g. right to information about one's health state and access to medical documentation, as well as right to receive a copy of information about health state of a juvenile staying in a penal institution – are still excessively and groundlessly limited by current provisions.

[40] Act on protection of mental health, which was passed by the Polish Parliament on August 19, 1994, is the first legal regulation related to treatment of mentally impaired people. It applies also to children suffering from mental disorders. The act has introduced a completely new concept: in order to place a child who has attained the age of 16 in a mental hospital, one has to obtain a consent of the child (with exception to cases when it is up to the court to decide). Age limit below which patient's consent for treatment should be obtained was lowered by 2 years as compared with common practice.

11. Contacts with the Outside World.   According to the law, juveniles have the right to contact with their families, friends and other persons by means of correspondence and visits. They receive visits of their family in the facility and may also visit their homes upon receiving special permission (as an award or in case of special accidents) or leave.

This particular right is seldom infringed in practice. Administration of resocialization centres encourages the communication of juveniles with the outside world, as it has an educational value. Personal contacts (and sometimes even correspondence) of juveniles with their families inside and outside detention facilities are nevertheless limited. It is often a result of indifference of families of detained juveniles, which neither write letters nor visit the child. Despite efforts of the personnel, it is difficult to preserve family ties .[41]

There are no impediments in case of juveniles who want to study outside the detention facility. However, this is not very common.

Individual short-time leaves are seriously limited, especially in case of educational centres for girls. Their personnel argued that this was due to the fact that they could get pregnant .[42]

Close analysis of reports shows that in many cases (especially in small towns) local communities have positive attitude towards children staying in resocialization institutions. Therefore, we believe that there is no reason to limit short-time leaves, especially in case of ECYs.

12. Right to Inviolability.   Children staying in resocialization centres are protected against acts infringing their inviolability committed by either their peers or personnel. It is assured by both legal regulations and practical control mechanisms. As far as wards are concerned, their behaviour is under permanent observation; and in case of personnel (teachers, educators and others), they control one another and may be subject to severe sanctions for infringement of ward's inviolability .[43]

Affrays, battery and other forms of infringement of inviolability by peer wards are usually a result of subculture existing in institutions for detained juveniles .[44] Effective struggle against that phenomenon is a real problem in some places. In contrast to prisons, usually a great number of wards staying in resocialization institutions take part in subculture. As a consequence of subcultural rules, wards who do not take part in it (so-called "squares") are

---

[41]   *SCR's report* p.75 and the next. According to the *Senate's report* juveniles who did not communicate with their families stated the following reasons for such state of affairs: poor financial condition, reluctance of the family, no family, no chance to visit the family, reluctance of the juvenile himself/herself (*ibid.* p.77).

[42]   T. Bulenda, A. Kremplewski, *Report on inspection., op.cit* p.26.

[43]   A person infringing ward's inviolability may be prosecuted for doing so. In the *Senate's report* there is a story of three educators working in a house of correction of intensified supervision who were accused of beating their foster-children. In two cases legal proceedings were discontinued and the third person was released under amnesty. *Ibid,* p.9.

[44]   *2. Foundation's report* p.16.

humiliated, beaten and exploited. Such conflicts usually take place at night, when the number of personnel on duty is limited.

Extreme cases of infringment of inviolability take place during riots or other forms of protest of wards .[45]

Despite efforts of the personnel, trying to provide proper safety measures, there are still situations when inviolability of wards is infringed.

Single blow or battery are the most common examples of infringment of ward's inviolability by the personnel. It happens in many institutions, but in some of them such conduct of the personnel is something common .[46] In other places such situations happen only ocassionally.

Lack of confidence of wards in the effectiveness of existing legal protection measures, as well as the fact, that they do not inform the head of the institution that they were hit or beaten further stimulate such infringements. When questioned about it, detained juveniles who were hit or beaten used to say that they had not talked about it since nobody would believe it and they would only involve themselves into further trouble .[47]

13. Awards and Punishments. Rules governing resocialization institutions usually set forth awards and punishments, as well as authorities competent to apply them. But description of conduct which should be awarded or which is a disciplinary infraction is rather vague .[48] Especially, lack of characteristics of the conduct constituting a disciplinary offence is a major transgression. It favours arbitrary awarding and punishing of the wards by the personnel. Lack of detailed procedures of awarding and punishing as well as of appealing from the imposed sanctions makes the situation even worse .[49]

Catalogue of sanctions includes the following: admonition, reprimand, informing parents and the court about improper conduct, denial or restriction of the contact with the outside people (excluding parents or guardians), stop-

---

[45] In 1993, in an HC in Grodzisk Wielkopolski (central Poland), a group of boys who were members of subculture barricaded themselves in a day-room on the second floor. They took a hostage (a boy who was not participating in the subculture), pull a grating out of the window and hang out the boy upside down. They threatened they would throw him out unless their demands were met. Order was restored by the antiterrorist brigade of the police. *SCR's report* pp. 67–68.

[46] According to *SCR's report* 42 out of 288 (14.5%) juveniles staying in 14 HCs and detention centres for juveniles have been hit or beaten by the personnel. In three institutions, more than 30% of the wards who were questioned said, that the personnel used "such methods". According to *Senate's report* 51% of the total of 980 wards who were questioned in 35 HCs and detention centres for juveniles said that they were subject of "beating and violence". *Ibid* p.57.

[47] *SCR's report* pp. 62–63.

[48] Usually the description is limited to the formula: "The following sanctions may be imposed for disciplinary infraction..."

[49] Only P.e.c. provides that one can appeal from the decision imposing disciplinary sanctions to penitentiary court.

ping of permissions to leave the facility for up to a month, suspension of the right to leave for 3 months and transfer to an institution of increased rigour.

Sometimes, also informal sanctions are inflicted (although the problem is diminishing). In one of the institutions, the personnel used to impose informal "punishment" by ordering the wards to stay in pyjamas all day long. Increased "punishment" included taking away trousers – the wards had to wear underwear only .[50] We found out that the personnel of another institution used to force insubordinate girls to wear "official" clothing. Most probably, the punishment was intended to stigmatize the ward.

14. Coercive Measures and Use of Force.   In contrast to penal institutions, there are no legal regulations concerning the use of force and coercive measures in case of juveniles staying in ECYs and HCs .[51] In practice, various methods to solve this problem were used by the administration. Representatives of the Senate Interventions Bureau found out that *contra legem* there was a confidential instruction allowing to use coercive measures against wards (e.g. placement in a solitary confinement, restraining belts, straitjackets) .[52]

15. Complaints.   Detained juveniles are not informed about methods of making complaints and authorities who are competent to receive them. Usually, internal rules governing educational centres and houses of correction just mention the right of the ward to make complaints.

Rules of carrying out penalty of deprivation of liberty provide detailed description of this right. Among ca 3.800 letters requesting intervention or legal assistance received by the Helsinki Foundation for Human Rights during the period of January 1992 – September 1994, there was not even one from a detained juvenile.

Also Spokesman for Civil Rights receives a very small number of letters with complaints from children (although he has been active and since 1988 and thus relatively well known). It shows that children (even older ones) either do not know their rights or do not believe that their complaint may change anything.

It should be mentioned, however, that last year (September 1993 – September 1994) the Committee for the Protection of the Rights of the Child received about 100 letters with various complaints from children and youth (the number of such letters increased after information about the organization and its address were published in the Polish edition of *Bravo*). Representatives of the Committee have found out, that telephone complaints or requests

---

[50] It was an institution for boys and there were women among its personnel (*2. Foundation report*).

[51] As a result of stating of this deficiency in the Senate report, Minister of Justice began (after discussion of politicians about juvenile delinquency) to prepare a regulation concerning this issue.

[52] *Senate report* p. 162 and the next.

for legal advise are less popular among children and youth (although phone number is published repeatedly in nationwide magazines).

16. Court Supervision In theory, ECYs and HCs are supervised by a judge sitting in a juvenile and family court (a judge of district court). But in practice, inspections of these institutions are conducted only occasionally.

Penal institutions are supervised by a penitentiary judge (of regional court) and there is no major negligence of this obligation. It is interesting to note, that every prisoner has the right to demand to talk to the penitentiary judge.

VIII. DISCUSSION AND CONCLUSIONS

1. As has been presented, there are still shortcomings and deficiencies related to the protection of the rights of the child in resocialization institutions – both in terms of legal system and practice.

   Analysis of the Polish law shows that the principles set forth in*UN Rules for the Protection of Juveniles Deprived of Their Liberty* have not been fully reflected in the regulations concerning placement of juveniles in resocialization institutions. For example, there are no legal regulations related to the following issues: use of coercive measures and force (with the exception for PIs), disciplinary proceedings, right to legal advise and the problem of employing psychiatrists and social assistants in resocialization institutions (in contrast to PIs). There is no clear declaration that the personnel is obligated to respect the ward's right to privacy.

   It seems that censorship of letters of children staying in HCs and PIs is inconsistent with Art.16 of *Convention on the Rights of the Child*.

   There is no regulation concerning the right of the child to request assistance of an interpreter.

2. Housing, accommodation, organizational and especially financial conditions do not help in the full observance of the rights of the child.

   Status of human rights is much worse in institutions for children and youth than in institutions for adults. Although prisons have become "civilized" (though they do not fully comply with Western standards), there is still a lot to do about institutions for children and youth. Children and youth staying in ECYs and HCs do not really know their rights. That applies even to the personnel of these institutions.

3. We believe that, poor organizational structure is another important factor which has negative effects on the protection of children's rights. The fact that the responsibility for institutions for children is shared by three central governmental bodies (Ministry of Justice, Ministry of National Education and Ministry of Health and Social Welfare), while these institutions have

rather local character, results in a formal attitude towards the issue of the rights of the child .[53]

4. Bad habits of the personnel, who got used to getting precise amounts of money from the "H.Q." are another obstacle. We have seen some places, however, where despite economic difficulties, the personnel – due to good cooperation with local authorities – was able to obtain flats for wards who were leaving the institution after getting mature.

5. We believe, that a wide educational programme intended to inform the society about the rights of the child should be implemented. Results of sociological polls confirm its necessity .[54] They show only the tip of the iceberg, that is generally the poor situation of the child in the family. It is interesting to note, that the declaration of the Polish government related to the rights set forth in Art.12–16 of the *Convention on the Rights of the Child* stated that these rights may be exercised by children "with respect for parental authority, Polish customs and tradition related to the place of the child inside and outside the family". The above mentioned declaration may be interpreted in several different manners, but the idea that one should not interfere in family matters (including dealing with children) is also a deep-rooted element of Polish tradition. Indifference of neighbours and reluctance of the police in case of cruelty to children by their parents or guardians is the evidence of that situation.

The principle set forth in the *Convention on the Rights of the Child* that one should consider the opinion of the child if it may freely express it depending on its age (Art.12(1) of the *Convention*) is reflected neither in legal regulations nor practice. Juveniles staying in resocialization institutions do not stand for their rights (they seldom make complaints or recourse to the law).

6. The rights and obligations of the juveniles, as well as the means of their protection should be determined more precisely in internal rules of resocialization institutions. There is a question, whether each ECY and HC should prepare its own rules (as it has been now) or there should be one standard set of rules for all institutions (as in case of PIs). Since attempts of resocialization institutions to prepare their own rules have been very inept, the second solution seems much better. This is even more so, since general outlines for statutes of various institutions are also deficient.

---

[53] In the Ministry of Justice, an organizational unit responsible for HCs is a part of the department of courts and notary's offices; thus, it has practically no meaning, being located next to "powerful neighbours". It is important when budget funds are divided.

[54] Question polls carried out in 1983–84 in a district of "intellectuals" in Warsaw showed that 82% of parents "slapped" their children; 67% hit them with hands; 38% "seriously spanked" them; 44% beat children with "a belt or other object". A. Piekarska, *Violence in the family.* Warsaw 1991; As quoted in: *Situation of children and youth (5–20-year-old) in Poland. Report*; Polish Foundation for Children and Youth, Warsaw 1993, pp.79–80.

ANNETTE JACOB

Monitoring Children's Rights in a Socio-educational Establishment

The Lyonnaise Society for Childhood and Adolescence

INTRODUCTION

With regard to the validity of this publication, my contribution is based on the hypothesis that if the UN Committee for the Rights of the Child fulfils an aim at monitoring on an international scale, this will heighten as a whole the responsibility of all at the educational establishments taking part in this conference i.e. those from States which ratified the United Nations Convention on the Rights of the Child.

Indeed, at the centre of each of these States, if one of the tasks of the elected politicians is to pass laws to bring national texts in line with the international ones, the public and private educational establishments have their own responsibilities, among others, informing children and young people, and to train them, and introduce them to exercise their rights on a daily basis.

This hypothesis takes note of opposition and legal-ideological arguments which have delayed the Convention from being applied legally on a nationwide scale.[1] It modestly proposes to demonstrate that the application of this convention is possible on the scale of an establishment housing 700 children and young people.

Let us go into more detail of institutions which are joining in this same dynamic, quoting particularly those with numerous NGOs, the French Support Council for Childrens Rights (Conseil Français des Droits de l'Enfant, COFRADE). The Lyonnaise Society for Childhood and Adolescence (SLEA) is also a member of this council, and this paper will concern the practical experience of this one association.[2]

E. Verhellen (ed.), Monitoring Children's Rights, 745–756.
© 1996 *Kluwer Law International. Printed in the Netherlands.*

I. THE INSTITUTIONAL FRAME OF THE SLEA

It was in November 1990, at the time of a European Conference dealing with children's rights within the protection systems of different countries[3] (organised by the SLEA because of its centenary) that a decision for the use of the convention in the educational and associated applications of the institution was made.

The present day experience takes place in an institution born under the 3rd republic, whose founders, we know, expanded on the main programme for the protection of childhood, which is still in force today under modernised forms in France.

On 24 July 1990 a law was passed to protect children who had been morally abandoned, and it was to ensure the establishment of this kind of protection that the SLEA, the lyonnaise society for the preservation of childhood was founded in 1890.[4]

100 years later, its leaders have a choice: to apply the United Nations Convention on children's rights in terms of continuing their aim of education, or to move closer towards children and young people in trouble.

II. NECESSARY CONDITIONS FOR THE APPLICATION OF CHILDREN'S RIGHTS (THEIR MONITORING)

– It is important that the association's board of directors clearly expresses their wish to take on the setting up of the convention in professionnal terms, and take the required steps to acheive this.
– This "political" desire is firmly written in the long-term plan of the society, and on every project.
– It is essential that this "wish" can rely on the support of all of the social-psychological, educational staff. The work on the history of an establishment has certainly been helped by the work stemming from conferences which gave a support to this venture.
– Finally it is necessary that an establishment can guarantee the quality of work, and of professionnal practice which can undergo a revision, an adaptation, or an innovation. The board of directors has created a committee made up of social-educational professionnals, and directors of the SLEA, as well as outside individuals.[5]

This board forms a kind of observatory, "watching over" the application of children's rights, recording the achievements, setting goals, proposing motions. Every member of the committee is a resourceful person, having a specific skill. Among its members a coordinator circulates information dealing with a particuliar subject, for example published legal documents (laws and case laws)[6]. This information is also broadcast to the different service sectors and establishments, by the members who represent them on the committee. The coordinator draws up reviews, and an annual report on the committee's work. He/she is also a board member for COFRADE.

III. THE THEORY IN PRACTICE: SOME APPLIED EXAMPLES

Generally the committee's work centres on the position of young people and children who, based on a judge's decision, and after examining the established rights for children in the convention, takes them away from their family. We can sum this up in a quotation taken from two authors[7] "Children and adolescents taken into care, is the subject of a collection of documents which guarantees the rights and the obligations of institutions, guardianships, magistrates and people in authority in the departement. But are there defined rights for fostered children?".

In the Rhône-Alpes region, M. Klajnberg, chief judge at the children's court in Grenoble, made an important transcript of the convention on the position of a fostered child. This gives the committee more of a choice in reference material. He observes that "the Convention reinforces a certain amount of laws already established in French law (for example articles 2 – 3 – 9 – 12 – 19 – 25), asking questions and introducing them again the universal norm".

Having worked on the whole document, the committee chose to question further the "new rights" (article 13 to 17), and to clarify the structuring of their implementation with educational and institutional practices. Why this? and I quote again M. Klajnberg[8] "Besides the physical protection that a child deserves, they take into account their identity, his or her ability to be a subject and participant in their own experiences, for instance, their social environment". This a totally democratic and educational objective.

Article 12 of the convention defines the right of child for individual expression, while articles 13–17 state freedom of expression, meeting and association, thoughts, religion, conscience, and the right for respect of their private life. We call them the "new rights" but are they really new? Their novelty lies in the fact that from now on they make up a universal standard.

At a conference[9] a magistrate said that "If minority in the legal sense of the word is a time of incapacity, the restriction on freedom that it imposes under the name of protection does not mean that a child does not have the same fundamental rights as an adult ". Consider the "republican theory which states that freedom should be law, its limitation and regulation the exception".[10] On the other hand, when these rights are established it is their putting into practice that falls short. He asks us to ask ourselves about our own way of perceiving freedom, and to arrange pedagogical and theraputic aims of protection and restriction".

Other authors demonstrate the lack of information of "users in the field of the protection of minors "no incompetence justifies this omission of information",[11] or reveals ignorance of the people working in this area (public service or associations) indeed it's the reluctance of some of them to call on the new code of cival procedure, published 1975. Also Ch. Vogt argues that "certain judges, and people working in the educational sector, branch away from the law and seriously undermine the rights and freedom of parents and minors".[12]

Aware of these problems and insufficiencies, the committee members defined their work aim in the framework of their mission of education and protection. To inform children's and adolescents of their rights to create favourable conditions to exercice these rights, to help them to grow up in terms of individual and joint freedom, to allow them to exercise their responsibilities, to learn about democracy, but also to have control over their own life. In this light, the convention is a very good educational tool, and the application of articles on the "new rights" gives the opportunity to learn about citizenship[13] as well as legal tool to develop to an equal degree where "the resorting to the law destroys completely classic social-educational or psycho-medical intervention towards children".[14] For judge Klajnberg, "this child would have knowledge of the law, so that he could insist on rights from the adults working in the institution, and knowledge of places which take these rights into account. This seems to him to be one of the essential supporting points to complement institutional thought processes, and could reinstate individual needs. However he recognizes that the application of these new rights poses some problems in establishments housing children and adolescents. In effect the new rights come into direct conflict with the rights of the adults working in the institution, who find themselves in a position of authority or responsability over the child; and the protection to which they have the right. Finally they disrupt again the current practices.

In professional fields, for example learning how to participate and about freedom of expression for children and adolescents, will force the tutor to develop collective practices. But according to Ch. Vogt[15] "the actual reinforcement of the teaching pattern, made legal by the leitmotive "taking care of oneself" resists the project of learning democracy and citizenship for young people".

A professor of educational sciences, Ph. Meirieu[16] awards pedagogue the task of "turning formal laws, into actual ones, of allowing spontaneous activities, mainly determined by social influences, of thoughtful activities; "The pedagogue succeeds in linking closely knowledge with problems that the pupils come up against, knowledge of the situation that they are living in. It succeeds in putting the pupils in a status, of being able to interrogate, understand, criticise and protest not only in the near future but now, in the classroom.

Jean Le Gal[17], lecturer in science and education at Nantes and in charge of childrens rights at the "Institute Cooperaty de l'Ecole Moderne" (ICEM), draws attention to "classes and co-operative schools which demonstrates the possibility of defining the contradiction between protection, and freedom in dialectic terms of a link between these two seemingly antagonistic situations. To quote one of the pioneers of new education, Freinet, 1923[18] writing in an educational review: "the known theory of rights and duties of the individual in a community is not enough: it is social practice that we must develop, so that man will know how to behave in many different situations in his life".

Another important reference: the works of the national education, who integrate the convention in their school practices (decree of 18 March 1991) relating to rights and obligations of pupils". Individual freedom, and joint expression in every respect are known to all pupils in public institutions. It is specified that exercising this freedom is written into an educational aim, and that it takes into account the age of the pupils "learning how to be a citizen, and about responsibility that must be practiced from the entry into secondary school to college where the number of pupils is at its maximum". These texts are of interest because of their content and originality to other establishments other than schools. This underlines one of the aims of COFRADE[19] "if school takes on a particular importance, notably that it is a compulsory and common passage for all children, it is not the only place or community concerned with the exercice of participation rights for children. The commune, village or the area in which the child is living, are places for young people where they can express themselves, meet others and associate". These documents are of equal interest to medical-social, and social institutions.

Finally in the field of legal and social protection for minors, the law establishes rights of expression and participation and certain documents established this before the convention. In this way the validity of the child's opinion on everything concerning him is written in the law of 06.06.1984 "applicable to family rights and the relationships of children with the services in charge of the protection of the family and children".

On the subject of educational assistance, the law of 04.06.1970 on parental authority state that the hearing of children is compulsary. This can be directly in front of a judge, and with the help of a lawyer. The inability to go to court doesnot apply to minors within legal protection.

The decree of 31.12.1991, relates to the advice board of the institutions, social and medical-social, mentioned in article 3 of the law of 30.06.1975, and anticipate that the users, children from 12 upwards are forcibly linked to the running of the establishment. Examining these documents in the prism of the convention, allows us to reread them, intepret them for children's rights and to judge the gap between what is said, and what is in fact happening. Some examples of the convention applied in professionnal practices. This application brings us up to date on the rights of expression and of the participation of children and adolescents, on their own behalf and of life in an institution, i.e. the participation of children and adolescents in their own placing.

The educational teams of the SLEA had involved the principal of consulting the child and adolescent in their practices well before the convention stated it, and associated both the child and adolescent in all decisions concerning him/her. But these must be revised, adjusted and modernised with reference to the new legal framework. This also gives a different meaning to the concept of "participation" in so far as this participation, formally granted by adults to children, now becomes a right for them.

Current practices
  – Participation in meetings concerning the weekly organization of the timetable, of leisure;
  – Participation in the managing of their own personal budget (clothes pocket money, leisure);
  – Participation in defining their own educational project, and of aims for their own placement;
  – Preparation of a report for the "children's judge", collection of the view points of the child and adolescent.

New practices (inspired by the work of judge Klajnberg)
  – The respect of the possibility of contradictory ideas in every decision made by the educational team concerning the placement of a child. The fostered child must have the right to speak to a neutral person from within the establishment in the case of conflict with their educator.
  – The expansion of formalities and procedures which guarantees the rights being written into interior ruling.
  – The taking into account of the collective voice of the young people. For example: a transport problem in a training establishment welcoming young adults and adolescents, taking a vote, creates a democratic process in a group where the tendency would normally be to follow the point of view of the strongest personalities. The shy or weak pupils would then have an opportunity to express their opinion, and the more dominant children would agree with whatever the majority voted.
  – The Convention forces a revision of educational projects for young adults. At 18 they are able to vote but what are their citizens' rights at this age established? How can we make them into adults, capable of being active citizens in their area or village, by developing training to citizenship (not only in terms of a job) well before the legal age.

Participation in institutional life
Elected representatives for the children and adolescents, elected by their peers are present at each establishment and institution which houses them. The main objective of this council is to join everyone associated with life at the institution, occupants, families, staff, and management. The council can give opinions, and make suggestions on anything to do with the running of the place. It is a learning place for children, to exercise their rights of expression and participation. There were 2 important pieces of work on behalf of the educational teams and young people:
  – the rewriting of interior rules in light of the convention;

– the organization of elections to set up a council.

To rewrite the interior ruling the educators were inspired by the work of 2 authors already quoted. M. Klajnberg who underlines the importance of formalising "institutional law" by written ones, the importance of adjusting the functioring of the rules of the "capability of the child to abide by them", and to explain to him/her the way in which these rules have been expanded on. Ch. Vogt (20) advises "maintaining the essence of the fundemental concept of the State' present day law, which examines every social event under the point of view of lively opposition, autonomy, freedom of subjects, that can be problematic, and on the other hand the obligations of those who are taking control of it, of knowing their responsibility of protecting under the perspective of autonomisation, and the need to guarantee a coherence of a provision of a service". Each child and teenagers taking part in the expansion of interior ruling received a booklet, outlining the rules for the running of the establishment, which they can refer to in case of problems or breach of rules. It makes up a reference plan, for adults, children and adolescents alike, of all subject under its rules, with respect for one another on the same charter.

This interior ruling, argues that a director (21) "helps both the educator and the trainer, in that it depersonalises their powers of position which are now no longer theirs but those of the institution".

"The effects of the adjustments, are also of benefit to the adolescent who due to these adjustments is placed in a better environment at the professional teaching and youth welcoming centre (CEPAJ).Within these boundaries he can evolve at his own rate and see that he can wait for us and we will wait for him, because our interior ruling apart from the rules for life, preludes the aim of our association, our educational orientations, and the questioning of an admission to the CEPAJ.

This permanent official ruling eliminates the victim status; it thus can become focus of all our care and attention. A subject acquires the status of a legal subject who takes responsibility for her actions.

An example of the respect for the contradictory and the right to be heard is the council for discipline

It sometimes happens that in the same institution, certain young people break the rules several times consecutively, because of violent and destructive behaviour. When there is a chance that the child might be expelled the council for discipline will meet up. J. Vinais, in his aforementioned report describes its purpose.

"This process which gathers all directors of the establishment together, as well as the educator, the child's trainer, the child, and a friend that he/she has chosen to defend him/herself, functions well enough to establish a plan of events which is proved correct in the sense that the young people have placed their trust in this council immediately. This involves detailed justifi-cations, questions, explanations which reveal problems within the institution.

Some children make amends, others confirm their situation but never with agressiveness, boastfulness or defiance. I conclude on my part that the young people of today, inspite of all the problems they pose, are prepared for this type of activity here and elsewhere.

This council also allows adults to explain their situation more clearly, and objectively than when the incident happened.

Even if finally we decide on another placing for the adolescent we will know better, as will the youth and the team – why, this why, not being considered at the time of the event. (We must note that of the 6 councils that have taken place, not one has expelled a pupil) Of course the decision lies with the judge. This discipline council, which tries to explain actions which are sometimes more serious than mentioned here, encourages the child to be an actor, not another focus of pressure, of social repression with this right to be heard. "The adolescent is no longer a piece of the institution" (22).

IV. THE NECESSITY OF LEGAL TRAINING

If the information mainly broadcast by the convention has self-training effects, it cannot replace organized training. This need for training was clearly expressed in a meeting of the committee for the "rights of the child" at SLEA in May 1994.

"This need is mainly a shared one" said Jean Le Gal (23) speaking on cooperatives classes "which are consistent with the rights written into the convention and educational end points". With a reference to his experience as a primary school teacher, Freinet clarifies "you have to be aware of the illusion of children capable of expressing themselves and of organising themselves by the one virtue that 'you are free' autonomy and individual responsibility are the outcome of a large training period in which adults have a crucial role in questioning the principal that 'theoretical and practical training of teachers must precede or accompany the practical changes, because their competence will depend on the success of attempts often difficult to control.'

The "education nationale" is in the processs of creating class elections. The minister for Social Affairs, had taken on commitments on the subject of training for the convention, but he was not there for the broadcast of the text. However this preoccupation is still topical. At the time of European Conference of ministers in charge of family affairs, the European council in July 1993 asked the question "with regard to your country, what is the political question linked to the theme of this conference that seems to be the most sensitive to you?"

France's representatives answered in the form of 2 questions:
- What teaching of the International Convention on the Rights of the Child can we give in a period of economic and merit crisis?
- What support can the state give in this context?

At the SLEA, a training project, from the needs expressed in the institution, is in the process of being set up.

The acquiring of legal knowledge directly relates to the development of a culture for the rights of the child, and favours the application of this culture by those concerned.

CONCLUSIONS

A political wish is to apply the CIDE on behalf of the board of directors of a social-educational institution of means at the disposal of professionals in the field, as well as the creation of an observatory type structure, in charge of stimulating, and watching over this application, as approved by the SLEA. At COFRADE and participation of its work and its commisions, such is the device of the right of the large site of harmonisation of institutional and professionnal pratices revised within the prism of the Convention.

The report of the experiment is presently being compiled. It shows that the exercising of freedom and rights by children and adolescents is perfectly compatible with the protection that is due to them. According to a director of the institution "all our work consists of changing an adolescent from a position of an object, under our protection to that of a social subject who is responsible for him/herself."

It is too early to carry out a detailed evalutation of the effects on young people. However we state that our agreement to participate relates to our own situation of the placement of life in an institution. In fact they express themselves much more easily when they feel heard. We also note a rebalancing of positions of power between adults and young people, and young people and adults.

A legal training for children and adolescents, as well as social workerss going to make up an important [art of the course. The training of those elected to the council of the institution is necessary in the manner of what is being done at school, or in the municipal childrens council (CME or CMEJ). The option of also choosing a training of collective expression of the whole of electing children is renforced by the results of a survey not yet published by CME.

These councils form one of the devices of the local and national policy dealing to do with the social participation of young people aged 10 to 25 (650 local administrative areas and 10 departments have CMES). Those who carried out this survey noted that there were different levels of participation, according to whether the young person was a voter or had been voted. "The young electors did not learn much outside the mechanisms of the elections and their role was restricted by the setting up of the council. The fate of the elected children is another thing. We can speak of a professionalism which swept through the young people who were elected, who learn to present projects, negotiate, and to unravel the role of adults."

Paul Fustier, in the course of his work for the commission, SLEA, observed that a collective expression training scheme was connected the effect of militarism which could develop among those young people who were elected to the institutional council and had an advantage over the non elected. During the aforementioned interview, P. Fustier clarifies his thoughts and presents the question in terms of direct democracy in institutions.

"Also the functioning will be parliamentary type. We would also have the elected on one side, and the pupils who are going to do their electoral tasks on the other side without them being directly involved. On the other hand, more and more establishments would succeed in carrying out procedures closer to direct democracy. It would also generate the "militant" situation which seems to me to be a situation of treatment that we do not use enough in France".

It seems to us that the 2 forms of democracy are being experimented with by young people, and they make up part of an education in citizenship, also an education on human rights as defined in the United Nations Convention on the Rights of the Child in it's article 29 b.

Notes

1. Quoting, on this subject, the judgements of the court of appeal, between March and July 1993, according to which this convention cannot be invoked in front of the law courts, and is only binding for the member States.
2. The Lyonnaise Society for Children and Adolescence, 14 quai Général Sarrail, 69006 LYON, is responsible for several establishments representing as a whole 700 children and young people and 450 staff employees. It is empowered by the legal minister, and General Consulate of the Rhône region, under the heading of legal protection of minors (law of 4th august 1970, title 11 and order of the 2nd february 1945). It also manages an institute, in agreement with the Social Security service, for re-education.
3. Records from a conference "childrens rights, what protection tomorrow", SLEA, Lierre et Coudrier, 350 p , 1991.
4. The SLEA entrusted the economic, social, and historic research department at the University II Lyon to work on its own history, published in the year of the conference. Dominique DESSERTINE, la Société lyonnaise for the preservation of childhood (1890–1990), Ed. ERES, Toulouse, 224 p , 1990.
5. The members of the committee
   Mr Bernet Rollande, Deputy manager in charge of education at the CEPAJ
   Mr Bonnet, Director, sociologist
   Mme Boucaud, Director of the institute for the rights of man, Lyon
   Mme Chefnau, Departmental manager, Family Welcoming
   Mme Chifflet, Deputy manager, Family Welcoming
   Mr Colin, Professor, lecturer in Medicine at University (criminology)
   Mr Fustier, Professor at Lyon II University, directory the psychological institute
   Mme Hannebelle, Director of S.L.E.A.
   Mme Jacob, in charge of delegation, coordination of the committee's work
   Mr Labopin, General manager of the association
   Mme Lagabe, Inspector for the A.E.F.
   Mme Monhard, Lawyer, specialised in children's law, bar of Lyon

Mr Penaud, Vice president in charge of the children's court Lyon
Mme Perrier, Director of centre for specalised education "Les Eaux Vives"
Mr Peycelon, Director, lawyer
Mr Redon, Departmental manager, educational, childrens home "Les Peupliers"
Mme Thiolliere, Psychologist
Melle Veydarier, in charge of the aim of the Conseil General.

6. There is no need for a complete bibliography in this paper, however here are a few basic references.
    - The works of COFRADE
    - 73 ideas, for the application in France of the United Nations convention for childrens rights, 1990. Report 1991–1992, 2 years after..., October 1992.
    - The IDEF publishes a monthly bulletin "IDEF's letter" and in 1992, edited an important book *"Children's Rights in France"*, A. Bouyx and J.P. Rosenczveig.
    - A monthly review, *"Children's Rights Journal"* regularly published.
7. J. Tomkiewicz, P. Vivet, *Spare the Rod, Spoil the Child, Paris*, 1991.
8. M. Klajnberg, *"The Rights of a Foster Child"*, CREAI Rhône-Alpes, Thomas Moore Centre (extracts from 21 March 1991 Lyon).
9. D. Cloupet, "Do we have to discuss rights in medical, educational and social establishments?", Extracts from a discussion, 1789–1989, *Child Adolescent and Freedom*, ENSP, 1989.
10. Quote from article 4 of the declaration of the rights of mankind 1789: "freedom is the power to do anything that doesnot harm another person, as well as the exercise of rights for every man which ensure that other members of society enjoy the same rights. These boundaries can only be determined by law".
11. M. Klajnberg, op. cit.
12. Ch. Vogt, *The Grammar of Institutions*. ENSP, 1992.
13. "Recognising the citizenship of children, is first of all to allow the development of each person in their individual dimensions, and in social dimensions; secondly to allow every child to understand the environment in which he lives, and to have a social life; finally to contribute to the social problems of his integration, that is to say taking account of what they say, feel", COFRADE, Report 1991–1992, p 80.
14. "The law against social exclusion", presentation of a journal *The Right of Young People*, in TSA, 22–10–1993.
15. Ch. Vogt, *Educational Function, the Relation in Dialectic Questions*. Ed, Matrice, 1985.
16. Ph. Meirieu, M. Develay, "Emile come back quickly,... they are going mad", ESF, p 101, 1992.
17. Jean Le GAL, Children's rights, freedom of expression, right to participate, doc. dactylog, pp 14 et 15.
18. In 1923, the terms "children's rights" were first mentioned by the International Society for the Protection of Children. In 1924, following this work, the "Société de Nations" adopted a declaration from Geneva on children's rights, like in principal "the declaration of the rights of citizens and of man". M.J. CHOMBART De LAUWE "the child and citizenship" 1789–1989 – The Child, Adolescent and their Freedom, ENSP, 1989.

19. Commission for "the rights and citizenship" COFRADE, Report 1991–1992, also, Marie-José Chombart De Lauwe "child's rights, in educational institution and on an estate", extracts from a discussion "the rights of the child what protection tomorrow?" SLEA, ed Lierre et Coudrier, p 78.
20. The author of the grammar of institutions already quoted, did a joint successive experiment professionally: an educational practice of the director specalising and practising psychoanalysis.
21. J. VINAIS, annuel report general meeting of the SLEA, May 1994, the children welcomed by the CEPAJ often have behaviour difficulties and are sometimes inclined to be violent and deviant.
22. Interview of Paul FUSTIER, a professor at the University of Lyon II. Director of the psychological institute.
23. Jean Le GAL, schooling at the time of the convention rights and childhood paradoxes and future of the convention, No. 138, January-March 1993.

ARIAN PANO

Human Rights of the Child in Residential Homes for Mentally Retarded Children in Albania

Albania, after overthrowing the communist dictatorship, starts looking more and more towards the European and North American example of a new society.

Because of sufferings in the past, people are more sensitive to new developments, especially in the field of human rights. For that reason, the Republic of Albania has started activities on human rights and become associated with several conventions and treaties – in February 1992 with the UN Convention of Children's Rights.

Still, the Albanian authorities consider "human rights" more than just an issue of agreement and cooperation, but also as a topic for political fight. Meanwhile, much of the convention was not taken into account and nothing was done for the bad situation of children and their rights and needs.

In the fall of 1993, when BBC and other foreign journalists, as well as the local papers "Koha Jone" and "Gazeta Shqiptare", brought to the attention of the public the horrible situation of the residential house for handicapped children in Berat (a town, located in the centre with 20,000 inhabitants). Changes were then introduced. The Ministry of Health of Albania ordered the closure of the centre for not being able to serve its function. The patients were moved to another centre in Tepelena (a town, located in the south, with 10,000 inhabitants). There, the residential house was situated on the edge of the town and hidden for public. The situation of the children was as bad as in Berat, and the augmentation of the number of patients deteriorated the situation: A 14-year-old girl died of freezing because of the lack of heating. Clothes and medicines were scarce. The staff was neglecting the suggestions for improvement from the centre.

Again, media and NGOs, and Human Rights activists, had to raise their voice in order to change the situation. The situation had chances to improve, due to humanitarian aid and volunteers that came to help. Children were split to other residential houses in Tirana, Shkodra, Durres and Korca.

Living conditions and related facilities, as well as medical and specialized care are better in the centre of Tirana where a Swiss project is responsible for the improvement of the facilities and the training of personnel. The objective

E. Verhellen (ed.), Monitoring Children's Rights, 757–760.
© 1996 *Kluwer Law International. Printed in the Netherlands.*

is to examine and evaluate the local facilities by using the criteria of the WHO Guidelines on Quality Assurance in Mental Health Care (Vol 1, 94.17) for the situation in Residential Houses. It will take some time to give the exact results, since the project will be finished by the end of this summer, but a rough observation indicates that the situation is far from good.

LEGAL BACKGROUND

A legal background is totally lacking in Albania. According to the answer that we got from the Ministry of Justice, Albania has no law that could defend or deal with mentally retarded children. Under the social point of view the only attempt forward is an administrative order issued by the Prime Minister of Albania, to replace a law that was operational in the communist period, with a few changes on the sum of welfare given to these children and their families. The provision takes care only for those children who suffer a heavy handicap and the amount of the financial support they get is about the same as the welfare that an unemployed person gets, which reaches up to 7–8 US$ per month (art 3). No other special service or treatment is given to these children.

LIVING CONDITIONS

In most cases the conditions are either bad or unappropriate space is available for the number of patients or children that are given shelter. The Berati Centre is under reconstruction since two years now, but the problems they have with the property of the land and other bureaucratic obstacles are delaying the end of the construction. The bureaucracy is still "killing the baby". In Tepelena the building had some reconstruction, but it was torn down soon afterward, because no maintenance and care were provided. In Korca and other places the buildings are old and although attempts are made to fix something, the situation has not been ameliorated. Specific information is available on request.

ADMINISTRATIVE ARRANGEMENTS

Being just a burden for all the governments, the residential centres for mentally retarded children/persons have always been neglected. In the past (i.e under the communist regime), they have been assigned to the Ministry of Health. The former Albanian Health Care System has been designed to meet the primary needs and try to prevent diseases, but the second stage treatment (i.e. specialized treatment services) was no priority. So children with a chronic need for medical and other care have always been treated badly in residential centres. The medical staff that has been assigned to the centres has had no training and has been sent to work as a punishment for stealing, non-professional behaviour, a different political view, etc. In other words they were send to be "reeducated" in a difficult position. It is understandable that their place of work has been described as a kind of small prison without bars. This impression is still the same.

With this legacy we entered the era of the "democracy". But the release of political prisoners did not mean the freedom and better treatment for these small creatures that were suffering under the same conditions. Evidently mentally retarded children have been always around us, somewhere behind the curtains of everyday life, but it seems that none wanted to let them in, and seriously wanted to take care of them, although merits of being a fighter of Human Rights were nice to everyone.

Examples of this mentality were Berat and Tepelena. Children were moved from a bad place to one that was worse, just to get them out of the attention of the public and their sensitivity. After being put under a big pressure from all sides, national as well as international, and after the death of the 14-year-old girl in Tepelena, the government was obliged to take some measures. The responsibility for all the residential houses were transferred to the Ministry of Labour and Social Welfare. Here they, in spite of good will, could not do much because of several reasons: the absence of a legal framework, where they could base and build their work on in the future; the staff that has not acquired training and is not sufficient in number, and had no previous experience, the bad condition of the buildings and the mentality where none showed concern for the neighbour. There are therefore no specialized services and educators for these children.

Under these conditions the Albanian Government is clearly violating most of the articles of the Convention that deal with legal background, living conditions and care.

In Shkoder local officials closed a mixed school attended partly by handicapped children. The building was given to one of the religious groups claimed it as a former property of the catholic church. Local officials arranged soon afterward the place for normal school pupils, but no solution was given for the mentally retarded children. It was only the firm protest of their parents and other sympathizers and Human Rights activists that made the officials promise another place for these children.

It is obvious that the living conditions, education, medical care etc. for all these children are scarce, but the biggest problem is that bureaucracy is moving very slowly in order to give a solution to the situation, and there is plenty of ignorance. Human Rights here are far from being met.

Suggestions for the Future

1. Information is very difficult to obtain and Human Rights of the Child to be taught and experienced. For this reason it is crucial that a Centre for Human Rights of the Child can be established in Albania. This will help to investigate and obtain knowledge of the situation and coordinate various attempts that are made in education, medical care, housing, social support etc.
2. More pressure must be put on the Albanian Government in order to address the issue of a specific bill of law on the defence of children, or incorporate provisions in existing laws.
3. Under the medical point of view, much needs to improve in terms of basic medical care, and priority must be given to specialized services for mentally retarded children.
4. The international community must be informed as well of the domestic opinion in order to help in this direction, because this is not considered as a priority for our economy.

FÉLICITÉ TALON AHOUANDOGBO

Enfants déplacés et placés auprès de tierces personnes (Vidomègon)

Au Bénin, en dehors des enfants qui sont devenus des enfants réfugiés du fait de certains troubles politico-sociaux, ethniques et du fait des guerres et autres cataclysmes – et qui sont séparés soit, de leur famille, soit de leurs communautés, etc., nous assistons à un autre phénomène: celui des enfants déplacés de leur milieu familial et qui sont placés auprès de tierces personnes que nous appelons "Vidomègon" et qui servent de domestiques.

Ce concept de "Vidomègon" ou enfants placés auprès de tierces personnes représente et définit une pratique de placement auprès de tierces personnes d'enfants surtout des fillettes de 5 à 12 ans avec le consentement de leurs parents. Elle est en cours dans la sous-région Ouest africaine (Bénin, Togo, Ghana).

Avant les temps modernes et compte tenu du mystique de la vie et de la notion, la famille élargie en Afrique et notamment au Bénin, il est de coutume de penser, de croire, de se comporter comme si l'éducation, la protection et l'entretien des enfants d'un membre du lignage familial incombaient à toutes les personnes capables de cette collectivité d'en assumer la responsabilité (cette notion a d'ailleurs été reprise par l'article 5 de la Convention Internationale du 20 novembre 1989 relative aux droits de l'enfant).

Avec l'apparition du colonialisme et la formation de l'élite intellectuelle, sociale, et administrative, les membres de la famille élargie qui ont réussi ne faisaient aucune objection à accepter de garder les enfants de ses parents restés dans les Zones rurales aux fins de les aider à être éduqués, instruits et à accéder à un métier en vue de leur insertion sociale une fois devenus adultes et pouvant mener une vie autonome et responsable.

Tout cela répond aux dispositions contenues dans la Convention de la Haye de 1961 sur la protection des enfants même si sur le plan interne les parents et les tuteurs ne se conforment pas de jure aux garanties juridiques sur la tutelle, la délégation d'autorité parentale ou de puissance paternelle et que sont établies à cet effet. (Notre Société est de tradition orale et il y a plus de 85% de la population qui est paysanne et il y a beaucoup d'analphabète).

Seulement, après la deuxième guerre mondiale et de nos jours, face aux problèmes économiques, à la mauvaise répartition des ressources de l'hu-

E. Verhellen (ed.), Monitoring Children's Rights, 761–763.
© 1996 *Kluwer Law International. Printed in the Netherlands.*

manité, aux problèmes structurels des Africains, au sous-développement du continent et à l'ascension des femmes à des métiers et au commerce, la pratique de placement d'enfants dans une famille d'accueil qui se voulait une pratique d'entraide basée sur la solidarité et l'affection s'est dégradée au point de dégénérer en un système vénal dans la plupart du temps qui consiste à se faire placer par des intermédiaires ou à aller chercher auprès des ruraux pour de l'argent que l'on verse souvent aux parents, des enfants mineurs aux fins d'exploitation de leur force de travail. En effet, il y a des enfants qui jouent le rôle de domestiques et sont employés pour accomplir des travaux domestiques pour lesquels on les épuise quand d'autres se voient confier des étales de marchandises qu'ils sont obligés de vendre en se promenant de maisons en maisons et cela les expose à la rue, à la violence sexuelle, à la prostitution.

Une enquête sur le terrain effectuée sous l'égide de l'UNICEF au cours de l'année 1994 a permis de relever que:

> Sur 155 ménages observés, 101 possèdent des Vidomègon, soit un taux de 69,4% pour Cotonou et 58,8% pour Porto-Novo.

Les ménagères-vendeuses constituent les principales utilisatrices de "Vidomègon"; 66% pour Cotonou et 40% à Porto-Novo.

Les conjoints de ces ménagères-vendeuses sont soit des fonctionnaires, soit des artisans tailleurs.

Le nombre des "Vidomègons" se compose surtout de filles de 10 à 14 ans dans la proportion de 80%.

D'autres enfants déplacés de leurs familles et milieux socio-culturels sont carrément envoyés dans des pays limitrophes (Nigéria, Gabon, Côte d'Ivoire), ou emmenés dans des pays européens avec des documents falsifiés (passeport et autres documents portant sur leur nom, leur filiation).

Il est ressorti des statistiques de l'enquête que 36% des enfants sont placés par leur géniteur ou leurs ascendants, 20% par des tuteurs.

De tout ce qui précède nous soutenons que ce sont des enfants dont on ne tient pas compte de leur intérêt supérieur et à qui leur droit à l'enfance est retiré.

Ils ne peuvent pas avoir droit à l'enseignement (article 28 de la Convention internationale du 20 novembre 1989).

Ce sont des enfants coupés de leurs familles et qui sont livrés parfois à un réseau de trafic d'enfants déportés vers d'autres pays sans espoir de retour pour aller constituer une force de travail servile et surexploitée au mépris:

– de la Convention No. 138 de la Conférence internationale du Travail du BIT de 1973 sur l'âge minimum d'admission à un emploi;

– de leur intérêt supérieur (art. 3, alinéa 1) de la Convention du 20 novembre 1989;

– des textes administratifs, légaux nationaux et internationaux existant qui protègent les enfants contre les abus, les exploitations et qui règlementent en un mot le travail de l'enfant de moins de 18 ans, de moins de 14 ans.

Ce sont des enfants qui sont pour la plupart victimes de toutes les formes de mauvais traitements ou d'exploitations (y compris de la violence sexuelle parfois).

En somme, cette pratique, que l'on aurait pu réglementer en limitant l'âge de l'enfant à placer auprès de tiers à l'âge de 14 ans par exemple, en instituant par ailleurs un système de filles ou d'enfants au pair en leur permettant de travailler pour autrui en fonction de leur force de travail sans que leur état de santé ne s'altère tout en ayant la possibilité d'accéder à une formation professionnelle en vue de s'assurer un avenir responsable, se maintient. Il se maintient au mépris des articles 3, 9, 11, 14, 18, 19, 20, 28, 31, 32, 34 et 36 de la Convention internationale du 20 Novembre 1989 relative aux droits des enfants qui ne sont pas appliqués par des pays qui l'ont pourtant ratifiée et qui portent sur:
- l'intérêt supérieur de l'enfant qui doit guider la prise de toute décision le concernant;
- le droit de l'enfant de vivre avec ses parents qui doivent l'élever sauf quand cela va justement contre cet "intérêt supérieur";
- la protection de l'enfant, surtout la scolarisation des fillettes en Afrique;
- son droit au repos et aux loisirs, le travail, le déplacement et le non-retour illicites de l'enfant.

Ce phénomène de "Vidomègon" et les conséquences négatives qui en découlent nous font poser également le problème évoqué par les articles 27 et 35 de la Convention internationale de 1989 sus-citée sur le rôle et le devoir des Etats Parties à ladite Convention qui doivent tout mettre en oeuvre pour:
- que tout enfant ait droit à un niveau de vie suffisant à son développement physique, mental, spirituel, moral et social;
- que la famille à laquelle est échue primordialement cette responsabilité soit capable de l'assumer;
- empêcher l'enlèvement, la vente ou la traite d'enfants.

Nous posons également le problème de l'aide Nord-Sud dégagé à travers les lignes de la Convention Internationale en son article 4.

Même si le Gouvernement Béninois a pris, dans le cadre de l'application de la convention (surtout, au fond de son article 28) des mesures pour rendre gratuit l'enseignement primaire des filles en zones rurales, il reste cependant beaucoup à faire.

En effet, il faudrait arriver à faire comprendre aux parents le bien fondé de l'enseignement primaire, dont peut bénéficier filles et garçons et l'égalité des charges dont ils disposent indifféremment.

Tout cela demande du temps car appelant comme changements de mentalité du peuple et exigeant beaucoup de courage et de détermination de la part de tous ceux qui ont accepté de servir de valeurs de transmission de message: faire accepter et appliquer les Droits de l'enfant.

PILAR ARNAIZ SÁNCHEZ

The Rights of People with Disabilities

I. INTRODUCTION

From the Universal Declaration of Human Rights of 1948 until now, the attention given to people with a disability has come a long way, although it is not yet fully implemented.

In the sixties, the world experienced profound social transformations: The French students' revolt of May 1968, the fight to achieve Civil Rights and to defend the dignity of the coloured people in the United States of America, the struggle of youth to set themselves free from classic colonialism and their peace impulses, are some examples.

The claims resulting from the changes created the vindications of discriminated groups, among such groups we find the people with disabilities, the parents associations, the educators and/or the rehabilitators. The institutions of people with disabilities who fought without great success for years at a local level, are now seen as a great force to be reckoned with.

Thanks to these mobilisations of the seventies we now have the "Declaration of Rights for the disabled" (1971) the "North-American Rehabilitation Act" (1973) proclaimed by the World Health Organization, and the "Declaration of Rights for the disabled" (1975).

During this decade, thus, the problems of people with disabilities reached an important level of diffusion and analysis, especially, in the northern hemisphere. A large number of research projects were carried out by the United Nations, in which for the first time many disabled people took part, making it into a worldwide programme with 1981 being designated "The year of disabled". The projects provided a visionary impulse for the programme of attention and reestablishment of the rights of people with disabilities. Hundreds of institutions were established which were grouped into federations with great influence and projection.

Under this great impulse the World Organisation for the Disabled was founded, in order to proclaim before the whole world the full rights of people with disabilities and the fact that they could represent themselves.

E. Verhellen (ed.), Monitoring Children's Rights, 765–773.

As a result of this process, in 1982 the United Nations declared the period 1983 to 1992: "the Decade of the disabled" and passed a programme for world-wide action "whose implementation was possible thanks to the interventions of people with different disabilities". This last document is of paramount importance, as it promotes from an international perspective, the measures for the prevention of disabilities, the rehabilitation and the realization of the objectives of equality and the full participation of the people with disabilities in social life and development. For the first time in history, a report revealed all kinds of details of the problems faced by these people whatever their disability, and showed all its dimensions.

It is important to mention the so-called "Third World" which has not followed the same course, due to its poverty status, and where the means of prevention, rehabilitation and equal opportunities still remain an aspiration.

In order to carry out an analysis and follow up of the "Decade of the Disabled", a meeting was held in Stockholm in 1987 organised by The Secretary General of The United Nations, in which many experts on the topic and people with disabilities took part. The fundamental conclusions can be summarized in three fundamental ideas:

1. The world action for the disabled shed light on a new stimulating model of work for the integration of these people.
2. The opportunities to stimulate the global execution of the World Action Programme, which this decade offered, were not exploited to full.
3. And little worldwide progress had been made, above all in those countries with limited resources, where people with disabilities were discriminated because of economic and social conditions, and to say the least, their conditions have actually deteriorated in the last five years.

The Council of Europe's Resolutions (92)6 put forward all these declarations to all its member states so that they could put to effect its development and political coherence for people with disabilities.

The following lines allow us to analyse in greater detail the above mentioned points.

II. THE PROTECTION OF THE RIGHTS OF PEOPLE WITH DISABILITIES

Despite the resolution and the changes in attitudes which have resulted from the previously indicated documents and proclamation of human rights which highlighted the equivalent value put on all the human lives, there still is important work left to be done with respect to the promulgation and fulfilment of the rights of people with disabilities. This is due to the fact that different resolutions which have been passed to improve the recognition of equal conditions for people with mental, physical or psychic deficiencies, have been based on old laws which determine the rights of these people and are not respected as they should be.

In general, the present declarations with respect to the rights of people with deficiencies are characterised as disperse and with variable accessibility. Thus, it is important, for example, to point out the confusion caused in defining these people's "deficiency", "disability", "handicap", the lack of a specific and common definition, and in not making a distinction between child, adult and adolescent.

Similarly, the declarations of rights at international level frequently suffer from a lack of precision, which hinders the exercising of these proclaimed rights, above all, when we are faced with a general conception of society which rewards people for their capacity, competitiveness and professional success.

If we start from the fact that a person relates himself to the social environment, interacting and interrelating with it, then we will come to an assumption that being a human can be considered as a "System of systems in a social environment".

Thus, when speaking about people we are referring to the projects of life and necessities which move around two axes: the personal axis and the social axis. The rights of people lie under the latter, that is to say, that each person must receive an answer to his/her capacities, so as not to discriminate against others for their personal characteristics.

When we talk about people with deficiencies we are talking about people – in many instances – who do not have a series of communicative, relational, motorial and cognitive capacities to the same degree as other people, and which prevents them from developing and putting into practice an array of abilities.

Nevertheless, we would like to mention that in the majority of cases, what impede the normal process of social development of these people are not these difficulties, but a series of conditions which influence their environment. This lack of support lead to the development of segregating ideas which are easily identifiable in our society.

Despite the application of normalisation principles (Wolfenberger, 1986), with respect to the realisation of physical integration, ways of naming or application, social relationship, equipment preparation, etc.., improved medical help, education, and service, among others, we still find many people living in institutions, stereotyping and attitudes, little integration and social participation, little primary education, hardly any professional formation and work formation, the lack of quality of services provided. This fact highlights the difficulty and anxiety of parents in their desire to give their children the best education. Finally, one should mention the lack of good social services.

Wolfensberger (1991) with respect to social services, points out the importance of these difficulties at present, given the economic and moral crisis which we are facing.

Although the rights of people with disabilities are – at least on paper – essentially the same as for any other person, there is no need to establish a separate form, and this fact determines the necessity to undertake a series of complementary measures. If it is true that the rights granted to people with disabilities are socially recognized and they are not questioned when formulated, the problem arises when one places them in family environment, in friendships, in professional life, etc... There is a natural tendency to deal with these problems as a second priority.

Reality indicates that people with disabilities are more vulnerable than other people with respect to their rights, which has led to the formulation of a series of specific rights for them, with the aim of defending their liberty and integrity as people (Teheran, 1968; Declaration of the Rights of the Mentally Disabled, 1971; Declaration of the Rights of the Disabled, 1975). Paradoxically, some fundamental rights such as the liberty of movement, liberty of expression, liberty of ownership, privacy, fear, own image, etc., are the ones which are not commonly respected or are left apart when using the argument that they cannot be applied in the case of people with disabilities; in other words in many cases the right is accepted, but in spite of this its realization has not yet been planned, as far as the disabled are concerned.

Coupled with these fundamental rights we can analyze others which are more related with activities of service and benefits from society. We are talking about rights such as: medical attention, education, transport, housing, employment, tutelage, etc., which arise directly from the principle of normalisation.

In this respect, we can point out the following: how often people over use medication, or the fact that we do not normally take into account how restrictive the environment may be. We do not guarantee sufficiently the right to receive attention or enjoy all the facilities that a person needs to improve his/her own condition depending on his/her ability, with the kind of guarantees which assure his/her social integration.

Considering these rights involves the reasonable possibility of reaching new goals progressively, and of counting on the freedom and the means to get them.

Although the majority of international institutions that take care of children (UNO, UNESCO, WHO, the Council of Europe, European Union) have tried to promote the rights of the disabled child within the frame of his/her competences, their so-called preoccupation has not brought about a clarification as a consequence, rather the dispersion continues to be the most outstanding characteristic. For that reason it is necessary to go on making an effort to try to persuade the governments, to ratify the existing conclusions.

Therefore, the disabled child has the right to a special protection with immediate priority according to judicial ordination. This right is based on the general principle of non-discrimination established in the majority of international instruments about people with deficit, which promotes equality of opportunities: the child with some disabilities should therefore benefit from some supplementary help and protection.

The psychic and physical needs are the ones which appear first in the life of a disabled person. This is why they must be assured with priority from the very beginning of life (Universal Declaration of Human Rights, art. 3).

The typical question that is posed with respect to this idea is to determine in which moment life begins, whether it starts at the very moment of conception, or at the birth. According to both theories, the child with a deficit is menaced in a double way during the gestation period: as every child, given the liberal laws of abortion, and as a disabled child, even when life is viable and there is no danger for the mother's life.

As regards the life of the disabled child it is important to take into account the respect for his/her physical integrity in those aspects related to cruel treatment and of experimentation (ill treatment from the family, electroshock, etc.).

From now on, we will analyse the main areas to be taken into account in the difficult task of protection of the rights of the disabled.

A. Health Needs

These needs are articulated around two axes:

1. To Prevent the Disability

This must be integrated in the series of general measures directed to prevent all those aspects related with the physical and psychic health of the person: vaccination, hygiene, improvement of life conditions, nourishment, pre- and post-birth assistance, protection of the mother's health during pregnancy, etc. This should be conducted to achieve a diagnosis which will be as precocious as possible of the person with the deficit.

2. The Treatments and Material help are also the Object of Certain Dispositions, and above all when the Treatments are Long-lasting and Expensive[1]

The existing declaration with respect to the rights of the disabled is characterised by being dispersed and having a variable importance. Thus, we can comment, for example, on the confusion about the nomenclature used to designate the disabled; or the lack of a specific and common definition; or the non-distinction between child, adolescent and adult.

---

[1] In this respect we should consult: *Le droit à la santé en tant que droit de l'homme.* A talk from 27th to 29th July, Academia de Derecho International ACADI, 1979.
– Article 12 of the International pact of Economic, social and cultural rights.
– Article 11 of The European Social Charter.
– OIT, Recommendation No.95, Art. 5.
– Report: The prevention of disability and the readaptation of disabled people, E/CN. 5/565, page 6 and 8

B. The Family

The family is the fundamental institution for the growth and development of children. Other institutions must help him, and so the family must only be substituted in case of need. Therefore, the family is decisive for the affective balance of the child, and it plays a main role in his/her socialisation, since the child, from the very first moment of his/her life develops his/her own personality, acquires habits and starts to form his/her own system of values.

This recognition of the family as the best situation in which the disabled child can develop himself is recorded in the Declaration of the Rights of the Mentally Disabled (art. 4), and in the Declaration of the Rights of the Disabled (art.9). These documents support the fact that people with mental deficiency or any other deficit should be interned only in extreme situations due to urgent needs.

In this important role of the family, we should take into account that, although the child with problems needs some special care and attention, there is no need to protect him to the point of dismissing or isolating him; we should rather try to integrate him in a normalised environment, basing his/her education on an essential vehicle for the development of his/her personal, social and intellectual autonomy.

The problem that disabled people face is that many times they are deprived of the right to get it wrong with the aim of protecting them. Or we make the development of their abilities more difficult, which, although reduced in number, can go further than what one may expect.

C. The Right to Education, Orientation and Vocational Training

Their education must be achieved in an environment which will be as normal as possible, with the aim of preventing their isolation and discrimination, and thus facilitating their social integration. This education must be as broad as possible in a stimulating educative medium and from the very first moment in which any change is detected. In this respect, we should highlight the three essential steps in the development of the disabled person: their early attention from the very first moment of life, their school life and the vocational training period.

1. Early Attention
It has been proved that early stimulation has reached a considerable increase during the last few years, due to the improvements that their application achieves from 0 years to 3 years of age.

The early attention programmes started in the sixties, and mainly during the seventies, and had as their goals:
- To identify the children with deficiencies in their development as soon as possible.

- To evaluate and test the developmental difficulties of these children.
- To foster the capabilities that disabled children possess.
- And to give these children the opportunity to develop and interact in an adequate environment.

2. School Life

The implicit principles in the movement of integration normalisation, sectorisation and individualisation which are present nowadays in school life, have the aim of defending, ruling and guaranteeing the educational process of the children with special educational needs.

Therefore, the attention given to these children will be focused so as to make up for their deficit and difficulties, using pedagogical methods, materials and specialised staff (integrated contexts, specific centres). That is why the following principles (MacMillan, 1982: 3,4) to get a schooling for everybody become the key issues:

- The right to an accurate procedure in the classification systems and location of children in schools.
- Protection against the use of discriminatory tests for their cultural and/or academic significance for some children.
- Location of the child in non-restrictive environments for his/her educational needs.
- And finally, these children must receive those individualised educational programmes which these children may need.

3. Vocational Training

This involves the right to orientation and vocational training, which has great importance, due to the fact that both are closely interrelated with the educational and reeducational values of employment, and the search for economic independence. To sum up, we should add the right to a job that of every individual has; which is, the duty to be useful, depending on the possibilities of each individual.

D. Social Integration and Preparation for Economic Independence

The right to social integration of adolescents with disability implies that they should be prepared for the exercise of a job, which will assure them of the best way to get economic independence. Reaching these rights implies that both the national and international communities accept the right to difference up to an adult age, pointing out that social integration must be considered as the last and fundamental goal in the life of these people.

This achievement depends on the application of the appropriate means and on the possibility of achieving their actual insertion in the labour world.

Therefore, adolescence introduces other needs which are added to the ones that the disabled child had previously. At present, the principle of equality of opportunities leads to a compensation for inequality by means of particular assistance. The vocational training that may later take shape in a job acquires now some fundamental dimensions. It must be considered as a basic principle of equality and access, under the same conditions as the rest of the people without deficit, from a merely remunerative point of view.

Measures should be taken to encourage employers to employ disabled people (European Social Charter, art.15,2) and likewise, sheltered workshops must be created. Nevertheless, we should not forget that, although these constitute a means of providing a job for the disabled, they represent a segregational measure and that this can be questioned.

III. CONCLUSION

As a conclusion to this piece of work, we should indicate that, although the application of rights to orientation and vocational training of the disabled is difficult, the problem of the acceptance of the disabled person (child, adolescent or adult) by the members of the community in which he is integrated may be even more difficult to be applied.

If we analyse up to what point people with deficiencies can choose their way of life, we will be able to decide whether we actually let them exercise their rights (which we legally recognise) in real life or not. Some aspects such as confidentiality, privacy, dignity, the use of personal effects, sexual intercourse, liberty of movement and communication, economic aspects, the defence against abuses or the negligences they suffer, demonstrate the attitudes that we normally adopt before them.

In the same way, we should think about the number of people who exercise some authority over the disabled. This will lead us to realise that their liberties and the exercise of their rights are diminished. In the same way as a series of authorities which make up the frame in which we can exercise our own liberties, falls on every person, so it is in the case of the mentally disabled, where the list is lengthened to a considerable extent.

Any country that wants to defend the rights of people with deficit should find it desirable to promote laws and demand their fulfilment by all the social strata, even via the judicial power. But it is perhaps of greater importance that society, that is, each one of us, maintains a permanent attitude of respect in our relationship with the disabled, which will allow them to express and make their desires, rights and own life come true.

Since the government is the only institution which has the power to apply the rights of the disabled and to demand that they be respected, it should mobilise its resources and coordinate actions in two axes:
- efficiency in the search for fulfilment of needs in close coordination with other administrative and social institutions;
- the implementations of measures directed at the structural adaptations in social and administrative institutions;

– and putting into practice the measures directed to adapt the environment with the aim of satisfying the rights to the quality of life of people with deficiencies.

As far as the international sphere is concerned, the obligation of cooperation is a primary objective and the recognition on the part of international community of the rights of children and, therefore, the rights of disabled children, is necessary.

Liberty, justice and peace in the world have the recognition of the intrinsic dignity and of the equal rights of all the members of the human family as their basis.

All countries and nations must make an effort, so that individuals as well as institutions, being constantly inspired, foster the respect for these rights, by means of teaching and education.

Declaration of Human Rights (1948)

REFERENCES

Assemblée Parlamentaire du Conseil de L'Europe (1990) *Recommandation 879* relative à une Charte européenne des droits de l'enfant.

Basoco, J.L. (1990) El ejercicio de los derechos de la persona con deficiencia mental en el marco del derecho positivo y la realidad social. *Zerbitzuan, 12/13*, 55–57.

Casas, F. (1992) La infancia española en el contexto europeo. *Infancia y Sociedad, 15*, 5–36.

Conferencia Internacional de Derechos Humanos (1968) *Proclamación de Teherán*.

Council of Europe. Committee of Ministres (1973) Resolution (73). *On the Socials Services for Physically or Mentally Handicapped Persons*. Adopted by Committee of Ministers on 19 January at the 217th meeting of the Ministers Deputies.

Council of Europe (1992) Texts Drawn-up by Council of Europe in the Field of Childhood Policies. Strasbourg, 7 December.

De la Villa Gil-Sagardo y Bengoechea, J.A. (1986) Propuestas sobre el derecho al trabajo. *Siglo Cero, 103*, 46–47.

Declaración Universal de los Derechos Humanos (1948).

Declaración de los Derechos del Retrasado Mental (1971).

Declaración de los Derechos de los Impedidos (1975).

Declaración de los Derechos del Niño (1959).

MacMillan, D., Keoghs, B. Y., Jones, R. (1986) Special Education Research in Mildly Handicapped Children. In Wittrock (Ed): *Handbook of Research on Teaching*. New York: MacMillan.

Naciones Unidas (1983) *Programa de acción mundial para las personas con discapacidad*. Madrid: Ministerio de Asuntos Sociales y Real Patronato de Prevención y de Atención a Personas con Minusvaía.

Torrelli, M. (1986) La protección de los derechos de los impedidos. *Siglo Cero, 105*, 42–55.

Verhellen, E. (1992) Los derechos del niño en Europa. *Infancia y Sociedad, 15*, 37-60.

Wolfensberger, W. (1991) Reflections on the lifetime in Human Services and Mental Retardation. *Mental Retardation*, Vol. 29(1).

MARC-G. SCHWEITZER and NIELLE PUIG-VERGÈS

The Child and Its Health:
Consent and Medical Interventions

Why, among the variety of questions surrounding child health and related
actions, have we chosen to focus on the issue of consent for medical interventions and health measures?

The clinical work we carry out with children and adolescents, as well
as the theoretical aspects developed in the framework of the GRECC-EDS
have sensitized us to the significance of *respect for the individual's wishes*
in every medical intervention, and to the difficulties surrounding this respect,
particularly with regard to the seeking of consent. These issues are even more
complex when it comes to children and adolescents.

I. CONSENT AND MINORITY

During the last few years, the patient's consent to a medical intervention has
become one of the rare preoccupations shared by jurists and doctors.

The *term "consent" originates in the legal field*: it does not belong to the
medical vocabulary since it has not been a longstanding feature in the history
of doctor-patient relations. Its definition, or rather its crystallisation emerged
slowly in France, building on a body of judicial precedents taking shape at
the beginning of the twentieth century. This movement was linked with the
widening of the field of medical experimentation and with the increase in
surgical interventions.

Thus, seeking consent for various health care techniques gradually became
an *obligation* for the practitioner. One prerequisite underlies this obligation:
the necessity of providing the patient with *information*, which has become a
real legal obligation. But the discussion and dialogue implied in this is generally only envisaged with capable adults (in the legal sense of the term).[3,18]

Seeking consent is not only a legal obligation, to which the practitioner
must conform, but it also *constitutes* – from our point of view – *above all a
moral obligation based on an ethical conception of another person*.[7] Prior
to each initiative involving a medical action, one must indeed consider each
person, whatever his/her age, not only as an object of health care, but as a
person directly implicated in a decisional process.

E. Verhellen (ed.), Monitoring Children's Rights, 775–783.
© 1996 *Kluwer Law International. Printed in the Netherlands.*

By consent, we imply taking into account respect for the person's wishes in the health care contract, if the person is able to express it; as a corollary it implies the possibility of refusal. Indeed, the freedom to oppose must be accepted for every person facing a medical intervention; for the respect of individual liberty requires it.[6]

Thus understood, consent becomes a behaviour or action that is part of the personal dynamic and the psychological economy of the person expressing it; since it has legal effects, this act of will also entails responsibility for the practitioner.

For the minor, however, *although consent remains an eminently personal act, it is systematically delegated to the parents or the legal representative.* This situation is even more paradoxical since the place occupied by the minor in civil society has evolved considerably during the last few years.

Whereas French law defines him as *incapable* on the legal level, for the last few years the minor has begun to enjoy a better recognition of his individuality and his rights. This was first expressed in the protection of his interests in legal decisions (for instance, in custody matters during divorce proceedings). Moreover, article 12 of the Convention on the Rights of the Child recognizes a genuine *right of individual expression* for the minor. The emerging unanimity on a widening legal recognition of rights of minors also goes hand in hand with a greater questioning of their penal responsibility.

How does this recognition of the right to individual expression relate to matters of health for minors and their relations with the health care system? Does the same situation prevail when it comes to minor persons absolutely requiring care and when minors themselves take the initiative to request a medical action (sometimes without their parents' knowledge)?

II. Capacity (in the legal sense) and ability to consent

Responding to these questions implies that we come back to the notions of competence and capacity.

On a more general level than the one we are dealing with, *provisions to protect the most vulnerable persons has been instituted by law*; this relates to persons who do not themselves possess the faculty to express themselves their opposition or their approval, due to their minority status or a state of unconsciousness. The law protects those whom their age or their mental state renders incapable of responding to the obligations of civil life, such as expressing valid consent; it recognizes two categories of incapable persons: in France these are minors of less than eighteen years of age (legal incapacity) and of protected persons of full legal age. This protection extends to the whole range of actions involved in civil life. However, it does not settle the question of levels of competence.[7]

Whether one refers to the adult, the elderly or the child, a common set of questions applies, which we have analysed in several previous papers; on the other hand, the responses call for a different analysis according to the age of the person concerned and of his ability to judge and to act.

The legal incapacity, which affects the minor is intended to protect him against himself. Due to his age, consent expressed by the minor is considered insufficiently free and enlightened; the minor is assumed to be unable to defend his interests on his own and must be subjected to a regime of legal protection. This legal protection ends with coming of age, the moment when the minor becomes fully capable on the legal level. His *ability to consent* to medical acts in particular is then recognized. But what does this ability imply?

On the legal level, the ability to consent refers to capacity alone, a condition necessary for the validity of civil acts (particularly contracts). Jurists distinguish the "capacity of use" (ability to become entitled to a right or an obligation) and the "capacity to exercise" (ability to assert a right one possesses, by oneself and alone, without having to be represented, nor assisted by a third party). For the jurist, capacity exists or it does not exist, there is no intermediate position.[8]

For the clinician, on the other hand, we consider that the notion of capacity is difficult to separate from the notion of ability; *capacity in fact depends on a number of abilities falling into place*. It implies the person's ability to perceive and understand what is said by another party, particularly information with respect to his state of health, as well as on the medical interventions envisaged. These preconditions are essential for the validity of consent and a large number of minors possess these abilities.[9]

In this perspective, the *consent to health care* is not reduced to an authorization given (or conceded) to a professional by a person of age or a minor, in a legal framework. We should remember that the legal framework, where a minor is concerned, always refers to the parent or his substitute. From our point of view, the consent to health care first of all has to be the expression of the individual's wishes; *as early as possible and as long as possible*, it is a matter of respecting these wishes within the limits defined by regulatory and legislative texts in force, but equally taking into account the specific rules of the medical profession.[10]

Concerning adolescents, some jurists accept the idea of a "civil pre-majority", others evoke the notion of "medical capacity of the minor". How should this be defined? As practitioners, we have to take into account not only the maturation of the minor's judgment, his capacity to form an opinion, but also of his family interactions, and of the possibility of differences between the minor's opinion and that of the parental authority.[7]

III. Capacity, Competence and Discernment

We believe it necessary to reconsider the notion of capacity in the legal sense and to relate it to cognitive-affective development. The capacity to consent must be understood not only on the legal level, but also in the sense of *competence which assumes a synthesis of cognitive processes*, particularly when access to medical care is concerned.

We also know that, even if we try to relate the ability to consent and the expression of will, it remains a delicate matter to determine the age when the minor psychologically attains these abilities.

Some clinicians make an analogy between capacity and autonomy in the actions of daily life. This corresponds with a tendency among educators, teachers and social workers in recent years to favour *personal autonomy*. This tendency sometimes takes on exaggerated proportions, because one expects the child to perform in areas of activity where it cannot yet do so. A few clinicians, on the other hand, prefer to focus on a link with the *level of reasoning acquired* (operational, concrete, abstract): this broad approach appears to us to be the most pertinent.

Some authors have attempted to define, by way of objective criteria, the notion of capacity, and suggested that it partially matches with the Anglo-Saxon term of competence (capacity of discernment). Capacity must not be treated as a general notion, since it applies each time to a precise object and to a specific moment.

On the other hand, *competence*, in the psychological sense of the term, is characterized by the fact that it develops, is modified and then regresses with age. It encompasses several elements: the capacity of comprehending the information provided; - the capacity to decide, to express a choice; - the modes of reasoning which underlie this ability to decide; - and finally, the ability to evaluate potential consequences this decision is likely to entail for oneself and for others.[6]

At the same time the question of the *freedom to decide for oneself* arises, taking into account the level of psycho-affective development, family interactions and the influence of the environment.

In order to be recognized by the practitioner, capacity as the capability to choose and to consent, assumes the integrity of individual psychological functioning, whether in the process of formation or development (child or adolescent) or whether it has reached a particular level of psychological maturity. It implies the exercise of judgment and assumes the continuity of thought processes, the permanence of mental representations and the integrity of memory, as well as the capacities of anticipation and projection into the future.

It calls for cognitive and specific conative functions; the first, "cognitive functions" refer to the processes of selection and processing of information, the second, "conative functions", refer to processes governing the orientation and control of behaviour. The integrity of these functions ensures the effective operation of discernment, the faculty of assessing things and circumstances.[9]

In this analysis and in clinical situations, we place special emphasis on the importance of the notion of *discernment* since this term also occupies a place in legislative provisions.

Historically, the question of discernment was first linked to the attribution of *criminal responsibility*, before its usage was reintroduced in connection with *civil responsibility*. The analysis of discernment then diminished among the concerns of judges and social interveners, to be replaced by the study of grounds, motives and motivations.

Moreover, the International Convention on the Rights of the Child (article 12) has carried over this term, stemming from criminal law, to areas relating to freedom of expression. On the other hand, nothing is said in relation to access to care. French law has also introduced the notions of discernment and faculty of discernment, including age, maturity and the degree of understanding, into recent clauses relating to civil status and the rights of the child (with a view to defence in legal proceedings).

Discernment remains, first of all, a capacity to distinguish good from evil, which appears in the minor at the age of reason. At the same time, legislators have not established the ages at which discernment is absent or present, either for civil or for criminal purposes. On the other hand, references are often made to the notions of maturation or reason, without indicating the age at which they are acquired. The difficulty facing the judge is to assess the age when discernment is acquired in a stable manner. This is a question which arises as well among clinicians with respect to other aspects of reasoning and judgment.

For us, as practitioners, discernment must be linked with the notions of maturity, awakening of awareness, degree of awareness and intellectuel level. Discernment guides the child's entire behaviour. In this perspective, access to medical care and to health care institutions raises specific questions for minors. It is essential to take into account the quality of discernment by the minor in order to understand the often transitory character of certain relational and psychological difficulties which may modify the forms of consent.[9]

The principle of express and free consent, an expression maintained in French law, assumes a capacity of discernment which has been internalized in a stable and lasting way. As practitioners, we would add other requirements to this. Thus, *a mastery of the language* is the guarantee for a level of understanding and for the *capacity* to express orally the wishes of the person concerned. Taking into account the oral expression of the minor's wishes is also linked with the assessment of his capacity to project into the future.

We would emphasize the importance of this *notion of projection into the future*, that is the possibility of anticipation, which the child and adolescent have some difficulty in performing. They often fear a development for the worse in an illness and they resort to denial. Thus, this faculty of anticipation, of projection into the future of a possible (and not fantasized) reality is a precondition of any act of consent.

IV. CONSENT TO HEALTH CARE AND DEVELOPMENT LEVELS

More than age, it is perhaps the development level reached which has to be taken into consideration in order to rule on the minor's competence to make up his mind on medical actions affecting him. This assessment depends on a pluridisciplinary analysis, which we believe should be carried out in full respect of ethical and deontological positions.[1,4]

The *analyses of psychological development* leads us to believe that capacity, as the competence to discern, or judge, is progressively established, allowing the child to form an opinion not only with respect to questions that concern him directly, but also in relation to various aspects of reality of the world surrounding him.

In order to analyse the ontogeny on which this capacity is based, it is necessary to assess the development level of various motivational areas, affective and cognitive, as well as their interrelationship with possible psychopathological phenomena affecting the activity of thinking. This assumes a knowledge of the development of cognitive, conative and affective functions. There are variations between individuals in each of the areas or functions examined, as well as non-homogenous stages of development (psychomotor, linguistic and social) within the same child.[7]

Thus, seeking consent cannot be a purely formal procedure, falling upon practitioners; seeking the support or the approval of the child or adolescent has to be undertaken after the practitioner has provided information and explanations. We consider a child, even a very young one, able to understand a certain number of pieces of information pertaining to his health. This has to be attuned to the child's level of language comprehension, which is generally better than his level of expression, including children with psychopathological disorders. We think that even a child in unfavourable conditions which hinder his competencies, and thus his capacity, may be able to form an opinion and express his will in circumstances and conditions (of independence) which remain to be assessed. Other issues must be clarified depending on developmental levels.

For the *young child*, the question arises of a relational development between the will and the maturation of individual competencies with respect to discernment and anticipation. More than the direct expression of will (which is observed very early on with the young child), it is a matter of apprehending the moment when the child becomes capable of an activity of choosing and deciding, and of specifying the fields where this activity is exercised. In practice, we observe that the acceptance of medical care by the young child depends on the quality of the relation established betweem him and the caregiver, his parents and the caregiver.

For *the older child*, the majority of research focusses on the determination of an age, at which consent could be sought, the age of seven often being the one most often mentioned. To us age does not appear to be an appropriate decisive criterion - above all one should refer to the notions of maturity and developmental level. It seems relevant to us to assess how the child integrates temporal organisation in his experience.

In *adolescence*, these questions take a special direction. Detailed research by genetic psychologists and pediatric-psychoanalysts have shown the evolution in reasoning modes (the transition from concrete to formal thinking) and thought mechanisms (the possibility of reappearance of modes of infantile functioning in certain areas). This evolution affects acts of will.

This maturative phase is also characterized by an intense reactivation of infantile conflicts before giving way to the reactivation of identification processes. At this point, it is appropriate to recall the increase of dysmorpho-phobic disorders in adolescence, which entail a particularization of consent from the moment when it comes to acts practised on the body.

During this period, the question of capacity to consent should in our view thus be treated according to: - the maturation of reasoning, which underlies the ability of judgment; - the possibility of forming an opinion which is based on the acquisition of discernment; and - the nature and the quality of family and social interactions which modify the image of oneself.[8]

V. IN FAVOUR OF THE PERSONAL INVOLVEMENT OF THE MINOR

As we already indicated, seeking the minor's view in the area of medical care, is not viewed positively by the law. The power of decision in matters of medical and surgical actions regarding the child is first attributed to his parents, then and subsidiarily to the doctor, and finally, in a marginal manner, to the minor himself. The legal incapacity of the minor leads directly back to parental authority and, for any medical act, makes obligatory the consent of parents, or, the legal representative.

Thus, in Canada, a person has to be at least sixteen years of age to be allowed to give his consent without the intervention of his parents; but the age limit below which a child's consent has to be supported by his parents' approval is deliberately not determined.

It appears to us that in France, many children and adolescents, if they were sufficiently informed (that is if health questions were explained to them) and if they had established a relationship of trust with the doctor, would be in a position to have a relevant view on health measures that concern them.

Notably, adolescents claim a position of autonomy and decision-making concerning not only access to the health care system, but also the orientation of their lives. It is worth noting that new legal arrangements and case law developments are tending to leave to the adolescent a growing participation. This is the case to the extent that the adolescent's view is increasingly solicited (and sometimes even required), even if it does not always have a decision-making value in all the domains of civil life, including the area of health. In view of this social fact, certain authors have proposed the idea of a civil pre-majority, others one of a medical autonomy for the minor, or of a civil capacity in "health", which is broader than the one assigned to him by common law.

For our part, we propose the idea of a *medical capacity of the minor*, this capacity being assessed on the psychological level with respect to discernment. The expression of individual wishes, consent and its corollary, the opposition to care, are above all individidual acts involving the person. Thus, in all issues concerning the minor's access to the health care system, it is first advisable to refer to the latter's consent, seeking the expression of his wishes, and not referring only to the consent of parents or legal representatives, even if this remains necessary on the legal level. In cases of conflict between the acceptance of a therapeutic proposal by the adolescent and refusal by his parents, or the contrary, a refusal of care by the adolescent and agreement of his parents, it is essential to consider first the minor's point of view, be it to favour a health care procedure, or be it to defer the beginning of care (except in a situation of great emergency). This attitude is only possible if the practitioner takes the greatest possible care in providing the necessary information to the child and his family to help them to move beyond the situation of a conflict.[7]

To conclude, it is worth recalling that in order for the procedures we suggest to be possible, the questions we have raised imply that the child develop in a context where he has access to the health care system.[2] In practice, we are aware that we have to combine our efforts in order for this to become an international reality.

REFERENCES

Collectif, *Le Secret professionnel et l'Hôpital*, premier guide juridique et pratique, Direction des Affaires Juridiques de l'Assistance Publique de Paris, 95 p., Doin éd.

Moutin P., Schweitzer M.G. (1994) *Crimes contre l'humanité*: aspects cliniques et théoriques. PUF Grenoble/Fond. Mémoire déportation, 129 p.

Pepper-Smith R. (1992) "Consent to a competency Assesment", *Int. Jnl. Law and Psychiatry*, *15*, 13–24.

Puig-Vergès N., Schweitzer M.G. (1992) *Face à la Souffrance: l'Ethique, la Liberté et la Loi*, in *Psychiatrie Française*, pp. 135–139, No. spécial mai.

Schubert D., "Informed Consent as a Source of Biais in Clinical Research", *Psychiatry research, 12*, 313–20.

Schweitzer M.G. (1986) Consentement et refus de soins à l'adolescence: expressions légales de la capacité de l'adolescent, D.U. Administration, Economie de la Santé. GRECC-EDS, Paris, 102 p.

Schweitzer M.G. (1994) Volonté et Droit de la Santé, étude critique, Doctorat en Droit et Sciences Politiques. GRECC-EDS, Paris, 802 p.

Schweitzer M.G., Puig-Vergès N. (1991) *Capacité de consentement à l'Adolescence*, in *La Raison psychiatrique et la raison Juridique*, Tome III, pp. 465–469.

Schweitzer M.G., Puig-Vergès N. (1992) "Consentement et troubles psychiques à l'adolescence. In J. Casselman (ed): *Law and Mental Health toward the Year 2001*", pp. 239–246. Leuwen, Belgique.

Schweitzer M.G., Puig-Vergès N. (1993) *Consentement et Urgences psychiatriques* in *Compte-rendus du Congrès de Psychiatrie et de Neurologie de langue française T IV*, pp. 535–542. Masson.

Silverman X.W.A. (1989) "The myth of Informed Consent: in daily practice and clinical trials. *Journal of Medical Ethics, 15*, 6–11.

JEROEN VAN NIEUWENHOVE

Abortion: A Right to Life for Unborn Children?

INTRODUCTION

The question to what extent the fetus enjoys the right to life is a highly controversial issue. This paper contains a brief overview both of the relevant provisions in some international human rights treaties and of important decisions of the supreme courts of the United States, Germany and Belgium and of the European Commission of Human Rights. Unlike many other legal issues, the case law contains very few common elements across the different legal orders. Although the difference in case law can be explained to a certain extent, it raises questions regarding the character of law and the way in which the social reality is qualified by lawyers. Actually, the abortion issue proves that law is unable to translate the continuous process of development of life in legal rules, because law is characterized by the need to draw lines and to distinguish between what is allowed and what is not forbidden. This binary character of law makes it even more difficult to accomplish a meaningful and constructive dialogue between the anti-abortion "pro-life" movement and the liberal "pro-choice" movement.

I. INTERNATIONAL HUMAN RIGHTS TREATIES

A. *The Universal Declaration of Human Rights (United Nations, December 10, 1948)*

Article 3 of the UDHR reads as follows: "*Everyone has the right to life, liberty and the security of person*". During the deliberations in the working group, some countries, like Chile and Lebanon, proposed a text affirming the right to life from the moment of conception. Other countries, like Denmark, the USA and the USSR, opposed this proposal, pointing out that a number of countries do not have laws against abortion and that the Declaration should only contain ideas that were acceptable to all members.

E. Verhellen (ed.), Monitoring Children's Rights, 785–795.
© 1996 *Kluwer Law International. Printed in the Netherlands.*

B. The International Covenant on Civil and Political Rights
(United Nations, December 16, 1966)

Article 6 § 1 of the ICCPR states: "*Every human being has the inherent right to life. This right shall be protected by law. No one shall be arbitrarily deprived of his life*". Some countries proposed a text affirming the right to life from the moment of conception. Other countries rejected this proposal for the same reasons as for the Declaration. They argued that abortion for medical reasons should not be banned by the Covenant and that it should not contain many details. The proposal of a text protecting life "at any stage of human development" was likewise rejected. Nevertheless, the word "person" that figured in the initial draft text, was replaced by the words "human being". Also, the words "inherent right to life" were used, apparently to appease the countries with a pro-life point of view. These alterations can be seen as a compromise between the pro-life and the pro-choice countries.

C. The International Convention on the Rights of the Child
(United Nations November 20, 1989)

Article 1 of the ICRC states that "*For the purposes of the present Convention, a child means every human being below the age of eighteen years unless, under the law applicable to the child, majority is attained earlier*". The initial draft of this article, defining a child as a human being from the moment of his birth to the age of 18 years, was abandoned in favour of a definition which does not exclude the unborn children (but which does not explicitly include them either). Proposals to define a child as every human being from its conception to the age of eighteen years were withdrawn before a vote could take place.

Article 6 reads: "*1. States Parties recognize that every child has the inherent right to life. 2. States Parties shall ensure to the maximum extent possible the survival and development of the child*".

One of the paragraphs of the preamble states: "*Bearing in mind that, as indicated in the Declaration of the Rights of the Child, "the child, by reason of his physical and mental immaturity, needs special safeguards and care including appropriate legal protection, before as well as after birth*"". It resulted from a proposal of an informal drafting group, composed of the Federal Republic of Germany, Ireland, Italy, the Netherlands, Poland, Sweden and the United States. The paragraph quoted from the Declaration of the Rights of the Child originated from an amendment introduced by the Philippines during the drafting of the Declaration, seeking to reach a compromise between pro-life and pro-choice countries. The preamble resembles a lightning conductor, to the extent that it satisfied pro-life countries. The pro-choice countries were satisfied as well because the words "before as well as after birth" do not mean the same as "from the moment of conception" and because the politically sensitive wordings do not occur in articles 1 or 6, but in the preamble which is not legally binding, but only sets out the general considerations and motivations for the adoption of the Convention by the States Parties.

D. The European Convention for the Protection of Human Rights and Fundamental Freedoms (Council of Europe, November 4, 1950)

Article 2 § 1 of the ECHR reads as follows: "*Everyone's right to life shall be protected by law*". The question whether "everyone" also includes the unborn child was not dealt with during the drafting of the ECHR. The case law of the European Commission of Human Rights concerning this question will be discussed later in this paper.

Until now, the European Court of Human Rights has not ruled on the question whether the unborn child enjoys the right to life, although it has had two opportunities to do so indirectly (viz. ECHR, October 29, 1992, *Open Door and Dublin Well Woman v. Ireland*, Vol. 246; June 21, 1988, *Plattform "Ärzte für das Leben" v. Austria*, Vol. 139).

The case law of the European Commission of Human Rights regarding this politically delicate question is characterized by judicial self-restraint. However, two important elements in its case law deserve a brief discussion. Firstly, the Commission considers punishing abortion on itself to be an admissible restriction of the right of privacy of the pregnant woman. It is unclear, however, at what point an anti-abortion legislation can no longer be justified by the second paragraph of article 8 ECHR. This leads us to a second element: does article 2 ECHR protect the unborn children? The Commission cautiously avoided this question, but ruled that, even if the fetus would enjoy a right to life, abortion is an admissible restriction of that right. By way of summary, one can say that at this point in its case law, the Commission will only condemn extremely repressive or extremely liberal abortion regulations.

Domestic courts also pronounced themselves on the applicability of article 2 on the unborn child. The Austrian Constititional Court held in 1974 that it does not apply to unborn children. The Belgian Court of Cassation took the opposite point of view in 1992, whereas the French Council of State occupies a middle position. This clearly illustrates that article 2 can be interpreted in many ways.

E. The American Convention on Human Rights (Organization of American States, November 22, 1969)

Article 4 of the ACHR states that "*Every person has the right to have his life respected. This right shall be protected by law and, in general, from the moment of conception. No one shall be arbitrarily deprived of his life*". The framers of the ACHR felt it necessary to include the principle that human life should be protected from the moment of conception. The words "in general" indicate, however, that certain exceptions are acceptable. Brazil and the U.S.A. declared that they interpret the provision of article 4 "as preserving to States Parties discretion with respect to the content of legislation in the light of their own social development, experience and similar factors". The ACHR was preceded by the American Declaration on the Rights and Duties of Man (ADRDM). Article 1 of the Declaration reads as follows: "*Every human being has the right to life, liberty and the security of his person*".

The Inter-American Commission on Human Rights ruled on the scope of article 4 of the ACHR (and article 1 of the ADRDM) in the case of "Baby Boy" (March 6, 1981). It concluded that the abortion regulation in the U.S.A. does not violate article 1 of the ADRDM (nor article 4 of the ACHR), because, according to the Commission, the framers of the ADRDM, when faced with the question of the scope of the right to life, chose not to adopt language which would clearly state that the fetus enjoys this right. The Commission added that the insertion of the words "*in general*" before the words "*from the moment of conception*" indicates that the framers of the ACHR did not want to extend the scope of the right to life in comparison with the ADRDM.

F. Conclusion

The human rights treaties offer no clear answer to the question whether the unborn child enjoys the right to life, because the wording of the relevant provisions is vague and because it most certainly was not the intention of the framers of the treaties to resolve the question in one way or another. Rather, the subtle changes in the wording of the preamble of the convention on the rights of the child indicate that neither states with a liberal abortion legislation nor states with a conservative abortion legislation wanted to ratify a treaty that contained the opposite. During the drafting of these treaties, representatives of different states (both pro-life and pro-choice) repeatedly pointed out that the text should be acceptable to all countries and that, if certain pro-life or pro-choice amendments were to be accepted, they would be unable to ratify the treaty. Some countries with a growing population and limited resources feared their freedom of action as to population control would be limited by certain pro-life amendments. The Convention on the Rights of the Child is a very good example of these evasive tactics concerning the right to life.

II. Case Law on Abortion

A. The United States Supreme Court

The U.S. Supreme Court has a long history of case law concerning abortion, which can be summarized as follows. The most famous case is *Roe v. Wade* (decided January 22, 1973), in which the recently "discovered" right to privacy was extended as to encompass the woman's right to decide whether or not to terminate her pregnancy. The Court cautiously avoided the question of when life begins: "We need not resolve the difficult question of when life begins. [...] It should be sufficient to note briefly the wide divergence of thinking on this most sensitive and difficult question." (410 US 159–160). Nevertheless, the Court also pointed out that "the word "person", as used in the Fourteenth Amendment, does not include the unborn" (410 US 158). In order to strike a balance between the right of privacy of the pregnant woman and the State interest of protecting the woman's health and the potential life of the fetus, the Court drew up a basic framework, which consists of two basic concepts: *quickening* (i.e. the moment of the first recognizable movement of the fetus *in utero*, approximately at the end of the first trimester) and *viability* (i.e. the moment when the fetus is potentially able to live outside the mother's womb, albeit with artificial aid). For the stage prior to the quickening of the fetus, the decision whether or not to terminate her pregnancy must be left to the woman and her attending physician. For the subsequent stage, the State may regulate the abortion procedure to assure the health of the mother. For the stage subsequent to viability, the State may also regulate abortion to promote its interest in the potentiality of human life, except where the preservation of the life or health of the mother is concerned.

In 1973, viability of the fetus before 28 weeks (approximately the end of the second trimester) was unusual. The *Roe* framework was a trimester framework, with complete freedom of appreciation for the pregnant woman in the first trimester (before quickening) and moderate freedom in the second trimester (before viablity). In a dissenting opinion to *City of Akron v. Akron Center for Reproductive Health, Inc.*, Justice O'Connor warned that fetal viability in the first trimester of pregnancy may be possible in the not too distant future. Considered from this viewpoint, the *Roe* framework is on a collision course with itself, due to the progress of medical science (462 US 457–458).

The nomination of more conservative judges by republican Presidents Reagan and Bush weakened the majority behind Roe and finally resulted in a partial overruling of the 1973 judgment. In the latest "big abortion case", *Planned Parenthood of Southeastern Pennsylvania v. Casey* (decided June, 29, 1992), the conservative majority gave a new, more restrictive interpretation of *Roe v. Wade*, leaving the basic elements intact, but at the same time giving more freedom to the State legislatures to limit the right of privacy of pregnant women. This could result in more restrictive abortion legislation in several states, thus indirectly encouraging "abortion tourism".

Furthermore, a new element was built in in the *Roe v. Wade* rationale: the "undue burden" criterion. This criterion was developed by Justice O'Connor in her sharp dissenting opinion in *City of Akron v. Akron Center for Reproductive Health, Inc.* (see 462 US 459–466). It essentially means that state regulation which imposes an undue burden on the pregnant woman, will be struck down. This will be the case when the state places a substantial obstacle in the path of a woman seeking an abortion of a nonviable fetus. A statute with this purpose is invalid because the means chosen by the state to further the interest in potential life must be calculated to inform the woman's free choice, not hinder it.

B. The German Bundesverfassungsgericht

The German Federal Supreme Court (Bundesverfassungsgericht) built up its case law concerning abortion from a totally different viewpoint than the U.S. Supreme Court. On February 25, 1975, the Federal Supreme Court declared unconstitutional the law of 1974 that liberalized abortion, for reasons totally different from those used by the U.S. Supreme Court. The right to life, which is explicitly enshrined in article 2 of the German Basic Law, extends to the unborn child from the fourteenth day after conception. Also, the State has an obligation to protect this right to life, which the Court deduced from article 1, first paragraph of the German Basic Law, which contains the obligation for the state to protect human dignity.

The crucial question of course is how far this obligation reaches in the case of abortion and what concrete measures should be undertaken by the state in order to fulfil its obligation.

First, the Court developed the so-called *Zumutbarkeitskriterium*, which actually is very similar to the undue burden test in U.S. Supreme Court case law. It essentially means that under certain circumstances or indications (*Indikationen*), one cannot reasonably expect the woman to carry out her pregnancy. Of course, the decision of the court depends on the indications which it judges to be of such a graveness that the undue burden criterion can be applied. The most important consequence is, however, that the Court explicitly rules out a legislation based on time limits (*Fristenregelung*), rather than on indications that may permit the woman to terminate her pregnancy (*Indikationenregelung*). The Court rejects a time limit-based framework (like the *Roe* framework) because it constitutes a lump-sum balancing of life against life and cannot be considered to constitute an adequate protection of the unborn life.

Secondly, the Court underlines that criminalizing abortion must be considered as the ultimate means. It seems to suggest that it would be preferable to avoid the *ultima ratio* of punishing the woman (or physician) when it is possible to accomplish the same goal (reducing or banning abortion) by means that are less drastic, such as counselling and helping women who are distressed and need medical, psychological, social or financial aid.

On May 28, 1993, the Bundesverfassungsgericht partially invalidated a new abortion law of 1992. The law of June 27, 1992 made first-trimester abortions possible for women who find themselves in "a state of distress" after counseling. The words "state of distress" are to some extent misleading, since the woman alone decides whether or not to have an abortion. One could describe the new law as a concealed time limit-based solution. The Court found counselling "as such" unsatisfactory in view of the State's obligation to protect human life. Counselling must be organized to convince the woman to carry her pregnancy to term and indications must be present in order to justify the decision to have an abortion. The bundesverfassungsgericht indicates that it would accept a more permissive abortion legislation under these conditions.

On August 21, 1995, a new abortion bill was enacted according to the principles set out by the Bundesverfassungsgericht.

C. The Belgian Court of Arbitration

On November 6, 1989 and March 29, 1990, respectively, the Senate and the Chamber of Belgium adopted a new bill which liberalized the abortion legislation. During the first twelve weeks of pregnancy, the woman can get an abortion when certain indications are present. One of these indications is "a state of distress". Since the woman is to be the sole judge of this state of distress, this legislation in practice amounts to a trimester solution. The late King Boudewijn I refused to sign the bill for moral reasons. In order to avoid a serious political and constitutional crisis, the Council of Ministers temporarily exercised the powers of the King and signed the bill.

On December 19, 1991, the Belgian Court of Arbitration held that the newly enacted law of April 3, 1990 was constitutional. The Court has, however, a limited scope of judicial review: in this case, it could only examine whether the liberalisation of abortion violated the principle of equality and could not decide upon the question whether the fetus enjoys a right to life and whether that right was violated. The Court of Arbitration held that the legislator has an obligation to protect the fetus, but that this obligation does not mean that unborn life should be treated in exactly the same way as children who are already born.

III. ANALYSIS

One of the paramount questions in the abortion debate is whether the fetus enjoys the right to life, or, as some call it, the right to be born.

The pro-life movement argues that the fetus constitutes human life. When the fetus is alive, when it is a person, it enjoys the right to life. This reasoning calls for two critical remarks.

Firstly, the distinction between human life and other forms of life cannot be drawn as sharply as one might think: animals are not legal persons, yet for some reason we find it to be morally desirable to punish ill-treatment of animals, especially of animals that *resemble* human beings in one way or another. Even destroying plants is considered to be a wrong which is punishable in some cases. Furthermore, empirical data reveal that the development from zygote to fetus to a born human is similar to a certain extent with the development from animal to man. I do not claim that the fetus resembles more an animal than a human person, nor do I pretend that killing an animal ought to be punished in the same way as killing a fetus, but I think that this reflection makes sense when dealing with fundamental ethical issues, such as the right to life.

Secondly, when we depart from the assumption that the fetus *is* life, is a legal person, we cannot avoid the question as to at which moment "inanimate" matter turns into "living" matter. Is the union of the *ovum* and the sperm cell this "magic moment"? If so, is it disrespectful to ask oneself why a five-year old animal is not a legal person, and a zygote so small it cannot be observed with the naked eye is? Is the moment of birth this magic moment? Is it perhaps quickening or viability? Is it ovulation or is it the ejaculation of sperm? Is it the implantation of the fertilized *ovum* in the womb? Is it the development of the heart, of the lungs, of the brains of the fetus?

This last consideration leads to another, more fundamental question on the way in which law translates (one could also say "mutates") reality into legal terms and into legal rules. The confrontation with the binary structure of the legal instruments is always very painful, especially in the abortion issue. "One is a legal person or one is not". The choice is very hard to make, because we know that the development of the fetus is a continuous process. Even though this process sometimes exhibits accelerated growth phases, it is, from a biological point of view, impossible to draw a line between "living" and "inanimate" matter.

Some pretend that a legal person can only exist from the moment of birth. Of course, it is an important stage in the development of human life, not in the least because the physical connection with the mother is disrupted, because the child has to breathe independently and receives its nutrition by its mouth. But there are many basic human features that were already present before birth. The same criticisms can be addressed to those who claim that the fetus is a legal person from the moment of conception. The artificial character of this claim cannot be illustrated in a better way than with a fragment of the pro-life pamphlet "Did you know?":

> You once were a fertilized ovum. A fertilized ovum? Yes! *You were then everything you are today.* Nothing has been added to the fertilized ovum you once were except nutrition.

Is not an ovum or a sperm cell life? One might assume that a living human cell is life as well. Considered from this point of view, destroying the ovary or the testicles might be looked at as destroying potential life. The main difference between a sperm cell or an ovum and a fertilized ovum, though, is that the latter *has a future – it might develop into a human being, but it is still growing.* To a certain extent, the growing process starts before fertilization, continues after birth and one can safely assume it is not completed until several years after birth.

Thus, choosing one "magical moment" in the development of the fetus from conception to birth is a misunderstanding, a treacherous misrepresentation of life itself, because this development is a continuous process with, admittedly, some critical moments, that fall short of being recognized as important enough to be called the one critical moment.

Lawyers, legislators and judges should adopt a more modest position towards this continuous development. Arguably the best solution would be to weigh the rights that are invoked to the benefit of the unborn child and the mother, and, to a lesser extent, of the father and other persons involved in the moral conflict that abortion constitutes.

Again, these reflections are not meant to criticize every existing abortion regulation. Rather, I want to point out that lawyers should keep in mind that when they are dealing with abortion, they are dealing with the question at what moment and under which conditions a continuous development of a fertilized ovum into a full-grown human being can be interrupted. Also, abortion is and will always be a weighing of different interests: interests of the woman, the fetus, the biological father, the husband, the family, the physician, the society... Each of these interests should be taken into account, albeit not on an equal base. It is obvious that the interests of the woman and the fetus are more important than, for example, those of the husband who happens not to be the biological father.

Of course, a legal rule cannot take into account every individual case – it must be an abstract rule, based on a political decision by an elected parliament and/or by a constitutional court. The problem of the legislative character of lengthy court decisions prescribing a rather detailed abortion regulation, which is designed by a small number of judges without much democratic legitimation, like the U.S. Supreme Court or the German Bundesverfassungsgericht, will not be discussed here.

This general and abstract character of law of course also applies to abortion laws. Therefore, the continuous process of developing life should be articulated in legal rules of conduct by striking a balance between the different interests in different phases of the development of the fetus. From this point of view, both time-limit solutions as well as indication solutions may constitute an adequate weighing of interests. Furthermore, a certain tendency towards moderate solutions can be perceived: in the U.S., the relatively liberal time-limit solution, contained in *Roe v. Wade*, appears to be moving in a more conservative direction, whereas in Germany, the existing relatively conservative indication solution is evolving in a more liberal direction.

ACKNOWLEDGEMENT

The author thanks Lisa Salas and Liesbet Van Nieuwenhove for valuable advice and comments.

REFERENCES

Abortion and the Status of the Fetus (1983) In: Bondeson, W.B., Engelhardt, H.T., Spicker, S.F. and Winship, D.H. (Eds), Dordrecht: D. Reidel Publishing, 351 p.

Brugger, W. (1987) "A Constitutional Duty to outlaw Abortion? A Comparative Analysis of the American and German Abortion Decisions". *Jahrbuch des öffenlichen Rechts der Gegenwart*, Band *36*, 49-66.

Cane, M.B. (1973) "Whose Right to Life? Implications of Roe v. Wade". *Family Law Quarterly*, 413-432.

de Blois, M. (1981) "Abortus en artikel 2 van de Europese Conventie voor de rechten van de mens". *Nederlands Juristenblad*, 141-150, with reaction from J.T.K. Bos (*ibidem*, 438–439) and reply from M. de Blois (*ibidem*, 439–440).

Davey, D.A.T. (1989) "The Right to Be Born". *Medicine and Law*, 475-482.

Ely, J.H. (1973) "The Wages of Crying Wolf: A Comment on Roe v. Wade". *Yale Law Journal*, 920-949.

Eser, A. (1994) "Abortion Law Reform in Germany in International Comparative Perspective". *European Journal of Health Law*, 15-34.

Esser, W. (1984) "Can Abortion Be Legally Justified?" *Medicine and Law*, 205-216.

Glendon, M.A. (1987) *Abortion and Divorce in Western Law*. Cambridge: Harvard University Press, 197 p.

Hermes, G. and Walther, S. (1993) "Schwangerschaftsabbruch zwischen Recht und Unrecht. Das zweite Abtreibungsurteil des BVerfG und seine Folgen". *Neue Juristische Wochenschrift*, 2337-2347.

Hoerster, N. (1991) "Föten, Menschen und "Speziesismus" – rechtsethisch betrachtet". *Neue Juristische Wochenschrift*, 2540-2542, with reaction from H. Tröndle, ("Zum Begriff des Menschseins", *ibidem*, 2542–2543).

Johnsen, D.E. (1986) "The Creation of Fetal Rights: Conflicts with Women's Constitutional Rights to Liberty, Privacy, and Equal Protection". *Yale Law Journal*, 599-625.

King, P.A. (1982) "The Juridical Status of the Fetus: A Proposal for Legal Protection of the Unborn". In: Schneider, C. E. and Vinovskis, M.E. (Eds): *The Law and Politics of Abortion*. Lexington (Mass.): Lexington Books, 81-121.

Leyshon, D.J. (1991) "Abortion: In Search of a Constitutional Doctrine". *Medicine and Law*, 155-183 and 219-234.

Levinson, B. (1993) "The Rights of the Unborn Child Seen through the Eyes of a Psychologist". *Medicine and Law*, 471-477.

Main, E.J. (1987) "The Relevance of a Biological Definition of Life to Fundamental Rights". *Medicine and Law*, 189-209.

Pinto, R. (1993) "La Cour Suprême américaine et l'avortement". *Revue de Droit Publique*, 907-938.

Regan, D.H. (1982) "Rewriting Roe v. Wade". In: Schneider, C.E. and Vinovskis, M.A. (Eds): *The Law and Politics of Abortion*. Lexington (Mass.), Lexington Books, 1-80.

Smits, P.W. (1992) *The Right to Life of the Unborn Child in International Documents, Decisions and Opinions*. Bedum: Scholma, 348 p.

Starck, Ch. (1993a) "Der verfassungsrechtliche Schutz des ungeborenen menschlichen Lebens. Zum zweiten Abtreibungsurteil des BVerfG". *Juristen Zeitung*, 816-822.

Starck, Ch. (1993b) "Abtreibung auf Grund Gewissensentscheidung?" *Juristen Zeitung*, 31-32.

Stürner, R. (1990) "Die Unverfügbarkeit ungeborenen menschlichen Lebens und die menschliche Selbstbestimmung". *Juristen Zeitung*, 709-724.

Tribe, L.H. (1990) *Abortion. The Clash of Absolutes*. New York: Norton, 270 p.

Tribe, L.H. (1973) "The Supreme Court 1972 Term. Foreword: Toward a Model of Roles in the Due Process of Life and Law". *Harvard Law Review*, 1-53.

Tröndle, H. (1995) "Das Schwangeren- und Familienhilfe-änderungsgesetz". *Neuwe Juristische Wochenschrift*, 3009–3019.

Tröndle, H. (1989) "Der Schutz des ungeborenen Lebens in unserer Zeit". *Zeitschrift für Rechtspolitik*, 54-61.

Williams, G. (1994) "The Fetus and the Right to Life". *Cambridge Law Journal*, 71-80.

Willems, J.C.M. (1990) "Het VN-Kinderverdrag en het recht op abortus". *Nederlands Juristenblad*, 776-778.

Wouters, M. (1993/94) "Het recht op leven en de strafbaarstelling van abortus. Twee bedenkingen bij een "terloops" cassatiearrest". *Rechtskundig Weekblad*, 458-463.

AUTHOR'S PUBLICATIONS ON ABORTION

"Zwangerschapsafbreking: afweging van rechten door Hoge Gerechtshoven". *Tijdschrift voor Bestuurswetenschappen en Publiekrecht*, 1992, 352-358.

"Zur Neuregelung des Schwangerschaftsrechts in Belgien und zur Rolle des belgischen Schiedshofs. Zugleich eine Anmerkung zur Entscheidung des belgischen Schiedshofes vom 19.12.1991 zum Schwangerschaftsabbruch". *Europäische Grundrechte Zeitschrift*, 1992, 340-344.

"Zwangerschapsafbreking en vrije meningsuiting" (annotation of ECHR, October 29, 1992, *Open Door and Dublin Well Woman v. Ireland*). *NJCM-Bulletin*, 1993, 700-715.

"Zwangerschapsafbreking: een delicate afweging van grondrechten" (in preparation).

DIETER WINDELS

Social and Educational Assistance for Children and their Mild Mental Retarded Parents

Recently, the Department of Special Education of the University of Ghent, in which we are active, conducted important research in Flanders into adults with a mild mental handicap.

Geert Van Hove[1] offered a theoretical framework with regard to supervised living for persons with a mild mental handicap. Eric Broekaert and Vicky Quinet[2] executed an evaluation research by order of the Flemish Government, Department of Welfare and Family, one year after the recognition of the services for supervised living (4/4/1990).

Services for supervised living are ambulatory centres which guide adults with a mild mental handicap, who are able to live independently. A social worker guides them for a restricted number of hours per week. This guidance concentrates mainly on problems with regard to budgetting, administrative problems, leisure, contacts with the social environment, and the like.

The programme of this conference states that children often are "invisible" in society. When they are counted, this always happens "in relation to" adults. This was confirmed by Broekaerts and Quinets research.

This research (1992) assessed the method of working of the services for supervised living through questionnaires that these services had to fill out, through individual index cards of the target group and through "time registration" with regard to the task of the counsellors. Concerning the target group, they selected 605 clients within the 32 recognized services for supervised living. Interesting was the fact that they also selected a number of 231 children, especially young children, from the data of the individual index cards.

RESULTS OF QUESTIONNAIRES

Recognized services 1992 (n=32)	605 clients
Effective in guidance in 1992	712 clients
Waiting list (n=19)	156 clients
Number of children (n=26)	*231 children*

E. Verhellen (ed.), Monitoring Children's Rights, 797–801.
© 1996 *Kluwer Law International. Printed in the Netherlands.*

Of these 231 children, 41 were placed under supervision of the special child welfare services, 9 resided within fostercare and 3 elsewhere; 178 children then lived with their parents. The researchers regarded this group of children rightly as a high-risk group.

In 1993 the Flemish Fund for social integration of people with a handicap, commissioned further investigation (3) into the situation of these children. Of the 36 services for supervised living, 26 reported that they were dealing with children. In all 302 children in guided families were reported. Of 285 children an information index card was drawn up. This resulted in the following data:

Age children	Number of children
Younger than 6	106
Between 6 and 18	152
Older than 18	27
Total	285

Children according to form of cohabitation

Form of cohabitation parents	Number
Single parents with children	57
Couples (both under guidance)	53
Couples (1 parent under guidance)	51

Further data with regard to the group of children between 6 and 18 established that 53,3% of these children were handicapped (especially mild mental retarded children). A large part received special education. More than 40% of these children did not reside at home, which suggests more problems than just the handicap. From the group of children younger than 6, 26,4% was placed under care. Several assistance bodies, such as juvenile courts, special child welfare services, services of the Flemish Fund for social integration, and the like, are involved with these problem families.

With regard to possible problems that occur when handicapped adults raise their children, Van Hove and Vermeire[4] stated in a paper (1991) a number of causes that can explain certain problems:

- A lot of these parents never knew a "model-family", they lack as it were an "education model".
- These parents have restricted cognitive skills, which causes a lack of insight in educational situations.
- Alot of parents lack a realistic view of education, which is expressed in a less adequate stimulation, especially in the field of language. These parents often experience problems in taking decisions, which results in uncertainty.
- These parents often act inconsistently.
- Often over-protection of the children is stated as a problem with these parents.

The article of Van Hove and Vermeire, as well as the research results of Broekaert and Quinet, establish that the situation of these children results in extra demands and tasks for the social workers of the services for supervised living. "It appears that the way of communicating between children and parents lacks in relational and educational aspects. Since we prefer to raise children in their natural environment, this environment must be guided and stimulated pedagogically. The task of social integration and the educational task go together."[2]

The present decree of 1991 with regard to the services for supervised living unfortunately disregards this problem. Apart from acting planning, the services are also expected to lend pedagogical family guidance, which requires special training and refresher courses for the social workers. A guidance methodology adapted to this population would be advisable.

In her licentiate's thesis[5] and later through a research grant of the Foundation Marie Delacroix, Veerle Wellens drew up, at the University of Ghent, a methodology of pedagogical assistance backed by video images. The project is based on the "Video home training-methodology" of the Foundation Spin in the Netherlands.

This concludes a survey of the data about research with regard to children and their mentally retarded parents in supervised living. In this research, these children suddenly became visible, yet in relation to their mentally retarded parents.

The research also indicated that alot of these families had to contend with serious problems. According to researchers this is a high-risk group; we could also argue that these families find themselves in a "problematic educational situation". The expression "problematic educational situation" originates from the orthopedagogical development of a theory and was first used by the Dutchman Ter Horst.[6] He defined the problematic educational situation as follows:

> This educational situation is experienced by the persons involved as almost without prospects. Without expert help from the outside, they are unnable to change the whole situation in such a way that it offers perspective. (Ter Horst, 1980)

At the centre of this definition is the whole situation, not only the child, not only the parents. The children, parents, educators, relatives, teachers, neighbours, social workers, the environment, are involved. When so-called "child-problems" do not occur, we obviously risk to give a central role to the parents in the problematical educational situation.

The parents play an important role in the development of the child; the norms, the morality, the therapeutical value of the family, views, are in turn dependent on a wider social context[7,8,9] (W. Van Damme, 1990; K. Raes, 1994; B. Spiecker & D. De Ruyter). According to Schoorl (1981) the educational context has to be brought under discussion.

In actual practice of the (youth) assistance, the factors directed at the child, or at the parents, are too often taken as point of departure. This view must be broadened through criteria development, so that the problematic educational situation can be defined more clearly, through specific methodology development for the complete approach of a problematic educational situation.

At this time, we are preparing a paper directed at the social workers of the services for supervised living. Through a qualitative study (in-depth interviews and participating observation) we would like to assess how they estimate the problematical educational situation, which initiatives they take, with which other services they collaborate in order to counsel these families as well as possible. In our opinion, alot of social workers experience difficulties in taking decisions, given the relationship based on trust they have with their clients. Furthermore, they have and want to continue the "specific" guidance tasks of supervised living. But often they are confronted with extremely difficult situations, that require adequate and consequent reactions. The objective is the development of a guideline, a way of assessment, so that social workers are able to define and approach a problematical educational situation more adequately.

A possible way of assesment has already been developed by Ter Horst (1977) in "Herstel van het gewone leven – translated as Recovery or Restoration of ordinary life".[6] He departs from the following question: "What can be done in everyday life to solve an educational situation that has come to a standstill and what can the educators do in order to re-establish ordinary life?". Starting from this question, they who have to deal with educational problems, can assess the situation on the basis of a series of questions with regard to the child, the parents-educators, the environment of the child and the reality behind the environment of the child. We would like to make this questionnaire subject of discussion with the social workers and to evaluate the utility for this specific target group.

Moreover, we would like to assess how the staff of services for supervised living respond to these educational problems: in which way are these problems being evaluated, how does one react to it (action planning), what is offered, what is one capable of, when does one appeal to other specialized services, how does one take decisions (f.i. about placing a child outside the family), which procedures are being followed.

We would process the data from these interviews according to a qualitative processing programme, Kwalitan. The interview data will also presented to a group of experts. The conclusions reached by Kwalitan will then be tested by the conclusions of the group of experts.

The Preamble of the Convention on the Rights of the Child states that to the family, as centre of society and the natural environment for the development and welfare of all its members and of children in particular, the necessary assistance has to be rendered. The elaboration of adapted methodologies forces itself upon us for this "new" way of assistance for mild retarded persons, and certainly for families, and these children in particular. In this context, we quote Michael Freeman[10] (1992) in "Taking children's rights more seriously: "If we are to make progress we have to recognize the moral integrity of children. We have to treat them as persons entitled to equal concern and respect and entitled to have both their present autonomy recognized and their capacity for future autonomy safeguarded. And this to recognize that children, particulary younger children, need nurture, care and protection. Children, must not, as Hafen (1977) puts it, be "abandoned" to their rights.

REFERENCES

Van Hove Geert (1992) "Begeleid Wonen van volwassenen met een lichte mentale handicap, Een theoretisch kader". Leuven, Belgium: Garant.

Broekaert Eric, Quinet Vicky (1992) "Begeleid Wonen van Volwassenen met een lichte mentale handicap, Evaluatiestudie op initiatief van de Gemeenschapsminister voor Gezin en Welzijn" Leuven, Belgium: Garant.

Bourgois N., Coudyser U., Gussé E. (1994) "Jaarwerk: onderzoek naar kinderlast in diensten voor begeleid wonen". University of Ghent, Belgium: Department of Special Education.

Van Hove G., Vermeire L. (1991) "Volwassenen met een mentale handicap als ouders: Pedagogische problematiek". *Tijdschrift Vereniging voor Orthopedagogiek, 10(3)*, Gent, Belgium.

Wellens Veerle (1992) "Verantwoorde begeleiding van de opvoedingsproblematiek van ouders met een lichte mentale handicap: Ondersteuning aan de hand van videobeelden". *VVO-info, 12(1)*, Gent, Belgium.

Ter Horst W. (1997) "Herstel van het gewone leven". In *Orthovisies*. Groningen, Netherlands: Wolters-Noordhoff.

Vandamme W. (1990) "Van Jeugdbescherming naar Bijzondere Jeugdbijstand, een nieuw imago met andere inhouden". Kortrijk, Belgium: Werktekst.

Raes K. (1994) "De morele betekenis van het vertoog over de rechten van het kind. Naar een differentiële mens- en maatschappijopvatting". In Verhellen E., et al. (Eds): *Kinderrechtengids*. Gent, Belgium: Mys en Breesch.

Spiecker B., De Ruyter D. (1993) "Desoriëntatie en houvast; opvoeden en volwassen worden in het fin de siècle". *Tijdschrift voor Orthopedagogiek, 32*.

Freeman M. (1992) "Taking children's rights more siriously", abstract. Bristol, United Kingdom.

DEEPAK KUMAR BEHERA

The Invisible Little Big Workforce: Plight of the Female Working Child in India

INTRODUCTION

Children constitute more than a minority group defined by an absence of rights. Adults and children might be considered as constituting classes in the sense of being social categories which exists principally by their economic opposition to each other, and in the ability of the dominant class (adults) to exploit economically the activities of the subordinate class (children) (Oldman, 1994: 44). It is in the interest of adult employees that children are occupied with a number of different activities, because it provides adults with gainful occupation (ibid: 44). Children who in every society are by definition excluded from the power game control childhood the least. In this power game over an invaluable and potent resource there is no room left for children themselves to have a say (Shamgar-Handelman, 1994: 253). The involuntary participation of young children in household work and family occupations deprives them of "childhood" and its many opportunities, including those for schooling, recreation and rest (Nayar, 1991: 37). Children are persons and must therefore be treated as unit of observation in the statistical sense, and childhood is a category and a social status and must thus be dealt with as our unit of analysis (Qvortrup, 1994: 6-7). Liberating children, at least conceptually would mean statistics and other information from children's point of view, which would make themselves visible (ibid: 6). Therefore statistics should be collected and research conducted in order to perceive the place of children in a given society and thus to redesign the picture of childhood. It is manifestly clear that children are working to a great extent, only the amount and the condition of that work are largely known. The extent to which children are really contributing needs much more documentation and interpretation (Qvortrup, 1991: 31).

Every fourth working child in the world is an Indian. India ranks first in the world for having the highest number of child workers. According to 1981 census, there were 263 million children in India comprising 39.5 per cent of

E. Verhellen (ed.), Monitoring Children's Rights, 803–816.
© 1996 *Kluwer Law International. Printed in the Netherlands.*

the total population of the country. The child labour force according to the same census was 13.59 million. The National Sample Survey figures of 1983 were 17.36 million and the Operation Group (a Baroda based organisation) figures of 1985 on child labour were 44 million. The reason for this sharp variation is that while the census counts only those children as workers who are engaged in economically productive work, the definition of child labour according to the Operation Research Group is more broad-based and includes all children between the age of 5 and 15 who are at productive work, may be paid or unpaid, and busy of any hour of the day within or outside the family (Khatu, 1983: 69). The availability of cheap, docile and non-unionised labour in India is in abundance. The prevalence of child labour is believed to be highest in Andhra Pradesh. Invariably wages of child labour are low, conditions of work are often sub-human (UNICEF 1990: 61).

While concern for working children predates the constitution of India, there has been no separate division of male and female child labour (Nayar, 1991: 37). The question has often arisen in discussion as to why the subject of female working child merits separate attention. The argument is advanced that children who work, of whichever sex they might be, should be the focus of research; it is implied that gender discrimination is sought to be observed where it does not exist. In fact, majority of the children who work in factories and mines are male children. Therefore it is invidious to speak of female working child when the burnt of exploitation is visibly borne by male children (Burra, 1988: 1).

I. OBJECTIVE

Contrary to the above argument this paper makes an attempt to justify the need for the study of the female working child of India as a separate and independent category. It is argued that the question of whether the female working child is discriminated against vis-a-vis the male working child is a matter which has to be settled by evidence and not one that can be answered a priori. By reviewing the available literature on the problem at hand, the paper seeks to raise some basic issues concerning the working girl child in India. It tries to highlight the differences in the situation of female working girl child and that of its male counterpart. It deals with the working girl child of both rural and urban settings. Aspects such as occupational health hazards, educational standard, parental attitude towards girl child labour, government acts and policies have been dealt with. Admittedly, the data are sparse, but the paper endeavours to address the issue of this little big workforce of India from a sociological perspective.

II. SOCIO-CULTURAL MILIEU

In India the value of domestic and household work is not properly computed since it does not bring in a wage and is not productively oriented. Thus it affects the attitudes of parents of female children and confers upon the latter a status that is lower than that of their male siblings. There are also a complex of socio-cultural reasons for which the girl child is undervalued by parents. Most girls start their lives with the disadvantage of being less welcome than boys. Each successive girl in the family is less welcome than the earlier one. The birth of a male child is an occasion of celebration while that of a girl child is greeted with silence. They are brought up so carelessly that very soon they begin to feel that they are the economic burden of the family. She is made to work very hard at home and outside but her economic contribution is never recongnised. So no value is placed on her need for education and as she grows up, her lack of education limits her opportunities in the labour market and she is relegated to low paid, unskilled jobs (Burra, 1988: 18).

III. SOME STATISTICS FROM GIRL CHILDREN'S POINT OF VIEW

Girl child labour in the country was estimated at 7.6 million by a survey conducted during July 1987 – June 1988. This information was given by labour and Welfare Minister in the Rajya Sabha on 16 March 1990. According to 1981 census approximately 11.2 million children were notified as "main workers" and 2.4 million as "marginal workers". "Main workers" were those who were involved in full-time economic activity and "marginal workers" were those who were not working full-time. One of the significant features is that in 1981, the percentage of girls employed as "main workers" was consistently higher than boys in almost all the categories of occupation. Boys were employed more as "marginal workers" than girls. The difference clearly indicates that girls are being pushed to employment for full time more than boys, which further reduces the educational and developmental opportunities for girls.

Similarly, a comparison of the Work Participation Rate (WPR) of male and female children shows that between 1971 and 1981 there has been an increase in the WPR of children is the percentage of child workers to the total child population. While the percentage of rural boys working fell between 1971 and 1981, it increased for girls. Between 1981 and 2001, it is projected that work participation among girls of 14 years and below will increase by 20 per cent (Nayar, 1990: 40).

IV. GIRL CHILD LABOUR

From a review of literature, it appears that there is a strong gender typing of roles in terms of the work the female and male child perform. Various studies in India indicate that the burden of household duties falls largely upon female child. Greater number of hours are put in by girls in domestic work when compared with boys, at a young age. By the age of 10-12 years girls may be engaged in domestic work for about eight hours per day and by the age of 15 years, they work for at least 10 hours per day (Nayar, 1991: 39). A major contrast among girls and boys engaged early in domestic, non-economic work is that while boys eventually move on to full time agricultural or wage labour, young girls continue to shoulder the burden of household tasks, from where they are relegated eventually to their roles as wives and mothers. In the Indian context, the evidence suggest that girls are engaged in low-paid or no-wage unskilled jobs which do not necessarily lead to skill formation. In the case of boys the jobs that they do are closely related to apprenticeship training and skill formation. Hence it has been rightly stated by Nayar (1991: 41) that girl child labour is a dead end.

A. *Rural Working Girl Child*

In fact, the bulk of the female working child population is to be found in the rural areas where they are engaged in looking after younger siblings, working, sweeping, washing clothes and utensil, grinding, fetching water, taking care of the domestic animals, preparing of dung-cakes and storing of the balance as manure, plastering the house-wall with cow dung, taking the mid-day meal to her father and brother in the field, bringing fuelwood from the forest, taking the domestic animal to the grazing field, etc. This releases adult and male children for more productive work. In the rural areas, little girls can be seen carrying small pots on their heads, following their mothers or elder sisters to the well and what, at first, is little more than play develops soon into a useful contribution to the volume of work which has to be done in every household. Girls accompany parents to the fields to help them in activities such as sowing, transplanting, weeding and harvesting, scaring away the birds. They also accompany their mothers to the market place with small loads on their heads and backs (Burra, 1988:5). It was estimated in 1985 that by the time she ceases to be a child, the girl in rural India would have contributed as assistance of Rs39,600/- in economic terms to her family (Joseph, 1991: 35). Jain's (1990:11) reporting on a 11 years old Mina girl will help us further to understand the burden of household task of an average working girl child of rural India.

> "Naini is a 11 years old Mina girl of Etrampura, a small village of 57 households in Bharatpur district of Rajasthan. Hers is a joint family of 9 which includes her parents, uncles, an aunt and a younger brother. The family owns 8 bighas of land – live by its procedure, occasionally hires

labour or hires itself out depending on the season. The father and the uncle plough and dig while Naini, her mother and her aunt weed, pack groundnut and cut grass.

Rising at about 6 in the morning, Naini's first task is to make cow-dung cakes for an hour. This is followed by going to the well to fetch water. Returning to the house she sweeps the courtyard in front. At 7.30 AM, she sieves the wheat flour, lights the fire and assists her mother to prepare *rotis*. The family sits down to eat *daliya* and *bajra* rotis in brass *thalis*.

It is Naini's task to clean utensils after breakfast. After packing some launch for the family, she sets out with her mother to the field which lies on the border of Mehtoli and Etrampura, about 3kms away. In september, a quarter of the field is covered with capsicum while the rest is being ploughed and got ready for the next crop. She and her mother are assigned the task of weeding the field. This she does from 9 to 12 noon, goes home with her mother to cook lunch while her father and her uncle remain behind and eat in the field.

She chops the potatoes while her mother prepares the *rotis*. After eating lunch, she washes the utensils and goes to the well to fill another pitcher of water. Having been done this for two years already, Naini pulls up the water with great ease.

From 2.45 in the afternoon Naini is seen again on her field, cutting the grass for her cattle. By 4 in the evening, she has collected a big bundle which she ties and carries home. This she deposits in the cattle-shed. Her uncle will cut it later and feed it to the cattle.

Adjoining their mud-huts, next to the cattle-shed, is a little store-room from where Naini takes out the cow-dung cakes which are prepared by her every morning and the firewood which she and her aunt had collected last week. With the help of these Naini fires the oven, and cooks *daliya*. She then sweeps the house for the second time. Preparation of food is usually done by her aunt. As she is very sick these days, this task is shared by Naini and her mother. Once dinner is ready and Naini's daily tasks have been completed, she finally finds half an hour to sit down and relax which she does chatting and teasing her brother chuttan, who has kept aside his books. At 7.30 when it is time for dinner, she serves *daliya*, boiled milk and bajra rotis to all the family. She then joins them for dinner which they eat under the light of an oil lamp."

Naini belongs to 70 per cent of girls, between ages of 5 and 14 in rural India, who do not go to school. Perhaps this will be so till their mothers and fathers earn enough to manage without their labour time, or there is a good free care centre for children where the sibling can be left; or where the firewood and water are nearby and affordable.

B. Urban Working Girl Child

Girl children are bonded not only in the rural sector but also in the urban informal sector (Kulkarni, 1983: 1855). The method of payment for children is usually the piece rate system which puts an enormous pressure upon the child. Significantly while the working child is visible in rural India, this is not so in the urban areas. In the urban sector they are found to be working in some concentration of child labour but not in others. Girls are found in large number in match industry of Tamilnadu (Nair, 1983), coir industry and home based industries like incense-making and papad preparation in Kerala (Jhabvale, 1980). They are involved in substantial number in beedi industry (Burra, 1981) and gem-polishing industry (Burra, 1988) of Jaipur (Rajasthan). Hundreds of girls are working in the lock industry of Aligarh, Uttar Pradesh (Burra, 1988), pottery industry of Khurja, the carpet industry of Jammu and Kashmir and the zari embroidery industry of Varanasi (Uttar Pradesh). In the brass-ware industry of Moradabad, polishing goods by hand is considered as *auraton ka kaam* or women's work. There is a clear-cut sex differentiation between the work that male and female children do in the coir industry. While both boys and girls are employed to rotate spinning wheel, cleaning and willowing the fiber, etc., but in the beating of husks one sees only girls, hardly ever a boy. The latter is possibly one of the messiest jobs (Gulati, n.d.: 27). A significant number of girl children are again engaged in the making of paper bags, garments, cotton-pot shelling, groundnut pod shelling, hand-embroidery, grain cleaning, block making, sub-assembling electrical and electronic items (Bhat, 1987: 30). Girls are again found in domestic service, rag-picking, newspaper-vending and so on (Karlekar, 1982; Juyal, 1985 and Patil, 1986). Most of these working girl children are essentially invisible children who do not go to work in factories and therefore do not come under the purview of the law. For reason of space, we only highlight the situation of working child in some selected industries.

MATCH INDUSTRY OF SIVAKASI

Female workers, both adult and children, are far more widely employed in the match industry than male workers – Girls outnumber boys 3 to 1. They are Universally employed in piece-rated work and are not used in any kind of work requiring supervisory capability (MISD, 1985). A girl child fills more frames per hour than an adult. The employer's quest for tender age fingers with dexterity to work fast on match sticks, has brought the real age of working girl children to 10 or even 9 (Abraham, 1991: 282). Children are waken up at 4 in the morning, are taken from their homes to their place of work. They never return until 9 PM. Piece work keep children bent over the match frames for 10 to 12 hours a day. The children and women work for about three hours more on returning home. Parents take advance loans against their children's wages, forcing them to keep working without pay. The only incentive for them are small gifts such as soap box, comb or bangles and an occasional screening of a film show (Moulik and Purushotham, 1982).

One reason for the large number of girl children in the match industry is that the work in this industry is poorly paid and does not lead to skill-formation. Interestingly, the bulk of the labour force here belongs to scheduled castes, where restrictions on the movements of females are not so severe. Thus Sivakasi affords an example where poverty forces children to work and cultural traditions allow girl children to participate in work outside the home.

GEM-POLISHING INDUSTRY OF JAIPUR

In this industry *bindai ka kaam* was traditionally a female job and even today 6,000 girls are to be found working there with their mothers. They pierce holes in beads for necklaces. But due to the increased international demand for gem stones, an ultra-sonic machine has been introduced to do the same work. Though it is a relatively simple gadget, nowhere in Jaipur are women seen doing this work on machines. The wages paid to men working on machines are five times more than that of women and girls doing the same job manually because the output of the latter is much less. Thus in the gem polishing industry of Jaipur women are clearly losing out to men over machines (Burra, 1988: 18).

KHADI INDUSTRY OF UTTAR PRADESH AND TAMILNADU

In this industry, a high proportion of spinners are girls and who have studied upto class-V and are waiting to be married. They earn about Rs.3/- to Rs.5/- a day, depending on their output, and save this money for dowry (Sinha, 1988). These contributions of girls are scarcely noticed and they are regarded as an economic burden, because their saving do not meet the requirements of dowry and the expenditure on their marriage and traditional post-marriage gifts (Nayar, 1991: 39).

BEEDI WORKERS OF NIZAMABAD (ANDRA PRADESH)

A report on *beedi* (Indian cigarette) workers of Nizamabad in Andra Pradesh states that the female children of this region rarely attend school. They stay at home to do the work their mothers can not do. And once they are sufficiently grown up they go to the factory to help their mothers. The adult female worker is paid at so low a rate that even in order to earn a pittance, she enlists the help of her female children (Burra, 1981: 19).

RAG-PICKERS OF BOMBAY AND BANGALORE CITIES

A substantial number of girl children are rag-pickers. Girl rag-pickers live in constant fear of sexual abuse. A rag-picker is one who makes his/her livelihood by picking up used waste papers, plastic scrap, rags, bottles, tins, metal pieces, discarded and broken containers from the dust bins, streets, garbage heaps and sell them to a nearby retailer. Rag-picking is not an easy way of making living even a meagre one. The rag-picker must have a certain sharpness for it is essential to chase a dump truck swiftly and be first on the line to glean the garbage. The rag-picker must also develop a knack for correctly ascertaining the content of a particular truck. Bangalore city has about 25,000 rag pickers – men, women, youth and children. Youngsters in the 8-20 age group form half of the number. They come mostly from Bangalore's slum and draught prone areas. Aiyer (1992) reports about the rag-pickers of Deonar. It is probably India's largest garbage dump, where an estimated 4,000 tons of trash from Bombay is strewn over five square kilometers of undulating land. Each day, a fleet of about 1,2000 trucks come to the site and the garbage they dump there provides a living of sorts to more than 15,000 rag-pickers, mostly women, teenagers and children as young as five year old girl Fahmida, the youngest in a family of seven.

"Fahmida is at the dump by 9 O'clock each morning along with her brother Salim, who is 17 year old. At an age when many of her more affluent contemporaries need help to tie their shoelaces, Fahmida swarms over each mound of garbage, picking out pieces of plastic, bottle caps and gunny. Every now and then, she adds whatever she has collected to a pile to which Salim also contributes his pickings (...). After the initial pushing and shoving to grab a choice piece of trash, serious gleaning begins with the rag pickers using an iron rod to dig into the garbage pile. When they are through, it is the turn of Fahmida and the other girl children, who sift through the garbage meticulously looking for less desirable but still saleable items.

At the end of the day, Fahmida and Salim take their collection to trader nearby, who weigh their offering and pay them at varying rates. If the rag-picker has not sorted out the trash into separate piles of plastic, polythene, paper and gunny sacking, then the rate is a flat 50 paise per kilogram (Aiyer, 1992: 9)."

DOMESTIC GIRL SERVANTS IN URBAN AREA

A special reference about domestic servants needs to be made. Quite a large number of girls are found to be engaged as servants in urban areas. Families find it convenient and economical to employ girls below 10 years for domestic chores. Such girls are readily available in the urban slum pockets. Her voice is feeble and her demands are relatively fewer than older domestic servants. She has no time limit, no specific job spelt out and no fixed wages. She is the bond slave of the family and the family takes pride and pleasure in owning her as girl servant of the family (Vasant, 1991: 67). In general the major work done by these girls are scrubbing the floors, cleaning the rooms, washing clothes, cleaning household utensils and in some cases cooking and serving of food. The other additional works are making beds for family members, fetching milk, escorting younger children to their schools, looking after the children, helping the housewife in the kitchen, looking after cattle or household pets (Kanungo, 1991: 222). It has been reported that girls domestic servants are bored and at risk of mental depression (Naidu and Parasuraman, 1985). They are often caught up in exploitative situation, especially when they are sexually abused by the males in the family.

Hence it is not only in the maintenance of the household but also in the engagement of productive work at home that the work of the female child goes unrecognised (Sing and Vittanen, 1987). If the work of women in home-based industry is invisible, this statement is more true, for their female children who help them in their work. In this section, the term "informalisation of employment" needs to be examined critically. This phrase refers to the response of the entrepreneurs in a competitive market by which they subcontract a number of jobs to dispersed households which are then performed by women and mainly their female children. This method of organisation of production is one way of evading stringent labour legislation.

V. WORKING GIRL CHILD AND EDUCATIONAL PROSPECTS

There is a close association between the work of young girls and that of their mothers. The mother might utilise her daughter's help in a part of her work in order to increase efficiency or wages. This may be especially true in the increasing number of female headed households in India. Because a daughter is of high utility to her mother in alleviating the heavy load of household work, child care and has the potential for paid labour, the mothers have somewhat negative attitude towards their education. This may be more so than the father's attitude. Evidence suggest that the girl children in India have received a raw deal in the matter of education (Kamat, 1973). In this regard they are treated as species of lower and secondary importance compared to boys. According to available statistics, girls in India are less in schools than boys. Fewer working girls attend school than boys. Very few complete primary education and only a small number can combine earning and learning. Studies have revealed that the drop out rate amongst girls is heavy (Bordia, 1986). Most working girls are illiterate. Long hours of work, the necessity at home to do household chores and mind younger siblings, reduce the possibility of any kind of schooling for girls.

Karlekar (1982: 126) in her study on women sweepers in Delhi states that female children are kept away from the educational process. Her respondents felt that daughters could help the family by looking after younger children so that mothers could be released for wage earning. If most mothers were somewhat motivated to keep their sons in school, fewer were so inclined for their daughters. Apart from the opportunity cost argument, women accepted the conventional sex stereotypes for their daughters; in addition they were pessimistic about the chances of their daughters achieving occupational or social mobility through education. Phoolbathi, a sweeper (respondent) told Karlekar that:

> "(...) nearly all our girls work as sweepers. Why should I waste my time and money on sending my daughters to school where she will learn nothing of use. ..... So why not put my girl to work so that she will learn something about our profession as well as be able to cook. My elder girl who is 15 years old will be married soon. Her mother-in-law will put her to cleaning latrines somewhere. Too much of schooling will only give girls big ideas, and then they will be beaten up by their husbands or be abused by their in-laws."

For every 100 boys who attend school in India there are only 55 girls. Enrollment of girls of 6-11 years is only 68 per cent in primary level. In group 11-14 years only 29 per cent girls attend school as against 54 per cent boys. In higher education there are only 40 girls for every 100 boys and in case of professional higher education the ratio is 15 girls for every 100 boys (Devasia and Devasia, 1991: 12-13).

VI. WORKING GIRL CHILDREN AND HEALTH HAZARDS

Childhood is the stage of personality development. Children in exploitative work are likely to suffer permanent adverse psychosocial consequences of the physical and emotional stress or work, combined with the denial of opportunity to play and interact fully with other children. Many of those children again become the victims of various occupational diseases.

Boudhiba (1982) reports that the girls who weave the magnificent carpet spend the entire day on narrow planks. They are unable to move and their work makes them adopt a squatting posture. Despite their youth, some children suffer from a form of ankylosis of the whole of the lower part of the torso. Many are sickly, suffering from tuberculosis or anemia. By the time they become adults, they are often round-shouldered and have deformed arms and legs. A large number of them are subsequently sterile or have very difficult pregnancies because of the fixed posture that they have had to adopt.

The *zari* embroidery industry where a large number of girls are working is another potentially hazardous industry. The eyesight of young girls working for 12-14 hours a day in the *zari* embroidery industry is reported to be damaged within a period of 5-8 years (Shah, 1985: 29). The effects of lead poisoning have been documented in *zari* brocade workers, who inhale very fine particles of zari (Banerji, 1979).

The *beedi* industry is another hazardous industry. In fact, *beedi* rolling leads the girl children to two types of occupational diseases. One is caused by the injurious effect of inhaling tobacco fume and the other is the result of long hours of continuous job. Diseases like TB, asthma, allergy and continuous cold belong to the former while backache, bodyache, stomach ache, gas trouble, piles and rheumatic complaints belong to the second category (Mohandas, 1980: 1522).

Similarly the girl children in the match industry work in extremely hazardous conditions. Iyengar (1980) states that children mixing chemicals in the boiler-room get lung fills of toxic fumes, suffer high degrees of intense heat and run the risk of being badly injured in fire accidents. Children who stamp frames on the metal sheet too suffer heat, toxic fumes and excessive strain on the arms and shoulders. Delay of a second can cause the entire frame to go up in roaring flames which could cause instant death. Fire accidents occur when match-heads rub against the friction side in the course of putting the box together too quickly. The children of match factories also complain of severe back – and neck-aches.

Severe malnutrition, anemia, hard labour, fatigue and inadequate sleep increase the girls susceptibility to infectious diseases. Rag picking girls are exposed to insanitary and infectious conditions (Nayar, 1991: 41). Because of the long incubation period of some diseases, it is difficult to convince people about the long term adverse effects of some occupations in which girl children are engaged (WHO, 1988).

VII. GOVERNMENT ACTS AND POLICIES

It is significant to note that neither the Employment of Children Act of 1938 nor the Child Labour (Prohibition and Regulation) Act of 1986 addresses the distinctive concerns of the female working child. Article 24 of the Indian constitution stresses that child labour is banned in factories, mines and hazardous employments and this is the premise on which the Child Labour (Prohibition and Regulation) Act, 1986 has been framed. It is important to point out here that majority of the girl workers, because of socio-cultural reasons, practise their trade at home. Very few are found to be working in factories and mines.

In case of hazardous employments, not much is known about hazardous work and the work "hazardous" itself has not been defined anywhere in the Act or in the Constitution.

The child labour (Prohibition and Regulation) Act of 1986 while designed to protect children working in industries only does so for those children who go out to work. The basic premise of labour legislation is that there must be an identifiable employer and an identifiable employee whose working conditions can be regulated and wage fixed. The Act explicitly denies protection to children working as part of family labour. With the exception of match industry where girls are visible workers, in almost all other industries, the girls are invisible workers and , as such, unprotected by the law. Majority of the child labour concentration areas having craft oriented home-based industries are inhabited by the Muslims. Whether it is gem-polishing industry of Jaipur, the lock industry of Aligarh, the carpet industry of Jammu and Kashmir or the zari embroidery of Varanasi, the constraint placed upon the muslim girl prevent her from going out of the house to work. Yet, there are large number of girl workers who practise their trade at home. The law is blind to their existence and deaf to their needs. In most cases they are not even recognised as workers by their own parents because their work is not directly remunerative even if it is productive. The girl child is seen as a helper and not as a worker in any of the industries where she is contributing her mite (Burra, 1988: 19). Sometimes, if the girl goes to work in a factory in place of her mother and is injured, she is not even paid compensation because she is seen as a stand-in for her mother. It is her mother who is supposed to be at work, but a lot of women (4 grade employees) enter their names on three or four muster and send their daughters in their place at a couple of factories. Thus in case of any injury, the owner does not give the daughter any compensation with the plea that her name is not even on the muster. Further the home-based piece rate workers are not included as workers in the Factories Act and so are not covered by most labour laws. Furthermore, most trades are not listed under the Minimum Wages Act and even where they are, home-based workers are not mentioned (Bhat, 1987: 30). Factory owners resort to giving work out on piece-rate wages to women at home because this is one way by which they can cut costs. Employers pay women low wages because they know that they will be helped by their children – mainly daughters. There is ample evidence to show that in part the exploitation of female child is directly a result of the exploitation of women (Barru, 1988: 14).

In pursuance of Constitutional mandates, the government of India has announced the formulation of a National Child Labour Policy. A child labour Technical Advisory Committee has been constituted to identify the hazardous processes and industries. The basic thrust of the National Child Labour Programme is to coordinate and intensify on-going developmental programmes for income generation and employment in child labour concentration areas. Thus aforesaid policy seeks to have a beneficial impact upon health, education and nutrition of the working child in a setting where different labour laws are better implemented. It covers only visible children and the policy, like the law, overlooks the female working child by default. When male working children receive the attention bestowed by governmental intervention, this will most likely reinforce in the minds of parents their already poor opinion of their female children. In turn, greater discrimination against them will follow (Nayar, 1991: 42).

VIII. Conclusions

Little girls, like their brothers, must be given their rights. First of all she must have a right to childhood – the right to be freed from working at a tender age. It is clear from the evidence presented above that there is significant differences in the situation of the female working child in India and that of its male counterpart. These differences manifest themselves in the gender typing of work. For a complex of socio-cultural reasons, the girl child is under-valued by parents. She is made to work very hard at home and outside but her economic contribution is never recognised. No value is placed on her need for education and as she grows up, her lack of education limit her opportunities in the labour market and she is relegated to low-paid, unskilled jobs. She undergoes deprivation related to very fact of her being as invisible home-based worker, who is usually not recognised as a worker at all, either by her own family or by the labour laws. She is the blind spot of child labour law, programme and policy. The legal system has been used as an effective tool in hands of the powerful sections to grant small concessions to the girl child. Devalued as a child, denied equal access to education and devoid of skills, she carries into her womanhood all the accumulated burden of her past.

Based upon our analysis, it is argued that there is special need for the study of this little big workforce as a separate category. More research is needed to illuminate the darkness that surrounds the working girl children in India.

References

Aiyer, V.S. (1992) "Living it Out in Garbage Fields." *Indian Express*: 1 March.

Banerji, S. (1979) *Child Labour in India*. London: Anti-Slavery Society.

Bhat, E. (1987) "The Invisibility of Home-Based Work: The Case of Piece Rate Workers in India." In Andrea M.Singh and Anita K.Vittanen (Eds): *Invisible Hands*. New Delhi: Sage publication.

Bordia, A. (1986) "Child Labour in India – Implications for Educational Planning." Paper presented at the ILO Regional Tripartite Workshop, Bangkok.

Boudhiba, A. (1982) Exploitation of Child Labour. Final Report. Special Rapporteur of the Sub-commission on prevention of Discrimination and protection of Minorities. New York: United Nation.

Burra, N. (1981) "Beedi Workers of Nizamabad," *Economic and Political Weekly*. 8 August.

Burra, N. (1988) "Out of Sight, Out of Mind: the Female Working Child in India." Paper presented at a workshop on "the Girl Child" for the SAARC, India International Centre, New Delhi.

Devasia, L. and Devasia, V.V. (1991) "The Struggle for Survival of the Girl Child." In L. Devasia and V.V. Devasia (Eds): *Girl Child in India*. New Delhi: Ashish Publishing House.

Gulati, L. Child Labour in Kerala's Coir Industry – Study of a few Selected Villages. Trivandrum: Centre for Development Studies (unpublished).

Iyengar, V.L. (1986) "Child Labour in the Match Units of Southern Tamilnadu." Paper presented at a Seminar on Child Labour in India. New Delhi: Indian Social Institute.

Jain, D. (1990) "Improving the Lot of Working Girl Child." *Kurukshetra*, 14 November.

Joseph, S. (1991) "Girl Child Worker – A Victim Invisible." *Kurukshetra*, August.

Juyal, B.N. et al. (1985) *Child Labour: The Twice Exploited*. Varanasi: Gandhian Institute of Studies.

Kamat, A.R. (1973) *The Education Situation and other Essays on Education*. New Delhi: People's Publishing House.

Kanungo, J. (1991) "The Young Girls Helping us in our Household Work." in R.N. Pati (Eds): *Rehabilitation of Child Labourers in India*. New Delhi: Asish Publishing House.

Karlekar, M. (1982) *Poverty and Women's Work*: A study of Sweeper Women in Delhi. New Delhi: Vikas Publishing House.

Khatu, K.K. et al. (1983) *Working Children in India*. Baroda: Operations Research Group.

M.I.D.S. (1985) *The Match Industry in Sivakasi, Sattur: Towards Removal of Child Labour*. Madras: Madras Institute of Development Studies.

Mohandas, M. (1980) "Beedi Workers in Kerala: Condition of Life and Work." *Ecomomic and Political Weekly, XV(36)*.

Moulik, T.K. and Purushotom, P. (1982) "The Match Industry in Sivakasi – A case study of Technology, Working conditions and Employments." *Economic and Political Weekly, XVII*.

Naidu, U.S. and Parasuraman, S. (1985) "Health Situation of Working Children in Greater Bombay," (WHO sponsored Study) Bombay : Tata Institute of Social Sciences (Mimeo).

Nair, R. (1983) "Education: Why do more girls drop out?" *Kurukshetra, XXXI(13)*.

Nayar, U.S. (1991) "Labour of the Indian Girl Child: Multi-Curse, Multi-Abuse and Multi-Neglect." *The Indian Journal of Social Work, L11(1)*.

Oldman, D. (1994) "Adult-Child Relations as Class Relations." In Jens Qvortrup et al. (Eds): *Childhood Matters – Social Theory, Practice and Politics*. England: Avebury.

Patil, B.R. (1986) "Child Workers in Bangalore – I." *Financial Express*, 3 January.

Qvortrup, J. (1991) Childhood as a Social Phenomenon – An Introduction to a series of National Reports (2 edn.). *Eurosocial Report 36/0*. Vienna: European Centre for Social Welfare Policy and Research.

Qvortrup, J. (1994) "Childhood Matters: An Introduction." In Jens Qvortrup et al. (Eds): *Childhood Matters – Social Theory, Practice and Politics*. England: Avebury.

Shah, P.M. (1985) "Alternative Health Approaches for the Health Care of Working Children." In P.M. Shah and N. Cantwell (Eds): *Child Labour: A Threat to Health and Development*. Geneva: Defence for Children International.

Shamgar-Handelaman, L. (1994) "To whom does Childhood belong?" In Jens Qvortrup et al. (Eds): *Childhood Matters Social Theory, Practice and Politics*. England: Avebury.

Singh, A.M. and Vittanen, A.K. (Eds) (1987) *Invisible Hands*. New Delhi: Sage Publication.

UNICEF (1990) *Children and Women in India: A Situation Analysis*.

Vasant, F. (1991) "Prevailing Conditions of Girl Child." In J.A. Williams (Eds): *An Anatomy of Girl Child*. Madras.

J. CHRISTOPHER DANIEL

Ethical Aberration in Using Children for Endorsing Consumer Products

A Cross Cultural Study

Children are born free and equal, yet often find a paradoxical mix of reception and uncertain future, hope and despair.They are the most powerless and vulnerable human beings whose needs are the most immediate.

In article 17(a) of the UN Convention of the Rights of the Child it is affirmed that the State shall encourage the mass media to disseminate information and materials of Social and Cultural benefit to the Child and (17e) encourage the development of appropriate guidelines for the protection of the child from information and material injuries to his or her well being. Further it is declared in article 34(c) of the UN Convention of the Rights of the Child, the States Parties undertake to protect the child from all forms of sexual exploitation and sexual abuse and in particular take all appropriate measures to prevent the exploitative use of children in pornographic performances and materials.

The Subject of the use of children in advertising is becoming a major concern in developed and developing countries. In fact, the use of children per se is not only a form of abuse but also as "exploitative human objects". While one is delighted to see children appearing in advertisements, how ethical is it to make them recommend Consumer Products especially those not directly meant for them? Do advertisements in which children appear, focus on encouraging healthy habits and positive attitudes among the children? Are these advertisements making developmental or anti developmental messages to children? "The World of Advertising continues to use children as objects and misuse to peddle all kinds of products." Most of the children have begun accepting advertising as part of their daily habit. They are often led to believe that they are immune to advertising because they are aware of its motives and it has become part of their life.

Hal Huninelstein (1984) cites a summary of "Social Science findings regarding children's cognitive development and its relation to advertising" by Jonathan Prince(1978) to the effect that at the age of five or Six, children have trouble distinguishing fantasy from reality and make believe from lying. They do not distinguish programs from advertisements, and may even prefer

E. Verhellen (ed.), Monitoring Children's Rights, 817–822.

the ads. Children at the age of 7-10 are most vulnerable to televised manipulation. By 10, this has begun to turn into the cynical view that "ads always lie". Young (1990) has observed that due to their lack of experience, young children have less resistance to advertising and it may be especially harmful because of their inability to distinguish it from other programming. He has further stated that the content of advertising has been subjected to much criticism. Stereotyping and the raising of children's expectations higher than they can be fulfilled might be stressed.

According to Brian M. Young (1990) "T.V. in general has also changed the image of the child in modern society and advertisements may amplify the change. In earlier times, children were regarded as 'Sweet' and 'different' - incapable of adult responses. Now there is a tendency to portray them as 'Kids' – Streetwise, amusing, interested in excitement and fast action. They are seen as living in an age of innocence – trusting, naive, uncritical. Adults who act upon this stereotype are likely to regard television advertising as unmitigated evil, seducing and taking advantage of the innocent and defenceless."

One study found that 79 percent of American mothers believed television commercials were misleading their children (Advertising: Views of Children, New York times, April 3, 1974). The most resented ads were those for junk foods, sugary cereals, flavoured vitamins and dangerous toys. In 1973, the Canadian Broadcasting Corporation agreed to drop all commercials from shows aimed at children age 12 or younger.

In Australia, the Broadcasting Control Board set up strict rules for children's advertising on T.V. Child actors in the ads must be well-mannered and respectful of their parents; children may not be urged to pressure their parents to buy a particular product; personalities and characters from children's programs may not endorse products; and no ad may imply that a product makes its power superiors to peers; or that the lack of a product could lead to ridicule. (Aussie Guidelines in Kidvid, "Variety", July 25, 1973). The Chairman of the U.S. Federal Trade Commission (1974), Lewis A. Engman called for tighter federal controls on premium offers, on commercials that exploit children and anxieties or their propensity to confuse reality and fantasy, on the use of hero figures, on advertisements for dangerous toys, on children's Vitamin commercials. He added "the advertiser who chooses a child audience as a target for his selling message is subject not only to the standards of truthful advertising; he is in my judgement, also bound to deal in complete fairness with his young viewers (New York Times, June 1974)."

The Government of France has banned using children for endorsing products in advertisements.

The use of children in pornographic elements is evident from the study conducted by the Institute for the Study of Media and Family, Haifa, Israel, as reported by the Israel Branch of W.C.I, 1989. It is reported that Israeli Advertising frequently combines use of babies and children with pornographic elements. Pornography in its different forms presents children as "Sexual objects", showing children who take sexual initiatives with adults and as persons who enjoy sexual abuse. The Advertisers in Israel use the pornographic elements in all mainstream media – newspapers, magazines, cinema etc. It is stated in Article 34(e) that the accumulative exposure to pictures of children as legitimate sexual objects has the potential to influence the perceptions of children as sexual partners. Most countries have established an advertising Code of Practice plus pertinent laws to guarantee their compliance. Nonetheless, cases of misleading and unethical advertisements which portray children are legendary.

METHODOLOGY

The method used in this study was content analysis. This is frequently used in the study of cross-cultural studies [Rice and Lu, 1988, Hong, Muderrisogh and Zinkhan, 1987, Frith and Wesson, 1991]. The unit of analysis was restricted to product advertisements containing children. For the purpose of this research, two general interest magazines namely "India Today" and "Frontline" published in India and Two American Magazines "TIME" and "Newsweek" were chosen for analysis. A total of 90 advertisements from "India Today" and "Frontline" and 30 advertisements from "TIME" and "Newsweek" were scanned. These advertisements were analysed in term of the texts including themes, informational contents and appeals. Advertisements which feature Single Child and Children in a group/family context during the period 1992–1993 were collected and used as the data sources for this study. Product wise classification of advertisements was made namely (1) Infant Milk Substitutes (2) Toiletries (3) Soft beverages (4) Electronics (5) Pharmaceuticals (6) Automotive (7) Domestic appliances (8) Toys and play materials (9) Textiles and Children's wear (10) Travel and Holiday Resorts (11) Confectionaries, and (12) Life Health Insurance.

DISCUSSION

Generally there are few similarities in the portrayals of children in advertisements. While ferreting out the issues of these magazines, it was found that there were only limited number of advertisements featuring children in the American magazines as compared to Indian magazines. It stands to reason that the use of children in products advertisements in the American magazines was restricted. Presumably, it might be due to the pressure given by Citizen groups and also the strict adherence of Advertising Codes followed by the Advertisers in the U.S. It is reported that these Action groups continue to push for strong regulations in this regard. But the Indiscriminate use of children in product advertisements in India is evident from the number of advertisements which portray both male and female children. There are no marked differences in the Indian as well as the US ads in terms of the role portrayals of children. The imaginary and magical role portrayals used in the ads from the US magazines are limited to a considerable extent and exaggeration of facts beyond all limits is conspicuous by its absence. In the Indian Magazines; male children are given important role portrayals in product advertisements whereas female children are given supplementary roles. Most of the adventurous roles are featured by male children whereas females are given submissive roles. Another interesting feature is the portrayal of a male child and a female child together in advertisements in a family context.

As regards the themes and appeals of advertisements showing children in Indian magazines it is evident that most of the advertisements feature role portrayals of children as models to enumerate the virtues of Chocolates, toffees, bubble gums, biscuits, food and energy drinks, which often distort the perception of child viewers. For undergoing James Bond, Superman or Spiderman like adventures or to win a boxing contest, children have to eat certain biscuits or drink certain energy drinks.

"I got it! shouts a tiny girl in a two-piece suit with a two-in-one in her hand. In another advertisement for Television, a young boy is portrayed as one with a tonsured head fitted with two horns of an animal and a long coiled tail making an appeal like 'Villians fighting in your living room', Cuddle up with a heroine in your bed room; Here's your chance to have all your romantic dreams come true."

The rampant exploitation of children in India in the World of advertising is potent when an advertiser went to a village and took a snap of a dirty girl. She was happy that she had been selected for an advertisement. However, she was horrified when she saw in the papers an advertisement carrying her picture. It said, "If you have a child like this, ours is the soap you should use."

In another advertisement of photocopying machine which is not directly meant for children, a School going boy makes a bold statement, "I refuse to go by the book anymore". It is noticed from another advertisement that a girl child recommending a movie of leading a South Indian Actor, which is not a film for children. We often see Indian children in the Advertisements for Refrigerators, Washing Machines etc.

Obviously enough, children can be easily carried into a fantasy world by portraying convincingly anything to them. So even harmful products can be sold to children if they are glamorously advertised. Furthermore, when children are shown in advertisements either as a Single Child or in a group/family context recommending certain products, child Viewers 'Continue' to buy them or pester their parents to buy for children for they (children) do not care about the nutritive value of the products. Their attraction is mainly centred around "taste" and "looks". There is a growing concern among parents that using children in the media for endorsing food products at least should not be allowed. Many Indian advertisements for food products make the following appeal "Would you like your child to grow strong, successful and intelligent? Then use our product. These advertisements carry visuals of a child "before" and "after" consuming the product. This kind of "magical formula" and emotional black mail of parents put them at their wits'end. These advertisements inject the fixed feeling in the minds of parents that if their children are not fed with product, they would not be as plumpy and strong or intelligent as the ones in the advertisement.

An analysis of 10 Indian advertisements of infant foods, milk substitutes and feeding bottles reveal the fact that the advertising texts, informational content, appeals and visuals images made in the containers of the products are glaring violations of the "Infant Milk substitutes, Feeding Bottles and Infant Foods [regulation of Production, Supply and Distribution] Act 1992. The Act prohibits "pictures of an infant or a woman or both, or have pictures or other graphic material, or phrases designed to increase the saleability. All these products carry disallowed pictures giving false messages. For instance, in the Commercial advertising of a famous brand of infant food, four babies are seen clamouring for it while another one tom toms the advantages of feeding bottle. Words like "full protein", complete food or energy food though out of bound, could be found widely.

It was found that in an Indian advertisement in which a child is seen asking "What shall we buy if we win this lottery?", to which her mother replies "First let us buy the lottery tickets!!!" In another advertisement for toothpaste, children are assured that they can eat any amount of Cake or Chocolate but their teeth would be protected by the use of the toothpaste.

In point of fact, the subject of children endorsing products in advertisements which are not directly meant for them or glamorising harmful products in advertisements meant for children deserves rapt attention because children are highly vulnerable. At the same time their sense of distinction is questionable since they do not have proper access to the right information. The norms of the Advertising Standards Council of India States, inter alia, that "advertisements addressed to children shall not contain anything which might result in their physical, mental or moral harm or which exploits their vulnerability".

Scientific evidences reveal the fact that products such as Chocolates containing Nickel, Soft drinks containing brominated Vegetable oil, certain noodles containing mono-Sodium glutamate are being endorsed by children in advertisements. How many parents are aware of the harmful effects these hazardous elements will have on their children? Should advertisements for such products, especially making children appear and endorse them, be banned? Is it not an exercise of misinformation made by commercial advertisers when proven facts are hidden or refuted? Aren't the product advertisements meant for children carrying dangerous anti-development messages?.

While certain countries in the West have banned using children for endorsing products in advertisements, in India there is no specific law which prohibits employing children to appear in product advertisements (which exceed the norms set by the Advertising Standards Council of India). The children (Pledging of Labour) Act, 1933 prohibits the making the agreements to pledge the labour of children, and the employment of children whose labour has been pledged under such an agreement. The Act extends to the whole of India. Child, under the Act means a person who is under the age of fifteen years. An agreement to pledge the labour of a child is void. There is an escaping proviso in the Act that consideration of any benefit other than reasonable wages to be paid for the child services and terminable at not more than a week's notice, is not an agreement within the meaning of agreement to pledge labour of a child under the Act. The Act is required to be amended to empower the competent authorities to exercise some sort of control so that indiscriminate use of children in advertisements and indiscreet endorsement of products by children could be prohibited, which would do more harm to society than good.

Advertisements featuring children to endorse consumer products encourage wrong priorities in life, bad habits, false and misleading claims, bad taste, wastefulness, simplemindness, rapid erosion of the positive aspects of indigenous culture and products, production and sales of luxurious, superfluous and harmful products while the basic needs of numerous disadvantaged children remain unfulfilled.

ANNE-MARIE POREYE-THYS

Exploitation and Violation of Children's Rights

An Action Carried out in Belgium since
January 1993 – INFOKIOSK Service and Pink Lines

Belgacom, the successor to R.T.T., has been offering for some time now a new service called "INFOKIOSK". Through this service, Belgacom rents its lines to companies or other persons for commercial purposes. Belgacom issues the invoices, but the profits are shared between Belgacom and the hirer.

If a telephone bill issued by Belgacom indicates BF40000 for "INFO" services for example, this amount is shared between Belgacom and the hirer. Of course, one must not forget the VAT, which represents a significant profit for the Ministry for Finance.

The Infokiosk service offers a "pink line" alongside the so-called serious ones.

The pink line is connected to a telephone number which generally replays a pre-recorded message, always erotic or pornographic, with a particular message being allocated to each specific number. These messages offer a whole series of possibilities, from soft to hard, ranging from sadomasochistic lines to exchange lines, to lines featuring teenagers, to party lines, or even to lines where one can leave one's phone number.

Infokiosk offers services other than the pink lines: stock exchange rates, some local radio stations, television games, etc. These lines all have the same prefix code – 077 – and the invoice indicates only "Infokiosk".

A company renting lines from Belgacom acquires the use of the pink lines and the others at the same time. The last page of the telephone directory contains the names of the impressive number of companies which rent the lines, but does not, of course, contain any mention of the pink lines. If one tries to telephone these companies, there is never any reply. On closer scrutiny of this last page of the telephone directory, one may notice that many of these companies have the same postal address: "Rue de la Presse", for example.

In Belgium, everybody, including children and teenagers, has access to these lines via private or public telephones. The cost of these calls is not clearly decipherable, and it is only with the help of a magnifying glass that one can decipher the cost (BF5.98 every 20 seconds). Therefore, nothing prevents a child or an adolescent from availing of these facilities in the

E. Verhellen (ed.), Monitoring Children's Rights, 823–828.
© 1996 *Kluwer Law International. Printed in the Netherlands.*

absence of their parents, facilities which are in principle reserved for adults. Of course the invoice will consequently be sent to the parents costed under "Infokiosk".

Telephone subscribers may, however, request cancellation of their access to "Infokiosk" and accordingly to the pink line, by means of payment of BF650 + VAT.

Why should action be carried out against this pink line?

Free commercial papers, newspapers and weekly magazines advertise a telephone number: 077. Allowing access to these lines by children and young people constitutes an abuse by the company and therefore ill-treatment of children. Minors, who are prohibited from entering brothels, are allowed free access to these lines, regardless of age, which surely constitutes an incitement to debauchery and an act of indecent exposure.

Infokiosk is a commercial enterprise, run by Belgacom for purposes of viability and increasing its turn-over, regardless of the consequences. The risks involved are not taken into account. Télé-Accueil Brussels, where the under-signed is responsible for the service "ill-treated children", has shown its civic-mindedness and has set out to protect youth against the dupery which is in constant evolution given the publicity allocated to it in the press.

A halt must be put to children becoming victims of exploitation by adults and these adult games damaging the lives of children. Politicians can only intervene if citizens and those working on the ground expose what they see, what they hear, what they notice. One may well imagine that it would be very difficult for Belgacom to abandon this special service if one looks at the enormous profits made by this company since the installation of the pink lines by the Infokiosk service (more than BF700million).

Services whose aim is to prevent ill-treatment and assist the victims of ill-treatment want to make the message clear that this practice raises a real danger for children.

At a time when more and more parents are spending longer periods away from the home for economic reasons, when more and more children are inclined to drop out of school, the facility of access to pink lines constitutes an additional danger in this climate of ill-treatment. How can certain children distinguish between the open condonation of paedophilia (as via the pink lines) and the prevention campaigns carried out in certain schools against pedophelia?

Many complaints have been made by parents to Télé-Accueil about the pink lines; parents confronted with enormous telephone bills (ranging from BF50000 to BF100000). Belgacom had cut off their telephones and the only way to get re-connected was to pay the bill. They were looking for help. How could they react towards Belgacom?

These parents also asked for assistance in coping with their children whose behaviour had suddenly changed. In general the complaints of the parents were that the school was deploring the deterioration in the children's schoolwork, that the children had suddenly become very aggressive towards their parents, that their language had changed, becoming more and more vulgar, even obscene, according to some parents.

Some parents reported that their children, whose access to the pink lines had been stopped, acted as if they had withdrawal symptoms. "She acts like a drug addict", stated one father. Some of these parents brought a court action against Belgacom. Some parents were able to talk to the school psychologist, together with their child. Others were too ashamed to lodge a complaint. Sex is still a taboo subject, and some parents feel unable to admit openly that their child has been manipulated by the adults who operate these pink lines.

In the Netherlands, where this practice has been widespread for several years now, groups similar to the A.A. have been set up to assist in the detoxification of pink line addicts.

The anti-pink line campaign was launched in January 1993, because a listener of Télé-Accueil drew our attention to an advertisement in a free commercial paper which was attempting to attract prospective readers; advertisements such as "horny schoolgirls" or "their first time" - "dial 077". These advertisements had definite paedophilic connotations.

When one dials the number, one can note that the message is pre-recorded, and that the voices are indeed those of young girls, who are acting out the scenario. "A young girl"...

Télé-Accueil (through the intermediary of AMADE) started warning the people professionally involved in the combat against ill-treatment of children. A joint action was set up. Each association involved sent a letter to the Public Prosecutors, to newspapers, to famous people and to various State authorities.

This letter, dated 18.02.93, exposed:
— The exploitation of children through pink lines, and the suggestive scenarios proposed in these pink lines;
— The accessibility of these telephone numbers 24 hours a day to all and sundry, including children and youngsters;
— The distribution of these telephone numbers, via normal communication networks (free commercial papers, newspapers, weekly magazines);
— The consequences of these practices, leading to paedophilia becoming a regular feature of normal life.

We petitioned:
— that all practices involving sexual utilisation of children in pink lines be stopped incessantly;
— that the contents of the messages be checked regularly and on the long term;
— that Belgacom be ordered to charge a fee for access to the pink lines and not the contrary, as is the case at present (A subscriber who wishes to have the "Infokiosk" line cut off must pay BF650 + VAT).

Newspapers and media broadcast widely our petition: La Libre Belgique, La Lanterne, La Meuse, Le Peuple, La Nouvelle Gazette, Le Vif Express, La Cité, En Marche, Flair, RTBF, RTL, Tele21, TV5 as well as some radio stations, broadcast our petition.

One free commercial newspaper, which had previously been advertising the pink line, reacted strongly, thanking us for our intercession, "our sense of enterprise, and our continual search for customers blinded us. But thanks to your intercession we have remedied the situation". And indeed, no further advertisement appeared in this paper.

Acknowledgements of receipt, reactions, intercessions, reminders, requests for aid, letters were forwarded to us from various Ministers, in particular from Guy Coëme, Minister for Communications, and Melchior Wathelet, Minister for Justice.

Belgacom, in a letter of 31.03.93, stated that it was not its function to judge the nature and the contents of telephone calls.

The Police of Brussels, on behalf of the Court of Mons, registered and recorded our action.

The Public Prosecutors of Neufchateau, Dinant and Huy informed us that they had acknowledged our action and would take the necessary steps to remedy the situation.

In June 1993, through the intermediary of Télé-Accueil, 600 persons sent a letter of protest against these pink lines to Mr Bessel Kok, Director of Belgacom.

In July 1993, Senator 't Serclaes, Head of the PSC Group, raised a question with the Minister of Communications, regarding the protection of minors in the use of the Belgacom network for telephone lines with sexual connotations. The media echoed this question.

On 13 July 1993, the Judicial Police of Brussels summoned the associations which had brought actions before the Public Prosecutor to a hearing (Télé-Accueil, AMADE, SOS Viol.).

In July 1993, Mrs Ernst de la Graete sent a written question to the European Commission regarding the pink lines. Around the same time, Swiss and Spanish newspapers published stories relating to disagreements in their countries between the telecommunications companies and their Departments for Justice.

In September 1993, Belgacom called a meeting between representatives of its company, Test Achats, the "serious" telephone lines, Télé-Accueil and a mediator. Each party expressed its point of view, which was not always shared. Télé-Accueil advocated the cause of ill-treated children. The participants in the meeting suggested certain guidelines, such as separate telephone numbers for pink lines and for other commercial lines, the suppression of pink lines via public call boxes, the creation of an Ethics Committee, similar to that set up in England, for example, the restriction of access by Belgacom to pink lines, free of charge. This latter point was a touchy one, given that there is no problem with vigilant parents, but that the problem arises particularly with the type of parents whom Télé-Accueil represents.

In November 1993 the Cabinet of the Minister for Justice, under the chairmanship of Mr Nouwynck, invited the various organisations to a round table conference. The participants were: representatives of the Ministers for Communications and for Justice, of Belgacom, of Test Achats, the legal Adviser to Mr Lelièvre – Youth Adviser, PSC Senator 't Serclaes, representatives of "Femmes Prévoyantes Socialistes" and of Télé-Accueil – Mrs Poreye and Attorney Thibaut de Maisières and Mr Van de Meulebroecke, legal expert, who was preparing an article for the Court newspaper.

At the end of the meeting, Mr Nouwynck presented a draft bill, aimed at a strict control of advertising for pink lines.

In December 1993, a vast legal inquiry was carried out all over Belgium. Roughly a thousand recorded tapes were seized. The Public Prosecutor promised that the persons principally responsible in the networks would be questioned without further delay.

Our action was geared thus towards informing the public in the first place of the danger of this practice, through the media and the press.

The action was centred around three levels:

technical level:
- That serious lines and pink lines have a different prefix code. It was hoped that this would materialise and become operational as of end 1994.
- The request that the subscribers who wished to have access to pink lines be charged for this facility instead of the opposite has been shelved by the responsible authorities.
- The request that the lines 077 no longer be available from public call boxes is materialising insofar as it is technically possible (Belgacom often uses technical problems as an excuse).

legal level:
- Matters are following their course. The "Renard" affair, which hit the headlines, most certainly helped to advance the issue. (A mother of an adolescent, a shopkeeper, whom Belgacom threatened to cut off her telephone because she had refused to pay an excessive telephone bill for Infokiosk, obtained a provisional court order forbidding the cutting off of her telephone).
- Around this time, one of the deputy directors of Belgacom, Mr Remiche, was charged with sexual abuse, incitement to debauchery and prostitution.

The third and legislative level, is the most important.
Measures to be taken:

- Only measures preventing advertising of pink lines can block the upsurge and proliferation of these lines. Why? Because neither technical measures nor judicial actions within the framework of the current penal code can brake this new evolution of the pornographic industry. Technically speaking, any laws imposed on Belgacom cannot be transposed to other telecommunication systems of other countries (France, United Kingdom), who exercise the right of exploitation in Belgium.
- On the other hand, can legal proceedings be instigated against companies which have access to Belgian lines, but which are based in the furthest corners of the earth (Australia, Singapore)? For example, Israel prohibited pink telephones. But the newspapers are full of advertisements for pink telephones located in other countries yet capable of communicating within that country.
- The preliminary draft bill, which would insert an additional Article in the Penal Code, would penalise any publicity, direct or indirect, aimed at advertising any office of sexual services.

This preliminary draft bill was submitted to the Council of State, which approved it. The Senate and the Chamber will vote in favour of it in the near future, thus ensuring that children will be safeguarded against certain adult games and pleasures detrimental to them.

LIEVE STAPPERS

Les droits de l'enfant dans le sport

PREAMBULE

Personne n'ignore à quel point la pratique régulière d'un sport est importante pour le développement physique, social et l'affirmation de la personnalité des enfants. La compétition sportive offre également aux enfants une possibilité fantastique de découvrir leurs possibilités, confrontées à des situations déterminées, de jauger leurs capacités de domination de soi, de faire preuve de tolérance vis-à-vis des autres.

A côté des nombreux aspects positifs que la pratique du sport de compétition peut apporter aux enfants, il faut toutefois tenir compte également de la méconnaissance de la spécificité propre des enfants dans ce milieu sportif. Le monde du sport est d'ailleurs un monde organisé et règlementé par les adultes où la spécificité de l'enfant peut être mise en péril.

La preuve que ces manques de considération à l'égard des enfants sont bien réels, nous est fournie par le fait qu'au cours de ces dernières années, on doit constater que de plus en plus de questions sont posées par les parents, les organisations de défense des intérêts de l'enfant et le monde scientifique. "L'importance accordée à la prestation fournie et la victoire n'est-elle pas exagérée, ce qui provoque un stress trop grand, un degré trop élevé d'entrainement et une agression sur le plan pédagogique? Les enfants ne sont-ils pas souvent dans le cadre de règlements fédéraux déterminées considérés comme de la marchandise et traités comme tels?"

Voilà les questions à côté de tant d'autres, qui ont été posées à trois organisations privées, Sporta, de BGJG (Bond van Grote en van Jonge Gezinnen) et NDO (Nationaal Diensten- en Onderzoekscentrum voor het Spelende Kind).

Suite à ces questions et soucises du bien-être de l'enfant pratiquant le sport, ces trois organisations ont lancé - au mois de mai - en Flandres un projet abordant les droits de l'enfant dans le milieu sportif.

Le climat pour entamer une telle action était d'ailleurs le plus favorable qu'il soit. Grâce à la convention de 1989 des Nations Unies concernant les droits de l'enfant, l'attention pour la place et les intérêts de l'enfant dans le monde sportif a été totalement accrue.

E. Verhellen (ed.), Monitoring Children's Rights, 829–834.

I. L'ACTION ELLE-MÊME

Nous retrouvons à différents endroits le souci en Belgique de l'acceuil de l'enfant dans le monde du sport et le respect de ses droits.

II. L'ACTION DE SPORTA, NDO ET BGJG

Ces trois organisations ont présenté le projet "les droits de l'enfant dans le monde du sport" lors d'une conférence de presse du 18/05/1993 en présence du Ministre de la Communauté Flamande compétant. Ce projet a vu le jour suite aux lettres de parents mécontents et scandalisés par les règlements des Fédérations où les enfants étaient considérés comme de la marchandise et traités comme tels. Cela concernait plus précisément les règlements de transfert de la KBBB (Koninklijke Belgische Basketbalbond) et de la KBVB (Koninklijke Belgische Voetbalbond).

Ce n'est pas par hasard que ces deux fédérations ont refusé d'adapter leur règlement au décret du 25 février 1975 constatant le statut du sportif non payé (d'application en Flandres). C'est par ce texte législatif que l'autorité essaie de lutter contre quelques abus dans le monde du sport. Le fait de lier quelqu'un sa vie durant à un club ou une fédération fait partie de ces excès, ce qui est en totale contradiction avec la liberté d'association, l'autorité parentale et le fait d'être membre à part entière d'une société.

Le fait que la problématique des transferts dans le sport en Belgique soit si actuelle en ce qui concerne les enfants, du fait de la convention de 1989 concernant les droits de l'enfant, puisse maintenant être combattue sur le plan juridique, a permis à ces trois organisations de mettre le doigt sur le caractère de respect ou non de l'enfant dans le sport. Il existe également d'autres atteintes au non respect de l'enfant dans le monde du sport liées à la personnalité des enfants eux-mêmes et qui sont totalement combattues tel que les entraînements physiques inadaptés, les prestations violentes, le fait de devoir rester assis souvent sur les bancs pour les moins bons joueurs, la manière dont les différents avec les enfants sont traités...

III. SERVICE TÉLÉPHONIQUE

Le projet commença par la mise en place d'un service téléphonique. Pendant une période de 6 semaines, chacun a pu prendre contact avec ces trois organisations pour dénoncer le non respect de la personnalité de l'enfant en matière sportive.

Ces informations ont permis à Sporta, NDO et BGJG, sur base d'éléments matériels, d'envisager des changements législatifs, règlementaires et de mentalité.

IV.   CHANGEMENTS LÉGISLATIFS

En vue de changements législatifs, des experts furent recrutés aussi bien des services proprement dits, du Bloso, du cabinet du Ministre Weckx que de la Communauté Flamande et bien entendu des gens sur le terrain.

Leur mission consistait à rendre effective la législation applicable à savoir le décret concernant le statut du sportif non payé. Ceci dans le cadre des droits et libertés élémentaires, en premier orde, du jeune sportif non payé. Le but en était d'empêcher les associations sportives d'ignorer plus longtemps ce décret. Monsieur Stéphane Van Mulders, conseiller juridique du déparement Bien-Etre, Santé et Culture du Ministère de la communauté flamande, dirigeait les activités du groupe de travail. Ces activités résultaient d'un projet de décret qui constaterait le statut du sportif non professionnel. Ce projet fut transmis au Ministre compétent et par ce dernier pour avis, au conseil supérieur flamand pour le sport. Cet avis a déjà été rendu. Les trois organisations espèrent que le Ministre introduira le plus rapidement possible ce projet de décret auprès du conseil de la Communauté flamande. Il est intéressant de remarquer dans les commentaires, qu'il est expressément renvoyé à la Convention des Nations Unies de 1989 concernant les droits de l'enfant. On doit constater que la protection des droits de l'enfant est une condition nécessaire prévue dans ce projet.

V.   MODIFICATIONS DE RÈGLEMENT

En ce qui concernent les modifications de règlement, différentes réunions ont été organisées avec les différentes fédérations de sport tel que la KBVB (Koninklijke Belgische Voetbalbond), la KBBB (Koninklijke Belgische Basketbalbond) et la VSF (Vlaamse Sportfederatie). Il fut clairement attirer l'attention des fédérations sur le fait que dans le monde du sport, l'intérêt de l'enfant devait primer sur les aspects sportifs et financiers du club de sport ou de la fédération de sport. Cet intérêt de l'enfant, dont celui-ci est le meilleur juge, est repris explicitement dans les articles 3 et 12 de la convention des Nations Unies. L'attention fut particulièrement attirée sur le fait que les fédérations de sport, si elles devaient faire comparaître des enfants devant des juridictions internes, devaient adapter ces comparutions à la spécificité propre des enfants.

Il est apparu que l'ambiance formaliste, la présence de nombreux membres de la commission, l'emploi solennel de la langue, la présence de la partie adverse... faisaient trop d'impression sur l'enfant. Ces procédures trop lourdes empêchent le mineur d'expliquer son point de vue.

C'est avant tout la pression de l'inérêt des médias pour ce projet que la KBVB a adapté son règlement pour les jeunes. Malgré ces adaptations la liberté de l'enfant de jouer dans le club de son choix n'est toujours pas garantie de manière optimale. Si un enfant contre la volonté de son club d'origine veut changer au profit d'un autre club, ce nouveau club devra toujours payer une certaine somme d'argent (15.000 F par saison jouée). On peut se demander à bon droit si de tels transferts ne tombent pas sous l'application 35 de la convention des Nations Unies laquelle interdit "le commerce ou la vente d'enfants".

Que se passe-t-il si le nouveau club ne paie pas le montant, l'enfant est alors souvent obligé de mettre fin à ses activités de football.

C'est ici un manquement à l'article 31 point 1 de la convention des Nations Unies, qui reconnaît le droit à la participation aux jeux.

Le règlement modifié pour les jeunes du KBBB est souvent moins en ligne de mire. Pourtant celui-ci est plus mauvais que celui de KBVB. Ce règlement prévoit la possibilité jusqu'à l'âge de 16 ans de prêter annuellement un joueur à un autre club moyennant le paiement d'un loyer de 15.000 F. Lorsqu'on atteint l'âge de 15 ans, on retourne à son club de départ et les tractations financières commencent.

VI. Changement de Mentalité

Pour les trois organisations il est clair que les modifications législatives et le changement de règlement ne sont pas suffisants.

Dans le monde du sport, les enfants doivent être approchés depuis leur propre milieu de vie. Ceci est clairement une question de mentalité. Pas seulement pour les clubs de sport ou fédérations de sport mais également pour les entraîneurs, parents, professeurs de sport,...

VII. Enquête

Les trois organisations sont d'avis qu'un meilleur examen des motivatons des enfants pour faire du sport, rendrait possible une meilleure introduction de l'enfant dans le monde du sport. En collaboration avec la facultés universitaires d'Anvers, département des sciences politiques et sociales, a demarré une enquête dans le monde du sport chez les enfants. Les résultats de cette enquête doivent avoir un impact chez tous les adressés du monde sportif et contribuera à une mentalité de respect de l'enfant dans le domaine du sport.

VIII. Offre de Formation

Les trois organisations découvraient dans le cadre de leur projet que dans les différentes formations pour entraîneurs auprès des jeunes, beaucoup d'attention était apportée à l'aspect de technqiues sportives ainsi qu'à l'aspect didactique. Il est fait à peine allusion à l'aspect pédagogique.

En collaboration avec le 'Vormingsdienst Kind en Samenleving' des conseils en formation spécifique ont été développés qui devraient contribuer à une meilleure formation des entraîneurs spécifiques pour les jeunes. Dans ce projet l'accent est mis sur l'élément pédagogique.

IX. L'ACTION DES PARENTS ET DES ENFANTS

Nous constatons que de nombreux parents qui estimaient que les droits de leurs enfants étaient baffouées dans le monde du sport s'adressaient directement au tribunaux. Ils n'attendaient pas des initiatives législatives mais entamaient eux-mêmes une action en ce sens. Ils n'acceptent plus que les clubs de sport sur base d'un règlement de transfert interne ne donnent pas l'autorisation à leurs enfants de jouer dans le club de leur choix. Cela concerne essentiellement les montants importants de transfert liés au déplacement vers un autre club. Ceci principalement dans le monde du football et du basket. Selon ces derniers, il n'est pas tenu compte des souhaits et des besoins de leurs enfants. Depuis l'entrée en vigueur de la convention des Nations Unies de 1989 sur le plan national concernant les droits de l'enfant, des décisions judiciaires furent régulièrement prononcées en matière de transfert d'enfants.

Différents clubs sportifs et fédérations de sport qui refusaient un transfert d'enfants ou qui liaient ce transfert à des conditions financières, ont été condamnés à prendre toutes mesures pour que l'enfant puisse s'affilier au club de son choix. Le juge s'appuie dans ce cas sur l'article 15 du traité garantissant le droit à la liberté d'association.

On retrouve dans une série de jugements un argument qui doit être mis en avant: l'intérêt du jeune sportif ou l'intérêt financier du club. Dans de nombreux cas l'accent est mis sur l'intérêt de l'enfant. Cependant il est rare que la jurisprudence renvoie explicitement aux articles de la convention des Nations Unies. Le juge tient cependant compte des souhaits de l'enfant et de ses parents et condamne le règlement de transfert.

A côté des actions individuelles des parents, d'autre s'associent dans une ASBL efficace pour lutter contre ces situations. L'ASBL Jeunesse, Liberté et Football L'ASBL Jeunesse, Liberté et Football a été créée en décembre 1992 à Liège. Cette ASBL réunit les parents qui s'estiment grugés par les règlements de transfert de la KBVB. Elle défend les intérêts et droits du jeune sportif via des avis, tractations ou assistance judiciaire pour ester en justice lorsqu'aucune autre solution n'a pu être trouvée. Cette association compte pour le moment pas moins de 800 membres, en Flandres et en Wallonie.

CONCLUSION

Il est singulier de remarquer comme le débat des sociétés concernant les droits de l'enfant dans le monde du sport, est influencé par la Convention des Nations Unies sur le droit de l'enfant, applicable au niveau national. Les atteintes aux droits de l'enfant au sein des Fédérations de sport existent depuis des années. L'intérêt du public quant à ce n'a jamais très important. Les arguments pour changer cet état sont confortés au niveau juridique par la Convention des Nations Unies.

A ce propos la Convention oblige le Ministre compétent dans le domaine des sports à prendre un point de vue clair, et ceci vis-à-vis des Fédérations de sport. Principalement, les Fédérations de sport (surtout la KBVB et la KBBB) qui sociétairement et politiquement jouent un rôle important. Des initiatives législatives furent également prises dans l'esprit de la convention. Des médias ont joué à ce propos un rôle très important. Les débats télévisés de même qu'à la radio furent organisés à côté de la presse écrite, avec des représentants de différentes disciplines (autorités académiques, avocats, sportifs, organisations des droits de l'enfance...). Sous l'influence de l'opinion publique, largement influencée par les médias, quelques Fédérations ont changé à contre coeur leurs règlements. Le chemin est cependant encore long avant que la spécificité de l'enfant soit complètement garantie dans le monde du sport. Les quelques changements en matière législative et de règlementation ne sont pas à eux seuls suffisants. Un changement de mentalité est avant tout nécessaire. Est-on totalement persuadé de la valeur des droits de l'enfant dans le sport ou les règlements sont-ils simplement modifiés sous pression des médias et le nombre important des procédures introduites devant le tribunal? Nous devons encore trop souvent constater que l'intérêt des enfants est finalement sacrifié pour des besoins financiers et politiques. Même si le débat sociétaire est déjà ouvert et si des initiatives législatives sont prises, les efforts des autorités restent insuffisants. Cela ressort du fait que le projet précité du décret n'est toujours pas voté, et du fait également que les questions pour développer des projets qui veulent promouvoir le respect de l'enfant dans le monde du sport et qui financièrement doivent être appuyés par les autorités, restent sans réponse.

Ce qui inquète de plus les trois organisations, c'est le fait que dans le rapport transmis par la Belgique aux Nations Unies, il n'est fait nullement mention du respect dû à l'enfant dans le sport. L'administration compétente est pourtant régulièrement informée des atteintes aux droits de l'enfant dans le monde du sport ainsi que des initiatives qui sont prises dans le cadre du projet "les droits de l'enfant dans le monde sportif".

ANNE-MARIE FRÉDÉRIC

Inégalité des droits de l'enfant et rôle de la femme

> Le monde matériel repose sur l'équilibre,
> le monde moral sur l'équité.
>
> (Hugo)

Le respect des droits de l'enfant implique une vision éducative attentive à ne marginaliser aucune catégorie d'enfants.

Or dans les villes de l'Union Européenne, l'évolution du logement et des coutumes risque de priver les minorités atopiques d'un logement adéquat à leurs besoins physiologiques. Ce risque semble inégalement contrôlé selon les pays.

Parallèlement, on constate que les textes des Nations Unies relatifs au logement ne sont pas identiques: du point de vue éducatif, ils sont plus favorables en anglais et en espagnol qu'en français.

Sans nous hasarder dans des développements médicaux, urbanistiques ou juridiques pour lesquels nous ne sommes nullement qualifiée, nous aborderons la question – certes modestement – dans une perspective simplement civique, en prenant pour exemple la Région bruxelloise et pour guide la philologie.

Posons-nous quatre questions.

I. QU'EST CE QUE LE "STATUS ATOPIQUE"?

La population humaine est génétiquement hétérogène. L'un des aspects de cette biodiversité est le "status atopique", qui désigne une prédisposition génétique à développer des allergies.

Par étymologie, *a*topique signifie en français "*in*habituel", en anglais "*un*usual" et en néerlandais "*on*gewoon". Les atopiques sont donc minoritaires par définition. Le "status atopique" se vérifie chez 25–30% de la population totale (atopiques latents). Au moins 10% de la population totale sont allergiques (atopiques connus) soit environ un atopique sur deux. Vu le brassage génétique, il peut évidemment y avoir un atopique dans n'importe quelle famille. L'atopie concerne donc la population tout entière.

E. Verhellen (ed.), Monitoring Children's Rights, 835–840.

Les atopiques sont sujets à devenir allergiques *si* l'environnement est producteur de risque et à souffrir par exemple d'allergie respiratoire ou d'asthme allergique.

Leur santé est liée à la qualité de l'air à l'intérieur des bâtiments à commencer par les logements. Pour le comprendre il suffit de penser au temps que le citadin y passe, notamment dans son enfance.

Les allergènes sont des substances non toxiques mais biologiquement étrangères, d'origine végétale (par exemple des allergènes polliniques) ou animale (par exemple les allergènes des acariens de la poussière de maison ou ceux des animaux domestiques). *A l'intérieur* des locaux, les atopiques perçoivent leur présence même à l'état de traces. Par contre, les trois quarts des gens ne les perçoivent pas puisqu'ils ne sont pas atopiques.

Outre cette sensibilité spécifique aux allergènes, les atopiques réagissent plus tôt et plus fort à la pollution atmosphérique (chimique). Ce sont donc de précieux bio-indicateurs et de bons modérateurs à l'égard de la pollution atmosphérique.

Pour terminer, nous ne saurions mieux faire que de citer à leur sujet le Dr. P. Gervais, professeur à la Faculté de Médecine Lariboisière - Saint-Louis, de Paris. Voici un extrait de la conclusion de son étude sur *Allergologie et écologie*.[1]

A la lecture de publications portant sur les conditions de vie de l'homme et le danger de certains produits chimiques, le médecin est frappé par le fait que les auteurs semblent toujours considérer l'homme comme un être uniforme, chaque être humain étant supposé réagir de la même façon aux différentes situations qui sont réalisées par l'évolution de la vie sociale.

En réalité, l'être humain présente une grande diversité génétique adapté, résultat du contact avec un environnement physique et immunologique très riche qui se révèle au cours d'une première enfance très dépendante, qui permet son développement ultérieur.

Dès maintenant, les médecins constatent que certains patients présentent des phénomènes d'intolérance dans les conditions actuelles de vie, principalement en fonction de leurs particularités immuno – allergologiques. L'étude de l'hypersensibilité allergique des atopiques nous a conduit à la notion nouvelle "d'organisme sentinelle" (op.cit., p. 135).

( ) La tentation peut être forte de négliger ces groupes apparemment plus fragiles dans l'établissement des normes de l'environnement, si l'on envisage seulement pour les choix économiques le coût apparent et immédiat de la pollution sur la santé générale.

---

[1] P. Gervais – *Allergologie et écologie*. Paris, Masson, 1976 (145 p.)

Il faut savoir que l'on accepte alors délibérément le sacrifice de ces personnes qui ont, en réalité, l'avantage biologique caché de réagir plus vite et plus fort aux substances nocives" (op.cit., p. 136).

II. Quels sont les Risques liés à la Standardisation Sommaire du Logement Urbain Actuel? Exemple de la Région Bruxelloise

Il faut évidemment que l'ensemble du logement reste *adéquat* pour l'ensemble de la population. Puisqu'une partie est *atopique*, il faut favoriser le *libre choix* de vivre dans des bâtiments à moindre risque allergique , notamment des bâtiments sans animaux allergisants (mammifères et oiseaux). Le logement doit être binaire.

De tout temps et jusque dans les années '30, la coutume assurait ce libre choix car le parc des logements était suffisamment individualisé: maisons unifamiliales et petits bâtiments à appartements.

Après la guerre, il y a eu une mutation: le logement a été de plus en plus concentré dans des bâtiments à habitations multiples, conçus dans une optique unitaire.

Ces bâtiments collectifs déterminent des microclimats intérieurs également à usage collectif, d'où des risques nouveaux liés à la qualité de l'air à l'intérieur. Ce sont les risques d'exposition forcée, parfois massive, aux allergènes des animaux vivant à l'intérieur. De plus, ces risques sont:
- répétitifs, dans les escaliers, couloirs, ascenseurs et autres parties communes;
- multipliés au prorata de la diversité des animaux, qui ont chacun leurs allergènes spécifiques: chats, chiens, hamsters ...

Imaginons un bâtiment de 100 appartements où vivent 100 familles dont la moitié détient des animaux à concurrence de 6. En tout, cela fait 300 animaux. Il est évident que l'autre moitié des appartements n'est pas adéquate pour des familles où il y a un atopique!

A partir des années '80, nouvelle standardisation: on trouve des textes de loi ou de règlements concernant les animaux et dont la formulation permet de tourner facilement les règlements existants, cela unilatéralement, sans concertation, en rupture avec la coutume et sans même penser à faire étudier l'impact d'une telle révolution.

La liberté de choisir un logement à moindre risque allergique devient de plus en plus aléatoire.

Ce paradoxe inhumain, apparu dans l'indifférence générale, a cependant *un* aspect positif, c'est de révéler un problème plus fondamental: une carence des droits humains.

L'étude des textes des Nations Unies relatifs au logement montre en effet que la Belgique est handicapée par rapport à d'autres pays européens, parce que les textes en anglais et en espagnol mentionnent en effet clairement le droit à un logement adéquat, tandis qu'en français les textes sont moins favorables.

La Belgique est également handicapée par rapport à la France, où la réflexion civique a pu se fonder sur la Constitution de 1946 dont le préambule mentionne que "(la Nation) garantit à tous, notamment à l'enfant ( ) la protection de la santé".[2] Par contre en Belgique, c'est tout récemment que le droit à la protection de la santé vient d'être inscrit dans la Constitution dans le cadre des droits économiques, sociaux et culturels (art. 23 de la Constitution coordonnée du 17 février 1994).

III. Quels sont les Risques liés aux Textes des Nations Unies?

Le "responsable" du handicap dont la Belgique est la victime depuis les années '40, c'est un hasard historique auquel l'étymologie n'est pas étrangère. On constate en effet que les textes des Nations Unies qualifient le logement inégalement selon la langue, au détriment du français: dans tous les textes anglais on trouve "adequate", dans tous les textes espagnols "adecuado", alors qu'en français "adéquat" est concurrencé par "suffisant".

A. Que signifie "Adéquat"?

"Adéquat" signifie "exactement proportionné à son objet, adapté à son but". L'étymologie montre que "adéquat" a la même racine que "équité": lat. "aequus" "égal". "Equité" désigne "la notion de la justice naturelle dans l'appréciation de ce qui est dû à chacun".[3]

"Adéquat" comporte effectivement des connotations d'équité, qui sont plus ou moins conscientes selon les personnes et qui s'expliquent par l'étymologie. A cet égard, il y a équivalence entre l'anglais "adequate, equity" et les langues romanes, par exemple l'espagnol "adecuado, equidad" et le français "adéquat, équité".

Le droit à un logement adéquat, c'est donc le droit à un logement exactement proportionné aux besoins fondamentaux de l'être humain, adapté à son but qui est d'abriter contre les intempéries et contre la pollution de l'air, et cela en tenant compte de la justice naturelle dans l'appréciation de ce qui est dû à chacun. "Adéquat" induit une réflexion large, méthodique, impartiale.

B. Inégalité des Textes des Nations-Unies

Dans la *Déclaration universelle des droits de l'homme* (1948, art. 25 relatif au niveau de vie et où il est déjà question du logement), on trouve en anglais

---

[2] D. Colas – *Textes constitutionnels français et étrangers.* (p. 777) Paris, Larousse, 1994. J.M. de Forges – *Le droit de la santé.* (pp. 5 et 8) Paris, P.U.F. (Que sais-je?), 1986.

[3] Le Petit Robert, 1993 et Littré, *Dictionnaire étymologique de la langue française* 1863 – 1873.

"adequate", en espagnol "adecuado" mais en français "suffisant". L'optique est donc plus étroite en français: sans "adéquat" il n'y a pas "équité".

Dans la *Déclaration des droits de l'enfant* (1959), le principe 4 mentionne effectivement le droit à un logement adéquat dans les trois langues européennes.

Toutefois, le texte est plus clair en anglais pour une raison liée à la langue même: la place de l'adjectif se rapportant à une série de termes énumérés. En anglais l'adjectif est en tête, alors qu'en français il est après le dernier terme de l'énumération, ce qui peut prêter à confusion.

Principle 4: The child shall have the right to adequate nutrition, housing, recreation and medical services.

Principe 4: L'enfant a droit à une alimentation, à un logement, à des loisirs et à des soins médicaux adéquats.

L'ambigüité du texte français apparaît notamment dans des documents éducatifs, par exemple des documents publiés par l'UNICEF; selon les textes, on trouve soit "L'enfant a droit à un logement" (UNICEF 1978) soit "L'enfant a droit à un logement adéquat (UNICEF 1971). L'ambigüité apparaît aussi dans des traductions en néerlandais.

Dans le *Pacte relatif aux droits économiques, sociaux et culturels* (1966, art. 11 relatif au niveau de vie), on trouve en anglais "the right of everyone to an adequate ( ) housing", en espagnol "el derecho de toda persona a un(a) vivienda adecuad(a)", mais en français" le droit de toute personne à ( ) un logement suffisant". En français, l'optique redevient plus étroite.

Enfin, la *Convention internationale des droits de l'enfant*, adoptée à New York par l'Assemblée générale des Nations Unies en 1989, ne mentionne pas le droit au logement. Dans son préambule, elle se réfère aux textes précédents, entérinant ainsi pour ainsi dire entre les enfants les inégalités selon la langue que nous avons signalées ci-avant. Les premières victimes sont les enfants de "status" inhabituel: les enfants atopiques, à commencer par les nouveau-nés et y compris les générations futures.

C. Le Problème Particulier des Pays Multilingues

De plus, cette inégalité selon la langue peut poser problème dans les pays multilingues au moment de l'inscription du droit au logement dans la Constitution. En Belgique, il y a effectivement eu un problème pour la Constitution de 1994 du fait qu'elle est trilingue et posait donc un problème d'équivalence entre 3 langues de familles différentes: une langue romane (le français) et deux langues germaniques (l'allemand et le néerlandais). Nous ne développerons pas ici cette question, qui est très spécifique.

IV. Conclusion: Comment pallier les Risques d'inégalité liés aux Textes des Nations Unies?

Ne peut-on pas faire inscrire le droit à un logement adéquat dans la *Convention internationale des droits de l'enfant*?

A cette fin et pour la surveillance, ne peut-on bénéficier – au moins au niveau européen – de la participation d'immuno-allergologues et autres spécialistes autorisés dans des matières médico-scientifiques connexes?

Pour la surveillance, au moins au niveau de la Belgique fédérale, nous avons l'intime conviction qu'une participation équitable des femmes serait dans l'intérêt général.

Pour des raisons socio-culturelles évidentes, elles sont les premiers agents de santé dans la famille, mieux informées que les hommes en ce qui concerne l'hygiène domestique favorable à l'enfant atopique (notamment par les revues féminines). Enfin, ayant elles-mêmes l'expérience d'une certaine discrimination, elles ont développé des modes d'analyse s'appliquant à différents domaines quotidiens. En attendant une démocratie paritaire, cette parité pourrait être partiellement réalisée par le biais de commissions attentives à la question.

FRANS W.P.M. NEDERSTIGT

"Broad Legal Assistance": Defence and Realization of Children's Rights

A Legal Assistance Project for Street Children in Rio de Janeiro

INTRODUCTION

In connection with my work-experience, early this year, at a legal assistance project for street children in Rio de Janeiro, I would like to draw your attention to the monitoring of children's rights in the Brazilian practice. For three months I have actively participated in the *Centro de Defesa e Garantia de Direitos Humanos: the Center for Defence and Guarantee of Human Rights*. This Brazilian Human Rights Center is functioning as a legal assistance project for street children under the Brazilian name *Projeto Legal* which means: Legal project as well as "fine" or "good" project. The project started in 1992 and is one of the forty projects of the *Brazilian Institute for Innovations in Social Health Care*, the IBISS.

In this contribution I will try to characterize the so-called concept of "broad legal assistance". Without doubt a very innovating way for a non governmental organization to shape the monitoring of children's rights in practice. By describing the objectives, structure and working-methods of the *Projeto Legal* I will demonstrate that "broad legal assistance" pays attention to the *defence* of children's rights as well as to the *realization* of children's rights. The *Projeto Legal* tries to construct a necessary bridge across the abyss between the rights of the child "on paper" on the one side, and the rights of the child in daily practice on the other side.

The proof of such a "bridge" being built by the *Projeto Legal*, will initially be delivered by analyzing the actual social and legal position of street children in Brazil. This analysis will enable us to derive the most important aspects of the street children phenomenon. Then we will focus on the objectives of the *Projeto Legal*, and conclude that they link up seamlessly to the nature of the problems street children face. After that, we will analyze the structure and

E. Verhellen (ed.), Monitoring Children's Rights, 841–851.
© 1996 *Kluwer Law International. Printed in the Netherlands.*

the working-methods of the *Projeto Legal* so that a kind of system-analysis will be completed. This means that the objectives postulated by the *Projeto Legal* are based on the problems pointed out in reality, and can be realized by means of a structure and the use of working-methods that link up to that reality.

Before I end this introduction, I would like to give you some grip on the concept of "broad legal assistance". The concept supposes an important distinction, which is also made by Verhellen,[1] between the *defensive* or *reactive* use of legal rights on the one side, and the *offensive* or *proactive* use of these rights on the other side. This is the same kind of difference that can be made between the *defence* of children's rights and the *realization* of children's rights.

I. The Actual Social and Legal Position of Street Children in Brazil

Estimations of UNICEF, that are based on a census taken in 1980, tell us that in Brazil more than 7 million children are living and working in the streets.[2] Obscure, however, is how strong family ties of these 7 million street children are, whether they only hang out on the streets during daytime, and therefore do not attend school, and, whether they also work on the streets, or even sleep on the streets during the night.

The *National Brazilian Street Children's Movement* (MNMMR) supposes that the vast majority does not actually sleep on the street. This majority, distinguished as children *in* the street, can be found in the streets during daytime and maintains mostly at least some contact with relatives. These children *in* the street do not attend school but instead work in the informal market and do what they can to earn some money: They guard or wash cars, shine shoes, sell candy, cigarettes, beg, deal drugs, prostitute themselves,[3] steal and commit other petty crimes. The minority of the street children that actually sleeps on the street are the so-called children *of* the street. Countings in 1992 made clear that in the city center of Rio de Janeiro about 1,100

---

[1] Verhellen, E., "The Search for the Achilles Heel: Monitoring of the UN Convention on the Rights of the Child", In: *Children's Rights: Monitoring Issues*, Verhellen, E., Spiesschaert, F. (eds.), Ghent: Mys & Breesch Publishers, 1994, p. 5.

[2] Myers, W., "Alternative Services for Street Children; The Brazilian Approach", In: *Combating Childlabour*, Bequelle, A., Boyden, J., Geneva: ILO-report, 1988, p. 126 (based on figures of 1980).

[3] According to estimations there are 600,000 Brazilian children working as prostitutes. Lemineur, M., *Child Prostitution in Brazil*, dissertation, 1991, p. 12.

children actually were sleeping on the street.[4] On the whole, the total number of children *of* the street in the city center of Rio de Janeiro is estimated 4,000.[5]

In order to describe the character of the problems encountered by street children in an honest and useful way, it is necessary that street children are not considered as an isolated segment of Brazilian society, but instead, are looked at as one of the most visible consequences of underlying problems. According to UNICEF the social and economic situation in Brazil, especially when related to its relatively high national income, is very tense or even explosive.[6] A UNICEF rapport of this year states that the poorest 40% of the Brazilian households earns only 7% of the total national income generated by all Brazilian households, while the richest 20% earn as much as 68% of the total national income.[7] Figures of 1989 show that as much as 75% of the Brazilian children were raised in households that could only spend one minimum salary or even less.[8] According to UNICEF a family needs at least two minimum salaries to fulfil the basic needs of the family members.[9] Small wonder that the extreme poverty in Brazil forces children living in the lowest social strata of society, to contribute to the family income in one way or another. School attendance, again no wonder, is very low in Brazil: Only 22% of the children who actually attend classes, finishes primary school.[10] Because children are often forced onto the street because of Brazil's extreme poverty and inequal distribution of wealth, it is wrong to raise the presence of children on the street as the main problem.

However, through a process of selective perception, almost the entire Brazilian society considers the street children phenomenon as the disease itself, instead of perceiving this phenomenon as a symptom of a disease. Many Brazilians do not consider street children as the victims of an unequal social and economic system, but stigmatize them as little criminals without any future, and hold them responsible for their own miserable living conditions.

---

[4] Heringer, R., Pereira Júnior, A., *Survey of Boys and Girls on the Streets of Rio de Janeiro*, Cadernos do IBASE 6, Rio de Janeiro: Instituto Brasileiro de Análises Sociais e Econômicas (IBASE), March 1992.

[5] Human Rights Watch / Americas, *Final Justice: Police and Death Squad Homicides of Adolescents in Brazil*, New York: Human Rights Watch, 1994, p. 8.

[6] UNICEF, *The State of the World's Children 1994*, Wallingford: Oxford University Press, 1994, pp. 64–81.

[7] Ibidem, p. 64. In the Netherlands these figures are respectively 20% for the poorest 40% of the households, and 38% for the richest 20% of all households. Ibidem, p. 65.

[8] Instituto Brasileiro de Geografia e Estatística (IBGE), *Crianças e Adolescentes: Indicadores Sociais, Volume 2, Indicadores Sociais*, Rio de Janeiro: IBGE, 1989. In April 1994 the minimum salary was about 65 US$. The minimum salary fluctuates, depending on the inflation percentage, between 110 US$ and 50 US$ per month.

[9] Cited in: Kranen, F. van, Bosco Feres, J., *Een Wet over, een Wet voor, een Wet van Kinderen: Straatkinderen in Brazilië, een Terreinverkenning*, mimeo, Amsterdam, maart 1991.

[10] UNICEF, *The State of the World's Children 1994*, Wallingford: Oxford University Press, 1994, p. 70.

A town-councillor of a provincial town in the southern, more wealthy, part of Brazil, and member of a respected political party, gave the following statement, during the public council meeting in March this year: "What alarms me is the youth-criminality. Everyone defends the minor, his human rights, the reception-house, and I don't know what else; But who defends the families of the people who were killed by these minors? (...) And what happens if a minor kills somebody? Then he is pitiful because he is a minor: Seventeen years old! For making children and for stealing they are old enough, but when it comes to responsibility for what they did, one is starting again about human rights. (...) I believe there is a saying that expresses all this in the best possible way: You have to kill them when they are small, so you don't have to bother about the grown-up."[11]

This shocking statement is a true real-life case, that does not stand on its own.[12] The example gives a good insight in the character of the street children's problems which nowadays exist in Brazil. We can distinguish the formal recognition of the existence of the rights of the child in theory, on the one side, and the brutal violation of these rights in daily practice, on the other side. This contrast shows itself in a most horrible way when we have a look at the number of homicides of adolescents in Brazil. If we are to believe the office of the Brazilian Public Prosecutor, between 1988 and 1991 a total of 5,644 children from the ages of 5 to 17, died a violent death. According to more recent figures supplied by the civil police, in Rio de Janeiro state alone in 1992 424 children under the age of 18 were victims of homicide, while 298 were killed already in the first six months of 1993.

The outspoken opinion of the town-councillor also highlights a phenomenon in Brazilian society which can be best described as the so-called "dehumanization of the street child image".[13] Street children are no longer perceived as children but as dangerous vermin, that has to be exterminated. Through such a negative street child image, the killing of street children is considered as "social cleansing" and even defended as being in the best interests of Brazilian society.

The rights of the Brazilian child in theory, however, are as good, or even better, as those mentioned in the UN Convention on the Rights of the Child. Especially when we have a look at Brazil's outstanding translation of these rights in a very progressive statute on the rights of the child and the adolescent.

---

[11] Lima, M. de, (PMDB), Sessão Ordinária do dia 3-3-1994, Câmara Municipal de Novo Hamburgo, Estado do Rio Grande do Sul, p. 6.

[12] An advertisement on the front page of the house-to-house newspaper "Hot List" (6 till 11-3-1994), edited in the south Brazilian provincial town "Londrina", stated: "Help to improve the living environment of our neighbourhood: Kill a juvenile law offender." Feldens, M., "Anúncio Convaca Comerciante a Exterminar Menor Infrator", → In: *Jornal do Brasil*, 9-3-1994.

[13] Fernandes, E., *Extrajudicial Execution of Children: Shortcomings of Social Citizenship and the Fallacy of Criminal Justice in Brazil*, Paper van Studie- en Informatiecentrum Mensenrechten (SIM), Utrecht, 1993, pp. 33–36.

This new law, the so-called ECA, came into force in 1990.[14] The ECA, that replaced the old "minor law"[15] dating from the time when Brazil was ruled by the military, defines children no longer as objects for assistance, but as subjects of rights.

The progressive ECA came into being mainly as a result of the pressure of a number of Brazilian NGOs that promote children's rights. The completion of the UN Convention on the Rights of the Child turned out to be an important tool to press for a new and updated national law on children's rights. The public outcry of indignation in the international community on the subject of the extermination of street children, made the democratic Brazilian government even more aware of the need for a hastily ratification of the UN Convention, and of the proclamation of a new statute on children's rights. So, the legal framework really changed for the better in Brazil.

However, the ECA is nicknamed as a "law for the next century" or as a "law for Switzerland" because many of the ambitious objectives seem impossible to realize in the short term, and therefore serve merely a symbolic goal. The implementation of the ECA indeed leaves much to be desired. I already mentioned the continuing killing of children in Brazil. But also the ratification of the UN Convention on the Rights of the Child in 1990, the Brazilian "Pact for Children" which was established as a result of the World Children Summit in New York in 1990, as well as the recommendations made by the parliamentary inquiry commission that, in 1992, investigated the killings of street children, or the introduction, early this year, of legal measures that were collected in a so-called "Package against Violence", failed to bring about any visible improvement in the situation of the Brazilian street children. A prominent journalist of the quality newspaper "Folha de São Paulo" concludes as follows: "On street children, the government's measures have been designed to stop what it calls the 'phenomenon of extermination', but this is treated in isolation from its social, economic and political roots. In this way the government never acknowledges responsibility for the millions of rejected children who roam Brazil's streets, and takes no measures to prevent yet more children taking to the streets."[16]

II. The Objectives of the Projeto Legal

The objectives of the *Projeto Legal* are based on the daily reality we just described. As we noticed, street children have to be considered as the symptom of a disease and not as the disease itself. The true disease consists of an enormously complicated web of social and economic problems, that forces the majority of the Brazilians to live on the edge. The only effective medicine

---

[14] Estatuto da Criança e do Adolescente (ECA), Lei 8.069/90.

[15] Código do Menor, Lei 6.697/79.

[16] Dimenstein, G., *Brazil: War on Children*, London: Latin American Bureau (LAB), 1991, p. 12.

to cure this disease is to set political priorities in favor of a structural solution of the street children phenomenon.

A structural improvement in the rights of the child can be reached by influencing the so-called superstructure of society. This means the search "for changes in culture, mentality and individual attitudes" in the words of Verhellen. He adds: "The philosophy which is reflected in public opinion is extremely important when it comes to improving children's living conditions. Disseminating information and expressing well-founded opinions are the best ways of influencing public opinion."[17] So, by doing this one can mobilize society and work on a more structural approach to the solution of the phenomenon of street children.

In its policy for 1994 the *Projeto Legal* has developed three concrete variables for action to promote the awakening of Brazilian society in its opinion concerning street children. The project distinguishes three so-called alliances to stimulate this process of awakening and emancipation:

The first, fundamental alliance is composed by the street children themselves. In this alliance one supposes that children's rights can be used in a process of emancipation. By awakening the street children's awareness of their marginal position in Brazilian society, and by confronting them with the rights they own as a consequence of the ECA, the *Projeto Legal* gives them a certain power of defence. This is likewise proclaimed in article 42 of the UN Convention on the Rights of the Child, that is known as the "know-your-rights" article.[18]

The second alliance, to be distinguished, is the so-called internal alliance which consists of the *Projeto Legal* itself. The role of the legal and social assistants must be approached critically. Especially a lawyer should not take the already existing legal reality as a fixed starting-point of his or her work, but instead should try to address the actual social and economic situation of street children. The lawyer, as a mediator between his or her client on the one hand, and the often conservatively interpreted ECA or criminal law, on the other hand, must not act as a paternalistic assistant. He must be someone who offers his or her client the possibility, by means of the legal confrontation, to awaken to the unjust situation the client is in.

Finally, the third alliance, is the so-called external alliance, by which is meant the remainder category known as the public opinion in general. One can think of political parties, political leaders, the police, the judiciary, the Brazilian Organization of Lawyers (OAB), the national and international media and various human rights organizations.

---

[17] Verhellen, E., "The Search for the Achilles Heel: Monitoring of the UN Convention on the Rights of the Child", In: *Children's Rights: Monitoring Issues*, Verhellen, E., Spiesschaert, F. (eds.), Ghent: Mys & Breesch Publishers, 1994, p. 6.

[18] Article 42 reads: "States Parties undertake to make the principles and provisions of the Convention widely known, by appropriate and active means, to adults and children alike."

Thus, promoting a change in awareness concerning the street children phenomenon is based on the recognition of "shared responsibility" in society. "So everybody shares some responsibility, and everybody is both part of the problem and of the solution, including street children, including us."[19]

The second main objective developed by the *Projeto Legal* is the realization of a direct improvement of the street children's living conditions. This objective can be justified easily by pointing at the almost universally accepted human rights idea, and more specifically by mentioning the UN Convention on the Rights of the Child, article 227 of the Brazilian Constitution[20] and, of course, the ECA. This objective can roughly be described as the granting of legal assistance, consisting of two complementary approaches. Two approaches that guard two different kinds of human rights.

The first approach is based on a defensive point of view. The *Projeto Legal* uses legal rights to provide legal assistance for street children in direct need. At the same time, the project denounces human rights violations. At stake are the so-called basic human rights of every human being, such as the right of physical integrity, the right to be protected from unlawful duress, discrimination and torture. These rights have to be considered as the universal property of every human being, if one is to speak about a life to be lived in dignity.

Besides this approach, the *Projeto Legal* uses legal rights also as an instrument for serving the interests of street children by improving their miserable living conditions. By using legal rights out of an offensive point of view, and by granting social and economic assistance to street children, it is possible to pursue the realization of the social and economic basic rights. The formal right to education as recognized in the ECA, for example, is a legal tool to press successfully for free education for children without a birth-certificate.

Concluding, we find that the two main objectives as formulated by the *Projeto Legal* consist of a strive for a changing attitude towards the street children phenomenon on the one hand, and the realization of a direct improvement of the street children's living conditions on the other hand. This can be typified as the concept of "broad legal assistance". Of course there exists no such thing as a perfect watershed between the two main objectives. On the contrary. The two objectives reinforce one another. For, a legal confrontation gives street children, and other actors involved, the opportunity to become aware of the unjust situation they are in. At the same time, however, this awakening, by means of public denouncements of the killing of street children, may result in

---

[19] Vanistendael, S., *Street Children: Problems or Persons*, Geneva: International Catholic Child Bureau, 1992, In: *Documentatiemap Straatkinderen*, DCI, InDRA, Amsterdam: DCI, InDRA, 1993, p. 21.

[20] Article 227 reads: "It is the duty of the family, society and the State to guarantee the child and the adolescent, with absolute priority, the rights to life, health, food, education, leisure, professional training, culture, dignity, respect, freedom, family and social life, and to protect them from all forms of negligence, discrimination, exploitation, cruelty and oppression."

a structural improvement of the street children's living conditions in the long term.

III. The Structure and the Working-methods of the Projeto Legal

We will find that the chosen structure and the working-methods used, constitute the missing links between the actual social and legal position of street children in Brazil, and the objectives formulated by the *Projeto Legal*.

Today, the *Projeto Legal* is organized in four legal assistance teams, each of which consists of a lawyer and a trainee, dealing all together with a total number of about 150 cases. Each team deals individually with the cases assigned to the team. Every week an evaluation meeting is held so problems can be discussed and solved together.

Alongside the four legal assistance teams, nowadays three social assistants accompany each client in their social, economic and psychological problems.

Recently, also a part-time journalist and a trainee have started to maintain contacts with the press, radio, television and several influential national and international organizations.

Within the organizational structure of the IBISS, the *Projeto Legal* maintains good contacts with the other independently functioning projects. Many clients of the *Projeto Legal* are also clients of other IBISS street children projects that focus on different kind of problems, as for example *Projeto Excola*, which means ex-glue sniffing project and school at the same time, *Sempre Viva*, a street girls project, and the *Projeto Programa* working with young male and female prostitutes.

On the municipal, regional and national level the *Projeto Legal* maintains many contacts with other NGOs working with children's and human rights. Besides these contacts, the *Projeto Legal* maintains also contacts with different segments of the local authorities. On the regional level the *Projeto Legal* has a seat in the *Council for Children's and Adolescents' Affairs* (CEDCA) and serves the interests of children in this political body out of an offensive point of view, by working together with other NGOs and authority agencies.

On the international level the *Projeto Legal* maintains regular contacts with respected human rights organizations such as *Amnesty International, Human Rights Watch / Americas* and the *Inter-American Commission for Human Rights of the Organization of American States* (OAS). The *Projeto Legal* also maintains good contacts with the organizations contributing to the work of the project like the Dutch organizations *Lawyers for Lawyers,* the *Street Children Brazil* foundation, and the German *Children Mission Fund.*

The working-method of the *Projeto Legal* can be divided in two main categories that link up very closely to the two main objectives of the project.

The first category contains the so-called political articulation that promotes the awakening and emancipation of (Brazilian) society. The variety in external contacts of the *Projeto Legal* we just mentioned, enables the project to denounce the miserable living conditions and human rights violations in public. On the macro level the influencing of public opinion in Brazil and the rest of the world, consists of actively spreading news-reports, the giving of interviews to newspapers, radio and television, and of course by writing reports for national and international human rights organizations.

In its policy for 1994 the *Projeto Legal* has formulated some active campaigning on different subjects. By actively influencing public opinion the project tries this year to initiate a public discussion on the role and responsibility of the judiciary in its approach of the street children phenomenon.

The political articulation on the micro level consists of daily consulting hours for street children and the personal accompaniment of clients. The marginal position the street child holds in Brazilian society, is always contrasted with the rights he or she owns in theory. This activist approach is practiced by giving information about the ECA, in schools in poor neighborhoods. The co-operators of the *Projeto Legal* also retrain themselves by organizing internal seminars dealing with problematic issues they encounter in their work.

The second category that can be distinguished in the working-method of the *Projeto Legal* is providing assistance, which consists of a legal and social component. This "symptom fighting" is directed towards a direct improvement of the street children's living conditions.

The free legal assistance the *Projeto Legal* is granting, consists of providing consulting hours, the accompaniment of clients during the legal process, including visits to police prisons, and the attendance of hearings of the suspect or witnesses. The lawyers also try, if possible, to be present during, or shortly after arrests of street children, in order to prevent provocation or power abuse by police officers, that may result in the harassment of imprisoned street children.

The social component of the assistance provided by the *Projeto Legal* is for the account of the three social assistants. More specifically, this means the visiting of family members whose son, daughter, brother or sister has been imprisoned or murdered. Such radical occurrences may cause not only serious psychological damage, but also signify the temporary or definite drying up of a part of the family-income. Apart from that, the social assistants provide probation and after-care services for children and adolescents who will have to adjust to their regained freedom. After-care services mean in practice that the social assistants try to restore family ties. The social assistants also help the children and adolescents to find a job by mediating with educational or housing projects of the IBISS, or other organizations. To create real opportunities for the released children and adolescents for building up a better life is a very difficult task, but therefore not less important.

Having said all this, let us try to evaluate the structure and the working-methods of the *Projeto Legal*.

The effectiveness of political articulation is hard to measure, and besides, it often shows visible results only in the longer term. Demonstrating the usefulness of political articulation, therefore, is only possible by mentioning some examples.

Different speech-making cases involving action taken by the *Projeto Legal,* reached the newspapers or were even reported on radio or television. The case of the murder of Marco Aurélio Fernandes that was judged in court, for example, got the interest of radio and television when two prime suspects turned out to be military police officers. This case, like another case, has also been mentioned in a recent report of the American Human Rights Organization *Human Rights Watch/ Americas.*[21] In the meantime one of the suspected military police officers has been convicted, while the Public Prosecutor, after consulting the *Projeto Legal,* decided to appeal in the case of the acquittal of the other.

Examples of direct improvement in the living conditions of individual street children, who were legally or socially assisted by the *Projeto Legal* are legion. A structural and permanent improvement of their living conditions however, is highly dependent on an intensive cooperation with other projects of the IBISS and other organizations working with street children. To free a child or an adolescent out of a police prison, or to prevent this of happening at all, is only the first step in the improvement of a child's living conditions, and remains often useless when it is not followed up by an after-care service.

Of course this does not mean that legal assistance cannot have a preventive function as well. The ending of impunity, for example, by getting the responsible murderers of children convicted, and the expelling of involved police officers from active duty, may result in changing (police) attitudes.

My final, and in fact most important question is to what extent "broad legal assistance" contributes in solving the street children phenomenon. Before we judge the effectiveness of the *Projeto Legal* as a development project, however, we have to conclude that the active strive for more respect of human rights, especially children's rights, at least gives the project a moral right to exist.

But a significant answer to the question of the effectiveness of the *Projeto Legal* cannot be founded on moral grounds only. What we really want to know is whether the *Projeto Legal* is successful? But how to solve the problem of defining criteria for success? In this respect I like to quote Vanistendael, a co-operator of the *International Catholic Child Bureau*:

> What do we call "success" in work with street children? (...) even if we can define our "success criteria" beyond doubt, what "success" can reasonably be expected? Let us make a comparison with physics. A light bulb uses less than 10% of its energy to produce light, hence 90% or more of its energy is wasted in heat. This is, therefore an extremely ineffective way of producing light, yet we use millions of light bulbs every day and we do

---

[21] Human Rights Watch / Americas, *Final Justice: Police and Death Squad Homicides of Adolescents in Brazil*, New York: Human Rights Watch, 1994. Marco Aurélio Fernandes, pp. 99–102; Edméia da Silva Euzébio, pp. 42–45.

not think twice about it. But what would we think of a project that "saves" only 10% of the children it takes in?[22]

In this respect, the functioning of the *Projeto Legal*, the second largest legal assistance project in Brazil, is indeed successful. We found that the daily reality with its variety of problems, matched the formulated objectives and the developed working-methods. Besides, the exemplary cases are very promising, justifying confidence in the results already achieved.

The recent extensions of the project and the growing number of cases, certainly show the need for effective legal assistance. But the *Projeto Legal* looks ahead and considers it necessary to develop serious initiatives for a structural approach of the street children phenomenon. By means of political articulation and the granting of social assistance the *Projeto Legal* broadened its initial field of activity. Therefore it is right to label the project as an innovative "broad legal assistance" project.

Legal assistance projects, like the *Projeto Legal*, already harvest due admiration. Because of these successes, the Dutch General Directorate for International Co-operation and Development decided to support the establishment of similar projects in Mali and the Ivory Coast.[23]

---

[22] Vanistendael, S., *Street Children: Problems or Persons*, Geneva: International Catholic Child Bureau, 1992, In: *Documentatiemap*, DCI, InDRA, Amsterdam: DCI, InDRA, 1993, p. 20.

[23] Information Service "Foreign Aid" of the Ministry of Foreign Affairs, *Kids 94*, volume 2, 1994, p. 4.

LYNETTE OCHOLA

The Undugu Society Approach in Dealing with Children at Risk to Abuse and Neglect

The escalating instances of child abuse and neglect is becoming a major problem in many countries of the world today. Children in especially difficult circumstances are denied their rights and rarely have protection against abuse and neglect.

Although many countries have ratified the Convention on the Rights of the Child, they have not incorporated the convention in their laws and neither do they have policies for the children in especially difficult circumstances like the street children.

There are certain cultural barriers that make it very easy for children's rights to be abused. In certain countries a child is to be seen and not to be heard. Thus children are not given a voice, they cannot express themselves and voice their feelings. Traditionally children have no rights.

None of the African countries have free and compulsory education, even when the education is free, there are usually hidden costs e.g., desks, chairs, uniform and other school levies. Most governments do not cater for remedial education (basic literacy, numeracy and some sort of job skills) and thus the right to education is abused.

Street children for instanstance rarely have protection against abuse and neglect. Perceived as an eye sore by many city officials they are often imprisoned and taken to juvenile court systems without any legal representation.

I. THE CHALLENGE

While on the streets the children's major preoccupations are begging, hawking, peddling of drugs and substances, and prostitution. Prostitution is very common among the group of street girls who are on the streets permanently. Girls of ages 8 years and above are actively involved in prostitution. Another phenomenon among the same category of girls is that they act as wives to parking boys. Gangs of these girls are co-habiting with boys of 14 years and above between tall buildings in the city centre. The parking boys are accorded all the treatment that befits a husband, including emotional and sexual

E. Verhellen (ed.), Monitoring Children's Rights, 853–866.

favours. In this setting there is a very strong sense of community and there is a recognised gang leader, often a man. The shift hovels (chuoms) which they live in are made of old polythene paper and cartons on both the roofs and the sides. To get in they have to literally crawl on their knees. They have no doors, windows or any form of ventilation. The children sleep on the ground and cover themselves with rugs and threadbare blankets which they may have collected from the streets and city estates.

The children have formed their own street-culture and are very protective over each other. We now have the third generation of street children; these are children of street children.

II. Background of the Undugu Society of Kenya

The Undugu Society of Kenya is an non-profit making organisation founded 21 years ago (1973) by a Dutch Priest Father Arnold Grol with the purpose of enhancing the quality of life of Nairobi's street boys, known as 'Parking Boys' through provision of food, shelter, recreation and education. The organisation has since grown and today it pursues a network of Community Development activities within targeted slum (or informal) settlements in and around Nairobi. The activities of Undugu are geared towards mobilization for socio-economic improvement. The organisation activities in these larger areas now focus on community mobilization, employment creation, small enterprise development, informal skills training, pursuit of affordable shelter, community health and nutrition.

Undugu has grown from a handful of dedicated beginners to an organisation which touches thousands of Kenyans lives today and has managed to improve the quality of living of the less fortunate, while protecting the rights of the many children in difficult circumstances.

Slum settlement around Nairobi offer the major breeding ground for street children and generate a variety of social conditions which lead to child abuse and neglect. The socio-economic status of the slum community is very poor. It is characterized by:

- Very poor overcrowded housing, poor sanitation, no drainage systems, no toilets, no privacy. This therefore poses a great danger to health.
- Very low income that hinders basic necessities.
- Unaffordable, inaccessible education for children by parents. They are unable to meet school requirements like uniforms, fees, harambee funds and other levies.

Most of Undugu's activities are centred around the child, the parents and the communities that the children come from. They are geared towards promoting the overall development of the child with an emphasis on family centred rehabilitation. It is Undugu's strong belief that the family institution is the best institution for any child.

III. UNDUGU'S APPROACH IN DEALING WITH CHILDREN AT RISK TO ABUSE AND NEGLECT (STREET CHILDREN)

It is estimated that there may be as many as 40.000 street children in Nairobi and 400.000 in Kenya as a whole. Many of these children have been robbed off their inherent joys of childhood and find themselves engaged in all sorts of activities such as begging, prostituting, collecting waste paper for recycling, trafficking drugs, hawking, working in homes as house-maids, in hotels and bars in order to fend for themselves and their families.

These children struggle with responsibilities and situations that are more suited to adulthood thus denying them a chance to be 'Children'. With the slum population growing at an annual rate of 10 per cent, it is conceivable that this number will continue to grow unless the cycle of poverty, family disruption and unwanted/abandoned children is broken.

Undugu's activities focuses particularly on the following:
- Intervention: better provision for the street children of effective and accessible information, guidance and services for promotion of health habitants, living conditions, the prevention of problems, and the treatment and rehabilitation of those in need.
- Educating communities on issues affecting their lives so as to change their negative attitudes towards life.
- Facilitating provision of education both formal and informal.
- Facilitating provision of skills training for street children and slum children as well as their parents and communities. And sensitizing/training them in skills needed to promote effective health care and healthy behaviour, change in attitudes and enhance their aspirations through training and education.
- Mobilization of youth and women groups within the slums into strong groups as a way of influencing attitudes, influencing policy making in their favour. Enhancing a sense of responsibility.
- Advocacy: creating awareness among the target communities as to their potential to change their own destiny to create an appropriate climate for policy and legislation to better meet the street children's needs.
- Upholding the rights of street children and stimulating them to exploit their latent talent by equipping them with better survival skills.
- Undugu is also committed to upholding the rights of street girls who are exposed to experiences which are often traumatic.

Undugu's efforts are regarded as a series of on-going experiments which are meant to stimulate the community in a way which will enable them in turn to discharge basic responsibilities towards their children and the society at large. By working in the slums of Nairobi particularly with the parents and communities that the street children came from and by making them self-reliant, Undugu aims at preventing more children from taking to the streets.

In the slums where most of the street children are produced, there is a definite lack of control on children due to lack of viable alternatives to occupy their free time. This makes it necessary for children to engage in illegal and unconventional means of income generation.

IV. THE UNDUGU APPROACH

To the authorities the street children represent a menace which must be removed from the streets and put in jail or remand home, to the public they represent the lowest class of human race, dirty, diseased and a source of embarassment to be despised and avoided.

Undugu works through a team of street workers who have sought to ask and then address themselves to the question as to why these young members of society (street boys and girls) continue to flock into the streets despite all the risks.

The street work team functions at three different levels namely Case work, Group work and Data collection. These activities are centred around street visits carried out every Tuesday, Thursday and Monday night.

A. Case Work

During street visits, attempts are made to identify problems specific to each child on individual basis. On other occasions, the children themselves volunteer information on what usually turns out to be acute personal problems. This often calls for crisis intervention which includes providing medical assistance for any number of ailments a majority of which are sexually transmitted diseases (STDs).

Once identified, the sick children are referred to the Mercy Sister Dispensary at Makandara or to the Crescent Medical Aid Centre at Pumwani. In the past few months about 100 girls and 40 boys have referred for medical attention for symptoms suspected to be those of HIV+ infection and STDs. Cases of STDs include gonorrhoea and syphilis (among others). AIDS is emerging as a problem requiring special and immediate attention especially because of the multifactional approach required to address it.

All other time, the street work team may have to visit juvenile courts and remand homes to arbitrate on behalf of the children who find themselves on the wrong side of the law.

B. Group Work

The street work project operates largely, as a group event. Each street visit involves discussions with the children in their own environment. On other occasions, it has proved equally useful to organise picnics and camping trips to take the children to different settings.

Special mention must be made of the 'African Heritage Group' of girls. These are prostitutes of about 15 years and above who practice their trade around the centre of Nairobi. It has been possible to organise these girls into a cohesive group which is training to participate in alternative income generating activities in such fields as mechanics, tailoring, and beauty/hair care.

Another instance of Undugu's impact is exemplified in a group of girls who meet at the Mathare Valley Programme Office. Here they are involved in activities such as embroidery, traditional dance, and bead work, taught and facilitated by volunteers interested in keeping girls occupied in alternative income generating activities and consequently off the streets. These girls have also been attending workshops organised by Undugu covering the areas of health, business, and family planning.

Drug taking, glue sniffing, marijuana smoking, petrol sniffing, and alcohol abuse sometimes go hand in hand with prostitution. The street work team has realized that to break the cycle of children on the streets, it is important to break their dependence on these intoxicants through counselling.

Undugu has also initiated a new strategy in which children are rehabilitated within a cohesive community in which Undugu is working. A child lives with a mother figure who has children close to the child's age. A child living with children on the streets lack a family set up, we can look forward to the older women within those communities to fulfil the role of a grandmother and give guidance and advice.

C. Data Collection – Street Girls Survey

The street work programme has seen a number of street children attain various levels of rehabilitation. It became clear that a way of quantifying our results was needed so that trends could be monitored. For this reason, data collection is included as the third element of the project.

It is intended that the administration of surveys be made periodically. This has already begun with the baseline survey carried out in February.

40 street girls aged 8–16 years were selected at random and formed the basis of the study. 5 of the girls were interviewed by means of a questionnaire in the streets while the rest were interviewed while on a picnic at Thika's Fourteen Falls. The questionnaire was designed to obtain information on the following.

– Demographic and biographic factors and family background.
– Educational history.
– Life style and daily activities.
– Prior contact and intervention received.
– Respondent's personality.

V. Summary of Survey Results

Most of the girls of our respondent population of 40 are between the ages of eight and twelve years. Close to 90 per cent of them come from households where their parents are suffering from physically and verbally damaging to the child who not only witnesses this abuse but is likely to have such abuse meted on to her as well.

Half of the girls originate from single parented households. 75 per cent of the girls are second or middle siblings. First born children may feel a greater obligation towards the family and fear leaving their siblings behind. Last born children may be lucky to have older siblings to look after them and are therefore less in a hurry to leave the home.

In 32 of the cases, the family resides in a one room house with five to ten people. Over half of the girls come from the slum areas of Nairobi with the majority from the Mathare Valley area. 80 per cent of the girls indicated that they receive two or three meals a day though the frequency of this and the content of the meal remain questionable. Many of the girls must search for food by their own means.

30 out of the 40 respondents have been to school but dropped out. The girls cited the inability to raise school fees as the primary reason for dropping out of school. In fact, it seems that the cost of school fees is responsible for inhibiting access of most children to education. This is especially evidenced by the fact that all but six of the children would like to go back to school or receive some sort of training. A few of the children mentioned peer pressure as one of the reasons for dropping out of school but lack of school fees remains the primary cause.

Most of the girls were introduced to the streets by friends. Only six came with family members. Three came on their own.

Once they arrive on the streets, the girls find a place to stay. Half of the respondents end up staying on the streets or behind hotels. 30 per cent end up in "chuoms" (groupings of children, both male and female) who stay in makeshift family units. These are often located in dark alleyways between buildings of the city centre. The boys within the chuoms tend to take responsibility for the security of the girls. This phenomenon illustrates that once on the streets, children still have a desire sense of belonging and safety which are found in a family.

90 percent of the respondents participate in income generating activities and find earning money in fact the primary factor for coming to the streets and staying there. Sometimes the children are sent by family members to search for work to send money home, others leave home opting to survive on their own to escape the intolerable levels of poverty and prostitution and hawking. Close to 80 per cent of the children earn up to Ksh. 100 a day while working on the streets. The income generated from these activities is spent on purchasing food and clothing.

While on the streets, these children experience problems of harassment from city authorities, physical and verbal abuse from other members of the society. As products of abusive households, it is difficult to ascertain the level of abuse which street children receive on the streets since to them violence and abuse is what they have known and therefore considered normal and expected behaviour.

Half of the respondents have someone on the streets to whom they can turn to in times of need. Most have permanent partners who are often referred to as "husbands". These are often older street boys who provide the girls with protection and make sure that they have sufficient food and medicines. Girls must in return accord the boys emotional and sexual favours. This marriage seems to be restricted to the chuoms for once out on the streets girls are free to do whatever they can to make money and prostitution is seen as a normal income generating activity.

Of those who claim to have a religious affiliation, most believe they have not in any way benefitted from it. Only 27 per cent say they use the church facilities while 8 per cent claim the church taught them how to pray. 68 per cent of the girls have been in official places of detention such as police cells, remand homes, juvenile courts and like institutions. They have experienced instances of being beaten, staying in unsanitary conditions which sometimes lead to infection and sleeping without beddings on the cold floor. Even after such experiences however, the children normally return to the same practices that originally implicated the need to earn money. The rest do not want to go home because they feel that they have more freedom on the street.

Asked what they would like to be when they grow up, 25 per cent said that they would like to do business. 20 percent said that they would like to be teachers and the remaining would like to be doctors, nurses, tailors and other skilled professionals. Almost all believe that the way to achieve this is through schooling and/or training. They recognise their schooling furthers their progress.

VI. THE UNDUGU PARKING BOYS PROGRAMME

Undugu has established centres where the boys after being counselled while on the streets and their most urgent needs being attended to are referred to. There are three centres for the boys namely, a reception centre, Eastleigh Community Home and Dandora Community Home. At these centres the children are offered shelter, food, clothing security, health, parental and brotherly love and a sense of belonging.

At the reception centre, the boys are also introduced to communial activities such as preparing their own meals, music, literacy classes, sports and gardening where they are encouraged to grow vegetables, fruits, trees and other crops on small pieces of land allocated to them.

The boys are given opportunities to join local schools and there have been many examples of boys who have excelled in their new opportunities. A total number of 5 boys have joined the universities. This is a clear indication of the potential of street children for growth and redemption once they are given the emotional support and opportunity to improve their lives.

VII. The Undugu Street Girls Programme

Through activities with parking boys in Nairobi, it became noticeable in the streets that there were also girls. Social workers begon reporting a great increase in their numbers in the late 1980's as the deteriorating living conditions in the slums led to a further breakdown of traditional African values which had normally found the daughters (who were unable to attend school) at home helping their mothers.

Whereas the survival tactics of the boys ranged from collecting scrap garbage for sale to offering 'parking services' to the shoppers, those of the girls were more or less limited to begging and prostitution. It soon became clear that child prostitution and its vicious cycle of sexually transmitted diseases, trauma and sexual abuse existed within the operational areas of Undugu's activities and that the problem of parking boys cannot be separated from that of street girls and child prostitution. The two had common sources in intolerable poverty and family disruptions.

In a way, the problem of street girls presents a much more ominous picture than that of street boys largely because girls are more vulnerable and face a higher frequency of sexual abuse and violence. The contract, suffer from and transmit sexually transmitted diseases. In the face of the AIDS epidemic they represent a definite time bomb.

The Street-girls programme was started for the purpose of guiding and developing girls in order to give them hope for tomorrow through training, counselling, provision of basic needs, community involvement, educational opportunities, medication and awareness.

Today there are 62 girls staying in a rented home in Rioki. Most of these girls have been placed in schools where they have proven to be as capable as any other students. At Rioki centre, girls receive counselling to help them overcome their past traumas. An emphasis on positive behaviour changes helps these girls realize their potential to achieve and lead decent lives.

At the centre the girls are also offered practical alternatives with a view to incalculating a sense of responsibility and self-reliance.

One of the main activities of the Undugu Street-girls programme is to impact assertive skills to the girls (how to say NO). We realize that the girls who are abused sexually and physically need empowerment, their self-esteem has to be increased and their selfrespect too.

The term 'NO' is very difficult for most of these girls especially the fact that it is interpreted differently. Some people say that when a women says 'no' she really means yes.

VIII. UNDUGU BASIC EDUCATION PROGRAMME

Undugu has since 1978 operated an informal schooling programme running parallel to the regular public education system in Kenya.

Undugu operates four schools located in the slums of Nairobi and offers numeracy skills and basic literacy. The UBEP curriculum runs over a four year period. In the first three years the children are taught basic numeracy i.e. how to read, write basic Maths, English and character development and in the fourth year, the learners are exposed to a variety of vocational skills for developments which include carpentry, tailoring, sheet metal work. These are skills considered to be marketable and applicable in the slums.

Upon completion the learners are encouraged to join the informal sector where they select a vocational skill to engage in.

IX. INFORMAL SECTOR TRAINING PROGRAMME

The learners go through trade identification workshops where they learn about the importance of trade by marketability, by cost and by ability to identify trainers in slum environments to ensure community involvement.

X. THE INTEGRATED APPROACH TO COMMUNITY DEVELOPMENT

Most of the children that Undugu works with come from the slums of Nairobi and have run away from abusive home situations which are prone to abuse and neglect. To uplift the living conditions of the children and those communities that they come from, Undugu uses an integrated approach.

The Undugu programmes in the major slums namely Kibera, Pumwani and Mathare strive to avail essentials to the communities in an integrated manner through social work and counselling, mobilization, sponsorship, business advisory, low cost housing, sanitation, community health care, informal skills, training/education, youth and women groups, urban agriculture, environmental concerns including waste recycling and appropriate technology.

XI. YOUTH GROUPS

Many youths in the slums fall into anti-social behaviour, mainly because they are idle. This is due to the high rate of school drop outs and unemployment.

In an effort to redirect their energies Undugu has struggled to promote youth activities mainly in the areas of sports and recreation. There are long established youth groups in boxing, football, tae-kwan-do and table tennis, young women are taught embroidery. Youth groups actively pursue interests in music and drama, acrobatics, dancing (cultural) and football. One group of youth has embarked on production of hand-curved curios for the local and export markets. They are assisted by the Undugu Export Unit.

XII. WOMEN GROUPS

Women groups are Undugu's central entry point into the community. Experience has shown that to uplift the community at large and to prevent children from running off to the streets, it is vital to improve the socio-economic standing of the women. This is done by providing them with ample opportunities, while offering them appropriate financial assistance to underwrite income generating ventures.

Kenya has one of the highest proportions of women in difficult circumstances in Africa. In low income areas the proportion is extremely high. In the Mathare slum, for instance it is estimated that between 70 and 80 per cent of all households are headed by women. Considering that they are among the poorest of Kenya's poor the implication for the children living in these areas is bleak.

To ensure that women play a central role, Undugu organises them into groups which subsequently define and pursue specific community needs.

Undugu stimulates the women to establish their own enterprises by:
- Taking them through business management courses where they are exposed to organisational, leadership and communication skills.
- Business advice on feasibility of business and drawing of business plans.

A number of groups have drawn up impressive business plans and are self reliant enough to act on their own. This indicates that the women have taken control of their own situation.

Most women groups are involved in activities such as building houses for rental or their own, water kiosks, traditional dancing, doll making and embroidery, production and sale of banana fibre products, kerosene selling.

XIII. PUBLIC AWARENESS CAMPAIGNS

Undugu is committed to upholding the rights of children in especially difficult circumstances, more specifically the street children.

In 1992, Undugu society carried out a month long campaign to sensitize the public and seek solutions to the plight of the children. Numerous events were organised with the intention of targeting different categories of society. Those targeted involved:

- Policy makers.
- Researchers, professional, academic.
- The general public, by offering them realities of life experiences of street children. For instance educating them of what the children do with the money, they are given by the public and why it is actually worsening the situation and also presenting ideas to them on how they can contribute to the solution seeking process.

The campaign reached out to both the children themselves and the public through a series of events and activities and a constant steam of media exposure which has continued.

Undugu also advocates for the protection of children against economic exploitation. Although it is sometimes necessary for a child to work, the conditions under which they work are very exploitative and thus abusive.

The children go to the street to assist their families but when one looks at the payment it is not worth it. There are cases where employees physically, sexually abuse the children with no or very little pay. Undugu through campaigns creates awareness/advocacy for change of attitudes towards any form of exploitation and abuse.

A new venture that Undugu is exploring at the moment is the child-to-child approach. Some rehabilitated children are used to educate their old street friends. They accompany the social workers to the streets and talk on issues like health, family planning, how to keep off the streets and ways to build up self-esteem.

The approach is proving effective because it appears that the children especially the girls listen and trust each other and are able to discuss certain issues much more freely with those of their own age groups.

Undugu is also in the process of establishing 'Child Rights Clubs' where children are made aware of their rights and discuss them openly.

XIV. Problems Encountered while Working with Neglected and Abused Children and Suggested Solutions

A. Poverty

When talking about poverty we have to talk about control i.e. control of resources, control of information, control of power (democratic power, power to decide). Economy of the rich and poor – The poor live on the rich but they have no control, the rich live on the poor and they have all the control. The work we are doing poses a challenge – it is an uphill task in that we have to build the bargaining power of the poor. We therefore need tools of the analysis, proper information, advocacy and techniques.

1. Ill Health

The children's eating habits are unhealthy in both quality and consistency. They collect food stuffs from garbage disposed off which is dangerous because it could be poisonous as well as unhygienic. The children may also go without food. They use tins to cook as their utensils which is also unhygienic. On the other hand the environment in which they live is very polluted. There is no sanitation as their 'houses' are unplanned-for structures. Consequently the place is so humid, and dirty.

This exposes the children to all sorts of diseases, the most common being scabies, worms, stomach and other skin diseases. They also suffer coughs and chest problems because the cold nights they spend out there. Their makeshift hovels normally give in the heavy storm.

2. Sexual Abuse

The girls are exposed to excessive sexual promiscuity. Consequently the girls contract all forms of STDs including the dreaded AIDS virus. In recent findings, out of 22 girls 21 were found to have one form of STD or the other. 5 were found to have contracted the AIDS causing virus. One had a baby at 13 years. Girls say that it is common to find a certain community who are very rich, picking them from the streets in big, posh vehicles luring them for sexual favours.

3. Psychological Disorders

The children are hardened by the street environment. Their hide and seek game with the police followed by frequent custody in remand homes make them devise survival technics. So in dealing with them one is dealing with young adults as opposed to children. They often operate at a higher level than their age.

4. Glue Sniffing/Drug Abuse

De-gluing and character development is necessary before the street children can be able to make up their minds about what they want.

Lack of physical strength inhibits choice of certain trades. This is usually as a result of overindulgence in drugs, poor physical growth and development, poor health due to lack of food, poor environment.

Lack of awareness: the public do not understand the plight of street children e.g. hospitals do not want to treat them, school head-teachers do not accept them, etc.

Problems of balancing between full-time training and looking for food for those boys and girls, previously bread-winners for themselves, their brothers, sisters or their children.

Capital to start up an enterprise is scarce or lacking, due to changing circumstances given the devaluation of the shilling and the escalating cost of living. Competition in the informal sector. Flooding of similar trades.

B. Drug Abuse

The children sniff glue and other intoxicating substances, thinner, tablets. These products are usually highly addictive and affect their mental ability leading to deviance in behaviour. In addition they abuse any other drugs that are available to the gangs. As a result the children are normally very violent. Often they are engaged in fights quarrels and insults, they are very temperamental.

C. The Prices of Drugs/Tablets

Tablets – Kshs. 1.00
Crablets – Kshs. 1.00
Thinner – Kshs. 65.00
Cocaine – Kshs. 110.00

The solution lies in understanding and addressing the factors that lead to child abuse and neglect. The problems are societal thus should be tackled by all members of society.

Sex education should be made a basic necessity to out of school youth since they are most involved in it. Youth living on the streets are involved in survival sex.

It is extremely difficult to discuss AIDS prevention without addressing the underlying issues that place youth at risk. Since sex for street children represents recreation, income and power, promoting healthier life styles and safer sexual behaviour requires tackling these underlying issues.

People should be made aware of the dangers facing their children especially those children who are neglected and abused so that they desist from creating situations that lead to the abuse and exploitation of the children.

Research should be done on the effect of drugs on the children and to lobby for certain policy shifts, then we should have our fact right.

Education and health services are inaccessible, unaffordable and irrelevant in most cases. Organisations should therefore network and collaborate over education matters and should also provide basic literacy, remedial and vocational training.

The fight against child abuse and neglect should be in a collaborated manner. There is a lack of coordination and information sharing among those organisations working with the children. The establishment of a method of networking is very important.

It is necessary to persuade government to honour the implementation of the Convention on the Rights of the Child and provide strict legal instruments to safeguard the same.

Governments should have regulations of conditions and remuneration of children working. Undugu creates through campaigning awareness/advocacy for a change of attitudes towards this kind of exploitation.

The Undugu Society programs related to street children have proved to be highly effective means of coping with the problems children face. The facilities and programs provide children with a realistic view of their situation, while building self-esteem and survival skills to sufficiently prepare them for their future. Slum locations of the offices as well as interaction with the children on the streets make Undugu accessible to the communities with which it is interacting. The programs have a high succes, a good sense of the problems present and the solutions available.

Nevertheless Undugu cannot reach every child in need and therefore needs the support and collaboration of other agencies (private and public). Certain policies affecting the children have to change and people need to be sensitized. Agencies working with the children should get involved in the political and economic decision making process.

MOULAYE TALL

Droits des jeunes vivant et travaillant dans les interstices du milieu urbain

L'accroissement de la pauvreté dans les villes africaines implique pour un grand nombre d'enfants et jeunes l'obligation de survivre en s'activant dans l'économie populaire urbaine. Ces jeunes tirent donc leurs ressources du milieu naturel d'évolution – la ville – de même que les jeunes pasteurs ou pêcheurs travaillent dans leurs milieux respectifs. L'économie populaire urbaine ou "secteur informel" est maintenant reconnue comme faisant partie intégrante de l'économie nationale. On ne peut donc plus la traiter de marginale, ni employer le terme marginaux pour ces jeunes et vieux, hommes ou femmes qui la pratiquent. Lorsque l'on parlera d'enfants travailleurs, cireurs, petites bonnes, pousse pousseurs, petites vendeuses, porteurs de marchés, gardiens de voiture, etc... on ne pourra les traiter de marginaux, et par conséquent imaginer des voies de réinsertion ou réhabilitation. Car l'on doit admettre qu'ils sont pleinement inserés dans le contexte socio-économique urbain de la décenie 1990–2000.

Il est par contre impératif de considerer le soutien qui doit leur être apporté, par les différents acteurs: état, environnement socio-culturel, associations populaires, ONG organismes internationaux, afin qu'ils puissent accéder à un minimum de services qu'ils sont en droit de révendiquer doublement, en tant qu'enfants, et en tant que travailleurs. Droit à la formation, à l'accès aux services de santé aux loisirs, au respect. Ceci implique un important effort d'adaptation de la société à la situation de ces enfants qui représentent une quantité importante. Cet effort ne se justifie pas seulement par une compassion à leur égard, mais doit être le remède pour la société au risque de gaspiller le potentiel considérable de ressource humaine pour le développement qu'ils constituent.

Une réflexion sur les droits de l'homme ne peut ignorer ces enfants et jeunes, elle doit les considerer comme une composante à part entière de la société, et comme tels ils doivent jouir du respect minimum et des droits qui appartiennent à tous les enfants. Devant la dureté de leur vie, le poids de la conjoncture et la lutte sans cesse croissante pour leur survie, ils font preuve d'une imagination et d'une lucidité sans par pareil, s'inventant du travail en exerçant des petits métiers. Ils sont vus par beaucoup, comme des voyous,

E. Verhellen (ed.), Monitoring Children's Rights, 867–869.

des voleurs et donc traités comme tels. Devant ces accusations les jeunes protestent. Ils reclament le droit au respect. Il est indispensable de bien saisir la diversion et les dangers de cette marginalisation psychologique. Le droit à l'identité peut constituer un élément dans la recherche solutions. Les jeunes se plaignent en dénonçant les difficultés avec la police, qui procède souvent à des rafles parfois avec violence, les garde à vue trop longues, sans motif réel, les incarcérations à durée non déterminée dans des centres de rééducation. L'inadéquation, voire l'absence de légalisation rend difficile le soutien des personnes et des institutions privées.

TERMINOLOGIE

Les termes "enfants *de ou dans* la rue" inventés en 1980 à Rio de Janeiro, sont aujourd'hui dépassés:
- parce qu'ils impliquent une appartenance d'origine à un milieu où nul enfant ne peut être conçu, la rue.
- parce qu'ils créent un amalgame entre situations différentes qui se rencontrent dans un même environnement.

Il existe parmi les enfants travailleurs, un groupe très minoritaire (quelques centaines à Bamako) qui évolue hors des structures familiales traditionnelles et qui sont victimes de la crise de ces structures. Beaucoup d'entre eux rencontrent des problèmes voire des discriminations de la part de leurs marâtres. Certains sont transfuges des écoles coraniques auxquelles ils ont été confiés, d'autres tout simplement sont en conflit avec un père trop sévère ou n'ayant pas suffisamment de temps à leurs consacrer. D'autres, enfin, se sont échappés à la suite d'un larcin qui est pourtant très courant chez des enfants de leur âge.

Hors de leur famille, ces enfants subsistent en se regroupant en bandes qui assurent, l'affection, la solidarité et l'autodéfense dans un milieu hostile.

Ils exercent des petits métiers, mais parfois sont poussés à des activités moins recommandables par la situation précaire dans laquelle ils évoluent.

Une stratégie d'appui global aux enfants travailleurs telle que évoquée plus haut pourrait leur permettre d'acquérir plus de sécurité, voir même faciliter leur retour en famille. Mais la tendance à l'exclusion qui prévaut dans le milieu urbain les pousse à un isolement croissant.

C'est tenant compte de ces éléments que l'on peut aboutir à une vision correcte des problèmes et des pistes de solution:
- tous les enfants travailleurs ont besoin d'un appui.
- les enfants qui connaissent un problème de rupture familiale (toujours temporaire dans la société africaine) méritent une attention particulière mais non exclusive.

Le risque que l'on rencontre dans la plupart des interventions qui se font dans ce domaine, est d'isoler la seconde catégorie car elle est plus dérangeante que la première de son contexte.

PROCESSUS D'AUTO-ORGANISATION EN AFRIQUE DE L'OUEST

Depuis deux années, un processus d'auto-organisation des enfants et jeunes travailleurs est mis en route dans les villes comme Bamako, Abidjan, Bouaké, Dakar. Cet élan d'organisation repond à un désir de ceux-ci de s'organiser mieux pour défendre leurs droits et augmenter leur revenus. A Bamako, l'A.J.A.P. (l'association des jeunes artisans pour le progrès) regroupe l'ensemble des cireurs et réparateurs de chaussures de la maison des artisans.

A Dakar, les bonnes (employées de maison) en participant au défilé du 1er mai entendaient faire savoir aux autorités et à l'opinion publique qu'elles étaient des travailleurs comme les autres.

Ce processus d'auto-organisation a abouti à la rencontre des enfants et jeunes travailleurs à Bouaké au mois de juillet 94.

Les douze droits des enfants et jeunes travailleurs:
– droit à une formation pour apprendre un métier;
– droit à rester au village (à ne pas s'exoder);
– droit à un recours et à une justice équitable, en cas de problèmes;
– droit à des repos de maladie;
– droit à être respectés;
– droit à être écoutés;
– droit à un travail léger et limité (adapté à nos âges et nos capacités);
– droit à des soins de santé;
– droit à apprendre, à lire et à écrire;
– droit à s'amuser, à jouer;
– droit à s'exprimer et à s'organiser;
– droit à exercer nos activités en sécurité.

Ces droits ont été identifiés par les enfants et jeunes travailleurs de quatre pays (Mali, Côte d'Ivoire, Sénégal et Burkina Faso) comme étant prioritaires à défendre pour eux. Une campagne de soutien a été lancée pour les soutenir. Les mécanismes de suivi mis en place par eux sous forme de calendrier suit son cours normal.

En conclusion, n'est-il pas plus facile de surveiller, défendre les droits de ceux qui se défendent eux-mêmes.

JAN VAN SUSTEREN

Approach of Homeless Young People

Concentrations of homeless youth we find mostly in the big cities. Recent research shows the number of these youths in The Netherlands to lie between six to seven thousand. Because they and/or their social environment and network do not function optimally and because there are not enough (temporary) solutions problems arise. The youngsters start sleeping rough and finally end up in the big cities. The nomadic existence is not the problem. The unwanted social effects like drug abuse, prostitution, health problems, suicide and delinquency are.

Various new methods of (youth) assistance point out that an individual "help-to-measure" and an optimal cooperation on the executional level of divers organisations in a network is the key to good results. These methods start from the assumption that "assistance should be as brief as possible, as light and as close to the environment as possible".[1]

Homeless youths often have shopped through all the possible forms of social support and assistance already. The assistance does not meet there needs and so they do not see the point of it any longer. Still we think the above mentioned starting points apply to them also.

I. THE METHOD

The method "Approach of homeless young people" is based on field experiences and has been developed in cooperation with field workers and other experts. The development has been made possible in collaboration with the Directorate of Youth Policy of the Ministry of Welfare, Health and Cultural Affairs, and the cities of The Hague, Rotterdam and Utrecht.

The method is divided into four stages. The first stage is passed through only once to become acquainted with the structure of the meeting places and with the social and service organisations of a city. The other three stages are passed through with each individual client. The definition we use for homeless youth is taken from two recent researches:[2]

---

[1] "Tussen droom en daad", Interdepartementale Werkgroep Ambulante en Preventieve Voorzieningen voor hulpverlening aan jeugdigen, Ministerie van W.V.C., Rijswijk, 1984.

[2] Dortmans, H. en H. de Bie, Thuisloze jongeren, met medewerking van M. Nuy, P. Heydendael en L. Geurts, Katholieke Universiteit Nijmegen, Instituut voor Sociale Geneeskunde,

E. Verhellen (ed.), Monitoring Children's Rights, 871–882.
© 1996 *Kluwer Law International. Printed in the Netherlands.*

Homeless youths are youngsters up to 25 years of age who have not had a fixed address since three months. In this time they have stayed at at least three different places.

Two groups are excluded: severe hard drug abusers and youngsters with severe psychiatric problems. Physical, psychological, medical and psychiatric problems are looked at by specialists on request of the T-Team.

II. THE BASICS

The assistance is focused on creating a good functioning social environment. The youths are being made an offer in the areas of housing/lodging, finances, education, work and the improvement of relations. In the method cooperation at the executional level is very important. Cooperation around the individual problems of young persons seems to be one of the best ways to get positive results quickly. A network of persons at the executional level of organisations working with or for homeless youth is created for this purpose. The help is offered as much as possible in the own social environment of the youths. We involve people of the different locations and meeting points of the youngster in question in solving the problems.

Also the former social environment is reactivated and we link up with people that are, or formerly were trusted by the client (V.I.P.s). If this is not possible, a new social environment is created together with the client. The areas that will be involved are: parents, (extended) family, friends, leisure activities, work, education and physical and mental health.

The client is followed as long as needed to reinstall sufficient adaptability and a stable social network to support him in a self-reliant continuation of his life. The basic principals of the method are:

– building up a network of contacts and cooperation with all organisations that have to do with homeless youngsters (welfare, police and justice departments, schools and education, health care, job centres, shelters, social work institutions, etc.); an optimum network cooperation between a T-Team and the different service and social organisations can offer each individual youngster a "help-to-measure" from the first contact up to the aftercare;
– seek out homeless youths at their meeting points and motivate and support them;
– approach the youngster person-to-person and intensely, build up (a relationship of) trust, make a thorough analysis of the past and present social environment of the youth and set out from his positive possibilities;

Nijmegen 1990 en Ploeg, J.D. v.d., J. Gaemers en P.H. Hoogendam, Zwervende jongeren, serie: Hedendaagse Jeugdzorg, Centrum Onderzoek Jeugdhulpverlening – R.U. Leiden, D.S.W.O. Press, Leiden, 1991.

- the help should as much as possible take place in the environment at which the problems arose; try to activate the past social network of the young person, make use of his (former) important persons (V.I.P.s). Ask them to help and support him; is this not possible create a new social environment together with the person in question;
- build up a good functioning social environment on the basis of the wishes, expectations and possibilities of the youngster; look at the family, the extended family, friends, work, school and the places where the young person spends his free time;
- the help should be consistent, step by step and of sufficient duration;
- work at and improve the responsibilities of each person involved (the youngster, the organisations and the V.I.P.s) by way of checkable agreements;
- follow and support the youngster until he has enough "loading and unloading capacity" and a (new) social environment, which is stable enough to support him to go on on his own;
- find solutions within normal and every day life situations and social possibilities, like a regular job, regular education, etcetera;
- provide good aftercare.

III. THE T-TEAM

The "Thuislozen-Team", T-Team, consists of four or five members. They are posted to the team from different service and social organisations. The tasks of the T-Team worker are:

- making contact with individual homeless youths by leaving desk and seeking out youths at their meeting points is essential;
- inspiring the confidence of the young person;
- stimulating his motivation;
- making a plan with a clear perspective together with the youth in question. The plan is a step by step plan and must have short and long term results. The short term results show the youngster the plan is achievable. Essential is to make a thorough social environment analysis, and to check if a youngster can and wants to go back to his past social environment/network;
- initialising, regulating and coordinating contacts with workers on the executional level of service and social organisations in the network to support and execute the plan: restoring the youth to his past social environment or build up a new one;
- monitor the progress;
- monitor the aftercare;
- spotting blank spaces in the network (for instance having no organisation in the network to finance directly and temporarily the bare essentials of a youth).

The T-Team worker is at the disposal of the client for 24 hours a day and 7 days a week. He can undertake direct action at any moment, can use his time very flexible and can intervene intensively up to 20 hours a week. In a contract is laid down that the worker has face-to-face contact with the youth for at least 12 hours a week. The remaining time is spend in behalf of the youth. The programme is limited in time. The T-Team worker works 4 to 8 weeks on a very personal basis with a youngster. Because of this he has a low caseload existing of 2 youths a month.

To tackle the problems of a youth we need a worker who does not stay put behind his desk, but who looks up the youths at their meeting places and attempts to make contact with them.

IV. The 4 stages of the method

A. Stage 1 – the Network of Contacts

This stage is passed through once to obtain a clear and overall picture of the macrostructure of the city and its service and social organisations and of all the meeting points of the target group in the city (street, gambling halls/game arcades, coffeeshops, boarding houses, railway stations, crises centres, centres for the homeless, etcetera).

We start the building up of a network of service and social organisations that have to do with homeless youngsters (welfare, police and justice departments, schools and education, health care, job centres, etcetera).

A T-Team worker has to be able to contact the right person to work at the problem of a youth as soon as possible. He has to be able to find people within an organisation or at a meeting point of youths, who have a good relationship with the target group. These persons can be VIPs or people who have a good overall view of the situation at a certain meeting point. They are important sources of information. These people we call "key-figures". For this reason it is important to have special attention officials at each organisation who can show you to the right person immediately. To accomplish this a network is started by way of a three-day training. This network consists of executive workers on an urban level, who, working within their organisation, become special attention officials who take special responsibility for the assistance of homeless youths.

The T-Team can consult them in the intervention period and can do business with them with regard to material needs. After the intervention period these special attention officials take over the guidance; they carry out the agreed plan of action.

A condition is that the special attention official, works since a considerable time at one of the below mentioned disciplines and has a good insight in the possibilities of the existing organisations in his field.

In the network of contacts the following organisations should be represented:

- ambulant and residential youth assistance;
- (day and night) shelters and crisis centres;
- police and justice departments;
- educational institutes;
- municipal services;
- social work services;
- housing departments;
- job centres and the employment exchange;
- health organisations (physical, psychological and psychiatric).

The network of contacts together with the T-Team is called the "problem solving network". The "problem solving network" is as broadly-based as possible (minimally 15 organisations, 20 participants) and meets once every two months. Main task is making homeless youngsters a fitting offer on the domains of work, education, health, etc.

While working for individual youngsters the network is expanded and strengthened by mutual contacts around the individual assistance. The tasks of the organisations in the network are:

- being a point of consultation to the T-Team worker on their own field;
- taking on that part of the plan worked out by the T-Team worker and the individual youngster which has to do with their field of work and is needed to support and execute the plan;
- taking on the necessary aftercare of that part of the plan;
- drawing attention to arising problems at an early stage and so trying to prevent youth to start sleeping rough.

Sleeping rough is a behavioural indicator, a consecutive problem. The basic problem often can be found within the family relationships. Therefore a systematic approach is very important. When a youngster wants to go back home and at least one of the parents wants this too a comparable intensive, person-to-person method can be offered to support the family.

B. Stage 2 – The intervention period: making contact and motivate

To the T-Team worker the intervention period is the most time- and labour-consuming period in the guidance of the individual youth. He has to make contact with the youngster, to gain his trust and to motivate him to work together at finding a place in society. The guidance is ambulant and intensive.

Homeless youth live in an almost constant state of crisis. Generally we see it as our task to get rid of a crisis. This method shows that a crisis can serve as a necessary, very important means of motivation. Often it is necessary to create a disturbance of the balance in order to bring about a change.

The main goal of the intervention period is to convert the problems of the youngster from a street rough behaviour into problem behaviour.

To stop the street rough behaviour preconditions have to be met. The most important are:

– having a permanent accomodation;
– having settled the finances;
– having (the prospect of) a job or going to school.

All problems are not resolved as yet, but the step is made by which the youth takes part again in the social system. By working systematically and stimulating the motivation of the youngster the street rough behaviour is broken.

The T-Team worker should not present himself as a social worker, but as a trustworthy mediator of the youth. It means to be committed, to go along actively with the life-style and environment of the youth in question. Proceeding from this involvement and this actively going along, realistic steps can be made. Because most of the homeless youths do not want to have to do anything anymore with the social work circuit, the strategy of a T-Team worker as a mediator (a go-between between the youth and the assistance) is a good approach. First of all the youth will not think at the moment of making contact: here is another social worker who will solve my problems for me in a trice. Secondly, when during the process of assistance problems arise with a service or social organisation the youth will more easily fall back on the T-Team worker; he will probably also tell more. Finally we concentrate on the positive points of the youth instead of on the negative ones.

Making contact

The T-Team worker visits the meeting places or he makes use of the people that are important to the youth, the VIPs. These persons can support the youth at building up his "new" social environment.

The VIPs have to be relations of the youth based on mutual trust, for whom the youth himself chooses. A requirement though is that these relations can offer a perspective of growth. The youth could for instance choose a VIP, who is part of the criminal scene. So a distinction has to be made between VIPs that may keep the youth in the circuit ("fungous" VIPs) and those that can help him to get out. Both are important to the youth, but the T-Team worker can not do business with them both. The fungous VIP does have to be involved in the process, otherwise the youth will (only) strengthen the relation with this person.

A VIP with growth perspective (for instance a neighbour or an uncle) can be given responsibilities, can be stimulated to do certain things. It is someone who takes care of the youth and who guides him a while, who talks with the youngster and puts him on his way.

Making/establishing contact takes three steps

Step 1. The T-Team worker attempts three to four times to make contact with a youngster within a period of two weeks. Not all youngsters are willing to talk straight away with just another social worker. If the attempts fail the team keeps an eye on the youth in question. The T-Team can not sit back and wait.

Important elements of making contact are:
- establishing contact and going along with the worker is environment of the youth, with his system and way of living, so the worker is able to think along with the youth and can start working together from his perspective;
- credibility and trust;
- temporary solutions for a few material problems, like housing and finances.

Step 2. Our methodical reasoning is: give the youth chances in the social system, so that in this way a change of behaviour can be brought about. We do not talk about the behaviour of the past, we talk about the current behaviour and the current motivation. The worker can only measure the behaviour and motivation of the youth on the basis of actual experiences in the field he is working in.

The past is important as background information. But we are only interested in the positive aspects of the past behaviour. At what moment did it go well with the youth, how and why? These aspects give us "acting mechanisms", that can be used in the new social environment we create. The negative aspects tend to confirm the problems. Visible steps keep the motivation strong, that is why short term goals are important. Youth often do not see the effects of long term goals, so they drop out. We have to explain again and again what the effects are of the things we do with them.

Step 3. The next step is formulating a plan of action by way of a thorough analysis of the social environment.

C. Stage 3 – The intervention period: social environment analysis and contract

To be able to formulate a good plan of action it is necessary to make a thorough analysis of the social environment of the youth. To this end the T-Team worker makes use of a model of analysis, in which the past, present and wished for situation of the youth are mapped:

- with regard to the past situation a picture is formed of the old social environment of the youth with its meeting points, relations and VIPs and of the physical and psychological problems from birth;
- with regard to the present situation a picture is formed of which conditions for a normal life in society are lacking and which are present, like for instance: finances; housing; education and/or work; social skills and a social network; psychological and physical well-being and legal status;
- for the wished for situation a time scaled plan of action with perspective is outlined (with temporary and structural goals) in order to meet the wishes, possibilities and expectations of the youngster and to build up a "new" social environment.

The mutual contract

We work towards a moment on which a satisfactory contact is made: the youth is motivated and puts his trust in the T-Team worker and a possible VIP. In short: the youth is willing. That moment will be reached with one youth only after three weeks, with another within a day.

At that moment a mutual contract is signed, in which the approach is written down as clearly as possible: what will the youth himself undertake, what will the T-Team worker and further assistance undertake.

Three routes are possible, of which two are laid down in the contract: the route for building up and strengthening (new) relationships and the school route, or the route for building up and strengthening (new) relationships and the job route.

If the contract is broken prematurely and it is confirmed that the problems have not been resolved satisfactorily a follow-up policy has to take place.

Summarized the contract:

- is mutually agreed upon and signed with agreements about commitments of both the youth and the assistance;
- has a plan of action with long and short term goals with regard to two routes;
- can be terminated by both parties.

D. Stage 4 – the Routes

The fourth and last stage, starting immediately after the 4 to 8 weeks of intensive ambulant assistance by the T-Team, consists of the execution of the plan of action. In this period several persons and organisations, varying from job centres, schools, youth assistance workers, social work services, guardians, health and municipal institutions take over the guidance and coaching of the youth, in accordance with the agreements of the mutual contract. They give guidance to the youngsters from their specific area of services together with other organisations in the network. The T-Team worker distances himself more and more from the youth. He monitors and checks at intervals how the youngster is coping. If the youth wants the T-Team worker to stay the mediator this can be arranged.

The network of contacts sees to:
- giving the T-Team a thorough feedback;
- a big as possible chance of succes of the routes;
- contacts and agreements with regard to the guidance of the social aspects and skills and the motivation of the youth;
- contacts and agreements with the youth with regard to his progress, the agreements and possible bottlenecks;
- contacts and agreements with the employer with regard to the initial period and possible further assistance on the workfloor;
- assistance and guidance for the youth and his (new) relations.

Together with the youngster the former/a new network of relations is made by:
- departing from the agreements in the contract;
- clearing up together the misunderstandings and the consecutive problems;
- working on the basic problem;
- spotting new arising problems as soon as possible;
- seeing to it the youth feels safe socially;
- working on the youngster's (social) skills.

Summarizing the most effective way of restoring the past social environment is: clear up the misunderstandings or the consecutive problems at the meeting point(s) where they occur. And in this way create peace in the social environment of the youth. Above all get the basic problem attended to. With that it is important that the youngster can be helped effectively only when there are good functioning networks with the social environment and the social network of the youth.

V. THE AFTERCARE

The plan of action is executed by the network of contacts. The T-Team evaluates the progress after a period of half a year and a year. On the basis of this evaluation the expectations of the youngster and involved persons can be adjusted. Also the approach of the service and social organisations can be adjusted as well as the method of the T-Team.

At a certain point the young person has enough confidence and a stable enough basis in his "new" social environment to function on his own in everyday life. At that moment the decision is made to stop the support and to end the mutual contract.

Together with the young person it is decided if some form of assistance is still necessary and which organisation takes over.

VI. THE FIRST RESULTS

At the end of 1993, rather more than a year after starting the A.T.J.-experiment (A.T.J. is short for "Aanpak Thuisloze Jeugd" = Approach of Homeless Young People), the first results of the T-Team guidance in The Hague, Rotterdam and Utrecht are measured by the S.C.O.-Kohnstamm Institute.[3]

143 youngsters have received guidance. Their average age at the start of the guidance is 19, varying from 13 to 34 years. 27% of them is of the female gender. 74% has the Dutch and 15% the Moroccan nationality. The percentage non-Dutch in The Hague is 42%, in Utrecht 22% and in Rotterdam 10%.

Other facts about the A.T.J.-population are:
- 90% of the youngsters is sleeping rough or has a temporary shelter;
- 73% has slept at four or more different places in the past period;
- 97% has not been to school in the past period;
- 73% has not worked for more than three months;
- 90% has no current job;
- 93% has no daily activities;
- 82% has no regular income;
- 63% shows signs of criminal behaviour;
- 80% has no contact with their father;
- 70% has no contact with their mother;
- 68% uses soft drugs on a regular basis;
- 80% is homeless for three months or longer.

When using the division of Van der Ploeg et al.[4] 13% of the A.T.J.-population must be regarded as moderately problematic, 48% as seriously problematic and 39% as severely problematic. There are significantly more seriously and severely problematic homeless youths in the A.T.J.-population than in the research of Van der Ploeg et al. Within the A.T.J.-population there are more severely problematic boys than girls.

The support of the T-Teams is aimed at guiding homeless youths to a socially acceptable social environment with perspective by realising (temporary)

---

[3] Gijtenbeek, J., Interimrapportage evaluatie "Aanpak Thuisloze Jeugd" 1993, Tussentijds verslag van de evaluatie van een nieuwe methodiek van hulpverlening, "Aanpak Thuisloze Jeugd", in Den Haag, Rotterdam en Utrecht, S.C.O.-rapport 358, I.S.B.N.: 90-6813-407-8, S.C.O.-Kohnstamm-Instituut, Amsterdam, 1994.

[4] Ploeg, J.D. van der, J. Gaemers en P.H. Hoogendam, Zwervende jongeren, serie: Hedendaagse Jeugdzorg, Centrum Onderzoek Jeugdhulpverlening – R.U. Leiden, D.S.W.O. Press, Leiden, 1991.

housing, tidying up the finances and, if possible, arrange meaningful daily activities (like school and/or work) and repairing and/or stimulating relationships. The process of guidance can be stopped by the youth or the T-Team worker before these goals are achieved; we call this a premature closure. We talk about a regular closure when the guidance is completed as planned. The guidance of 117 (82%) youngsters of the population of 143 is closed at the end of 1993. In 35 (30%) of the cases the closure was premature and in 82 (70%) of the cases the closure was regular.

When comparing the aforementioned division in moderately, seriously and severely problematic youths there are no differences found in premature and regular closures. As yet it has to be stated that the approach is not group specific.

Premature closure

In 35 cases the closure of the T-Team guidance was premature. Reasons are: insufficient cooperation of the youth (9 times), refusal of further guidance by the youth (9 times), drug abuse (6 times), enduring criminal behaviour (4 times), detention (4 times) and psychiatric problems (3 times).

In the cases of premature closure because of detention the aim is to pick up the guidance again after the detention period.

Regular closure

95% of the youngsters of whom the guidance ends with a regular closure has (temporary) housing: 35% has his own room or apartment, 22% lives with their parents, family or friends, 18% lives in an institution and 16% has found accomodation at a supervised housingproject.

The finances of 88% of the youngsters are settled; for one youngster it turned out not to be possible and for the others guidance with regard to this aspect was not necessary. Realising work or schooling turns out to be more difficult than finding living arrangements and settling the finances. At the closure of the guidance 32% of the youngsters has a job, 20% receives a form of training or goes to school, 7% has a job and goes to school and 39% has no job nor attends any kind of schooling.

Judicial matters of 37% of the youngsters are resolved during the guidance. For 59% of the ATJ-population this was not necessary.

Only six youths indicate during the guidance they do not want to repair their former relationships. The remaining youths (93%) make a start with this; notably with their parents and brothers and sisters. Looking at the situation of the youths three months after the regular closure of the T-Team guidance, mid september 1993 this applies to 58 youths, for 46 (79%) of them the situation has not changed in a negative way. Two youngsters have become homeless again, 1 is in prison and of 8 youths no particulars are known.

Six months after regular closure of the guidance, this applies to 28 youths, the situation of 16 youngsters has stabilised, 1 youth has become homeless again and of 11 youths no information is known.

At the start of 1996 the final results of the A.T.J.-experiment have been published. They don't differ from the first results. 400 homeless youngsters have received T-Team assistance. A year after regular closure of the guidance 77 out of 100 youngsters still maintain their new found place in society.

The same results have been obtained with comparable projects aimed at delinquent youth.

At this moment new T-Teams have started their work in seven other Dutch cities. For about two years Bureau INSTAP also has a "help-to-measure" project in Moscow, Russia, to keep multi problem families together and to prevent out of home placement of children.

Results, brochures and video-material of the methods are available.

APPENDIX

Bureau INSTAP

The last fifteen years Bureau INSTAP has developed several methods for and given courses to executive workers of organisations who work with and for young people in problem situations.

We have developed a method for schools and other institutions to prevent children getting into trouble, an approach of homeless youth and an approach of young people committing criminal acts.

Two main goals in our methods are:
1. In a region of about 50,000 people we bring together all executive workers who work with youngsters of the target group, like police, family doctors, Social Workers, teachers, etc. With them we start a network. The problem solving network. We train this network to strengthen the cooperation between social work, neighbourhood centres, police, schools, health care, etc. and the meeting points of the youngsters, in a town, a quarter of a town, a neighbourhood or a regional area.
2. We help young people individually and very intensive.

DARIJA REMETA

Children Victims of War in the Republic of Croatia

The Republic of Croatia as a legal successor of the former Yugoslavia adopted the Convention on the Rights of the Child in its legal system by the Notification act in December 8th, 1991.

In November 1993, Croatia made its first report about the Convention on the Rights of the Child and an additional special Report on the violations of the Convention on the Rights of the Child during the war in the republic of Croatia.

We considered that we had to do it separately, because we wished to inform organisations and individuals world-wide, and especially the Committee for the Rights of the Child about the flagrant violations of basic children's rights in Europe in the end of the 20th century.

In this short report I shall inform what has happened with the children in Croatia during the war and how the Convention was violated and is still violated now. 247 children were killed, most of them during the first year of the war. Most children got killed in the area of East Slavonia, because families didn't want to leave their homes, and later they could not leave this part of Croatia. The causes of death were air-raids, shelling, shooting and explosions.

Article 6 of the Convention guarantees the right to life to every child.

What does this number of 247 killed children mean for our country in comparison with the USA or Germany? In correlation with the total number of inhabitants we can see from next example:

	Croatia	USA	Germany
Inhabitants	4.784.265	226.504.825	61.657.945
Killed children	247	11.325	3.083

In the same time a huge number of children were wounded (947).

We have now 12 children with 100% invalidity, 2 with 90%, 14 with 80%, 70 with 70% and so on. Some of them are still in rehabilitation and for some of them we don't know if they will stay as severe disabled children.

E. Verhellen (ed.), Monitoring Children's Rights, 883–885.
© 1996 Kluwer Law International. Printed in the Netherlands.

Articles 6, 19 and 24 of the Convention talk about the right to life, adequate medical help and protection of all forms of violence (physical and psychical).

For 52 children we don't know where they are, they are missing. Some of them, 30, now are more than 18 years old.

During the war 4.273 children lost one parent and 54 lost both of them; 10 children whose parents were killed got injured in the same shooting incident.

We have 986 children whose parents are missing. They didn't hear about them from the beginning of the war. The right of children to their own families is violated (Article 16 and 19 of the Convention on the Rights of the Child).

During the war a significant number of children were forced to exile. In the period of only two and a half months (from October to December 1991), 172.268 children were displaced.

Upon the arrival of the UN Peace-Keeping Forces at the beginning of 1992, and the suspension of most violent hostilities, some of them returned to their homes.

About 25% of them have been poorly accommodated in refugee centres, where several generations of families live together in one room without appropriate sanitary conditions. These children were deprived of their right to home, family life, education and natural environment.

According to the latest data of April 27, 1994, 71.976 displaced children were registered.

Now we have children with serious psychological problems. The children in their growing up period are still unable to apply various compensatory mechanisms aimed at helping in dealing with traumatic experiences. At the same time they have to confront the previously unknown situations: the changing relations within the family and neighbours; their friends have become their enemies, and finally, their home does not belong to them any more.

Living with stress-affected parents is another problem. A parent who finds it difficult to live up to new living conditions is not only unable to give an appropriate support to his child, but often is either aggressive or depressed and thus inflicts an additional stress on a child.

As a result we have now more and more children who come in our Trauma centre with sleeping disorders, learning disorders, phobias, communication disorders, eating disorders, and so on.

It is very difficult sometimes to help them because we don't know what to tell them, when their fathers will come back, when they will go back to their destroyed homes, we can't plan future with them.

So the Convention is still violated, because they still have not their homes, they are still waiting for their parents, mostly the fathers, they still live in very dangerous parts (first front lines).

During the war 15 health institutions for children were destroyed, and 14 were damaged.

8 children's homes were destroyed and damaged, 3 reformatory homes, and 5 homes for handicapped children were totally destroyed.

128 kindergartens, 335 elementary schools and 56 high schools and dormitories were destroyed or damaged.

From the European Conference we expect condemnation of such acts, and international intervention in offering help to children.

CONCLUSION

- The children are the most helpless victims of the war.
- The professionals gathered at the European Conference on Monitoring Children's Rights are willing and ready to cooperate to improve the living conditions of children but for the moment this is not enough.
- It is a must that the politicians and the statesmen fulfil their part of responsibility to ensure peace in the world and to cease children's suffering.

E.A. PEETERS, P. IDENBURG and E. WILLEMSE

Declaration of Amsterdam: A Summary

The "Conference on the Rights of Children in Armed Conflict" was held on 20 and 21 June 1994 in the City Hall of Amsterdam. This two-day conference was organized by International Dialogues Foundation (IDF) together with the Netherlands Committee for UNICEF and Defence for Children International (DCI). Academics and practitioners in the fields of humanitarian law, the rights of the child, development cooperation, humanitarian relief assistance and UN peacekeeping participated in the "Conference on the Rights of Children in Armed Conflict". The Conference was chaired by Prof. Dr. G.H. Aldrich, Professor of International Law at Leyden State University. Dr. Th.A. van Baarda, scholar of International Humanitarian Law, served as its General Secretary. At the conclusion of the Conference the participants committed themselves to the urgent improvement of the situation of children in armed conflict. Their intentions were proclaimed in the "Declaration and Recommendations on the Rights of Children in Armed Conflict" ("Declaration of Amsterdam").

The "Declaration of Amsterdam" provides recommendations concerning child-victims of war in particular and the humanitarian protection and assistance of civilians in general. This initiative is in line with the resolution 48/157 of the UN General Assembly, requesting the Secretary General of the United Nations to initiate a study into the means of improving the protection of children in armed conflicts. The epidemic character of civil war-like conflicts with its enormous number of child-victims makes the further strengthening of the international legal instruments for their protection a matter of the greatest urgency.

The "Declaration of Amsterdam" is based on, and refers where possible to, existing international humanitarian law, including the Geneva Conventions on the Protection of the Victims of War and the Convention on the Rights of the Child.

Among the basic principles explicitly confirmed by the Declaration are the principles that child-victims of war shall be among the first to receive protection and relief and the recognition of the family as the basic unit of society.

The family unity shall be respected by all governmental and non-governmental organisations during the armed conflict and its aftermath. No sep-

E. Verhellen (ed.), Monitoring Children's Rights, 887–890.

aration shall take place between siblings and their parents or permanent care-givers. Children include every human being up to the age of eighteen years.

The Declaration explicitly reconfirms the fundamental distinction between civilian and military objects and objectives. Children shall be respected as civilians and in all situations of armed conflict children shall not be made subject of attack. Children shall neither be recruited in armed forces nor allowed to take part in hostilities. The present internationally recognized definition of a child carries the maximum age of fifteen years; this should be raised to eighteen.

All children up to the age of eighteen should receive education in schools or in other institutions. Education shall be given in accordance with the cultural, linguistic or religious identity of the children concerned and the wishes of their parents or guardians.

In order to limit the psycho-social stress and traumatic effects of armed conflict on children, additional measures should be taken in the field of humanitarian assistance and protection.

Prior to the imminent outbreak of hostilities such measures may include the precautionary and voluntary temporary evacuation of children from danger zones accompanied by at least one parent or adult member of the family. During hostilities these measures may include the establishment of health centres and services to help parents and children; the opportunity for children and their parents to maintain personal relations through correspondence; the establishment of local cease-fires; hospital zones, "zones of tranquillity" for humanitarian purposes and evacuation from besieged or encircled areas in accordance with the present Declaration or the Geneva Conventions and Protocols.

During the hostilities and their aftermath they may include tracing facilities for dislocated parents, families and children and reuniting dislocated children with their parents and family members.

The Conference recommends that the above measures be included in relief programmes. Neutral states and humanitarian organisations established in neutral states, should support the measures recommended as far as feasible and appropriate, through local humanitarian organisations.

The Declaration indicates several special categories of child-victims of war that shall be given special treatment. A broad category is that of unaccompanied children. For them a legal custodian should be appointed if the parents are unknown or cannot be found within a limited period of time. All children who have been separated from their parents or guardians must be registered and fully documented in order to facilitate the tracing.

A child who is pregnant as the result of rape or other sexual abuse should, under the law of the land, have the same rights as an adult woman. Every effort shall be made to prevent the danger of stigmatisation of children born as the result of rape. Due consideration should be given to the possibility of secret delivery and the adoption of these children.

THE ISSUE OF CHILDREN BORN AS THE RESULT OF RAPE IN PARTICULAR DESERVES MENTIONING, AS IT REPRESENTS THE FIRST CODIFICATION OF THE ISSUE IN INTERNATIONAL HUMANITARIAN LAW

Abuse of adoption should be prevented. The declaration supports the UNHCR/UNICEF joint statement on "The Evacuation of Children from Conflict Areas" of 1992 and the "Convention on the Protection of Children and Cooperation in Respect of Inter-Country adoption" of 1993. The UNHCR/UNICEF statement expresses that adoption should not be considered if the parents might still be alive; if it is against the express wishes of the child or the parent and if reasonable time (at least two years) has passed to allow for tracing information to be gathered. Staying with relatives in extended family units is to be preferred. State governments, humanitarian and human rights organisations should monitor closely the risk of trafficking of children during and after the end of hostilities.

Institutions should keep records and share information relating to any enquiries made by private individuals or non-humanitarian agencies to organise private adoptions and/or evacuations of children.

The Declaration strongly supports the appointment of a Special Rapporteur on the Protection of Children in Armed Conflict.

The Special Rapporteur could solicit and transmit information from and to governmental, inter-governmental and non-governmental sources, and respond effectively. The Special Rapporteur may as well make his good offices and expertise available to the government or authorities concerned, in order to advise on the improvement of children's humanitarian rights. He may make specific and general recommendations to the authorities concerned.

Among the general recommendations on humanitarian protection and assistance of civilians are recommendations on the rights of safe and timely access for impartial humanitarian organisations. Their actions should be facilitated by governmental and inter-governmental authorities.

There is an urgent need to control and outlaw indiscriminate forms of warfare that maim and kill children. The Declaration recommends that there should be a total ban on the production, stockpiling, transfer, and use of anti-personnel mines.

All states concerned should take the present Declaration into account when applying or interpreting international humanitarian law.

PURPOSE

The "Declaration of Amsterdam" will be distributed among government-agencies and relevant humanitarian, military and educational institutions. In order to raise awareness amongst the young of the plight of children in armed conflict, a "popular version" of the "Declaration of Amsterdam" will be published by DCI, Amsterdam.

International Dialogues Foundation is an independent organisation that strives to advance the position of oppressed peoples and minorities by means of international dialogue. That dialogue is stimulated by IDF through the organization of conferences and the publication of various documents and reports. Raising awareness of the plight of children in armed conflict has over the years been and continues to be an important objective of International Dialogues Foundation.

***

NOTE: The report of the "Conference on the Rights of Children in Armed Conflict" including the complete text of the "Declaration of Amsterdam", can be ordered – preferably in writing – at the Secretariat of International Dialogues Foundation. The price is US $ 20 and can be paid by Eurocheque (no other cheques) to International Dialogues Foundation. Or by instructing your bank to transfer the amount due to the account 43.69.87.708 (ABN AMRO Bank, Amsterdam) of International Dialogues Foundation.

JANE GREEN SCHALLER

Protection of Children and their Health During Times of War

In recent years great advances have been made in protecting the world's children against some of their oldest and most common enemies: respiratory disease, diarrheal disease, infectious disease, and malnutrition. But unfortunately no great progress has been made in protecting the world's children from two other ancient enemies: war and violence. Indeed war is now emerging as a major disease – a major cause of childhood mortality and morbidity – a disease which affects children in too many countries of the world today. UNICEF estimates that in the last decade, 2 million children have died in wars, 4–5 million have been physically disabled by wars, more than 5 million have been forced into refugee camps around the world, and more than 12 million children have been left homeless.[1]

Most wars used to be conducted with armies fighting armies, and soldiers fighting soldiers. Civilians were in principal protected. It is estimated that in World War I only 5% of casualties were civilians. In World War II, 50% of casualties were civilians. However in the many large and small wars which have occurred since World War II, the vast majority of casualties, an estimated 80–90% of them, have been civilians, many of them children. Indeed civilians rather than soldiers seem to have now become the major targets of war.[1,2]

Wars affect the health of children in many ways, using a broad definition of health which includes not only physical well being but also mental and social well being. Considerations of the family, the community, and the educational system are of great importance in this regard. Direct effects of war on children include death, injury, disability, physical and sexual abuse, detention, loss of families through death or separation, displacement from homes and countries, and psychological trauma. Indirect effects of war on children include poverty, poor living conditions, poor nutrition, poor health care, poor education, disruption of normal life, loss of family life and recreation and safety, discrimination on religious and ethnic grounds, and exploitation as child soldiers, child laborers, and child prostitutes.

Discussions of children and war are often difficult because the topic of war has many political implications, whereas the topics of children and child well being should not be politicized. Those of us with the ability, the authority, and

E. Verhellen (ed.), Monitoring Children's Rights, 891–898.

the ethical and professional responsibilities to care for and protect children must not allow our professions to become politicized so that we fail to act on behalf of children. Indeed our professions and our responsibilities for children must transcend politics. Furthermore, our concerns for children must go further than the borders of our own houses, villages, cities, states, and countries. As professionals and as human beings we share a common responsibility for the well being of children everywhere. The unfortunate children of the world who are caught up in wars are not "somebody else's children"; they are our children too.

I would like to tell you now about an ongoing project which is attempting to address the broad health issues of children in war: Workshops on Child Health in Countries of the Former Yugoslavia. This project has been sponsored and supported by the National Research Council/Institute of Medicine/National Academy of Science of the United States, by Tufts University in Boston/Medford, Masachusetts, and by UNICEF in former Yugoslavia. So far we have held two workshops, in March and November 1994.[3,4] These workshops have involved the leaders in pediatrics and children's medicine from Bosnia-Herzegovina, Croatia, Macedonia, Serbia, and Slovenia; and respresentatives of American, European, and International Pediatric Societies and academic institutions.

Why was former Yugoslavia chosen as a site for this kind of project? There are, sadly, many possible sites where one could study the impact of war on children. Former Yugoslavia is unfortunately now a tragic laboratory of war, and one where health statistics were known before the war and where health statistics will be known again after the war. What is happening in this part of the world can be documented. We fully realize that there could, regrettably, be many other places for such a project, and we do not in any way imply that any one place is more important than any other.

I am only sorry that my colleagues from these countries cannot be here today to speak to you directly. I will attempt to speak for them, using their own words spoken in March 1994. Their descriptions of what happens to children in times of war are very moving, and tell more of the situations than I could ever tell myself.

Pediatrician – Bosnia-Herzegovina

"Before the war our children were free. They had a wonderful life. They were well fed and well dressed; they wore Levis brought from Trieste. They had good kindergartens; they learned languages and heard fairy tales. They had toys, played with dolls and model railways. They listened to the latest music, and played on computers. They fished in the waters of the Bosnia River.

Now a new kind of child lives with us. Our children are old. They are children with sad eyes. When they look up, they see chimneys with no smoke coming out. At school, instead of computers, they are given bits of newspaper on which to write assignments. Their schools are still bright, but the children share the space with 40,000 refugees.

The children live a different life now. They no longer think like before, and neither do we. We have no hygienic materials, no soap, little clean water. And as for music, our children listen now only to the music of war. Instead of Bach or Beethoven, they hear the sounds of shells. Instead of fairy tales, they go to sleep thinking of food. The piano now is not for music, but for selling in order to buy things to eat.

Children worry about their parents at the front. Often, when they go to school now – it is underground. They do not fish in the river any longer, because all the fish have been eaten. Our children are no longer charmed by the cooing of the pigeons, because all of the pigeons have been eaten. In the evening our children worry if their parents will come home again, if their mothers or fathers will be able to go on taking care of them.

Let me tell you something about the state of health before the war. We had regional hospitals, and a well organized general hospital with specialists. We had good health care for school-age and pre-school children. We had intensive care and excellent surgical capacity. We were able to perform most medical and surgical care. Eighty-five percent of all births were in hospital. Now we cannot provide even basic health care. Out of our twenty-one incubators, only three are working. The mortality of our babies is much worse now. Our equipment is ruined by electrical failures, the lack of spare parts, and the impossibility of maintenance. We see malignant tumors grow. We see children die with cardiac diseases. By far the most tragic are refugee children. They suffer the effects of psychological trauma. They suffer from rape and maiming, from hepatitis and digestive tract diseases. We see children with arms and legs missing. I have seen a child who sat holding a part of her face in her hands.

Yet these same maimed children sit in wheelchairs in the corridors in the evenings and play their games. They have hope. We must help them in their hope. We must think about the future of these children. Out of these children, we must create a new people. Our children ask you to help us in bringing peace again. And we must restore respect for the United Nations Convention on the Rights of the Child."

TRAUMA SURGEON – BOSNIA-HERZEGOVINA

"Bosnia and Hezegovina are unfortunately universities of war now. We have 800,000 refugees and 2 million displaced persons. In Bosnia there have been 143,000 persons killed, 16,500 of them children. In Sarajevo there have been 10,000 people killed, 1600 of them children. In Bosnia there have been 162,500 people injured, 34,000 of them children. In Sarajevo there have been 58,000 people injured, 15,000 of them children. In Bosnia, there have been 9,000 disabled, 1820 of them children. In Sarajevo, there have been 1680 people disabled, 340 of them children.

We surgeons would be very happy if we didn't have to do what we have to do now every day. The youngest patient on whom I amputated a limb was a 4-month old baby. We surgeons don't want to have to do this kind of work.

Our children had a past. They have no present. We must find them a future."

PEDIATRICIAN – CROATIA

"Many problems for children have resulted from the war in Croatia of 1991–1992:

First was the loss of life and injury. Official figures listed 236 children killed, and 802 gravely wounded. These figures will probably go up by 20% when all data are factored in. The majority were victims of firearms and artillery and land mines.

Psychological symptoms have occurred in both children and in the local populations. The most frequent symptoms we find in these children are sadness, depression, tearfulness, physical tension, sleep disturbances, fears, withdrawn behavior, irritability, and detachment behavior.

In addition to direct injuries, the war caused severe displacement of populations. In 1992, over 700,000 people were forced out of their homes, about 15% of the total Croatian population. The situation in Croatia was made more difficult by the arrival of 280,000 refugees from Bosnia. 47% of these refugees are children. Half of the homeless are children. 10% of our total population are refugees. On March 16th, 1994 there were 492,636 registered displaced and refugee persons. Of that number, 241,014 are from Croatia and 251,622 from Bosnia-Herzegovina. We estimate the total, including unregistered persons, at 530,061.

At our hospital, in the first six months of 1993, 10 to 15% of all our medical services were given to displaced children and little refugees, mostly from Bosnia and Herzegovina. In some Divisions up to 50% of the children were and still are from Bosnia and Herzegovina.

Another effect of the war has been the destruction of infrastructure. 15 Croatian hospitals have been totally destroyed; 14 partially. Schools and pediatric clinics have also been destroyed.

We all look forward to peace, but we must realize that these wars have caused terrible destruction and terrible damage to child health. When peace comes, it will take more than signatures on a treaty to restore the health of our children."

PSYCHIATRIST – BOSNIA-HERZEGOVINA

"The largest concentration camp in the world has 300,000 residents. It is cut off from civilization in an unprecedented way. It is hidden from the world. It is the city of Sarajevo. Our people live every minute, because they know they could be killed every minute. We are facing an epidemic of psychological disorders. The damage to our buildings and equipment exceeds 50 million dollars. Our Children's Clinic has been destroyed. Our Psychiatric Clinic has been hit 14 times by mortars. Two of our nurses and one of our doctors have been killed. Several of our patients have been wounded. Our Medical University continues to function and to graduate doctors in spite of all this. We teach in the dark and give shorter lectures.

We are turning toward the future. We are developing programs. One is called "Recovery from War". We propose to develop a post-graduate course on human rights. Such training will be very important in the post-war period. Sad to say, Bosnia-Herzegovina will be a great laboratory for the study of the effects of war. Out of what we have learned, we hope to create a better system of health protection and protection for children.

Our people are scattered all over the world. Those who have remained have suffered intensely. We want our children to return home."

PEDIATRICIAN – SERBIAN CONTROLLED AREA FORMERLY IN CROATIA:

"The place of children's toys has been taken over by toy bombs and guns, sometimes even by real bombs and guns. Instead of stories, children hear the sounds of shellling. Family weekend trips and outings have given place to running for shelter as shells fall. Children less and less dare to play at street corners or in parks, or to visit their friends' homes as all children are eager to do.

The health protection of the mother and child is among the first victims of war. War has gone on in our land for three years now. Preventive measures to protect and promote the health of mothers and children are next to impossible now. Treatment of sick, wounded and exhausted mothers and children takes place in very difficult circumstances, with inappropriate accommodation and inadequate equipment, not to mention severe rationing of medicine, medical supplies and food.

The war has brought about increased morbidity and mortality of children. Premature births are more frequent and perinatal mortality has gone up in our entire area. This results from stressed living conditions of pregnant women, the lack of prenatal care and inadequate care of newborns in the ward, due to shortages of medicine, medical supplies, oxygen and disinfectants.

The principal causes of death of children in 1993 were inadequate living conditions at home, or in shelters; late arrivals to the hospital due to petrol shortages; lack of medicine and food shortages. A great number of children suffer from psychosocial traumas. Instances of gastrointestinal disease have increased. Instances of hepatitis have been recorded among school children and at refugee centers. Lack of medicines, medical and laboratory supplies, vaccines and food continue to be a very serious problem."

PEDIATRICIAN – SERBIAN CONTROLLED AREA FORMERLY IN BOSNIA-HERZEGOVINA

"In our area we have one million people, 100,000 of whom are refugees. Our problems with refugees are similar to those of other regions. We also suffer from the direct consequences of war.

We have not had electricity for months in a row. Through the entire winter our hospital was without central heating. Newborn babies died in our hospital because we did not have the oxygen that they needed so desperately. We have only 6 incubators, so we sometimes must put three premature babies in the same one.

Malignant disorders are a big problem. We have had no cytotoxic drugs for the past two years and as a result 8 children died last year. We have noted increases in respiratory infections, iron deficiency anemia, asthmatic attacks, rickets, gastroenteritis, tuberculosis and diabetes. We detect increases in prematurity rates, perinatal mortality, and congenital anomalies. Inadequate care is available to pregnant women. We have mental health problems among children."

PSYCHIATRIST – SERBIA

"From the very beginning of this war, we were aware that the psychosocial consequences of the war might be as important and deleterious as the immediate traumatic consequences. We, as child psychiatrists, are aware that the traumatic experiences in childhood may alter and influence the development of personality, the cognitive emotional development. But, even more dangerous, such traumatic events may affect the development of consciousness of a whole nation. We are aware that three generations are needed to overcome the effects of early childhood trauma of hatred, retaliation, and revenge claims. Therefore, we think that this situation is very dangerous. The groups at the highest risk for the development of mental health disorders are the group of children who have experienced directly the war stresses, those children who have witnessed the killing of their parents, the wounding of themselves. The majority of these children in my region are to be found among refugee children. A second group of theses children suffering due to the difficulties in the functioning of the families which are affected by the economic crisis and unemployment. A third group of children are those which are suffering because of difficulties to provide health and social care to our children in the current situation."

PSYCHIATRIST – SLOVENIA

"My personal experience is very important for the philosophy of my work. I survived the Second World War. My mother was Jewish. My parents worked in the Partisan movement. I must say that what helped me most was to see that the world was not only bad. I was left in the care of very simple peasants in Slavonia (Croatia). They were good to me. The saved me. I survived because of their kindness, because of their noble sentiment and morale. I think that for all of us it is so important to give a manifestation of good will to help these refugee children now and to change their view of the world. I think for the future this is the most important thing, more so than psychotherapy."

PEDIATRICIAN – SERBIA

"Before the war, we had a high standard of living, and very good health care for all. Now, everything has changed. Fewer than 30% of children have an adequate financial status and receive good private care and everything they need. About 30% have less money than they need, and very often if a family has an ill child, they have to give all of their earnings for the month for medical care. More than 30% do not have enough food and money for medicine, and these are the people who are most often acutely and chronically ill. In the worst scenario are children wo are refugees. They also have problems of stress and emotional trauma.

In my hospital we now have all sorts of restrictions. Our patients are very ill, and the death rate is higher. Patients are undernourished. Frequently we do not have medicine for our children with sepsis, leukemia, and hemophilia. The food in the hospital is inadequate. Heating fuel in winter did not arrive on time and our hospital was so cold that we could not examine a child. Many of our instruments are not working, and we have shortages of all types of materials. Nearly every child in my region is suffering to some degree, physically or mentally."

COMMENTARY

What is the future of this project? First of all it is heartening that the participants wish to continue their participation. A third workshop is planned for the Spring of 1995. To prepare for that meeting, working groups have been established to address the topics of mental halth, child protection, trauma, primary health care, and restoration of a health care system for children.

This type of project attempts to bring professionals actively into the protection of children. There are human rights treaties and international humanitarian laws that should serve to protect children during times of war [5,6,7,8] Of these, the Convention on the Rights of the Child speaks specifically to the needs of children. There are also codes of professional ethics which should govern the way doctors and other professionals behave.[9] Unfortunately none of these laws, standards, or codes has served adequately to protect the children of former Yugoslavia, or the chiildren of other recent wars.

It is apparent that international human rights lawyers cannot by themselves effect the protection of children in war and other difficult circumstances. The front line of such protection must exist at a community level and must involve those persons who have direct contact with children and who bear responsibility for their care and nurture. Such persons include doctors, teachers, social workers, religious leaders, community leaders, and so forth. Such professionals must be educated about the rights of children and about their own professional responsibilities in this regard, and should develop their roles and assume their responsibilities in the protection of and the rehabilitation of the children in their communities.

One of our colleagues from Bosnia-Herzegovina has stated this very well:

We all want very much to give our children who have been so wounded by these wars a better future. In my thinking about my own country, I realize that we as pediatricians have to stand in a mutual front line against war and cope with the gathered hatred which is destroying us, to decrease this hatred through our conversations and our professional and human ideals. It is important that we teach our children how to love people again and bring back their childhoods. We have to change the world so that our children will be safe again. Only knowledge and wisdom and human caring say enough. Material things can always die in smoke and fire. We have all learned that any rich man can become poor very quickly. But our ideals and our concerns for our children cannot and must not be so easily lost.

REFERENCES

The State of the World's Children (1995) UNICEF Report. New York: Oxford University Press.

Schaller J.G. and Nightingale E.O. (1992) Children and childhoods: Hidden Casualties of War and Civil Unrest [editorial]. *JAMA 268(5)* 642–644.

Schaller J.G. (Chairman, Organizing Committee) (1995) The Impact of War on Child Health in the Countries of the Former Yugoslavia: a workshop summary. Institute of Medicine, in collaboration with Office of International Affairs, National Research Council. Washington: National Academy Press.

Schaller J.G. (Chairman, Organizing Committee) (1995) The Impact of War on Child Health in the Countries of the Former Yugoslavia: Interim Workshop. UNICEF and Tufts University.

The Geneva Conventions of August 12, 1949, International Committee of the Red Cross, Geneva.

Protocols Additional to the Geneva Conventions of August 12, 1949.

Reisman W.M. and Antoniou C.T. (1994) *The Laws of War*: a comprehensive collection of primary documents on international laws governing armed conflict. New York: Random House.

The Convention on the Rights of the Child. Adopted by the General Assembly of the United Nations, November 20, 1989.

Stover E. and Nightingale E.O. (Eds) (1985) *The Breaking of Bodies and Minds*. New York: WH Freeman and Company.

APPENDICES

UN Convention on the Rights of the Child

PREAMBLE

The States Parties to the present Convention.

Considering that in accordance with the principles proclaimed in the Charter of the United Nations, recognition of the inherent dignity and of the equal and inalienable rights of all members of the human family is the foundation of freedom, justice and peace in the world,

Bearing in mind that the peoples of the United Nations have, in the Charter, reaffirmed their faith in fundamental human rights and in the dignity and worth of the human person, and have determined to promote social progress and better standards of life in larger freedom,

Recognizing that the United Nations has, in the Universal Declaration of Human Rights (3) and in the International Covenants on Human Rights, (4) proclaimed and agreed that everyone is entitled to all the rights and freedoms set forth therein, without distinction of any kind, such as race, colour, sex, language, religion, political or other opinion, national or social origin, property, birth or other status,

Recalling that, in the Universal Declaration of Human Rights, the United Nations has proclaimed that childhood is entitled to special care and assistance,

Convinced that the family, as the fundamental group of society and the natural environment for the growth and well-being or all its members and particularly children, should be afforded the necessary protection and assistance so that it can fully assume its responsibilities within the community,

Recognizing that the child, for the full and harmonious development of his or her personality, should grow up in a family environment, in an atmosphere of happiness, love and understanding,

Considering that the child should be fully prepared to live an individual life in society, and brought up in the spirit of the ideals proclaimed in the Charter of the United Nations, and in particular in the spirit of peace, tolerance, freedom, equality and solidarity,

Bearing in mind that the need to extend particular care to the child has been stated in the Geneva Declaration of the Rights of the Child of 1924(5) and in the Declaration of the Rights of the Child adopted by the General Assembly on 20 November 1959(2) and recognized in the Universal Declaration of Human Rights, in the International Covenant on Civil and Political Rights (in particular in articles 23 and 24), (4) in the International Covenant on Economic, Social and Cultural Rights (in particular in

E. Verhellen (ed.), Monitoring Children's Rights, 901–918.
© 1996 *Kluwer Law International. Printed in the Netherlands.*

article 10) (4) and in the statutes and relevant instruments of specialized agencies and international organizations concerned with the welfare of children,

Bearing in mind that, as indicated in the Declaration of the Rights of the Child, "the child, by reason of his physical and mental immaturity, needs special safeguards and care, including appropriate legal protection, before as well as after birth", (6)

Recalling the provisions of the Declaration on Social and Legal Principles relating to the Protection and Welfare of Children, with Special Reference to Foster Placement and Adoption Nationally and Internationally, (7) the United Nations Standard Minimum Rules for the Administration of Juvenile Justice (The Beijing Rules); (8) and the Declaration on the Protection of Women and Children in Emergency and Armed Conflict, (9)

Recognizing that, in all countries in the world, there are children living in exceptionally difficult conditions, and that such children need special consideration,

Taking due account of the importance of the traditions and cultural values of each people for the protection and harmonious development of the child,

Recognizing the importance of international co-operation for improving the living conditions of children in every country, in particular in the developing countries,

Have agreed as follows:

PART I

Article 1

For the purposes of the present Convention, a child means every human being below the age of eighteen years unless, under the law applicable to the child, majority is attained earlier.

Article 2

1. States Parties shall respect and ensure the rights set forth in the present Convention to each child within their jurisdiction without discrimination of any kind, irrespective of the child's or his or her parent's or legal guardian's race, colour, sex, language, religion, political or other opinion, national, ethnic or social origin, property, disability, birth or other status.
2. States Parties shall take all appropriate measures to ensure that the child is protected against all forms of discrimination or punishment on the basis of the status, activities, expressed opinions, or beliefs of the child's parents, legal guardians, or family members.

Article 3

1. In all actions concerning children, whether undertaken by public or private social welfare institutions, courts of law, administrative authroties or legislative bodies, the best interests of the child shall be a primary consideration.
2. States Parties undertake to ensure the child such protection and care as is necessary for his or her well-being, taking into account the rights and duties of his or her parents, legal guardians, or other individuals legally responsible for him

or her, and, to this end, shall take all appropriate legislative and administrative measures.

3. States Parties shall ensure that the institutions, services and facilities responsible for the care or protection of children shall conform with the standards established by competent authorities, particularly in the areas of safety, health, in the number and suitability of their staff, as well as competent supervision.

Article 4

States Parties shall undertake all appropriate legislative, administrative, and other measures for the implementation of the rights recognized in the present Convention. With regard to economic, social and cultural rights, States Parties shall undertake such measures to the maximum extent of their available resources and, where needed, within the framework of international co-operation.

Article 5

States Parties shall respect the responsibilities, rights and duties of parents or, where applicable, the members of the extended family or community as provided for by local custom, legal guardians or other persons legally responsible for the child, to provide, in a manner consistent with the evolving capacities of the child, appropriate direction and guidance in the exercise by the child of the rights recognized in the present Convention.

Article 6

1. States Parties recognize that every child has the inherent right to life.
2. States Parties shall ensure to the maximum extent possible the survival and development of the child.

Article 7

1. The child shall be registered immediately after birth and shall have the right from birth to a name, the right to acquire a nationality and, as far as possible, the right to know and be cared for by his or her parents.
2. States Parties shall ensure the implementation of these rights in accordance with their national law and their obligations under the relevant international instruments in this field, in particular where the child would otherwise be stateless.

Article 8

1. States Parties undertake to respect the right of the child to preserve his or her identity, including nationality, name and family relations as recognized by law without unlawful interference.
2. Where a child is illegally deprived of some or all of the elements of his or her identity, States Parties shall provide appropriate assistance and protection, with a view to speedily re-establishing his or her identity.

Article 9

1. States Parties shall ensure that a child shall not be separated from his or her parents against their will, except when competent authorities subject to judicial review determine, in accordance with applicable law and procedures, that such separation is necessary for the best interests of the child. Such determination may be necessary in a particular case such as one involving abuse or neglect of the child by the parents, or one where the parents are living separately and a decision must be made as to the child's place of residence.
2. In any proceedings pursuant to paragraph 1 of the present article, all interested parties shall be given an opportunity to participate in the proceedings and make their views known.
3. States Parties shall respect the right of the child who is separated from one or both parents to maintain personal relations and direct contact with both parents on a regular basis, except if it is contrary to the child's best interests.
4. Where such separation results from any action initiated by a State Party, such as the detention, imprisonment, exile, deportation or death (including death arising from any cause while the person is in the custody of the State) of one or both parents or of the child, that State Party shall, upon request, provide the parents, the child or, if appropriate, another member of the family with the essential information concerning the whereabouts of the absent member(s) of the family unless the provision of the information would be detrimental to the well-being of the child. States Parties shall further ensure that the submission of such a request shall of itself entail no adverse consequence for the person(s) concerned.

Article 10

1. In accordance with the obligation of States Parties under article 9, paragraph 1, applications by a child or his or her parents to enter or leave a State Party for the purpose of family reunification shall be dealt with by States Parties in a positive, humane and expeditious manner. States Parties shall further ensure that the submission of such a request shall entail no adverse consequences for the applicants and for the members of their family.
2. A child whose parents reside in different States shall have the right to maintain on a regular basis, save in exceptional circumstances, personal relations and direct contacts with both parents. Towards that end and in accordance with the obligation of States Parties under article 9, paragraph 2. States Parties shall respect the right of the child and his or her parents to leave and country, including their own, and to enter their own country. The right to leave any country shall be subject only to such restrictions as are prescribed by law and which are necessary to protect the national security, public order (*ordre public*), public health or morals or the rights and freedoms of others and are consistent with the other rights recognized in the present Convention.

Article 11

1. States Parties shall take measures to combat the illicit transfer and non-return of children abroad.

2. To this end, States Parties shall promote the conclusion of bilateral or multilaterial agreements or accession to existing agreements.

Article 12

1. States Parties shall assure to the child who is capable of forming his or her own views the right to express those views freely in all matters affecting the child, the views of the child being given due weight in accordance with the age and maturity of the child.
2. For this purpose, the child shall in particular be provided the opportunity to be heard in any judicial and administrative proceedings affecting the child, either directly, or through a representative or an appropriate body, in a manner consistent with the procedural rules of national law.

Article 13

1. The child shall have the right to freedom of expression; this right shall include freedom to seek, receive and impart information and ideas of all kinds, regardless of frontiers, either orally, in writing or in print, in the form of art, or through any other media of the child's choice.
2. The exercise of this right may be subject to certain restrictions, but these shall only be such as are provided by law and are necessary:
    (a) For respect of the rights or reputations of others; or
    (b) For the protection of national security or of public order (*ordre public*), or of public health or morals.

Article 14

1. States Parties shall respect the right of the child to freedom of thought, conscience and religion.
2. States Parties shall respect the rights and duties of the parents and, when applicable, legal guardians, to provide direction to the child in the exercise of his or her right in a manner consistent with the evolving capacities of the child.
3. Freedom to manifest one's religion or beliefs may be subject only to such limitations as are prescribed by law and are necessary to protect public safety, order, health or morals, or the fundamental rights and freedoms of others.

Article 15

1. States Parties recognize the rights of the child to freedom of association and to freedom of peaceful assembly.
2. No restrictions may be placed on the exercise of these rights other than those imposed in conformity with the law and which are necessary in a democratic society in the interests of national security or public safety, public order (*ordre public*), the protection of public health or morals or the protection of the rights and freedoms of others.

Article 16

1. No child shall be subjected to arbitrary or unlawful interference with his or her privacy, family, home or correspondence, nor to unlawful attacks on his or her honour and reputation.
2. The child has the right to the protection of the law against such interference or attacks.

Article 17

States Parties recognize the important function performed by the mass media and shall ensure that the child has access to information and material from a diversity of national and international sources, especially those aimed at the promotion of his or her social, spiritual and moral well-being and physical and mental health. To this end, States Parties shall:
  (a) Encourage the mass media to disseminate information and material of social and cultural benefit to the child and in accordance with the spirit of article 29;
  (b) Enfcourage international co-operation in the production, exchange and dissemination of such information and material from a dviersity of cultural, national and international sources;
  (c) Encourage the production and dissemination of children's books;
  (d) Encourage the mass media to have particular regard to the linguistic needs of the child who belongs to a minority group or who is indigenous;
  (e) Encourage the development of appropriate guidelines for the protection of the child from information and material injurious to his or her well-being, bearing in mind the provisions of articles 13 and 18.

Article 18

1. States Parties shall use their best efforts to ensure recognition of the principle that both parents have common responsibilities for the upbringing and development of the child. Parents or, as the case may be, legal guardians, have the primary responsibility for the upbringing and development of the child. The best interests of the child will be their basic concern.
2. For the purpose of guaranteeing and promoting the rights set forth in the present Convention, States Parties shall render appropriate assistance to parents and legal guardians in the performance of their child-rearing responsibilities and shall ensure the development of institutions, facilities and services for the care of children.
3. States Parties shall take all appropriate measures to ensure that children of working parents have the right to benefit from child-care services and facilities for which they are eligible.

Article 19

1. States Parties shall take all appropriate legislative, administrative, social and educational measures to protect the child from all forms of physical or mental violence, injury of abuse, neglect or negligent treatment, maltreatment or exploita-

tion, including sexual abuse, while in the care of parent(s), legal guardian(s) or any other person who has the care of the child.

2. Such protective measures should, as appropriate, include effective procedures for the establishment of social programmes to provide necessary support for the child and for those who have the care of the child, as well as for other forms of prevention and for identification, reporting, referral, investigation, treatment and follow-up of instances of child maltreatment described heretofore, and, as appropriate, for judicial involvement.

Article 20

1. A child temporarily or permanently deprived of his or her family environment, or in whose own best interests cannot be allowed to remain in that environment, shall be entitled to special protection and assistance provided by the State.
2. States Parties shall in accordance with their national laws ensure alternative care for such a child.
3. Such care could include, *inter alia*, foster placement, *kafalab* or Islamic law, adoption or if necessary placement in suitable institutions for the care of children. When considering solutions, due regard shall be paid to the desirability of continuity in a child's upbringing and to the child's ethnic, religious, cultural and linguistic background.

Article 21

States Parties that recognize and/or permit the system of adoption shall ensure that the best interests of the child shall be the paramount consideration and they shall:
  (a) Ensure that the adoption of a child is authorized only by competent authorities who determine, in accordance with applicable law and procedures and on the basis of all partiment and reliable information, that the adoption is permissible in view of the child's status concerning parents, relatives and legal guardians and that, if required, the persons concerned have given their informed consent to the adoption on the basis of such counselling as may be necessary;
  (b) Recognize that inter-country adoption may be considered as an alternative means of child's care, if the child cannot be placed in a foster or an adoptive family or cannot in any suitable manner be cared for in the child's country of origin;
  (c) Ensure that the child concerned by inter-country adoption enjoys safeguards and standards equivalent to those existing in the case of national adoption;
  (d) Take all appropriate measures to ensure that, in intercountry adoption, the placement does not result in improper financial gain for those involved in it;
  (e) Promote, where appropriate, the objectives of the present article by concluding bilateral or multilateral arrangements or agreements, and endeavour, within this framework, to ensure that the placement of the child in another country is carried out by competent authorities or organs.

Article 22

1. States Parties shall take appropriate measures to ensure that a child who is seeking refugee status or who is considered a refugee in accordance with applicable

international or domestic law and procedures shall, whether unaccompanied or accompanid by his or her parents or by any other person, receive appropriate protection and humanitarian assistance in the enjoyment of applicable rights set forth in the present Convention and in other international human rights of humanitarian instruemnts to which the said States are Parties.

2. For this purpose, States Parties shall provide, as they consider appropriate, co-operation in any efforts by the United Nations and other competent intergovernmental organizations or non-governmental organizations co-operating with the United Nations to protect and assist such a child and to trace the parents or other members of the family of any refugee child in order to obtain information necessary for reunification with his or her family. In cases where no parents or other members of the family can be found, the child shall be accorded the same protection as any other child permanently or temporarily deprived of his or her family environment for any reason, as set forth in the present Convention.

Article 23

1. States Parties recognize that a mentally or physically disabled child should enjoy a full and decent life, in conditions which ensure dignity, promote self-reliance and facilitate the child's active participation in the community.

2. States Parties recognize the right of the disabled child to special care and shall encourage and ensure the extension, subject to available resources, to the eligible child and those responsible for his or her care, of assistance for which application is made and which is appropriate to the child's condition and to the circumstances of the parents or others caring for the child.

3. Recognizing the special needs of a disabled child, assistance extended in accordance with paragraph 2 of the present article shall be provided free of charge, whenever possible, taking into account the financial resources of the aprents or others caring for the child, and shall be designed to ensure that the disabled child has effective access to and receives education, training, health care services, rehabilitation services, preparation for employment and recreation opportunities in a manner conducive to the child's achieving the fullest possible social integration and individual development, including his or her cultural and spiritual development.

4. States Parties shall promote, in the spirit of international co-operation, the exchange of appropriate information in the field of preventive health care and of medical, psychological and functional treatment of disabled children, including dissemination of and access to information concerning methods of rehabilitation, education and vocational services, with the aim of enabling States Parties to improve their capabilities and skills and to widen their experience in these areas. In this regard, particular account shall be taken of the needs of developing countries.

Article 24

1. States Parties recognize the right of the child to the enjoyment of the highest attainable standard of health and to facilities for the treatment of illness and rehabilitation of health. States Parties shall strive to ensure that no child is deprived of his or her right of access to such health care services.

2. States Parties pursue full implementation of this right and, in particular, shall take appropriate measures:
  (a) To diminish infant and child mortality;
  (b) To ensure the provision of necessary medical assistance and health care to all children with emphasis on the development of primary health care;
  (c) To combat disease and malnutrition, including within the framework of primary health care, through, *inter alia*, the applciation of readily available technology and through the provision of adequate nutritious foods and clean drinkingwater, taking into consideration the dangers and risks of environmental pollution;
  (d) To ensure appropriate pre-natal and post-natal health care for mothers;
  (e) To ensure that all segments of society, in particular parents and children, are informed, have access to education and are supported in the use of basic knowledge of child health and nutrition, the advantages of breast-feeding, hygiene and environmental sanitation and the prevention of accidents;
  (f) To develop preventive health care, guidance for parents and family planning education and services.
3. States Parties shall take all effective and appropriate measures with a view to abolishing traditional practices prejudicial to the healt of children.
4. States Parties undertake to promote and encourage international co-operation with a view to achieving progressively the full realization of the right recognized in the present article. In this regard, particular account shall be taken of the needs of developing countries.

Article 25

States Parties recognize the right of a child who has been placed by the competent authorities for the purpose of care, protection or treatment of his or her physical or mental health, to a periodic review of the treatment provided to the child and all other circumstances relevant to his or her placement.

Article 26

1. States Parties shall recognize for every child the right to benefit from social security, including social insurance, and shall take the necessary measures to achieve the full realization of this right in accordance with their national law.
2. The benefits should, where appropriate, be granted, taking into account the resources and the circumstances of the child and persons having responsibility for the maintenance of the child, as well as any other consideration relevant to an application for benefits made by or on behalf of the child.

Article 27

1. States Parties recognize the right of every child to a standard of living adequate for the child's physical, mental, spiritual, moral and social development.
2. The parent(s) or others responsible for the child have the primary responsibility to secure, within their abilities and financial capacities, the conditions of living necessary for the child's development.

3. States Parties, in accordance with national conditions and within their means, shall take appropriate measures to assist parents and others responsible for the child to implement this right and shall in case of need provide material assistance and support programmes, particularly with regard to nutrition, clothing and housing.
4. States Parties shall take all appropriate measures to secure the recovery of maintenance for the child from the parents or other persons having financial responsibility for the child, both within the State Party and from abroad. In particular, where the person having financial responsibility for the child lives in a State different from that of the child, States Parties shall promote the accession to international agreements of the conclusion of such agreements, as well as the making of other appropriate arrangements.

Article 28

1. States Parties recognize the right of the child to education, and with a view to achieving this right progressively and on the basis of equal opportunity, they shall, in particular:
    (a) Make primary education compulsory and available free to all;
    (b) Encourage the development of different forms of secondary education, including general and vocational education, make them available and accessible to every child, and take appropriate measures such as the introduction of free education and offering financial assistance in case of need;
    (c) Make higher education accessible to all on the basis of capacity by every appropriate means;
    (d) Make educational and vocational information and guidance available and accessible to all children;
    (e) Take measures to encourage regular attendance at schools and the reduction of drop-out rates.
2. States Parties shall take all appropriate measures to ensure that school discipline is administered in a manner consistent with the child's human dignity and in conformity with the present Convention.
3. States Parties shall promote and encourage international co-operation in matters relating to education, in particular with a view to contributing to the elimination of ignorance and illiteracy throughout the world and facilitating access to scientific and technical knowledge and modern teaching methods. In this regard, particular account shall be taken of the needs of developing countries.

Article 29

1. States Parties agree that the education of the child shall be directed to:
    (a) The development of the child's personality, talents and mental and physical abilities to their fullest potential;
    (b) The development of respect for human rights and fundamental freedoms, and for the principles enshrined in the Charter of the United Nations;
    (c) The development of respect for the child's parents, his or her own cultural identity, language and values, for the national values of the country in which the child is living, the country from which he or she may originate, and for civilizations different from his or her own;

(d) The preparation of the child for responsible life in a free society, in the spirit of understanding, peace, tolerance, equality of sexes, and friendship among all peoples, ethnic, national and religious groups and persons of indigenous origin;

(e) The development of respect for the natural environment.

2. No part of the present article or article 28 shall be construed so as to interfere with the liberty of individuals and bodies to establish and direct educational institutions, subject always to the observance of the principles set forth in paragraph 1 of the present article and to the requirements that the education given in such institutions shall conform to such minimum standards as may be laid down by the State.

Article 30

In those States in which ethnic, religious or linguistic minorities or persons of indigenous origin exist, a child belonging to such a minority or who is indigenous shall not be denied the right, in community with other members of his or her group, to enjoy his or her own culture, to profess and practise his or her own religion, or to use his or her own language.

Article 31

1. States Parties recognize the right of the child to rest and leisure, to engage in play and recreational activities appropriate to the age of the child and to participate freely in cultural life and the arts.

2. States Parties shall respect and promote the right of the child to participate fully in cultural and artistic life and shall encourage the provision of appropriate and equal opportunities for cultural, artistic, recreational and leisure activity.

Article 32

1. States Parties recognize the right of the child to be protected from economic exploitation and from performing any work that is likely to be hazardous or to interfere with the child's education, or to be harmful to the child's health or physical, mental, spiritual, moral or social development.

2. States Parties shall take legislative, administrative, social and educational measures to ensure the implementation of the present article. To this end, and having regard to the relevant provisions of other international instruments, States Parties shall in particular:

(a) Provide for a minimum age or minimum ages for admission to employment;

(b) Provide for appropriate regulation of the hours and conditions of employment;

(c) Provide for appropriate penalties or other sanctions to ensure the effective enforcement of the present article.

Article 33

States Parties shall take all appropriate measures, including legislative, administrative, social and educational measures, to protect children from the illicit use of narcotic drugs and psychotropic substances as defined in the relevant international treaties, and to prevent the use of children in the illicit production and trafficking of such substances.

Article 34

States Parties undertake to protect the child from all forms of sexual exploitation and sexual abuse. For these purposes, States Parties shall in particular take all appropriate national, bilateral and multilateral measures to prevent:
(a) The inducement or coercion of a child to engage in any unlawful sexual activity;
(b) The exploitative use of children in prostitution or other unlawful sexual practices;
(c) The exploitative use of children in pornographic performances and materials.

Article 35

States Parties shall take all appropriate national, bilateral and multilateral measures to prevent the abduction of, the sale of or traffic in children for any purpose or in any form.

Article 36

States Parties shall protect the child against all other forms of exploitation prejudicial to any aspects of the child's welfare.

Article 37

States Parties shall ensure that:
(a) No child shall be subjected to torture or other cruel, inhuman or degrading treatment or punishment. Neither capital punishment nor life imprisonment without possibility of release shall be imposed for offences committed by persons below eighteen years of age;
(b) No child shall be deprived of his or her liberty unlawfully or arbitrarily. The arrest, detention or imprisonment of a child shall be in conformity with the law and shall be used only as a measure of last resort and for the shortest appropriate period of time;
(c) Every child deprived of liberty shall be treated with humanity and respect for the inherent dignity of the human person, and in a manner which takes into account the needs of persons of his or her age. In particular, every child deprived of liberty shall be separated from adults unless it is considered in the child's best interest not to do so and shall have the right to maintain contact with his or her family through correspondence and visits, save in exceptional circumstances;
(d) Every child deprived of his or her liberty shall have the right to prompt access to legal and other appropriate assistance, as well as the right to challenge the legality of the deprivation of his or her liberty before a court or other competent, independant and impartial authority, and to a prompt decision on any such action.

Article 38

1. States Parties undertake to respect and to ensure respect for rules of international humanitarian law applicable to them in armed conflicts which are relevant to the child.
2. States Parties shall take all feasible measures to ensure that persons who have not attained the age of fifteen years do not take a direct part in hostilities.
3. States Parties shall refrain from recruiting any person who has not attained the age of fifteen years into their armed forces. In recruiting among those persons who have attained the age of fifteen years but who have not attained the age of eighteen years, States Parties shall endeavour to give priority to those who are oldest.
4. In accordance with their obligations under international humanitarian law to protect the civilian population in armed conflicts, States Parties shall take all feasible measures to ensure protection and care of children who are affected by an armed conflict.

Article 39

States Parties shall take all appropriate measures to promote physical and psychological recovery and social reintegration of a child victim of: any form of neglect, exploitation, or abuse; torture or any other form of cruel, inhuman or degrading treatment or punishment; or armed conflicts. Such recovery and reintegration shall take place in an environment which fosters the health, self-respect and dignity of the child.

Article 40

1. States Parties recognize the right of every child alleged as, accused or, or recognized as having infringed the penal law to be treated in a manner consistent with the promotion of the child's sense of dignity and worth, which reinforces the child's respect for the human rights and fundamental freedoms of others and which takes into account the child's age and the desirability of promoting the child's reintegration and the child's assuming a constructive role in society.
2. To this end, and having regard to the relevant provisions of international instruments, States Parties shall, in particular, ensure that:
   (a) No child shall be alleged as, be accused of, or recognized as having infringed the penal law by reason of acts or omissions that were not prohibited by national or international law at the time they were committed;
   (b) Every child alleged as or accusd of having infringed the penal law has at least the following guarantees:
      (i) To be presumed innocent until proven guilty according to law;
      (ii) To be informed promptly and directly of the charges against him or her, and, if appropriate, through his or her parents or legal guardians, and to have legal or other appropriate assistance in the preparation and presentation of his or her defence;
      (iii) To have the matter determined without delay by a competent, independent and impartial authority or judicial body in a fair hearing according to law, in the presence of legal or other appropriate assistance and, unless it is considered not to be in the best interest of the

child, in particular, taking into account his or her age or situation, his or her parents or legal guardians;

(iv) Not to be compelled to give testimony or to confess guilt; to examine or have examind adverse witnesses and to obtain the participation and examination of witnesses on his or her behalf under conditions of equality;

(v) If considered to have infringed the penal law, to have this decision and any measures imposed in consequence thereof reviewed by a higher comptent, independent and impartial authority or judicial body according to law;

(vi) To have the free assistance of an interpreter if the child cannot understand or speak the language used;

(vii) To have his or her privacy fully respect at all stages of the proceedings.

3. States Parties shall seek to promote the establishment of laws, procedures, authorities and institutions specifically applicable to children alleged as, accused of, or recognized as having infringed the penal law, and, in particular:

(a) The establishment of a minimum age below which children shall be presumed not to have the capacity to infringe the penal law;

(b) Whenever appropriate and desirable, measures for dealing with such children without resorting to judicial proceedings, providing that human rights and lgal safeguards are fully respected.

4. A variety of dispositions, such as care, guidance and supervision orders; counselling; probation; foster care; education and vocational training programmes and other alternatives to institutional care shall be available to ensure that children are dealt with in a manner appropriate to their well-being and proportionate both to their circumsances and the offence.

Article 41

Nothing in the present Convention shall affect any provisions which are more conducive to the realization of the rights of the child and which may be contained in:

(a) The law of a State Party; or

(b) International law in force for that State.

PART II

Article 42

States Parties undertake to make the principles and provisions of the Convention widely known, by appropriate and active means, to adults and children alike.

Article 43

1. For the purpose of examining the progress made by States Parties in achieving the realization of the obligations undertaken in the present Convention, there shall be established a Committee on the Rights of the Child, which shall carry out the functions hereinafter provided.

2. The Committee shall consist of ten experts of high moral standing and recognized competence in the field covered by this Convention. Te members of the Committee shall be elected by States Parties from among their nationals and shall serve in their personal capacity, consideration being given to equitable geographical distribution, as well as to the principal legal systems.

3. The members of the Committee shall be elected by secret ballot from a list of persons nominated by States Parties. Each State Party may nominate one person from among its own nationals.

4. The initial election to the Committee shall be held no later than six months after the data of the entry into force of the present Convention and thereafter every second year. At least four months before the date of each election, the Secretary-General of the United Nations shall address a letter to States Parties inviting them to submit their nominations within two months. The Secretary-General shall subsequently prepare a lit in alphabetical order of all persons thus nominated, indicating States Parties which have nominated them, and shall submit it to the States Parties to the present Convention.

5. The elections shall be held at meetings of States Parties convened by the Secretary-General at United Nations Headquarters. At those meetings, for which two thirds of States Parties shall constitute a quorum, the persons elected to the Committee shall be those who obtain the largest number of votes and an absolute majority of the votes of the representatives of States Parties present and voting.

6. The members of the Committee shall be lected for a term of four years. They shall be eligible for reelection if renominated. The term of five of the members elected at the first election shall expire at the end of two years; immediately after the first election, the names of these five members shall be chosen by lot by the Chairman of the meeting.

7. If a member of the Committee dies or resigns or declares that for any other cause he or she can no longer perform the duties of the Committee, the State Party which nominated the member shall appoint another expert from among its nationals to serve for the remainder of the term, subject to the approval of the Committee.

8. The Committee shall establish its own rules of procedure.

9. The Committee shall elect its officers for a period of two years.

10. The meetings of the Committee shall normally be held at United Nations Headquarters or at any other convenient place as determined by the Committee. The Committee shall normally meet annually. The duration of the meetings of the Committee shall be determined, and reviewed, if necessary, by a meeting of the States Parties to the present Convention subject to the approval of the General Assembly.

11. The Secretary-General of the United Nations shall provide the necessary staff and facilities for the effective performance of the functions of the Committee under the present Convention.

12. With the approval of the General Assembly, the members of the Committee established under the present Convention shall receive emoluments from United Nations resources on such terms and conditions as the Assembly may decide.

Article 44

1. States Parties undertake to submit to the Committee, through the Secretary-General of the United Nations, reports on the measures they have adopted which give effect to the rights recognized herein and on the progress made on the enjoyment of those rights:
    (a) Within two years of the entry into force of the Convention for the State Party concerned;
    (b) Thereafter every five years.
2. Reports made under the present article shall indicate factors and difficulties, if any, affecting the degree of fulfilment of the obligations under the present Convention. Reports shall also contain sufficient information to provide the Committee with a comprehensive understanding of the implementation of the Convention in the country concerned.
3. A State Party which has submitted a comprehensive initial report to the Committee need not, in its subsequent reports submitted in accordance with paragraph 1 (b) of the present article, repeat basic information previously provided.
4. The Committee may request from States Parties further information relevant to the implementation of the Convention.
5. The Committee shall submit to the General Assembly, through the Economic and Social Council, every two years, reports on its activities.
6. States Parties make their reports widely available to the publc in their own countries.

Article 45

In order to foster the effective implementation of the Convention and to encourage international co-operation in the field covered by the Convention:
  (a) The specialized agencies, the United Nations Children's Fund, and other United Nations organs shall be entitled to be represented at the consideration of the implementation of such provisions of the present Convention as fall within the scope of their mandate. The Committee may invite the specialzied agencies, the United Nations Children's Fund and other competent bodies as it may consider appropriate to provide expert advice on the implementation of the Convention in areas falling within the scope of their respective mandates. The Committee may invite the specialized agencies, the United Nations organs to submit reports on the implementation of the Convention in areas falling within the scope of their activities;
  (b) The Committee shall transmit, as it may consider appropriate, to the specialized agencies, the United Nations Children's Fund and other competent bodies, any reports from States Parties that contain a request, or indicate a need, for technical advice or assistance, along with the Committee's observations and suggestions, if any, on these requests or indications;
  (c) The Committee may recommend to the General Assembly to request the Secretary-General to undertake on its behalf studies on specific issues relating to the rights of the child;
  (d) The Committee may make suggestions and general recommendations based on information received pursuant to articles 44 and 45 of the present Convention. Such suggestions and general recommendations shall be transmitted to any

State Party concerned and reported to the General Assembly, together with comments, if any, from States Parties.

PART III

Article 46

The present Convention shall be open for signature by all States.

Article 47

The present Convention is subject to ratification. Instruments of ratification shall be deposited with the Secretary-General of the United Nations.

Article 48

The present Convention shall remain open for accession by any State. The instruments of accession shall be deposited with the Secretary-General of the United Nations.

Article 49

1. The present Convention shall enter into force on the thirtieth day following the day of deposit with the Secretary-General of the United Nations of the twentieth instrument of ratification of accession.
2. For each State ratifying or acceding to the Convention after the deposit of the twentieth instrument of ratification or accession, the Convention shall enter into force on the thirtieth day after the deposit by such State of its instrument of ratification or accession.

Article 50

1. Any State Party may propose an amendment and file it with the Secretary-General of the United Nations. The Secretary-General shall thereupon communicate the proposed amendment to States Parties, with a request that they indicate whether they favour a conference of States Parties for the purpose of considering and voting upon the proposals. In the event that, within four months from the data of such communication, at least one third of the States Parties favour such a conference, the Secretary-General shall convene the conference under the auspices of the United Nations. Any amendment adopted by a majority of States Parties present and voting at the conference shall be submitted to the General Assembly for approval.
2. An amendment adopted in accordance with paragraph 1 of the present article shall enter into force when it has been approved by the General Assembly of the United Nations and accepted by a two-thirds majority of States Parties.
3. When an amendment enters into force, it shall be binding on those States Parties which have accepted it, other States Parties still being bound by the provisions of the present Convention and any earlier amendments which they have accepted.

Article 51

1. The Secretary-General of the United Nations shall receive and circulate to all States the text of reservations made by States at the time of ratification or accession.
2. A reservation incompatible with the object and purpose of the present Convention shall not be permitted.
3. Reservations may be withdrawn at any time by notification to that effect addressed to the Secretary-General of the United Nations, who shall then inform all States. Such notification shall take effect on the date on which it is received by the Secretary-General.

Article 52

A State Party may denounce the present Convention by written notification to the Secretary-General of the United Nations. Denunciation becomes effective one year after the date of receipt of the notification by the Secretary-General.

Article 53

The Secretary-General of the United Nations is designated as the depositary of the present Convention.

Article 54

The original of the present Convention, of which the Arabic, Chinese, English, French, Russian and Spanish texts are equally authentic, shall be deposited with the Secretary-General of the United Nations.

In witness thereof the undersigned plenipotentiaries, being duly authorized thereto by their respective Governments, have signed the present Convention.

The present Convention was signed by the following States:

Albania, Algeria, Austria, Bangladesh, Belgium, Brazil, Burkina Faso, Beylorussia, Chile, Columbia, Costa Rica, Ivory Coast, Cuba, Denmark, Dominica, Ecuador, El Salvador, Finland, France, Gabon, Germany (Federal Republic of), Greece, Guatemala, Guinea-Bissau, Haiti, Iceland, Indonesia, Italy, Jamaica, Kenya, Lebanon, Mali, Malta, Mauritania, Mexico, Mongolia, Morocco, Nepal, Netherlands, Niger, Nigeria, Norway, Panama, Peru, Philippines, Poland, Portugal, Romania, Rwanda, Saint Kitts-Nevis, Senegal, Spain, Sri Lanka, Surinam, Sweden, Togo, USSR, Uruguay, Venezuela, Vietnam, Yugoslavia, Ghana, Egypt, Gambia, Nicaragua, Sierra Leone, Yemen, Angola, Grenada, Ukraine, Tunisia, Belize, Bolivia, Zimbabwe, Hungary, Zaïre, Luxembourg, Paraguay, Barbados, Madagscar, United Kingdom, Holy See, Benin, Liberia, Burundi, Canada, Bulgaria, Honduras, Tanzania, Butan, Kuwait, Argentina, Israel, Sudan, Central African Republic, Dominican Republic, Uganda, Lesotho, Maldives, Australia, Swaziland, Korea (Democratic People's Republic), China, Jordan, Turkey, Syria, Pakistan, Japan, Cameroun, Korea (Republic), Namibia, Afghanistan, Chad, Comoro, Czechoslovakia, Djibouti, Guyana, Ireland, Liechtenstein, Mozambique, Papua New Guinea, Saint Lucia, Samoa, Trinidad and Tobago, Vanuatu, Zambia, New Zealand, Cyprus, GDR.

Council of Europe

Parliamentary Assembly

RECOMMENDATION 1121 (1990) ON THE RIGHTS OF CHILDREN

The Assembly,

1. Recalling that a society's vitality depends on the opportunities it offers its younger generation for growth and development in safety, self-realisation, solidarity and peace;
2. Considering that children, that is human beings who have not attained their majority, are in need of special assistance, care and protection, and considering that the parents' primary responsibility needs to be reasserted and canoot be called into question;
3. Considering that children, for the full and harmonious development of their personality, should grow up in an atmosphere of happiness, love and understanding;
4. Considering that the right of children to special protection imposes obligations on society and on the adults normally dealing with them such as parents, teachers, social workers, doctors and others;
5. Considering that, in addition to the right to be protected, children have rights they may independently exercise themselves – even against opposing adults;
6. Considering that parental powers and the authority of other adults on children are derived from a duty for protection and should exist only as long as they are necessary for the protection of the person and property of the child;
7. Considering that these powers decline as the child matures and that a child is subsequently able to exercise an increasing number of rights;
8. Considering that there is much uncertainty about the rights people under age have or may enjoy, and that it is highly desirable that all member states grant full legal capacity at the same age;
9. Considering that young persons, more and more frequently, travel, study and work abroad, and that, for this reason, coherent action and legislation are desirable in Council of Europe member states in respect of the rights of the child;
10. Welcoming the adoption of the Convention on the Rights of the Child by the General Assembly of the United Nations in November 1989;
11. Recalling its Recommendations 874 (1979) on a European Charter on the Rights of the Child, 1071 (1988) on child welfare and 1074 (1988) on family policy;

E. Verhellen (ed.), Monitoring Children's Rights, 919–921.

12. Recalling Recommendation No. R (88) 16 of the Committee of Ministers to member states on ratifying and improving the implementation of the conventions and agreements concluded within the Council of Europe in the field of private law, notably the conventions which protect the interests of the child;

13. Recommends that the Committe of Ministers:

  A. invite member states:
   i. in so far as they have not yet done so, to sign and ratify:
      a. the European Social Charter (1961, European Treaty Series, No. 35), and, in particular, to accept Article 7 thereof on the protection of children and young people, Article 17 on the protection of mothers and children and Article 19, paragraph 6, on family reunion, and to ensure that the standards therein are fully enforced;
      b. the European Convention on the Adoption of Children (1967, European Treaty Series, No. 580;
      c. the European Convention on the Legal Status of Children Born out of Wedlock (1975, European Treaty Series, No. 85);
      d. the European Convention on Recognition and Enforcement of Decisions concerning Custody of Children and on Restoation of Custody of Children (1980, European Treaty Series, No. 105);
      e. International Labour Organisation (ILO) Convention No. 138 on the Minimum Age of Admission to Employment (1973);
   ii. to envisage, if they have not yet done so, the appointment of a special ombudsman for children, who could inform them on their rights, counsel them, intervene and, possibly, take legal action on their behalf;
   iii. to do whatever they can in favour of the rapid ratification and implementation of the United Nations Convention on the Rights of the Child:

  B. instruct the competent steering committees to examine the possibility of drawing up an appropriate legal instrument of the Council of Europe in order to complete the United Nations Convention on the Rights of the Child, and, in particular, to instruct the Steering Committee for Human Rights (CDDH) to consider the possibility of elaborating an additional protocol to the European Convention on Human Rights concerning the rights of the child;

  C. arrange for the above-mentioned European legal instrument to embody not only the civil and political rights of children but also their economic and social rights, and accordingly instruct the Steering Committee for Human Rights to collaborate with other committees in the various sectors concerned, such as the social and employment sectors;

  D. instruct the European Committee on Legal Co-operation (CDCJ), or another appropriate intergovernmental expert committee, to make a full study on the position of children in courts and on the acts a minor is entitled to accomplish before the age of full legal capacity, with a view to arriving at common European positions;

E. convene a small group of highly competent independent experts to study
    how children may exercise the fundamental rights which have been granted
    to them by such international instruments as the European Convention on
    Human Rights and the European Social Charter;

F. better inform children of the rights they have;

G. establish co-ordination to ensure the systematic study of rights of chil-
    dren and co-operation with other international organisations such as the
    European Community, the International Labour organisation, The Hague
    Conference on Private International Law and non-governmental organisa-
    tions.

European Charter of Rights of the Child

Resolution A3-0172/92

RESOLUTION ON A EUROPEAN CHARTER OF RIGHTS OF THE CHILD

The European Parliament,

– having regard to the motions for resolutions by:
  (a) Mr Casini and others on the European Charter of Rights of the Child (B3-0035/90),
  (b) Mrs Ceci and others on the sexual exploitation of children, child pornography and prostitution, and trade in children in Europe (B3/0505/90),
  (c) Mr Ferri on improved child protection, with particular reference to children who have disappeared (B3/2166/90),
  (d) Mr Sisó Cruellas on child abuse (B3/1669/91),
– having regard to the petitions:
  (a) No 430/90, by Mrs Kaloudaki (Greek) on behalf of the Independent Women's Movement on the sexual abuse of children by their fathers; and
  (b) No 588/90 by Mr Alan Milburn (British) on child pornography and child sexual abuse,
– having regard to its resolution of 12 July 1990 on the Convention of the Rights of the Child[1] and its resolution of 13 December 1991 on the problems of children in the European Community,[2]
– having regard to its resolution of 12 April 1989 adopting the Declaration of fundamental rights and freedoms[3]
– having regard to its resolution of 26 May 1989 on the abduction of children,[4]
– having regard to its resolution of 13 May 1986 on a European Charter for children in hospital,[5]

---

[1] OJ No C 231, 17.9.1990, p. 170.
[2] OJ No C 13, 20.1.1992, p. 534.
[3] OJ No C 120, 16.5.1989, p. 51.
[4] OJ No C 158, 26.6.1989, p. 391.
[5] OJ No C 148, 16.6.1986, p. 37.

E. Verhellen (ed.), Monitoring Children's Rights, 923–930.
© 1996 *Kluwer Law International. Printed in the Netherlands.*

- having regard to Council Regulation (EEC) No 1612/68 on freedom of movement for workers within the Community;[6] Commission Regulation (EEC) No
1251/70 on the right of workers to remain in the territory of a Member State
after having been employed in that State;[7] and Council Directives 90/364/EEC
on the right of residence, 90/365/EEC on the right of residence for employees
and self-employed persons who have ceased their occupational activity and
90/366/EEC on the right of residence for students,[8]
- having regard to Council Directive 77/486/EEC on the education of the children
of migrant workers,[9]
- having regard to the United Nations Convention on the Rights of the Child of
20 November 1989,
- having regard to the European Convention on Human Rights,
- having regard to the Council of Europe's Convention 105 on recognition and
enforcement of decisions concerning custody of children and on restoration of
custody of children and the 1980 Convention of The Hague on civil aspects of
the abduction of minors,
- having regard to the report of the Committee on Legal Affairs and Citizens'
Rights and the opinion of the Committee on Women's Rights (A3-0172/92),

    A. whereas every individual's childhood and family and social background to
a great extent determine his or her subsequent life as an adult,
    B. stressing in particular the fundamental role of the family and its stability
in ensuring the harmonious and balanced development of the child,
    C. whereas children constitute one of the msot vulnerable sections of the
population, whose specific needs must be satisfied and safeguarded,
    D. whereas many international texts have recognized that these needs give
rise to a number of rights for children which in turn entail obligations for
parents, the State and society in general,

1. Recalls that in its resolutions of 12 July 1990 and 13 December 1991 it called
on the Member States conditionally to become parties to the United Nations
Convention of 1989 on the Rights of the Child;
2. Considers that as soon as all EC member States have ratified the Convention
the European Community should also become party to it;
3. Takes the view, however, that children in the Community have certain specific
problems and that they will be affected in particular by some of the consequences
of European integration and the completion of the single market;
4. Believes therefore that specific Community instruments, derived from the United Nations Convention on the Rights of the Child, should be introduced to deal
with the special problems that European integration will create for under-age
children and for which there are no provisions in the legislation of the Member
States;
5. Requests the legal Affairs Committee of the parliamentary Assembly of the
Council of Europe to step up its work on family law, in particular its work
on the applicability of the Convention on Human Rights to children, and to

---

[6] OJ No L 257, 19.10.1968, p. 2.
[7] OJ No L 142, 30.6.1970, p. 24.
[8] OJ No L 180, 13.7.1990, pp. 26 to 30.
[9] OJ No L 199, 6.8.1977, p. 32.

consider the option of appending a supplementary protocol to the Convention containing special provisions on the rights of the child;

6. Calls on the Member States to appoint a children's ombudsman, qualified in each country to safeguard children's rights and interests, deal with their requests and complaints, monitor the application of laws protecting children, and inform and guide the public authorities in their work to uphold children's rights;

7. Calls also on the competent Community authority to appoint a children's ombudsman, with the same powers, at Community level;

8. Calls on the Commission to submit, on the one hand, specific proposals for appropriate actions in favour of a policy on the family, and on the other a draft Community Charter of Rights of the Child containing a minimum of basic principles and using the following definitions:

8.1. The term "child" is taken to mean any human being under the age of 18 unless, by virtue of the national laws applicable to him, as he has already reached the age of majority. For purposes of criminal law the age of 18 shall be considered the minimum age of criminal responsibility.

8.2. Any child who is a citizen of the European Community must enjoy all the rights listed in this Charter in accordance with the procedures laid down in national legislation and the principles of Community law.

8.3. Any child, irrespective of his origin, who is dependent on a national of Member State who is or has been employed or resides in another member State, must, in that territory, benefit from all those rights and advantages which his family enjoys by virtue of Community legislation on freedom of movement for workers and the right of residence.

8.4. Children from third countries, whose parents lawfully reside in a Member State of the Community, and refugees or stateless children recognized as such who reside in that Member State, must be able to enjoy in that state the rights listed in this Charter in accordance with national laws and without prejudice to restrictions on any of these rights which may derive from Community law.

8.5. No child may be the subject, in the territory of the Community, of any discrimination on the basis of his or his parents' nationality, family background, sexual orientation, race, colour, sex, language, social origin, religion, belief, state of health or other circumstance.

8.6. Children from third countries, whose parents lawfully reside in a Member State must enjoy the same treatment in that State as the nationals of that State, in the spheres referred to in the association or cooperation agreements concluded between the Community and such third countries.

8.7. The provisions of this Charter may under no circumstances restrict children's rights and freedoms as recognized in national laws or in international instruments to which the States are party.

8.8. Every child has the right to life. If the parents or persons responsible for the child are not in a position to ensure his survival and development, the State must guarantee him the necessary protection and care and a decent minimum of resources and take steps to encourage and facilitate the provision of this care by individuals or families willing to do so, or, if this is not possible, via direct intervention by the authorities.

8.9. Every child must be registered after birth and shall be entitled to a name and a nationality. Any child who at the time of his birth is not entitled to the nationality of his parents or of one of them, must be able to acquire the nationality of the

State in whose territory he was born, provided that this eventuality is covered by the legislation of that State.

8.10. Every child shall be entitled to protection of his identity and, if appropriate, be allowed to know certain circumstances regarding his biological origin, subject to the restrictions imposed by national laws to protect the rights of third persons. Steps must be taken to lay down the conditions under which the child is to be given information regarding his biological origin and to protect the child from the divulging of this information by third persons.

8.11. Every child has the right to parents, or if he has no parents, to persons or institutions to replace them. The father and mother shall be jointly responsible for his development and education. It is the parents' prime responsibility, within the limits of their financial resources, to give the child a decent life and the means to satisfy his needs. The State must provide parents with appropriate assistance to fulfil their responsibilities, in the form of social institutions, services and facilities. Working parents must also be entitled to leave of absence to care for their children.

8.12. If the parents die, the Member States shall set up the machinery necessary to safeguard the future of the orphaned children. The wishes of the deceased parents shall be given priority if they have been expressed and it is feasible to comply with then. The Member States shall take responsibility for this and shall take the necessary steps to keep orphans from the same family together and avoid separating them under any circumstances. The Member States shall also set up centres to accommodate orphaned children.

8.13. If the parents live apart, are legally separated or divorced or their marriage is declared null and void, the child shall have the right to maintain direct and permanent contact with both parents, who both have the same obligations, even if one of them lives in another country, unless the competent authorities in the Member State concerned declare this to be incompatible with safeguard the child's interests. Appropriate measures must be adopted as soon as possible to prevent either of the parents or a third person from abducting children, unlawfully holding them or failing to hand them over, either in a Member State or in a third country. The legal procedures put in place must be capable of resolving disputes economically and speedily, and be easily enforceable throughout the Community.

8.14. Any decision regarding a child taken by its family, the administrative authorities or the courts must have as its prime aim the protection and safeguarding of the child's interests. To this end, provided that it involves no risk or prejudice to him, the child must be heard as soon as he is old enough and reaches sufficient intellectual maturity, regarding all decisions affecting him. So as to assist the competent persons to reach a decision, the child must in particular be heard in all proceedings and decisions involving a change in the exercise of parental authority, the allocation of care or custory, the appointment of a legal guardian, his adoption or placing in a home, educational institution or reintegration into society. For this purpose the Attorney-General's office shall be party to all proceedings and its chief role shall be to safeguard the child's rights and interests.

8.15. Any child who has one or both parents in prison must be allowed to maintain contact with them. Young children living with their mothers in prisons must have the benefit of suitabel facilities and care. The Member State shall guarantee that such children attend school outside the prison.

8.16. As far as possible and in accordance with national legislation and international agreements, Member States must promote the adoption of children in their territory, subject to the authorization of their parents or guardians or following effective abandonment for a period fixed by law. All legislation enacted in this connection must give priority to the interests of the child. Abandoned children and other children definitively or temporarily deprived of a family environment must under all circumstances be given special protection and help.

8.17. Every child is entitled to live with his natural, legal or adoptive parents.
Any child, whether or not a national of a Member State, shall be entitled:
 (a) to settle with his father or mother who is a national of a Member State in the territory of the Member State in which he or she is or has been employed;
 (b) to reside in the territory of another Member State in which his father or mother has right of residence, in accordance with any of the provisions on this right laid down in Community legislation. In accordance with their national laws the Member States shall allow children from third countries to join their parent or parents who are citizens of third countries, if they lawfully reside in the territory of a Member State of the Community. Children must also be allowed to be reunited with their parents, even if the granting of the right of residence or nationality to the latter is subject to administrative or legal procedures.

8.18. Every child who is a national of a Member State shall be entitled to move freely throughout the territory of the Community, to leave it and to return when he wishes, subject in all cases to respect for the rights and obligations inherent in parental authority.

8.19. Every child has the right to physical and moral integrity. Where a child is subjected to torture or to inhuman, cruel or degrading treatment by any public or private person, such treatment shall be considered an especially aggravating circumstance. The Member States shall give special protection to any child who suffers torture, ill-treatment, brutality or exploitation at the hands of members of his family or the persons responsible for looking after him. Furthermore, the member States shall ensure that such children continue their education and that they receive suitable treatment to facilitate their reintegration into society.

8.20. The Community and the Member States shall include in their development aid programmes specific projects for cooperation with third countries to combat both organized crime involving minors and brutal and repressive treatment of children.

8.21. Every child shall have the right to conscientious objection, in accordance with the laws in force in the Member States. No child under the age of eighteen shall be obliged to participate directly in warfare or other forms of armed conflict.

8.22. Every child shall have the right to freedom. No child may be unlawfully or arbitrarily detained or held incommunicado.

8.23. Every child shall have the right to legal security. Children accused of a crime are entitled to all the guarantees of a hearing in accordance with the due process of law, including the right to special and appropriate legal assistance in preparing their defence. If a child is found guilty of a crime, efforts shall be made to prevent his being deprived of his freedom or detained in a prison for adults. In this case, the child shall be given access to suitable treatment provided by specialized staff aimed at reeducating him and subsequently reintegrating him into society.

8.24. Every child shall have the right to receive and impart information and to express his opinion. To this end he shall be entitled to form associations provided this does not prejudice the rights of third persons or contravene provisions laid down on this subject in national legislation.

8.25. Every child has the right to freedom of conscience, thought and religion without prejudice to the responsibilities laid down in national law in these areas for the child's parents or guardians.

8.26. In order to protect minors, there should be stricter controls on the activities of sects or new religious movements that can have an undesirable impact on children's education and cultural and social integration, along with adherence to Recommendation 1178 of the Council of Europe of 5 February 1992 which calls in particular for the syllabus of the system of general education to include concrete information on the major religions and their principal variants, on the principles of the comparative study of religion, and on ethics and personal and social rights.

8.27. Every child has the right to have his own culture, to practise his own religion or beliefs and to use his own language.

8.28. Every child has the right to leisure, play and voluntary participation in sports activities. He must also be able to take part in social, cultural and artistic activities.

8.29. Every child has the right not to be subjected by third persons to unjustified interference in his or his family's private life or unlawful attacks on his honour.

8.30. Every child shall have the right to health. Every child shall be entitled to a non-polluted environment, clean accommodation and healthy nutrition. No child may be subjected to unnecessary medical treatment or scientific or therapeutic experiments, nor may he be subjected to tests to detect possible illnesses without due authorization from his parents or the persons responsible for him. No child may be the subject of discriminatory treatment, on grounds of illness, in centres providing family or health care.

8.31. The European Charter for Children in Hospital contained in Parliament;s resolution of 13 May 1986[10] should be included as an annex to the European Charter of Rights of the Child; the Commission should submit specific proposals to this end.

8.32. Children shall be protected from sexual illnesses and shall be provided with sex education and the necessary medical attention, including measures relating to birth control, information on birth control methods and the prevention of sexually-transmitted diseases in circumstances of respect for philosophical and religious convictions.

8.33. Every child shall be entitled to benefit from appropriate social services in connection with family life, education and reintegration into society.

8.34. Every child shall be entitled to benefit from social security benefits in accordance with the rules laid down in national legislation.

8.35. All children in the Community shall be guaranteed equal opportunities with respect to access to education and social security.

8.36. Every disabled child shall be entitled to:

---

[10] OJ No C 148, 16.6.1986, p. 37.

    (a) receive special care and attention;
    (b) receive appropriate education and vocational training that will permit his social integration, either in an ordinary establishment or in a specialist establishment;
    (c) take part in social, cultural and sporting activities. Any child with a disability must have access to a job commensurate with his aspirations, training and abilities.

8.37. Every child is entitled to receive education. The Member States shall ensure that every child receives free and compulsory primary education. They shall adopt the necessary measures to guarantee access opportunities for all to secondary and university education. Children's education must, as well as preparing them for working life, also encourage the development of their personality and promote respect for human rights and the national cultural differences of other countries or regions and the eradication of racism and xenophobia. Such education must include instruction in the routines of political and industrial relations activity. The admission of a child to any establishment which receives public funding must not depend on the economic situation of his parents, their social, racial or ethnic origin, sexual orientation or their religious beliefs or lack of them. Every child shall be entitled to receive appropriate sex education and information. A child's schooling may not be affected or interrupted because of an illness which is not infectious or contagious for other children. Member States shall make particular efforts to protect children, in accordance with their age, from pornographic and violent messages.

8.38. Every child who is a national of a Member State shall in particular be entitled to:
    (a) receive, on the territory of that State, education in the language or one of the languages of that Member State:
    (b) receive free education in the territory of another Member State where one of the parents, who is a national of a Member State, is or has been engaged in paid employment in any of the official languages of the host state: each Member· State shall also encourage, as far as possible, the teaching of one of its languages to children who are nationals of that State but who reside in another Member State;
    (c) move to the member State of his choice to pursue his studies subject to the conditions laid down in Directive 90/366/EEC[11] on the right of residence of students.

8.39. Every child must be protected against any form of economic exploitation. No child may engage in any kind of work which endangers his health, development, psychology or right to basic education. No child may be employed full time before the age of sixteen and under no circumstances before completing his compulsory schooling. The laws of the Member States must be harmonized and brought into line with the national law which provides most protection for children regarding *inter alia* the following points:
    (a) the minimum age for admission to employment;
    (b) the definition of and conditions for all possible exceptions to this rule, in particular exceptions relating to what is considered as light work, work in entertainment and the arts, work in family businesses, temporary work in companies or vocational training schools in educational programmes, or seasonal work;

---

[11] OJ No L 180, 13.7.1990, p. 30.

    (c) no child shall be employed in work involving the use of dangerous substances, underground work, night work or work involving overtime;

    (d) the conditions under which work liable to endanger their health, education or cause psychological or physical exhaustion shall be prohibited.

8.40. Every child over sixteen engaged in work shall be entitled to decent and adequate remuneration. If he has a job equivalent to that of an adult and under the same conditions, he must be given equal treatment as regards pay, access to vocational training, social security, working conditions and rules on health and safety. Every child shall on leaving the education system have the right to adequate assistance in seeking employment in the event of unemployment, in particular long-term unemployment.

8.41. Every child must be protected against all forms of sexual slavery, violence or exploitation. Appropriate measures shall be taken to prevent any child from being abducted, sold or exploited for the purposes of prostitution or pornography in the territory of the Community and to prevent anyone within the Community facilitating or endorsing the sexual exploitation of children outside the territory of the Community.

8.42. Every child must be protected against drug abuse. Member States shall therefore be obliged to promote information campaigns on the risks of drug use, prevention and rehabilitation, in terms which are accessible to children's intelligence and not hurtful to their sensibilities.

8.43. Every child must be protected against the excesses of advertising, in such a way as to avoid both the use of images of children themselves in forms harmful to their dignity.

8.44. Children from third countries who apply for refugee status in a Member State must be given due protection and assistance in that State whilst their application is being considered.

8.45. Member States shall implement and render effective the rights enshrined in the Charter by means of laws, administrative provisions, expenditure commitments and other suitable forms of intervention.

   9. Instructs its President to forward this resolution to the Commission, the Council and the Council of Europe.

Name Index

Subject Index